RAND McNALLY
New Universal World Atlas

RAND McNALLY
New Universal World Atlas

CONTENTS

USING THE ATLAS ....v - vii

WORLD TIME ZONES viii

REFERENCE MAPS ....1 – 160
Map Symbols and Index Map.................. 1
World ....2 – 3

Europe ....4 – 5
Northern Europe ....6 – 7
British Isles...............................8 – 9
Central Europe ....10 – 11
Belgium, Netherlands,
    and Luxembourg 12
Switzerland 13
France and the Alps ....14 – 15
Spain and Portugal ....16 – 17
Italy ....18 – 19
Southeastern Europe ....20 – 21
Baltic and Moscow Regions ....22 – 23

Asia...................................24 – 25
Northwest Asia ....26 – 27
Northeast Asia ....28 – 29
China, Japan, and Korea..............30 – 31
Northeastern China
    and Korea ....32 – 33
Eastern and
    Southeastern China ....34 – 35
Japan ....36 – 37
Southeastern Asia.....................38 – 39
Myanmar, Thailand,
    and Indochina ....40 – 41
India, Pakistan, and
    Southwestern Asia ....42 – 43
Northern India and Pakistan ....44 – 45
Southern India and Sri Lanka 46
Southern Arabian Peninsula. 47
The Middle East ....48 – 49
Israel and Southern Lebanon ......50 – 51

Africa...................................52 – 53
Western North Africa ....54 – 55
Eastern North Africa ....56 – 57
Southern Africa ....58 – 59
Egypt and Sudan.......................60 – 61
Northwestern Africa ....62 – 63
West Africa ....64 – 65
Southern Africa
    and Madagascar ....66 – 67

Australia ....68 – 69
Eastern Australia ....70 – 71
New Zealand................................72

Antarctica...................................73

South America ....74 – 75
Northern South America ....76 – 77
Southern South America 78
Southeastern Brazil 79
Central Argentina and Chile ....80 – 81
Peru, Bolivia, and
    Western Brazil ....82 – 83

Colombia, Ecuador,
    Venezuela, and Guyana ....84 – 85

North America ....86 – 87
Middle America
    and Caribbean ....88 – 89
Mexico ....90 – 91
Central America ....92 – 93
Caribbean Region ....94 – 95

Canada ....96 – 97
Alberta 98
British Columbia 99
Manitoba 100
New Brunswick, Nova Scotia,
    and Prince Edward Island...............101
Newfoundland 102
Ontario 103
Quebec 104
Saskatchewan 105

United States of America ....106 – 107
Alabama 108
Alaska 109
Arizona.................................110
Arkansas 111
California 112
Colorado 113
Connecticut...............................114
Delaware 115
Florida 116
Georgia 117
Hawaii 118
Idaho 119
Illinois 120
Indiana 121
Iowa 122
Kansas.................................123
Kentucky 124
Louisiana 125
Maine 126
Maryland 127
Massachusetts 128
Michigan 129
Minnesota 130
Mississippi 131
Missouri 132
Montana 133
Nebraska.................................134
Nevada.................................135
New Hampshire 136
New Jersey 137
New Mexico 138
New York 139
North Carolina 140
North Dakota 141
Ohio 142
Oklahoma 143
Oregon 144
Pennsylvania 145
Rhode Island 146
South Carolina 147
South Dakota 148

Tennessee 149
Texas 150
Utah 151
Vermont 152
Virginia 153
Washington 154
West Virginia 155
Wisconsin 156
Wyoming 157

Pacific and Indian Oceans ......158 – 159

Atlantic Ocean 160

INDEX TO REFERENCE MAPS 161

Rand McNally
New Universal World Atlas

Published exclusively for Barnes & Noble Inc.
Copyright © 1994 by Rand McNally & Company.
Second Printing 1995.

Library of Congress Cataloging -in-Publication Data
Rand McNally and Company.
    Rand McNally new universal world atlas.
        p.   cm.
    Includes index.
    ISBN 0-526-83717-6
    1. Atlases. I. Title II. Title: New universal world atlas.
G1021.R4875   1994   <G&M>
912--dc20

94-3532
CIP
MAP

USING THE ATLAS

MAPS AND ATLASES

Satellite images of the world (figure 1) constantly give us views of the shape and size of the earth. It is hard, therefore, to imagine how difficult it once was to ascertain the look of our planet. Yet from early history we have evidence of humans trying to work out what the world actually looked like.

Twenty-five hundred years ago, on a tiny clay tablet the size of a hand, the Babylonians inscribed the earth as a flat disk (figure 2) with Babylon at the center. The section of the Cantino map of 1502 (figure 3) is an example of a *portolan* chart used by mariners to chart the newly discovered Americas. Handsome and useful maps have been produced by many cultures. The Mexican map drawn in 1583 marks hills with wavy lines and roads with footprints between parallel lines (figure 4). The methods and materials used to create these maps were dependent upon the technology available, and their accuracy suffered considerably. A modern topographic map (figure 5), as well as those in this atlas, shows the detail and accuracy that cartographers are now able to achieve. They benefit from our ever-increasing technology, including satellite imagery and computer assisted cartography.

In 1589 Gerardus Mercator used the word *atlas* to describe a collection of maps. Atlases now bring together not only a variety of maps but an assortment of tables and other reference material as well. They have become a unique and indispensable reference for graphically defining the world and answering the question *where*. Only on a map can the countries, cities, roads, rivers, and lakes covering a vast area be simultaneously viewed in their relative locations. Routes between places can be traced, trips planned, boundaries of neighboring states and countries examined, distances between places measured, the meandering of rivers and streams and the sizes of lakes visualized—and remote places imagined.

FIGURE 1

FIGURE 4

FIGURE 2

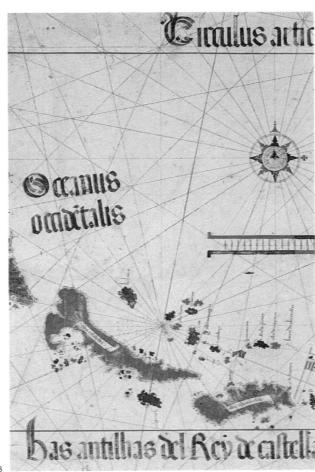

FIGURE 3

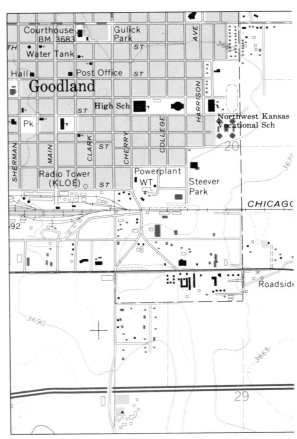

FIGURE 5

SEQUENCE OF THE MAPS

The world is made up of seven major landmasses: the continents of Europe, Asia, Africa, Antarctica, Australia, South America, and North America (figure 6). The maps in this atlas follow this continental sequence. To allow for the inclusion of detail, each continent is broken down into a series of maps, and this grouping is arranged so that as consecutive pages are turned, a continuous successive part of the continent is shown. Larger-scale maps are used for regions of greater detail (having many cities, for example) or for areas of global significance.

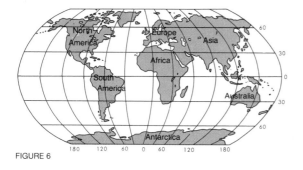

FIGURE 6

GETTING THE INFORMATION

An atlas can be used for many purposes, from planning a trip to finding hot spots in the news and supplementing world knowledge. To realize the potential of an atlas the user must be able to:

1. Find places on the maps
2. Measure distances
3. Determine directions
4. Understand map symbols

FINDING PLACES

One of the most common and important tasks facilitated by an atlas is finding the location of a place in the world. A river's name in a book, a city mentioned in the news, or a vacation spot may prompt your need to know where the place is located. The illustrations and text below explain how to find Yangon (Rangoon), Myanmar.

1. Look up the place-name in the index at the back of the atlas. Yangon, Myanmar can be found on the map on page 38, and it can be located on the map by the letter-number key *B2* (figure 7).

Yangguanpu, China	C4	34
Yangjia, China	I7	32
Yangjiang, China	G9	30
Yangkoushi, China	G7	34
Yangliuqing, China	D5	32
Yanglousi, China	F2	34
Yangon (Rangoon), Mya.	B2	38
Yangp'yŏng, S. Kor.	F15	32
Yangquan, China	F1	32
Yangsan, S. Kor.	H17	32
Yangshuling, China	B6	32
Yangtze see Chang, stm., China	E10	30
Yangxiaodian, China	D5	34
Yangyang, S. Kor.	E16	32
Yangzhou, China	C8	34
Yanheying, China	C7	32
Yanji, China	A17	32
Yankdók, N. Kor.	D14	32

FIGURE 7

2. Turn to the map of Southeastern Asia found on page 38. Note that the letters *A* through *H* and the numbers *1* through *11* appear in the margins of the map.

3. To find Yangon, on the map, place your left index finger on *B* and your right index finger on *2*. Move your left finger across the map and your right finger down the map. Your fingers will meet in the area in which Yangon is located (figure 8).

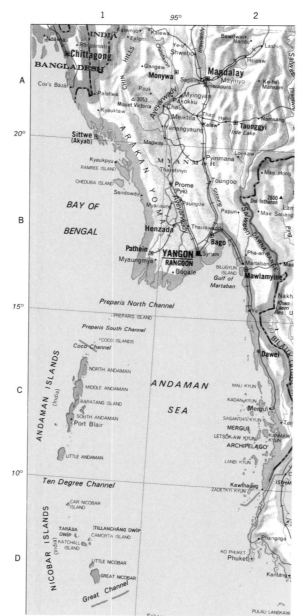

FIGURE 8

MEASURING DISTANCES

In planning trips, determining the distance between two places is essential, and an atlas can help in travel preparation. For instance, to determine the approximate distance between Paris and Rouen, France, follow these three steps:

1. Lay a slip of paper on the map on page 14 so that its edge touches the two cities. Adjust the paper so one corner touches Rouen. Mark the paper directly at the spot where Paris is located (figure 9).

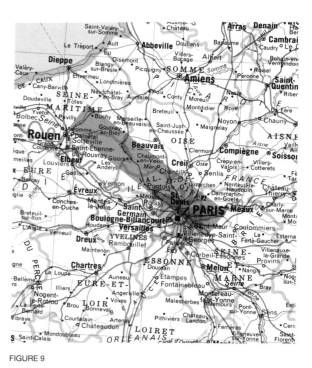

FIGURE 9

2. Place the paper along the scale of miles beneath the map. Position the corner at 0 and line up the edge of the paper along the scale. The pencil mark on the paper indicates Rouen is between 50 and 100 miles from Paris (figure 10).

3. To find the exact distance, move the paper to the right so that the pencil mark is at 100 on the scale. The corner of the paper stands on the fourth 5-mile unit on the scale. This means that the two towns are 50 plus 20, or 70 miles apart (figure 11).

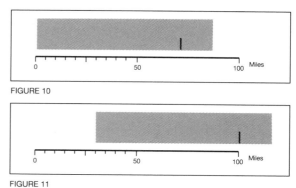

FIGURE 10

FIGURE 11

DETERMINING DIRECTION

Most of the maps in the atlas are drawn so that when oriented for normal reading, north is at the top of the map, south is at the bottom, west is at the left, and east is at the right. Most maps have a series of lines drawn across them—the lines of *latitude* and *longitude*. Lines of latitude, or *parallels* of latitude, are drawn east and west. Lines of longitude, or *meridians* of longitude, are drawn north and south (figure 12).

Parallels and meridians appear as either curved or straight lines. For example, in the section of the map of Europe (figure 13) the parallels of latitude appear as curved lines. The meridians of longitude are straight lines that come together toward the top of the map. Latitude and longitude lines help locate places on maps. Parallels of latitude are numbered in degrees north and south of the *Equator*. Meridians of longitude are numbered in degrees east and west of a line called the *Prime Meridian*, running through Greenwich, England, near London. Any place on earth can be located by the latitude and longitude lines running through it.

To determine directions or locations on the map, you must use the parallels and meridians. For example, suppose you want to know which is farther north, Bergen, Norway, or Stockholm, Sweden. The map in figure 13 shows that Stockholm is south of the 60° parallel of latitude and Bergen is north of it. Bergen is farther north than Stockholm. By looking at the meridians of longitude, you can determine which city is farther east. Bergen is approximately 5° east of the 0° meridian (Prime Meridian), and Stockholm is almost 20° east of it. Stockholm is farther east than Bergen.

UNDERSTANDING MAP SYMBOLS

In a very real sense, the whole map is a symbol, representing the world or a part of it. It is a reduced representation of the earth; each of the world's features—cities, rivers, etc.—is represented on the map by a symbol. Map symbols may take the form of points, such as dots or squares (often used for cities, capital cities, or points of interest), or lines (roads, railroads, rivers). Symbols may also occupy an area, showing extent of coverage (terrain, forests, deserts). They seldom look like the feature they represent and therefore must be identified and interpreted. For instance, the maps in this atlas define political units by a colored line depicting their boundaries. Neither the colors nor the boundary lines are actually found on the surface of the earth, but because countries and states are such important political components of the world, strong symbols are used to represent them. The Map Symbols page in this atlas identifies the symbols used on the maps.

FIGURE 12

FIGURE 13

World Time Zones

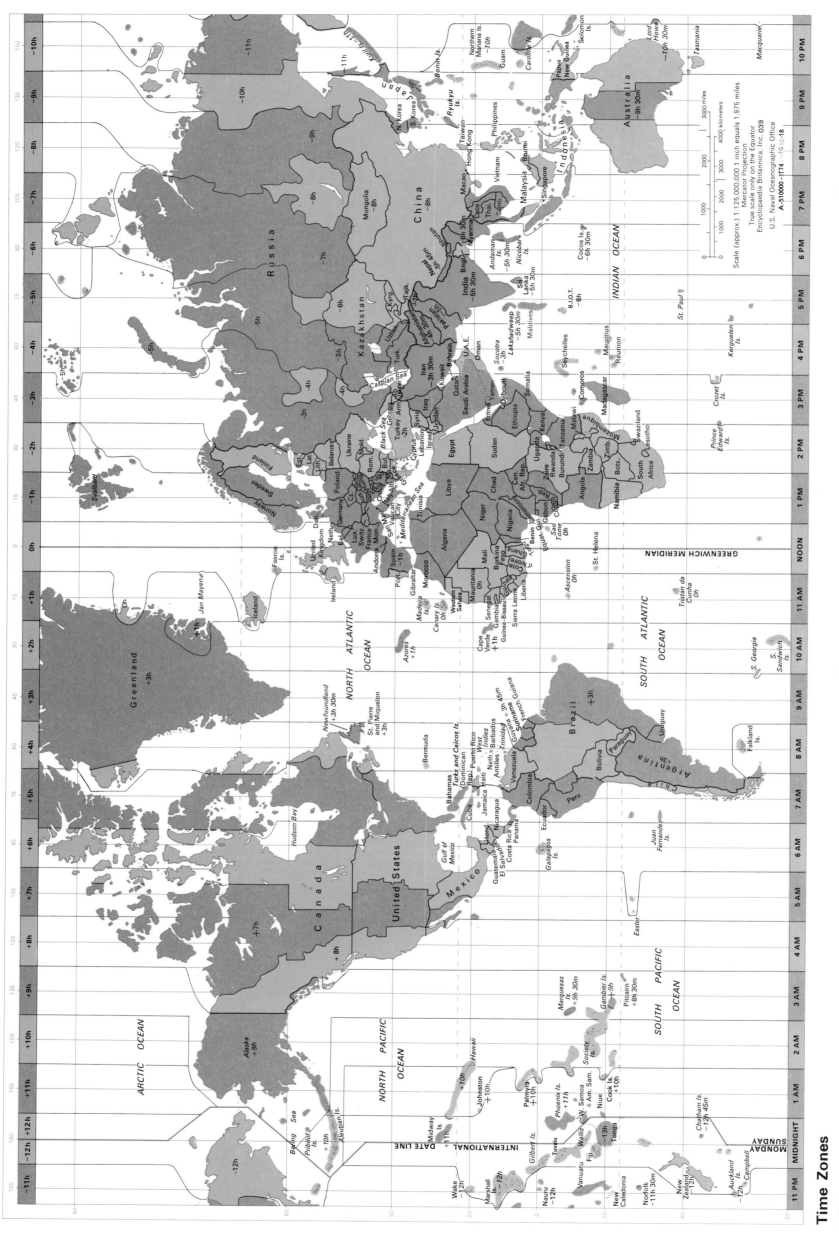

Scale (approx.) 1:125,000,000 1 inch equals 1,975 miles
Mercator Projection
True scale only on the Equator
Encyclopaedia Britannica, Inc. Q39
U.S. Naval Oceanographic Office
A-510000-1T74 · 10-18

The standard time zone system, fixed by international agreement and by law in each country, is based on a theoretical division of the globe into 24 zones of 15° longitude each. The mid-meridian of each zone fixes the hour for the entire zone. The zero time zone extends 7½° east and 7½° west of the Greenwich meridian, 0° longitude. Since the earth rotates toward the east, time zones to the west of Greenwich are earlier, to the east, later.
Plus and minus hours at the top of the map are added to or subtracted from local time to find Greenwich time. Local standard time can be determined for any area in the world by adding one hour for each time zone counted in an easterly direction from one's own, or by subtracting one hour for each zone counted in a westerly direction. To separate one day from the next, the 180th meridian has been designated as the international date line. On both sides of the line the time of day is the same, but west of the line it is one day later than it is to the east. Countries which adhere to the international zone system adopt the zone applicable to their location. Some countries, however, establish time zones based on political boundaries, or adopt the time zone of a neighboring unit. For all or part of the year some countries also advance their time by one hour, thereby utilizing more daylight hours each day

Time Zones

Standard time zone of even-numbered hours from Greenwich time

Standard time zone of odd-numbered hours from Greenwich time

Time varies from the standard time zone by half an hour

Time varies from the standard time zone by other than half an hour

h m   hours, minutes

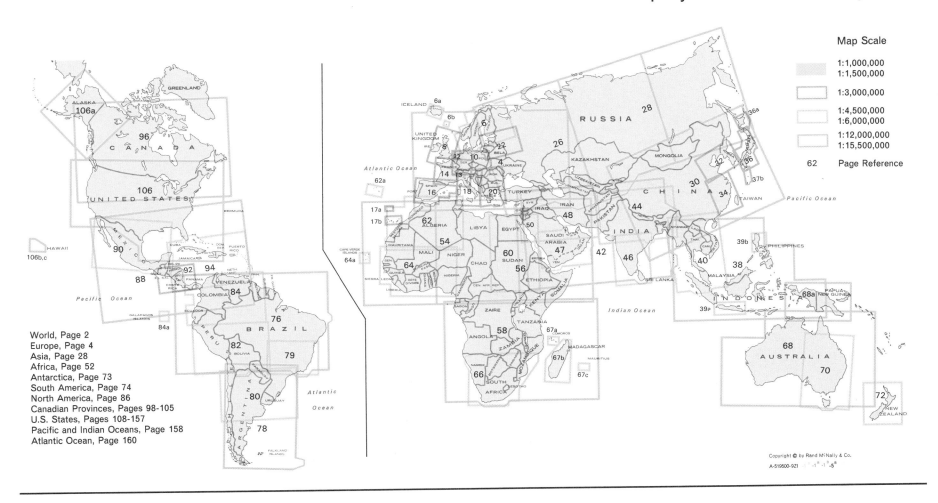

World, Page 2
Europe, Page 4
Asia, Page 28
Africa, Page 52
Antarctica, Page 73
South America, Page 74
North America, Page 86
Canadian Provinces, Pages 98–105
U.S. States, Pages 108–157
Pacific and Indian Oceans, Page 158
Atlantic Ocean, Page 160

Map Scale

	1:1,000,000 1:1,500,000
	1:3,000,000
	1:4,500,000 1:6,000,000
	1:12,000,000 1:15,500,000
62	Page Reference

World Maps Symbols

Inhabited Localities

The size of type indicates the relative economic and political importance of the locality

Écommoy	Lisieux	**Rouen**
Trouville	**Orléans**	**PARIS**
Bi'r Safājah °	Oasis	

The symbol represents the population of the locality

1:1,000,000–1:6,000,000	1:12,000,000–1:15,500,000	1:24,000,000–1:48,000,000
• 0—10,000	• 0—50,000	• 0—100,000
○ 10,000—25,000	◉ 50,000—100,000	◉ 100,000—1,500,000
◉ 25,000—100,000	⊡ 100,000—250,000	■ >1,500,000
⊡ 100,000—250,000	⊡ 250,000—1,000,000	
▣ 250,000—1,000,000	■ >1,000,000	
■ >1,000,000		

English or second official language names are shown in reduced size lettering. Historical or other alternate names in the local language are shown in parentheses.

Urban Area (Area of continuous industrial, commercial, and residential development)

Capitals of Political Units

BUDAPEST	Independent Nation
Cayenne	Dependency (Colony, protectorate, etc.)
Recife	State, Province, County, Oblast, etc.

Political Boundaries

International (First-order political unit)

	Demarcated and Undemarcated
	Disputed de jure
	Indefinite or Undefined
	Demarcation Line

Internal

	State, Province, etc. (Second-order political unit)
MURCIA	Historical Region (No boundaries indicated)
GALAPAGOS (Ecuador)	Administering Country

Transportation

	Primary Road
	Secondary Road
	Minor Road, Trail
	Railway
Canal du Midi	Navigable Canal
	Bridge
	Tunnel
TO MALMÖ	Ferry

Hydrographic Features

	Shoreline
	Undefined or Fluctuating Shoreline
Amur	River, Stream
	Intermittent Stream
	Rapids, Falls
	Irrigation or Drainage Canal
	Reef
The Everglades	Swamp
RIMO GLACIER	Glacier
L. Victoria	Lake, Reservoir
Tuz Gölü	Salt Lake
	Intermittent Lake, Reservoir
	Dry Lake Bed
(395)	Lake Surface Elevation

Topographic Features

Matterhorn △ 4478	Elevation Above Sea Level
76 ▽	Elevation Below Sea Level
Mount Cook ▲ 3764	Highest Elevation in Country
133 ▼	Lowest Elevation in Country
Khyber Pass ⊒ 1067	Mountain Pass

Elevations are given in meters.
The highest and lowest elevations in a continent are underlined

	Sand Area
	Lava
	Salt Flat

State, Province Maps Symbols

⊙	Capital
○	County Seat
▲	Military Installation
△	Point of Interest
+	Mountain Peak

	International Boundary
	State, Province Boundary
	County Boundary
	Railroad
	Road
	Urban Area

1

ARCTIC OCEAN

Barents Sea
Hammerfest
Murmansk

ZEML'A FRANCA-IOSIFA
NOVAJA ZEML'A
Karskoje more

NOVOSIBIRSKIJE OSTROVA
more Laptevych

Dikson
Chatanga
Tiksi

Noril'sk
Igarka
Verchojansk
Arctic Circle

Jenisej
Salechard
Vorkuta

Lena
Jakutsk

Anadyr'

SWEDEN
FINLAND
HELSINKI
Ladožskoje ozero
SANKT-PETERBURG
GT. PETERSBURG
STOCKHOLM EST.
LITH.
BELARUS
MOSKVA
Niznij Novgorod
Perm'
Jekaterinburg
Čel'abinsk
Omsk
Novosibirsk

RUSSIA

Lensk
Irkutsk
Krasnojarsk
ozero Bajkal
Cita

Ochotsk
Nikolajevsk
Magadan
Sea of Okhotsk

Bering Sea
Petropavlovsk-Kamčatskij
ALEUTIAN IS. (U.S.)

DENMARK
POLAND
WARSZAWA
UKRAINE
KYYIV
Volgograd
Volga
Astrachan'
gora El'brus 5642
Samara
Ural
Orsk
KAZAKHSTAN
Karaganda
ALTAJ
Chabarovsk
OSTROV SACHALIN
KURIL'SKIJE OSTROVA

CZECH REP.
WIEN
HUNG.
BUDAPEST
BUCUREŞTI
BEOGRAD
Milano
BUL.
SOFIJA
Black Sea
Aral Sea
UZBEKISTAN
TAŠKENT
ALMA-ATA
Ürümqi
MONGOLIA
ULaanbaatar
Harbin
Vladivostok
Sapporo
International Date Line

ITALY
ROMA
Napoli
GREECE
ATHINAI
İstanbul
ANKARA
TURKEY
ARM. AZERB.
BAKI
TURKMENISTAN
TADZ.
KYRG.
TIEN SHAN
Shache
GOBI
Hohhot
BEIJING PEKING
Shenyang
N. KOREA
P'YONGYANG
S. KOREA
SEOUL
Pusan
JAPAN
Sendai
HONSHŪ

MALTA
Mediterranean Sea
TARĀBULUS
TRIPOLI
TUNIS
SYRIA
LEB.
ISR.
JORDAN
BAGHDĀD
IRAQ
KUWAIT
TEHRĀN
Eşfahān
IRAN
AFGHANISTAN
Islāmābād
Rawalpindi
Lahore
HIMALAYAS
Lhasa
CHINA
Lanzhou
Xi'an
Chengdu
Chongqing
Wuhan
Nanjing
SHANGHAI
Changsha
Fuzhou
Dalian
Qingdao
Yellow Sea
ŌSAKA
TŌKYŌ
Fukuoka
Sea of Japan

LIBYA
EGYPT
Al-Iskandariyah
Alexandria
AL-QĀHIRAH
CAIRO
Aswān
SAUDI
AR-RIYĀD
QATAR
UNITED ARAB EMIRATES
OMAN
Masqat
Karāchi
PAKISTAN
New Delhi
DELHI
Kāthmāndau
Mount Everest 8848
NEPAL
BNGL.
DHAKA
MYANMAR
Kunming
Guangzhou
HONG KONG (U.K.)
T'AIPEI
TAIWAN
NANSEI-SHOTŌ
OGASAWARA-GUNTŌ (Japan)
PACIFIC
WAKE ISLAND (U.S.)

ARABIA
Red Sea
Makkah
Sana
ERITREA
YEMEN
'Adan
DJIBOUTI
Djibouti
SUQUTRĀ (Yam.)
GĒS GWARDAFUY
Arabian Sea
Tropic of Cancer
Ahmadābād
INDIA
BOMBAY
Hyderābād
Bay of Bengal
YANGON
Bangalore
Madras
CALCUTTA
ANDAMAN ISLANDS (India)
KRUNG THEP
BANGKOK
THAILAND
VIETNAM
Thanh Pho Ho Chi Minh
Phnum Penh
MANILA
PHILIPPINES
GUAM (U.S.)
NORTHERN MARIANA ISLANDS (U.S.)
OCEAN
MARSHALL ISLANDS

NIGER
CHAD
AL-KHARTŪM
SUDAN
Kano
N'Djamena
CEN. AFR. REP.
Bangui
ADIS ABEBA
ETHIOPIA
SOMALIA
Muqdisho
SEYCHELLES
MALDIVES
SRI LANKA
COLOMBO
Cochin
NICOBAR ISLANDS (India)
South China Sea
MALAYSIA
KUALA LUMPUR
SINGAPORE
BRUNEI
Davao
PALAU (T.T.P.I.)
FEDERATED STATES OF MICRONESIA
MICRONESIA

CAMEROON
Yaoundé
GABON
CONGO
ZAIRE
RWANDA
BURUNDI
Bujumbura
KAMPALA
UGANDA
KENYA
NAIROBI
Lake Victoria
Kilimanjaro 5895
Mombasa
Medan
SUMATRA
Palembang
JAKARTA
JAWA
Surabaya
BORNEO
Ujungpandang
SULAWESI
INDONESIA
TIMOR
PAPUA NEW GUINEA
Mount Wilhelm 4509
NEW GUINEA
Port Moresby
KIRIBATI
NAURU
TUVALU
SOLOMON ISLANDS
Equator

Brazzaville
KINSHASA
LUANDA
Lobito
ANGOLA
ZAMBIA
Lusaka
Lubumbashi
TANZANIA
DAR ES SALAAM
Zanzibar
DODOMA
Lake Tanganyika
Lake Nyasa
BRITISH INDIAN OCEAN TERRITORY
INDIAN
OCEAN
COCOS ISLANDS (Aust.)
CHRISTMAS ISLAND (Austl.)
Darwin
CAPE YORK
Gulf of Carpentaria
Cairns
Coral Sea
NEW CALEDONIA (Fr.)
VANUATU
Suva
FIJI
MELANESIA

NAMIBIA
Windhoek
Walvis Bay
BOTSWANA
Saborone
ZIMBABWE
HARARE
Zambezi
MOZAMBIQUE
Mozambique Channel
MADAGASCAR
ANTANANARIVO
MAURITIUS
RÉUNION (Fr.)
Tropic of Capricorn
Alice Springs
AUSTRALIA
Rockhampton
Brisbane
NORFOLK ISLAND (Austl.)

SOUTH AFRICA
PRETORIA
Johannesburg
MAPUTO
SWAZILAND
LESOTHO
Durban
CAPE TOWN
CAPE AGULHAS
Port Elizabeth
Perth
Darling
Adelaide
Canberra
Sydney
Melbourne
Mount Kosciusko 2228
TASMANIA
Hobart
Tasman Sea
NEW ZEALAND
NORTH ISLAND
Auckland
Wellington
SOUTH ISLAND
Christchurch

ÎLES KERGUÉLEN (Fr.)

SOUTHERN
OCEAN

Antarctic Circle
ENDERBY LAND
WILKES LAND

Copyright © by Rand McNally & Co.
Map prepared by Rand McNally & Co.
A-510000-264

TICA

Kilometers 0 1000 2000 3000 Km.
Statute Miles 0 1000 2000 3000 Mi.

One centimeter represents 750 kilometers.
One inch represents approximately 1200 miles.
Robinson Projection
Scale 1:75,000,000

3

Kilometers

Statute Miles

Scale 1:12,000,000

One centimeter represents 120 kilometers.
One inch represents approximately 190 miles.

Miller Oblated Stereographic Projection

5

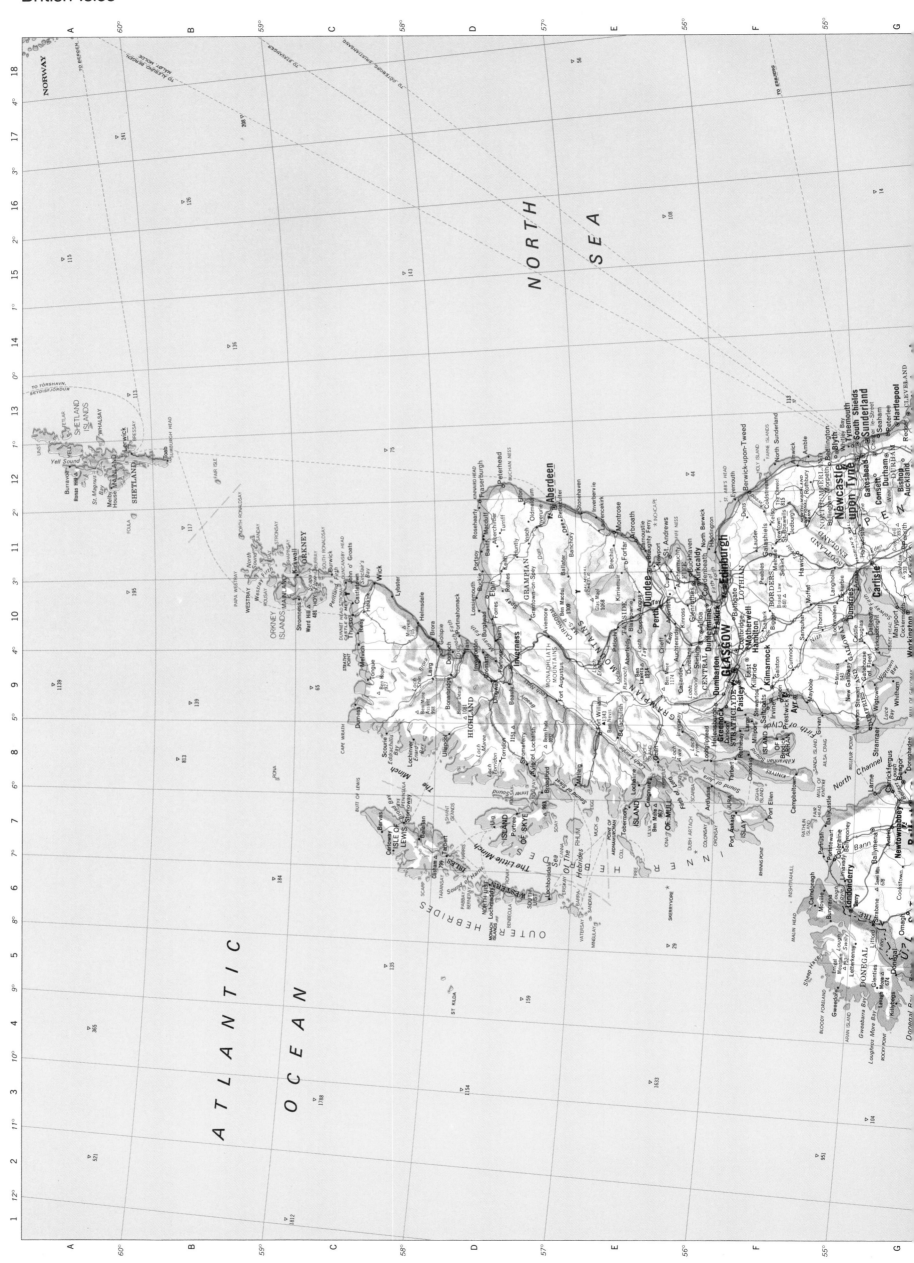

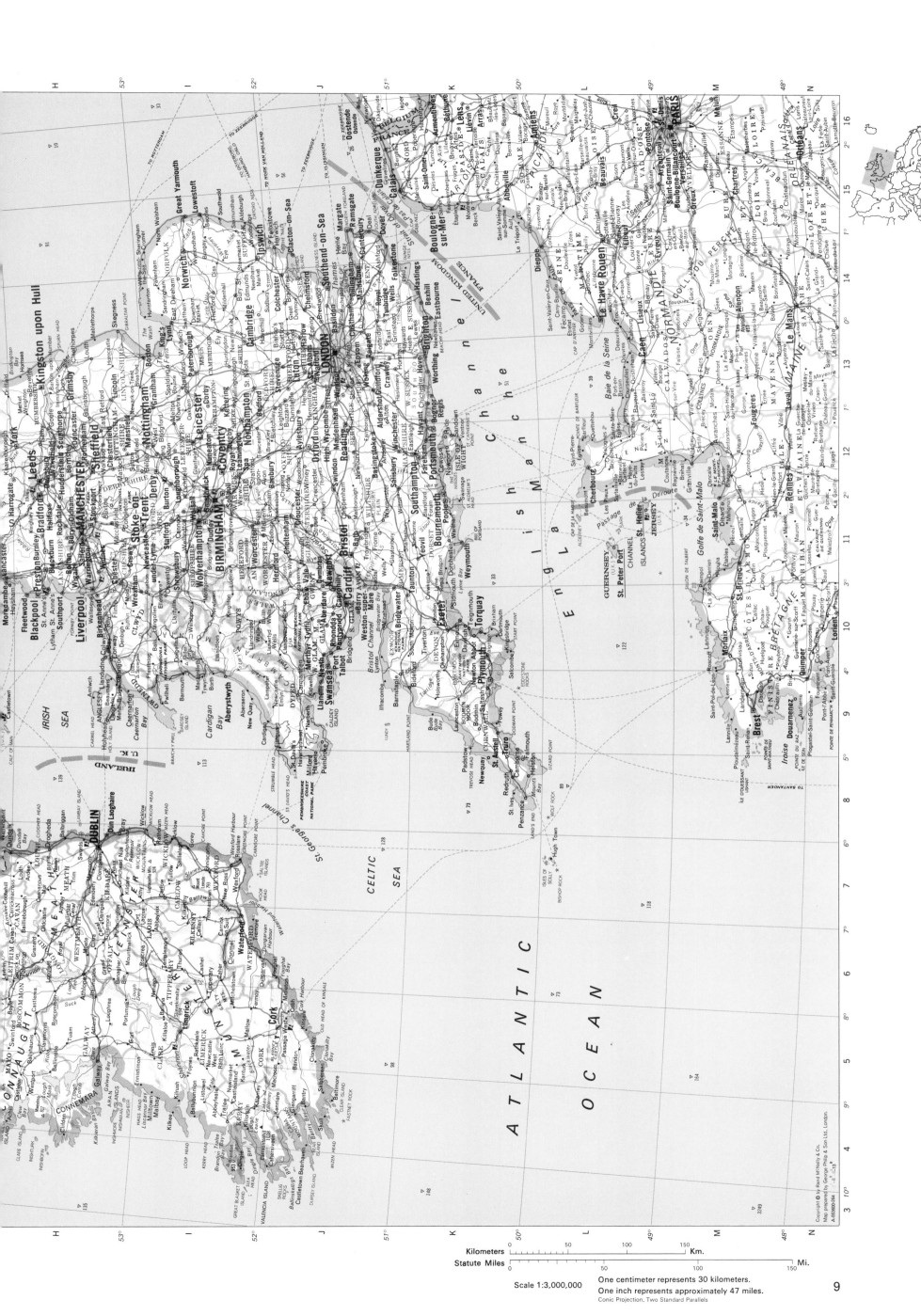

Kilometers

Statute Miles

Scale 1:3,000,000

One centimeter represents 30 kilometers.
One inch represents approximately 47 miles.
Conic Projection, Two Standard Parallels

Kilometers 0   50   100   150   Km.

Statute Miles 0   50   100   150   Mi.

Scale 1:3,000,000   One centimeter represents 30 kilometers.
One inch represents approximately 47 miles.
Conic Projection, Two Standard Parallels.

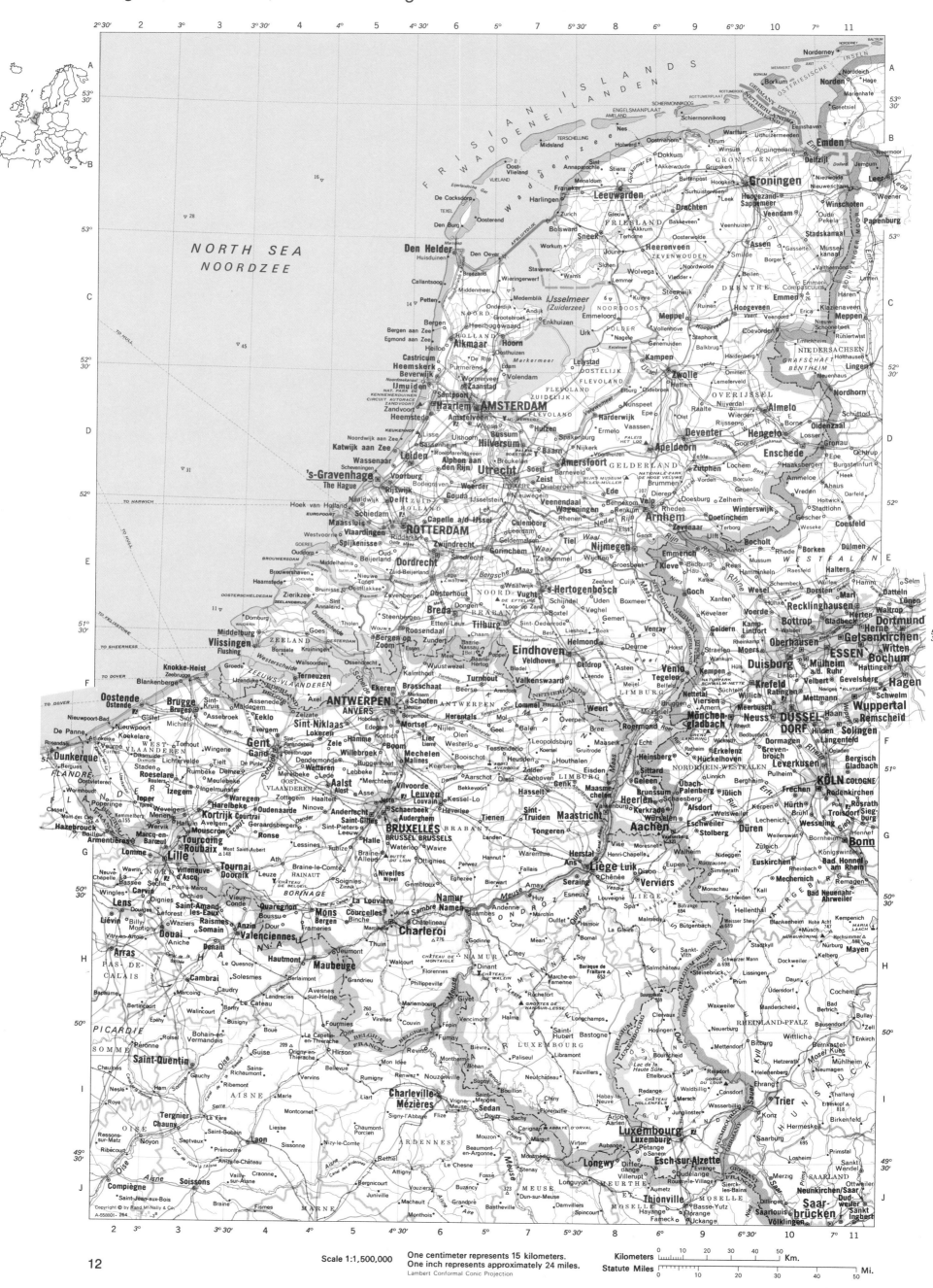

Scale 1:1,500,000
One centimeter represents 15 kilometers.
One inch represents approximately 24 miles.
Lambert Conformal Conic Projection

Kilometers
Statute Miles

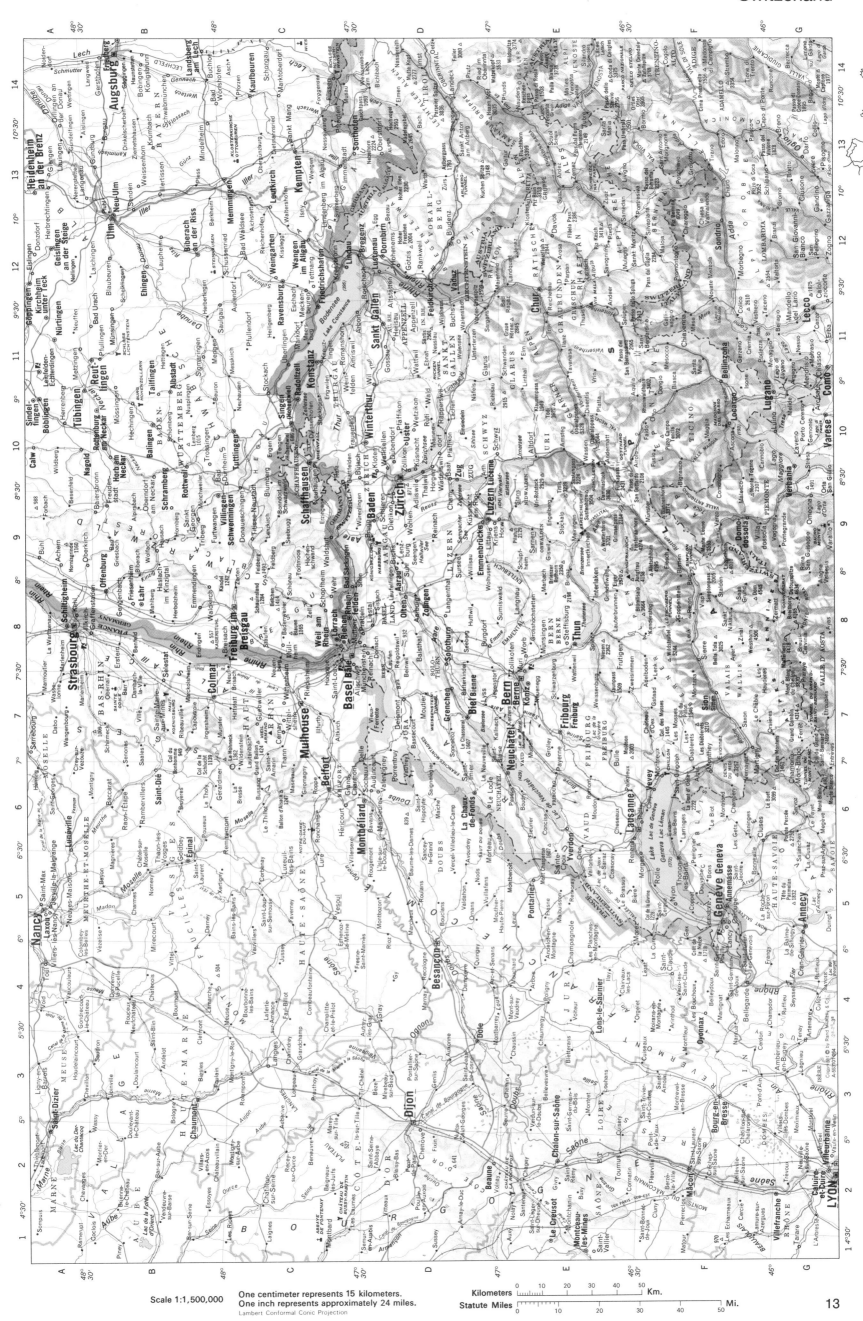

Scale 1:1,500,000
One centimeter represents 15 kilometers.
One inch represents approximately 24 miles.
Lambert Conformal Conic Projection

Kilometers
Statute Miles

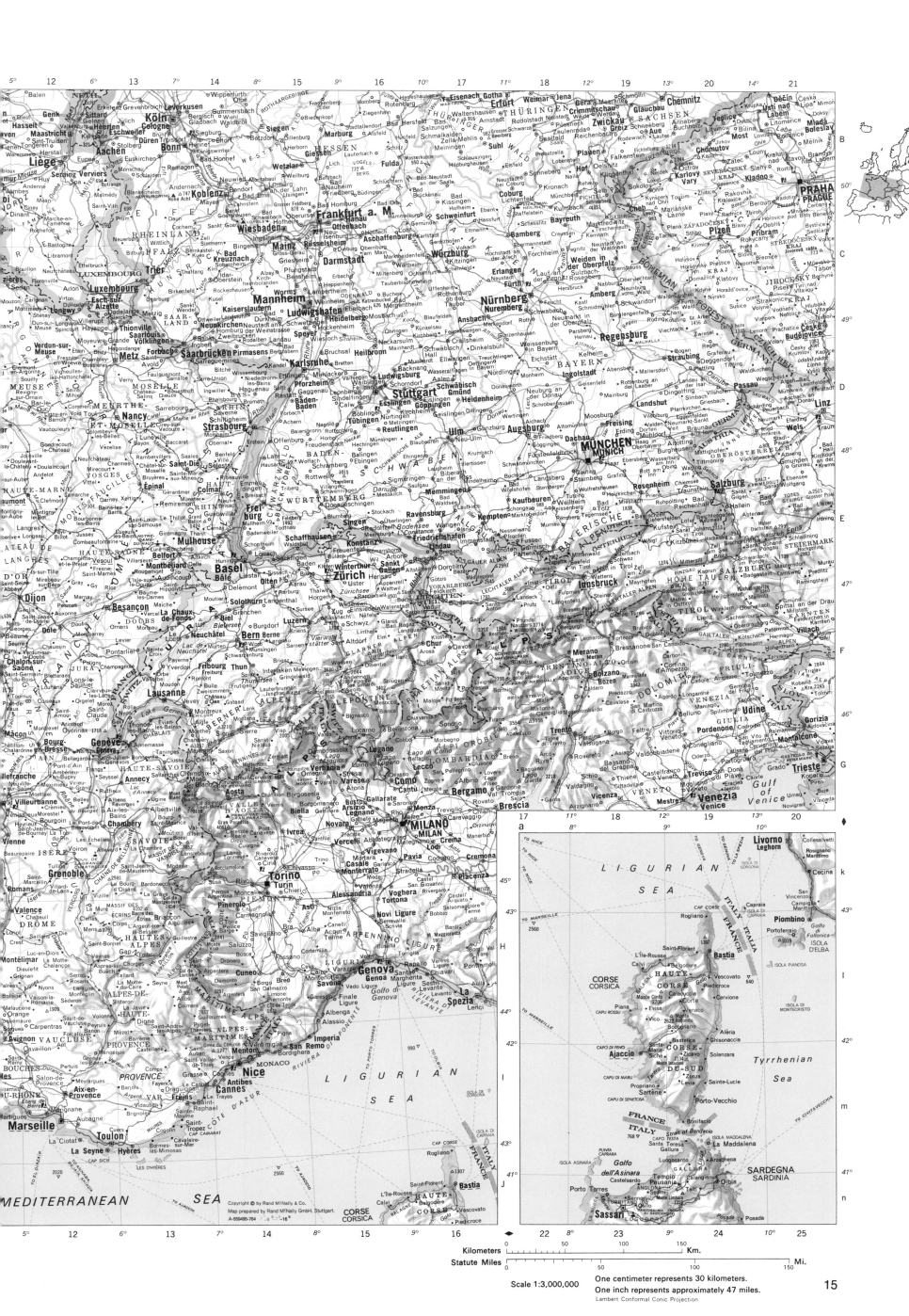

Kilometers

Statute Miles

Scale 1:3,000,000
One centimeter represents 30 kilometers.
One inch represents approximately 47 miles.
Lambert Conformal Conic Projection

15

MEDITERRANEAN SEA

Golfe du Lion

ILLES BALEARS
BALEARIC ISLANDS

MENORCA
MINORCA

MALLORCA
MAJORCA

Palma

BALEARS

ATLANTIC OCEAN

ARQUIPÉLAGO DA MADEIRA
MADEIRA ISLANDS
(Portugal)

Funchal

MADEIRA

PORTO SANTO

ILHAS DESERTAS

ISLAS CANARIAS
CANARY ISLANDS
(Spain)

LA PALMA

TENERIFE

Santa Cruz de Tenerife

GRAN CANARIA

Las Palmas de
Gran Canaria

GOMERA

HIERRO

LANZAROTE

Arrecife

FUERTEVENTURA

WESTERN SAHARA

ATLANTIC OCEAN

ALGERIA
ALGÉRIE

Wahran
Oran

Kilometers
Statute Miles

Scale 1:3,000,000   One centimeter represents 30 kilometers.
One inch represents approximately 47 miles.
Conic Projection, Two Standard Parallels

17

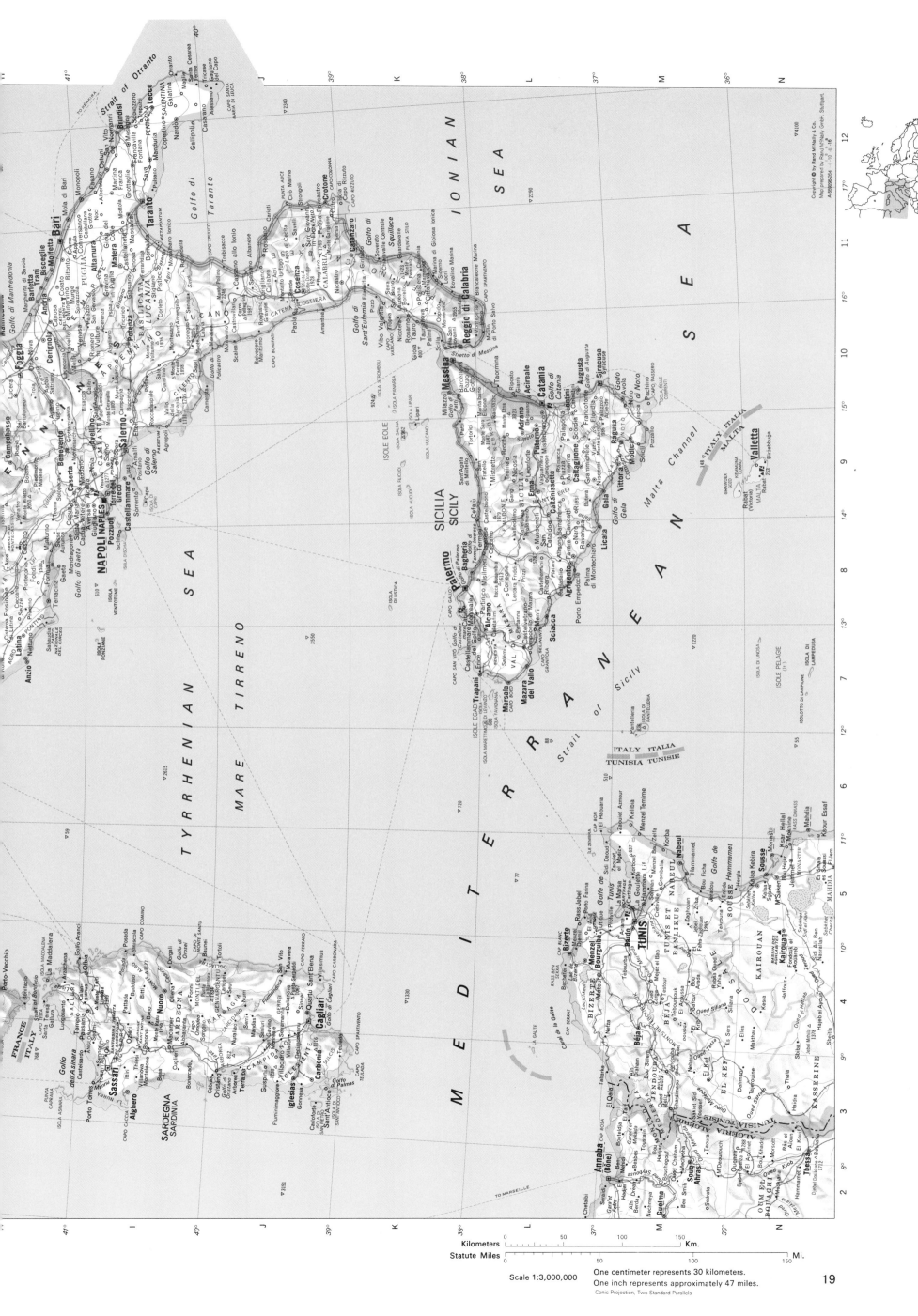

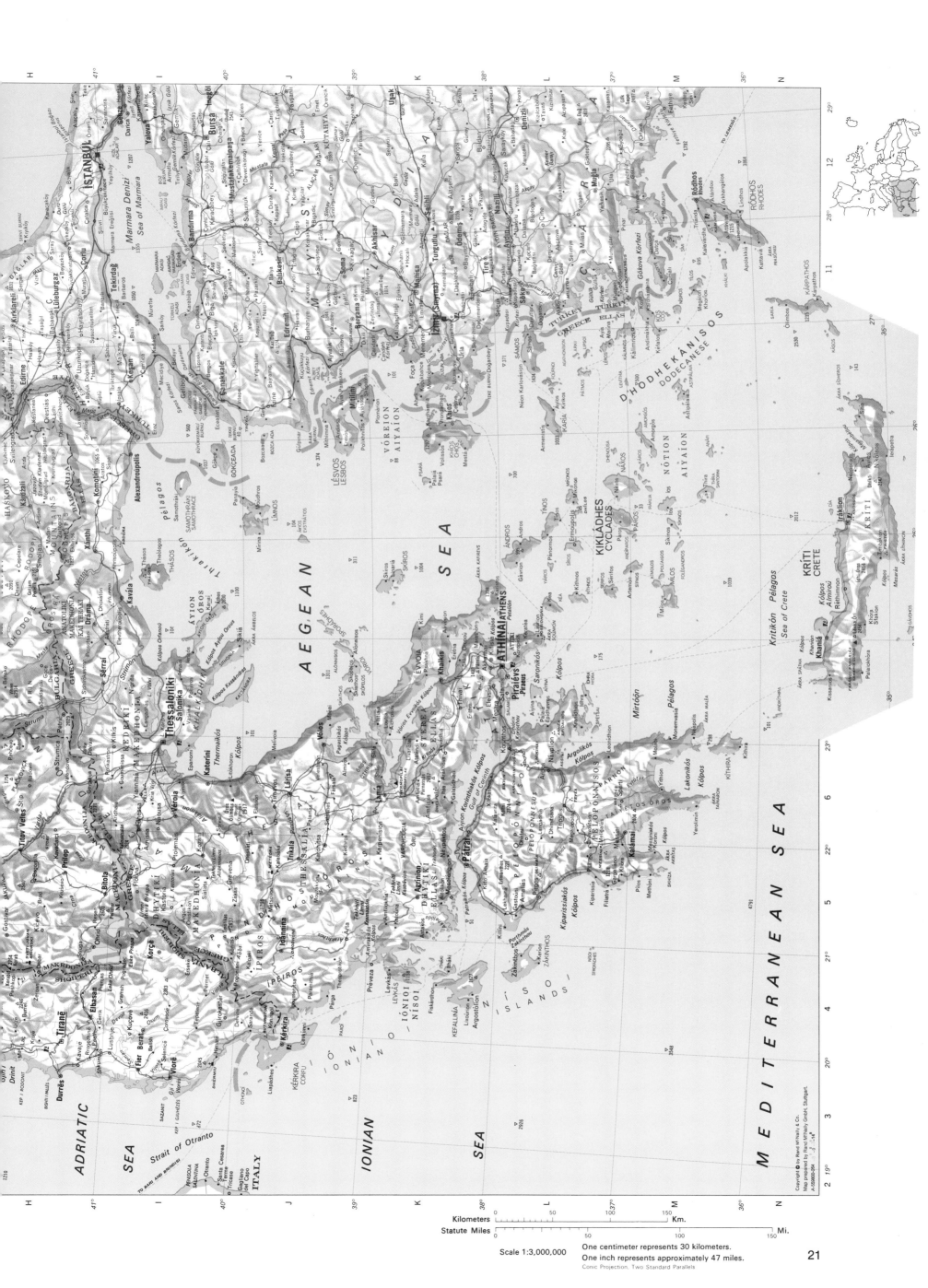

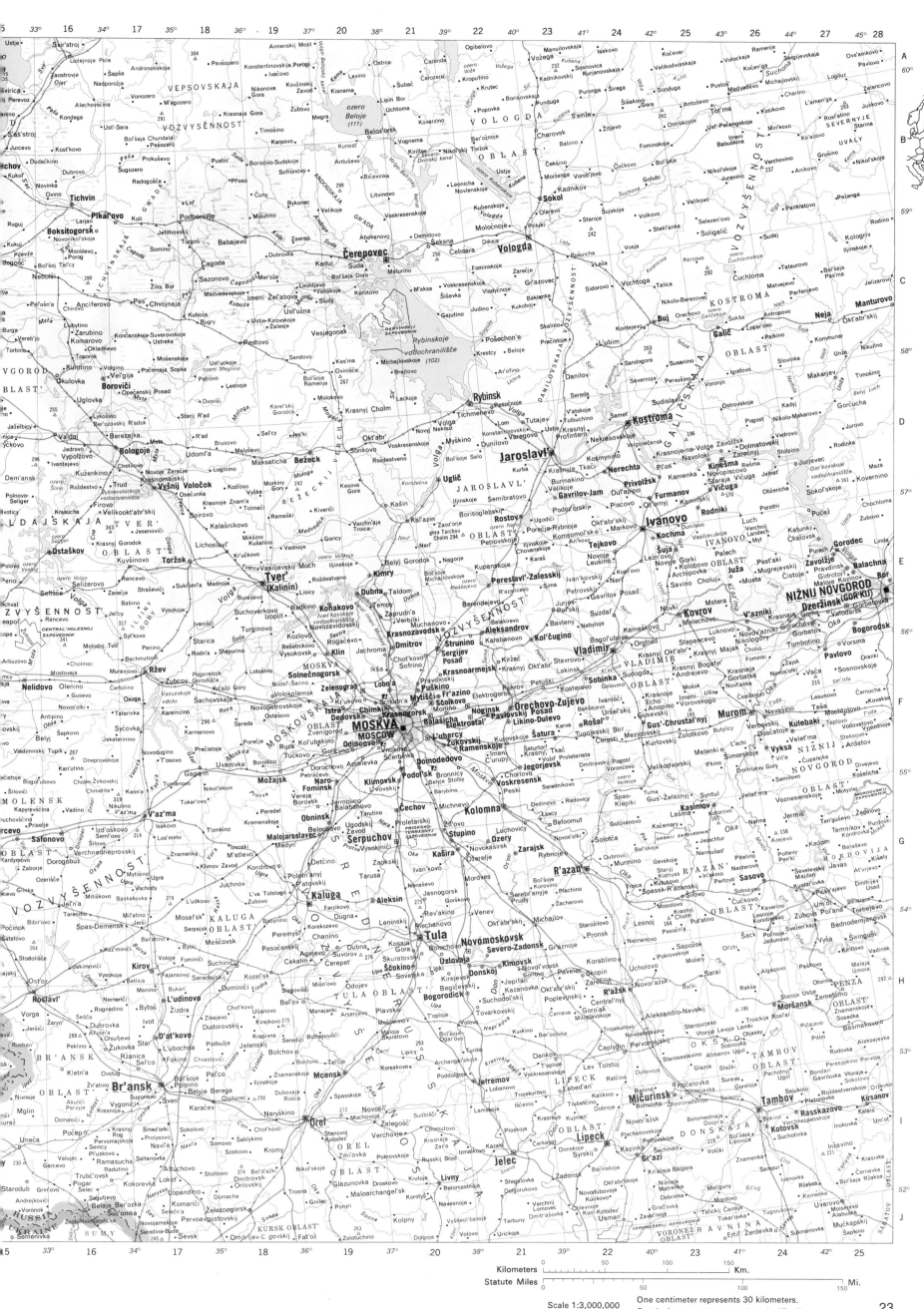

Kilometers

Statute Miles

Scale 1:3,000,000   One centimeter represents 30 kilometers.
                     One inch represents approximately 47 miles.
                     Lambert Conformal Conic Projection

23

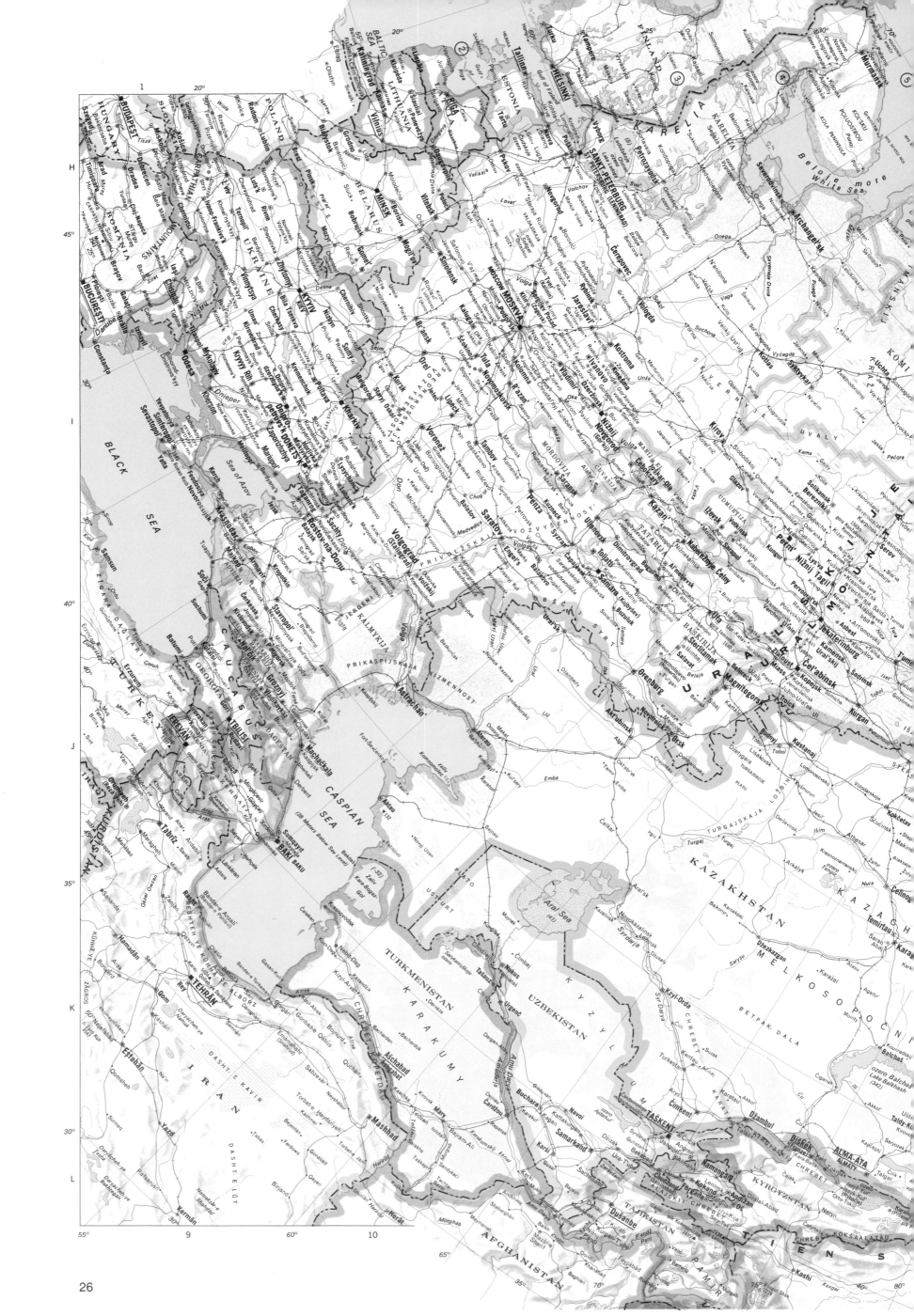

Kilometers

Statute Miles

Scale 1:12,000,000   One centimeter represents 120 kilometers.
One inch represents approximately 190 miles.
Lambert Conformal Conic Projection

Copyright © by Rand McNally & Co.
Map prepared by Esselte Map Service AB, Stockholm.
A-579594-264

Scale 1:12,000,000
One centimeter represents 120 kilometers.
One inch represents approximately 190 miles.
Lambert Conformal Conic Projection

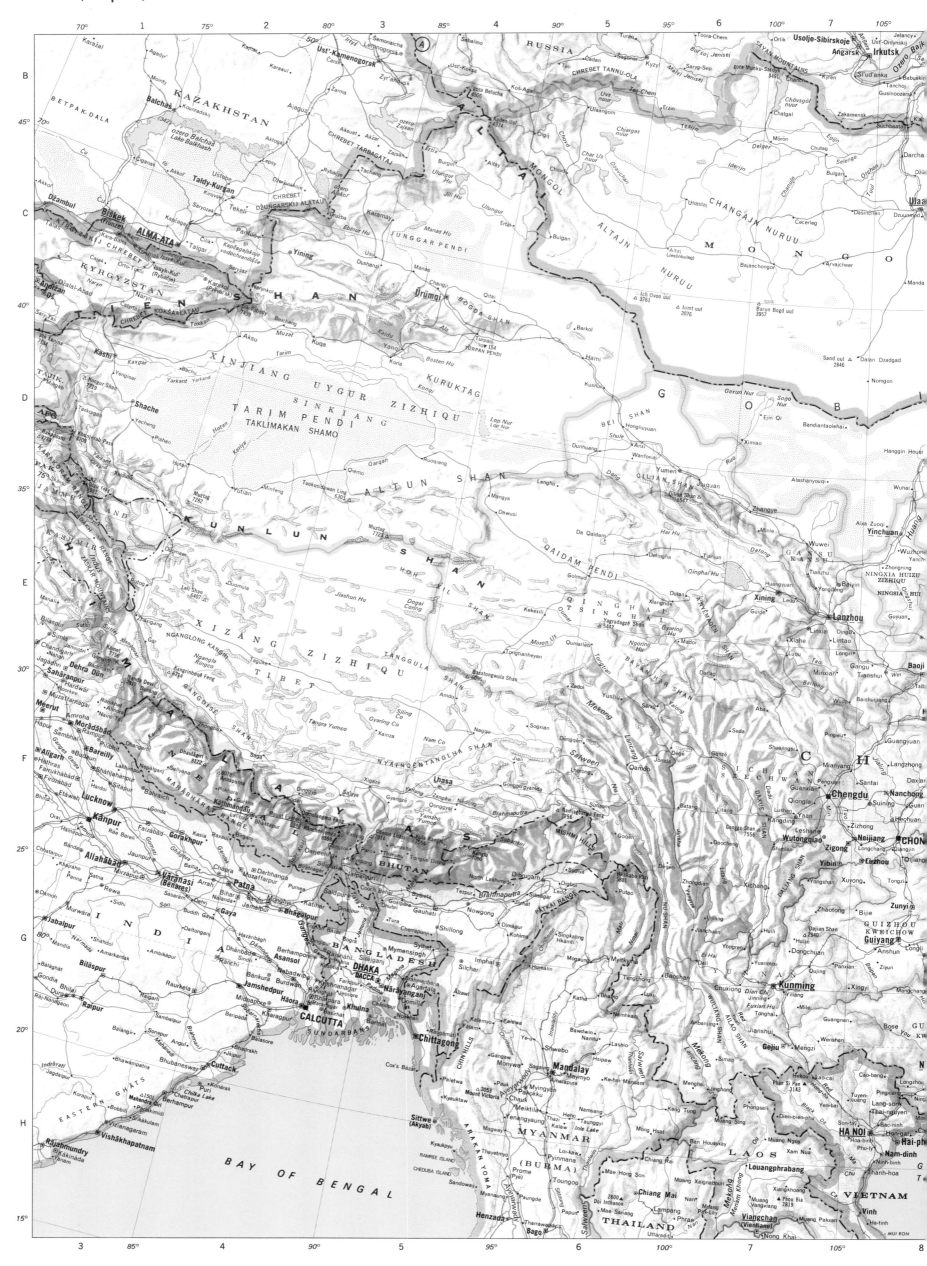

Kilometers
0   200   400   600   Km.

Statute Miles
0   200   400   600   Mi.

Scale 1:12,000,000
One centimeter represents 120 kilometers.
One inch represents approximately 190 miles.
Lambert Conformal Conic Projection

Copyright © by Rand McNally & Co.
Map prepared by Esselte Map Service AB, Stockholm.
A-569700-264

31

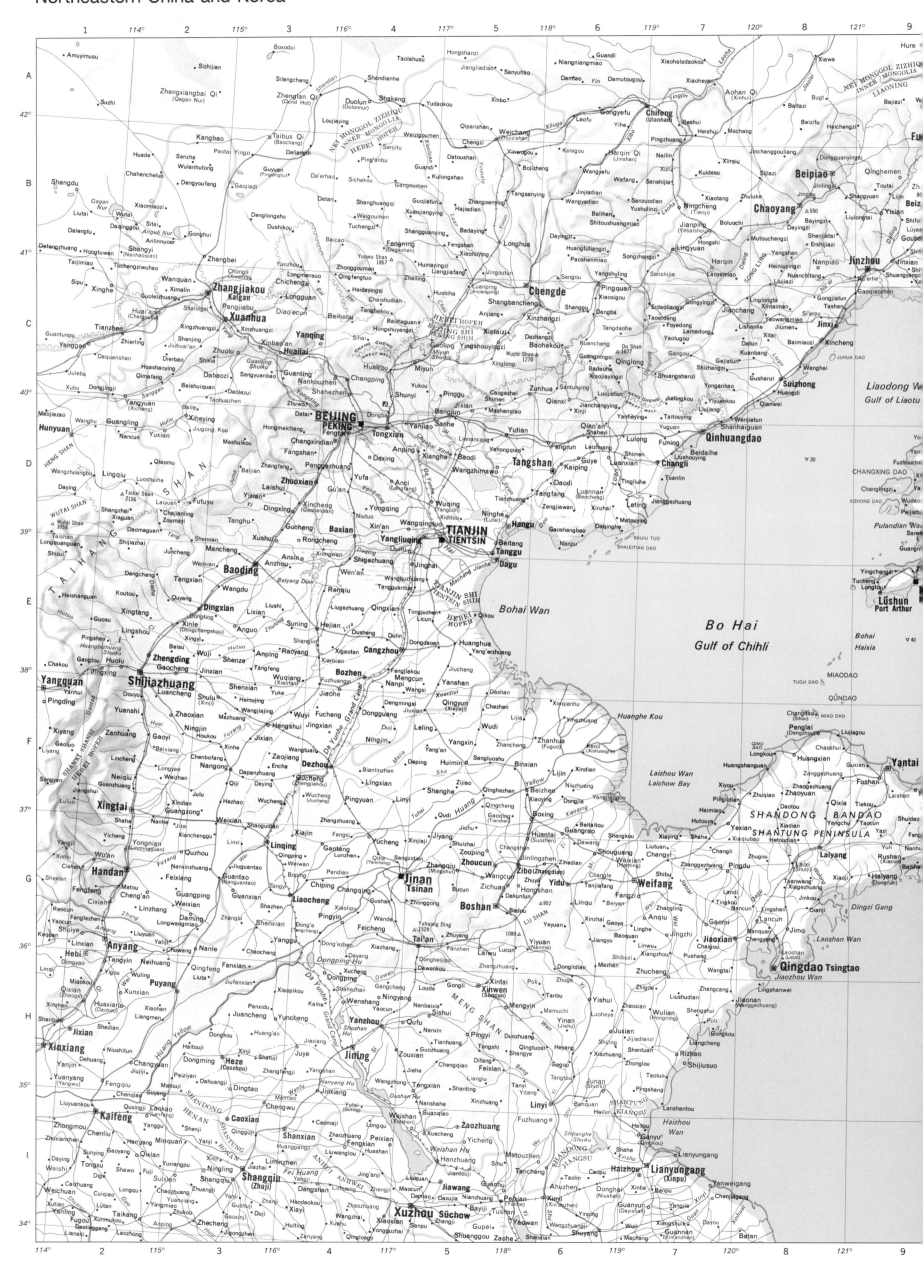

33

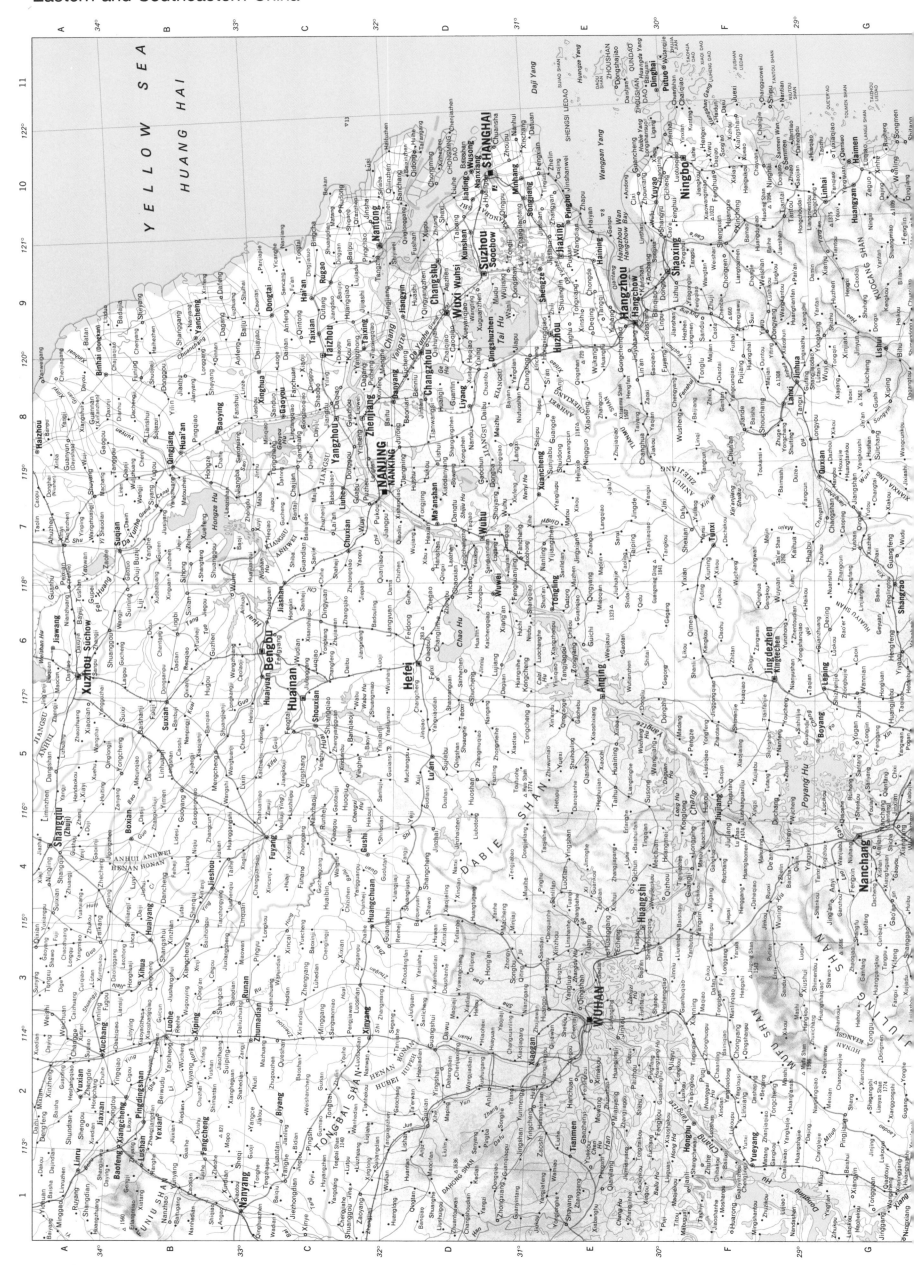

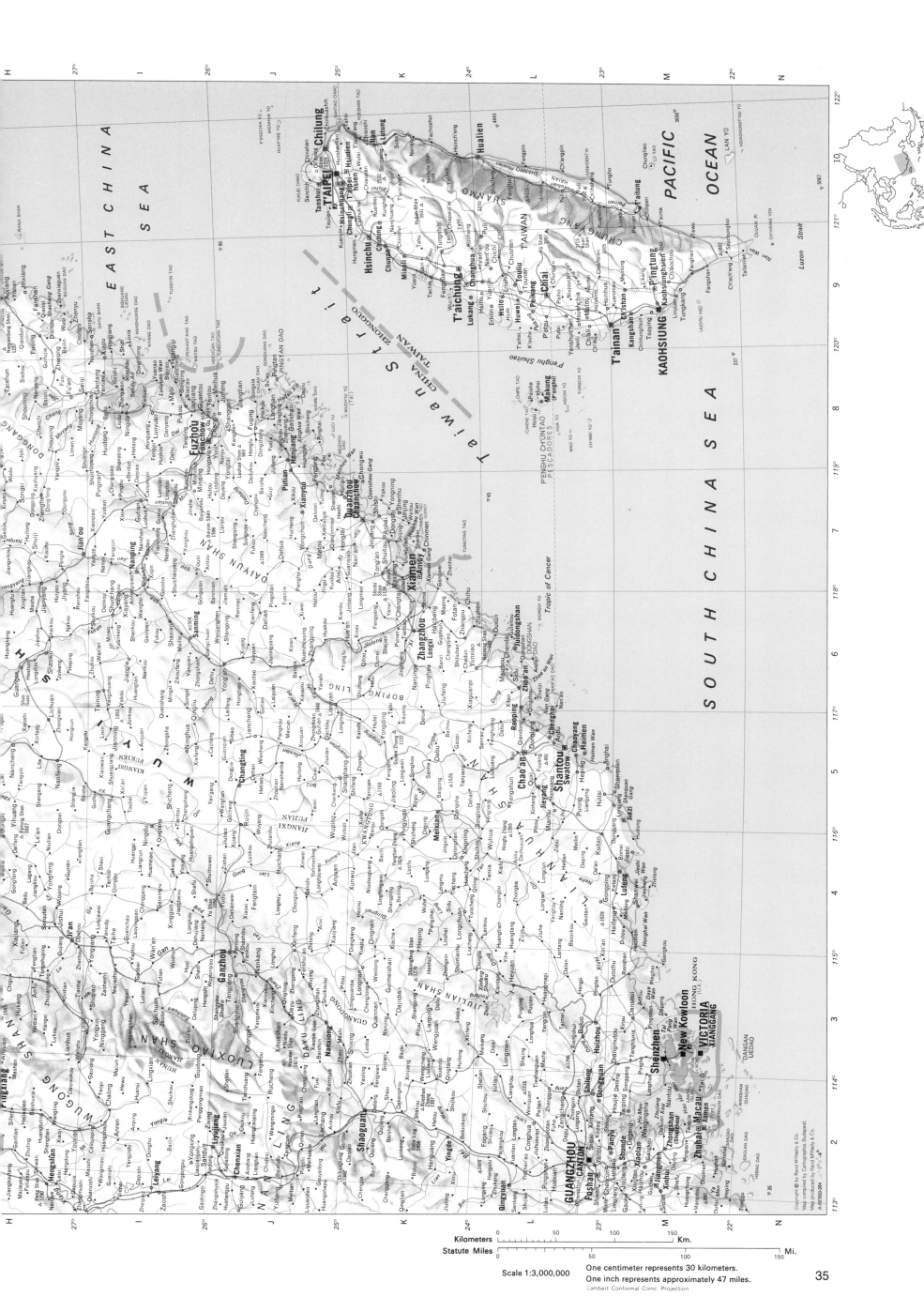

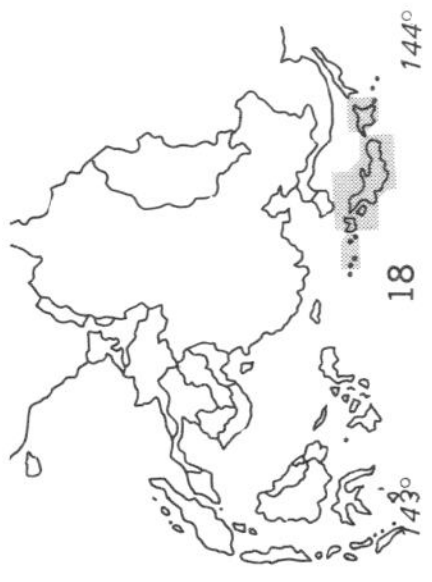

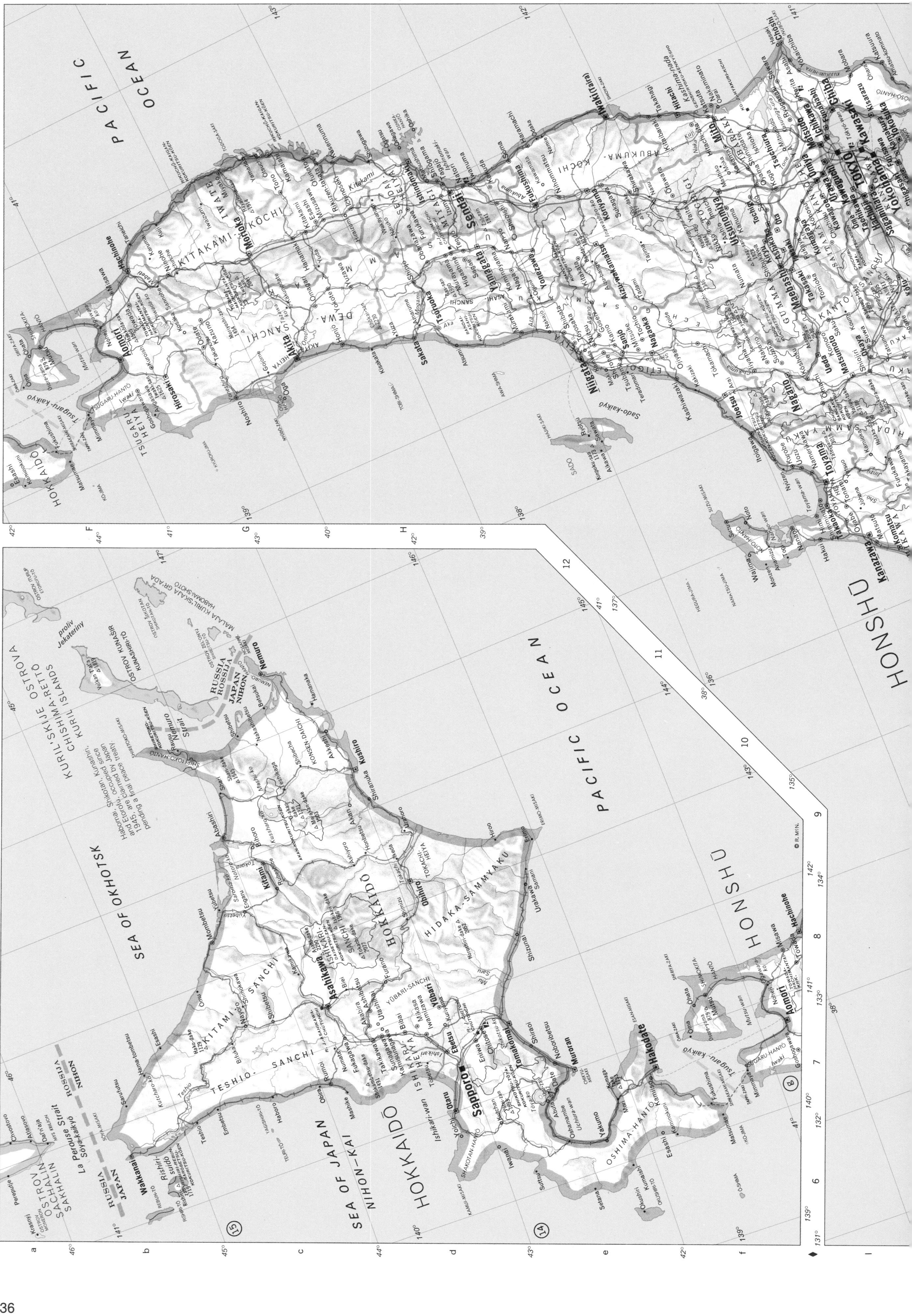

Japan

PACIFIC OCEAN

SEA OF OKHOTSK

SEA OF JAPAN
NIHON-KAI

PACIFIC OCEAN

HOKKAIDŌ

HONSHŪ

KURIL'SKIJE OSTROVA
CHISHIMA-RETTŌ
KURIL ISLANDS

proliv Jekaterdiny

RUSSIA
ROSSIJA
JAPAN
NIHON

La Perouse Strait
Soya-kaikyo
RUSSIA NIHON
JAPAN

OSTROV SACHALIN
SAKHALIN

Wakkanai

Rishiri
Rebun

Teshio-Sanchi

KITAMI-SANCHI

Asahikawa

ISHIKARI-SANCHI

Otaru
Sapporo
Ebetsu
Tomakomai
Muroran
Hakodate
OSHIMA-HANTŌ

Tsugaru-kaikyō

HIDAKA-SAMMYAKU

TOKACHI-HEIYA
Obihiro
Kushiro

Nemuro
Nemuro Strait

Aomori
Hachinohe

TSUGARU-HANTŌ

Habomai, Shikotan, Kunashir
and Etorofu occupied since Japan
since 1945, are a final peace treaty
pending a final peace treaty.

KOCHI
KITAKAMI
IWATE
Morioka
KITAKAMI-KOCHI

DEWA-SANCHI
Akita
Hirosaki
Aomori
HOKKAIDŌ
TSUGARU-HEIYA

SENDAI
Sendai
MIYAGI

YAMAGATA
Yamagata
Yonezawa

Niigata
ECHIGO
Sado-kaikyō
SADO
Sakata
Tsuruoka

Nagaoka
Sanjō

Joetsu

Toyama
Nagano
Matsumoto
Uda
KANTŌ
GUMMA
Maebashi
Takasaki
Utsunomiya
Ashikaga
Ōta
Fukushima
Koriyama
Aizuwakamatsu
ABUKUMA-KOCHI
Hitachi

Chōshi
Chiba
TOKYO
Kawasaki
Yokohama
Yokosuka
Ichikawa

HONSHŪ

Kanazawa
Komatsu

PACIFIC OCEAN

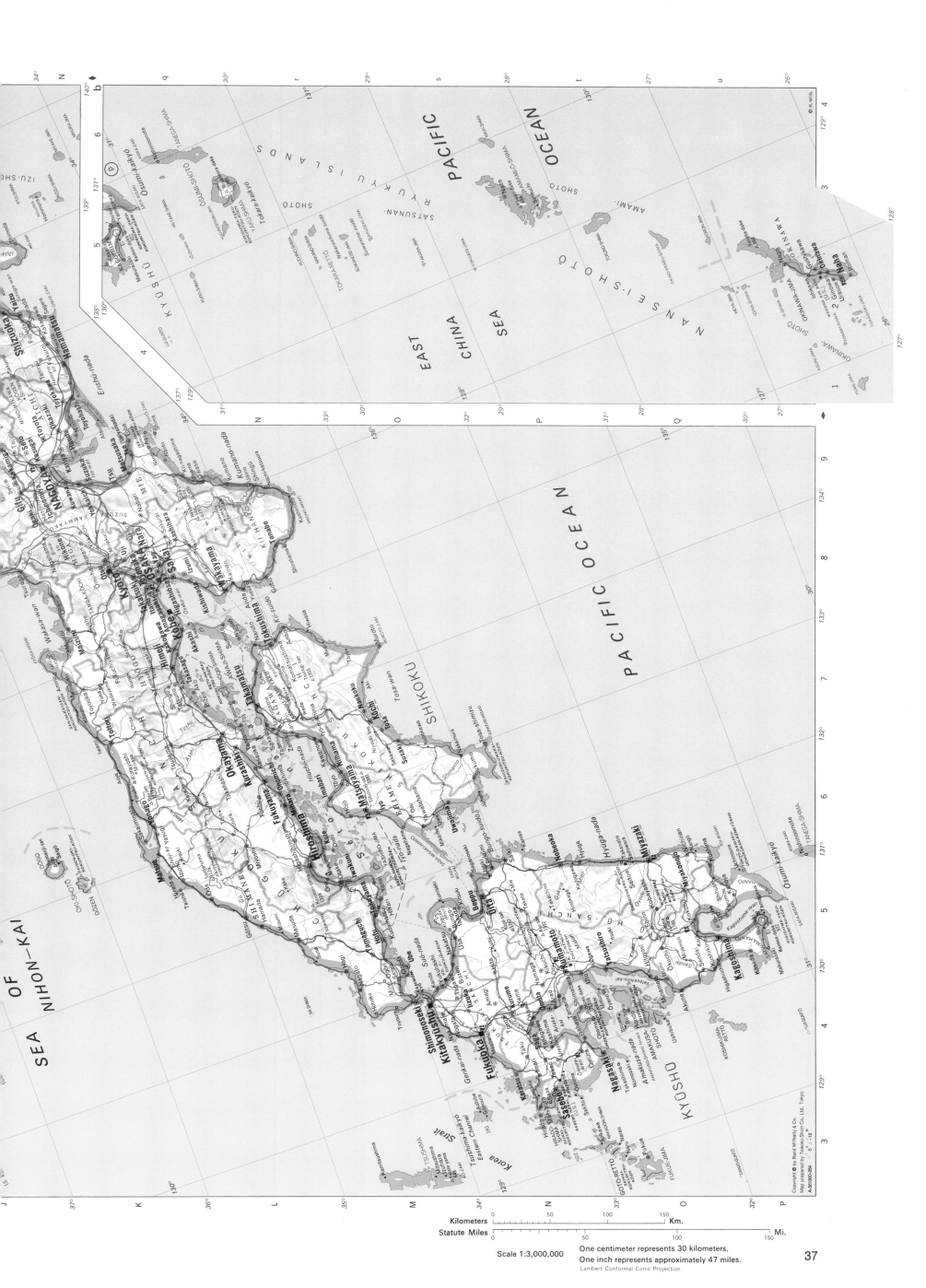

SEA OF NIHON-KAI

PACIFIC OCEAN

EAST CHINA SEA

RYUKYU ISLANDS

PACIFIC OCEAN

KYŪSHŪ

SHIKOKU

NAGOYA
OSAKA
Kyōto
Kōbe
Himeji
Okayama
Hiroshima
Tottori
Matsue
Shimonoseki
Kitakyūshū
Fukuoka
Sasebo
Nagasaki
Kumamoto
Kagoshima
Miyazaki
Beppu
Ōita
Matsuyama
Takamatsu
Tokushima
Kōchi
Tokushima
Wakayama
Ube
Yamaguchi

OKINAWA
Naha

Kilometers 0 50 100 150 Km.

Statute Miles 0 50 100 150 Mi.

Scale 1:3,000,000

One centimeter represents 30 kilometers.
One inch represents approximately 47 miles.

Lambert Conformal Conic Projection

Copyright © by Rand McNally & Co.
Map prepared by Teikoku-Shoin Co., Ltd., Tokyo.
A-561900-264

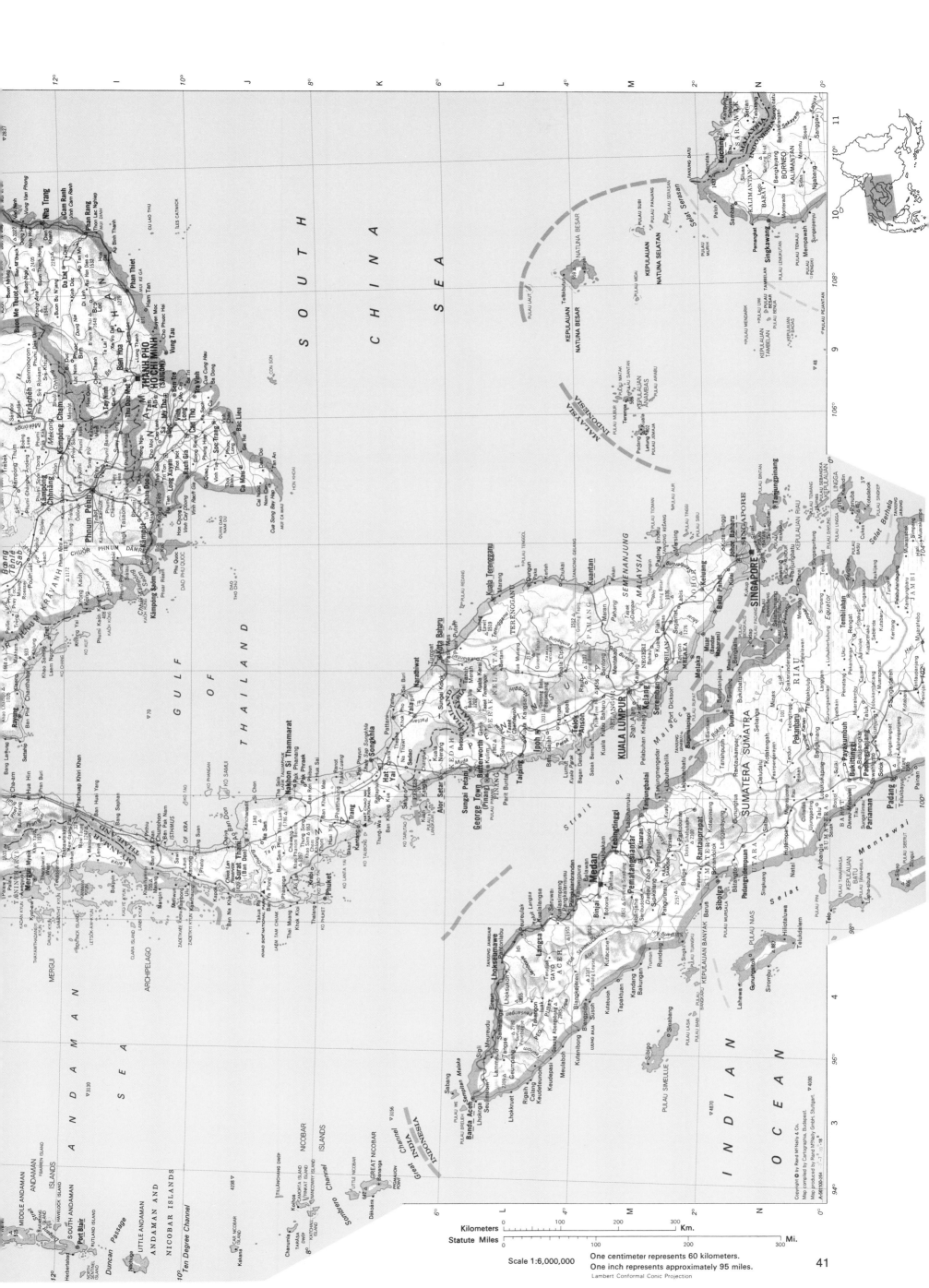

Kilometers
0   200   400   600   Km.

Statute Miles
0   200   400   600   Mi.

Scale 1:12,000,000
One centimeter represents 120 kilometers.
One inch represents approximately 190 miles.
Lambert Conformal Conic Projection

43

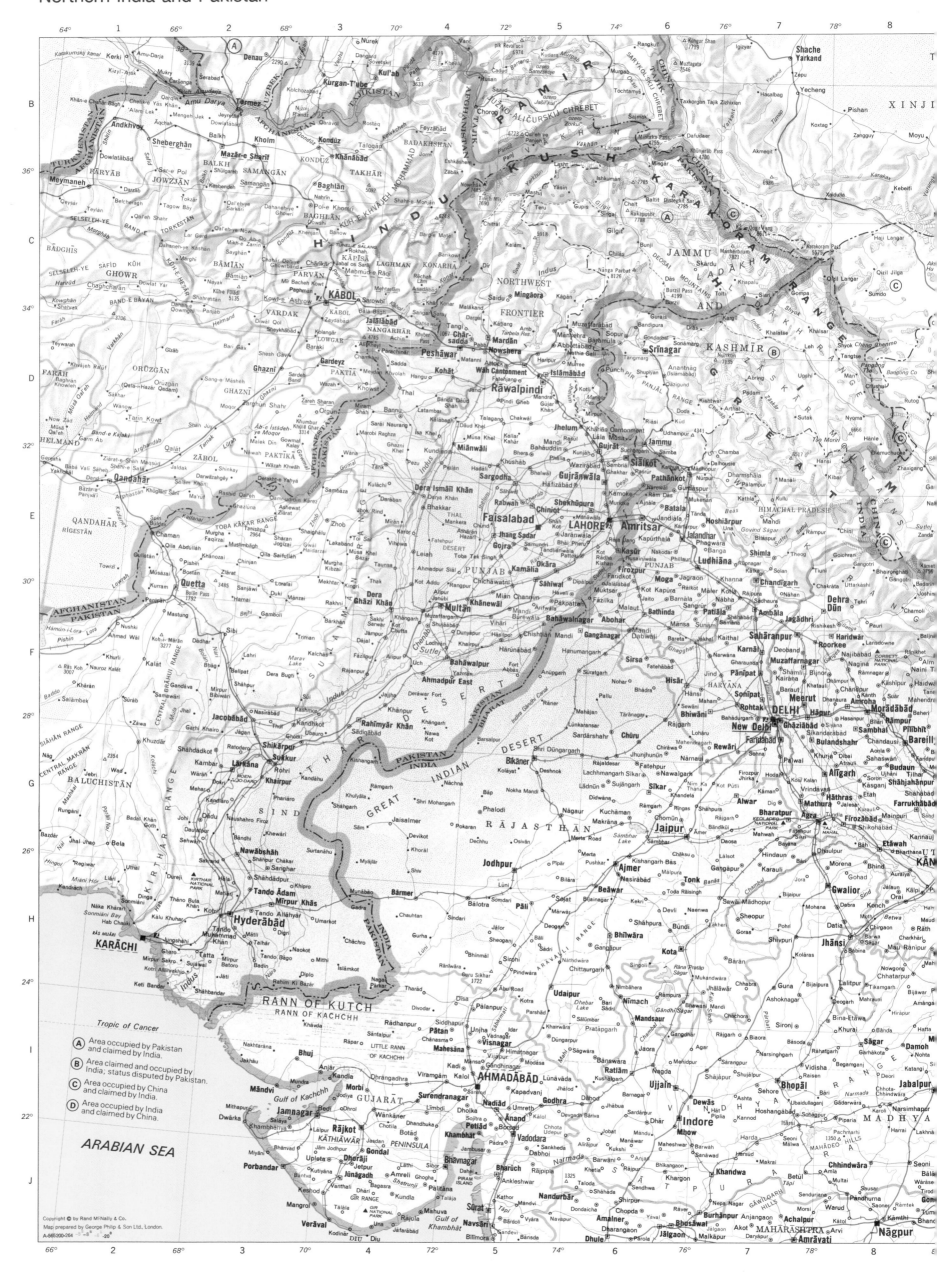

BAY OF BENGAL

Kilometers
Statute Miles

One centimeter represents 60 kilometers.
One inch represents approximately 95 miles.

Scale 1:6,000,000
Lambert Conformal Conic Projection

45

Southern India and Sri Lanka

Kilometers 0 100 200 300 Km.

Statute Miles 0 100 200 300 Mi.

Scale 1:6,000,000

One centimeter represents 60 kilometers.
One inch represents approximately 95 miles.
Lambert Conformal Conic Projection

Copyright © by Rand McNally & Co.
Map prepared by George Philip & Son Ltd., London.
A-565300-264

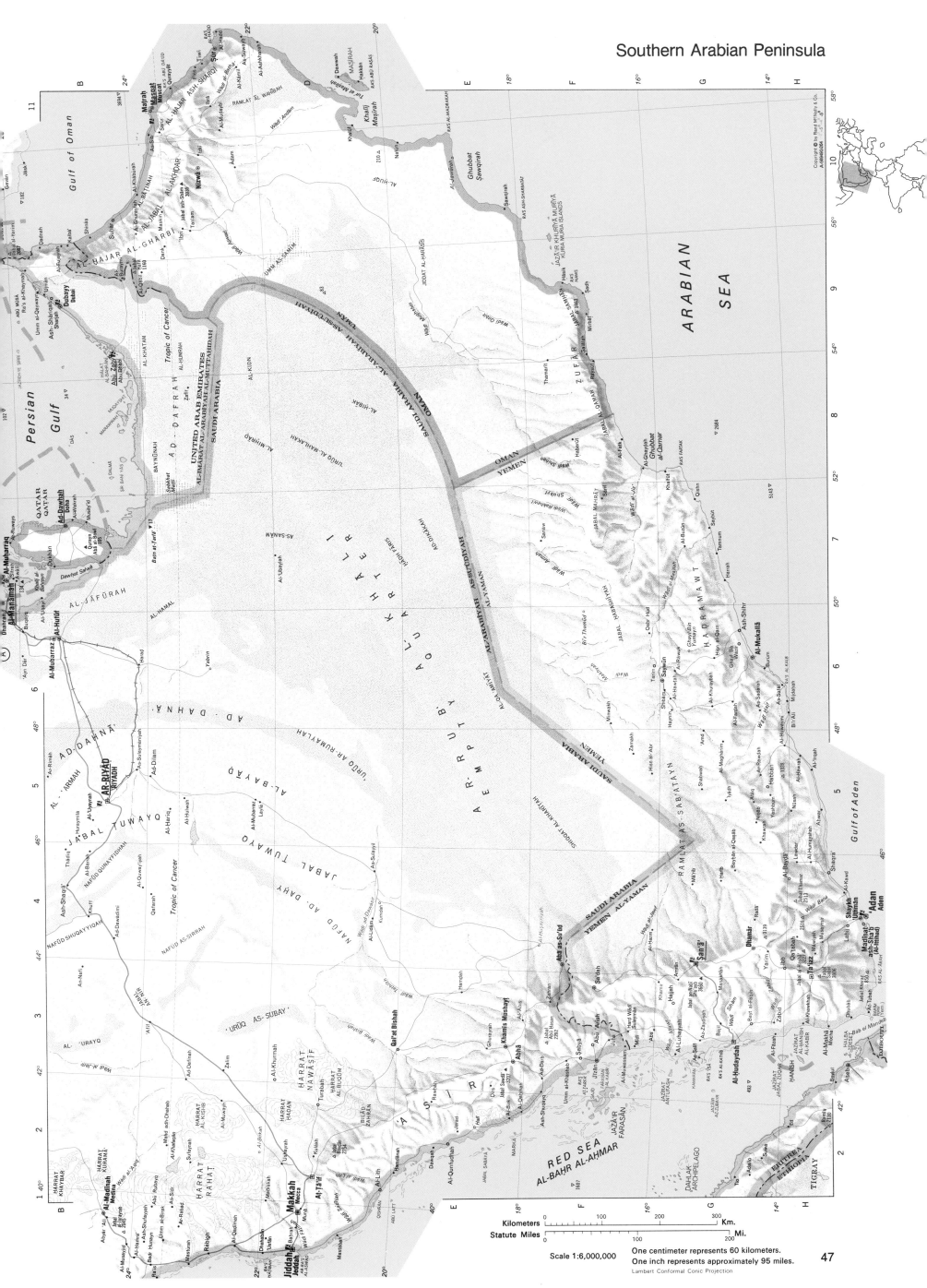

Southern Arabian Peninsula

ARABIAN SEA

Gulf of Oman

Persian Gulf

RUB' AL KHALI

AD-DAHNĀ'

Gulf of Aden

RED SEA
AL-BAḤR AL-AḤMAR

Makkah Mecca

Al-Madīnah Medina

AR-RIYĀḌ RIYADH

Ṣan'ā'

'Adan Aden

Kilometers   100   200   300 Km.
Statute Miles   100   200 Mi.

Scale 1:6,000,000

One centimeter represents 60 kilometers.
One inch represents approximately 95 miles.

Lambert Conformal Conic Projection

47

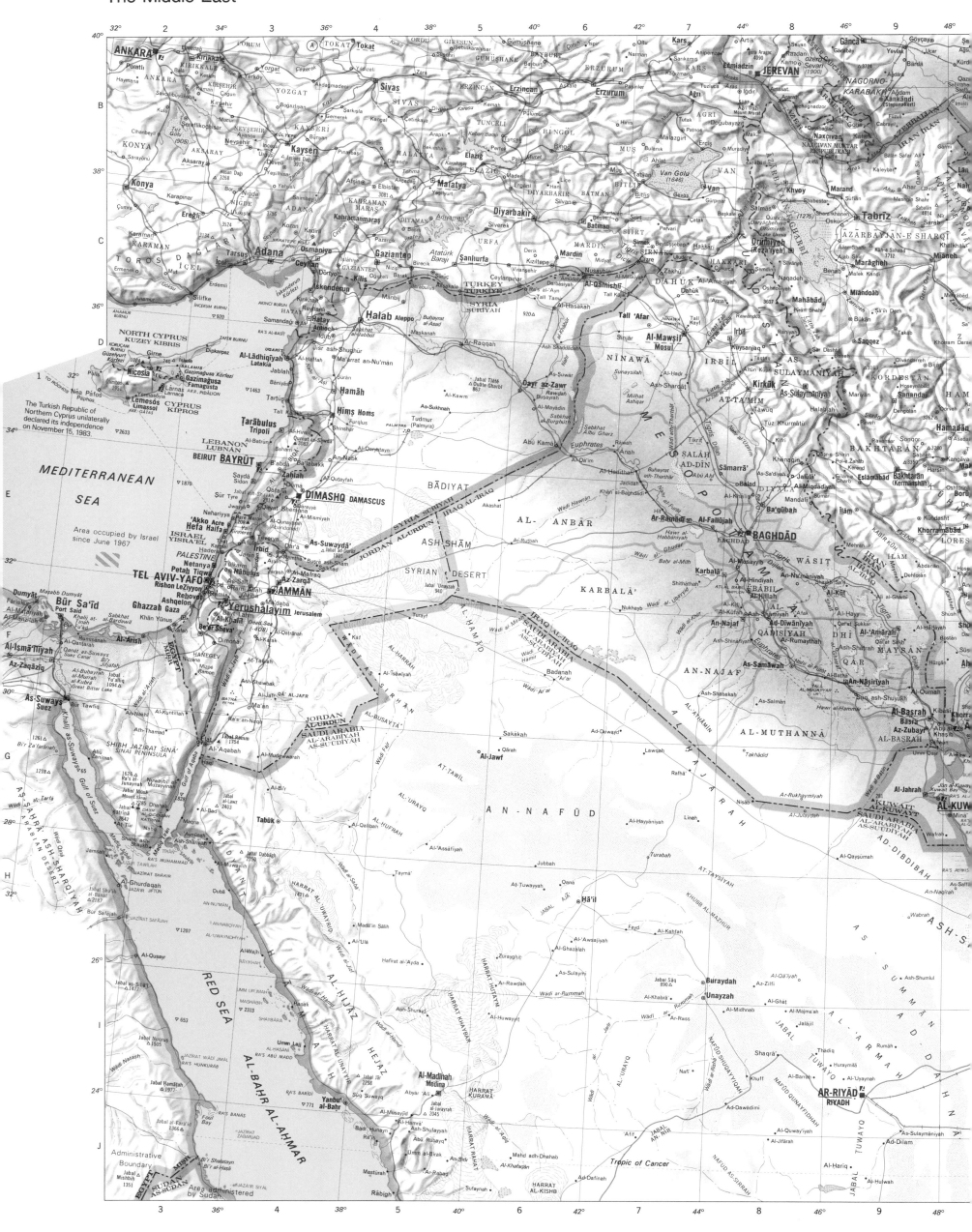

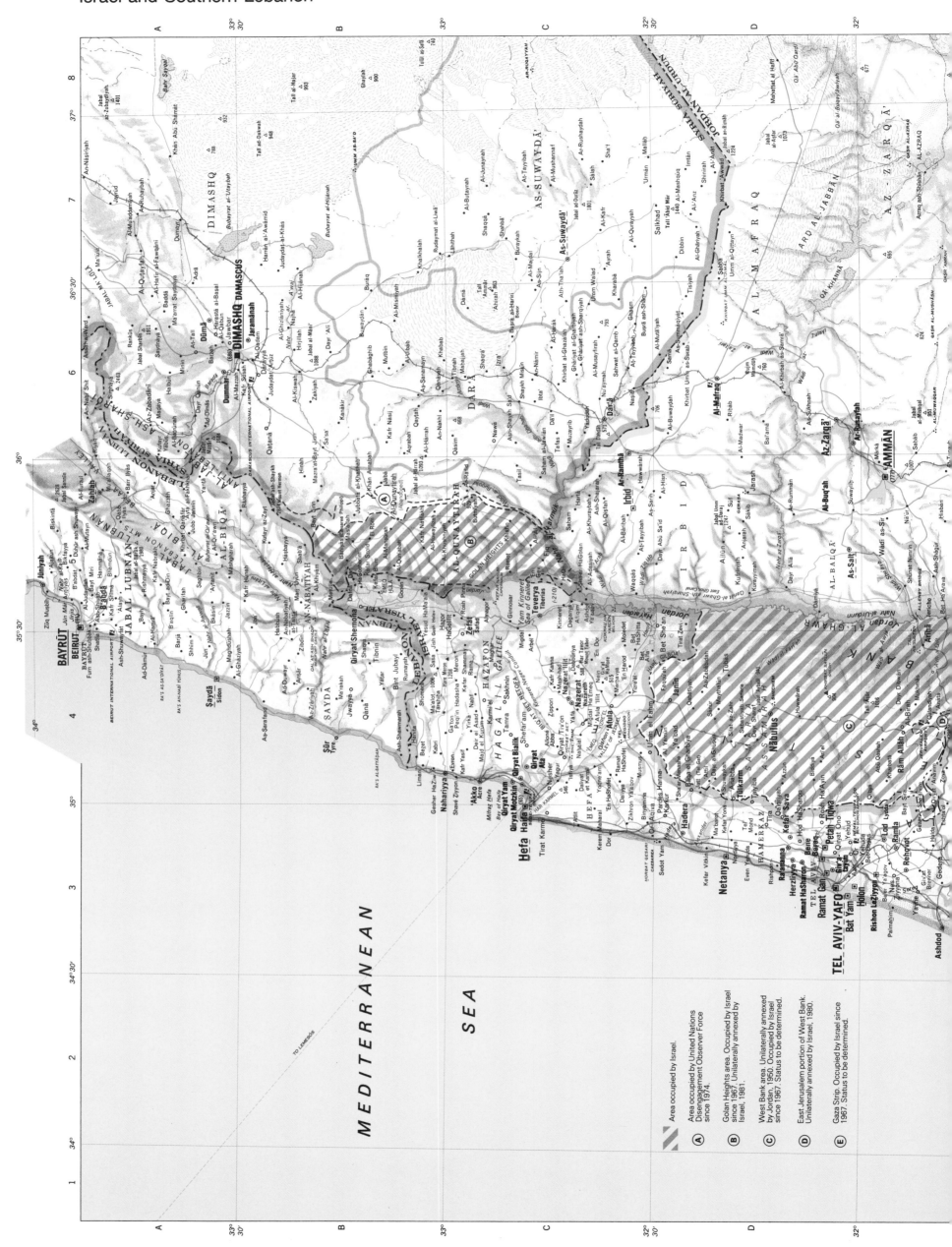

Israel and Southern Lebanon

Area occupied by Israel.

(A) Area occupied by United Nations
Disengagement Observer Force
since 1974.

(B) Golan Heights area. Occupied by Israel
since 1967. Unilaterally annexed by
Israel, 1981.

(C) West Bank area. Unilaterally annexed
by Jordan, 1950. Occupied by Israel
since 1967. Status to be determined.

(D) East Jerusalem portion of West Bank.
Unilaterally annexed by Israel, 1980.

(E) Gaza Strip. Occupied by Israel since
1967. Status to be determined.

Kilometers |⊢⊢⊢⊢⊢⊢| 0 10 20 30 40 50 Km.

Statute Miles ⊢⊢⊢⊢⊢| 0 10 20 30 40 50 Mi.

One centimeter represents 10 kilometers.
One inch represents approximately 16 miles.

Scale 1:1,000,000

Lambert Conformal Conic Projection

51

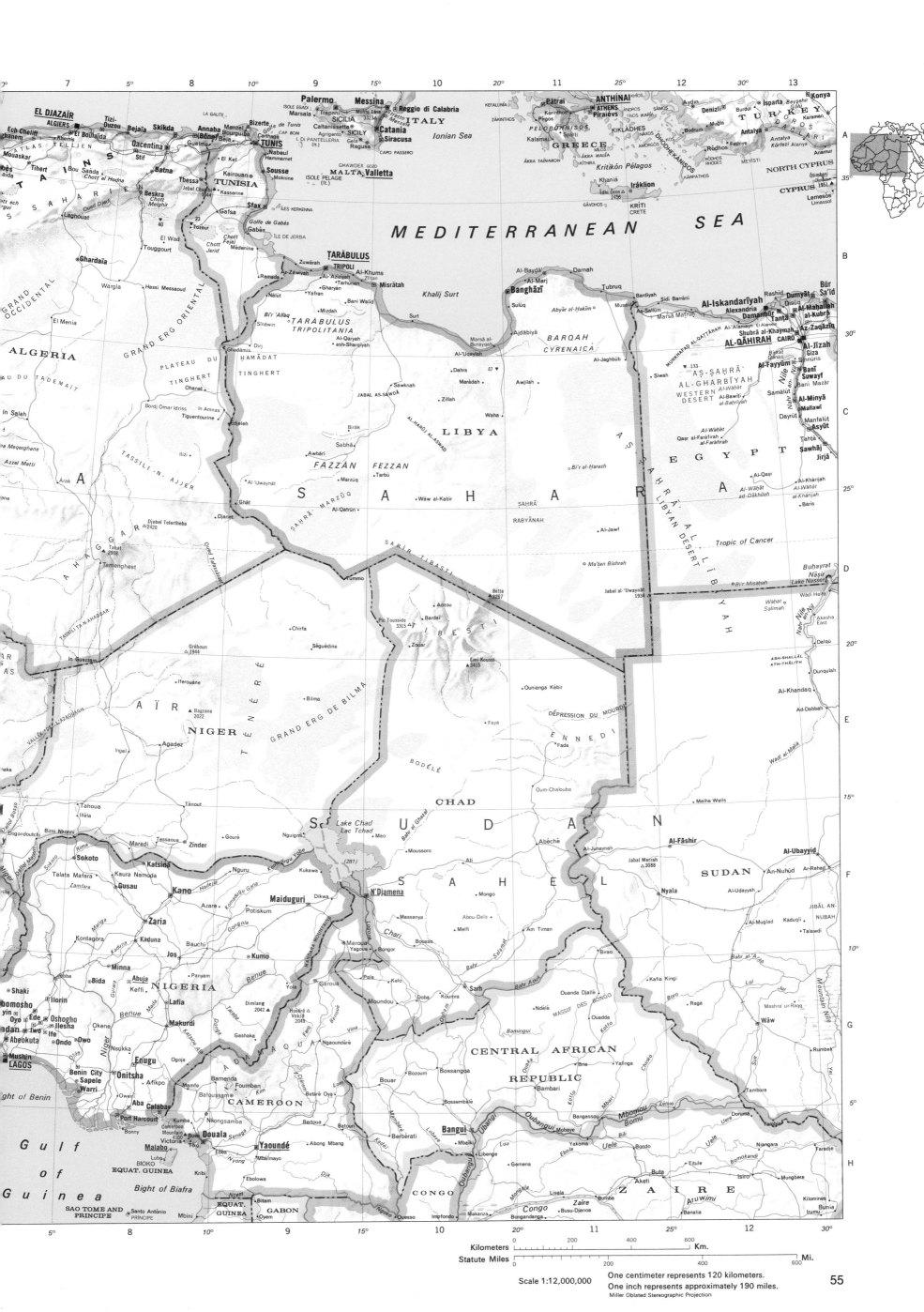

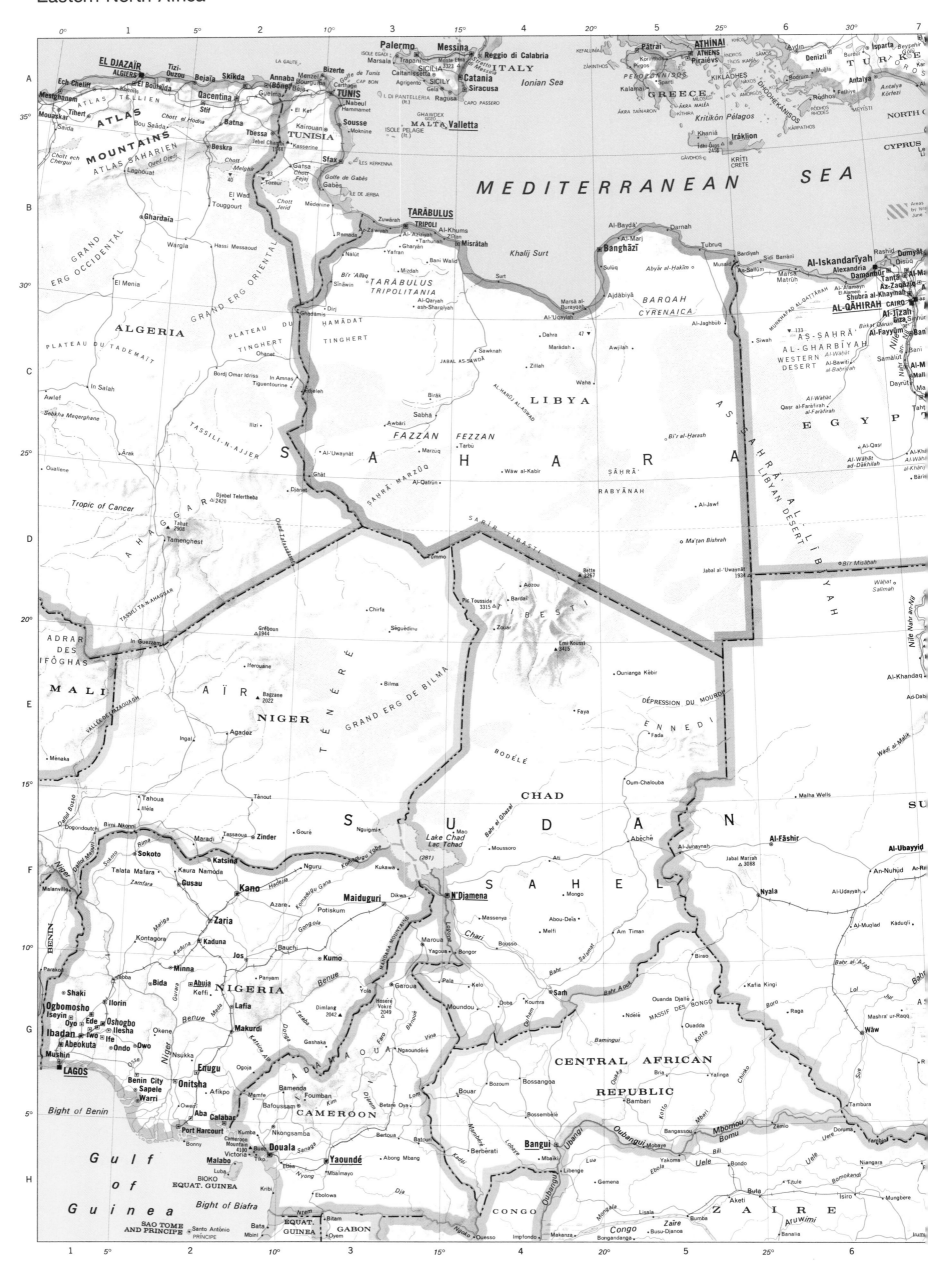

Copyright ○ by Rand McNally & Co.
Map prepared by Esselte Map Service AB, Stockholm.
A-589391 -264   -24°

Kilometers 0   200   400   600   Km.
Statute Miles 0   200   400   600   Mi.

Scale 1:12,000,000
One centimeter represents 120 kilometers.
One inch represents approximately 190 miles.
Miller Oblated Stereographic Projection

Map labels

Latitude/Longitude (top): 35° 7 40° 8 45° 9 50° 10 55° 11

Row labels (right): B C D E F G

SOMALIA
Baraawe
Lach Dera
Almadow
Afmadow
Mado Gashi
Jilib
Jamaame
Kismaayo
Jumboo
Buur Gaabo
Garissa
Kolbio
Bura
Kipini
Pate Island
Lamu
Malindi

Equator

KENYA
NAIROBI
Nakuru
Nanyuki
Meru
Isiolo
Eldoret
Kitale
Mount Elgon
Kisumu
Kericho
Kisii
Thika
Machakos
Kitui
Konza
Magadi
Mount Kilimanjaro 5895
Mount Meru 4565
Arusha
Moshi
Voi
Tsavo
Galana
Mombasa
Mackinnon Road
Same
Lushoto
Wete
PEMBA
Tanga
Korogwe
Pangani

INDIAN OCEAN

MASAI STEPPE
SERENGETI PLAIN
Lake Natron
Lake Manyara
Lake Eyasi
Mwadui
Shinyanga
Singida
Kondoa
Mpwapwa
Wami
Morogoro
Dodoma
Zanzibar
ZANZIBAR
Bagamoyo
DAR ES SALAAM
TANZANIA
Iringa
Kilosa
Mikumi
MAFIA ISLAND
Kilindoni
Sao Hill
Mahenge
Great Ruaha
Utete
Kilwa Kivinje
Njombe
Rungwa
Matandu
Liwale
Lindi
Mikindani
Mtwara
CABO DELGADO
Masasi
Songea
Tunduru
Nachingwea
Palma
Ruvuma
Mocímboa da Praia

SEYCHELLES
PRASLIN ISLAND
LA DIGUE
SILHOUETTE
Victoria
MAHÉ ISLAND
AMIRANTE ISLANDS (Sey.)
ÎLE DESROCHES (Sey.)
PLATTE ISLAND (Sey.)
ALPHONSE ISLAND (Sey.)
COETIVY ISLAND (Sey.)

PROVIDENCE ISLAND (Sey.)
ALDABRA ISLAND (Sey.)
COSMOLEDO I. (Sey.)
SAINT PIERRE ISLAND (Sey.)
CERF ISLAND (Sey.)
ASSUMPTION ISLAND (Sey.)
ASTOVE ISLAND (Sey.)
FARQUHAR GROUP (Sey.)
AGALEGA ISLANDS (Mauritius)

MALAWI
Lake Nyasa
Lake Malawi
Karonga
Livingstonia
Mzuzu
Nkhata Bay
LIKOMA
Lichinga
Lilongwe
Mangochi
Lake Chilwa
Zomba
Blantyre
Spitwa 3002
Mulanje
Thyolo

COMOROS
Moroni
NJAZIDJA
Mutsamudu
Fomboni
NZWANI
MWALI
MAYOTTE (Fr.)
Dzaoudzi
ARCHIPEL DES COMORES
ÎLES GLORIEUSES (Fr.)
CAP D'AMBRE
CAP SAINT-SÉBASTIEN
Antsiranana
NOSY MITSIO
NOSY BE
Hell-Ville
Ambilobe
Vohimarina
Ambanja
Ambato
MASSIF DU TSARATANANA
Maromokotro 2876
Sambava
NOSY LAVA
Analalava
Bealanana
Doany
Andapa
Antalaha

MOZAMBIQUE
Ibo
Quissanga
Pemba
Montepuez
Maúa
Namapa
Lúrio
Nacala
Nampula
Moçambique
Mogincual
Angoche
ILHA ANGOCHE
Quinga
Moma
Pebane
Mocuba
Namacurra
Quelimane
Sena
Vila Fontes
Zambeze
Dondo
Beira
Nova Sofala
Mocímboa
Bandula
Manica
Chimoio
Inhaminga
Chinde

Baie de Narinda
Befandriana
Port-Berge
Antsohihy
Sofia
Mandritsara
Maroantsetra
PRESQU'ÎLE DE MASOALA
CAP EST
NOSY BORAHA
Ambodifototra
Andilamena
Mampikony
Mananara
Analalava

MADAGASCAR
Mahajanga
CAP SAINT-ANDRÉ
Lac Kinkony
Soalala
Marovoay
Tsaratanana
Maevatanana
Helodranon' i Mahajamba
NOSY CHESTERFIELD (Madg.)
Besalampy
ÎLE JUAN DE NOVA (Fr.)
Tambohorano
Morafenobe
Maintirano
NOSY BARREN
Andriamena
Lac Alaotra
Fenoarivo Atsinanana
ANTANANARIVO
Ankazobe
Tsiroanomandidy
Ankavandra
Vohibinany
Toamasina
Ambatondrazaka
Bela
Tsiribihina
Miandrivazo
ANKARATRA
Ambatolampy
Vatomandry
Antsirabe
Belo
Mahabo
Malaimbandy
Mahanoro
Morondava
Ambositra
Nosy Varika
Mandabe
Manja
Mananjary
Fianarantsoa
Morombe
Mangoky
Beroroha
Ankazoabo
Ambalavao
Pic Boby 2658
Manakara
Ihosy
Toliara
Betroka
Farafangana
Vangaindrano
Betioky
Midongy Sud
Ampanihy
Bekily
Androka
Tsihombe
Ambovombe
Faradofay
CAP SAINTE-MARIE

Tropic of Capricorn

ÎLE TROMELIN (Fr.)
Port Louis
Curepipe
Mahébourg
MAURITIUS
Le Port
Saint-Paul
Saint-Denis
Saint-Pierre
RÉUNION
MASCARENE ISLANDS

BASSAS DA INDIA (Fr.)
ILHA DO BAZARUTO
PONTA SÃO SEBASTIÃO
Vilanculos
ÎLE EUROPA (Fr.)
CAP SAINT-VINCENT
Nova Mambone
Bartolomeu Dias
PONTA DA BARRA FALSA
Massinga
PONTA DA BARRA
Inhambane
Maxixe
Funhalouro
Morrumbene
Manjacaze
Inharrime
Xai-Xai

INDIAN OCEAN

Mozambique Channel
Betsiboka

Copyright © by Rand McNally & Co.
Map prepared by Esselte Map Service AB, Stockholm.
A-589200-264

Latitude/Longitude (bottom): 35° 7 40° 8 45° 9 50° 10 55° 11 60°

Kilometers   0   200   400   600   Km.
Statute Miles   0   200   400   600   Mi.

Scale 1:12,000,000   One centimeter represents 120 kilometers.
One inch represents approximately 190 miles.
Miller Oblated Stereographic Projection

59

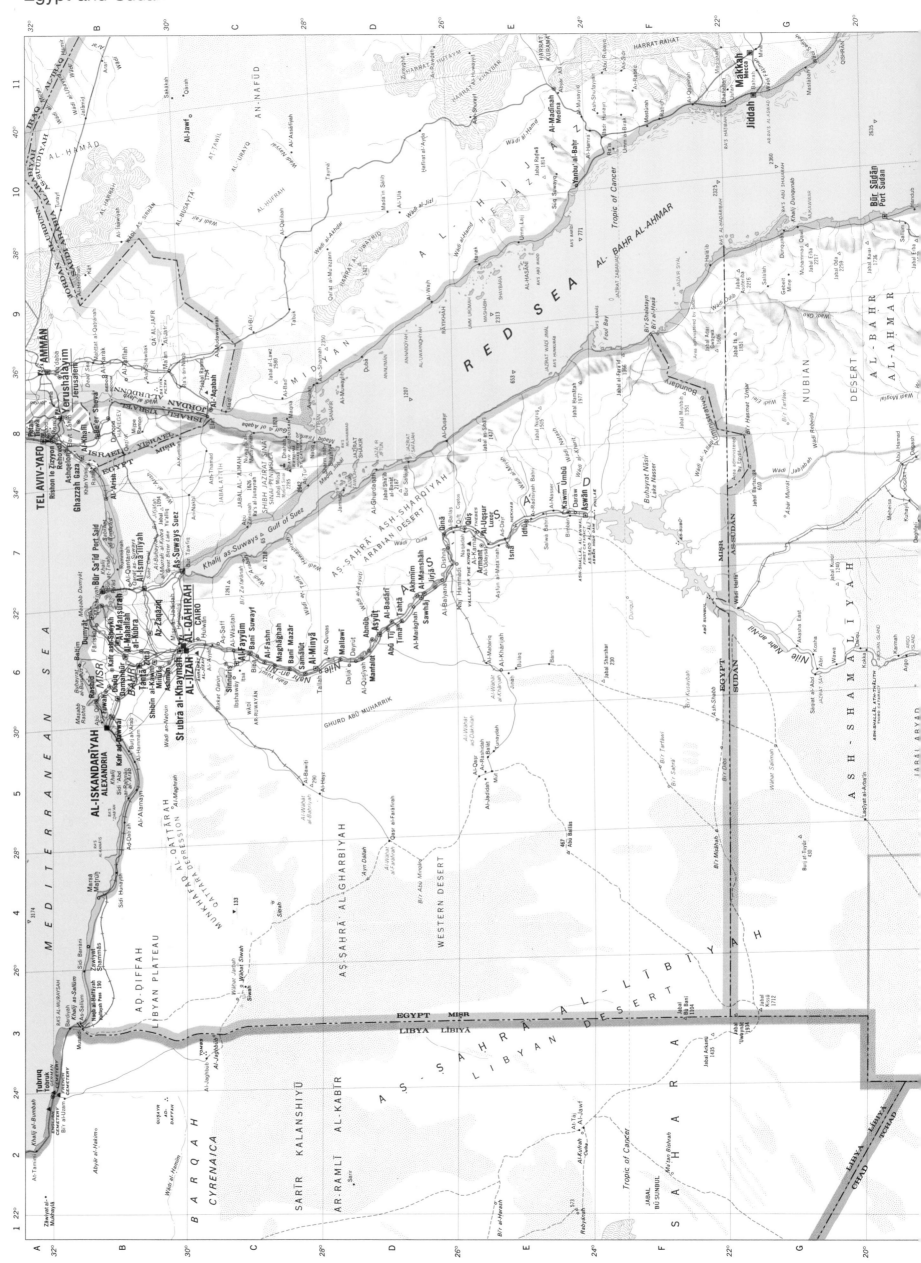

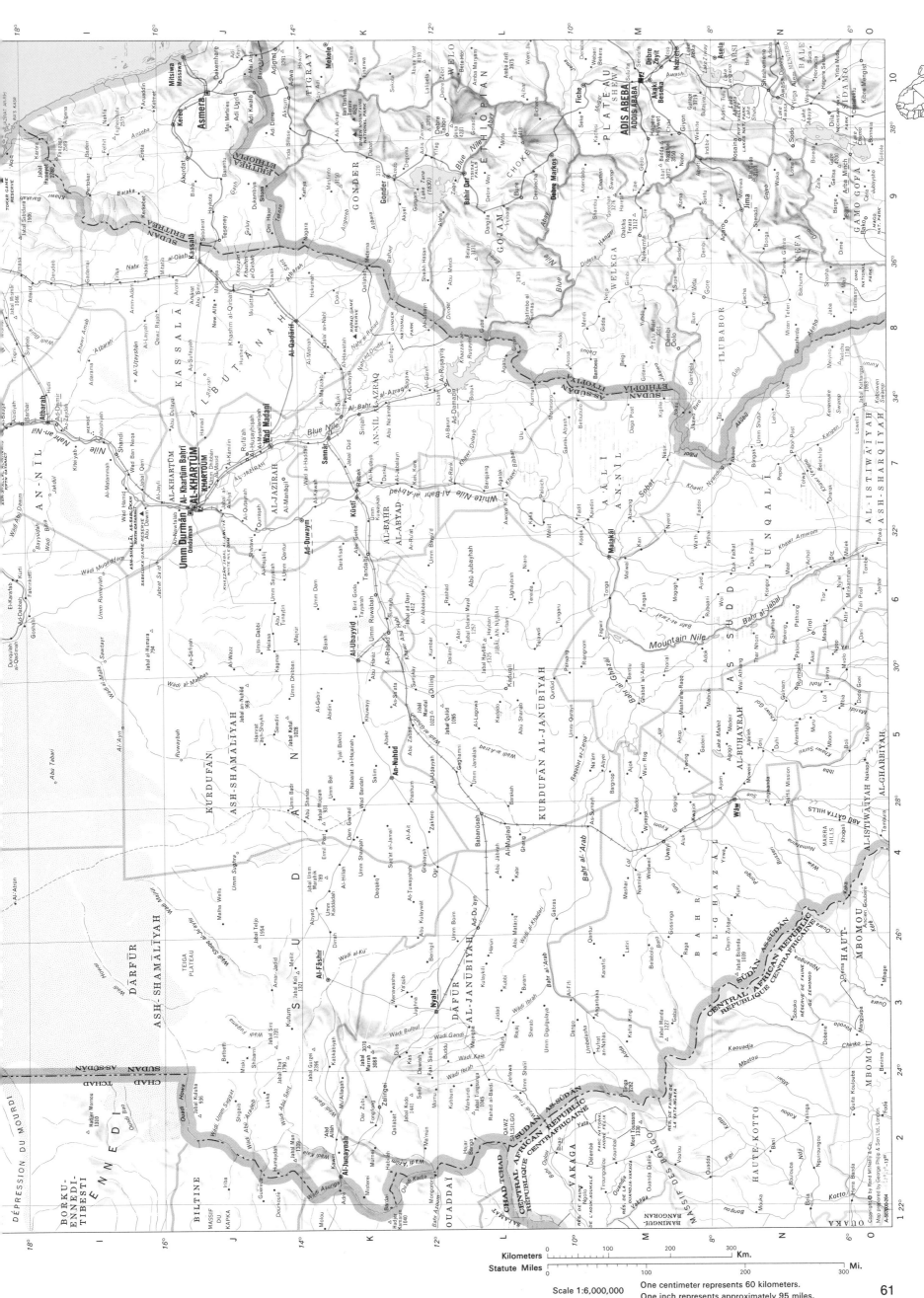

Kilometers
0 100 200 300 Km.

Statute Miles
0 100 200 300 Mi.

Scale 1:6,000,000

One centimeter represents 60 kilometers.
One inch represents approximately 95 miles.

Lambert Azimuthal Equal-Area Projection

61

ATLANTIC
OCEAN

CORVO
FLORES
Santa Cruz
das Flores
GRACIOSA
Santa Cruz
da Graciosa
SÃO JORGE
TERCEIRA
Praia da Vitória
Angra do Heroísmo
FAIAL
Velas
2351
Horta
São Mateus
Ponta do Pico
PICO

A
Ç
O
R
E
S
(Port.)

SÃO MIGUEL
Ribeira Grande
Povoação
Ponta
Delgada

Vila do Porto
SANTA MARIA

© R. MₙN.

ATLANTIC

OCEAN

Western Sahara has been
occupied by Morocco.

ARQUIPÉLAGO
DA MADEIRA
MADEIRA ISLANDS
(Port.)
PORTO SANTO
Pico Ruivo
1862
Funchal
Machico
MADEIRA
ILHAS DESERTAS

4660

ISLAS CANARIAS
CANARY ISLANDS
CANARY (Sp.)

ILHAS SELVAGENS
(Mad. Is.)

ISLA
ALEGRANZA
ISLA GRACIOSA
678
LANZAROTE
Arrecife
ISLA DE LOBOS

LA PALMA
Los
Llanos
PARQ. NAC. DE LA
CALDERA DE TABURIENTE
Santa Cruz
de la Palma
2426
Pico de la Cruz
La Orotava
TENERIFE
San Cristóbal
de la Laguna
Santa Cruz de Tenerife
724
Puerto del Rosario
FUERTEVENTURA

3715
Pico del Teide
PARQ. NAC.
DEL TEIDE
GOMERA
San Sebastián
de la Gomera
San Miguel
San Nicolás
Arucas
Las Palmas
de Gran Canaria
1949
Teide
GRAN CANARIA

Valverde
HIERRO
FERRO

CAP JUBY
Tarfaya

CAP BOJADOR

Dakhla

Khlij Oued edh
Dheheb
Tropic of Cancer

Imilili

Golfe de
Cintra

CAP
BARBAS

OCEAN

CÓRDOBA
Serpa
Almodôvar
Odemira
Lora
del Río
Guadalquivir
Cortegana
Aracena
Écija
BEJA
Bollullos par
del Condado
Valverde del
Camino
Sevilla
Lagos
Faro
Vila Real de
Santo António
Huelva
Morón
de la Frontera
Antequera
CABO DE
SÃO VICENTE
Golfo de
Cádiz
CABO DE
SANTA MARIA
Jerez
de la Frontera
Ronda
Arcos de
la Frontera
Marbe
Cádiz
Estep
CABO TRAFALGAR
Algeciras
La Línea
Gibraltar
CAP SPARTEL
Strait of Gibraltar
1242
Tanger
Ceuta (Sp.)
Tangier
Tétouan
Asilah
Bou Ahmed
Al-Hoc
LIXUS
Chaouen
Larache
Ksar-el-
Kebir
RIF
Jebel
Tidirhine
Souk Larbat Gharb
Karia-ba-
Mohammed
Salé
Kenitra
Fès
Rabat
Meknès
Mohammedia
(Fedala)
Khemisset
CASABLANCA
DAR-EL-BEIDA
Azemmour
Berrechid
El-Jadida
(Mazagan)
Settat
Khouribga
Oued-Zem
Safi
Youssoufia
Benguerir
Essaouira
(Mogador)
Marrakech
Agadir
Taroudant

WESTERN SAHARA

LA'YOUN

El Aaiun
(La'youn)

As Saguia al Hamra

Smara

Lemsid

Sebkhat
Aridal

ZEMMOUR

Galtat Zemmour

Sabkhat
Aghzoumal

Bir Enzaran

MOROCCO AL-MAGREB

Hawza
Al Mahbas

Bir Mogrein
(Fort-Trinquet)
701

55

TIRES

Sebkhet ej Jill
Fdérik
Zouérat
Kediet ej Jill

Sebkhet Oumm ed
Droûs Telli

Sebkhet Oumm ed
Droûs Guebli

Sebkha de
Rhallamane

EL HAMMAMI

TIRIS ZEMMOUR

EL KHATT

WESTERN SAHARA
Techlé
MAURITANIA MAURITANIE

DAKHLET
NOUÂDHIBOU

Nouâdhibou
La Guêra Cansado
RAS NOUÂDHIBOU
RAS AGÂDIR

PARC NATIONAL DU
BANC D'ARGUIN

INCHIRI

Passe de
Ouarârda
Choûm

Sebkhet
Chemchâm

485 Guelb er
Richât

Ouadâne

Atâr

ADRAR

Chinguetti

ALGERIA ALGÉRIE
MAURITANIA MAURITANIE

MCHERRAH

EL EGLAB

Ain Ben Tili

TIGUESMAT

Touassine

Agâraktem

EL Mreiti

KAHEL

MALI MAURITANIE

KREB EN NAGA

GUIDI

AFTOUT

HAMÁDA EL HARICHA

Taoudenni

EL KHNÁCHICH

HODH ECH
CHARGUI

TOMBOU

Copyright © by Rand McNally & Co.
Map prepared by George Philip & Son Ltd. London.
A-589791-264

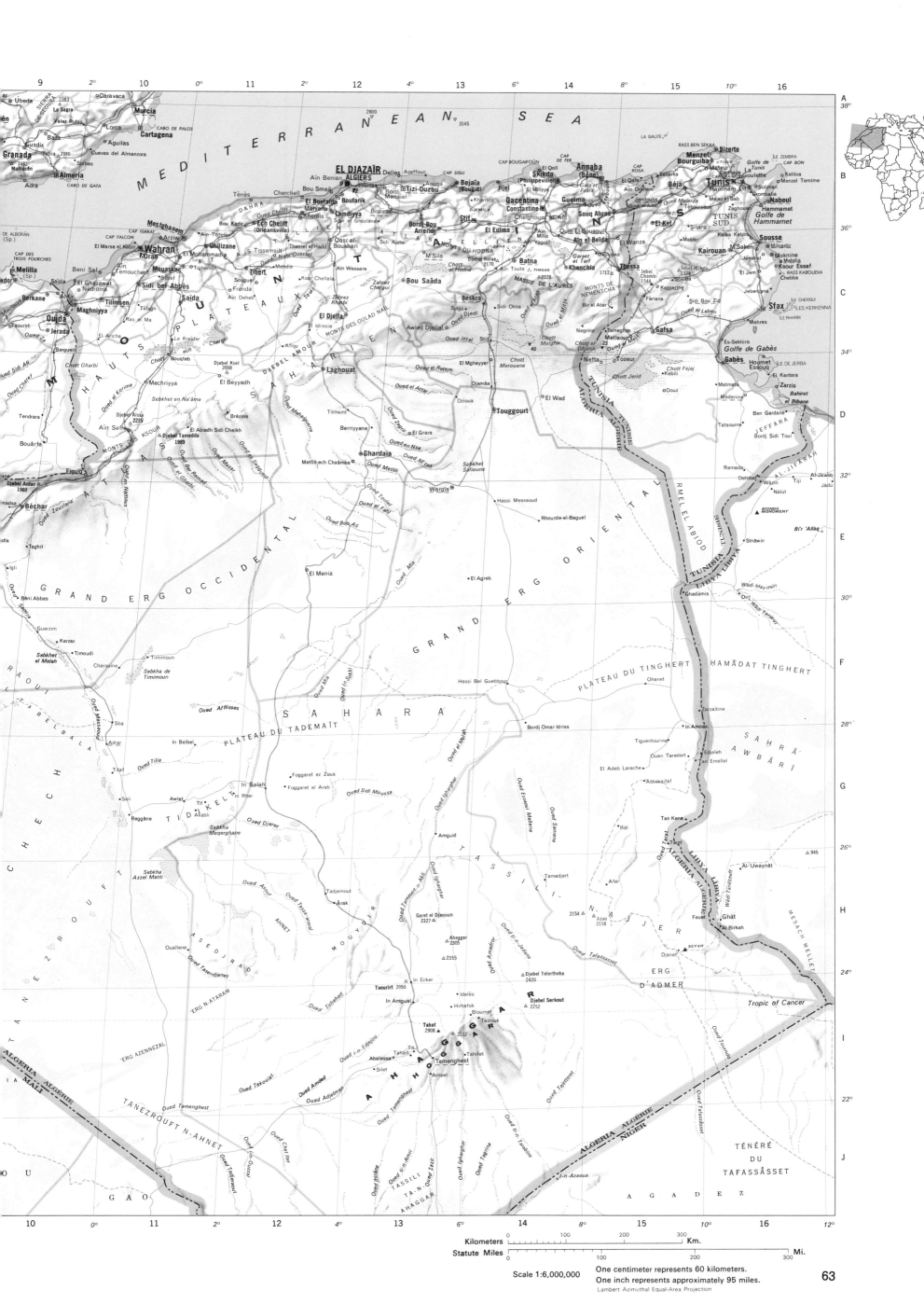

West Africa

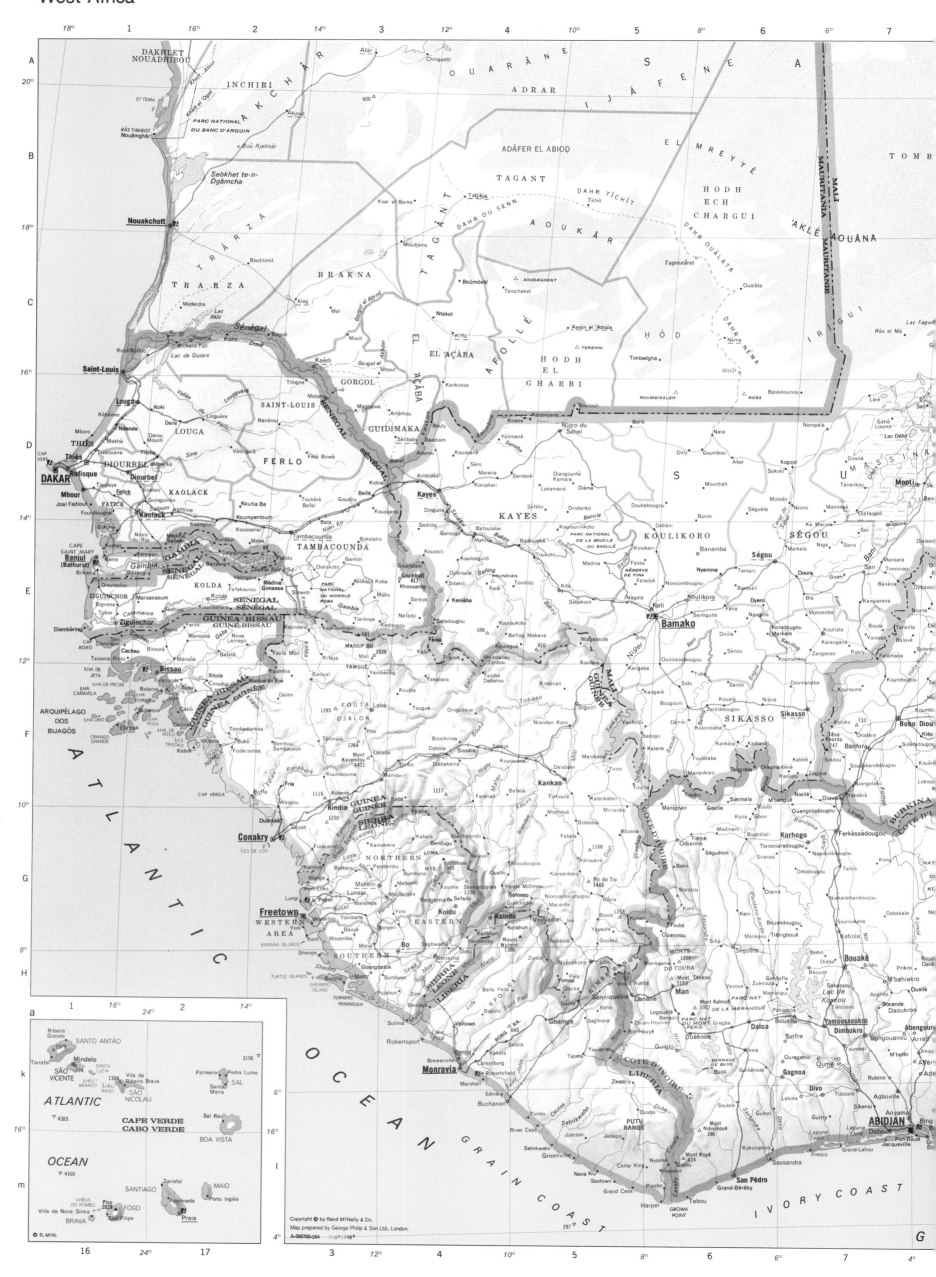

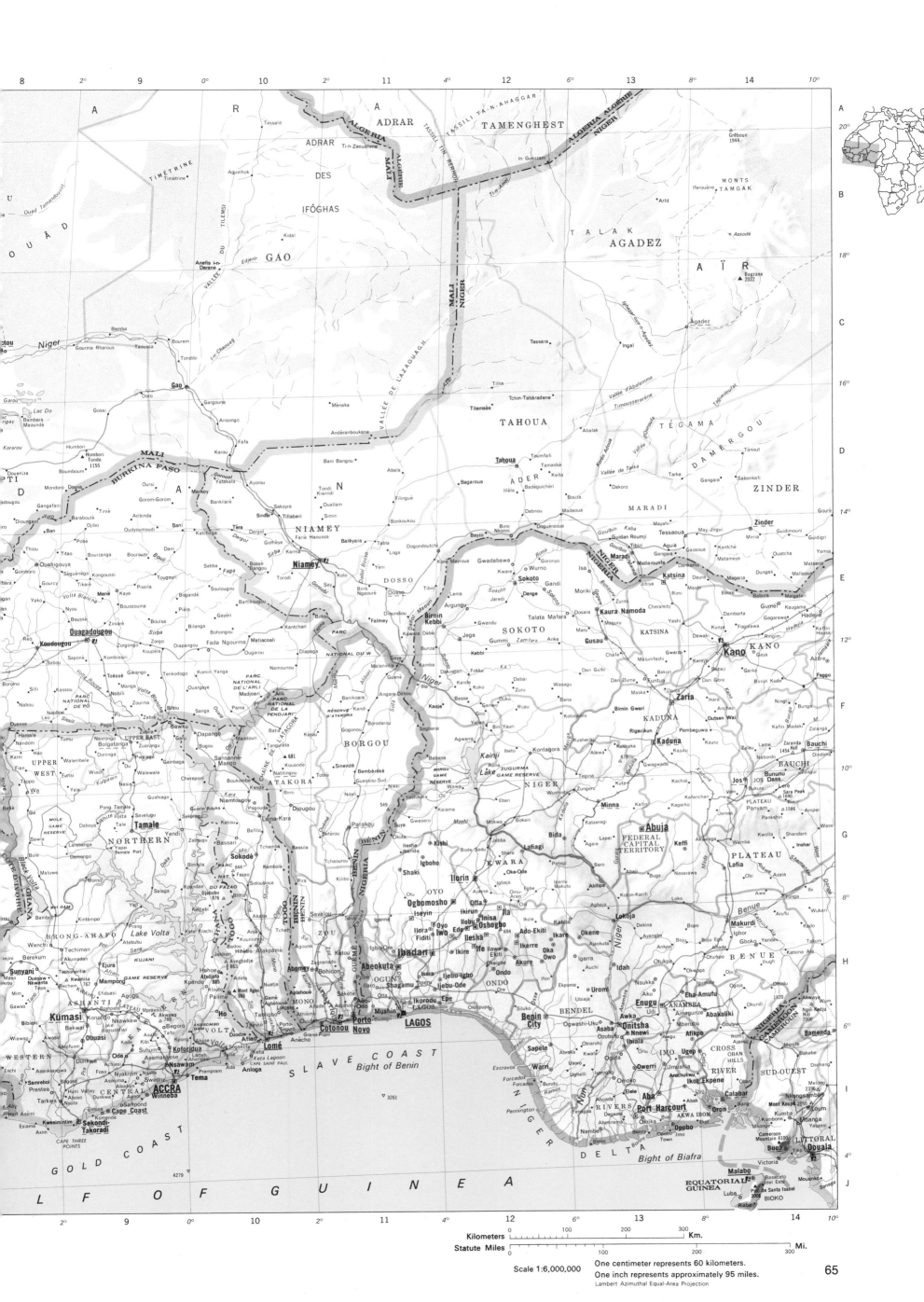

Kilometers | | 100 | 200 | 300 | Km.

Statute Miles | | 100 | 200 | 300 | Mi.

Scale 1:6,000,000

One centimeter represents 60 kilometers.
One inch represents approximately 95 miles.

Lambert Azimuthal Equal-Area Projection

Australia

68

Map Labels

Seas and Oceans
a Sea
Coral Sea
Solomon Sea
PACIFIC OCEAN
Tasman Sea
Gulf of Carpentaria
Bass Strait
Torres Strait

New Guinea / Papua
NEW GUINEA
PAPUA NEW GUINEA
Port Moresby
Papua
OWEN STANLEY RANGE
Mount Victoria 4035
Kokoda
Garara
Popondetta
Wanigela
Rigo
Abau
Esa'ala
Samarai
Milne Bay
D'ENTRECASTEAUX ISLANDS
Kulumadau
Muyua Island
LOUISIADE ARCHIPELAGO
MISIMA I.
Tagula Island
Yela Island
Long Reef

Solomon Islands
SOLOMON ISLANDS
Solomon Sea
VELLA LAVELLA
RANONGGA
GIZO
KOLOMBANGARA
NEW GEORGIA
VANGUNU
RUSSELL ISLANDS
GUADALCANAL
Mt. Makarakomburu 2447
Honiara 160°
Tulaghi
SANTA ISABEL
CHOISEUL
RENDOVA
KIRIWINA ISLANDS
Losuia
RENNELL

Cape York Peninsula / Queensland (northern)
CAPE YORK PENINSULA
CAPE YORK
GREAT BARRIER REEF
Daru
Boigu Island
Saibai Island
Moa Island
Warrior Reefs
Prince of Wales Island
Thursday Island
Endeavour Strait
Bamaga
Cape Grenville
Osprey Reef
Weipa
Albatross Bay
Duifken Point
Archer Bay
Aurukun
Cape Keer-Weer
Coen
Musgrave
Coleman
Laura
Cooktown
Bougainville Reef
Cape Melville
Iron Range
Cape York
Wenlock

Gulf of Carpentaria region
Cape Wessel
Wessel Islands
Buckingham Bay
The English Companys Islands
Cape Arnhem
Cape Grey
Groote Eylandt
Cape Beatrice
Limmen Bight
Maria Island
Sir Edward Pellew Group
Vanderlin Island
Borroloola
Mornington Island
Wellesley Islands
Bentinck Island
Barkly Tableland
Nicholson
Burketown
Normanton
Karumba
Croydon
Staaten
Gilbert
Gregory Range
Mitchell

Queensland (interior and coast)
QUEENSLAND
GREAT DIVIDING RANGE
GREAT ARTESIAN BASIN
Cairns
Cape Grafton
Atherton
Mareeba
Chillagoe
Innisfail
Bartle Frere 1622
Ravenshoe
Einasleigh
Forsayth
Greenvale
Ingham
Halifax Bay
Hinchinbrook Island
Townsville
Cape Cleveland
Charters Towers
Ayr
Home Hill
Pentland
Bowen
Collinsville
Proserpine
Cumberland Islands
Richmond
Hughenden
Netherdale
Mackay
Northumberland Isles
Cape Palmerston
Winton
Aramac
Clermont
Sarina
Broad Sound
Blair Athol
Connors Ra.
Denham Range
Townshend Island
Swain Reefs
Longreach
Ilfracombe
Barcaldine
Emerald
Rockhampton
Yeppoon
Keppel Bay
Capricorn Group
Blackall
Alpha
Nogoa
Springsure
Mount Morgan
Gladstone
Port Curtis
Curtis Island
Bunker Group
Theodore
Biloela
Monto
Tropic of Capricorn
Thomson
Barcoo
Yaraka
Windorah
Adavale
Augathella
Taroom
Childers
Bundaberg
Hervey Bay
Fraser Island
Sandy Cape
Charleville
Mitchell
Injune
Roma
Maryborough
Murgon
Gympie
Quilpie
Bulloo
Paroo
Wyandra
Miles
Kingaroy
Wondai
Nambour
Cunnamulla
Thargomindah
Charleville
Warrego
Moonie
Dalby
Nanango
Kilcoy
Mount Kangaroo 1146
Toowoomba
Brisbane
Ipswich
Southport
Moreton Island
North Stradbroke Island
Warwick
Goondiwindi
Stanthorpe
Cape Byron
Ballina

Coral Sea reefs and islands
HOLMES REEF
WILLIS GROUP (Austl.)
CHILCOTT ISLAND (Austl.)
DIAMOND ISLETS (Austl.)
FLINDERS REEFS
MALAY REEF
LIHOU REEF AND CAYS
TREGOSSE ISLETS (Austl.)
ABINGTON REEFS
MARION REEF
MELLISH REEF
ÎLES CHESTERFIELD (N. Cal.)
ÎLE DE SABLE (N. Cal.)
KENN REEF
CAYE DE L'OBSERVATOIRE (N. Cal.)
RÉCIFS BELLONA
SAUMAREZ REEF
WRECK REEF
BIRD ISLET (Austl.)
CATO ISLAND
MIDDLETON REEF
ELIZABETH REEF
LORD HOWE ISLAND (N.S.W.)
BALLS PYRAMID (N.S.W.)
INDISPENSABLE REEFS

New South Wales
NEW SOUTH WALES
GREAT DIVIDING RANGE
Tenterfield
Casino
Lismore
Murwillumbah
Inglewood
Glen Innes
Grafton
Maclean
Coffs Harbour
Armidale
Moree
Narrabri
Gunnedah
Tamworth
Kempsey
Smoky Cape
Walgett
Coonamble
Coonabarabran
Gilgandra
Port Macquarie
Taree
Bourke
Nyngan
Narromine
Dubbo
Wellington
Mudgee
Singleton
Maitland
Newcastle
Sugarloaf Point
Gosford
Cobar
Condobolin
Lake Cargelligo
Forbes
Orange
Bathurst
Lithgow
Katoomba
Parramatta
SYDNEY
Campbelltown
Wollongong
Broken Hill
Menindee
Wilcannia
Ivanhoe
Hillston
West Wyalong
Young
Cowra
Bowral
Nowra
Jervis Bay
Tilpa
Darling
Olary
Balranald
Hay
Griffith
Leeton
Narrandera
Cootamundra
Junee
Yass
Goulburn
Queanbeyan
Wagga Wagga
Gundagai
Tumut
Lake Hume

Australian Capital Territory
Canberra
A.C.T.

Victoria
VICTORIA
Mildura
Swan Hill
Kerang
Deniliquin
Echuca
Shepparton
Benalla
Wangaratta
Albury
Bendigo
Castlemaine
Ballarat
MELBOURNE
Geelong
Moe
Port Phillip Bay
Sale
Traralgon
Morwell
Bairnsdale
Orbost
Ninety Mile Beach
Wonthaggi
Foster
Wilsons Promontory
Mount Bogong 1986
SNOWY MTNS
Cooma
Bombala
Eden
Cape Howe
Point Hicks
Horsham
Stawell
Ararat
Hamilton
Portland
Cape Nelson
Warrnambool
Colac
Port Fairy
Port Campbell
Cape Otway
Phillip Island
South East Point
Bordertown

South Australia (partial)
AUSTRALIA
SIMPSON DESERT
STURT STONY DESERT
STRZELECKI CREEK
Lake Eyre North
Lake Eyre South
Marree
Innamincka
Cooper Creek
Oodnadatta
Copley
Woomera
Lake Torrens
Lake Frome
Lake Blanche
Lake Callabonna
Tibooburra
Milparinka
Lake Gairdner
Lake Macfarlane
Port Augusta
Quorn
Hawker
N. FLINDERS RANGE
Saint Mary Peak 1180
Pimba
Kimba
Iron Knob
Whyalla
Port Pirie
Peterborough
Jamestown
Burra
Gawler
SAWLER RANGES
Port Lincoln
EYRE PENINSULA
Cowell
Wallaroo
Kadina
Spencer Gulf
Gulf Saint Vincent
Elizabeth
Adelaide
Murray Bridge
Pinnaroo
Loxton
Renmark
Wentworth
Kingston Southeast
Naracoorte
Penola
Millicent
Mount Gambier
Cape Jaffa
YORKE PENINSULA
CAPE SPENCER
Investigator Strait
KANGAROO ISLAND
Victor Harbor
Encounter Bay
Lake Alexandrina

Tasmania
TASMANIA
Bass Strait
King Island
Flinders Island
Furneaux Group
Cape Barren Island
Hunter Island
Cape Grim
Smithton
Burnie
Devonport
Ulverstone
Beaconsfield
Scottsdale
Launceston
Saint Marys
Mount Ossa 1617
Queenstown
Zeehan
Strahan
Cape Sorell
New Norfolk
Huonville
Geeveston
Hobart
Port Arthur
Maria Island
Freycinet Peninsula
South West Cape
South East Cape
Low Rocky Point
Sandy Cape
Banks Strait

Scale / Legend
Kilometers   0   200   400   Km.
Statute Miles   0   200   400   600   Mi.
Scale 1:12,000,000
One centimeter represents 120 kilometers.
One inch represents approximately 190 miles.
Lambert Conformal Conic Projection

Grid coordinates (margins)
Top: 135° · 7 · 140° · 8 · 145° · 9 · 150° · 10 · 155° · 11
Left/Right: A · B · 15° · C · 20° · D · Tropic of Capricorn · 25° · E · 30° · F · 165° · 35° · G · 40° · H
Bottom: 135° · 7 · 140° · 8 · 145° · 10 · 155° · 11 · 160° · 12 · 165°

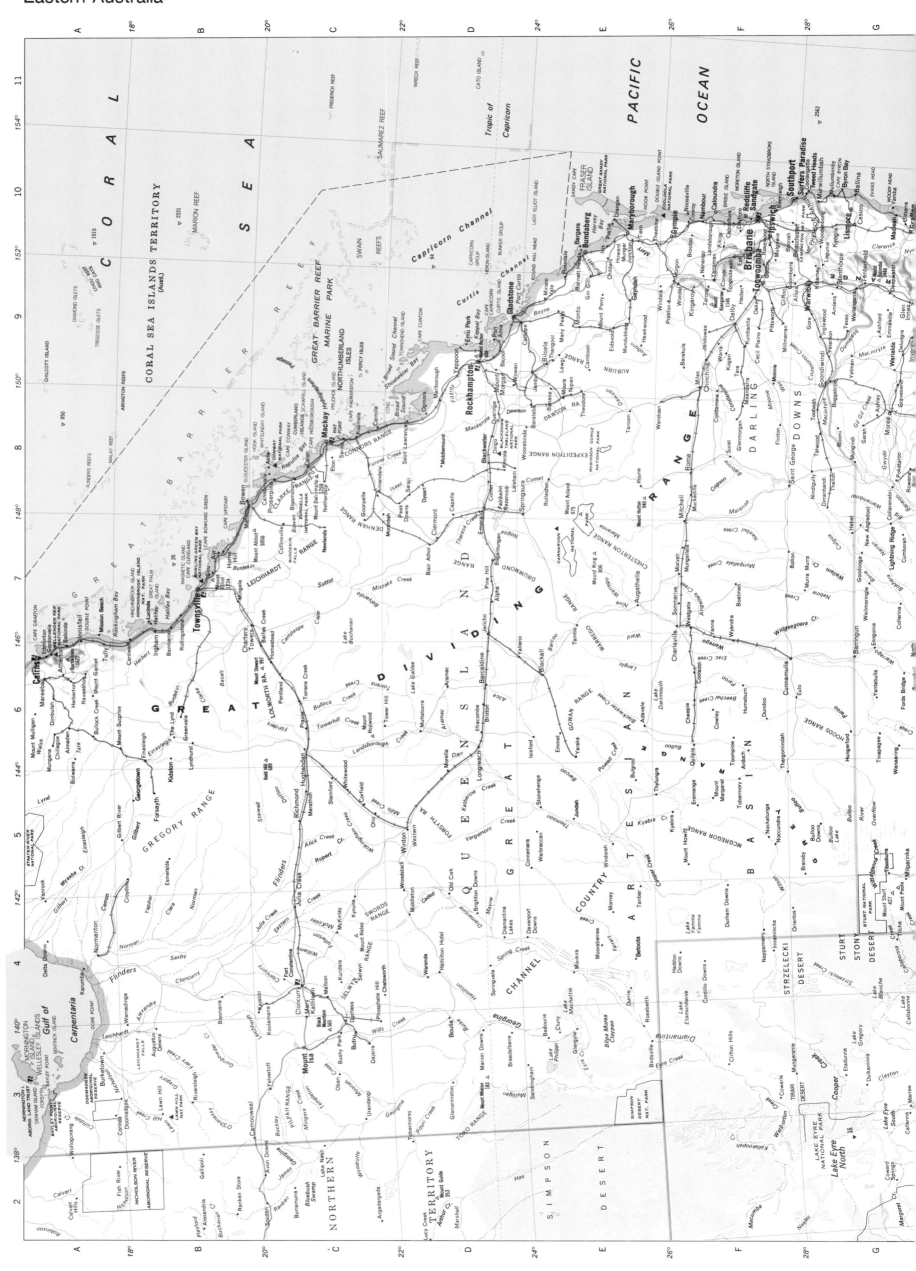

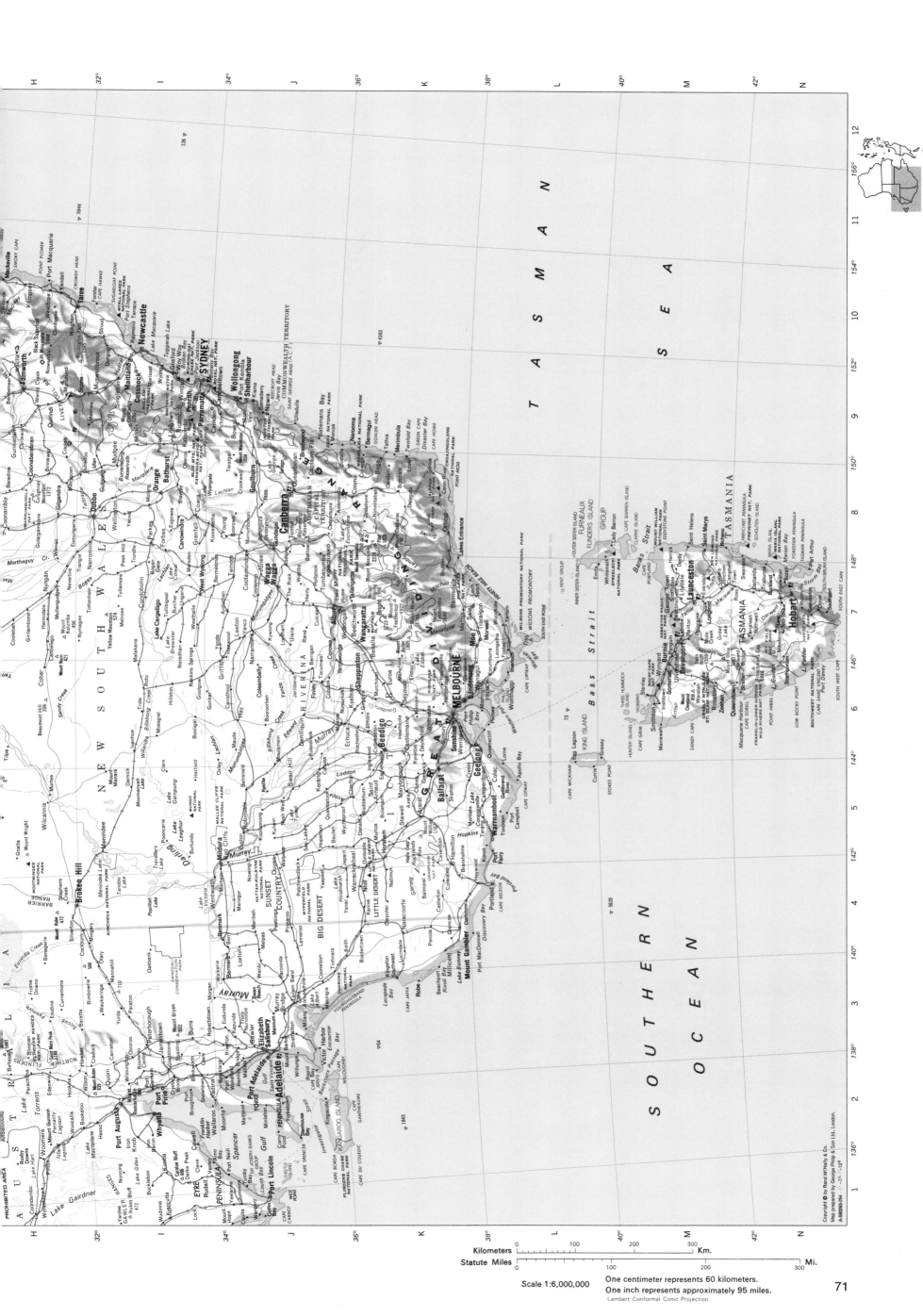

Kilometers 0 100 200 300 Km.

Statute Miles 0 100 200 300 Mi.

Scale 1:6,000,000
One centimeter represents 60 kilometers.
One inch represents approximately 95 miles.
Lambert Conformal Conic Projection

Copyright © by Rand McNally & Co.
Map prepared by George Philip & Son, Ltd., London.
A-590293-254

New Zealand

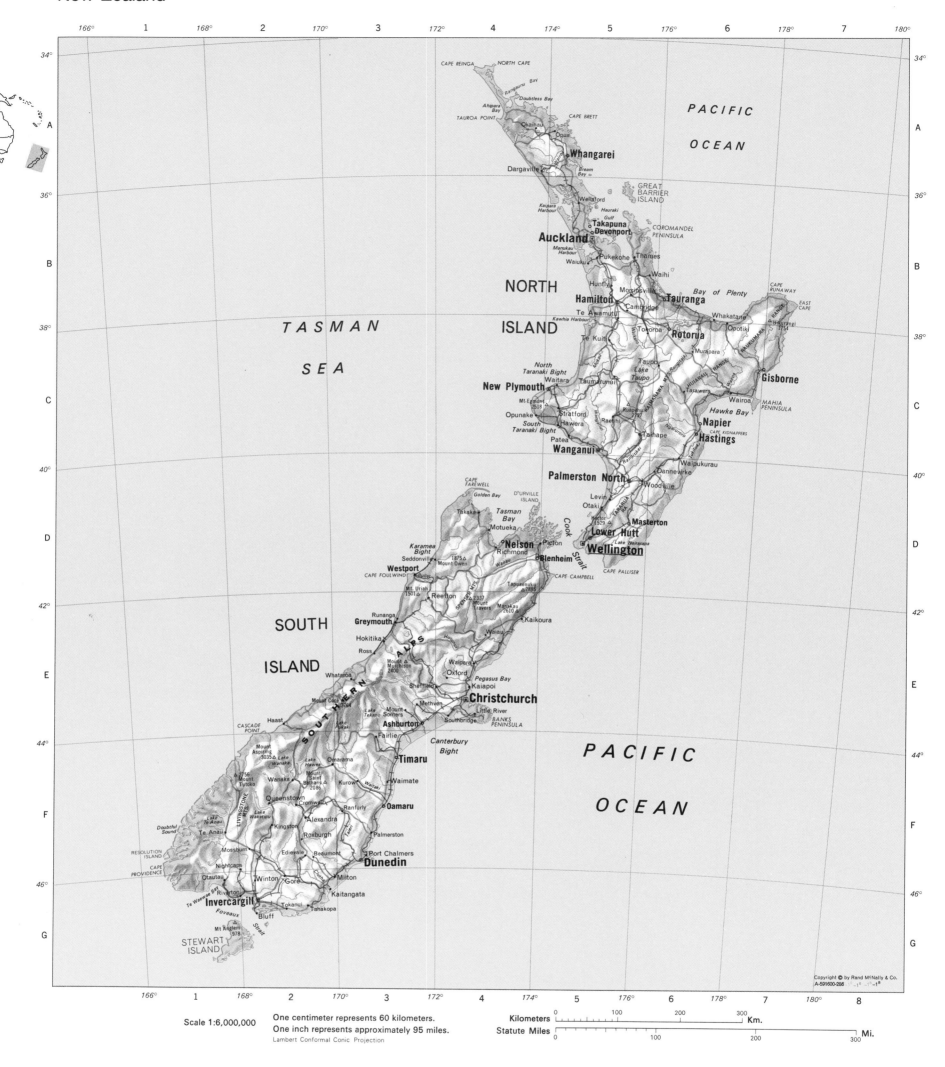

TASMAN

SEA

NORTH

ISLAND

SOUTH

ISLAND

PACIFIC

OCEAN

Copyright © by Rand McNally & Co.
A-591600-288

Scale 1:6,000,000

One centimeter represents 60 kilometers.
One inch represents approximately 95 miles.
Lambert Conformal Conic Projection

Kilometers
Statute Miles

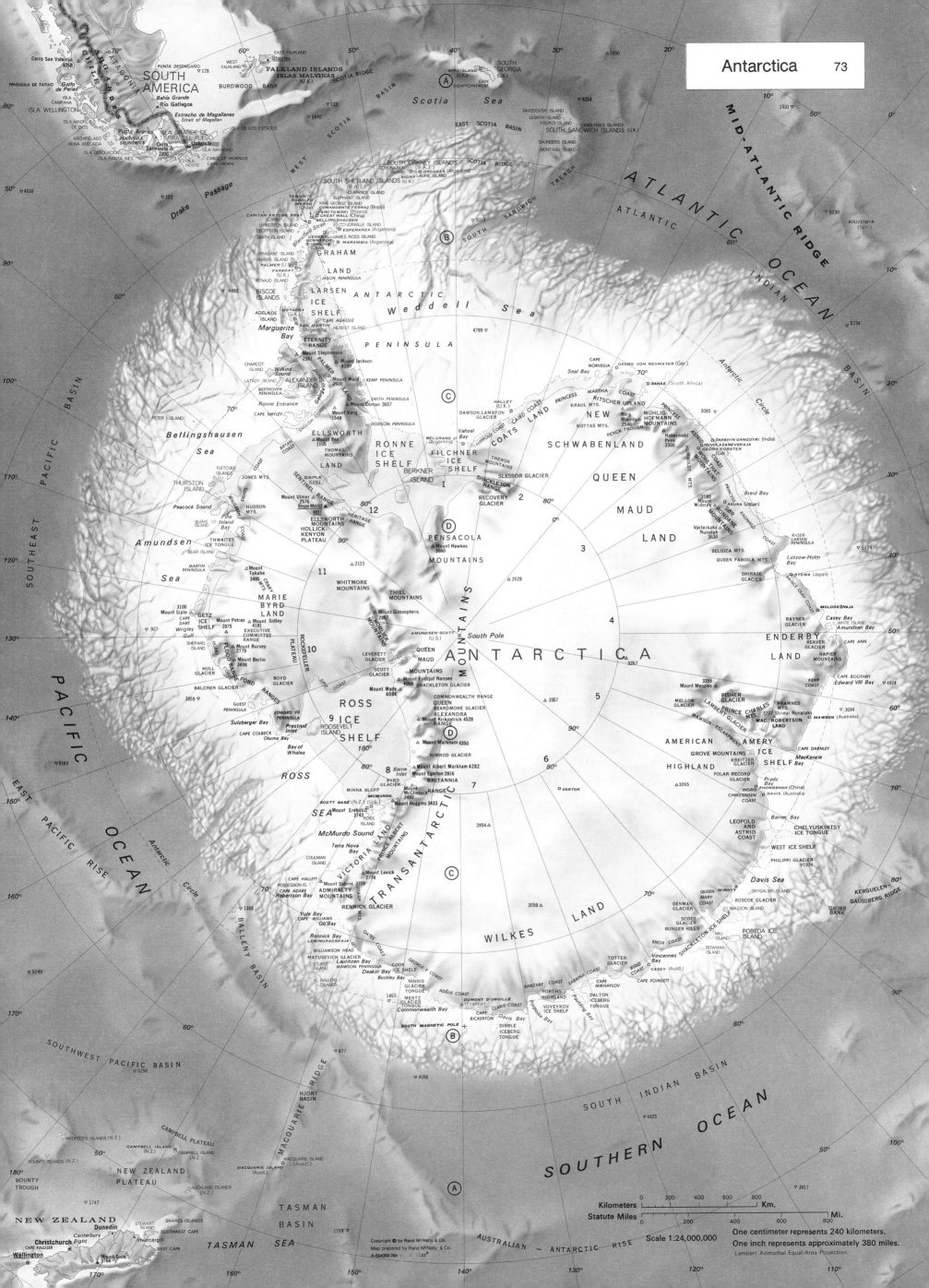

Scale 1:24,000,000

One centimeter represents 240 kilometers.
One inch represents approximately 380 miles.

Lambert Azimuthal Equal-Area Projection

Copyright © by Rand McNally & Co.
Map prepared by Rand McNally & Co.
A-594000-764

ATLANTIC OCEAN

NORTH AMERICA

UNITED STATES

ROCKY MTS. GREAT PLAINS

APPALACHIAN MOUNTAINS

NORTH AMERICA

Cheyenne · North Platte · Omaha · Des Moines · CHICAGO · CLEVELAND · Pittsburgh · NEW YORK · PHILADELPHIA · Baltimore · WASHINGTON · Norfolk · Richmond · Raleigh · Charlotte · Charleston · Columbia · Savannah · Jacksonville · Charleston · Cincinnati · Indianapolis · Louisville · St. Louis · Kansas City · Wichita · Denver · Albuquerque · Santa Fe · Oklahoma City · Little Rock · Memphis · Nashville · Chattanooga · Birmingham · Atlanta · Montgomery · Jackson · Mobile · New Orleans · Shreveport · Dallas · Fort Worth · Houston · San Antonio · Laredo · Brownsville · Tampa · Miami

OZARK PLATEAU · EDWARDS PLATEAU · El Paso

Missouri · Ohio · Wabash · Tennessee · Mississippi · Colorado · Brazos · Rio Grande / Bravo

Mt. Mitchell 2038 · CAPE HATTERAS · CAPE LOOKOUT · CAPE FEAR · CAPE CANAVERAL · CAPE SABLE · Lake Okeechobee · Chesapeake Bay · LONG ISLAND · GEORGES BANK

AZORES PLATEAU · AZORES (Port.) · FLORES · SÃO MIGUEL · TERCEIRA · SANTA MARIA · PICO

Great Meteor Tablemount 269

CAPE VERDE BASIN · SARGASSO SEA · MID-ATLANTIC RIDGE

NORTH AMERICAN BASIN

BERMUDA (U.K.) · BERMUDA RISE

Tropic of Cancer

BAHAMAS · GRAND BAHAMA BANK · GREAT BAHAMA BANK · ELEUTHERA · ANDROS · Nassau · SAN SALVADOR · CAT ISLAND · GREAT INAGUA · BLAKE PLATEAU · BLAKE RIDGE

CUBA · La Habana / Havana · Santiago de Cuba · Guantánamo · ISLA DE LA JUVENTUD · CAYMAN ISLANDS (U.K.) · CAYMAN TRENCH

HISPANIOLA · HAITI · Port-au-Prince · DOMINICAN REPUBLIC · Santo Domingo · PUERTO RICO (U.S.) · San Juan · PUERTO RICO TRENCH · Windward Passage · Mona Passage

JAMAICA · Kingston

WEST INDIES · LESSER ANTILLES · GREATER ANTILLES · LEEWARD ISLANDS · WINDWARD ISLANDS · NETHERLANDS ANTILLES · VIRGIN ISLANDS · ANTIGUA AND BARBUDA · GUADELOUPE (Fr.) · DOMINICA · MARTINIQUE (Fr.) · SAINT LUCIA · BARBADOS · Bridgetown · SAINT VINCENT AND THE GRENADINES · GRENADA · MONTSERRAT (U.K.)

TRINIDAD AND TOBAGO · Port of Spain · TRINIDAD · TOBAGO

CARIBBEAN SEA · COLOMBIAN BASIN · VENEZUELAN BASIN · YUCATAN BASIN

ARUBA · CURAÇAO · BONAIRE

GULF OF MEXICO · Straits of Florida · Canal de Yucatán · Gulf of Honduras

MEXICO · CIUDAD DE MÉXICO / MEXICO CITY · Guadalajara · Torreón · Monterrey · Matamoros · Saltillo · Tampico · Veracruz · Puebla · Acapulco · Oaxaca · Villahermosa · Mérida · SIERRA MADRE ORIENTAL · SIERRA MADRE DEL SUR · YUCATAN PENINSULA · Bahía de Campeche · Golfo de Tehuantepec · Laguna de Chapala

BELIZE · Belize City · Belmopan · GUATEMALA · Guatemala · HONDURAS · Tegucigalpa · EL SALVADOR · San Salvador · NICARAGUA · Managua · Lago de Nicaragua · COSTA RICA · San José · PANAMA · Panamá · Colón · Canal de Panamá · Golfo de Panamá · ISTMO DE PANAMÁ · Bluefields · Lago de Managua

MIDDLE AMERICA TRENCH · TEHUANTEPEC · GUATEMALA BASIN · COCOS RIDGE · ISLA DEL COCO (C.R.) · ISLA DE MALPELO (Col.) · CARNEGIE RIDGE · PANAMA BASIN · COLÓN RIDGE

Equator

ISLA SANTIAGO · ISLA SANTA CRUZ · ISLA SAN CRISTÓBAL · ISLA ISABELA · ISLA FERNANDINA · ARCHIPIÉLAGO DE COLÓN / GALÁPAGOS ISLANDS (Ec.)

SOUTH AMERICA

COLOMBIA · SANTA FE DE BOGOTÁ · Medellín · Cali · Barranquilla · Cartagena · Cúcuta · Bucaramanga · Manizales · Buenaventura · CORDILLERA OCCIDENTAL · CORDILLERA ORIENTAL · ANDES

VENEZUELA · CARACAS · Maracaibo · Barquisimeto · Barcelona · Ciudad Bolívar · Ciudad Guayana · San Cristóbal · San Fernando de Atabapo · Puerto Ayacucho · Lago de Maracaibo · PAKARAIMA MTS · Mount Roraima 2875 · LLANOS · Orinoco · Apure · Meta · Negro

GUYANA · Georgetown · SURINAME · Paramaribo · FRENCH GUIANA · Cayenne · TUMUC-HUMAC MTS · Essequibo · Courantyne · Corentyne

ECUADOR · Quito · Guayaquil · Cuenca · Esmeraldas · Golfo de Guayaquil · Chimborazo 6310 · Cayambe 5790

PERU · LIMA · Trujillo · Chiclayo · Iquitos · Cerro de Pasco · Callao · Cusco · Nevado Huascarán 6768 · PERU-CHILE TRENCH

BRAZIL · SELVAS · Belém · Manaus · Fortaleza · Teresina · São Luís · Natal · João Pessoa · Recife · Maceió · Aracaju · Salvador · Campina Grande · Caruaru · Penedo · Juàzeiro · Paulistana · Parnaíba · ILHA DE MARAJÓ · ILHA DO BANANAL · CHAPADA DAS MANGABEIRAS · SA. DO CACHIMBO · Pico das Almas 1832 · Pico da Neblina 3014

Amazon / Amazonas · Rio Negro · Madeira · Tapajós · Xingu · Tocantins · Araguaia · Branco · Japurá · Juruá · Purus · Içá · Napo · Marañón · Ucayali · Mamoré · Beni · Putumayo · São Francisco · Parnaíba

CABO ORANGE · CABO MAGUARI · CAPO DE SÃO ROQUE · ATOL DAS ROCAS · ILHA FERNANDO DE NORONHA (Braz.)

Equator

MATO GROSSO

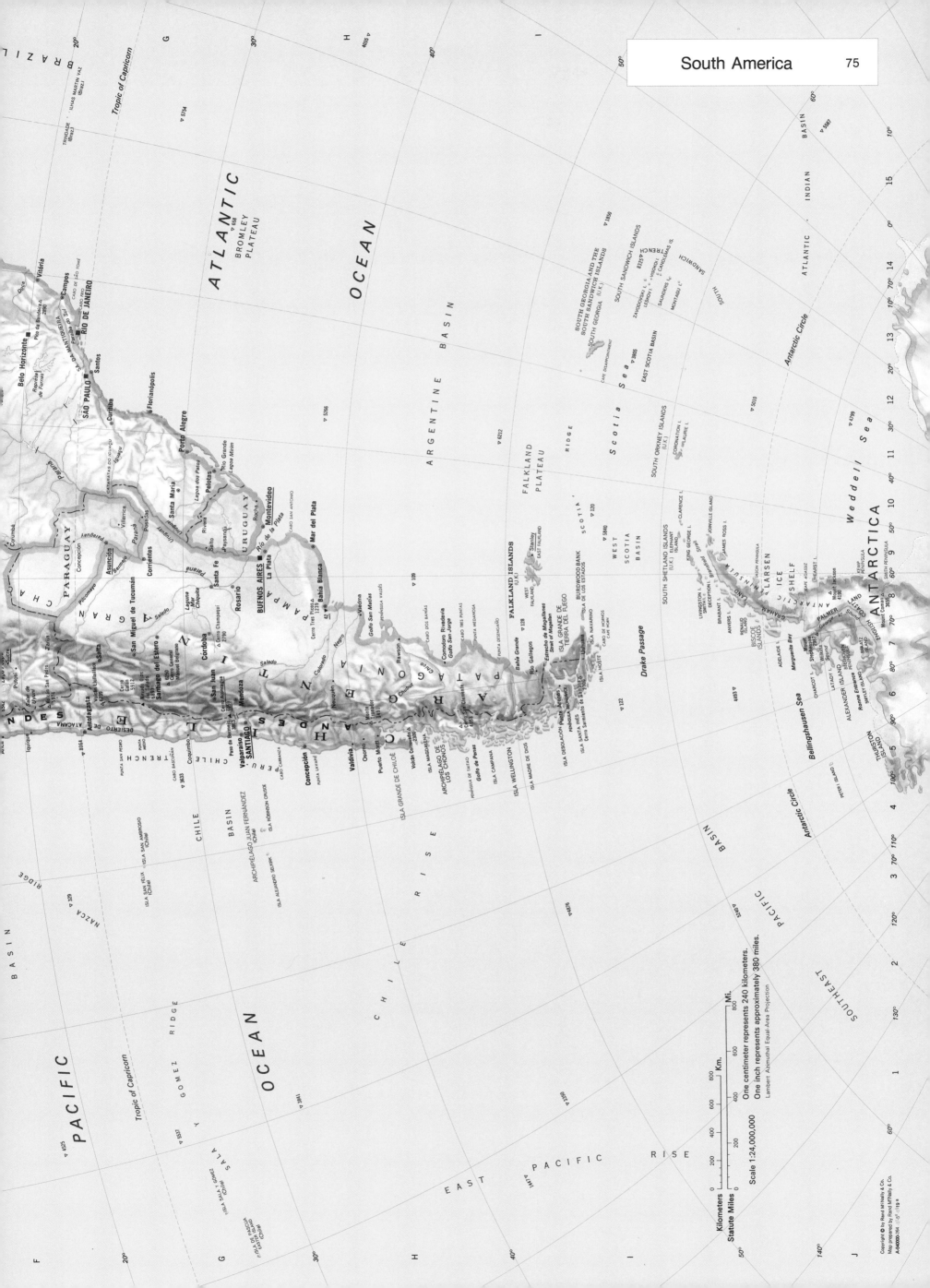

ATLANTIC

OCEAN

BROMLEY
PLATEAU

ARGENTINE BASIN

SOUTH GEORGIA AND THE
SOUTH SANDWICH ISLANDS

SOUTH SANDWICH ISLANDS

SOUTH GEORGIA (U.K.)

Scotia Sea

FALKLAND
PLATEAU

FALKLAND ISLANDS
(U.K.)

WEST
SCOTIA
BASIN

SOUTH ORKNEY ISLANDS
(U.K.)

Drake Passage

SOUTH SHETLAND ISLANDS
(U.K.)

Weddell Sea

ANTARCTICA

ANTARCTIC CIRCLE

Bellingshausen Sea

Antarctic Circle

BRAZIL

Tropic of Capricorn

Vitória

Campos

RIO DE JANEIRO

Belo Horizonte

SÃO PAULO

Santos

Curitiba

Florianópolis

Porto Alegre

Rio Grande

Pelotas

Santa Maria

PARAGUAY

Asunción

Concepción

Corrientes

URUGUAY

Rivera

Salto

Paysandú

Montevideo

Río de la Plata

La Plata

BUENOS AIRES

Rosario

Santa Fe

Córdoba

San Miguel de Tucumán

Santiago del Estero

Salta

Antofagasta

DESIERTO DE ATACAMA

Mendoza

San Juan

SANTIAGO

Valparaíso

Concepción

Valdivia

Puerto Montt

ISLA GRANDE DE CHILOÉ

CHILE

ANDES

PATAGONIA

Bahía Blanca

Mar del Plata

Viedma

Comodoro Rivadavia

Río Gallegos

Punta Arenas

Ushuaia

TIERRA DEL FUEGO

CAPE HORN

PACIFIC

OCEAN

NAZCA RIDGE

CHILE BASIN

GOMEZ RIDGE

Tropic of Capricorn

CHILE RISE

EAST PACIFIC RISE

SOUTHEAST PACIFIC BASIN

Kilometers
Statute Miles

Mi.

Km.

One centimeter represents 240 kilometers.
One inch represents approximately 380 miles.

Lambert Azimuthal Equal-Area Projection

Scale 1:24,000,000

Copyright © by Rand McNally & Co.
Map prepared by Rand McNally & Co.

Kilometers

Statute Miles

Scale 1:12,000,000

One centimeter represents 120 kilometers.
One inch represents approximately 190 miles.
Oblique Conformal Conic Projection

Copyright © by Rand McNally & Co.
Map prepared by Esselte Map Service AB, Stockholm.
A-649100-264

Kilometers

Statute Miles

Scale 1:12,000,000   One centimeter represents 120 kilometers.
One inch represents approximately 190 miles.

ATLANTIC

OCEAN

Kilometers
0   100   200   300   Km.

Statute Miles
0   100   200   300   Mi.

Scale 1:6,000,000
Oblique Conic Conformal Projection

One centimeter represents 60 kilometers.
One inch represents approximately 95 miles.

79

Scale 1:6,000,000
One centimeter represents 60 kilometers.
One inch represents approximately 95 miles.
Oblique Conic Conformal Projection

Kilometers
Statute Miles

Mexico

90

Kilometers

Statute Miles

Scale 1:6,000,000
One centimeter represents 60 kilometers.
One inch represents approximately 95 miles.
Lambert Conformal Conic Projection

Caribbean Region

Kilometers

Statute Miles

Scale 1:12,000,000

One centimeter represents 120 kilometers.
One inch represents approximately 190 miles.

Lambert Conformal Conic Projection

Alberta

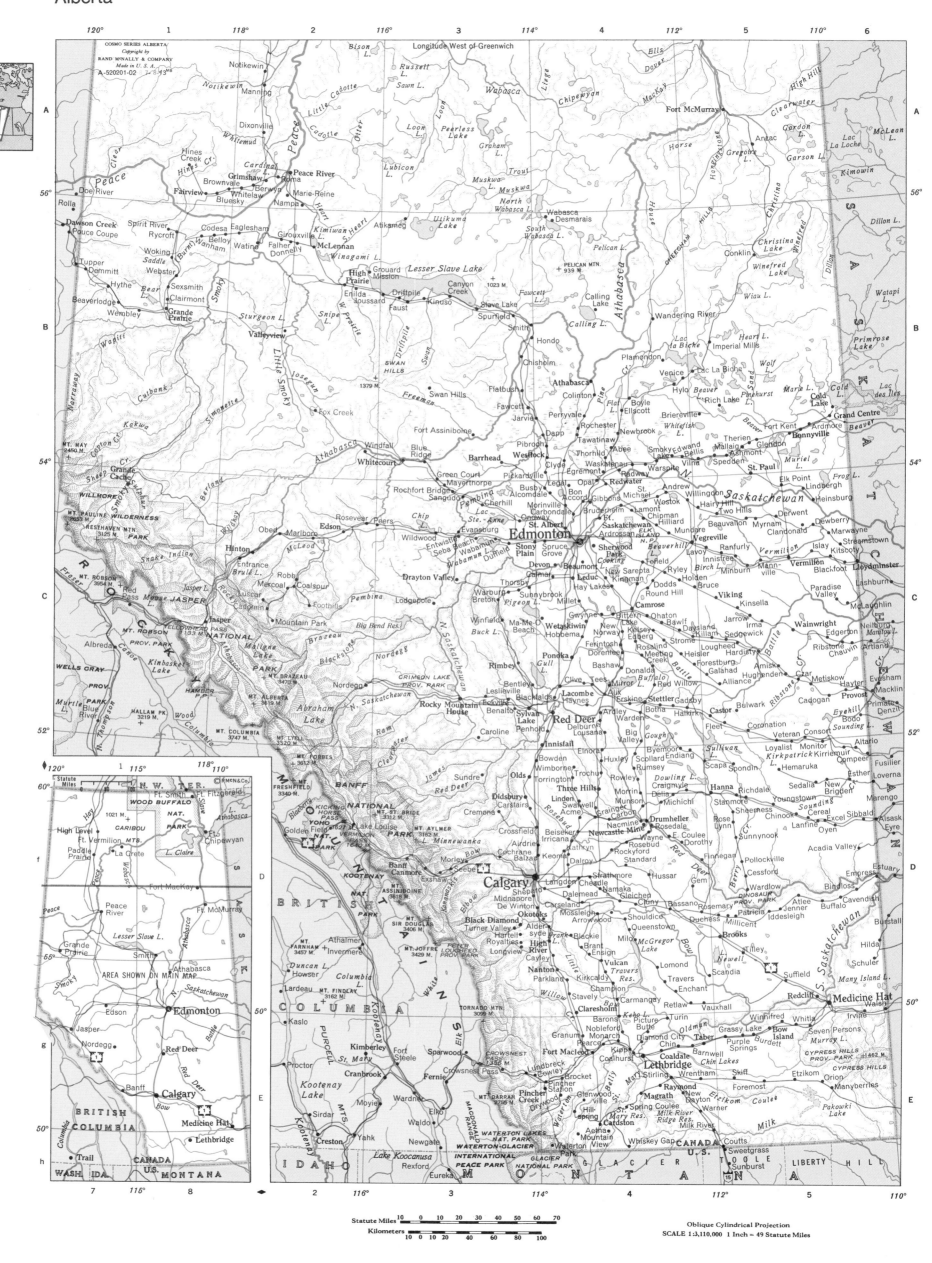

Oblique Cylindrical Projection
SCALE 1:4,255,000 1 Inch = 67 Statute Miles

Statute Miles 10 0 10 20 30 40 50 60 70 80 90 100

Kilometers 10 0 10 20 40 60 80 100 120 140

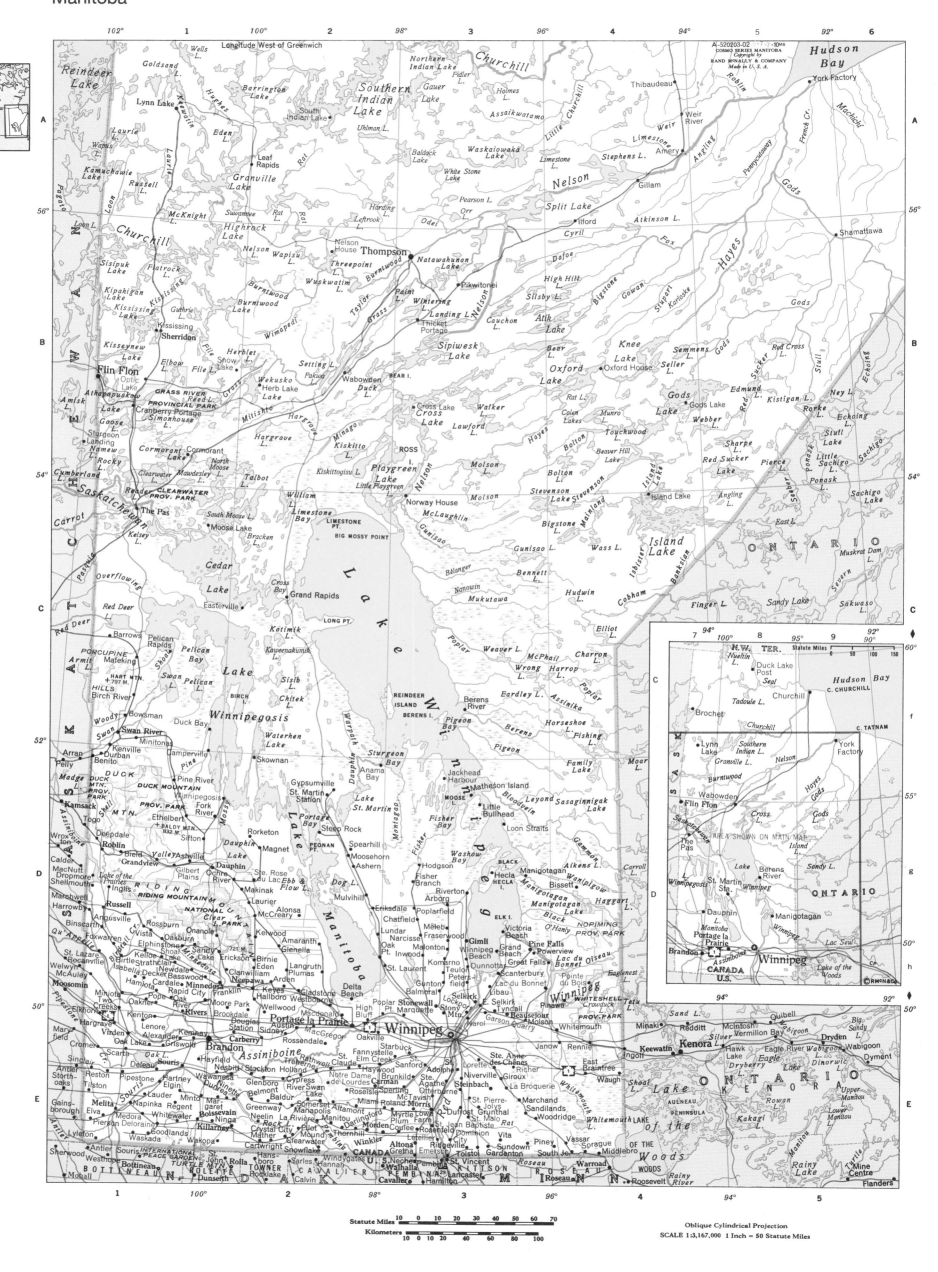

Oblique Cylindrical Projection
SCALE 1:3,167,000   1 Inch = 50 Statute Miles

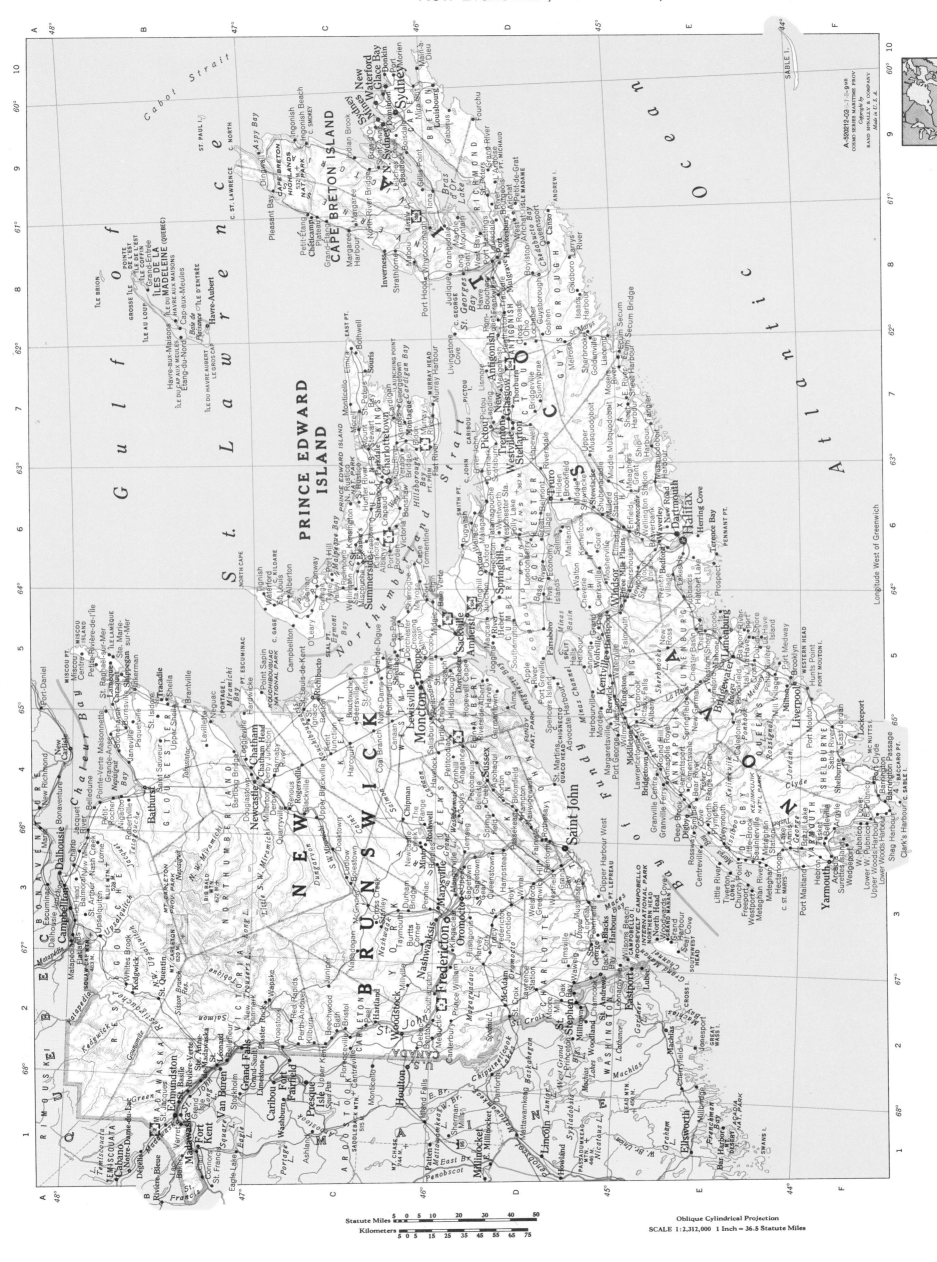

Oblique Cylindrical Projection
SCALE 1:2,312,000 1 Inch = 36.5 Statute Miles

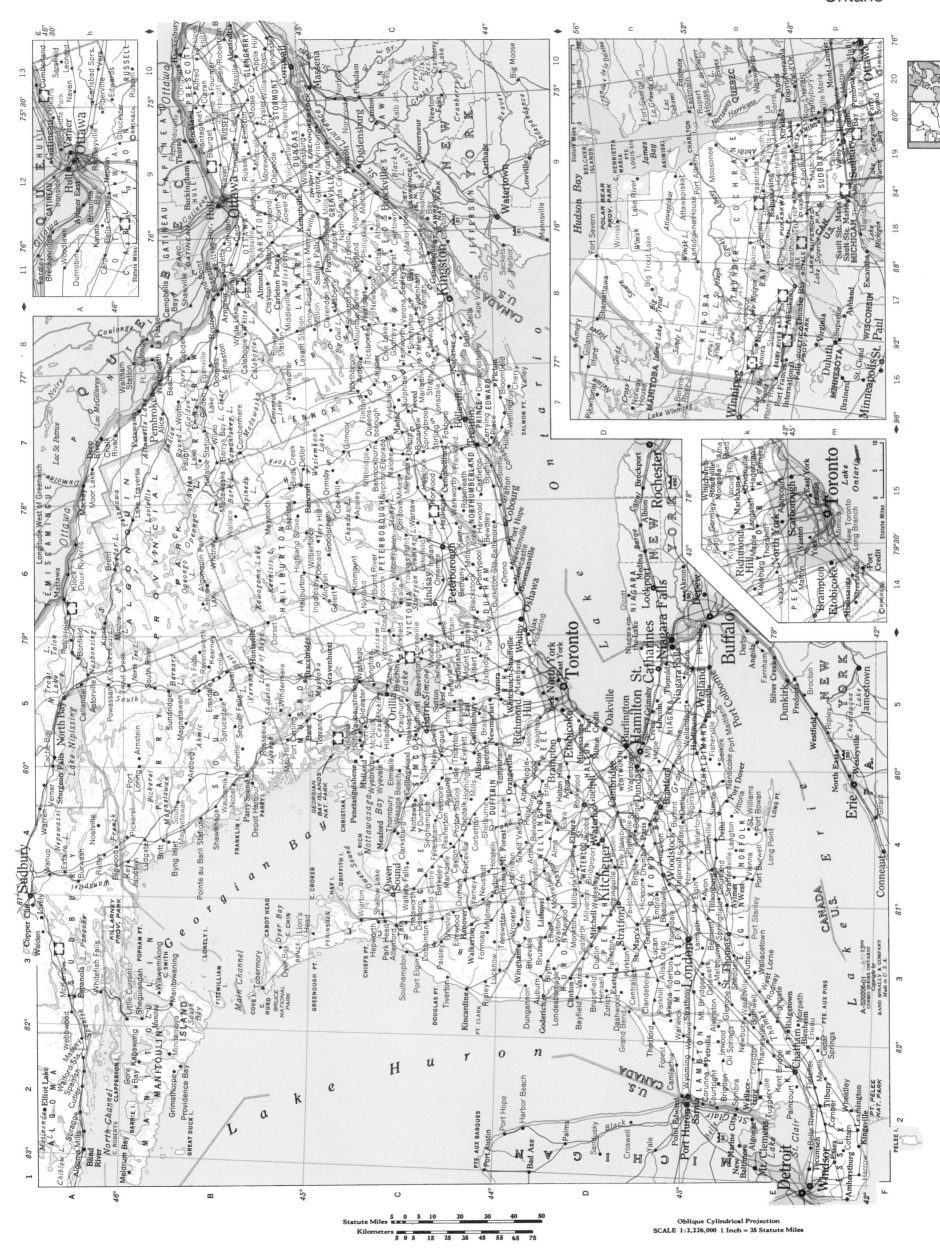

Statute Miles 5 0 5 10   20   30   40   50

Kilometers 5 0 5 15   25   35   45   55   65   75

Oblique Cylindrical Projection
SCALE 1:2,226,000 1 Inch = 35 Statute Miles

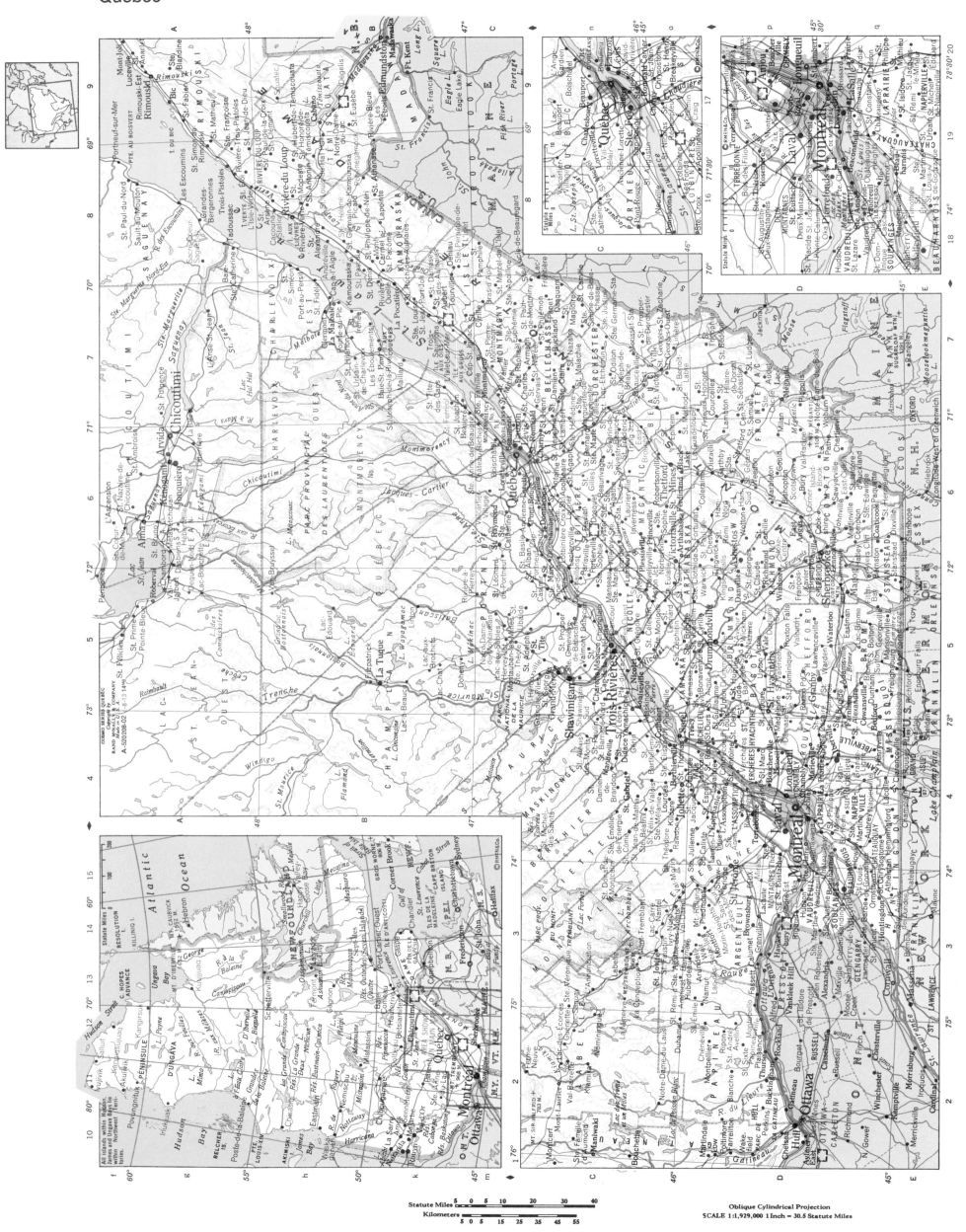

Statute Miles 5 0 5 10 20 30 40
Kilometers 5 0 5 15 25 35 45 55

Oblique Cylindrical Projection
SCALE 1:1,929,000 1 Inch = 30.5 Statute Miles

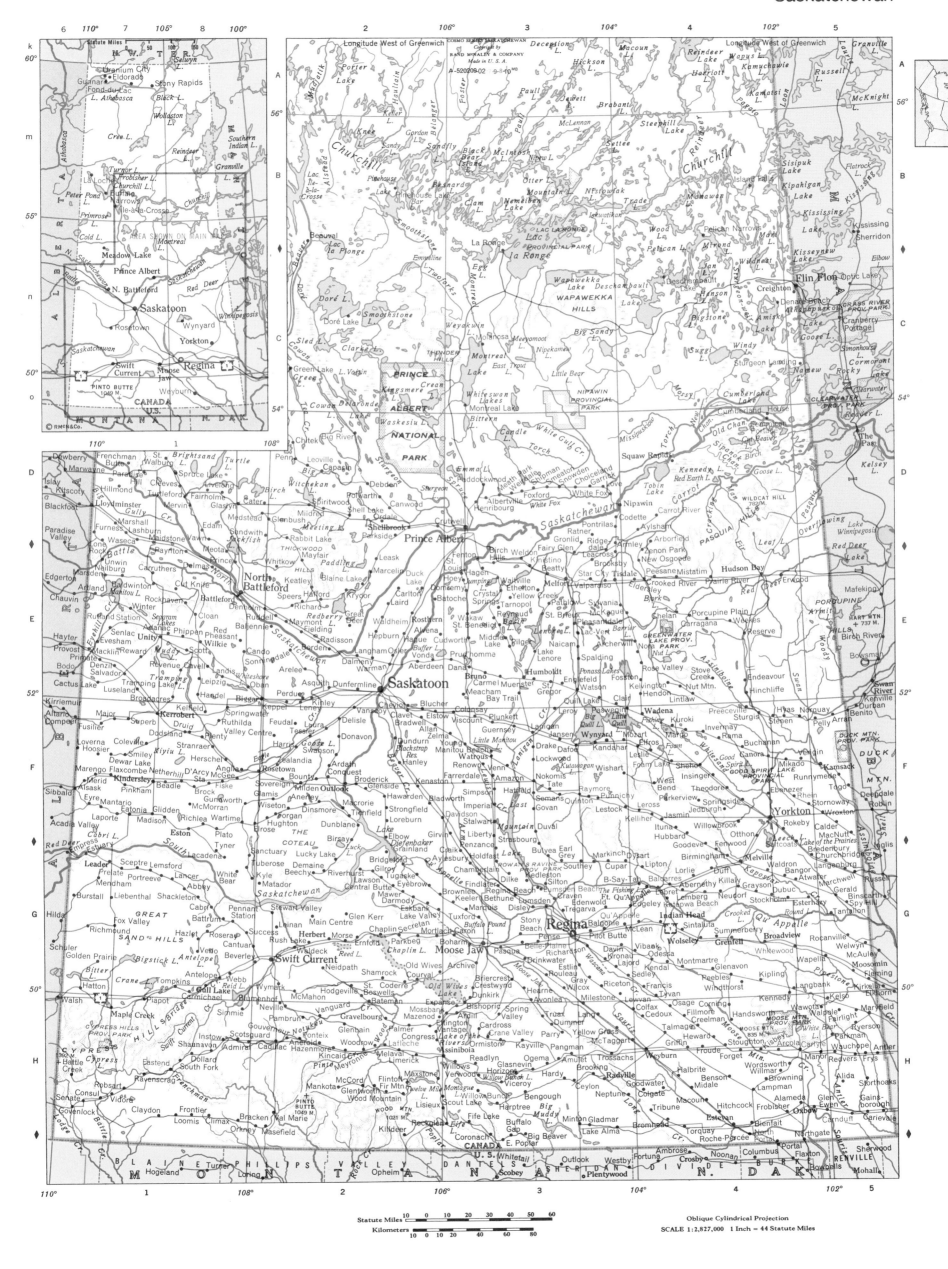

Saskatchewan

United States of America

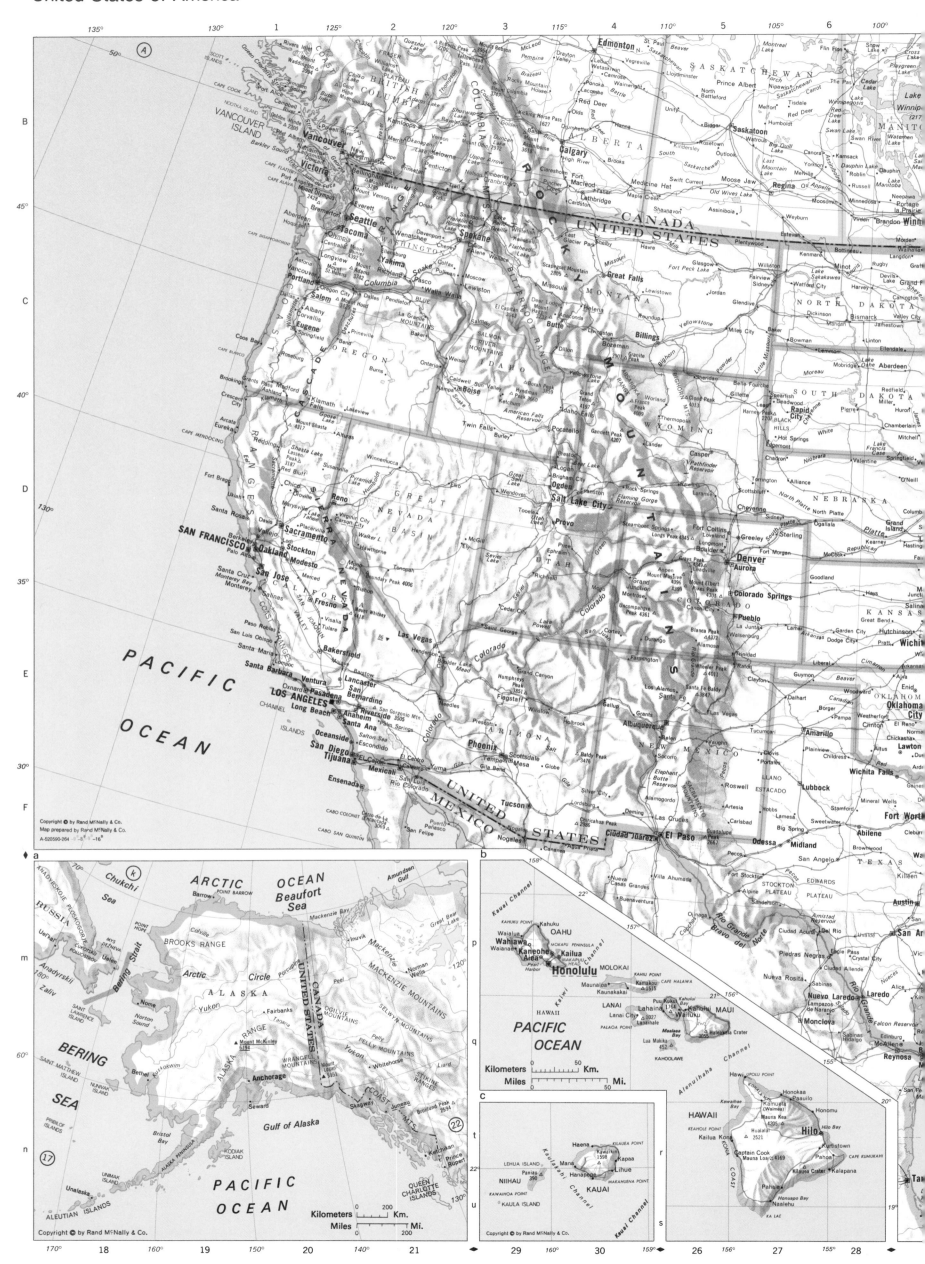

Kilometers ⊢⊢⊢⊢⊢⊢⊢⊢ Km.

Statute Miles ⊢⊢⊢⊢⊢⊢⊢⊢ Mi.

Scale 1:12,000,000   One centimeter represents 120 kilometers.
One inch represents approximately 190 miles.
Albers Conical Equal-Area Projection

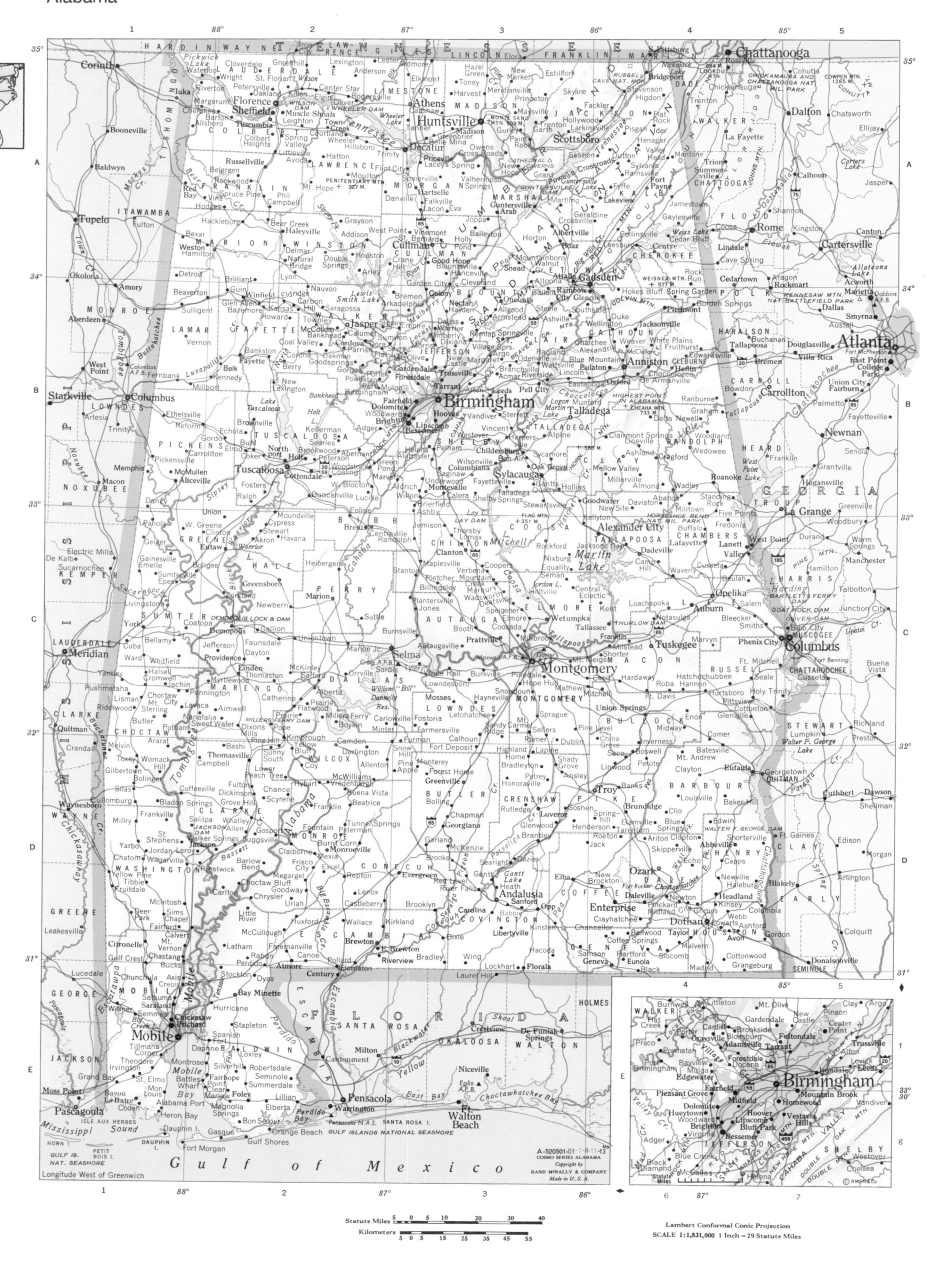

Statute Miles
Kilometers

A-520501-01
COSMO SERIES ALABAMA
Copyright by
RAND McNALLY & COMPANY
Made in U.S.A.

Lambert Conformal Conic Projection
SCALE 1:1,831,000   1 Inch = 29 Statute Miles

Longitude West of Greenwich

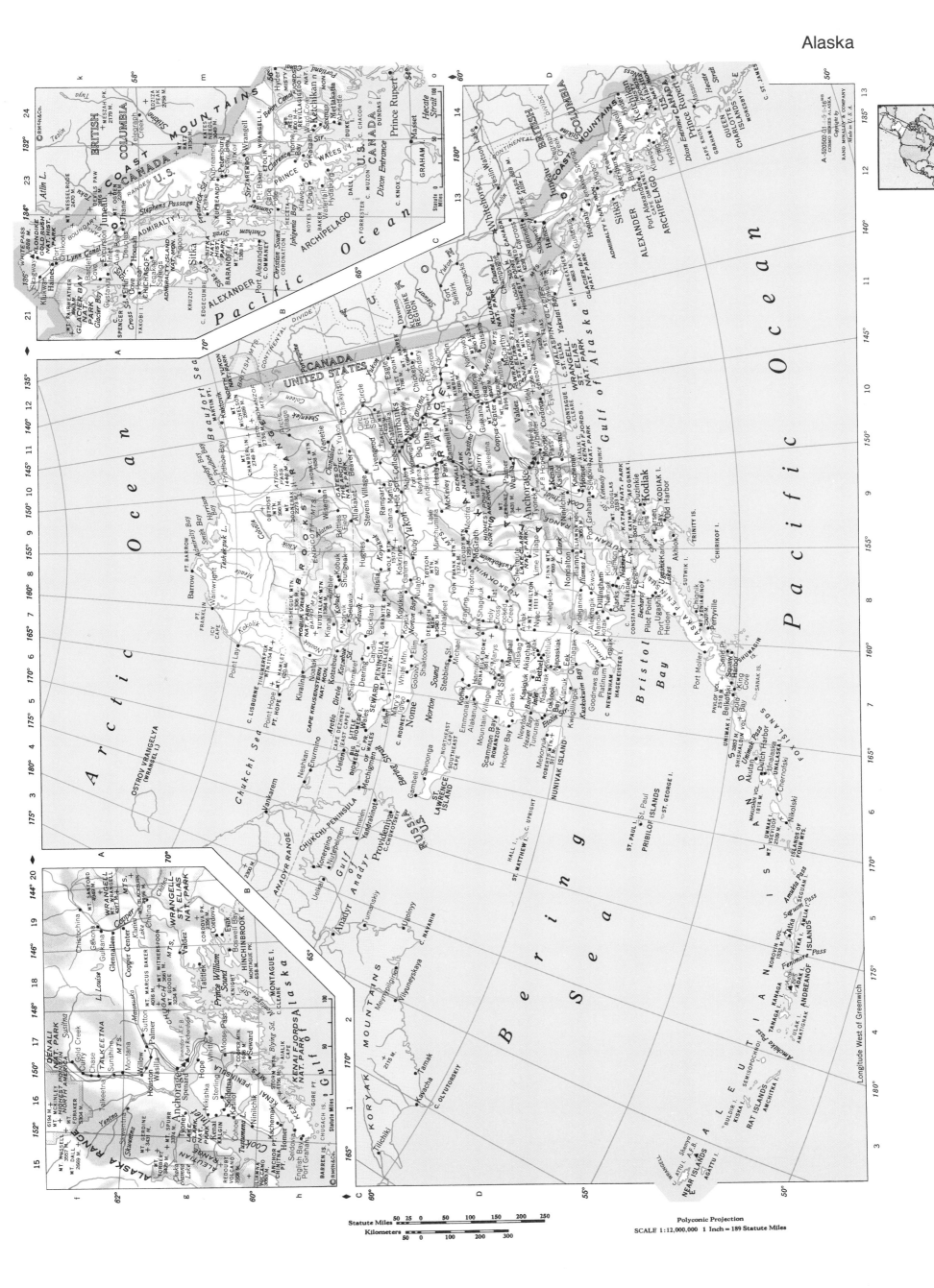

Polyconic Projection
SCALE 1:12,000,000   1 Inch = 189 Statute Miles

Statute Miles
Kilometers

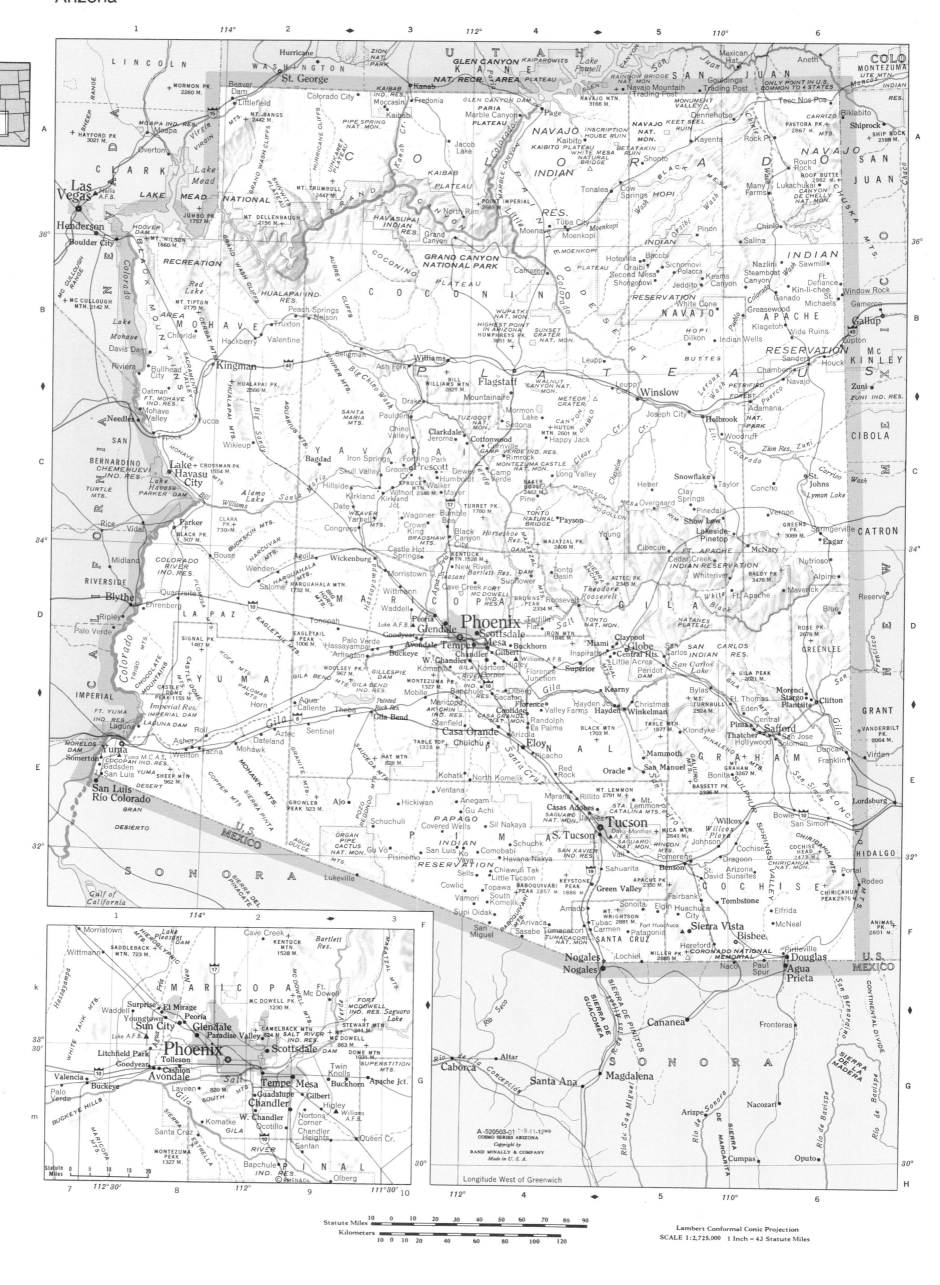

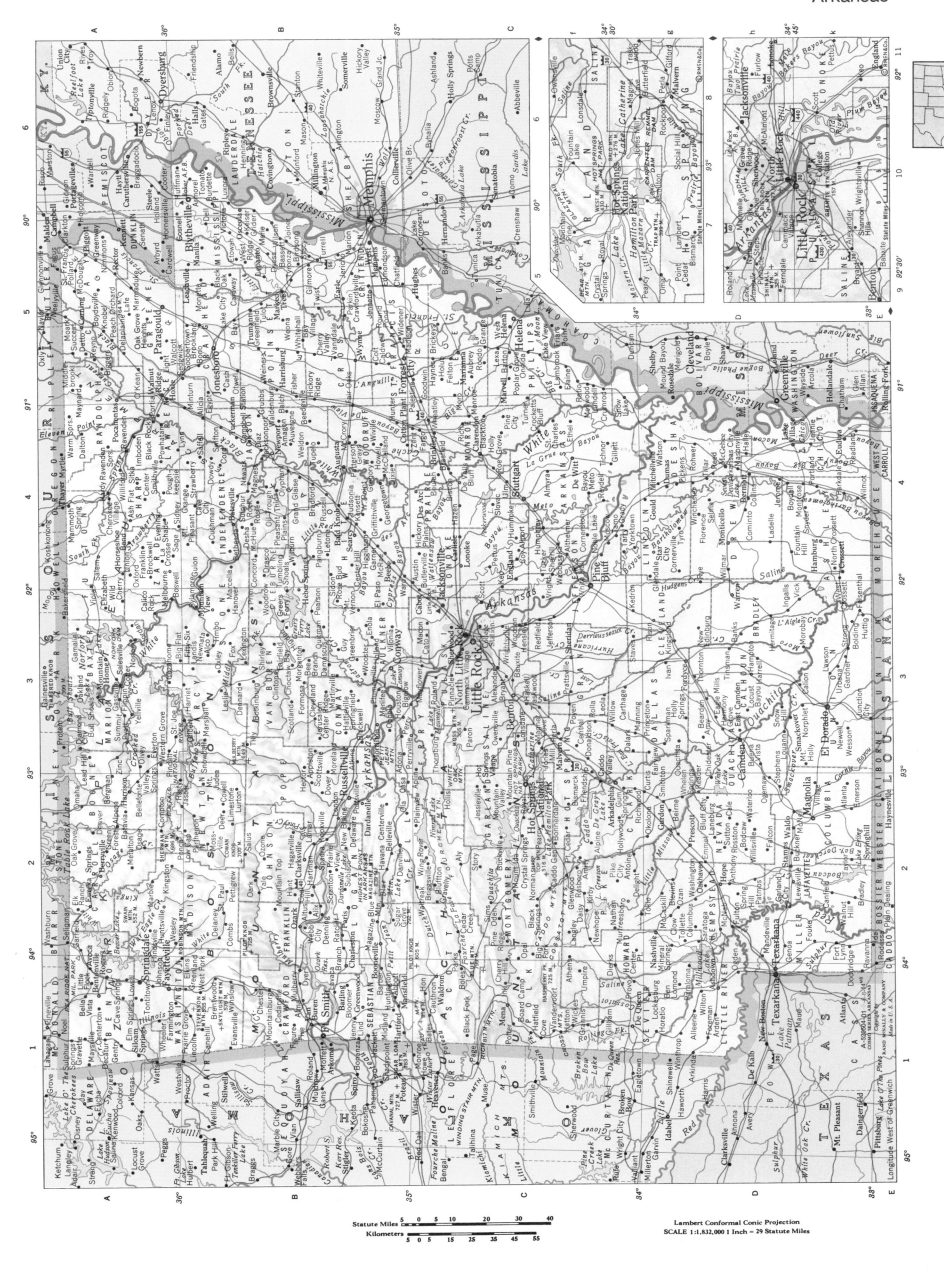

Statute Miles 5 0 5 10 20 30 40
Kilometers 5 0 5 15 25 35 45 55

Lambert Conformal Conic Projection
SCALE 1:1,832,000 1 Inch = 29 Statute Miles

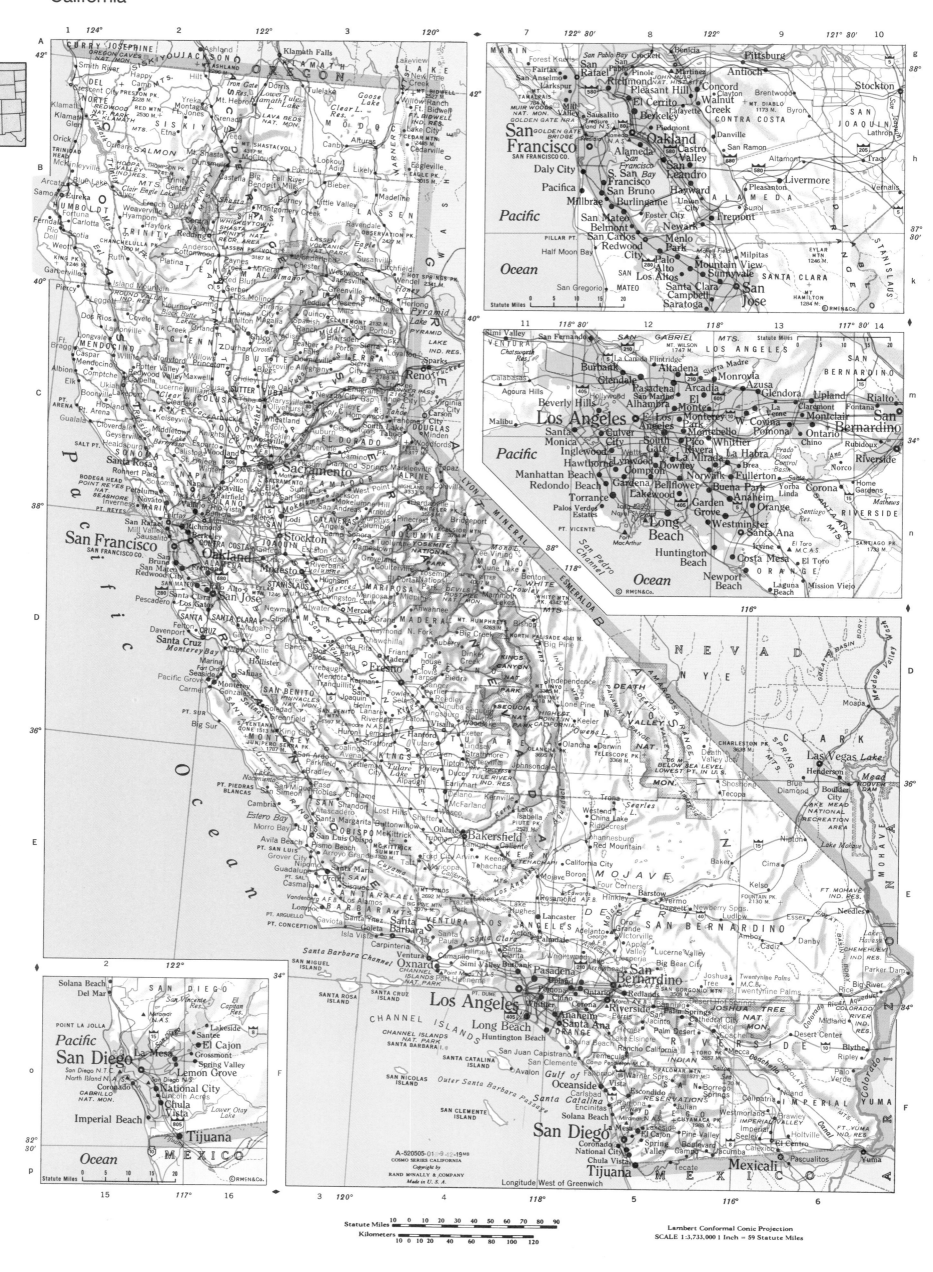

California

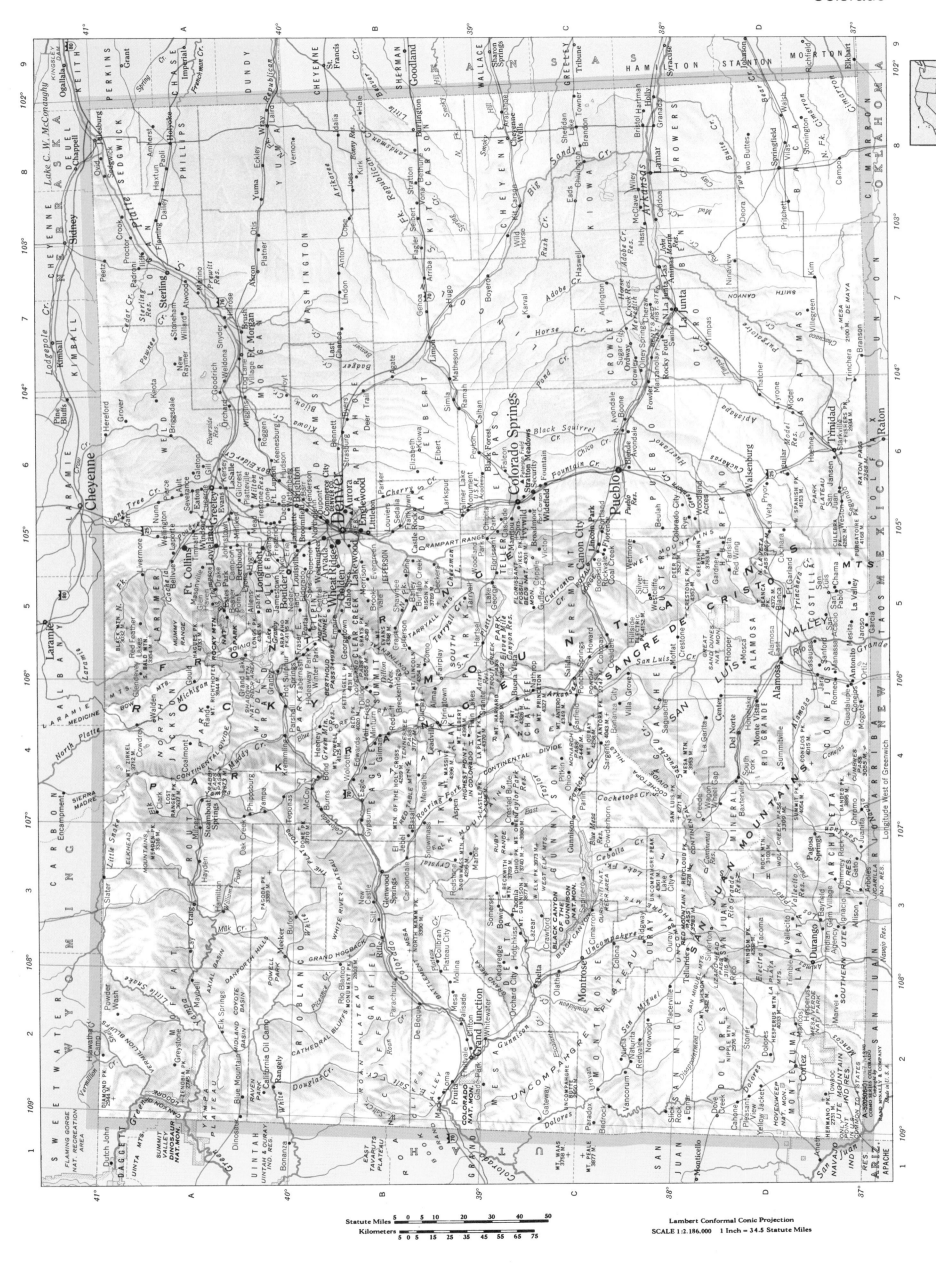

Statute Miles 5 0 5 10 20 30 40 50

Kilometers 5 0 5 15 25 35 45 55 65 75

Lambert Conformal Conic Projection
SCALE 1:2,186,000   1 Inch = 34.5 Statute Miles

Connecticut

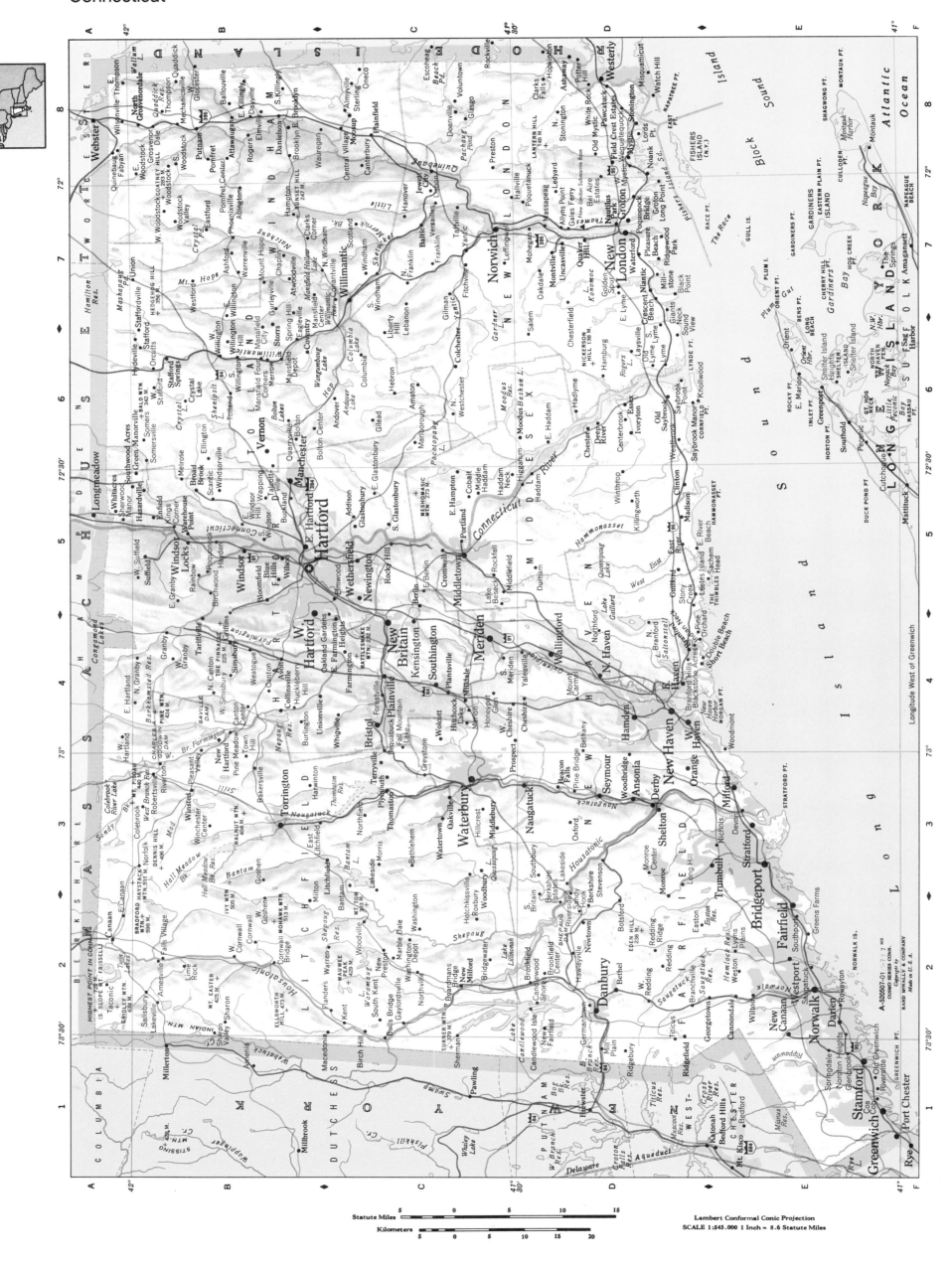

Statute Miles

Kilometers

Lambert Conformal Conic Projection
SCALE 1:545,000 1 Inch = 8.6 Statute Miles

A-520507-01—7/7 MB
COPYRIGHT BY
RAND MCNALLY & COMPANY
Made in U.S.A.

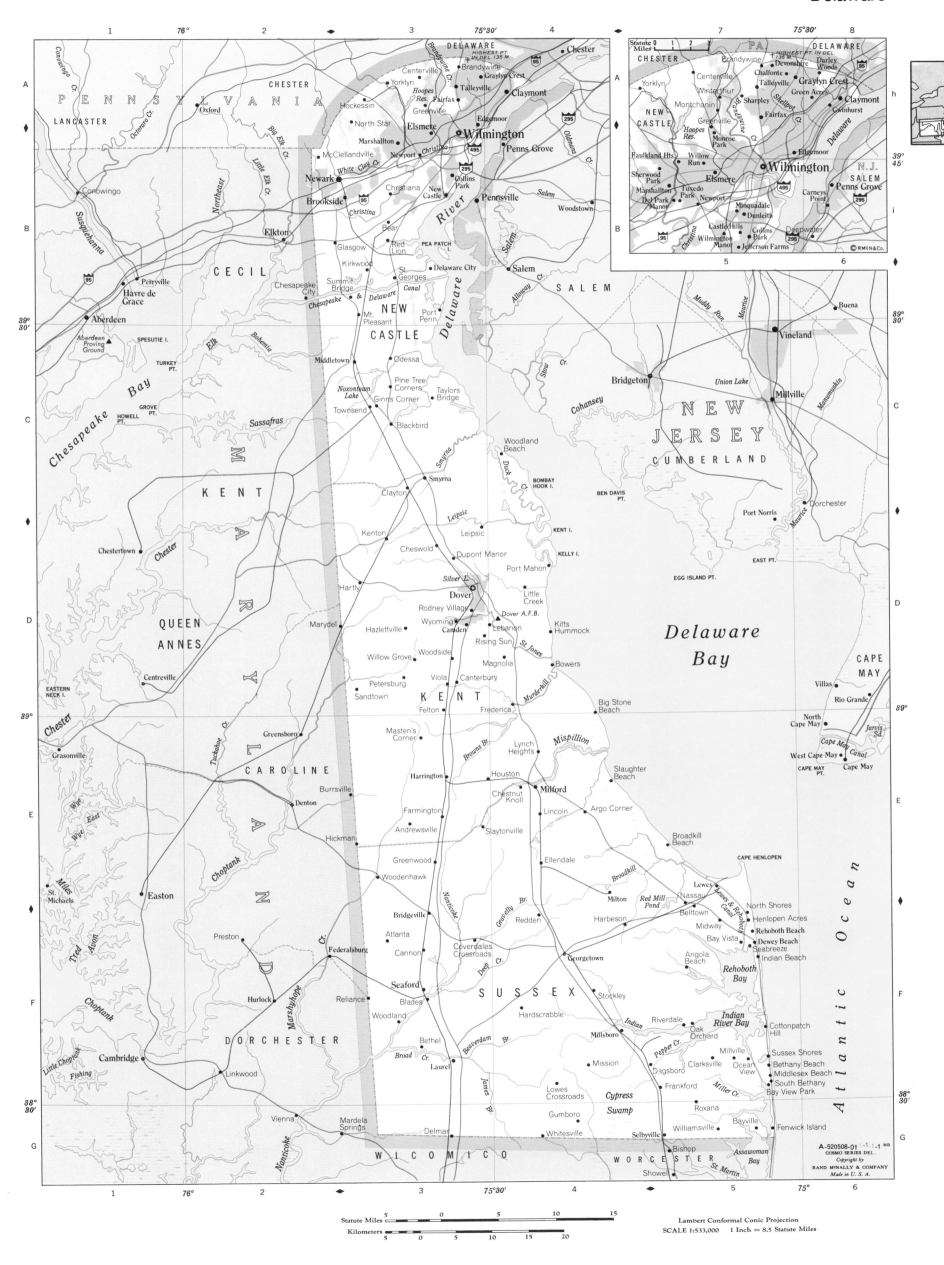

Delaware

Florida

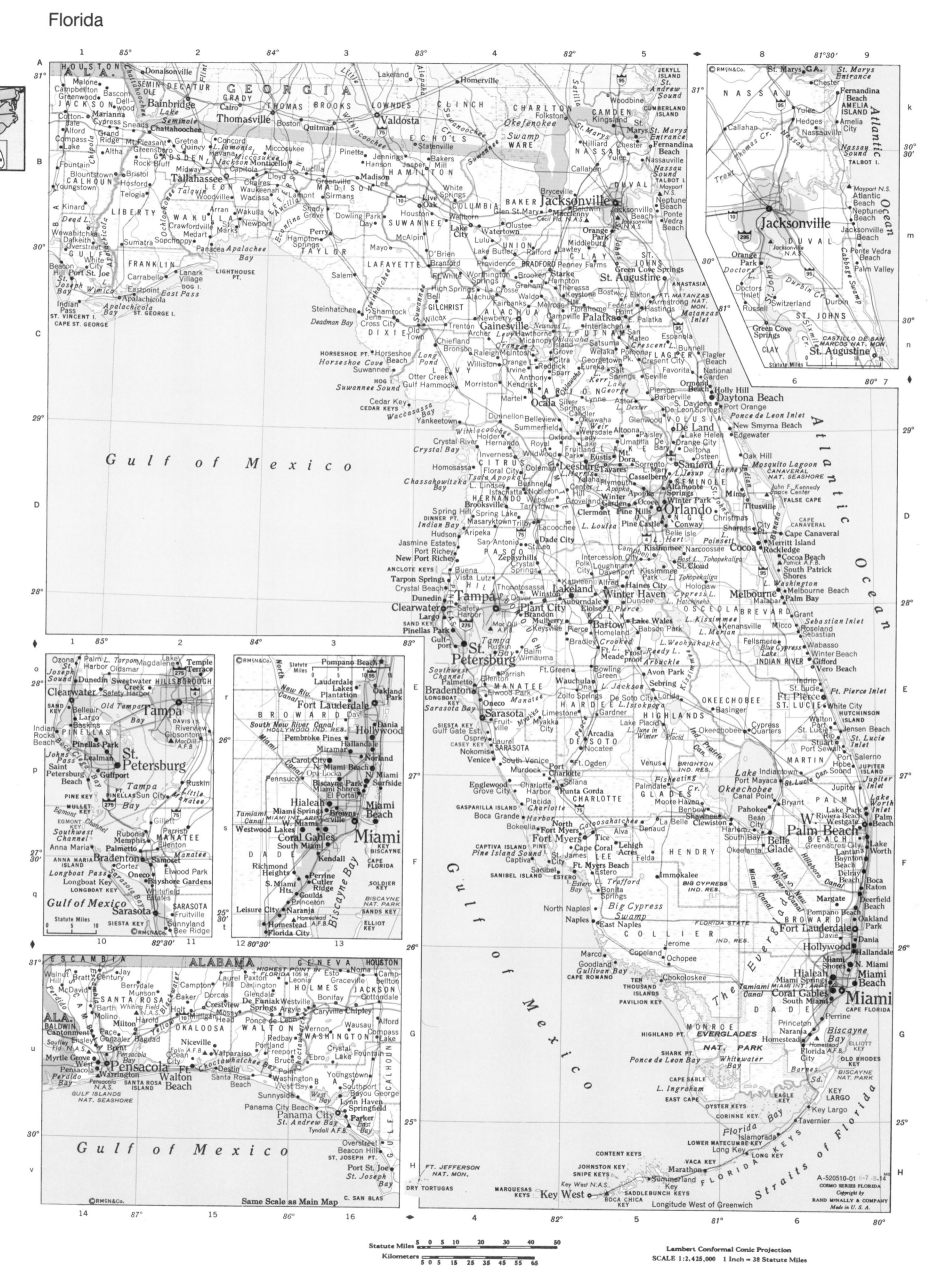

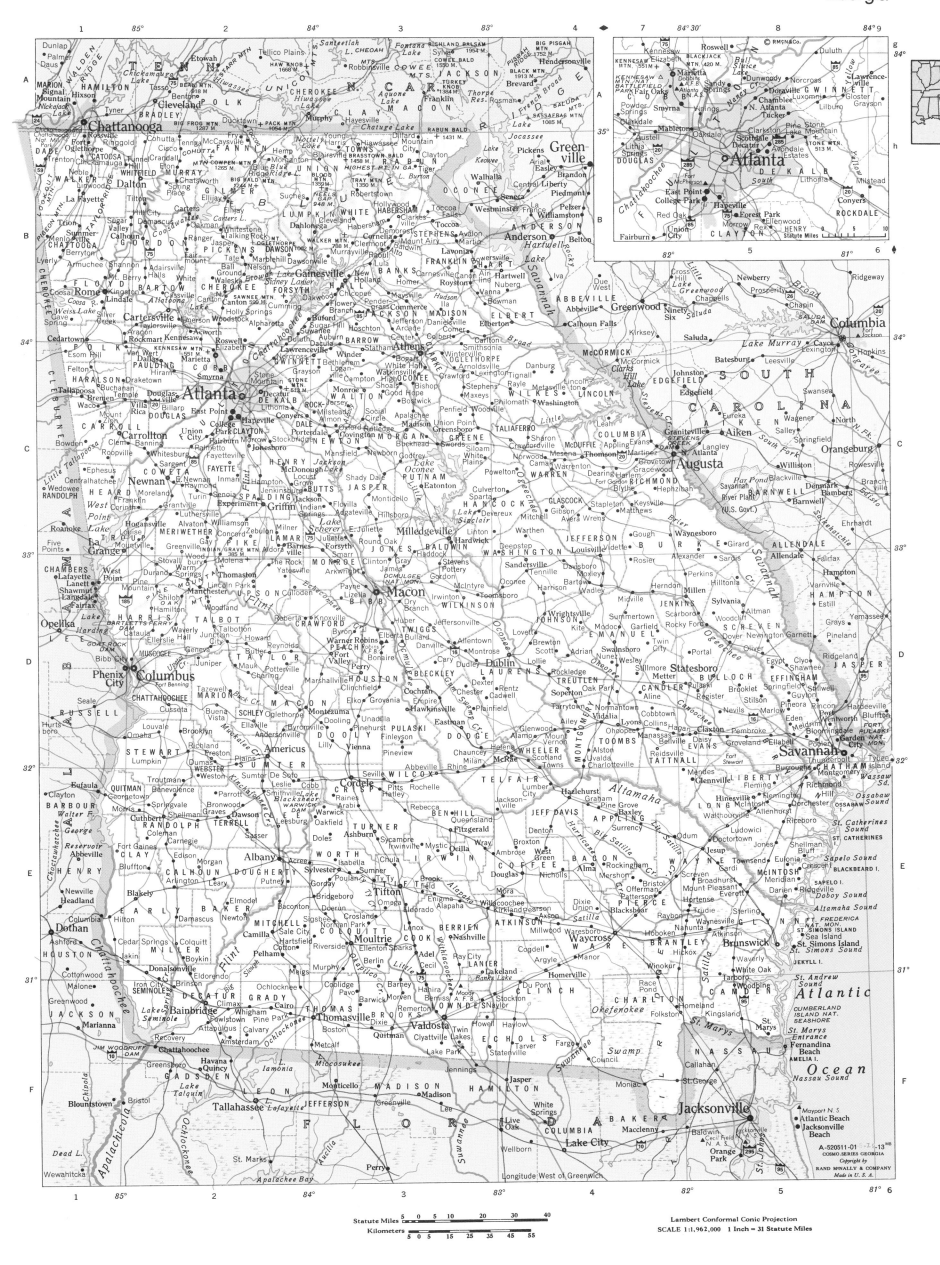

Lambert Conformal Conic Projection
SCALE 1:1,962,000   1 Inch = 31 Statute Miles

Hawaii

HAWAIIAN ISLANDS

Pacific Ocean

KURE MIDWAY IS. (U.S.A.) PEARL AND HERMES REEF

LISIANSKI I.
LAYSAN I.
MARO REEF
GARDNER PINNACLES
FRENCH FRIGATE SHOALS
NECKER I.
NIHOA

KAUAI
OAHU
MOLOKAI
MAUI
HAWAII
Honolulu
Hilo

Tropic of Cancer
Int. Date Line
JOHNSTON ATOLL

Statute Miles
150   300

KAUAI

KAUAI COUNTY
Lihue
Kapaa
Wailua
Hanamaulu
Kalaheo
Koloa
Hanapepe
Waimea
Kekaha
Mana
Anahola
Kilauea
Hanalei
Wainiha
Haena
Princeville
Puhi
Lawai
Eleele

KAWAIKINI 1598 M.
Kaulakahi Channel
Hanalei Bay
Wailua Bay
Nawiliwili Bay
MAKAHUENA PT.
MAKAHA PT.
MANA PT.
KAWAIHOA PT.
PUEO PT.

NIIHAU
LEHUA I.
PANIAU 390 M.
Kaumakani

OAHU

HONOLULU COUNTY
Honolulu
Pearl City
Waipahu
Waianae
Nanakuli
Ewa Beach
Aiea
Kailua
Kaneohe
Waimanalo
Waialua
Wahiawa
Haleiwa
Laie
Hauula
Kahana
Kahuku

KAENA PT.
BARBERS PT.
DIAMOND HEAD
KOKO HEAD
MAKAPUU HEAD
KAALA 1231 M.
WAIANAE RANGE
Kahuku Pt.

MOLOKAI

KALAWAO COUNTY
MAUI COUNTY
Kaunakakai
Hoolehua
Kualapuu
Maunaloa
Halawa
Kalaupapa
Kamalo
Puukolii

KAMAKOU 1515 M.
CAPE HALAWA
ILIO PT.
LAAU PT.
KALAUPAPA PT.

LANAI

LANAI CITY
Lanai City

PALAOA PT.
LANAIHALE 1027 M.
Kaumalapau

KAHOOLAWE

KEALAIKAHIKI PT.

MAUI

MAUI COUNTY
Wailuku
Kahului
Lahaina
Paia
Kihei
Makawao
Pukalani
Hana
Haiku
Kula
Keanae
Napili
Waiehu
Keokea

HALEAKALA 3055 M.
HALEAKALA NATIONAL PARK
HALEAKALA CRATER
KAUIKI HEAD
PAPAWAI PT.
MCGREGOR PT.

HAWAII

HAWAII COUNTY
Hilo
Kailua Kona
Kealakekua
Captain Cook
Honokaa
Waimea
Kapaau
Hawi
Kamuela
Pahala
Naalehu
Volcano
Pahoa
Keaau
Papaikou
Honomu
Laupahoehoe
Mountainview
Kurtistown
Glenwood
Kaumana
Hookena
Kainaliu
Holualoa
Honaunau
Milolii
Waiohinu
Keaukaha

MAUNA KEA (VOL.) 4205 M. HIGHEST POINT IN HAWAII
MAUNA LOA (VOL.) 4169 M.
HUALALAI 2521 M.
KILAUEA CRATER
HAWAII VOLCANOES NATIONAL PARK
KILAUEA 1247 M.
PUU WAAWAA 1726 M.
KOHALA MTS.
KAU DESERT
UPOLU PT.
KALAE
KA LAE
APUA PT.
KUMUKAHI
LELEIWI PT.
KALOLI PT.
Kalana Homesteads
PUUKOHOLA HEIAU NATIONAL HISTORIC SITE
CITY OF REFUGE HONAUNAU NATIONAL HISTORICAL PARK
Kawaihae
Kalaoa
Kalapana
Kaimu
Opihikao
Kukuihaele
Paauilo
Paauhau
Ookala
Ninole
Papaaloa
Hakalau
Pepeekeo
Keauhou
Keahole Pt.
Napoopoo
Keei
Kai Malino
Puako
Kiholo Bay
Keawaula Bay
Honuapo Bay
Kaalualu Bay
Pohue Bay
Kealakekua Bay
Kauna Pt.

Alenuihaha Channel
Kaiwi Channel
Kalohi Channel
Auau Channel
Pailolo Channel
Kealaikahiki Channel
Kaulakahi Channel
Kauai Channel
Kaieiewaho Channel
Kailua Bay
Kaneohe Bay
Waimanalo Bay
Mamala Bay
Kaneohe Bay

Longitude West of Greenwich

Lambert Conformal Conic Projection
SCALE 1:2,000,000   1 Inch = 32 Statute Miles

Statute Miles
5 0 5 10 20 30 40 50
Kilometers
5 0 5 10 20 30 40 50 60

A-500512-01   COSMO SERIES HAWAIIAN ST.   RAND MCNALLY & COMPANY   Copyright by   Made in U.S.A.

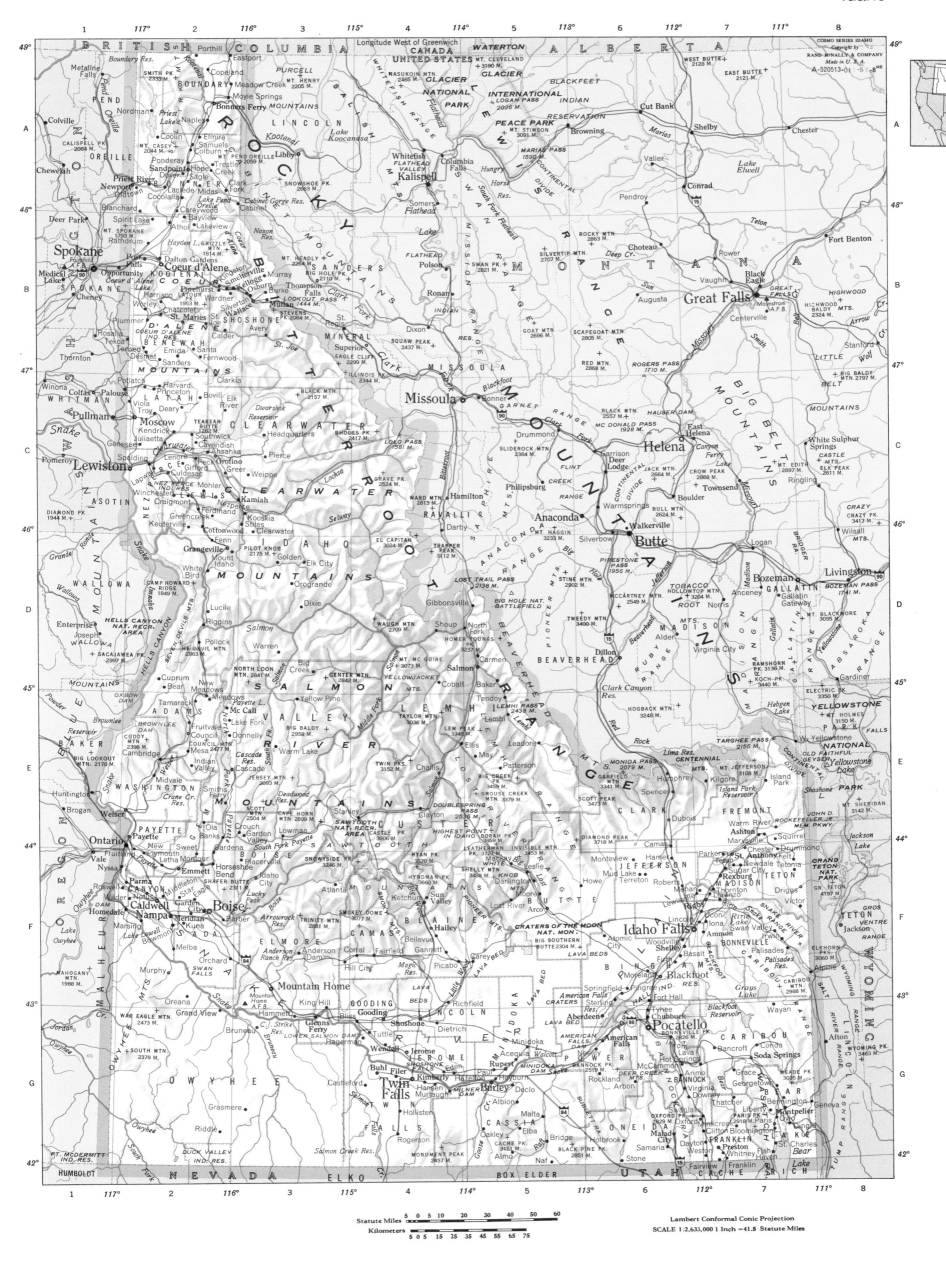

Lambert Conformal Conic Projection
SCALE 1:2,633,000 1 Inch =41.5 Statute Miles

Statute Miles

Kilometers

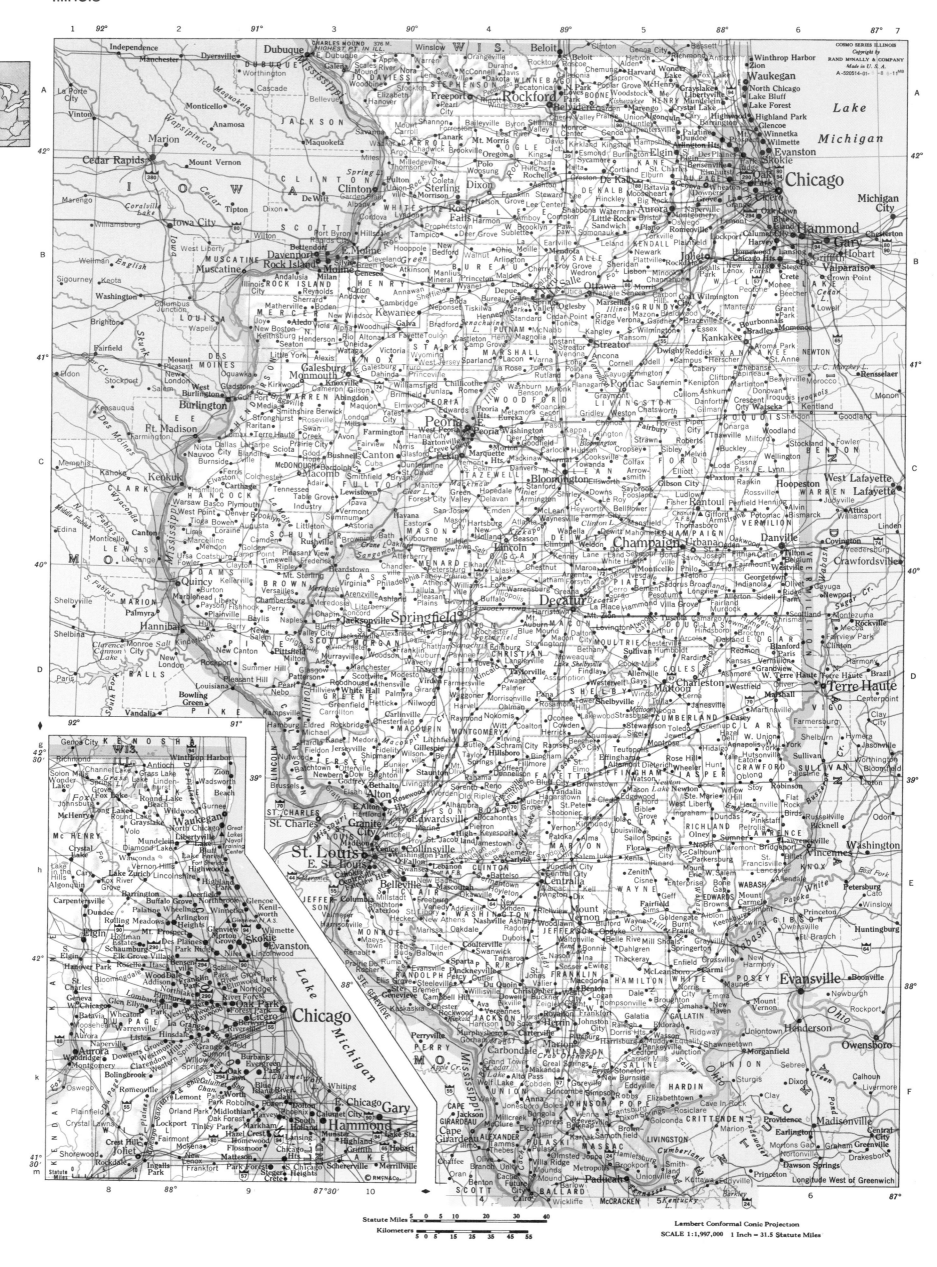

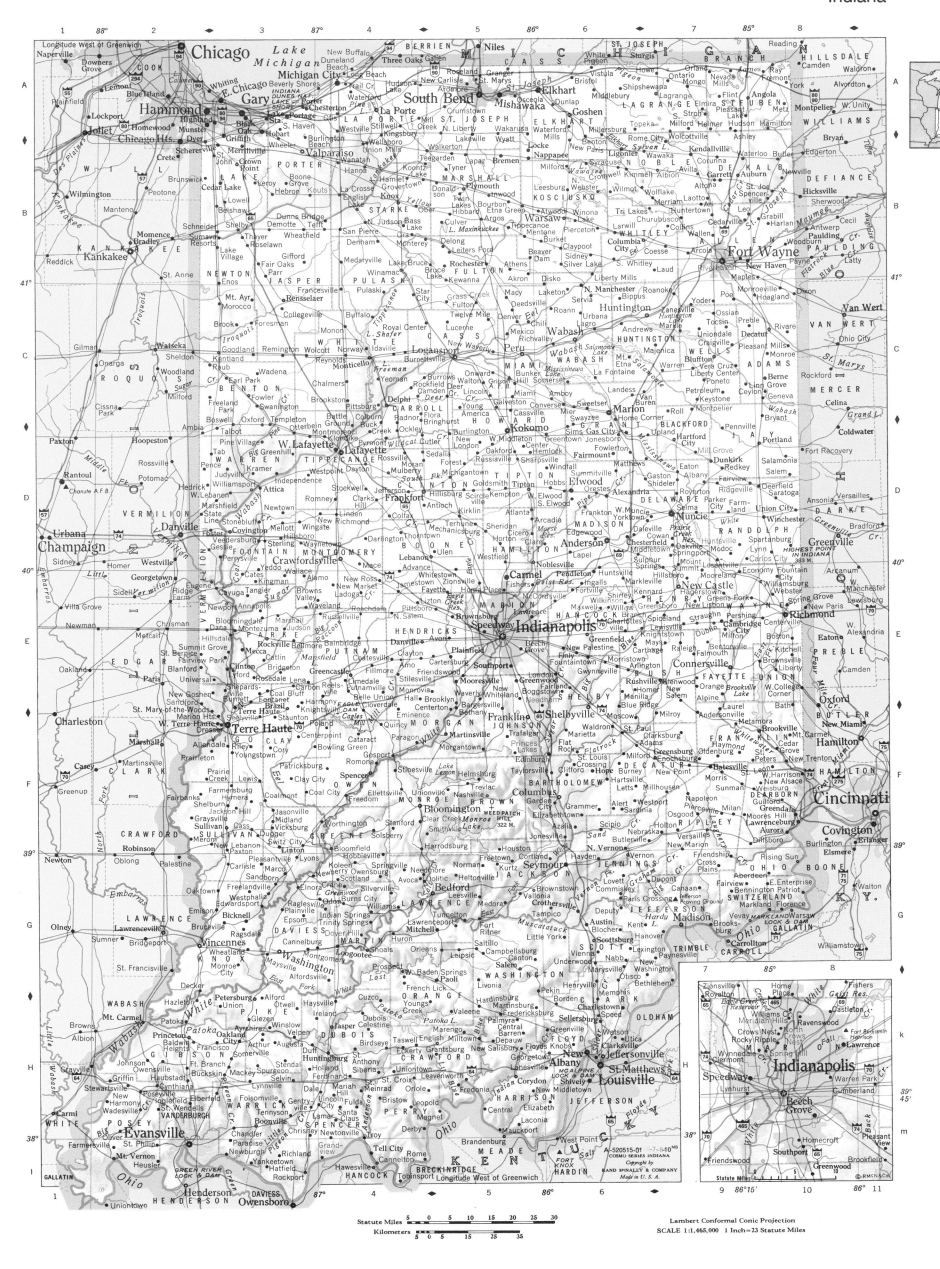

Indiana

Iowa

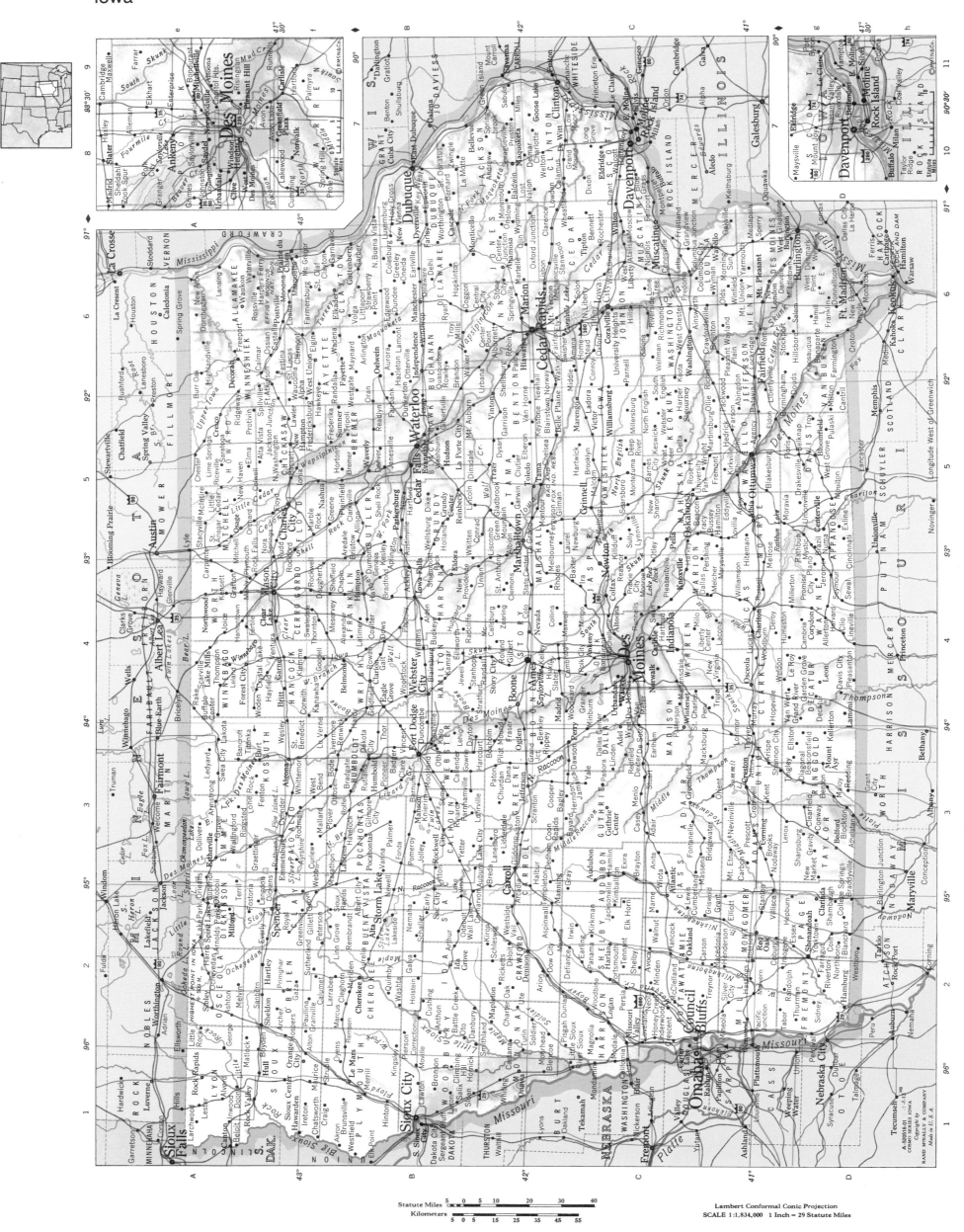

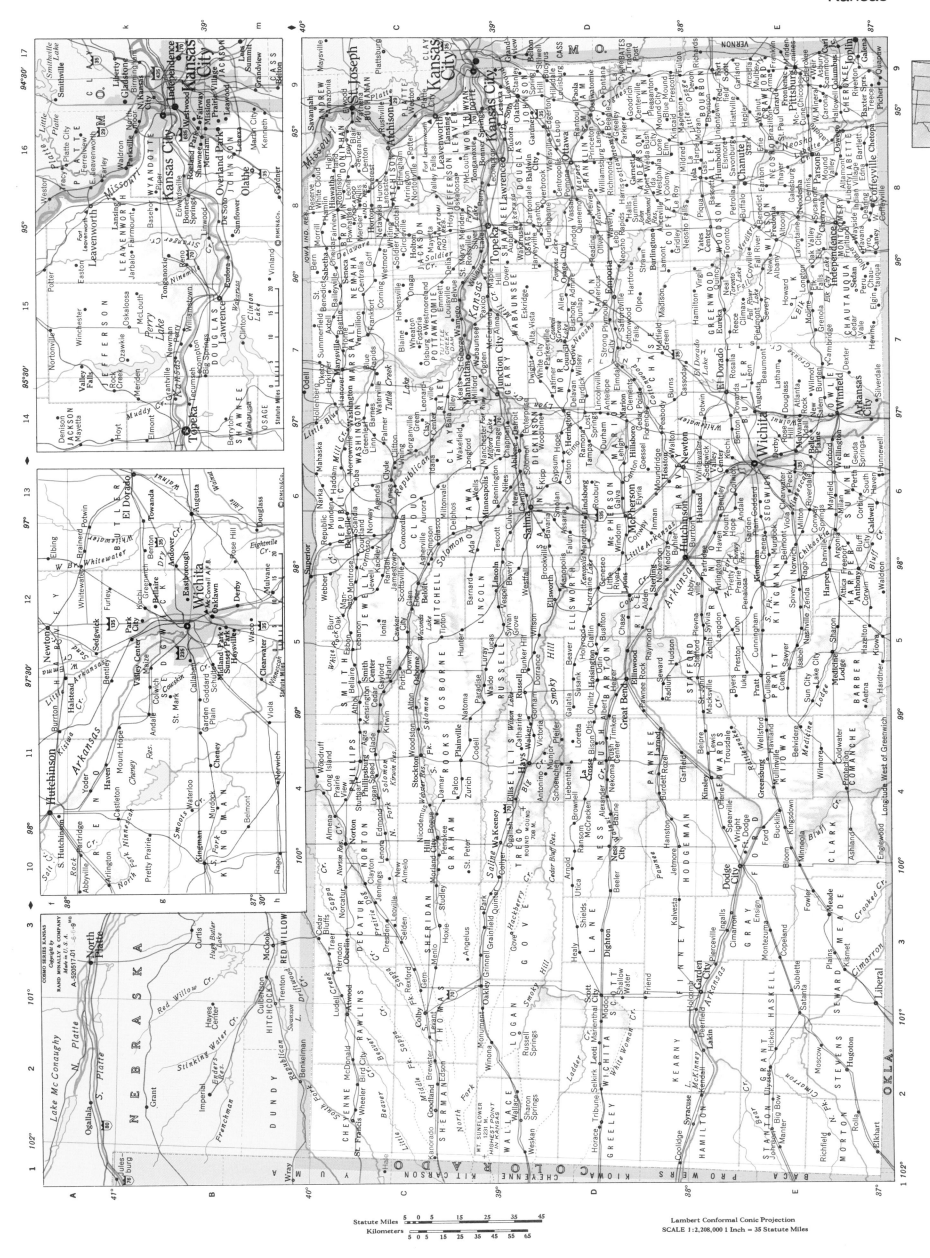

Statute Miles
Kilometers

Lambert Conformal Conic Projection
SCALE 1:2,208,000 1 Inch = 35 Statute Miles

Kentucky

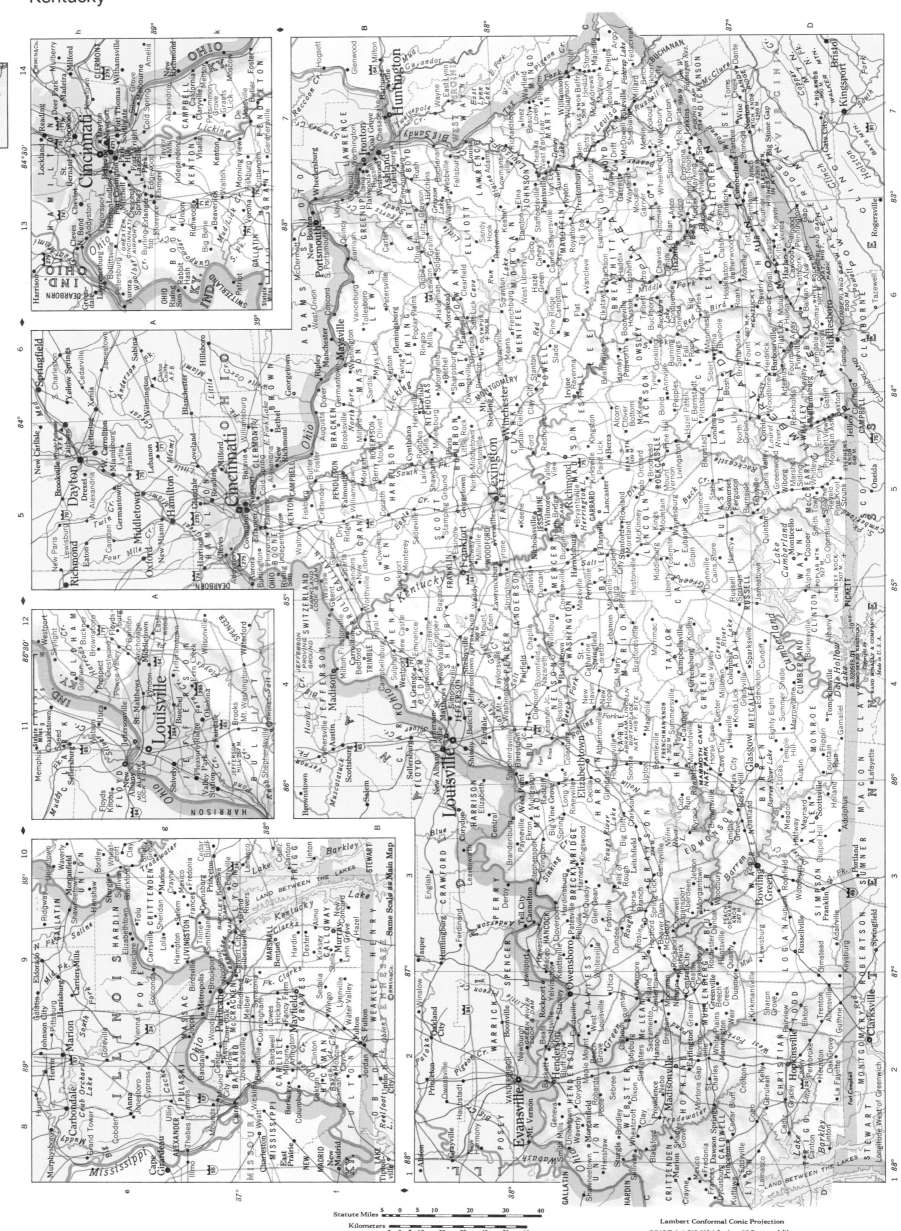

Lambert Conformal Conic Projection
SCALE 1:1,738,000 1 Inch = 27 Statute Miles

Statute Miles
Kilometers

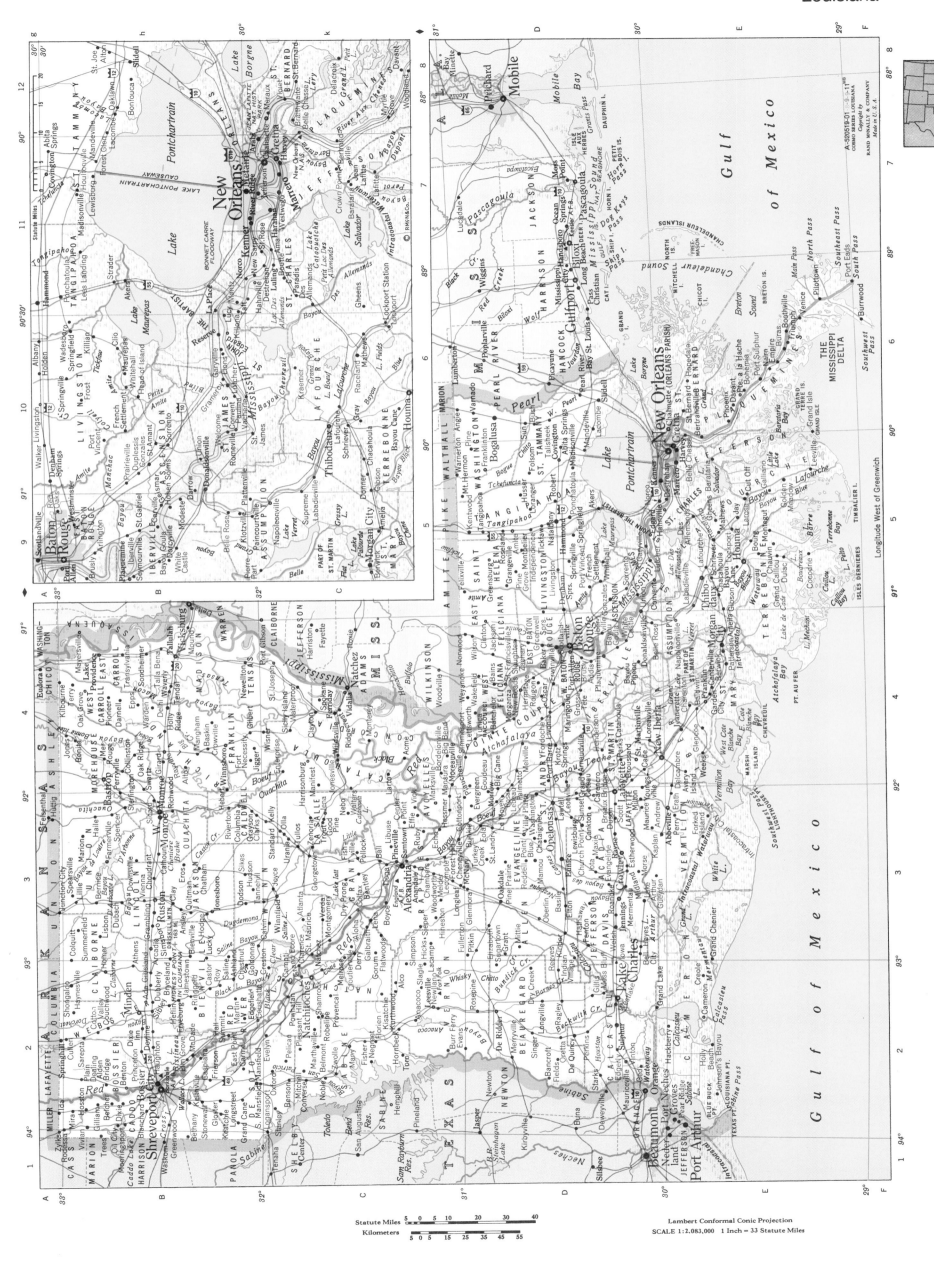

Lambert Conformal Conic Projection
SCALE 1:2,083,000   1 Inch = 33 Statute Miles

Statute Miles
Kilometers

Maine

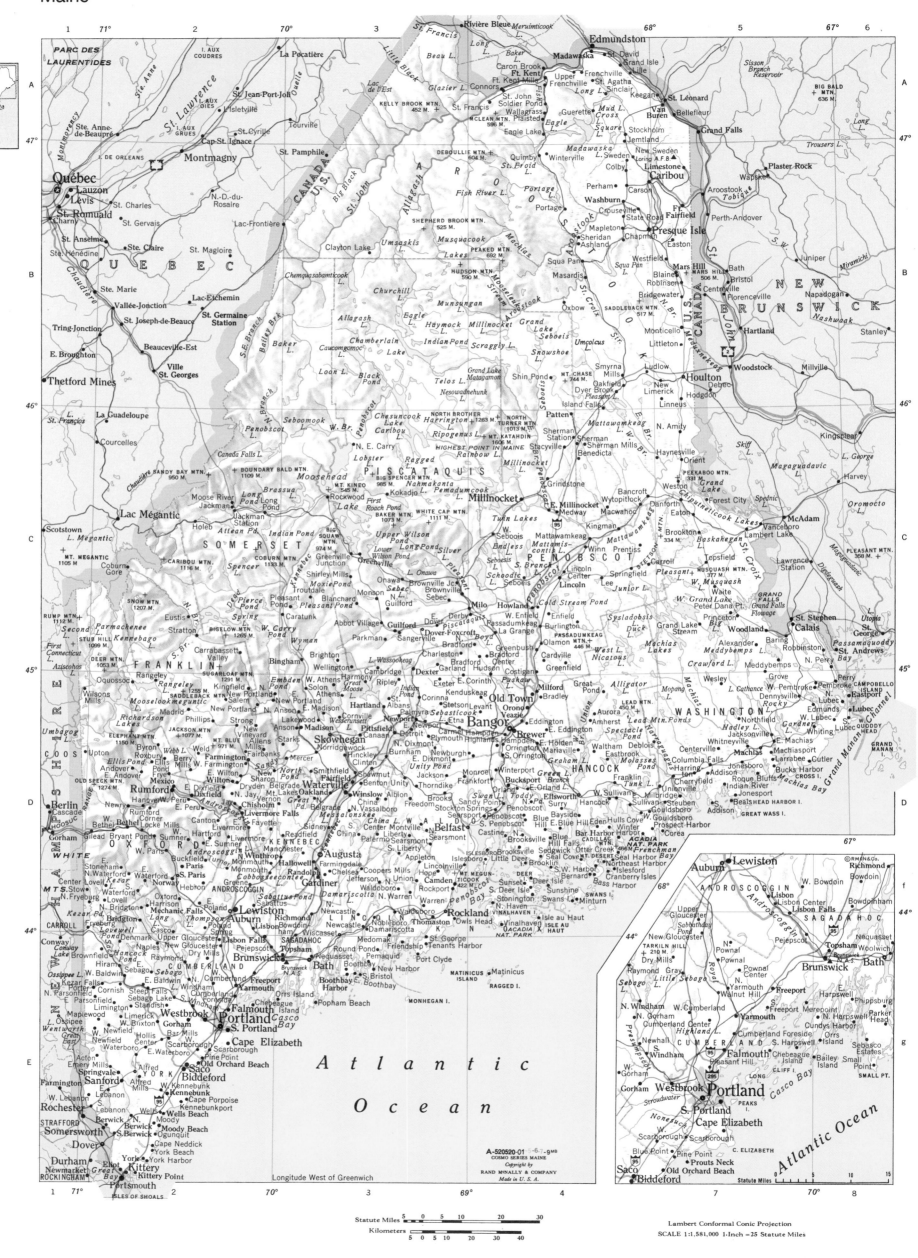

Statute Miles

Kilometers

Lambert Conformal Conic Projection
SCALE 1:985,000 1 Inch = 15.5 Statute Miles

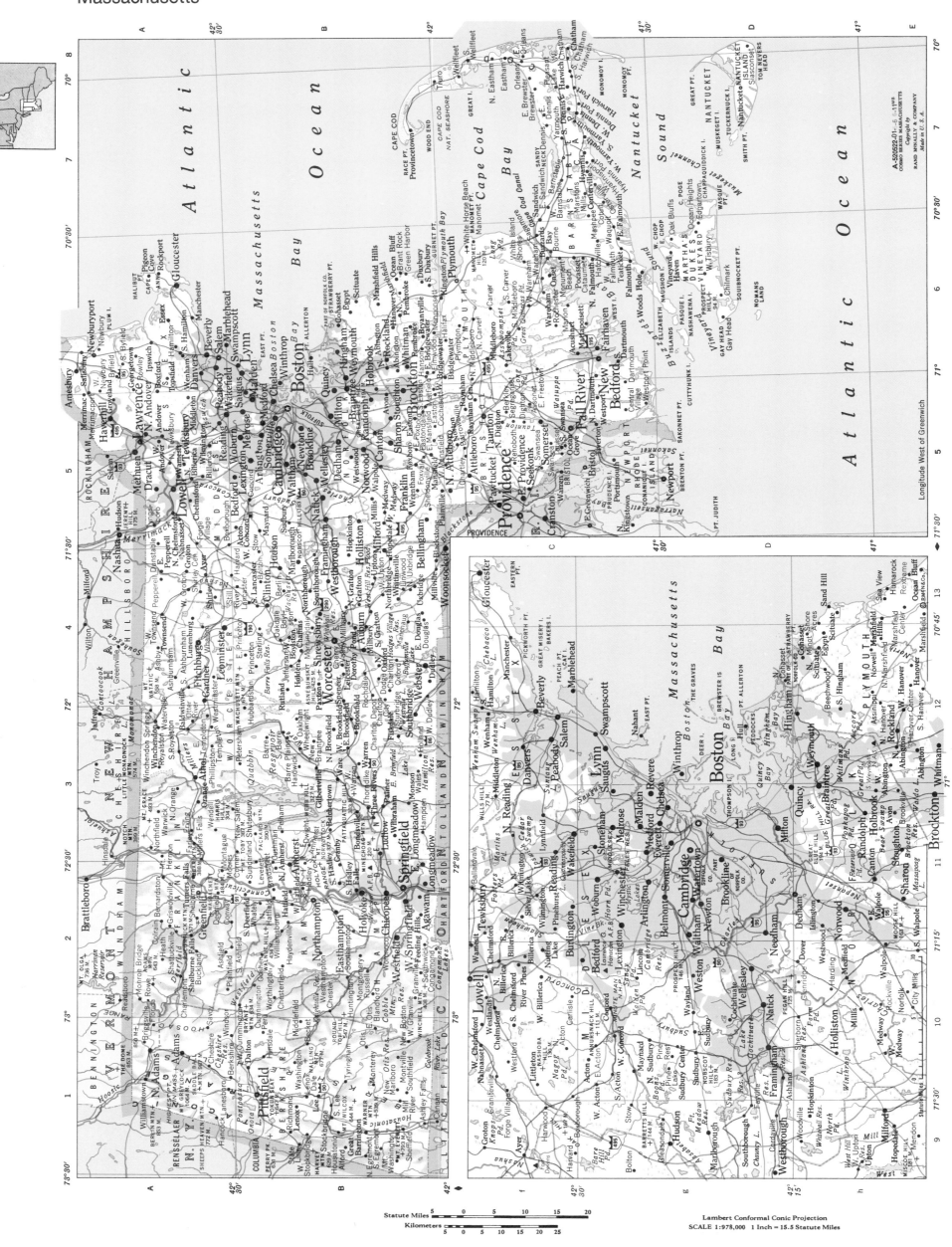

Statute Miles

Kilometers

Lambert Conformal Conic Projection
SCALE 1:978,000   1 Inch = 15.5 Statute Miles

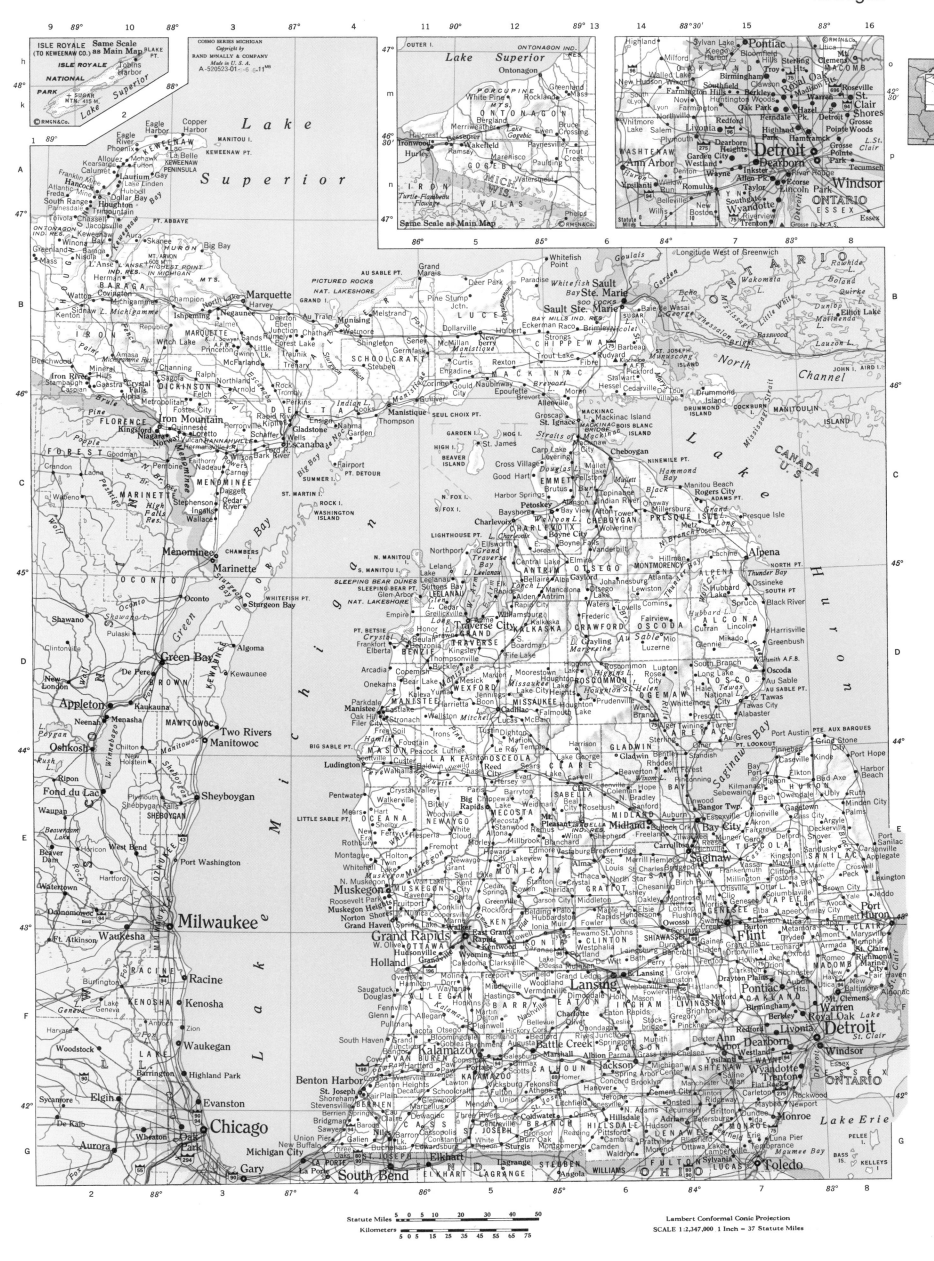

Statute Miles

Kilometers

Lambert Conformal Conic Projection
SCALE 1:2,347,000 1 Inch = 37 Statute Miles

Minnesota

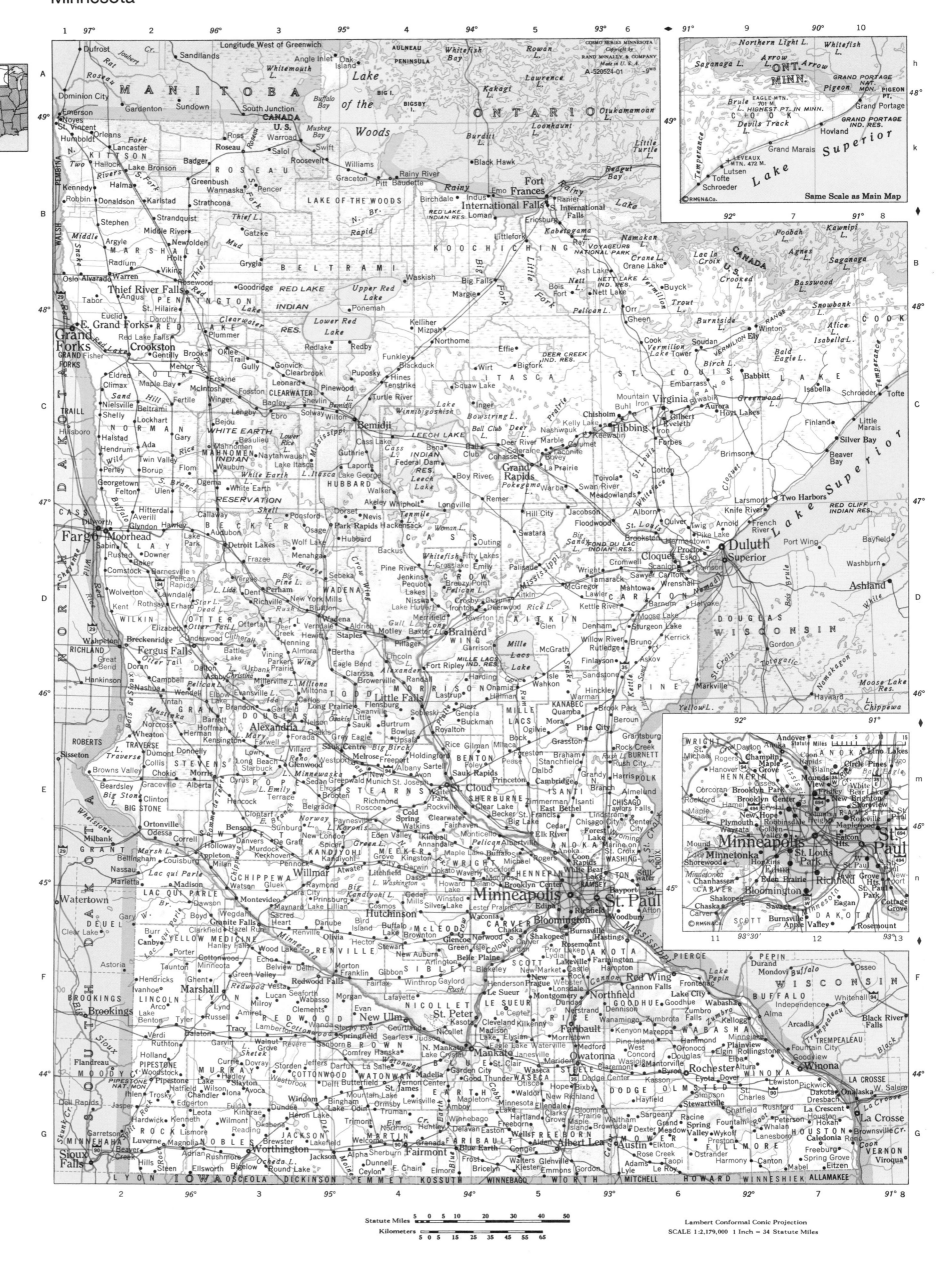

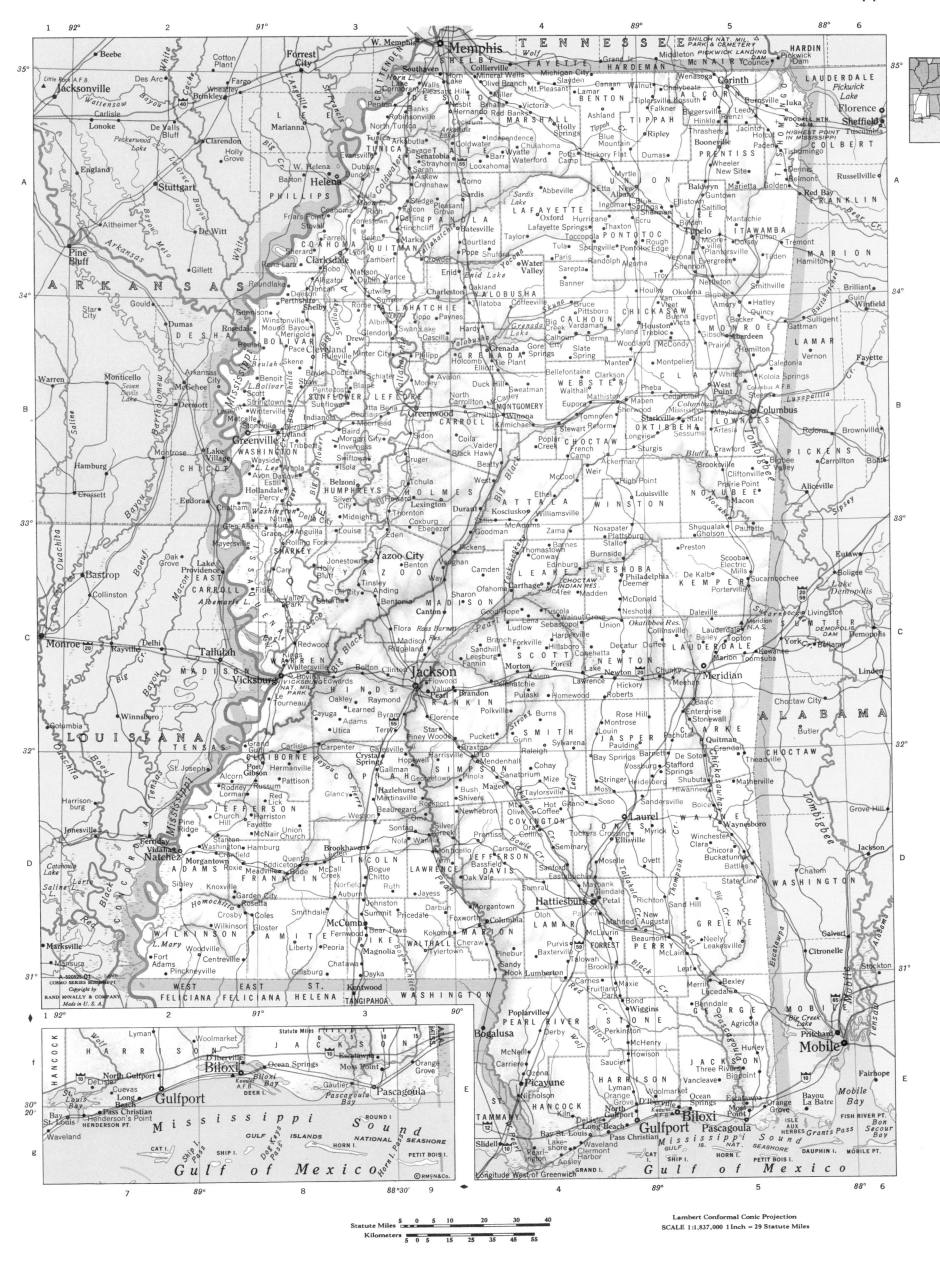

Mississippi

Lambert Conformal Conic Projection
SCALE 1:1,837,000 1 Inch = 29 Statute Miles

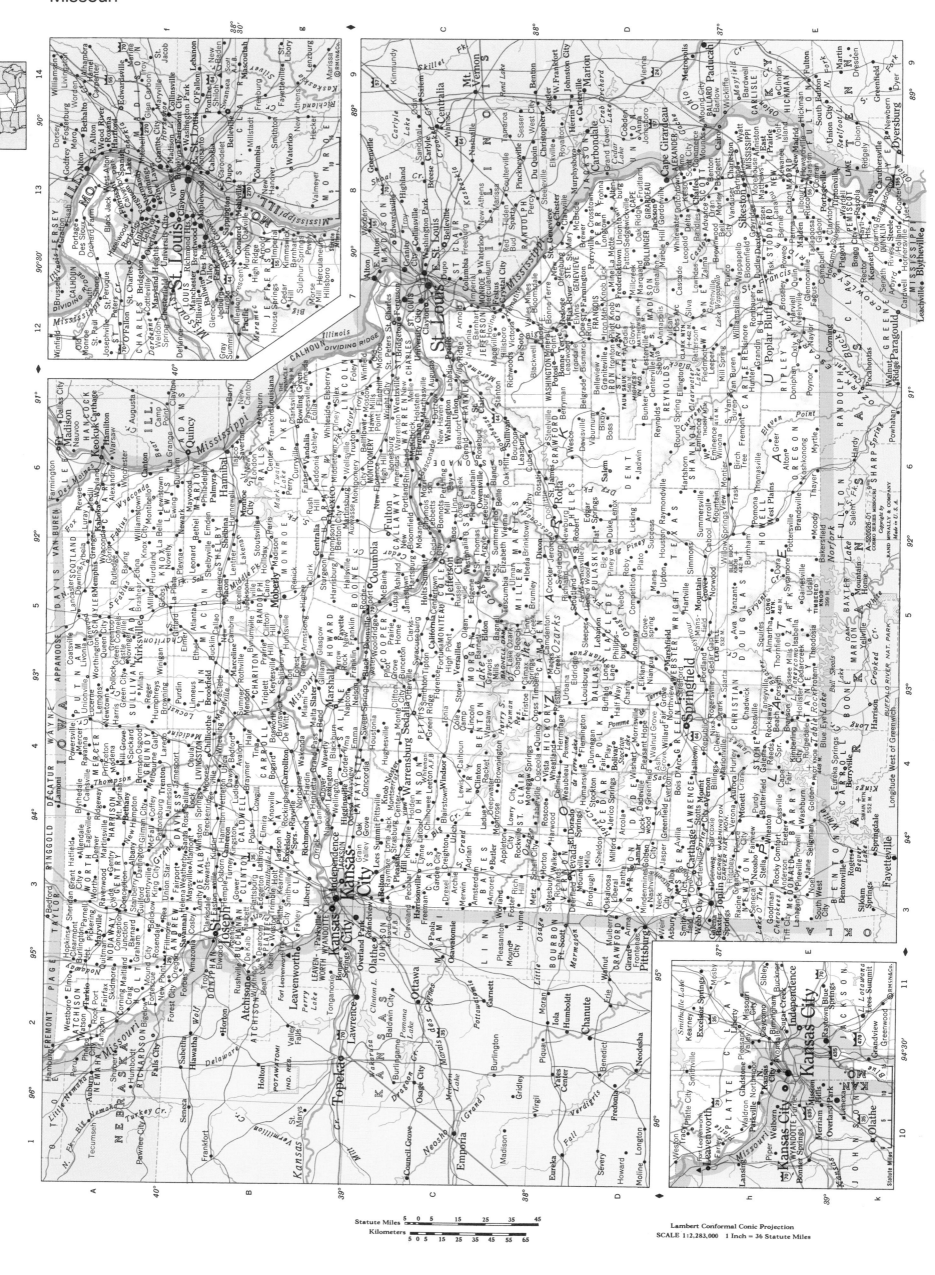

Statute Miles

Kilometers

Lambert Conformal Conic Projection
SCALE 1:2,283,000   1 Inch = 36 Statute Miles

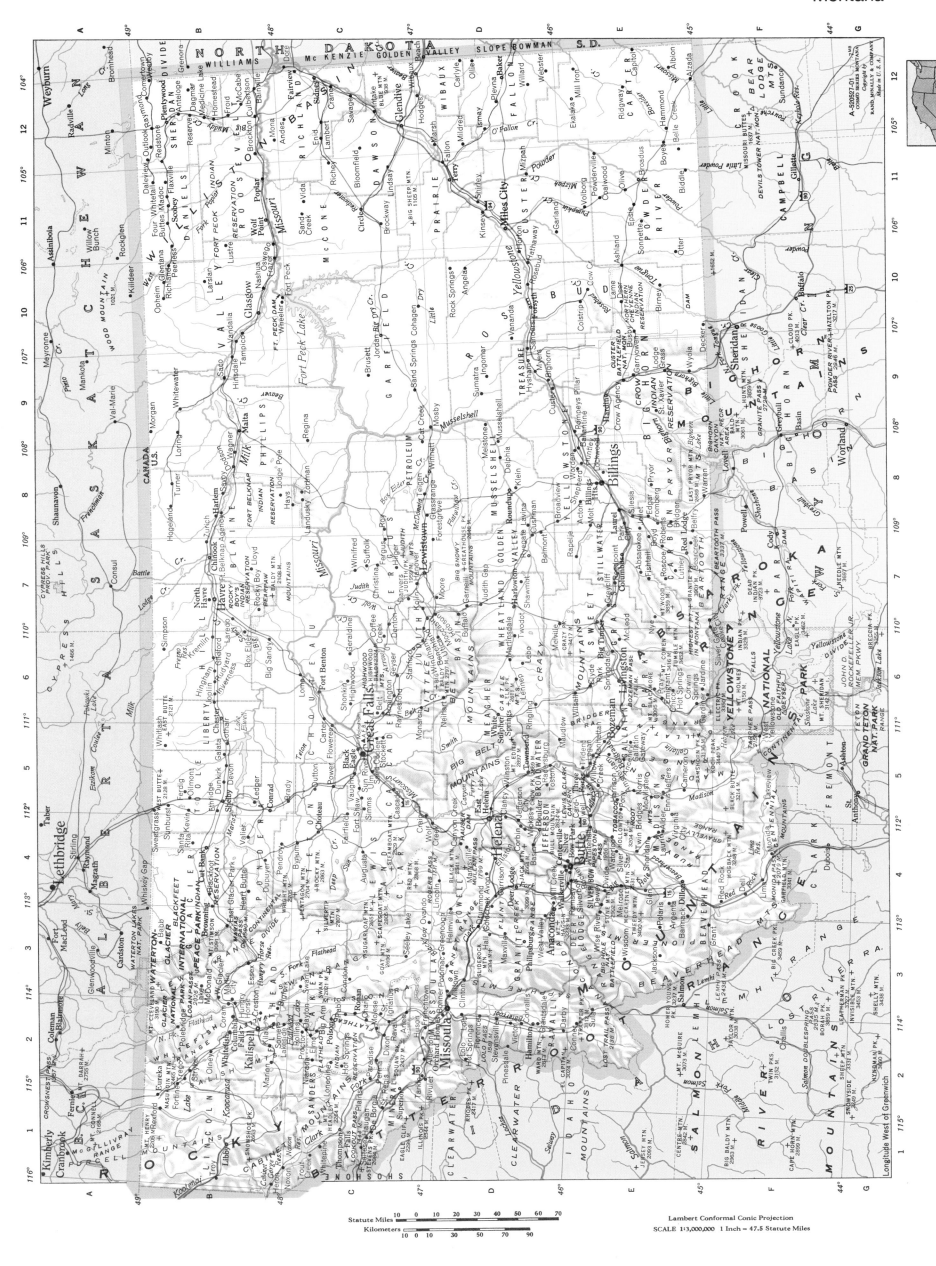

Statute Miles
Kilometers

Lambert Conformal Conic Projection
SCALE 1:3,000,000   1 Inch = 47.5 Statute Miles

Nebraska

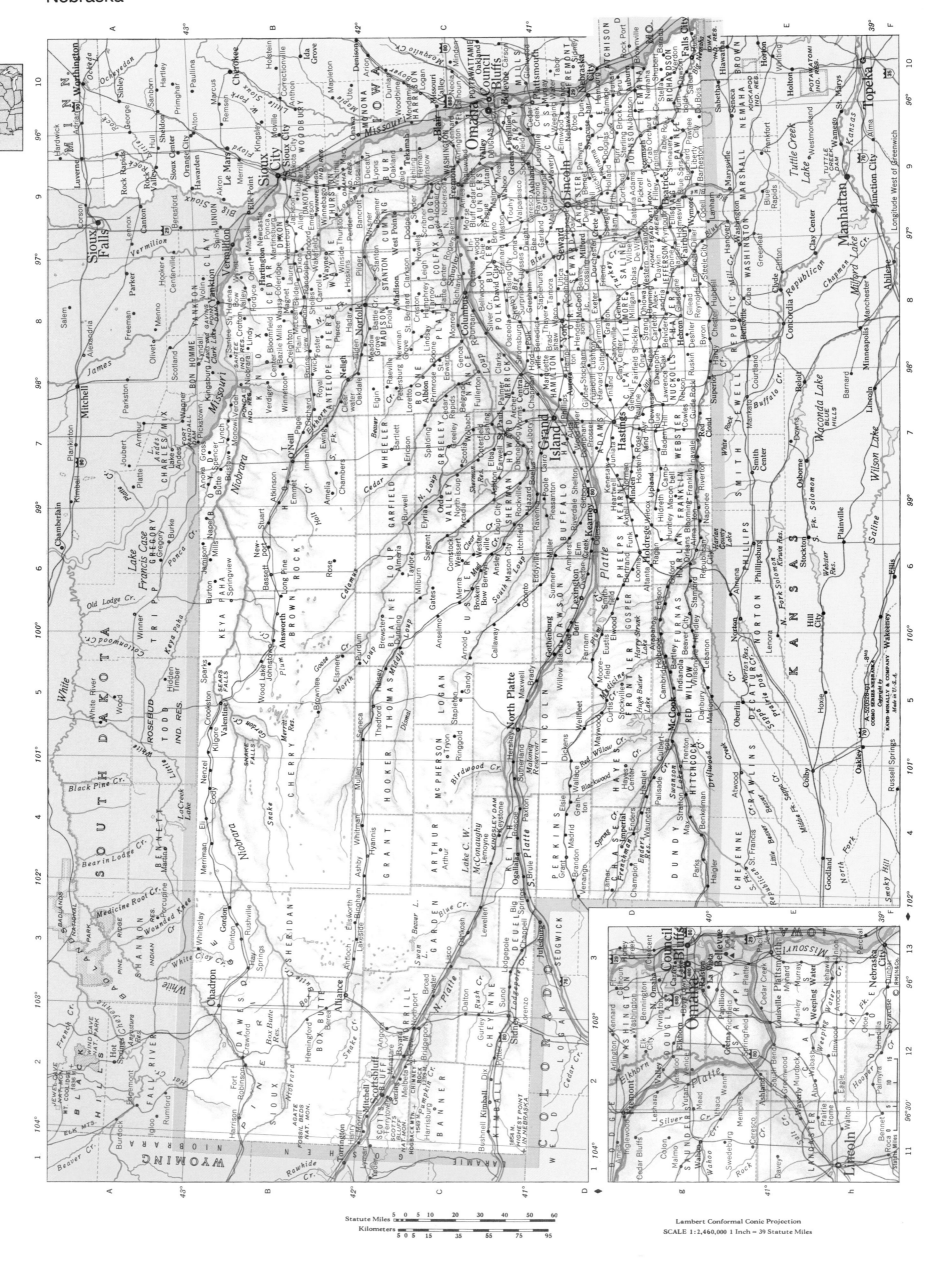

Statute Miles 5 0 5 10 20 30 40 50 60
Kilometers 5 0 5 15 35 55 75 95

Lambert Conformal Conic Projection
SCALE 1:2,460,000 1 Inch = 39 Statute Miles

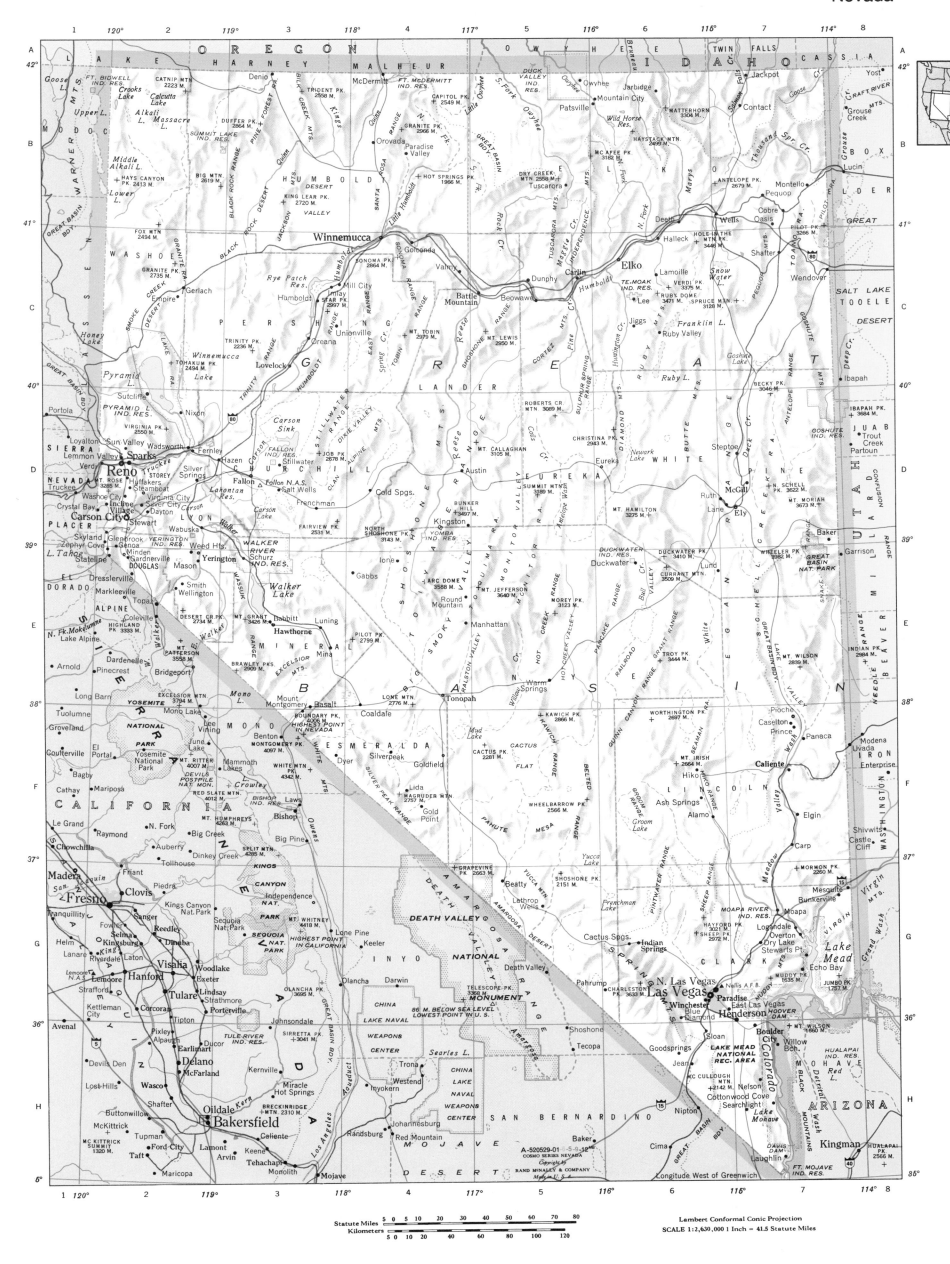

Statute Miles
Kilometers

Lambert Conformal Conic Projection
SCALE 1:2,630,000 1 Inch = 41.5 Statute Miles

New Hampshire

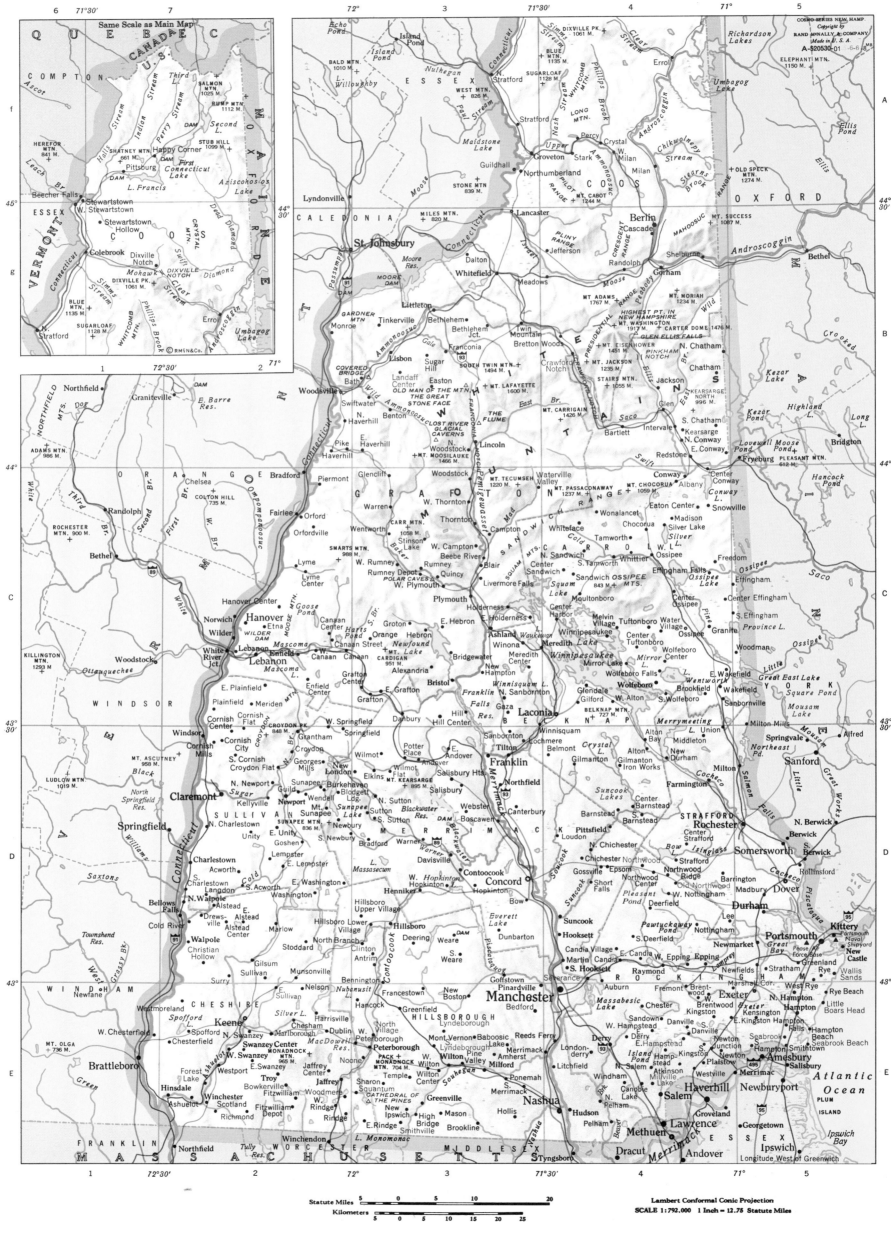

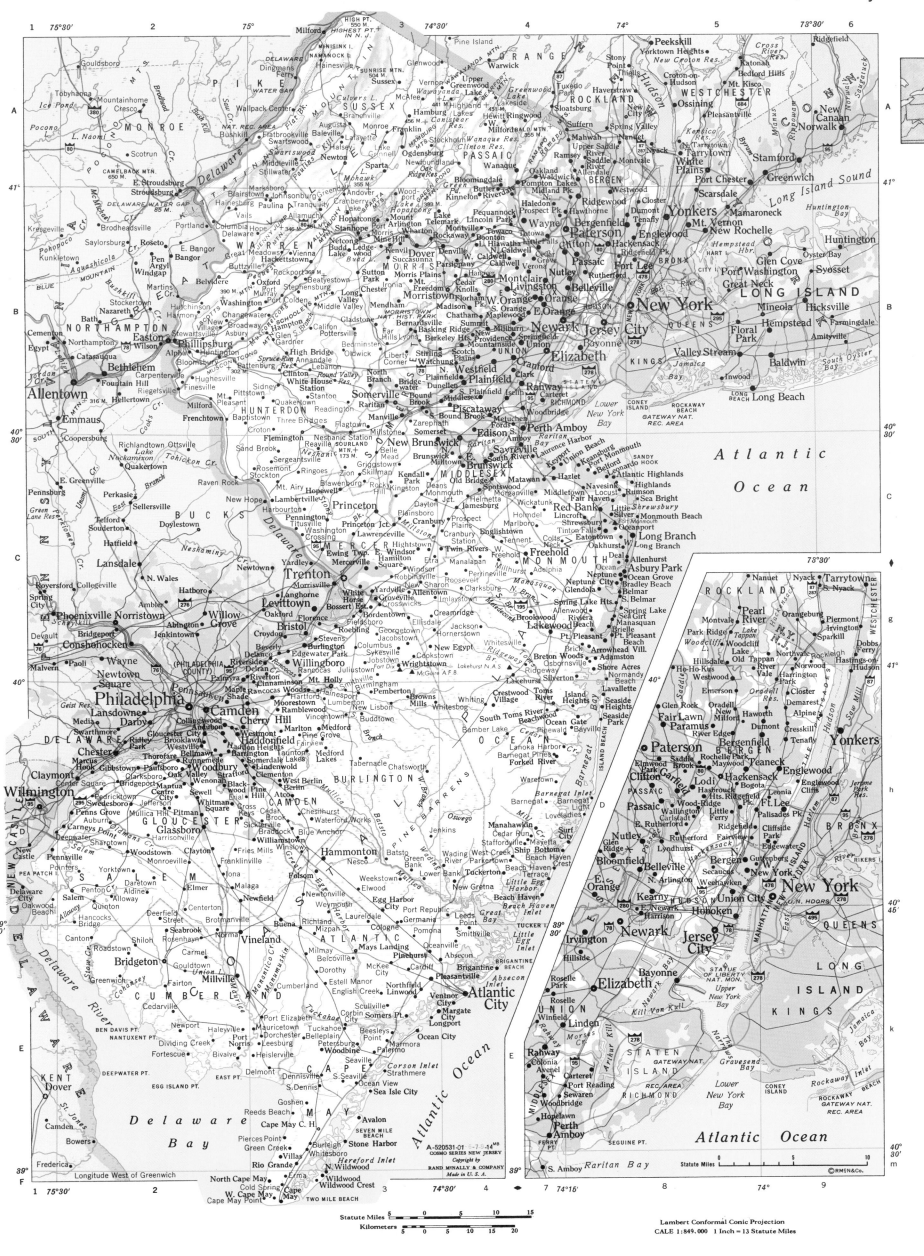

New Jersey

New Mexico

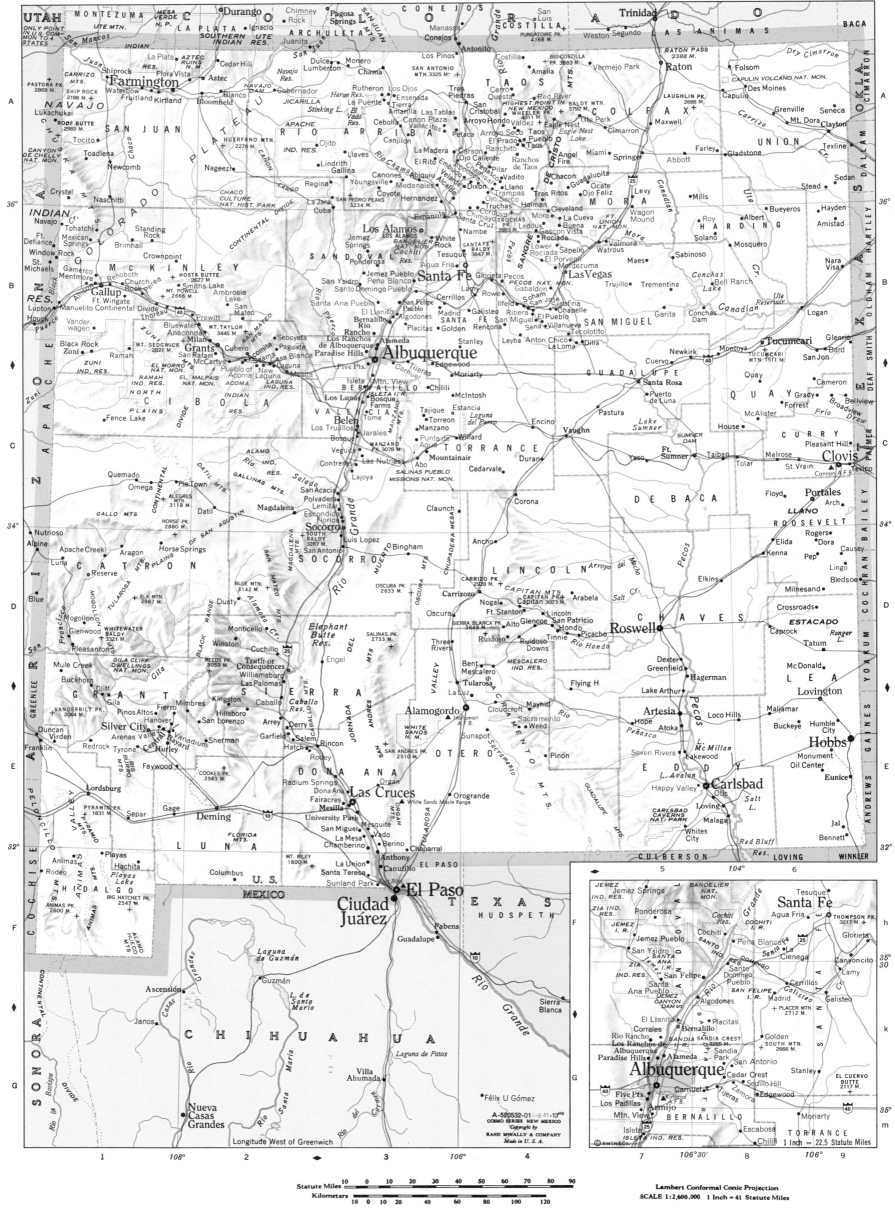

Statute Miles
10 0 10 20 30 40 50 60 70 80 90

Kilometers
10 0 10 20 40 60 80 100 120

A-520532-01 · 8-11-13 M6
COSMO SERIES NEW MEXICO
Copyright by
RAND McNALLY & COMPANY
Made in U.S.A.

Lambert Conformal Conic Projection
SCALE 1:2,600,000   1 Inch = 41 Statute Miles

Santa Fe
Inset: 1 Inch = 22.5 Statute Miles

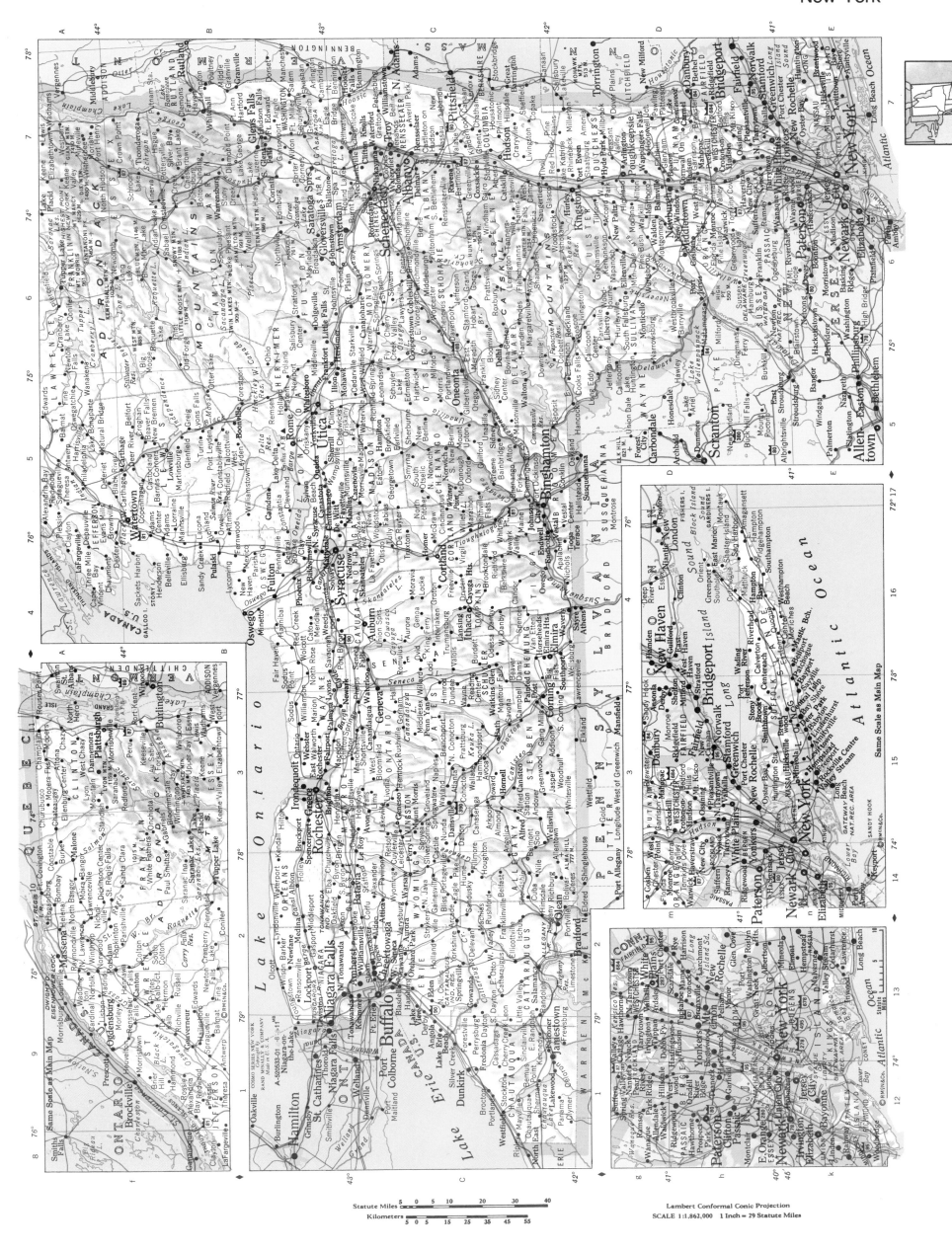

Statute Miles 5 0 5 10   20   30   40
Kilometers 5 0 5 15   25   35 45   55

Lambert Conformal Conic Projection
SCALE 1:1,862,000   1 Inch = 29 Statute Miles

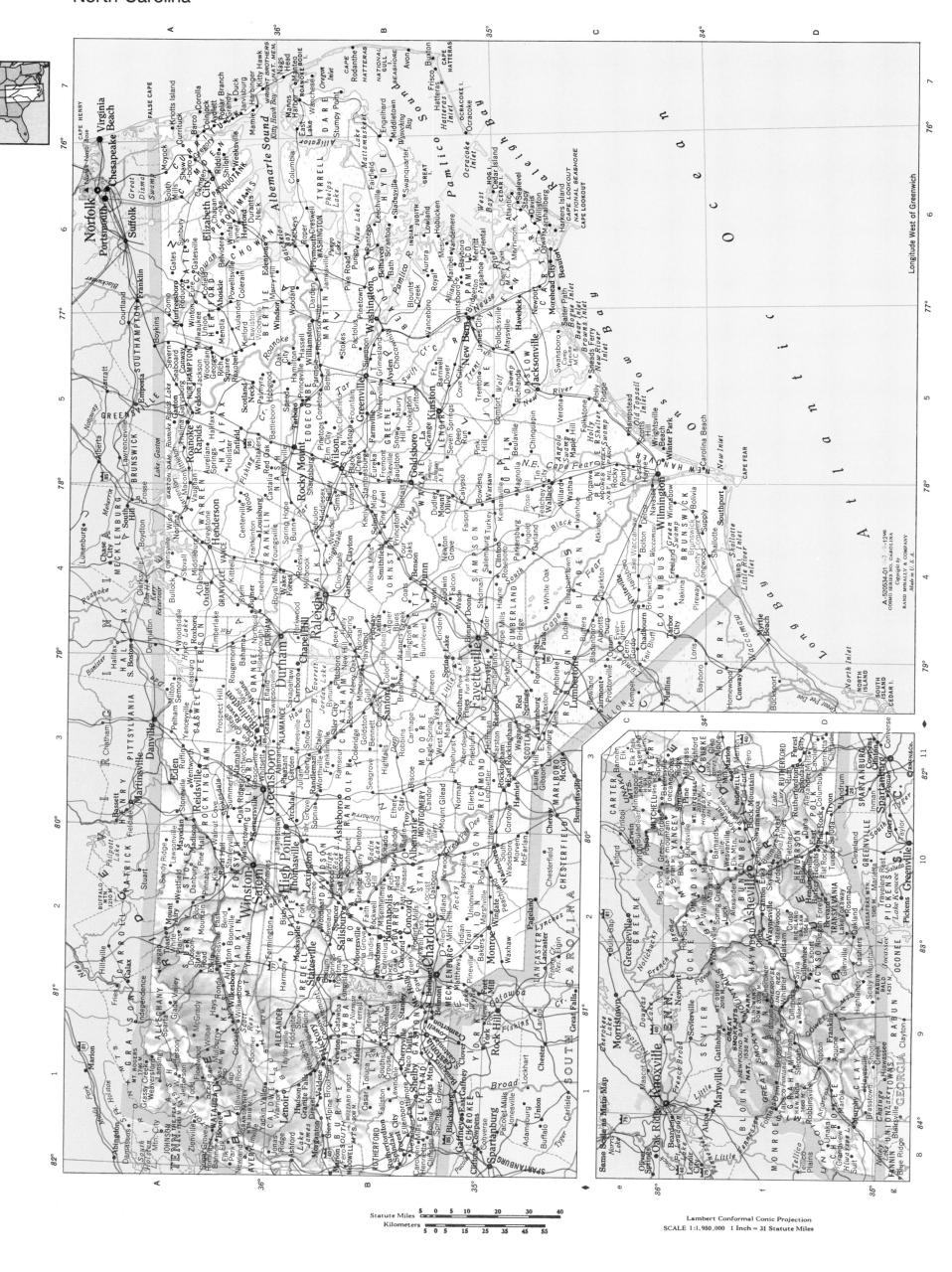

Statute Miles
Kilometers

Lambert Conformal Conic Projection
SCALE 1:1,950,000 1 Inch = 31 Statute Miles

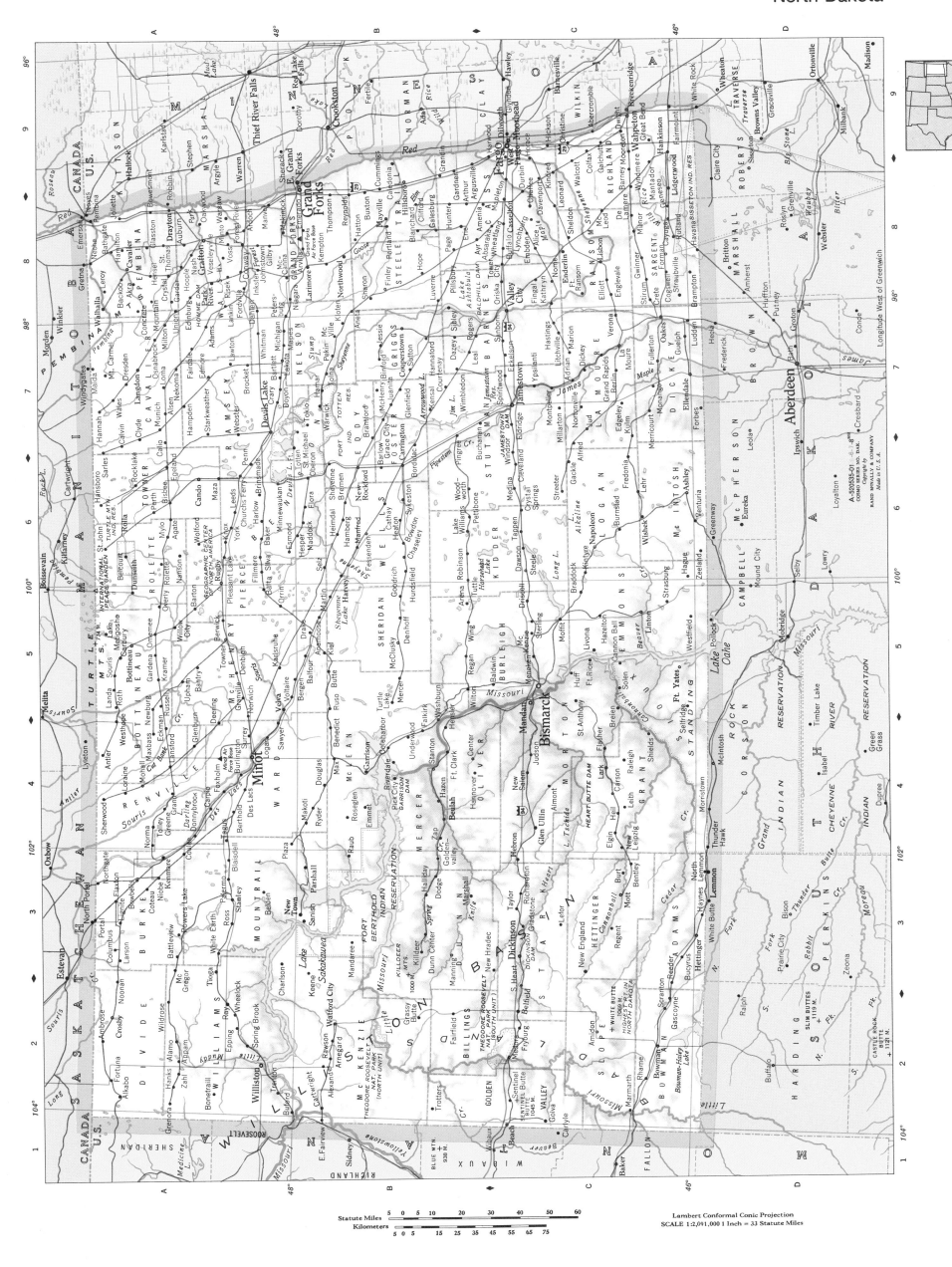

Lambert Conformal Conic Projection
SCALE 1:2,091,000 1 Inch = 33 Statute Miles

Statute Miles
Kilometers

Ohio

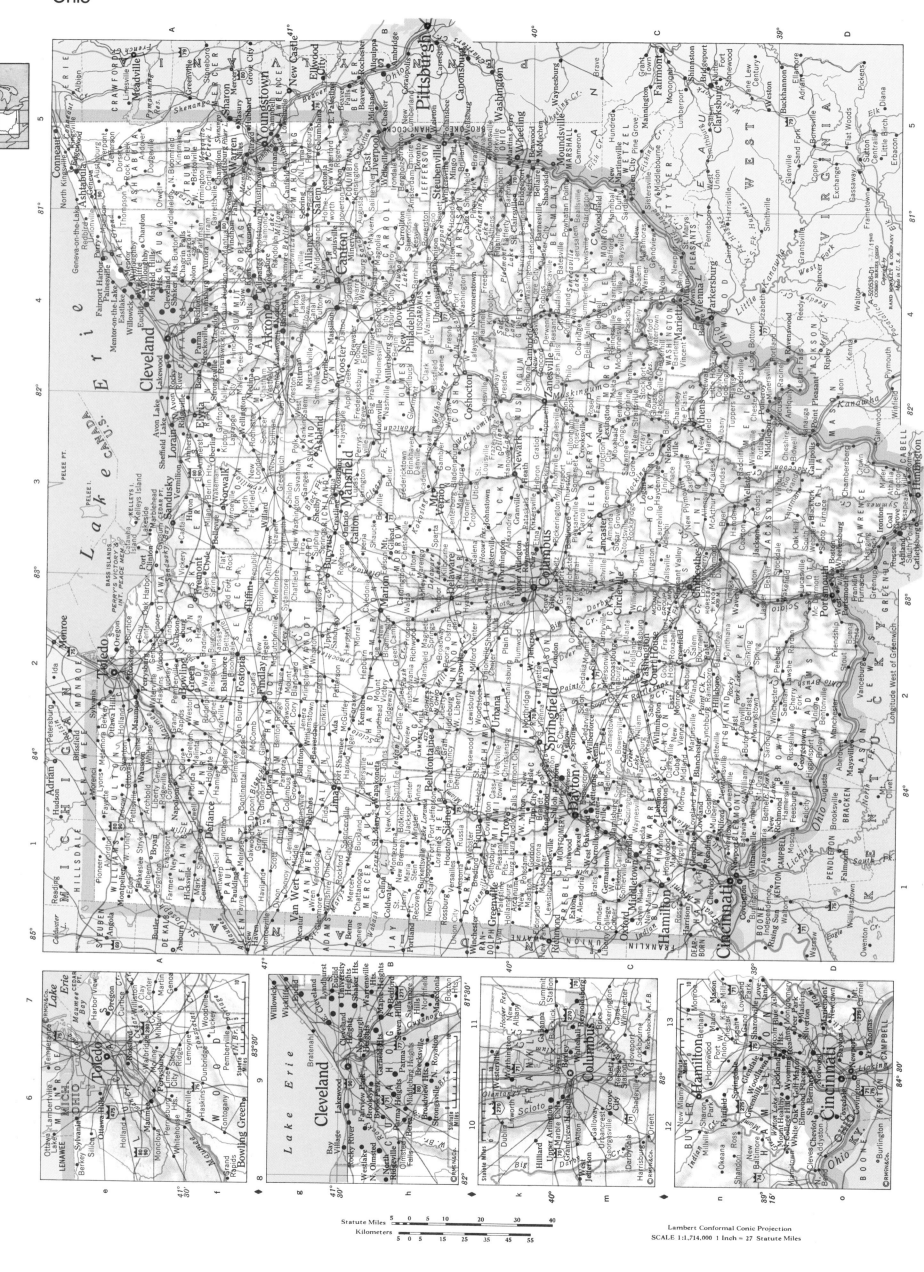

Lambert Conformal Conic Projection
SCALE 1:1,714,000 1 Inch = 27 Statute Miles

Statute Miles
Kilometers

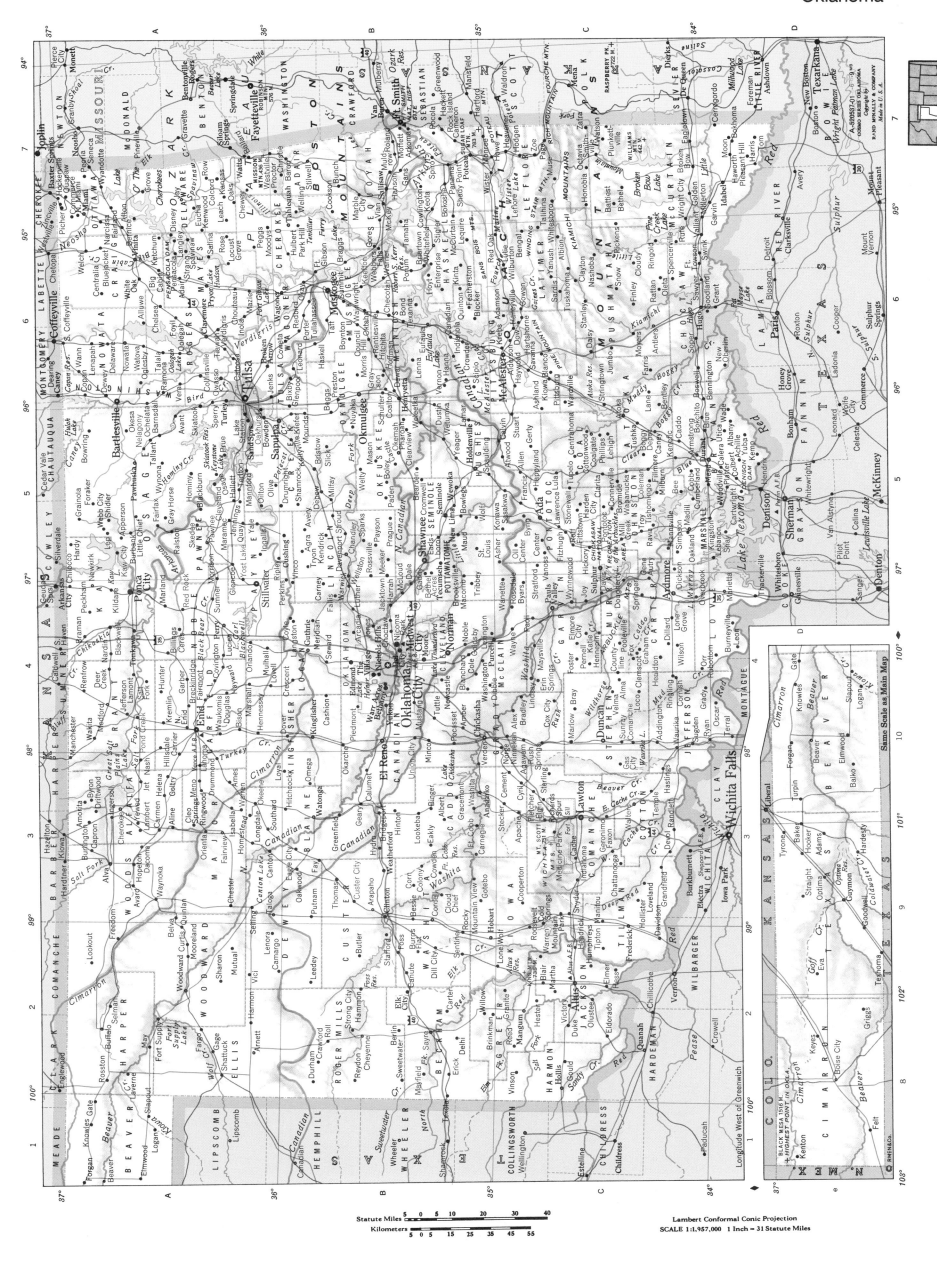

Lambert Conformal Conic Projection
SCALE 1:1,957,000 1 Inch = 31 Statute Miles

Statute Miles 5 0 5 10 20 30 40
Kilometers 5 0 5 15 25 35 45 55

Oregon

Lambert Conformal Conic Projection
SCALE 1:2,329,000   1 Inch = 37 Statute Miles

Statute Miles
Kilometers

RAND M^cNALLY & COMPANY
Copyright by
COSMO SERIES OREGON
A-520538-01 — 7/6-10^MM
Made in U.S.A.

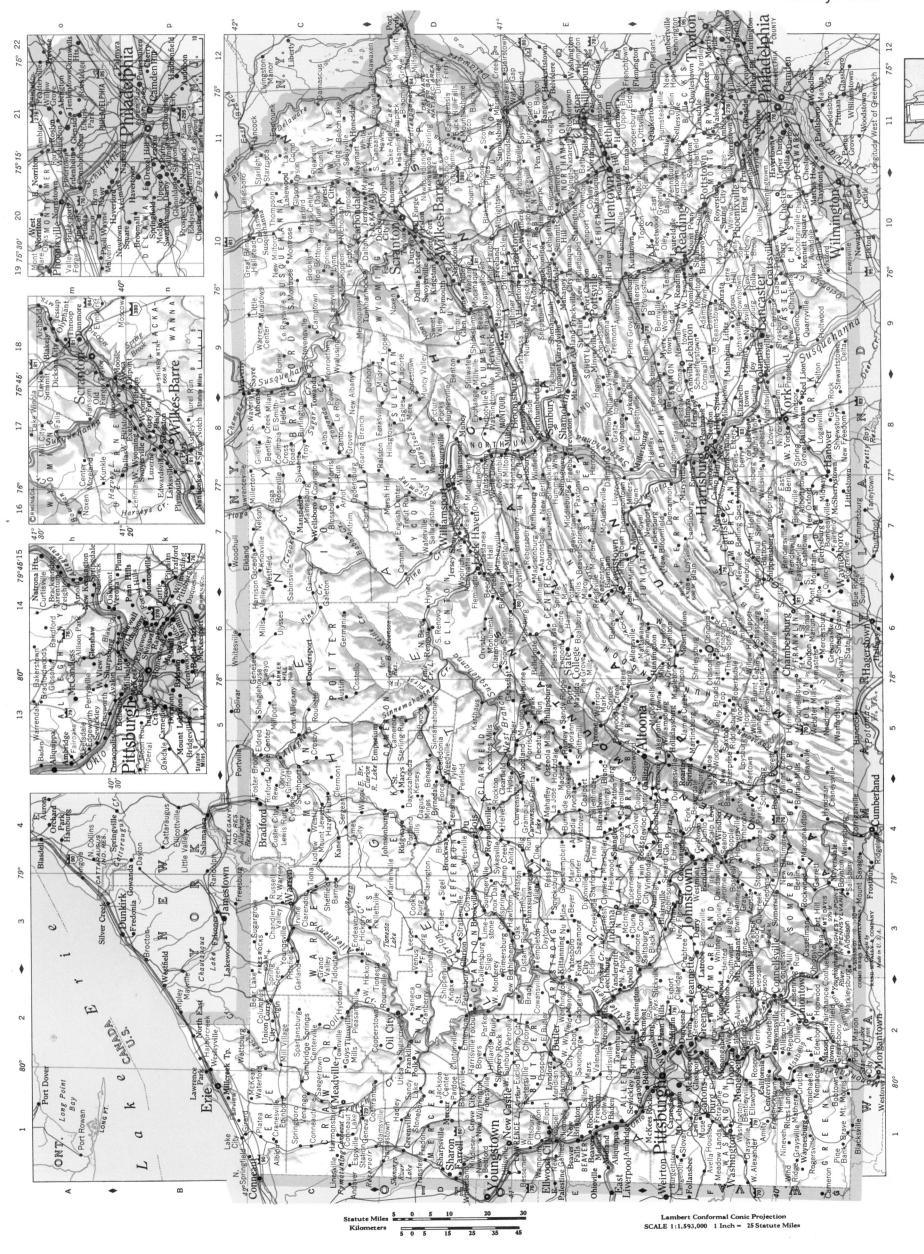

Statute Miles
Kilometers

Lambert Conformal Conic Projection
SCALE 1:1,593,000   1 Inch = 25 Statute Miles

Rhode Island

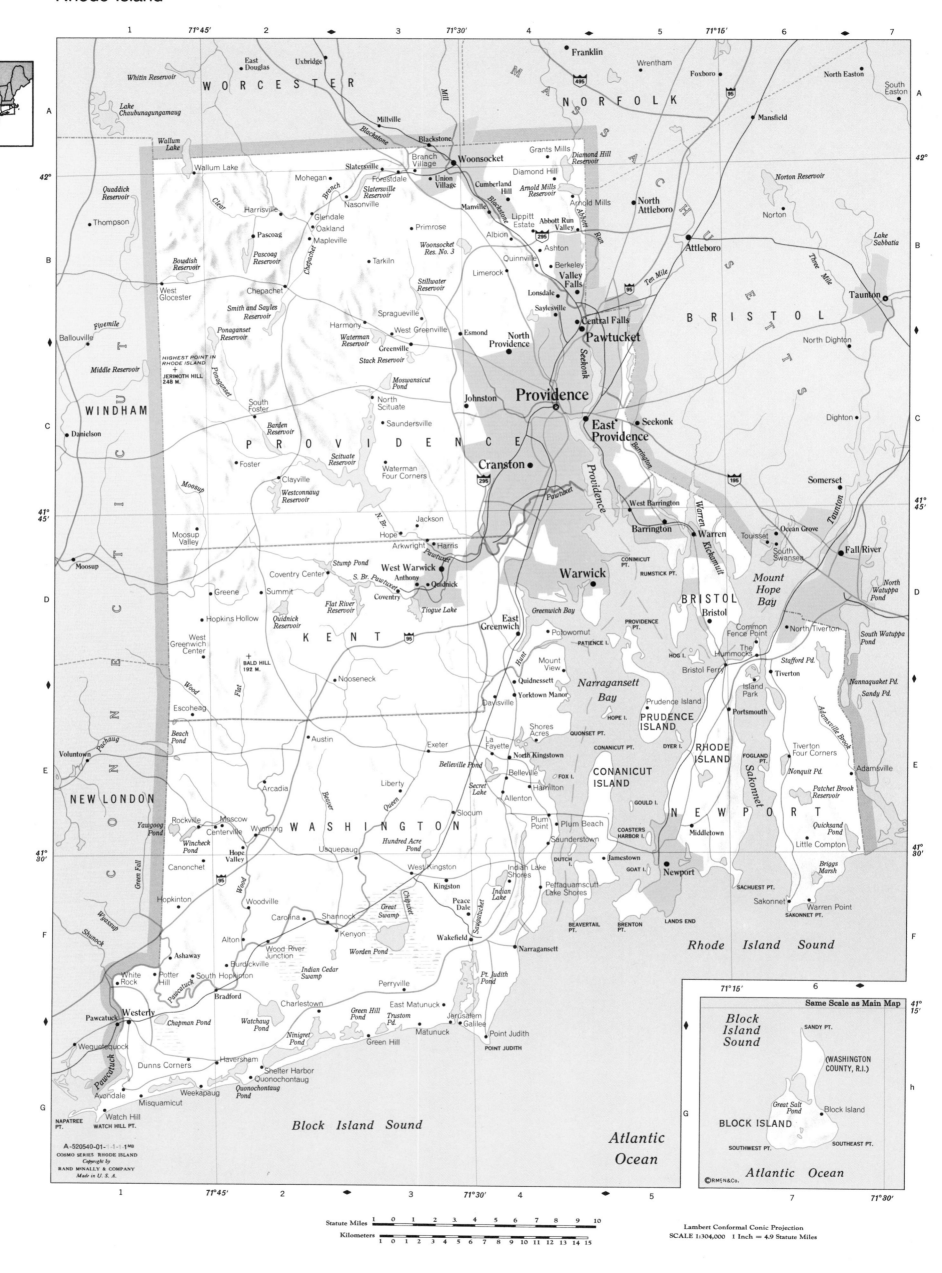

WORCESTER

Whitin Reservoir • East Douglas • Uxbridge • Franklin • Wrentham • Foxboro • North Easton • South Easton

Lake Chaubunagungamaug

NORFOLK

Quaddick Reservoir • Thompson

Millville • Blackstone • Mansfield • North Attleboro • Norton Reservoir • Norton • Lake Sabbatia

Wallum Lake • Slatersville • Branch Village • Woonsocket • Grants Mills • Diamond Hill Reservoir

Mohegan • Forestdale • Union Village • Cumberland Hill • Diamond Hill • Arnold Mills Reservoir • Arnold Mills • North Attleboro • Attleboro

Harrisville • Glendale • Nasonville • Manville • Lippitt Estate • Abbott Run Valley • Taunton

Pascoag • Oakland • Mapleville • Primrose • Albion • Quinnville • Ashton • Berkeley • Valley Falls • BRISTOL

Bowdish Reservoir • Pascoag Reservoir • Tarkiln • Woonsocket Res. No. 3 • Limerock • Lonsdale • Saylesville • Three Mile

West Glocester • Stillwater Reservoir • Central Falls • Pawtucket • North Dighton

Smith and Sayles Reservoir • Spragueville • Esmond • North Providence • Seekonk • Dighton

Chepachet • Harmony • West Greenville • Johnston • Providence • East Providence • Seekonk • Somerset

Ponaganset Reservoir • Waterman Reservoir • Greenville • Stack Reservoir • Cranston • Barrington • Warren • Ocean Grove • Fall River

HIGHEST POINT IN RHODE ISLAND + JERIMOTH HILL 248 M.

South Foster • Moswansicut Pond • West Barrington • Kickamuit • Mount Hope Bay • North Watuppa Pond

PROVIDENCE • North Scituate • Saundersville • Barrington • Warren • South Swansea

Foster • Barden Reservoir • Scituate Reservoir • Waterman Four Corners • CONIMICUT PT. • RUMSTICK PT. • BRISTOL • Bristol • North Tiverton • South Watuppa Pond

Clayville • Westconnaug Reservoir • Jackson • PROVIDENCE PT. • Common Fence Point • The Hummocks • Stafford Pd. • Tiverton • Nannaquaket Pd. • Sandy Pd.

Moosup • Moosup Valley • Hope • Arkwright • Harris • Greenwich Bay • PATIENCE I. • Prudence Island • Bristol Ferry • Island Park • Portsmouth • Adamsville Brook • Tiverton Four Corners

Danielson • West Greenwich Center • Stump Pond • West Warwick • Anthony • Quidnick • Warwick • HOG I. • PRUDENCE ISLAND • FOGLAND PT. • Adamsville

Greene • Coventry Center • S. Br. Pawtuxet • Coventry • Tiogue Lake • East Greenwich • Potowomut • QUONSET PT. • RHODE ISLAND • Nonquit Pd.

Hopkins Hollow • Summit • Flat River Reservoir • Mount View • Quidnessett • CONANICUT PT. • DYER I. • CONANICUT ISLAND • Patchet Brook Reservoir

Quidnick Reservoir • BALD HILL 192 M. • Nooseneck • Davisville • Yorktown Manor • La Fayette • North Kingstown • FOX I. • Quicksand Pond

Escoheag • Wood • Flat • Austin • Exeter • Shores Acres • Belleville • Hamilton • GOULD I. • NEWPORT • Little Compton

Beach Pond • Arcadia • Liberty • Queen • Slocum • Allenton • Plum Beach • Middletown

WASHINGTON • Belleville Pond • Secret Lake • Plum Point • Saunderstown • COASTERS HARBOR I. • Middletown

Voluntown • Rockville • Moscow • Wyoming • Hundred Acre Pond • West Kingston • DUTCH I. • Jamestown • Sachuest Pt.

Yawgoog Pond • Centerville • Usquepaug • GOAT I. • Newport

Wincheck Pond • Hope Valley • Kingston • Indian Lake Shores • Pettaquamscutt Lake Shores • Little Compton

Canonchet • Woodville • Peace Dale • Indian Lake • BEAVERTAIL PT. • BRENTON PT. • LANDS END • Warren Point

Hopkinton • Carolina • Shannock • Kenyon • Great Swamp • Wakefield • Narragansett • SACHUEST PT. • SAKONNET PT.

Ashaway • Alton • Wood River Junction • Worden Pond • Pt. Judith Pond

Burdickville • Indian Cedar Swamp • Perryville • East Matunuck • Jerusalem • Galilee • Point Judith

White Rock • Potter Hill • South Hopkinton • Bradford • Charlestown • Green Hill Pond • Trustom Pd. • Matunuck • POINT JUDITH

Westerly • Chapman Pond • Watchaug Pond • Green Hill • Pawcatuck

Weguetequock • Ninigret Pond • Haversham • Shelter Harbor

Dunns Corners • Quonochontaug • Quonochontaug Pond

NAPATREE PT. • Watch Hill • WATCH HILL PT. • Avondale • Weekapaug • Misquamicut

Rhode Island Sound

Block Island Sound

Atlantic Ocean

A-520540-01-·-1-·-1-1-1 ᴹᴹ
COSMO SERIES RHODE ISLAND
Copyright by
RAND McNALLY & COMPANY
Made in U.S.A.

Statute Miles 1 0 1 2 3 4 5 6 7 8 9 10
Kilometers 1 0 1 2 3 4 5 6 7 8 9 10 11 12 13 14 15

Lambert Conformal Conic Projection
SCALE 1:304,000   1 Inch = 4.9 Statute Miles

Block Island Sound

Block Island Sound

Block Island Sound — Same Scale as Main Map

SANDY PT.

(WASHINGTON COUNTY, R.I.)

Great Salt Pond • Block Island

BLOCK ISLAND

SOUTHWEST PT. • SOUTHEAST PT.

©RMcN&Co.

Atlantic Ocean

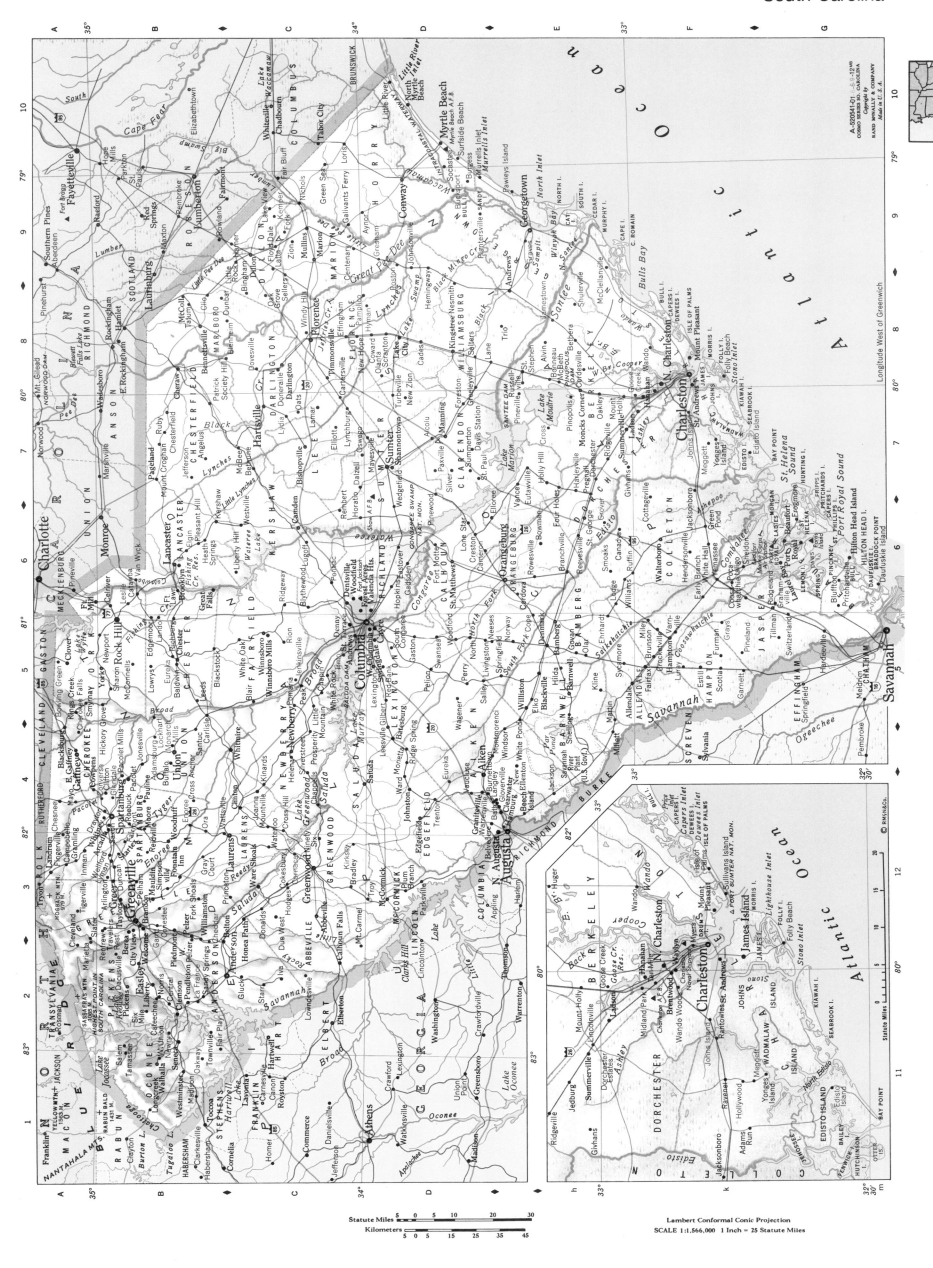

Lambert Conformal Conic Projection
SCALE 1:1,566,000   1 Inch = 25 Statute Miles

Statute Miles
Kilometers

South Dakota

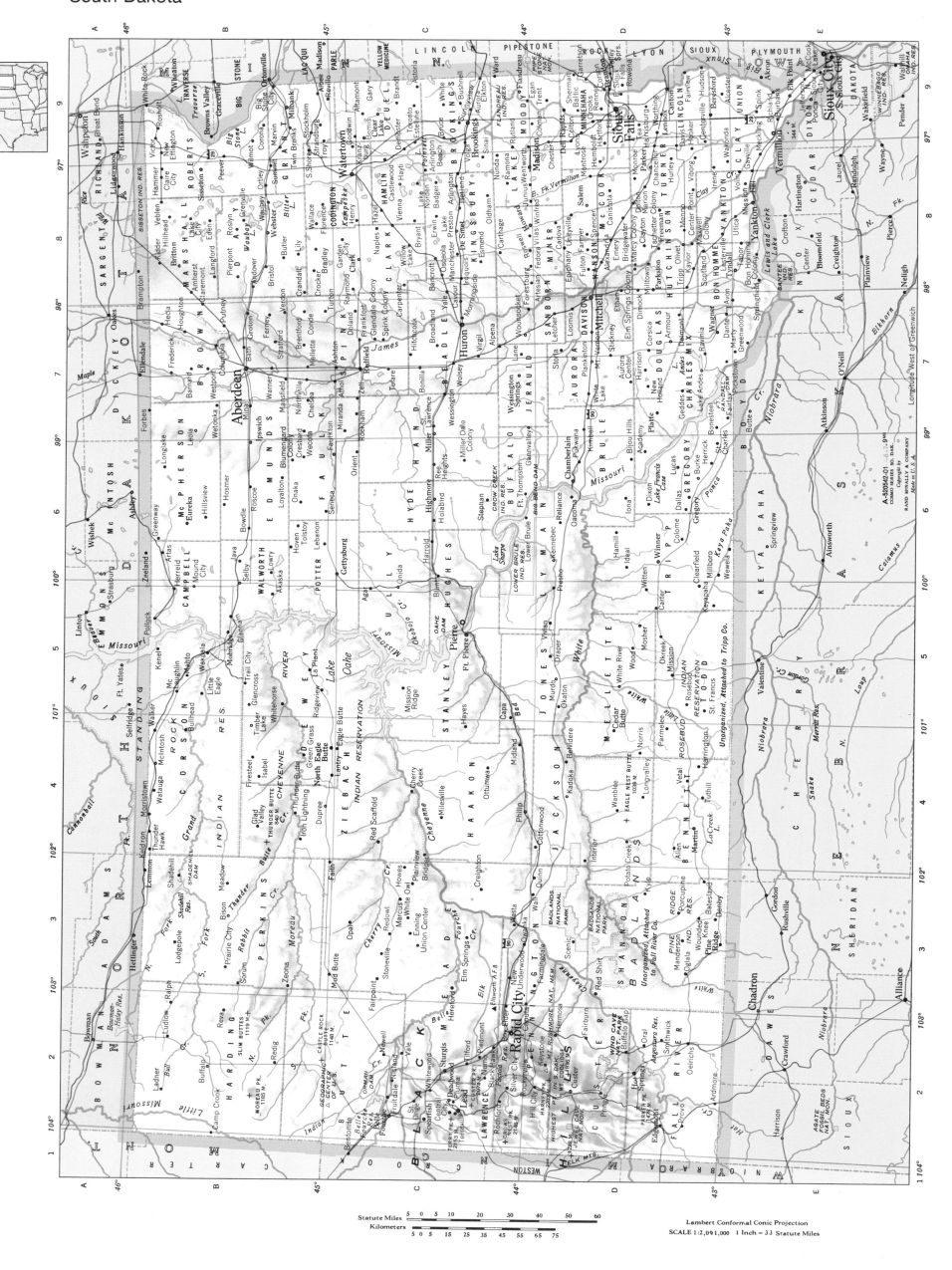

Statute Miles

Kilometers

Lambert Conformal Conic Projection
SCALE 1:2,091,000   1 Inch = 33 Statute Miles

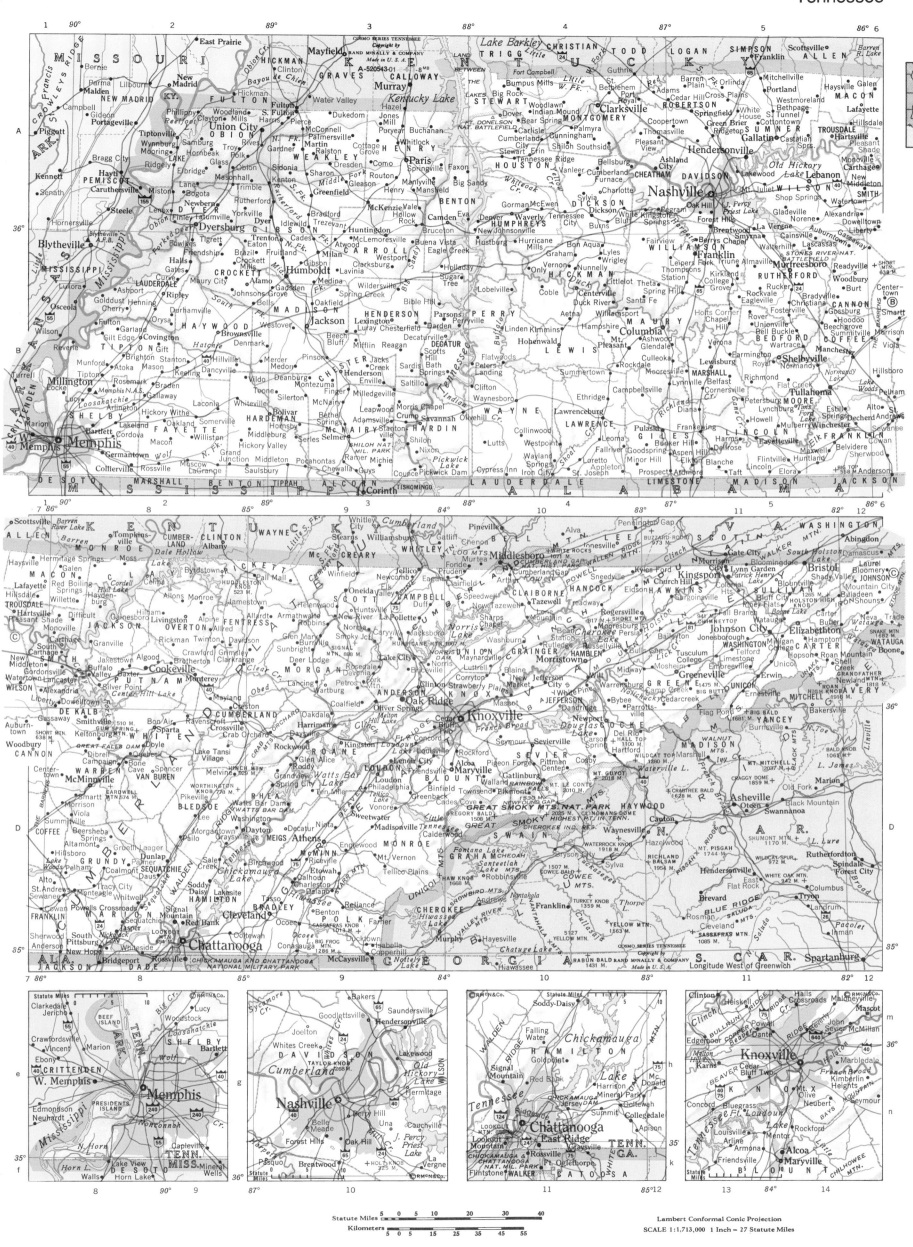

Texas

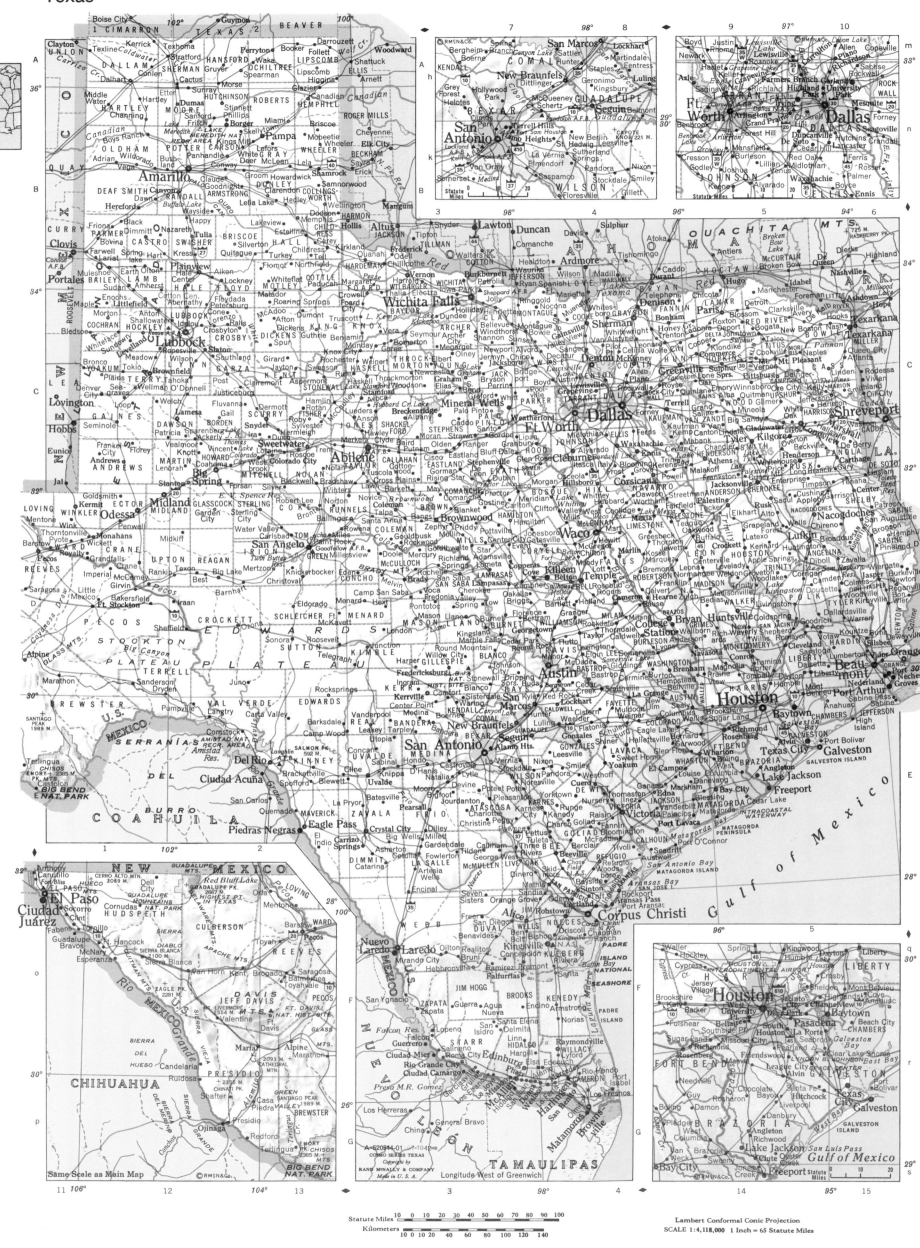

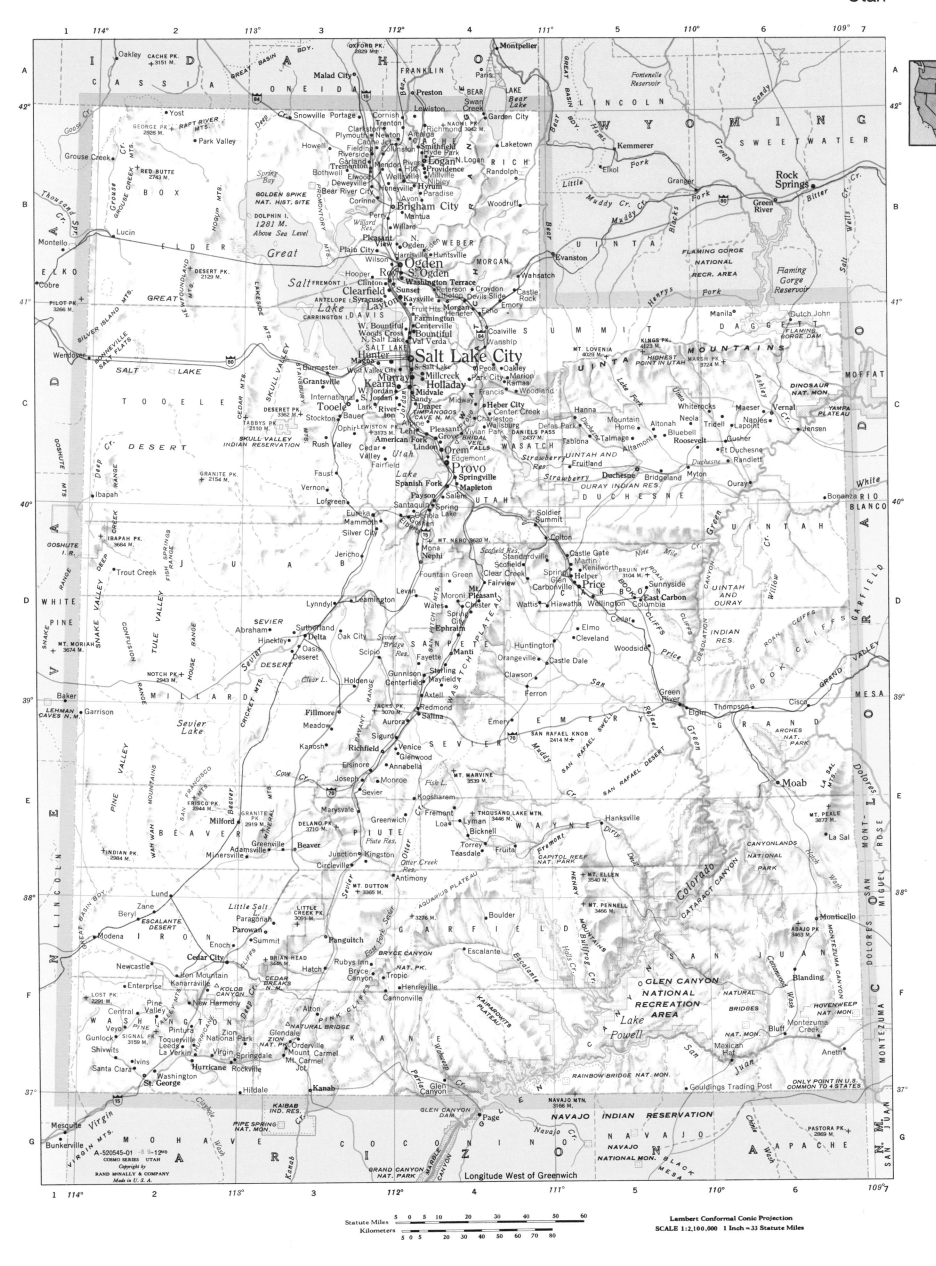

Statute Miles 5 0 5 10 20 30 40 50 60
Kilometers 5 0 5 20 40 60 70 80

Lambert Conformal Conic Projection
SCALE 1:2,100,000 1 Inch = 33 Statute Miles

A-520545-01 -8 8-12MB
COSMO SERIES UTAH
Copyright by
RAND McNALLY & COMPANY
Made in U.S.A.

Longitude West of Greenwich

Vermont

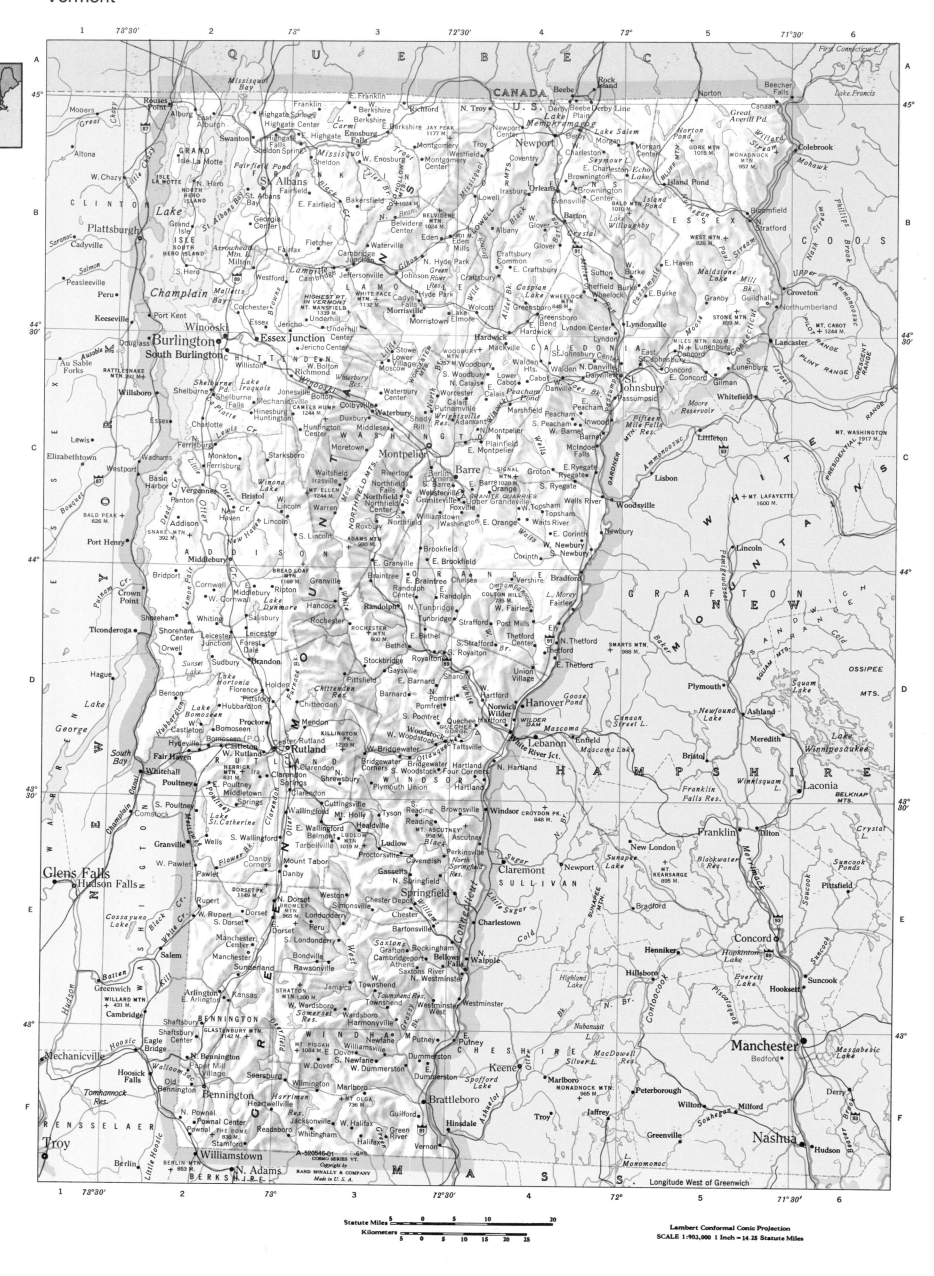

Statute Miles

Kilometers

Lambert Conformal Conic Projection
SCALE 1:903,000 1 Inch = 14.25 Statute Miles

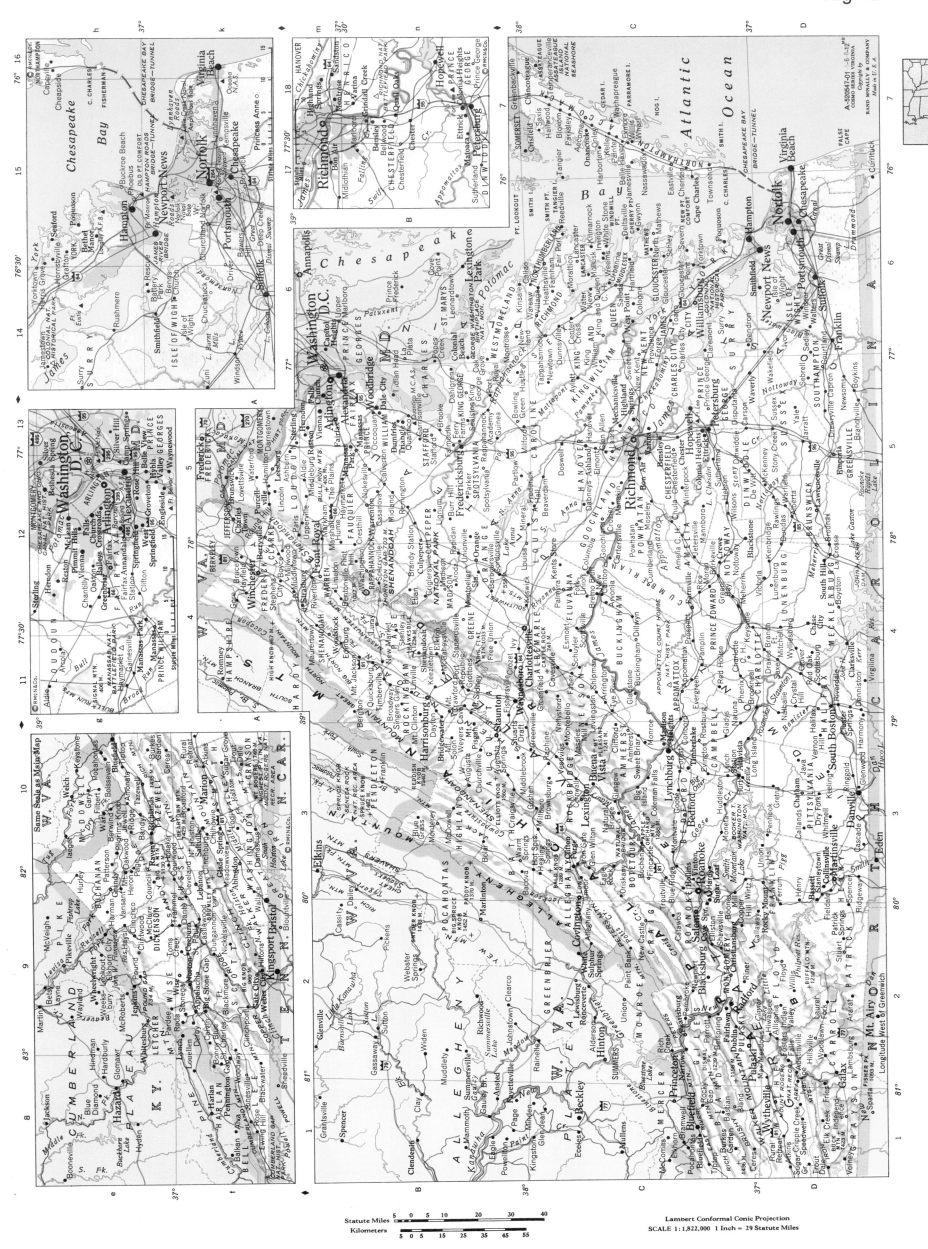

Lambert Conformal Conic Projection
SCALE 1:1,822,000   1 Inch = 29 Statute Miles

Statute Miles
Kilometers

Washington

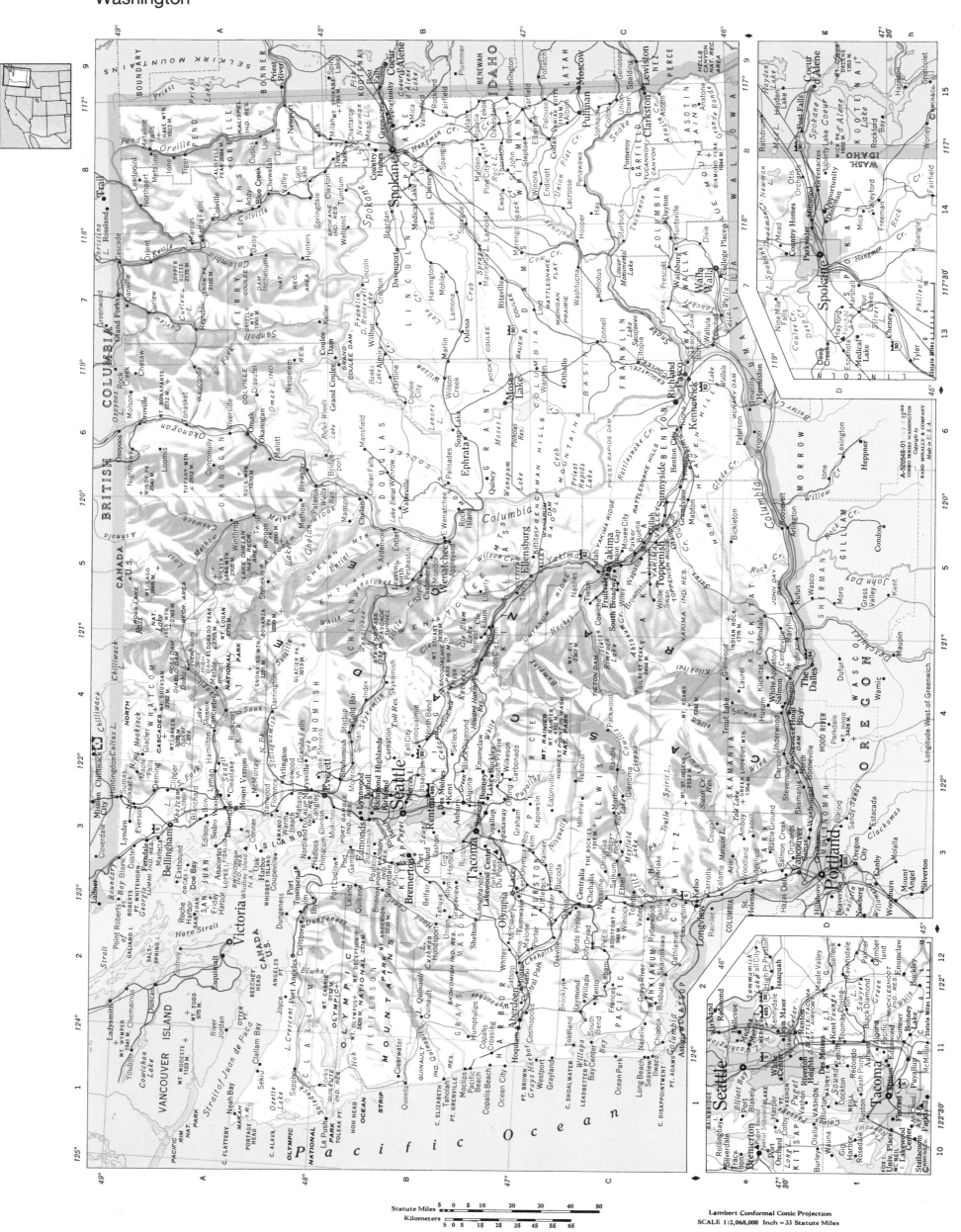

Statute Miles 5 0 5 10 20 30 40 50
Kilometers 5 0 5 15 25 35 45 55 65

Lambert Conformal Conic Projection
SCALE 1:2,068,000 Inch = 33 Statute Miles

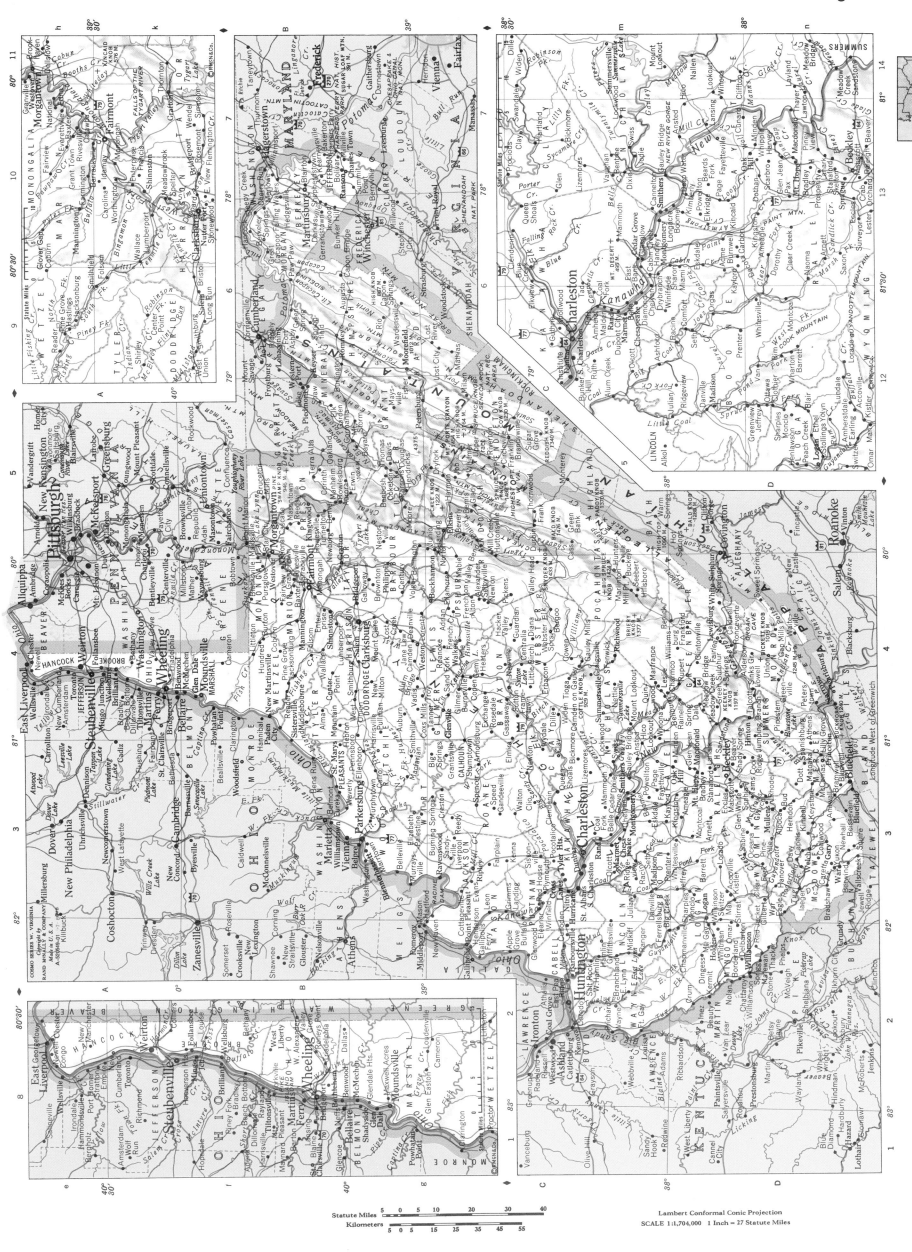

Lambert Conformal Conic Projection
SCALE 1:1,704,000   1 Inch = 27 Statute Miles

Statute Miles 5 0 5 10 20 30 40
Kilometers 5 0 5 15 25 35 45 55

Wisconsin

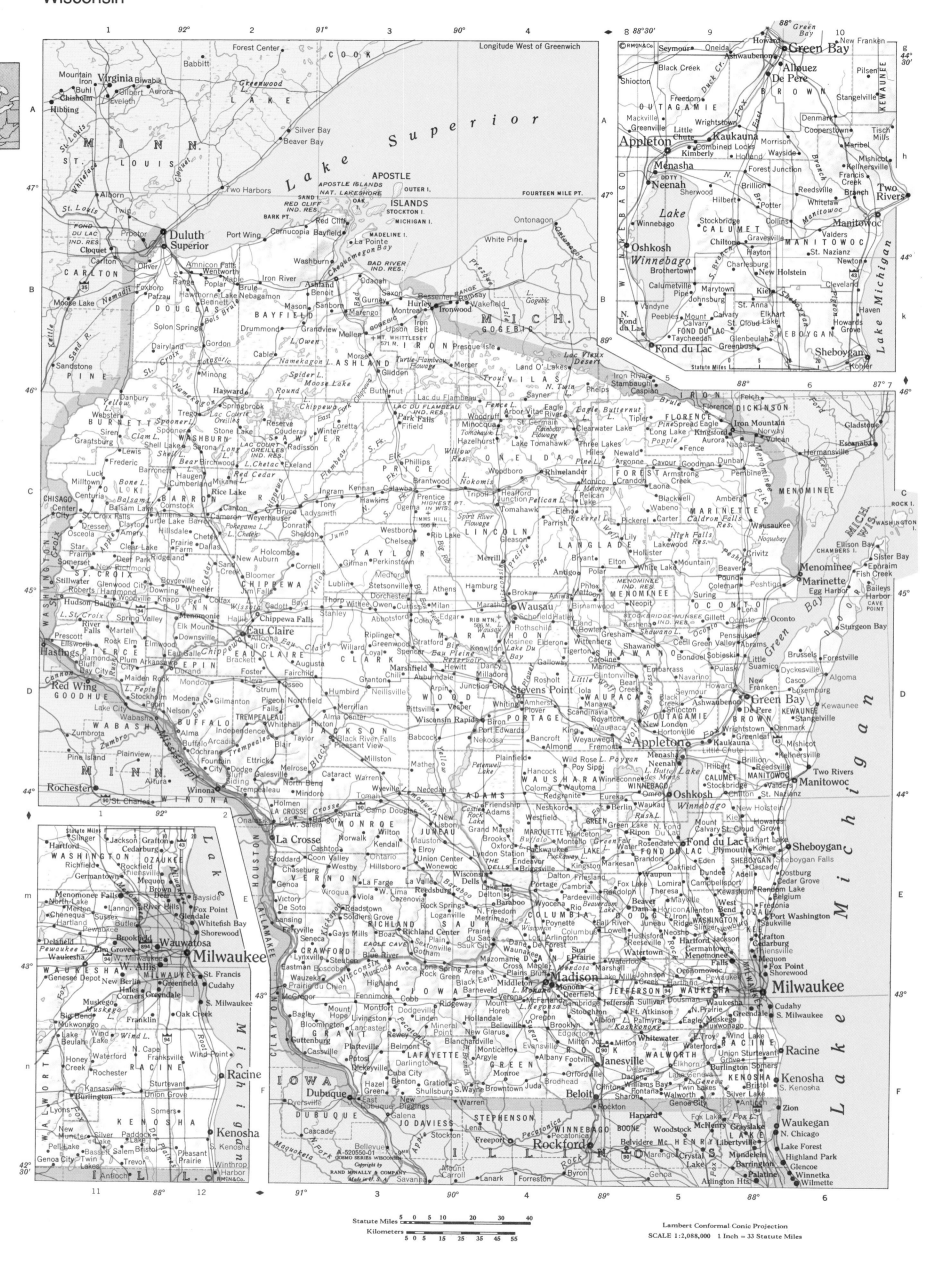

Statute Miles 5 0 5 10   20   30   40
Kilometers 5 0 5 15 25 35 45 55

Lambert Conformal Conic Projection
SCALE 1:2,088,000   1 Inch = 33 Statute Miles

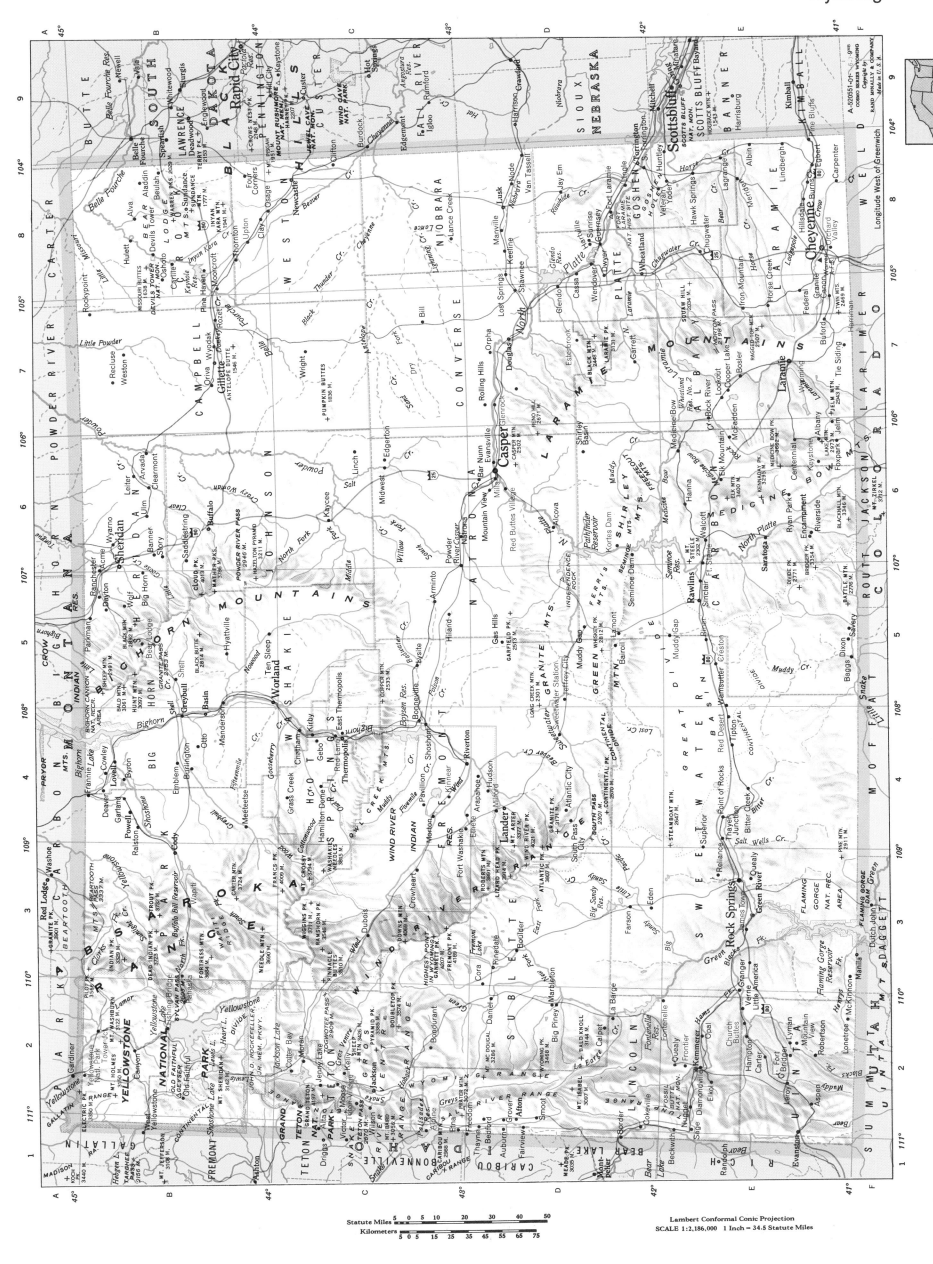

Statute Miles 5 0 5 10 20 30 40 50
Kilometers 5 0 5 15 25 35 45 55 65 75

Lambert Conformal Conic Projection
SCALE 1:2,186,000 1 Inch = 34.5 Statute Miles

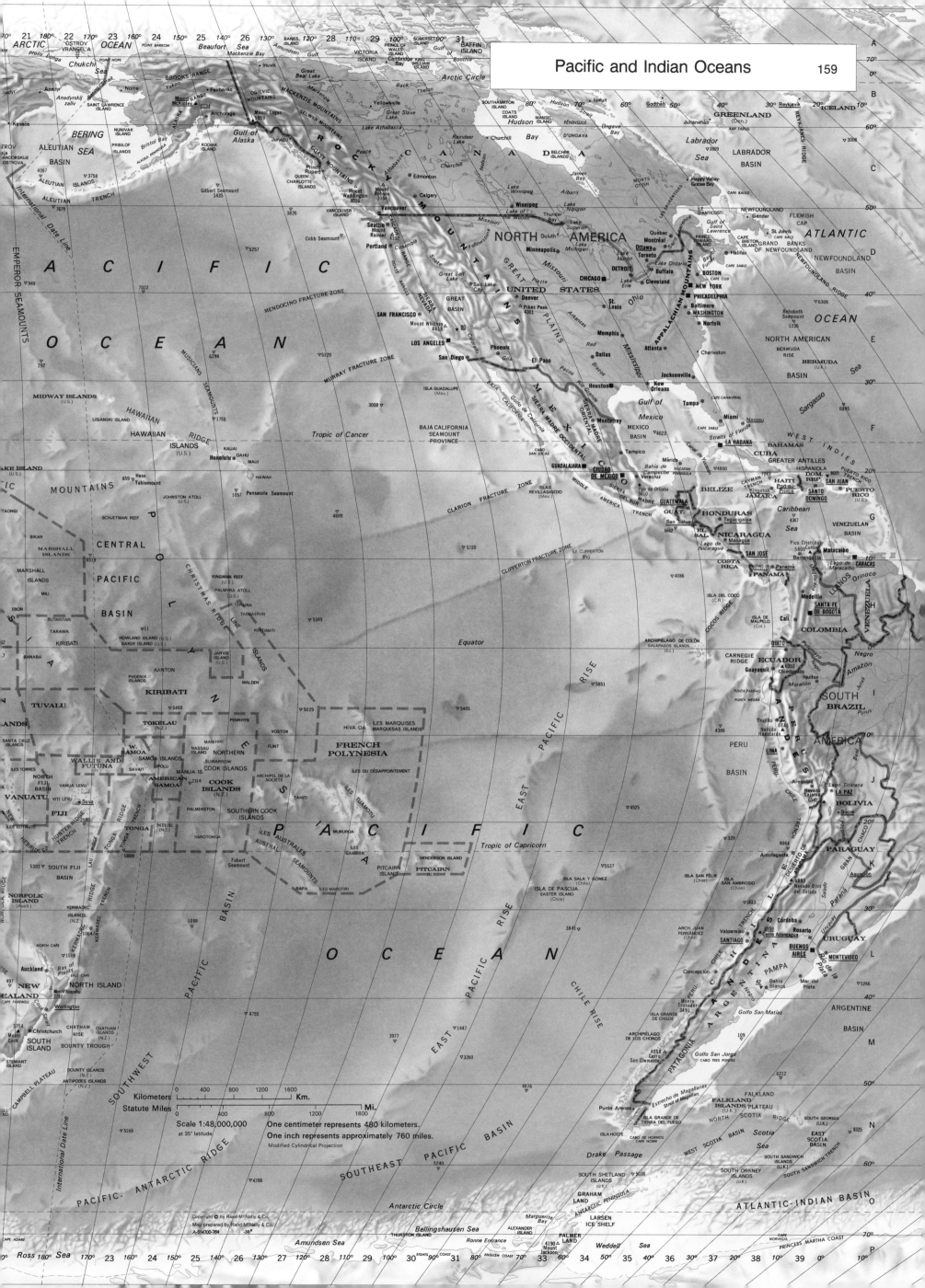

Copyright © by Rand McNally & Co.
Map prepared by Rand McNally & Co.
A-914700-764

Kilometers
Statute Miles
Scale 1:48,000,000
at 35° latitude
One centimeter represents 480 kilometers.
One inch represents approximately 760 miles.
Modified Cylindrical Projection

Kilometers

Statute Miles

Scale 1:48,000,000
at 35° latitude.
Modified Cylindrical Projection

One centimeter represents 480 kilometers.
One inch represents approximately 760 miles.

Index to World Reference Maps

Introduction to the Index

This universal index includes in a single alphabetical list approximately 40,000 names of features that appear on the reference maps. Each name is followed by the name of the country or continent in which it is located, a map-reference key and a page reference.

Names The names of cities appear in the index in regular type. The names of all other features appear in *italics*, followed by descriptive terms (hill, mtn., state) to indicate their nature.

Names that appear in shortened versions on the maps due to space limitations are spelled out in full in the index. The portions of these names omitted from the maps are enclosed in brackets — for example, Acapulco [de Juárez].

Abbreviations of names on the maps have been standardized as much as possible. Names that are abbreviated on the maps are generally spelled out in full in the index.

Country names and names of features that extend beyond the boundaries of one country are followed by the name of the continent in which each is located. Country designations follow the names of all other places in the index. The locations of places in the United States, Canada, and the United Kingdom are further defined by abbreviations that indicate the state, province, or political division in which each is located.

All abbreviations used in the index are defined in the List of Abbreviations below.

Alphabetization Names are alphabetized in the order of the letters of the English alphabet. Spanish *ll* and *ch*, for example, are not treated as distinct letters. Furthermore, diacritical marks are disregarded in alphabetization — German or Scandinavian *ä* or *ö* are treated as *a* or *o*.

The names of physical features may appear inverted, since they are always alphabetized under the proper, not the generic, part of the name, thus: 'Gibraltar, Strait of'. Otherwise every entry, whether consisting of one word or more, is alphabetized as a single continuous entity. 'Lakeland', for example, appears after 'La Crosse' and before 'La Salle'. Names beginning with articles (Le Havre, Den Helder, Al Manşūrah) are not inverted. Names beginning 'St.', 'Ste.' and 'Sainte' are alphabetized as though spelled 'Saint'.

In the case of identical names, towns are listed first, then political divisions, then physical features. Entries that are completely identical are listed alphabetically by country name.

Map-Reference Keys and Page References The map-reference keys and page references are found in the last two columns of each entry.

Each map-reference key consists of a letter and number. The letters appear along the sides of the maps. Lowercase letters indicate reference to inset maps. Numbers appear across the tops and bottoms of the maps.

Map reference keys for point features, such as cities and mountain peaks, indicate the locations of the symbols. For extensive areal features, such as countries or mountain ranges, locations are given for the approximate centers of the features. Those for linear features, such as canals and rivers, are given for the locations of the names.

The page number generally refers to the main map for the country in which the feature is located. Page references to two-page maps always refer to the left-hand page.

List of Abbreviations

Afg.	Afghanistan	C.V.	Cape Verde	Jam.	Jamaica	N. Ire., U.K.	Northern Ireland, U.K.	Sri L.	Sri Lanka
Afr.	Africa	Cyp.	Cyprus	Jord.	Jordan	N.J., U.S.	New Jersey, U.S.	*state*	state, republic, canton
Ak., U.S.	Alaska, U.S.	Czech Rep.	Czech Republic	Kaz.	Kazakhstan	N. Kor.	North Korea	St. Hel.	St. Helena
Alb.	Albania	D.C., U.S.	District of Columbia, U.S.	Kir.	Kiribati	N.M., U.S.	New Mexico, U.S.	St. K./N	St. Kitts and Nevis
Alg.	Algeria	De., U.S.	Delaware, U.S.	Ks., U.S.	Kansas, U.S.	N. Mar. Is.	Northern Mariana Islands	St. Luc.	St. Lucia
Alta., Can.	Alberta, Can.	Den.	Denmark	Kuw.	Kuwait			*stm.*	stream (river, creek)
Am. Sam.	American Samoa	*dep.*	dependency, colony	Ky., U.S.	Kentucky, U.S.	Nmb.	Namibia	S. Tom./P.	Sao Tome and Principe
anch.	anchorage	*depr.*	depression	Kyrg.	Kyrgyzstan	Nor.	Norway	St. P./M.	St. Pierre and Miquelon
And.	Andorra	*dept.*	department, district	*l.*	lake, pond	Norf. I.	Norfolk Island		
Ang.	Angola	*des.*	desert	La., U.S.	Louisiana, U.S.	N.S., Can.	Nova Scotia, Can.	*strt.*	strait, channel, sound
Ant.	Antarctica	Dji.	Djibouti	Lat.	Latvia	Nv., U.S.	Nevada, U.S.	St. Vin.	St. Vincent and the Grenadines
Antig.	Antigua and Barbuda	Dom.	Dominica	Leb.	Lebanon	N.W. Ter., Can.	Northwest Territories, Can.	Sud.	Sudan
Ar., U.S.	Arkansas, U.S.	Dom. Rep.	Dominican Republic	Leso.	Lesotho	N.Y., U.S.	New York, U.S.	Sur.	Suriname
Arg.	Argentina	Ec.	Ecuador	Lib.	Liberia	N.Z.	New Zealand	*sw.*	swamp, marsh
Arm.	Armenia	El Sal.	El Salvador	Liech.	Liechtenstein	Oc.	Oceania	Swaz.	Swaziland
Aus.	Austria	Eng., U.K.	England, U.K.	Lith.	Lithuania	Oh., U.S.	Ohio, U.S.	Swe.	Sweden
Austl.	Australia	Eq. Gui.	Equatorial Guinea	Lux.	Luxembourg	Ok., U.S.	Oklahoma, U.S.	Switz.	Switzerland
Az., U.S.	Arizona, U.S.	Erit.	Eritrea	Ma., U.S.	Massachusetts, U.S.	Ont., Can.	Ontario, Can.	Tai.	Taiwan
Azer.	Azerbaijan	*est.*	estuary			Or., U.S.	Oregon, U.S.	Taj.	Tajikistan
b.	bay, gulf, inlet, lagoon	Est.	Estonia	Mac.	Macedonia	Pa., U.S.	Pennsylvania, U.S.	Tan.	Tanzania
Bah.	Bahamas	Eth.	Ethiopia	Madag.	Madagascar	Pak.	Pakistan	T./C. Is.	Turks and Caicos Islands
Bahr.	Bahrain	Eur.	Europe	Malay.	Malaysia	Pan.	Panama	*ter.*	territory
Barb.	Barbados	Faer. Is.	Faeroe Islands	Mald.	Maldives	Pap. N. Gui.	Papua New Guinea	Thai.	Thailand
B.A.T.	British Antarctic Territory	Falk. Is.	Falkland Islands	Man., Can.	Manitoba, Can.	Para.	Paraguay	Tn., U.S.	Tennessee, U.S.
B.C., Can.	British Columbia, Can.	Fin.	Finland	Marsh. Is.	Marshall Islands	P.E.I., Can.	Prince Edward Island, Can.	Tok.	Tokelau
Bdi.	Burundi	Fl., U.S.	Florida, U.S.	Mart.	Martinique			Trin.	Trinidad and Tobago
Bel.	Belgium	*for.*	forest, moor	Maur.	Mauritania	*pen.*	peninsula		
Bela.	Belarus	Fr.	France	May.	Mayotte	Phil.	Philippines	Tun.	Tunisia
Ber.	Bermuda	Fr. Gu.	French Guiana	Md., U.S.	Maryland, U.S.	Pit.	Pitcairn	Tur.	Turkey
Bhu.	Bhutan	Fr. Poly.	French Polynesia	Me., U.S.	Maine, U.S.	*pl.*	plain, flat	Turk.	Turkmenistan
B.I.O.T.	British Indian Ocean Territory	F.S.A.T.	French Southern and Antarctic Territory	Mex.	Mexico	*plat.*	plateau, highland	Tx., U.S.	Texas, U.S.
Bngl.	Bangladesh			Mi., U.S.	Michigan, U.S.	Pol.	Poland	U.A.E.	United Arab Emirates
Bol.	Bolivia	Ga., U.S.	Georgia, U.S.	Micron.	Federated States of Micronesia	Port.	Portugal		
Boph.	Bophuthatswana	Gam.	Gambia			P.R.	Puerto Rico	Ug.	Uganda
Bos.	Bosnia and Herzegovina	Gaza	Gaza Strip	Mid. Is.	Midway Islands	*prov.*	province, region	U.K.	United Kingdom
		Geor.	Georgia	*mil.*	military installation	Que., Can.	Quebec, Can.	Ukr.	Ukraine
Bots.	Botswana	Ger.	Germany	Mn., U.S.	Minnesota, U.S.	*reg.*	physical region	Ur.	Uruguay
Braz.	Brazil	Gib.	Gibraltar	Mo., U.S.	Missouri, U.S.	*res.*	reservoir	U.S.	United States
Bru.	Brunei	Golan	Golan Heights	Mol.	Moldova	Reu.	Reunion	Ut., U.S.	Utah, U.S.
Br. Vir. Is.	British Virgin Islands	Grc.	Greece	Mon.	Monaco	*rf.*	reef, shoal	Uzb.	Uzbekistan
Bul.	Bulgaria	Gren.	Grenada	Mong.	Mongolia	R.I., U.S.	Rhode Island, U.S.	Va., U.S.	Virginia, U.S.
Burkina	Burkina Faso	Grnld.	Greenland	Monts.	Montserrat	Rom.	Romania	*val.*	valley, watercourse
c.	cape, point	Guad.	Guadeloupe	Mor.	Morocco	Rw.	Rwanda	Vat.	Vatican City
Ca., U.S.	California, U.S.	Guat.	Guatemala	Moz.	Mozambique	S.A.	South America	Ven.	Venezuela
Cam.	Cameroon	Gui.	Guinea	Mrts.	Mauritius	S. Afr.	South Africa	Viet.	Vietnam
Camb.	Cambodia	Gui.-B.	Guinea-Bissau	Ms., U.S.	Mississippi, U.S.	Sask., Can.	Saskatchewan, Can.	V.I.U.S.	Virgin Islands (U.S.)
Can.	Canada	Guy.	Guyana	Mt., U.S.	Montana, U.S.			*vol.*	volcano
Cay. Is.	Cayman Islands	Hi., U.S.	Hawaii, U.S.	*mth.*	river mouth or channel	Sau. Ar.	Saudi Arabia	Vt., U.S.	Vermont, U.S.
Cen. Afr. Rep.	Central African Republic	*hist.*	historic site, ruins			S.C., U.S.	South Carolina, U.S.	Wa., U.S.	Washington, U.S.
		hist. reg.	historic region	*mtn.*	mountain	*sci.*	scientific station	Wal./F.	Wallis and Futuna
Christ. I.	Christmas Island	H.K.	Hong Kong	*mts.*	mountains	Scot., U.K.	Scotland, U.K.	Wi., U.S.	Wisconsin, U.S.
C. Iv.	Cote d'Ivoire	Hond.	Honduras	Mwi.	Malawi	S.D., U.S.	South Dakota, U.S.	W. Sah.	Western Sahara
clf.	cliff, escarpment	Hung.	Hungary	Mya.	Myanmar	Sen.	Senegal	W. Sam.	Western Samoa
co.	county, parish	*i.*	island	N.A.	North America	Sey.	Seychelles	*wtfl.*	waterfall
Co., U.S.	Colorado, U.S.	Ia., U.S.	Iowa, U.S.	N.B., Can.	New Brunswick, Can.	Sing.	Singapore	W.V., U.S.	West Virginia, U.S.
Col.	Colombia	Ice.	Iceland			S. Geor.	South Georgia	Wy., U.S.	Wyoming, U.S.
Com.	Comoros	*ice*	ice feature, glacier	N.C., U.S.	North Carolina, U.S.	S. Kor.	South Korea	Yugo.	Yugoslavia
cont.	continent	Id., U.S.	Idaho, U.S.	N. Cal.	New Caledonia	S.L.	Sierra Leone	Yukon, Can.	Yukon Territory, Can.
C.R.	Costa Rica	Il., U.S.	Illinois, U.S.	N. Cyp.	North Cyprus	Slvk.	Slovakia		
Cro.	Croatia	In., U.S.	Indiana, U.S.	N.D., U.S.	North Dakota, U.S.	Slvn.	Slovenia	Zam.	Zambia
Ct., U.S.	Connecticut, U.S.	Indon.	Indonesia	Ne., U.S.	Nebraska, U.S.	S. Mar.	San Marino	Zimb.	Zimbabwe
ctry.	country	I. of Man	Isle of Man	Neth.	Netherlands	Sol. Is.	Solomon Islands		
		Ire.	Ireland	Neth. Ant.	Netherlands Antilles	Som.	Somalia		
		is.	islands	Newf., Can.	Newfoundland, Can.	Sp. N. Afr.	Spanish North Africa		
		Isr.	Israel	N.H., U.S.	New Hampshire, U.S.				
		Isr. Occ.	Israeli Occupied Territories	Nic.	Nicaragua				
				Nig.	Nigeria				

Index

A

Name	Map Ref.	Page
Aachen, Ger.	E6	10
Aalen, Ger.	G10	10
Aalst (Alost), Bel.	G5	12
Aarau, Switz.	D9	13
Aarburg, Switz.	D8	13
Aare, stm., Switz.	C9	13
Aba, China	E7	30
Aba, Nig.	I13	64
Abā as-Su'ūd, Sau. Ar.	F4	47
Abaco, i., Bah.	A6	94
Abacou, Pointe, c., Haiti	E8	94
Ābādān, Iran	F10	48
Ābādeh, Iran	F12	48
Abadia dos Dourados, Braz.	E5	79
Abadiânia, Braz.	D4	79
Abadla, Alg.	E9	62
Abaeté, Braz.	E6	79
Abaetetuba, Braz.	D9	76
Abagnar Qi, China	C10	30
Abaí, Para.	D11	80
Abaj, Kaz.	H12	26
Abajo Peak, mtn., Ut., U.S.	F6	151
Abakaliki, Nig.	H14	64
Abakan, Russia	G10	28
Abancay, Peru	E5	82
Abasolo, Mex.	E10	90
Abay see Blue Nile, stm., Afr.	K7	60
Abaya, Lake, l., Eth.	N9	60
Abaza, Russia	G16	26
Abbaye, Point, c., Mi., U.S.	B2	129
Abbeville, Fr.	B8	14
Abbeville, Al., U.S.	D4	108
Abbeville, Ga., U.S.	E3	117
Abbeville, La., U.S.	E3	125
Abbeville, S.C., U.S.	C3	147
Abbeville, co., S.C., U.S.	C2	147
Abbey, Sask., Can.	G1	105
Abbiategrasso, Italy	D3	18
Abbotsford, Wi., U.S.	D3	156
Abbottābād, Pak.	C5	44
Abbott Run Valley, R.I., U.S.	B4	146
'Abd Allāh, Sud.	K2	60
Abdulino, Russia	G8	26
Abe, Lake, l., Afr.	F9	56
Abéché, Chad	F5	56
Abejorral, Col.	E5	84
Abelek, Kaz.	N5	60
Abengourou, C. Iv.	H8	64
Abeokuta, Nig.	H11	64
Abercrombie, N.D., U.S.	C9	141
Aberdeen, Sask., Can.	E2	105
Aberdeen, S. Afr.	I7	66
Aberdeen, Scot., U.K.	D11	8
Aberdeen, Id., U.S.	G6	119
Aberdeen, Md., U.S.	A5	127
Aberdeen, Ms., U.S.	B5	131
Aberdeen, N.C., U.S.	B3	140
Aberdeen, S.D., U.S.	B7	148
Aberdeen, Wa., U.S.	C2	154
Abernant, Al., U.S.	B2	108
Abernethy, Sask., Can.	G4	105
Abert, Lake, l., Or., U.S.	E6	144
Abhā, Sau. Ar.	E3	47
Abhar, Iran	C10	48
Abidjan, C. Iv.	I7	64
Abilene, Ks., U.S.	D6	123
Abilene, Tx., U.S.	C3	150
Abingdon, Il., U.S.	C3	120
Abingdon, Md., U.S.	B5	127
Abingdon, Va., U.S.	f10	153
Abington, Ma., U.S.	B6	128
Abington [Township], Pa., U.S.	o21	145
Abiquiu, N.M., U.S.	A3	138
Abita Springs, La., U.S.	D5	125
Abitibi, stm., Ont., Can.	o19	103
Abitibi, Lake, l., Can.	G17	96
Abiy Adi, Eth.	K10	60
Abnūb, Egypt	D6	60
Abohar, India	E6	44
Abomey, Benin	H10	64
Abony, Hung.	H20	10
Abou-Deïa, Chad	F4	56
Abraham Lincoln Birthplace National Historic Site, hist., Ky., U.S.	C4	124
Abrantes, Port.	F3	16
Abra Pampa, Arg.	B6	80
Abre-Campo, Braz.	F7	79
Ábrego, Col.	C6	84
'Abrī, Sud.	L6	60
Abruzzi, prov., Italy	G8	18
Absaroka Range, mts., U.S.	F7	157
Absarokee, Mt., U.S.	E7	133
Absecon, N.J., U.S.	E4	137
Abşeron Yarımadası, pen., Azer.	A11	48
Abū 'Arīsh, Sau. Ar.	F3	47
Abu Dhabi see Abū Zaby, U.A.E.	B9	47
Abū Gelba, Sud.	K6	60
Abū Hamad, Sud.	H7	60
Abuja, Nig.	G13	64
Abū Jubayhah, Sud.	L6	60
Abū Kamāl, Syria	D8	48
Abū Mūsá, i., Asia	I13	48
Abuná (Abunã), stm., S.A.	C8	82
Abū Na'āmah, Sud.	K8	60
Abū Shajarah, Ra's, c., Sud.	G9	60
Abū Tīj, Egypt	D6	60
Abū Tunaytīn, Sud.	J6	60
Abū Zaby, U.A.E.	B9	47
Abyad, Sud.	K4	60
Acadia, co., La., U.S.	D3	125
Acadia National Park, Me., U.S.	D4	126
Acajutla, El Sal.	D5	92
Acámbaro, Mex.	G9	90
Acandí, Col.	C4	84
Acaponeta, Mex.	F7	90
Acapulco [de Juárez], Mex.	I10	90
Acarai Mountains, mts., S.A.	G14	84
Acaraú, Braz.	D10	76
Acarí, Peru	F4	82
Acarigua, Ven.	C8	84
Acatlán de Juárez, Mex.	G8	90
Acatlán de Osorio, Mex.	H10	90
Acay, Nevado de, mtn., Arg.	C5	80
Acayucan, Mex.	I12	90
Accokeek, Md., U.S.	C3	127
Accomack, co., Va., U.S.	C7	153
Accoville, W.V., U.S.	D3	155
Accra, Ghana	I9	64
Acerra, Italy	I9	18
Acevedo, Arg.	G8	80
Achacachi, Bol.	G7	82
Achalpur, India	J7	44
Achar, Ur.	G10	80
Acheng, China	B12	30
Achill Island, i., Ire.	H3	8
Achiras, Arg.	G6	80
Ačinsk, Russia	F10	28
Acireale, Italy	L10	18
Ackerman, Ms., U.S.	B4	131
Ackley, Ia., U.S.	B4	122
Acklins, i., Bah.	C8	94
Acme, Alta., Can.	D4	98
Acme, Wy., U.S.	B6	157
Acobamba, Peru	E4	82
Acomayo, Peru	E6	82
Acomita, N.M., U.S.	B2	138
Aconchi, Mex.	C4	90
Aconcagua, Cerro, mtn., Arg.	G3	80
Açores (Azores), is., Port.	k19	62a
Acoyapa, Nic.	F9	92
Acqui Terme, Italy	E3	18
Acre see 'Akko, Isr.	C4	50
Acre, state, Braz.	C6	82
Acre, stm., S.A.	C8	82
Acton, Ma., U.S.	B5	128
Acton, Mt., U.S.	E8	133
Acton Vale, Que., Can.	D5	104
Actopan, Mex.	G10	90
Acushnet, Ma., U.S.	C6	128
Acworth, Ga., U.S.	B2	117
Ada, Mn., U.S.	C2	130
Ada, Oh., U.S.	B2	142
Ada, Yugo.	D4	20
Ada, co., Id., U.S.	F2	119
Adaba, Eth.	N10	60
Adair, Ia., U.S.	C3	122
Adair, co., Ia., U.S.	C3	122
Adair, co., Ky., U.S.	C4	124
Adair, co., Mo., U.S.	A5	132
Adair, co., Ok., U.S.	B7	143
Adairsville, Ga., U.S.	B2	117
Adairville, Ky., U.S.	D3	124
Adak Island, i., Ak., U.S.	E4	109
Adamantina, Braz.	F3	79
Adamaoua, mts., Afr.	G9	54
Adami Tulu, Eth.	N10	60
Adams, Ma., U.S.	A1	128
Adams, Mn., U.S.	G6	130
Adams, Ne., U.S.	D9	134
Adams, N.D., U.S.	A7	141
Adams, Wi., U.S.	E4	156
Adams, co., Co., U.S.	B6	113
Adams, co., Id., U.S.	E2	119
Adams, co., Il., U.S.	D2	120
Adams, co., In., U.S.	C8	121
Adams, co., Ia., U.S.	C3	122
Adams, co., Ms., U.S.	D2	131
Adams, co., Ne., U.S.	D7	134
Adams, co., N.D., U.S.	C3	141
Adams, co., Oh., U.S.	D2	142
Adams, co., Pa., U.S.	G7	145
Adams, co., Wa., U.S.	B7	154
Adams, co., Wi., U.S.	D4	156
Adams, Mount, mtn., N.H., U.S.	B4	136
Adams, Mount, mtn., Wa., U.S.	C4	154
Adams Bridge, rf., Asia	H5	46
Adamsville, Al., U.S.	f7	108
Adamsville, R.I., U.S.	E6	146
Adamsville, Tn., U.S.	B3	149
'Adan (Aden), Yemen	H4	47
Adana, Tur.	C3	48
Adarama, Sud.	I9	60
Adare, Cape, c., Ant.	C8	73
Adarot, Sud.	I9	60
Ad-Damazin, Sud.	L8	60
Ad-Dāmir, Sud.	I7	60
Ad-Dammām, Sau. Ar.	A7	47
Ad-Dawhah (Doha), Qatar	I11	48
Ad-Diffah (Libyan Plateau), plat., Afr.	B3	60
Ad-Dilam, Sau. Ar.	C5	47
Addis, La., U.S.	D4	125
Addis Ababa see Adis Abeba, Eth.	G8	56
Addison, Al., U.S.	A2	108
Addison, Ct., U.S.	C5	114
Addison, Il., U.S.	k8	120
Addison, Me., U.S.	D5	126
Addison, N.Y., U.S.	C3	139
Addison, Vt., U.S.	C2	152
Ad-Dīwānīyah, Iraq	F8	48
Ad-Du'ayn, Sud.	L4	60
Ad-Duwaym, Sud.	J7	60
Adel, Ga., U.S.	E3	117
Adel, Ia., U.S.	C3	122
Adelaide, Austl.	J3	70
Adelaide Island, i., Ant.	B12	73
Adélie Coast, Ant.	B7	73
Aden see 'Adan, Yemen	H4	47
Aden, Gulf of, b.	F10	56
Adger, Al., U.S.	B2	108
Adige, stm., Italy	D7	18
Adigrat, Eth.	J10	60
Adi Keyih, Erit.	J10	60
Adi Kwala, Erit.	J10	60
Ādīlābād, India	C5	46
Adirondack Mountains, mts., N.Y., U.S.	A6	139
Adis Abeba (Addis Ababa), Eth.	M10	60
Adis Zemen, Eth.	K9	60
Adi Ugri, Erit.	J10	60
Adıyaman, Tur.	C5	48
Adjud, Rom.	C11	20
Adliswil, Switz.	D10	13
Admiralty Bay, b., Ak., U.S.	A9	109
Admiralty Island, i., Ak., U.S.	m22	109
Admiralty Islands, is., Pap. N. Gui.	k16	68a
Admiralty Mountains, mts., Ant.	C8	73
Adobe Acres, N.M., U.S.	*B3	138
Ado-Ekiti, Nig.	H12	64
Adok, Sud.	M6	60
Adolfo López Mateos, Mex.	C6	90
Ādoni, India	E4	46
Ado-Odo, Nig.	H11	64
Adra, Spain	I8	16
Adrano, Italy	L9	18
Adrar, Alg.	C6	54
Adrār, reg., Maur.	J4	62
Adria, Italy	D7	18
Adrian, Ga., U.S.	D4	117
Adrian, Mi., U.S.	G6	129
Adrian, Mn., U.S.	G3	130
Adrian, Mo., U.S.	C3	132
Adrianople see Edirne, Tur.	H10	20
Adriatic Sea, Eur.	G11	4
Advance, In., U.S.	D4	121
Advance, Mo., U.S.	D8	132
Adwa, Eth.	J10	60
Adygea see Adygeja, state, Russia	I6	26
Adygeja, state, Russia	I6	26
Aegean Sea, Eur.	J8	20
Afghanistan (Afghānestān), ctry., Asia	C8	42
Afgooye, Nic.	H10	56
Afikpo, Nig.	I13	64
Aflou, Alg.	C12	62
Afognak Island, i., Ak., U.S.	D9	109
Afonso Claudio, Braz.	F8	79
Africa	G9	52
Afsluitdijk, Neth.	B7	12
Afton, Ia., U.S.	C3	122
Afton, Mn., U.S.	F6	130
Afton, Ok., U.S.	A7	143
Afton, Wy., U.S.	D2	157
'Afula, Isr.	C4	50
Afyon, Tur.	H14	4
Agadez, Niger	C13	64
Agadir, Mor.	E6	62
Agadyr', Kaz.	H12	26
Agaro, Eth.	N9	60
Agartala, India	I14	44
Agaru, Sud.	L8	60
Agattu Island, i., Ak., U.S.	E2	109
Agawam, Ma., U.S.	B2	128
Agboville, C. Iv.	I7	64
Ağdam, Azer.	B9	48
Agejevo, Russia	G19	22
Agen, Fr.	H7	14
Agency, Mo., U.S.	B3	132
Aghā Jārī, Iran	F10	48
Aginskoje, Russia	G14	28
Agogo, Sud.	N5	60
Agouna, Benin	H10	64
Agoura Hills, Ca., U.S.	m11	112
Āgra, India	G8	44
Agrado, Col.	F5	84
Ağrı Dağı (Mount Ararat), mtn., Tur.	B8	48
Agrigento, Italy	L8	18
Agrínion, Grc.	K5	20
Agryz, Russia	F8	26
Agua, Volcán de, vol., Guat.	C4	92
Aguachica, Col.	C6	84
Aguada de Pasajeros, Cuba	C4	94
Aguadas, Col.	E5	84
Aguadilla, P.R.	E11	94
Aguadulce, Pan.	C2	84
Agua Fria, N.M., U.S.	B3	138
Agua Fria, stm., Az., U.S.	D3	110
Aguaí, Braz.	G5	79
Aguanaval, stm., Mex.	E8	90
Agua Prieta, Mex.	B5	90
Aguaray, Arg.	B7	80
Aguascalientes, Mex.	G8	90
Águas Formosas, Braz.	D8	79
Agua Vermelha, Represa de, res., Braz.	E3	79
Agudos, Braz.	G4	79
Aguié, Niger	E13	64
Aguila, Az., U.S.	D2	110
Aguilar, Co., U.S.	D6	113
Águilas, Spain	H10	16
Aguja, Punta, c., Peru	A1	82
Agulhas, Cape, c., S. Afr.	J5	66
Agustín Codazzi, Col.	B6	84
Ahaggar (Hoggar), mts., Alg.	I13	62
Ahar, Iran	B9	48
Ahaus, Ger.	C7	10
Ahlen, Ger.	D7	10
Ahmadābād, India	I5	44
Ahmadnagar, India	C3	46
Ahmadpur East, Pak.	F4	44
Ahmar Mountains, mts., Eth.	G9	56
Ahome, Mex.	E5	90
Ahoskie, N.C., U.S.	A6	140
Ahuacatlán, Mex.	G7	90
Ahuachapán, El Sal.	D5	92
Ahumada, Mex.	B6	90
Ahväz, Iran	F10	48
Aiea, Hi., U.S.	B4	118
Aigle, Switz.	F6	13
Aiguá, Ur.	H11	80
Aihui, China	A12	30
Aija, Peru	C3	82
Aiken, S.C., U.S.	D4	147
Aiken, co., S.C., U.S.	D4	147
Ailsa Craig, Ont., Can.	D3	103
Aimogasta, Arg.	E5	80
Aimorés, Braz.	E8	79
Aïn Benian, Alg.	B12	62
Aïn Berda, Alg.	M2	18
Aïn Deheb, Alg.	C11	62
Aïn el Beïda, Alg.	C14	62
Aïn Milia, Alg.	B14	62
Aïn Sefra, Alg.	D10	62
Ainsworth, Ne., U.S.	B6	134
Aïn Tedelès, Alg.	B11	62
Aïn Témouchent, Alg.	C10	62
Aïn Touta, Alg.	C13	62
Aïn Wessara, Alg.	C12	62
Aipe, Col.	F5	84
Aïr, mts., Niger	C14	64
Airdrie, Alta., Can.	D3	98
Airão, Braz.	H12	84
Aire-sur-l'Adour, Fr.	I6	14
Airolo, Switz.	E10	13
Aisne, stm., Fr.	C10	14
Aitape, Pap. N. Gui.	F11	38
Aitkin, Mn., U.S.	D5	130
Aitkin, co., Mn., U.S.	D5	130
Aitolikón, Grc.	K5	20
Aiud, Rom.	C7	20
Aix-en-Provence, Fr.	I12	14
Aix-les-Bains, Fr.	G12	14
Aíyion, Grc.	K6	20
Āīzawl, India	I15	44
Aizkraukle, Lat.	E8	22
Aizpute, Lat.	E4	22
Aizu-wakamatsu, Japan	J14	36
Ajaccio, Fr.	m23	15a
Ajaguz, Kaz.	H8	28
Ajax, Ont., Can.	D6	103
Ajdābiyā, Libya	B5	56
Ajibar, Eth.	L10	60
'Ajlūn, Jord.	D5	50
Ajmer, India	G6	44
Ajo, Az., U.S.	E3	110
Ajtos, Bul.	G11	20
Akaki Beseka, Eth.	M10	60
'Akasha East, Sud.	G6	60
Akashi, Japan	M9	36
Akbou, Alg.	B13	62
Aketi, Zaire	H5	56
Akharnaí, Grc.	K7	20
Akhisar, Tur.	K11	20
Akhmīm, Egypt	D6	60
Akiachak, Ak., U.S.	C7	109
Akiak, Ak., U.S.	C7	109
Akita, Japan	H15	36
Akjoujt, Maur.	B2	64
'Akko (Acre), Isr.	C4	50
Aklavik, N.W. Ter., Can.	C5	96
Akola, India	B4	46
Akop, Sud.	M5	60
Akordat, Erit.	E8	56
Akot, India	B4	46
Akranes, Ice.	B2	6a
Akrítas, Ákra, c., Grc.	M5	20
Akron, Al., U.S.	C2	108
Akron, Co., U.S.	A7	113
Akron, In., U.S.	B5	121
Akron, Ia., U.S.	B1	122
Akron, N.Y., U.S.	B2	139
Akron, Oh., U.S.	A4	142
Akron, Pa., U.S.	F9	145
Aksaray, Tur.	B3	48
Akşehir, Tur.	H14	4
Aksu, China	C3	30
Aksum, Eth.	J10	60
Aktau, Kaz.	I8	26
Akt'ubinsk, Kaz.	G9	26
Akureyri, Ice.	B4	6a
Akutan, Ak., U.S.	E6	109
Akwanga, Nig.	G14	64
Alabama, state, U.S.	C3	108
Alabama, stm., Al., U.S.	D2	108
Alabaster, Al., U.S.	B3	108
Al-'Abbāsīyah, Sud.	K6	60
Alacant, Spain	G11	16
Alachua, Fl., U.S.	C4	116
Alachua, co., Fl., U.S.	C4	116
Alagoa Grande, Braz.	E11	76
Alagoinhas, Braz.	B9	79
Al-Ait, Sud.	K4	60
Alajuela, Lago, res., Pan.	H15	92
Alakanuk, Ak., U.S.	C7	109
Al-'Alamayn, Egypt	B5	60
Al-'Amārah, Iraq	F9	48
Alameda, Sask., Can.	H4	105
Alameda, Ca., U.S.	h8	112
Alameda, N.M., U.S.	B3	138
Alameda, co., Ca., U.S.	D3	112
Alamein see Al-'Alamayn, Egypt	B5	60
Alamo, Ga., U.S.	D4	117
Alamo, Nv., U.S.	F6	135
Alamo, Tn., U.S.	B2	149
Alamo, Tx., U.S.	F3	150
Alamo Heights, Tx., U.S.	E3	150
Alamogordo, N.M., U.S.	E4	138
Álamos, Mex.	D5	90
Álamos, stm., Mex.	C7	90
Alamosa, Co., U.S.	D5	113
Alamosa, co., Co., U.S.	D5	113
Alamosa, stm., Co., U.S.	D4	113
Åland (Ahvenanmaa), is., Fin.	K16	6
Alang, Pan.	I12	92
Alaotra, Lac, l., Madag.	p23	67b
Alapaha, Ga., U.S.	E3	117
Alapaha, stm., U.S.	E3	117
Alapajevsk, Russia	F10	26
Alarcón, Embalse de, res., Spain	F9	16
Alaska, state, U.S.	C9	109
Alaska, Gulf of, b., Ak., U.S.	D10	109
Alaska Peninsula, pen., Ak., U.S.	D8	109
Alaska Range, mts., Ak., U.S.	C9	109
Alassio, Italy	E3	18
Alatyr', Russia	G7	26
Alausí, Ec.	I3	84
Alba, Italy	E3	18
Albacete, Spain	G10	16
Albania (Shqipëri), ctry., Eur.	G12	4
Albano Laziale, Italy	H7	18
Albany, Austl.	G3	68
Albany, P.E.I., Can.	C6	101
Albany, Ga., U.S.	E2	117
Albany, In., U.S.	D7	121
Albany, Ky., U.S.	D4	124
Albany, Mn., U.S.	E4	130
Albany, Mo., U.S.	A3	132
Albany, N.Y., U.S.	C7	139
Albany, Or., U.S.	C3	144
Albany, Wi., U.S.	F4	156
Albany, co., N.Y., U.S.	C6	139
Albany, co., Wy., U.S.	E7	157
Albany, stm., Ont., Can.	o18	103
Al-Baq'ah, Jord.	D5	50
Al-Barun, Sud.	L7	60
Al-Basrah (Basra), Iraq	F9	48
Al-Baydā, Libya	B5	56
Al-Bayḍā', Yemen	G4	47
Albemarle, N.C., U.S.	B2	140
Albemarle, co., Va., U.S.	C4	153
Albemarle Sound, strt., N.C., U.S.	A6	140
Albenga, Italy	E3	18
Alberdi, Para.	D9	80
Albert, Fr.	C9	14
Albert, Lake, l., Afr.	A6	58
Albert, Mount, mtn., Alta., Can.	C2	98
Albert City, Ia., U.S.	B3	122
Alberta, prov., Can.	C4	98
Alberta, Mount, mtn., Alta., Can.	C2	98
Albert Lea, Mn., U.S.	G5	130
Albert Markham, Mount, mtn., Ant.	D8	73
Albert Nile, stm., Ug.	H7	56
Alberton, P.E.I., Can.	C5	101
Alberton, Mt., U.S.	C2	133
Albertson, N.Y., U.S.	k13	139
Albertville, Fr.	G13	14
Albertville, Al., U.S.	A3	108
Albertville, Mn., U.S.	E5	130
Albia, Ia., U.S.	C5	122
Albin, Wy., U.S.	E8	157
Albina, Sur.	B8	76
Albion, Id., U.S.	G5	119
Albion, Il., U.S.	E5	120
Albion, In., U.S.	B7	121
Albion, Mi., U.S.	F6	129
Albion, Ne., U.S.	C7	134
Albion, N.Y., U.S.	B2	139
Albion, Pa., U.S.	B1	145
Albion, R.I., U.S.	B4	146
Albion, Wa., U.S.	C8	154
Alborán, Isla de, i., Spain	J8	16
Alborán Sea	I8	16
Ålborg, Den.	M11	6
Alborz, Reshteh-ye Kūhhā-ye (Elburz Mountains), mts., Iran	C12	48
Albuquerque, N.M., U.S.	B3	138
Alburg, Vt., U.S.	B2	152
Albury, Austl.	K7	70
Alca, Peru	F5	82
Alcalá de Guadaira, Spain	H6	16
Alcalá de Henares, Spain	E8	16
Alcalde, N.M., U.S.	A3	138
Alcamo, Italy	L7	18
Alcañiz, Spain	D11	16
Alcântara, Braz.	D10	76
Alcántara, Embalse de, res., Spain	F5	16
Alcantarilla, Spain	H10	16
Alcázar de San Juan, Spain	F8	16
Alcester, S.D., U.S.	D9	148
Alcira (Gegena), Arg.	G6	80
Alcoa, Tn., U.S.	D10	149
Alcobaça, Braz.	D9	79
Alcoi, Spain	G11	16
Alcona, co., Mi., U.S.	D7	129
Alcorn, co., Ms., U.S.	A5	131
Alcorta, Arg.	G8	80
Alcova, Wy., U.S.	D6	157
Alda, Ne., U.S.	D7	134
Aldabra Islands, i., Sey.	C9	58
Aldama, Mex.	F10	90
Aldan, Russia	F17	28
Aldan, stm., Russia	F18	28
Alden, Ia., U.S.	B4	122
Alden, Mn., U.S.	G5	130
Alder, Mt., U.S.	E4	133
Aldershot, Eng., U.K.	J13	8
Alderson, W.V., U.S.	D4	155
Aldrich, Al., U.S.	B3	108
Aledo, Il., U.S.	B3	120
Aleg, Maur.	B2	64
Alegre, Braz.	F8	79
Alegrete, Braz.	E10	80
Alejandro Roca, Arg.	G7	80
Alejandro Selkirk, Isla, i., Chile	H6	74
Alejo Ledesma, Arg.	G8	80
Aleksandrov-Nevskij, Russia	H23	22
Aleksandrov, Russia	G8	26
Aleksandrov Gaj, Russia	G7	26
Aleksandrovsk-Sachalinskij, Russia	G20	28
Aleksejevka, Russia	G12	26
Aleksejevka, Russia	G5	26
Aleksin, Russia	G20	22
Aleksinac, Yugo.	F5	20
Além Paraíba, Braz.	F7	79
Alençon, Fr.	D7	14
Alenquer, Braz.	D8	76
Alentejo, hist. reg., Port.	G3	16
Alenuihaha Channel, strt., Hi., U.S.	C5	118
Aleppo see Halab, Syria	C4	48
Alert, N.W. Ter., Can.	A13	86
Alert Bay, B.C., Can.	D4	99
Alès, Fr.	H11	14
Alessandria, Italy	E3	18
Ålesund, Nor.	J10	6
Aletschhorn, mtn., Switz.	F9	13
Aleutian Islands, is., Ak., U.S.	E3	109
Aleutian Range, mts., Ak., U.S.	D9	109
Aleutian Trench	D3	86
Alevina, mys, c., Russia	F22	28
Alexander, Man., Can.	E1	100
Alexander, co., Il., U.S.	F4	120
Alexander, N.C., U.S.	B1	140
Alexander Archipelago, is., Ak., U.S.	D12	109
Alexander Bay, S. Afr.	G3	66
Alexander City, Al., U.S.	C4	108
Alexander Island, i., Ant.	C12	73
Alexandra, N.Z.	F2	72
Alexandra Falls, wtfl, N.W. Ter., Can.	D9	96
Alexandretta see İskenderun, Tur.	C4	48
Alexandria, Ont., Can.	B10	103
Alexandria see Al-Iskandarīyah, Egypt	B5	60
Alexandria, Rom.	F9	20
Alexandria, In., U.S.	D6	121
Alexandria, Ky., U.S.	B5	124
Alexandria, La., U.S.	C3	125
Alexandria, Mn., U.S.	E3	130
Alexandria, N.H., U.S.	C3	136
Alexandria, S.D., U.S.	D8	148
Alexandria, Tn., U.S.	A5	149
Alexandria, Va., U.S.	B5	153
Alexandroúpolis, Grc.	I9	20
Alexis, Il., U.S.	B3	120
Alfalfa, co., Ok., U.S.	A3	143
Al-Fāshir, Sud.	K3	60
Al-Fashn, Egypt	C6	60
Al-Fāw, Iraq	G10	48
Al-Fayyūm, Egypt	C6	60
Alfeld, Ger.	D9	10
Alfenas, Braz.	F6	79
Al-Fīfī, Sud.	L3	60
Alföld, pl., Hung.	H20	10
Alford, Ont., Can.	B10	103
Alfred, Me., U.S.	E2	126
Alfred, N.Y., U.S.	C3	139
Alga, Kaz.	H9	26
Algarrobal, Chile	E3	80
Algarrobo, Chile	G3	80
Algarve, hist. reg., Port.	H3	16
Al-Gebir, Sud.	K5	60
Algeciras, Spain	I6	16
Algemesí, Spain	F11	16
Algena, Erit.	I10	60
Alger, co., Mi., U.S.	B4	129
Algeria (Algérie), ctry., Afr.	C7	54
Alghero, Italy	I3	18
Al-Ghurdaqah, Egypt	D7	60
Algiers see El Djazaïr, Alg.	B12	16
Alginet, Spain	F11	16
Algodones, N.M., U.S.	B3	138
Algoma, Wi., U.S.	D6	156
Algona, Ia., U.S.	A3	122
Algona, Wa., U.S.	B3	154
Algonac, Mi., U.S.	F8	129
Algonquin, Il., U.S.	A5	120
Algood, Tn., U.S.	C8	149
Algorta, Spain	B8	16
Algorta, Ur.	G10	80
Al Hajeb, Mor.	D8	62
Alhama de Murcia, Spain	H10	16
Alhambra, Ca., U.S.	m12	112
Al-Hammām, Egypt	B5	60
Al-Hariq, Sau. Ar.	C5	47
Alhaurín el Grande, Spain	I7	16
Al-Hawrah, Yemen	H5	47
Al-Hawtah, Yemen	G6	47
Al-Hayy, Iraq	F9	48
Al-Hijāz, reg., Sau. Ar.	I5	48
Al-Hillah, Iraq	F8	48
Al-Hisn, Jord.	D5	50
Al-Hoceïma, Mor.	A6	54
Al-Hudaydah, Yemen	G3	47
Al-Hufūf, Sau. Ar.	B6	47
Al-Husayhişah, Sud.	J7	60
'Alīabād, Iran	C13	48
Äli Bayramlı, Azer.	B10	48
Alice, Tx., U.S.	F3	150
Alice Springs, Austl.	D6	68
Aliceville, Al., U.S.	B1	108
Alida, Sask., Can.	H5	105
Aligarh, India	G8	44
Alīgūdarz, Iran	E10	48
Aliquippa, Pa., U.S.	E1	145
Al-Iskandarīyah (Alexandria), Egypt	B5	60
Al-Ismā'īlīyah, Egypt	B7	60
Aliwal North, S. Afr.	H8	66
Alix, Alta., Can.	C4	98
Al-Jawf, Libya	E2	56
Al-Jawf, Sau. Ar.	G5	48
Al-Jazīrah, reg., Sud.	J6	60
Al-Jubayl, Sau. Ar.	A6	47
Al-Jubayn, Sud.	K8	60
Al-Junaynah, Sud.	K2	60
Aljustrel, Port.	H3	16
Al-Karābah, Sud.	H7	60
Al-Karak, Jord.	F5	50
Al-Kawah, Sud.	K7	60
Al-Khalīl (Hebron), W.B.	E4	50
Al-Khārijah, Egypt	E6	60
Al-Kharţūm (Khartoum), Sud.	J7	60
Al-Kharţūm Baḥrī, Sud.	J7	60
Al-Khubar, Sau. Ar.	A7	47
Al-Khums, Libya	B3	56
Al-Khurmah, Sau. Ar.	D3	47
Alkmaar, Neth.	C6	12
Al-Kūt, Iraq	E8	48

Name	Map Ref.	Page
Al-Kuwayt, Kuw.	G9	48
Al-Lādhiqīyah (Latakia), Syria	D3	48
Allagash, stm., Me., U.S.	B3	126
Al-Lagowa, Sud.	L5	60
Allahābād, India	H9	44
Allamakee, co., Ia., U.S.	A6	122
Allan, Sask., Can.	F2	105
Allanmyo, Mya.	E3	40
Allardt, Tn., U.S.	C9	149
Allatoona Lake, res., Ga., U.S.	B2	117
Allegan, Mi., U.S.	F5	129
Allegan, co., Mi., U.S.	F5	129
Allegany, co., Md., U.S.	k13	127
Allegany, co., N.Y., U.S.	C2	139
Alleghany, co., N.C., U.S.	A1	140
Alleghany, co., Va., U.S.	C2	153
Allegheny, co., Pa., U.S.	E2	145
Allegheny, stm., U.S.	E2	145
Allegheny Mountain, mts., U.S.	B3	153
Allegheny Plateau, plat., U.S.	E1	145
Allegheny Reservoir, res., U.S.	B4	145
Allemands, Lac Des, l., La., U.S.	E5	125
Allen, Ok., U.S.	C5	143
Allen, Tx., U.S.	C4	150
Allen, Tx., U.S.	m10	150
Allen, co., In., U.S.	B7	121
Allen, co., Ks., U.S.	E8	123
Allen, co., Ky., U.S.	D3	124
Allen, co., La., U.S.	D3	125
Allen, co., Oh., U.S.	B1	142
Allendale, N.J., U.S.	A4	137
Allendale, S.C., U.S.	E5	147
Allendale, co., S.C., U.S.	F5	147
Allende, Mex.	C9	90
Allen Park, Mi., U.S.	p15	129
Allenspark, Co., U.S.	A5	113
Allenton, R.I., U.S.	E4	146
Allentown, Pa., U.S.	E11	145
Alleppey, India	H4	46
Aller, stm., Ger.	C9	10
Allerton, Point, c., Ma., U.S.	B6	128
Allgäuer Alpen, mts., Eur.	E17	14
Allgood, Al., U.S.	B3	108
Alliance, Ne., U.S.	B3	134
Alliance, Oh., U.S.	B4	142
Alligator, stm., N.C., U.S.	B6	140
Allison, Ia., U.S.	B5	122
Allison Park, Pa., U.S.	h14	145
Alliston [Beeton Tecumseth and Tottenham], Ont., Can.	C5	103
Al-Līth, Sau. Ar.	D2	47
Alloa, Scot., U.K.	E10	8
Allora, Austl.	G9	70
Allouez, Wi., U.S.	h9	156
Allumette Lake, l., Can.	B7	103
Allyn, Wa., U.S.	B3	154
Alma, N.B., Can.	D5	101
Alma, Que., Can.	A6	104
Alma, Ar., U.S.	B1	111
Alma, Ga., U.S.	E4	117
Alma, Ks., U.S.	C7	123
Alma, Mi., U.S.	E6	129
Alma, Ne., U.S.	D6	134
Alma-Ata (Almaty), Kaz.	I13	26
Almada, Port.	G2	16
Almadén, Spain	G7	16
Al-Madīnah (Medina), Sau. Ar.	B1	47
Al-Mafāzah, Sud.	K8	60
Al-Mafraq, Jord.	D6	50
Al-Mahallah al-Kubrā, Egypt	B6	60
Al-Makhā' (Mocha), Yemen	H3	47
Almalyk, Uzb.	I11	26
Al-Manāmah, Bahr.	H11	48
Almansa, Spain	G10	16
Al-Manshāh, Egypt	D6	60
Al-Mansūrah, Egypt	B6	60
Al-Manzilah, Egypt	F1	48
Al-Marāghah, Egypt	D6	60
Al-Marj, Libya	B5	56
Almassora, Spain	F11	16
Al-Matammah, Sud.	I7	60
Al-Matarīyah, Egypt	B7	60
Al-Mawsil (Mosul), Iraq	C7	48
Al-Mayādīn, Syria	D6	48
Al-Mazār, Jord.	F5	50
Al-Mazra'ah, Jord.	F5	50
Almeirim, Port.	F3	16
Almelo, Neth.	D10	12
Almena, Ks., U.S.	C4	123
Almenara, Braz.	D8	79
Almendralejo, Spain	G5	16
Almería, Spain	I9	16
Al'metjevsk, Russia	G8	26
Almirante, Pan.	F7	120
Almont, Mi., U.S.	F7	129
Almonte, Ont., Can.	B8	103
Almonte, Spain	H5	16
Al-Mubarraz, Sau. Ar.	B6	47
Al-Mudawwarah, Jord.	G3	48
Al-Muglad, Sud.	L4	60
Al-Muharraq, Bahr.	H11	48
Al-Mukallā, Yemen	G6	47
Almuñécar, Spain	I8	16
Al-Musallamīyah, Sud.	J7	60
Almyra, Ar., U.S.	C4	111
Aloha, Or., U.S.	h12	144
Alonsa, Man., Can.	D2	100
Alor Setar, Malay.	K6	40
Alpachiri, Arg.	I7	80
Alpena, Ar., U.S.	A2	111
Alpena, Mi., U.S.	C7	129
Alpena, co., Mi., U.S.	C7	129
Alpharetta, Ga., U.S.	B2	117
Alpine, Az., U.S.	D6	110
Alpine, Tx., U.S.	o13	150
Alpine, Ut., U.S.	C4	151
Alpine, Wy., U.S.	C1	157
Alpine, co., Ca., U.S.	C4	112
Alpinópolis, Braz.	F5	79
Alps, mts., Eur.	F10	4
Al-Qadārif, Sud.	J8	60
Al-Qāhirah (Cairo), Egypt	B6	60
Al-Qāmishlī, Syria	C6	48
Al-Qantarah, Egypt	B7	60
Al-Qatīf, Sau. Ar.	A7	47
Al-Qatrānah, Jord.	F6	50
Al-Quds see Yerushalayim, Isr.	E4	50
Al-Qunaytirah, Syria	B5	50
Al-Qunfudhah, Sau. Ar.	E2	47
Al-Qusayr, Egypt	D8	60
Al-Qūsīyah, Egypt	D6	60
Al-Qutayfah, Syria	A7	50
Al-Qutaynah, Sud.	J7	60
Alsace, hist. reg., Fr.	D14	14
Alsask, Sask., Can.	F1	105
Alstead, N.H., U.S.	D2	136
Alta, Ia., U.S.	B2	122
Altadena, Ca., U.S.	m12	112
Alta Gracia, Arg.	F6	80
Altagracia, Ven.	B7	84
Altagracia de Orituco, Ven.	C9	84
Altai, mts., Asia	H16	26
Altaj, state, Russia	G15	26
Altamaha, stm., Ga., U.S.	E4	117
Altamira, Braz.	D8	76
Altamont, Il., U.S.	D5	120
Altamont, Ks., U.S.	E8	123
Altamont, Or., U.S.	E5	144
Altamont, Tn., U.S.	D8	149
Altamonte Springs, Fl., U.S.	D5	116
Altamura, Italy	I11	18
Altar, Mex.	B4	90
Altar, Desierto de, des., Mex.	B3	90
Altata, Mex.	E6	90
Alta Verapaz, dept., Guat.	B4	92
Alta Vista, Ks., U.S.	D7	123
Altavista, Va., U.S.	C3	153
Altay see Altaj, state, Russia	G15	26
Altdorf, Switz.	E10	13
Altenburg, Ger.	E12	10
Altheimer, Ar., U.S.	C4	111
Altiplano, plat., S.A.	F5	79
Altkirch, Fr.	E14	14
Alto, Ga., U.S.	B3	117
Alto, N.M., U.S.	D4	138
Alto Araguaia, Braz.	D2	79
Alto Garças, Braz.	D2	79
Alton, Il., U.S.	E3	120
Alton, Ia., U.S.	B2	122
Alton, Mo., U.S.	E6	132
Alton, N.H., U.S.	D4	136
Altona, Man., Can.	E3	100
Alton Bay, N.H., U.S.	D4	136
Altoona, Al., U.S.	A3	108
Altoona, Ia., U.S.	C4	122
Altoona, Ks., U.S.	E8	123
Altoona, Pa., U.S.	E5	145
Altoona, Wi., U.S.	D2	156
Alto Paraguai, Braz.	F13	82
Alto Paraná, dept., Para.	I12	82
Alto Parnaíba, Braz.	E9	76
Alto Río Senguer, Arg.	F2	78
Altstätten, Switz.	D12	13
Altun Shan, mts., China	D4	30
Altus, Ar., U.S.	B2	111
Altus, Ok., U.S.	C2	143
Altus Reservoir, res., Ok., U.S.	C2	143
Al-Ubayyid, Sud.	K6	60
Al-Udayyah, Sud.	K5	60
Alūksne, Lat.	D10	22
Alum Creek, W.V., U.S.	m12	155
Al-Uqsur (Luxor), Egypt	E7	60
Alva, Ok., U.S.	A3	143
Alvarado, Mex.	H12	90
Alvarães, Braz.	I10	84
Álvaro Obregón, Presa, res., Mex.	D5	90
Alvdal, Nor.	J12	6
Alvear, Arg.	E10	80
Alvernia, Mount, hill, Bah.	B7	94
Alvesta, Swe.	M14	6
Alvin, Tx., U.S.	E15	150
Alvinópolis, Braz.	F7	79
Alvinston, Ont., Can.	E3	103
Alwar, India	G7	44
Al-Wāsitah, Egypt	J6	60
Al-Wazz, Sud.	J6	60
Alxa Zuoqi, China	D8	30
Alytus, Lith.	G7	22
Alzamaj, Russia	F11	28
Alzira (Alcira), Spain	F11	16
Amadjuak Lake, l., N.W. Ter., Can.	C18	96
Amador, co., Ca., U.S.	C3	112
Amagasaki, Japan	M10	36
Amagunze, Nig.	H13	64
Amahai, Indon.	F8	38
Åmål, Swe.	L13	6
Amaliás, Grc.	L5	20
Amambaí, Braz.	G1	79
Amambay, dept., Para.	B10	80
Amapá, Braz.	D9	74
Amapá, Braz.	C8	76
Amapala, Hond.	D7	92
Amapala, Punta de, c., El Sal.	D7	92
Amaranth, Braz.	E10	76
Amaranth, Man., Can.	D2	100
Amarapura, Mya.	D4	40
Amargosa, Braz.	B9	79
Amargosa, stm., U.S.	D5	112
Amargosa Desert, des., U.S.	G5	135
Amargosa Range, mts., U.S.	G5	135
Amarillo, Tx., U.S.	B2	150
'Amar Jadīd, Sud.	J3	60
Amasya, Tur.	G15	4
Amatique, Bahía de, b., N.A.	B6	92
Amatitlán, Guat.	C4	92
Amatitlán, Lago de, l., Guat.	C4	92
Amazon (Solimões) (Amazonas), stm., S.A.	D7	76
Amazonas, state, Braz.	H10	84
Amazonas, dept., Col.	H7	84
Amazonas, dept., Peru	A2	82
Amazonas, ter., Ven.	F9	84
Ambakaka, Madag.	t22	67b
Ambala, India	E7	44
Ambalavao, Madag.	r22	67b
Ambanja, Madag.	n23	67b
Ambararata, Madag.	o23	67b
Ambargasta, Salinas de, pl., Arg.	E6	80
Ambato, Ec.	H3	84
Ambatolampy, Madag.	q22	67b
Ambatondrazaka, Madag.	p23	67b
Ámbelos, Ákra, c., Grc.	J7	20
Amberg, Ger.	F11	10
Ambergris Cay, i., Belize	H16	90
Ambérieu-en-Bugey, Fr.	G12	14
Ambert, Fr.	G10	14
Ambilobe, Madag.	n23	67b
Ambinanindrano, Madag.	r23	67b
Ambler, Ak., U.S.	B8	109
Ambler, Pa., U.S.	F11	145
Ambo, Peru	D3	82
Amboahangy, Madag.	t22	67b
Ambodiriana, Madag.	p23	67b
Ambohidray, Madag.	q23	67b
Amboise, Fr.	E7	14
Ambon, Indon.	F8	38
Ambositra, Madag.	r22	67b
Ambovombe, Madag.	t22	67b
Amboy, Il., U.S.	B4	120
Ambre, Cap d', c., Madag.	m23	67b
Ambridge, Pa., U.S.	E1	145
Ambunti, Pap. N. Gui.	F11	38
Amderma, Russia	D10	26
Amdo, China	D5	30
Ameca, Mex.	G7	90
Ameca, stm., Mex.	G7	90
Amecameca [de Juárez], Mex.	H10	90
Ameland, i., Neth.	B8	12
Amelia, La., U.S.	E4	125
Amelia, co., Va., U.S.	C4	153
Amelia Court House, Va., U.S.	C5	153
American, stm., Ca., U.S.	C3	112
Americana, Braz.	G5	79
American Falls, Id., U.S.	G6	119
American Falls Reservoir, res., Id., U.S.	F5	119
American Fork, Ut., U.S.	C4	151
American Highland, plat., Ant.	B21	73
American Samoa, dep., Oc.	G1	2
Americus, Ga., U.S.	D2	117
Americus, Ks., U.S.	D7	123
Amersfoort, Neth.	D7	12
Amery, Wi., U.S.	C1	156
Amery Ice Shelf, Ant.	B5	73
Ames, Ia., U.S.	B4	122
Amesbury, Ma., U.S.	A6	128
Ámfissa, Grc.	K6	20
Amherst, N.S., Can.	D5	101
Amherst, Ma., U.S.	B2	128
Amherst, N.H., U.S.	E3	136
Amherst, N.Y., U.S.	C2	139
Amherst, Oh., U.S.	A3	142
Amherst, Va., U.S.	C3	153
Amherst, co., Va., U.S.	C3	153
Amherstdale, W.V., U.S.	n12	155
Amiens, Fr.	C9	14
Amili, China	F16	44
Amīndīvi Islands, is., India	G2	46
Aminuis, Nmb.	D4	66
Amirante Islands, is., Sey.	C10	58
Amisk Lake, l., Sask., Can.	C4	105
Amite, La., U.S.	D5	125
Amite, co., Ms., U.S.	D3	131
Amite, stm., La., U.S.	D5	125
Amity, Ar., U.S.	C2	111
Amity, Or., U.S.	B3	144
Amityville, N.Y., U.S.	E7	139
'Ammān, Jord.	E5	50
Ammon, Id., U.S.	F7	119
Ammonoosuc, stm., N.H., U.S.	B3	136
Amne Machin Shan see A'nyêmaqên Shan, mts., China	D6	30
Amnok-kang (Yalu), stm., Asia	C13	32
Ämol, Iran	C12	48
Amory, Ms., U.S.	B5	131
Amos, Que., Can.	k11	104
Amoy see Xiamen, China	K7	34
Ampanihy, Madag.	t21	67b
Amparo, Braz.	G5	79
Amparo, Nevado, mtn., Peru	F6	82
Ampombiantambo, Madag.	n23	67b
Amposta, Spain	E12	16
Amrāvati, India	J7	44
Amreli, India	J4	44
Amritsar, India	E6	44
Amroha, India	F8	44
Amsterdam, Neth.	D6	12
Amsterdam, S. Afr.	F10	66
Amsterdam, N.Y., U.S.	C6	139
Amsterdam, Île, i., F.S.A.T.	L11	158
Amstetten, Aus.	G14	10
Am Timan, Chad	F5	56
Amu Darya (Amudarja), stm., Asia	B2	44
Amundsen Gulf, b., N.W. Ter., Can.	B8	96
Amundsen-Scott, sci., Ant.	D10	73
Amundsen Sea, Ant.	C11	73
Amur (Heilong), stm., Asia	B14	30
Anaco, Ven.	C10	84
Anaconda, Mt., U.S.	D4	133
Anaconda Range, mts., Mt., U.S.	E3	133
Anacortes, Wa., U.S.	A3	154
Anacostia, stm., U.S.	C4	127
Anadarko, Ok., U.S.	B3	143
Anadyr', Russia	E27	28
Anadyrskij zaliv, b., Russia	E28	28
Anaheim, Ca., U.S.	F5	112
Anahim Lake, B.C., Can.	C5	99
Anahola, Hi., U.S.	A2	118
Anáhuac, Mex.	C6	90
Anahuac, Tx., U.S.	E5	150
Ánai Mudi, mtn., India	G4	46
Analalava, Madag.	o22	67b
Ana María, Golfo de, b., Cuba	D5	94
Anamoose, N.D., U.S.	B5	141
Anamosa, Ia., U.S.	B6	122
Anamur, Tur.	H14	4
Ānand, India	I5	44
Anandale, La., U.S.	C3	125
Ananea, Peru	F7	82
Anan'yiv, Ukr.	B13	20
Anápolis, Braz.	D4	79
Anastácio, Braz.	F1	79
Añatuya, Arg.	E7	80
Anbu, China	L5	34
Ancash, dept., Peru	C3	82
Ancaster, Ont., Can.	D4	103
Anchang, China	E9	34
Anchorage, Ak., U.S.	C10	109
Anchorage, Ky., U.S.	g11	124
Anchor Point, Ak., U.S.	D9	109
Anci (Langfang), China	D4	32
Ancienne-Lorette, Que., Can.	C6	104
Ancón, Peru	D3	82
Ancona, Italy	F8	18
Ancón de Sardinas, Bahía de, b., S.A.	G3	84
Ancud, Chile	E2	78
Ancud, Golfo de, b., Chile	E2	78
Anda, China	B12	30
Andacollo, Arg.	I3	80
Andahuaylas, Peru	E5	82
Andale, Ks., U.S.	D5	80
Andalgalá, Arg.	D5	80
Åndalsnes, Nor.	J10	6
Andalucía, prov., Spain	H7	16
Andalusia, Al., U.S.	D3	108
Andalusia, Il., U.S.	B3	120
Andaman Islands, is., India	H2	40
Andaman Sea, Asia	I3	40
Andamarca, Peru	D4	82
Andamooka, Austl.	H2	70
Andapa, Madag.	o23	67b
Andaraí, Braz.	B8	79
Andenes, Nor.	G15	6
Andermatt, Switz.	E10	13
Andernach, Ger.	E7	10
Anderson, Ak., U.S.	C10	109
Anderson, In., U.S.	D6	121
Anderson, Mo., U.S.	E3	132
Anderson, S.C., U.S.	B2	147
Anderson, co., Ks., U.S.	D8	123
Anderson, co., Ky., U.S.	C4	124
Anderson, co., S.C., U.S.	B2	147
Anderson, co., Tn., U.S.	C9	149
Anderson, co., Tx., U.S.	D5	150
Anderson, stm., N.W. Ter., Can.	C7	96
Anderson Ranch Reservoir, res., Id., U.S.	F3	119
Andersonville, Ga., U.S.	D2	117
Andes, Col.	E5	84
Andes, mts., S.A.	G8	74
Andhra Pradesh, state, India	D5	46
Andimeshk, Iran	E10	48
Andīzān, Uzb.	I12	26
Andkhvoy, Afg.	B1	44
Andong, S. Kor.	G16	32
Andorra, And.	C13	16
Andorra, ctry., Eur.	G8	4
Andover, Ks., U.S.	g12	123
Andover, Me., U.S.	D2	126
Andover, Ma., U.S.	A5	128
Andover, Mn., U.S.	m12	130
Andover, N.H., U.S.	D3	136
Andøya, i., Nor.	G14	6
Andradina, Braz.	F3	79
Andranopasy, Madag.	r20	67b
Andreanof Islands, is., Ak., U.S.	E4	109
Andreapol', Russia	E15	22
Andrejevka, Russia	F24	22
Andrew, Alta., Can.	C4	98
Andrew, co., Mo., U.S.	B3	132
Andrews, In., U.S.	C6	121
Andrews, N.C., U.S.	f9	140
Andrews, S.C., U.S.	E8	147
Andrews, Tx., U.S.	C1	150
Andrews, co., Tx., U.S.	C1	150
Andrews Air Force Base, mil., Md., U.S.	C4	127
Andria, Italy	H11	18
Andriamena, Madag.	p22	67b
Androka, Madag.	t21	67b
Andros, i., Bah.	B6	94
Androscoggin, co., Me., U.S.	D2	126
Androscoggin, stm., Me., U.S.	D2	126
Andrychów, Pol.	F19	10
Andújar, Spain	G7	16
Anécho, Togo	H10	64
Anegada Passage, strt., N.A.	E13	94
Aneta, N.D., U.S.	B8	141
Aneto, Pico de, mtn., Spain	C12	16
Anfeng, China	C9	34
Anfeng, China	B9	34
Anfu, China	H3	34
Angamos, Punta, c., Chile	A3	80
Ang'angxi, China	B11	30
Angao, China	B1	34
Angara, stm., Russia	F17	26
Angara-Débou, Benin	F11	64
Angarbaka, Sud.	M3	60
Angarsk, Russia	G12	28
Ángel, Salto (Angel Falls), wtfl, Ven.	E11	84
Ángel de la Guarda, Isla, i., Mex.	C3	90
Angeles, Phil.	n19	39b
Angel Falls see Ángel, Salto, wtfl, Ven.	E11	84
Angelina, co., Tx., U.S.	D5	150
Angelina, stm., Tx., U.S.	D5	150
Angels Camp, Ca., U.S.	C3	112
Angermünde, Ger.	B13	10
Angers, Fr.	E6	14
Angical, Braz.	B6	79
Angicos, Braz.	E11	76
Angier, N.C., U.S.	B4	140
Ängk Tasaôm, Camb.	I8	40
Angle Inlet, Mn., U.S.	A3	130
Anglesey, i., Wales, U.K.	H9	8
Angleton, Tx., U.S.	E5	150
Angmagssalik, Grnld.	C16	86
Angoche, Moz.	E7	66
Angol, Chile	I2	80
Angola, In., U.S.	A8	121
Angola, ctry., Afr.	D3	58
Angoon, Ak., U.S.	D13	109
Angora see Ankara, Tur.	B2	48
Angoram, Pap. N. Gui.	F11	38
Angostura, Mex.	E5	90
Angostura, Presa de la, res., Mex.	I13	90
Angoulême, Fr.	G7	14
Angra dos Reis, Braz.	G7	79
Angren, Uzb.	I12	26
Anguilla, Ms., U.S.	C3	131
Anguilla, dep., N.A.	E13	94
Anguille, Cape, c., Newf., Can.	E2	102
Anguo, China	E3	32
Anhai, China	K7	34
Anhui (Anhwei), prov., China	E10	30
Aniak, Ak., U.S.	C8	109
Aniche, Fr.	H3	12
Anina, Rom.	D5	20
Anita, Ia., U.S.	C3	122
Anivorano, Madag.	q23	67b
Anji, China	E8	34
Anjou, Que., Can.	p19	104
Anjŭ, N. Kor.	D13	32
Ankang, China	E8	30
Ankara, Tur.	B2	48
Ankarimbelo, Madag.	r22	67b
Ankavandra, Madag.	q21	67b
Ankazoabo, Madag.	s21	67b
Ankazobe, Madag.	q22	67b
Ankeny, Ia., U.S.	C4	122
Ankilimalinika, Madag.	s20	67b
Ankpa, Nig.	H13	64
Anlu, China	E2	34
Anna, Il., U.S.	F4	120
Anna, Lake, res., Va., U.S.	B5	153
Annaba (Bône), Alg.	B14	62
Annaberg-Buchholz, Ger.	E13	10
An-Nabk, Syria	D4	48
An-Nafūd, des., Sau. Ar.	G6	48
An-Najaf, Iraq	F8	48
Anna Maria, Fl., U.S.	p10	116
Annamitique, Chaîne, mts., Asia	F9	40
Annandale, Mn., U.S.	E4	130
Annandale, Va., U.S.	g12	153
Annapolis, Md., U.S.	C5	127
Annapolis, co., N.S., Can.	E4	101
Annapolis Junction, Md., U.S.	B4	127
Annapolis Royal, N.S., Can.	E4	101
Annapŭrna, mtn., Nepal	F10	44
Ann Arbor, Mi., U.S.	F7	129
Anna Regina, Guy.	D13	84
Anne Arundel, co., Md., U.S.	B4	127
Annecy, Fr.	G13	14
Annemasse, Fr.	F13	14
Anniston, Al., U.S.	B4	108
Annobón, i., Eq. Gui.	B1	58
Annonay, Fr.	G11	14
An-Nuhūd, Sud.	K5	60
Annville, Pa., U.S.	F8	145
Anoka, Mn., U.S.	E5	130
Anoka, co., Mn., U.S.	E5	130
Anori, Braz.	I12	84
Anping, China	D4	32
Anpu, China	E6	34
Anqing, China	E10	30
Anqiu, China	G7	32
Ansbach, Ger.	F10	10
Anse-d'Hainault, Haiti	E7	94
Anserma, Col.	E5	84
Anshan, China	B10	32
Anshun, China	F8	30
Ansley, Ne., U.S.	C6	134
Anson, Me., U.S.	D3	126
Anson, co., N.C., U.S.	B2	140
Ansong, S. Kor.	F15	32
Ansongo, Mali	D10	64
Ansted, W.V., U.S.	C3	155
Anta, Peru	E5	82
Antabamba, Peru	F5	82
Antalaha, Madag.	o24	67b
Antalya, Tur.	H14	4
Antananarivo, Madag.	q22	67b
Antanetibe, Madag.	q22	67b
Antarctica	D5	73
Antarctic Peninsula, pen., Ant.	B12	73
Antelope, co., Ne., U.S.	B7	134
Antelope Island, i., Ut., U.S.	B3	151
Antelope Peak, mtn., Nv., U.S.	B7	135
Antequera, Para.	A5	80
Antequera, Spain	H7	16
Antevamena, Madag.	r21	67b
Anthony, Ks., U.S.	E5	123
Anthony, N.M., U.S.	F3	138
Anthony, R.I., U.S.	D3	146
Anthony, Tx., U.S.	o11	150
Anti-Atlas, mts., Mor.	E6	62
Antibes, Fr.	I14	14
Anticosti, Île d', i., Que., Can.	k14	104
Antietam National Battlefield, hist., Md., U.S.	B2	127
Antigo, Wi., U.S.	C4	156
Antigonish, N.S., Can.	D8	101
Antigua and Barbuda, ctry., N.A.	F14	94
Antigua Guatemala, Guat.	C4	92
Antiguo Morelos, Mex.	F10	90
Anti-Lebanon see Sharqī, Al-Jabal ash- mts., Asia	A6	50
Antioch see Hatay, Tur.		
Antioch, Ca., U.S.	h9	112
Antioch, Il., U.S.	A5	120
Antioquia, Col.	D5	84
Antioquia, dept., Col.	E5	84
Antipodes Islands, is., N.Z.	M21	158
Antizana, vol., Ec.	H3	84
Antlers, Ok., U.S.	C6	143
Antofagasta, Chile	A3	80
Antofagasta, prov., Chile	B4	80
Antofalla, Volcán, vol., Arg.	C5	80
Antón, Pan.	C2	84
Antongila, Helodrano, b., Madag.	o23	67b
Antonina, Braz.	C14	80
Antônio Prado, Braz.	E13	80
Antonito, Co., U.S.	D5	113
Antou, China	I7	34
Antrim, N. Ire., U.K.	G7	8
Antrim, N.H., U.S.	D3	136
Antrim, co., Mi., U.S.	C5	129
Antropovo, Russia	C26	22
Antsalova, Madag.	q21	67b
Antsirabe, Madag.	q22	67b
Antsiranana, Madag.	n23	67b
Antsla, Est.	D9	22
Antsohihy, Madag.	o22	67b
Antwerp see Antwerpen, Bel.	F5	12
Antwerpen (Anvers), Bel.	F5	12
Antwerpen, prov., Bel.	F6	12
Anxi, China	C6	30
Anxi, China	J7	34
Anxin, China	E3	32
Anyama, C. Iv.	I7	64
Anyang, China	G2	32
A'nyêmaqên Shan, mts., China	D6	30
Anyi, China	G4	34
Anyuan, China	H2	34
Anzac, Alta., Can.	A5	98
Anžero-Sudžensk, Russia	F15	26
Anzhen, China	D9	34
Anzhou, China	E3	32
Anzin, Fr.	B10	14
Anzio, Italy	H7	18
Anzóategui, state, Ven.	C10	84
Aohan Qi (Xinhui), China	A7	32
Aoji, N. Kor.	A18	32
Aojiang, China	H9	34
Aomori, Japan	G15	36
Aosta, Italy	D2	18
Apa, stm., S.A.	B10	80
Apache, Ok., U.S.	C3	143
Apache, co., Az., U.S.	B6	110
Apache Junction, Az., U.S.	m9	110
Apalachee Bay, b., Fl., U.S.	B2	116
Apalachicola, Fl., U.S.	C2	116
Apalachicola, stm., Fl., U.S.	B1	116
Apalachicola Bay, b., Fl., U.S.	C2	116
Apanas, Laguna de, res., Nic.	D9	92
Apaporis, stm., S.A.	H7	84
Aparri, Phil.	I19	39b
Apaseo El Grande, Mex.	G9	90
Apatin, Yugo.	D2	20
Apatity, Russia	D4	26
Apatzingán de la Constitución, Mex.	H8	90
Apaxtla de Castrejón, Mex.	H10	90
Apeldoorn, Neth.	D8	12
Apennines see Appennino, mts., Italy	F7	18
Apex, N.C., U.S.	B4	140
Api, mtn., Nepal	F9	44
Apia, W. Sam.	G1	2
Apiaí, Braz.	C14	80
Apizaco, Mex.	H10	90
Aplao, Peru	G5	82
Aplington, Ia., U.S.	B5	122
Apo, Mount, mtn., Phil.	D8	38
Apodaca, Mex.	D11	90
Apohan... N.B., Can.	D4	101
Apolda, Ger.	D11	10
Apolinario Saravia, Arg.	C6	80
Apollo, Pa., U.S.	E2	145
Apolo, Bol.	F7	82
Apopka, Fl., U.S.	D5	116
Apopka, Lake, l., Fl., U.S.	D5	116
Apostle Islands, is., Wi., U.S.	A3	156
Apostle Islands National Lakeshore, Wi., U.S.	A3	156
Apóstoles, Arg.	D11	80
Apostolove, Ukr.	I9	153
Appalachia, Va., U.S.	f9	153
Appalachian Mountains, mts., N.A.	C11	106
Appanoose, co., Ia., U.S.	D5	122
Appennino (Apennines), mts., Italy	F7	18
Appenzell, Switz.	D11	13
Applegate, Or., U.S.	E3	144
Apple Orchard Mountain, mtn., Va., U.S.	C3	153
Appleton, Mn., U.S.	E2	130
Appleton, Wi., U.S.	D5	156
Appleton City, Mo., U.S.	C3	132
Apple Valley, Ca., U.S.	E5	112
Apple Valley, Mn., U.S.	n12	130
Appleyard, Wa., U.S.	B5	154
Appling, Ga., U.S.	C4	117
Appling, co., Ga., U.S.	E4	117
Appomattox, Va., U.S.	C4	153
Appomattox, co., Va., U.S.	C4	153
Appomattox, stm., Va., U.S.	C4	153
Appomattox Court House National Historical Park, Va., U.S.	C4	153
Aprelevka, Russia	F20	22
Apt, Fr.	I12	14
Apucarana, Braz.	G3	79
Apure, state, Ven.	D8	84
Apure, stm., Ven.	D9	84
Apurímac, dept., Peru	E5	82
Apurímac, stm., Peru	E5	82
Aqaba, Gulf of, b.	I5	60
Aquidauana, Braz.	F1	79
Aquiles Serdán, Mex.	C7	90
Aquin, Haiti	E11	94
Ara, India	H11	44
'Arab, Bahr al-, stm., Sud.	M4	60
'Arab, Shatt al-, stm., Asia	k11	153
Arabi, La., U.S.	k11	125
Arabian Desert see Sharqī, As-Sahrā' ash-, des., Egypt	D7	60
Arabian Peninsula, pen., Asia	G5	24
Arabian Sea	G4	24
Aracaju, Braz.	F11	76
Aracati, Braz.	D11	76

Name	Map Ref.	Page
Araçatuba, Braz.	F3	79
Aracruz, Braz.	E8	79
Araçuaí, Braz.	D7	79
Arad, Rom.	C5	20
Arafura Sea	I17	158
Aragarças, Braz.	C2	79
Aragon, Ga., U.S.	B1	117
Aragón, prov., Spain	D10	16
Aragua, state, Ven.	B9	84
Araguaçu, Braz.	B4	79
Aragua de Barcelona, Ven.	C10	84
Araguaia, stm., Braz.	E9	76
Araguari, Braz.	E4	79
Araguatins, Braz.	E9	76
Arāk, Iran	D10	48
Arakan Yoma, mts., Mya.	E3	40
Aral Sea, Asia	H10	26
Aral'sk, Kaz.	H10	26
Aramac, Austl.	D6	70
Aramari, Braz.	B9	79
Aramtalla, Sud.	N5	60
Ãrān, Iran	D11	48
Aranda de Duero, Spain	D8	16
Arandas, Mex.	G8	90
Aran Islands, is., Ire.	H4	8
Aranjuez, Spain	E8	16
Aransas, co., Tx., U.S.	E4	150
Aransas Bay, b., Tx., U.S.	E4	150
Aransas Pass, Tx., U.S.	F4	150
Arao, Japan	O5	36
Arapaho, Ok., U.S.	B3	143
Arapahoe, Ne., U.S.	D6	134
Arapahoe, co., Co., U.S.	B6	113
Arapiraca, Braz.	E11	76
Arapongas, Braz.	G3	79
Arapoti, Braz.	H4	79
Araranguá, Braz.	E14	80
Araraquara, Braz.	F4	79
Araras, Braz.	G5	79
Ararat, Austl.	K5	70
Ararat, Mount see Ağrı Dağı, mtn., Tur.	B8	48
Arauca, Col.	D7	84
Arauca, dept., Col.	D7	84
Arauca, stm., S.A.	D9	84
Araucária, Braz.	C14	80
Arauco, Chile	I2	80
Arauco, Golfo de, b., Chile	I2	80
Araújos, Braz.	E6	79
Araure, Ven.	C8	84
Araxá, Braz.	E5	79
Araya, Ven.	B10	84
Araya, Punta de, c., Ven.	B10	84
Arba Minch, Eth.	N9	60
Arboga, Swe.	L14	6
Arbois, Fr.	F12	14
Arbon, Switz.	C11	13
Arborfield, Sask., Can.	D4	105
Arborg, Man., Can.	D3	100
Arbroath, Scot., U.K.	E11	8
Arbuckle Mountains, mts., Ok., U.S.	C4	143
Arbuckles, Lake of the, res., Ok., U.S.	C5	143
Arbyrd, Mo., U.S.	E7	132
Arcachon, Fr.	H5	14
Arcade, Ga., U.S.	B3	117
Arcadia, N.S., Can.	E3	101
Arcadia, Ca., U.S.	m12	112
Arcadia, Fl., U.S.	E5	116
Arcadia, In., U.S.	D5	121
Arcadia, La., U.S.	B3	125
Arcadia, Mo., U.S.	D7	132
Arcadia, Ne., U.S.	C6	134
Arcadia, S.C., U.S.	B4	147
Arcadia, Wi., U.S.	D2	156
Arcanum, Oh., U.S.	C1	142
Arcata, Ca., U.S.	B1	112
Arc Dome, mtn., Nv., U.S.	E4	135
Arcelia, Mex.	H9	90
Archangel'sk, Russia	E6	26
Archbald, Pa., U.S.	m18	145
Archbold, Oh., U.S.	A1	142
Archdale, N.C., U.S.	B3	140
Archer, co., Tx., U.S.	C3	150
Archerwill, Sask., Can.	E4	105
Arches National Park, Ut., U.S.	E6	151
Archie, Mo., U.S.	C3	132
Archuleta, co., Co., U.S.	D3	113
Arco, Id., U.S.	F5	119
Arcola, Sask., Can.	H4	105
Arcola, Il., U.S.	D5	120
Arcola, Ms., U.S.	B3	131
Arcos, Braz.	F6	79
Arcos de la Frontera, Spain	I6	16
Arcoverde, Braz.	E11	76
Arctic Bay, N.W. Ter., Can.	B15	96
Arctic Ocean	A1	86
Arcturus, Zimb.	A10	66
Ardabīl, Iran	B10	48
Ardakān, Iran	E12	48
Ardatov, Russia	F26	22
Arden, Man., Can.	D2	100
Ardennes, reg., Eur.	E5	10
Ardlethan, Austl.	J7	70
Ardmore, Alta., Can.	B5	98
Ardmore, Al., U.S.	A3	108
Ardmore, In., U.S.	A5	121
Ardmore, Ok., U.S.	C4	143
Ardmore, Pa., U.S.	F11	145
Ardmore, Tn., U.S.	B5	149
Ardsley, N.Y., U.S.	g13	139
Areado, Braz.	F5	79
Arecibo, P.R.	E11	94
Areia Branca, Braz.	D11	76
Arena, Point, c., Ca., U.S.	C2	112
Arenac, co., Mi., U.S.	D7	129
Arenápolis, Braz.	F13	82
Arenas Valley, N.M., U.S.	E1	138
Arendal, Nor.	L11	6
Arenillas, Ec.	I2	84
Arenys de Mar, Spain	D14	16
Arequipa, Peru	G6	82
Arequipa, dept., Peru	F5	82
Arequito, Arg.	G8	80
Arezzo, Italy	F6	18
Argadargada, Austl.	C2	70
Arganda, Spain	E8	16
Argelès-Gazost, Fr.	I7	14
Argelès-sur-Mer, Fr.	J10	14
Argenta, Il., U.S.	D5	120
Argentan, Fr.	D6	14
Argentina, ctry., S.A.	C4	78
Argentino, Lago, l., Arg.	G2	78
Argenton-sur-Creuse, Fr.	F8	14
Argeș, stm., Rom.	E9	20
Arghandāb, stm., Afg.	D2	44
Argo, Sud.	H6	60
Argonia, Ks., U.S.	E6	123
Argonne, reg., Fr.	C12	14
Árgos, Grc.	L6	20
Argos, In., U.S.	B5	121
Argostólion, Grc.	K4	20
Arguello, Point, c., Ca., U.S.	E3	112
Argun' (Ergun), stm., Asia.	G16	28
Argyle, Lake, res., Austl.	C5	68
Århus, Den.	M12	6
Ariana, Tun.	M5	18
Arias, Arg.	G7	80
Arica, Chile	H6	82
Arichat, N.S., Can.	D8	101
Arid, Cape, c., Austl.	F4	68
Arīhā (Jericho), W.B.	E4	50
Arima, Trin.	I14	94
Arimo, Id., U.S.	G6	119
Ario de Rosales, Mex.	H9	90
Aripuanã, Braz.	C11	82
Aripuanã, stm., Braz.	B11	82
Ariquemes, Braz.	C10	82
'Arīsh, Wādī al-, val., Egypt	B7	60
Aristazabal Island, i., B.C., Can.	C3	99
Ariton, Al., U.S.	D4	108
Arivaca, Az., U.S.	F4	110
Arivonimamo, Madag.	q22	67b
Arizaro, Salar de, pl., Arg.	B9	80
Arizgoiti, Spain	B9	16
Arizona, state, U.S.	C3	110
Arizona Sunsites, Az., U.S.	F6	110
Arizpe, Mex.	B4	90
Arjay, Ky., U.S.	D6	124
Arjeplog, Swe.	H15	6
Arjona, Col.	B5	84
Arkabutla Lake, res., Ms., U.S.	A4	131
Arkadelphia, Ar., U.S.	C2	111
Arkalyk, Kaz.	G11	26
Arkansas, co., Ar., U.S.	C4	111
Arkansas, state, U.S.	C3	111
Arkansas, stm., U.S.	D8	106
Arkansas City, Ar., U.S.	D4	111
Arkansas City, Ks., U.S.	E6	123
Arkhangelsk see Archangel'sk, Russia	E6	26
Arklow, Ire.	I7	8
Arkoma, Ok., U.S.	B7	143
Arkona, Kap, c., Ger.	A13	10
Arlbergpass, Aus.	D13	13
Arles, Fr.	I11	14
Arlington, Ga., U.S.	E2	117
Arlington, In., U.S.	E6	121
Arlington, Ks., U.S.	E5	123
Arlington, Ma., U.S.	B5	128
Arlington, Mn., U.S.	F4	130
Arlington, Ne., U.S.	C9	134
Arlington, N.Y., U.S.	D7	139
Arlington, S.D., U.S.	C8	148
Arlington, Tn., U.S.	B2	149
Arlington, Tx., U.S.	n9	150
Arlington, Vt., U.S.	E2	152
Arlington, Va., U.S.	B5	153
Arlington, Wa., U.S.	A3	154
Arlington, co., Va., U.S.	g12	153
Arlington, Lake, res., Tx., U.S.	n9	150
Arlington Heights, Il., U.S.	A5	120
Arlit, Niger	B13	64
Arlon (Aarlen), Bel.	I8	12
Arma, Ks., U.S.	E9	123
Armada, Mi., U.S.	F8	129
Armageddon see Tel Megiddo, hist., Isr.	C4	50
Armant, Egypt	E7	60
Armavir, Russia	H6	26
Armenia, Col.	E5	84
Armenia, ctry., Asia	I6	26
Armentières, Fr.	B9	14
Armería, Mex.	H8	90
Armero, Col.	E5	84
Armidale, Austl.	H9	70
Armijo, N.M., U.S.	k7	138
Armorel, Ar., U.S.	B6	111
Armour, S.D., U.S.	D7	148
Armstrong, Arg.	G8	80
Armstrong, B.C., Can.	D8	99
Armstrong, Ia., U.S.	A3	122
Armstrong, co., Pa., U.S.	E2	145
Armstrong, co., Tx., U.S.	B2	150
Arnaudville, La., U.S.	D4	125
Arnedo, Spain	C9	16
Arnett, W.V., U.S.	D3	155
Arnhem, Neth.	E8	12
Arnhem, Cape, c., Austl.	B7	68
Arnhem Land, reg., Austl.	B6	68
Arno, stm., Italy	F5	18
Arno Bay, Austl.	I2	70
Arnold, Md., U.S.	B4	127
Arnold, Mn., U.S.	D6	130
Arnold, Mo., U.S.	C7	132
Arnold, Ne., U.S.	C5	134
Arnold, Pa., U.S.	h14	145
Arnold Mills, R.I., U.S.	B4	146
Arnold's Cove, Newf., Can.	E4	102
Arnolds Park, Ia., U.S.	A2	122
Arnprior, Ont., Can.	B8	103
Arnsberg, Ger.	D8	10
Arnstadt, Ger.	E10	10
Aroa, Ven.	B8	84
Aroab, Nmb.	F4	66
Aroostook, N.B., Can.	C2	101
Aroostook, co., Me., U.S.	B4	126
Aros, stm., Mex.	C5	90
Arosa, Switz.	E12	13
Ar-Rahad, Sud.	K6	60
Arraial do Cabo, Braz.	G7	79
Arraias, Braz.	B5	79
Ar-Ramādī, Iraq	C4	48
Ar-Ramthā, Jord.	C5	50
Arran, Island of, i., Scot., U.K.	F8	8
Ar-Rank, Sud.	L7	60
Ar-Raqqah, Syria	D5	48
Arras, Fr.	B9	14
Ar-Rayyān, Qatar	I11	48
Arrecife, Spain	o27	17b
Arrecifes, Arg.	H8	80
Arriaga, Mex.	I13	90
Ar-Riyāḍ (Riyadh), Sau. Ar.	B5	47
Arroio Grande, Braz.	G12	80
Arrowrock Reservoir, res., Id., U.S.	F3	119
Arroyito, Arg.	F7	80
Arroyo Grande, Ca., U.S.	E3	112
Arroyo Hondo, N.M., U.S.	A4	138
Arroyo Seco, Arg.	G8	80
Arroyo Seco, N.M., U.S.	A4	138
Ar-Rub' al-Khālī (Empty Quarter), des., Asia	D7	47
Ar-Rusayfah, Jord.	D6	50
Ar-Rusayris, Sud.	L8	60
Arsenjev, Russia	I18	28
Arsenjevo, Russia	H19	22
Árta, Grc.	J4	20
Arteaga, Mex.	H8	90
Artemisa, Cuba	C3	94
Artemus, Ky., U.S.	D6	124
Artesia, N.M., U.S.	E5	138
Arth, Switz.	D10	13
Arthabaska, Que., Can.	C6	104
Arthur, Ont., Can.	D4	103
Arthur, Il., U.S.	D5	120
Arthur, N.D., U.S.	B8	141
Arthur, co., Ne., U.S.	C4	134
Arthur, Lake, res., Pa., U.S.	E1	145
Arthur's Town, Bah.	B7	94
Artibonite, stm., Haiti	E8	94
Artigas, Ur.	F10	80
Art'om, Russia	I18	28
Art'omovsk, Russia	G10	28
Art'omovskij, Russia	F10	26
Artsyz, Ukr.	C13	20
Artvin, Tur.	G16	4
Aru, Kepulauan, is., Indon.	G9	38
Aruanã, Braz.	C3	79
Aruba, dep., N.A.	H9	94
Arunāchal Pradesh, state, India	F16	44
Aruppukkottai, India	H5	46
Arusha, Tan.	B7	58
Aruwimi, stm., Zaire	H6	56
Arvada, Co., U.S.	B5	113
Arvajcheer, Mong.	B7	30
Arvidsjaur, Swe.	I16	6
Arvika, Swe.	L13	6
Arvin, Ca., U.S.	E4	112
Arvon, Mount, mtn., Mi., U.S.	B2	129
Arvonia, Va., U.S.	C4	153
Arvorezinha, Braz.	E12	80
Arxan, China	H15	28
Arys, stm., Kaz.	I11	26
Arys', Kaz.	I11	26
Arzamas, Russia	F6	26
Arziw, Alg.	C10	62
Aš, Czech Rep.	E12	10
Aša, Russia	F9	26
Asad, Buhayrat al-, res., Syria	C5	48
Asahikawa, Japan	d17	36a
Asamankese, Ghana	I9	64
Asansol, India	I12	44
Asbest, Russia	F10	26
Asbury Park, N.J., U.S.	C4	137
Ascensión, Mex.	B6	90
Ascension, co., La., U.S.	D5	125
Ascensión, i., St. Hel.	I5	52
Aschabad (Ashgabat), Turk.	J9	26
Aschaffenburg, Ger.	F9	10
Aschersleben, Ger.	D11	10
Ascoli Piceno, Italy	G8	18
Ascona, Switz.	F10	13
Ascope, Peru	B2	82
Ascutney, Vt., U.S.	E4	152
Aseb, Erit.	H3	47
Asela, Eth.	N10	60
Åsele, Swe.	I15	6
Asenovgrad, Bul.	G8	20
Ashaway, R.I., U.S.	F1	146
Ashburn, Ga., U.S.	E3	117
Ashburton, N.Z.	E3	72
Ashburton, stm., Austl.	D3	68
Ashcroft, B.C., Can.	D7	99
Ashdod, Isr.	E3	50
Ashdown, Ar., U.S.	D1	111
Ashe, co., N.C., U.S.	A1	140
Asheboro, N.C., U.S.	B3	140
Ashern, Man., Can.	D2	100
Asheville, N.C., U.S.	f10	140
Ash Flat, Ar., U.S.	A4	111
Ashford, Al., U.S.	D4	108
Ashford, W.V., U.S.	m12	155
Ash Fork, Az., U.S.	B3	110
Ash Grove, Mo., U.S.	D4	132
Ashikaga, Japan	K14	36
Ashkhabad see Aschabad, Turk.	J9	26
Ashland, Al., U.S.	B4	108
Ashland, Il., U.S.	D3	120
Ashland, Ks., U.S.	E4	123
Ashland, Ky., U.S.	B7	124
Ashland, Me., U.S.	B4	126
Ashland, Ma., U.S.	g10	128
Ashland, Mo., U.S.	C5	132
Ashland, Mt., U.S.	E10	133
Ashland, N.H., U.S.	C3	136
Ashland, Oh., U.S.	B3	142
Ashland, Or., U.S.	E4	144
Ashland, Pa., U.S.	E9	145
Ashland, Va., U.S.	C5	153
Ashland, Wi., U.S.	B3	156
Ashland, co., Oh., U.S.	B3	142
Ashland, co., Wi., U.S.	B3	156
Ashland, Mount, mtn., Or., U.S.	E4	144
Ashland City, Tn., U.S.	A4	149
Ashley, N.D., U.S.	C6	141
Ashley, Oh., U.S.	B2	142
Ashley, co., Ar., U.S.	D4	111
Ashley, stm., S.C., U.S.	n17	145
Ashmore Islands, is., Austl.	B4	68
Ashmont, Alta., Can.	B4	98
Ashqelon, Isr.	E3	50
Ash-Shaqrā', Sau. Ar.	B4	47
Ash-Shāriqah (Sharjah), U.A.E.	B9	47
Ash-Shaṭrah, Iraq	F9	48
Ash-Shihr, Yemen	G6	47
Ash-Shurayk, Sud.	H7	60
Ashtabula, Oh., U.S.	A5	142
Ashtabula, co., Oh., U.S.	A5	142
Ashton, S. Afr.	I5	66
Ashton, Id., U.S.	E7	119
Ashton, Il., U.S.	B4	120
Ashton, Md., U.S.	B3	127
Ashton, R.I., U.S.	B4	146
Ashuelot, N.H., U.S.	E2	136
Ashuelot, stm., N.H., U.S.	E2	136
Ashville, Al., U.S.	B3	108
Ashville, Oh., U.S.	C3	142
Ashwaubenon, Wi., U.S.	D5	156
Asia	D11	24
Asia Minor, hist. reg., Tur.	H14	4
Asilah, Mor.	C7	62
Asino, Russia	F9	28
'Asīr, reg., Sau. Ar.	E2	47
Asmara see Asmera, Erit.	E8	56
Asmera, Erit.	E8	56
Asosa, Eth.	F7	56
Asotin, Wa., U.S.	C8	154
Asotin, co., Wa., U.S.	C8	154
Asp, Col., U.S.	G11	16
Aspen, Co., U.S.	B4	113
Aspen Butte, mtn., Or., U.S.	E4	144
Aspen Hill, Md., U.S.	B3	127
Aspermont, Tx., U.S.	C2	150
Aspinwall, Pa., U.S.	k14	145
Asquith, Sask., Can.	E2	105
As-Saff, Egypt	C6	60
As-Sāfī, Jord.	F5	50
As-Ṣāfiyah, Sud.	J6	60
Assai, Braz.	G3	79
As-Salt, Jord.	D5	50
Assam, state, India	G15	44
As-Samāwah, Iraq	F8	48
Assateague Island, i., U.S.	D7	127
Assateague Island National Seashore, U.S.	D7	127
Assawoman Bay, b., Md., U.S.	D7	127
Assende, Bel.	F4	12
Assiniboia, Sask., Can.	H2	105
Assiniboine, stm., Can.	E2	100
Assiniboine, Mount, mtn., Can.	D3	98
Assis, Braz.	G3	79
Assisi, Italy	F7	18
As-Sudd, reg., Sud.	N6	60
As-Sulaymānīyah, Iraq	D8	48
As-Sumayh, Sud.	M4	60
Assumption, Il., U.S.	D4	120
Assumption, co., La., U.S.	E4	125
As-Suwaydā', Syria	C7	50
As-Suways (Suez), Egypt	C7	60
Asti, Italy	E3	18
Astorga, Braz.	G3	79
Astorga, Spain	C5	16
Astoria, Il., U.S.	C3	120
Astoria, Or., U.S.	A3	144
Astrachan', Russia	F17	4
Asturias, prov., Spain	B5	16
Asunción, Para.	C10	80
Asunción Mita, Guat.	G3	92
Asunción Nochixtlán, Mex.	I11	90
Aswān, Egypt	D7	60
Asyūṭ, Egypt	C6	60
Atacama, prov., Chile	D3	80
Atacama, Desierto de, des., Chile	G8	74
Atacama, Puna de, plat., S.A.	C5	80
Atacama, Salar de, pl., Chile	B4	80
Atakpamé, Togo	H10	64
Atalándi, Grc.	K7	20
Atalaya, Pan.	I14	92
Atār, Maur.	A3	64
Atascadero, Ca., U.S.	E3	112
Atascosa, co., Tx., U.S.	E3	150
Atasu, Kaz.	H12	26
'Atbarah, Sud.	I7	60
Atbasar, Kaz.	G11	26
Atchafalaya, stm., La., U.S.	D4	125
Atchafalaya Bay, b., La., U.S.	E4	125
Atchison, Ks., U.S.	C8	123
Atchison, co., Ks., U.S.	C8	123
Atchison, co., Mo., U.S.	A2	132
Aterau, Kaz.	H8	26
Ath (Aat), Bel.	G4	12
Athabasca, Alta., Can.	B4	98
Athabasca, stm., Alta., Can.	f8	98
Athabasca, Lake, l., Can.	m7	105
Athena, Or., U.S.	B8	144
Athens, Ont., Can.	C9	103
Athens see Athínai, Grc.	L7	20
Athens, Al., U.S.	A3	108
Athens, Ga., U.S.	C3	117
Athens, Il., U.S.	D4	120
Athens, Mi., U.S.	F5	129
Athens, N.Y., U.S.	C7	139
Athens, Oh., U.S.	C3	142
Athens, Pa., U.S.	C8	145
Athens, Tn., U.S.	D9	149
Athens, Tx., U.S.	C5	150
Athens, W.V., U.S.	D3	155
Athens, Wi., U.S.	C3	156
Athens, co., Oh., U.S.	C3	142
Atherton, Austl.	A6	70
Athiémé, Benin	H10	64
Athínai (Athens), Grc.	L7	20
Athlone, Ire.	H6	8
Athol, Ma., U.S.	A3	128
Ati, Chad	F4	56
Atico, Peru	G5	82
Atiquizaya, El Sal.	E4	92
Atitlán, Lago de, l., Guat.	C3	92
Atitlán, Volcán, vol., Guat.	C3	92
Atkarsk, Russia	G7	26
Atkins, Ar., U.S.	B3	111
Atkins, Va., U.S.	f11	153
Atkinson, Il., U.S.	B3	120
Atkinson, N.H., U.S.	E4	136
Atkinson, Ne., U.S.	B7	134
Atkinson, co., Ga., U.S.	E4	117
Atlanta, Ga., U.S.	C2	117
Atlanta, Il., U.S.	C4	120
Atlanta, In., U.S.	D5	121
Atlanta, Tx., U.S.	C5	150
Atlantic, Ia., U.S.	C2	122
Atlantic, co., N.J., U.S.	E3	137
Atlantic Beach, Fl., U.S.	m9	116
Atlantic City, N.J., U.S.	E4	137
Atlantic Highlands, N.J., U.S.	C4	137
Atlántico, dept., Col.	B5	84
Atlantic Ocean	I11	160
Atlantic Peak, mtn., Wy., U.S.	D3	157
Atlántida, dept., Hond.	B7	92
Atlas Mountains, mts., Afr.	B6	54
Atlas Saharien, mts., Alg.	D11	62
Atlas Tellien, mts., Alg.	C11	62
Atlin, B.C., Can.	m16	99
Atlin Lake, l., Can.	E6	96
Atmore, Al., U.S.	D2	108
Atocha, Bol.	I8	82
Atoka, Ok., U.S.	C5	143
Atoka, Tn., U.S.	B2	149
Atoka, co., Ok., U.S.	C5	143
Atoka Reservoir, res., Ok., U.S.	C5	143
Atoyac de Álvarez, Mex.	I9	90
Atoyaquillo, stm., Mex.	I11	90
Atrato, stm., Col.	D4	84
Aṭ-Ṭafīlah, Jord.	G5	50
At-Ṭā'if, Sau. Ar.	D2	47
Attala, co., Ms., U.S.	B4	131
Attalla, Al., U.S.	A3	108
Attapu, Laos	G9	40
Attawapiskat, stm., Ont., Can.	n18	103
Attica, In., U.S.	D3	121
Attica, Ks., U.S.	E5	123
Attica, N.Y., U.S.	C2	139
Attir, Sud.	N6	60
Attleboro, Ma., U.S.	C5	128
Attock, Pak.	D4	44
Attu Island, i., Ak., U.S.	E2	109
Atuel, stm., Arg.	H5	80
Atuel, Bañados del, sw., Arg.	I5	80
Atuntaqui, Ec.	G3	84
Atwater, Ca., U.S.	D3	112
Atwater, Mn., U.S.	E4	130
Atwood, Ont., Can.	D3	103
Atwood, Il., U.S.	D5	120
Atwood, Tn., U.S.	B3	149
Auau Channel, strt., Hi., U.S.	C5	118
Aubagne, Fr.	I12	14
Aube, stm., Fr.	D11	14
Aubigny-sur-Nère, Fr.	E9	14
Auburn, Al., U.S.	C4	108
Auburn, Ca., U.S.	C3	112
Auburn, Ga., U.S.	B3	117
Auburn, Il., U.S.	D4	120
Auburn, In., U.S.	B7	121
Auburn, Ks., U.S.	D8	123
Auburn, Ky., U.S.	D3	124
Auburn, Me., U.S.	D2	126
Auburn, Ma., U.S.	B4	128
Auburn, Mi., U.S.	E6	129
Auburn, Ne., U.S.	D10	134
Auburn, N.H., U.S.	D4	136
Auburn, N.Y., U.S.	C4	139
Auburn, Wa., U.S.	B3	154
Auburn, Wy., U.S.	D1	157
Auburndale, Fl., U.S.	D5	116
Auburn Heights, Mi., U.S.	F7	129
Aubusson, Fr.	G9	14
Auce, Lat.	E5	22
Auch, Fr.	I7	14
Auckland, N.Z.	B5	72
Auckland Islands, is., N.Z.	N20	158
Audincourt, Fr.	E13	14
Audrain, co., Mo., U.S.	B6	132
Audubon, Ia., U.S.	C3	122
Audubon, N.J., U.S.	D2	137
Audubon, co., Ia., U.S.	C3	122
Aue, Ger.	E12	10
Augathella, Austl.	E7	70
Auglaize, co., Oh., U.S.	B1	142
Auglaize, stm., Oh., U.S.	A1	142
Augsburg, Ger.	G10	10
Augusta, Austl.	F3	68
Augusta, Italy	L10	18
Augusta, Ar., U.S.	B4	111
Augusta, Ga., U.S.	C5	117
Augusta, Ks., U.S.	E7	123
Augusta, Ky., U.S.	B6	124
Augusta, Me., U.S.	D3	126
Augusta, Mt., U.S.	C4	133
Augusta, Wi., U.S.	D2	156
Augusta, co., Va., U.S.	B3	153
Augustów, Pol.	B22	10
Aulander, N.C., U.S.	A5	140
Aulneau Peninsula, pen., Ont., Can.	E4	100
Ault, Co., U.S.	A6	113
Aumsville, Or., U.S.	k12	144
Aurangābād, India	C4	46
Auray, Fr.	E4	14
Aurelia, Ia., U.S.	B2	122
Aurich, Ger.	B7	10
Auriflama, Braz.	F3	79
Aurillac, Fr.	H9	14
Aurora, Ont., Can.	C5	103
Aurora, Co., U.S.	B6	113
Aurora, Il., U.S.	B5	120
Aurora, In., U.S.	F8	121
Aurora, Mn., U.S.	C6	130
Aurora, Mo., U.S.	E4	132
Aurora, Ne., U.S.	D7	134
Aurora, N.C., U.S.	B6	140
Aurora, Oh., U.S.	A4	142
Aurora, S.D., U.S.	C9	148
Aurora, Ut., U.S.	E4	151
Aurora, co., S.D., U.S.	D7	148
Aurukun, Austl.	B8	68
Aus, Nmb.	F3	66
Au Sable, stm., Mi., U.S.	D6	129
Ausable, stm., N.Y., U.S.	f11	139
Au Sable Point, c., Mi., U.S.	D7	129
Auschwitz see Oświęcim, Pol.	E19	10
Austell, Ga., U.S.	h7	117
Austin, Man., Can.	E2	100
Austin, Mn., U.S.	G6	130
Austin, Nv., U.S.	D4	135
Austin, Tx., U.S.	D4	150
Austin, co., Tx., U.S.	E4	150
Austintown, Oh., U.S.	A5	142
Australes, Îles, is., Fr. Poly.	K24	158
Australia, ctry., Oc.	D7	68
Australian Capital Territory, ter., Austl.	G9	68
Austria (Österreich), ctry., Eur.	F10	4
Autauga, co., Al., U.S.	C3	108
Autaugaville, Al., U.S.	C3	108
Autazes, Braz.	I13	84
Autlán de Navarro, Mex.	H7	90
Autun, Fr.	F11	14
Auvergne, hist. reg., Fr.	G9	14
Auxerre, Fr.	E10	14
Auxier, Ky., U.S.	C7	124
Auxonne, Fr.	E12	14
Auxvasse, Mo., U.S.	B6	132
Auyán Tepuy, mtn., Ven.	E11	84
Auzangate, Nevado, mtn., Peru	E6	82
Ava, Mo., U.S.	E5	132
Avallon, Fr.	E10	14
Avalon, Ca., U.S.	F4	112
Avalon, Pa., U.S.	h13	145
Avalon Peninsula, pen., Newf., Can.	E5	102
Avaré, Braz.	G4	79
Aveiro, Port.	E3	16
Avelgem, Bel.	G3	12
Avellaneda, Arg.	E9	80
Avellaneda, Arg.	H9	80
Avellino, Italy	I9	18
Avenal, Ca., U.S.	E3	112
Avenel, N.J., U.S.	k7	137
Aversa, Italy	I9	18
Avery, co., N.C., U.S.	e11	140
Avezzano, Italy	G8	18
Avignon, Fr.	I11	14
Ávila, Spain	E7	16
Avilés, Spain	B6	16
Avilla, In., U.S.	B7	121
Aviston, Il., U.S.	E4	120
Avoca, Ia., U.S.	C2	122
Avoca, Pa., U.S.	m18	145
Avola, Italy	M10	18
Avon, Ct., U.S.	B4	114
Avon, Il., U.S.	C3	120
Avon, Ma., U.S.	B5	128
Avon, Mn., U.S.	E4	130
Avon, N.Y., U.S.	C3	139
Avon, Oh., U.S.	A3	142
Avon, S.D., U.S.	E7	148
Avon, stm., Eng., U.K.	J11	8
Avon, stm., Eng., U.K.	I12	8
Avondale, Az., U.S.	D3	110
Avondale, Co., U.S.	C6	113
Avondale, Pa., U.S.	h10	132
Avondale Estates, Ga., U.S.	h8	117
Avon Downs, Austl.	C2	70
Avon Lake, Oh., U.S.	A3	142
Avonlea, Sask., Can.	G3	105
Avon Park, Fl., U.S.	E5	116
Avoyelles, co., La., U.S.	C3	125
Avranches, Fr.	D5	14
Awasa, Eth.	N10	60
Awash, Eth.	G9	56
Awbārī, Libya	C3	56
Awjilah, Libya	C3	56
Awka, Nig.	G7	64
Aworo Kit, Sud.	L7	60
Axel Heiberg Island, i., N.W. Ter., Can.	B15	86
Axis, Al., U.S.	E1	108
Axtell, Ks., U.S.	C7	123
Axtell, Ne., U.S.	D6	134
Ayabaca, Peru	J3	84
Ayacucho, Arg.	I9	80
Ayacucho, Peru	E4	82
Ayacucho, dept., Peru	E4	82
Ayamonte, Spain	H4	16
Ayapel, Col.	C5	84
Ayaviri, Peru	F6	82
Ayden, N.C., U.S.	B5	140
Aydın, Tur.	L11	20
Ayer, Ma., U.S.	A4	128
Ayers Rock, mtn., Austl.	E6	68
Ayeyarwady (Irrawaddy), stm., Mya.	F3	40
Ayía Paraskeví, Grc.	J10	20
Ayiássos, Grc.	J10	20
Áyios Nikólaos, Grc.	N9	20
Aylesbury, Eng., U.K.	J13	8
Aylesford, N.S., Can.	D5	101
Aylmer, Mount, mtn., Alta., Can.	D3	98
Aylmer East, Que., Can.	D2	104
Aylmer West, Ont., Can.	E4	103
Ayom, Sud.	N5	60
'Ayoûn el 'Atroûs, Maur.	C5	64
Ayr, Austl.	B7	70
Ayr, Scot., U.K.	F9	8
Ayton, Ont., Can.	D4	103
Ayutla, Mex.	G7	90
Ayutla de los Libres, Mex.	I10	90
Ayvalık, Tur.	J10	20
Āzamgarh, India	G10	44
Azángaro, Peru	F6	82
Azaouagh, Vallée de l', val., Afr.	D11	64
Azare, Nig.	F15	64
Āẕar Shahr, Iran	C8	48
Azazga, Alg.	B13	62
Azemmour, Mor.	D6	62
Azerbaijan, ctry., Asia	I7	26
Azle, Tx., U.S.	n9	150
Azogues, Ec.	I3	84
Azores see Açores, is., Port.	k19	62a
Azov, Russia	H5	26
Azov, Sea of, Eur.	H5	26
Azpeitia, Spain	B9	16
Azrou, Mor.	D6	62
Aztec, N.M., U.S.	A2	138
Azua, Dom. Rep.	E9	94
Azuaga, Spain	G6	16
Azuay, prov., Ec.	I3	84
Azuero, Península de, pen., Pan.	D2	84
Azul, Arg.	I9	80
Azul, Cerro, (Mtn. Hond.)	C6	92
Azur, Côte d', Fr.	I14	14
Azurduy, Bol.	H9	82
Azusa, Ca., U.S.	m13	112
Az-Zabadānī, Syria	A6	50
Az-Zahrān (Dhahran), Sau. Ar.	A7	47

Name	Map Ref.	Page
Az-Zaqāzīq, Egypt	B6	60
Az-Zarqā', Jord.	D6	50
Az-Zāwiyah, Libya	B3	56
Az-Zubayr, Iraq	F9	48

B

Name	Map Ref.	Page
Baalbek see Ba'Labakk, Leb.	D4	48
Baar, Switz.	D10	13
Baarle-Hertog (Baerle-Duc), Bel.	F6	12
Babahoyo, Ec.	H3	84
Babailiqiao, China	C7	34
Babajevo, Russia	B18	22
Babanūsah, Sud.	L4	60
Babbie, Al., U.S.	D3	108
Babbitt, Mn., U.S.	C7	130
Babbitt, Nv., U.S.	E3	135
Bab el Mandeb see Mandeb, Bab el, strt.	H3	47
Babine, stm., B.C., Can.	B4	99
Babine Lake, l., B.C., Can.	B5	99
Bābol, Iran	C12	48
Bābol Sar, Iran	C12	48
Baboosic Lake, N.H., U.S.	E3	136
Baboquivari Mountains, mts., Az., U.S.	F4	110
Baboquivari Peak, mtn., Az., U.S.	F4	110
Babuškin, Russia	G13	28
Babuyan Islands, is., Phil.	B7	38
Babylon, N.Y., U.S.	n15	139
Baca, co., Co., U.S.	D8	113
Bacabal, Braz.	D10	76
Bacadéhuachi, Mex.	C5	90
Bacău, Rom.	C10	20
Bac Can, Viet.	C8	40
Baccarat, Fr.	D13	14
Bacerac, Mex.	B5	90
Bac Giang, Viet.	D9	40
Bachaquero, Ven.	C7	84
Bacharden, Turk.	J9	26
Bachi, China	K4	34
Bachiniva, Mex.	C6	90
Back, stm., N.W. Ter., Can.	C13	96
Bačka Palanka, Yugo.	D3	20
Bačka Topola, Yugo.	D3	20
Back Bay, N.B., Can.	D3	101
Backbone Mountain, mtn., U.S.	m12	127
Backnang, Ger.	G9	10
Backstairs Passage, strt., Austl.	J2	70
Bac Lieu, Viet.	J8	40
Bac Ninh, Viet.	D9	40
Bacolod, Phil.	C7	38
Bacon, co., Ga., U.S.	E4	117
Baconton, Ga., U.S.	E2	117
Bacoor, Phil.	n19	39b
Bácum, Mex.	D4	90
Bad, stm., S.D., U.S.	C5	148
Badagara, India	G3	46
Badajia, China	B9	34
Badajoz, Spain	G5	16
Badalona, Spain	D14	16
Badanah, Sau. Ar.	F6	48
Badaohao, China	B9	32
Bad Axe, Mi., U.S.	E8	129
Baddeck, N.S., Can.	C9	101
Baden, Erit.	I9	60
Baden, Switz.	D9	13
Baden, Pa., U.S.	E1	145
Baden-Baden, Ger.	G8	10
Baden-Württemberg, state, Ger.	G8	10
Badgastein, Aus.	H13	10
Badger, Newf., Can.	D3	102
Bad Harzburg, Ger.	D10	10
Bad Hersfeld, Ger.	E9	10
Badin, N.C., U.S.	B2	140
Badin Lake, res., N.C., U.S.	B2	140
Bad Kreuznach, Ger.	F7	10
Badlands, hills, S.D., U.S.	D3	148
Badlands National Park, S.D., U.S.	D3	148
Bad Nauheim, Ger.	E8	10
Bad Oeynhausen, Ger.	C8	10
Bad Pyrmont, Ger.	D9	10
Bad Ragaz, Switz.	D12	13
Bad Salzuflen, Ger.	C8	10
Bad Tölz, Ger.	H11	10
Baena, Spain	H7	16
Baependi, Braz.	F6	79
Bafatá, Gui.-B.	F2	64
Baffin Bay, b., N.A.	B13	86
Baffin Island, i., N.W. Ter., Can.	C18	96
Bafoulabé, Mali	E4	64
Bafoussam, Cam.	G9	54
Bafwasende, Zaire	A5	58
Bagaces, C.R.	G9	92
Bāgalkot, India	D3	46
Bagansiapiapi, Indon.	M6	40
Bagawi, Sud.	K8	60
Bagdad see Baghdād, Iraq		
Bagdad, Az., U.S.	C2	110
Bagé, Braz.	F11	80
Baggs, Wy., U.S.	E5	157
Baghdad, Iraq	E8	48
Bagheria, Italy	K8	18
Baghlān, Afg.	B3	44
Bagley, Mn., U.S.	C3	130
Bagnères-de-Bigorre, Fr.	I7	14
Bagnères-de-Luchon, Fr.	J7	14
Bagnols-sur-Cèze, Fr.	H11	14
Bago (Pegu), Mya.	F4	40
Bagrationovsk, Russia	G3	22
Baguio, Phil.	m19	39b
Bagzane, mtn., Niger	C14	64
Bahamas, ctry., N.A.	D9	88
Baharampur, India	H13	44
Bahāwalnagar, Pak.	F5	44
Bahāwalpur, Pak.	F4	44
Bahia, Braz.	B7	79
Bahía, Islas de la, is., Hond.	A8	92
Bahía Blanca, Arg.	J7	80
Bahir Dar, Eth.	L9	60
Bahraich, India	G9	44
Bahrain (Al-Bahrayn), ctry., Asia	D5	42
Baia Mare, Rom.	B7	20
Baia Sprie, Rom.	B7	20
Baicheng, China	B11	30

Name	Map Ref.	Page
Baicheng, China	C3	30
Baie-Comeau, Que., Can.	k13	104
Baie-d'Urfé, Que., Can.	q19	104
Baie-Saint-Paul, Que., Can.	B7	104
Baie Verte, Newf., Can.	D3	102
Baihebu, China	C4	32
Baiju, China	B9	34
Baikal, Lake see Bajkal, ozero, l., Russia	G13	28
Baile Átha Cliath see Dublin, Ire.	H7	8
Bailén, Spain	G8	16
Băileşti, Rom.	E7	20
Bailey, co., Tx., U.S.	B1	150
Bailey Island, Me., U.S.	g8	126
Baileys Crossroads, Va., U.S.	g12	153
Baimaguan, China	C4	32
Baimashi, China	F7	34
Bainbridge, Ga., U.S.	F2	117
Bainbridge, In., U.S.	E4	121
Bainbridge Island, i., Wa., U.S.	e10	154
Bain-de-Bretagne, Fr.	E5	14
Baipu, China	C9	34
Bairnsdale, Austl.	K7	70
Bairoil, Wy., U.S.	D5	157
Baisha, China	E10	40
Baishanji, China	B5	34
Baitu, China	D8	34
Baixa Grande, Braz.	A8	79
Baiyin, China	D7	30
Baja, Hung.	I18	10
Baja California, state, Mex.	C2	90
Baja California, pen., Mex.	C3	90
Baja California Sur, state, Mex.	E4	90
Bajanchongor, Mong.	B7	30
Baja Verapaz, dept., Guat.	B4	92
Bajdarackaja guba, b., Russia	D11	26
Bajiazi, China	B11	32
Bajimba, Mount, mtn., Austl.	G10	70
Bajkal, ozero (Lake Baikal), l., Russia	G13	28
Bajmak, Russia	G9	26
Bajo Boquete, Pan.	C1	84
Bajos de Haina, Dom. Rep.	E9	94
Bajram-Ali, Turk.	J10	26
Bakel, Sen.	D3	64
Baker, La., U.S.	D4	125
Baker, Mt., U.S.	D12	133
Baker, Nv., U.S.	D7	135
Baker, Or., U.S.	C9	144
Baker, co., Fl., U.S.	B4	116
Baker, co., Ga., U.S.	E2	117
Baker, co., Or., U.S.	C9	144
Baker, Mount, mtn., Wa., U.S.	A4	154
Baker Island, i., Oc.	H22	158
Baker Lake, N.W. Ter., Can.	D13	96
Baker Mountain, mtn., Me., U.S.	C3	126
Bakersfield, Ca., U.S.	E4	112
Bakersville, Vt., U.S.	B3	152
Bākhtarān (Kermānshāh), Iran	D9	48
Bakı (Baku), Azer.	I7	26
Bako, Eth.	O9	60
Baku see Bakı, Azer.	I7	26
Bakun, China	D9	44
Balabac Strait, strt., Asia	D6	38
Balabanovo, Russia	F19	22
Balachna, Russia	E26	22
Balaguer, Spain	D12	16
Balakirevo, Russia	E21	22
Balaklava, Austl.	J3	70
Balakovo, Russia	G7	26
Bālā Morghāb, Afg.	D17	48
Balāngīr, India	B7	46
Balašicha, Russia	F20	22
Balašov, Russia	G6	26
Balassagyarmat, Hung.	G19	10
Balaton, Mn., U.S.	F3	130
Balaton, l., Hung.	I17	10
Balbina, Reprêsa, res., Braz.	H13	84
Balboa, Pan.	I15	92
Balbriggan, Ire.	H7	8
Balcanoona, Austl.	H3	70
Balcarce, Arg.	I9	80
Balcarres, Sask., Can.	G4	105
Balchaš, Kaz.	H12	26
Balchaš, ozero (Lake Balkhash), l., Kaz.	H12	26
Bald Knob, Ar., U.S.	B4	111
Bald Knob, mtn., Va., U.S.	c3	153
Bald Knob, mtn., W.V., U.S.	C5	155
Baldur, Man., Can.	E2	100
Baldwin, Ga., U.S.	B3	117
Baldwin, La., U.S.	E4	125
Baldwin, Pa., U.S.	k14	145
Baldwin, Wi., U.S.	D1	156
Baldwin, co., Al., U.S.	E2	108
Baldwin, co., Ga., U.S.	C3	117
Baldwin City, Ks., U.S.	D8	123
Baldwinsville, N.Y., U.S.	B4	139
Baldwyn, Ms., U.S.	A5	131
Baldy Mountain, mtn., Man., Can.	D1	100
Baldy Mountain, mtn., N.M., U.S.	A4	138
Baldy Peak, mtn., Az., U.S.	D6	110
Balearic Islands see Balears, Illes, is., Spain	F15	16
Balears, Illes, is., Spain	F15	16
Balears (Balearic Islands), prov., Spain	F15	16
Baleine, Rivière à la, stm., Que., Can.	g13	104
Balej, Russia	G15	28
Bāleshwar, India	J12	44
Baléyara, Niger	E11	64
Balfate, Hond.	B8	92
Balgonie, Sask., Can.	G3	105
Bali, Laut (Bali Sea), Indon.	G6	38
Balıkesir, Tur.	J11	20
Balikpapan, Indon.	F6	38
Balimo, Pap. N. Gui.	G11	38
Balingen, Ger.	G8	10
Balkan Mountains see Stara Planina, mts., Eur.	G8	20

Name	Map Ref.	Page
Balkan Peninsula, pen., Eur.	D9	52
Balkaria see Kabardino-Balkarija, state, Russia	I6	26
Balkh, Afg.	B2	44
Balkh, stm., Afg.	B2	44
Balkhash, Lake see Balchaš, ozero, l., Kaz.	H12	26
Ballantine, Mt., U.S.	E8	133
Ballard, co., Ky., U.S.	e8	124
Balleny Islands, is., Ant.	B8	73
Ball Ground, Ga., U.S.	B2	117
Ballia, India	H11	44
Ballina, Austl.	G10	70
Ballina, Ire.	G4	8
Ballinger, Tx., U.S.	D3	150
Ballston Spa, N.Y., U.S.	B7	139
Ballwin, Mo., U.S.	f12	132
Balmoral, Man., Can.	D3	100
Balmoral, N.B., Can.	B3	101
Balmville, N.Y., U.S.	D6	139
Baloži, Lat.	E7	22
Balranald, Austl.	J5	70
Bálsamo, Braz.	F2	79
Balsas, Braz.	E9	76
Balsas, stm., Mex.	H8	90
Balsthal, Switz.	D8	13
Balta, Ukr.	H3	26
Baltasar Brum, Ur.	F10	80
Bălţi, Mol.	H3	26
Baltic, Ct., U.S.	C7	114
Baltic, S.D., U.S.	D9	148
Baltic Sea, Eur.	M16	6
Baltijsk, Russia	G2	22
Baltım, Egypt	B6	60
Baltimore, Md., U.S.	B4	127
Baltimore, Oh., U.S.	C3	142
Baltimore, co., Md., U.S.	B4	127
Baltimore Highlands, Md., U.S.	h11	127
Balvi, Lat.	D10	22
Balykši, Kaz.	H8	26
Balzar, Ec.	H3	84
Bam, Iran	B9	40
Bama, China	B9	40
Bamako, Mali	E5	64
Bambara Maoundé, Mali	D8	64
Bambari, Cen. Afr. Rep.	G5	56
Bamberg, Ger.	F10	10
Bamberg, S.C., U.S.	E5	147
Bamberg, co., S.C., U.S.	E5	147
Bambezi, Zimb.	C9	66
Bambuí, Braz.	F6	79
Bamenda, Cam.	I15	64
Banaba, i., Kir.	I20	158
Bananal, Ilha do, i., Braz.	F8	76
Banana River, b., Fl., U.S.	D6	116
Banās, Ra's c., Egypt	F8	60
Banat, hist. reg., Eur.	D4	20
Bancroft, Ont., Can.	B7	103
Bancroft, Id., U.S.	G7	119
Bancroft, Ia., U.S.	A3	122
Bancroft, Ne., U.S.	B9	134
Bānda, India	H9	44
Banda, Laut (Banda Sea), Indon.	G8	38
Banda Aceh, Indon.	L3	40
Banda del Río Salí, Arg.	D6	80
Bandama, stm., C. Iv.	H7	64
Bandar see Machilipatnam, India	D6	46
Bandar-e 'Abbās, Iran	H14	48
Bandar-e Anzalī (Bandar-e Pahlavī), Iran	C10	48
Bandar-e Būshehr, Iran	G11	48
Bandar-e Khomeynī (Bandar-e Shāhpūr), Iran	F10	48
Bandar-e Māh Shahr, Iran	F10	48
Bandar-e Torkeman, Iran	C10	48
Bandar Seri Begawan, Bru.	E5	38
Bandeira, Pico da, mtn., Braz.	F8	79
Bandeirantes, Braz.	E1	79
Bandeirantes, Braz.	G3	79
Bandera, Arg.	E7	80
Bandera, co., Tx., U.S.	E3	150
Banderas, Bahía de, b., Mex.	G7	90
Bandiagara, Mali	D8	64
Bandırma, Tur.	I11	20
Bandon, Or., U.S.	D2	144
Ban Don, Ao, b., Thai.	J5	40
Bandundu, Zaire	B3	58
Bandung, Indon.	j13	39a
Banes, Cuba	D7	94
Banff, Scot., U.K.	D11	8
Banff, Alta., Can.	D2	98
Banff National Park, Alta., Can.	D2	98
Banfora, Burkina	F7	64
Bangalore, India	F4	46
Bangaon, India	I13	44
Bangassou, Cen. Afr. Rep.	H5	56
Banghāzī, Libya	B5	56
Bangil, Indon.	j16	39a
Bangjun, China	D5	32
Bangka, Pulau, i., Indon.	F4	39a
Bangkalan, Indon.	j16	39a
Bangkok see Krung Thep, Thai.	H6	40
Bangladesh, ctry., Asia	E13	42
Bangor, N. Ire., U.K.	G8	8
Bangor, Wales, U.K.	H9	8
Bangor, Me., U.S.	D4	126
Bangor, Mi., U.S.	F4	129
Bangor, Pa., U.S.	E11	145
Bangor, Wi., U.S.	E3	156
Bangor Township, Mi., U.S.	E7	129
Bangui, Cen. Afr. Rep.	H4	56
Bangweulu, Lake, l., Zam.	D5	58
Bani, Burkina	D9	64
Bani, Dom. Rep.	E9	94
Bani, stm., Mali	E7	64
Banī Mazār, Egypt	C6	60
Banī Suwayf, Egypt	C6	60
Bāniyās, Golan	B4	50
Banja Luka, Bos.	E12	18
Banjarmasin, Indon.	F5	38
Banjul (Bathurst), Gam.	E1	64
Bankas, Indon.	D8	64

Name	Map Ref.	Page
Bankhead Lake, res., Al., U.S.	B2	108
Banks, co., Ga., U.S.	B3	117
Banks Island, i., B.C., Can.	C2	99
Banks Island, i., N.W. Ter., Can.	B8	96
Banks Lake, res., Wa., U.S.	B6	154
Banks Peninsula, pen., N.Z.	E4	72
Banks Strait, strt., Austl.	M8	70
Bānkura, India	I12	44
Bann, stm., N. Ire., U.K.	G7	8
Banner, co., Ne., U.S.	C2	134
Banning, Ca., U.S.	F5	112
Bannock, co., Id., U.S.	G6	119
Bannock Peak, mtn., Id., U.S.	F6	119
Bannu, Pak.	D4	44
Baños, Ec.	H3	84
Ban Pong, Thai.	H5	40
Banqiao, China	E9	34
Banqiaoji, China	C5	34
Banquan, China	H6	32
Banshi, China	J4	34
Banská Bystrica, Slvk.	G19	10
Bānswāra, India	I6	44
Banyoles, Spain	C14	16
Baoding, China	E3	32
Baofeng, China	B2	34
Bao Ha, Viet.	C8	40
Baohekou, China	C6	32
Baoji, China	E8	30
Bao Lac, Viet.	I9	40
Baonian, China	D8	34
Baoshan, China	D10	34
Baoshan, China	B5	40
Baoting, China	H8	30
Baotou, China	C8	30
Baowei, China	C9	40
Baoxinji, China	C4	34
Baoying, China	B8	34
Barabinsk, Russia	B9	14
Baraboo, Wi., U.S.	E4	156
Baracaldo, Spain	B9	16
Baracoa, Cuba	D7	94
Baradero, Arg.	G8	80
Baradine, Austl.	H8	70
Baraga, Mi., U.S.	B2	129
Baraga, co., Mi., U.S.	B2	129
Bārah, Sud.	K6	60
Barahona, Dom. Rep.	E9	94
Baran', Bela.	G13	22
Bārānagar, India	I13	44
Baranoa, Col.	B5	84
Baranof Island, i., Ak., U.S.	m22	109
Baranoviči, Bela.	H9	22
Barataria, La., U.S.	E5	125
Barataria Bay, b., La., U.S.	E6	125
Baraut, India	F7	44
Baraya, Col.	F5	84
Barbacena, Braz.	F7	79
Barbacoas, Col.	G3	84
Barbados, ctry., N.A.	H15	94
Barbar, Sud.	H7	60
Barbastro, Spain	C12	16
Barbate de Franco, Spain	I6	16
Barbeau Peak, mtn., N.W. Ter., Can.	A12	86
Barber, co., Ks., U.S.	E5	123
Barbers Point, c., Hi., U.S.	B3	118
Barberton, Oh., U.S.	A4	142
Barberton, S. Afr.	E10	66
Barbezieux, Fr.	G6	14
Barbour, co., Al., U.S.	D4	108
Barbour, co., W.V., U.S.	B4	155
Barboursville, W.V., U.S.	C2	155
Barbourville, Ky., U.S.	D6	124
Barcaldine, Austl.	D6	70
Barce see Al-Marj, Libya	B5	56
Barcellona Pozzo di Gotto, Italy	K10	18
Barcelona, Spain	D14	16
Barcelona, Ven.	B10	84
Barcelos, Braz.	H11	84
Barcoo, stm., Austl.	E5	70
Bärdä, Azer.	A9	48
Bardaï, Chad	K1	60
Barddhamān, India	I12	44
Bardejov, Slvk.	F21	10
Bardera, Som.	M5	60
Bardo, Tun.	M4	18
Bardstown, Ky., U.S.	C4	124
Bardwell, Ky., U.S.	f9	124
Bareilly, India	F8	44
Barents Sea, Eur.	B4	24
Bargersville, In., U.S.	E5	121
Bar Harbor, Me., U.S.	D4	126
Bari, Italy	H11	18
Barillas, Guat.	F2	92
Barima-Waini, prov., Guy.	D13	84
Barinas, Ven.	C7	84
Barinas, state, Ven.	C8	84
Baring, Cape, c., N.W. Ter., Can.	B9	96
Barinitas, Ven.	C7	84
Bariri, Braz.	G4	79
Barisal, Bngl.	I14	44
Barisan, Pegunungan, mts., Indon.	F3	38
Barito, stm., Indon.	F5	38
Barkley, Lake, res., U.S.	f10	124
Barkley Sound, strt., B.C., Can.	E5	99
Barkly Tableland, plat., Austl.	C7	68
Barkly West, S. Afr.	G5	66
Barkol, China	C5	30
Bārlād, Rom.	C11	20
Bar-le-Duc, Fr.	D12	14
Barlee, Lake, l., Austl.	E3	68
Barletta, Italy	H11	18
Barling, Ar., U.S.	B1	111
Barlow, Ky., U.S.	e8	124
Bärmer, India	H4	44
Bar Mills, Me., U.S.	E2	126
Barnard, co., Al., U.S.	G14	26

Name	Map Ref.	Page
Barnes, co., N.D., U.S.	B7	141
Barnesboro, Pa., U.S.	E4	145
Barnesville, Ga., U.S.	C2	117
Barnesville, Mn., U.S.	D2	130
Barnesville, Oh., U.S.	C4	142
Barnhart, Mo., U.S.	C7	132
Barnsdall, Ok., U.S.	A5	143
Barnstable, Ma., U.S.	C7	128
Barnstable, co., Ma., U.S.	C7	128
Barnstead, N.H., U.S.	D4	136
Bar Nunn, Wy., U.S.	D6	157
Barnwell, Alta., Can.	E4	98
Barnwell, S.C., U.S.	E5	147
Barnwell, co., S.C., U.S.	E5	147
Barons, Alta., Can.	E4	98
Barqah (Cyrenaica), hist. reg., Libya	C2	60
Barques, Pointe aux, c., Mi., U.S.	D8	129
Barquisimeto, Ven.	B8	84
Barra, Braz.	F10	76
Barra, Ponta da, c., Moz.	D12	66
Barra da Estiva, Braz.	B7	79
Barra do Bugres, Braz.	F13	82
Barra do Corda, Braz.	E9	76
Barra do Cuanza, Ang.	C2	58
Barra do Garças, Braz.	C2	79
Barra do Mendes, Braz.	A7	79
Barra do Piraí, Braz.	G7	79
Barra do Ribeiro, Braz.	F13	80
Barra Mansa, Braz.	G6	79
Barranca, Peru	A3	82
Barrancabermeja, Col.	D6	84
Barrancas, Ven.	C11	84
Barrancas, Ven.	C7	84
Barranqueras, Arg.	D9	80
Barranquilla, Col.	B5	84
Barras, Braz.	D10	76
Barre, Vt., U.S.	C4	152
Barre, Ma., U.S.	B3	128
Barreal, Arg.	F4	80
Barreiras, Braz.	B6	79
Barreirinha, Braz.	I14	84
Barreiro, Port.	G2	16
Barreiros, Braz.	E11	76
Barretos, Braz.	F4	79
Barrett, W.V., U.S.	D3	155
Barrhead, Alta., Can.	B3	98
Barrie, Ont., Can.	C5	103
Barrière, B.C., Can.	D7	99
Barrier Range, mts., Austl.	H4	70
Barrington, Il., U.S.	A5	120
Barrington, N.H., U.S.	D5	136
Barrington, N.J., U.S.	D2	137
Barrington Passage, N.S., Can.	F4	101
Barro Alto, Braz.	C4	79
Barron, Wi., U.S.	C2	156
Barron, co., Wi., U.S.	C2	156
Barron Lake, Mi., U.S.	G4	129
Barrow, Ak., U.S.	A8	109
Barrow, co., Ga., U.S.	B3	117
Barrow, Point, c., Ak., U.S.	A8	109
Barrow Creek, Austl.	D6	68
Barrow-in-Furness, Eng., U.K.	G10	8
Barrows, Man., Can.	C1	100
Barrow Strait, strt., N.W. Ter., Can.	B13	96
Barry, Il., U.S.	D2	120
Barry, co., Mi., U.S.	F5	129
Barry, co., Mo., U.S.	E4	132
Barrys Bay, Ont., Can.	B7	103
Bārsi, India	C3	46
Barsinghausen, Ger.	C9	10
Barstow, Ca., U.S.	E5	112
Bar-sur-Aube, Fr.	D11	14
Bar-sur-Seine, Fr.	D11	14
Bartholomew, co., In., U.S.	F6	121
Bartica, Guy.	D13	84
Bartle Frere, mtn., Austl.	A6	143
Bartlesville, Ok., U.S.	A6	143
Bartlett, N.H., U.S.	B4	136
Bartlett, Tx., U.S.	D4	150
Barton, Vt., U.S.	B4	152
Barton, co., Ks., U.S.	D5	123
Barton, co., Mo., U.S.	D3	132
Bartonville, Il., U.S.	C4	120
Bartoszyce, Pol.	A20	10
Bartow, Fl., U.S.	E5	116
Bartow, Ga., U.S.	C4	117
Bartow, co., Ga., U.S.	B2	117
Barú, Volcán, vol., Pan.	C1	84
Baruun-Urt, Mong.	B9	30
Barwon, stm., Austl.	G8	70
Barybino, Russia	F20	22
Baryš, Russia	G7	26
Basalt, Co., U.S.	B4	113
Basalt, Id., U.S.	F6	119
Basankusu, Zaire	A3	58
Basarabeasca, Mol.	C12	20
Basawul, Afg.	C4	44
Bascuñán, Cabo, c., Chile	B2	80
Basehor, Ks., U.S.	k16	123
Basel (Bâle), Switz.	C8	13
Bashaw, Alta., Can.	C4	98
Bashi Channel, strt., Asia	G11	30
Bashkortostan see Baškirija, state, Russia	G9	26
Basile, La., U.S.	D3	125
Basilicata, prov., Italy	I11	18
Basin, Mt., U.S.	D4	133
Basin, Wy., U.S.	B4	157
Basīrhāt, India	I13	44
Basoko, Zaire	A4	58
Basque Lands see Euskal Herriko, prov., Spain	B9	16
Basra see Al-Başrah, Iraq	F9	48
Bassano, Alta., Can.	D4	98
Bassano del Grappa, Italy	D6	18
Bassar, Togo	G6	64
Bassecourt, Switz.	D7	13
Bassein, mth., Mya.	F3	40
Bassein, India	C2	46
Basse-Terre, Guad.	F14	94
Basse-Terre, St. K/N.	F13	94
Basse-Terre, i., Guad.	F14	94

Name	Map Ref.	Page
Bassett, Ne., U.S.	B6	134
Bassett, Va., U.S.	D3	153
Basse-Yutz, Fr.	J9	12
Bass Harbor, Me., U.S.	D4	126
Bassila, Benin	G10	64
Bass Islands, is., Oh., U.S.	A3	142
Bass Lake, In., U.S.	B4	121
Bass Strait, strt., Austl.	L6	70
Basswood Lake, l., Mn., U.S.	B7	130
Basti, India	G10	44
Bastia, Fr.	I16	14
Bastogne (Bastenaken), Bel.	H8	12
Bastrop, La., U.S.	B4	125
Bastrop, Tx., U.S.	D4	150
Bastrop, co., Tx., U.S.	D4	150
Basutoland see Lesotho, ctry., Afr.	G5	58
Bata, Eq. Gui.	A1	58
Bataan Peninsula, pen., Phil.	n19	39b
Batabanó, Golfo de, b., Cuba	C3	94
Bataguassu, Braz.	F2	79
Bataiporã, Braz.	G2	79
Batajsk, Russia	H5	26
Batala, India	E6	44
Batan, China	A9	34
Batangas, Phil.	o19	39b
Batan Islands, is., Phil.	A7	38
Batatais, Braz.	F5	79
Batavia, Il., U.S.	B5	120
Batavia, N.Y., U.S.	C2	139
Bâtdâmbâng, Camb.	H7	40
Batemans Bay, Austl.	J9	70
Bates, co., Mo., U.S.	C3	132
Batesburg, S.C., U.S.	D4	147
Batesville, Ar., U.S.	B4	111
Batesville, In., U.S.	F7	121
Batesville, Ms., U.S.	A4	131
Bath, N.B., Can.	C2	101
Bath, Ont., Can.	C8	103
Bath, Eng., U.K.	J11	8
Bath, Me., U.S.	E3	126
Bath, N.H., U.S.	B3	136
Bath, N.Y., U.S.	C3	139
Bath, Pa., U.S.	E11	145
Bath, S.C., U.S.	D4	147
Bath, co., Ky., U.S.	B6	124
Bath, co., Va., U.S.	B3	153
Bathinda, India	E6	44
Bathsheba, Barb.	H15	94
Bathurst, Austl.	I8	70
Bathurst, N.B., Can.	B4	101
Bathurst see Banjul, Gam.	E1	64
Bathurst Island, i., N.W. Ter., Can.	A12	96
Batman, Tur.	C6	48
Batna, Alg.	C14	62
Baton Rouge, La., U.S.	D4	125
Batouri, Cam.	H9	54
Batrā (Petra), hist., Jord.	H4	50
Batticaloa, Sri L.	I6	46
Battle, stm., Can.	F10	96
Battle Creek, Ia., U.S.	B2	122
Battle Creek, Mi., U.S.	F5	129
Battle Creek, Ne., U.S.	C8	134
Battleford, Sask., Can.	E1	105
Battle Ground, In., U.S.	C4	121
Battle Ground, Wa., U.S.	D3	154
Battle Lake, Mn., U.S.	D3	130
Battle Mountain, Nv., U.S.	C5	135
Batumi, Geor.	I6	26
Batu Pahat, Malay.	N7	40
Baturité, Braz.	D11	76
Bat Yam, Isr.	D3	50
Baubau, Indon.	G7	38
Bauchi, Nig.	F14	64
Baudette, Mn., U.S.	B4	130
Bauld, Cape, c., Newf., Can.	C4	102
Baume-les-Dames, Fr.	E13	14
Baures, stm., Bol.	E10	82
Baurú, Braz.	G4	79
Bauska, Lat.	E7	22
Bautzen, Ger.	D14	10
Bauxite, Ar., U.S.	C3	111
Bavaria see Bayern, state, Ger.	F11	10
Bavispe, stm., Mex.	C5	90
Bawku, Ghana	F9	64
Bawlf, Alta., Can.	C4	98
Baxian, China	D4	32
Baxley, Ga., U.S.	E4	117
Baxter, Mn., U.S.	D4	130
Baxter, Tn., U.S.	C8	149
Baxter, co., Ar., U.S.	A3	111
Baxter Springs, Ks., U.S.	E9	123
Bay, co., Fl., U.S.	u16	116
Bay, co., Mi., U.S.	E7	129
Bayamo, Cuba	D6	94
Bayamón, P.R.	E11	94
Bayano, Lago, res., Pan.	C3	84
Bayard, N.M., U.S.	E1	138
Bayard, Ne., U.S.	C2	134
Bay Bulls, Newf., Can.	E5	102
Bayburt, Tur.	A6	48
Bay City, Mi., U.S.	E7	129
Bay City, Tx., U.S.	E5	150
Bay de Verde, Newf., Can.	D5	102
Baydhabo, Som.	H9	54
Bayerische Alpen, mts., Eur.	H11	10
Bayern, state, Ger.	F11	10
Bayfield, Ont., Can.	D3	103
Bayfield, Wi., U.S.	B3	156
Bayfield, co., Wi., U.S.	B2	156
Bayiji, China	A6	34
Baylor, co., Tx., U.S.	C3	150
Bay Minette, Al., U.S.	E2	108
Bayonne, Fr.	I5	14
Bayonne, N.J., U.S.	B4	137
Bayou D'Arbonne Lake, res., La., U.S.	B3	125
Bayou La Batre, Al., U.S.	E1	108
Bayport, Mn., U.S.	E6	130
Bayport, N.Y., U.S.	n15	139
Bayreuth, Ger.	F11	10

Name	Map Ref.	Page
Bay Ridge, Md., U.S.	C5	127
Bay Roberts, Newf., Can.	E5	102
Bayrūt (Beirut), Leb.	A5	50
Bay Saint Louis, Ms., U.S.	E4	131
Bay Shore, N.Y., U.S.	E7	139
Bayshore Gardens, Fl., U.S.	q10	116
Bayside, Wi., U.S.	m12	156
Bays Mountain, mtn., Tn., U.S.	C10	149
Bay Springs, Ms., U.S.	D4	131
Bayt Laḩm (Bethlehem), W.B.	E4	50
Baytown, Tx., U.S.	E5	150
Bayview, Al., U.S.	f7	108
Bayview, Id., U.S.	B2	119
Bay Village, Oh., U.S.	h9	142
Bayzo, Niger	E12	64
Baza, Spain	H9	16
Be, Nosy, i., Madag.	n23	67b
Beach, Il., U.S.	h9	120
Beach, N.D., U.S.	C1	141
Beachburg, Ont., Can.	B8	103
Beachville, Ont., Can.	D4	103
Beachwood, N.J., U.S.	D4	137
Beacon, N.Y., U.S.	D7	139
Beacon Falls, Ct., U.S.	D3	114
Beaconsfield, Austl.	M7	70
Beaconsfield, Que., Can.	q19	104
Beadle, co., S.D., U.S.	C7	148
Bealanana, Madag.	o23	67b
Beals, Me., U.S.	D5	126
Bear, De., U.S.	B3	115
Bear, stm., U.S.	B3	151
Bear Creek, Al., U.S.	A2	108
Bearden, Ar., U.S.	D3	111
Beardstown, Il., U.S.	C3	120
Bear Lake, co., Id., U.S.	G7	119
Bear Lake, l., U.S.	A4	151
Bear Mountain, mtn., Ar., U.S.	f7	111
Bear River, N.S., Can.	E4	101
Bear River City, Ut., U.S.	B3	151
Beartooth Pass, Wy., U.S.	B3	157
Beartooth Range, mts., U.S.	E7	133
Bear Town, Ms., U.S.	D3	131
Beasain, Spain	B9	16
Beata, Cabo, c., Dom. Rep.	F9	94
Beata, Isla, i., Dom. Rep.	F9	94
Beatrice, Al., U.S.	D2	108
Beatrice, Ne., U.S.	D9	134
Beatrice, Zimb.	B10	66
Beatty, Nv., U.S.	G5	135
Beattyville, Ky., U.S.	C6	124
Beaucaire, Fr.	I11	14
Beaudesert, Austl.	F10	70
Beaufort, N.C., U.S.	C6	140
Beaufort, S.C., U.S.	G6	147
Beaufort, co., N.C., U.S.	B5	140
Beaufort, co., S.C., U.S.	G6	147
Beaufort Sea, N.A.	B5	86
Beaufort West, S. Afr.	I6	66
Beaugency, Fr.	E8	14
Beauharnois, Que., Can.	D4	104
Beaumont, Alta., Can.	C4	98
Beaumont, Ms., U.S.	D5	131
Beaumont, Tx., U.S.	D5	150
Beaune, Fr.	E11	14
Beauport, Que., Can.	n17	104
Beaupré, Que., Can.	B7	104
Beaupréau, Fr.	E5	14
Beauregard, co., La., U.S.	D2	125
Beausejour, Man., Can.	D3	100
Beauvais, Fr.	C9	14
Beauval, Sask., Can.	B2	105
Beaver, Ok., U.S.	A1	143
Beaver, Pa., U.S.	E1	145
Beaver, Ut., U.S.	E3	151
Beaver, W.V., U.S.	D3	155
Beaver, co., Ok., U.S.	e10	143
Beaver, co., Pa., U.S.	E1	145
Beaver, co., Ut., U.S.	E2	151
Beaver, stm., U.S.	F11	96
Beaver, stm., U.S.	B2	105
Beaver, stm., U.S.	A2	143
Beaverbank, N.S., Can.	E6	101
Beaver City, Ne., U.S.	D6	134
Beavercreek, Oh., U.S.	C1	142
Beaver Crossing, Ne., U.S.	D8	134
Beaver Dam, Ky., U.S.	C3	124
Beaver Dam, Wi., U.S.	E5	156
Beaverdam Lake, res., Wi., U.S.	E5	156
Beaverdell, B.C., Can.	E8	99
Beaver Falls, Pa., U.S.	E1	145
Beaverhead, co., Mt., U.S.	E3	133
Beaverhead, stm., Mt., U.S.	E4	133
Beaverhead Mountains, mts., U.S.	D5	119
Beaverhill Lake, l., Alta., Can.	C4	98
Beaver Island, i., Mi., U.S.	C5	129
Beaver Lake, res., Ar., U.S.	A2	111
Beaverlodge, Alta., Can.	B1	98
Beāwar, India	G6	44
Bebedouro, Braz.	F4	79
Becal, Mex.	G14	90
Bécancour, Que., Can.	C5	104
Bečej, Yugo.	D4	20
Béchar, Alg.	E9	62
Beckemeyer, Il., U.S.	E4	120
Becker, co., Mn., U.S.	D3	130
Beckham, co., Ok., U.S.	B2	143
Beckley, W.V., U.S.	D3	155
Beckum, Ger.	D8	10
Becky Peak, mtn., Nv., U.S.	D7	135
Bédarieux, Fr.	I10	14
Bedele, Eth.	M9	60
Bedford, N.S., Can.	E6	101
Bedford, Que., Can.	D5	104
Bedford, In., U.S.	G5	121
Bedford, Ia., U.S.	D3	122
Bedford, Ky., U.S.	B4	124
Bedford, N.H., U.S.	E3	136
Bedford, Oh., U.S.	A4	142
Bedford, Pa., U.S.	F4	145
Bedford, Va., U.S.	C3	153
Bedford, Wy., U.S.	D2	157
Bedford, co., Pa., U.S.	G4	145
Bedford, co., Tn., U.S.	B5	149
Bedford, co., Va., U.S.	C3	153
Bedford Hills, N.Y., U.S.	D7	139
Bedfordshire, co., Eng., U.K.	I13	8
Bee, co., Tx., U.S.	E4	150
Beebe, Ar., U.S.	B4	111
Beebe Plain, Vt., U.S.	A4	152
Beecher, Il., U.S.	B6	120
Beech Grove, In., U.S.	E5	121
Beech Island, S.C., U.S.	E4	147
Beechwood, N.B., Can.	C2	101
Beechworth, Austl.	K7	70
Beechy, Sask., Can.	G2	105
Beemer, Ne., U.S.	C9	134
Beenleigh, Austl.	F10	70
Bee Ridge, Fl., U.S.	q11	116
Beersheba see Be'ér Sheva', Isr.	F3	50
Be'ér Sheva (Beersheba), Isr.	F3	50
Beeville, Tx., U.S.	E4	150
Befandriana, Madag.	o23	67b
Befotaka, Madag.	s22	67b
Bega, Austl.	K8	70
Beggs, Ok., U.S.	B5	143
Begičevskij, Russia	H21	22
Begoml', Bela.	G11	22
Begoro, Ghana	H9	64
Begusarai, India	H12	44
Behbahān, Iran	F11	48
Behshahr, Iran	C12	48
Bei'an, China	B12	30
Beida see Al-Bayḑā', Libya	B5	56
Beidaihe, China	D7	32
Beigi, Eth.	M8	60
Beihai, China	D10	40
Beijing (Peking), China	D4	32
Beijing Shi (Peking Shih), China	C10	30
Beikan, China	C10	34
Beiling, China	K4	34
Beipiao, China	B8	32
Beira, Moz.	B12	66
Beira Baixa, hist. reg., Port.	F4	16
Beira Litoral, hist. reg., Port.	E3	16
Beirut see Bayrūt, Leb.	A5	50
Beiseker, Alta., Can.	D4	98
Beitang, China	D5	32
Beitbridge, Zimb.	D10	66
Beizhen, China	B9	32
Beja, Port.	G4	16
Béja, Tun.	M4	18
Bejaïa (Bougie), Alg.	B13	62
Béjar, Spain	E6	16
Bejuco, Pan.	C3	84
Bekabad, Uzb.	I11	26
Bekdaš, Turk.	I8	26
Békés, Hung.	I21	10
Békéscsaba, Hung.	I21	10
Bekily, Madag.	t21	67b
Bekoji, Eth.	N10	60
Bekodoka, Madag.	p21	67b
Bekwai, Ghana	H9	64
Bela, India	H9	44
Bela, Pak.	G2	44
Belabolo, Sud.	M3	60
Bela Crkva, Yugo.	E5	20
Bel Air, Md., U.S.	A5	127
Belaja Ber'ozka, Russia	I16	22
Bel Alton, Md., U.S.	D4	127
Belarus, ctry., Eur.	E13	4
Belau see Palau, ctry., Oc.	H17	158
Bela Vista, Braz.	B10	80
Bela Vista, Braz.	D4	79
Bela Vista do Paraíso, Braz.	G3	79
Bełchatów, Pol.	D19	10
Belcher Islands, is., N.W. Ter., Can.	E17	96
Belchertown, Ma., U.S.	B3	128
Belden, Ms., U.S.	A5	131
Belding, Mi., U.S.	E5	129
Beled Weyne, Som.	H10	56
Belém, Braz.	D9	76
Belen, Arg.	D5	80
Belén, Para.	B10	80
Belen, N.M., U.S.	C3	138
Belén, Ur.	F10	80
Belén de Escobar, Arg.	H9	80
Belfair, Wa., U.S.	B3	154
Belfast, S. Afr.	E10	66
Belfast, N. Ire., U.K.	G8	8
Belfast, Me., U.S.	D3	126
Belfield, N.D., U.S.	C2	141
Belford, N.J., U.S.	C4	137
Belfort, Fr.	E13	14
Belfry, Ky., U.S.	C7	124
Belfry, Mt., U.S.	E8	133
Belgaum, India	E3	46
Belgium, Wi., U.S.	E6	156
Belgium, ctry., Eur.	E8	4
Belgorod, Russia	G5	26
Belgrade, Mn., U.S.	E3	130
Belgrade, Mt., U.S.	E5	133
Belgrade see Beograd, Yugo.	E4	20
Belgrade Lakes, Me., U.S.	D3	126
Belhaven, N.C., U.S.	B6	140
Belington, W.V., U.S.	B5	155
Belize, ctry., N.A.	I15	90
Belize City, Belize	I15	90
Belknap, co., N.H., U.S.	C3	136
Belknap Crater, crat., Or., U.S.	C5	144
Bell, co., Ky., U.S.	D6	124
Bell, co., Tx., U.S.	D4	150
Bellac, Fr.	F8	14
Bella Coola, B.C., Can.	C4	99
Bellaire, Ks., U.S.	g12	123
Bellaire, Oh., U.S.	C5	142
Bellaire, Tx., U.S.	r14	150
Bellamy, Al., U.S.	C1	108
Bellary, India	E4	46
Bella Unión, Ur.	F10	80
Bella Vista, Arg.	B5	80
Bella Vista, Arg.	E9	80
Bella Vista, Arg.	D6	80
Bella Vista, Para.	B10	80
Bella Vista, Ar., U.S.	A1	111
Bellbrook, Oh., U.S.	C1	142
Belle, Mo., U.S.	C6	132
Belle, W.V., U.S.	C3	155
Belleair, Fl., U.S.	p10	116
Belle Chasse, La., U.S.	E5	125
Belledune, N.B., Can.	B4	101
Bellefontaine, Oh., U.S.	B2	142
Bellefonte, Ar., U.S.	A2	111
Bellefonte, Pa., U.S.	E6	145
Belle Fourche, S.D., U.S.	C2	148
Belle Fourche, stm., U.S.	C3	148
Bellegarde, Fr.	F12	14
Belle Glade, Fl., U.S.	F6	116
Belle-Île, i., Fr.	E3	14
Belle Isle, i., Newf., Can.	C4	102
Belle Isle, Strait of, strt., Newf., Can.	C3	102
Belleisle Creek, N.B., Can.	D4	101
Belle Meade, Tn., U.S.	g10	149
Belleoram, Newf., Can.	E4	102
Belle Plaine, Ia., U.S.	C5	122
Belle Plaine, Ks., U.S.	E6	123
Belle Plaine, Mn., U.S.	F5	130
Belle River, Ont., Can.	E2	103
Belleview, Fl., U.S.	C4	116
Belle View, Va., U.S.	g12	153
Belleville, Ont., Can.	C7	103
Belleville, Ar., U.S.	B2	111
Belleville, Il., U.S.	E4	120
Belleville, Ks., U.S.	C6	123
Belleville, Mi., U.S.	p15	129
Belleville, N.J., U.S.	B4	137
Belleville, Wi., U.S.	F4	156
Belleville-sur-Saône, Fr.	F11	14
Bellevue, Id., U.S.	F4	119
Bellevue, Ia., U.S.	B7	122
Bellevue, Ky., U.S.	h13	124
Bellevue, Mi., U.S.	F5	129
Bellevue, Ne., U.S.	C10	134
Bellevue, Oh., U.S.	A3	142
Bellevue, Pa., U.S.	F1	145
Bellevue, Wa., U.S.	e11	154
Belley, Fr.	G12	14
Bellflower, Ca., U.S.	n12	112
Bellingham, Ma., U.S.	B5	128
Bellingham, Wa., U.S.	A3	154
Bellingshausen Sea, Ant.	C11	73
Bellinzona, Switz.	F11	13
Bellmawr, N.J., U.S.	D2	137
Bello, Col.	D5	84
Bellows Falls, Vt., U.S.	E4	152
Bellport, N.Y., U.S.	n16	139
Bells, Tn., U.S.	B2	149
Belluno, Italy	C7	18
Bell Ville, Arg.	G7	80
Bellville, Tx., U.S.	E4	150
Bellvue, Co., U.S.	A5	113
Bellwood, Il., U.S.	k9	120
Bellwood, Ne., U.S.	C8	134
Bellwood, Pa., U.S.	E5	145
Bellwood, Va., U.S.	n18	153
Belmar, N.J., U.S.	C4	137
Belmond, Ia., U.S.	B4	122
Belmont, Man., Can.	E2	100
Belmont, N.S., Can.	D6	101
Belmont, Ont., Can.	E3	103
Belmont, Ca., U.S.	h8	112
Belmont, Ms., U.S.	A5	131
Belmont, N.H., U.S.	D4	136
Belmont, N.C., U.S.	B1	140
Belmont, Vt., U.S.	E3	152
Belmont, W.V., U.S.	B3	155
Belmont, co., Oh., U.S.	C4	142
Belmonte, Braz.	C9	79
Belmopan, Belize	I15	90
Bel-Nor, Mo., U.S.	f13	132
Belo, Madag.	q21	67b
Beloeil, Que., Can.	D4	104
Belogorsk, Russia	G17	28
Belo Horizonte, Braz.	E7	79
Beloit, Ks., U.S.	C5	123
Beloit, Wi., U.S.	F4	156
Beloje, ozero, l., Russia	A20	22
Beloje more (White Sea), Russia	D5	26
Belomorsk, Russia	E4	26
Beloomut, Russia	G22	22
Beloozersk, Bela.	I8	22
Beloreck, Russia	G9	26
Belorečensk, Russia	I5	26
Belorussia see Belarus, ctry., Eur.	E13	4
Belousovo, Russia	F19	22
Bel'ov, Russia	H19	22
Belovo, Russia	G9	28
Beloz'orsk, Russia	A20	22
Belpre, Oh., U.S.	C4	142
Belt, Mt., U.S.	C6	133
Belterra, Braz.	D7	76
Belton, Mo., U.S.	C3	132
Belton, S.C., U.S.	B3	147
Belton, Tx., U.S.	D4	150
Belton Lake, res., Tx., U.S.	D4	150
Beltrán, Arg.	D6	80
Beltsville, Md., U.S.	B4	127
Belucha, gora, mtn., Asia	H15	26
Beluchistān, hist. reg., Asia	G17	48
Belvedere, Il., U.S.	A5	120
Belyj, Russia	F15	22
Belyje Berega, Russia	H17	22
Belyje Stolby, Russia	F20	22
Belyniči, Bela.	H12	22
Belzoni, Ms., U.S.	B3	131
Bemavo, Madag.	r21	67b
Bement, Il., U.S.	D5	120
Bemidji, Mn., U.S.	C4	130
Benāb, Iran	C9	48
Benagerie, Austl.	H4	70
Benahmed, Mor.	D7	62
Benalla, Austl.	K6	70
Benares see Vārānasi, India	H10	44
Ben Arous, Tun.	B16	62
Benavente, Spain	C6	16
Ben Badis, Alg.	K11	16
Benbrook, Tx., U.S.	n9	150
Bencubbin, Austl.	F3	68
Bend, Or., U.S.	C5	144
Bendigo, Austl.	K6	70
Bene Beraq, Isr.	C3	50
Benedict, Md., U.S.	C4	127
Benevento, Italy	H9	18
Benewah, co., Id., U.S.	B2	119
Benfeld, Fr.	D14	14
Bengal, Bay of, b., Asia	J14	44
Ben Gardane, Tun.	D16	62
Bengbu, China	C6	34
Benghazi see Banghāzī, Libya	B5	56
Bengkulu, Indon.	F3	38
Bengough, Sask., Can.	H3	105
Benguela, Ang.	D2	58
Benguerir, Mor.	D7	62
Benham, Ky., U.S.	D7	124
Ben Hill, co., Ga., U.S.	E3	117
Beni, Zaire	A5	58
Beni, dept., Bol.	E9	82
Beni, stm., Bol.	D9	82
Béni Abbas, Alg.	E9	62
Benicarló, Spain	E12	16
Benicia, Ca., U.S.	C2	112
Beni-Mellal, Mor.	D7	62
Benin (Bénin), ctry., Afr.	G7	54
Benin, Bight of, Afr.	G7	54
Benin City, Nig.	H12	64
Beni Saf, Alg.	J10	16
Benito, Man., Can.	D1	100
Benito Juárez, Arg.	I9	80
Benjamin Constant, Braz.	J7	84
Benjamin Hill, Mex.	B4	90
Benkelman, Ne., U.S.	D4	134
Benld, Il., U.S.	D4	120
Ben Mehidi, Alg.	M2	18
Bennet, Ne., U.S.	D9	134
Bennett, Co., U.S.	B6	113
Bennett, co., S.D., U.S.	D4	148
Bennettsville, S.C., U.S.	B8	147
Bennington, Ks., U.S.	C6	123
Bennington, Ne., U.S.	g12	134
Bennington, N.H., U.S.	D3	136
Bennington, Vt., U.S.	F2	152
Bennington, co., Vt., U.S.	E2	152
Benniu, China	D8	34
Benoit, Ms., U.S.	B2	131
Benoni, S. Afr.	G9	66
Bénoué (Benue), stm., Afr.	G9	54
Benque Viejo del Carmen, Belize	I15	90
Bensenville, Il., U.S.	B6	120
Bensley, Va., U.S.	C5	153
Ben-Slimane, Mor.	D7	62
Benson, Az., U.S.	F5	110
Benson, Mn., U.S.	E3	130
Benson, N.C., U.S.	B4	140
Benson, co., N.D., U.S.	A6	141
Bent, co., Co., U.S.	D7	113
Bentinck Island, i., Austl.	C7	68
Bentiu, Sud.	M5	60
Bentley, Alta., Can.	C3	98
Bentleyville, Pa., U.S.	F1	145
Bento Gonçalves, Braz.	E13	80
Benton, Ar., U.S.	C3	111
Benton, Il., U.S.	E5	120
Benton, Ks., U.S.	E6	123
Benton, Ky., U.S.	f9	124
Benton, La., U.S.	B2	125
Benton, Mo., U.S.	D8	132
Benton, Tn., U.S.	B7	149
Benton, co., Ar., U.S.	A1	111
Benton, co., In., U.S.	C3	121
Benton, co., Ia., U.S.	B5	122
Benton, co., Mn., U.S.	E4	130
Benton, co., Ms., U.S.	A4	131
Benton, co., Mo., U.S.	C4	132
Benton, co., Or., U.S.	C3	144
Benton, co., Tn., U.S.	A3	149
Benton, co., Wa., U.S.	C6	154
Benton City, Wa., U.S.	C6	154
Benton Harbor, Mi., U.S.	F4	129
Benton Heights, Mi., U.S.	F4	129
Bentonville, Ar., U.S.	A1	111
Ben Tre, Viet.	I9	40
Benue (Bénoué), stm., Afr.	G8	54
Benwood, W.V., U.S.	f8	155
Benxi (Penhsi), China	B11	32
Benzie, co., Mi., U.S.	D4	129
Beograd (Belgrade), Yugo.	E4	20
Beowawe, Nv., U.S.	C5	135
Beppu, Japan	N6	36
Berat, Alb.	I3	20
Beravina, Madag.	q21	67b
Berbera, Som.	F10	56
Berbérati, Cen. Afr. Rep.	H4	56
Berbice, stm., Guy.	D14	84
Berchtesgaden, Ger.	H13	10
Berdsk, Russia	G8	28
Berdyans'k, Ukr.	H5	26
Berdyčiv, Ukr.	H3	26
Berea, Ky., U.S.	C5	124
Berea, Oh., U.S.	A4	142
Berea, S.C., U.S.	B3	147
Berehomet, Ukr.	A9	20
Berehove, Ukr.	G22	22
Berens, stm., Can.	C3	100
Berens River, Man., Can.	C3	100
Beresford, S.D., U.S.	D9	148
Berezino, Bela.	H11	22
Berezniki, Russia	F9	26
Berga, Spain	C13	16
Bergama, Tur.	J11	20
Bergamo, Italy	D4	18
Bergen, Nor.	K9	6
Bergen [auf Rügen], Ger.	A13	10
Bergenfield, N.J., U.S.	E5	12
Bergen op Zoom, Neth.	E5	12
Bergerac, Fr.	H7	14
Bergisch Gladbach, Ger.	E7	10
Bergman, Ar., U.S.	A2	111
Bergues, Fr.	B9	14
Bering Sea	—	86
Bering Strait, strt.	m18	106a
Berkane, Mor.	C9	62
Berkeley, Ca., U.S.	f13	132
Berkeley, Mo., U.S.	f13	132
Berkeley, co., S.C., U.S.	E7	147
Berkeley, co., W.V., U.S.	B6	155
Berkeley Springs, W.V., U.S.	B6	155
Berkley, Mi., U.S.	F7	129
Berkner Island, i., Ant.	C1	73
Berks, co., Pa., U.S.	F9	145
Berkshire, co., Eng., U.K.	J12	8
Berkshire Hills, hills, Ma., U.S.	B1	128
Berlin, Ct., U.S.	C5	114
Berlin, Md., U.S.	D7	127
Berlin, N.H., U.S.	B4	136
Berlin, N.J., U.S.	D3	137
Berlin, Pa., U.S.	G4	145
Berlin, Wi., U.S.	E5	156
Berlin Corners, Vt., U.S.	C3	152
Berlin Lake, res., Oh., U.S.	A4	142
Bermejillo, Mex.	E8	90
Bermejo, stm., Arg.	F5	80
Bermejo, stm., S.A.	C9	80
Bermejo, Paso del, S.A.	G3	80
Bermeo, Spain	B9	16
Bermuda, dep., N.A.	B12	88
Bern (Berne), Switz.	E7	13
Bernalillo, N.M., U.S.	B3	138
Bernalillo, co., N.M., U.S.	C3	138
Bernardsville, N.J., U.S.	B3	137
Bernasconi, Arg.	I7	80
Bernau bei Berlin, Ger.	C13	10
Bernay, Fr.	C7	14
Bernburg, Ger.	D11	10
Berne, In., U.S.	C8	121
Berner Alpen, mts., Switz.	F7	13
Bernice, La., U.S.	B3	125
Bernie, Mo., U.S.	E8	132
Bernina, Passo del, Switz.	F13	13
Beromünster, Switz.	H8	10
Berón de Astrada, Arg.	D10	80
Beroroha, Madag.	r21	67b
Beroun, Czech Rep.	F14	10
Ber'oza, Bela.	I7	22
Ber'ozovo, Russia	I1	26
Berrechid, Mor.	D7	62
Berri, Austl.	J4	70
Berrien, co., Ga., U.S.	E3	117
Berrien, co., Mi., U.S.	F4	129
Berrien Springs, Mi., U.S.	G4	129
Berriyyane, Alg.	D12	62
Berry, Al., U.S.	B2	108
Berryessa, Lake, res., Ca., U.S.	C2	112
Berry Hill, Tn., U.S.	g10	149
Berry Islands, is., Bah.	B6	94
Berrys Chapel, Tn., U.S.	B5	149
Berryville, Ar., U.S.	A2	111
Berryville, Va., U.S.	A5	153
Bershad', Ukr.	A13	20
Berthierville, Que., Can.	C4	104
Berthold, N.D., U.S.	A4	141
Berthoud, Co., U.S.	A5	113
Berthoud Pass, Co., U.S.	B5	113
Bertie, co., N.C., U.S.	A5	140
Bertoua, Cam.	H9	54
Bertrand, Mo., U.S.	E8	132
Bertrand, Ne., U.S.	D6	134
Berwick, N.S., Can.	D5	101
Berwick, La., U.S.	E4	125
Berwick, Me., U.S.	E2	126
Berwick, Pa., U.S.	D9	145
Berwind, W.V., U.S.	D3	155
Berwyn, Alta., Can.	A2	98
Berwyn, Il., U.S.	k9	120
Berwyn, Pa., U.S.	o20	145
Besalampy, Madag.	p21	67b
Besançon, Fr.	E13	14
Besbes, Alg.	M2	18
Bešenkoviči, Bela.	F12	22
Beskid Mountains, mts., Eur.	F20	10
Beskra, Alg.	C13	62
Besni, Tur.	C4	48
Bessarabia, hist. reg., Mol.	C12	20
Bessemer, Al., U.S.	B3	108
Bessemer, Mi., U.S.	n11	129
Bessemer City, N.C., U.S.	B1	140
Betafo, Madag.	q22	67b
Bethal, S. Afr.	F9	66
Bethalto, Il., U.S.	E3	120
Bethanien, Nmb.	F3	66
Bethany, Ont., Can.	C6	103
Bethany, Il., U.S.	D5	120
Bethany, Mo., U.S.	A3	132
Bethany, Ok., U.S.	B4	143
Bethany, W.V., U.S.	A4	155
Bethel, Ak., U.S.	C7	109
Bethel, Ct., U.S.	D2	114
Bethel, Me., U.S.	D2	126
Bethel, N.C., U.S.	B5	140
Bethel, Oh., U.S.	D1	142
Bethel, Vt., U.S.	D3	152
Bethel Acres, Ok., U.S.	B5	143
Bethel Park, Pa., U.S.	k14	145
Bethel Springs, Tn., U.S.	B3	149
Bethesda, Md., U.S.	C3	127
Bethlehem, S. Afr.	G5	66
Bethlehem, Ct., U.S.	C3	114
Bethlehem, N.H., U.S.	B3	136
Bethlehem, Pa., U.S.	E11	145
Bethlehem see Bayt Laḩm, W.B.	E4	50
Béthune, Sask., Can.	G3	105
Béthune, Fr.	B9	14
Betioky, Madag.	s21	67b
Betong, Thai.	L6	40
Betoota, Austl.	E4	70
Betroka, Madag.	s22	67b
Betsiboka, stm., Madag.	p22	67b
Betsy Layne, Ky., U.S.	C7	124
Bette, Mt., Libya	D4	56
Bettendorf, Ia., U.S.	C7	122
Beulah, Co., U.S.	C6	113
Beulah, N.D., U.S.	B4	141
B. Everett Jordan Lake, res., N.C., U.S.	B3	140
Beverley Head, c., Newf.	D2	102
Beverly, Ma., U.S.	A6	128
Beverly, W.V., U.S.	C5	155
Beverly Hills, Ca., U.S.	m12	112
Beverly Shores, In., U.S.	A4	121
Beverwijk, Neth.	D6	12
Bexar, co., Tx., U.S.	E3	150
Bexley, Oh., U.S.	m11	142
Beypazarı, Tur.	G14	4
Bežeck, Russia	D19	22
Béziers, Fr.	I10	14
Bezmein, Turk.	B15	48
Bhadrak, India	J12	44
Bhāgalpur, India	H12	44
Bhakkar, Pak.	E4	44
Bhaktapur, Nepal	G11	44
Bhamo, Mya.	B4	40
Bhandāra, India	J8	44
Bharatpur, India	G7	44
Bharatpur, India	G11	44
Bharūch, India	J5	44
Bhātpāra, India	I13	44
Bhāvnagar, India	J5	44
Bhilai, India	J9	44
Bhind, India	G8	44
Bhilwāra, India	H6	44
Bhiwandi, India	C2	46
Bhiwāni, India	F7	44
Bhopāl, India	I7	44
Bhubaneshwar, India	J11	44
Bhuj, India	I3	44
Bhusāwal, India	J6	44
Bhutan (Druk-Yul), ctry., Asia	D13	42
Bia, Phou, mtn., Laos	E7	40
Biafra, Bight of, Afr.	H8	54
Biała Podlaska, Pol.	C23	10
Białogard, Pol.	A16	10
Białystok, Pol.	B23	10
Biarritz, Fr.	I5	14
Biasca, Switz.	F10	13
Bibā, Egypt	C6	60
Bibb, co., Al., U.S.	C2	108
Bibb, co., Ga., U.S.	D3	117
Biberach an der Riss, Ger.	G9	10
Bicas, Braz.	F7	79
Bicaz, Rom.	C10	20
Bichena, Eth.	L10	60
Bickle Knob, mtn., W.V., U.S.	C5	155
Bicknell, In., U.S.	G3	121
Bicske, Hung.	H18	10
Bīd, India	C3	46
Bida, Nig.	G13	64
Bīdar, India	D4	46
Biddeford, Me., U.S.	E2	126
Biel (Bienne), Switz.	D7	13
Bielawa, Pol.	E16	10
Bielefeld, Ger.	C8	10
Bielersee, l., Switz.	D7	13
Biella, Italy	D3	18
Bielsko-Biała, Pol.	F19	10
Bielsk Podlaski, Pol.	C23	10
Bienfait, Sask., Can.	H4	105
Bien Hoa, Viet.	I9	40
Bienville, co., La., U.S.	B2	125
Biga, Tur.	I11	20
Big Bay De Noc, b., Mi., U.S.	C4	129
Big Belt Mountains, mts., Mt., U.S.	D5	133
Big Bend, Wi., U.S.	n11	156
Big Bend National Park, Tx., U.S.	E1	150
Big Black, stm., Me., U.S.	B3	126
Big Black, stm., Ms., U.S.	C3	131
Big Butt, mtn., Tn., U.S.	C11	149
Big Costilla Peak, mtn., N.M., U.S.	A4	138
Big Cypress Swamp, sw., Fl., U.S.	F5	116
Big Darby Creek, stm., Oh., U.S.	C2	142
Big Delta, Ak., U.S.	C10	109
Big Eau Pleine, stm., Wi., U.S.	D3	156
Big Eau Pleine Reservoir, res., Wi., U.S.	D4	156
Bigelow, Ar., U.S.	B3	111
Bigelow, Mount, mtn., Me., U.S.	C2	126
Big Flats, N.Y., U.S.	C4	139
Bigfork, Mt., U.S.	B2	133
Bigfork, Mn., U.S.	C5	130
Biggar, Sask., Can.	E1	105
Biggers, Ar., U.S.	A5	111
Big Horn, co., Mt., U.S.	E9	133
Big Horn, co., Wy., U.S.	B4	157
Bighorn, stm., U.S.	E8	133
Bighorn Lake, res., U.S.	E8	133
Bighorn Mountains, mts., U.S.	B5	157
Big Lake, Mn., U.S.	E5	130
Big Lake, Tx., U.S.	D2	150
Big Lake, l., Me., U.S.	C5	126
Big Lost, stm., Id., U.S.	F5	119
Big Mossy Point, c., Man., Can.	C2	100
Big Muddy, stm., Il., U.S.	F4	120
Big Nemaha, stm., Ne., U.S.	D10	134
Bignona, Sen.	E1	64
Big Piney, Wy., U.S.	D2	157
Bigpoint, Ms., U.S.	E5	131
Big Rapids, Mi., U.S.	E5	129
Big River, Sask., Can.	D2	105
Big Sable Point, c., Mi., U.S.	D4	129
Big Sandy, Mt., U.S.	B6	133
Big Sandy, Tn., U.S.	A3	149
Big Sandy, Tx., U.S.	C5	150
Big Sandy, stm., Az., U.S.	C2	110
Big Sandy, stm., U.S.	B7	155
Big Sandy, stm., Wy., U.S.	D3	157
Big Sandy Creek, stm., Co., U.S.	C8	113
Big Sioux, stm., U.S.	E9	148
Big Spring, Tx., U.S.	C2	150
Big Springs, Ne., U.S.	C3	134
Big Spruce Knob, mtn., W.V., U.S.	C4	155
Big Stone, co., Mn., U.S.	E2	130
Big Stone City, S.D., U.S.	B9	148
Big Stone Gap, Va., U.S.	f9	153
Big Stone Lake, l., U.S.	E2	130
Big Sur, Ca., U.S.	D3	112
Big Sunflower, stm., Ms., U.S.	B3	131
Big Thompson, stm., Co., U.S.	A5	113
Big Timber, Mt., U.S.	E7	133
Biguaçu, Braz.	B7	80
Big Valley, Alta., Can.	C4	98
Big Wills Creek, stm., Al., U.S.	A3	108
Big Wood, stm., Id., U.S.	F4	119
Bihać, Bos.	E10	18
Bihār, India	H11	44
Bihār, state, India	H11	44
Bijagós, Arquipélago dos, is., Gui.-B.	F1	64
Bijār, Iran	D9	48

Name	Map Ref.	Page
Bijeljina, Bos.	E3	20
Bijie, China	F8	30
Bijou Creek, stm., Co., U.S.	B6	113
Bijsk, Russia	G9	28
Bīkāner, India	F5	44
Bikeqi, China	C9	30
Bikin, Russia	H18	28
Bikini, atoll, Marsh. Is.	G20	158
Bilac, Braz.	F3	79
Bilāspur, India	I10	44
Bila Tserkva, Ukr.	H4	26
Bilauktaung Range, mts., Asia	H5	40
Bilbao, Spain	B9	16
Bilhorod-Dnistrovs'kyy, Ukr.	H4	26
Bilian, China	G9	34
Bilin, Mya.	F4	40
Bílina, Czech Rep.	E13	10
Billabong Creek, stm., Austl.	J6	70
Billerica, Ma., U.S.	A5	128
Billings, Mo., U.S.	D4	132
Billings, Mt., U.S.	E8	133
Billings, co., N.D., U.S.	B2	141
Billings Heights, Mt., U.S.	E8	133
Billom, Fr.	G10	14
Bill Williams, stm., Az., U.S.	C1	110
Bill Williams Mountain, mtn., Az., U.S.	B3	110
Bilma, Niger	E9	54
Biloela, Austl.	E9	70
Biloxi, Ms., U.S.	E5	131
Biltmore Forest, N.C., U.S.	f10	140
Bilyayivka, Ukr.	C14	20
Bimini Islands, is., Bah.	B5	94
Binche, Bel.	H5	12
Bindura, Zimb.	E6	58
Binford, N.D., U.S.	B7	141
Binga, Monte, mtn., Afr.	B11	66
Bingara, Austl.	G9	70
Bingen, Ger.	F7	10
Bingen, Wa., U.S.	D4	154
Binger, Ok., U.S.	B3	143
Bingham, Me., U.S.	C3	126
Bingham, co., Id., U.S.	F6	119
Binghamton, N.Y., U.S.	C5	139
Bingöl, Tur.	B6	48
Binhai (Dongkan), China	A8	34
Binjai, Indon.	M5	40
Binscarth, Man., Can.	D1	100
Bintimani, mtn., S.L.	G4	64
Bint Jubayl, Leb.	B4	50
Binyang, China	C10	40
Biobío, prov., Chile	I3	80
Biobío, stm., Chile	I2	80
Bioko, i., Eq. Gui.	J14	64
Birātnagar, Nepal	F4	30
Birch Hills, Sask., Can.	E3	105
Birch Island, B.C., Can.	D8	99
Birch River, Man., Can.	C1	100
Birch Tree, Mo., U.S.	E6	132
Birchy Bay, Newf., Can.	D4	102
Bird City, Ks., U.S.	C2	123
Bird Island, Mn., U.S.	F4	130
Birdsboro, Pa., U.S.	F10	145
Birdum, Austl.	C6	68
Birecik, Tur.	C4	48
Bir el Ater, Alg.	C15	62
Bir Enzaran, W. Sah.	I3	62
Birigui, Braz.	F3	79
Birjand, Iran	E15	48
Birkenhead, Eng., U.K.	H10	8
Birmingham, Eng., U.K.	I12	8
Birmingham, Al., U.S.	B3	108
Birmingham, Mi., U.S.	F7	129
Bîr Mogreïn (Fort-Trinquet), Maur.	H5	62
Birni Nkonni, Niger	E12	64
Birnin Kudu, Nig.	F14	64
Birobidžan, Russia	H18	28
Birobijan see Jevrej, state, Russia	H18	28
Birsk, Russia	F9	26
Birtle, Man., Can.	D1	100
Bisbee, Az., U.S.	F6	110
Biscarrosse, Fr.	H5	14
Biscay, Bay of, b., Eur.	H3	14
Biscayne, Key, i., Fl., U.S.	s13	116
Biscayne Bay, b., Fl., U.S.	G6	116
Biscayne National Monument, Fl., U.S.	G6	116
Biscayne Park, Fl., U.S.	s13	116
Bisceglie, Italy	H11	18
Biscoe, Ar., U.S.	C4	111
Biscoe, N.C., U.S.	B3	140
Bisha, Erit.	J9	60
Bishkek see Biškek, Kyrg.	I12	26
Bisho, S. Afr.	I8	66
Bishop, Ca., U.S.	D4	112
Bishop, Tx., U.S.	F4	150
Bishop Auckland, Eng., U.K.	G12	8
Bishop's Falls, Newf., Can.	D4	102
Bishopville, S.C., U.S.	C7	147
Biškek (Frunze), Kyrg.	I12	26
Bislig, Phil.	D8	38
Bismarck, Mo., U.S.	D7	132
Bismarck, N.D., U.S.	C5	141
Bismarck Archipelago, is., Pap. N. Gui.	k16	68a
Bismarck Range, mts., Pap. N. Gui.	m15	68a
Bismarck Sea, Pap. N. Gui.	m15	68a
Bismuna, Laguna, b., Nic.	C11	92
Bison, D.D., U.S.	B3	148
Bissau, Gui.-B.	F3	54
Bissikrima, Gui.	F4	64
Bissorã, Gui.-B.	E2	64
Bistineau, Lake, res., La., U.S.	B2	125
Bistrița, Rom.	B8	20
Bitam, Gabon	A2	58
Bitche, Fr.	C14	14
Bitlis, Tur.	B7	48
Bitola, Mac.	H5	20
Bitonto, Italy	H11	18
Bitter Creek, stm., Wy., U.S.	E4	157
Bitterroot, stm., Mt., U.S.	D2	133
Bitterroot Range, mts., U.S.	B3	119
Bitung, Indon.	E8	38
Bituruna, Braz.	D13	80
Biwabik, Mn., U.S.	C6	130
Biwa-ko, l., Japan	L11	36
Bixby, Ok., U.S.	B6	143
Biyang, China	C2	34
Bizerte, Tun.	L4	18
Bjala Slatina, Bul.	F7	20
Bjelovar, Cro.	D11	18
Bla, Mali	E7	64
Black (Lixian) (Da), stm., Asia	D8	40
Black, stm., Az., U.S.	D5	110
Black, stm., Ar., U.S.	B4	111
Black, stm., La., U.S.	C4	125
Black, stm., Mi., U.S.	E8	129
Black, stm., S.C., U.S.	D8	147
Black, Bayou, stm., La., U.S.	E5	125
Blackall, Austl.	E6	70
Blackburn, Mount, mtn., Ak., U.S.	C11	109
Black Butte, mtn., Mt., U.S.	F5	133
Black Canyon, val., Co., U.S.	C3	113
Black Canyon City, Az., U.S.	C3	110
Black Canyon of the Gunnison National Monument, Co., U.S.	C3	113
Black Creek, B.C., Can.	E5	99
Black Creek, Wi., U.S.	D5	156
Black Creek, stm., S.C., U.S.	B7	147
Black Diamond, Alta., Can.	D3	98
Black Diamond, Wa., U.S.	B4	154
Blackduck, Mn., U.S.	C4	130
Black Eagle, Mt., U.S.	C5	133
Black Earth, Wi., U.S.	E4	156
Blackfalds, Alta., Can.	C4	98
Black Forest, Co., U.S.	C6	113
Black Forest see Schwarzwald, mts., Ger.	G8	10
Black Hawk, S.D., U.S.	C2	148
Black Hawk, co., Ia., U.S.	B5	122
Black Hills, mts., U.S.	C2	148
Blackie, Alta., Can.	D4	98
Black Lake, Que., Can.	C6	104
Black Lake, l., Mi., U.S.	C6	129
Black Lake, l., N.Y., U.S.	f9	139
Black Mesa, mtn., Ok., U.S.	e8	143
Black Mountain, N.C., U.S.	f10	140
Black Mountain, mtn., Mt., U.S.	D4	133
Black Mountains, mts., Az., U.S.	B1	110
Blackpool, Eng., U.K.	H10	8
Black River Falls, Wi., U.S.	D3	156
Black Rock, Ar., U.S.	A4	111
Black Rock, N.M., U.S.	B1	138
Blacksburg, S.C., U.S.	A4	147
Blacksburg, Va., U.S.	C2	153
Black Sea	G15	4
Blacks Fork, stm., U.S.	E3	157
Blacks Harbour, N.B., Can.	D3	101
Blackshear, Ga., U.S.	E4	117
Blackstone, Ma., U.S.	B4	128
Blackstone, Va., U.S.	C5	153
Blackstone, stm., R.I., U.S.	B4	146
Blackville, N.B., Can.	C4	101
Blackville, S.C., U.S.	E5	147
Black Volta (Volta Noire), stm., Afr.	G6	54
Black Warrior, stm., Al., U.S.	C2	108
Blackwater, stm., Ire.	I5	8
Blackwater, stm., Va., U.S.	D6	153
Blackwell, Ok., U.S.	A4	143
Blackwood, N.J., U.S.	D2	137
Bladen, co., N.C., U.S.	C4	140
Bladenboro, N.C., U.S.	C4	140
Bladensburg, Md., U.S.	f9	127
Blades, De., U.S.	F3	115
Blagodarnyj, Russia	H6	26
Blagoevgrad, Bul.	G7	20
Blagoveščensk, Russia	G17	28
Blain, Fr.	E5	14
Blaine, Me., U.S.	B5	126
Blaine, Mn., U.S.	m12	130
Blaine, Tn., U.S.	C10	149
Blaine, Wa., U.S.	A3	154
Blaine, co., Id., U.S.	F4	119
Blaine, co., Mt., U.S.	B7	133
Blaine, co., Ne., U.S.	C6	134
Blaine, co., Ok., U.S.	B3	143
Blaine, co., Sask., Can.	E2	105
Blair, Ne., U.S.	C9	134
Blair, Ok., U.S.	C2	143
Blair, W.V., U.S.	n12	155
Blair, co., Pa., U.S.	E5	145
Blair Athol, Austl.	D8	70
Blairstown, Ia., U.S.	C5	122
Blairsville, Ga., U.S.	B2	117
Blairsville, Pa., U.S.	F3	145
Blakely, Ga., U.S.	E2	117
Blakely, Pa., U.S.	m18	145
Blake Point, c., Mi., U.S.	h10	129
Blanc, Mont (Monte Bianco), mtn., Eur.	G13	14
Blanca, Co., U.S.	D5	113
Blanca, Bahía, b., Arg.	J7	80
Blanca, Sierra, mtn., Tx., U.S.	o12	150
Blanca Peak, mtn., Co., U.S.	D5	113
Blanchard, La., U.S.	B2	125
Blanchard, Ok., U.S.	B4	143
Blanchard, stm., Oh., U.S.	A1	142
Blanchester, Oh., U.S.	C2	142
Blanco, co., Tx., U.S.	D3	150
Blanco, Cabo, c., C.R.	H9	92
Blanco, Cape, c., Or., U.S.	E2	144
Bland, Mo., U.S.	C6	132
Bland, co., Va., U.S.	C1	153
Blanding, Ut., U.S.	F6	151
Blanes, Spain	D14	16
Blangy-sur-Bresle, Fr.	C8	14
Blankenberge, Bel.	F3	12
Blankenburg, Ger.	D10	10
Blankenheim, Ger.	E6	10
Blantyre, Mwi.	E7	58
Blasdell, N.Y., U.S.	C2	139
Blaye-et-Sainte-Luce, Fr.	G6	14
Bleckley, co., Ga., U.S.	D3	117
Bledsoe, co., Tn., U.S.	D8	149
Blende, Co., U.S.	C6	113
Blenheim, Ont., Can.	E3	103
Blenheim, N.Z.	D4	72
Blennerhassett, W.V., U.S.	B3	155
Blind River, Ont., Can.	A2	103
Blissfield, Mi., U.S.	G7	129
Blitar, Indon.	k16	39a
Block Island, R.I., U.S.	h7	146
Block Island, i., R.I., U.S.	h7	146
Block Island Sound, strt., U.S.	G2	146
Bloemfontein, S. Afr.	G8	66
Bloemhof, S. Afr.	F7	66
Blois, Fr.	E8	14
Blönduós, Ice.	B3	6a
Bloodsworth Island, i., Md., U.S.	D5	127
Bloodvein, stm., Can.	D3	100
Bloomer, Wi., U.S.	C2	156
Bloomfield, Ont., Can.	D7	103
Bloomfield, Ct., U.S.	B5	114
Bloomfield, In., U.S.	F4	121
Bloomfield, Ia., U.S.	D5	122
Bloomfield, Ky., U.S.	C4	124
Bloomfield, Mo., U.S.	E8	132
Bloomfield, Ne., U.S.	B8	134
Bloomfield, N.J., U.S.	h8	137
Bloomfield, N.M., U.S.	A2	138
Bloomfield Hills, Mi., U.S.	o15	129
Bloomingdale, Ga., U.S.	D5	117
Bloomingdale, Il., U.S.	k8	120
Bloomingdale, N.J., U.S.	A4	137
Bloomingdale, Tn., U.S.	C11	149
Blooming Prairie, Mn., U.S.	G5	130
Bloomington, Il., U.S.	C4	120
Bloomington, In., U.S.	F4	121
Bloomington, Mn., U.S.	F5	130
Bloomsburg, Pa., U.S.	E9	145
Blora, Indon.	j15	39a
Blount, co., Al., U.S.	B3	108
Blount, co., Tn., U.S.	D10	149
Blountstown, Fl., U.S.	B1	116
Blountsville, Al., U.S.	A3	108
Blountville, Tn., U.S.	C11	149
Blowing Rock, N.C., U.S.	A1	140
Bludenz, Aus.	H9	10
Blue, stm., Ok., U.S.	C5	143
Blue Ash, Oh., U.S.	o13	142
Blue Creek, Al., U.S.	g6	108
Blue Creek, W.V., U.S.	m13	155
Blue Diamond, Nv., U.S.	G6	135
Blue Earth, Mn., U.S.	G4	130
Blue Earth, co., Mn., U.S.	G4	130
Blue Earth, stm., Mn., U.S.	G4	130
Bluefield, Va., U.S.	C1	153
Bluefield, W.V., U.S.	D3	155
Bluefields, Nic.	H9	92
Bluefields, Bahía de, b., Nic.	F11	92
Blue Grass, Ia., U.S.	C7	122
Blue Hill, Me., U.S.	D4	126
Blue Hill, Ne., U.S.	D7	134
Blue Hills, Ct., U.S.	B5	114
Blue Island, Il., U.S.	B6	120
Blue Mound, Il., U.S.	D4	120
Blue Mountain, Ms., U.S.	A4	131
Blue Mountain, mtn., N.M., U.S.	D2	138
Blue Mountain, mtn., N.Y., U.S.	B6	139
Blue Mountain, mtn., Pa., U.S.	F6	145
Blue Mountain Peak, mtn., Jam.	E6	94
Blue Mountains, mts., U.S.	B3	106
Blue Nile (Al-Baḥr al-Azraq) (Abay), stm., Afr.	F7	56
Blue Point, Me., U.S.	g7	126
Blue Rapids, Ks., U.S.	C7	123
Blue Ridge, Alta., Can.	B3	98
Blue Ridge, Va., U.S.	C3	153
Blue Ridge, mts., U.S.	D10	106
Blue Ridge Summit, Pa., U.S.	G7	145
Blue River, B.C., Can.	C8	99
Blue Springs, Mo., U.S.	h11	132
Blue Springs, Ne., U.S.	D9	134
Bluestone Lake, res., U.S.	D4	155
Bluewater, N.M., U.S.	B2	138
Bluewell, W.V., U.S.	D3	155
Bluff City, Tn., U.S.	C11	149
Bluff Park, Al., U.S.	g7	108
Bluffton, In., U.S.	C7	121
Bluffton, Oh., U.S.	B2	142
Blumenau, Braz.	D14	80
Blunt, S.D., U.S.	C6	148
Bly, Or., U.S.	E5	144
Blyth, Ont., Can.	D3	103
Blythe, Ca., U.S.	F6	112
Blytheville, Ar., U.S.	B6	111
Bo, S.L.	H4	64
Boaco, Nic.	E9	92
Boaco, dept., Nic.	E9	92
Boa Esperança, Braz.	F6	79
Boalsburg, Pa., U.S.	E6	145
Boardman, Oh., U.S.	A5	142
Boardman, Or., U.S.	B7	144
Boatman, Austl.	F8	70
Boa Vista, Braz.	F12	84
Boa Vista, i., C.V.	m17	64a
Boaz, Al., U.S.	A3	108
Bobai, China	C10	40
Bobcaygeon, Ont., Can.	C6	103
Böblingen, Ger.	G9	10
Bobo Dioulasso, Burkina	F7	64
Bobonong, Bots.	C7	66
Bobrujsk, Bela.	H12	22
Boca Chica Key, i., Fl., U.S.	H5	116
Boca do Acre, Braz.	C8	82
Boca Raton, Fl., U.S.	F6	116
Bocas del Toro, Pan.	C1	84
Bocas del Toro, prov., Pan.	I12	92
Bocas del Toro, Archipiélago de, is., Pan.	H12	92
Bochnia, Pol.	F20	10
Bocholt, Ger.	D6	10
Bocholt, Ger.	D7	10
Boconó, Ven.	C7	84
Bodegraven, Neth.	D6	12
Boden, Swe.	I17	6
Bodensee (Lake Constance), l., Eur.	E16	14
Bodināyakkanūr, India	G4	46
Bodø, Nor.	H14	6
Bodrum, Tur.	L11	20
Boende, Zaire	B4	58
Boeo, Capo, c., Italy	L7	18
Boerne, Tx., U.S.	E3	150
Bone, Teluk, b., Indon.	F7	38
Boeuf, stm., La., U.S.	C4	125
Boeuf, Bayou, stm., La., U.S.	D3	125
Bogale, Mya.	F3	40
Bogalusa, La., U.S.	D6	125
Bogart, Ga., U.S.	C3	117
Boger City, N.C., U.S.	B1	140
Bogol'ubovo, Russia	E23	22
Bogong, Mount, mtn., Austl.	K7	70
Bogorodick, Russia	H21	22
Bogorodsk, Russia	E26	22
Bogotá see Santa Fe de Bogota, Col.	E5	84
Bogota, N.J., U.S.	h8	137
Bogotol, Russia	F9	28
Bogué, Maur.	E3	64
Bogue Chitto, Ms., U.S.	D3	131
Bogue Chitto, stm., U.S.	D5	125
Boguševsk, Bela.	G13	22
Bo Hai (Gulf of Chihli), b., China	E8	32
Bohain-en-Vermandois, Fr.	C10	14
Bohemia see Čechy, hist. reg., Czech Rep.	F14	10
Bohemian Forest, mts., Eur.	F12	10
Bohicon, Benin	H11	64
Bohol, i., Phil.	D7	38
Bohol Sea, Phil.	D7	38
Boiestown, N.B., Can.	C3	101
Boiling Springs, N.C., U.S.	B1	140
Boiling Springs, Pa., U.S.	F7	145
Bois Blanc Island, i., Mi., U.S.	C6	129
Boischâtel, Que., Can.	C6	104
Bois-des-Filion, Que., Can.	p19	104
Boise, Id., U.S.	F2	119
Boise, co., Id., U.S.	F3	119
Boise City, Ok., U.S.	e8	143
Boissevain, Man., Can.	E1	100
Boissevain, Va., U.S.	e10	153
Bojeador, Cape, c., Phil.	I19	39b
Bojnūrd, Iran	C14	48
Bojonegoro, Indon.	j15	39a
Bokani, Nig.	G12	64
Boké, Gui.	F2	64
Boksitogorsk, Russia	B16	22
Bolaños, stm., Mex.	F8	90
Bolaños de Calatrava, Spain	G8	16
Bolbec, Fr.	C7	14
Bole, China	B4	30
Boli, China	B13	30
Boli, Sud.	N5	60
Bolingbrook, Il., U.S.	k8	120
Bolívar, Col.	E4	84
Bolivar, Mo., U.S.	D4	132
Bolivar, Tn., U.S.	B3	149
Bolívar, state, Ven.	D11	84
Bolívar, prov., Ec.	H3	84
Bolívar, dept., Col.	C5	84
Bolivar, co., Ms., U.S.	B3	131
Bolívar, Pico, mtn., Ven.	C7	84
Bolivia, ctry., S.A.	F8	74
Bollène, Fr.	H11	14
Bollinger, co., Mo., U.S.	D7	132
Bollullos par del Condado, Spain	H5	16
Bolobo, Zaire	B3	58
Bolochovo, Russia	G20	22
Bologna, Italy	E6	18
Bologoje, Russia	D17	22
Bolonchén de Rejón, Mex.	G15	90
Bolotnoje, Russia	F14	26
Bolovens, Plateau des, plat., Laos	G9	40
Bol'šaja Ižora, Russia	B12	22
Bol'šaja Murta, Russia	F16	26
Bol'ševik, Bela.	I13	22
Bol'ševik, ostrov, i., Russia	B12	28
Bol'šoj L'achovskij, ostrov, i., Russia	C20	28
Bolton, Ms., U.S.	C3	131
Bolzano (Bozen), Italy	C6	18
Boma, Zaire	C2	58
Bomaderry, Austl.	J9	70
Bombala, Austl.	K8	70
Bombay, India	C2	46
Bom Despacho, Braz.	E6	79
Bom Jardim de Goiás, Braz.	D2	79
Bom Jesus da Lapa, Braz.	B7	79
Bom Jesus de Goiás, Braz.	E4	79
Bomoseen, Vt., U.S.	D2	152
Bomoseen, Lake, l., Vt., U.S.	D2	152
Bom Retiro, Braz.	D14	80
Bom Sucesso, Braz.	G3	79
Bomu (Mbomou), stm., Afr.	H5	56
Bon, Cap, c., Tun.	L6	18
Bon Accord, Alta., Can.	C4	98
Bon Air, Va., U.S.	C5	153
Bonaire, i., Neth. Ant.	H10	94
Bonanza, Nic.	C10	92
Bonanza Peak, mtn., Wa., U.S.	A5	154
Bonao, Dom. Rep.	E9	94
Bonaparte, stm., B.C., Can.	D7	99
Bonaparte Archipelago, is., Austl.	B5	68
Bonasila Dome, mtn., Ak., U.S.	C7	109
Bonavista, Newf., Can.	D5	102
Bonavista, Cape, c., Newf., Can.	D5	102
Bonavista Bay, b., Newf., Can.	D5	102
Bond, Ms., U.S.	E4	131
Bond, co., Il., U.S.	E4	120
Bondeno, Italy	E6	18
Bondo, Zaire	H5	56
Bondoukou, C. Iv.	G8	64
Bondsville, Ma., U.S.	B3	128
Bonduel, Wi., U.S.	D5	156
Bondurant, Ia., U.S.	C4	122
Bondurant, Wy., U.S.	C2	157
Bone, Teluk, b., Indon.	F7	38
Bonete, Cerro, mtn., Arg.	D4	80
Bonete Chico, Cerro, mtn., Arg.	E4	80
Bonga, Eth.	N9	60
Bongor, Chad	F4	56
Bongouanou, C. Iv.	H7	64
Bonham, Tx., U.S.	C4	150
Bonifacio, Strait of, strt., Eur.	J17	6
Bonifay, Fl., U.S.	u16	116
Bonita Springs, Fl., U.S.	F5	116
Bonito, Braz.	I13	82
Bonn, Ger.	E7	10
Bonne Bay, b., Newf., Can.	D3	102
Bonners Ferry, Id., U.S.	A2	119
Bonner Springs, Ks., U.S.	C9	123
Bonne Terre, Mo., U.S.	D7	132
Bonneval, Fr.	D8	14
Bonneville, Fr.	F13	14
Bonneville, co., Id., U.S.	F7	119
Bonneville Peak, mtn., Id., U.S.	F6	119
Bonneville Salt Flats, pl., Ut., U.S.	C2	151
Bonney Lake, Wa., U.S.	B3	154
Bonnie Doone, N.C., U.S.	B4	140
Bonny, Nig.	I13	64
Bonnyville, Alta., Can.	B5	98
Bon Secour, Al., U.S.	E2	108
Bonthe, S.L.	H3	64
Bookaloo, Austl.	H2	70
Boola, Gui.	G5	64
Boom, Bel.	F5	12
Boomer, W.V., U.S.	C3	155
Boonah, Austl.	G10	70
Boone, Co., U.S.	C6	113
Boone, Ia., U.S.	B4	122
Boone, N.C., U.S.	A1	140
Boone, co., Ar., U.S.	A2	111
Boone, co., Il., U.S.	A5	120
Boone, co., In., U.S.	D4	121
Boone, co., Ia., U.S.	B3	122
Boone, co., Ky., U.S.	B5	124
Boone, co., Mo., U.S.	B5	132
Boone, co., Ne., U.S.	C7	134
Boone, co., W.V., U.S.	C3	155
Boone, co., Ia., U.S.	B4	122
Booneville, Ar., U.S.	B2	111
Booneville, Ms., U.S.	A5	131
Boonsboro, Md., U.S.	A2	127
Boonton, N.J., U.S.	B4	137
Boonville, Ca., U.S.	C2	112
Boonville, In., U.S.	H3	121
Boonville, Mo., U.S.	C5	132
Boonville, N.C., U.S.	A2	140
Boonville, N.Y., U.S.	B5	139
Boorama, Som.	G9	56
Boothbay Harbor, Me., U.S.	E3	126
Boothia, Gulf of, b., N.W. Ter., Can.	B14	96
Boothia Peninsula, pen., N.W. Ter., Can.	B14	96
Bophuthatswana, hist. reg., S. Afr.	F7	66
Boquerón, Pan.	I12	92
Boquerón, dept., Para.	B8	80
Boquillas del Carmen, Mex.	C8	90
Bor, Russia	E26	22
Bor, Sud.	N6	60
Bor, Tur.	C3	48
Bor, Yugo.	E6	20
Boraha, Nosy, i., Madag.	p23	67b
Borah Peak, mtn., Id., U.S.	E5	119
Borås, Swe.	M13	6
Borāzjān, Iran	G11	48
Borba, Braz.	J13	84
Bordeaux, Fr.	H6	14
Borden, Sask., Can.	E2	105
Borden, co., Tx., U.S.	C2	150
Borderland, W.V., U.S.	D2	155
Bordentown, N.J., U.S.	C3	137
Bordertown, Austl.	K4	70
Bordj Bou Arreridj, Alg.	B12	62
Bordj Menaïel, Alg.	B12	62
Borg (Porvoo), Fin.	K19	6
Borger, Tx., U.S.	B2	150
Borgholm, Swe.	M15	6
Borgne, Lake, b., La., U.S.	D6	125
Borgosesia, Italy	D3	18
Borisoglebsk, Russia	G6	26
Borisoglebskij, Russia	D22	22
Borisov, Bela.	G11	22
Borja, Swe.	M13	6
Borken, Ger.	D6	10
Börlänge, Swe.	K14	6
Borna, Ger.	E6	79?
Borneo (Kalimantan), i., Asia	N11	40
Bornholm, i., Den.	I8	6
Boromo, Burkina	N14	6
Borovići, Russia	C16	22
Borovsk, Russia	F19	22
Borrazópolis, Braz.	G3	79
Borriana, Spain	F11	16
Borroloola, Austl.	C7	68
Borşa, Rom.	B8	20
Borşa, Rom.	M8	20
Bort-les-Orgues, Fr.	G9	14
Boruca, C.R.	H11	92
Borūjen, Iran	F11	48
Borūjerd, Iran	E10	48
Bor'ja, Russia	G15	28
Bosanska Dubica, Bos.	D11	18
Bosanska Gradiška, Bos.	D11	18
Bosanski Novi, Bos.	D11	18
Bosanski Šamac, Bos.	D2	20
Bose, China	C9	40
Boshan, China	D5	32
Bosna, stm., Bos.	E13	18
Bosnia and Herzegovina, ctry., Eur.	G11	4
Bosporus see İstanbul Boğazı, strt., Tur.	H13	20
Bosque, co., Tx., U.S.	D3	138?
Bosque Farms, N.M., U.S.	C3	138
Bossangoa, Cen. Afr. Rep.	G4	56
Bossé Bangou, Niger	H5	56
Bossier, co., La., U.S.	B2	125
Bossier City, La., U.S.	B2	125
Bosten Hu, l., China	C4	30
Boston, Eng., U.K.	I13	8
Boston, Ga., U.S.	F3	117
Boston, Ma., U.S.	B5	128
Boston Bay, b., Ma., U.S.	B6	128
Boston Mountains, mts., Ar., U.S.	B2	111
Boswell, In., U.S.	C3	121
Boteti, stm., Bots.	C6	66
Botetourt, co., Va., U.S.	C3	153
Bothaville, S. Afr.	F8	66
Bothnia, Gulf of, b., Eur.	J17	6
Bothwell, Ont., Can.	E3	103
Botoşani, Rom.	B10	20
Botrange, mtn., Bel.	H9	12
Botswana, ctry., Afr.	F4	58
Bottineau, N.D., U.S.	A5	141
Bottineau, co., N.D., U.S.	A4	141
Botucatu, Braz.	G4	79
Botwood, Newf., Can.	D4	102
Bouaké, C. Iv.	H7	64
Bouar, Cen. Afr. Rep.	G4	56
Bou Arada, Tun.	M4	18
Bouârfa, Mor.	D10	62
Boucherville, Que., Can.	D4	104
Bouctouche, N.B., Can.	C5	101
Boudry, Switz.	E6	13
Boufarik, Alg.	B12	62
Bougainville, i., Pap. N. Gui.	I19	158
Bougouni, Mali	F6	64
Bou Hadjar, Alg.	M3	18
Bou Hajar, Tun.	N5	18
Bouïra, Alg.	B12	62
Boujad, Mor.	D7	62
Bou Kadir, Alg.	B11	62
Bou Khadra, Alg.	N3	18
Boulder, Co., U.S.	A5	113
Boulder, Mt., U.S.	D4	133
Boulder, co., Co., U.S.	A5	113
Boulder City, Nv., U.S.	H7	135
Boulevard Heights, Md., U.S.	f9	127
Boulia, Austl.	D3	70
Boulogne-Billancourt, Fr.	D9	14
Boulogne-sur-Mer, Fr.	B8	14
Boulsa, Burkina	E9	64
Bouly, Maur.	D4	64
Bouna, C. Iv.	G8	64
Boundary, co., Id., U.S.	A2	119
Boundary Bald Mountain, mtn., Me., U.S.	C2	126
Boundary Bay, b., Wa., U.S.	A3	154
Boundary Peak, mtn., Nv., U.S.	F3	135
Bound Brook, N.J., U.S.	B3	137
Bountiful, Ut., U.S.	C4	151
Bounty Islands, is., N.Z.	M21	158
Bouqteb, Alg.	C11	62
Boura, Mali	E7	64
Bourbon, In., U.S.	B5	121
Bourbon, Mo., U.S.	C6	132
Bourbon, co., Ks., U.S.	E9	123
Bourbon, co., Ky., U.S.	B5	124
Bourbon-Lancy, Fr.	F10	14
Bourbonnais, Il., U.S.	B6	120
Bourem, Mali	C9	64
Bourg, La., U.S.	E5	125
Bourganeuf, Fr.	G8	14
Bourg-en-Bresse, Fr.	F12	14
Bourges, Fr.	E9	14
Bourgogne (Burgundy), hist. reg., Fr.	E11	14
Bourgoin, Fr.	G12	14
Bourg-Saint-Andéol, Fr.	H11	14
Bourg-Saint-Maurice, Fr.	G13	14
Bourke, Austl.	H6	70
Bournemouth, Eng., U.K.	K12	8
Bou Saâda, Alg.	C13	62
Bou Salem, Tun.	M3	18
Bouse, Az., U.S.	D2	110
Bou Smail, Alg.	B12	62
Bouteldja, Alg.	M3	18
Boutilimit, Maur.	C2	64
Boutte, La., U.S.	k11	125
Bouvetøya, i., Ant.	A3	73
Bouza, Niger	D13	64
Bøverdal, Nor.	K11	6
Bovey, Mn., U.S.	C5	130
Bovill, Id., U.S.	C2	119
Bovina, Tx., U.S.	B1	150
Bovril, Arg.	F9	80
Bow, N.H., U.S.	D3	136
Bow, stm., Alta., Can.	D4	98
Bowbells, N.D., U.S.	A3	141
Bowden, Alta., Can.	D3	98
Bowdle, S.D., U.S.	B6	148
Bowdoinham, Me., U.S.	D3	126
Bowdon, Ga., U.S.	C1	117
Bowen, Arg.	H5	80
Bowen, Austl.	C8	70
Bowie, Md., U.S.	C4	127
Bowie, Tx., U.S.	C4	150
Bowie, co., Tx., U.S.	C5	150
Bow Island, Alta., Can.	E5	98
Bowling Green, Fl., U.S.	E5	116
Bowling Green, Ky., U.S.	D3	124
Bowling Green, Mo., U.S.	B6	132
Bowling Green, Oh., U.S.	A2	142
Bowling Green, Va., U.S.	B5	153
Bowman, Ga., U.S.	B3	117
Bowman, N.D., U.S.	C2	141
Bowman, S.C., U.S.	E6	147
Bowman, co., N.D., U.S.	C2	141
Bowman-Haley Lake, res., N.D., U.S.	C2	141
Bowral, Austl.	J9	70
Bowsman, Man., Can.	C1	100
Box Elder, S.D., U.S.	C2	148
Box Elder, Mt., U.S.	B6	133
Box Elder, co., Ut., U.S.	B2	151
Box Elder Creek, stm., Co., U.S.	A6	113
Box Elder Creek, stm., Co., U.S.	A6	128
Boxford, Ma., U.S.	A5	128
Boxian, China	B4	34
Boxtel, Neth.	E7	12
Boyacá, dept., Col.	E6	84
Boyang, China	G5	34
Boyce, La., U.S.	C3	125
Boyceville, Wi., U.S.	C1	156
Boyd, Mn., U.S.	F2	130
Boyd, co., Ky., U.S.	B7	124
Boyd, co., Ne., U.S.	B7	134

Name	Map Ref.	Page
Boyer, stm., Ia., U.S.	C2	122
Boyertown, Pa., U.S.	F10	145
Boyle, Alta., Can.	B4	98
Boyle, Ms., U.S.	B3	131
Boyle, co., Ky., U.S.	C5	124
Boyne City, Mi., U.S.	C6	129
Boynton Beach, Fl., U.S.	F6	116
Boysen Reservoir, res., Wy., U.S.	C4	157
Boys Town, Ne., U.S.	g12	134
Bozeman, Mt., U.S.	E5	133
Bozen see Bolzano, Italy	C6	18
Bozhen, China	E4	32
Bra, Italy	E2	18
Brabant, prov., Bel.	G6	12
Brač, Otok, i., Cro.	F11	18
Bracciano, Lago di, l., Italy	G7	18
Bracebridge, Ont., Can.	B5	103
Bracken, co., Ky., U.S.	B5	124
Brackenridge, Pa., U.S.	h15	145
Braço do Norte, Braz.	E14	80
Brad, Rom.	C6	20
Braddock, Pa., U.S.	k14	145
Braddock Heights, Md., U.S.	B2	127
Bradenton, Fl., U.S.	E4	116
Bradford, Ar., U.S.	B4	111
Bradford, N.H., U.S.	D3	136
Bradford, Oh., U.S.	B1	142
Bradford, Pa., U.S.	C4	145
Bradford, R.I., U.S.	F2	146
Bradford, Tn., U.S.	A3	149
Bradford, Vt., U.S.	D4	152
Bradford, co., Fl., U.S.	C4	116
Bradford, co., Pa., U.S.	C8	145
Bradford [West Gwillimbury], Ont., Can.	C5	103
Bradley, Ar., U.S.	D2	111
Bradley, Il., U.S.	B6	120
Bradley, Me., U.S.	D4	126
Bradley, W.V., U.S.	D3	155
Bradley, co., Ar., U.S.	D3	111
Bradley, co., Tn., U.S.	D9	149
Bradley Beach, N.J., U.S.	C4	137
Brady, Tx., U.S.	D3	150
Braeside, Ont., Can.	B8	103
Braga, Port.	D3	16
Bragado, Arg.	H8	80
Bragança, Braz.	D9	76
Bragança, Port.	D5	16
Bragança Paulista, Braz.	G5	79
Braham, Mn., U.S.	E5	130
Brāhmanbāria, Bngl.	I14	44
Brahmapur, India	C8	46
Brahmaputra (Yarlung), stm., Asia	G15	44
Braich y Pwll, c., Wales, U.K.	I9	8
Braidwood, Austl.	J8	70
Braidwood, Il., U.S.	B5	120
Brăila, Rom.	D11	20
Braine-l'Alleud (Eigenbrakel), Bel.	G5	12
Braine-le-Comte ('s-Gravenbrakel), Bel.	G5	12
Brainerd, Mn., U.S.	D4	130
Braintree, Ma., U.S.	B5	128
Brakwater, Nmb.	D3	66
Brampton, Ont., Can.	D5	103
Bramsche, Ger.	C7	10
Bramwell, W.V., U.S.	D3	155
Branch, co., Mi., U.S.	G5	129
Branchland, W.V., U.S.	C2	155
Branch Village, R.I., U.S.	B3	146
Branchville, S.C., U.S.	E6	147
Branco, stm., Braz.	H12	84
Brandberg, mtn., Nmb.	C2	66
Brandenburg, Ger.	C12	10
Brandenburg, Ky., U.S.	C3	124
Brandenburg, state, Ger.	C13	10
Brandon, Man., Can.	E2	100
Brandon, Fl., U.S.	E4	116
Brandon, Ms., U.S.	C4	131
Brandon, S.C., U.S.	B3	147
Brandon, S.D., U.S.	D9	148
Brandon, Vt., U.S.	D2	152
Brandsen, Arg.	H9	80
Brandvlei, S. Afr.	H5	66
Brandýs nad Labem, Czech Rep.	E14	10
Brandywine, Md., U.S.	C4	127
Branford, Ct., U.S.	D4	114
Branford Hills, Ct., U.S.	D4	114
Braniewo, Pol.	A19	10
Bransfield Strait, strt., Ant.	B12	73
Br'ansk, Russia	H17	22
Branson, Mo., U.S.	E4	132
Brantford, Ont., Can.	D4	103
Brantley, Al., U.S.	D3	108
Brantley, co., Ga., U.S.	E4	117
Brant Rock, Ma., U.S.	B6	128
Brantville, N.B., Can.	B5	101
Branxholme, Austl.	K4	70
Bras-d'Or, N.S., Can.	C9	101
Bras d'Or Lake, l., N.S., Can.	D9	101
Brasiléia, Braz.	D7	82
Brasília, Braz.	C5	79
Brasília de Minas, Braz.	D6	79
Brașov, Rom.	D9	20
Brasstown Bald, mtn., Ga., U.S.	B3	117
Bratislava, Slvk.	G17	10
Bratsk, Russia	F12	28
Bratskoje vodochranilišče, res., Russia	F18	26
Brattleboro, Vt., U.S.	F3	152
Braunau [am Inn], Aus.	G13	10
Braunschweig (Brunswick), Ger.	C10	10
Brava, Costa, Spain	D15	16
Brava, Punta, c., Ur.	H10	80
Bravo del Norte (Rio Grande), stm., N.A.	F6	106
Brawley, Ca., U.S.	F6	112
Brawley Peaks, mts., Nv., U.S.	E3	135
Braxton, co., W.V., U.S.	C4	155
Bray, Ire.	H7	8
Bray, Ok., U.S.	C4	143
Braymer, Mo., U.S.	B4	132
Brazeau, stm., Alta., Can.	C2	98
Brazil, In., U.S.	E3	121
Brazil (Brasil), ctry., S.A.	F8	76
Brazoria, co., Tx., U.S.	E5	150
Brazos, co., Tx., U.S.	D4	150
Brazos, stm., Tx., U.S.	D4	150
Brazzaville, Congo	B3	58
Brčko, Bos.	E2	20
Brea, Ca., U.S.	n13	112
Bread Loaf Mountain, mtn., Vt., U.S.	D3	152
Brea Pozo, Arg.	E7	80
Breathitt, co., Ky., U.S.	C6	124
Breaux Bridge, La., U.S.	D4	125
Breaza, Rom.	D9	20
Brechin, Scot., U.K.	E11	8
Breckenridge, Co., U.S.	B4	113
Breckenridge, Mi., U.S.	E6	129
Breckenridge, Mn., U.S.	D2	130
Breckenridge, Tx., U.S.	C3	150
Breckinridge, co., Ky., U.S.	C3	124
Brecksville, Oh., U.S.	A4	142
Břeclav, Czech Rep.	G16	10
Brecon, Wales, U.K.	J10	8
Breda, Neth.	E6	12
Bredasdorp, S. Afr.	J5	66
Bredenbury, Sask., Can.	G4	105
Breese, Il., U.S.	E4	120
Bregenz, Aus.	H9	10
Breidafjördur, b., Ice.	B2	6a
Brejo, Braz.	D10	76
Brejões, Braz.	B9	79
Bremen, Ger.	B8	10
Bremen, Ga., U.S.	C1	117
Bremen, In., U.S.	B5	121
Bremer, co., Ia., U.S.	B5	122
Bremerhaven, Ger.	B8	10
Bremerton, Wa., U.S.	B3	154
Brenham, Tx., U.S.	D4	150
Brenner Pass, Eur.	H11	10
Brent, Al., U.S.	C2	108
Brent, Fl., U.S.	u14	116
Brenton Point, c., R.I., U.S.	F5	146
Brentwood, Ca., U.S.	h9	112
Brentwood, Md., U.S.	f9	127
Brentwood, Mo., U.S.	f13	132
Brentwood, N.H., U.S.	E4	136
Brentwood, N.Y., U.S.	E7	139
Brentwood, Pa., U.S.	k14	145
Brentwood, S.C., U.S.	k11	147
Brentwood, Tn., U.S.	A5	149
Brescia, Italy	D8	18
Breslau see Wrocław, Pol.	D17	10
Bressuire, Fr.	F6	14
Brest, Bela.	C23	10
Brest, Fr.	D2	14
Bretagne (Brittany), hist. reg., Fr.	D3	14
Breteuil, Fr.	C9	14
Breton, Alta., Can.	C3	98
Breton Islands, is., La., U.S.	E6	125
Breton Sound, strt., La., U.S.	E6	125
Brett, Cape, c., N.Z.	A5	72
Bretten, Ger.	F8	10
Breukelen, Neth.	D7	12
Brevard, N.C., U.S.	f10	140
Brevard, co., Fl., U.S.	E6	116
Breves, Braz.	D8	76
Brewarrina, Austl.	G7	70
Brewer, Me., U.S.	D4	126
Brewster, Oh., U.S.	B4	142
Brewster, Wa., U.S.	A6	154
Brewster, co., Tx., U.S.	E1	150
Brewster, Kap, c., Grnld.	B17	86
Brewster Islands, is., Ma., U.S.	g12	128
Brewton, Al., U.S.	D2	108
Bria, Cen. Afr. Rep.	N1	60
Briançon, Fr.	H13	14
Briare, Fr.	E9	14
Briceni, Mol.	A11	20
Briceville, Tn., U.S.	C9	149
Brick [Township], N.J., U.S.	C4	137
Bridgehampton, N.Y., U.S.	n16	139
Bridgeport, Al., U.S.	A4	108
Bridgeport, Ct., U.S.	E3	114
Bridgeport, Il., U.S.	E6	120
Bridgeport, Mi., U.S.	E7	129
Bridgeport, Ne., U.S.	C2	134
Bridgeport, Oh., U.S.	B5	142
Bridgeport, Pa., U.S.	o20	145
Bridgeport, Tx., U.S.	C4	150
Bridgeport, Wa., U.S.	B6	154
Bridgeport, W.V., U.S.	B4	155
Bridger, Mt., U.S.	E8	133
Bridgeton, Mo., U.S.	C7	132
Bridgeton, N.J., U.S.	E2	137
Bridgetown, Austl.	F3	68
Bridgetown, Barb.	H15	94
Bridgetown, N.S., Can.	E4	101
Bridgeville, De., U.S.	F3	115
Bridgeville, Pa., U.S.	k13	145
Bridgewater, N.S., Can.	E5	101
Bridgewater, Me., U.S.	B5	126
Bridgewater, Ma., U.S.	C6	128
Bridgewater, N.J., U.S.	B3	137
Bridgewater, S.D., U.S.	D8	148
Bridgewater, Vt., U.S.	D3	152
Bridgewater, Va., U.S.	B4	153
Bridgman, Mi., U.S.	G4	129
Bridgton, Me., U.S.	D2	126
Bridgwater, Eng., U.K.	J10	8
Brielle, N.J., U.S.	C4	137
Brienne-le-Château, Fr.	D11	14
Brienz, Switz.	E9	13
Brienzersee, l., Switz.	E9	13
Briery Knob, mtn., W.V., U.S.	C4	155
Briey, Fr.	C12	14
Brig, Switz.	F9	13
Brigantine, N.J., U.S.	E4	137
Brigham City, Ut., U.S.	B3	151
Bright, Austl.	K7	70
Brighton, Ont., Can.	C7	103
Brighton, Eng., U.K.	K13	8
Brighton, Al., U.S.	B3	108
Brighton, Co., U.S.	B6	113
Brighton, Il., U.S.	D3	120
Brighton, Ia., U.S.	C6	122
Brighton, Mi., U.S.	F7	129
Brighton, N.Y., U.S.	B3	139
Brighton, Tn., U.S.	B2	149
Brignoles, Fr.	I13	14
Brikama, Gam.	E1	64
Brilliant, Al., U.S.	A2	108
Brillion, Wi., U.S.	D5	156
Brilon, Ger.	D8	10
Brindisi, Italy	I12	18
Brinkley, Ar., U.S.	C4	111
Brinnon, Wa., U.S.	B3	154
Brioude, Fr.	G10	14
Brisbane, Austl.	F10	70
Briscoe, co., Tx., U.S.	B2	150
Bristol, N.B., Can.	C2	101
Bristol, Eng., U.K.	J11	8
Bristol, Co., U.S.	C8	113
Bristol, Ct., U.S.	C4	114
Bristol, In., U.S.	A6	121
Bristol, N.H., U.S.	C3	136
Bristol, R.I., U.S.	D5	146
Bristol, S.D., U.S.	B8	148
Bristol, Tn., U.S.	C11	149
Bristol, Vt., U.S.	C2	152
Bristol, Va., U.S.	f9	153
Bristol, co., Ma., U.S.	C5	128
Bristol, co., R.I., U.S.	D5	146
Bristol Bay, b., Ak., U.S.	D7	109
Bristol [Township], Pa., U.S.	F12	145
Bristow, Ok., U.S.	B5	143
Britânia, Braz.	C3	79
Britannia Beach, B.C., Can.	E6	99
British Antarctic Territory, dep., S.A.	B1	73
British Columbia, prov., Can.	C6	99
British Honduras see Belize, ctry., N.A.	I15	90
British Indian Ocean Territory, dep., Afr.	J8	24
British Virgin Islands, dep., N.A.	E12	94
Brits, S. Afr.	E8	66
Britstown, S. Afr.	H6	66
Britt, Ia., U.S.	A4	122
Brittany see Bretagne, hist. reg., Fr.	D3	14
Britton, S.D., U.S.	B8	148
Brive-la-Gaillarde, Fr.	G8	14
Brno, Czech Rep.	F16	10
Broad, stm., S.C., U.S.	C5	147
Broad Brook, Ct., U.S.	B5	114
Broadkill Beach, De., U.S.	E5	115
Broadus, Mt., U.S.	E11	133
Broadview, Sask., Can.	G4	105
Broadview Heights, Oh., U.S.	h9	142
Broadwater, co., Mt., U.S.	D5	133
Broadway, Va., U.S.	B4	153
Brocēni, Lat.	E5	22
Brochet, Man., Can.	f7	100
Brockport, N.Y., U.S.	B3	139
Brockton, Ma., U.S.	B5	128
Brockton, Mt., U.S.	B12	133
Brockville, Ont., Can.	C9	103
Brockway, Pa., U.S.	D4	145
Brodhead, Ky., U.S.	C5	124
Brodhead, Wi., U.S.	F4	156
Brodnica, Pol.	B19	10
Broken Arrow, Ok., U.S.	A6	143
Broken Bow, Ne., U.S.	C6	134
Broken Bow, Ok., U.S.	C7	143
Broken Bow Lake, res., Ok., U.S.	C7	143
Broken Hill, Austl.	H4	70
Brokopondo Stuwmeer, res., Sur.	C7	76
Bromptonville, Que., Can.	D6	104
Bronnicy, Russia	F21	22
Bronson, Mi., U.S.	G5	129
Bronx, co., N.Y., U.S.	E7	139
Bronxville, N.Y., U.S.	h13	139
Brook, In., U.S.	C3	121
Brooke, co., W.V., U.S.	A4	155
Brookfield, N.S., Can.	D6	101
Brookfield, Ct., U.S.	D2	114
Brookfield, Il., U.S.	k9	120
Brookfield, Ma., U.S.	B3	128
Brookfield, Mo., U.S.	B4	132
Brookfield, Wi., U.S.	m11	156
Brookfield Center, Ct., U.S.	D2	114
Brookhaven, Ms., U.S.	D3	131
Brookhaven, W.V., U.S.	h11	155
Brookings, Or., U.S.	E2	144
Brookings, S.D., U.S.	C9	148
Brookings, co., S.D., U.S.	C9	148
Brookland, Ar., U.S.	B5	111
Brooklet, Ga., U.S.	D5	117
Brookline, Ma., U.S.	B5	128
Brookline, N.H., U.S.	E3	136
Brooklyn, N.S., Can.	E5	101
Brooklyn, Ct., U.S.	B8	114
Brooklyn, In., U.S.	E5	121
Brooklyn, Ia., U.S.	C5	122
Brooklyn, Ms., U.S.	D4	131
Brooklyn, Oh., U.S.	h9	142
Brooklyn, S.C., U.S.	B6	147
Brooklyn Center, Mn., U.S.	E5	130
Brooklyn Park, Md., U.S.	h11	127
Brooklyn Park, Mn., U.S.	m12	130
Brookneal, Va., U.S.	C4	153
Brook Park, Oh., U.S.	h9	142
Brookport, Il., U.S.	F5	120
Brooks, Alta., Can.	D5	98
Brooks, Ky., U.S.	g11	124
Brooks, Me., U.S.	D3	126
Brooks, co., Ga., U.S.	F3	117
Brooks, co., Tx., U.S.	F3	150
Brookside, Al., U.S.	f7	108
Brookside, De., U.S.	B3	115
Brooks Range, mts., Ak., U.S.	B9	109
Brookston, In., U.S.	C4	121
Brooksville, Fl., U.S.	D4	116
Brooksville, Ky., U.S.	B5	124
Brooksville, Ms., U.S.	B5	131
Brookville, In., U.S.	F8	121
Brookville, Oh., U.S.	C1	142
Brookville, Pa., U.S.	D3	145
Brookville Lake, res., In., U.S.	E7	121
Brookwood, Al., U.S.	B2	108
Brookwood, N.J., U.S.	C4	137
Broomall, Pa., U.S.	p20	145
Broome, Austl.	C4	68
Broome, co., N.Y., U.S.	C5	139
Broomfield, Co., U.S.	B5	113
Brossard, Que., Can.	q20	104
Brou, Fr.	D8	14
Broussard, La., U.S.	D4	125
Broward, co., Fl., U.S.	F6	116
Browerville, Mn., U.S.	D4	130
Brown, co., Il., U.S.	D3	120
Brown, co., In., U.S.	F5	121
Brown, co., Ks., U.S.	C8	123
Brown, co., Mn., U.S.	F4	130
Brown, co., Ne., U.S.	B6	134
Brown, co., Oh., U.S.	D2	142
Brown, co., S.D., U.S.	B7	148
Brown, co., Tx., U.S.	D3	150
Brown, co., Wi., U.S.	D6	156
Brown City, Mi., U.S.	E8	129
Brown Deer, Wi., U.S.	m12	156
Brownfield, Tx., U.S.	C1	150
Browning, Mt., U.S.	B3	133
Brownlee Reservoir, res., U.S.	C10	144
Brownsburg, Que., Can.	D3	104
Brownsburg, In., U.S.	E5	121
Brownsdale, Mn., U.S.	G6	130
Browns Mills, N.J., U.S.	D3	137
Brownstown, In., U.S.	G5	121
Browns Valley, Mn., U.S.	E2	130
Brownsville, Fl., U.S.	s13	116
Brownsville, Ky., U.S.	C3	124
Brownsville, Or., U.S.	C4	144
Brownsville, Pa., U.S.	F2	145
Brownsville, Tn., U.S.	B2	149
Brownsville, Tx., U.S.	G4	150
Brownton, Mn., U.S.	F4	130
Brownton, W.V., U.S.	B4	155
Brownville, Me., U.S.	C3	126
Brownville Junction, Me., U.S.	C3	126
Brownwood, Tx., U.S.	D3	150
Broxton, Ga., U.S.	E4	117
Bruay-en-Artois, Fr.	B9	14
Bruce, Ms., U.S.	B4	131
Bruce, Mount, mtn., Austl.	D3	68
Bruce Peninsula, pen., Ont., Can.	B3	103
Bruceton, Tn., U.S.	A3	149
Bruchsal, Ger.	F8	10
Bruck an der Mur, Aus.	H15	10
Bruderheim, Alta., Can.	C4	98
Brugg, Switz.	D9	13
Brugge (Bruges), Bel.	F3	12
Brugge-Gent, Kanaal, Bel.	F3	12
Brühl, Ger.	E6	10
Brule, Ne., U.S.	C4	134
Brule, co., S.D., U.S.	D6	148
Brumadinho, Braz.	F6	79
Brumado, Braz.	C8	79
Brumath, Fr.	D14	14
Brundidge, Al., U.S.	D4	108
Bruneau, stm., U.S.	G3	119
Brunei, ctry., Asia	E5	38
Bruno, Sask., Can.	E3	105
Brunswick see Braunschweig, Ger.	C10	10
Brunswick, Ga., U.S.	E5	117
Brunswick, Me., U.S.	E3	126
Brunswick, Md., U.S.	B2	127
Brunswick, Mo., U.S.	B4	132
Brunswick, Oh., U.S.	A4	142
Brunswick, co., N.C., U.S.	C4	140
Brunswick, co., Va., U.S.	D5	153
Brunswick, Peninsula, pen., Chile	G2	78
Bruntál, Czech Rep.	F17	10
Brus, Laguna de, b., Hond.	B10	92
Brush, Co., U.S.	A7	113
Brus Laguna, Hond.	B10	92
Brusly, La., U.S.	D4	125
Brusque, Braz.	D14	80
Brussels see Bruxelles, Bel.	G5	12
Brussels, Ont., Can.	D3	103
Bruxelles (Brussel) (Brussels), Bel.	G5	12
Bruyères, Fr.	D13	14
Bryan, Oh., U.S.	A1	142
Bryan, Tx., U.S.	D4	150
Bryan, co., Ga., U.S.	D5	117
Bryan, co., Ok., U.S.	D5	143
Bryansk see Br'ansk, Russia	H17	22
Bryans Road, Md., U.S.	C3	127
Bryant, Ar., U.S.	C3	111
Bryant, S.D., U.S.	C8	148
Bryant Pond, Me., U.S.	D2	126
Bryce Canyon National Park, Ut., U.S.	F3	151
Bryn Mawr, Wa., U.S.	e11	154
Brzeg, Pol.	E17	10
B-Say-Tah, Sask., Can.	G4	105
Buba, Gui.-B.	F2	64
Būbiyān, i., Kuw.	G10	48
Bucaramanga, Col.	D6	84
Buccaneer Archipelago, is., Austl.	C4	68
Buchanan, Sask., Can.	F4	105
Buchanan, Lib.	I4	64
Buchanan, Ga., U.S.	C1	117
Buchanan, Mi., U.S.	G4	129
Buchanan, Va., U.S.	C3	153
Buchanan, co., Ia., U.S.	B6	122
Buchanan, co., Mo., U.S.	B3	132
Buchanan, co., Va., U.S.	e9	153
Buchans, Newf., Can.	D3	102
Buchara, Uzb.	J10	26
Bucharest see București, Rom.	E10	20
Buchholz, Ger.	B9	10
Buchs, Switz.	D11	13
Buckatunna, Ms., U.S.	D5	131
Buckeye, Az., U.S.	D3	110
Buckeye Lake, Oh., U.S.	C3	142
Buckfield, Me., U.S.	D2	126
Buckhannon, W.V., U.S.	C4	155
Buckhaven, Scot., U.K.	E10	8
Buckie, Scot., U.K.	D11	8
Buckingham, Que., Can.	D2	104
Buckingham, co., Va., U.S.	C4	153
Buckinghamshire, co., Eng., U.K.	J13	8
Buckland, Ak., U.S.	B7	109
Buckley, Wa., U.S.	B3	154
Bucklin, Ks., U.S.	E4	123
Bucklin, Mo., U.S.	B5	132
Buck Mountain, mtn., Va., U.S.	D1	153
Buckner, Ar., U.S.	D2	111
Buckner, Mo., U.S.	h11	132
Bucks, co., Pa., U.S.	F11	145
Bucksport, Me., U.S.	D4	126
Bucksport, S.C., U.S.	D9	147
Bucoda, Wa., U.S.	C3	154
Bucun, China	G5	32
București (Bucharest), Rom.	E10	20
Bucyrus, Oh., U.S.	B3	142
Bud, W.V., U.S.	D3	155
Budapest, Hung.	H19	10
Budaun, India	F8	44
Bude, Ms., U.S.	D3	131
Budogošč', Russia	B15	22
Bud'onnovsk, Russia	I6	26
Budweis see České Budějovice, Czech Rep.	G14	10
Buea, Cam.	I14	64
Buena, N.J., U.S.	D3	137
Buena, Wa., U.S.	C5	154
Buena Esperanza, Arg.	H6	80
Buena Park, Ca., U.S.	n12	112
Buenaventura, Col.	F4	84
Buenaventura, Mex.	C6	90
Buena Vista, Bol.	G10	82
Buena Vista, Para.	D10	80
Buena Vista, Co., U.S.	C4	113
Buena Vista, Fl., U.S.	D4	116
Buena Vista, Ga., U.S.	D2	117
Buena Vista, Va., U.S.	C3	153
Buena Vista, co., Ia., U.S.	B2	122
Buenópolis, Braz.	D6	79
Buenos Aires, Arg.	H9	80
Buenos Aires, C.R.	H11	92
Buenos Aires, prov., Arg.	I8	80
Buenos Aires, Lago (Lago General Carrera), l., S.A.	F2	78
Buerarema, Braz.	C9	79
Buffalo, Ia., U.S.	C7	122
Buffalo, Mn., U.S.	E5	130
Buffalo, Mo., U.S.	D4	132
Buffalo, N.Y., U.S.	C2	139
Buffalo, Ok., U.S.	A2	143
Buffalo, S.C., U.S.	B4	147
Buffalo, S.D., U.S.	B2	148
Buffalo, W.V., U.S.	C3	155
Buffalo, Wi., U.S.	D2	156
Buffalo, Wy., U.S.	B6	157
Buffalo, co., Ne., U.S.	D6	134
Buffalo, co., S.D., U.S.	C6	148
Buffalo, co., Wi., U.S.	D2	156
Buffalo, stm., Ar., U.S.	B3	111
Buffalo, stm., Tn., U.S.	B4	149
Buffalo, stm., Wi., U.S.	D2	156
Buffalo Bill Reservoir, res., Wy., U.S.	B3	157
Buffalo Center, Ia., U.S.	A4	122
Buffalo Grove, Il., U.S.	h9	120
Buffalo Lake, Mn., U.S.	F4	130
Buford, Ga., U.S.	B2	117
Bug, stm., Eur.	E12	4
Buga, Col.	F4	84
Buga, Nig.	G13	64
Bugojno, Bos.	E12	18
Bugt, China	A8	32
Bugul'ma, Russia	G8	26
Buguruslan, Russia	G8	26
Buhl, Id., U.S.	G4	119
Buhl, Mn., U.S.	C6	130
Buhler, Ks., U.S.	D6	123
Buhuși, Rom.	C10	20
Buies Creek, N.C., U.S.	B4	140
Builth Wells, Wales, U.K.	I10	8
Buin, Chile	G3	80
Buir Nuur, l., Asia	B10	30
Buj, Russia	C24	22
Bujnaksk, Russia	I7	26
Bujumbura, Bdi.	B5	58
Bukačača, Russia	G15	28
Bukama, Zaire	C5	58
Būkān, Iran	C9	48
Bukavu, Zaire	B5	58
Bukittinggi, Indon.	O6	40
Bukovina, hist. reg., Eur.	B9	20
Bülach, Switz.	C10	13
Bulan, Ky., U.S.	C6	124
Bulandshahr, India	F7	44
Bulawayo, Zimb.	C9	66
Bulgan, Mong.	B7	30
Bulgaria (Bălgarija), ctry., Eur.	G13	4
Bulki, Eth.	N9	60
Bullas, Spain	G10	16
Buller, Mount, mtn., Austl.	K7	70
Bullfinch, Austl.	F3	68
Bullhead, S.D., U.S.	B4	148
Bullhead City, Az., U.S.	B1	110
Bullitt, co., Ky., U.S.	C4	124
Bulloch, co., Ga., U.S.	D5	117
Bullock, co., Al., U.S.	C4	108
Bulloo, stm., Austl.	G5	70
Bull Run, stm., Va., U.S.	g11	153
Bulls Bay, b., S.C., U.S.	F8	147
Bulls Gap, Tn., U.S.	C10	149
Bull Shoals, Ar., U.S.	A3	111
Bull Shoals Lake, res., U.S.	A3	111
Bulnes, Chile	I2	80
Bultfontein, S. Afr.	G8	66
Bumba, Zaire	A4	58
Bunbury, Austl.	F3	68
Buncombe, co., N.C., U.S.	f10	140
Bundaberg, Austl.	E10	70
Bünde, Ger.	C8	10
Būndi, India	H6	44
Bunia, Zaire	A6	58
Bunker Group, is., Austl.	D10	70
Bunker Hill, Il., U.S.	D4	120
Bunker Hill, In., U.S.	C5	121
Bunker Hill, W.V., U.S.	B6	155
Bunker Hill, W.V., U.S.	m12	155
Bunker Hill, mtn., Nv., U.S.	D4	135
Bunkerville, Nv., U.S.	G7	135
Bunkie, La., U.S.	D3	125
Bunnell, Fl., U.S.	C5	116
Bunyolo, Spain	F11	16
Buon Me Thuot, Viet.	H10	40
Buram, Sud.	L3	60
Buras, La., U.S.	E6	125
Buraydah, Sau. Ar.	H7	48
Burbank, Ca., U.S.	E4	112
Burbank, Il., U.S.	k9	120
Burbank, Wa., U.S.	C7	154
Burcher, Austl.	I7	70
Burco, Som.	G10	56
Burdekin, stm., Austl.	B7	70
Burden, Ks., U.S.	E7	123
Burdett, Alta., Can.	E5	98
Burdickville, R.I., U.S.	F2	146
Burdur, Tur.	H14	4
Bure, Eth.	L9	60
Bureau, co., Il., U.S.	B4	120
Büren, Ger.	D8	10
Burgas, Bul.	G11	20
Burgaw, N.C., U.S.	C5	140
Burg [bei Magdeburg], Ger.	C11	10
Burgdorf, Switz.	D8	13
Burgenland, state, Aus.	H16	10
Burgeo, Newf., Can.	E3	102
Burgersdorp, S. Afr.	H8	66
Burgin, Ky., U.S.	C5	124
Burgos, Spain	C8	16
Burgundy see Bourgogne, hist. reg., Fr.	E11	14
Burhaniye, Tur.	J10	20
Burhānpur, India	J7	44
Buri, Braz.	G4	79
Burica, Punta, c., N.A.	I12	92
Burin, Newf., Can.	E4	102
Burin Peninsula, pen., Newf., Can.	E4	102
Buri Ram, Thai.	G7	40
Buritama, Braz.	F3	79
Buriti Alegre, Braz.	E4	79
Buritizeiro, Braz.	D6	79
Burjassot, Spain	F11	16
Burjatija, state, Russia	G14	28
Burkburnett, Tx., U.S.	B3	150
Burke, S.D., U.S.	D6	148
Burke, co., Ga., U.S.	C4	117
Burke, co., N.C., U.S.	B1	140
Burke, co., N.D., U.S.	A3	141
Burke Channel, strt., B.C., Can.	C4	99
Burkesville, Ky., U.S.	D4	124
Burketown, Austl.	A3	70
Burkina Faso, ctry., Afr.	F6	54
Burk's Falls, Ont., Can.	B5	103
Burleigh, co., N.D., U.S.	C5	141
Burleson, Tx., U.S.	n9	150
Burleson, co., Tx., U.S.	D4	150
Burley, Id., U.S.	G5	119
Burlingame, Ca., U.S.	h8	112
Burlingame, Ks., U.S.	D8	123
Burlington, Newf., Can.	D3	102
Burlington, Ont., Can.	D5	103
Burlington, Co., U.S.	B8	113
Burlington, Ia., U.S.	D6	122
Burlington, Ks., U.S.	D8	123
Burlington, Ky., U.S.	A5	124
Burlington, Me., U.S.	C4	126
Burlington, Ma., U.S.	f11	128
Burlington, N.J., U.S.	C3	137
Burlington, N.C., U.S.	A3	140
Burlington, N.D., U.S.	A4	141
Burlington, Vt., U.S.	C2	152
Burlington, Wa., U.S.	A3	154
Burlington, Wi., U.S.	F5	156
Burlington, Wy., U.S.	B4	157
Burlington, co., N.J., U.S.	D3	137
Burlington Beach, In., U.S.	B3	121
Burlington Junction, Mo., U.S.	A2	132
Burma see Myanmar, ctry., Asia	A2	38
Burnaby, B.C., Can.	E6	99
Burnet, Tx., U.S.	D3	150
Burnet, co., Tx., U.S.	D3	150
Burnett, co., Wi., U.S.	C1	156
Burnham, Pa., U.S.	E6	145
Burnie, Austl.	M6	70
Burnley, Eng., U.K.	H11	8
Burns, Or., U.S.	D7	144
Burns, Tn., U.S.	A4	149
Burns, Wy., U.S.	E8	157
Burns Flat, Ok., U.S.	B2	143
Burnside, Ky., U.S.	D5	124
Burns Lake, B.C., Can.	B5	99
Burnsville, Mn., U.S.	F5	130
Burnsville, Ms., U.S.	A5	131
Burnsville, N.C., U.S.	f10	140
Burnsville, W.V., U.S.	C4	155
Burnt Islands, Newf., Can.	E2	102
Burnt Mills, Lake, l., Va., U.S.	k14	153
Burra, Austl.	I3	70
Burrton, Ks., U.S.	D6	123
Bursa, Tur.	I13	20
Būr Safājah, Egypt	D7	60
Būr Sa'īd (Port Said), Egypt	B7	60
Burstall, Sask., Can.	G1	105
Būr Sūdān (Port Sudan), Sud.	H9	60
Burt, co., Ne., U.S.	C9	134
Burt Lake, l., Mi., U.S.	C6	129
Burton, Mi., U.S.	F7	129
Burtts Corner, N.B., Can.	C3	101
Buru, i., Indon.	F8	38
Burundi, ctry., Afr.	B6	58
Burwell, Ne., U.S.	C6	134
Bury, Que., Can.	D6	104
Buryatia see Burjatija, state, Russia	G14	28
Bury Saint Edmunds, Eng., U.K.	I14	8
Busby, Mt., U.S.	E10	133
Bushkill, Pa., U.S.	D11	145
Bushnell, Fl., U.S.	D4	116
Bushnell, Il., U.S.	C3	120
Bushtyna, Ukr.	A7	20
Busko Zdrój, Pol.	E20	10
Busselton, Austl.	F3	68
Bussum, Neth.	D7	12
Busto Arsizio, Italy	D3	18
Buta, Zaire	H5	56
Butajira, Eth.	M10	60
Butare, Rw.	B5	58
Bute Inlet, b., B.C., Can.	D5	99
Butha Qi, China	B11	30
Butiá, Braz.	F13	80
Butler, Al., U.S.	C1	108
Butler, Ga., U.S.	D2	117
Butler, In., U.S.	B8	121
Butler, Ky., U.S.	B5	124
Butler, Mo., U.S.	C3	132
Butler, N.J., U.S.	B4	137
Butler, Pa., U.S.	E2	145
Butler, Wi., U.S.	m11	156
Butler, co., Al., U.S.	D3	108
Butler, co., Ia., U.S.	B5	122
Butler, co., Ks., U.S.	E7	123
Butler, co., Ky., U.S.	C3	124
Butler, co., Mo., U.S.	E7	132
Butler, co., Ne., U.S.	C8	134
Butler, co., Oh., U.S.	C1	142
Butler, co., Pa., U.S.	E2	145
Butner, N.C., U.S.	A4	140
Butru, Austl.	C3	70

Name	Map Ref.	Page
Butte, Mt., U.S.	E4	133
Butte, Ne., U.S.	B7	134
Butte, co., Ca., U.S.	C3	112
Butte, co., Id., U.S.	F5	119
Butte, co., S.D., U.S.	C2	148
Butte des Morts, Lake, l., Wi., U.S.	D5	156
Butte du Lion, hist., Bel.	G5	12
Butterworth, Malay.	L6	40
Butts, co., Ga., U.S.	C3	117
Butuan, Phil.	D8	38
Butzbach, Ger.	E8	10
Buurgplaatz, mtn., Lux.	H9	12
Buxtehude, Ger.	B9	10
Buxton, N.C., U.S.	B7	140
Buxton, N.D., U.S.	B8	141
Buzançais, Fr.	F8	14
Buzău, Rom.	D10	20
Búzi, stm., Moz.	B12	66
Buzuluk, Russia	G8	26
Buzzards Bay, Ma., U.S.	C6	128
Buzzards Bay, b., Ma., U.S.	C6	128
Bychov, Bela.	H13	22
Bydgoszcz, Pol.	B18	10
Byelorussia see Belarus, ctry., Eur.	E13	4
Byers, Co., U.S.	B6	113
Byesville, Oh., U.S.	C4	142
Byhalia, Ms., U.S.	A4	131
Bylas, Az., U.S.	D5	110
Bylot Island, i., N.W. Ter., Can.	B17	96
Byng, Ok., U.S.	C5	143
Byrdstown, Tn., U.S.	C8	149
Byron, Ga., U.S.	D3	117
Byron, Il., U.S.	A4	120
Byron, Mn., U.S.	F6	130
Byron, Wy., U.S.	B4	157
Byron, Cape, c., Austl.	G10	70
Byron Bay, Austl.	G10	70
Bytom (Beuthen), Pol.	E18	10
Bytoš', Russia	H17	22

C

Name	Map Ref.	Page
Caacupé, Para.	C10	80
Caaguazú, Para.	C10	80
Caaguazú, dept., Para.	C11	80
Caála, Ang.	D3	58
Caapucú, Para.	D10	80
Caarapó, Braz.	G1	79
Caazapá, Para.	D10	80
Caazapá, dept., Para.	D10	80
Cabaiguán, Cuba	C5	94
Caballo Reservoir, res., N.M., U.S.	E2	138
Cabana, Peru	C2	82
Cabanatuan, Phil.	n19	39b
Cabano, Que., Can.	B9	104
Cabarrus, co., N.C., U.S.	B2	140
Cabeceiras, Braz.	C5	79
Cabedelo, Braz.	E12	76
Cabell, co., W.V., U.S.	C2	155
Cabezas, Bol.	H10	82
Cabildo, Arg.	J8	80
Cabimas, Ven.	B7	84
Cabin Creek, W.V., U.S.	m13	155
Cabinda, Ang.	C2	58
Cabinda, dept., Ang.	C2	58
Cabinet Gorge Reservoir, res., U.S.	B1	133
Cabinet Mountains, mts., Mt., U.S.	B1	133
Cabin John, Md., U.S.	C3	127
Cabo, Braz.	E11	76
Cabo Frio, Braz.	G7	79
Cabo Gracias a Dios, Nic.	C11	92
Cabool, Mo., U.S.	D5	132
Caboolture, Austl.	F10	70
Cabora Bassa Dam, Moz.	E6	58
Caborca, Mex.	B3	90
Cabot, Ar., U.S.	C3	111
Cabot, Vt., U.S.	C4	152
Cabot Strait, strt., Can.	G20	96
Cabra, Spain	H7	16
Cabri, Sask., Can.	G1	105
Cabuyal, C.R.	G9	92
Caçador, Braz.	D13	80
Čačak, Yugo.	F4	20
Cacaohatán, Mex.	C2	92
Caçapava, Braz.	G6	79
Caçapava do Sul, Braz.	F12	80
Cacapon, stm., W.V., U.S.	B6	155
Cacequi, Braz.	E11	80
Cáceres, Braz.	G13	82
Cáceres, Col.	D5	84
Cáceres, Spain	F5	16
Cacharí, Arg.	I9	80
Cache, Ok., U.S.	C3	143
Cache, co., Ut., U.S.	B4	151
Cache, stm., Ar., U.S.	C4	111
Cache Bay, Ont., Can.	A5	103
Cache Creek, B.C., Can.	D7	99
Cache la Poudre, stm., Co., U.S.	A5	113
Cache Peak, mtn., Id., U.S.	G5	119
Cacheu, Gui.-B.	E1	64
Cachí, Arg.	C5	80
Cachimbo, Serra do, mts., Braz.	C13	82
Cachoeira Alta, Braz.	E3	79
Cachoeira do Sul, Braz.	F12	80
Cachoeiras de Macacu, Braz.	G7	79
Cachoeiro de Itapemirim, Braz.	F8	79
Caconda, Ang.	D3	58
Caçu, Braz.	E3	79
Caculé, Braz.	C7	79
Čadan, Russia	G16	26
Caddo, Ok., U.S.	C5	143
Caddo, co., La., U.S.	B2	125
Caddo, co., Ok., U.S.	B3	143
Caddo, stm., Ar., U.S.	C2	111
Caddo Lake, res., U.S.	B2	125
Caddo Mountains, mtn., Ar., U.S.	C2	111
Caddo Valley, Ar., U.S.	C2	111
Cadereyta de Jiménez, Mex.	E9	90
Cadillac, Mi., U.S.	D5	129
Cádiz, Spain	I5	16
Cadiz, Ky., U.S.	D2	124
Cadiz, Oh., U.S.	B4	142
Cádiz, Golfo de, b., Eur.	I4	16
Cadott, Wi., U.S.	D2	156
Cadys Falls, Vt., U.S.	B3	152
Caen, Fr.	C6	14
Caesar Creek Lake, res., Oh., U.S.	C2	142
Cæsarea see Qesari, Ḥorbat, hist., Isr.	C3	50
Caetanópolis, Braz.	E6	79
Caeté, Braz.	E7	79
Caetité, Braz.	C7	79
Cafayate, Arg.	D6	80
Cagayan, stm., Phil.	I19	39b
Cagayan de Oro, Phil.	D7	38
Cagliari, Italy	J4	18
Cagnes, Fr.	I14	14
Čagoda, Russia	B18	22
Cagua, Ven.	B9	84
Caguas, P.R.	E11	94
Cahaba, stm., Al., U.S.	C2	108
Cahokia, Il., U.S.	E3	120
Cahors, Fr.	H8	14
Cahul, Mol.	H3	26
Caiapônia, Braz.	D3	79
Caibarién, Cuba	C5	94
Caicara de Orinoco, Ven.	D9	84
Caicara de Orinoco, Ven.	G11	88
Caicedonia, Col.	E5	84
Caicó, Braz.	E11	76
Caicos Islands, is., T./C. Is.	D9	94
Caicos Passage, strt., N.A.	C8	94
Cailloma, Peru	F6	82
Cairns, Austl.	A6	70
Cairo see Al-Qāhirah, Egypt	B6	60
Cairo, Ga., U.S.	F2	117
Cairo, Il., U.S.	F4	120
Cairo, Ne., U.S.	D7	134
Cajabamba, Peru	B2	82
Cajacay, Peru	D3	82
Cajamarca, Peru	B2	82
Cajamarca, dept., Peru	B2	82
Cajatambo, Peru	D3	82
Cajàzeiras, Braz.	E11	76
Čajkovskij, Russia	F8	26
Cajuru, Braz.	F5	79
Čakovec, Cro.	C11	18
Calabar, Nig.	I14	64
Calabasas, Ca., U.S.	m11	112
Calabozo, Ven.	C9	84
Calabria, prov., Italy	J11	18
Calahorra, Spain	C10	16
Calais, Fr.	B8	14
Calais, Me., U.S.	C5	126
Calais, Pas de (Strait of Dover), strt., Eur.	J15	8
Calama, Chile	B4	80
Calamar, Col.	B5	84
Călărași, Mol.	B12	20
Călărași, Rom.	E11	20
Calarcá, Col.	E5	84
Calatayud, Spain	D10	16
Calaveras, co., Ca., U.S.	C3	112
Calca, Peru	E6	82
Calcasieu, co., La., U.S.	D2	125
Calcasieu, stm., La., U.S.	D2	125
Calcasieu Lake, l., La., U.S.	E2	125
Calcasieu Pass, strt., La., U.S.	E2	125
Calceta, Ec.	H2	84
Calchaquí, Arg.	E8	80
Calçoene, Braz.	C8	76
Calcutta, India	I13	44
Caldas, Braz.	F5	79
Caldas, Col.	D5	84
Caldas, dept., Col.	E5	84
Caldas Novas, Braz.	D4	79
Caldera, Chile	D3	80
Calderwood, Tn., U.S.	D10	149
Caldwell, Ar., U.S.	B5	111
Caldwell, Id., U.S.	F2	119
Caldwell, Ks., U.S.	E6	123
Caldwell, N.J., U.S.	B4	137
Caldwell, Tx., U.S.	D4	150
Caldwell, co., Ky., U.S.	C2	124
Caldwell, co., La., U.S.	B3	125
Caldwell, co., Mo., U.S.	B3	132
Caldwell, co., N.C., U.S.	B1	140
Caldwell, co., Tx., U.S.	E4	150
Caledon, Ont., Can.	D5	103
Caledonia, Belize	H15	90
Caledonia, N.S., Can.	E4	101
Caledonia, Mn., U.S.	G7	130
Caledonia, Ms., U.S.	B5	131
Caledonia, co., Vt., U.S.	C4	152
Calella, Spain	D14	16
Calera, Al., U.S.	B3	108
Calera, Ok., U.S.	D5	143
Caleufú, Arg.	H6	80
Calexico, Ca., U.S.	F6	112
Calgary, Alta., Can.	D3	98
Calhan, Co., U.S.	B6	113
Calhoun, Ga., U.S.	B2	117
Calhoun, Ky., U.S.	C2	124
Calhoun, co., Al., U.S.	B4	108
Calhoun, co., Ar., U.S.	D3	111
Calhoun, co., Fl., U.S.	B1	116
Calhoun, co., Ga., U.S.	E2	117
Calhoun, co., Il., U.S.	D3	120
Calhoun, co., Ia., U.S.	B3	122
Calhoun, co., Mi., U.S.	F5	129
Calhoun, co., Ms., U.S.	B4	131
Calhoun, co., S.C., U.S.	D6	147
Calhoun, co., Tx., U.S.	E4	150
Calhoun, co., W.V., U.S.	C3	155
Calhoun City, Ms., U.S.	B4	131
Calhoun Falls, S.C., U.S.	C2	147
Cali, Col.	F4	84
Calico Rock, Ar., U.S.	A3	111
Calicut, India	G3	46
Caliente, Nv., U.S.	F7	135
California, Md., U.S.	D4	127
California, Mo., U.S.	C5	132
California, Pa., U.S.	F2	145
California, state, U.S.	D4	112
California, Golfo de, b., Mex.	D4	90
California Aqueduct, Ca., U.S.	E4	112
California City, Ca., U.S.	E5	112
Calilegua, Arg.	B6	80
Calimere, Point, c., India	G5	46
Calingasta, Arg.	F4	80
Calion, Ar., U.S.	D3	111
Callahan, co., Tx., U.S.	C3	150
Callao, Peru	E3	82
Callaway, Ne., U.S.	C6	134
Callaway, co., Mo., U.S.	C6	132
Callosa de Segura, Spain	G11	16
Calloway, co., Ky., U.S.	f9	124
Calmar, Alta., Can.	C4	98
Calmar, Ia., U.S.	A6	122
Calobre, Pan.	I14	92
Caloosahatchee, stm., Fl., U.S.	F5	116
Caloundra, Austl.	F10	70
Caltagirone, Italy	L9	18
Caltanissetta, Italy	L9	18
Calumet, co., Wi., U.S.	D5	156
Calumet, Lake, l., Il., U.S.	k9	120
Calumet City, Il., U.S.	B6	120
Calunda, Ang.	D4	58
Calvert, Al., U.S.	D1	108
Calvert, co., Md., U.S.	C4	127
Calvert City, Ky., U.S.	e9	124
Calvert Island, i., B.C., Can.	D3	99
Calverton, N.Y., U.S.	n16	139
Calverton Park, Mo., U.S.	f13	132
Calvi, Fr.	I23	15a
Calvillo, Mex.	G8	90
Calvinia, S. Afr.	H4	66
Calw, Ger.	G8	10
Camaçari, Braz.	B9	79
Camacupa, Ang.	D3	58
Camagüey, Cuba	D6	94
Camaiore, Italy	F5	18
Camajuaní, Cuba	C5	94
Camamu, Braz.	B9	79
Camaná, Peru	G5	82
Camanche, Ia., U.S.	C7	122
Camano Island, i., Wa., U.S.	A3	154
Camapuã, Braz.	E1	79
Camaquã, Braz.	F13	80
Camargo, Bol.	I9	82
Camargo, Mex.	D7	90
Camargue, reg., Fr.	I11	14
Camarillo, Ca., U.S.	E4	112
Camarón, Cabo, c., Hond.	A9	92
Camas, Spain	H5	16
Camas, Wa., U.S.	D3	154
Camas, co., Id., U.S.	F4	119
Ca Mau, Viet.	J8	40
Ca Mau, Mui, c., Viet.	J8	40
Cambará, Braz.	G3	79
Cambodia (Kâmpŭchéa), ctry., Asia	C4	38
Camboriú, Braz.	D14	80
Cambrai, Fr.	B10	14
Cambria, Ca., U.S.	E3	112
Cambria, co., Pa., U.S.	E4	145
Cambrian Mountains, mts., Wales, U.K.	I10	8
Cambridge, Ont., Can.	D4	103
Cambridge, N.Z.	B5	72
Cambridge, Eng., U.K.	I14	8
Cambridge, Id., U.S.	E2	119
Cambridge, Il., U.S.	B3	120
Cambridge, Ia., U.S.	C4	122
Cambridge, Md., U.S.	C5	127
Cambridge, Ma., U.S.	B5	128
Cambridge, Mn., U.S.	E5	130
Cambridge, Ne., U.S.	D5	134
Cambridge, Oh., U.S.	B4	142
Cambridge, Vt., U.S.	B3	152
Cambridge, Wi., U.S.	F4	156
Cambridge Bay, N.W. Ter., Can.	C11	96
Cambridge City, In., U.S.	E7	121
Cambridgeshire, co., Eng., U.K.	I13	8
Cambridge Springs, Pa., U.S.	C1	145
Cambuí, Braz.	G5	79
Camden, Austl.	J9	70
Camden, Al., U.S.	D2	108
Camden, Ar., U.S.	D3	111
Camden, De., U.S.	D3	115
Camden, In., U.S.	D3	126
Camden, Me., U.S.	C4	131
Camden, Ms., U.S.	D2	137
Camden, N.J., U.S.	B5	139
Camden, N.Y., U.S.	C1	142
Camden, Oh., U.S.	C6	147
Camden, S.C., U.S.	A3	149
Camden, Tn., U.S.	E4	150
Camden, co., Ga., U.S.	F5	117
Camden, co., Mo., U.S.	C5	132
Camden, co., N.J., U.S.	D3	137
Camden, co., N.C., U.S.	A6	140
Camdenton, Mo., U.S.	D5	132
Camelback Mountain, mtn., Az., U.S.	k9	110
Camels Hump, mtn., Vt., U.S.	C3	152
Camenca, Mol.	A12	20
Cameron, Az., U.S.	B4	110
Cameron, La., U.S.	E2	125
Cameron, Mo., U.S.	B3	132
Cameron, Tx., U.S.	D4	150
Cameron, W.V., U.S.	B4	155
Cameron, Wi., U.S.	C2	156
Cameron, co., La., U.S.	E2	125
Cameron, co., Pa., U.S.	D5	145
Cameron, co., Tx., U.S.	F4	150
Cameroon (Cameroun), ctry., Afr.	G9	54
Cameroon Mountain, mtn., Cam.	I14	64
Cametá, Braz.	D9	76
Camilla, Ga., U.S.	E2	117
Camiña, Chile	H7	82
Cammack Village, Ar., U.S.	C3	111
Camocim, Braz.	D10	76
Camooweal, Austl.	B3	70
Camp, co., Tx., U.S.	C5	150
Campana, Arg.	H9	80
Campania, prov., Italy	I9	18
Campbell, Ca., U.S.	k8	112
Campbell, Fl., U.S.	D5	116
Campbell, Mo., U.S.	E7	132
Campbell, Ne., U.S.	D7	134
Campbell, Oh., U.S.	A5	142
Campbell, co., Ky., U.S.	B5	124
Campbell, co., S.D., U.S.	B5	148
Campbell, co., Tn., U.S.	C9	149
Campbell, co., Va., U.S.	C3	153
Campbell, co., Wy., U.S.	B7	157
Campbell, Cape, c., N.Z.	D5	72
Campbellford, Ont., Can.	C7	103
Campbell Hill, hill, Oh., U.S.	B2	142
Campbell Island, i., N.Z.	N20	158
Campbellsburg, Ky., U.S.	B4	124
Campbellsport, Wi., U.S.	E5	156
Campbellsville, Ky., U.S.	C4	124
Campbellton, N.B., Can.	A3	101
Campbellton, Newf., Can.	D4	102
Campbelltown, Austl.	J9	70
Campeche, Mex.	H14	90
Campeche, state, Mex.	H14	90
Campeche, Bahía de, b., Mex.	H12	90
Campechuela, Cuba	D6	94
Camperdown, Austl.	L5	70
Camperville, Man., Can.	D1	100
Cam Pha, Viet.	D9	40
Camp Hill, Al., U.S.	C4	108
Camp Hill, Pa., U.S.	F8	145
Câmpina, Rom.	D9	20
Campina Grande, Braz.	E11	74
Campina Grande, Braz.	E11	76
Campinas, Braz.	G5	79
Campina Verde, Braz.	E4	79
Campion, Co., U.S.	A5	113
Camp Lejeune Marine Corps Base, mil., N.C., U.S.	C5	140
Campoalegre, Col.	F5	84
Campobasso, Italy	H9	18
Campobello Island, i., N.B., Can.	E3	101
Campo Belo, Braz.	F6	79
Campo de Criptana, Spain	F8	16
Campo Erê, Braz.	D12	80
Campo Gallo, Arg.	D7	80
Campo Grande, Arg.	D11	80
Campo Grande, Braz.	F1	79
Campo Largo, Arg.	D8	80
Campo Largo, Braz.	C14	80
Campo Maior, Braz.	D10	76
Campo Mourão, Braz.	H2	79
Campo Novo, Braz.	D12	80
Campo Quijano, Arg.	C6	80
Campos, Braz.	F8	79
Campos Altos, Braz.	E5	79
Campo Santo, Arg.	C6	80
Campos Belos, Braz.	B5	79
Campos do Jordão, Braz.	G6	79
Campos Gerais, Braz.	F6	79
Campos Novos, Braz.	D13	80
Camp Pendleton Marine Corps Base, mil., Ca., U.S.	F5	112
Camp Point, Il., U.S.	C2	120
Camp Springs, Md., U.S.	f9	127
Campti, La., U.S.	C2	125
Campton, N.H., U.S.	C3	136
Câmpulung, Rom.	D9	20
Câmpulung Moldovenesc, Rom.	B9	20
Camp Verde, Az., U.S.	C4	110
Cam Ranh, Viet.	I10	40
Camrose, Alta., Can.	C4	98
Canaan, Ct., U.S.	A2	114
Canaan, Me., U.S.	D3	126
Canaan, N.H., U.S.	C2	136
Canaan, Vt., U.S.	A5	152
Canaan Street, N.H., U.S.	C2	136
Canada, ctry., N.A.	D13	96
Cañada de Gómez, Arg.	G8	80
Canadian, co., Ok., U.S.	B3	143
Canadian, stm., U.S.	D6	106
Çanakkale, Tur.	I10	20
Çanakkale Boğazı (Dardanelles), strt., Tur.	I10	20
Canal Flats, B.C., Can.	D10	99
Canal Fulton, Oh., U.S.	B4	142
Canals, Arg.	G7	80
Canal Winchester, Oh., U.S.	C3	142
Canandaigua, N.Y., U.S.	C3	139
Canandaigua Lake, l., N.Y., U.S.	C3	139
Cananea, Mex.	B4	90
Cananéia, Braz.	C15	80
Canápolis, Braz.	E4	79
Cañar, Ec.	I3	84
Cañar, prov., Ec.	I3	84
Canarias, Islas (Canary Islands), is., Spain	o25	17b
Canary Islands see Canarias, Islas, is., Spain	C3	54
Cañas, C.R.	G9	92
Canastota, N.Y., U.S.	B5	139
Canatlán, Mex.	E7	90
Canaveral, Cape, c., Fl., U.S.	D6	116
Canaveral National Seashore, Fl., U.S.	D6	116
Canavieiras, Braz.	C9	79
Cañazas, Pan.	C2	84
Canberra, Austl.	J8	70
Canby, Mn., U.S.	F2	130
Canby, Or., U.S.	B4	144
Cancale, Fr.	D5	14
Cancún, Mex.	G16	90
Cancún, Punta, c., Mex.	D1	94
Candeias, Braz.	B9	79
Candeias, Braz.	F6	79
Candela, Mex.	D9	90
Candelaria, Arg.	D11	80
Candelaria, Arg.	G6	80
Candelária, Braz.	E12	80
Candia, N.H., U.S.	D4	136
Candiac, Que., Can.	q19	104
Cândido de Abreu, Braz.	C13	80
Candler, co., Ga., U.S.	D4	117
Candlewood, Lake, l., Ct., U.S.	D1	114
Candlewood Isle, Ct., U.S.	D2	114
Candlewood Shores, Ct., U.S.	D2	114
Cando, N.D., U.S.	A6	141
Cane, stm., La., U.S.	C2	125
Canela, Braz.	E13	80
Canelones, Ur.	H10	80
Cañete, Chile	I2	80
Caney, Ks., U.S.	E8	123
Caney Fork, stm., Tn., U.S.	C8	149
Canfield, Oh., U.S.	A5	142
Cangallo, Peru	E4	82
Cangkuang, Tanjung, c., Indon.	j12	39a
Canguçu, Braz.	F12	80
Cangzhou, China	E4	32
Canicattì, Italy	L8	18
Canindeyú, dept., Para.	C11	80
Canisteo, stm., N.Y., U.S.	C3	139
Canistota, S.D., U.S.	D8	148
Cañitas de Felipe Pescador, Mex.	F8	90
Canmore, Alta., Can.	D3	98
Cannelton, In., U.S.	I4	121
Cannelton, W.V., U.S.	m13	155
Cannes, Fr.	I14	14
Canning, N.S., Can.	D5	101
Cannon, co., Tn., U.S.	B5	149
Cannon, stm., Mn., U.S.	F5	130
Cannon Ball, N.D., U.S.	C5	141
Cannonball, stm., N.D., U.S.	C5	141
Cannon Beach, Or., U.S.	B3	144
Cannondale, Ct., U.S.	E2	114
Cannon Falls, Mn., U.S.	F6	130
Cannonsburg, Ky., U.S.	B7	124
Cannonsville Reservoir, res., N.Y., U.S.	C5	139
Canoas, Braz.	E13	80
Canoinhas, Braz.	D13	80
Canon, Ga., U.S.	B3	117
Canon City, Co., U.S.	C5	113
Canonsburg, Pa., U.S.	F1	145
Canora, Sask., Can.	F4	105
Canosa [di Puglia], Italy	H11	18
Canossa, hist., Italy	E5	18
Canowindra, Austl.	I8	70
Canso, N.S., Can.	D8	101
Cantabria, prov., Spain	B7	16
Cantábrica, Cordillera, mts., Spain	B6	16
Cantagalo, Braz.	F7	79
Cantaura, Ven.	C10	84
Canterbury, N.B., Can.	D2	101
Canterbury, Eng., U.K.	J15	8
Canterbury, De., U.S.	D3	115
Canterbury, N.H., U.S.	D3	136
Canterbury Bight, N.Z.	F4	72
Can Tho, Viet.	I8	40
Canton see Guangzhou, China	L2	34
Canton, Ct., U.S.	B4	114
Canton, Ga., U.S.	B2	117
Canton, Il., U.S.	C3	120
Canton, Ks., U.S.	D6	123
Canton, Me., U.S.	D2	126
Canton, Ma., U.S.	B5	128
Canton, Ms., U.S.	C3	131
Canton, Mo., U.S.	A6	132
Canton, N.Y., U.S.	f9	139
Canton, N.C., U.S.	f10	140
Canton, Oh., U.S.	B4	142
Canton, Pa., U.S.	C8	145
Canton, S.D., U.S.	D9	148
Canton, Tx., U.S.	C5	150
Cantonment, Fl., U.S.	u14	116
Cantù, Italy	D4	18
Cañuelas, Arg.	H9	80
Canutama, Braz.	B9	82
Canutillo, Tx., U.S.	o11	150
Canwood, Sask., Can.	D2	105
Canyon, Tx., U.S.	B2	150
Canyon, co., Id., U.S.	F2	119
Canyon City, Or., U.S.	C8	144
Canyon Creek, Alta., Can.	B3	98
Canyon de Chelly National Monument, Az., U.S.	A6	110
Canyon Ferry Lake, res., Mt., U.S.	D5	133
Canyon Lake, Tx., U.S.	E3	150
Canyonlands National Park, Ut., U.S.	E6	151
Canyonville, Or., U.S.	E3	144
Caoqiao, China	D8	34
Caoxian, China	I3	32
Cap, Pointe du, c., St. Luc.	G14	94
Capac, Mi., U.S.	F8	129
Čapajevsk, Russia	G7	26
Capanema, Braz.	C12	80
Capão Bonito, Braz.	H4	79
Capatárida, Ven.	B7	84
Cap-aux-Meules, Que., Can.	B8	101
Cap-de-la-Madeleine, Que., Can.	C5	104
Cape Barren Island, i., Austl.	M8	70
Cape Breton Island, i., N.S., Can.	C9	101
Cape Broyle, Newf., Can.	E5	102
Cape Canaveral, Fl., U.S.	D6	116
Cape Charles, Va., U.S.	C6	153
Cape Coast, Ghana	I9	64
Cape Cod Bay, b., Ma., U.S.	C7	128
Cape Cod Canal, Ma., U.S.	C6	128
Cape Cod National Seashore, Ma., U.S.	C7	128
Cape Coral, Fl., U.S.	F5	116
Cape Dorset, N.W. Ter., Can.	D17	96
Cape Elizabeth, Me., U.S.	E2	126
Cape Fear, stm., N.C., U.S.	C4	140
Cape Girardeau, Mo., U.S.	D8	132
Cape Girardeau, co., Mo., U.S.	D8	132
Cape Hatteras National Seashore, N.C., U.S.	B7	140
Capelinha, Braz.	D7	79
Capelle [aan den IJssel], Neth.	E6	12
Capelongo, Ang.	D3	58
Cape Lookout National Seashore, N.C., U.S.	C6	140
Cape May, N.J., U.S.	F3	137
Cape May, co., N.J., U.S.	E3	137
Cape May Court House, N.J., U.S.	E3	137
Cape Neddick, Me., U.S.	E2	126
Cape Porpoise, Me., U.S.	E2	126
Cape Ray, Newf., Can.	E2	102
Capernaum see Kefar Naḥum, hist., Isr.	C5	50
Cape Sable Island, i., N.S., Can.	F4	101
Cape Town (Kaapstad), S. Afr.	I4	66
Cape Verde (Cabo Verde), ctry., Afr.	E2	54
Cape York Peninsula, pen., Austl.	B8	68
Cap-Haïtien, Haiti	E8	94
Capilla del Monte, Arg.	F6	80
Capinópolis, Braz.	E4	79
Capinota, Bol.	G8	82
Capinzal, Braz.	D13	80
Capira, Pan.	C3	84
Capitan, N.M., U.S.	D4	138
Capitán Bado, Para.	B11	80
Capitán Bermúdez, Arg.	G8	80
Capitán Meza, Para.	D11	80
Capitan Peak, mtn., N.M., U.S.	D4	138
Capitán Sarmiento, Arg.	H9	80
Capitol Heights, Ia., U.S.	e8	122
Capitol Heights, Md., U.S.	C4	127
Capitol Reef National Park, Ut., U.S.	E4	151
Capivari, Braz.	G5	79
Čaplygin, Russia	H22	22
Cap-Pelé, N.B., Can.	C5	101
Capreol, Ont., Can.	p19	103
Capri, Isola di, i., Italy	I9	18
Capricorn, Cape, c., Austl.	D9	70
Capricorn Group, is., Austl.	D10	70
Caprivi Zipfel (Caprivi Strip), hist. reg., Nmb.	A6	66
Cap-Rouge, Que., Can.	n17	104
Cap-Saint-Ignace, Que., Can.	B7	104
Captain Cook, Hi., U.S.	D6	118
Captains Flat, Austl.	J8	70
Capua, Italy	H9	18
Caquetá, ter., Col.	G5	84
Caquetá (Japurá), stm., S.A.	H7	84
Carabobo, state, Ven.	J10	94
Caracal, Rom.	E8	20
Caracaraí, Braz.	G12	84
Caracas, Ven.	B9	84
Caraguatatuba, Braz.	G6	79
Caraguatay, Para.	C10	80
Carajás, Braz.	E8	76
Carandaí, Braz.	F7	79
Carangola, Braz.	F7	79
Caransebeş, Rom.	D6	20
Carapeguá, Para.	C10	80
Caraquet, N.B., Can.	B5	101
Caráquez, Ec.	H2	84
Caratasca, Laguna de, b., Hond.	B11	92
Caratinga, Braz.	E7	79
Carauari, Braz.	J9	84
Caravaca, Spain	G10	16
Caravelas, Braz.	D9	79
Caravelí, Peru	F5	82
Caraway, Ar., U.S.	B5	111
Caraz, Peru	C3	82
Carazinho, Braz.	E12	80
Carazo, dept., Nic.	F8	92
Carberry, Man., Can.	E2	100
Carbo, Mex.	C4	90
Carbon, Alta., Can.	D4	98
Carbon, co., Mt., U.S.	E7	133
Carbon, co., Pa., U.S.	E10	145
Carbon, co., Ut., U.S.	D5	151
Carbon, co., Wy., U.S.	E5	157
Carbondale, Co., U.S.	B3	113
Carbondale, Il., U.S.	F4	120
Carbondale, Ks., U.S.	D8	123
Carbondale, Pa., U.S.	C10	145
Carbonear, Newf., Can.	E5	102
Carbon Hill, Al., U.S.	B2	108
Carbonia, Italy	J3	18
Carbonville, Ut., U.S.	D5	151
Carcaixent, Spain	F11	16
Carcarañá, Arg.	G8	80
Carcassonne, Fr.	I9	14
Carchi, prov., Ec.	G3	84
Carcross, Yukon, Can.	D6	96
Cárdenas, Cuba	C4	94
Cárdenas, Mex.	I13	90
Cárdenas, Mex.	F10	90
Cardiff, Wales, U.K.	J10	8
Cardigan, P.E.I., Can.	C7	101
Cardigan Bay, b., Wales, U.K.	I9	8
Cardinal, Ont., Can.	C9	103
Cardona, Ur.	G10	80
Cardoso, Braz.	F4	79
Cardston, Alta., Can.	E4	98
Cardwell, Mo., U.S.	E7	132
Čardžou, Turk.	J10	26
Carei, Rom.	B6	20
Careiro, Braz.	I13	84
Carencro, La., U.S.	D3	125
Carentan, Fr.	C5	14
Caretta, W.V., U.S.	D3	155
Carey, Id., U.S.	F5	119
Carey, Oh., U.S.	B2	142
Carhaix-Plouguer, Fr.	D3	14
Carhuaz, Peru	C3	82
Carhué, Arg.	I7	80
Cariacica, Braz.	F8	79
Cariaco, Golfo de, b., Ven.	B10	84
Cariamanga, Ec.	J3	84
Caribbean Sea	G8	94
Cariboo Mountains, mts., B.C., Can.	C7	99
Caribou, Me., U.S.	B5	126
Caribou, co., Id., U.S.	G7	119
Caribou Mountain, mtn., Me., U.S.	C2	126
Carichic, Mex.	D6	90
Carievale, Sask., Can.	H5	105
Carignan, Fr.	C12	14
Carinhanha, Braz.	C7	79
Carini, Italy	K8	18
Caripe, Ven.	B11	84
Caripito, Ven.	B11	84
Carleton, Mi., U.S.	F7	129
Carleton, Mount, mtn., N.B., Can.	B3	101
Carleton Place, Ont., Can.	B8	103
Carlin, Nv., U.S.	C5	135
Carlinville, Il., U.S.	D4	120
Carlisle, Eng., U.K.	G11	8
Carlisle, Ar., U.S.	C4	111
Carlisle, In., U.S.	G3	121
Carlisle, Ia., U.S.	C4	122
Carlisle, Ky., U.S.	B5	124
Carlisle, Oh., U.S.	C1	142
Carlisle, Pa., U.S.	F7	145
Carlisle, co., Ky., U.S.	f8	124
Carl Junction, Mo., U.S.	D3	132
Carlópolis, Braz.	G4	79
Carlos Barbosa, Braz.	E13	80
Carlos Casares, Arg.	H8	80
Carlos Chagas, Braz.	D8	79
Carlos Pellegrini, Arg.	G8	80
Carlos Reyles, Ur.	G10	80
Carlos Tejedor, Arg.	H7	80

Name — Map Ref. — Page

Carlow, Ire. I7 8
Carlow, co., Ire. I7 8
Carlsbad see Karlovy Vary, Czech Rep. E12 10
Carlsbad, Ca., U.S. F5 112
Carlsbad, N.M., U.S. E5 138
Carlsbad Caverns National Park, N.M., U.S. E5 138
Carlstadt, N.J., U.S. h8 137
Carlton, Mn., U.S. D6 130
Carlton, Or., U.S. B3 144
Carlton, co., Mn., U.S. D6 130
Carlyle, Sask., Can. H4 105
Carlyle, Il., U.S. E4 120
Carlyle Lake, res., Il., U.S. E4 120
Carmacks, Yukon, Can. D5 96
Carmagnola, Italy E2 18
Carman, Man., Can. E2 100
Carmangay, Alta., Can. D4 98
Carmanville, Newf., Can. D4 102
Carmaux, Fr. H9 14
Carmel, Ca., U.S. D3 112
Carmel, In., U.S. E5 121
Carmel, Me., U.S. D3 126
Carmel, N.Y., U.S. D7 139
Carmel, Mount see Karmel, Har, mtn., Isr. C4 50
Carmelo, Ur. H9 80
Carmen, Ur. G10 80
Carmen, Isla, i., Mex. E4 90
Carmen, Isla del, i., Mex. H14 90
Carmen de Areco, Arg. H9 80
Carmen de Patagones, Arg. E4 78
Carmi, Il., U.S. E5 120
Carmo do Paranaíba, Braz. E5 79
Carmo do Rio Verde, Braz. C4 79
Carmona, Spain H6 16
Carmópolis de Minas, Braz. F6 79
Carnarvon, Austl. D2 68
Carnarvon, S. Afr. H6 66
Carnatic, hist. reg., India G10 42
Carnation, Wa., U.S. B4 154
Carnduff, Sask., Can. H5 105
Carnegie, Ok., U.S. B3 143
Carnegie, Pa., U.S. F1 145
Carnegie, Lake, l., Austl. E4 68
Carney, Md., U.S. B4 127
Carneys Point, N.J., U.S. D2 137
Carnoustie, Scot., U.K. E11 8
Carnsore Point, c., Ire. I7 8
Caro, Mi., U.S. E7 129
Carol City, Fl., U.S. s13 116
Carolina, Braz. E9 76
Carolina, R.I., U.S. F2 146
Carolina, W.V., U.S. k10 155
Carolina Beach, N.C., U.S. C5 140
Caroline, Alta., Can. C3 98
Caroline, co., Md., U.S. C6 127
Caroline, co., Va., U.S. C5 153
Caroline Islands, is., Oc. H18 158
Caroní, stm., Ven. C11 84
Carora, Ven. B7 84
Carouge, Switz. F5 13
Carpathian Mountains, mts., Eur. F12 4
Carpaţii Meridionali, mts., Rom. D8 20
Carpentaria, Gulf of, b., Austl. B7 68
Carpenter, Wy., U.S. E8 157
Carpentersville, Il., U.S. A5 120
Carpentras, Fr. H12 14
Carpi, Italy E5 18
Carpinteria, Ca., U.S. E4 112
Carrara, Italy E5 18
Carrauntoohil, mtn., Ire. J4 8
Carrboro, N.C., U.S. B3 140
Carriacou, i., Gren. H14 94
Carriere, Ms., U.S. E4 131
Carrier Mills, Il., U.S. F5 120
Carrigan, Mount, mtn., N.H., U.S. B4 136
Carrillo, C.R. H9 92
Carrington, N.D., U.S. B6 141
Carrington Island, i., Ut., U.S. C3 151
Carrizal Bajo, Chile E3 80
Carrizo Mountain, mtn., N.M., U.S. D4 138
Carrizozo, N.M., U.S. D4 138
Carroll, Ia., U.S. B3 122
Carroll, co., Ar., U.S. A2 111
Carroll, co., Ga., U.S. C1 117
Carroll, co., Il., U.S. A4 120
Carroll, co., In., U.S. C4 121
Carroll, co., Ia., U.S. B3 122
Carroll, co., Ky., U.S. B4 124
Carroll, co., Md., U.S. A3 127
Carroll, co., Ms., U.S. B4 131
Carroll, co., Mo., U.S. B4 132
Carroll, co., N.H., U.S. C4 136
Carroll, co., Oh., U.S. B4 142
Carroll, co., Tn., U.S. B3 149
Carroll, co., Va., U.S. D2 153
Carrollton, Al., U.S. B1 108
Carrollton, Ga., U.S. C1 117
Carrollton, Il., U.S. D3 120
Carrollton, Ky., U.S. B4 124
Carrollton, Mi., U.S. E7 129
Carrollton, Mo., U.S. B4 132
Carrollton, Oh., U.S. B4 142
Carrollton, Tx., U.S. n10 150
Carrot, stm., Can. D4 105
Carrot River, Sask., Can. D4 105
Carry Falls Reservoir, res., N.Y., U.S. f10 139
Čaršanga, Turk. B1 44
Carseland, Alta., Can. D4 98
Carson, Ia., U.S. C2 122
Carson, N.D., U.S. C4 141
Carson, Wa., U.S. D4 154
Carson, co., Tx., U.S. B2 150
Carson, stm., Nv., U.S. D2 135
Carson City, Mi., U.S. E6 129
Carson City, Nv., U.S. D2 135
Carson Lake, l., Nv., U.S. D3 135
Carson Sink, l., Nv., U.S. D3 135
Carson Spring, Tn., U.S. D10 149
Carstairs, Alta., Can. D3 98
Cartagena, Chile G3 80
Cartagena, Col. B5 84
Cartagena, Spain H11 16
Cartago, Col. E5 84
Cartago, C.R. H11 92
Cartaxo, Port. F3 16
Carter, co., Ky., U.S. B6 124
Carter, co., Mo., U.S. E7 132
Carter, co., Mt., U.S. E12 133
Carter, co., Ok., U.S. C4 143
Carter, co., Tn., U.S. C11 149
Carter Dome, mtn., N.H., U.S. B4 136
Carteret, N.J., U.S. B4 137
Carteret, co., N.C., U.S. C6 140
Carter Lake, Ia., U.S. C2 122
Cartersville, Ga., U.S. B2 117
Carterville, Il., U.S. F4 120
Carterville, Mo., U.S. D3 132
Carthage, Ar., U.S. C3 111
Carthage, Il., U.S. C2 120
Carthage, In., U.S. E6 121
Carthage, Ms., U.S. C4 131
Carthage, Mo., U.S. D3 132
Carthage, N.Y., U.S. B5 139
Carthage, Tn., U.S. C8 149
Carthage, Tx., U.S. C5 150
Carthage, hist., Tun. M5 18
Cartier Islands, is., Austl. B4 68
Cartwright, Man., Can. E2 100
Cartwright, Newf., Can. B3 102
Cartwright, Ok., U.S. D5 143
Caruaru, Braz. E11 76
Carúpano, Ven. B11 84
Carutapera, Braz. D9 76
Caruthersville, Mo., U.S. E8 132
Carver, Mn., U.S. F5 130
Carver, co., Mn., U.S. F5 130
Carville, La., U.S. h9 125
Carvin, Fr. B9 14
Cary, Il., U.S. A5 120
Cary, N.C., U.S. B4 140
Caryville, Tn., U.S. C9 149
Casablanca (Dar-el-Beida), Mor. D7 62
Casa Blanca, N.M., U.S. B2 138
Casa Branca, Braz. F5 79
Casa Grande, Az., U.S. E4 110
Casale Monferrato, Italy D3 18
Casanare, state, Col. E6 84
Casanare, stm., Col. D7 84
Casas Adobes, Az., U.S. E5 110
Casas Grandes, stm., Mex. B6 90
Casbas, Arg. I7 80
Cascade, Co., U.S. C6 113
Cascade, Id., U.S. E2 119
Cascade, Ia., U.S. B6 122
Cascade, Mt., U.S. C5 133
Cascade, co., Mt., U.S. C5 133
Cascade Locks, Or., U.S. B5 144
Cascade Range, mts., N.A. C2 106
Cascade Reservoir, res., Id., U.S. E3 119
Cascais, Port. G2 16
Cascavel, Braz. C12 80
Cascina, Italy F5 18
Casco, Me., U.S. D2 126
Casco Bay, b., Me., U.S. E3 126
Caserta, Italy H9 18
Casey, Il., U.S. D6 120
Casey, co., Ky., U.S. C5 124
Casey, Mount, mtn., Id., U.S. A2 119
Cashion, Az., U.S. m8 110
Cashmere, Wa., U.S. B5 154
Casilda, Arg. G8 80
Casino, Austl. G10 70
Casiquiare, stm., Ven. F9 84
Čáslav, Czech Rep. F15 10
Casma, Peru C2 82
Čašniki, Bela. G12 22
Casper, Wy., U.S. D6 157
Caspian Sea I8 26
Cass, co., Il., U.S. D3 120
Cass, co., In., U.S. C5 121
Cass, co., Ia., U.S. C3 122
Cass, co., Mi., U.S. G4 129
Cass, co., Mn., U.S. D4 130
Cass, co., Mo., U.S. C3 132
Cass, co., Ne., U.S. D9 134
Cass, co., N.D., U.S. C8 141
Cass, co., Tx., U.S. C5 150
Cass, stm., Mi., U.S. E7 129
Cassai (Kasai), stm., Afr. C4 58
Cass City, Mi., U.S. E7 129
Casselberry, Fl., U.S. D5 116
Casselman, Ont., Can. B9 103
Casselton, N.D., U.S. C8 141
Cássia, Braz. F5 79
Cassia, co., Id., U.S. G5 119
Cassiar, B.C., Can. m17 99
Cassiar Mountains, mts., Can. E7 96
Cassidy, B.C., Can. f12 99
Cassilândia, Braz. E3 79
Cassino, Italy H8 18
Cass Lake, Mn., U.S. C4 130
Cass Lake, l., Mn., U.S. C4 130
Cassopolis, Mi., U.S. G4 129
Cassville, Ga., U.S. B2 117
Cassville, Mo., U.S. E4 132
Cassville, Wi., U.S. F3 156
Castellammare [di Stabia], Italy I9 18
Castelli, Arg. I10 80
Castelló de la Plana, Spain F11 16
Castelnaudary, Fr. I8 14
Castelo, Braz. F8 79
Castelo Branco, Port. F4 16
Castelsarrasin, Fr. H8 14
Castelvetrano, Italy L7 18
Castilho, Braz. F3 79
Castilla, Peru A1 82
Castilla-La Mancha, prov., Spain F8 16
Castilla-León, prov., Spain D6 16
Castillos, Ur. H12 80
Castine, Me., U.S. D4 126
Castleberry, Al., U.S. D2 108
Castle Dale, Ut., U.S. D4 151
Castle Dome Peak, mtn., Az., U.S. D1 110
Castle Douglas, Scot., U.K. G10 8
Castlegar, B.C., Can. E9 99
Castle Hills, De., U.S. i7 115
Castlemaine, Austl. K6 70
Castle Point, Mo., U.S. f13 132
Castle Rock, Co., U.S. B6 113
Castle Rock, Wa., U.S. C3 154
Castle Rock Lake, res., Wi., U.S. E4 156
Castleton, Vt., U.S. D2 152
Castlewood, S.D., U.S. C8 148
Castlewood, Va., U.S. f9 153
Castor, Alta., Can. C5 98
Castres, Fr. I9 14
Castricum, Neth. C6 12
Castries, St. Luc. G14 94
Castro, Braz. C13 80
Castro, Chile E2 78
Castro, co., Tx., U.S. B1 150
Castro Valley, Ca., U.S. h8 112
Castrovirreyna, Peru E4 82
Casupá, Ur. H11 80
Caswell, co., N.C., U.S. A3 140
Catacamas, Hond. C9 92
Catacaos, Peru A1 82
Catacocha, Ec. J3 84
Cataguases, Braz. F7 79
Catahoula, co., La., U.S. C4 125
Catahoula Lake, l., La., U.S. C3 125
Catalão, Braz. E5 79
Catalina, Newf., Can. D5 102
Catalonia see Catalunya, prov., Spain D13 16
Catalunya, prov., Spain D13 16
Catamarca, prov., Arg. D5 80
Catamayo, Ec. I3 84
Catanduva, Braz. F4 79
Catania, Italy L10 18
Catanzaro, Italy K11 18
Catarama, Ec. H3 84
Catarroja, Spain F11 16
Catasauqua, Pa., U.S. E11 145
Catawba, co., N.C., U.S. B1 140
Catawba, stm., S.C., U.S. B6 147
Catedral, Cerro, hill, Ur. H11 80
Cathedral City, Ca., U.S. F5 112
Cathlamet, Wa., U.S. C2 154
Cat Island, i., Bah. B7 94
Cat Island, i., Ms., U.S. E4 131
Catlettsburg, Ky., U.S. B7 124
Catlin, Il., U.S. C6 120
Catoche, Cabo, c., Mex. G16 90
Catoctin Mountain, mtn., U.S. B2 127
Cato Island, i., Austl. D11 70
Catonsville, Md., U.S. B4 127
Catoosa, Ok., U.S. A6 143
Catoosa, co., Ga., U.S. B1 117
Catriló, Arg. I7 80
Catron, co., N.M., U.S. D1 138
Catskill, N.Y., U.S. C7 139
Catskill Mountains, mts., N.Y., U.S. C6 139
Cattaraugus, co., N.Y., U.S. C2 139
Cattolica, Italy F7 18
Catu, Braz. B9 79
Caubvick, Mount (Mont d'Iberville), mtn., Can. f9 102
Cauca, dept., Col. F4 84
Cauca, stm., Col. D5 84
Caucasia, Col. C5 84
Caucasus, mts. I6 26
Caucete, Arg. F4 80
Caudry, Fr. B10 14
Čaunskaja guba, b., Russia D25 28
Cauquenes, Chile H2 80
Caura, stm., Ven. D10 84
Căuşani, Mol. C13 20
Caussade, Fr. H8 14
Čausy, Bela. H13 22
Cauto, stm., Cuba D6 94
Cavaillon, Fr. I12 14
Cavalaire-sur-Mer, Fr. I13 14
Cavalier, N.D., U.S. A8 141
Cavalier, co., N.D., U.S. A7 141
Cavan, co., Ire. H6 8
Cave City, Ar., U.S. B4 111
Cave City, Ky., U.S. C4 124
Cave Creek, Az., U.S. D4 110
Cave In Rock, Il., U.S. F5 120
Cave Junction, Or., U.S. E3 144
Cavelo, Ang. A4 66
Cavendish, Vt., U.S. E3 152
Cave Run Lake, res., Ky., U.S. B6 124
Cave Spring, Ga., U.S. B1 117
Cave Spring, Va., U.S. C2 153
Cave Springs, Ar., U.S. A1 111
Cavetown, Md., U.S. A2 127
Cavite, Phil. n19 39b
Cawker City, Ks., U.S. C5 123
Cawood, Ky., U.S. D6 124
Cawston, B.C., Can. E8 99
Caxambu, Braz. F6 79
Caxias, Braz. D10 76
Caxias do Sul, Braz. E13 80
Caxito, Ang. C2 58
Cayambe, Ec. G3 84
Cayambe, vol., Ec. G4 84
Cayce, S.C., U.S. D5 147
Cayenne, Fr. Gu. C8 76
Cayey, P.R. E11 94
Cayley, Alta., Can. D4 98
Cayman Brac, i., Cay. Is. E5 94
Cayman Islands, dep., N.A. E4 94
Cayman Trench H11 86
Cayuga, In., U.S. E3 121
Cayuga, co., N.Y., U.S. C4 139
Cayuga Heights, N.Y., U.S. C4 139
Cayuga Lake, l., N.Y., U.S. C4 139
Cazenovia, N.Y., U.S. C5 139
Ceará, state, Braz. E10 76
Ceará-Mirim, Braz. E11 76
Cebaco, Isla De, i., Pan. D2 84
Čeboksary, Russia F7 26
Cebollatí, Ur. G12 80
Cebu, Phil. C7 38
Cebu, i., Phil. C7 38
Čecerleg, Mong. B7 30
Čečersk, Bela. I13 22
Čechov, Russia F20 22
Čechy, hist. reg., Czech Rep. F14 10
Cecil, co., Md., U.S. A6 127
Cecilia, Ky., U.S. C4 124
Cecina, Italy F5 18
Cedar, co., Ia., U.S. C6 122
Cedar, co., Mo., U.S. D4 132
Cedar, co., Ne., U.S. B8 134
Cedar, stm., U.S. C6 122
Cedar Bluff, Al., U.S. A4 108
Cedar Bluffs, Ne., U.S. C9 134
Cedar Bluff Two, Tn., U.S. D9 149
Cedar Breaks National Monument, Ut., U.S. F3 151
Cedarburg, Wi., U.S. E6 156
Cedar City, Ut., U.S. F2 151
Cedar Creek, stm., N.D., U.S. C3 141
Cedar Creek Lake, res., Tx., U.S. C4 150
Cedar Crest, N.M., U.S. k8 138
Cedaredge, Co., U.S. C3 113
Cedar Falls, Ia., U.S. B5 122
Cedar Grove, N.J., U.S. B4 137
Cedar Grove, W.V., U.S. C3 155
Cedar Grove, Wi., U.S. E6 156
Cedar Hill, Mo., U.S. g12 132
Cedar Hill, Tx., U.S. n10 150
Cedarhurst, N.Y., U.S. k13 139
Cedar Lake, In., U.S. B3 121
Cedar Lake, res., Man., Can. C1 100
Cedar Park, Tx., U.S. D4 150
Cedar Point, c., Oh., U.S. e7 142
Cedar Point, c., Oh., U.S. A3 142
Cedar Rapids, Ia., U.S. C6 122
Cedar Rapids, Ne., U.S. C7 134
Cedar Springs, Mi., U.S. E5 129
Cedartown, Ga., U.S. B1 117
Cedar Vale, Ks., U.S. E7 123
Cedarville, Oh., U.S. C2 142
Cedros, Hond. C7 92
Cedros, Isla, i., Mex. C2 90
Ceduna, Austl. F6 68
Ceerigaabo, Som. F10 56
Cefalù, Italy K9 18
Čegdomyn, Russia G18 28
Cegléd, Hung. H19 10
Cehegín, Spain G10 16
Čel'abinsk, Russia F10 26
Celaya, Mex. G9 90
Celebes see Sulawesi, i., Indon. F7 38
Celebes Sea, Asia E7 38
Čeleken, Turk. J8 26
Celendín, Peru B2 82
Celestún, Mex. G14 90
Celina, Oh., U.S. B1 142
Celina, Tn., U.S. C8 149
Celinograd, Kaz. G12 26
Celje, Slvn. C10 18
Čelkar, Kaz. H9 26
Celle, Ger. C10 10
Celtic Sea, Eur. J7 8
Čel'uskin, mys, c., Russia B18 26
Centenario, Arg. J4 80
Centenário do Sul, Braz. G3 79
Centennial, Wy., U.S. E6 157
Center, Co., U.S. D4 113
Center, Mo., U.S. B6 132
Center, N.D., U.S. B4 141
Center, Tx., U.S. D5 150
Center Barnstead, N.H., U.S. D4 136
Centerbrook, Ct., U.S. D6 114
Center Conway, N.H., U.S. C4 136
Centereach, N.Y., U.S. n15 139
Centerfield, Ut., U.S. D4 151
Center Harbor, N.H., U.S. C4 136
Center Hill Lake, res., Tn., U.S. C8 149
Center Moriches, N.Y., U.S. n16 139
Center Ossipee, N.H., U.S. C4 136
Center Point, Al., U.S. f7 108
Center Point, Ia., U.S. B6 122
Center Rutland, Vt., U.S. D2 152
Center Sandwich, N.H., U.S. C4 136
Centerton, Ar., U.S. A1 111
Center Tuftonboro, N.H., U.S. C4 136
Centerville, Ar., U.S. B2 111
Centerville, De., U.S. A3 115
Centerville, In., U.S. E8 121
Centerville, Ia., U.S. D5 122
Centerville, Ma., U.S. C7 128
Centerville, Oh., U.S. C1 142
Centerville, Pa., U.S. F2 145
Centerville, S.D., U.S. D9 148
Centerville, Tn., U.S. B4 149
Centerville, Ut., U.S. C4 151
Central, N.M., U.S. E1 138
Central, S.C., U.S. B2 147
Central, dept., Para. C10 80
Central, Cordillera, mts., Col. E5 84
Central, Cordillera, mts., C.R. G10 92
Central, Massif, mts., Fr. G10 14
Central African Republic, ctry., Afr. G5 56
Central Butte, Sask., Can. G2 105
Central City, Co., U.S. B5 113
Central City, Il., U.S. E4 120
Central City, Ia., U.S. B6 122
Central City, Ky., U.S. C2 124
Central City, Ne., U.S. C7 134
Central Falls, R.I., U.S. B4 146
Central Heights, Az., U.S. D5 110
Centralia, Il., U.S. E4 120
Centralia, Ks., U.S. C7 123
Centralia, Mo., U.S. B5 132
Centralia, Wa., U.S. C3 154
Centralina, Braz. E4 79
Central Islip, N.Y., U.S. n15 139
Central Park, Wa., U.S. C2 154
Central Point, Or., U.S. E4 144
Central Village, Ct., U.S. C8 114
Centre, Al., U.S. A4 108
Centre, co., Pa., U.S. E6 145
Centreville, N.B., Can. C2 101
Centreville, Al., U.S. C2 108
Centreville, Il., U.S. E3 120
Centreville, Md., U.S. B5 127
Centreville, Mi., U.S. G5 129
Centreville, Ms., U.S. D2 131
Century, Fl., U.S. u14 116
Cenxi, China C11 40
Cepu, Indon. j15 39a
Ceram see Seram, i., Indon. F8 38
Ceram Sea see Seram, Laut, Indon. F8 38
Cereal, Alta., Can. D5 98
Ceredo, W.V., U.S. C2 155
Čeremchovo, Russia G14 26
Čerepanovo, Russia G10 26
Čerepovec, Russia B20 22
Ceres, Arg. E8 80
Ceres, Braz. C4 79
Ceres, S. Afr. I4 66
Ceres, Ca., U.S. D3 112
Ceresco, Ne., U.S. C9 134
Céret, Fr. J9 14
Cereté, Col. C5 84
Cerf Island, i., Sey. C10 58
Cerignola, Italy H10 18
Čerikov, Bela. H14 22
Čerkessk, Russia I6 26
Čerlak, Russia G12 26
Čern', Russia H19 22
Čern'achovsk (Insterburg), Russia G4 22
Cernavodă, Rom. E12 20
Cernay, Fr. E14 14
Černogorsk, Russia G10 28
Černyševskij, Russia E14 28
Cerralvo, Mex. D10 90
Cerralvo, Isla, i., Mex. E5 90
Cerrillos, Arg. C6 80
Cerrillos, N.M., U.S. B3 138
Cerritos, Mex. F9 90
Cerro, N.M., U.S. A4 138
Cerro Azul, Arg. D11 80
Cerro Azul, Braz. C14 80
Cerro Azul, Mex. G11 90
Cerro Azul, Peru E3 82
Cerro Chato, Ur. G11 80
Cerro de Pasco, Peru D3 82
Cerro Gordo, Il., U.S. D5 120
Cerro Gordo, co., Ia., U.S. A4 122
Cerro Largo, Braz. E11 80
Cerrón Grande, Embalse, res., El Sal. C5 92
Cerros Colorados, Embalse, res., Arg. J4 80
Čerskogo, chrebet, mts., Russia E21 28
Červen', Bela. H11 22
Cesar, dept., Col. C6 84
Cesena, Italy E7 18
Cesenatico, Italy E7 18
Cēsis, Lat. D8 22
Česká Lípa, Czech Rep. E14 10
České Budějovice, Czech Rep. G14 10
Český Krumlov, Czech Rep. G14 10
Češskaja guba, b., Russia D7 26
Cessnock, Austl. I9 70
Cetinje, Yugo. G2 20
Ceuta, Sp. N. Afr. C8 62
Ceyhan, Tur. C3 48
Ceylon, Sask., Can. H3 105
Ceylon, Mn., U.S. G4 130
Chaanling, China F2 34
Chabarovsk, Russia H19 28
Chabás, Arg. G8 80
Chablis, Fr. E10 14
Chacabuco, Arg. H8 80
Chachani, Nevado, mtn., Peru G6 82
Chachoengsao, Thai. H6 40
Chaco, prov., Arg. D8 80
Chaco, dept., Para. H11 82
Chacon, N.M., U.S. A4 138
Chacon, Cape, c., Ak., U.S. n24 109
Chad (Tchad), ctry., Afr. E4 56
Chad, Lake (Lac Tchad), l., Afr. F3 56
Chadbourn, N.C., U.S. C4 140
Chadron, Ne., U.S. B3 134
Chaeryŏng, N. Kor. E13 32
Chaffee, Mo., U.S. D8 132
Chaffee, co., Co., U.S. C4 113
Chaffin, Ma., U.S. B4 128
Chāgai Hills, hills, Asia G18 48
'Chaghcharān, Afg. C1 44
Chagny, Fr. F11 14
Chagos Archipelago, is., B.I.O.T. J8 24
Chagrin Falls, Oh., U.S. A4 142
Chahal, Guat. B5 92
Chaiqiao, China F10 34
Chaiyaphum, Thai. G7 40
Chajarí, Arg. F10 80
Chajian, China C7 34
Chajiaqiao, China A9 34
Chakasija, state, Russia G15 26
Chākdaha, India I13 44
Chakwāl, Pak. D5 44
Chala, Peru F4 82
Chalatenango, El Sal. C6 92
Chalchuapa, El Sal. D5 92
Chalengkou, China B15 44
Chaleur Bay, b., Can. B4 101
Chalfonte, De., U.S. h7 115
Chalhuanca, Peru F5 82
Chaling, China I2 34
Chālisgaon, India B3 46
Chalk River, Ont., Can. A7 103
Challapata, Bol. H8 82
Challenger Deep G18 158
Challis, Id., U.S. E4 119
Chalmers, In., U.S. C4 121
Chalmette, La., U.S. E6 125
Châlons-sur-Marne, Fr. D11 14
Chalon-sur-Saône, Fr. F11 14
Chaltel, Cerro (Monte Fitzroy), mtn., S.A. F2 78
Chālūs, Iran C11 48
Chama, Co., U.S. D5 113
Chama, N.M., U.S. A3 138
Chama, Rio, stm., N.M., U.S. A3 138
Chaman, Pak. E2 44
Chamberino, N.M., U.S. E3 138
Chamberlain, S.D., U.S. D6 148
Chamberlin, Mount, mtn., Ak., U.S. B10 109
Chambers, Az., U.S. B6 110
Chambers, co., Al., U.S. C4 108
Chambers, co., Tx., U.S. E5 150
Chambersburg, Pa., U.S. G6 145
Chambers Island, i., Wi., U.S. C6 156
Chambéry, Fr. G12 14
Chambi, Jebel, mtn., Tun. C15 62
Chamblee, Ga., U.S. h8 117
Chambly, Que., Can. D4 104
Chamcook, N.B., Can. D2 101
Chame, Pan. I15 92
Chamelecón, stm., Hond. B6 92
Chamical, Arg. F5 80
Chamisal, N.M., U.S. A4 138
Chamonix-Mont-Blanc, Fr. G13 14
Champagne Castle, mtn., Afr. G9 66
Champagnole, Fr. F12 14
Champaign, Il., U.S. C5 120
Champaign, co., Il., U.S. C5 120
Champaign, co., Oh., U.S. B2 142
Champasak, Laos G8 40
Champerico, Guat. C3 92
Champion, Alta., Can. D4 98
Champion, Oh., U.S. A5 142
Champlin, Mn., U.S. m12 130
Champotón, Mex. H14 90
Chañaral, Chile D3 80
Chancay, Peru D3 82
Chanco, Chile H2 80
Chandalar, stm., Ak., U.S. B10 109
Chandausi, India F8 44
Chandeleur Islands, is., La., U.S. E7 125
Chandeleur Sound, strt., La., U.S. E6 125
Chandīgarh, India E7 44
Chandler, Que., Can. k14 104
Chandler, Az., U.S. D4 110
Chandler, In., U.S. H3 121
Chandler, Ok., U.S. B5 143
Chandler Heights, Az., U.S. m9 110
Chandrapur, India C5 46
Chandyga, Russia E19 28
Chang (Yangtze), stm., China E10 30
Changane, stm., Moz. D11 66
Chang Cheng (Great Wall), hist., China C4 32
Changchou see Zhangzhou, China K6 34
Changchow see Changzhou, China D8 34
Changchun, China C12 30
Changde, China F9 30
Change Islands, Newf., Can. D4 102
Changhua, Tai. K9 34
Changji, China C4 30
Changli, China D7 32
Changsha, China G2 34
Changshan, China G7 34
Changshu, China D9 34
Changting, China J5 34
Changuinola, Pan. H12 92
Changxing, China D8 34
Changyŏn, N. Kor. E13 32
Changzhi, China D9 30
Changzhou (Changchow), China D8 34
Chanhassen, Mn., U.S. n11 130
Chanka, ozero (Xingkai Hu), l., Asia B13 30
Channahon, Il., U.S. B5 120
Channel Country, reg., Austl. E4 70
Channel Islands, is., Eur. L11 8
Channel Islands, is., Ca., U.S. F4 112
Channel Islands National Park, Ca., U.S. F4 112
Channel Lake, Il., U.S. H8 120
Channel-Port-aux-Basques, Newf., Can. E2 102
Channelview, Tx., U.S. r14 150
Chantang, China B6 34
Chanthaburi, Thai. H7 40
Chantilly, Fr. C9 14
Chantilly, Va., U.S. g12 153
Chanty-Mansijsk, Russia E11 26
Chanute, Ks., U.S. E8 123
Chao'an, China L5 34
Chao Phraya, stm., Thai. G6 40
Chaoshui, China F8 32
Chaouen, Mor. C8 62
Chaoyang, China B8 32
Chaoyang, China L5 34
Chaoyangchuan, China A17 32
Chapada dos Guimarães, Braz. F14 82
Chapala, Mex. G8 90
Chapala, Laguna de, l., Mex. G8 90
Chaparral, Col. F5 84
Chaparral, N.M., U.S. E3 138
Chapecó, Braz. D12 80
Chapel Hill, N.C., U.S. B3 140
Chapel Hill, Tn., U.S. B5 149
Chaplin, Sask., Can. G2 105
Chaplin Lake, l., Sask., Can. G2 105
Chapman, Ks., U.S. D6 123
Chapman, Cape, c., N.W. Ter., Can. C15 96
Chapmanville, W.V., U.S. D2 155
Chappaquiddick Island, i., Ma., U.S. D7 128
Chappell, Ne., U.S. C3 134
Chaqui, Bol. H9 82
Charadai, Arg. D9 80
Charagua, Bol. H10 82
Charalá, Col. D6 84
Charaña, Bol. G7 82
Charata, Arg. D8 80
Charcas, Mex. F9 90
Chardon, Oh., U.S. A4 142
Charenton, La., U.S. E4 125
Chārīkār, Afg. C3 44
Chariton, Ia., U.S. C4 122
Chariton, co., Mo., U.S. B4 132
Chariton, stm., U.S. A5 132
Charleroi, Bel. H5 12
Charleroi, Pa., U.S. F2 145
Charles, co., Md., U.S. C3 127
Charles, stm., Ma., U.S. B5 128
Charles, Cape, c., Va., U.S. C6 153
Charlesbourg, Que., Can. n17 104
Charles City, Ia., U.S. A5 122
Charles City, co., Va., U.S. C5 153
Charles Mix, co., S.D., U.S. D7 148
Charles Mound, hill, Il., U.S. A3 120
Charleston, Ar., U.S. B1 111
Charleston, Il., U.S. D5 120
Charleston, Ms., U.S. A3 131
Charleston, Mo., U.S. E8 132
Charleston, Or., U.S. D2 144
Charleston, S.C., U.S. F8 147
Charleston, Tn., U.S. D9 149

Name	Map Ref.	Page

Charleston, W.V., U.S. . . . C3 155
Charleston, co., S.C., U.S. F8 147
Charleston Peak, mtn., Nv., U.S. . . . G6 135
Charlestown, St. K./N. . . F13 94
Charlestown, In., U.S. . . . H6 121
Charlestown, N.H., U.S. . . D2 136
Charlestown, R.I., U.S. . . F2 146
Charles Town, W.V., U.S. . B7 155
Charleville, Austl. F7 70
Charleville-Mézières, Fr. . . C11 14
Charlevoix, Mi., U.S. . . . C5 129
Charlevoix, co., Mi., U.S. . C5 129
Charlieu, Fr. . . . F11 14
Charlo, N.B., Can. . . . B3 101
Charlo, Mt., U.S. . . . C2 133
Charlotte, Mi., U.S. . . . F6 129
Charlotte, N.C., U.S. . . . B2 140
Charlotte, Tn., U.S. . . . A4 149
Charlotte, Vt., U.S. . . . C2 152
Charlotte, co., Fl., U.S. . . F5 116
Charlotte, co., Va., U.S. . . C4 153
Charlotte Amalie, V.I.U.S. . E12 94
Charlotte Harbor, Fl., U.S. . F4 116
Charlotte Hall, Md., U.S. . . D4 127
Charlottesville, Va., U.S. . . B4 153
Charlottetown, P.E.I., Can. . C6 101
Charlton, co., Ga., U.S. . . F4 117
Charmco, W.V., U.S. . . . D3 155
Charmes, Fr. . . . D13 14
Charny, Que., Can. . . . C6 104
Charovsk, Russia . . . B23 22
Chārsadda, Pak. . . . C4 44
Charters Towers, Austl. . . D8 70
Chartres, Fr. . . . D8 14
Chasavjurt, Russia . . . G17 4
Chascomús, Arg. . . . H9 80
Chase, B.C., Can. . . . D8 99
Chase, Ks., U.S. . . . D5 123
Chase, co., Ks., U.S. . . . D7 123
Chase, co., Ne., U.S. . . . D4 134
Chase, Mount, mtn., Me., U.S. . . . B4 126
Chase City, Va., U.S. . . . D4 153
Chaska, Mn., U.S. . . . F5 130
Chatangskij zaliv, b., Russia C13 28
Châteaubriant, Fr. . . . E5 14
Château d'Oex, Switz. . . . F7 13
Château-du-Loir, Fr. . . . E7 14
Châteaudun, Fr. . . . D8 14
Château-Gontier, Fr. . . . E6 14
Châteauguay, Que., Can. . . D4 104
Châteaulin, Fr. . . . D2 14
Château-Renault, Fr. . . . E9 14
Château-Richer, Que., Can. . C6 104
Châteauroux, Fr. . . . F8 14
Château-Thierry, Fr. . . . C10 14
Châtellerault, Fr. . . . F7 14
Chatfield, Mn., U.S. . . . G6 130
Chatham, N.B., Can. . . . B4 101
Chatham, Ont., Can. . . . E2 103
Chatham, Il., U.S. . . . D4 120
Chatham, Ma., U.S. . . . C8 128
Chatham, N.J., U.S. . . . B4 137
Chatham, Va., U.S. . . . D3 153
Chatham, co., Ga., U.S. . . E5 117
Chatham, co., N.C., U.S. . . B3 140
Chatham Islands, is., . . . M22 158
Chatham Strait, strt., Ak., U.S. . . . m22 109
Châtillon-sur-Seine, Fr. . . E11 14
Chatom, Al., U.S. . . . D1 108
Chatsworth, Ga., U.S. . . . B2 117
Chatsworth, Il., U.S. . . . C5 120
Chatsworth, Zimb. . . . B10 66
Chattahoochee, Fl., U.S. . . B2 116
Chattahoochee, co., Ga., U.S. . . . D2 117
Chattahoochee, stm., U.S. . . E1 117
Chattanooga, Tn., U.S. . . . D8 149
Chattaroy, W.V., U.S. . . . D2 155
Chattooga, co., Ga., U.S. . . B1 117
Chattooga, stm., U.S. . . . B1 147
Chaudière, stm., Que., Can. . C7 104
Chau Doc, Viet. . . . I8 40
Chaumont, Fr. . . . D12 14
Chauncey, Oh., U.S. . . . C3 142
Chauny, Fr. . . . C10 14
Chautauqua, N.Y., U.S. . . . C1 139
Chautauqua, co., Ks., U.S. . E7 123
Chautauqua, co., N.Y., U.S. C1 139
Chautauqua Lake, l., N.Y., U.S. . . . C1 139
Chauvigny, Fr. . . . F7 14
Chauvin, Alta., Can. . . . C5 98
Chauvin, La., U.S. . . . E5 125
Chavarría, Arg. . . . E9 80
Chaves, co., N.M., U.S. . . D5 138
Cheaha Mountain, mtn., Al., U.S. . . . B4 108
Cheatham, co., Tn., U.S. . . A4 149
Cheb, Czech Rep. . . . E12 10
Chebanse, Il., U.S. . . . C6 120
Chebba, Tun. . . . C16 62
Chebeague Island, Me., U.S. . . . E2 126
Cheboygan, Mi., U.S. . . . C6 129
Cheboygan, co., Mi., U.S. . C6 129
Chech'on, S. Kor. . . . F16 32
Checotah, Ok., U.S. . . . B6 143
Chedabucto Bay, b., N.S., Can. . . . D8 101
Cheduba Island, i., Mya. . . E2 40
Cheektowaga, N.Y., U.S. . . C2 139
Chegutu, Zimb. . . . B10 66
Chehalis, Wa., U.S. . . . C2 154
Chehalis, stm., Wa., U.S. . . C2 154
Cheju, S. Kor. . . . E12 30
Cheju-do, i., S. Kor. . . . E12 30
Chelan, Wa., U.S. . . . B5 154
Chelan, co., Wa., U.S. . . . B4 154
Chelan, Lake, l., Wa., U.S. . A5 154
Chelan Mountains, mts., Wa., U.S. . . . A5 154
Chelelektu, Eth. . . . N10 60
Chelghoum el Aïd, Alg. . . B14 62
Chéliff, Oued, stm., Alg. . . B11 62
Chełm, Pol. . . . D23 10
Chetmno, Pol. . . . B18 10
Chelmsford, Ma., U.S. . . . A5 128
Chelsea, Que., Can. . . . D2 104
Chelsea, Al., U.S. . . . g7 108
Chelsea, Ma., U.S. . . . B5 128
Chelsea, Mi., U.S. . . . F6 129

Chelsea, Ok., U.S. . . . A6 143
Chelsea, Vt., U.S. . . . D4 152
Chelyabinsk see Čel'abinsk, Russia . . . F10 26
Chelyan, W.V., U.S. . . . C3 155
Chemax, Mex. . . . G16 90
Chemnitz, Ger. . . . E12 10
Chemung, co., N.Y., U.S. . . C4 139
Chemung, stm., Pa., U.S. . . C8 145
Chemung Lake, l., Ont., Can. . . . C6 103
Chenāb, stm., Asia . . . E5 44
Chenango, co., N.Y., U.S. . . C5 139
Chenango, stm., N.Y., U.S. . C5 139
Chenango Bridge, N.Y., U.S. . . . C5 139
Cheney, Ks., U.S. . . . E6 123
Cheney, Wa., U.S. . . . B8 154
Cheneyville, La., U.S. . . . C3 125
Chengde, China . . . C5 32
Chengdu, China . . . E7 30
Chenghai, China . . . L5 34
Chengjiang, China . . . B7 40
Chengshan Jiao, c., China . . F10 32
Chengtu see Chengdu, China . . . E7 30
Chengzitan, China . . . D10 32
Chenoa, Il., U.S. . . . C5 120
Chenoweth, Or., U.S. . . . B5 144
Chenxian, China . . . J1 34
Chepachet, R.I., U.S. . . . B2 146
Chepén, Peru . . . B2 82
Chepes, Arg. . . . F5 80
Chepo, Pan. . . . C3 84
Chequamegon Bay, b., Wi., U.S. . . . B3 156
Cher, stm., Fr. . . . E8 14
Cheraw, Co., U.S. . . . C7 113
Cheraw, S.C., U.S. . . . B8 147
Cherbourg, Fr. . . . C5 14
Cherchell, Alg. . . . B12 62
Chergui, Chott ech, l., Alg. . C11 62
Cherkasy, Ukr. . . . H4 26
Cherníhiv, Ukr. . . . G4 26
Chernivtsi, Ukr. . . . A9 20
Chernobyl see Chornobyl', Ukr. . . . G4 26
Cherokee, Al., U.S. . . . A2 108
Cherokee, Ia., U.S. . . . B2 122
Cherokee, Ks., U.S. . . . E9 123
Cherokee, Ok., U.S. . . . A3 143
Cherokee, co., Al., U.S. . . A4 108
Cherokee, co., Ga., U.S. . . B2 117
Cherokee, co., Ia., U.S. . . B2 122
Cherokee, co., Ks., U.S. . . E9 123
Cherokee, co., N.C., U.S. . . f8 140
Cherokee, co., Ok., U.S. . . B6 143
Cherokee, co., S.C., U.S. . . A4 147
Cherokee, co., Tx., U.S. . . D5 150
Cherokee Lake, res., Tn., U.S. . . . C10 149
Cherokees, Lake O' The, res., Ok., U.S. . . . A7 143
Cherokee Village, Ar., U.S. . A4 111
Cherquenco, Chile . . . J2 80
Cherry, co., Ne., U.S. . . . B4 134
Cherry Creek, S.D., U.S. . . C4 148
Cherry Creek, stm., S.D., U.S. . . . C3 148
Cherryfield, Me., U.S. . . . D5 126
Cherry Hill, N.J., U.S. . . . D2 137
Cherryvale, Ks., U.S. . . . E8 123
Cherry Valley, Ar., U.S. . . B5 111
Cherry Valley, Il., U.S. . . . A5 120
Cherryville, N.C., U.S. . . . B1 140
Chervonohrad, Ukr. . . . G2 26
Chesaning, Mi., U.S. . . . E6 129
Chesapeake, Va., U.S. . . . D6 153
Chesapeake, W.V., U.S. . . C3 155
Chesapeake Bay, b., U.S. . . D11 106
Chesapeake Bay Bridge-Tunnel, Va., U.S. . . . D7 153
Chesapeake Beach, Md., U.S. . . . C4 127
Chesapeake Ranch Estates, Md., U.S. . . . D5 127
Cheshire, Ct., U.S. . . . D4 114
Cheshire, co., Eng., U.K. . . H11 8
Cheshire, co., N.H., U.S. . . E2 136
Chesley, Ont., Can. . . . C3 103
Chesnee, S.C., U.S. . . . A4 147
Chester, Eng., U.K. . . . H11 8
Chester, Ct., U.S. . . . D6 114
Chester, Ga., U.S. . . . D3 117
Chester, Id., U.S. . . . F7 119
Chester, Il., U.S. . . . F4 120
Chester, Mt., U.S. . . . B6 133
Chester, Ne., U.S. . . . D8 134
Chester, N.H., U.S. . . . E4 136
Chester, N.Y., U.S. . . . D6 139
Chester, Pa., U.S. . . . G11 145
Chester, S.C., U.S. . . . B5 147
Chester, Vt., U.S. . . . E3 152
Chester, Va., U.S. . . . C5 153
Chester, W.V., U.S. . . . A4 155
Chester, co., Pa., U.S. . . . G10 145
Chester, co., S.C., U.S. . . B5 147
Chester, co., Tn., U.S. . . . B3 149
Chester, stm., Md., U.S. . . B5 127
Chester Basin, N.S., Can. . . E5 101
Chester Depot, Vt., U.S. . . E3 152
Chesterfield, In., U.S. . . . D6 121
Chesterfield, Mo., U.S. . . . f12 132
Chesterfield, N.H., U.S. . . E2 136
Chesterfield, S.C., U.S. . . B7 147
Chesterfield, co., S.C., U.S. . B7 147
Chesterfield, co., Va., U.S. . C5 153
Chesterfield, Îles, is., N. Cal. . . . C11 68
Chesterfield Inlet, N.W. Ter., Can. . . . D14 96
Chester-le-Street, Eng., U.K. . . . G12 8
Chesterton, In., U.S. . . . A3 121
Chestertown, Md., U.S. . . B5 127
Chesterville, Ont., Can. . . B9 103
Cheswick, Pa., U.S. . . . h14 145
Chetek, Wi., U.S. . . . C2 156
Chéticamp, N.S., Can. . . . C8 101
Chetopa, Ks., U.S. . . . E8 123
Chetumal, Mex. . . . H15 90
Chetumal, Bahía, b., N.A. . . H15 90
Chetwynd, B.C., Can. . . . B7 99
Chevak, Ak., U.S. . . . C6 109
Cheviot, Oh., U.S. . . . C1 142

Chevreuil, Point, c., La., U.S. . . . E4 125
Chevy Chase, Md., U.S. . . C3 127
Chew Bahir (Lake Stefanie), l., Afr. . . . H8 56
Chewelah, Wa., U.S. . . . A8 154
Cheyenne, Ok., U.S. . . . B2 143
Cheyenne, Wy., U.S. . . . E8 157
Cheyenne, co., Co., U.S. . . C8 113
Cheyenne, co., Ks., U.S. . . C2 123
Cheyenne, co., Ne., U.S. . . C2 134
Cheyenne, stm., U.S. . . . C4 148
Cheyenne Wells, Co., U.S. . C8 113
Chhapra, India . . . H11 44
Chhatarpur, India . . . H8 44
Chhindwāra, India . . . I8 44
Chiai, Tai. . . . L9 34
Chiang Mai, Thai. . . . E5 40
Chiang Rai, Thai. . . . E5 40
Chiapa de Corzo, Mex. . . . I13 90
Chiapas, state, Mex. . . . I14 90
Chiari, Italy . . . D4 18
Chiasso, Switz. . . . G11 13
Chiautla de Tapia, Mex. . . H10 90
Chiavari, Italy . . . E4 18
Chiba, Japan . . . L15 36
Chibougamau, Que., Can. . . k12 104
Chibuto, Moz. . . . E11 66
Chicago, Il., U.S. . . . B6 120
Chicago Heights, Il., U.S. . . B6 120
Chicago Sanitary and Ship Canal, Il., U.S. . . . k8 120
Chichagof Island, i., Ak., U.S. . . . m22 109
Chicheng, China . . . C3 32
Chichén Itzá, hist., Mex. . . G15 90
Chichester, Eng., U.K. . . . K13 8
Chichibu, Japan . . . L14 36
Chichica, Pan. . . . I13 92
Chichicastenango, Guat. . . C3 92
Chichigalpa, Nic. . . . E7 92
Chichimilá, Mex. . . . G15 90
Chickahominy, stm., Va., U.S. . . . C5 153
Chickamauga, Ga., U.S. . . B1 117
Chickamauga Lake, res., Tn., U.S. . . . D8 149
Chickasaw, Al., U.S. . . . E1 108
Chickasaw, co., Ia., U.S. . . A5 122
Chickasaw, co., Ms., U.S. . . B5 131
Chickasawhay, stm., Ms., U.S. . . . D5 131
Chickasha, Ok., U.S. . . . B4 143
Chiclana de la Frontera, Spain . . . I5 16
Chiclayo, Peru . . . B2 82
Chico, Ca., U.S. . . . C3 112
Chico, stm., Arg. . . . E3 78
Chico, stm., Arg. . . . F3 78
Chicopee, Ga., U.S. . . . B3 117
Chicopee, Ma., U.S. . . . B2 128
Chicoutimi, Que., Can. . . . A6 104
Chicxulub, Mex. . . . G15 90
Chidester, Ar., U.S. . . . D2 111
Chiefland, Fl., U.S. . . . C4 116
Chiemsee, l., Ger. . . . H12 10
Chieri, Italy . . . D2 18
Chifeng (Ulanhad), China . . A7 32
Chigasaki, Japan . . . L14 36
Chignahuapan, Mex. . . . H10 90
Chignecto, Cape, c., N.S., Can. . . . D5 101
Chignecto Bay, b., Can. . . D5 101
Chihli, Gulf of see Bo Hai, b., China . . . E8 32
Chihsi see Jixi, China . . . B13 30
Chihuahua, Mex. . . . C6 90
Chihuahua, state, Mex. . . C6 90
Chihuahuan Desert, des., N.A. . . . F9 86
Chikindzonot, Mex. . . . G15 90
Chilakalúrupet, India . . . D6 46
Chilapa de Álvarez, Mex. . . I10 90
Chilca, Peru . . . E3 82
Chilca, Peru . . . E4 82
Childers, Austl. . . . E10 70
Childersburg, Al., U.S. . . . B3 108
Childress, Tx., U.S. . . . B2 150
Childress, co., Tx., U.S. . . C2 150
Chile, ctry., S.A. . . . F2 78
Chile Chico, Chile . . . E5 80
Chilecito, Arg. . . . B2 82
Chilete, Peru . . . B2 82
Chilhowie, Va., U.S. . . . f10 153
Chilika Lake, l., India . . . C8 46
Chililabombwe (Bancroft), Zam. . . . D5 58
Chilko, stm., B.C., Can. . . D6 99
Chillán, Chile . . . I2 80
Chillar, Arg. . . . I9 80
Chillicothe, Il., U.S. . . . C4 120
Chillicothe, Mo., U.S. . . . B4 132
Chillicothe, Oh., U.S. . . . C3 142
Chilliwack, B.C., Can. . . . E7 99
Chillon, hist., Switz. . . . F6 13
Chillum, Md., U.S. . . . f9 127
Chiloé, Isla Grande de, i., Chile . . . E2 78
Chilok, Russia . . . G14 28
Chiloquin, Or., U.S. . . . E5 144
Chilpancingo de los Bravo, Mex. . . . I10 90
Chilton, Wi., U.S. . . . D5 156
Chilton, co., Al., U.S. . . . C3 108
Chilung, Tai. . . . J10 34
Chilwa, Lake, l., Afr. . . . E7 58
Chimacum, Wa., U.S. . . . A3 154
Chimaltenango, Guat. . . . C4 92
Chimaltenango, dept., Guat. . C4 92
Chimayo, N.M., U.S. . . . A4 138
Chimbas, Arg. . . . F3 80
Chimborazo, prov., Ec. . . . H3 84
Chimborazo, vol., Ec. . . . H3 84
Chimbote, Peru . . . C2 82
Chimkent see Čimkent, Kaz. . . . I11 26
Chimki, Russia . . . F20 22
Chimney Rock, mtn., Ne., U.S. . . . C2 134
Chimoio, Moz. . . . B11 66
Chimpay, Arg. . . . J5 80
China, Mex. . . . E10 90
China, Me., U.S. . . . D3 126
China (Zhongguo), ctry., Asia . . . D8 30

China Grove, N.C., U.S. . . B2 140
China Lake, Ca., U.S. . . . E5 112
Chinandega, Nic. . . . E7 92
Chinandega, dept., Nic. . . E8 92
Chinati Peak, mtn., Tx., U.S. . . . p12 150
Chincha Alta, Peru . . . E3 82
Chinchaga, stm., Can. . . . E9 96
Chincheros, Peru . . . E5 82
Chinchilla, Austl. . . . F9 70
Chinchiná, Col. . . . E5 84
Chincoteague, Va., U.S. . . C7 153
Chincoteague Bay, b., U.S. . D7 127
Chinde, Moz. . . . B13 66
Chindwin, stm., Mya. . . . C3 40
Chingola, Zam. . . . D5 58
Chinguetti, Maur. . . . A3 64
Chinhae, S. Kor. . . . H16 32
Chin Hills, hills, Mya. . . . C2 40
Chinhoyi, Zimb. . . . E6 58
Chiniot, Pak. . . . E5 44
Chinju, S. Kor. . . . H16 32
Chinkiang see Zhenjiang, China . . . E10 30
Chinle, Az., U.S. . . . A6 110
Chinmen, China . . . K7 34
Chinmen Tao, i., Tai. . . . K7 34
Chino, Ca., U.S. . . . F5 112
Chinook, Mt., U.S. . . . B7 133
Chinook, Wa., U.S. . . . C2 154
Chinook, Lake, res., Or., U.S. . . . C5 144
Chino Valley, Az., U.S. . . . C3 110
Chinsali, Zam. . . . D6 58
Chinú, Col. . . . C5 84
Chioggia, Italy . . . D7 18
Chios see Khíos, Grc. . . . K10 20
Chipata, Zam. . . . D6 58
Chipinge, Zimb. . . . C11 66
Chipita Park, Co., U.S. . . . C6 113
Chipley, Fl., U.S. . . . u16 116
Chipman, N.B., Can. . . . C4 101
Chippewa, co., Mi., U.S. . . B6 129
Chippewa, co., Mn., U.S. . . E3 130
Chippewa, co., Wi., U.S. . . C2 156
Chippewa, stm., Wi., U.S. . . D2 156
Chippewa, Lake, l., Wi., U.S. . . . C2 156
Chippewa Falls, Wi., U.S. . . D2 156
Chiquimula, Guat. . . . C5 92
Chiquimula, dept., Guat. . . C5 92
Chiquimulilla, Guat. . . . C4 92
Chiquinquirá, Col. . . . E6 84
Chiricahua Mountains, mts., Az., U.S. . . . F6 110
Chiricahua Peak, mtn., Az., U.S. . . . F6 110
Chiriquí, Pan. . . . I12 92
Chiriquí, prov., Pan. . . . I12 92
Chiriquí, Golfo de, b., Pan. . I12 92
Chiriquí, Laguna de, b., Pan. . . . H12 92
Chiriquí Grande, Pan. . . . I12 92
Chirripó, Cerro, mtn., C.R. . H11 92
Chisago, co., Mn., U.S. . . E6 130
Chisago City, Mn., U.S. . . E6 130
Chisholm, Mn., U.S. . . . C6 130
Chishtián Mandi, Pak. . . . F5 44
Chişinău (Kishinev), Mol. . . B12 20
Chislavičì, Russia . . . G15 22
Chisos Mountains, mts., Tx., U.S. . . . E1 150
Chist'akovo see Torez, Ukr. . F15 4
Chitembo, Ang. . . . D3 58
Chitradurga, India . . . E4 46
Chitrāl, Pak. . . . C4 44
Chitré, Pan. . . . D2 84
Chittagong, Bngl. . . . I14 44
Chittaurgarh, India . . . H6 44
Chittenango, N.Y., U.S. . . B5 139
Chittenden, Vt., U.S. . . . D3 152
Chittenden, co., Vt., U.S. . . C2 152
Chittoor, India . . . F5 46
Chíuchíu, Chile . . . A3 80
Chiuta, Lake, l., Afr. . . . D7 58
Chivacoa, Ven. . . . B8 84
Chivasso, Italy . . . D2 18
Chivay, Peru . . . F6 82
Chivhu, Zimb. . . . B10 66
Chivilcoy, Arg. . . . H8 80
Chixoy (Salinas), stm., N.A. . J14 90
Chixoy, Embalse, res., Guat. . . . B4 92
Chobe, stm., Afr. . . . A7 66
Choch'iwŏn, S. Kor. . . . G15 32
Chocó, dept., Col. . . . D4 84
Chocolate Mountains, mts., Ca., U.S. . . . F6 112
Chocontá, Col. . . . E6 84
Chocope, Peru . . . B2 82
Chocorua, N.H., U.S. . . . C4 136
Choctaw, Ok., U.S. . . . B4 143
Choctaw, co., Al., U.S. . . . C1 108
Choctaw, co., Ms., U.S. . . B4 131
Choctaw, co., Ok., U.S. . . D6 143
Choctawhatchee Bay, b., Fl., U.S. . . . u15 116
Chodžejli, Uzb. . . . I9 26
Chodzież, Pol. . . . C16 10
Choele-Choel, Arg. . . . J6 80
Choiseul, i., Sol.Is. . . . I19 158
Choix, Mex. . . . D5 90
Cholet, Fr. . . . E6 14
Cholmsk, Russia . . . H20 28
Cholula [de Rivadabia], Mex. . . . H10 90
Choluteca, Hond. . . . D7 92
Choluteca, dept., Hond. . . D7 92
Choluteca, stm., Hond. . . . D8 92
Choma, Zam. . . . A5 66
Chomo Lhāri, mtn., Asia . . G13 44
Chomutov, Czech Rep. . . . E13 10
Chomutovo, Russia . . . I20 22
Chon Buri, Thai. . . . H6 40
Chone, Ec. . . . H2 84
Ch'ŏngjin, N. Kor. . . . B17 32
Ch'ŏngju, N. Kor. . . . D13 32

Ch'ŏngju, S. Kor. . . . G15 32
Chongqing, China . . . F8 30
Chongru, China . . . H9 34
Chongzuo, China . . . G8 30
Chŏnju, S. Kor. . . . H15 32
Chonos, Archipiélago de los, is., Chile . . . F2 78
Chontaleña, Cordillera, mts., Nic. . . . F10 92
Chontales, dept., Nic. . . . E9 92
Chop, Ukr. . . . A6 20
Chopinzinho, Braz. . . . C12 80
Choptank, stm., Md., U.S. . . C6 127
Chorlovo, Russia . . . F21 22
Chorog, Taj. . . . J12 26
Ch'osan, N. Kor. . . . C13 32
Chōshi, Japan . . . L15 36
Choshui, stm., Tai. . . . L9 34
Chosica, Peru . . . D3 82
Chos Malal, Arg. . . . I3 80
Chota, Peru . . . B2 82
Choteau, Mt., U.S. . . . C4 133
Chotimsk, Bela. . . . H15 22
Chot'kovo, Russia . . . E21 22
Chotynec, Russia . . . H18 22
Chouteau, Ok., U.S. . . . A6 143
Chouteau, co., Mt., U.S. . . B5 133
Chovd, Mong. . . . B5 30
Chövsgöl Nuur, l., Mong. . . A7 30
Chowan, co., N.C., U.S. . . A6 140
Chowan, stm., N.C., U.S. . . A6 140
Chowchilla, Ca., U.S. . . . D3 112
Chowchilla, stm., Ca., U.S. . D3 112
Chrisman, Il., U.S. . . . D6 120
Christchurch, N.Z. . . . E4 72
Christian, co., Il., U.S. . . . D4 120
Christian, co., Ky., U.S. . . D2 124
Christian, co., Mo., U.S. . . E4 132
Christian, S. Afr. . . . F7 66
Christiana, De., U.S. . . . B3 115
Christiansburg, Va., U.S. . . C2 153
Christiansted, V.I.U.S. . . . F12 94
Christina, stm., De., U.S. . . B3 115
Christina Peak, mtn., Nv., U.S. . . . D6 135
Christmas Island, dep., Oc. . H4 38
Christopher, Il., U.S. . . . F4 120
Chromtau, Kaz. . . . G9 26
Chrudim, Czech Rep. . . . F15 10
Chrzanów, Pol. . . . E19 10
Chubbuck, Id., U.S. . . . G6 119
Chubut, stm., Arg. . . . E3 78
Chudžand (Leninabad), Taj. . I11 26
Chugach Mountains, mts., Ak., U.S. . . . g18 109
Chugwater, Wy., U.S. . . . E8 157
Chukchi Sea . . . C2 86
Chula Vista, Ca., U.S. . . . F5 112
Chulucanas, Peru . . . A1 82
Chulumani, Bol. . . . G8 82
Chumbicha, Arg. . . . E5 80
Chunan, Tai. . . . K9 34
Ch'unch'ŏn, S. Kor. . . . F15 32
Chunchula, Al., U.S. . . . E1 108
Chungju, S. Kor. . . . G15 32
Chungking see Chongqing, China . . . F8 30
Chungli, Tai. . . . K10 34
Ch'ungmu, S. Kor. . . . I16 32
Chunhuhux, Mex. . . . H15 90
Chuŏr Phnum Krâvanh, mts., Asia . . . H7 40
Chupaca, Peru . . . E4 82
Chuquibamba, Peru . . . G5 82
Chuquicamata, Chile . . . B4 80
Chuquisaca, dept., Bol. . . H9 82
Chur, Switz. . . . E12 13
Churachandpur, India . . . H6 44
Churchbridge, Sask., Can. . . G5 105
Church Hill, Tn., U.S. . . . C11 149
Churchill, Man., Can. . . . f9 100
Churchill, co., Nv., U.S. . . D3 135
Churchill, stm., Newf., Can. . h9 100
Churchill, stm., Can. . . . f8 100
Churchill, Cape, c., Man., Can. . . . f9 100
Churchill Falls, wtfl, Newf., Can. . . . h8 100
Church Point, N.S., Can. . . E3 101
Church Point, La., U.S. . . . D3 125
Church Rock, N.M., U.S. . . B1 138
Churu, India . . . F6 44
Churubusco, In., U.S. . . . B7 121
Churuguara, Ven. . . . B8 84
Chuska Mountains, mts., Az., U.S. . . . A6 110
Chuvashia see Čuvašija, state, Russia . . . F7 26
Chuwang, China . . . B6 40
Chuxiong, China . . . G12 30
Chuy, Ur. . . . G7 26
Chvalynsk, Russia . . . C17 22
Chvojnaja, Russia . . . C12 20
Ciadâr Lunga, Mol. . . . C12 20
Cianorte, Braz. . . . G2 79
Cibecue, Az., U.S. . . . C5 110
Cibola, co., N.M., U.S. . . B2 138
Cibolo, co., Tx., U.S. . . . E5 121...

Čirčik, Uzb. . . . I11 26
Circle, Mt., U.S. . . . C11 133
Circle Pines, Mn., U.S. . . . m12 130
Circleville, Oh., U.S. . . . C3 142
Cirebon, Indon. . . . j14 39a
Ciremay, Gunung, mtn., Indon. . . . j14 39a
Čirpan, Bul. . . . G9 20
Cisco, Tx., U.S. . . . C3 150
Ciskei, hist. reg., S. Afr. . . I8 66
Cisneros, Col. . . . D5 84
Cistern Point, c., Bah. . . . C6 94
Čistopol', Russia . . . F8 26
Čita, Russia . . . G14 28
Citac, Nevado, mtn., Peru . . E4 82
Citronelle, Al., U.S. . . . D1 108
Citrus, co., Fl., U.S. . . . D4 116
Città di Castello, Italy . . . F7 18
City of Refuge National Historical Park, Hi., U.S. . D5 118
City View, S.C., U.S. . . . B3 147
Ciudad Acuña, Mex. . . . C9 90
Ciudad Altamirano, Mex. . . H9 90
Ciudad Bolívar, Ven. . . . C11 84
Ciudad Bolivia, Ven. . . . C7 84
Ciudad Camargo, Mex. . . . D10 90
Ciudad Constitución, Mex. . E4 90
Ciudad del Carmen, Mex. . . H14 90
Ciudad del Este, Para. . . . C11 80
Ciudad del Maíz, Mex. . . . F10 90
Ciudad de México (Mexico City), Mex. . . . H10 90
Ciudad Guayana, Ven. . . . C11 84
Ciudad Guzmán, Mex. . . . H8 90
Ciudad Hidalgo, Mex. . . . H9 90
Ciudad Juárez, Mex. . . . B6 90
Ciudad Lerdo, Mex. . . . E8 90
Ciudad Madero, Mex. . . . F11 90
Ciudad Mante, Mex. . . . F10 90
Ciudad Manuel Doblado, Mex. . . . G9 90
Ciudad Miguel Alemán, Mex. . . . D10 90
Ciudad Obregón, Mex. . . . D5 90
Ciudad Ojeda (Lagunillas), Ven. . . . B7 84
Ciudad Piar, Ven. . . . D11 84
Ciudad Real, Spain . . . G8 16
Ciudad Rodrigo, Spain . . . E5 16
Ciudad Tecún Umán, Guat. . C2 92
Ciudad Trujillo see Santo Domingo, Dom. Rep. . . E10 94
Ciudad Valles, Mex. . . . G10 90
Ciudad Victoria, Mex. . . . F10 90
Ciutadella, Spain . . . E15 16
Civitanova Marche, Italy . . F8 18
Civitavecchia, Italy . . . G6 18
Cizre, Tur. . . . C7 48
C.J. Strike Reservoir, res., Id., U.S. . . . G3 119
Clackamas, Or., U.S. . . . h12 144
Clackamas, co., Or., U.S. . . B4 144
Clacton-on-Sea, Eng., U.K. . J15 8
Claflin, Ks., U.S. . . . D5 123
Claiborne, co., La., U.S. . . B2 125
Claiborne, co., Ms., U.S. . . D3 131
Claiborne, co., Tn., U.S. . . C10 149
Clair, N.B., Can. . . . B1 101
Claire, Lake, l., Alta., Can. . f8 98
Clair Engle Lake, res., Ca., U.S. . . . B2 112
Clairmont, Alta., Can. . . . B1 98
Clairton, Pa., U.S. . . . F2 145
Clallam, co., Wa., U.S. . . . B1 154
Clallam Bay, Wa., U.S. . . . A1 154
Clanton, Al., U.S. . . . C3 108
Clanwilliam, S. Afr. . . . I4 66
Clara City, Mn., U.S. . . . F3 130
Clare, Austl. . . . I3 70
Clare, Mi., U.S. . . . E6 129
Clare, co., Ire. . . . I4 8
Clare, co., Mi., U.S. . . . E6 129
Claremont, Ca., U.S. . . . m13 112
Claremont, N.H., U.S. . . . D2 136
Claremore, Ok., U.S. . . . A6 143
Claremorris, Ire. . . . H4 8
Clarence, Mo., U.S. . . . B5 132
Clarence Strait, strt., Austl. . B6 68
Clarence Strait, strt., Ak., U.S. . . . n23 109
Clarence Town, Bah. . . . C7 94
Clarendon, Ar., U.S. . . . C4 111
Clarendon, Tx., U.S. . . . B2 150
Clarendon, Vt., U.S. . . . D3 152
Clarendon, co., S.C., U.S. . D7 147
Clarendon Hills, Il., U.S. . . k9 120
Clarenville, Newf., Can. . . D4 102
Claresholm, Alta., Can. . . D4 98
Clarinda, Ia., U.S. . . . D2 122
Clarion, Ia., U.S. . . . B4 122
Clarion, Pa., U.S. . . . D3 145
Clarion, co., Pa., U.S. . . . D3 145
Clarion, stm., Pa., U.S. . . . D2 145
Clarión, Isla, i., Mex. . . . H2 90
Clark, S.D., U.S. . . . C8 148
Clark, N.J., U.S. . . . k8 137
Clark, co., Ar., U.S. . . . C2 111
Clark, co., Id., U.S. . . . E6 119
Clark, co., Il., U.S. . . . D6 120
Clark, co., In., U.S. . . . H6 121
Clark, co., Ks., U.S. . . . E4 123
Clark, co., Ky., U.S. . . . C5 124
Clark, co., Mo., U.S. . . . A5 132
Clark, co., Nv., U.S. . . . G7 135
Clark, co., Oh., U.S. . . . C2 142
Clark, co., S.D., U.S. . . . C8 148
Clark, co., Wa., U.S. . . . D3 154
Clark, co., Wi., U.S. . . . D3 156
Clark, Point, c., Ont., Can. . C3 103
Clarkdale, Az., U.S. . . . C3 110
Clarkdale, Ga., U.S. . . . h7 117
Clarke, co., Al., U.S. . . . D2 108
Clarke, co., Ga., U.S. . . . C3 117
Clarke, co., Ia., U.S. . . . C4 122
Clarke, co., Ms., U.S. . . . C5 131
Clarke, co., Va., U.S. . . . A4 153
Clarkesville, Ga., U.S. . . . B3 117
Clarkfield, Mn., U.S. . . . F3 130
Clark Fork, Id., U.S. . . . A2 119
Clark Fork, stm., U.S. . . . C1 133
Clarks, La., U.S. . . . B3 125
Clarksburg, Ont., Can. . . . C4 103
Clarksburg, Md., U.S. . . . B3 127

Name — Map Ref. — Page

Clarksburg, W.V., U.S. B4 155
Clarksdale, Ms., U.S. A3 131
Clark's Harbour, N.S., Can. F4 101
Clarks Hill, In., U.S. D4 121
Clarks Hill Lake, res., U.S. E10 106
Clarkson, Ky., U.S. C3 124
Clarkson, Ne., U.S. C8 134
Clarks Summit, Pa., U.S. m18 145
Clarkston, Ga., U.S. h8 117
Clarkston, Ut., U.S. B3 151
Clarkston, Wa., U.S. C8 154
Clarksville, Ar., U.S. B2 111
Clarksville, De., U.S. F5 115
Clarksville, In., U.S. H6 121
Clarksville, Ia., U.S. B5 122
Clarksville, Tn., U.S. A4 149
Clarksville, Tx., U.S. C5 150
Clarksville, Va., U.S. D4 153
Clarkton, Mo., U.S. E8 132
Clatskanie, Or., U.S. A3 144
Clatsop, co., Or., U.S. A3 144
Clavet, Sask., Can. F2 105
Clawson, Mi., U.S. o15 129
Claxton, Ga., U.S. D5 117
Clay, Ky., U.S. C2 124
Clay, W.V., U.S. C3 155
Clay, co., Al., U.S. B4 108
Clay, co., Ar., U.S. A5 111
Clay, co., Fl., U.S. B5 116
Clay, co., Ga., U.S. E2 117
Clay, co., Il., U.S. E5 120
Clay, co., In., U.S. F3 121
Clay, co., Ia., U.S. A2 122
Clay, co., Ks., U.S. C6 123
Clay, co., Ky., U.S. C6 124
Clay, co., Mn., U.S. D2 130
Clay, co., Ms., U.S. B5 131
Clay, co., Mo., U.S. B3 132
Clay, co., Ne., U.S. D7 134
Clay, co., N.C., U.S. f9 140
Clay, co., S.D., U.S. E8 148
Clay, co., Tn., U.S. C8 149
Clay, co., Tx., U.S. C3 150
Clay, co., W.V., U.S. C3 155
Clay Center, Ks., U.S. C6 123
Clay Center, Ne., U.S. D7 134
Clay City, Il., U.S. E5 120
Clay City, In., U.S. F3 121
Clay City, Ky., U.S. C6 124
Clayhatchee, Al., U.S. D4 108
Claymont, De., U.S. A4 115
Claypool, Az., U.S. D5 110
Clay Springs, Az., U.S. C5 110
Clayton, Al., U.S. D4 108
Clayton, Ca., U.S. h9 112
Clayton, De., U.S. C3 115
Clayton, Ga., U.S. B3 117
Clayton, In., U.S. E4 121
Clayton, La., U.S. C4 125
Clayton, Mo., U.S. f13 132
Clayton, N.J., U.S. D2 137
Clayton, N.M., U.S. A6 138
Clayton, N.C., U.S. B4 140
Clayton, co., Ga., U.S. C2 117
Clayton, co., Ia., U.S. B6 122
Clear Boggy Creek, stm., Ok., U.S. C5 143
Clear Creek, W.V., U.S. n13 155
Clear Creek, co., Co., U.S. B5 113
Cleare, Cape, c., Ak., U.S. D10 109
Clearfield, Ky., U.S. B6 124
Clearfield, Pa., U.S. D5 145
Clearfield, Ut., U.S. B3 151
Clearfield, co., Pa., U.S. D5 145
Clearlake, Ca., U.S. C2 112
Clear Lake, Ia., U.S. A4 122
Clear Lake, S.D., U.S. C9 148
Clearlake, Wa., U.S. A3 154
Clear Lake, Wi., U.S. C1 156
Clear Lake, res., Ca., U.S. C2 112
Clearmont, Wy., U.S. B6 157
Clearview City, Ks., U.S. g12 123
Clearwater, Fl., U.S. E4 116
Clearwater, Ks., U.S. E6 123
Clearwater, Ne., U.S. B7 134
Clearwater, S.C., U.S. E4 147
Clearwater, co., Id., U.S. C3 119
Clearwater, co., Mn., U.S. C3 130
Clearwater, stm., Can. A5 98
Clearwater, stm., Id., U.S. C2 119
Clearwater Mountains, mts., Id., U.S. C2 119
Cleburne, Tx., U.S. C4 150
Cleburne, co., Al., U.S. B4 108
Cleburne, co., Ar., U.S. B3 111
Cle Elum, Wa., U.S. B5 154
Clementon, N.J., U.S. D3 137
Clementsport, N.S., Can. E4 101
Clemmons, N.C., U.S. A2 140
Clemson, S.C., U.S. B2 147
Clendenin, W.V., U.S. C3 155
Cleona, Pa., U.S. F9 145
Clermont, Austl. D7 70
Clermont, Que., Can. B7 104
Clermont, Fr. C9 14
Clermont, Fl., U.S. D5 116
Clermont, co., Oh., U.S. C1 142
Clermont-Ferrand, Fr. G10 14
Cleveland, Al., U.S. A3 108
Cleveland, Ga., U.S. B3 117
Cleveland, Ms., U.S. B3 131
Cleveland, N.M., U.S. A4 138
Cleveland, Oh., U.S. A4 142
Cleveland, Ok., U.S. A5 143
Cleveland, Tn., U.S. D9 149
Cleveland, Tx., U.S. D5 150
Cleveland, Wi., U.S. k10 156
Cleveland, co., Eng., U.K. G12 8
Cleveland, co., Ar., U.S. D3 111
Cleveland, co., N.C., U.S. B1 140
Cleveland, co., Ok., U.S. B4 143
Cleveland, Mount, mtn., Mt., U.S. B3 133
Cleveland Heights, Oh., U.S. A4 142
Clevelândia, Braz. D12 80
Clever, Mo., U.S. D4 132
Cleves, Oh., U.S. o12 142
Clew Bay, b., Ire. H4 8
Clewiston, Fl., U.S. F6 116
Clifford, Ont., Can. D4 103
Cliffside Park, N.J., U.S. h9 137
Clifton, Az., U.S. D6 110
Clifton, Co., U.S. B2 113
Clifton, Il., U.S. C6 120
Clifton, Ks., U.S. C6 123
Clifton, N.J., U.S. B4 137
Clifton, Tn., U.S. B4 149
Clifton, Tx., U.S. D4 150
Clifton Forge, Va., U.S. C3 153
Clifton Knolls, N.Y., U.S. C7 139
Climax, Sask., Can. H1 105
Clinch, co., Ga., U.S. F4 117
Clinch, stm., U.S. D9 149
Clinchco, Va., U.S. e9 153
Clinch Mountain, mtn., U.S. C10 149
Clingmans Dome, mtn., U.S. D10 149
Clint, Tx., U.S. o11 150
Clinton, B.C., Can. D7 99
Clinton, Ont., Can. D3 103
Clinton, Ar., U.S. B3 111
Clinton, Ct., U.S. D5 114
Clinton, Il., U.S. C5 120
Clinton, In., U.S. E3 121
Clinton, Ia., U.S. C7 122
Clinton, Ky., U.S. f9 124
Clinton, La., U.S. D4 125
Clinton, Me., U.S. D3 126
Clinton, Md., U.S. C4 127
Clinton, Ma., U.S. B4 128
Clinton, Mi., U.S. F7 129
Clinton, Ms., U.S. C3 131
Clinton, Mo., U.S. C4 132
Clinton, N.C., U.S. C4 140
Clinton, Ok., U.S. B3 143
Clinton, S.C., U.S. C4 147
Clinton, Tn., U.S. C9 149
Clinton, Ut., U.S. B3 151
Clinton, Wa., U.S. B3 154
Clinton, Wi., U.S. F5 156
Clinton, co., Il., U.S. E4 120
Clinton, co., In., U.S. D4 121
Clinton, co., Ia., U.S. C7 122
Clinton, co., Ky., U.S. D4 124
Clinton, co., Mi., U.S. F6 129
Clinton, co., Mo., U.S. B3 132
Clinton, co., N.Y., U.S. f11 139
Clinton, co., Oh., U.S. C2 142
Clinton, co., Pa., U.S. D6 145
Clinton Lake, res., Il., U.S. C5 120
Clintonville, Wi., U.S. D5 156
Clintwood, Va., U.S. e9 153
Clio, Al., U.S. D4 108
Clio, Mi., U.S. E7 129
Clipperton, Île, atoll, Oc. F3 88
Clisson, Fr. E5 14
Clive, Alta., Can. C4 98
Clive, Ia., U.S. e8 122
Clodomira, Arg. D6 80
Cloncurry, Austl. C4 70
Clonmel, Ire. I6 8
Cloppenburg, Ger. C8 10
Cloquet, Mn., U.S. D6 130
Clorinda, Arg. C10 80
Closter, N.J., U.S. B5 137
Clothier, W.V., U.S. n12 155
Cloud, co., Ks., U.S. C6 123
Cloudcroft, N.M., U.S. E4 138
Cloud Peak, mtn., Wy., U.S. B5 157
Clover, S.C., U.S. A5 147
Cloverdale, Al., U.S. A2 108
Cloverdale, In., U.S. E4 121
Cloverport, Ky., U.S. C3 124
Clovis, Ca., U.S. D4 112
Clovis, N.M., U.S. C6 138
Cluj-Napoca, Rom. C7 20
Cluny, Fr. F11 14
Cluses, Fr. F13 14
Clute, Tx., U.S. r14 150
Clyde, Alta., Can. B4 98
Clyde, Ks., U.S. C6 123
Clyde, Oh., U.S. A3 142
Clyde, Tx., U.S. C3 150
Clyde, stm., Scot., U.K. F10 8
Clyde, Firth of, est., Scot., U.K. F8 8
Clyde Park, Mt., U.S. E6 133
Clyde River, N.W. Ter., Can. B19 96
Coachella, Ca., U.S. F5 112
Coachella Canal, Ca., U.S. F6 112
Coahoma, co., Ms., U.S. A3 131
Coahuila, state, Mex. C8 90
Coal, co., Ok., U.S. C5 143
Coal City, Il., U.S. B5 120
Coalcomán de Matamoros, Mex. H8 90
Coaldale, Alta., Can. E4 98
Coal Fork, W.V., U.S. C3 155
Coalgate, Ok., U.S. C5 143
Coal Grove, Oh., U.S. D3 142
Coal Harbour, B.C., Can. D4 99
Coal Hill, Ar., U.S. B2 111
Coalhurst, Alta., Can. E4 98
Coaling, Al., U.S. B2 108
Coalinga, Ca., U.S. D3 112
Coalmont, Tn., U.S. D8 149
Coalville, Ut., U.S. C4 151
Coalwood, W.V., U.S. D3 155
Coamo, P.R. E11 94
Coaraci, Braz. C9 79
Coari, Braz. J11 84
Coast Mountains, mts., N.A. E6 96
Coast Ranges, mts., U.S. C2 106
Coatbridge, Scot., U.K. F9 8
Coatepeque, Guat. C3 92
Coatesville, Pa., U.S. G10 145
Coaticook, Que., Can. D6 104
Coats, N.C., U.S. B4 140
Coats Island, i., N.W. Ter., Can. D16 96
Coats Land, reg., Ant. C2 73
Coatzacoalcos, Mex. H12 90
Cobalt, Ont., Can. p19 103
Cobán, Guat. B4 92
Cobar, Austl. H6 70
Cobb, co., Ga., U.S. C2 117
Cobberas, Mount, mtn., Austl. K8 70
Cobble Hill, B.C., Can. g12 99
Cobble Mountain Reservoir, res., Ma., U.S. B2 128
Cobden, Ont., Can. B8 103
Cobden, Il., U.S. F4 120
Cobh, Ire. J5 8
Cobija, Bol. D7 82
Cobleskill, N.Y., U.S. C6 139
Cobourg, Ont., Can. D6 103
Cobourg Peninsula, pen., Austl. B6 68
Cobram, Austl. J6 70
Cobre, Barranca del, val., Mex. D6 90
Coburg, Ger. E10 10
Coburg, Or., U.S. C3 144
Cocentaina, Spain G11 16
Cochabamba, Bol. G8 82
Cochabamba, dept., Bol. G9 82
Cochin, India H10 42
Cochise, co., Az., U.S. F5 110
Cochise Head, mtn., Az., U.S. E6 110
Cochiti, N.M., U.S. h8 138
Cochituate, Ma., U.S. g10 128
Cochran, Ga., U.S. D3 117
Cochran, co., Tx., U.S. C1 150
Cochrane, Alta., Can. D3 98
Cochrane, Ont., Can. o19 103
Cochrane, stm., Can. E12 96
Cochrane, Lago (Lago Pueyrredón), l., S.A. F2 78
Cocke, co., Tn., U.S. D10 149
Cockeysville, Md., U.S. B4 127
Cockrell Hill, Tx., U.S. n10 150
Coclé, prov., Pan. I14 92
Coco, stm., N.A. G3 94
Coco, Cayo, i., Cuba C5 94
Coco, Isla del, i., C.R. G7 88
Cocoa, Fl., U.S. D6 116
Cocoa Beach, Fl., U.S. D6 116
Coco Channel, strt., Asia C1 38
Coco Islands, is., Mya. G2 40
Coconino, co., Az., U.S. B3 110
Coconino Plateau, plat., Az., U.S. B3 110
Cocos, Braz. C6 79
Cocos (Keeling) Islands, dep., Oc. K10 24
Cocula, Mex. G8 90
Cod, Cape, c., Ma., U.S. C7 128
Codajás, Braz. I11 84
Coden, Al., U.S. E1 108
Codette, Sask., Can. D3 105
Codington, co., S.D., U.S. C8 148
Codó, Braz. D10 76
Codogno, Italy D4 18
Codpa, Chile H7 82
Cody, Wy., U.S. B3 157
Coeburn, Va., U.S. f9 153
Coeroeni (Corentyne), stm., S.A. F14 84
Coetivy Island, i., Sey. C11 58
Coeur d'Alene, Id., U.S. B2 119
Coeur d'Alene, stm., Id., U.S. B2 119
Coeur d'Alene Lake, res., Id., U.S. B2 119
Coeur d'Alene Mountains, mts., Id., U.S. B2 119
Coffee, co., Al., U.S. D3 108
Coffee, co., Ga., U.S. E4 117
Coffee, co., Tn., U.S. B5 149
Coffeeville, Al., U.S. D1 108
Coffeeville, Ms., U.S. B4 131
Coffey, co., Ks., U.S. D8 123
Coffeyville, Ks., U.S. E8 123
Coffs Harbour, Austl. H10 70
Cofre de Perote, Cerro, mtn., Mex. H11 90
Cognac, Fr. G6 14
Cogolin, Fr. I13 14
Cohasset, Ma., U.S. B6 128
Cohasset, Mn., U.S. C5 130
Cohoes, N.Y., U.S. C7 139
Coiba, Isla de, i., Pan. D2 84
Coig, stm., Arg. G2 78
Coihaique, Chile F2 78
Coimbatore, India G4 46
Coimbra, Port. E3 16
Coín, Spain I7 16
Coipasa, Lago, l., Bol. H7 82
Coipasa, Salar de, pl., S.A. H7 82
Čojbalsan, Mong. B9 30
Cojedes, state, Ven. C8 84
Cojutepeque, El Sal. D6 92
Cokato, Mn., U.S. E4 130
Coke, co., Tx., U.S. D2 150
Coker, Al., U.S. B2 108
Cokeville, Wy., U.S. D2 157
Colac, Austl. L5 70
Colatina, Braz. E8 79
Colbeck, Cape, c., Ant. C9 73
Colbert, Ok., U.S. D5 143
Colbert, co., Al., U.S. A2 108
Colbert Heights, Al., U.S. A2 108
Colborne, Ont., Can. C7 103
Colbún, Chile H3 80
Colby, Ks., U.S. C2 123
Colby, Wi., U.S. D3 156
Colchester, Eng., U.K. J14 8
Colchester, Ct., U.S. C6 114
Colchester, Il., U.S. C3 120
Colchester, Vt., U.S. B2 152
Cold Lake, Alta., Can. B5 98
Cold Spring, Ky., U.S. A5 124
Cold Spring, Mn., U.S. E4 130
Coldwater, Ont., Can. C5 103
Coldwater, Ks., U.S. E4 123
Coldwater, Mi., U.S. G5 129
Coldwater, Ms., U.S. A4 131
Coldwater, Oh., U.S. B1 142
Coldwater, stm., Ms., U.S. A3 131
Cole, co., Mo., U.S. C5 132
Colebrook, N.H., U.S. g7 136
Cole Camp, Mo., U.S. C4 132
Coleman, Mi., U.S. E6 129
Coleman, Tx., U.S. D3 150
Coleman, co., Tx., U.S. D3 150
Coleraine, Austl. K4 70
Coleraine, Mn., U.S. C5 130
Coleridge, Ne., U.S. B8 134
Coles, co., Il., U.S. D5 120
Coles, Punta, c., Peru G6 82
Colesberg, S. Afr. H7 66
Coleville, Sask., Can. F1 105
Colfax, In., U.S. D4 121
Colfax, Ia., U.S. C4 122
Colfax, La., U.S. C3 125
Colfax, Wa., U.S. C8 154
Colfax, Wi., U.S. D2 156
Colfax, co., Ne., U.S. C8 134
Colfax, co., N.M., U.S. A5 138
Colhué Huapi, Lago, l., Arg. F3 78
Colima, Mex. H8 90
Colima, state, Mex. H8 90
Colima, Nevado de, mtn., Mex. H8 90
Colinas, Braz. E10 76
College, Ak., U.S. B10 109
Collegedale, Tn., U.S. h11 149
College Park, Ga., U.S. C2 117
College Park, Md., U.S. C4 127
College Place, Wa., U.S. C7 154
College Station, Ar., U.S. C3 111
College Station, Tx., U.S. D4 150
Collegeville, In., U.S. C3 121
Collegeville, Pa., U.S. F11 145
Collerina, Austl. G7 70
Colleton, co., S.C., U.S. F6 147
Collie, Austl. F3 68
Collier, co., Fl., U.S. F5 116
Collier Bay, b., Austl. C4 68
Colliers, W.V., U.S. f8 155
Collierville, Tn., U.S. B2 149
Collin, co., Tx., U.S. C4 150
Collingdale, Pa., U.S. p20 145
Collingswood, N.J., U.S. D2 137
Collingsworth, co., Tx., U.S. B2 150
Collingwood, Ont., Can. C4 103
Collins, Ms., U.S. D4 131
Collins Park, De., U.S. B3 115
Collinsville, Austl. C7 70
Collinsville, Al., U.S. A4 108
Collinsville, Ct., U.S. B4 114
Collinsville, Il., U.S. E4 120
Collinsville, Ms., U.S. C5 131
Collinsville, Ok., U.S. A6 143
Collinsville, Va., U.S. D3 153
Collinwood, Tn., U.S. B4 149
Collipulli, Chile I2 80
Colman, S.D., U.S. D9 148
Colmar, Fr. D14 14
Colmar Manor, Md., U.S. f9 127
Colmenar Viejo, Spain E8 16
Colnett, Cabo, c., Mex. B1 90
Colo, Ia., U.S. B4 122
Cologne see Köln, Ger. E6 10
Coloma, Mi., U.S. F4 129
Colômbia, Braz. F4 79
Colombia, Col. F5 84
Colombia, ctry., S.A. C4 76
Colombo, Braz. C14 80
Colombo, Sri L. I5 46
Colome, S.D., U.S. D6 148
Colón, Arg. G8 80
Colón, Arg. G9 80
Colón, Cuba C4 94
Colón, Pan. C3 84
Colon, Mi., U.S. G5 129
Colón, prov., Pan. I14 92
Colón, dept., Hond. B9 92
Colón, Archipiélago de (Galapagos Islands), is., Ec. m15 85a
Colón, Isla, i., Pan. H12 92
Colonia Caroya, Arg. F6 80
Colonia del Sacramento, Ur. H10 80
Colonia Dora, Arg. E7 80
Colonia Elisa, Arg. D9 80
Colonial Beach, Va., U.S. B6 153
Colonial Heights, Tn., U.S. C11 149
Colonial Heights, Va., U.S. C5 153
Colonial National Historical Park, Va., U.S. C6 153
Colonias Unidas, Arg. D9 80
Colonie, N.Y., U.S. C7 139
Colonsay, Sask., Can. F3 105
Colony, Ks., U.S. D8 123
Colorado, C.R. G11 92
Colorado, co., Tx., U.S. E4 150
Colorado, state, U.S. B5 113
Colorado, stm., Arg. J7 80
Colorado, stm., N.A. E4 106
Colorado, stm., Tx., U.S. D3 150
Colorado City, Az., U.S. A3 110
Colorado City, Co., U.S. D6 113
Colorado City, Tx., U.S. C2 150
Colorado Plateau, plat., U.S. B4 110
Colorado River Aqueduct, Ca., U.S. F6 112
Colorado Springs, Co., U.S. C6 113
Colotlán, Mex. F8 90
Colquechaca, Bol. H8 82
Colquitt, Ga., U.S. E2 117
Colquitt, co., Ga., U.S. E3 117
Colstrip, Mt., U.S. E10 133
Colt, Ar., U.S. B5 111
Coltauco, Chile H3 80
Colton, S.D., U.S. D9 148
Columbia, Al., U.S. D4 108
Columbia, Il., U.S. E3 120
Columbia, Ky., U.S. C4 124
Columbia, Md., U.S. B4 127
Columbia, Ms., U.S. D4 131
Columbia, Mo., U.S. C5 132
Columbia, Pa., U.S. F9 145
Columbia, S.C., U.S. C5 147
Columbia, Tn., U.S. B4 149
Columbia, co., Ar., U.S. D2 111
Columbia, co., Fl., U.S. B4 116
Columbia, co., Ga., U.S. C4 117
Columbia, co., N.Y., U.S. C7 139
Columbia, co., Or., U.S. B3 144
Columbia, co., Pa., U.S. D9 145
Columbia, co., Wa., U.S. C7 154
Columbia, co., Wi., U.S. E4 156
Columbia, stm., N.A. B2 106
Columbia, Cape, c., N.W. Ter., Can. A12 86
Columbia, Mount, mtn., Can. C2 98
Columbia City, In., U.S. B7 121
Columbia City, Or., U.S. B4 144
Columbia Falls, Me., U.S. D5 126
Columbia Falls, Mt., U.S. B2 133
Columbia Heights, Mn., U.S. m12 130
Columbia Mountains, mts., B.C., Can. C7 99
Columbiana, Al., U.S. B3 108
Columbiana, Oh., U.S. B5 142
Columbiana, co., Oh., U.S. B5 142
Columbus, Ga., U.S. D2 117
Columbus, In., U.S. F6 121
Columbus, Ks., U.S. E9 123
Columbus, Ms., U.S. B5 131
Columbus, Mt., U.S. E7 133
Columbus, Ne., U.S. C8 134
Columbus, N.M., U.S. F2 138
Columbus, Oh., U.S. C2 142
Columbus, Tx., U.S. E4 150
Columbus, Wi., U.S. E4 156
Columbus, co., N.C., U.S. C4 140
Columbus Grove, Oh., U.S. B1 142
Columbus Junction, Ia., U.S. C6 122
Columbus Point, c., Bah. B7 94
Colusa, Ca., U.S. C2 112
Colusa, co., Ca., U.S. C2 112
Colville, Wa., U.S. A8 154
Colville, stm., Ak., U.S. B9 109
Colville, stm., Wa., U.S. A8 154
Colvos Passage, strt., Wa., U.S. f10 154
Colwich, Ks., U.S. E6 123
Colwood, B.C., Can. h12 99
Comacchio, Italy E7 18
Comal, co., Tx., U.S. E3 150
Comala, Mex. H8 90
Comalapa, Guat. C4 92
Comalcalco, Mex. H13 90
Comanche, Ok., U.S. C4 143
Comanche, Tx., U.S. D3 150
Comanche, co., Ks., U.S. E4 123
Comanche, co., Ok., U.S. C3 143
Comanche, co., Tx., U.S. D3 150
Comandante Fontana, Arg. C9 80
Comandante Nicanor Otamendi, Arg. J10 80
Comarapa, Bol. G9 82
Comayagua, Hond. C7 92
Comayagua, dept., Hond. C7 92
Combahee, stm., S.C., U.S. F6 147
Combarbalá, Chile F3 80
Comber, Ont., Can. E2 103
Combined Locks, Wi., U.S. h9 156
Combs, Ky., U.S. C6 124
Comer, Ga., U.S. B3 117
Comilla, Bngl. I14 44
Comiso, Italy M9 18
Comitan de Dominguez, Mex. I13 90
Commentry, Fr. F9 14
Commerce, Ga., U.S. B3 117
Commerce, Ok., U.S. A7 143
Commerce, Tx., U.S. C5 150
Commerce City, Co., U.S. B6 113
Commercy, Fr. D12 14
Common Fence Point, R.I., U.S. D6 146
Como, Italy D4 18
Como, Ms., U.S. A4 131
Como, Lago di, l., Italy C4 18
Comodoro Rivadavia, Arg. F3 78
Comores, Archipel des, is., Afr. D8 58
Comorin, Cape, c., India H4 46
Comoros (Comores), ctry., Afr. D8 58
Comox, B.C., Can. E5 99
Compiègne, Fr. C9 14
Compostela, Mex. G7 90
Compton, Ca., U.S. n12 112
Comrat, Mol. C12 20
Comstock, Mi., U.S. F5 129
Conakry, Gui. G3 64
Conanicut Island, i., R.I., U.S. E5 146
Concarán, Arg. G6 80
Concarneau, Fr. E3 14
Conceição da Barra, Braz. E9 79
Conceição das Alagoas, Braz. E4 79
Conceição do Almeida, Braz. B9 79
Conceição do Araguaia, Braz. E9 76
Conceição do Mato Dentro, Braz. E7 79
Concepción, Arg. E10 80
Concepción, Arg. D6 80
Concepción, Bol. G10 82
Concepción, Chile I2 80
Concepción, Para. B10 80
Concepción, dept., Para. B10 80
Concepción, Bahía, b., Mex. D4 90
Concepción, Volcán, vol., Nic. F9 92
Concepción de la Sierra, Arg. D11 80
Concepcion del Oro, Mex. E9 90
Concepción del Uruguay, Arg. G9 80
Concepción Huista, Guat. B3 92
Conception, Point, c., Ca., U.S. E3 112
Conception Bay, b., Newf., Can. E5 102
Conception Bay South, Newf., Can. E5 102
Conchas Dam, N.M., U.S. B5 138
Conchas Lake, res., N.M., U.S. B5 138
Conche, Newf., Can. C4 102
Conches-en-Ouche, Fr. D7 14
Concho, Az., U.S. C6 110
Concho, co., Tx., U.S. D3 150
Conchos, stm., Mex. E10 90
Conchos, stm., Mex. C7 90
Concord, Ca., U.S. h8 112
Concord, Ma., U.S. B5 128
Concord, N.H., U.S. D3 136
Concord, N.C., U.S. B2 140
Concord, Tn., U.S. D9 149
Concord, Vt., U.S. C5 152
Concord, stm., Ma., U.S. A5 128
Concordia, Arg. F9 80
Concórdia, Braz. D12 80
Concordia, Mex. F6 90
Concordia, Ks., U.S. C6 123
Concordia, Mo., U.S. C4 132
Concordia, co., La., U.S. C4 125
Concrete, Wa., U.S. A4 154
Conde, Braz. A10 79
Condé, Fr. D6 14
Condeúba, Braz. C8 79
Condobolin, Austl. I7 70
Condom, Fr. I7 14
Conecuh, co., Al., U.S. D2 108
Conecuh, stm., U.S. D3 108
Conegliano, Italy D7 18
Conejos, co., Co., U.S. D4 113
Coney Island (part of New York), N.Y., U.S. k13 139
Congamond, Ma., U.S. B2 128
Congamond Lakes, l., U.S. A4 114
Congaree, stm., S.C., U.S. D6 147
Congo, ctry., Afr. B3 58
Congo (Zaire) (Zaïre), stm., Afr. C2 58
Congo Basin, Afr. H9 52
Congress, Az., U.S. C3 110
Conjeeveram see Kānchipuram, India G10 42
Connaught, hist. reg., Ire. H4 8
Conneaut, Oh., U.S. A5 142
Connecticut, state, U.S. C5 114
Connecticut, stm., U.S. C12 106
Connell, Wa., U.S. C7 154
Connellsville, Pa., U.S. F2 145
Connersville, In., U.S. E7 121
Conover, N.C., U.S. B1 140
Conowingo, Md., U.S. A5 127
Conquest, Sask., Can. F2 105
Conquista, Braz. E5 79
Conrad, Ia., U.S. B5 122
Conrad, Mt., U.S. B5 133
Conroe, Tx., U.S. D5 150
Conselheiro Lafaiete, Braz. F7 79
Conselheiro Pena, Braz. E8 79
Conshohocken, Pa., U.S. F11 145
Consolación del Sur, Cuba C3 94
Con Son, is., Viet. J9 40
Consort, Alta., Can. C5 98
Constance, Lake see Bodensee, l., Eur. E16 14
Constanța, Rom. E12 20
Constantine see Qacentina, Alg. B14 62
Constantine, Mi., U.S. G5 129
Constantinople see İstanbul, Tur. H12 20
Constitución, Chile H2 80
Constitución, Ur. F10 80
Consuegra, Spain F8 16
Contamana, Peru B4 82
Contoocook, N.H., U.S. D3 136
Contoocook, stm., N.H., U.S. D3 136
Contra Costa, co., Ca., U.S. D3 112
Contratación, Col. D6 84
Contrecoeur, Que., Can. D4 104
Contumazá, Peru B2 82
Converse, In., U.S. C6 121
Converse, S.C., U.S. B4 147
Converse, co., Wy., U.S. C7 157
Conway, Ar., U.S. B3 111
Conway, Fl., U.S. D5 116
Conway, Mo., U.S. D5 132
Conway, N.H., U.S. C4 136
Conway, Pa., U.S. E1 145
Conway, S.C., U.S. D9 147
Conway, co., Ar., U.S. B3 111
Conway Springs, Ks., U.S. E6 123
Conyers, Ga., U.S. C2 117
Cook, Mn., U.S. C6 130
Cook, co., Ga., U.S. E3 117
Cook, co., Il., U.S. B6 120
Cook, co., Mn., U.S. k9 130
Cook, Mount, mtn., N.Z. E3 72
Cooke, co., Tx., U.S. C4 150
Cookes Peak, mtn., N.M., U.S. E2 138
Cookeville, Tn., U.S. C8 149
Cook Inlet, b., Ak., U.S. D9 109
Cook Islands, dep., Oc. H2 2
Cook Point, c., Md., U.S. C5 127
Cookshire, Que., Can. D6 104
Cookson, Ok., U.S. B7 143
Cook Strait, strt., N.Z. D5 72
Cooktown, Austl. C9 68
Coolah, Austl. H8 70
Coolangatta, Austl. G10 70
Coolgardie, Austl. F4 68
Coolidge, Az., U.S. E4 110
Coolidge, Ga., U.S. E3 117
Coolin, Id., U.S. A2 119
Cooma, Austl. K8 70
Coonabarabran, Austl. H8 70
Coonamble, Austl. H8 70
Coon Rapids, Ia., U.S. C3 122
Coon Rapids, Mn., U.S. E5 130
Cooper, co., Mo., U.S. C5 132
Cooper Creek, stm., Austl. G3 70
Cooper Mountain, mtn., Ak., U.S. g17 109
Coopersburg, Pa., U.S. F11 145
Coopers Mills, Me., U.S. D3 126
Cooperstown, N.Y., U.S. C6 139
Cooperstown, N.D., U.S. B7 141
Coopersville, Mi., U.S. E5 129
Coos, co., N.H., U.S. A4 136
Coos, co., Or., U.S. D2 144
Coosa, co., Al., U.S. C3 108
Coosa, stm., U.S. C3 108
Coosada, Al., U.S. C3 108
Coosawhatchie, stm., S.C., U.S. F5 147
Coos Bay, Or., U.S. D2 144
Cootamundra, Austl. J8 70
Copacabana, Bol. G7 82
Copacabana, Col. D5 84
Copainalá, Mex. I13 90
Copalis Beach, Wa., U.S. B1 154
Copán, Hond. C5 92
Copan, Ok., U.S. A6 143
Copán, dept., Hond. C6 92
Copenhagen see København, Den. N13 6
Copetonas, Arg. J8 80
Copiah, co., Ms., U.S. D3 131
Copiapó, Chile D3 80
Coplay, Pa., U.S. E10 145
Copley, Austl. H3 70
Copper, stm., Ak., U.S. C11 109
Copperas Cove, Tx., U.S. D4 150
Copper Canyon see Cobre, Barranca del, val., Mex. D6 90
Copper Center, Ak., U.S. C10 109
Copper Harbor, Mi., U.S. A3 129
Coppermine, N.W. Ter., Can. C9 96
Coquille, Or., U.S. D2 144
Coquimbo, Chile E3 80
Coquimbo, prov., Chile F3 80
Corabia, Rom. F8 20
Coração de Jesus, Braz. D6 79

Name	Map Ref.	Page
Coração de Maria, Braz.	B9	79
Coracora, Peru	F5	82
Coral Gables, Fl., U.S.	G6	116
Coral Harbour, N.W. Ter., Can.	D16	96
Coral Sea, Oc.	J19	158
Coral Sea Islands Territory, ter., Austl.	B9	70
Coralville, Ia., U.S.	C6	122
Coralville Lake, res., Ia., U.S.	C5	122
Coram, Mt., U.S.	B2	133
Coraopolis, Pa., U.S.	E1	145
Corato, Italy	H11	18
Corbeil-Essonnes, Fr.	D9	14
Corbin, Ky., U.S.	D5	124
Corcoran, Ca., U.S.	D4	112
Corcoran, Mn., U.S.	m11	130
Corcovado, Golfo, b., Chile	E2	78
Cordeiro, Braz.	G7	79
Cordele, Ga., U.S.	E3	117
Cordell, Ok., U.S.	B3	143
Cordell Hull Lake, res., Tn., U.S.	C8	149
Cordillera, dept., Para.	C10	80
Cordisburgo, Braz.	E6	79
Córdoba, Arg.	F6	80
Córdoba, Mex.	H11	90
Córdoba, Spain	H7	16
Córdoba, prov., Arg.	F7	80
Córdoba, dept., Col.	C5	84
Córdova, Peru	F4	82
Cordova, Al., U.S.	B2	108
Cordova, Ak., U.S.	C10	109
Cordova, N.M., U.S.	A4	138
Cordova, N.C., U.S.	C3	140
Corea, Me., U.S.	D5	126
Corentyne (Corantijn) (Coeroeni), stm., S.A.	E14	84
Corfu see Kérkira, Grc.	J3	20
Corfu see Kérkira, i., Grc.	J3	20
Coria, Spain	F5	16
Coria del Río, Spain	H5	16
Coribe, Braz.	B6	79
Corinna, Austl.	A3	70
Corinne, Me., U.S.	D3	126
Corinne, Ut., U.S.	B3	151
Corinth see Kórinthos, Grc.	L6	20
Corinth, Ms., U.S.	A5	131
Corinth, N.Y., U.S.	B7	139
Corinth, Gulf of see Korinthiakós Kólpos, b., Grc.	K6	20
Corinto, Braz.	E6	79
Corinto, Nic.	E7	92
Cork, Ire.	J5	8
Cork, co., Ire.	I5	8
Corleone, Italy	L8	18
Çorlu, Tur.	H11	20
Cornelia, Ga., U.S.	B3	117
Cornélio Procópio, Braz.	G3	79
Cornelius, N.C., U.S.	B2	140
Cornelius, Or., U.S.	g11	144
Cornell, Wi., U.S.	C2	156
Corner Brook, Newf., Can.	D3	102
Cornersville, Tn., U.S.	B5	149
Corneta, Punta, c., Mex.	J11	90
Corning, Ar., U.S.	A5	111
Corning, Ca., U.S.	C2	112
Corning, Ia., U.S.	D3	122
Corning, N.Y., U.S.	C3	139
Cornish, Me., U.S.	E2	126
Cornish Flat, N.H., U.S.	D2	136
Corno Grande, mtn., Italy	G8	18
Cornville, Az., U.S.	C4	110
Cornwall, Ont., Can.	B10	103
Cornwall, Pa., U.S.	F9	145
Cornwall, co., Eng., U.K.	K9	8
Cornwallis Island, i., N.W. Ter., Can.	A14	96
Cornwall on Hudson, N.Y., U.S.	D6	139
Coro, Ven.	B8	84
Coro, Golfete de, b., Ven.	I10	94
Corocoro, Bol.	G7	82
Coroico, Bol.	G8	82
Coromandel, Braz.	E5	79
Coromandel Coast, India	F6	46
Coromandel Peninsula, pen., N.Z.	B5	72
Corona, Ca., U.S.	F5	112
Coronach, Sask., Can.	H3	105
Coronado, Ca., U.S.	F5	112
Coronation, Alta., Can.	C5	98
Coronda, Arg.	F8	80
Coronel, Chile	I2	80
Coronel Bogado, Para.	D10	80
Coronel Dorrego, Arg.	J8	80
Coronel Du Graty, Arg.	D8	80
Coronel Fabriciano, Braz.	E7	79
Coronel Moldes, Arg.	C6	80
Coronel Moldes, Arg.	G4	80
Coronel Murta, Braz.	D7	79
Coronel Oviedo, Para.	C10	80
Coronel Pringles, Arg.	I8	80
Coronel Sapucaia, Braz.	G1	80
Coronel Suárez, Arg.	I8	80
Coronel Vidal, Arg.	I10	80
Coronel Vivida, Braz.	C12	80
Coronie, dept., Sur.	E14	84
Coropuna, Nevado, mtn., Peru	F5	82
Corowa, Austl.	K7	70
Corozal, Belize	H15	90
Corozal, Col.	C5	84
Corpus, Arg.	D11	80
Corpus Christi, Tx., U.S.	F4	150
Corral, Chile	D7	78
Corral de Bustos, Arg.	G7	80
Corrales, N.M., U.S.	k7	138
Correctionville, Ia., U.S.	B2	122
Correntina, Braz.	B6	79
Corrib, Lough, l., Ire.	H4	8
Corrientes, Arg.	D9	80
Corrientes, prov., Arg.	I5	84
Corrientes, stm., S.A.	I5	84
Corrientes, Cabo, c., Col.	A4	84
Corrientes, Cabo, c., Mex.	G7	90
Corriganville, Md., U.S.	k13	127
Corry, Pa., U.S.	C2	145
Corse (Corsica), i., Fr.	I24	15a
Corse, Cap, c., Fr.	k24	15a
Corsica, S.D., U.S.	D7	148
Corsica see Corse, i., Fr.	I24	15a
Corsicana, Tx., U.S.	C4	150
Corson, co., S.D., U.S.	B4	148
Cortazar, Mex.	G9	90
Corte, Fr.	I24	15a
Cortés, dept., Hond.	B6	92
Cortez, Co., U.S.	D2	113
Cortez, Fl., U.S.	q10	116
Cortez, Sea of see California, Golfo de, b., Mex.	D4	90
Cortland, Il., U.S.	B5	120
Cortland, Ne., U.S.	D9	134
Cortland, N.Y., U.S.	C4	139
Cortland, Oh., U.S.	A5	142
Cortland, co., N.Y., U.S.	C4	139
Çorum, Tur.	J12	20
Corumbá, Braz.	H13	82
Corumbá de Goiás, Braz.	C4	79
Corumbaíba, Braz.	E4	79
Coruña, Mi., U.S.	F6	129
Corupire, Braz.	F11	76
Corvallis, Mt., U.S.	D2	133
Corvallis, Or., U.S.	C3	144
Corydon, In., U.S.	H5	121
Corydon, Ia., U.S.	D4	122
Corydon, Ky., U.S.	C2	124
Coryell, co., Tx., U.S.	D4	150
Corzuela, Arg.	D8	80
Cosamaloapan [de Carpio], Mex.	H12	90
Cosenza, Italy	J11	18
Coshocton, Oh., U.S.	B4	142
Coshocton, co., Oh., U.S.	B4	142
Cosigüina, Punta, c., Nic.	E7	92
Cosmopolis, Wa., U.S.	C2	154
Cosne-Cours-sur-Loire, Fr.	E9	14
Cosquín, Arg.	F6	80
Costa Mesa, Ca., U.S.	n13	112
Costa Rica, ctry., N.A.	G10	92
Costa Rica, Mex.	E6	90
Costilla, co., Co., U.S.	D5	113
Cotabato, Phil.	D7	38
Cotagaita, Bol.	I9	82
Cotahuasi, Peru	F4	82
Coteau-Landing, Que., Can.	D3	104
Coteaux, Haiti	E7	94
Cote d'Ivoire (Ivory Coast), ctry., Afr.	G5	54
Cotegipe, Braz.	B6	79
Cotentin, pen., Fr.	C5	14
Cotija de la Paz, Mex.	H8	90
Cotonou, Benin	H11	64
Cotopaxi, prov., Ec.	H3	84
Cotopaxi, vol., Ec.	H3	84
Cottage Grove, Mn., U.S.	n13	130
Cottage Grove, Or., U.S.	D3	144
Cottam, Ont., Can.	E2	103
Cottbus, Ger.	D14	10
Cotter, Ar., U.S.	A3	111
Cottle, co., Tx., U.S.	B2	150
Cottleville, Mo., U.S.	f12	132
Cottondale, Al., U.S.	B2	108
Cotton Plant, Ar., U.S.	B4	111
Cottonport, La., U.S.	C3	125
Cotton Valley, La., U.S.	B2	125
Cottonwood, Al., U.S.	D4	108
Cottonwood, Az., U.S.	C3	110
Cottonwood, Id., U.S.	C2	119
Cottonwood, Mn., U.S.	F3	130
Cottonwood, co., Mn., U.S.	F3	130
Cottonwood, stm., Ks., U.S.	D7	123
Cottonwood Cove, Nv., U.S.	H7	135
Cottonwood Falls, Ks., U.S.	D7	123
Cotulla, Tx., U.S.	E3	150
Coudersport, Pa., U.S.	C5	145
Coulee City, Wa., U.S.	B6	154
Coulee Dam, Wa., U.S.	B7	154
Coulee Dam National Recreation Area, Wa., U.S.	A7	154
Coulommiers, Fr.	D10	14
Coulterville, Il., U.S.	E4	120
Counce, Tn., U.S.	B3	149
Council, Id., U.S.	E2	119
Council Bluffs, Ia., U.S.	C2	122
Council Grove, Ks., U.S.	D7	123
Country Homes, Wa., U.S.	B8	154
Coupeville, Wa., U.S.	A3	154
Courcelles, Bel.	H5	12
Courland see Kurzeme, hist. reg., Lat.	E5	22
Courtenay, B.C., Can.	E5	99
Courtland, Ont., Can.	E4	103
Courtland, Al., U.S.	A2	108
Courtland, Va., U.S.	D5	153
Coushatta, La., U.S.	B2	125
Coutances, Fr.	C5	14
Coutts, Alta., Can.	E5	98
Couvin, Bel.	H5	12
Cove, Ar., U.S.	C1	111
Covedale, Oh., U.S.	o12	142
Coventry, Eng., U.K.	I12	8
Coventry, Ct., U.S.	B6	114
Coventry, R.I., U.S.	D3	146
Coventry, Vt., U.S.	B4	152
Cove Point, c., Md., U.S.	D5	127
Coverdale Crossroads, De., U.S.	F3	115
Covilhã, Port.	E4	16
Covina, Ca., U.S.	m13	112
Covington, Ga., U.S.	C3	117
Covington, In., U.S.	D3	121
Covington, Ky., U.S.	A5	124
Covington, La., U.S.	D5	125
Covington, Oh., U.S.	B1	142
Covington, Tn., U.S.	B2	149
Covington, Va., U.S.	C3	153
Covington, co., Al., U.S.	D3	108
Covington, co., Ms., U.S.	D4	131
Cowan, Tn., U.S.	B5	149
Cowansville, Que., Can.	D5	104
Coward, S.C., U.S.	D8	147
Cowarts, Al., U.S.	D4	108
Cowdenbeath, Scot., U.K.	E10	8
Cowell, Austl.	I2	70
Cowen, W.V., U.S.	C4	155
Cowen, Mount, mtn., Mt., U.S.	E6	133
Coweta, Ok., U.S.	B6	143
Coweta, co., Ga., U.S.	C2	117
Cow Head, Newf., Can.	D3	102
Cowichan Bay, B.C., Can.	g12	99
Cowley, Alta., Can.	E3	98
Cowley, Wy., U.S.	B4	157
Cowley, co., Ks., U.S.	E7	123
Cowlington, Ok., U.S.	B7	143
Cowlitz, co., Wa., U.S.	C2	154
Cowlitz, stm., Wa., U.S.	C3	154
Cowpasture, stm., Va., U.S.	B3	153
Cowpens, S.C., U.S.	A4	147
Cowra, Austl.	I8	70
Coxim, Braz.	E1	79
Coxsackie, N.Y., U.S.	C7	139
Cox's Bāzār, Bngl.	J14	44
Cox's Cove, Newf., Can.	D2	102
Coyaguama, Cerro, mtn., Arg.	B5	80
Coyuca de Benítez, Mex.	I9	90
Coyuca de Catalán, Mex.	H9	90
Cozad, Ne., U.S.	D6	134
Cozumel, Mex.	G16	90
Cozumel, Isla, i., Mex.	G16	90
Crab Orchard, Ky., U.S.	C5	124
Crab Orchard, Tn., U.S.	D9	149
Crab Orchard, W.V., U.S.	n13	155
Crab Orchard Lake, res., Il., U.S.	F4	120
Crabtree Mills, Que., Can.	D4	104
Cradock, S. Afr.	I7	66
Crafton, Pa., U.S.	k13	145
Craig, Ak., U.S.	D13	109
Craig, Co., U.S.	A3	113
Craig, co., O., U.S.	A6	143
Craig, co., Va., U.S.	C2	153
Craighead, co., Ar., U.S.	B5	111
Craigmont, Id., U.S.	C2	119
Craigsville, Va., U.S.	B3	153
Craigsville, W.V., U.S.	C4	155
Craik, Sask., Can.	F3	105
Crailsheim, Ger.	F10	10
Craiova, Rom.	E7	20
Cramerton, N.C., U.S.	B1	140
Cranberry Lake, l., N.Y., U.S.	A6	139
Cranberry Portage, Man., Can.	B1	100
Cranbrook, B.C., Can.	E10	99
Crandon, Wi., U.S.	C5	156
Crane, Mo., U.S.	E4	132
Crane, Tx., U.S.	D1	150
Crane, co., Tx., U.S.	D1	150
Cranford, N.J., U.S.	B4	137
Cranston, R.I., U.S.	C4	146
Craon, Fr.	E6	14
Crapaud, P.E.I., Can.	C6	101
Crater Lake, l., Or., U.S.	E4	144
Crater Lake National Park, Or., U.S.	E4	144
Craters of the Moon National Monument, Id., U.S.	F5	119
Crateús, Braz.	E10	76
Craven, Sask., Can.	G3	105
Craven, co., N.C., U.S.	B5	140
Crawford, Ga., U.S.	C3	117
Crawford, Ms., U.S.	B5	131
Crawford, Ne., U.S.	B2	134
Crawford, co., Ar., U.S.	B1	111
Crawford, co., Ga., U.S.	D3	117
Crawford, co., Il., U.S.	D6	120
Crawford, co., In., U.S.	H4	121
Crawford, co., Ia., U.S.	B2	122
Crawford, co., Ks., U.S.	E9	123
Crawford, co., Mi., U.S.	D6	129
Crawford, co., Mo., U.S.	D6	132
Crawford, co., Oh., U.S.	B3	142
Crawford, co., Pa., U.S.	C1	145
Crawford, co., Wi., U.S.	E3	156
Crawford Bay, B.C., Can.	E9	99
Crawford Notch State Park, N.H., U.S.	B4	136
Crawfordsville, Ar., U.S.	B5	111
Crawfordsville, In., U.S.	D4	121
Creede, Co., U.S.	D4	113
Creedmoor, N.C., U.S.	A4	140
Creek, co., Ok., U.S.	B5	143
Creel, Mex.	D6	90
Cree Lake, l., Sask., Can.	m7	105
Creemore, Ont., Can.	C4	103
Creighton, Sask., Can.	C5	105
Creighton, Ne., U.S.	B8	134
Creighton, Pa., U.S.	h14	145
Creil, Fr.	C9	14
Crema, Italy	D4	18
Cremona, Alta., Can.	D3	98
Cremona, Italy	D3	18
Crenshaw, Ms., U.S.	A3	131
Crenshaw, co., Al., U.S.	D3	108
Creola, Al., U.S.	E1	108
Cres, Otok, i., Cro.	E9	18
Cresaptown, Md., U.S.	k13	127
Crescent, Ok., U.S.	B4	143
Crescent, Or., U.S.	D5	144
Crescent City, Ca., U.S.	B1	112
Crescent City, Fl., U.S.	C5	116
Crescent Springs, Ky., U.S.	h13	124
Cresco, Ia., U.S.	A5	122
Crespo, Arg.	G8	80
Cresskill, N.J., U.S.	h9	137
Crest Hill, Il., U.S.	k8	120
Crested Butte, Co., U.S.	C4	113
Crestline, Oh., U.S.	B3	142
Creston, B.C., Can.	E9	99
Creston, Ia., U.S.	C3	122
Crestone Peak, mtn., Co., U.S.	D5	113
Crestview, Fl., U.S.	u15	116
Crestview, Hi., U.S.	g10	118
Crestwood, Ky., U.S.	B4	124
Crestwood Village, N.J., U.S.	D4	137
Creswell, N.C., U.S.	B6	140
Creswick, Austl.	K5	70
Crete, Il., U.S.	B6	120
Crete, Ne., U.S.	D9	134
Crete see Kríti, i., Grc.	N8	20
Creus, Cap de, c., Spain	C15	16
Creve Coeur, Il., U.S.	C4	120
Crevillent, Spain	G11	16
Crewe, Eng., U.K.	H11	8
Crewe, Va., U.S.	C4	153
Criciúma, Braz.	E14	80
Cricket, N.C., U.S.	A1	140
Cridersville, Oh., U.S.	B1	142
Crieff, Scot., U.K.	E10	8
Crikvenica, Cro.	D9	18
Crimean Peninsula see Kryms'kyy pivostriv, pen., Ukr.	H4	26
Crimmitschau, Ger.	E12	10
Cripple Creek, Co., U.S.	C5	113
Crisfield, Md., U.S.	E6	127
Crisp, co., Ga., U.S.	E3	117
Crissiumal, Braz.	D11	80
Cristalândia, Braz.	F9	76
Cristalina, Braz.	D5	79
Cristóbal Colón, Pico, mtn., Col.	B6	84
Crittenden, Ky., U.S.	B5	124
Crittenden, co., Ar., U.S.	B5	111
Crittenden, co., Ky., U.S.	e9	124
Crivitz, Wi., U.S.	C6	156
Crna Gora, state, Yugo.	G2	20
Croatia, ctry., Eur.	F11	4
Crocker, Mo., U.S.	D5	132
Crockett, Tx., U.S.	D5	150
Crockett, Tn., U.S.	B2	149
Crockett, co., Tn., U.S.	B2	149
Crockett, co., Tx., U.S.	D2	150
Crofton, Ky., U.S.	C2	124
Crofton, Md., U.S.	B4	127
Crofton, Ne., U.S.	B8	134
Croix, Lac la, l., Mn., U.S.	B6	130
Croker, Cape, c., Austl.	B6	68
Croker, Cape, c., Ont., Can.	C4	103
Croker Island, i., Austl.	B6	68
Cromona, Ky., U.S.	C7	124
Cromwell, Ct., U.S.	C5	114
Cromwell, In., U.S.	B6	121
Crook, co., Or., U.S.	C6	144
Crook, co., Wy., U.S.	B8	157
Crooked Island, i., Bah.	C7	94
Crooked Island Passage, strt., Bah.	C7	94
Crooked Lake, l., Mn., U.S.	B6	130
Crooks, S.D., U.S.	D9	148
Crookston, Mn., U.S.	C2	130
Crooksville, Oh., U.S.	C3	142
Crosby, Mn., U.S.	D5	130
Crosby, N.D., U.S.	A2	141
Crosby, co., Tx., U.S.	C2	150
Cross, co., Ar., U.S.	B5	111
Cross City, Fl., U.S.	C3	116
Crossett, Ar., U.S.	D4	111
Crossfield, Alta., Can.	D3	98
Cross Lake, Man., Can.	B3	100
Crosslake, Mn., U.S.	D4	130
Cross Lanes, W.V., U.S.	C3	155
Cross Plains, Tn., U.S.	A5	149
Cross Plains, Wi., U.S.	E4	156
Crossville, Al., U.S.	A4	108
Crossville, Il., U.S.	E5	120
Crossville, Tn., U.S.	D8	149
Croswell, Mi., U.S.	E8	129
Crothersville, In., U.S.	G6	121
Crotone, Italy	J12	18
Croton-on-Hudson, N.Y., U.S.	D7	139
Crow, stm., Mn., U.S.	E4	130
Crow Agency, Mt., U.S.	E9	133
Crowder, Ms., U.S.	A3	131
Crowell, Tx., U.S.	B3	150
Crowley, La., U.S.	D3	125
Crowley, co., Co., U.S.	C7	113
Crowley, Lake, res., Ca., U.S.	n9	150
Crown Point, In., U.S.	B3	121
Crown Point, La., U.S.	k11	125
Crownpoint, N.M., U.S.	B1	138
Crowsnest Pass, Alta., Can.	E3	98
Crowsnest Pass, Can.	E3	98
Crows Nest Peak, mtn., S.D., U.S.	C2	148
Croydon, Austl.	B5	70
Croydon, Eng., U.K.	J12	8
Croydon, Pa., U.S.	F12	145
Crozet, Va., U.S.	B4	153
Crozet, Archipel, is., F.S.A.T.	M9	158
Crucero, Peru	F6	82
Cruces, Cuba	C4	94
Cruger, Ms., U.S.	B3	131
Crump, Tn., U.S.	B3	149
Cruz, Cabo, c., Cuba	E6	94
Cruz Alta, Arg.	G8	80
Cruz Alta, Braz.	E12	80
Cruz del Eje, Arg.	F6	80
Cruzeiro, Braz.	G6	79
Cruzeiro do Oeste, Braz.	G3	79
Cruzeiro do Sul, Braz.	B5	82
Cruzília, Braz.	F6	79
Crysler, Ont., Can.	B9	103
Crystal, Mn., U.S.	m12	130
Crystal Bay, Nv., U.S.	D1	135
Crystal City, Man., Can.	E2	100
Crystal City, Mo., U.S.	C7	132
Crystal City, Tx., U.S.	E3	150
Crystal Falls, Mi., U.S.	B2	129
Crystal Lake, Ct., U.S.	B6	114
Crystal Lake, Fl., U.S.	u16	116
Crystal Lake, Il., U.S.	A5	120
Crystal Lake, l., Mi., U.S.	D4	129
Crystal Lawns, Il., U.S.	k8	120
Crystal River, Fl., U.S.	D4	116
Crystal Springs, Ms., U.S.	D3	131
Csongrád, Hung.	I20	10
Cúa, Ven.	B9	84
Cuajinicuilapa, Mex.	I10	90
Cuamba, Moz.	D7	58
Cuando (Kwando), stm., Afr.	D4	58
Cuango (Kwango), stm., Afr.	C3	58
Cuanza, stm., Ang.	C3	58
Cuareim (Quaraí), stm., S.A.	F10	80
Cuatrociénegas, Mex.	D8	90
Cuauhtémoc, Mex.	C6	90
Cuautitlán [de Romero Rubio], Mex.	H10	90
Cuba, Il., U.S.	C3	120
Cuba, Mo., U.S.	C6	132
Cuba, N.M., U.S.	A3	138
Cuba, N.Y., U.S.	C2	139
Cuba, ctry., N.A.	C5	94
Cuba City, Wi., U.S.	F3	156
Cubango (Okavango), stm., Afr.	E3	58
Cubero, N.M., U.S.	B2	138
Cuchara, Co., U.S.	D5	113
Cuchloma, Russia	C25	22
Cúcuta, Col.	C6	84
Cudahy, Wi., U.S.	F6	156
Cuddalore, India	G5	46
Cuddapah, India	E5	46
Čudovo, Russia	B14	22
Cudworth, Sask., Can.	E3	105
Cue, Austl.	E3	68
Cuenca, Ec.	I3	84
Cuenca, Spain	E9	16
Cuencamé [de Ceniceros], Mex.	E8	90
Cuernavaca, Mex.	H10	90
Cuero, Tx., U.S.	E4	150
Cuers, Fr.	I13	14
Cueto, Cuba	D7	94
Cuetzalan del Progreso, Mex.	G11	90
Cugir, Rom.	D7	20
Cuiabá, Braz.	F13	82
Cuiabá, Braz.	C4	79
Cuicatlán, Mex.	I11	90
Cuijk, Neth.	E8	12
Cuilapa, Guat.	C4	92
Cuilco, Guat.	B3	92
Cuilco (Grijalva), stm., N.A.	B3	92
Cuilo (Kwilu), stm., Afr.	C3	58
Cuíto, stm., Ang.	B5	66
Cuito-Cuanavale, Ang.	E3	58
Cuitzeo, Laguna de, l., Mex.	H9	90
Čukotskij poluostrov, pen., Russia	D28	28
Culberson, co., Tx., U.S.	o12	150
Culberson, Mt., U.S.	B12	133
Culbertson, Ne., U.S.	D5	134
Culebra, Isla de, i., P.R.	E12	94
Culebra Peak, mtn., Co., U.S.	D5	113
Culgoa, stm., Austl.	G7	70
Culiacán, Mex.	E6	90
Culiacancito, Mex.	E6	90
Culijón, Nevado, mtn., Peru	F7	82
Cullen, La., U.S.	B2	125
Cullera, Spain	F11	16
Cullinan, S. Afr.	E9	66
Cullman, Al., U.S.	A3	108
Cullman, co., Al., U.S.	A3	108
Culloden, W.V., U.S.	C2	155
Cullowhee, N.C., U.S.	f9	140
Culpeper, Va., U.S.	B5	153
Culpeper, co., Va., U.S.	B5	153
Culver, In., U.S.	B5	121
Culver, Or., U.S.	C5	144
Čulym, Russia	F14	26
Cumaná, Ven.	B10	84
Cumberland, B.C., Can.	E5	99
Cumberland, Ky., U.S.	D7	124
Cumberland, Md., U.S.	k13	127
Cumberland, Wi., U.S.	C2	156
Cumberland, co., Il., U.S.	D5	120
Cumberland, co., Ky., U.S.	D4	124
Cumberland, co., Me., U.S.	E2	126
Cumberland, co., N.J., U.S.	E2	137
Cumberland, co., N.C., U.S.	C4	140
Cumberland, co., Pa., U.S.	F7	145
Cumberland, co., Tn., U.S.	D8	149
Cumberland, co., Va., U.S.	C4	153
Cumberland, stm., U.S.	D9	106
Cumberland, Lake, res., Ky., U.S.	D5	124
Cumberland Center, Me., U.S.	g7	126
Cumberland Foreside, Me., U.S.	E2	126
Cumberland Gap, U.S.	D6	124
Cumberland Gap National Historical Park, U.S.	D6	124
Cumberland Hill, R.I., U.S.	B4	146
Cumberland House, Sask., Can.	D4	105
Cumberland Island National Seashore, Ga., U.S.	F5	117
Cumberland Islands, is., Austl.	C8	70
Cumberland Lake, l., Sask., Can.	C4	105
Cumberland Mountain, mtn., Tn., U.S.	C9	149
Cumberland Plateau, plat., U.S.	D8	149
Cumbres Pass, Co., U.S.	D4	113
Cumbria, co., Eng., U.K.	G11	8
Cuming, co., Ne., U.S.	C8	134
Cumming, Ga., U.S.	B2	117
Cummins, Austl.	J1	70
Cumpas, Mex.	B5	90
Çumra, Tur.	C2	48
Cunard, W.V., U.S.	m13	155
Cunco, Chile	D2	78
Cuncumén, Chile	F3	80
Cundinamarca, dept., Col.	E5	84
Cunene (Kunene), stm., Afr.	E2	58
Cuneo, Italy	E2	18
Cunha Porã, Braz.	D12	80
Cunnamulla, Austl.	G6	70
Cunningham, Ks., U.S.	E5	123
Cunningham, Ky., U.S.	f9	124
Cupar, Sask., Can.	G3	105
Cupica, Golfo de, b., Col.	D4	84
Curaçá, Braz.	E11	76
Curaçao, i., Neth. Ant.	H10	94
Curacautín, Chile	I3	80
Curanilahue, Chile	I2	80
Curaray, stm., S.A.	H5	84
Curepipe, Mrts.	v18	67c
Curepto, Chile	H2	80
Curiapo, Ven.	C12	84
Curicó, Chile	H3	80
Curitiba, Braz.	C14	80
Curitibanos, Braz.	D13	80
Curiúva, Braz.	H3	79
Curnamona, Austl.	H3	70
Currais Novos, Braz.	E11	76
Current, stm., U.S.	A5	111
Current Mountain, mtn., Nv., U.S.	E6	135
Currie, Nv., U.S.	A5	135
Currituck, co., N.C., U.S.	A6	140
Curry, co., N.M., U.S.	C6	138
Curry, co., Or., U.S.	E2	144
Curtea de Argeş, Rom.	D8	20
Curtis, Ne., U.S.	D5	134
Curtisville, Pa., U.S.	E2	145
Curuçá, Braz.	D9	76
Curuguaty, Para.	C11	80
Cururupu, Braz.	D10	76
Curuzú Cuatiá, Arg.	E9	80
Curvelo, Braz.	E6	79
Curwensville, Pa., U.S.	E4	145
Curwood, Mount, mtn., Mi., U.S.	B2	129
Cusco, Peru	E6	82
Cusco, dept., Peru	E5	82
Cushing, Ok., U.S.	B5	143
Cushman, Ar., U.S.	B4	111
Čusovoj, Russia	F9	26
Cusseta, Ga., U.S.	D2	117
Custer, Mt., U.S.	D9	133
Custer, S.D., U.S.	D2	148
Custer, Wa., U.S.	A3	154
Custer, co., Co., U.S.	C5	113
Custer, co., Id., U.S.	E4	119
Custer, co., Mt., U.S.	D11	133
Custer, co., Ne., U.S.	C6	134
Custer, co., Ok., U.S.	B2	143
Custer, co., S.D., U.S.	D2	148
Custer Battlefield National Monument, Mt., U.S.	E9	133
Custer Peak, mtn., S.D., U.S.	C2	148
Cut Bank, Mt., U.S.	B4	133
Cut Bank Creek, stm., N.D., U.S.	A4	141
Cutervo, Peru	B2	82
Cuthbert, Ga., U.S.	E2	117
Cut Knife, Sask., Can.	E1	105
Cutler Ridge, Fl., U.S.	s13	116
Cut Off, La., U.S.	E5	125
Cutral-Có, Arg.	J4	80
Cuttack, India	J11	44
Čuvašija, state, Russia	F7	26
Cuxhaven, Ger.	B8	10
Cuyahoga, co., Oh., U.S.	A4	142
Cuyahoga, stm., Oh., U.S.	A4	142
Cuyahoga Falls, Oh., U.S.	A4	142
Cuyuni, stm., S.A.	D13	84
Cuyuni-Mazaruni, prov., Guy.	D12	84
C.W. McConaughy, Lake, res., Ne., U.S.	C4	134
Cyclades see Kikládhes, is., Grc.	L9	20
Cynthiana, In., U.S.	H2	121
Cynthiana, Ky., U.S.	B5	124
Cypress River, Man., Can.	E2	100
Cyprus, ctry., Asia	H14	4
Cyprus, North (Kuzey Kıbrıs), ctry., Asia	H14	4
Cyril, Ok., U.S.	C3	143
Czech Republic (Česká Republika), ctry., Eur.	F11	4
Częstochowa, Pol.	E19	10

D

Name	Map Ref.	Page
Dabat, Eth.	K9	60
Dabeiba, Col.	D4	84
Dabnou, Niger	D12	64
Dabola, Gui.	F4	64
Dacca see Dhaka, Bngl.	I14	44
Dachau, Ger.	G11	10
Dacono, Co., U.S.	A6	113
Dacula, Ga., U.S.	C3	117
Dade, co., Fl., U.S.	G6	116
Dade, co., Ga., U.S.	B1	117
Dade, co., Mo., U.S.	D4	132
Dade City, Fl., U.S.	D4	116
Dadeville, Al., U.S.	C4	108
Dādra and Nagar Haveli, ter., India	B2	46
Dādu, Pak.	G2	44
Daet, Phil.	n20	39b
Dagana, China	M2	34
Daga Post, Sud.	M7	60
Dagda, Lat.	E10	22
Dagestan, state, Russia	I7	26
Daggett, co., Ut., U.S.	C6	151
Daghfalī, Sud.	H7	60
Dagsboro, De., U.S.	F5	115
Dagu, China	E5	32
Dagupan, Phil.	m19	39b
Da Hinggan Ling, mts., China	B11	30
Dahlak Archipelago, is., Erit.	G2	47
Dahlonega, Ga., U.S.	B3	117
Dahmani, Tun.	N3	18
Dāhod, India	I6	44
Dahomey see Benin, ctry., Afr.	G7	54
Dahūk, Iraq	C7	48
Daimiel, Spain	F8	16
Daireaux, Arg.	I8	80
Dairen see Dalian, China	E9	32
Dajabón, Dom. Rep.	E9	94
Dajarra, Austl.	D1	68
Dakar, Sen.	D1	62
Dakhla, W. Sah.	D13	64
Dakoro, Niger	F5	130
Dakota, co., Mn., U.S.	F5	130
Dakota, co., Ne., U.S.	B9	134
Dakota City, Ia., U.S.	B3	122
Dakota City, Ne., U.S.	B9	134
Đakovica, Yugo.	G4	20
Dalaba, Gui.	F3	64
Da Lat, Viet.	I10	40
Dalby, Austl.	F9	70
Dale, Nor.	K9	6
Dale, co., Al., U.S.	D4	108
Dale City, Va., U.S.	B5	153
Dale Hollow Lake, res., U.S.	C8	149
Daleville, Al., U.S.	D4	108
Daleville, In., U.S.	D7	121
Dalhart, Tx., U.S.	A1	150
Dalhousie, N.B., Can.	A3	101
Dali, China	B6	40
Dalian (Dairen), China	E9	32
Daljā', Egypt	C12	60
Dall, Mount, mtn., Ak., U.S.	F15	109
Dallam, co., Tx., U.S.	A1	150
Dallas, Ga., U.S.	C2	117
Dallas, N.C., U.S.	B1	140
Dallas, Or., U.S.	C3	144
Dallas, Pa., U.S.	D10	145
Dallas, S.D., U.S.	D6	148
Dallas, Tx., U.S.	C4	150
Dallas, Wi., U.S.	C2	156
Dallas, co., Al., U.S.	C2	108
Dallas, co., Ar., U.S.	D3	111
Dallas, co., Ia., U.S.	C3	122
Dallas, co., Mo., U.S.	D4	132
Dallas, co., Tx., U.S.	n10	150
Dallas Center, Ia., U.S.	C4	122
Dallastown, Pa., U.S.	G8	145
Dalmacija, hist. reg., Eur.	F11	18

Name — Map Ref. — Page

Dalmacio Vélez Sarsfield, Arg. ... G7 80
Dalmatia see Dalmacija, hist. reg., Eur. ... F11 18
Dalmeny, Sask., Can. ... E2 105
Dal'negorsk, Russia ... I19 28
Dal'nerečensk, Russia ... H18 28
Daloa, C. Iv. ... H6 64
Dalton, Ga., U.S. ... B2 117
Dalton, Ma., U.S. ... B1 128
Dalton Gardens, Id., U.S. ... B2 119
Daly, stm., Austl. ... B6 68
Daly City, Ca., U.S. ... h8 112
Daly Waters, Austl. ... C6 68
Damān, ter., India ... B2 46
Damanhūr, Egypt ... B6 60
Damariscotta, Me., U.S. ... D3 126
Damascus see Dimashq, Syria ... A6 50
Damascus, Md., U.S. ... B3 127
Damascus, Va., U.S. ... f10 153
Damāvand, Qolleh-ye, mtn., Iran ... D12 48
Damba, Ang. ... C3 58
Dam Gamad, Sud. ... K4 60
Dāmghān, Iran ... C13 48
Damietta see Dumyāt, Egypt ... B6 60
Dammartin-en-Goële, Fr. ... C9 14
Damoh, India ... I8 44
Dampier, Austl. ... D3 68
Dampier Archipelago, is., Austl. ... D3 68
Dan, stm., U.S. ... D3 153
Dana, In., U.S. ... E3 121
Da Nang, Viet. ... F10 40
Danbury, Ct., U.S. ... D2 114
Danbury, N.H., U.S. ... C3 136
Danby, Vt., U.S. ... E3 152
Dandenong, Austl. ... K6 70
Dandong, China ... C12 32
Dandridge, Tn., U.S. ... C10 149
Dan Dume, Nig. ... F13 64
Dane, stm., Wi., U.S. ... E4 156
Danforth, Me., U.S. ... C5 126
Dangila, Eth. ... L9 60
Dangriga, Belize ... I15 90
Dangtu, China ... D7 34
Dania, Fl., U.S. ... F6 116
Daniel, Wy., U.S. ... D2 157
Daniels, co., Mt., U.S. ... B11 133
Daniel's Harbour, Newf., Can. ... C3 102
Danielson, Ct., U.S. ... B8 114
Daniels Pass, Ut., U.S. ... C4 151
Danilov, Russia ... C23 22
Dänizkänan, Azer. ... A10 48
Dankov, Russia ... H22 22
Danlí, Hond. ... C8 92
Dannemora, N.Y., U.S. ... f11 139
Dannevirke, N.Z. ... D6 72
Dannhauser, S. Afr. ... G10 66
Dansville, N.Y., U.S. ... C3 139
Dante, Va., U.S. ... f9 153
Danube, stm., Eur. ... G13 4
Danubyu, Mya. ... F3 40
Danvers, Il., U.S. ... C4 120
Danvers, Ma., U.S. ... A6 128
Danville, Que., Can. ... D5 104
Danville, Ar., U.S. ... B2 111
Danville, Ca., U.S. ... h9 112
Danville, Il., U.S. ... C6 120
Danville, In., U.S. ... E4 121
Danville, Ia., U.S. ... D6 122
Danville, Ky., U.S. ... C5 124
Danville, N.H., U.S. ... E4 136
Danville, Pa., U.S. ... E8 145
Danville, Vt., U.S. ... C4 152
Danville, Va., U.S. ... D3 153
Danville, W.V., U.S. ... C3 155
Danyang, China ... C8 34
Danzig see Gdańsk, Pol. ... A18 10
Daoukro, C. Iv. ... H8 64
Dapango, Togo ... F10 64
Daphne, Al., U.S. ... E2 108
Da Qaidam, China ... B16 44
Daqqāq, Sud. ... K4 60
Dar'ā, Syria ... C6 50
Dārāb, Iran ... G13 48
Darabani, Rom. ... A10 20
Darāw, Egypt ... E7 60
Dārayyā, Syria ... B6 50
Darbhanga, India ... G11 44
D'Arbonne, Bayou, stm., La., U.S. ... B3 125
Darby, Mt., U.S. ... D2 133
Darby, Pa., U.S. ... G11 145
Darchan, Mong. ... B8 30
Dardanelle, Ar., U.S. ... B2 111
Dardanelle Lake, res., Ar., U.S. ... B2 111
Dardanelles see Çanakkale Boğazı, strt., Tur. ... I10 20
Dare, co., N.C., U.S. ... B7 140
Dar-el-Beïda see Casablanca, Mor. ... D7 62
Dar es Salaam, Tan. ... C7 58
Dargan-Ata, Turk. ... I10 26
Dargaville, N.Z. ... A4 72
Darien, Ct., U.S. ... E2 114
Darien, Ga., U.S. ... E5 117
Darien, Wi., U.S. ... F5 156
Darién, Serranía del, mts. ... C4 84
Dārjiling, India ... G13 44
Darke, co., Oh., U.S. ... B1 142
Darley Woods, De., U.S. ... h8 115
Darling, S. Afr. ... I4 66
Darling, stm., Austl. ... I5 70
Darling, Lake, res., N.D., U.S. ... A4 141
Darling Downs, reg., Austl. ... F9 70
Darlingford, Man., Can. ... E2 100
Darlington, In., U.S. ... D4 121
Darlington, S.C., U.S. ... C8 147
Darlington, Wi., U.S. ... F3 156
Darlington, co., S.C., U.S. ... C8 147
Darmstadt, Ger. ... F8 10
Darnah, Libya ... B5 56
Darnétal, Fr. ... C8 14
Darnley Cape, c., Ant. ... B20 73
Darrah, Mount, mtn., Can. ... E3 98
Darregueira, Arg. ... I7 80
Darrington, Wa., U.S. ... A4 154
Dart, Cape, c., Ant. ... C10 73
Dartmoor, for., Eng., U.K. ... K9 8

Dartmouth, N.S., Can. ... E6 101
Daru, Pap. N. Gui. ... A8 68
Daruvar, Cro. ... D12 18
Darwin, Austl. ... B6 68
Dashaping, China ... F2 34
Dasiji, China ... B4 34
Dassel, Mn., U.S. ... E4 130
Datil, N.M., U.S. ... C2 138
D'at'kovo, Russia ... H17 22
Datong, China ... C9 30
Datu, Tanjung, c., Asia ... M10 40
Daugava (Zapadnaja Dvina), stm., Eur. ... E7 22
Daugavpils, Lat. ... F9 22
Daule, Ec. ... H3 84
Daule, Ec. ... G2 84
Daule, stm., Ec. ... H2 84
Dauphin, Man., Can. ... D1 100
Dauphin, co., Pa., U.S. ... F8 145
Dauphin Island, Al., U.S. ... E1 108
Daura, Nig. ... E14 64
Dāvangere, India ... E3 46
Davao, Phil. ... D8 38
Davao Gulf, b., Phil. ... D8 38
Davenport, Ia., U.S. ... C7 122
Davenport, Ne., U.S. ... D8 134
Davenport, Ok., U.S. ... B5 143
Davenport, Wa., U.S. ... B7 154
David, Pan. ... C1 84
David City, Ne., U.S. ... C8 134
Davidson, N.C., U.S. ... B2 140
Davidson, co., N.C., U.S. ... B2 140
Davidson, co., Tn., U.S. ... A5 149
Davie, Fl., U.S. ... F6 116
Davie, co., N.C., U.S. ... B2 140
Daviess, co., In., U.S. ... G3 121
Daviess, co., Ky., U.S. ... C2 124
Daviess, co., Mo., U.S. ... B3 132
Davis, Ca., U.S. ... C3 112
Davis, Ok., U.S. ... C4 143
Davis, W.V., U.S. ... B5 155
Davis, co., Ia., U.S. ... D5 122
Davis, co., Ut., U.S. ... C3 151
Davis, Mount, mtn., Pa., U.S. ... G3 145
Davis Inlet, Newf., Can. ... g9 102
Davis Mountains, mts., Tx., U.S. ... o12 150
Davison, Mi., U.S. ... E7 129
Davison, co., S.D., U.S. ... D7 148
Davisville, R.I., U.S. ... E4 146
Davlekanovo, Russia ... G9 26
Davos, Switz. ... E12 13
Dawei (Tavoy), Mya. ... G5 40
Dawes, co., Ne., U.S. ... B2 134
Dawson, Yukon, Can. ... D5 96
Dawson, Ga., U.S. ... E2 117
Dawson, Mn., U.S. ... F2 130
Dawson, co., Ga., U.S. ... B2 117
Dawson, co., Mt., U.S. ... C11 133
Dawson, co., Ne., U.S. ... D6 134
Dawson, co., Tx., U.S. ... C1 150
Dawson, Mount, mtn., B.C., Can. ... D9 99
Dawson Creek, B.C., Can. ... B7 99
Dawson Springs, Ky., U.S. ... C2 124
Dax, Fr. ... I5 14
Daxian, China ... E8 30
Daxing, China ... D4 32
Day, co., S.D., U.S. ... B8 148
Daye, China ... E3 34
Daylesford, Austl. ... K6 70
Daym Zubayr, Sud. ... N4 60
Dayr Abū Sa'īd, Jord. ... C5 50
Dayr az-Zawr, Syria ... D6 48
Dayrūt, Egypt ... D6 60
Daysland, Alta., Can. ... C4 98
Dayton, Id., U.S. ... G6 119
Dayton, In., U.S. ... D4 121
Dayton, Ia., U.S. ... B3 122
Dayton, Ky., U.S. ... h14 124
Dayton, Md., U.S. ... B4 127
Dayton, Mn., U.S. ... m12 130
Dayton, Nv., U.S. ... D2 135
Dayton, Oh., U.S. ... C1 142
Dayton, Or., U.S. ... B3 144
Dayton, Tn., U.S. ... D8 149
Dayton, Tx., U.S. ... D5 150
Dayton, Va., U.S. ... B4 153
Dayton, Wa., U.S. ... C8 154
Daytona Beach, Fl., U.S. ... C5 116
Dayu, China ... J3 34
Da Yunhe (Grand Canal), China ... E10 30
Dayville, Ct., U.S. ... B8 114
De Aar, S. Afr. ... H7 66
Dead Sea (Al-Bahr al-Mayyit) (Yam HaMelah), l., Asia ... F4 50
Deadwood, S.D., U.S. ... C2 148
Deaf Smith, co., Tx., U.S. ... B1 150
Deal, Eng., U.K. ... J15 8
Deale, Md., U.S. ... C4 127
Dean Channel, strt., B.C., Can. ... C4 99
Deán Funes, Arg. ... F6 80
Dearborn, Mi., U.S. ... F7 129
Dearborn, co., In., U.S. ... F7 121
Dearborn Heights, Mi., U.S. ... p15 129
Dearing, Ks., U.S. ... E8 123
De Armanville, Al., U.S. ... B4 108
Deary, Id., U.S. ... C2 119
Dease Strait, strt., N.W. Ter., Can. ... C11 96
Death Valley, val., Ca., U.S. ... D5 112
Death Valley National Monument, U.S. ... D5 112
Deauville, Fr. ... C7 14
Deaver, Wy., U.S. ... B4 157
De Baca, co., N.M., U.S. ... C5 138
Debar, Mac. ... H4 20
De Bary, Fl., U.S. ... D5 116
Debden, Sask., Can. ... D2 105
De Beque, Co., U.S. ... B2 113
Dębica, Pol. ... E21 10
Deblin, Pol. ... D21 10
Debrecen, Hung. ... H21 10
Debre Markos, Eth. ... L9 60
Debre Tabor, Eth. ... L10 60
Debre Zeyit, Eth. ... M10 60
Decatur, Al., U.S. ... A3 108

Decatur, Ar., U.S. ... A1 111
Decatur, Ga., U.S. ... C2 117
Decatur, Il., U.S. ... D5 120
Decatur, In., U.S. ... C8 121
Decatur, Mi., U.S. ... F5 129
Decatur, Ms., U.S. ... C4 131
Decatur, Ne., U.S. ... B9 134
Decatur, Tn., U.S. ... D9 149
Decatur, Tx., U.S. ... C4 150
Decatur, co., Ga., U.S. ... F2 117
Decatur, co., In., U.S. ... F6 121
Decatur, co., Ia., U.S. ... D4 122
Decatur, co., Ks., U.S. ... C3 123
Decatur, co., Tn., U.S. ... B3 149
Decatur, Lake, res., Il., U.S. ... D5 120
Decaturville, Tn., U.S. ... B3 149
Decazeville, Fr. ... H9 14
Deccan, plat., India ... D5 46
Deception Island, i., Ant. ... B12 73
Decherd, Tn., U.S. ... B5 149
Děčín, Czech Rep. ... E14 10
Decize, Fr. ... F10 14
Decker Lake, B.C., Can. ... B5 99
Decorah, Ia., U.S. ... A6 122
Dedham, Ma., U.S. ... B5 128
De Doorns, S. Afr. ... I4 66
Dédougou, Burkina ... E8 64
Dedovsk, Russia ... F20 22
Dee, stm., U.K. ... H10 8
Dee, stm., Scot., U.K. ... D11 8
Deep Brook, N.S., Can. ... E4 101
Deep Creek Lake, res., Md., U.S. ... K12 127
Deep Fork, stm., Ok., U.S. ... B5 143
Deep River, Ont., Can. ... A7 103
Deep River, Ct., U.S. ... D6 114
Deer Creek Indian Reservation, Mn., U.S. ... C5 130
Deerfield, Il., U.S. ... h9 120
Deerfield, Ks., U.S. ... E2 123
Deerfield, N.H., U.S. ... D4 136
Deerfield, Wi., U.S. ... E4 156
Deerfield, stm., U.S. ... A2 128
Deerfield Beach, Fl., U.S. ... F6 116
Deer Isle, i., Me., U.S. ... D4 126
Deer Isle, Me., U.S. ... D4 126
Deer Lake, Newf., Can. ... D3 102
Deer Lodge, Mt., U.S. ... D4 133
Deer Lodge, co., Mt., U.S. ... E3 133
Deer Mountain, mtn., Me., U.S. ... C2 126
Deer Park, N.Y., U.S. ... n15 139
Deer Park, Oh., U.S. ... o13 142
Deer Park, Tx., U.S. ... r14 150
Deer Park, Wa., U.S. ... B8 154
Deer River, Mn., U.S. ... C5 130
Deer Trail, Co., U.S. ... B6 113
Deeth, Nv., U.S. ... B6 135
Defiance, Oh., U.S. ... A1 142
Defiance, co., Oh., U.S. ... A1 142
De Forest, Wi., U.S. ... E4 156
De Funiak Springs, Fl., U.S. ... u15 116
Dégelis, Que., Can. ... B9 104
Deggendorf, Ger. ... G12 10
Dehiwala-Mount Lavinia, Sri L. ... I5 46
Dehra Dūn, India ... E8 44
Dehri, India ... H11 44
Dehua, China ... J7 34
Dehui, China ... C12 30
Dej, Rom. ... B7 20
Dejnau, Turk. ... J10 26
De Kalb, Il., U.S. ... B5 120
De Kalb, Ms., U.S. ... C5 131
De Kalb, co., Al., U.S. ... A4 108
De Kalb, co., Ga., U.S. ... C2 117
De Kalb, co., Il., U.S. ... B5 120
De Kalb, co., In., U.S. ... B7 121
De Kalb, co., Mo., U.S. ... B3 132
De Kalb, co., Tn., U.S. ... D8 149
Dekemhare, Erit. ... J10 60
Delafield, Wi., U.S. ... m11 156
De Land, Fl., U.S. ... C5 116
Delano, Ca., U.S. ... E4 112
Delano, Mn., U.S. ... E5 130
Delano Peak, mtn., Ut., U.S. ... E3 151
Delareyville, S. Afr. ... F7 66
Delaronde Lake, l., Sask., Can. ... C2 105
Delavan, Il., U.S. ... C4 120
Delavan, Wi., U.S. ... F5 156
Delaware, Ont., Can. ... E3 103
Delaware, Oh., U.S. ... B2 142
Delaware, co., In., U.S. ... D7 121
Delaware, co., Ia., U.S. ... B6 122
Delaware, co., N.Y., U.S. ... C5 139
Delaware, co., Oh., U.S. ... B2 142
Delaware, co., Ok., U.S. ... A7 143
Delaware, co., Pa., U.S. ... G11 145
Delaware, state, U.S. ... D3 115
Delaware, stm., U.S. ... E2 137
Delaware, stm., Ks., U.S. ... C8 123
Delaware Bay, b., U.S. ... D11 106
Delaware City, De., U.S. ... B3 115
Delaware Water Gap, Pa., U.S. ... E11 145
Delaware Water Gap, N.J., U.S. ... B2 137
Delaware Water Gap National Recreation Area, U.S. ... B2 137
Delbarton, W.V., U.S. ... D2 155
Delburne, Alta., Can. ... C4 98
Delcambre, La., U.S. ... E4 125
Del Campillo, Arg. ... H6 80
Delegate, Austl. ... K8 70
Delémont, Switz. ... D7 13
Delfinópolis, Braz. ... F5 79
Delfzijl, Neth. ... B10 12
Delgado, El Sal. ... D5 92
Delgado, Cabo, c., Moz. ... D8 58
Delhi, India ... F7 44
Delhi, La., U.S. ... B4 125
Delhi, N.Y., U.S. ... C6 139
Delhi, ter., India ... F7 44
Delicias, Mex. ... C7 90
Delight, Ar., U.S. ... C2 111
Delisle, Sask., Can. ... F2 105
De Lisle, Ms., U.S. ... E4 131
Delitzsch, Ger. ... D12 10
Delle, Fr. ... E14 14

Dellenbaugh, Mount, mtn., Az., U.S. ... A2 110
Delles, Alg. ... B12 62
Dell Rapids, S.D., U.S. ... D9 148
Del Mar, Ca., U.S. ... o15 112
Delmar, De., U.S. ... G3 115
Delmar, Md., U.S. ... D6 127
Delmar, N.Y., U.S. ... C7 139
Delmarva Peninsula, pen., U.S. ... D11 106
Delmenhorst, Ger. ... B8 10
Del Norte, Co., U.S. ... D4 113
Del Norte, co., Ca., U.S. ... B2 112
De-Longa, ostrova, is., Russia ... B22 28
Delphi see Dhelfoí, hist., Grc. ... K6 20
Delphos, Ks., U.S. ... C6 123
Delphos, Oh., U.S. ... B1 142
Delran, N.J., U.S. ... C3 137
Delray Beach, Fl., U.S. ... F6 116
Del Rio, Tx., U.S. ... E2 150
Delson, Que., Can. ... q19 104
Delta, Co., U.S. ... C2 113
Delta, Oh., U.S. ... A2 142
Delta, Ut., U.S. ... D3 151
Delta, co., Co., U.S. ... C3 113
Delta, co., Mi., U.S. ... C3 129
Delta, co., Tx., U.S. ... C5 150
Delta, reg., Ms., U.S. ... B3 131
Delta Amacuro, ter., Ven. ... C12 84
Delta Downs, Austl. ... A4 70
Delta Junction, Ak., U.S. ... C10 109
Deltaville, Va., U.S. ... C6 153
Deltona, Fl., U.S. ... D5 116
Delyatyn, Ukr. ... A8 20
Dem'ansk, Russia ... D15 22
Demarest, N.J., U.S. ... h9 137
Demba, Zaire ... C4 58
Dembecha, Eth. ... L9 60
Dembi, Eth. ... M9 60
Dembi Dolo, Eth. ... M8 60
Demidov, Russia ... F14 22
Deming, N.M., U.S. ... E2 138
Demirci, Tur. ... J12 20
Demopolis, Al., U.S. ... C2 108
Demorest, Ga., U.S. ... B3 117
Demotte, In., U.S. ... B3 121
Denain, Fr. ... B10 14
Denali National Park, Ak., U.S. ... C9 109
Denare Beach, Sask., Can. ... C5 105
Denbigh, Wales, U.K. ... H10 8
Dender (Dendre), stm., Bel. ... G4 12
Dendermonde (Termonde), Bel. ... F5 12
Dengshahe, China ... D10 32
Denham Springs, La., U.S. ... D5 125
Den Helder, Neth. ... C6 12
Dénia, Spain ... G12 16
Deniliquin, Austl. ... J6 70
Denison, Ia., U.S. ... B2 122
Denison, Tx., U.S. ... C4 150
Denizli, Tur. ... L13 20
Denmark, Austl. ... F3 68
Denmark, S.C., U.S. ... E5 147
Denmark, Wi., U.S. ... D6 156
Denmark (Danmark), ctry., Eur. ... D10 4
Denmark Strait, strt. ... B4 52
Dennehotso, Az., U.S. ... A6 110
Dennis, Ma., U.S. ... C7 128
Dennison, Oh., U.S. ... B4 142
Dennis Port, Ma., U.S. ... C7 128
Denny Terrace, S.C., U.S. ... C5 147
Denpasar, Indon. ... G6 38
Dent, co., Mo., U.S. ... D6 132
Denton, Md., U.S. ... C6 127
Denton, N.C., U.S. ... B2 140
Denton, Tx., U.S. ... C4 150
Denton, co., Tx., U.S. ... C4 150
D'Entrecasteaux Islands, is., Pap. N. Gui. ... A10 68
Dentsville, S.C., U.S. ... C6 147
Denver, Co., U.S. ... B6 113
Denver, Ia., U.S. ... B5 122
Denver, Pa., U.S. ... F9 145
Denver, co., Co., U.S. ... B6 113
Denver City, Tx., U.S. ... C1 150
Denville, N.J., U.S. ... B4 137
Denzil, Sask., Can. ... E1 105
Deoghar, India ... H12 44
Deoria, India ... G10 44
De Pere, Wi., U.S. ... D5 156
Depew, N.Y., U.S. ... C2 139
Depoe Bay, Or., U.S. ... C2 144
Depok, Indon. ... j13 39a
Depue, Il., U.S. ... B4 120
Dêqên, China ... F6 30
De Queen, Ar., U.S. ... C1 111
De Quincy, La., U.S. ... D2 125
Dera Ghāzi Khān, Pak. ... E4 44
Dera Ismāīl Khān, Pak. ... E4 44
Derbent, Russia ... I7 26
Derby, Eng., U.K. ... I12 8
Derby, Ct., U.S. ... D3 114
Derby, Ks., U.S. ... E6 123
Derby Line, Vt., U.S. ... A4 152
Derbyshire, co., Eng., U.K. ... H12 8
Derecske, Hung. ... H21 10
De Ridder, La., U.S. ... D2 125
Derma, Ms., U.S. ... B4 131
Dermott, Ar., U.S. ... D4 111
Dernieres, Isles, is., La., U.S. ... E5 125
Derry see Londonderry, N. Ire., U.K. ... F6 8
Derry, N.H., U.S. ... E4 136
Derry, Pa., U.S. ... F3 145
Derventa, Bos. ... E1 20
Derwood, Md., U.S. ... B3 127
Deržavinsk, Kaz. ... G11 26
Desaguadero, stm., Arg. ... G5 80
Desaguadero, stm., Bol. ... G7 82
Des Allemands, La., U.S. ... E5 125
Des Arc, Ar., U.S. ... C4 111
Descartes, Fr. ... F7 14
Deschambault, Que., Can. ... C6 104

Deschambault Lake, Sask., Can. ... C4 105
Deschambault Lake, l., Sask., Can. ... C4 105
Deschutes, co., Or., U.S. ... D5 144
Deschutes, stm., Or., U.S. ... B6 144
Dese, Eth. ... F8 56
Deseado, stm., Arg. ... F3 78
Deseret Peak, mtn., Ut., U.S. ... C3 151
Deseronto, Ont., Can. ... C7 103
Desert Creek Peak, mtn., Nv., U.S. ... E2 135
Desert Hot Springs, Ca., U.S. ... F5 112
Desha, Ar., U.S. ... B4 111
Desha, co., Ar., U.S. ... D4 111
Deshler, Ne., U.S. ... D8 134
Deshler, Oh., U.S. ... A2 142
Des Lacs, stm., N.D., U.S. ... A4 141
Desloge, Mo., U.S. ... D7 132
Desmarais, Alta., Can. ... B4 98
Des Moines, Ia., U.S. ... C4 122
Des Moines, Wa., U.S. ... B3 154
Des Moines, co., Ia., U.S. ... D6 122
Des Moines, stm., U.S. ... D5 122
Desolación, Isla, i., Chile ... J7 74
De Smet, S.D., U.S. ... C8 148
De Soto, Il., U.S. ... F4 120
De Soto, Ia., U.S. ... C3 122
De Soto, Ks., U.S. ... D9 123
De Soto, Mo., U.S. ... C7 132
De Soto, co., Fl., U.S. ... E5 116
De Soto, co., La., U.S. ... B2 125
De Soto, co., Ms., U.S. ... A3 131
Des Peres, Mo., U.S. ... f13 132
Des Plaines, Il., U.S. ... A6 120
Des Plaines, stm., U.S. ... k8 120
Desroches, Île, i., Sey. ... C10 58
Dessau, Ger. ... D12 10
Destin, Fl., U.S. ... u15 116
Destrehan, La., U.S. ... E5 125
Desvres, Fr. ... B8 14
Dete, Zimb. ... B8 66
Detmold, Ger. ... D8 10
Detroit, Mi., U.S. ... F7 129
Detroit Lakes, Mn., U.S. ... D3 130
Deuel, co., Ne., U.S. ... C3 134
Deuel, co., S.D., U.S. ... C9 148
Deutsche Bucht, b., Ger. ... A7 10
Deux-Montagnes, Que., Can. ... p19 104
Deux Montagnes, Lac des, l., Que., Can. ... q19 104
Deva, Rom. ... D6 20
De Valls Bluff, Ar., U.S. ... C4 111
Dévaványa, Hung. ... H20 10
Deventer, Neth. ... D9 12
DeView, Bayou, stm., Ar, U.S. ... B4 111
Devils Island see Diable, Île du, i., Fr. Gu. ... B8 76
Devils Lake, N.D., U.S. ... A7 141
Devils Postpile National Monument, Ca., U.S. ... D4 112
Devils Tower National Monument, Wy., U.S. ... B8 157
Devine, Tx., U.S. ... E3 150
DeVola, Oh., U.S. ... C4 142
Devon, Alta., Can. ... C4 98
Devon, co., Eng., U.K. ... K10 8
Devon Island, i., N.W. Ter., Can. ... B11 86
Devonport, Austl. ... M7 70
Devonport, N.Z. ... B5 72
Devonshire, De., U.S. ... h7 115
Devoto, Arg. ... F7 80
Dewar, Ok., U.S. ... B6 143
Dewās, India ... I7 44
Dewberry, Alta., Can. ... C5 98
Dewey, Az., U.S. ... C3 110
Dewey, Ok., U.S. ... A6 143
Dewey, co., Ok., U.S. ... B2 143
Dewey, co., S.D., U.S. ... B4 148
De Witt, Ar., U.S. ... C4 111
De Witt, Ia., U.S. ... C7 122
De Witt, Mi., U.S. ... F6 129
De Witt, Ne., U.S. ... D9 134
De Witt, N.Y., U.S. ... B4 139
De Witt, co., Il., U.S. ... C5 120
De Witt, co., Tx., U.S. ... E4 150
Dexter, Me., U.S. ... C3 126
Dexter, Mi., U.S. ... F7 129
Dexter, Mo., U.S. ... E8 132
Dexter, N.M., U.S. ... D5 138
Dezfūl, Iran ... E10 48
Dezhou, China ... F4 32
Dežņeva, mys, c., Russia ... D30 28
Dháfni, Grc. ... L6 20
Dhahran see Az-Zahrān, Sau. Ar. ... A7 47
Dhaka, Bngl. ... I14 44
Dhamār, Yemen ... G4 47
Dhamtari, India ... J10 44
Dhanbād, India ... I12 44
Dharmavaram, India ... E4 46
Dhaulpur, India ... G7 44
Dhawlāgiri, mtn., Nepal ... F10 44
Dhelfoí, hist., Grc. ... K6 20
Dhībān, Jord. ... E5 50
Dhodhekánisos (Dodecanese), is., Grc. ... M10 20
Dhorāji, India ... J4 44
Dhubri, India ... G13 44
Dhule, India ... J6 44
Diable, Île du, i., Fr. Gu. ... B8 76
Diablo, Canyon, val., Az., U.S. ... C4 110
Diablo, Mount, mtn., Ca., U.S. ... h9 112
Diablo, Pico del, mtn., Mex. ... B2 90
Diablotins, Morne, mtn., Dom. ... G14 94
Diamante, Arg. ... G8 80
Diamantina, Braz. ... E7 79
Diamantina, stm., Austl. ... F3 70
Diamond City, Ar., U.S. ... A3 111
Diamond Head, crat., Hi., U.S. ... B4 118
Diamond Hill, R.I., U.S. ... B5 146
Diamond Islets, is., Austl. ... A9 70
Diamond Lake, Il., U.S. ... h9 120

Diamondville, Wy., U.S. ... E2 157
Diangounté Kamara, Mali ... D5 64
Dianópolis, Braz. ... F9 76
Diapaga, Burkina ... E10 64
Diaz, Ar., U.S. ... B4 111
D'Iberville, Ms., U.S. ... E5 131
Dibete, Bots. ... D8 66
Diboll, Tx., U.S. ... D5 150
Dibrugarh, India ... G16 44
Dickens, co., Tx., U.S. ... C2 150
Dickenson, co., Va., U.S. ... e9 153
Dickerson, Md., U.S. ... B3 127
Dickey, co., N.D., U.S. ... C7 141
Dickinson, N.D., U.S. ... C3 141
Dickinson, co., Ia., U.S. ... A2 122
Dickinson, co., Ks., U.S. ... D6 123
Dickinson, co., Mi., U.S. ... B3 129
Dickson, Ok., U.S. ... C5 143
Dickson, Tn., U.S. ... A4 149
Dickson, co., Tn., U.S. ... A4 149
Dickson City, Pa., U.S. ... D10 145
Didsbury, Alta., Can. ... D3 98
Die, Fr. ... H12 14
Diébougou, Burkina ... F8 64
Dieciocho de Julio, Ur. ... G12 80
Diefenbaker, Lake, res., Sask., Can. ... F2 105
Diego de Almagro, Chile ... D3 80
Diego Garcia, i., B.I.O.T. ... J8 24
Diego Ramírez, Islas, is., Chile ... H3 78
Dien Bien Phu, Viet. ... D7 40
Dieppe, N.B., Can. ... C5 101
Dieppe, Fr. ... C8 14
Dierks, Ar., U.S. ... C1 111
Dietikon, Switz. ... D9 13
Dieuze, Fr. ... D13 14
Differdange, Lux. ... I8 12
Digby, N.S., Can. ... E4 101
Dighton, Ks., U.S. ... D3 123
Digne, Fr. ... H13 14
Digoin, Fr. ... F10 14
Dijon, Fr. ... E12 14
Dike, Ia., U.S. ... B5 122
Dikhil, Dji. ... F9 56
Dikson, Russia ... C8 28
Dikwa, Nig. ... F9 64
Dila, Eth. ... N10 60
Dili, Indon. ... G8 38
Dillard, Or., U.S. ... D3 144
Dilley, Tx., U.S. ... E3 150
Dilling, Sud. ... K5 60
Dillingham, Ak., U.S. ... D8 109
Dillon, Co., U.S. ... B4 113
Dillon, Mt., U.S. ... E4 133
Dillon, S.C., U.S. ... C9 147
Dillon, co., S.C., U.S. ... C9 147
Dillon Lake, res., Oh., U.S. ... B3 142
Dillsboro, In., U.S. ... F7 121
Dillsburg, Pa., U.S. ... F7 145
Dilolo, Zaire ... D4 58
Dilworth, Mn., U.S. ... D2 130
Dimashq (Damascus), Syria ... A6 50
Dimitrovgrad, Russia ... G7 26
Dimlang, mtn., Nig. ... G9 54
Dimmit, co., Tx., U.S. ... E3 150
Dimmitt, Tx., U.S. ... B1 150
Dimona, Isr. ... F4 50
Dinājpur, Bngl. ... H13 44
Dinan, Fr. ... D4 14
Dinant, Bel. ... H6 12
Dinara (Dinaric Alps), mts., Eur. ... F11 18
Dinard, Fr. ... D4 14
Dinaric Alps see Dinara, Eur. ... F11 18
Dindigul, India ... G4 46
Dinghai, China ... E11 34
Dingle Bay, b., Ire. ... I3 8
Dingnan, China ... K3 34
Dingshuzhen, China ... D8 34
Dinguiraye, Gui. ... F4 64
Dingxian, China ... E2 32
Dingyuan, China ... C6 34
Dinh Lap, Viet. ... D9 40
Dinosaur, Co., U.S. ... A1 113
Dinosaur National Monument, U.S. ... C6 151
Dinsmore, Sask., Can. ... F2 105
Dinuba, Ca., U.S. ... D4 112
Dinwiddie, co., Va., U.S. ... C5 153
Dioïla, Mali ... E6 64
Dionísio, Braz. ... E7 79
Dionísio Cerqueira, Braz. ... D12 80
Dioundiou, Niger ... E11 64
Diourbel, Sen. ... D1 64
Diplog, Phil. ... D7 38
Dire Dawa, Eth. ... G9 56
Diriamba, Nic. ... F9 92
Dirk Hartog Island, i., Austl. ... E2 68
Dirrah, Sud. ... K4 60
Dirranbandi, Austl. ... G8 70
Dirty Devil, stm., Ut., U.S. ... E5 151
Disappointment, Cape, c., Wa., U.S. ... C1 154
Disappointment, Lake, l., Austl. ... D4 68
Disentis, Switz. ... E10 13
Dishman, Wa., U.S. ... g14 154
Dishnā, Egypt ... D12 60
Disko, i., Grnld. ... C14 86
Disna, Bela. ... F11 22
Disraëli, Que., Can. ... D6 104
District of Columbia, dept., U.S. ... f8 127
Distrito Federal, dept., Braz. ... C5 79
Distrito Federal, dept., Ven. ... B9 84
Disūq, Egypt ... B6 60
Divalá, Pan. ... I12 92
Divernon, Il., U.S. ... D4 120
Divide, co., N.D., U.S. ... A2 141
Divino, Braz. ... F7 79
Divinópolis, Braz. ... F6 79
Divisor, Serra do (Cordillera Ultraoriental), plat., S.A. ... C5 82
Divriği, Tur. ... B4 48
Dixfield, Me., U.S. ... D2 126
Dixie, W.V., U.S. ... C3 155
Dixie, co., Fl., U.S. ... C3 116
Dix Mountain, mtn., N.Y., U.S. ... A7 139
Dixon, Ca., U.S. ... C3 112

Name	Map Ref.	Page
Dixon, Il., U.S.	B4	120
Dixon, Ky., U.S.	C2	124
Dixon, Mo., U.S.	D5	132
Dixon, N.M., U.S.	A4	138
Dixon, Wy., U.S.	E5	157
Dixon, co., Ne., U.S.	B9	134
Diyarbakır, Tur.	C6	48
Djakarta see Jakarta, Indon.	j13	39a
Djamâa, Alg.	D13	62
Djambala, Congo	B2	58
Djema, Cen. Afr. Rep.	N3	60
Djénné, Mali	E7	64
Djibo, Burkina	D9	64
Djibouti, Dji.	F9	56
Djibouti, ctry., Afr.	F9	56
Djougou, Benin	G10	64
Dmitrija Lapteva, proliv, strt., Russia	C20	22
Dmitrijevka, Russia	I23	22
Dmitrijev-L'govskij, Russia	I18	22
Dmitrov, Russia	E20	22
Dmitrovsk-Orlovskij, Russia	I18	22
Dnepropetrovsk see Dnipropetrovs'k, Ukr.	H4	26
Dnieper, stm., Eur.	H4	26
Dniester see Dnister, stm., Eur.	H3	26
Dniprodzerzhyns'k, Ukr.	H4	26
Dnipropetrovs'k, Ukr.	H4	26
Dnister (Nistru), stm., Eur.	H3	26
Dno, Russia	D12	22
Doaktown, N.B., Can.	C3	101
Doba, Chad	E4	56
Dobane, Cen. Afr. Rep.	N3	60
Dobbs Ferry, N.Y., U.S.	g13	139
Dobele, Lat.	E6	22
Döbeln, Ger.	D13	10
Doberai, Jazirah, pen., Indon.	F9	38
Doboj, Bos.	E2	20
Dobr'anka, Russia	F9	26
Dobrič, Bul.	F11	20
Dobrinka, Russia	I23	22
Dobruja, hist. reg., Eur.	E12	20
Dobruš, Bela.	I14	22
Doce, stm., Braz.	E8	79
Docena, Al., U.S.	f7	108
Doctor Arroyo, Mex.	F9	90
Doddridge, co., W.V., U.S.	B4	155
Dodecanese see Dhodhekánisos, is., Grc.	M10	20
Dodge, Ne., U.S.	C9	134
Dodge, co., Ga., U.S.	D3	117
Dodge, co., Mn., U.S.	G6	130
Dodge, co., Ne., U.S.	C9	134
Dodge, co., Wi., U.S.	E5	156
Dodge Center, Mn., U.S.	F6	130
Dodge City, Ks., U.S.	E3	123
Dodgeville, Wi., U.S.	F3	156
Dodola, Eth.	N10	60
Dodoma, Tan.	C7	58
Dodsland, Sask., Can.	F1	105
Doerun, Ga., U.S.	E3	117
Doe Run, Mo., U.S.	D7	132
Doetinchem, Neth.	E9	12
Dog Island, i., Anguilla	E13	94
Do Gonbadān, Iran	F11	48
Dogondoutchi, Niger	E12	64
Doğubayazıt, Tur.	B8	48
Doha see Ad-Dawhah, Qatar	B7	47
Dokšicy, Bela.	G10	22
Doland, S.D., U.S.	C7	148
Dolbeau, Que., Can.	k12	104
Dol-de-Bretagne, Fr.	D5	14
Dole, Fr.	E12	14
Dolega, Pan.	C1	84
Dolgoje, Russia	I20	22
Dolinsk, Russia	H20	28
Dolisie, Congo	B2	58
Dolomite, Al., U.S.	B3	108
Dolores, Arg.	I10	80
Dolores, Guat.	I15	90
Dolores, Co., U.S.	D2	113
Dolores, Ur.	G9	80
Dolores, co., Co., U.S.	D2	113
Dolores, stm., U.S.	E7	151
Dolores Hidalgo, Mex.	G9	90
Dolphin and Union Strait, strt., N.W. Ter., Can.	C9	96
Dolton, Il., U.S.	k9	120
Domažlice, Czech Rep.	F12	10
Dombarovskij, Russia	G9	26
Dombås, Nor.	J11	6
Dom Cavati, Braz.	E7	79
Domeyko, Cordillera, mts., Chile	B4	80
Domfront, Fr.	D6	14
Domingos Martins, Braz.	F8	79
Dominica, ctry., N.A.	G14	94
Dominican Republic (República Dominicana), ctry., N.A.	E9	94
Dominica Passage, strt., N.A.	G14	94
Dominion, N.S., Can.	C9	101
Dominion City, Man., Can.	E3	100
Domodedovo, Russia	F20	22
Domodossola, Italy	C3	18
Domoni, Com.	I16	67a
Dom Pedrito, Braz.	F11	80
Dom Silvério, Braz.	F7	79
Don, stm., Russia	H6	26
Don, stm., Scot., U.K.	D11	8
Dona Ana, N.M., U.S.	E3	138
Dona Ana, co., N.M., U.S.	E2	138
Donalda, Alta., Can.	C4	98
Donaldson, Ar., U.S.	C3	111
Donaldsonville, La., U.S.	D4	125
Donalsonville, Ga., U.S.	E2	117
Donaueschingen, Ger.	H8	10
Don Benito, Spain	G6	16
Doncaster, Eng., U.K.	H12	8
Dondo, Moz.	B12	66
Dondra Head, c., Sri L.	J6	44
Donduşeni, Mol.	A11	20
Donegal, Ire.	G5	8
Donegal, co., Ire.	G5	8
Donegal Bay, b., Ire.	G5	8
Doneraile, S.C., U.S.	C8	147
Donets'k, Ukr.	H5	26
Dong, stm., China	L6	34
Dongara, Austl.	E2	68
Dongba, China	D8	34
Dongchuan, China	A7	40
Dongdaoan, China	E5	32
Dong'ezhen, China	G4	32
Dongfang (Basuo), China	E10	40
Dongfeng, China	A13	32
Dongguan, China	L2	34
Dongshi, China	K7	34
Dongtai, China	C9	34
Dongting Hu, l., China	G1	34
Dongyang, China	F9	34
Dongzhi, China	E5	34
Doniphan, Mo., U.S.	E7	132
Doniphan, Ne., U.S.	D7	134
Doniphan, co., Ks., U.S.	C8	123
Donji Vakuf, Bos.	E12	18
Donkin, N.S., Can.	C10	101
Donley, co., Tx., U.S.	B2	150
Donna, Tx., U.S.	F3	150
Donnacona, Que., Can.	C6	104
Donnellson, Ia., U.S.	D6	122
Donnelly, Alta., Can.	B2	98
Donner Pass, Ca., U.S.	C3	112
Donora, Pa., U.S.	F2	145
Donostia (San Sebastián), Spain	B10	16
Donskoj, Russia	H21	22
Doolittle, Mo., U.S.	D6	132
Dooly, co., Ga., U.S.	D3	117
Doomadgee, Austl.	A3	70
Doonerak, Mount, mtn., Ak., U.S.	B9	109
Door, co., Wi., U.S.	D6	156
Dora, Al., U.S.	B2	108
Doraville, Ga., U.S.	h8	117
Dorchester, N.B., Can.	D5	101
Dorchester, Ne., U.S.	D8	134
Dorchester, co., Md., U.S.	D5	127
Dorchester, co., S.C., U.S.	E7	147
Dordogne, stm., Fr.	H8	14
Dordrecht, Neth.	E6	12
Doré Lake, l., Sask., Can.	C2	105
Dores do Indaiá, Braz.	E6	79
Dorion-Vaudreuil, Que., Can.	q18	104
Dormont, Pa., U.S.	k13	145
Dornbirn, Aus.	H9	10
Dorochovo, Russia	F19	22
Dorogobuž, Russia	G16	22
Dorohoi, Rom.	B10	20
Dorothy, W.V., U.S.	n13	155
Dorr, Mi., U.S.	F5	129
Dorset, Vt., U.S.	E2	152
Dorset, co., Eng., U.K.	K11	8
Dorset Peak, mtn., Vt., U.S.	E2	152
Dorsey, Md., U.S.	B4	127
Dortmund, Ger.	D7	10
Dorton, Ky., U.S.	C7	124
Dörtyol, Tur.	C4	48
Do Rūd, Iran	E10	48
Dorval, Que., Can.	q19	104
Dos Bahías, Cabo, c., Arg.	E3	78
Dosčatoje, Russia	F25	22
Dos Hermanas, Spain	H6	16
Dos Quebradas, Col.	E5	84
Dothan, Al., U.S.	D4	108
Dotnuva, Lith.	F6	22
Douai, Fr.	B10	14
Douala, Cam.	I14	64
Douarnenez, Fr.	D2	14
Double Beach, Ct., U.S.	D4	114
Double Springs, Al., U.S.	A2	108
Douentza, Mali	D8	64
Dougherty, co., Ga., U.S.	E2	117
Douglas, I. of Man	G9	8
Douglas, Ga., U.S.	E4	117
Douglas, Wy., U.S.	D7	157
Douglas, co., Co., U.S.	B6	113
Douglas, co., Ga., U.S.	C2	117
Douglas, co., Il., U.S.	D5	120
Douglas, co., Ks., U.S.	D8	123
Douglas, co., Mn., U.S.	E3	130
Douglas, co., Mo., U.S.	E5	132
Douglas, co., Ne., U.S.	C9	134
Douglas, co., Nv., U.S.	E2	135
Douglas, co., Or., U.S.	D3	144
Douglas, co., S.D., U.S.	D7	148
Douglas, co., Wa., U.S.	B6	154
Douglas, co., Wi., U.S.	B2	156
Douglas, Mount, mtn., Ak., U.S.	D9	109
Douglas Channel, strt., B.C., Can.	C3	99
Douglas Lake, res., Tn., U.S.	D10	149
Douglass, Ks., U.S.	E7	123
Douglas Station, Man., Can.	E2	100
Douglastown, N.B., Can.	B4	101
Douglasville, Ga., U.S.	C2	117
Doullens, Fr.	B9	14
Doumanaba, Mali	F7	64
Dourados, Braz.	G1	79
Dourdan, Fr.	D9	14
Douro (Duero), stm., Eur.	D4	16
Dousman, Wi., U.S.	E5	156
Douz, Tun.	D15	62
Dove Creek, Co., U.S.	D2	113
Dover, Austl.	N7	70
Dover, Eng., U.K.	J15	8
Dover, Ar., U.S.	B2	111
Dover, De., U.S.	D3	115
Dover, Fl., U.S.	D4	116
Dover, Ma., U.S.	h10	128
Dover, N.H., U.S.	D5	136
Dover, N.J., U.S.	B3	137
Dover, Oh., U.S.	B4	142
Dover, Tn., U.S.	A4	149
Dover, Strait of (Pas de Calais), strt., Eur.	J15	8
Dover Air Force Base, mil., De., U.S.	D4	115
Dover-Foxcroft, Me., U.S.	C3	126
Dowagiac, Mi., U.S.	G4	129
Dowlatābād, Afg.	B1	44
Downers Grove, Il., U.S.	B5	120
Downey, Ca., U.S.	n12	112
Downey, Id., U.S.	G6	119
Downingtown, Pa., U.S.	F10	145
Downs, Ks., U.S.	C5	123
Dows, Ia., U.S.	B4	122
Doylestown, Oh., U.S.	B4	142
Doylestown, Pa., U.S.	F11	145
Doyline, La., U.S.	B2	125
Dozier, Al., U.S.	D3	108
Drâa, Oued, val., Afr.	F5	62
Dracena, Braz.	F3	79
Dracut, Ma., U.S.	A5	128
Drăgăşani, Rom.	E8	20
Dragons Mouths, strt.	B12	84
Draguignan, Fr.	I13	14
Drain, Or., U.S.	D3	144
Drake, Sask., Can.	F3	105
Drake, Co., U.S.	A5	113
Drake, N.D., U.S.	B5	141
Drakensberg, mts., Afr.	F9	66
Drake Passage, strt.	J8	74
Drake Peak, mtn., Or., U.S.	E4	144
Drakesboro, Ky., U.S.	C2	124
Dráma, Grc.	H8	20
Drammen, Nor.	L12	6
Drau (Drava) (Dráva), stm., Eur.	C8	18
Drava (Drau) (Dráva), stm., Eur.	D13	18
Drayton, Ont., Can.	D4	103
Drayton, N.D., U.S.	A8	141
Drayton, S.C., U.S.	B4	147
Drayton Plains, Mi., U.S.	F7	129
Drayton Valley, Alta., Can.	C3	98
Drean, Alg.	M2	18
Drenthe, prov., Neth.	C10	12
Dresden, Ont., Can.	E2	103
Dresden, Ger.	D13	10
Dresden, Tn., U.S.	A3	149
Dresslerville, Nv., U.S.	E2	135
Dreux, Fr.	D8	14
Drew, Ms., U.S.	B3	131
Drew, co., Ar., U.S.	D4	111
Drexel, Mo., U.S.	C3	132
Drexel, N.C., U.S.	B1	140
Drexel, Oh., U.S.	C1	142
Drift, Ky., U.S.	C7	124
Driftpile, Alta., Can.	B3	98
Driggs, Id., U.S.	F7	119
Drin, stm., Alb.	H3	20
Drina, stm., Eur.	E3	20
Drinit, Gjiri i b., Alb.	H3	20
Driskill Mountain, hill, La., U.S.	B3	125
Drobeta-Turnu Severin, Rom.	E6	20
Drochia, Mol.	A11	20
Drogheda, Ire.	H7	8
Drogičin, Bela.	I8	22
Drohobych, Ukr.	H2	26
Drumheller, Alta., Can.	D4	98
Drummond, Mt., U.S.	D3	133
Drummond Island, i., Mi., U.S.	C7	129
Drummondville, Que., Can.	D5	104
Drumright, Ok., U.S.	B5	143
Druskininkai, Lith.	G6	22
Družba, Kaz.	H14	26
Drybranch, W.V., U.S.	m13	155
Dry Cimarron, stm., U.S.	A6	138
Dryden, Ont., Can.	o16	103
Dryden, N.Y., U.S.	C4	139
Dry Mills, Me., U.S.	E2	126
Dry Ridge, Ky., U.S.	B5	124
Dry Tortugas, is., Fl., U.S.	H5	116
Dschang, Cam.	I15	64
Duarte, Pico, mtn., Dom. Rep.	E9	94
Duartina, Braz.	G4	79
Dubai see Dubayy, U.A.E.	B9	47
Dubăsari (Dubesar), Mol.	B13	20
Dubăsari, Lacul, res., Mol.	B13	20
Dubawnt Lake, l., N.W. Ter., Can.	D12	96
Dubayy (Dubai), U.A.E.	B9	47
Dubbo, Austl.	I8	70
Dübendorf, Switz.	D10	13
Dublin (Baile Átha Cliath), Ire.	H7	8
Dublin, Ga., U.S.	D4	117
Dublin, In., U.S.	E7	121
Dublin, N.H., U.S.	E2	136
Dublin, Oh., U.S.	k10	142
Dublin, Tx., U.S.	C3	150
Dublin, Va., U.S.	C2	153
Dublin, co., Ire.	H7	8
Dubna, Russia	E20	22
Dubois, Id., U.S.	E6	119
Dubois, In., U.S.	H4	121
Dubois, Wy., U.S.	C3	157
Dubois, co., In., U.S.	H4	121
Du Bois, Pa., U.S.	D4	145
Dubovka, Russia	H6	26
Dubréka, Gui.	G3	64
Dubrovka, Russia	G13	22
Dubrovnik, Cro.	G2	20
Dubrovno, Bela.	G13	22
Dubuque, Ia., U.S.	B7	122
Dubuque, co., Ia., U.S.	B7	122
Duchcov, Czech Rep.	E13	10
Duchesne, Ut., U.S.	C5	151
Duchesne, co., Ut., U.S.	C5	151
Duchess, Alta., Can.	D5	98
Duchovščina, Russia	F15	22
Duck, stm., Tn., U.S.	B4	149
Duck Bay, Man., Can.	C1	100
Duck Hill, Ms., U.S.	B4	131
Duck Lake, Sask., Can.	E2	105
Duckwater Peak, mtn., Nv., U.S.	E6	135
Dudelange, Lux.	J9	12
Duderstadt, Ger.	D10	10
Dudinka, Russia	D9	28
Dudley, Ma., U.S.	B4	128
Duékoué, C. Iv.	H6	64
Duenweg, Mo., U.S.	D3	132
Duero (Douro), stm., Eur.	D5	16
Due West, S.C., U.S.	C3	147
Dufourspitze, mtn., Eur.	F3	13
Dugger, In., U.S.	F3	121
Dugi Otok, i., Cro.	E10	18
Duisburg, Ger.	D6	10
Duitama, Col.	E6	84
Dukes, co., Ma., U.S.	D6	128
Duk Fadiat, Sud.	N6	60
Dukhān, Qatar	B7	47
Dukla Pass, Eur.	F21	10
Dūkštas, Lith.	F9	22
Duku, Nig.	F12	64
Dulce, N.M., U.S.	A2	138
Dulce, stm., Arg.	F7	80
Dulce, Golfo, b., C.R.	I11	92
Dulkaninna, Austl.	G3	70
Duluth, Ga., U.S.	B2	117
Duluth, Mn., U.S.	D6	130
Dūmā, Syria	A6	50
Dumaguete, Phil.	D7	38
Dumas, Ar., U.S.	D4	111
Dumas, Tx., U.S.	B2	150
Dumbarton, Scot., U.K.	F9	8
Dumfries, Scot., U.K.	F10	8
Dumfries, Va., U.S.	B5	153
Duminiči, Russia	H18	22
Dumont, Ia., U.S.	B5	122
Dumont, N.J., U.S.	B5	137
Dumyāt, Egypt	B6	60
Dumyāt, Maşabb, mth., Egypt	F1	48
Dunaharaszti, Hung.	H19	10
Dunakeszi, Hung.	H19	10
Dunaújváros, Hung.	I18	10
Dunbar, W.V., U.S.	C3	155
Duncan, B.C., Can.	E6	99
Duncan, Az., U.S.	E6	110
Duncan, Ne., U.S.	C8	134
Duncan, Ok., U.S.	C4	143
Duncan, S.C., U.S.	B3	147
Duncan Lake, res., B.C., Can.	D9	99
Duncansby Head, c., Scot., U.K.	C10	8
Duncanville, Tx., U.S.	n10	150
Dundalk, Ont., Can.	C4	103
Dundalk, Ire.	G7	8
Dundalk, Md., U.S.	B4	127
Dundas, Ont., Can.	D5	103
Dundas Island, i., B.C., Can.	B2	99
Dundee, S. Afr.	G10	66
Dundee, Scot., U.K.	E11	8
Dundee, Fl., U.S.	D5	116
Dundee, Il., U.S.	A5	120
Dundee, Mi., U.S.	G7	129
Dundee, Or., U.S.	h11	144
Dundurn, Sask., Can.	F2	105
Dundy, co., Ne., U.S.	D4	134
Dunedin, N.Z.	F3	72
Dunedin, Fl., U.S.	D4	116
Dunellen, N.J., U.S.	B4	137
Dunfermline, Scot., U.K.	E10	8
Dungog, Austl.	I9	70
Dungun, Malay.	L7	40
Dunham, Que., Can.	D5	104
Dunhua, China	C12	30
Dunkerque, Fr.	A9	14
Dunkerton, Ia., U.S.	B5	122
Dunkirk see Dunkerque, Fr.	A9	14
Dunkirk, In., U.S.	D7	121
Dunkirk, N.Y., U.S.	C1	139
Dunklin, co., Mo., U.S.	E7	132
Dunkwa, Ghana	I9	64
Dún Laoghaire, Ire.	H7	8
Dunlap, Il., U.S.	C4	120
Dunlap, Ia., U.S.	C2	122
Dunlap, Tn., U.S.	D8	149
Dunleary see Dún Laoghaire, Ire.	H7	8
Dunleith, De., U.S.	i7	115
Dunmore, Pa., U.S.	D10	145
Dunn, N.C., U.S.	B4	140
Dunn, co., N.D., U.S.	B3	141
Dunn, co., Wi., U.S.	D2	156
Dunnellon, Fl., U.S.	C4	116
Dunnottar, Man., Can.	D3	100
Dunnville, Ont., Can.	E5	103
Dunqulah, Sud.	H6	60
Dunqulah al-Qadīmah, Sud.	H6	60
Dunseith, N.D., U.S.	A5	141
Dun-sur-Auron, Fr.	F9	14
Dunville, Newf., Can.	E5	102
Dunwoody, Ga., U.S.	h8	117
Duolun (Dolonnur), China	A4	32
Duolundabohuer, China	D15	44
Duomaer, China	E2	30
Duozhu, China	M3	34
Du Page, co., Il., U.S.	B5	120
Du Page, stm., Il., U.S.	k8	120
Duplin, co., N.C., U.S.	C5	140
Dupnica, Bul.	G7	20
Dupont, Pa., U.S.	n18	145
Du Pont, W.V., U.S.	m13	155
Dupont City, W.V., U.S.	m12	155
Dupont Manor, De., U.S.	D3	115
Dupree, S.D., U.S.	B4	148
Duque de Caxias, Braz.	G7	79
Duquesne, Pa., U.S.	k14	145
Du Quoin, Il., U.S.	E4	120
Durack Ranges, mts., Austl.	C5	68
Durance, stm., Fr.	I12	14
Durand, Il., U.S.	A4	120
Durand, Mi., U.S.	F6	129
Durand, Wi., U.S.	D2	156
Durango, Mex.	E7	90
Durango, Spain	B9	16
Durango, Co., U.S.	D3	113
Durango, state, Mex.	E7	90
Durant, Ia., U.S.	C7	122
Durant, Ms., U.S.	B4	131
Durant, Ok., U.S.	D5	143
Durazno, Ur.	G10	80
Durban, S. Afr.	G10	66
Düren, Ger.	E6	10
Durg, India	J9	44
Durgāpur, India	I12	44
Durham, Ont., Can.	C4	103
Durham, Eng., U.K.	G11	8
Durham, Ca., U.S.	C3	112
Durham, Ct., U.S.	D5	114
Durham, N.H., U.S.	D5	136
Durham, N.C., U.S.	A4	140
Durham, co., Eng., U.K.	G12	8
Durham, co., N.C., U.S.	A4	140
Durlești, Mol.	B12	20
Durmitor, mtn., Yugo.	F3	20
Durrës, Alb.	H3	20
D'Urville, Tanjung, c., Indon.	F10	38
D'Urville Island, i., N.Z.	D4	72
Dušanbe, Taj.	J11	26
Dushan, China	B9	40
Dushanbe see Dušanbe, Taj.	J11	26
Düsseldorf, Ger.	D6	10
Dutchess, co., N.Y., U.S.	D7	139
Dutch Harbor, Ak., U.S.	E6	109
Dutiwe, Bots.	D6	66
Dutton, Ont., Can.	E3	103
Dutton, Mt., U.S.	C5	133
Duval, co., Fl., U.S.	B5	116
Duval, co., Tx., U.S.	F3	150
Duyun, China	A9	40
Dvinskaja guba, b., Russia	I26	6
Dvůr Králové [nad Labem], Czech Rep.	E15	10
Dwight, Il., U.S.	B5	120
Dwight D. Eisenhower Lock, N.Y., U.S.	f9	139
Dworshak Reservoir, res., Id., U.S.	C3	119
Dyer, Ar., U.S.	B1	111
Dyer, In., U.S.	A2	121
Dyer, Nv., U.S.	F3	135
Dyer, Tn., U.S.	A3	149
Dyer, co., Tn., U.S.	A2	149
Dyer, Cape, c., N.W. Ter., Can.	C20	96
Dyersburg, Tn., U.S.	A2	149
Dyersville, Ia., U.S.	B6	122
Dyess, Ar., U.S.	B5	111
Dyje (Thaya), stm., Eur.	G16	10
Dysart, Sask., Can.	G3	105
Dysart, Ia., U.S.	B5	122
Džalal-Abad, Kyrg.	I12	26
Žambul, Kaz.	I12	26
Dzaoudzi, May.	I16	67a
Džebel, Turk.	B13	48
Dzemul, Mex.	G15	90
Dzeržinsk, Bela.	H10	22
Dzeržinsk, Russia	E26	22
Dzětygara, Kaz.	G10	26
Džezkazgan, Kaz.	H11	26
Dzhankoy, Ukr.	H4	26
Dzierżoniów (Reichenbach), Pol.	E16	10
Dzilam González, Mex.	G15	90
Dzitás, Mex.	G15	90
Dzitbalché, Mex.	G14	90
Džizak, Uzb.	I11	26
Dzungarian Basin see Junggar Pendi, China	B4	30
Džungarskij Alatau, chrebet, mts., Asia	H8	28
Džusaly, Kaz.	H10	26
Dzuunmod, Mong.	B8	30

E

Name	Map Ref.	Page
Eads, Co., U.S.	C8	113
Eagan, Mn., U.S.	n12	130
Eagar, Az., U.S.	C6	110
Eagle, Co., U.S.	B4	113
Eagle, Id., U.S.	F2	119
Eagle, Ne., U.S.	D9	134
Eagle, Wi., U.S.	F5	156
Eagle, co., Co., U.S.	B4	113
Eagle, stm., Newf., Can.	B2	102
Eagle Butte, S.D., U.S.	C4	148
Eagle Creek Reservoir, res., In., U.S.	E5	121
Eagle Grove, Ia., U.S.	B4	122
Eagle Lake, Me., U.S.	A4	126
Eagle Lake, Mn., U.S.	F5	130
Eagle Lake, Tx., U.S.	E4	150
Eagle Lake, l., Me., U.S.	A4	126
Eagle Mountain, mtn., Mn., U.S.	k9	130
Eagle Mountain Lake, res., Tx., U.S.	m9	150
Eagle Pass, Tx., U.S.	E2	150
Eagle Peak, mtn., Tx., U.S.	o12	150
Eagle Point, Or., U.S.	E4	144
Eagle River, Wi., U.S.	C4	156
Eagletown, Ok., U.S.	C7	143
Eagle, Ar., U.S.	B5	111
Earl Grey, Sask., Can.	G3	105
Earlham, Ia., U.S.	C3	122
Earlimart, Ca., U.S.	E4	112
Earlington, Ky., U.S.	C2	124
Earlville, Il., U.S.	B5	120
Earlville, Ia., U.S.	B6	122
Early, Ia., U.S.	B2	122
Early, co., Ga., U.S.	E2	117
Earth, Tx., U.S.	B1	150
Easley, S.C., U.S.	B2	147
East Alstead, N.H., U.S.	E2	136
East Alton, Il., U.S.	E3	120
East Andover, N.H., U.S.	D3	136
East Angus, Que., Can.	D6	104
East Arlington, Vt., U.S.	E2	152
East Aurora, N.Y., U.S.	C2	139
East Baldwin, Me., U.S.	E2	126
East Bank, W.V., U.S.	m13	155
East Barre, Vt., U.S.	C4	152
East Baton Rouge, co., La., U.S.	D4	125
East Berbice-Corentyne, prov., Guy.	E13	84
East Bernard, Tx., U.S.	E4	150
East Bernstadt, Ky., U.S.	C5	124
East Bethel, Mn., U.S.	E5	130
East Bethel, Vt., U.S.	D3	152
East Billerica, Ma., U.S.	f11	128
East Boothbay, Me., U.S.	E3	126
East Borough, Ks., U.S.	g12	123
East Brewton, Al., U.S.	D2	108
East Bridgewater, Ma., U.S.	B6	128
East Brimfield Lake, res., Ma., U.S.	B3	128
East Brooklyn, Ct., U.S.	B8	114
East Brunswick, N.J., U.S.	C4	137
East Burke, Vt., U.S.	B5	152
East Camden, Ar., U.S.	D3	111
East Canaan, Ct., U.S.	A3	114
East Candia, N.H., U.S.	D4	136
East Cape, c., N.Z.	B7	72
East Carbon, Ut., U.S.	D5	151
East Carroll, co., La., U.S.	B4	125
East Chicago, In., U.S.	A3	121
East China Sea, Asia	E11	30
East Cleveland, Oh., U.S.	g9	142
East Corinth, Me., U.S.	C4	126
East Cote Blanche Bay, b., La., U.S.	E4	125
East Derry, N.H., U.S.	E4	136
East Detroit, Mi., U.S.	p16	129
East Dorset, Vt., U.S.	E2	152
East Douglas, Ma., U.S.	B4	128
East Dubuque, Il., U.S.	A3	120
East Eddington, Me., U.S.	D4	126
Eastend, Sask., Can.	H1	105
Easter Island see Pascua, Isla de, i., Chile	G4	74
Eastern Bay, b., Md., U.S.	C5	127
Eastern Ghāts, mts., India	F5	46
Eastern Neck Island, i., Md., U.S.	B5	127
East Falkland, i., Falk. Is.	G5	78
East Falmouth, Ma., U.S.	C6	128
East Feliciana, co., La., U.S.	D4	125
East Flat Rock, N.C., U.S.	f10	140
Eastford, Ct., U.S.	B7	114
East Frisian Islands see Ostfriesische Inseln, is., Ger.	B7	10
East Gaffney, S.C., U.S.	A4	147
East Glacier Park, Mt., U.S.	B3	133
East Granby, Ct., U.S.	B5	114
East Grand Forks, Mn., U.S.	C2	130
East Grand Rapids, Mi., U.S.	F5	129
East Greenville, Pa., U.S.	F10	145
East Greenwich, R.I., U.S.	D4	146
East Hampstead, N.H., U.S.	E4	136
East Hampton, Ct., U.S.	C5	114
Easthampton, Ma., U.S.	B2	128
East Hartford, Ct., U.S.	B5	114
East Hartland, Ct., U.S.	B4	114
East Haven, Ct., U.S.	D4	114
East Helena, Mt., U.S.	D5	133
East Jordan, Mi., U.S.	C5	129
East Kilbride, Scot., U.K.	F9	8
East Kingston, N.H., U.S.	E5	136
Eastlake, Oh., U.S.	A4	142
Eastland, Tx., U.S.	C3	150
Eastland, co., Tx., U.S.	C3	150
East Lansing, Mi., U.S.	F6	129
East Las Vegas, Nv., U.S.	G6	135
East Lempster, N.H., U.S.	D2	136
East Liverpool, Oh., U.S.	B5	142
East London (Oos-Londen), S. Afr.	I8	66
East Longmeadow, Ma., U.S.	B2	128
East Los Angeles, Ca., U.S.	m12	112
East Lyme, Ct., U.S.	D7	114
East Lynn Lake, res., W.V., U.S.	C2	155
East Machias, Me., U.S.	D5	126
East Madison, Me., U.S.	D3	126
Eastmain-Opinaca, Réservoir, res., Que., Can.	h11	104
Eastman, Ga., U.S.	D3	117
East Matunuck, R.I., U.S.	F3	146
East Middlebury, Vt., U.S.	D2	152
East Millinocket, Me., U.S.	C4	126
East Moline, Il., U.S.	B3	120
East Montpelier, Vt., U.S.	C4	152
East Naples, Fl., U.S.	F5	116
East Newnan, Ga., U.S.	C2	117
East Nishnabotna, stm., Ia., U.S.	C2	122
East Norriton, Pa., U.S.	o20	145
East Olympia, Wa., U.S.	C3	154
Easton, Ks., U.S.	k15	123
Easton, Me., U.S.	B5	126
Easton, Md., U.S.	C5	127
Easton, Ma., U.S.	B5	128
Easton, Pa., U.S.	E11	145
East Orange, N.J., U.S.	B4	137
East Orleans, Ma., U.S.	C8	128
Eastover, S.C., U.S.	D6	147
East Palatka, Fl., U.S.	C5	116
East Palestine, Oh., U.S.	B5	142
East Pea Ridge, W.V., U.S.	C2	155
East Peoria, Il., U.S.	C4	120
East Pepperell, Ma., U.S.	A4	128
East Petersburg, Pa., U.S.	F9	145
East Pittsburgh, Pa., U.S.	k14	145
East Point, Ga., U.S.	C2	117
East Point, c., P.E.I., Can.	C8	101
East Point, c., Ma., U.S.	B6	128
Eastport, Newf., Can.	D5	102
Eastport, Me., U.S.	D6	126
East Poultney, Vt., U.S.	D2	152
East Prairie, Mo., U.S.	E8	132
East Providence, R.I., U.S.	C4	146
East Quogue, N.Y., U.S.	n16	139
East Ridge, Tn., U.S.	h11	149
East River, Ct., U.S.	D5	114
East Rockingham, N.C., U.S.	C3	140
East Rutherford, N.J., U.S.	h8	137
East Saint Louis, Il., U.S.	E3	120
East Sebago, Me., U.S.	E2	126
East Selkirk, Man., Can.	D3	100
East Siberian Sea see Vostočno-Sibirskoje more, Russia	C23	28
Eastsound, Wa., U.S.	A3	154
East Spencer, N.C., U.S.	B2	140
East Stroudsburg, Pa., U.S.	D11	145
East Sullivan, N.H., U.S.	E2	136
East Swanzey, N.H., U.S.	E2	136
East Tawas, Mi., U.S.	D7	129
East Thermopolis, Wy., U.S.	C4	157
East Troy, Wi., U.S.	F5	156
East Vestal, N.Y., U.S.	C4	139
East View, N.Y., U.S.	k10	139
East Wallingford, Vt., U.S.	E3	152
East Walpole, Ma., U.S.	h11	128
East Washington, Pa., U.S.	F1	145
East Waterboro, Me., U.S.	E2	126
East Wenatchee, Wa., U.S.	B5	154
East Wilton, Me., U.S.	D2	126
East Windsor, Ct., U.S.	B5	114
East York, Ont., Can.	D5	103
Eaton, Co., U.S.	A6	113
Eaton, In., U.S.	D7	121
Eaton, Oh., U.S.	C1	142
Eaton, co., Mi., U.S.	F6	129
Eatonia, Sask., Can.	G1	105
Eaton Rapids, Mi., U.S.	F6	129
Eatonton, Ga., U.S.	C3	117
Eatontown, N.J., U.S.	C4	137
Eatonville, Wa., U.S.	C3	154
Eau Claire, Wi., U.S.	D2	156
Eau Claire, co., Wi., U.S.	D2	156
Eau Claire, Lac à l', l., Que., Can.	g11	104
Eauze, Fr.	I7	14
Ebano, Mex.	F10	90

Name	Map Ref.	Page
Ebbw Vale, Wales, U.K.	J10	8
Ebenezer, Sask., Can.	F4	105
Ebensburg, Pa., U.S.	F4	145
Eberswalde, Ger.	C13	10
Ebetsu, Japan	d16	36a
Eboli, Italy	I10	18
Ebolowa, Cam.	H9	54
Ebony, Nmb.	D2	66
Ebro (Ebre), stm., Spain	E12	16
Eccles, W.V., U.S.	n13	155
Echaporã, Braz.	G3	79
Ech Cheliff (Orléansville), Alg.	B11	62
Echo Bay, Nv., U.S.	G7	135
Echols, co., Ga., U.S.	F4	117
Echuca, Austl.	K6	70
Écija, Spain	H6	16
Eckernförde, Ger.	A9	10
Eckhart Mines, Md., U.S.	k13	127
Eckville, Alta., Can.	C3	98
Eclectic, Al., U.S.	C3	108
Economy, Pa., U.S.	*h13	145
Ecorse, Mi., U.S.	p15	129
Écrins, Barre des, mtn., Fr.	H13	14
Ecru, Ms., U.S.	A4	131
Ector, co., Tx., U.S.	D1	150
Ecuador, ctry., S.A.	D3	76
Edam, Sask., Can.	D1	105
Edam, Neth.	C7	12
Eddy, co., N.M., U.S.	E5	138
Eddy, co., N.D., U.S.	B7	141
Eddystone, Pa., U.S.	p20	145
Eddyville, Ia., U.S.	C5	122
Eddyville, Ky., U.S.	e9	124
Ede, Nig.	H12	64
Edéa, Cam.	H9	54
Edéia, Braz.	D4	79
Eden, Austl.	K8	70
Eden, Ga., U.S.	D5	117
Eden, Id., U.S.	G4	119
Eden, N.Y., U.S.	C2	139
Eden, N.C., U.S.	A3	140
Eden, Wy., U.S.	D3	157
Eden Prairie, Mn., U.S.	n12	130
Edenton, N.C., U.S.	A6	140
Eden Valley, Mn., U.S.	E4	130
Edenwold, Sask., Can.	G3	105
Edfu see Idfū, Egypt	E7	60
Edgar, Ne., U.S.	D8	134
Edgar, Wi., U.S.	D4	156
Edgar, co., Il., U.S.	D6	120
Edgartown, Ma., U.S.	D6	128
Edgecombe, co., N.C., U.S.	B5	140
Edgefield, S.C., U.S.	D4	147
Edgefield, co., S.C., U.S.	D4	147
Edgeley, N.D., U.S.	C7	141
Edgemere, Md., U.S.	B5	127
Edgemont, S.D., U.S.	D2	148
Edgemoor, De., U.S.	A3	115
Edgeøya, i., Sval.	B3	24
Edgerton, Alta., Can.	C5	98
Edgerton, Ks., U.S.	D8	123
Edgerton, Mn., U.S.	G2	130
Edgerton, Mo., U.S.	B3	132
Edgerton, Oh., U.S.	A1	142
Edgerton, Wi., U.S.	F4	156
Edgerton, Wy., U.S.	C6	157
Edgewater, Al., U.S.	f7	108
Edgewater, Fl., U.S.	D6	116
Edgewater, Md., U.S.	C4	127
Edgewater, N.J., U.S.	h9	137
Edgewater Park, N.J., U.S.	C3	137
Edgewood, In., U.S.	D6	121
Edgewood, Ia., U.S.	B6	122
Edgewood, Ky., U.S.	h13	124
Edgewood, Md., U.S.	B5	127
Edgewood, N.M., U.S.	B3	138
Edgewood, Oh., U.S.	A5	142
Edgewood, Pa., U.S.	k14	145
Edgewood, Wa., U.S.	f11	154
Édhessa, Grc.	I6	20
Edina, Mn., U.S.	F5	130
Edina, Mo., U.S.	A5	132
Edinboro, Pa., U.S.	C1	145
Edinburg, Il., U.S.	D4	120
Edinburg, N.D., U.S.	A8	141
Edinburg, Tx., U.S.	F3	150
Edinburg, Va., U.S.	B4	153
Edinburgh, Scot., U.K.	F10	8
Edinburgh, In., U.S.	F6	121
Edirne, Tur.	H10	20
Edison, Ga., U.S.	E2	117
Edison, N.J., U.S.	B4	137
Edisto, stm., S.C., U.S.	E6	147
Edisto Island, i., S.C., U.S.	F7	147
Edmond, Ok., U.S.	B4	143
Edmonds, Wa., U.S.	B3	154
Edmonson, co., Ky., U.S.	C3	124
Edmonton, Austl.	A6	70
Edmonton, Alta., Can.	C4	98
Edmonton, Ky., U.S.	D4	124
Edmore, N.D., U.S.	A7	141
Edmunds, co., S.D., U.S.	B6	148
Edmundston, N.B., Can.	B1	101
Edna, Ks., U.S.	E8	123
Edna, Tx., U.S.	E4	150
Edremit, Tur.	J11	20
Edson, Alta., Can.	C2	98
Eduardo Castex, Arg.	H6	80
Edward, Lake, l., Afr.	B5	58
Edwards, Ms., U.S.	C3	131
Edwards, co., Il., U.S.	E5	120
Edwards, co., Ks., U.S.	E4	123
Edwards, co., Tx., U.S.	E2	150
Edwards Air Force Base, mil., Ca., U.S.	E5	124
Edwardsville, Il., U.S.	E4	120
Edwardsville, Ks., U.S.	k16	123
Edwardsville, Pa., U.S.	n17	145
Edward VII Peninsula, pen., Ant.	C9	73
Eek, Ak., U.S.	C7	109
Eeklo, Bel.	F4	12
Eel, stm., In., U.S.	C6	121
Eel, stm., In., U.S.	F3	121
Effingham, Il., U.S.	D5	120
Effingham, Ks., U.S.	C8	123
Effingham, co., Ga., U.S.	D5	117
Effingham, co., Il., U.S.	D5	120
Egadi, Isole, is., Italy	L7	18
Egan Range, mts., Nv., U.S.	E7	135
Eganville, Ont., Can.	B7	103
Eger see Cheb, Czech Rep.	E12	10
Eger, Hung.	H20	10
Egersund, Nor.	L10	6
Egg Harbor City, N.J., U.S.	D3	137
Egg Island Point, c., N.J., U.S.	E2	137
Egilsstaðir, Ice.	B6	6a
Eglin Air Force Base, mil., Fl., U.S.	u15	116
Egmont, Mount, mtn., N.Z.	C4	72
Egmont Bay, b., P.E.I., Can.	C5	101
Egypt (Misr), ctry., Afr.	C7	56
Egypt, Lake of, res., Il., U.S.	F5	120
Ehrenberg, Az., U.S.	D1	110
Eibar, Spain	B9	16
Eidsvold, Austl.	E9	70
Eiger, mtn., Switz.	E9	13
Eight Degree Channel, strt., Asia	I2	46
Eighty Mile Beach, Austl.	C4	68
Eildon, Austl.	K6	70
Einasleigh, stm., Austl.	A5	70
Einbeck, Ger.	D9	10
Eindhoven, Neth.	F7	12
Einsiedeln, Switz.	D10	13
Eirunepé, Braz.	B7	82
Eisenach, Ger.	E10	10
Eisenhower, Mount, mtn., N.H., U.S.	B4	136
Eisenhüttenstadt, Ger.	C14	10
Eisenstadt, Aus.	H16	10
Eišiškés, Lith.	G8	22
Eisleben, Ger.	D11	10
Eivissa, Spain	G13	16
Eivissa (Ibiza), i., Spain	G13	16
Ejea de los Caballeros, Spain	C10	16
Ejeda, Madag.	t21	67b
Ejido, Ven.	C7	84
Ejutla de Crespo, Mex.	I11	90
Ekalaka, Mt., U.S.	E12	133
Ekibastuz, Kaz.	H12	28
Eksjö, Swe.	M14	6
El Aaiún (La'youn), W. Sah.	G4	62
El Abiadh Sidi Cheikh, Alg.	D11	62
El Aguilar, Arg.	B6	80
Elaine, Ar., U.S.	C5	111
El Alamein see Al-'Alamayn, Egypt	B5	60
El Aouinet, Alg.	N2	18
El Arahal, Spain	H6	16
Elat, Isr.	I3	50
Elazığ, Tur.	B5	48
Elba, Al., U.S.	D3	108
Elba, Isola d', i., Italy	G5	18
El Banco, Col.	C6	84
Elbasan, Alb.	H4	20
El Baúl, Ven.	C8	84
Elbe (Labe), stm., Eur.	B9	10
Elberfeld, In., U.S.	H3	121
Elbert, co., Co., U.S.	B6	113
Elbert, co., Ga., U.S.	B4	117
Elbert, Mount, mtn., Co., U.S.	B4	113
Elberta, Al., U.S.	E2	108
Elberta, Ga., U.S.	D3	117
Elberton, Ga., U.S.	B4	117
Elbeuf, Fr.	C8	14
El Beyyadh, Alg.	D11	62
Elbistan, Tur.	B4	48
Elbląg (Elbing), Pol.	A19	10
El Boulaïda, Alg.	B12	62
Elbow, Sask., Can.	F2	105
Elbow Lake, Mn., U.S.	E3	130
El'brus, gora, mtn., Russia	I6	26
Elburn, Il., U.S.	B5	120
El Cajon, Ca., U.S.	F5	112
El Cajón, Embalse, res., Hond.	B7	92
El Calafate, Arg.	G2	78
El Callao, Ven.	D12	84
El Campo, Tx., U.S.	E4	150
El Carmen de Bolívar, Col.	C5	84
El Carril, Arg.	B6	80
El Centro, Ca., U.S.	F6	112
El Cerrito, Col.	F4	84
El Cerro, Bol.	G11	82
El Chile, Montaña, mtn., Hond.	C8	92
El Cocuy, Col.	D6	84
El Colorado, Arg.	D9	80
El Cóndor, Cerro, mtn., Arg.	D4	80
Elda, Spain	G11	16
Eldersburg, Md., U.S.	B4	127
El Djazaïr (Algiers), Alg.	B12	62
El Djelfa, Alg.	C12	62
Eldon, P.E.I., Can.	C7	101
Eldon, Ia., U.S.	D5	122
Eldon, Mo., U.S.	C5	132
Eldora, Ia., U.S.	B4	122
Eldorado, Arg.	D11	80
Eldorado, Braz.	C14	80
El Dorado, Mex.	E6	90
El Dorado, Ar., U.S.	D3	111
Eldorado, Il., U.S.	F5	120
El Dorado, Ks., U.S.	E7	123
El Dorado, Ven.	D12	84
El Dorado, co., Ca., U.S.	C3	112
Eldorado Peak, mtn., Wa., U.S.	A4	154
Eldorado Springs, Co., U.S.	B5	113
El Dorado Springs, Mo., U.S.	D3	132
Eldoret, Kenya	A7	58
Eldridge, Ia., U.S.	C7	122
Eleanor, W.V., U.S.	C3	155
Electra, Tx., U.S.	C3	150
Elefantes, Rio dos (Olifants), stm., Afr.	E11	66
Elektrogorsk, Russia	F21	22
Elektrostal', Russia	F21	22
Elephant Butte Reservoir, res., N.M., U.S.	D2	138
Elephant Mountain, mtn., Me., U.S.	D2	126
El Eulma, Alg.	B13	62
Eleuthera, i., Bah.	B6	94
Eleven Point, stm., U.S.	A4	111
Elevsís, Grc.	K7	20
El Ferrol del Caudillo, Spain	B3	16
Elfrida, Az., U.S.	F6	110
Elfros, Sask., Can.	F4	105
El Fuerte, Mex.	D5	90
El Galpón, Arg.	C6	80
El Ghazawet, Alg.	C10	62
Elgin, Scot., U.K.	D10	8
Elgin, Il., U.S.	A5	120
Elgin, Mn., U.S.	F6	130
Elgin, Ne., U.S.	C7	134
Elgin, N.D., U.S.	C4	141
Elgin, Ok., U.S.	C3	143
Elgin, Or., U.S.	B9	144
Elgin, Tx., U.S.	D4	150
Elgon, Mount, mtn., Afr.	A6	58
El Grara, Alg.	D13	62
El Hadjar, Alg.	M2	18
Elhovo, Bul.	G10	20
El Ídolo, Isla, i., Mex.	G11	90
El Idrissia, Alg.	C12	62
Elim, Ak., U.S.	C7	109
Elisabethville see Lubumbashi, Zaire	D5	58
Elista, Russia	H6	26
Elizabeth, Austl.	J7	70
Elizabeth, Co., U.S.	B6	113
Elizabeth, N.J., U.S.	B4	137
Elizabeth, W.V., U.S.	B3	155
Elizabeth City, N.C., U.S.	A6	140
Elizabeth Islands, is., Ma., U.S.	D6	128
Elizabethton, Tn., U.S.	C11	149
Elizabethtown, Ky., U.S.	C4	124
Elizabethtown, N.C., U.S.	C4	140
Elizabethtown, Pa., U.S.	F8	145
El-Jadida (Mazagan), Mor.	D6	62
El Jebel, Co., U.S.	B3	113
El Jem, Tun.	N5	18
Elk, Pol.	B22	10
Elk, co., Ks., U.S.	E7	123
Elk, co., Pa., U.S.	D4	145
Elk, stm., W.V., U.S.	C3	155
Elkader, Ia., U.S.	B6	122
El-Karafah, Sud.	H6	60
Elk City, Id., U.S.	D3	119
Elk City, Ok., U.S.	B2	143
El Kef, Tun.	M3	18
El-Kelâa-des-Srarhna, Mor.	D7	62
El Kerma, Alg.	J11	16
Elkford, B.C., Can.	D10	99
Elk Grove, Ca., U.S.	C3	112
Elk Grove Village, Il., U.S.	h9	120
Elkhart, In., U.S.	A6	121
Elkhart, Ks., U.S.	E2	123
Elkhart, co., In., U.S.	A6	121
Elkhart Lake, Wi., U.S.	E6	156
Elkhorn, Man., Can.	E1	100
Elk Horn, Ia., U.S.	C2	122
Elkhorn, Ne., U.S.	g12	134
Elkhorn, Wi., U.S.	F5	156
Elkhorn, stm., Ne., U.S.	B7	134
Elkhorn City, Ky., U.S.	C7	124
Elkin, N.C., U.S.	A2	140
Elkins, Ar., U.S.	A1	111
Elkins, W.V., U.S.	C5	155
Elkland, Pa., U.S.	C7	145
Elk Mountain, Wy., U.S.	E6	157
Elk Mountain, mtn., N.M., U.S.	D1	138
Elk Mountains, mts., U.S.	D1	148
Elko, Nv., U.S.	C6	135
Elko, co., Nv., U.S.	B6	135
El Kouif, Alg.	N3	18
Elk Point, Alta., Can.	C5	98
Elk Point, S.D., U.S.	E9	148
Elk Rapids, Mi., U.S.	D5	129
Elkridge, Md., U.S.	B4	127
Elk River, Mn., U.S.	E5	130
Elkton, Ky., U.S.	D2	124
Elkton, Md., U.S.	A6	127
Elkton, S.D., U.S.	C9	148
Elkton, Va., U.S.	B4	153
Elkview, W.V., U.S.	m13	155
Elkville, Il., U.S.	F4	120
Ellaville, Ga., U.S.	D2	117
Ellen, Mount, mtn., Ut., U.S.	E5	151
Ellen, Mount, mtn., Vt., U.S.	C3	152
Ellenboro, W.V., U.S.	B3	155
Ellendale, N.D., U.S.	C7	141
Ellensburg, Wa., U.S.	C5	154
Ellenton, Fl., U.S.	E4	116
Ellenville, N.Y., U.S.	D6	139
Ellershouse, N.S., Can.	E6	101
Ellerslie, Md., U.S.	k13	127
Ellesmere Island, i., N.W. Ter., Can.	A11	86
Ellettsville, In., U.S.	F4	121
Ellice Islands see Tuvalu, ctry., Oc.	G24	2
Ellichpur see Achalpur, India	J7	44
Ellicott City, Md., U.S.	B4	127
Ellijay, Ga., U.S.	B2	117
Ellington, Ct., U.S.	B6	114
Ellington, Mo., U.S.	D7	132
Ellinwood, Ks., U.S.	D5	123
Elliot Lake, Ont., Can.	A2	103
Elliott, S.C., U.S.	C8	147
Elliott, co., Ky., U.S.	B6	124
Ellis, Ks., U.S.	D4	123
Ellis, co., Ks., U.S.	D4	123
Ellis, co., Ok., U.S.	A2	143
Ellis, co., Tx., U.S.	C4	150
Elliston, Newf., Can.	D5	102
Elliston, Va., U.S.	C2	153
Ellisville, Ms., U.S.	D4	131
Ellisville, Mo., U.S.	f12	132
Ellore see Elūru, India	F11	42
Ellsworth, Man., Can.	E2	100
Ellsworth, Me., U.S.	D4	126
Ellsworth, Ks., U.S.	D5	123
Ellsworth, Wi., U.S.	D1	156
Ellsworth, co., Ks., U.S.	D5	123
Ellsworth Land, reg., Ant.	C7	73
Ellsworth Mountains, mts., Ant.	C12	73
Ellwangen, Ger.	G10	10
Ellwood City, Pa., U.S.	E1	145
Elma, Wa., U.S.	C2	154
El Mahdia, Tun.	N5	18
El Malah, Alg.	J10	16
El Manteco, Ven.	D11	84
El Marsa el Kebir, Alg.	C10	62
Elm City, N.C., U.S.	B5	140
Elm Creek, Man., Can.	E2	100
Elm Creek, Ne., U.S.	D6	134
Elmendorf Air Force Base, mil., Ak., U.S.	C10	109
El Menia, Alg.	E12	62
El Mghayyar, Alg.	D13	62
Elm Grove, Wi., U.S.	m11	156
Elmhurst, Il., U.S.	B6	120
El Milagro, Arg.	F6	80
El Miliyya, Alg.	B14	62
Elmina, Ghana	I9	64
Elmira, N.Y., U.S.	C4	139
El Mirage, Az., U.S.	k8	110
Elmira Heights, N.Y., U.S.	C4	139
Elmont, N.Y., U.S.	k13	139
El Monte, Ca., U.S.	m12	112
Elmore, Austl.	K6	70
Elmore, Al., U.S.	C3	108
Elmore, Mn., U.S.	G4	130
Elmore, co., Al., U.S.	C3	108
Elmore, co., Id., U.S.	F3	119
Elmsdale, N.S., Can.	E6	101
Elmshorn, Ger.	B9	10
Elm Springs, Ar., U.S.	A1	111
Elmvale, Ont., Can.	C5	103
Elmwood, Il., U.S.	C3	120
Elmwood, Ne., U.S.	D9	134
Elmwood Park, Il., U.S.	k9	120
Elmwood Park, N.J., U.S.	h8	137
Elmwood Place, Oh., U.S.	o13	142
Elne, Fr.	J9	14
El Nihuil, Arg.	H4	80
Elnora, Alta., Can.	D4	98
Elnora, In., U.S.	G3	121
Elon College, N.C., U.S.	A3	140
Elora, Ont., Can.	D4	103
El Oro, Ec.	I3	84
Elortondo, Arg.	G8	80
Elorza, Ven.	D8	84
Eloy, Az., U.S.	E4	110
Eloy Alfaro, Ec.	I3	84
El Palmar, Ven.	D12	84
El Pao, Ven.	C11	84
El Paraíso, Hond.	D8	92
El Paraíso, dept., Hond.	C8	92
El Paso, Il., U.S.	C4	120
El Paso, Tx., U.S.	o11	150
El Paso, co., Co., U.S.	C6	113
El Paso, co., Tx., U.S.	o11	150
Elphinstone, Man., Can.	D1	100
El Piquete, Arg.	B6	80
El Pital, Cerro, mtn., N.A.	C5	92
El Portal, Fl., U.S.	s13	116
El Porvenir, Peru	C2	82
El Prado, N.M., U.S.	A4	138
El Prat de Llobregat, Spain	D14	16
El Progreso, Hond.	B7	92
El Progreso, dept., Guat.	C4	92
El Puerto de Santa María, Spain	I5	16
El Qala, Alg.	B15	62
El Qoll, Alg.	B14	62
El Quebrachal, Arg.	C6	80
El Reno, Ok., U.S.	B4	143
Elrod, Al., U.S.	B2	108
Elrose, Sask., Can.	F1	105
Elroy, Wi., U.S.	E3	156
Elsa, Tx., U.S.	F3	150
El Salto, Mex.	F7	90
El Salvador, ctry., N.A.	D6	92
El Samán de Apure, Ven.	D8	84
Elsberry, Mo., U.S.	B7	132
El Seibo, Dom. Rep.	E10	94
Elsinore, Ut., U.S.	E3	151
Elsmere, De., U.S.	B3	115
Elsmere, Ky., U.S.	B5	124
El Sombrero, Ven.	C9	84
Elst, Neth.	E8	12
El Tala, Arg.	C6	80
El Tigre, Ven.	C10	84
El Tigre, Isla, i., Hond.	D7	92
El Tocuyo, Ven.	C8	84
Elton, La., U.S.	D3	125
El Toro, Ca., U.S.	n13	112
El Tránsito, Chile	E3	80
El Trébol, Arg.	G8	80
El Triunfo, Hond.	D7	92
Elūru, India	D6	46
Elva, Est.	C9	22
El Valle, Pan.	C2	84
Elvas, Port.	G4	16
El Vendrell, Spain	D13	16
El Viejo, Nic.	E7	92
El Vigía, Ven.	C7	84
Elvins, Mo., U.S.	D7	132
El Wad, Alg.	D14	62
El Wanza, Alg.	C15	62
Elwell, Lake, res., Mt., U.S.	B5	133
Elwood, In., U.S.	D6	121
Elwood, Ks., U.S.	C9	123
Elwood, Ne., U.S.	D6	134
Elwood, Ut., U.S.	B3	151
Elx, Spain	G11	16
Ely, Mn., U.S.	C7	130
Ely, Nv., U.S.	D7	135
Elyria, Oh., U.S.	A3	142
Elysburg, Pa., U.S.	E8	145
Emāmshahr (Shāhrūd), Iran	C13	48
Emanuel, co., Ga., U.S.	D4	117
Emba, Kaz.	H9	26
Emba, stm., Kaz.	H9	26
Embarcación, Arg.	B6	80
Embarras, stm., Il., U.S.	D6	120
Embro, Ont., Can.	D4	103
Embrun, Fr.	H13	14
Emden, Ger.	B7	10
Emerald, Austl.	D8	70
Emerson, Man., Can.	E3	100
Emerson, Ar., U.S.	D2	111
Emerson, Ga., U.S.	B2	117
Emerson, Ne., U.S.	B9	134
Emery, S.D., U.S.	D8	148
Emery, co., Ut., U.S.	E5	151
Emiliano Zapata, Mex.	I14	90
Emilia-Romagna, prov., Italy	E5	18
Emine, nos, c., Bul.	G11	20
Eminence, Ky., U.S.	B4	124
Eminence, Mo., U.S.	D6	132
Emirdağ, Tur.	H14	20
Emmaus, Pa., U.S.	E11	145
Emmaville, Austl.	G9	70
Emmen, Neth.	C10	12
Emmendingen, Ger.	G7	10
Emmerich, Ger.	D6	10
Emmet, Ar., U.S.	D2	111
Emmet, co., Ia., U.S.	A3	122
Emmet, co., Mi., U.S.	C6	129
Emmetsburg, Ia., U.S.	A3	122
Emmett, Id., U.S.	F2	119
Emmitsburg, Md., U.S.	A3	127
Emmonak, Ak., U.S.	C7	109
Emmons, co., N.D., U.S.	C5	141
Emory Peak, mtn., Tx., U.S.	E1	150
Empalme, Mex.	D4	90
Empangeni, S. Afr.	G10	66
Empedrado, Arg.	D9	80
Empire, Co., U.S.	B5	113
Empire, Nv., U.S.	C2	135
Empoli, Italy	F5	18
Emporia, Ks., U.S.	D7	123
Emporia, Va., U.S.	D5	153
Emporium, Pa., U.S.	D5	145
Empty Quarter see Ar-Rub' al-Khālī, des., Asia	D7	47
Ems, stm., Ger.	B7	10
Emsdetten, Ger.	C7	10
Emsworth, Pa., U.S.	h13	145
Emure-Ekiti, Nig.	H12	64
Encampment, Wy., U.S.	E6	157
Encantado, Braz.	E13	80
Encarnación, Para.	D11	80
Encinitas, Ca., U.S.	F5	112
Encontrados, Ven.	C6	84
Encruzilhada, Braz.	C8	79
Encruzilhada do Sul, Braz.	F12	80
Ende, Indon.	G7	38
Endeavour, Sask., Can.	E4	105
Enderby, B.C., Can.	D8	99
Enderby Land, reg., Ant.	C8	141
Enderlin, N.D., U.S.	C8	141
Endicott, N.Y., U.S.	C4	139
Endicott Mountains, mts., Ak., U.S.	B9	109
Endwell, N.Y., U.S.	C4	139
Ene, stm., Peru	D4	82
Enewetak, atoll, Marsh. Is.		
Enfield, N.S., Can.	E6	101
Enfield (Thompsonville), Ct., U.S.	B5	114
Enfield, Me., U.S.	C4	126
Enfield, N.H., U.S.	C2	136
Enfield, N.C., U.S.	A5	140
Engaño, Cabo, c., Dom. Rep.	E10	94
Engelberg, Switz.	E9	13
Engel's, Russia	G7	26
England, Ar., U.S.	C4	111
England, ter., U.K.	I12	8
Englee, Newf., Can.	C3	102
Englefeld, Sask., Can.	E3	105
Englefield, Cape, c., N.W. Ter., Can.	C15	96
Engleside, Va., U.S.	g12	153
Englewood, Co., U.S.	B6	113
Englewood, Fl., U.S.	F4	116
Englewood, N.J., U.S.	B5	137
Englewood, Oh., U.S.	C1	142
Englewood, Tn., U.S.	D9	149
Englewood Cliffs, N.J., U.S.	h9	137
English, In., U.S.	H5	121
English Channel (La Manche), strt., Eur.	K12	8
Enid, Ok., U.S.	A4	143
Enid Lake, res., Ms., U.S.	A4	131
Enigma, Ga., U.S.	E3	117
Enka, N.C., U.S.	f10	140
Enna, Italy	L9	18
Ennedi, plat., Chad	E5	56
Ennis, Mt., U.S.	E5	133
Ennis, Tx., U.S.	C4	150
Enns, Aus.	G14	10
Enns, stm., Aus.	G14	10
Enoch, Ut., U.S.	F2	151
Enola, Pa., U.S.	F8	145
Enon, S.C., U.S.	n13	112
Enoree, S.C., U.S.	B4	147
Enoree, stm., S.C., U.S.	B3	147
Enosburg Falls, Vt., U.S.	B3	152
Enriquillo, Lago, l., Dom. Rep.	E9	94
Enschede, Neth.	D10	12
Ensenada, Mex.	B1	90
Enshi, China	E8	30
Ensley, Fl., U.S.	u14	116
Enterprise, Al., U.S.	D4	108
Enterprise, Ks., U.S.	D6	123
Enterprise, Or., U.S.	B9	144
Enterprise, Ut., U.S.	F2	151
Enterprise, W.V., U.S.	B4	155
Entiat, Wa., U.S.	B5	154
Entiat, Lake, l., Wa., U.S.	B5	154
Entre Rios, Braz.	C9	79
Entre Ríos, prov., Arg.	F9	80
Entre-Rios de Minas, Braz.	F6	79
Entwistle, Alta., Can.	C3	98
Enugu, Nig.	H13	64
Enumclaw, Wa., U.S.	C4	154
Envigado, Col.	D5	84
Envira, Braz.	B4	82
Eólie, Isole, is., Italy	K9	18
Epe, Nig.	H11	64
Épernay, Fr.	C10	14
Ephesus see Efes, Tur.	L11	20
Ephraim, Ut., U.S.	D4	151
Ephrata, Pa., U.S.	F9	145
Ephrata, Wa., U.S.	B6	154
Épinal, Fr.	D13	14
Epira, Guy.	E13	84
Epirus see Ípeiros, hist. reg., Grc.	J4	20
Epokiro, Nmb.	C4	66
Epping, N.H., U.S.	D5	136
Epping, Eng., U.K.	J13	8
Epsom, Eng., U.K.	J12	8
Epworth, Ia., U.S.	B7	122
Eqlīd, Iran	F12	48
Equatorial Guinea, ctry., Afr.	H8	54
Erath, La., U.S.	E3	125
Erath, co., Tx., U.S.	C3	150
Erciş, Tur.	B6	48
Erciyes Dağı, mtn., Tur.	B3	48
Érd, Hung.	H18	10
Erdene, Mong.	C9	30
Erebus, Mount, mtn., Ant.	C9	73
Ereğli, Tur.	C3	48
Erenhot, China	C9	30
Erexim, Braz.	D12	80
Erfurt, Ger.	E11	10
Ergun (Argun), stm., Asia	A11	30
Erice, Italy	K7	18
Erick, Ok., U.S.	B2	143
Erickson, B.C., Can.	E9	99
Erickson, Man., Can.	D2	100
Erie, Co., U.S.	A5	113
Erie, Il., U.S.	B3	120
Erie, Ks., U.S.	E8	123
Erie, Pa., U.S.	B1	145
Erie, co., N.Y., U.S.	C2	139
Erie, co., Oh., U.S.	A3	142
Erie, co., Pa., U.S.	C1	145
Erie, Lake, l., N.A.	C10	106
Erie Canal, N.Y., U.S.	B5	139
Eriksdale, Man., Can.	D2	100
Erimo-misaki, c., Japan	f18	36a
Erin, Ont., Can.	D4	103
Erin, Tn., U.S.	A4	149
Eritrea, ctry., Afr.	E8	56
Erjiazhen, China	C10	34
Erkelenz, Ger.	D6	10
Erlangen, Ger.	F11	10
Erlanger, Ky., U.S.	A5	124
Ermelo, S. Afr.	F9	66
Ermoúpolis, Grc.	L8	20
Erne, Lower Lough, l., N. Ire., U.K.	G6	8
Ernée, Fr.	D6	14
Erode, India	G4	44
Erota, Erit.	I9	60
Er-Rachidia, Mor.	C8	62
Erskine, Alta., Can.	C4	98
Erstein, Fr.	D14	14
Ertil', Russia	J23	22
Eruwa, Nig.	H11	64
Erwin, N.C., U.S.	B4	140
Erwin, Tn., U.S.	C11	149
Erzincan, Tur.	B5	48
Erzurum, Tur.	B6	48
Esbjerg, Den.	N11	6
Escalante, Ut., U.S.	F4	151
Escalante, stm., Ut., U.S.	F4	151
Escambia, co., Al., U.S.	D2	108
Escambia, co., Fl., U.S.	u14	116
Escambia, stm., Fl., U.S.	u14	116
Escanaba, Mi., U.S.	C3	129
Escanaba, stm., Mi., U.S.	B3	129
Escárcega, Mex.	H14	90
Escarpada Point, c., Phil.	B18	39b
Escatawpa, Ms., U.S.	E5	131
Escaut (Schelde), stm., Eur.	I8	12
Esch-sur-Alzette, Lux.	I8	12
Eschwege, Ger.	D10	10
Eschweiler, Ger.	E6	10
Escobal, Pan.	H15	92
Escondido, Ca., U.S.	F5	112
Escondido, stm., Nic.	E11	92
Escuinapa de Hidalgo, Mex.	F7	90
Escuintla, Guat.	C4	92
Escuintla, dept., Guat.	C3	92
Escuminac, Point, c., N.B., Can.	B5	101
Eşfahān (Isfahan), Iran	E11	48
Esfarāyen, Iran	C14	48
Eshowe, S. Afr.	G10	66
Esigodini, Zimb.	C9	66
Esk, Austl.	F10	70
Eskilstuna, Swe.	L15	6
Eskimo Point, N.W. Ter., Can.	D14	96
Eskişehir, Tur.	H14	4
Eskridge, Ks., U.S.	D7	123
Eslāmābād, Iran	D9	48
Eslāmshahr, Iran	D11	48
Esmeralda, Cuba	D5	94
Esmeralda, co., Nv., U.S.	F4	135
Esmeraldas, Ec.	G3	84
Esmeraldas, prov., Ec.	G3	84
Esmeraldas, stm., Ec.	G3	84
Esmond, R.I., U.S.	B3	146
Esneux, Bel.	G8	12
Espalion, Fr.	H9	14
Espanola, Ont., Can.	A3	103
Española, N.M., U.S.	B3	138
Esparza, C.R.	H10	92
Espera Feliz, Braz.	F8	79
Esperance, Austl.	F4	68
Esperança, Braz.	E11	76
Esperanza, Arg.	F8	80
Esperanza, Mex.	D5	90
Espinal, Col.	E5	84
Espinhaço, Serra do, mts., Braz.	C7	79
Espinho, Port.	D3	16
Espírito Santo, state, Braz.	E8	79
Espíritu Santo, Isla, i., Mex.	F5	90
Espita, Mex.	G15	90
Espoo (Esbo), Fin.	K19	6
Espumoso, Braz.	E12	80
Esquel, Arg.	E2	78
Esquimalt, B.C., Can.	g12	99
Esquina, Arg.	F9	80
Essaouira (Mogador), Mor.	E6	62
Essen, Bel.	F5	12
Essen, Ger.	D7	10
Essequibo, stm., Guy.	E13	84
Essequibo Islands-West Demerara, prov., Guy.	D13	84
Essex, Ont., Can.	E2	103
Essex, Ct., U.S.	D6	114
Essex, Md., U.S.	B5	127
Essex, Vt., U.S.	C2	152
Essex, co., Eng., U.K.	J14	8
Essex, co., Ma., U.S.	A5	128
Essex, co., N.J., U.S.	B4	137
Essex, co., N.Y., U.S.	B7	139
Essex, co., Vt., U.S.	B5	152
Essex, co., Va., U.S.	C6	153
Essex Junction, Vt., U.S.	C2	152
Essexville, Mi., U.S.	E7	129
Esslingen, Ger.	G9	10
Es-Suki, Sud.	K7	60
Estados, Isla de los, i., Arg.	J8	74
Estahbān, Iran	G13	48
Estância, Braz.	F11	76
Estanislao del Campo, Arg.	C8	80
Estcourt, S. Afr.	G9	66
Este, Italy	D6	18

Name	Map Ref.	Page
Esteio, Braz.	E13	80
Estelí, Nic.	D8	92
Estelí, dept., Nic.	D8	92
Estella, Spain	C9	16
Estelline, S.D., U.S.	C9	148
Estepa, Spain	H7	16
Estepona, Spain	I6	16
Esterhazy, Sask., Can.	G4	105
Estes Park, Co., U.S.	A5	113
Estevan, Sask., Can.	H4	105
Estherville, Ia., U.S.	A3	122
Estill, S.C., U.S.	F5	147
Estill, co., Ky., U.S.	C6	124
Estill Springs, Tn., U.S.	C8	122
Estonia (Eesti), ctry., Eur.	E13	4
Estrela, Braz.	E13	80
Estrela, mtn., Port.	E4	16
Estremadura, hist. reg., Port.	F3	16
Esztergom, Hung.	H18	10
Etadunna, Austl.	G3	70
Etah, India	G8	44
Étain, Fr.	C12	14
Étampes, Fr.	D9	14
Étaples, Fr.	B8	14
Etāwah, India	G8	44
Etchojoa, Mex.	D5	90
Ethan, S.D., U.S.	D8	148
Ethel, W.V., U.S.	n12	155
Ethelbert, Man., Can.	D1	100
Ethete, Wy., U.S.	C4	157
Ethiopia (Ityopiya), ctry., Afr.	G8	56
Etna, N.H., U.S.	C2	136
Etna, Pa., U.S.	k14	145
Etna, Wy., U.S.	C1	157
Etna, Monte, vol., Italy	L10	18
Etna Green, In., U.S.	B5	121
Etobicoke, Ont., Can.	D5	103
Etolin Island, i., Ak., U.S.	m23	109
Etosha Pan, pl., Nmb.	B3	66
Etowah, Tn., U.S.	D9	149
Etowah, co., Al., U.S.	A3	108
Etowah, stm., Ga., U.S.	B2	117
Ettelbruck, Lux.	I9	12
Ettlingen, Ger.	G8	10
Ettrick, Va., U.S.	C5	153
Eu, Fr.	B8	14
Euclid, Oh., U.S.	A4	142
Eucumbene, Lake, res., Austl.	K8	70
Eudora, Ar., U.S.	D4	111
Eudora, Ks., U.S.	D8	123
Eufaula, Al., U.S.	D4	108
Eufaula, Ok., U.S.	B6	143
Eufaula Lake, res., Ok., U.S.	C3	144
Eugene, Or., U.S.	C3	144
Eugenio Bustos, Arg.	G4	80
Eunice, La., U.S.	D3	125
Eunice, N.M., U.S.	E6	138
Eupen, Bel.	G9	12
Euphrates (Firat) (Nahr al-Furāt), stm., Asia	F9	48
Eupora, Ms., U.S.	B4	131
Eureka, Ca., U.S.	B1	112
Eureka, Il., U.S.	C4	120
Eureka, Ks., U.S.	E7	123
Eureka, Mo., U.S.	f12	132
Eureka, Mt., U.S.	B1	133
Eureka, Nv., U.S.	D6	135
Eureka, S.C., U.S.	B5	147
Eureka, S.D., U.S.	B6	148
Eureka, Ut., U.S.	D3	151
Eureka, co., Nv., U.S.	D5	135
Eureka Springs, Ar., U.S.	A2	111
Euroa, Austl.	K6	70
Europa Point, c., Gib.	I6	16
Europe	C9	52
Europoort, Neth.	E5	12
Euskal Herriko, prov., Spain	B9	16
Euskirchen, Ger.	E6	10
Eustis, Fl., U.S.	D5	116
Eustis, Ne., U.S.	D5	134
Eutaw, Al., U.S.	C2	108
Eutsuk Lake, l., B.C., Can.	C4	99
Eva, Al., U.S.	A3	108
Evangeline, co., La., U.S.	D3	125
Evans, Co., U.S.	A6	113
Evans, Ga., U.S.	C4	117
Evans, W.V., U.S.	C3	155
Evans, co., Ga., U.S.	D5	117
Evans, Mount, mtn., Co., U.S.	B5	113
Evansburg, Alta., Can.	C3	98
Evans City, Pa., U.S.	E1	145
Evansdale, Ia., U.S.	B5	122
Evanston, Il., U.S.	A6	120
Evanston, Wy., U.S.	E2	157
Evansville, In., U.S.	I2	121
Evansville, Wi., U.S.	F4	156
Evansville, Wy., U.S.	D6	157
Evarts, Ky., U.S.	D6	124
Evart, Mi., U.S.	E5	129
Eveleth, Mn., U.S.	C6	130
Evening Shade, Ar., U.S.	A4	111
Everest, Mount (Qomolangma Feng), mtn., Asia	G12	44
Everett, Ont., Can.	C5	103
Everett, Ma., U.S.	g11	128
Everett, Pa., U.S.	F5	145
Everett, Wa., U.S.	B3	154
Everett, Mount, mtn., Ma., U.S.	B1	128
Everglades National Park, Fl., U.S.	G5	116
Evergreen, Al., U.S.	D3	108
Evergreen, Co., U.S.	B5	113
Evergreen Park, Il., U.S.	k9	120
Everly, Ia., U.S.	A2	122
Everson, Wa., U.S.	A3	154
Évian-les-Bains, Fr.	F13	14
Évora, Port.	G4	16
Évreux, Fr.	C8	14
Évry, Fr.	D9	14
E.V. Spence Reservoir, res., Tx., U.S.	D2	150
Évvoia, i., Grc.	K7	20
Ewa, Hi., U.S.	B3	118
Ewa Beach, Hi., U.S.	B3	118
Ewing, Ne., U.S.	B7	134
Ewing Township, N.J., U.S.	C3	137
Exaltación, Bol.	E9	82
Excel, Al., U.S.	D2	108
Excelsior Springs, Mo., U.S.	B3	132
Exeter, Ont., Can.	D3	103
Exeter, Eng., U.K.	K10	8
Exeter, Ca., U.S.	D4	112
Exeter, Mo., U.S.	E4	132
Exeter, Ne., U.S.	D8	134
Exeter, N.H., U.S.	E5	136
Exeter, Pa., U.S.	D10	145
Exira, Ia., U.S.	C3	122
Exmore, Va., U.S.	C7	153
Exmouth, Eng., U.K.	K10	8
Exmouth Gulf, b., Austl.	D2	68
Experiment, Ga., U.S.	C2	117
Exploits, stm., Newf., Can.	D3	102
Exshaw, Alta., Can.	D3	98
Extremadura, prov., Spain	F5	16
Exuma Cays, is., Bah.	B6	94
Exuma Sound, strt., Bah.	B6	94
Eyebrow, Sask., Can.	G2	105
Eyota, Mn., U.S.	G6	130
Eyre, Austl.	F5	68
Eyre North, Lake, l., Austl.	G2	70
Eyre Peninsula, pen., Austl.	I1	70
Eyre South, Lake, l., Austl.	G2	70

F

Name	Map Ref.	Page
Fabens, Tx., U.S.	o11	150
Fábrega, Cerro, mtn., Pan.	H12	92
Fabriano, Italy	F7	18
Facatativá, Col.	E5	84
Fada, Chad	M7	60
Fada Ngourma, Burkina	E10	64
Fadit, Sud.	M7	60
Faenza, Italy	E6	18
Faeroe Islands (Føroyar), dep., Eur.	D8	6b
Fafa, Mali	D10	64
Făgăraş, Rom.	D8	20
Fagernes, Nor.	K11	6
Fairacres, N.M., U.S.	E3	138
Fairbank, Ia., U.S.	B5	122
Fairbanks, Ak., U.S.	C10	109
Fairborn, Oh., U.S.	C1	142
Fairburn, Ga., U.S.	C2	117
Fairbury, Il., U.S.	C5	120
Fairbury, Ne., U.S.	D8	134
Fairchance, Pa., U.S.	G2	145
Fairdale, Ky., U.S.	B4	124
Fairfax, Ca., U.S.	C2	112
Fairfax, De., U.S.	A3	115
Fairfax, Mn., U.S.	F4	130
Fairfax, Mo., U.S.	A2	132
Fairfax, Ok., U.S.	A5	143
Fairfax, S.C., U.S.	F5	147
Fairfax, Vt., U.S.	B2	152
Fairfax, Va., U.S.	B5	153
Fairfax, co., Va., U.S.	B5	153
Fairfield, Al., U.S.	B3	108
Fairfield, Ca., U.S.	C2	112
Fairfield, Ct., U.S.	E2	114
Fairfield, Id., U.S.	F4	119
Fairfield, Il., U.S.	E5	120
Fairfield, Ia., U.S.	C6	122
Fairfield, Me., U.S.	D3	126
Fairfield, Mt., U.S.	C5	133
Fairfield, Ne., U.S.	D7	134
Fairfield, Oh., U.S.	n12	142
Fairfield, Tx., U.S.	D4	150
Fairfield, co., Ct., U.S.	D2	114
Fairfield, co., Oh., U.S.	C3	142
Fairfield, co., S.C., U.S.	C5	147
Fairfield Bay, Ar., U.S.	B3	111
Fair Grove, Mo., U.S.	D4	132
Fair Grove, N.C., U.S.	B2	140
Fairhaven, Ma., U.S.	C6	128
Fair Haven, N.J., U.S.	C4	137
Fair Haven, Vt., U.S.	D2	152
Fairhope, Al., U.S.	E2	108
Fairland, In., U.S.	E6	121
Fairland, Ok., U.S.	A7	143
Fair Lawn, N.J., U.S.	h8	137
Fairlawn, Va., U.S.	C2	153
Fairlea, W.V., U.S.	D4	155
Fairlee, Vt., U.S.	D2	152
Fairmont, Mn., U.S.	G4	130
Fairmont, N.C., U.S.	C3	140
Fairmont, W.V., U.S.	B4	155
Fairmount, Ga., U.S.	B2	117
Fairmount, In., U.S.	D6	121
Fairmount, N.D., U.S.	C9	141
Fairmount Heights, Md., U.S.	f9	127
Fair Oaks, Ga., U.S.	h7	117
Fairoaks, Pa., U.S.	h13	145
Fair Plain, Mi., U.S.	F4	129
Fairplay, Co., U.S.	B5	113
Fairport, N.Y., U.S.	B3	139
Fairport Harbor, Oh., U.S.	A4	142
Fairvale, N.B., Can.	D4	101
Fairview, Alta., Can.	A1	98
Fairview, Mt., U.S.	C12	133
Fairview, N.J., U.S.	h8	137
Fairview, Ok., U.S.	A3	143
Fairview, Pa., U.S.	B1	145
Fairview, Tn., U.S.	B4	149
Fairview, Ut., U.S.	D4	151
Fairview, W.V., U.S.	B4	155
Fairview, Wy., U.S.	D2	157
Fairview Heights, Il., U.S.	E3	120
Fairview Park, In., U.S.	E3	121
Fairview Park, Oh., U.S.	g9	142
Fairway, Ks., U.S.	k16	123
Faisalabad, Pak.	E5	44
Faith, S.D., U.S.	B3	148
Faiyum see Al-Fayyūm, Egypt	C6	60
Faizābād, India	G10	44
Fajardo, P.R.	E12	94
Fakfak, Indon.	F9	38
Faku, China	A11	32
Falaise, Fr.	D6	14
Falam, Mya.	C2	40
Falcón, state, Ven.	B8	84
Falconer, N.Y., U.S.	C1	139
Falcon Heights, Mn., U.S.	n12	130
Falcon Heights, Or., U.S.	E5	144
Falești, Mol.	B11	20
Falfurrias, Tx., U.S.	F3	150
Falher, Alta., Can.	B2	98
Falkensee, Ger.	C13	10
Falkirk, Scot., U.K.	E10	8
Falkland, B.C., Can.	D8	99
Falkland Islands, dep., S.A.	G5	78
Falkville, Al., U.S.	A3	108
Fall Branch, Tn., U.S.	C11	149
Fallbrook, Ca., U.S.	F5	112
Fall City, Wa., U.S.	B4	154
Fall Creek, Wi., U.S.	D2	156
Fall Mountain Lake, Ct., U.S.	C4	114
Fallon, Mt., U.S.	D11	133
Fallon, Nv., U.S.	D3	135
Fallon, co., Mt., U.S.	D12	133
Fall River, Ma., U.S.	C5	128
Fall River, co., S.D., U.S.	D2	148
Falls, co., Tx., U.S.	D4	150
Falls Church, Va., U.S.	g12	153
Falls City, Ne., U.S.	D10	134
Falls City, Or., U.S.	C3	144
Fallston, Md., U.S.	A5	127
Falmouth, N.S., Can.	E5	101
Falmouth, Jam.	E6	94
Falmouth, Ky., U.S.	B5	124
Falmouth, Me., U.S.	E2	126
Falmouth, Ma., U.S.	C6	128
Falmouth, Va., U.S.	B5	153
Fălticeni, Rom.	B10	20
Famaillá, Arg.	D6	80
Famatina, Arg.	E5	80
Fana, Mali	E6	64
Fanambana, Madag.	n24	67b
Fanchon, Pointe, c., Haiti	E7	94
Fanchuan, China	B1	34
Fancy Farm, Ky., U.S.	f9	124
Fangak, Sud.	M6	60
Fangcheng, China	B1	34
Fangdao, China	H7	34
Fangxi, China	G3	34
Fanipol', Bela.	H10	22
Fannin, co., Ga., U.S.	B2	117
Fannin, co., Tx., U.S.	C4	150
Fanny Bay, B.C., Can.	E5	99
Fano, Italy	F8	18
Fan Si Pan, mtn., Viet.	C7	40
Fanxian, China	H3	32
Faradofay, Madag.	t22	67b
Farafangana, Madag.	s22	67b
Farāh, Afg.	E17	48
Farah, Gui.	F4	64
Farasān, Jazā'ir, is., Sau. Ar.	F2	47
Faratsiho, Madag.	q22	67b
Farewell, Cape, c., N.Z.	D4	72
Fargo, Ga., U.S.	F4	117
Fargo, N.D., U.S.	C9	141
Faribault, Mn., U.S.	F5	130
Faribault, co., Mn., U.S.	G4	130
Färiskūr, Egypt	B6	60
Farley, Ia., U.S.	B6	122
Farmer City, Il., U.S.	C5	120
Farmers Branch, Tx., U.S.	n10	150
Farmersburg, In., U.S.	F3	121
Farmerville, La., U.S.	B3	125
Farmingdale, Me., U.S.	D3	126
Farmingdale, N.J., U.S.	A1	111
Farmington, Ar., U.S.	C4	114
Farmington, Ct., U.S.	C3	120
Farmington, Il., U.S.	D2	126
Farmington, Ia., U.S.	p15	129
Farmington, Me., U.S.	F5	130
Farmington, Mn., U.S.	D7	132
Farmington, Mo., U.S.	D4	136
Farmington, N.H., U.S.	A1	138
Farmington, N.M., U.S.	C4	151
Farmington, Ut., U.S.	B4	114
Farmington, stm., Ct., U.S.	o15	129
Farmington Hills, Mi., U.S.	D7	121
Farmland, In., U.S.	B5	140
Farmville, N.C., U.S.	C4	153
Farmville, Va., U.S.	D5	104
Farnham, Que., Can.	H4	16
Faro, Port.	D10	58
Farquhar Group, is., Sey.	D1	145
Farrell, Pa., U.S.	G8	44
Farrukhābād, India	D3	157
Farson, Wy., U.S.	L10	6
Farsund, Nor.	G8	47
Fartak, Ra's c., Yemen	D15	86
Farvel, Kap, c., Grnld.	G12	48
Fasā, Iran	I12	18
Fasano, Italy	G6	44
Fatehpur, India	D1	64
Fatick, Sen.	F3	16
Fátima, Port.	I18	22
Fat'ož, Russia	B6	148
Faulk, co., S.D., U.S.	i7	115
Faulkland, De., U.S.	B3	111
Faulkner, co., Ar., U.S.	B6	148
Faulkton, S.D., U.S.	C13	14
Faulquemont, Fr.	B5	153
Fauquier, co., Va., U.S.	H14	6
Fauske, Nor.	B3	98
Faust, Alta., Can.	L8	18
Favara, Italy	G13	14
Faverges, Fr.	B2	6a
Faxaflói, b., Ice.	G3	79
Faxinal, Braz.	E12	80
Faxinal do Soturno, Braz.	E4	56
Faya, Chad	B2	108
Fayette, Al., U.S.	B6	122
Fayette, Ia., U.S.	D2	131
Fayette, Ms., U.S.	B5	132
Fayette, Mo., U.S.	B2	108
Fayette, co., Al., U.S.	C2	117
Fayette, co., Ga., U.S.	D5	120
Fayette, co., Il., U.S.	E7	121
Fayette, co., In., U.S.	B6	122
Fayette, co., Ia., U.S.	B5	124
Fayette, co., Ky., U.S.	C2	142
Fayette, co., Oh., U.S.	G2	145
Fayette, co., Pa., U.S.	B2	149
Fayette, co., Tn., U.S.	E4	150
Fayette, co., Tx., U.S.	C3	155
Fayette, co., W.V., U.S.	B3	108
Fayetteville, Al., U.S.	A1	111
Fayetteville, Ar., U.S.	C2	117
Fayetteville, Ga., U.S.	B5	139
Fayetteville, N.Y., U.S.	B4	140
Fayetteville, N.C., U.S.	G6	145
Fayetteville, Pa., U.S.	B5	149
Fayetteville, Tn., U.S.	C3	155
Fayetteville, W.V., U.S.	D3	79
Fazenda Nova, Braz.	C3	56
Fazzān (Fezzan), hist. reg., Libya	I4	62
Fdérik, Maur.		
Fear, Cape, c., N.C., U.S.	D5	140
Feather, stm., Ca., U.S.	C3	112
Feathertop, Mount, mtn., Austl.	K7	70
Fécamp, Fr.	C7	14
Federación, Arg.	F10	80
Federalsburg, Md., U.S.	C6	127
Feeding Hills, Ma., U.S.	B2	128
Fehérgyarmat, Hung.	H22	10
Fehmarn, i., Ger.	A11	10
Fehmarn Belt, strt., Eur.	A11	10
Feijó, Braz.	C6	82
Feira de Santana, Braz.	B9	79
Feixiang, China	G2	32
Feldbach, Aus.	I15	10
Feldkirch, Aus.	H9	10
Felix, Cape, c., N.W. Ter., Can.	C13	96
Felixlândia, Braz.	E6	79
Felixstowe, Eng., U.K.	J15	8
Fellbach, Ger.	G9	10
Fellsmere, Fl., U.S.	E6	116
Felton, Ca., U.S.	D2	112
Felton, De., U.S.	D3	115
Feltre, Italy	C6	18
Femund, l., Nor.	J12	6
Fenelon Falls, Ont., Can.	C6	103
Fengcheng, China	C12	32
Fengcheng, China	G4	34
Fengfeng, China	G2	32
Fenghuanging, China	D6	34
Fengxin, China	G3	34
Fengyang, China	E10	30
Fengyüan, Tai.	K9	34
Fengzhen, China	C9	30
Fennimore, Wi., U.S.	F3	156
Fenoarivo Atsinanana, Madag.	p23	67b
Fenshui'ao, China	J3	34
Fenton, Mi., U.S.	F7	129
Fentress, co., Tn., U.S.	C9	149
Feodosiya, Ukr.	H5	26
Fer, Point au, c., La., U.S.	E4	125
Ferdinand, In., U.S.	H4	121
Fergana, Uzb.	I12	26
Fergus, co., Mt., U.S.	C7	133
Fergus Falls, Mn., U.S.	D2	130
Ferguson, Ky., U.S.	C5	124
Ferguson, Mo., U.S.	C7	132
Fériana, Tun.	C15	62
Ferkéssédougou, C. Iv.	G7	64
Ferlo, Vallée du, val., Sen.	D2	64
Ferme-Neuve, Que., Can.	C2	104
Fermeuse, Newf., Can.	E5	102
Fermo, Italy	F8	18
Fermont, Que., Can.	h13	104
Fernández, Arg.	D7	80
Fernandina Beach, Fl., U.S.	B5	116
Fernando de la Mora, Para.	C10	80
Fernando de Noronha, Ilha, i., Braz.	D12	76
Fernandópolis, Braz.	F3	79
Fernando Póo see Bioko, i., Eq. Gui.	J14	64
Fern Creek, Ky., U.S.	g11	124
Ferndale, Md., U.S.	B4	127
Ferndale, Mi., U.S.	P15	129
Ferndale, Pa., U.S.	F4	145
Ferndale, Wa., U.S.	A3	154
Fernie, B.C., Can.	E10	99
Fernley, Nv., U.S.	D2	135
Fern Ridge Lake, res., Or., U.S.	C3	144
Fernwood, Id., U.S.	B2	119
Fernwood, Ms., U.S.	D3	131
Ferrara, Italy	E6	18
Ferreñafe, Peru	B2	82
Ferriday, La., U.S.	C4	125
Ferrisburg, Vt., U.S.	C2	152
Ferron, Ut., U.S.	D4	151
Ferrum, Va., U.S.	D2	153
Ferry, co., Wa., U.S.	A7	154
Ferry Farms, Va., U.S.	B5	153
Ferryland, Newf., Can.	E5	102
Fertile, Mn., U.S.	C2	130
Fès, Mor.	C8	62
Fessenden, N.D., U.S.	B6	141
Festus, Mo., U.S.	C7	132
Feteşti, Rom.	E11	20
Fethiye, Tur.	M13	20
Feuilles, Rivière aux, stm., Que., Can.	g12	104
Feyzābād, Afg.	B4	44
Fez see Fès, Mor.	C8	62
Fiambalá, Arg.	D5	80
Fianarantsoa, Madag.	r22	67b
Fiche, Eth.	M10	60
Fichtelberg, mtn., Ger.	E12	10
Ficksburg, S. Afr.	G5	66
Fidalgo Island, i., Wa., U.S.	A3	154
Fidenza, Italy	E5	18
Fieldale, Va., U.S.	D3	153
Fier, Alb.	I3	20
Figueira da Foz, Port.	E3	16
Figueres, Spain	C14	16
Figuig, Mor.	D10	62
Fiji, ctry., Oc.	H24	2
Filchner Ice Shelf, Ant.	C1	73
Filer, Id., U.S.	G4	119
Filingué, Niger	D11	64
Fillmore, Sask., Can.	H4	105
Fillmore, Ca., U.S.	E4	112
Fillmore, Ut., U.S.	E3	151
Fillmore, co., Mn., U.S.	G6	130
Fillmore, co., Ne., U.S.	D8	134
Findlay, Oh., U.S.	A2	142
Fingoè, Moz.	E7	68
Finke, stm., Austl.	D13	4
Finland (Suomi), ctry., Eur.	C13	4
Finland, Gulf of, b., Eur.	L20	6
Finley, Austl.	J6	70
Finley, N.D., U.S.	B8	141
Finley, Tn., U.S.	A2	149
Finney, co., Ks., U.S.	D3	123
Finsteraarhorn, mtn., Switz.	E9	13
Finsterwalde, Ger.	D13	10
Fiq, Golan	C5	50
Fircrest, Wa., U.S.	f10	154
Fluvanna, co., Va., U.S.	B4	153
Fly, stm.	m15	68a
Foam Lake, Sask., Can.	F4	105
Foard, co., Tx., U.S.	B3	150
Foča, Bos.	F2	20
Firenze (Florence), Italy	F6	18
Firestone, Co., U.S.	A6	113
Firmat, Arg.	G8	80
Firminópolis, Braz.	D3	79
Firminy, Fr.	G11	14
Firozābād, India	G8	44
Firozpur, India	E6	44
First Connecticut Lake, l., N.H., U.S.	f7	136
Firth, Id., U.S.	F6	119
Firth, Ne., U.S.	D9	134
Firūzābād, Iran	G12	48
Fish (Vis), stm., Nmb.	F3	66
Fisher, Il., U.S.	C5	120
Fisher, Mn., U.S.	C2	130
Fisher, co., Tx., U.S.	C2	150
Fisher Branch, Man., Can.	D3	100
Fishers, In., U.S.	E5	121
Fishers Island, i., N.Y., U.S.	m16	139
Fishersville, Va., U.S.	B4	153
Fishing Bay, b., Md., U.S.	D5	127
Fiskdale, Ma., U.S.	B3	128
Fismes, Fr.	C10	14
Fitchburg, Ma., U.S.	A4	128
Fitzgerald, Ga., U.S.	E3	117
Fitzroy, stm., Austl.	C4	68
Fitzroy, Monte (Cerro Chaltel), mtn., S.A.	F2	78
Fitzwilliam, N.H., U.S.	E2	136
Fitzwilliam Depot, N.H., U.S.	E2	136
Five Points, N.M., U.S.	B3	138
Fkih-Ben-Salah, Mor.	D7	62
Flagler, Co., U.S.	B7	113
Flagler, co., Fl., U.S.	C5	116
Flagler Beach, Fl., U.S.	C5	116
Flagstaff, Az., U.S.	B4	110
Flaming Gorge Reservoir, res., U.S.	E3	157
Flanagan, Il., U.S.	C5	120
Flanders (Flandre), hist. reg., Eur.	G2	12
Flandreau, S.D., U.S.	C9	148
Flasher, N.D., U.S.	C4	141
Flathead, co., Mt., U.S.	B2	133
Flathead Lake, l., Mt., U.S.	C2	133
Flat Lick, Ky., U.S.	D6	124
Flatonia, Tx., U.S.	E4	150
Flat River, Mo., U.S.	D7	132
Flat Rock, Mi., U.S.	F7	129
Flat Rock, N.C., U.S.	f10	140
Flattery, Cape, c., Wa., U.S.	A1	154
Flatwoods, Ky., U.S.	B7	124
Fleetwood, Pa., U.S.	F10	145
Fleming, Co., U.S.	A8	113
Fleming, co., Ky., U.S.	B6	124
Fleming-Neon, Ky., U.S.	C7	124
Flemingsburg, Ky., U.S.	B6	124
Flensburg, Ger.	A9	10
Fletcher, N.C., U.S.	f10	140
Fletcher, Ok., U.S.	C3	143
Fleurance, Fr.	I7	14
Fleur-de-Lys, Newf., Can.	C3	102
Fleurier, Switz.	E6	13
Flevoland, prov., Neth.	D7	12
Flin Flon, Man., Can.	B1	100
Flinders, Austl.	A4	70
Flinders Island, i., Austl.	M8	70
Flint, Mi., U.S.	E7	129
Flint, stm., Ga., U.S.	E2	117
Flint City, Al., U.S.	A3	108
Flippin, Ar., U.S.	A3	111
Flomaton, Al., U.S.	D2	108
Flora, Il., U.S.	E5	120
Flora, In., U.S.	C4	121
Flora, Ms., U.S.	C3	131
Florala, Al., U.S.	D3	108
Floral City, Fl., U.S.	D4	116
Flora Vista, N.M., U.S.	A1	138
Florence see Firenze, Italy	F6	18
Florence, Al., U.S.	A2	108
Florence, Az., U.S.	D4	110
Florence, Co., U.S.	C5	113
Florence, Ks., U.S.	D7	123
Florence, Ky., U.S.	A5	124
Florence, Ms., U.S.	C3	131
Florence, Mt., U.S.	D2	133
Florence, Or., U.S.	D2	144
Florence, S.C., U.S.	C8	147
Florence, co., S.C., U.S.	C8	147
Florence, co., Wi., U.S.	C5	156
Florencia, Col.	G5	84
Floresta, Braz.	E11	76
Flores, Braz.	E11	76
Flores, i., Indon.	G7	38
Flores, i., Port.	k18	62a
Flores, Laut (Flores Sea), Indon.	G7	38
Flores da Cunha, Braz.	E13	80
Floresta Azul, Braz.	C9	79
Floresti, Mol.	B12	20
Floresville, Tx., U.S.	E3	150
Floriano, Braz.	E10	76
Florianópolis, Braz.	D14	80
Florida, Col.	F4	84
Florida, Cuba	D5	94
Florida, Ur.	H10	80
Florida, state, U.S.	G6	116
Florida, Cape, c., Fl., U.S.	G6	116
Florida, Straits of, strt., N.A.	B4	94
Florida Bay, b., Fl., U.S.	H6	116
Floridablanca, Col.	D6	84
Florida Keys, is., Fl., U.S.	H6	116
Florido, stm., Mex.	D7	90
Flórina, Grc.	I5	20
Florissant, Co., U.S.	C5	113
Florissant, Mo., U.S.	f13	132
Florø, Nor.	K6	6
Flossmoor, Il., U.S.	k9	120
Flourtown, Pa., U.S.	o21	145
Flovilla, Ga., U.S.	C3	117
Flowery Branch, Ga., U.S.	B3	117
Flowood, Ms., U.S.	C3	131
Floyd, Ia., U.S.	A5	122
Floyd, co., Ga., U.S.	B1	117
Floyd, co., In., U.S.	H6	121
Floyd, co., Ky., U.S.	C7	124
Floyd, co., Tx., U.S.	B2	150
Floyd, co., Va., U.S.	D2	153
Floydada, Tx., U.S.	B2	150
Floyds Knobs, In., U.S.	H6	121
Flushing, Mi., U.S.	E7	129
Focşani, Rom.	D11	20
Foggia, Italy	H10	18
Fogo, i., C.V.	m16	64a
Fogo, Newf., Can.	D4	102
Fogo Island, i., Newf., Can.	D4	102
Fohnsdorf, Aus.	H14	10
Foix, Fr.	J8	14
Fokino, Russia	H17	22
Foley, Al., U.S.	E2	108
Foley, Mn., U.S.	E5	130
Foligno, Italy	G7	18
Folkestone, Eng., U.K.	J15	8
Folkston, Ga., U.S.	F4	117
Follansbee, W.V., U.S.	A4	155
Follonica, Italy	G5	18
Folly Beach, S.C., U.S.	F8	147
Folsom, Ca., U.S.	C3	112
Fomboni, Com.	l15	67a
Fonda, Ia., U.S.	B3	122
Fond du Lac, co., Wi., U.S.	E5	156
Fond du Lac Indian Reservation, Mn., U.S.	D6	130
Fondi, Italy	H8	18
Fonseca, Golfo de, b., N.A.	D7	92
Fontainebleau, Fr.	D9	14
Fontana, Arg.	D9	80
Fontana, Ca., U.S.	m14	112
Fontana, Wi., U.S.	F5	156
Fontana Lake, res., N.C., U.S.	f9	140
Fontanelle, Ia., U.S.	C3	122
Fonte Boa, Braz.	I9	84
Fontenelle Reservoir, res., Wy., U.S.	D2	157
Fontur, c., Ice.	A6	6a
Foochow see Fuzhou, China	I8	34
Foraker, Mount, mtn., Ak., U.S.	f16	109
Forbach, Fr.	C13	14
Forbes, Austl.	I8	70
Forchheim, Ger.	F11	10
Ford, co., Il., U.S.	C5	120
Ford, co., Ks., U.S.	E4	123
Ford City, Ca., U.S.	E4	112
Fordoche, La., U.S.	D4	125
Fords, N.J., U.S.	B4	137
Fords Prairie, Wa., U.S.	C2	154
Fordville, N.D., U.S.	A8	141
Fordyce, Ar., U.S.	D3	111
Forel, Mont, mtn., Grnld.	C16	86
Foreman, Ar., U.S.	D1	111
Foremost, Alta., Can.	E5	98
Forest, Ont., Can.	D2	103
Forest, Ms., U.S.	C4	131
Forest, co., Pa., U.S.	C3	145
Forest, co., Wi., U.S.	C5	156
Forest Acres, S.C., U.S.	C6	147
Forestburg, Alta., Can.	C4	98
Forest City, Ia., U.S.	A4	122
Forest City, N.C., U.S.	B1	140
Forest City, Pa., U.S.	C11	145
Forestdale, Al., U.S.	B3	108
Forestdale, R.I., U.S.	B3	146
Forest Dale, Vt., U.S.	D2	152
Forest Grove, Or., U.S.	B3	144
Forest Hill, Tx., U.S.	n9	150
Forest Hills, Pa., U.S.	k14	145
Forest Hills, Tn., U.S.	A5	149
Forest Lake, Mn., U.S.	E6	130
Forest Park, Ga., U.S.	h8	117
Forest Park, Il., U.S.	k9	120
Forfar, Scot., U.K.	E11	8
Forked Deer, stm., Tn., U.S.	B2	149
Forkland, Al., U.S.	C2	108
Forks, Wa., U.S.	B1	154
Forlì, Italy	E7	18
Formentera, i., Spain	G13	16
Formiga, Braz.	F6	79
Formosa, Arg.	D9	80
Formosa, Braz.	C5	79
Formosa, prov., Arg.	C9	80
Formosa see Taiwan, ctry., Asia	L9	34
Forney, Tx., U.S.	C4	150
Forrest, Il., U.S.	C5	120
Forrest, co., Ms., U.S.	D4	131
Forrest City, Ar., U.S.	B5	111
Forreston, Il., U.S.	A4	120
Forsayth, Austl.	B5	70
Forst, Ger.	D14	10
Forster, Austl.	I10	70
Forsyth, Ga., U.S.	C3	117
Forsyth, Il., U.S.	D5	120
Forsyth, Mo., U.S.	E4	132
Forsyth, Mt., U.S.	D10	133
Forsyth, co., Ga., U.S.	B2	117
Forsyth, co., N.C., U.S.	A2	140
Fort Adams, Ms., U.S.	D2	131
Fortaleza, Braz.	D11	76
Fort Ashby, W.V., U.S.	B6	155
Fort Atkinson, Wi., U.S.	F5	156
Fort Beaufort, S. Afr.	I8	66
Fort Belknap Agency, Mt., U.S.	B8	133
Fort Belvoir, mil., Va., U.S.	g12	153
Fort Bend, co., Tx., U.S.	E5	150
Fort Benning, mil., Ga., U.S.	D1	117
Fort Benton, Mt., U.S.	C6	133
Fort Bragg, Ca., U.S.	C2	112
Fort Bragg, mil., N.C., U.S.	H2	121
Fort Branch, In., U.S.	E2	157
Fort Bridger, Wy., U.S.	C9	134
Fort Calhoun, Ne., U.S.	r22	67b
Fort-Carnot, Madag.	f8	98
Fort Chipewyan, Alta., Can.	B3	143
Fort Cobb Reservoir, res., Ok., U.S.	A5	113
Fort Collins, Co., U.S.	o13	150
Fort Coulonge, Que., Can.		
Fort Davis, Tx., U.S.	o13	150
Fort Davis National Historic Site, hist., Az., U.S.	o13	150
Fort Defiance, Az., U.S.	B6	110
Fort-de-France, Mart.	G14	94
Fort Deposit, Al., U.S.	D3	108
Fort Dix, mil., N.J., U.S.	C3	137
Fort Dodge, Ia., U.S.	B3	122
Fort Dodge, Ks., U.S.	E4	123
Forteau, Newf., Can.	C3	102
Fort Edward, N.Y., U.S.	B7	139

Name	Map Ref.	Page
Fort Erie, Ont., Can.	E6	103
Fortescue, stm., Austl.	D3	68
Fort Fairfield, Me., U.S.	B5	126
Fort Frances, Ont., Can.	o16	103
Fort Franklin, N.W. Ter., Can.	C8	96
Fort Fraser, B.C., Can.	B5	99
Fort Gaines, Ga., U.S.	E1	117
Fort Garland, Co., U.S.	D5	113
Fort Gay, W.V., U.S.	C2	155
Fort Gibson, Ok., U.S.	B6	143
Fort Gibson Lake, res., Ok., U.S.	A6	143
Fort Good Hope, N.W. Ter., Can.	C7	96
Fort Gordon, mil., Ga., U.S.	C4	117
Fort Greely, mil., Ak., U.S.	C10	109
Forth, Firth of, b., Scot., U.K.	E11	8
Fort Hall, Id., U.S.	F6	119
Fort Huachuca, mil., Az., U.S.	F5	110
Fort Jefferson National Monument, Fl., U.S.	H4	116
Fort Kent, Me., U.S.	A4	126
Fort Knox, mil., Ky., U.S.	B4	124
Fort-Lamy see N'Djamena, Chad	F4	56
Fort Laramie, Wy., U.S.	D8	157
Fort Lauderdale, Fl., U.S.	F6	116
Fort Leavenworth, mil., Ks., U.S.	C9	123
Fort Lee, N.J., U.S.	B5	137
Fort Liard, N.W. Ter., Can.	D8	96
Fort Loudoun Lake, res., Tn., U.S.	D9	149
Fort Lupton, Co., U.S.	A6	113
Fort MacKay, Alta., Can.	f8	98
Fort Macleod, Alta., Can.	E4	98
Fort Madison, Ia., U.S.	D6	122
Fort McClellan, mil., Al., U.S.	B4	108
Fort McHenry National Monument And Historic Shrine, Md., U.S.	g11	127
Fort McMurray, Alta., Can.	A5	98
Fort McPherson, N.W. Ter., Can.	C6	96
Fort Meade, Fl., U.S.	E5	116
Fort Meade, mil., Md., U.S.	B4	127
Fort Mill, S.C., U.S.	A6	147
Fort Mitchell, Al., U.S.	C4	108
Fort Mitchell, Ky., U.S.	h13	124
Fort Morgan, Co., U.S.	A7	113
Fort Myers, Fl., U.S.	F5	116
Fort Myers Beach, Fl., U.S.	F5	116
Fort Nelson, B.C., Can.	m18	99
Fort Norman, N.W. Ter., Can.	D7	96
Fort Oglethorpe, Ga., U.S.	B1	117
Fort Payne, Al., U.S.	A4	108
Fort Peck, Mt., U.S.	B10	133
Fort Peck Lake, res., Mt., U.S.	C9	133
Fort Pierce, Fl., U.S.	E6	116
Fort Pierce Inlet, b., Fl., U.S.	E6	116
Fort Pierre, S.D., U.S.	C5	148
Fort Portal, Ug.	A6	58
Fort Providence, N.W. Ter., Can.	D9	96
Fort Qu'Appelle, Sask., Can.	G4	105
Fort Resolution, N.W. Ter., Can.	D10	96
Fort Richardson, mil., Ak., U.S.	C10	109
Fort Saint James, B.C., Can.	B5	99
Fort Saint John, B.C., Can.	A7	99
Fort Saskatchewan, Alta., Can.	C4	98
Fort Scott, Ks., U.S.	E9	123
Fort-Ševčenko, Kaz.	I8	26
Fort Shawnee, Oh., U.S.	B1	142
Fort Sill, mil., Ok., U.S.	C3	143
Fort Simpson, N.W. Ter., Can.	D8	96
Fort Smith, N.W. Ter., Can.	D10	96
Fort Smith, Ar., U.S.	B1	111
Fort Stanton, N.M., U.S.	D4	138
Fort Stewart, mil., Ga., U.S.	D5	117
Fort Stockton, Tx., U.S.	D1	150
Fort Sumner, N.M., U.S.	C5	138
Fort Sumter National Monument, S.C., U.S.	k12	147
Fort Thomas, Ky., U.S.	h14	124
Fort Thompson, S.D., U.S.	C6	148
Fort Totten, N.D., U.S.	B7	141
Fortuna, Ca., U.S.	B1	112
Fortune, Newf., Can.	E4	102
Fortune Bay, b., Newf., Can.	E4	102
Fort Valley, Ga., U.S.	D3	117
Fort Vermilion, Alta., Can.	f7	98
Fortville, In., U.S.	E6	121
Fort Wainwright, mil., Ak., U.S.	C10	109
Fort Walton Beach, Fl., U.S.	u15	116
Fort Washakie, Wy., U.S.	C4	157
Fort Washington, Pa., U.S.	o21	145
Fort Washington Forest, Md., U.S.	C4	127
Fort Wayne, In., U.S.	B7	121
Fort William, Scot., U.K.	E8	8
Fort Wingate, N.M., U.S.	B1	138
Fort Worth, Tx., U.S.	C4	150
Fort Wright, Ky., U.S.	h13	124
Forty Fort, Pa., U.S.	D10	145
Fort Yukon, Ak., U.S.	B10	109
Foshan, China	L2	34
Fossano, Italy	E2	18
Foss Reservoir, res., Ok., U.S.	B2	143
Fosston, Mn., U.S.	C3	130
Foster, co., N.D., U.S.	B6	141
Foster City, Ca., U.S.	h8	112
Foster Village, Hi., U.S.	g10	118
Fostoria, Oh., U.S.	A2	142
Fougamou, Gabon	B2	58
Fougères, Fr.	D5	14
Fouke, Ar., U.S.	D2	111
Foulwind, Cape, c., N.Z.	D3	72
Fouman, Cam.	G9	54
Foumbouni, Com.	k15	67a
Foundiougne, Sen.	D1	64
Fountain, Co., U.S.	C6	113
Fountain, co., In., U.S.	D3	121
Fountain City, In., U.S.	E8	121
Fountain City, Wi., U.S.	D2	156
Fountain Green, Ut., U.S.	D4	151
Fountain Hill, Pa., U.S.	E11	145
Fountain Inn, S.C., U.S.	B3	147
Fourche LaFave, stm., Ar., U.S.	C2	111
Fourche Mountain, mtn., Ar., U.S.	C2	111
Fourmies, Fr.	B11	14
Fourmile, Ky., U.S.	D6	124
Four Mountains, Islands of, is., Ak., U.S.	E6	109
Four Oaks, N.C., U.S.	B4	140
Foux, Cap à, c., Haiti	E8	94
Foveaux Strait, strt., N.Z.	G1	72
Fowler, Co., U.S.	C6	113
Fowler, In., U.S.	C3	121
Fowler, Ks., U.S.	E3	123
Fowlerville, Mi., U.S.	F6	129
Fox, stm., U.S.	B5	120
Fox, stm., U.S.	A6	132
Fox, stm., Wi., U.S.	D5	156
Foxboro, Ont., Can.	C7	103
Foxboro, Ma., U.S.	B5	128
Fox Creek, Alta., Can.	B2	98
Foxe Basin, b., N.W. Ter., Can.	C17	96
Foxe Channel, strt., N.W. Ter., Can.	D16	96
Foxe Islands, is., Ak., U.S.	E6	109
Fox Islands, is., Ak., U.S.	A5	120
Fox Lake, Il., U.S.	E5	157
Fox Lake, Wi., U.S.	E5	156
Foxpark, Wy., U.S.	E6	157
Fox Point, Wi., U.S.	E6	156
Fox River Grove, Il., U.S.	h8	120
Fox Valley, Sask., Can.	G1	105
Foxville, Vt., U.S.	C4	152
Foxwarren, Man., Can.	D1	100
Foxworth, Ms., U.S.	D4	131
Foyle, Lough, b., Eur.	F6	8
Foz do Cunene, Ang.	E2	58
Foz do Iguaçu, Braz.	C11	80
Frackville, Pa., U.S.	E9	145
Fraile Muerto, Ur.	G11	80
Framingham, Ma., U.S.	B5	128
Franca, Braz.	F5	79
Franca-Iosifa, Zeml'a (Franz Josef Land), is., Russia	A6	24
Francavilla Fontana, Italy	I12	18
France, ctry., Eur.	F8	4
Francés Viejo, Cabo, c., Dom. Rep.	E10	94
Francesville, In., U.S.	C4	121
Franceville, Gabon	B2	58
Francis, Sask., Can.	G4	105
Francis, Lake, l., N.H., U.S.	f7	136
Francis Case, Lake, res., S.D., U.S.	D6	148
Francisco Beltrão, Braz.	D12	80
Francisco I. Madero, Mex.	E8	90
Francisco I. Madero, Mex.	E7	90
Francisco Morazán, dept., Hond.	C7	92
Francisco Murguía, Mex.	E8	90
Francisco Sá, Braz.	D7	79
Francistown, Bots.	C8	66
Franconia, N.H., U.S.	B3	136
Franconia Notch, N.H., U.S.	B3	136
Francs Peak, mtn., Wy., U.S.	C3	157
Frankenmuth, Mi., U.S.	E7	129
Frankford, Ont., Can.	C7	103
Frankford, De., U.S.	F5	115
Frankfort, S. Afr.	F9	66
Frankfort, S. Afr.	I8	66
Frankfort, Il., U.S.	m9	120
Frankfort, In., U.S.	D4	121
Frankfort, Ks., U.S.	C7	123
Frankfort, Ky., U.S.	B5	124
Frankfort, Mi., U.S.	D4	129
Frankfort, N.Y., U.S.	B5	139
Frankfurt am Main, Ger.	E8	10
Frankfurt an der Oder, Ger.	C14	10
Franklin, Ga., U.S.	C1	117
Franklin, Id., U.S.	G7	119
Franklin, In., U.S.	F5	121
Franklin, Ks., U.S.	E9	123
Franklin, Ky., U.S.	D3	124
Franklin, La., U.S.	E4	125
Franklin, Ma., U.S.	B5	128
Franklin, Ne., U.S.	D7	134
Franklin, N.H., U.S.	D3	136
Franklin, N.J., U.S.	A3	137
Franklin, N.C., U.S.	f9	140
Franklin, Oh., U.S.	C1	142
Franklin, Pa., U.S.	D2	145
Franklin, Tn., U.S.	B5	149
Franklin, Tx., U.S.	D6	153
Franklin, Va., U.S.	D6	153
Franklin, W.V., U.S.	C5	155
Franklin, Wi., U.S.	n11	156
Franklin, co., Al., U.S.	A2	108
Franklin, co., Fl., U.S.	C2	116
Franklin, co., Ga., U.S.	B3	117
Franklin, co., Id., U.S.	G7	119
Franklin, co., Il., U.S.	E4	120
Franklin, co., In., U.S.	F7	121
Franklin, co., Ia., U.S.	B4	122
Franklin, co., Ks., U.S.	D8	123
Franklin, co., Ky., U.S.	B5	124
Franklin, co., La., U.S.	B4	125
Franklin, co., Me., U.S.	C2	126
Franklin, co., Ma., U.S.	A2	128
Franklin, co., Mo., U.S.	C6	132
Franklin, co., Ms., U.S.	D3	131
Franklin, co., N.Y., U.S.	f10	139
Franklin, co., N.C., U.S.	A4	140
Franklin, co., Oh., U.S.	B2	142
Franklin, co., Pa., U.S.	G6	145
Franklin, co., Tn., U.S.	B5	149
Franklin, co., Tx., U.S.	C5	150
Franklin, co., Vt., U.S.	B2	152
Franklin, co., Va., U.S.	D3	153
Franklin, co., Wa., U.S.	C6	154
Franklin D. Roosevelt Lake, res., Wa., U.S.	B7	154
Franklin Falls Reservoir, res., N.H., U.S.	C3	136
Franklin Grove, Il., U.S.	B4	120
Franklin Park, Il., U.S.	k9	120
Franklin Park, Pa., U.S.	*h13	145
Franklinton, La., U.S.	D5	125
Franklinton, N.C., U.S.	A4	140
Frankton, In., U.S.	D6	121
Franktown, Co., U.S.	B6	113
Frankville, N.S., Can.	D8	101
Frannie, Wy., U.S.	B4	157
Franz Josef Land see Franca Iosifa, Zeml'a, is., Russia	A6	24
Frascati, Italy	H7	18
Fraser, Co., U.S.	B5	113
Fraser, stm., B.C., Can.	E7	99
Fraser, Mount, mtn., Can.	C8	99
Fraserburg, S. Afr.	H5	66
Fraser Island, i., Austl.	E10	70
Fraser Lake, B.C., Can.	B5	99
Frauenfeld, Switz.	C10	13
Fray Bentos, Ur.	G9	80
Fray Marcos, Ur.	H11	80
Frazee, Mn., U.S.	D3	130
Frazer, Mt., U.S.	B10	133
Fr'azino, Russia	F21	22
Frederic, Wi., U.S.	C1	156
Frederica, De., U.S.	D4	115
Fredericia, Den.	N11	6
Frederick, Co., U.S.	A6	113
Frederick, Md., U.S.	B3	127
Frederick, Ok., U.S.	C2	143
Frederick, co., Md., U.S.	B3	127
Frederick, co., Va., U.S.	A4	153
Fredericksburg, Ia., U.S.	B5	122
Fredericksburg, Tx., U.S.	D3	150
Fredericksburg, Va., U.S.	B5	153
Fredericktown, Mo., U.S.	D7	132
Fredericktown, Oh., U.S.	B3	142
Frederico Westphalen, Braz.	D12	80
Fredericton, N.B., Can.	D3	101
Fredericton Junction, N.B., Can.	D3	101
Frederikshavn, Den.	M12	6
Frederiksted, V.I.U.S.	F12	94
Fredonia, Az., U.S.	A3	110
Fredonia, Ks., U.S.	E8	123
Fredonia, N.Y., U.S.	C1	139
Fredonia, Wi., U.S.	E6	156
Fredrikstad, Nor.	L12	6
Freeborn, co., Mn., U.S.	G5	130
Freeburg, Il., U.S.	E4	120
Freedom, N.H., U.S.	C4	136
Freedom, Pa., U.S.	E1	145
Freedom, Wy., U.S.	D2	157
Freehold, N.J., U.S.	C4	137
Freeland, Mi., U.S.	E6	129
Freeland, Pa., U.S.	D10	145
Freelandville, In., U.S.	G3	121
Freels, Cape, c., Newf., Can.	E5	102
Freels, Cape, c., Newf., Can.	D5	102
Freeman, S.D., U.S.	D8	148
Freemansburg, Pa., U.S.	E11	145
Freeport, Bah.	A5	94
Freeport, N.S., Can.	E3	101
Freeport, Il., U.S.	A4	120
Freeport, Me., U.S.	E2	126
Freeport, N.Y., U.S.	n15	139
Freeport, Pa., U.S.	E2	145
Freeport, Tx., U.S.	E5	150
Freer, Tx., U.S.	F3	150
Freestone, co., Tx., U.S.	D4	150
Freetown, P.E.I., Can.	C6	101
Freetown, S.L.	G3	64
Freetown, In., U.S.	G5	121
Freiberg, Ger.	E13	10
Freiburg [im Breisgau], Ger.	H7	10
Freirina, Chile	E3	80
Freising, Ger.	G11	10
Freistadt, Aus.	G14	10
Freital, Ger.	D13	10
Fréjus, Fr.	I13	14
Fremantle, Austl.	F3	68
Fremont, Ca., U.S.	D2	112
Fremont, In., U.S.	A8	121
Fremont, Ia., U.S.	C5	122
Fremont, Mi., U.S.	E5	129
Fremont, Ne., U.S.	C9	134
Fremont, N.H., U.S.	E4	136
Fremont, N.C., U.S.	B5	140
Fremont, Oh., U.S.	A2	142
Fremont, co., Co., U.S.	C5	113
Fremont, co., Id., U.S.	E7	119
Fremont, co., Ia., U.S.	D2	122
Fremont, co., Wy., U.S.	C4	157
Fremont Peak, mtn., Wy., U.S.	C3	157
French Broad, stm., U.S.	D10	149
Frenchburg, Ky., U.S.	C6	124
French Guiana (Guyane français), dep.	C8	76
French Island, i., Austl.	L6	70
French Lick, In., U.S.	G4	121
Frenchman Bay, b., Me., U.S.	D4	126
French Polynesia, dep., Oc.	H3	2
French Southern and Antarctic Territories, dep., Afr.	M10	158
Frenchville, Me., U.S.	A4	126
Frenda, Alg.	C11	62
Freshfield, Mount, mtn., Can.	D2	98
Fresnillo, Mex.	F8	90
Fresno, Ca., U.S.	D4	112
Fresno, co., Ca., U.S.	D4	112
Freyre, Arg.	F7	80
Friars Point, Ms., U.S.	A3	131
Frías, Arg.	E6	80
Fribourg (Freiburg), Switz.	E7	13
Friday Harbor, Wa., U.S.	A2	154
Fridley, Mn., U.S.	m12	130
Fridtjof Nansen, Mount, mtn., Ant.	D9	73
Friedberg, Ger.	G10	10
Friedberg, Ger.	E8	10
Friedrichshafen, Ger.	H9	10
Friend, Ne., U.S.	D8	134
Friendship, N.Y., U.S.	C2	139
Friendship, Tn., U.S.	B3	149
Friendsville, Tn., U.S.	D9	149
Friendswood, Tx., U.S.	r14	150
Friesach, Aus.	I14	10
Friesland, prov., Neth.	B8	12
Frio, co., Tx., U.S.	E3	150
Frio, stm., Tx., U.S.	E3	150
Frio, Cabo, c., Braz.	G7	79
Friona, Tx., U.S.	B1	150
Frisco, Co., U.S.	B4	113
Frisco City, Al., U.S.	D2	108
Frisian Islands, is., Eur.	E9	4
Frissell, Mount, mtn., U.S.	A2	114
Friuli-Venezia-Giulia, prov., Italy	C7	18
Frolovo, Russia	H6	26
Fromberg, Mt., U.S.	E8	133
Frome, Lake, l., Austl.	H3	70
Frontenac, Ks., U.S.	E9	123
Frontera, Mex.	H13	90
Frontera, Mex.	D9	90
Frontier, Wy., U.S.	E2	157
Frontier, co., Ne., U.S.	D5	134
Front Range, mts., Co., U.S.	A5	113
Front Royal, Va., U.S.	B4	153
Frosinone, Italy	H8	18
Frostburg, Md., U.S.	k13	127
Frostproof, Fl., U.S.	E5	116
Fruita, Co., U.S.	B2	113
Fruitdale, Al., U.S.	D1	108
Fruit Heights, Ut., U.S.	B4	151
Fruitland, Id., U.S.	F2	119
Fruitland, Md., U.S.	D6	127
Fruitland, N.M., U.S.	A1	138
Fruitland Park, Fl., U.S.	D5	116
Fruitvale, B.C., Can.	E9	99
Fruitvale, Wa., U.S.	C5	154
Fruitville, Fl., U.S.	E4	116
Frunze see Bishkek, Kyrg.	I12	26
Frutal, Braz.	F4	79
Frutigen, Switz.	E8	13
Frýdek-Místek, Czech Rep.	F18	10
Fryeburg, Me., U.S.	D2	126
Fuchū, stm., China	F8	34
Fuding, China	H9	34
Fuego, Volcán de, vol., Guat.	C4	92
Fuerte, stm., Mex.	D5	90
Fuerte Olimpo, Para.	I13	82
Fuerteventura, i., Spain	o26	17b
Fuji, Japan	L13	36
Fujian (Fukien), prov., China	F10	30
Fujieda, Japan	M13	36
Fujin, China	B13	30
Fujinomiya, Japan	L13	36
Fuji-san (Fujiyama), vol., Japan	L13	36
Fujisawa, Japan	L14	36
Fujiyama see Fuji-san, vol., Japan	L13	36
Fuji-yoshida, Japan	L13	36
Fukou, China	I6	34
Fukuchiyama, Japan	L10	36
Fukui, Japan	K11	36
Fukuoka, Japan	N5	36
Fukushima, Japan	J15	36
Fukuyama, Japan	M8	36
Fulacunda, Gui.-B.	F2	64
Fūlādī, Kūh-e, mtn., Afg.	C2	44
Fulda, Ger.	E9	10
Fulda, Mn., U.S.	G3	130
Fulechang, China	B8	40
Fuling, China	F8	30
Fullerton, Ca., U.S.	n13	112
Fullerton, Ne., U.S.	C8	134
Fulton, Il., U.S.	B3	120
Fulton, Ky., U.S.	f9	124
Fulton, Ms., U.S.	A5	131
Fulton, Mo., U.S.	C6	132
Fulton, N.Y., U.S.	B4	139
Fulton, co., Ar., U.S.	A4	111
Fulton, co., Ga., U.S.	C2	117
Fulton, co., Il., U.S.	C3	120
Fulton, co., In., U.S.	B5	121
Fulton, co., Ky., U.S.	f8	124
Fulton, co., N.Y., U.S.	B6	139
Fulton, co., Oh., U.S.	A1	142
Fulton, co., Pa., U.S.	G6	145
Fultondale, Al., U.S.	f7	108
Fumay, Fr.	C11	14
Fumel, Fr.	H7	14
Funabashi, Japan	L14	36
Funchal, Port.	m21	17a
Fundación, Col.	B5	84
Fundy, Bay of, b., Can.	D4	101
Funing, China	B8	34
Funkstown, Md., U.S.	A2	127
Funtua, Nig.	F13	64
Fuquay-Varina, N.C., U.S.	B4	140
Furmanov, Russia	D24	22
Furnas, co., Ne., U.S.	D6	134
Furnas, Represa de, res., Braz.	F5	79
Furneaux Group, is., Austl.	L8	70
Fürstenfeldbruck, Ger.	G11	10
Fürstenwalde, Ger.	C14	10
Fürth, Ger.	F10	10
Furukawa, Japan	I15	36
Fury and Hecla Strait, strt., N.W. Ter., Can.	C15	96
Fusagasugá, Col.	E5	84
Fushan, China	D9	34
Fushun, China	B11	32
Futuyu, China	D2	32
Fuwah, Egypt	B6	60
Fuxi, China	J2	34
Fuxian, China	D8	30
Fuxian (Wafangdian), China	D10	32
Fuxin, China	A9	32
Fuyang, China	C4	34
Fuyu, China	B11	30
Fuzhou (Foochow), China	I8	34
Fuzhou, China	G5	34
Fyffe, Al., U.S.	A4	108
Fyn, i., Den.	N12	6

G

Name	Map Ref.	Page
Gaalkacyo, Som.	G10	56
Gabbs, Nv., U.S.	E4	135
Gabela, Ang.	D2	58
Gabès, Tun.	C16	62
Gabès, Golfe de, b., Tun.	C16	62
Gabir, Sud.	M3	60
Gabon, ctry., Afr.	B2	58
Gaborone, Bots.	E7	66
Gabriola, B.C., Can.	f12	99
Gabrovo, Bul.	G9	20
Gackle, N.D., U.S.	C6	141
Gadag, India	E3	46
Gadsden, Al., U.S.	A3	108
Gadsden, Az., U.S.	E1	110
Gadsden, co., Fl., U.S.	B2	116
Gaeta, Italy	H8	18
Gaeta, Golfo di, b., Italy	H8	18
Gaffney, S.C., U.S.	A4	147
Gafsa, Tun.	C15	62
Gagarin, Russia	F18	22
Gage, co., Ne., U.S.	D9	134
Gagetown, N.B., Can.	D3	101
Gaggenau, Ger.	G8	10
Gaghamni, Sud.	L5	60
Gagnoa, C. Iv.	H7	64
Gahanna, Oh., U.S.	k11	142
Gaillac, Fr.	I8	14
Gaillon, Fr.	C8	14
Gaines, co., Tx., U.S.	C1	150
Gainesboro, Tn., U.S.	C8	149
Gainesville, Al., U.S.	C1	108
Gainesville, Fl., U.S.	C4	116
Gainesville, Ga., U.S.	B3	117
Gainesville, Mo., U.S.	E5	132
Gainesville, Tx., U.S.	C4	150
Gainesville, Va., U.S.	g11	153
Gainsborough, Sask., Can.	H5	105
Gairdner, Lake, l., Austl.	F7	68
Gaithersburg, Md., U.S.	B3	127
Gaixian, China	C10	32
Gajny, Russia	E19	22
Galán, Cerro, mtn., Arg.	C5	80
Galapagos Islands see Colón, Archipiélago de, is., Ec.	m15	85a
Galashiels, Scot., U.K.	F11	8
Galați, Rom.	D12	20
Galatia, Il., U.S.	F5	120
Galatina, Italy	I13	18
Galax, Va., U.S.	D2	153
Galena, Ak., U.S.	C8	109
Galena, Il., U.S.	A3	120
Galena, Ks., U.S.	E9	123
Galena, Md., U.S.	B5	127
Galena Park, Tx., U.S.	r14	150
Galesburg, Il., U.S.	C3	120
Galesburg, Mi., U.S.	F5	129
Gales Ferry, Ct., U.S.	D7	114
Galesville, Wi., U.S.	D2	156
Galič, Russia	C25	22
Galicia, prov., Spain	C3	16
Galicia, hist. reg., Eur.	F12	4
Galilee, R.I., U.S.	F3	146
Galilee, Sea of see Kinneret, Yam, l., Isr.	C5	50
Galiléia, Braz.	E8	79
Galion, Oh., U.S.	B3	142
Galiuro Mountains, mts., Az., U.S.	E5	110
Gallant, Al., U.S.	B3	108
Gallarate, Italy	D3	18
Gallatin, Mo., U.S.	B4	132
Gallatin, Tn., U.S.	C5	149
Gallatin, co., Il., U.S.	F5	120
Gallatin, co., Ky., U.S.	B5	124
Gallatin, co., Mt., U.S.	E5	133
Gallatin, stm., Mt., U.S.	E5	133
Gallatin Gateway, Mt., U.S.	E5	133
Galle, Sri L.	I6	46
Gallia, co., Oh., U.S.	C3	142
Galliano, La., U.S.	E5	125
Gallina, N.M., U.S.	A3	138
Gallinas, Punta, c., Col.	A7	84
Gallipoli, Italy	I12	18
Gallipoli see Gelibolu, Tur.	I10	20
Gallipoli Peninsula see Gelibolu Yanmadası, pen., Tur.	I10	20
Gallipolis, Oh., U.S.	C3	142
Gallitzin, Pa., U.S.	F4	145
Gällivare, Swe.	H17	6
Gallup, N.M., U.S.	B1	138
Galt, Ca., U.S.	C3	112
Galtat Zemmour, W. Sah.	H4	62
Galva, Il., U.S.	B4	120
Galva, Ks., U.S.	D6	123
Galveston, In., U.S.	C5	121
Galveston, co., Tx., U.S.	E5	150
Galveston Bay, b., Tx., U.S.	E5	150
Galveston Island, i., Tx., U.S.	E5	150
Gálvez, Arg.	G8	80
Galway, Ire.	H4	8
Galway, co., Ire.	H4	8
Galway Bay, b., Ire.	H4	8
Gamagōri, Japan	M12	36
Gamarra, Col.	C6	84
Gambela, Eth.	M8	60
Gambell, Ak., U.S.	C5	109
Gambia, ctry., Afr.	F3	54
Gambia (Gambie), stm., Afr.	F3	54
Gambier, Îles, is., Fr. Poly.	K26	158
Gambo, Newf., Can.	D4	102
Gamboa, Pan.	J2	84
Gamboma, Congo	B3	58
Gambrills, Md., U.S.	B4	127
Gamerco, N.M., U.S.	B1	138
Ganado, Az., U.S.	B6	110
Ganado, Tx., U.S.	E4	150
Gananoque, Ont., Can.	C8	103
Ganāveh, Iran	C4	44
Gäncä, Azer.	I7	26
Gancevichi, Bela.	I9	22
Ganda, Ang.	D2	58
Gandak, stm., India	G11	44
Gandhi Sāgar, res., India	H6	44
Gandia, Spain	G11	16
Gandu, Braz.	B9	79
Gangānagar, India	F5	44
Ganges, B.C., Can.	g12	99
Ganges (Ganga) (Padma), stm., Asia	I13	44
Gang Mills, N.Y., U.S.	C3	139
Gangtok, India	G13	44
Gangu, China	E8	30
Gannett Peak, mtn., Wy., U.S.	C3	157
Gansu (Kansu), prov., China	D7	30
Gantt, S.C., U.S.	B3	147
Ganxi, China	G7	34
Ganzhou, China	J3	34
Ganzê, China	E7	30
Gao, Mali	C9	64
Gaobe, China	M1	34
Gaokeng, China	H2	34
Gaoling, China	C5	32
Gaona, Arg.	C6	80
Gaoshan, China	J8	34
Gaoua, Burkina	F8	64
Gaoyou, China	H13	34
Garachiné, Pan.	C3	84
Garanhuns, Braz.	E11	76
Garber, Ok., U.S.	A4	143
Garça, Braz.	G4	79
Garda, Lago di, l., Italy	D5	18
Garden, co., Ne., U.S.	C3	134
Gardena, Ca., U.S.	n12	112
Garden City, Al., U.S.	A3	108
Garden City, Ga., U.S.	D5	117
Garden City, Id., U.S.	F2	119
Garden City, Ks., U.S.	E3	123
Garden City, Mi., U.S.	p15	129
Garden City, Mo., U.S.	C3	132
Gardendale, Al., U.S.	B3	108
Garden Grove, Ca., U.S.	n13	112
Garden Plain, Ks., U.S.	E6	123
Garden Valley, Id., U.S.	F3	119
Gardeyz, Afg.	D3	44
Gardiner, Mt., U.S.	E6	133
Gardiner, Me., U.S.	D3	126
Gardiners Island, i., N.Y., U.S.	m16	139
Gardner, Il., U.S.	B5	120
Gardner, Ks., U.S.	D9	123
Gardner, Ma., U.S.	A4	128
Gardner Canal, strt., B.C., Can.	C3	99
Gardnerville, Nv., U.S.	E2	135
Gareśnica, Cro.	D11	18
Garfield, Ar., U.S.	A2	111
Garfield, N.J., U.S.	h8	137
Garfield, Wa., U.S.	B8	154
Garfield, co., Co., U.S.	B2	113
Garfield, co., Mt., U.S.	C9	133
Garfield, co., Ne., U.S.	C6	134
Garfield, co., Ok., U.S.	A4	143
Garfield, co., Ut., U.S.	F4	151
Garfield, co., Wa., U.S.	C8	154
Garfield Heights, Oh., U.S.	h9	142
Garfield Mountain, mtn., Mt., U.S.	F4	133
Gargouna, Mali	D10	64
Garibaldi, Braz.	E13	80
Garibaldi, Or., U.S.	B3	144
Garibaldi, Mount, mtn., B.C., Can.	E6	99
Garko, Nig.	F14	64
Garland, Ar., U.S.	D2	111
Garland, Tx., U.S.	n10	150
Garland, Ut., U.S.	B3	151
Garland, co., Ar., U.S.	C2	111
Garm, Taj.	J12	26
Garmisch-Partenkirchen, Ger.	H11	10
Garnavillo, Ia., U.S.	B6	122
Garner, Ia., U.S.	A4	122
Garner, N.C., U.S.	B4	140
Garnett, Ks., U.S.	D8	123
Garonne, stm., Eur.	H6	14
Garoua, Cam.	G9	54
Garrard, co., Ky., U.S.	C5	124
Garretson, S.D., U.S.	D9	148
Garrett, In., U.S.	B7	121
Garrett, co., Md., U.S.	k12	127
Garrettsville, Oh., U.S.	A4	142
Garrison, Ky., U.S.	B6	124
Garrison, N.D., U.S.	B4	141
Garrison, Tx., U.S.	D5	150
Garson Quarry, Man., Can.	D3	100
Garub, Nmb.	F3	66
Garut, Indon.	j13	39a
Garvin, co., Ok., U.S.	C4	143
Garwood, Tx., U.S.	E4	150
Gary, In., U.S.	B3	121
Gary, W.V., U.S.	D3	155
Garyarsa, China	E9	44
Garyville, La., U.S.	D5	125
Garza, co., Tx., U.S.	C2	150
Garzón, Col.	F5	84
Gas, co., Ks., U.S.	E8	123
Gas City, In., U.S.	D6	121
Gasconade, co., Mo., U.S.	C6	132
Gasconade, stm., Mo., U.S.	C6	132
Gascoyne, stm., Austl.	E2	68
Gas Hills, Wy., U.S.	D5	157
Gaspar, Braz.	D14	80
Gaspé, Que., Can.	k14	104
Gassaway, W.V., U.S.	C4	155
Gassville, Ar., U.S.	A3	111
Gaston, In., U.S.	D7	121
Gaston, S.C., U.S.	D5	147
Gaston, co., N.C., U.S.	B1	140
Gaston, Lake, res., U.S.	A5	140
Gastonia, N.C., U.S.	B1	140
Gata, Cabo de, c., Spain	I9	16
Gátas, Akrotírion, c., Cyp.	B3	50
Gatčina, Russia	B13	22
Gate City, Va., U.S.	f9	153
Gates, N.Y., U.S.	B3	139
Gates, co., N.C., U.S.	A6	140
Gateshead, Eng., U.K.	G12	8
Gates of the Arctic National Park, Ak., U.S.	B9	109
Gatesville, Tx., U.S.	D4	150
Gateway, Co., U.S.	C2	113
Gatineau, Que., Can.	D2	104
Gatineau, stm., Que., Can.	D2	104
Gatlinburg, Tn., U.S.	D10	149
Gatton, Austl.	F10	70
Gatún, Esclusas de, Pan.	H15	92
Gatún, Lago, res., Pan.	H15	92
Gauley, stm., W.V., U.S.	C3	155
Gauley Bridge, W.V., U.S.	C3	155
Gautier, Ms., U.S.	E5	131
Gavà, Spain	D14	16
Gävle, Swe.	K15	6

Name	Map Ref.	Page

Gavrilov-Jam, Russia D22 22
Gavrilov Posad, Russia . . . E23 22
Gawler, Austl. J3 70
Gaya, India H11 44
Gay Head, c., Ma., U.S. . . D6 128
Gaylord, Mi., U.S. C6 129
Gaylord, Mn., U.S. F4 130
Gayndah, Austl. E9 70
Gayville, S.D., U.S. E8 148
Gaza see Ghazzah, Gaza . . F3 48
Gaziantep, Tur. C4 48
Gazimağusa (Famagusta),
   N. Cyp. D2 48
Gbangbatok, S.L. H3 64
Gbarnga, Lib. H5 64
Gbongan, Nig. H12 64
Gdańsk (Danzig), Pol. . . . A18 10
Gdańsk, Gulf of, b., Eur. . . A19 10
Gdov, Russia C10 22
Gdyel, Alg. J11 16
Gdynia, Pol. A18 10
Gearhart, Or., U.S. A3 144
Gearhart Mountain, mtn.,
   Or., U.S. E6 144
Geary, N.B., Can. D3 101
Geary, Ok., U.S. B3 143
Geary, co., Ks., U.S. D7 123
Geauga, co., Oh., U.S. . . . A4 142
Gebeit Mine, Sud. G9 60
Gebze, Tur. I13 20
Gecha, Eth. N8 60
Gedo, Eth. M9 60
Geel, Bel. F7 12
Geelong, Austl. L6 70
Geesthacht, Ger. B10 10
Gegong, China E6 34
Geislingen, Ger. G9 10
Geistown, Pa., U.S. F4 145
Gejiatun, China C7 32
Geju (Kokiu), China C7 40
Gela, Italy L9 18
Gelderland, prov., Neth. . . D8 12
Geldrop, Neth. F8 12
Gelibolu, Tur. I10 20
Gelibolu Yarımadası
   (Gallipoli Peninsula), pen.,
   Tur. I10 20
Gelsenkirchen, Ger. D7 10
Gem, co., Id., U.S. E2 119
Gemena, Zaire H4 56
Gemlik, Tur. I13 20
Genale (Jubba), stm., Afr. . G9 56
General Acha, Arg. I6 80
General Alvear, Arg. I8 80
General Alvear, Arg. H5 80
General Arenales, Arg. . . . H8 80
General Belgrano, Arg. . . . H9 80
General Cabrera, Arg. G7 80
General Campos, Arg. . . . F9 80
General Carrera, Lago
   (Lago Buenos Aires), l.,
   S.A. F2 78
General Daniel Cerri, Arg. . J7 80
General Enrique Martínez,
   Ur. G12 80
General Eugenio A. Garay,
   Para. C10 80
General Galarza, Arg. G9 80
General Güemes, Arg. . . . C6 80
General Guido, Arg. I10 80
General José de San
   Martín, Arg. D9 80
General Juan José Rios,
   Mex. E5 90
General Juan Madariaga,
   Arg. I10 80
General La Madrid, Arg. . . I8 80
General Lavalle, Arg. I10 80
General Levalle, Arg. H7 80
General Manuel Belgrano,
   Cerro, mtn., Arg. E5 80
General O'Brien, Arg. H8 80
General Pico, Arg. H7 80
General Pinedo, Arg. D8 80
General Pinto, Arg. H8 80
General Roca, Arg. J5 80
General San Martín, Arg. . . I7 80
General San Martín, Arg. . . H9 80
General Santos, Phil. D8 38
General Terán, Mex. E10 90
General Viamonte (Los
   Toldos), Arg. H8 80
General Villegas, Arg. H7 80
Genesee, Id., U.S. C2 119
Genesee, Mi., U.S. E7 129
Genesee, co., Mi., U.S. . . . E7 129
Genesee, co., N.Y., U.S. . . B2 139
Genesee, stm., N.Y., U.S. . B3 120
Geneseo, Il., U.S. C3 139
Geneseo, N.Y., U.S. F13 14
Geneva see Genève, Switz.
Geneva, Al., U.S. D4 108
Geneva, Il., U.S. B5 120
Geneva, In., U.S. C8 121
Geneva, Ne., U.S. D8 134
Geneva, N.Y., U.S. C4 139
Geneva, Oh., U.S. A5 142
Geneva, co., Al., U.S. D4 108
Geneva, Lake, l., Eur. . . . F13 14
Genève (Geneva), Switz. . . F5 13
Gengma, China C5 40
Genk, Bel. G8 12
Genlis, Fr. E12 14
Genoa see Genova, Italy . . E3 18
Genoa, Il., U.S. A5 120
Genoa, Ne., U.S. C8 134
Genoa, Nv., U.S. D2 135
Genoa, Oh., U.S. A2 142
Genoa City, Wi., U.S. F5 156
Genola, Ut., U.S. D4 151
Genova (Genoa), Italy . . . E3 18
Genova, Golfo di, b., Italy . E3 18
Gent (Gand), Bel. F4 12
Gentry, Ar., U.S. A1 111
Gentry, co., Mo., U.S. A3 132
Geok-Tepe, Turk. B14 48
George, S. Afr. I6 66
George, Ia., U.S. A2 122
George, co., Ms., U.S. . . . E5 131
George, Cape, c., N.S.,
   Can. D8 101
George, Lake, l., U.S. C5 116
George, Lake, l., N.Y., U.S. . B7 139
Georges Bank E9 86
George Town, Austl. M7 70
Georgetown, P.E.I., Can. . . C7 101
George Town, Cay. Is. . . . E4 94
Georgetown, Gam. E2 64
Georgetown, Guy. D13 84
George Town (Pinang),
   Malay. L6 40
Georgetown, St. Vin. H14 94
Georgetown, Co., U.S. . . . B5 113
Georgetown, Ct., U.S. . . . D2 114
Georgetown, De., U.S. . . . F4 115
Georgetown, Ga., U.S. . . . E1 117
Georgetown, Id., U.S. G7 119
Georgetown, Il., U.S. D6 120
Georgetown, In., U.S. H6 121
Georgetown, Ky., U.S. . . . B5 124
Georgetown, Ma., U.S. . . . A6 128
Georgetown, Oh., U.S. . . . D2 142
Georgetown, S.C., U.S. . . . E9 147
Georgetown, Tx., U.S. . . . D4 150
Georgetown, co., S.C., U.S. E9 147
George VI Sound, strt., Ant. C12 73
George Washington
   Birthplace National
   Monument, Va., U.S. . . . B6 153
Georgia, ctry., Asia I6 26
Georgia, state, U.S. D3 117
Georgiana, Al., U.S. D3 108
Georgian Bay, b., Ont.,
   Can. B3 103
Georgijevsk, Russia I6 26
Georgina, stm., Austl. . . . D3 70
Gera, Ger. E12 10
Geral, Serra, clf., Braz. . . . D14 80
Gerald, Sask., Can. G5 105
Gerald, Mo., U.S. C6 132
Geraldine, Al., U.S. A4 108
Geraldine, Mt., U.S. C6 133
Geraldton, Austl. E2 68
Geraldton, Ont., Can. o18 103
Gérardmer, Fr. D13 14
Gereshk, Afg. E1 44
Gering, Ne., U.S. C2 134
Gerlach, Nv., U.S. C2 135
Gerlachovský štít, mtn.,
   Slvk. F20 10
Germantown, Il., U.S. E4 120
Germantown, Md., U.S. . . . B3 127
Germantown, Oh., U.S. . . . C1 142
Germantown, Tn., U.S. . . . B2 149
Germantown, Wi., U.S. . . . E5 156
Germany (Deutschland),
   ctry., Eur. E9 4
Germiston, S. Afr. F9 66
Gernika-Lumo (Guernica y
   Luno), Spain B9 16
Geronimo, Ok., U.S. C3 143
Gervais, Or., U.S. B4 144
Getafe, Spain E8 16
Gettysburg, Pa., U.S. G7 145
Gettysburg, S.D., U.S. . . . C6 148
Getulina, Braz. F4 79
Getúlio Vargas, Braz. D12 80
Gex, Fr. F13 14
Ghadāmis, Libya E15 62
Ghāghara, stm., Asia G10 44
Ghana, ctry., Afr. G6 54
Ghanzi, Bots. C5 66
Gharbīyah, As-Şahrā' al-
   (Western Desert), des.,
   Egypt D4 60
Ghardaïa, Alg. D12 62
Ghardimaou, Tun. M3 18
Gharig, Sud. L4 60
Gharyān, Libya H16 62
Ghāt, Libya B3 56
Ghawdex (Gozo), i., Malta. M9 18
Ghawr ash-Sharqīyah,
   Qanāt al- (East Ghor
   Canal), Jord. D5 50
Ghazāl, Baḩr al-, stm., Sud. M5 60
Ghāziābād, India F7 44
Ghāzīpur, India H10 44
Ghaznī, Afg. D3 44
Ghazzah (Gaza), Gaza . . . F4 12
Ghent see Gent, Bel. F4 12
Gheorgheni, Rom. C9 20
Gherla, Rom. B7 20
Ghilizane, Alg. C11 62
Ghūrīān, Afg. D16 48
Giant Mountain, mtn., N.Y.,
   U.S. A7 139
Giant's Castle, mtn., Afr. . . G9 66
Giants Neck, Ct., U.S. . . . D7 114
Gibara, Cuba D6 94
Gibbon, Mn., U.S. F4 130
Gibbon, Ne., U.S. D7 134
Gibbons, Alta., Can. C4 98
Gibbstown, N.J., U.S. . . . D2 137
Gibeon, Nmb. E3 66
Gibraltar, Gib. I6 16
Gibraltar, dep., Eur. H6 4
Gibraltar, Strait of (Estrecho
   de Gibraltar), strt. J6 16
Gibsland, La., U.S. B2 125
Gibson, La., U.S. E5 125
Gibson, co., In., U.S. H2 121
Gibson, co., Tn., U.S. A3 149
Gibsonburg, Oh., U.S. . . . A2 142
Gibson City, Il., U.S. C5 120
Gibson Desert, des., Austl. . D5 68
Gibsonia, Pa., U.S. E2 145
Gibsons, B.C., Can. E6 99
Gibsonton, Fl., U.S. p11 116
Gibsonville, N.C., U.S. . . . A3 140
Giddings, Tx., U.S. D4 150
Gidole, Eth. O9 60
Gidrotfort, Russia E9 14
Gien, Fr. E8 10
Gifford, Fl., U.S. E6 116
Gifhorn, Ger. C10 10
Gifu, Japan L11 36
Gijduan, Col. F5 84
Gijón, Spain B6 16
Gila, N.M., U.S. E1 138
Gila, co., Az., U.S. D5 110
Gila, stm., Az., U.S. E4 106
Gila Bend, Az., U.S. E3 110
Gila Bend Mountains, mts.,
   Az., U.S. D2 110
Gilbert, Az., U.S. E3 103
Gilbert, Ia., U.S. B4 122
Gilbert, Mn., U.S. C6 130
Gilbert, W.V., U.S. h13 139
Gilbert Peak, mtn., Wa.,
   U.S. C4 154
Gilbert Plains, Man., Can. . D1 100
Gilbertsville, Ky., U.S. f9 124
Gilbertsville, Pa., U.S. . . . F10 145
Gilbertville, Ia., U.S. B5 122
Gilby, N.D., U.S. A8 141
Gilchrist, co., Fl., U.S. . . . C4 116
Gilcrest, Co., U.S. A6 113
Gildford, Mt., U.S. B6 133
Giles, co., Tn., U.S. B4 149
Giles, co., Va., U.S. H8 70
Gilgandra, Austl. . . . .
Gilgit, Pak. C6 44
Gillam, Man., Can. A4 100
Gillespie, Il., U.S. D4 120
Gillespie, co., Tx., U.S. . . . D3 150
Gillett, Ar., U.S. C4 111
Gillett, Wi., U.S. D5 156
Gillette, Wy., U.S. B7 157
Gilliam, co., Or., U.S. B6 144
Gilman, Il., U.S. C5 120
Gilman, Vt., U.S. C5 152
Gilmanton, N.H., U.S. . . . D4 136
Gilmanton Iron Works, N.H.,
   U.S. D4 136
Gilmer, Tx., U.S. C5 150
Gilmer, co., Ga., U.S. B2 117
Gilmer, co., W.V., U.S. . . . C4 155
Gilmore, Ar., U.S. B5 111
Gilpin, co., Co., U.S. B5 113
Gilroy, Ca., U.S. D3 112
Gilsum, N.H., U.S. D2 136
Giltner, Ne., U.S. D7 134
Giluwe, Mount, mtn., Pap.
   N. Gui. m15 68a
Gimbi, Eth. M8 60
Gimie, Mount, mtn., St. Luc. H14 94
Gimli, Man., Can. D3 100
Ginir, Eth. G9 56
Gioia del Colle, Italy I11 18
Girard, Il., U.S. D4 120
Girard, Ks., U.S. E9 123
Girard, Oh., U.S. A5 142
Girard, Pa., U.S. B1 145
Girardot, Col. E5 84
Girardville, Pa., U.S. E9 145
Girīdīh, India H12 44
Girne, N. Cyp. D2 48
Giromagny, Fr. E13 14
Girona, Spain D14 16
Gironde, est., Fr. G6 14
Girouxville, Alta., Can. . . . B2 98
Giru, Austl. B7 70
Giruá, Braz. E11 80
Gisborne, N.Z. C7 72
Gisors, Fr. C8 14
Giugliano [in Campania],
   Italy I9 18
Giulianova, Italy G8 18
Giurgiu, Rom. F9 20
Giv'atayim, Isr. D3 50
Givet, Fr. B11 14
Givors, Fr. G11 14
Givry, Fr. F11 14
Giyon, Eth. M9 60
Giza see Al-Jīzah, Egypt . . B2 60
Gizycko, Pol. A21 10
Gjirokastër, Alb. I4 20
Gjoa Haven, N.W. Ter.,
   Can. C13 96
Gjøvik, Nor. K12 6
Gjuhëzës, Kep i, c., Alb. . . I3 20
Glace Bay, N.S., Can. . . . C10 101
Glacier, co., Mt., U.S. . . . B3 133
Glacier Bay, b., Ak., U.S. . . k21 109
Glacier Bay National Park,
   Ak., U.S. D12 109
Glacier National Park, Mt.,
   U.S. B2 133
Glacier Peak, mtn., Wa.,
   U.S. A4 154
Gladbach see
   Mönchengladbach, Ger. . D6 10
Gladbrook, Ia., U.S. B5 122
Glade Park, Co., U.S. B2 113
Glades, co., Fl., U.S. F5 116
Glade Spring, Va., U.S. . . . f10 153
Gladewater, Tx., U.S. C5 150
Gladstone, Austl. D9 70
Gladstone, Austl. I3 70
Gladstone, Man., Can. . . . D2 100
Gladstone, Mi., U.S. C4 129
Gladstone, Mo., U.S. h10 132
Gladstone, Or., U.S. B4 144
Gladwin, Mi., U.S. E6 129
Gladwin, co., Mi., U.S. . . . D6 129
Glåma, stm., Nor. K12 6
Glarner Alpen, mts., Switz. . E10 13
Glarus, Switz. D11 13
Glasco, Ks., U.S. C6 123
Glascock, co., Ga., U.S. . . C4 117
Glasford, Il., U.S. C4 120
Glasgow, Scot., U.K. F9 8
Glasgow, Ky., U.S. D4 124
Glasgow, Mo., U.S. B5 132
Glasgow, Mt., U.S. B10 133
Glasgow, Va., U.S. C3 153
Glasgow, W.V., U.S. m13 155
Glaslyn, Sask., Can. D1 105
Glassboro, N.J., U.S. D2 137
Glasscock, co., Tx., U.S. . . D2 150
Glastenbury Mountain, mtn.,
   Vt., U.S. F2 152
Glastonbury, Ct., U.S. . . . C5 114
Glauchau, Ger. E12 10
Glazov, Russia F8 26
Glazunovka, Russia I19 22
Gleason, Tn., U.S. A3 149
Gleichen, Alta., Can. D4 98
Glen Allan, Ms., U.S. B2 131
Glen Allen, Va., U.S. C5 153
Glenavon, Sask., Can. . . . G4 105
Glenboro, Man., Can. E2 100
Glenbrook, Nv., U.S. D2 135
Glenburn, N.D., U.S. A4 141
Glen Burnie, Md., U.S. . . . B4 127
Glen Canyon, val., U.S. . . . G4 151
Glencoe, Austl. K4 70
Glencoe, Ont., Can. E3 103
Glencoe, Al., U.S. B4 108
Glencoe, Il., U.S. A6 120
Glencoe, Mn., U.S. F4 130
Glen Cove, N.Y., U.S. h13 139
Glendale, Az., U.S. D3 110
Glendale, Ca., U.S. m12 112
Glendale, Ms., U.S. D4 131
Glendale, Oh., U.S. C1 142
Glendale, Or., U.S. E3 144
Glendale, R.I., U.S. B2 146
Glendale, S.C., U.S. B4 147
Glen Dale, W.V., U.S. B4 155
Glendale, Wi., U.S. m12 156
Glendale Heights, W.V.,
   U.S. g8 155
Glendive, Mt., U.S. C12 133
Glendo, Wy., U.S. D7 157
Glendon, Alta., Can. B5 98
Glendora, Ca., U.S. m13 112
Glendo Reservoir, res., Wy.,
   U.S. D8 157
Glen Elder, Ks., U.S. C5 123
Glenella, Man., Can. D2 100
Glen Ellyn, Il., U.S. k8 120
Glenham, N.Y., U.S. D7 139
Glen Innes, Austl. G9 70
Glen Jean, W.V., U.S. D3 155
Glen Lyon, Pa., U.S. D9 145
Glenmora, La., U.S. D3 125
Glenn, co., Ca., U.S. C2 112
Glennallen, Ak., U.S. f19 109
Glenns Ferry, Id., U.S. . . . G3 119
Glenolden, Pa., U.S. p20 145
Glenormiston, Austl. D3 70
Glenpool, Ok., U.S. B5 143
Glen Raven, N.C., U.S. . . . A3 140
Glen Ridge, N.J., U.S. . . . h8 137
Glen Rock, N.J., U.S. h8 137
Glenrock, Wy., U.S. D7 157
Glens Falls, N.Y., U.S. . . . B7 139
Glenside, Pa., U.S. F11 145
Glen Ullin, N.D., U.S. C4 141
Glenview, Il., U.S. h9 120
Glenville, Mn., U.S. G5 130
Glenville, W.V., U.S. C4 155
Glenwood, Newf., Can. . . . D4 102
Glenwood, Ar., U.S. C2 111
Glenwood, Ga., U.S. D4 117
Glenwood, Ia., U.S. C2 122
Glenwood, Mn., U.S. E3 130
Glenwood, N.M., U.S. . . . D1 138
Glenwood, Va., U.S. D3 153
Glenwood City, Wi., U.S. . . C1 156
Glenwood Springs, Co.,
   U.S. B3 113
Glenwoodville, Alta., Can. . E4 98
Glidden, Ia., U.S. B3 122
Glide, Or., U.S. D3 144
Gliwice (Gleiwitz), Pol. . . . E18 10
Globe, Az., U.S. D5 110
Głogów, Pol. D16 10
Glória de Dourados, Braz. . G1 79
Gloster, Ms., U.S. h12 103
Gloucester, Ont., Can. . . .
Gloucester, Eng., U.K. . . . J11 8
Gloucester, Ma., U.S. A6 128
Gloucester, co., N.J., U.S. . D2 137
Gloucester, co., Va., U.S. . C6 153
Gloucester City, N.J., U.S. . D2 137
Gloucester Point, Va., U.S. . C6 153
Gloucestershire, co., Eng.,
   U.K. J11 8
Glouster, Oh., U.S. C3 142
Glover, Vt., U.S. B4 152
Glovers Reef, rf., Belize . . I16 90
Gloversville, N.Y., U.S. . . . B6 139
Glovertown, Newf., Can. . . D4 102
Gloverville, S.C., U.S. C4 147
Głubokoje, Bela. F10 22
Glusk, Bela. I11 22
Glyndon, Mn., U.S. D2 130
Glynn, co., Ga., U.S. E5 117
Gmelinka, Russia E6 117
Gmunden, Aus. H13 10
Gnalta, Austl. H5 70
Gniezno, Pol. C17 10
Gnjilane, Yugo. G5 20
Goa, state, India E2 46
Goascorán, stm., N.A. . . . D7 92
Goat Mountain, mtn., Mt.,
   U.S. C3 133
Goba, Eth. G9 56
Gobabis, Nmb. D4 66
Gobernador Gregores, Arg. F2 78
Gobernador Ingeniero
   Valentín Virasoro, Arg. . E10 80
Gobernador Juan E.
   Martínez, Arg. E9 80
Gobi, des., Asia C7 30
Gobō, Japan H7 20
Goch, Ger. D6 10
Gochas, Nmb. E4 66
Godāvari, stm., India D6 46
Goddard, Ks., U.S. E6 123
Goderich, Ont., Can. D3 103
Godfrey, Il., U.S. E3 120
Godhavn, Grnld. C18 86
Godhra, India I5 44
Godoy Cruz, Arg. G4 80
Gods, stm., Man., Can. . . . A5 100
Gods Lake, l., Man., Can. . B4 100
Godthåb, Grnld. C14 86
Godwin Austen see K2,
   mtn., Asia C7 44
Goes, Neth. E4 12
Goessel, Ks., U.S. D6 123
Goffstown, N.H., U.S. D3 136
Gogebic, co., Mi., U.S. . . . n12 129
Gogol, Braz. D7 79
Goiana, Braz. E4 79
Goianápolis, Braz. C4 79
Goiandira, Braz. C4 79
Goiânia, Braz. C3 79
Goiás, state, Braz. B4 79
Goiatuba, Braz. I9 79
Goio-Erê, Braz. C12 80
Gol, Nor. K11 6
Golconda, Nv., U.S. C4 135
Gold Bar, Wa., U.S. B4 154
Gold Beach, Or., U.S. . . . E2 144
Golden, B.C., Can. D9 99
Golden, Co., U.S. B5 113
Golden Beach, Md., U.S. . . C4 127
Golden City, Mo., U.S. . . . D3 132
Goldendale, Wa., U.S. . . . D5 154
Golden Gate Bridge, Ca.,
   U.S. h7 112
Golden Hinde, mtn., B.C.,
   Can. E5 99
Golden Meadow, La., U.S. . E5 125
Golden Spike National
   Historic Site, hist., Ut.,
   U.S. B3 151
Golden Valley, Mn., U.S. . . n12 130
Golden Valley, co., Mt.,
   U.S. D7 133
Golden Valley, co., N.D.,
   U.S. B2 141
Goldfield, Ia., U.S. B4 122
Goldfield, Nv., U.S. F4 135
Gold Hill, Or., U.S. E3 144
Goldsboro, N.C., U.S. . . . B5 140
Goldsby, Ok., U.S. D3 68
Goldsworthy, Austl. B14 10
Goleniów, Pol. E4 112
Goleta, Ca., U.S. I11 92
Golfito, C.R. o13 142
Golf Manor, Oh., U.S. . . . E4 150
Goliad, co., Tx., U.S. F19 22
Golicyno, Russia D5 30
Golmud, China E11 48
Golpāyegān, Iran u14 116
Golynki, Russia G14 22
Golyšmanovo, Russia F11 26
Goma, Zaire B5 58
Gomel', Bela. I14 22
Gomera, i., Spain o23 17b
Gómez Farías, Mex. C6 90
Gómez Palacio, Mex. E8 90
Gonaïves, Haiti E8 94
Gonâve, Golfe de la, b.,
   Haiti E8 94
Gonâve, Île de la, i., Haiti . E8 94
Gonbad-e Qābūs, Iran . . . C13 48
Gonda, India G9 44
Gondal, India J4 44
Gonder, Eth. K9 60
Gondia, India J9 44
Gönen, Tur. I11 20
Gongchenqiao, China E9 34
Gongga Shan, mtn., China . F7 30
Gongola, stm., Nig. F9 54
Gongxian, China E9 34
Gonzales, La., U.S. D5 125
Gonzales, Tx., U.S. E4 150
Gonzales, co., Tx., U.S. . . E4 150
González, Mex. F10 90
González, Fl., U.S. u14 116
González Chaves, Arg. . . . J8 80
González Moreno, Arg. . . . H7 80
Goochland, co., Va., U.S. . . C5 153
Goodhope Bay, Ak., U.S. . . A3 108
Good Hope, Al., U.S. . . . .
Good Hope, Cape of, c., S.
   Afr. J4 66
Good Hope Mountain, mtn.,
   B.C., Can. D5 99
Goodhue, co., Mn., U.S. . . F6 130
Gooding, Id., U.S. G4 119
Gooding, co., Id., U.S. . . . F4 119
Goodland, In., U.S. C3 121
Goodland, Ks., U.S. C2 123
Goodlettsville, Tn., U.S. . . . g10 149
Goodman, Ms., U.S. C4 131
Goodman, Wi., U.S. C5 156
Goodnews Bay, Ak., U.S. . . D7 109
Goodsprings, Al., U.S. . . . B2 108
Goodsprings, Nv., U.S. . . . H6 135
Goodview, Mn., U.S. F7 130
Goodwater, Al., U.S. B3 108
Goodwell, Ok., U.S. e9 143
Goodyear, Az., U.S. D3 110
Goombalie, Austl. G6 70
Goondiwindi, Austl. G9 70
Goose Bay, b., Newf., Can. B10 102
Goose Creek, S.C., U.S. . . F7 147
Goose Lake, l., U.S. B3 112
Göppingen, Ger. G9 10
Gorakhpur, India G10 44
Goražde, Bos. F2 20
Gorbatovka, Russia E26 22
Gordo, Al., U.S. B2 108
Gordon, Al., U.S. D4 108
Gordon, Ga., U.S. D3 117
Gordon, Ne., U.S. B3 134
Gordon, co., Ga., U.S. . . . B2 117
Gordonsville, Tn., U.S. . . . C8 149
Gordonsville, Va., U.S. . . . B4 153
Gordonvale, Austl. A6 70
Gore, Eth. M8 60
Gore, N.Z. G2 72
Gore Bay, Ont., Can. B2 103
Gorgān, Iran C13 48
Gorgona, Eth. K9 60
Gorham, Me., U.S. E2 126
Gorham, N.H., U.S. B4 136
Gori, Geor. I6 26
Gorinchem, Neth. E7 12
Gorizia, Italy D8 18
Gor'kovskoje
   vodochranilišče, res.,
   Russia D26 22
Gorky see Nižnij Novgorod,
   Russia E27 22
Gorlice, Pol. F21 10
Görlitz, Ger. D14 10
Gorn'ackij, Russia D10 26
Gornji Milanovac, Yugo. . . E4 20
Gorno-Altajsk, Russia G9 28
Gornozavodsk, Russia . . . E25 22
Gorochovec, Russia E26 22
Gorodec, Russia D26 22
Gorodeja, Bela. H9 22
Gorodišče, Bela. H8 22
Gorodok, Bela. F12 22
Goroka, Pap. N. Gui. G12 38
Gorontalo, Indon. E7 38
Goršečnoje, Russia I21 22
Górowo Iławeckie
   (Landsberg an der
   Warthe), Pol. I9 10
Gosford, Austl. I6 70
Goshabi, Sud. A6 121
Goshen, In., U.S. D6 136
Goshen, N.Y., U.S. D6 139
Goshen, Ut., U.S. D5 157
Goshen, co., Wy., U.S. . . . D8 157
Gosnell, Ar., U.S. B6 111
Gosper, co., Ne., U.S. . . . D6 134
Gosport, In., U.S. F4 121
Gossas, Sen. D1 64
Gossi, Mali D9 64
Gossville, N.H., U.S. D4 136
Gostivar, Mac. H4 20
Gostyń, Pol. D17 10
Gostynin, Pol. C19 10
Göta älv, stm., Swe. M13 6
Göteborg (Gothenburg),
   Swe. M12 6
Gotemba, Japan L13 36
Gotha, Ger. E10 10
Gothenburg see Göteborg,
   Swe. M12 6
Gothenburg, Ne., U.S. . . . D5 134
Göttingen, Ger. D9 10
Gouda, Neth. D6 12
Goudge, Arg. H4 80
Gough Island, i., St. Hel. . . M6 52
Gouin, Réservoir, res.,
   Que., Can. k12 104
Goulburn, Austl. J8 70
Goulburn Islands, is., Austl. B6 68
Gould, Ar., U.S. C4 111
Goulding, Fl., U.S. u14 116
Goulds, Fl., U.S. s13 116
Goulimime, Mor. F5 62
Goundam, Mali D7 64
Gourdon, Fr. H8 14
Gouré, Niger E15 64
Gourin, Fr. D3 14
Gourma Rharous, Mali . . . C9 64
Gournay-en-Bray, Fr. C8 14
Gouverneur, N.Y., U.S. . . . f9 139
Govan, Sask., Can. F3 105
Gove, co., Ks., U.S. D3 123
Governador Valadares,
   Braz. E8 79
Governor's Harbour, Bah. . B6 94
Govind Ballabh Pant Sāgar,
   res., India H10 44
Gowanda, N.Y., U.S. C2 139
Gower, Mo., U.S. B3 132
Gowrie, Ia., U.S. B3 122
Goya, Arg. E9 80
Göyçay, Azer. I7 26
Gozo see Ghawdex, i.,
   Malta M9 18
Graaff-Reinet, S. Afr. I7 66
Grabill, In., U.S. B8 121
Gračanica, Bos. E2 20
Grace, Id., U.S. G7 119
Graceville, Fl., U.S. u16 116
Graceville, Ga., U.S. C4 117
Gracewood, Ga., U.S. . . . C4 117
Gracias, Hond. C6 92
Gracias a Dios, dept.,
   Hond. B10 92
Gracias a Dios, Cabo, c.,
   N.A. B11 92
Gradačac, Bos. E2 20
Grady, Ar., U.S. C4 111
Grady, co., Ga., U.S. F2 117
Grady, co., Ok., U.S. C4 143
Graettinger, Ia., U.S. A3 122
Grafton, Austl. G10 70
Grafton, Ont., Can. D6 103
Grafton, Il., U.S. E3 120
Grafton, N.D., U.S. A8 141
Grafton, Oh., U.S. A3 142
Grafton, Vt., U.S. E3 152
Grafton, W.V., U.S. h15 153
Grafton, Wi., U.S. E6 156
Grafton, co., N.H., U.S. . . . C3 136
Graham, N.C., U.S. A3 140
Graham, Tx., U.S. C3 150
Graham, co., Az., U.S. . . . E5 110
Graham, co., Ks., U.S. . . . C4 123
Graham, co., N.C., U.S. . . f9 140
Graham, Mount, mtn., Az.,
   U.S. E6 110
Graham Island, i., B.C.,
   Can. C1 99
Graham Lake, l., Me., U.S. . D4 126
Graham Land, reg., Ant. . . B12 73
Grahamstown, S. Afr. I8 66
Grahn, Ky., U.S. B6 124
Grainger, co., Tn., U.S. . . . C10 149
Grain Valley, Mo., U.S. . . . B3 132
Grajaú, Braz. E9 76
Grajewo, Pol. B22 10
Gramado, Braz. E13 80
Gramalote, Col. D6 84
Grambling, La., U.S. B3 125
Gramercy, La., U.S. h10 125
Grammichele, Italy L9 18
Grampian Mountains, mts.,
   Scot., U.K. E9 8
Granada, Nic. F9 92
Granada, Spain H8 16
Granada, dept., Nic. F8 92
Granada, Co., U.S. C4 150
Granbury, Que., Can. D5 104
Granby, Co., U.S. A5 113
Granby, Ct., U.S. B4 114
Granby, Mo., U.S. E3 132
Granby, Lake, res., Co.,
   U.S. A5 113
Gran Canaria, i., Spain . . . o25 17b
Gran Chaco, pl., S.A. A4 113
Grand, co., Co., U.S. A4 113
Grand, co., Ut., U.S. E6 151
Grand, stm., Ont., Can. . . . D4 103
Grand, stm., Mi., U.S. F5 129
Grand, stm., Mo., U.S. . . . A3 132
Grand, stm., S.D., U.S. . . . B4 148
Grand Bahama, i., Bah. . . . A5 94
Grand Bank, Newf., Can. . . E4 102
Grand Banks of
   Newfoundland E14 86
Grand-Bassam, C. Iv. I8 64
Grand Bay, N.B., Can. . . . D3 101
Grand Bay, Al., U.S. E1 108
Grand Bend, Ont., Can. . . D3 103
Grand Blanc, Mi., U.S. . . . F7 129
Grand Caillou, La., U.S. . . E5 125
Grand Canal see Da Yunhe,
   China E10 30
Grand Canal, Ire. H6 8
Grand Canyon, Az., U.S. . . A3 110
Grand Canyon, val., Az.,
   U.S. A3 110

Name	Map Ref.	Page
Grand Canyon National Park, Az., U.S.	B3	110
Grand Cayman, i., Cay. Is.	E4	94
Grand Centre, Alta., Can.	B5	98
Grand Coteau, La., U.S.	D3	125
Grand Coulee, Wa., U.S.	B6	154
Grand Coulee Dam, Wa., U.S.	B6	154
Grand-Couronne, Fr.	C8	14
Grande, stm., Bol.	G9	82
Grande, stm., Braz.	E3	79
Grande, Bahía, Arg.	G3	78
Grande, Rio (Bravo del Norte), stm., N.A.	F7	106
Grande-Anse, N.B., Can.	B4	101
Grande Cache, Alta., Can.	C1	98
Grande de Matagalpa, stm., Nic.	D11	92
Grande de Santiago, stm., Mex.	G7	90
Grande de Tarija, stm., S.A.	J9	82
Grande de Térraba, stm., C.R.	I11	92
Grande-Digue, N.B., Can.	C5	101
Grande do Gurupá, Ilha, i., Braz.	D8	76
Grande Prairie, Alta., Can.	B1	98
Grand Erg de Bilma, des., Niger	E9	54
Grand Erg Occidental, des., Alg.	E11	62
Grand Erg Oriental, des., Alg.	E14	62
Grande rivière de la Baleine, stm., Que., Can.	g11	104
Grande Ronde, stm., U.S.	C8	154
Grandes, Salinas, pl., Arg.	F6	80
Grand-Étang, N.S., Can.	C8	101
Grande-Terre, i., Guad.	F14	94
Grand Falls (Grand-Sault), N.B., Can.	B2	101
Grand Falls, wtfl, Me., U.S.	C5	126
Grand Falls [-Windsor], Newf., Can.	D4	102
Grandfather Mountain, mtn., N.C., U.S.	A1	140
Grandfield, Ok., U.S.	C3	143
Grand Forks, B.C., Can.	E8	99
Grand Forks, N.D., U.S.	B8	141
Grand Forks, co., N.D., U.S.	B8	141
Grand Harbour, N.B., Can.	E3	101
Grand Haven, Mi., U.S.	E4	129
Grand Island, Ne., U.S.	D7	134
Grand Island, i., Mi., U.S.	B4	129
Grand Isle, La., U.S.	E6	125
Grand Isle, Me., U.S.	A4	126
Grand Isle, Vt., U.S.	B2	152
Grand Isle, co., Vt., U.S.	B2	152
Grand Isle, i., La., U.S.	E6	125
Grand Junction, Co., U.S.	B2	113
Grand Junction, Ia., U.S.	B3	122
Grand Lake, Co., U.S.	A5	113
Grand Lake, l., N.B., Can.	D3	101
Grand Lake, l., Newf., Can.	D3	102
Grand Lake, l., La., U.S.	E3	125
Grand Lake, l., La., U.S.	E6	125
Grand Lake, l., Oh., U.S.	B1	142
Grand Ledge, Mi., U.S.	F6	129
Grand Manan Island, i., N.B., Can.	E3	101
Grand Marais, Mn., U.S.	k9	130
Grand Meadow, Mn., U.S.	G6	130
Grand-Mère, Que., Can.	C5	104
Grand-Popo, Benin	H10	64
Grand Portage, Mn., U.S.	k10	130
Grand Portage Indian Reservation, Mn., U.S.	k10	130
Grand Portage National Monument, Mn., U.S.	h10	130
Grand Prairie, Tx., U.S.	n10	150
Grand Pré, N.S., Can.	D5	101
Grand Rapids, Mi., U.S.	F5	129
Grand Rapids, Mn., U.S.	C5	130
Grand-Saint-Bernard, Col du, Eur.	G7	13
Grand-Saint-Bernard, Tunnel du, Eur.	G14	14
Grand Teton, mtn., Wy., U.S.	C2	157
Grand Teton National Park, Wy., U.S.	C2	157
Grand Traverse, co., Mi., U.S.	D5	129
Grand Traverse Bay, b., Mi., U.S.	C5	129
Grand Turk, T./C. Is.	D9	94
Grand Valley, Ont., Can.	D4	103
Grandview, Man., Can.	D1	100
Grand View, Id., U.S.	G2	119
Grandview, In., U.S.	I4	121
Grandview, Mo., U.S.	C3	132
Grandview, Wa., U.S.	C6	154
Grandview Heights, Oh., U.S.	m10	142
Grandville, Mi., U.S.	F5	129
Grand Wash Cliffs, clf, Az., U.S.	B2	110
Granger, In., U.S.	A5	121
Granger, Wa., U.S.	C5	154
Granger, Wy., U.S.	E3	157
Grangeville, Id., U.S.	D2	119
Granisle, B.C., Can.	B4	99
Granite, Ok., U.S.	C2	143
Granite, co., Mt., U.S.	D3	133
Granite City, Il., U.S.	E3	120
Granite Falls, Mn., U.S.	F3	130
Granite Falls, N.C., U.S.	B1	140
Granite Falls, Wa., U.S.	A4	154
Granite Lake, res., Newf., Can.	D3	102
Granite Pass, Wy., U.S.	B5	157
Granite Peak, mtn., Mt., U.S.	E7	133
Granite Peak, mtn., Nv., U.S.	B4	135
Granite Quarry, N.C., U.S.	B2	140
Graniteville, S.C., U.S.	D4	147
Graniteville, Vt., U.S.	C4	152
Grannis, Ar., U.S.	C1	111
Granollers, Spain	D14	16
Gran Paradiso, mtn., Italy	D2	18
Gran Sasso d'Italia, mts., Italy	G8	18
Grant, Al., U.S.	A3	108
Grant, Ne., U.S.	D4	134
Grant, co., Ar., U.S.	C3	111
Grant, co., In., U.S.	D6	121
Grant, co., Ks., U.S.	E2	123
Grant, co., Ky., U.S.	B5	124
Grant, co., La., U.S.	C3	125
Grant, co., Mn., U.S.	E2	130
Grant, co., Ne., U.S.	C4	134
Grant, co., N.M., U.S.	E1	138
Grant, co., N.D., U.S.	C4	141
Grant, co., Ok., U.S.	A4	143
Grant, co., Or., U.S.	C7	144
Grant, co., S.D., U.S.	B8	148
Grant, co., Wa., U.S.	B6	154
Grant, co., W.V., U.S.	B5	155
Grant, co., Wi., U.S.	F3	156
Grant, Mount, mtn., Nv., U.S.	E3	135
Grant City, Mo., U.S.	A3	132
Grant Park, Il., U.S.	B6	120
Grants, N.M., U.S.	B2	138
Grantsburg, Wi., U.S.	C1	156
Grants Pass, Or., U.S.	E3	144
Grantsville, Ut., U.S.	C3	151
Grantsville, W.V., U.S.	C3	155
Grant Town, W.V., U.S.	B4	155
Grantville, Ga., U.S.	C2	117
Granum, Alta., Can.	E4	98
Granville, Fr.	D5	14
Granville, Il., U.S.	B4	120
Granville, N.Y., U.S.	B7	139
Granville, N.D., U.S.	A5	141
Granville, Oh., U.S.	B3	142
Granville, W.V., U.S.	h11	155
Granville, co., N.C., U.S.	A4	140
Granville Ferry, N.S., Can.	E4	101
Granville Lake, l., Man., Can.	A1	100
Grapeview, Wa., U.S.	B3	154
Grapevine, Tx., U.S.	C4	150
Grasonville, Md., U.S.	C5	127
Grass, stm., N.Y., U.S.	f9	139
Grasse, Fr.	I13	14
Grass Lake, Il., U.S.	h8	120
Grass Valley, Ca., U.S.	C3	112
Grassy Lake, Alta., Can.	E5	98
Grates Point, c., Newf., Can.	D5	102
Gratiot, co., Mi., U.S.	E6	129
Gravatá, Braz.	E11	76
Gravelines, Fr.	B9	14
Gravel Ridge, Ar., U.S.	h10	111
Gravenhurst, Ont., Can.	C5	103
Graves, co., Ky., U.S.	f9	124
Gravette, Ar., U.S.	A1	111
Gravina in Puglia, Italy	I11	18
Gray, Fr.	E12	14
Gray, Ga., U.S.	C3	117
Gray, Ky., U.S.	D5	124
Gray, La., U.S.	k10	125
Gray, Me., U.S.	g7	126
Gray, co., Ks., U.S.	E3	123
Gray, co., Tx., U.S.	B2	150
Grayland, Wa., U.S.	C1	154
Grayling, Mi., U.S.	D6	129
Graylyn Crest, De., U.S.	A3	115
Grays Harbor, co., Wa., U.S.	B2	154
Grays Harbor, b., Wa., U.S.	C1	154
Grayslake, Il., U.S.	A5	120
Grayson, Sask., Can.	G4	105
Grayson, Ky., U.S.	B7	124
Grayson, co., Ky., U.S.	C3	124
Grayson, co., Tx., U.S.	C4	150
Grayson, co., Va., U.S.	D1	153
Grays Peak, mtn., Co., U.S.	B5	113
Gray Summit, Mo., U.S.	g12	132
Graysville, Al., U.S.	f7	108
Graysville, Tn., U.S.	D8	149
Grayville, Il., U.S.	E5	120
Graz, Aus.	H15	10
Gr'azi, Russia	I22	22
Gr'azovec, Russia	C23	22
Greasewood, Az., U.S.	B6	110
Great Artesian Basin, Austl.	E5	70
Great Barrier Island, i., N.Z.	B5	72
Great Barrier Reef, rf., Austl.	C9	68
Great Barrington, Ma., U.S.	B1	128
Great Basin, U.S.	C3	106
Great Basin National Park, Nv., U.S.	E7	135
Great Bay, b., N.J., U.S.	D4	137
Great Bear Lake, l., N.W. Ter., Can.	C8	96
Great Bend, Ks., U.S.	D5	123
Great Britain, i., U.K.	E7	4
Great Cacapon, W.V., U.S.	B6	155
Great Channel, strt., Asia	K3	40
Great Dismal Swamp, sw., U.S.	D6	153
Great Divide Basin, Wy., U.S.	E4	157
Great Dividing Range, mts., Austl.	E9	68
Great Egg Harbor, stm., N.J., U.S.	D3	137
Greater Antilles, is., N.A.	D7	94
Greater Sunda Islands, is., Asia	F5	38
Great Exuma, i., Bah.	C7	94
Great Falls, Mt., U.S.	C5	133
Great Falls, S.C., U.S.	B6	147
Great Falls, wtfl, Md., U.S.	B3	127
Great Inagua, i., Bah.	D8	94
Great Indian Desert (Thar Desert), des., Asia	G4	44
Great Karroo, plat., S. Afr.	I6	66
Great Lakes Naval Training Center, mil., Il., U.S.	h9	120
Great Miami, stm., U.S.	C1	142
Great Neck, N.Y., U.S.	h13	139
Great Nicobar, i., India	K2	40
Great Pee Dee, stm., U.S.	D9	147
Great Plains, pl., N.A.	E9	86
Great Point, c., Ma., U.S.	D7	128
Great Ruaha, stm., Tan.	C7	58
Great Sacandaga Lake, l., N.Y., U.S.	C6	139
Great Saint Bernard Pass see Grand-Saint-Bernard, Col du, Eur.	G7	13
Great Salt Lake, l., Ut., U.S.	B3	151
Great Salt Lake Desert, des., Ut., U.S.	C2	151
Great Salt Plains Lake, res., Ok., U.S.	A3	143
Great Sand Dunes National Monument, Co., U.S.	D5	113
Great Sandy Desert, des., Austl.	D4	68
Great Slave Lake, l., N.W. Ter., Can.	D10	96
Great Smoky Mountains, mts., U.S.	B8	149
Great Smoky Mountains National Park, U.S.	B8	149
Great Valley, val., U.S.	C2	153
Great Victoria Desert, des., Austl.	E5	68
Great Village, N.S., Can.	D6	101
Great Wall see Chang Cheng, hist., China	C4	32
Great Yarmouth, Eng., U.K.	I15	8
Great Zab (Büyükzap) (Az-Zāb al-Kabīr), stm., Asia	C7	48
Grecia, C.R.	G10	92
Greece, N.Y., U.S.	B3	139
Greece (Ellás), ctry., Eur.	H12	4
Greeley, Co., U.S.	A6	113
Greeley, Ne., U.S.	C7	134
Greeley, co., Ks., U.S.	D2	123
Greeley, co., Ne., U.S.	C7	134
Green, Or., U.S.	D3	144
Green, co., Ky., U.S.	C4	124
Green, co., Wi., U.S.	F4	156
Green, stm., U.S.	D5	106
Green, stm., U.S.	A11	143
Green, stm., U.S.	F3	152
Green, stm., Il., U.S.	B4	120
Green, stm., Ky., U.S.	C2	124
Green Acres, De., U.S.	h8	115
Greenacres, Wa., U.S.	B8	154
Greenacres City, Fl., U.S.	F6	116
Greenback, Tn., U.S.	D9	149
Green Bay, Wi., U.S.	D6	156
Green Bay, b., U.S.	D3	129
Greenbelt, Md., U.S.	C4	127
Greenbriar, Va., U.S.	g12	153
Greenbrier, Ar., U.S.	B3	111
Green Brier, Tn., U.S.	A5	149
Greenbrier, co., W.V., U.S.	D4	155
Greenbrier, stm., W.V., U.S.	D4	155
Greenbush, Mn., U.S.	B2	130
Greencastle, In., U.S.	E4	121
Greencastle, Pa., U.S.	G6	145
Green City, Mo., U.S.	A5	132
Green Cove Springs, Fl., U.S.	C5	116
Greendale, In., U.S.	F8	121
Greendale, Wi., U.S.	F6	156
Greene, Ia., U.S.	B5	122
Greene, Me., U.S.	D2	126
Greene, co., Al., U.S.	C1	108
Greene, co., Ar., U.S.	A5	111
Greene, co., Ga., U.S.	C3	117
Greene, co., Il., U.S.	D3	120
Greene, co., In., U.S.	F4	121
Greene, co., Ia., U.S.	B3	122
Greene, co., Ms., U.S.	D5	131
Greene, co., Mo., U.S.	D4	132
Greene, co., N.Y., U.S.	C6	139
Greene, co., N.C., U.S.	B5	140
Greene, co., Oh., U.S.	C2	142
Greene, co., Pa., U.S.	G1	145
Greene, co., Tn., U.S.	C11	149
Greene, co., Va., U.S.	B4	153
Greeneville, Tn., U.S.	C11	149
Greenfield, Ca., U.S.	D3	112
Greenfield, In., U.S.	E6	121
Greenfield, Ia., U.S.	C3	122
Greenfield, Ma., U.S.	A2	128
Greenfield, Mo., U.S.	D4	132
Greenfield, N.H., U.S.	E3	136
Greenfield, Oh., U.S.	C2	142
Greenfield, Tn., U.S.	A3	149
Greenfield, Wi., U.S.	n12	156
Greenfield Plaza, Ia., U.S.	e8	122
Green Forest, Ar., U.S.	A2	111
Green Harbor, Ma., U.S.	B6	128
Greenhill, Al., U.S.	A2	108
Greenhills, Oh., U.S.	n12	142
Green Lake, Sask., Can.	D2	105
Green Lake, Wi., U.S.	E5	156
Green Lake, co., Wi., U.S.	E4	156
Greenland, Ar., U.S.	B1	111
Greenland, N.H., U.S.	D5	136
Greenland (Kalaallit Nunaat), dep., N.A.	B15	86
Greenland Sea	B20	86
Greenlee, co., Az., U.S.	D6	110
Green Mountains, mts., Vt., U.S.	F2	152
Greenock, Pa., U.S.	F2	145
Green Peter Lake, res., Or., U.S.	C4	144
Green Pond, Al., U.S.	B2	108
Green River, Ut., U.S.	E5	151
Green River, Wy., U.S.	E3	157
Green River Lake, res., Ky., U.S.	C4	124
Green River Reservoir, res., Vt., U.S.	B3	152
Green Rock, Il., U.S.	B3	120
Greensboro, Al., U.S.	C2	108
Greensboro, Ga., U.S.	C3	117
Greensboro, Md., U.S.	C6	127
Greensboro, N.C., U.S.	A3	140
Greensburg, In., U.S.	F7	121
Greensburg, Ks., U.S.	E4	123
Greensburg, Ky., U.S.	C4	124
Greensburg, Pa., U.S.	F2	145
Greensville, co., Va., U.S.	D5	153
Greentown, In., U.S.	D6	121
Greenup, Il., U.S.	D5	120
Greenup, Ky., U.S.	B7	124
Greenup, co., Ky., U.S.	B7	124
Greenvale, Austl.	B6	70
Green Valley, Az., U.S.	F5	110
Greenville, Lib.	I5	64
Greenville, Al., U.S.	D3	108
Greenville, Ca., U.S.	B3	112
Greenville, De., U.S.	A3	115
Greenville, Il., U.S.	E4	120
Greenville, Ky., U.S.	C2	124
Greenville, Me., U.S.	C3	126
Greenville, Mi., U.S.	E5	129
Greenville, Ms., U.S.	B2	131
Greenville, N.H., U.S.	E3	136
Greenville, N.C., U.S.	B5	140
Greenville, Oh., U.S.	B1	142
Greenville, Pa., U.S.	D1	145
Greenville, R.I., U.S.	C3	146
Greenville, S.C., U.S.	B3	147
Greenville, Tx., U.S.	C4	150
Greenville, co., S.C., U.S.	B3	147
Greenville Junction, Me., U.S.	C3	126
Greenwich, Ct., U.S.	E1	114
Greenwood, B.C., Can.	E8	99
Greenwood, De., U.S.	B1	111
Greenwood, In., U.S.	E5	121
Greenwood, La., U.S.	B2	125
Greenwood, Ms., U.S.	B3	131
Greenwood, Mo., U.S.	k11	132
Greenwood, Ne., U.S.	D9	134
Greenwood, S.C., U.S.	C3	147
Greenwood, Wi., U.S.	D3	156
Greenwood, co., Ks., U.S.	E7	123
Greenwood, co., S.C., U.S.	C3	147
Greenwood, Lake, res., S.C., U.S.	C4	147
Greenwood Lake, N.Y., U.S.	D6	139
Greer, S.C., U.S.	B3	147
Greer, co., Ok., U.S.	C2	143
Gu Achi, Az., U.S.	E3	110
Guachochi, Mex.	D6	90
Guaçuí, Braz.	F8	79
Guadalajara, Mex.	G8	90
Guadalajara, Spain	E8	16
Guadalcanal, i., Sol.Is.	I20	158
Guadalquivir, stm., Spain	H6	16
Guadalupe, C.R.	H10	92
Guadalupe, Mex.	E9	90
Guadalupe, Peru	B2	82
Guadalupe, Az., U.S.	m9	110
Guadalupe, Ca., U.S.	E3	112
Guadalupe, co., N.M., U.S.	C5	138
Guadalupe, co., Tx., U.S.	E4	150
Guadalupe [Bravos], Mex.	B6	90
Guadalupe Mountains, mts., U.S.	o12	150
Guadalupe Mountains National Park, Tx., U.S.	o12	150
Guadalupe Peak, mtn., Tx., U.S.	o12	150
Guadalupe Victoria, Mex.	E7	90
Guadalupita, N.M., U.S.	A4	138
Guadeloupe, dep., N.A.	F14	94
Guadeloupe Passage, strt., N.A.	F14	94
Guadiana, stm., Eur.	H4	16
Guadix, Spain	H8	16
Guaíba, Braz.	F13	80
Guaíra, Braz.	F4	79
Guaíra, Braz.	C11	80
Guairá, dept., Para.	C10	80
Guajará-Mirim, Braz.	D9	82
Gualaca, Pan.	C1	84
Gualaceo, Ec.	I3	84
Gualán, Guat.	B5	92
Gualaquiza, Ec.	I3	84
Gualeguay, Arg.	G9	80
Gualeguay, stm., Arg.	G9	80
Gualeguaychú, Arg.	G9	80
Guam, dep., Oc.	F22	2
Guaminí, Arg.	I7	80
Guamúchil, Mex.	E5	90
Guanacaste, Cordillera de, mts., C.R.	G9	92
Guanaja, Isla de, i., Hond.	A9	92
Guanajay, Cuba	C3	94
Guanajuato, Mex.	G9	90
Guanajuato, state, Mex.	G9	90
Guanambi, Braz.	C7	79
Guanare, Ven.	C8	84
Guanbuqiao, China	F3	34
Guandacol, Arg.	E4	80
Guandanghu, China	E2	34
Guandian, China	C7	34
Guane, Cuba	C2	94
Guang'an, China	E8	30
Guangde, China	E8	34
Guangdong (Kwangtung), prov., China	G9	30
Guanghua, China	E9	30
Guangrao, China	D10	30
Guangxi Zhuangzu Zizhiqu (Kwangsi Chuang), prov., China	G8	30
Guangyuan, China	E8	30
Guangzhou (Canton), China	L2	34
Guanhães, Braz.	E7	79
Guano, Ec.	H3	84
Guantánamo, Cuba	D7	94
Guantao (Nanguantao), China	G3	32
Guanxian, China	E7	30
Guanzhuang, China	F2	32
Guapí, Col.	F4	84
Guapiara, Braz.	H4	79
Guápiles, C.R.	G11	92
Guaporé, Braz.	E13	80
Guaporé (Itenes), stm., S.A.	E10	82
Guaqui, Bol.	G7	82
Guarabira, Braz.	E11	76
Guaraçaí, Braz.	F3	79
Guaraci, Braz.	F4	79
Guaranda, Ec.	H3	84
Guaraniaçu, Braz.	B12	80
Guarani das Missões, Braz.	B11	80
Guarapari, Braz.	F8	79
Guarapuava, Braz.	B13	80
Guararé, Pan.	D2	84
Guaratinguetá, Braz.	G6	79
Guaratuba, Braz.	C14	80
Guarico, state, Ven.	C9	84
Guárico, Embalse del, res., Ven.	C9	84
Guarulhos, Braz.	G5	79
Guasave, Mex.	E5	90
Guasdualito, Ven.	D7	84
Guasipati, Ven.	D12	84
Guastalla, Italy	E5	18
Guatemala, Guat.	C4	92
Guatemala, dept., Guat.	C4	92
Guatemala, ctry., N.A.	E6	88
Guateque, Col.	E6	84
Guatimozín, Arg.	G7	80
Guatraché, Arg.	I7	80
Guaviare, ter., Col.	F6	84
Guaviare, stm., Col.	F8	84
Guaxupé, Braz.	F5	79
Guayama, P.R.	F11	94
Guayaquil, Ec.	I3	84
Guayaquil, Golfo de, b., S.A.	I2	84
Guayaramerín, Bol.	D9	82
Guayas, prov., Ec.	H2	84
Guayas, stm., Ec.	I3	84
Guaymas, Mex.	D4	90
Guazacapán, Guat.	C4	92
Gubacha, Russia	F9	26
Gubbio, Italy	F7	18
Guben, Ger.	D14	10
Gubin, Pol.	D14	10
Gubkin, Russia	G5	26
Gudermes, Russia	I7	26
Gudiváda, India	F5	46
Gudivättam, India	F5	46
Guebwiller, Fr.	E14	14
Guelph, Ont., Can.	D4	103
Guérande, Fr.	E4	14
Guercif, Mor.	C9	62
Guéret, Fr.	F8	14
Guernsey, Sask., Can.	F3	105
Guernsey, Wy., U.S.	D8	157
Guernsey, co., Oh., U.S.	B4	142
Guernsey, dep., Eur.	F7	4
Guerrero, Mex.	C6	90
Guerrero, state, Mex.	I9	90
Guessou-Sud, Benin	F11	64
Guia Lopes da Laguna, Braz.	I13	82
Guibes, Nmb.	F3	66
Guichón, Ur.	G10	80
Guidan Roumji, Niger	E13	64
Guidimouni, Niger	E14	64
Guiding, China	A9	40
Guiglo, C. Iv.	H6	64
Guild, N.H., U.S.	D2	136
Guildford, Eng., U.K.	J13	8
Guilford, Ct., U.S.	D5	114
Guilford, co., N.C., U.S.	A3	140
Guilin (Kweilin), China	B11	40
Guimarães, Port.	D3	16
Guin, Al., U.S.	B2	108
Guinea (Guinée), ctry., Afr.	F4	54
Guinea, Gulf of, b., Afr.	H7	52
Guinea-Bissau (Guiné-Bissau), ctry., Afr.	F3	54
Güines, Cuba	C3	94
Guînes, Fr.	B8	14
Guingamp, Fr.	D3	14
Guiping, China	C11	40
Güira de Melena, Cuba	C3	94
Guiratinga, Braz.	D2	79
Güiria, Ven.	B11	84
Guixi, China	G6	34
Guixian, China	C10	40
Guiyang (Kweiyang), China	A9	40
Guizhou (Kweichow), prov., China	F8	30
Gujarāt, state, India	I4	44
Gujrānwāla, Pak.	D6	44
Gujrāt, Pak.	D6	44
Gulbarga, India	D4	46
Gulbene, Lat.	D9	22
Gulf, co., Fl., U.S.	C1	116
Gulf Gate Estates, Fl., U.S.	E4	116
Gulf Islands National Seashore, U.S.	E5	131
Gulfport, Fl., U.S.	E4	116
Gulfport, Ms., U.S.	E4	131
Gulf Shores, Al., U.S.	E2	108
Gulgong, Austl.	I8	70
Gulistan, Uzb.	I11	26
Gull Lake, Sask., Can.	G1	105
Gull Lake, l., Alta., Can.	C4	98
Gumare, Bots.	B6	66
Gummersbach, Ger.	D7	10
Gummi, Nig.	E12	64
Gümüşhane, Tur.	A5	48
Guna, India	H7	44
Gundagai, Austl.	J8	70
Gungu, Zaire	C3	58
Gunisao, stm., Man., Can.	C3	100
Gunnbjørn Fjeld, mtn., Grnld.	C17	86
Gunnedah, Austl.	H9	70
Gunnison, Co., U.S.	C4	113
Gunnison, Ut., U.S.	D4	151
Gunnison, co., Co., U.S.	C3	113
Gunnison, stm., Co., U.S.	C2	113
Gunpowder Neck, c., Md., U.S.	B5	127
Gunpowder River, b., Md., U.S.	B5	127
Guntakal, India	E4	46
Guntersville, Al., U.S.	A3	108
Guntersville Lake, res., Al., U.S.	A3	108
Gunton, Man., Can.	D3	100
Guntown, Ms., U.S.	A5	131
Guntūr, India	D6	46
Gunungsitoli, Indon.	N4	40
Gupei, China	I5	32
Gurdon, Ar., U.S.	D2	111
Guri, Embalse de, res., Ven.	D11	84
Gurjevsk, Russia	G13	22
Gurjevsk, Russia	G3	22
Gurley, Al., U.S.	A3	108
Gurnee, Il., U.S.	A6	120
Gurupá, Braz.	D8	76
Gurupi, Braz.	B4	79
Gusau, Nig.	E13	64
Gus'-Chrustal'nyj, Russia	F23	22
Gusev, Russia	G5	22
Gusevskij, Russia	F23	22
Gushanzi, China	C8	32
Gushi, China	C4	34
Gushikawa, Japan	u2	37b
Gusinoozersk, Russia	G13	28
Gustavus, Ak., U.S.	D12	109
Güstrow, Ger.	B12	10
Gütersloh, Ger.	D8	10
Guthrie, Ky., U.S.	D2	124

Name	Map Ref.	Page
Guthrie, Ok., U.S.	B4	143
Guthrie, W.V., U.S.	m12	155
Guthrie, co., Ia., U.S.	C3	122
Guthrie Center, Ia., U.S.	C3	122
Gutian, China	I7	34
Gutiérrez Zamora, Mex.	G11	90
Guttenberg, Ia., U.S.	B6	122
Guttenberg, N.J., U.S.	h8	137
Gutu, Zimb.	B10	66
Guwāhāti, India	G14	44
Guyana, ctry., S.A.	B7	76
Guyandotte, stm., W.V., U.S.	C2	155
Guymon, Ok., U.S.	e9	143
Guyot, Mount, mtn., U.S.	D10	149
Guysborough, N.S., Can.	D8	101
Guyton, Ga., U.S.	D5	117
Gvardejsk, Russia	G4	22
Gwa, Mya.	F3	40
Gwadabawa, Nig.	E12	64
Gwādar, Pak.	I17	48
Gwai, Zimb.	B8	66
Gwalior, India	G8	44
Gwanda, Zimb.	C9	66
Gwardafuy, Gees, c., Som.	F11	56
Gweru, Zimb.	B9	66
Gweta, Bots.	C7	66
Gwinhurst, De., U.S.	h8	115
Gwinn, Mi., U.S.	B3	129
Gwinner, N.D., U.S.	C8	141
Gwinnett, co., Ga., U.S.	C2	117
Gydanskaja guba, b., Russia	C13	26
Gyirong, China	F11	44
Gympie, Austl.	F10	70
Gyobingauk, Mya.	E3	40
Gyöngyös, Hung.	H19	10
Győr, Hung.	H17	10
Gypsum, Co., U.S.	B4	113
Gypsumville, Man., Can.	D2	100
Gyula, Hung.	I21	10
H		
Haakon, co., S.D., U.S.	C4	148
Haaltert, Bel.	G5	12
Haapajärvi, Fin.	J19	6
Haapamäki, Fin.	J19	6
Haapsalu, Est.	C6	22
Ha'Arava (Wādī al-Jayb), val., Asia	H4	50
Haarlem, Neth.	D6	12
Habbān, Yemen	G5	47
Habermehl Peak, mtn., Ant.	C3	73
Habersham, co., Ga., U.S.	B3	117
Habiganj, Bngl.	H14	44
Hachinohe, Japan	G16	36
Hachiōji, Japan	L14	36
Hacienda Miravalles, C.R.	G9	92
Hackensack, N.J., U.S.	B4	137
Hackett, Ar., U.S.	B1	111
Hackettstown, N.J., U.S.	B3	137
Hackleburg, Al., U.S.	A2	108
Hadalīya, Sud.	I9	60
Haddam, Ct., U.S.	D5	114
Haddock, Ga., U.S.	C3	117
Haddonfield, N.J., U.S.	D2	137
Haddon Heights, N.J., U.S.	D2	137
Hadejia, Nig.	E14	64
Hadera, Isr.	D3	50
Hadlock, Wa., U.S.	A3	154
Ha Dong, Viet.	D8	40
Hadramawt, reg., Yemen	G6	47
Haeju, N. Kor.	E13	32
Haenam, S. Kor.	I14	32
Hafford, Sask., Can.	E2	105
Hafnarfjördur, Ice.	B3	6a
Hafun, Ras, c., Som.	F11	56
Hagan, Ga., U.S.	D5	117
Hagen, Ger.	D7	10
Hagensborg, B.C., Can.	C4	99
Hagere Hiywet, Eth.	M9	60
Hagere Selam, Eth.	N10	60
Hagerman, Id., U.S.	G4	119
Hagerman, N.M., U.S.	D5	138
Hagerstown, In., U.S.	E7	121
Hagerstown, Md., U.S.	A2	127
Hagetmau, Fr.	I6	14
Haggin, Mount, mtn., Mt., U.S.	D3	133
Hagondange, Fr.	C13	14
Hague, Sask., Can.	E2	105
Hague, Cap de la, c., Fr.	C5	14
Haguenau, Fr.	D14	14
Hahira, Ga., U.S.	F3	117
Hahnville, La., U.S.	E5	125
Haicheng, China	C10	32
Hai Duong, Viet.	D9	40
Haifa see Hefa, Isr.	C4	50
Haifeng, China	M4	34
Haikang (Leizhou), China	D11	40
Haikou, China	D11	40
Haiku, Hi., U.S.	C5	118
Hā'il, Sau. Ar.	H6	48
Hailar, China	B10	30
Hailey, Id., U.S.	F4	119
Haileybury, Ont., Can.	p20	103
Haileyville, Ok., U.S.	C6	143
Hailong (Meihekou), China	A13	32
Hailun, China	B12	30
Haimen, China	L5	34
Haimen, China	G10	34
Hainan, prov., China	H8	30
Hainan Dao, i., China	E10	40
Hainaut, prov., Bel.	G4	12
Haines, Ak., U.S.	D12	109
Haines City, Fl., U.S.	D5	116
Haines Junction, Yukon, Can.	D5	96
Hai Phong, Viet.	D9	40
Haiti (Haïti), ctry., N.A.	E8	94
Haitou, China	I7	32
Haizhou, China	A8	34
Hajdúböszörmény, Hung.	H21	10
Hajdúnánás, Hung.	H21	10
Hājīpur, India	H11	44
Hajjah, Yemen	G3	47
Hajnówka, Pol.	C7	10
Hakodate, Japan	f15	36a
Halab (Aleppo), Syria	C4	48
Halachó, Mex.	G14	90
Halaula, Hi., U.S.	C6	118
Halawa, Cape, c., Hi., U.S.	B5	118
Halawa Heights, Hi., U.S.	g10	118
Halberstadt, Ger.	D11	10
Haldimand, Ont., Can.	E5	103
Haldwāni, India	F8	44
Hale, co., Al., U.S.	C2	108
Hale, co., Tx., U.S.	B2	150
Haleakala Crater, crat., Hi., U.S.	C5	118
Haleakala National Park, Hi., U.S.	C6	118
Haleiwa, Hi., U.S.	B3	118
Hales Corners, Wi., U.S.	n11	156
Halethorpe, Md., U.S.	B4	127
Haleyville, Al., U.S.	A2	108
Half Moon Bay, Ca., U.S.	k8	112
Halfway, Md., U.S.	A2	127
Haliburton, Ont., Can.	B6	103
Halifax, Austl.	B7	70
Halifax, N.S., Can.	E6	101
Halifax, Va., U.S.	D4	153
Halifax, co., N.C., U.S.	A5	140
Halifax, co., Va., U.S.	D4	153
Haliimaile, Hi., U.S.	C5	118
Hall, co., Ga., U.S.	B3	117
Hall, co., Ne., U.S.	D7	134
Hall, co., Tx., U.S.	B2	150
Hallam Peak, mtn., B.C., Can.	C8	99
Hallandale, Fl., U.S.	G6	116
Halla-san, mtn., S. Kor.	E12	30
Halle (Hal), Bel.	G5	12
Halle, Ger.	D11	10
Hallein, Aus.	H13	10
Halliday, N.D., U.S.	B3	141
Hallie, Wi., U.S.	D2	156
Hall in Tirol, Aus.	H11	10
Hallock, Mn., U.S.	B2	130
Hallowell, Me., U.S.	D3	126
Halls, Tn., U.S.	B2	149
Hallsberg, Swe.	L14	6
Halls Creek, Austl.	C5	68
Halls Crossroads, Tn., U.S.	m14	149
Hallstavik, Swe.	K16	6
Hallsville, Mo., U.S.	B5	132
Halmahera, i., Indon.	E8	38
Halmahera, Laut (Halmahera Sea), Indon.	F8	38
Halmstad, Swe.	M13	6
Halsey, Or., U.S.	C3	144
Halstead, Ks., U.S.	E6	123
Haltern, Ger.	D7	10
Haltiatunturi, mtn., Eur.	G17	6
Halton Hills, Ont., Can.	D5	103
Hamadān, Iran	D10	48
Hamah, Syria	D4	48
Hamamatsu, Japan	M12	36
Hamar, Nor.	K12	6
Hamblen, co., Tn., U.S.	C10	149
Hamburg, Ger.	B9	10
Hamburg, Ar., U.S.	D4	111
Hamburg, Ia., U.S.	D2	122
Hamburg, N.Y., U.S.	C2	139
Hamburg, Pa., U.S.	E10	145
Hamden, Ct., U.S.	D4	114
Häme, prov., Fin.	K19	6
Hämeenlinna, Fin.	K19	6
Hamel, Mn., U.S.	m11	130
Hameln, Ger.	C9	10
Hamersley Range, mts., Austl.	D3	68
Hamhŭng, N. Kor.	D15	32
Hami, China	C5	30
Hamilton, Austl.	K5	70
Hamilton, Ber.	B12	88
Hamilton, Ont., Can.	D5	103
Hamilton, N.Z.	B5	72
Hamilton, Scot., U.K.	F9	8
Hamilton, Al., U.S.	A2	108
Hamilton, Il., U.S.	C2	120
Hamilton, In., U.S.	A8	121
Hamilton, Ms., U.S.	B5	131
Hamilton, Mo., U.S.	B3	132
Hamilton, Mt., U.S.	D2	133
Hamilton, N.Y., U.S.	C5	139
Hamilton, Oh., U.S.	C1	142
Hamilton, Tx., U.S.	D3	150
Hamilton, Va., U.S.	A5	153
Hamilton, co., Fl., U.S.	B3	116
Hamilton, co., Il., U.S.	E5	120
Hamilton, co., In., U.S.	D5	121
Hamilton, co., Ia., U.S.	B4	122
Hamilton, co., Ks., U.S.	E2	123
Hamilton, co., Ne., U.S.	D7	134
Hamilton, co., N.Y., U.S.	B6	139
Hamilton, co., Oh., U.S.	C1	142
Hamilton, co., Tn., U.S.	D8	149
Hamilton, co., Tx., U.S.	D3	150
Hamilton, Mount, mtn., Nv., U.S.	D6	135
Hamilton Dome, Wy., U.S.	C4	157
Hamilton Hotel, Austl.	D4	70
Hamilton Sound, strt., Newf., Can.	D4	102
Hamilton Square, N.J., U.S.	C3	137
Hamina, Fin.	K20	6
Hamiota, Man., Can.	D1	100
Hamlet, In., U.S.	B4	121
Hamlet, N.C., U.S.	C3	140
Hamlin, W.V., U.S.	C2	155
Hamlin, Tx., U.S.	C2	150
Hamlin, co., S.D., U.S.	D7	148
Hamm, Ger.	D7	10
Hammamet, Alg.	N2	18
Hammamet, Tun.	M5	18
Hammamet, Golfe de, b., Tun.	M5	18
Hammam Lif, Tun.	M5	18
Hammār, Hawr al-, l., Iraq	F9	48
Hamme, Bel.	F5	12
Hammerfest, Nor.	F18	6
Hammond, In., U.S.	A2	121
Hammond, La., U.S.	D5	125
Hammond, Wi., U.S.	D1	156
Hammonton, N.J., U.S.	D3	137
Hampden, Newf., Can.	D3	102
Hampden, Me., U.S.	D4	126
Hampden, co., Ma., U.S.	B2	128
Hampden Highlands, Me., U.S.	D4	126
Hampshire, Il., U.S.	A5	120
Hampshire, co., Eng., U.K.	J12	8
Hampshire, co., Ma., U.S.	B2	128
Hampshire, co., W.V., U.S.	B6	155
Hampstead, Md., U.S.	A4	127
Hampstead, N.H., U.S.	E4	136
Hampton, N.B., Can.	D4	101
Hampton, Ar., U.S.	D3	111
Hampton, Ga., U.S.	C2	117
Hampton, Ia., U.S.	B4	122
Hampton, Ne., U.S.	D8	134
Hampton, N.H., U.S.	E5	136
Hampton, S.C., U.S.	F5	147
Hampton, Tn., U.S.	C11	149
Hampton, Va., U.S.	C6	153
Hampton, co., S.C., U.S.	F5	147
Hampton Bays, N.Y., U.S.	n16	139
Hampton Beach, N.H., U.S.	E5	136
Hampton Falls, N.H., U.S.	E5	136
Hamra, As Saquia al, val., W. Sah.	G4	62
Hams Fork, stm., Wy., U.S.	E2	157
Hamtramck, Mi., U.S.	p15	129
Hana, Hi., U.S.	C6	118
Hanahan, S.C., U.S.	F7	147
Hanalei, Hi., U.S.	A2	118
Hanamaki, Japan	H16	36
Hanamaulu, Hi., U.S.	B2	118
Hanapepe, Hi., U.S.	B2	118
Hanau, Ger.	E8	10
Hâncești, Mol.	C12	20
Hanceville, Al., U.S.	A3	108
Hancock, Me., U.S.	D4	126
Hancock, Md., U.S.	A1	127
Hancock, Mi., U.S.	A2	129
Hancock, Mn., U.S.	E3	130
Hancock, N.H., U.S.	E3	136
Hancock, co., Ga., U.S.	C3	117
Hancock, co., Il., U.S.	C2	120
Hancock, co., In., U.S.	E6	121
Hancock, co., Ia., U.S.	A4	122
Hancock, co., Ky., U.S.	C3	124
Hancock, co., Me., U.S.	D4	126
Hancock, co., Ms., U.S.	E4	131
Hancock, co., Oh., U.S.	A2	142
Hancock, co., Tn., U.S.	C10	149
Hancock, co., W.V., U.S.	A4	155
Hand, co., S.D., U.S.	C6	148
Handa, Japan	M11	36
Handan, China	G2	32
Handub, Sud.	H9	60
HaNegev (Negev Desert), reg., Isr.	G3	50
Hanford, Ca., U.S.	D4	112
Hangchow see Hangzhou, China	E9	34
Hanggin Houqi, China	C8	30
Hangö (Hanko), Fin.	L18	6
Hangu, China	D5	32
Hangzhou (Hangchow), China	E9	34
Hangzhou Wan (Hangchow Bay), b., China	E10	34
Hanjiang, China	J8	34
Hankey, S. Afr.	I7	66
Hankinson, N.D., U.S.	C9	141
Hanko see Hangö, Fin.	L18	6
Hankow see Wuhan, China	E3	34
Hanley, Sask., Can.	F2	105
Hanna, Alta., Can.	D5	98
Hanna, Wy., U.S.	E6	157
Hanna City, Il., U.S.	C4	120
Hannibal, Mo., U.S.	B6	132
Hannover, Ger.	C9	10
Ha Noi, Viet.	D8	40
Hanover, Ont., Can.	C3	103
Hanover, Il., U.S.	A3	120
Hanover, In., U.S.	G7	121
Hanover, Ks., U.S.	C7	123
Hanover, Ma., U.S.	D2	126
Hanover, Mn., U.S.	m11	130
Hanover, N.H., U.S.	C2	136
Hanover, N.M., U.S.	E1	138
Hanover, Pa., U.S.	G8	145
Hanover, co., Va., U.S.	C5	153
Hanover Park, Il., U.S.	k8	120
Hansen, Id., U.S.	G4	119
Hansford, co., Tx., U.S.	A2	150
Hanson, Ma., U.S.	B6	128
Hanson, co., S.D., U.S.	D8	148
Hant's Harbour, Newf., Can.	D5	102
Hantsport, N.S., Can.	D5	101
Hanumangarh, India	F6	44
Hanzhong, China	I5	32
Hanzhuang, China	I13	44
Hāora, India	C2	117
Hapeville, Ga., U.S.	E5	138
Happy Valley, N.M., U.S.	B1	102
Happy Valley-Goose Bay, Newf., Can.	F7	44
Hāpur, India	k11	125
Harahan, La., U.S.	C1	117
Haralson, co., Ga., U.S.	A10	66
Harare (Salisbury), Zimb.	F4	115
Harbeson, De., U.S.	B12	30
Harbin, China	E2	144
Harbor, Or., U.S.	E8	129
Harbor Beach, Mi., U.S.	C6	129
Harbor Springs, Mi., U.S.	E4	102
Harbour Breton, Newf., Can.	E5	102
Harbour Grace, Newf., Can.	D2	110
Harcuvar Mountains, mts., Az., U.S.	K10	6
Hardangerfjorden, Nor.	E5	116
Hardee, co., Fl., U.S.	G5	147
Hardeeville, S.C., U.S.	B3	149
Hardeman, co., Tn., U.S.	B2	150
Hardeman, co., Tx., U.S.	D3	12
Harderwijk, Neth.	D3	120
Hardin, Il., U.S.	f9	124
Hardin, Ky., U.S.	B4	132
Hardin, Mo., U.S.	E9	133
Hardin, Mt., U.S.	F5	120
Hardin, co., Il., U.S.	C4	124
Hardin, co., Ia., U.S.	B4	122
Hardin, co., Ky., U.S.	C4	124
Hardin, co., Oh., U.S.	B2	142
Hardin, co., Tn., U.S.	B3	149
Hardin, co., Tx., U.S.	D5	150
Harding, S. Afr.	H9	66
Harding, co., N.M., U.S.	B5	138
Harding, co., S.D., U.S.	B2	148
Harding, Lake, res., U.S.	C4	108
Hardinsburg, Ky., U.S.	C3	124
Hardisty, Alta., Can.	C5	98
Hardoi, India	G9	44
Hardwick, Ga., U.S.	C3	117
Hardwick, Vt., U.S.	C4	152
Hardy, Ar., U.S.	A4	111
Hardy, co., W.V., U.S.	B6	155
Hare Bay, Newf., Can.	D4	102
Hare Bay, b., Newf., Can.	C4	102
Harer, Eth.	G9	56
Hareto, Eth.	M9	60
Harford, co., Md., U.S.	A5	127
Hargeysa, Som.	G9	56
Hari, stm., Indon.	F3	38
Haridwār, India	F8	44
Harihar, India	E3	46
Harīrūd (Tedžen), stm., Asia	C16	48
Harkers Island, N.C., U.S.	C6	140
Harlan, In., U.S.	B8	121
Harlan, Ia., U.S.	C2	122
Harlan, Ky., U.S.	D6	124
Harlan, co., Ky., U.S.	D6	124
Harlan, co., Ne., U.S.	D6	134
Harlan County Lake, res., Ne., U.S.	E6	134
Harlem, Fl., U.S.	F6	116
Harlem, Ga., U.S.	C4	117
Harlem, Mt., U.S.	B8	133
Harlingen, Tx., U.S.	F4	150
Harlowton, Mt., U.S.	D7	133
Harmanli, Bul.	H9	20
Harmon, co., Ok., U.S.	C2	143
Harmony, In., U.S.	E3	121
Harmony, Me., U.S.	D3	126
Harmony, Mn., U.S.	G6	130
Harmony, R.I., U.S.	B3	146
Harnett, co., N.C., U.S.	B4	140
Harney, co., Or., U.S.	D7	144
Harney Lake, l., Or., U.S.	D7	144
Harney Peak, mtn., S.D., U.S.	D2	148
Härnösand, Swe.	J15	6
Haro Strait, strt., Wa., U.S.	A2	154
Harper, Lib.	I6	64
Harper, Ks., U.S.	E5	123
Harper, co., Ks., U.S.	E5	123
Harper, co., Ok., U.S.	A2	143
Harpers Ferry, W.V., U.S.	B7	155
Harpers Ferry National Historical Park, W.V., U.S.	B7	155
Harpersville, Al., U.S.	B3	108
Harpeth, stm., Tn., U.S.	A5	149
Harqin Qi (Jinshan), China	B6	32
Harquahala Mountain, mtn., Az., U.S.	D2	110
Harquahala Mountains, mts., Az., U.S.	D2	110
Harrah, Ok., U.S.	B4	143
Harricana, stm., Can.	F17	96
Harriman, Tn., U.S.	D9	149
Harriman Reservoir, res., Vt., U.S.	F3	152
Harrington, De., U.S.	E3	115
Harrington, Me., U.S.	D5	126
Harrington Park, N.J., U.S.	h9	137
Harris, Sask., Can.	F2	105
Harris, Mn., U.S.	E6	130
Harris, R.I., U.S.	D3	146
Harris, co., Ga., U.S.	D2	117
Harris, co., Tx., U.S.	E5	150
Harrisburg, Ar., U.S.	B5	111
Harrisburg, Il., U.S.	F5	120
Harrisburg, Or., U.S.	C3	144
Harrisburg, Pa., U.S.	F8	145
Harrisburg, S.D., U.S.	D9	148
Harrismith, S. Afr.	G9	66
Harrison, Ar., U.S.	A2	111
Harrison, Me., U.S.	D2	126
Harrison, Mi., U.S.	D6	129
Harrison, N.J., U.S.	k8	137
Harrison, N.Y., U.S.	h13	139
Harrison, Oh., U.S.	C1	142
Harrison, Tn., U.S.	h11	149
Harrison, co., In., U.S.	H5	121
Harrison, co., Ia., U.S.	C2	122
Harrison, co., Ky., U.S.	B5	124
Harrison, co., Ms., U.S.	E4	131
Harrison, co., Mo., U.S.	A3	132
Harrison, co., Oh., U.S.	B4	142
Harrison, co., Tx., U.S.	C5	150
Harrison, co., W.V., U.S.	B4	155
Harrison, Cape, c., Newf., Can.	g10	102
Harrisonburg, Va., U.S.	B4	153
Harrison Hot Springs, B.C., Can.	f14	99
Harrison Lake, l., B.C., Can.	E7	99
Harriston, Ont., Can.	D4	103
Harristown, Il., U.S.	D4	120
Harrisville, N.H., U.S.	E2	136
Harrisville, R.I., U.S.	B2	146
Harrisville, W.V., U.S.	B3	155
Harrodsburg, Ky., U.S.	C5	124
Harrogate, Eng., U.K.	G11	8
Harrow, Ont., Can.	E2	103
Harrowsmith, Ont., Can.	C8	103
Harry S. Truman Reservoir, res., Mo., U.S.	C4	132
Hart, Mi., U.S.	E4	129
Hart, co., Ga., U.S.	B4	117
Hart, co., Ky., U.S.	C4	124
Hartford, Al., U.S.	D4	108
Hartford, Ct., U.S.	B5	114
Hartford, Il., U.S.	E3	120
Hartford, Ia., U.S.	C4	122
Hartford, Ks., U.S.	D8	123
Hartford, Ky., U.S.	C3	124
Hartford, Mi., U.S.	F4	129
Hartford, S.D., U.S.	D9	148
Hartford, Vt., U.S.	D4	152
Hartford, Wi., U.S.	E5	156
Hartford, co., Ct., U.S.	B4	114
Hartford City, In., U.S.	D7	121
Hartington, Ne., U.S.	B8	134
Hartland, Me., U.S.	D3	126
Hartland, Wi., U.S.	E5	156
Hartley, Ia., U.S.	A2	122
Hartley, co., Tx., U.S.	B1	150
Hartman, Ar., U.S.	B2	111
Hartney, Man., Can.	E1	100
Hartselle, Al., U.S.	A3	108
Hartshorne, Ok., U.S.	C6	143
Hartsville, S.C., U.S.	C7	147
Hartsville, Tn., U.S.	A5	149
Hartville, Oh., U.S.	B4	142
Hartville, Wy., U.S.	D8	157
Hartwell, Ga., U.S.	B4	117
Hartwell Lake, res., U.S.	B1	147
Harvard, Il., U.S.	A5	120
Harvard, Ne., U.S.	D7	134
Harvard, Mount, mtn., Co., U.S.	C4	113
Harvest, Al., U.S.	A3	108
Harvey, N.B., Can.	D3	101
Harvey, Il., U.S.	B6	120
Harvey, La., U.S.	E5	125
Harvey, Mi., U.S.	B3	129
Harvey, N.D., U.S.	B6	141
Harvey, W.V., U.S.	n13	155
Harvey, co., Ks., U.S.	D6	123
Harwich, Ma., U.S.	C7	128
Harwinton, Ct., U.S.	B3	114
Harwood, N.D., U.S.	C9	141
Haryāna, state, India	F7	44
Harz, mts., Ger.	D10	10
Hasbrouck Heights, N.J., U.S.	h8	137
Hasenkamp, Arg.	F9	80
Haskell, Ar., U.S.	C3	111
Haskell, Ok., U.S.	B6	143
Haskell, Tx., U.S.	C3	150
Haskell, co., Ks., U.S.	E3	123
Haskell, co., Ok., U.S.	B6	143
Haskell, co., Tx., U.S.	C3	150
Haskovo, Bul.	H9	20
Hassan, India	F4	46
Hassayampa, stm., Az., U.S.	D3	110
Hasselt, Bel.	G7	12
Hassi el Ghella, Alg.	J10	16
Hassi Mameche, Alg.	J12	16
Hassi Messaoud, Alg.	E13	62
Hässleholm, Swe.	M13	6
Hastings, Ont., Can.	C7	103
Hastings, N.Z.	C6	72
Hastings, Eng., U.K.	K14	8
Hastings, Mi., U.S.	F5	129
Hastings, Mn., U.S.	F6	130
Hastings, Ne., U.S.	D7	134
Hastings-on-Hudson, N.Y., U.S.	h13	139
Hatay, Tur.	C4	48
Hatch, N.M., U.S.	E2	138
Hatchet Lake, N.S., Can.	E6	101
Hatfield, Ar., U.S.	C1	111
Hatfield, In., U.S.	I3	121
Hatfield, Pa., U.S.	F11	145
Hathras, India	G8	44
Ha Tinh, Viet.	E8	40
Hato Mayor [del Rey], Dom. Rep.	E10	94
Hatteras, N.C., U.S.	B7	140
Hatteras, Cape, c., N.C., U.S.	B7	140
Hattiesburg, Ms., U.S.	D4	131
Hatton, N.D., U.S.	B8	141
Hatvan, Hung.	H19	10
Haubstadt, In., U.S.	H2	121
Haugesund, Nor.	L9	6
Haughton, La., U.S.	B2	125
Haut, Isle au, i., Me., U.S.	D4	126
Haut Atlas, mts., Mor.	E7	62
Hautmont, Fr.	B10	14
Havana see La Habana, Cuba	C3	94
Havana, Ar., U.S.	B2	111
Havana, Il., U.S.	C3	120
Havasu, Lake, res., U.S.	C1	110
Havelock, N.B., Can.	D4	101
Havelock, Ont., Can.	C7	103
Havelock, N.C., U.S.	C6	140
Haverford [Township], Pa., U.S.	o20	145
Haverhill, Ma., U.S.	A5	128
Haverhill, N.H., U.S.	B2	136
Haverstraw, N.Y., U.S.	D7	139
Havířov, Czech Rep.	F18	10
Havlíčkův Brod, Czech Rep.	F15	10
Havre, Mt., U.S.	B7	133
Havre Boucher, N.S., Can.	D8	101
Havre de Grace, Md., U.S.	A5	127
Havre North, Mt., U.S.	B7	133
Hawaii, co., Hi., U.S.	D6	118
Hawaii, state, U.S.	C5	118
Hawaii, i., Hi., U.S.	D6	118
Hawaiian Islands, is., Hi., U.S.	m14	118
Hawaiian Ridge	F22	158
Hawaii Volcanoes National Park, Hi., U.S.	D6	118
Hawarden, Ia., U.S.	A1	122
Hawea, Lake, l., N.Z.	F2	72
Hawera, N.Z.	C5	72
Hawesville, Ky., U.S.	C3	124
Hawi, Hi., U.S.	C6	118
Hawick, Scot., U.K.	F11	8
Hawke, Cape, c., Austl.	I10	70
Hawke Bay, b., N.Z.	C6	72
Hawker, Austl.	H3	70
Hawkesbury, Ont., Can.	B10	103
Hawkins, co., Tn., U.S.	C11	149
Hawkinsville, Ga., U.S.	D3	117
Haw Knob, mtn., U.S.	D9	149
Hawk Springs, Wy., U.S.	E8	157
Hawley, Mn., U.S.	D2	130
Hawley, Pa., U.S.	D11	145
Hawleyville, Ct., U.S.	D2	114
Haw River, N.C., U.S.	A3	140
Hawthorne, Fl., U.S.	C4	116
Hawthorne, Nv., U.S.	E3	135
Hawthorne, N.J., U.S.	B4	137
Hawzen, Eth.	K10	60
Haxtun, Co., U.S.	A8	113
Hay, Austl.	J6	70
Hay, stm., Austl.	D7	68
Hay, stm., Can.	E9	96
Hay, Cape, c., N.W. Ter., Can.	B10	96
Hayange, Fr.	C13	14
Hayden, Az., U.S.	E5	110
Hayden, Co., U.S.	A3	113
Hayden Lake, l., Id., U.S.	B2	119
Hayes, co., Ne., U.S.	D4	134
Hayes, Mount, mtn., Ak., U.S.	C10	109
Hayfield, Mn., U.S.	G6	130
Hayford Peak, mtn., Nv., U.S.	G6	135
Haykota, Erit.	J9	60
Hay Lakes, Alta., Can.	C4	98
Haynesville, La., U.S.	B2	125
Hayneville, Al., U.S.	C3	108
Hays, Ks., U.S.	D4	123
Hays, Mt., U.S.	C8	133
Hays, co., Tx., U.S.	D3	150
Hay Springs, Ne., U.S.	B3	134
Haysville, Ks., U.S.	g12	123
Hayti, Mo., U.S.	E8	132
Hayti, S.D., U.S.	C8	148
Hayti Heights, Mo., U.S.	E8	132
Hayvoron, Ukr.	A13	20
Hayward, Wi., U.S.	B2	156
Hayward, Man., Can.	E2	100
Haywood, co., N.C., U.S.	f9	140
Haywood, co., Tn., U.S.	B2	149
Hazard, Ky., U.S.	C6	124
Hazardville, Ct., U.S.	B5	114
Hazārībāg, India	I11	44
Hazebrouck, Fr.	B9	14
Hazel Crest, Il., U.S.	k9	120
Hazel Dell, Wa., U.S.	D3	154
Hazel Green, Al., U.S.	A3	108
Hazel Green, Wi., U.S.	F3	156
Hazel Park, Mi., U.S.	p15	129
Hazelton, B.C., Can.	B4	99
Hazelton, Id., U.S.	G4	119
Hazelton, N.D., U.S.	C5	141
Hazelwood, N.C., U.S.	f10	140
Hazen, Ar., U.S.	C4	111
Hazen, N.D., U.S.	B4	141
Hazlehurst, Ga., U.S.	E4	117
Hazlehurst, Ms., U.S.	D3	131
Hazlet, N.J., U.S.	C4	137
Hazleton, Ia., U.S.	B6	122
Hazleton, Pa., U.S.	E10	145
Headland, Al., U.S.	D4	108
Healdsburg, Ca., U.S.	C2	112
Healdton, Ok., U.S.	C4	143
Healesville, Austl.	K6	70
Healy, Ak., U.S.	C10	109
Heard, co., Ga., U.S.	C1	117
Heard Island, i., Austl.	N11	158
Hearne, Tx., U.S.	D4	150
Hearst, Ont., Can.	o19	103
Heart, stm., N.D., U.S.	C3	141
Heart's Content, Newf., Can.	E5	102
Heath, Oh., U.S.	B3	142
Heatherton, N.S., Can.	D8	101
Heavener, Ok., U.S.	C7	143
Hebbronville, Tx., U.S.	F3	150
Hebei (Hopeh), prov., China	D10	30
Heber, Az., U.S.	C5	110
Heber City, Ut., U.S.	C4	151
Heber Springs, Ar., U.S.	B3	111
Hébertville, Que., Can.	A6	104
Hebi, China	H2	32
Hebrides, is., Scot., U.K.	D6	4
Hebron, N.S., Can.	F3	101
Hebron, In., U.S.	B3	121
Hebron, Ky., U.S.	h13	124
Hebron, Me., U.S.	D2	126
Hebron, Ne., U.S.	D8	134
Hebron, N.D., U.S.	C3	141
Hebron see Al-Khalīl, W.B.	E4	50
Hecate Strait, strt., B.C., Can.	C2	99
Hecelchakán, Mex.	G14	90
Hechi, China	B10	40
Hechuan, China	E8	30
Hecla, S.D., U.S.	B7	148
Hecla Island, i., Man., Can.	D3	100
Hector, Mn., U.S.	F4	130
He Devil, mtn., Id., U.S.	D2	119
Hedley, B.C., Can.	E7	99
Hedrick, Ia., U.S.	C5	122
Heerenveen, Neth.	C8	12
Heerlen, Neth.	G8	12
Hefa (Haifa), Isr.	C4	50
Hefei, China	D6	34
Heflin, Al., U.S.	B4	108
Hegang, China	B13	30
Heichengzi, China	A9	32
Heidelberg, Ger.	F8	10
Heidelberg, S. Afr.	F9	66
Heidelberg, Ms., U.S.	D5	131
Heidenheim, Ger.	F10	10
Heidrick, Ky., U.S.	D6	124
Heilbron, S. Afr.	F8	66
Heilbronn, Ger.	F9	10
Heilong (Amur), stm., Asia	A12	30
Heilongjiang (Heilungkiang), prov., China	B12	30
Heimaey, i., Ice.	C3	6a
Heishan, China	B10	32
Hejian, China	E4	32
Hekla, vol., Ice.	C4	6a
Hekou, China	C7	40
Helena, Ar., U.S.	C5	111
Helena, Ga., U.S.	D4	117
Helena, Mt., U.S.	D4	133
Helena, Oh., U.S.	A2	142
Helendale, Ca., U.S.	E5	112
Helensburgh, Scot., U.K.	E9	8
Helgoland, i., Ger.	A7	10
Hellertown, Pa., U.S.	E11	145
Hellín, Spain	G10	16
Hells Canyon, val., U.S.	B10	144
Hell-Ville, Madag.	n23	67b
Helmand, stm., Asia	D1	44
Helmond, Neth.	F8	12
Helmstedt, Ger.	C11	10
Helper, Ut., U.S.	D5	151
Helsingborg, Swe.	M13	6
Helsingfors see Helsinki, Fin.	K19	6
Helsingør (Elsinore), Den.	M13	6
Helsinki (Helsingfors), Fin.	K19	6

Name	Map Ref.	Page

Helvecia, Arg. F8 80
Hematite, Mo., U.S. C7 132
Hemel Hempstead, Eng.,
U.K. J13 8
Hemet, Ca., U.S. F5 112
Hemingford, Ne., U.S. B2 134
Hemlock, Mi., U.S. E6 129
Hemphill, co., Tx., U.S. . . . B2 150
Hempstead, N.Y., U.S. n15 139
Hempstead, Tx., U.S. D4 150
Hempstead, co., Ar., U.S. . . D2 111
Henagar, Al., U.S. A4 108
Henan (Honan), prov., China E9 30
Henderson, Arg. I8 80
Henderson, Co., U.S. B6 113
Henderson, Ky., U.S. C2 124
Henderson, La., U.S. D4 125
Henderson, Mn., U.S. F5 130
Henderson, Ne., U.S. D8 134
Henderson, Nv., U.S. G7 135
Henderson, N.C., U.S. A4 140
Henderson, Tn., U.S. B3 149
Henderson, Tx., U.S. C5 150
Henderson, W.V., U.S. C2 155
Henderson, co., Il., U.S. . . . C3 120
Henderson, co., Ky., U.S. . . C2 124
Henderson, co., N.C., U.S. . f10 140
Henderson, co., Tn., U.S. . . B3 149
Henderson, co., Tx., U.S. . . C5 150
Henderson Island, i., Pit. . . K27 158
Henderson's Point, Ms.,
U.S. g7 131
Hendersonville, N.C., U.S. . . f10 140
Hendersonville, Tn., U.S. . . A5 149
Hendricks, Mn., U.S. F2 130
Hendricks, co., In., U.S. . . . E4 121
Hendry, co., Fl., U.S. F5 116
Henefer, Ut., U.S. C4 151
Hengelo, Neth. D10 12
Hengshan, China H1 34
Hengshui, China F3 32
Hengxian, China C10 40
Hengyang, China F9 30
Henlawson, W.V., U.S. n12 155
Henlopen, Cape, c., De.,
U.S. E5 115
Hennaya, Alg. K10 16
Hennebont, Fr. E3 14
Hennef, Ger. E7 10
Hennenman, S. Afr. F8 66
Hennessey, Ok., U.S. A4 143
Henniker, N.H., U.S. D3 136
Henning, Mn., U.S. D3 130
Henning, Tn., U.S. B2 149
Henrico, co., Va., U.S. C5 153
Henrietta, N.C., U.S. B1 140
Henrietta Maria, Cape, c.,
Ont., Can. n19 103
Henry, Il., U.S. B4 120
Henry, co., Al., U.S. D4 108
Henry, co., Ga., U.S. C2 117
Henry, co., Il., U.S. B3 120
Henry, co., In., U.S. E7 121
Henry, co., Ia., U.S. C6 122
Henry, co., Ky., U.S. B4 124
Henry, co., Mo., U.S. C4 132
Henry, co., Oh., U.S. A1 142
Henry, co., Tn., U.S. A3 149
Henry, co., Va., U.S. D3 153
Henryetta, Ok., U.S. B6 143
Henry Kater, Cape, c., N.W.
Ter., Can. C19 96
Henry Mountains, mts., Ut.,
U.S. E5 151
Henrys Fork, stm., U.S. . . . E2 157
Henryville, In., U.S. G6 121
Hensall, Ont., Can. D3 103
Hensley, Ar., U.S. C3 111
Hentiesbaai, Nmb. D2 66
Henty, Austl. J7 70
Henzada, Mya. F3 40
Hepburn, Sask., Can. E2 105
Hephzibah, Ga., U.S. C4 117
Heping, China K3 34
Heppenheim, Ger. F8 10
Heppner, Or., U.S. B7 144
Hepu (Lianzhou), China . . . D10 40
Heqiao, China D8 34
Herāt, Afg. D17 48
Herbert, Sask., Can. G2 105
Herculaneum, Mo., U.S. . . . C7 132
Heredia, C.R. G10 92
Hereford, Tx., U.S. B1 150
Hereford and Worcester,
co., Eng., U.K. I11 8
Herentals, Bel. F6 12
Herford, Ger. C8 10
Herington, Ks., U.S. D7 123
Herisau, Switz. D11 13
Herkimer, N.Y., U.S. B6 139
Herkimer, co., N.Y., U.S. . . B5 139
Hermann, Mo., U.S. C6 132
Hermano Peak, mtn., Co.,
U.S. D2 113
Hermantown, Mn., U.S. . . . D6 130
Herminie, Pa., U.S. F2 145
Herminone, S. Afr. J4 66
Hermiston, Or., U.S. B7 144
Hermitage, Newf., Can. . . . E4 102
Hermitage, Ar., U.S. D3 111
Hermitage Bay, b., Newf.,
Can. E3 102
Hermon, Mount see
Shaykh, Jabal ash-, mtn.,
Asia B5 50
Hermosillo, Mex. C4 90
Hernandarias, Para. C11 80
Hernando, Arg. G7 80
Hernando, Fl., U.S. D4 116
Hernando, Ms., U.S. A4 131
Hernando, co., Fl., U.S. . . . D4 116
Herndon, Va., U.S. B5 153
Heroica Zitácuaro, Mex. . . . H9 90
Heron Lake, Mn., U.S. G3 130
Herradura, Arg. D9 80
Herreid, S.D., U.S. B5 148
Herrera, Arg. E7 80
Herrera, prov., Pan. I14 92
Herrin, Il., U.S. F4 120
Herring Cove, N.S., Can. . . E6 101
Herscher, Il., U.S. B5 120
Hershey, Ne., U.S. C5 134
Hershey, Pa., U.S. F8 145
Herstal, Bel. G8 12

Hertford, N.C., U.S. A6 140
Hertford, co., N.C., U.S. . . . A5 140
Hertfordshire, co., Eng.,
U.K. J13 8
Hervey Bay, b., Austl. E10 70
Herzliyya, Isr. D3 50
Heshangqiao, China A2 34
Hesperia, Ca., U.S. E5 112
Hesston, Ks., U.S. D6 123
Hettinger, N.D., U.S. D3 141
Hettinger, co., N.D., U.S. . . C3 141
Hettstedt, Ger. D11 10
Heves, Hung. H20 10
Hewitt, Tx., U.S. D4 150
Heyburn, Id., U.S. G5 119
Heywood, Austl. L7 70
Heyworth, Il., U.S. C5 120
Heze (Caozhou), China . . . H3 32
Hialeah, Fl., U.S. G6 116
Hiawatha, Ia., U.S. B6 122
Hiawatha, Ks., U.S. C8 123
Hibbing, Mn., U.S. C6 130
Hickam Air Force Base,
mil., Hi., U.S. g10 118
Hickman, Ky., U.S. f8 124
Hickman, Ne., U.S. D9 134
Hickman, co., Ky., U.S. . . . f8 124
Hickman, co., Tn., U.S. . . . B4 149
Hickory, N.C., U.S. B1 140
Hickory, co., Mo., U.S. D4 132
Hickory Flat, Ms., U.S. A4 131
Hickory Ridge, Ar., U.S. . . . B5 111
Hicksville, N.Y., U.S. E7 139
Hicksville, Oh., U.S. A1 142
Hico, W.V., U.S. C3 155
Hidalgo, Mex. E10 90
Hidalgo, Mex. E9 90
Hidalgo, Tx., U.S. F3 150
Hidalgo, state, Mex. G10 90
Hidalgo, co., N.M., U.S. . . . F1 138
Hidalgo, co., Tx., U.S. F3 150
Hidalgo del Parral, Mex. . . . D7 90
Hidrolândia, Braz. D4 79
Hierro (Ferro), i., Spain . . . p22 17b
Higashiōsaka, Japan M10 36
Higbee, Mo., U.S. B5 132
Higganum, Ct., U.S. D5 114
Higgins Lake, l., Mi., U.S. . . D6 129
Higginsville, Mo., U.S. B4 132
High Bluff, Man., Can. D2 100
Highgate Falls, Vt., U.S. . . . B2 152
High Knob, mtn., Va., U.S. . . A4 153
Highland, Il., U.S. E4 120
Highland, In., U.S. A3 121
Highland, Ks., U.S. C8 123
Highland, N.Y., U.S. D7 139
Highland, co., Oh., U.S. . . . C2 142
Highland, co., Va., U.S. . . . B3 153
Highland Lakes, N.J., U.S. . A4 137
Highland Park, Il., U.S. A6 120
Highland Park, Mi., U.S. . . . p15 129
Highland Park, Tx., U.S. . . . n10 150
Highlands, N.J., U.S. C5 137
Highlands, Tx., U.S. r14 150
Highlands, co., Fl., U.S. . . . E5 116
Highland Springs, Va., U.S. . C5 153
High Level, Alta., Can. f7 98
Highmore, S.D., U.S. C6 148
High Point, N.C., U.S. B2 140
High Prairie, Alta., Can. . . . B2 98
High Ridge, Mo., U.S. g12 132
High River, Alta., Can. D4 98
High Rock Lake, res., N.C.,
U.S. B2 140
High Spire, Pa., U.S. F8 145
High Springs, Fl., U.S. C4 116
Hightstown, N.J., U.S. C3 137
Highwood, Il., U.S. A6 120
High Wycombe, Eng., U.K. . J13 8
Higuera de Zaragoza, Mex. . E5 90
Higüero, Punta c., P.R. E11 94
Higüey, Dom. Rep. E10 94
Hiiumaa, i., Est. C4 34
Hiko, Nv., U.S. F6 135
Hikone, Japan L11 36
Hilbert, Wi., U.S. D5 156
Hildale, Ut., U.S. F3 151
Hilden, N.S., Can. D6 101
Hildesheim, Ger. C9 10
Hildreth, Ne., U.S. D6 134
Hill, co., Mt., U.S. B6 133
Hill, co., Tx., U.S. D4 150
Hillaby, Mount, mtn. Barb. . F4 133
Hill City, Ks., U.S. C4 123
Hill City, S.D., U.S. D2 148
Hillcrest Heights, Md., U.S. . C4 127
Hilliard, Fl., U.S. B5 116
Hilliard, Oh., U.S. k10 142
Hillsboro, Al., U.S. A2 108
Hillsboro, Il., U.S. D4 120
Hillsboro, Ks., U.S. D6 123
Hillsboro, Mo., U.S. C7 132
Hillsboro, N.H., U.S. D3 136
Hillsboro, N.D., U.S. B8 141
Hillsboro, Oh., U.S. C2 142
Hillsboro, Or., U.S. B4 144
Hillsboro, Tx., U.S. C4 150
Hillsboro, Wi., U.S. E3 156
Hillsboro Canal, Fl., U.S. . . F6 116
Hillsborough, N.B., Can. . . . D5 101
Hillsborough, N.C., U.S. . . . A3 140
Hillsborough, co., Fl., U.S. . E4 116
Hillsborough, co., N.H., U.S. E3 136
Hillsborough Bay, b., P.E.I.,
Can. C6 101
Hillsborough Upper Village,
N.H., U.S. D3 136
Hillsburgh, Ont., Can. D4 103
Hillsdale, Mi., U.S. G6 129
Hillsdale, N.J., U.S. g8 137
Hillsdale, co., Mi., U.S. . . . G6 129
Hillside, N.J., U.S. k8 137
Hillsville, Va., U.S. D2 153
Hilo, Hi., U.S. D6 118
Hilton, N.Y., U.S. B3 139
Hilton Head Island, S.C.,
U.S. G6 147
Hilton Head Island, i., S.C.,
U.S. G6 147
Hilversum, Neth. D7 12
Himāchal Pradesh, state,
India E7 44

Himalayas, mts., Asia F11 44
Himeji, Japan M9 36
Himi, Japan K11 36
Ḩims (Homs), Syria D4 48
Hinche, Haiti E8 94
Hinchinbrook Island, i.,
Austl. B7 70
Hinchinbrook Island, i., Ak.,
U.S. g18 109
Hinckley, Il., U.S. B5 120
Hinckley, Mn., U.S. D6 130
Hinckley, Ut., U.S. D3 151
Hindaun, India G7 44
Hinds, co., Ms., U.S. C3 131
Hindu Kush, mts., Asia . . . B4 44
Hindupur, India F4 46
Hines, Or., U.S. D7 144
Hinesburg, Vt., U.S. C2 152
Hines Creek, Alta., Can. . . . A1 98
Hineston, La., U.S. C3 125
Hinganghāt, India B5 46
Hingham, Ma., U.S. B6 128
Hingham Bay, b., Ma., U.S. . g12 128
Hingol, stm., Pak. H1 44
Hinis, Tur. B6 48
Hinnøya, i., Nor. G14 6
Hinsdale, Il., U.S. k9 120
Hinsdale, Mt., U.S. B9 133
Hinsdale, N.H., U.S. E2 136
Hinsdale, co., Co., U.S. . . . D3 113
Hinton, Alta., Can. C2 98
Hinton, Ia., U.S. B1 122
Hinton, Ok., U.S. B3 143
Hinton, W.V., U.S. D4 155
Hipólito Yrigoyen, Arg. G5 80
Hīrākud Reservoir, res.,
India B7 46
Hiram, Ga., U.S. C2 117
Hiram, Me., U.S. E2 126
Hiratsuka, Japan L14 36
Hirosaki, Japan G15 36
Hiroshima, Japan M7 36
Hirson, Fr. C11 14
Hisār, India F6 44
Hispaniola, i., N.A. E9 94
Hita, Japan N5 36
Hitachi, Japan K15 36
Hitchcock, Tx., U.S. r14 150
Hitchcock, co., Ne., U.S. . . D4 134
Hitchcock Lake, Ct., U.S. . . C4 114
Hitra, i., Nor. J11 6
Hiva Oa, i., Fr. Poly. I26 158
Hiwassee, stm., Tn., U.S. . . D9 149
Hiwassee Lake, res., N.C.,
U.S. f8 140
Hkakabo Razi, mtn., Mya. . . F6 30
Hlaikikulu, Swaz. F10 66
Hlohovec, Slvk. G17 10
Hlučin, Czech Rep. F18 10
Hlyboka, Ukr. A9 20
Ho, Ghana H10 64
Hoa Binh, Viet. D8 40
Hoagland, In., U.S. C8 121
Hobart, Austl. N7 70
Hobart, In., U.S. A3 121
Hobart, Ok., U.S. B2 143
Hobbs, N.M., U.S. E6 138
Hobe Sound, Fl., U.S. E6 116
Hoboken, N.J., U.S. k8 137
Hoboken, N.M., U.S. D7 133
Hockessin, De., U.S. A3 115
Hocking, co., Oh., U.S. C3 142
Hocking, stm., Oh., U.S. . . . C3 142
Hockley, co., Tx., U.S. C1 150
Hodeida see Al-Ḩudaydah,
Yemen G3 47
Hodgdon, Me., U.S. B5 126
Hodgeman, co., Ks., U.S. . . D4 123
Hodgenville, Ky., U.S. C4 124
Hodgeville, Sask., Can. . . . G2 105
Hódmezővásárhely, Hung. . I20 10
Hodonín, Czech Rep. G17 10
Hoek van Holland, Neth. . . E5 12
Hoeryong, N. Kor. A17 32
Hof, Ger. E11 10
Hoffman Estates, Il., U.S. . . h8 120
Höfn, Ice. B6 6a
Hofors, Swe. K15 6
Hōfu, Japan M6 36
Hofuf see Al-Huḟūf, Sau. Ar. I10 48
Hogback Mountain, mtn.,
Mt., U.S. F4 133
Hoggar see Ahaggar, mts.,
Alg. I13 62
Hohenwald, Tn., U.S. B4 149
Hoher Dachstein, mtn., Aus. H13 10
Hohe Tauern, mts., Aus. . . H12 10
Hohhot, China C9 30
Hohoe, Ghana H10 64
Hoisington, Ks., U.S. D5 123
Hokah, Mn., U.S. G7 130
Hoke, co., N.C., U.S. B3 140
Hokes Bluff, Al., U.S. B4 108
Hokkaidō, i., Japan d17 36a
Holbrook, Az., U.S. C5 110
Holbrook, Ma., U.S. B5 128
Holcomb, Ks., U.S. E3 123
Holden, Alta., Can. C4 98
Holden, Ma., U.S. B4 128
Holden, Mo., U.S. C3 132
Holden, W.V., U.S. D2 155
Holdenville, Ok., U.S. B5 143
Holderness, N.H., U.S. C3 136
Holdfast, Sask., Can. G3 105
Holdrege, Ne., U.S. D6 134
Hole in the Mountain Peak,
mtn., Nv., U.S. C6 135
Holguín, Cuba D6 94
Hollabrunn, Aus. G16 10
Holladay, Ut., U.S. C4 151
Holland, Man., Can. E2 100
Holland, In., U.S. H3 121
Holland, Mi., U.S. F4 129
Hollandale, Ms., U.S. B3 131
Hollandsbird Island, i., Nmb. C1 66
Hollidaysburg, Pa., U.S. . . . F5 145
Hollins, Va., U.S. C3 153
Hollis, N.H., U.S. E3 136
Hollis, Ok., U.S. C2 143
Hollister, Ca., U.S. D3 112
Hollister, Mo., U.S. E4 132
Holliston, Ma., U.S. B5 128
Hollow Rock, Tn., U.S. A3 149

Hollowtop Mountain, mtn.,
Mt., U.S. E4 133
Holly, Co., U.S. C8 113
Holly, Mi., U.S. F7 129
Holly Grove, Ar., U.S. C4 111
Holly Hill, Fl., U.S. C5 116
Holly Hill, S.C., U.S. E7 147
Holly Pond, Al., U.S. A3 108
Holly Springs, Ga., U.S. . . . B2 117
Holly Springs, Ms., U.S. . . . A4 131
Hollywood, Al., U.S. A4 108
Hollywood (part of Los
Angeles), Ca., U.S. m12 112
Hollywood, Fl., U.S. F6 116
Hollywood, Md., U.S. D4 127
Hollywood, S.C., U.S. k11 147
Holman, N.W. Ter., Can. . . B9 96
Holman, N.M., U.S. A4 138
Holmen, Wi., U.S. E2 156
Holmes, co., Fl., U.S. u16 116
Holmes, co., Ms., U.S. B3 131
Holmes, co., Oh., U.S. B4 142
Holmestrand, Nor. L12 6
Holmsund, Swe. I18 6
Holon, Isr. D3 50
Holstein, Ia., U.S. B2 122
Holston, stm., Tn., U.S. . . . C11 149
Holt, Al., U.S. B2 108
Holt, Mi., U.S. F6 129
Holt, co., Mo., U.S. A2 132
Holt, co., Ne., U.S. B7 134
Holt Lake, res., Al., U.S. . . . B2 108
Holton, Ks., U.S. C8 123
Holualoa, Hi., U.S. D6 118
Holy Cross, Ak., U.S. C8 109
Holy Cross, Mountain of
the, mtn., Co., U.S. B4 113
Holyoke, Co., U.S. A8 113
Holyoke, Ma., U.S. B2 128
Holyoke Range, hills, Ma.,
U.S. B2 128
Holyrood, Ks., U.S. D5 123
Holzminden, Ger. D9 10
Homalin, Mya. B3 40
Homburg, Ger. F7 10
Homecroft, In., U.S. m10 121
Homedale, Id., U.S. F2 119
Home Gardens, Ca., U.S. . . n14 112
Home Hill, Austl. B7 70
Homeland, Fl., U.S. E5 116
Homer, Ak., U.S. D9 109
Homer, Ga., U.S. B3 117
Homer, Il., U.S. C6 120
Homer, La., U.S. B2 125
Homer, Mi., U.S. F6 129
Homer, Ne., U.S. B9 134
Homer, N.Y., U.S. C4 139
Homer City, Pa., U.S. E3 145
Homerville, Ga., U.S. E4 117
Homestead, Fl., U.S. G6 116
Homestead, Pa., U.S. k14 145
Homestead National
Monument of America,
Ne., U.S. D9 134
Homewood, Al., U.S. g7 108
Homewood, Il., U.S. B6 120
Homewood, Oh., U.S. C1 142
Hominy, Ok., U.S. A5 143
Homochitto, stm., Ms., U.S. D2 131
Homosassa, Fl., U.S. D4 116
Homs see Ḩims, Libya B3 56
Homs see Ḩims, Syria D4 48
Honawar, Va., U.S. e10 153
Honaunau, Hi., U.S. D6 118
Honda, Col. E5 84
Hondo, N.M., U.S. D4 138
Hondo, Tx., U.S. E3 150
Hondo, stm., N.A. H15 90
Hondo, Rio, stm., N.M.,
U.S. D4 138
Honduras, ctry., N.A. B8 92
Honduras, Cabo de, c.,
Hond. A8 92
Honduras, Gulf of, b., N.A. . E7 88
Honea Path, S.C., U.S. . . . C3 147
Honesdale, Pa., U.S. C11 145
Honey Brook, Pa., U.S. . . . F10 145
Honeoye Bay, B.C., Can. . . E9 99
Honeypot Glen, Ct., U.S. . . C4 114
Honeyville, Ut., U.S. B3 151
Honfleur, Fr. C7 14
Hon Gai, Viet. D9 40
Hong'an, China D3 34
Hongch'ŏn, S. Kor. F15 32
Honghu, China F2 34
Hongjiang, China H2 34
Honglai, China J7 34
Hongliuyuan, China C6 30
Hongwŏn, N. Kor. C15 32
Hongxingqiao, China E8 34
Hongze Hu, l., China B7 34
Honiara, Sol. Is. I19 158
Honjō, Japan K13 36
Honokaa, Hi., U.S. C6 118
Honokahua, Hi., U.S. B5 118
Honolulu, Hi., U.S. B4 118
Honolulu, co., Hi., U.S. . . . B3 118
Honomu, Hi., U.S. D6 118
Honŏ, i., Japan g9 118
Honshū, i., Japan K13 36
Hood, co., Tx., U.S. C4 150
Hood, Mount, mtn., Or.,
U.S. B5 144
Hood Canal, b., Wa., U.S. . B2 154
Hoodoo Peak, mtn., Wa.,
U.S. A5 154
Hood River, Or., U.S. B5 144
Hood River, co., Or., U.S. . B5 144
Hoodsport, Wa., U.S. B2 154
Hooker, Ok., U.S. e9 143
Hooker, co., Ne., U.S. C4 134
Hooksett, N.H., U.S. D4 136
Hoonah, Ak., U.S. D12 109
Hooper, Ne., U.S. C9 134
Hooper Bay, Ak., U.S. C6 109
Hoopeston, Il., U.S. C6 120
Hoople, N.D., U.S. A8 141
Hoosac Range, mts., U.S. . A1 128
Hoosic, stm., U.S. C7 139
Hoosick Falls, N.Y., U.S. . . C7 139
Hoover, Al., U.S. B3 108
Hoover Dam, U.S. G7 135

Hoover Reservoir, res., Oh.,
U.S. B3 142
Hooverson Heights, W.V.,
U.S. f8 155
Hopatcong, N.J., U.S. B3 137
Hopatcong, Lake, l., N.J.,
U.S. A3 137
Hope, B.C., Can. E7 99
Hope, Ar., U.S. D2 111
Hope, In., U.S. F6 121
Hope, Ks., U.S. D6 123
Hope, N.D., U.S. B8 141
Hopedale, Newf., Can. . . . g9 102
Hopedale, Ma., U.S. B4 128
Hopefield, S. Afr. I4 66
Hopelchén, Mex. H15 90
Hopes Advance, Cap, c.,
Que., Can. f13 102
Hopetoun, Austl. J5 70
Hopetown, S. Afr. G7 66
Hope Valley, R.I., U.S. E2 146
Hopewell, N.S., Can. D7 101
Hopewell, Va., U.S. C5 153
Hopewell Cape, N.B., Can. . D5 101
Hopi Indian Reservation,
Az., U.S. A5 110
Hopkins, Mn., U.S. n12 130
Hopkins, Mo., U.S. A3 132
Hopkins, S.C., U.S. D6 147
Hopkins, co., Ky., U.S. . . . C2 124
Hopkins, co., Tx., U.S. C5 150
Hopkinsville, Ky., U.S. D2 124
Hopkinton, Ia., U.S. B6 122
Hopkinton, Ma., U.S. B4 128
Hopkinton, N.H., U.S. D3 136
Hopkinton, R.I., U.S. F1 146
Hopland, Ca., U.S. C2 112
Hopland Bouchard, Arg. . . . H7 80
Hopwood, Pa., U.S. G2 145
Hoquiam, Wa., U.S. C2 154
Horace, N.D., U.S. C9 141
Horatio, Ar., U.S. D1 111
Horconcitos, Pan. I12 92
Hørgen, Switz. D10 13
Horicon, Wi., U.S. E5 156
Horine, Mo., U.S. C7 132
Horizontina, Braz. D11 80
Horlivka, Ukr. H5 20
Hormuz, Strait of, strt., Asia H14 48
Horn, Aus. G15 10
Horn, c., Ice. A2 6a
Horn, Cape see Hornos,
Cabo de, c., Chile H3 78
Hornell, N.Y., U.S. C3 139
Hornersville, Mo., U.S. . . . E7 132
Horn Island, i., Ms., U.S. . . E5 131
Horn Lake, Ms., U.S. A3 131
Hornos, Cabo de (Cape
Horn), c., Chile H3 78
Horodenka, Ukr. A9 20
Horqin Youyi Qianqi, China B11 30
Horqueta, Para. B10 80
Horry, co., S.C., U.S. D10 147
Horse Cave, Ky., U.S. C4 124
Horse Creek, Wy., U.S. . . . E7 157
Horseheads, N.Y., U.S. . . . C4 139
Horsens, Den. N11 6
Horseshoe Bend, Ar., U.S. . A4 111
Horseshoe Bend, Id., U.S. . F2 119
Horsham, Austl. K5 70
Horton, Ks., U.S. C8 123
Hortonville, Wi., U.S. D5 156
Hosaina, Eth. N9 60
Hoschton, Ga., U.S. B3 117
Hoshangābād, India I7 44
Hoshiārpur, India E6 44
Hosmer, B.C., Can. E10 99
Hosmer, S.D., U.S. B6 148
Hospet, India E4 46
Hoste, Isla, i., Chile H3 78
Hotan, China D2 30
Hotchkiss, Co., U.S. C3 113
Hotevilla, Az., U.S. B5 110
Hot Spring, co., Ar., U.S. . . C2 111
Hot Springs, Mt., U.S. C2 133
Hot Springs, S.D., U.S. . . . D2 148
Hot Springs, co., Wy., U.S. . C4 157
Hot Springs National Park,
Ar., U.S. C2 111
Hot Springs National Park,
Ar., U.S. C2 111
Hot Springs Village, Ar.,
U.S. C2 111
Hot Sulphur Springs, Co.,
U.S. A4 113
Houck, Az., U.S. B6 110
Houghton, Mi., U.S. A2 129
Houghton, co., Mi., U.S. . . B2 129
Houghton Lake, l., Mi., U.S. D6 129
Houghton Lake, Mi., U.S. . . D6 129
Houghton Lake Heights,
Mi., U.S. D6 129
Houjie, China M2 34
Houlka, La., U.S. A4 131
Houlton, Me., U.S. B5 126
Houma, China D9 30
Houma, La., U.S. E5 125
House Springs, Mo., U.S. . . g12 132
Houston, De., U.S. E3 115
Houston, Mn., U.S. G7 130
Houston, Ms., U.S. B4 131
Houston, Tx., U.S. E5 150
Houston, co., Al., U.S. D4 108
Houston, co., Ga., U.S. . . . D3 117
Houston, co., Mn., U.S. . . . G7 130
Houston, co., Tn., U.S. . . . A4 149
Houston, co., Tx., U.S. D5 150
Houston, Lake, res., Tx.,
U.S. r14 150
Houtman Abrolhos, is.,
Austl. E2 68
Hoven, S.D., U.S. B6 148
Hovd, Mong. B6 30
Howard, Ks., U.S. E7 123
Howard, S.D., U.S. C8 148
Howard, Wi., U.S. D5 156
Howard, co., Ar., U.S. C1 111
Howard, co., In., U.S. C5 121
Howard, co., Ia., U.S. A5 122
Howard, co., Md., U.S. B4 127
Howard, co., Mo., U.S. . . . B5 132
Howard, co., Ne., U.S. C7 134

Howard, co., Tx., U.S. C2 150
Howard City, Mi., U.S. E5 129
Howard Lake, Mn., U.S. . . . E4 130
Howards Grove-Millersville,
Wi., U.S. E6 156
Howe, In., U.S. A7 121
Howell, Mi., U.S. F7 129
Howell, co., Mo., U.S. E6 132
Howells, Ne., U.S. C8 134
Howe Sound, strt., B.C.,
Can. E6 99
Howick, S. Afr. G10 66
Howitt, Mount, mtn., Austl. . K7 70
Howland, Me., U.S. C4 126
Howland Island, i., Oc. H22 158
Hoxie, Ar., U.S. A5 111
Hoxie, Ks., U.S. C3 123
Höxter, Ger. D9 10
Høyanger, Nor. K10 6
Hoyerswerda, Ger. D14 10
Hoyt, N.B., Can. D3 101
Hoyt, Ks., U.S. C8 123
Hoyt Lakes, Mn., U.S. C6 130
Hradec Králové, Czech
Rep. E15 10
Hranice, Czech Rep. F17 10
Hronov, Czech Rep. E16 10
Hrubieszów, Pol. E23 10
Hsilo, Tai. L9 34
Hsinchu, Tai. K9 34
Hsinchuang, Tai. J10 34
Hsintien, Tai. K10 34
Hsipaw, Mya. C4 40
Hua'an, China J6 34
Huacheng, China K4 34
Huacho, Peru D3 82
Huachuca City, Az., U.S. . . F5 110
Huaco, Arg. F4 80
Huacrachuco, Peru C3 82
Huadian, China C12 30
Hua Hin, Thai. H5 40
Huai, stm., China C6 34
Huai'an, China B8 34
Huaibin, China C4 34
Huaide, China C11 30
Huailai, China C3 32
Huainan, China C6 34
Huaining, China E5 34
Huaiyang, China B3 34
Huaiyuan, China C6 34
Huajuapan de León, Mex. . I11 90
Hualapai Mountains, mts.,
Az., U.S. C2 110
Hualapai Peak, mtn., Az.,
U.S. B2 110
Hualgayoc, Peru B2 82
Hualien, Tai. L10 34
Huallaga, stm., Peru A4 82
Huallanca, Peru C3 82
Huambo (Nova Lisboa),
Ang. D3 58
Huancabamba, Peru A2 82
Huancané, Peru F7 82
Huancavelica, Peru E4 82
Huancavelica, dept., Peru . E4 82
Huancayo, Peru E4 82
Huang (Yellow), stm., China D10 30
Huangchuan, China C4 34
Huangdu, China D10 34
Huanggang, China E3 34
Huangguoshu, China A8 40
Huanghua, China E5 32
Huangqi, China I8 34
Huangqiao, China C9 34
Huangshi, China E4 34
Huanguelén, Arg. I8 80
Huangyan, China G10 34
Huangyuan, China D7 30
Huanjiang, China B10 40
Huanta, Peru E4 82
Huánuco, Peru C4 82
Huánuco, dept., Peru C4 82
Huanuni, Bol. H8 82
Huara, Chile H7 82
Huaral, Peru D3 82
Huaráz, Peru C3 82
Huariaca, Peru D4 82
Huarina, Bol. G7 82
Huascarán, Nevado, mtn.,
Peru C3 82
Huasco, Chile E3 80
Huashi, China D9 34
Huatabampo, Mex. D5 90
Huatong, China C9 32
Huauchinango, Mex. G10 90
Huautla, Mex. H11 90
Huaxian, China L2 34
Huayin, China D3 82
Huayna Potosí, Nevado,
mtn., Bol. G7 82
Huaytará, Peru E4 82
Huayunca, Nevado, mtn.,
Peru F5 82
Hubbard, Ia., U.S. B4 122
Hubbard, Oh., U.S. A5 142
Hubbard, Or., U.S. B4 144
Hubbard, co., Mn., U.S. . . . C4 130
Hubbard Creek Lake, res.,
Tx., U.S. C3 150
Hubbards, N.S., Can. E5 101
Hubbell, Mi., U.S. A2 129
Hubei (Hupeh), prov., China E9 30
Hubli-Dhārwār, India E3 46
Huddersfield, Eng., U.K. . . H12 8
Hūdī, Sud. I8 60
Hudiksvall, Swe. K15 6
Hudson, Que., Can. D3 104
Hudson, Co., U.S. A6 113
Hudson, Fl., U.S. D4 116
Hudson, Il., U.S. C5 120
Hudson, In., U.S. A7 121
Hudson, Ia., U.S. B5 122
Hudson, Ks., U.S. D5 123
Hudson, Ma., U.S. G6 129
Hudson, N.H., U.S. E4 136
Hudson, N.Y., U.S. C7 139
Hudson, N.C., U.S. B1 140
Hudson, Oh., U.S. A4 142
Hudson, S.D., U.S. D9 148
Hudson, Wi., U.S. D1 156
Hudson, Wy., U.S. D4 157
Hudson, co., N.J., U.S. . . . B4 137
Hudson, stm., U.S. E7 139

Name	Map Ref.	Page
Hudson, Lake, res., Ok., U.S.	A6	143
Hudson Bay, Sask., Can.	E4	105
Hudson Bay, b., Can.	D15	96
Hudson Falls, N.Y., U.S.	B7	139
Hudson Hope, B.C., Can.	A6	99
Hudson Lake, In., U.S.	A4	121
Hudson Strait, strt., Can.	D18	96
Hudsonville, Mi., U.S.	F5	129
Hudspeth, co., Tx., U.S.	o12	150
Hue, Viet.	F9	40
Huehuetán, Mex.	B2	92
Huehuetenango, Guat.	B3	92
Huehuetenango, dept., Guat.	B3	92
Huejutla de Reyes, Mex.	G10	90
Huelva, Spain	H5	16
Huentelauquén, Chile	F3	80
Huerfano, co., Co., U.S.	D5	113
Huesca, Spain	C11	16
Huetamo de Núñez, Mex.	H9	90
Hueytown, Al., U.S.	g6	108
Huffakers, Nv., U.S.	D2	135
Huggins, Mount, mtn., Ant.	C8	73
Hugh Butler Lake, res., Ne., U.S.	D5	134
Hughenden, Austl.	C6	70
Hughenden, Alta., Can.	C5	98
Hughes, Ar., U.S.	C5	111
Hughes, co., Ok., U.S.	B5	143
Hughes, co., S.D., U.S.	C5	148
Hughesville, Md., U.S.	C4	127
Hughesville, Pa., U.S.	D8	145
Hugli, stm., India	J12	44
Hugo, Co., U.S.	B7	113
Hugo, Mn., U.S.	m13	130
Hugo, Ok., U.S.	C6	143
Hugo Lake, res., Ok., U.S.	C6	143
Hugoton, Ks., U.S.	E2	123
Hugou, China	B6	34
Huichang, China	J4	34
Huichapan, Mex.	G10	90
Hŭich'ŏn, N. Kor.	C14	32
Huila, dept., Col.	F5	84
Huila, Nevado del, mtn., Col.	F4	84
Huili, China	A7	40
Huillapima, Arg.	E6	80
Huimin, China	F5	32
Huinan (Chaoyang), China	A14	32
Huinca Renancó, Arg.	H6	80
Huiting, China	I4	32
Huitzuco de los Figueroa, Mex.	H10	90
Huixtla, Mex.	J13	90
Huiyang, China	A5	38
Huize, China	A7	40
Huizen, Neth.	D7	12
Huizhou, China	L3	34
Hukeng, China	H3	34
Hukuntsi, Bots.	E5	66
Hulan, China	B12	30
Hulett, Wy., U.S.	B8	157
Hull, Que., Can.	D2	104
Hull see Kingston upon Hull, Eng., U.K.	H13	8
Hull, Ia., U.S.	A1	122
Hull, Ma., U.S.	B6	128
Ḥulwān, Egypt	C6	60
Humacao, P.R.	E12	94
Humahuaca, Arg.	B6	80
Humaitá, Braz.	B10	82
Humaitá, Para.	D9	80
Humansdorp, S. Afr.	J7	66
Humansville, Mo., U.S.	D4	132
Humber, stm., Eng., U.K.	H13	8
Humberside, co., Eng., U.K.	H13	8
Humble, Tx., U.S.	E5	150
Humboldt, Sask., Can.	E3	105
Humboldt, Az., U.S.	C3	110
Humboldt, Ia., U.S.	B3	122
Humboldt, Ks., U.S.	E8	123
Humboldt, Ne., U.S.	D10	134
Humboldt, S.D., U.S.	D8	148
Humboldt, Tn., U.S.	B3	149
Humboldt, co., Ca., U.S.	B2	112
Humboldt, co., Ia., U.S.	B3	122
Humboldt, co., Nv., U.S.	B3	135
Humboldt, stm., Nv., U.S.	C3	135
Humeburn, Austl.	F6	70
Humenné, Slvk.	G21	10
Humnoke, Ar., U.S.	C4	111
Humphrey, Ar., U.S.	C4	111
Humphrey, Ne., U.S.	C8	134
Humphreys, co., Ms., U.S.	B3	131
Humphreys, co., Tn., U.S.	A4	149
Humphreys Peak, mtn., Az., U.S.	B4	110
Húnaflói, b., Ice.	B3	6a
Hunan, prov., China	F9	30
Hunchun, China	A18	32
Hunedoara, Rom.	D6	20
Hungary (Magyarország), ctry., Eur.	F12	4
Hŭngnam, N. Kor.	D15	32
Hungry Horse, Mt., U.S.	B2	133
Hungry Horse Reservoir, res., Mt., U.S.	B3	133
Huningue, Fr.	E14	14
Hunjiang (Badaojiang), China	B14	32
Hunt, co., Tx., U.S.	C4	150
Hunter, N.D., U.S.	B8	141
Hunterdon, co., N.J., U.S.	B3	137
Hunter Island, i., Austl.	M6	70
Hunter Island, i., B.C., Can.	D3	99
Hunter Mountain, mtn., N.Y., U.S.	C6	139
Hunter River, P.E.I., Can.	C6	101
Huntersfield Mountain, mtn., N.Y., U.S.	C6	139
Huntertown, In., U.S.	B7	121
Huntingburg, In., U.S.	H4	121
Huntingdon, B.C., Can.	f13	99
Huntingdon, Que., Can.	D3	104
Huntingdon, Pa., U.S.	F6	145
Huntingdon, Tn., U.S.	A3	149
Huntingdon, co., Pa., U.S.	F5	145
Huntington, Ar., U.S.	B1	111
Huntington, In., U.S.	C7	121
Huntington, N.Y., U.S.	E7	139
Huntington, Ut., U.S.	D5	151
Huntington, W.V., U.S.	C2	155
Huntington, co., In., U.S.	C6	121
Huntington Beach, Ca., U.S.	F4	112
Huntington Lake, res., In., U.S.	C7	121
Huntington Woods, Mi., U.S.	p15	129
Huntingtown, Md., U.S.	C4	127
Huntland, Tn., U.S.	B5	149
Huntley, Il., U.S.	A5	120
Huntley, Mt., U.S.	E8	133
Huntly, N.Z.	B5	72
Huntsville, Ont., Can.	B5	103
Huntsville, Al., U.S.	A3	108
Huntsville, Ar., U.S.	A2	111
Huntsville, Mo., U.S.	B5	132
Huntsville, Tn., U.S.	C9	149
Huntsville, Tx., U.S.	D5	150
Huntsville, Ut., U.S.	B4	151
Hunucmá, Mex.	G15	90
Hunyuan, China	D1	32
Huon Gulf, b., Pap. N. Gui.	m16	68a
Huoqiu, China	C5	34
Huotong, China	I8	34
Hurd, Cape, c., Ont., Can.	B3	103
Hure Qi, China	A9	32
Hurley, Ms., U.S.	E5	131
Hurley, N.M., U.S.	E1	138
Hurley, N.Y., U.S.	D6	139
Hurley, S.D., U.S.	D8	148
Hurley, Wi., U.S.	B3	156
Hurlock, Md., U.S.	C6	127
Huron, Oh., U.S.	A3	142
Huron, S.D., U.S.	C7	148
Huron, co., Mi., U.S.	E7	129
Huron, co., Oh., U.S.	A3	142
Huron, stm., Mi., U.S.	p14	129
Huron, Lake, l., N.A.	C10	106
Huron Mountains, hills, Mi., U.S.	B3	129
Hurricane, Ut., U.S.	F2	151
Hurricane, W.V., U.S.	C2	155
Hurstbridge, Austl.	K6	70
Hurt, Va., U.S.	C3	153
Hurtsboro, Al., U.S.	C4	108
Husheib, Sud.	J8	60
Huşi, Rom.	C12	20
Hustisford, Wi., U.S.	E5	156
Hutchinson, Ks., U.S.	D6	123
Hutchinson, Mn., U.S.	F4	130
Hutchinson, co., S.D., U.S.	D8	148
Hutchinson, co., Tx., U.S.	B2	150
Hutouya, China	F7	32
Huttig, Ar., U.S.	D3	111
Huttwil, Switz.	D8	13
Huwei, Tai.	L9	34
Huxley, Ia., U.S.	C4	122
Huzhou, China	E9	34
Hvannadalshnúkur, mtn., Ice.	B5	6a
Hvar, Otok, i., Cro.	F11	18
Hwange, Zimb.	B8	66
Hwang Ho see Huang, stm., China	D10	30
Hwangju, N. Kor.	E13	32
Hyannis, Ma., U.S.	C7	128
Hyannis Port, Ma., U.S.	C7	128
Hyattsville, Md., U.S.	C4	127
Hyattville, Wy., U.S.	B5	157
Hybla Valley, Va., U.S.	g12	153
Hyco Lake, res., N.C., U.S.	A3	140
Hydaburg, Ak., U.S.	D13	109
Hyde, co., N.C., U.S.	B6	140
Hyde, co., S.D., U.S.	C6	148
Hyde Park, N.Y., U.S.	D7	139
Hyde Park, Ut., U.S.	B4	151
Hyde Park, Vt., U.S.	B3	152
Hyderābād, India	D5	46
Hyderābād, Pak.	H3	44
Hydeville, Vt., U.S.	D2	152
Hydro, Ok., U.S.	B3	143
Hydrographers Passage, strt., Austl.	C8	70
Hyères, Fr.	I13	14
Hyères, Îles d', is., Fr.	B18	16
Hyesan, N. Kor.	B16	32
Hygiene, Co., U.S.	A5	113
Hyland, stm., Can.	D7	96
Hymera, In., U.S.	F3	121
Hyndman Peak, mtn., Id., U.S.	F4	119
Hyrum, Ut., U.S.	B4	151
Hysham, Mt., U.S.	D9	133
Hythe, Alta., Can.	B1	98

I

Name	Map Ref.	Page
Iacanga, Braz.	F4	79
Iaciara, Braz.	C5	79
Iaco (Yaco), stm., S.A.	C7	82
Iaçu, Braz.	B8	79
Iaeger, W.V., U.S.	D3	155
Ialomiţa, stm., Rom.	E11	20
Iapu, Braz.	E7	79
Iaşi, Rom.	B11	20
Ibadan, Nig.	H11	64
Ibagué, Col.	E5	84
Ibaiti, Braz.	G3	79
Ibans, Laguna de, b., Hond.	B10	92
Ibapah Peak, mtn., Ut., U.S.	D2	151
Ibarra, Ec.	G3	84
Ibarreta, Arg.	C9	80
Ibb, Yemen	G4	47
Ibbenbüren, Ger.	C7	10
Iberia, Mo., U.S.	C5	132
Iberia, co., La., U.S.	E4	125
Ibérica, Península, pen., Eur.	E6	52
Iberville, Que., Can.	D4	104
Iberville, co., La., U.S.	D4	125
Iberville, Mont d' (Mount Caubvick), mtn., Can.	g14	104
Ibiá, Braz.	E5	79
Ibicaraí, Braz.	C9	79
Ibicuí, Braz.	C9	79
Ibicuy, Arg.	G9	80
Ibiraci, Braz.	F5	79
Ibiraçu, Braz.	E8	79
Ibirama, Braz.	D14	80
Ibirapuã, Braz.	D8	79
Ibirataia, Braz.	C9	79
Ibirubá, Braz.	E12	80
Ibitinga, Braz.	F4	79
Ibo, Moz.	D8	58
Ibotirama, Braz.	B7	79
'Ibrī, Oman	C10	47
Ibshawāy, Egypt	C6	60
Ica, Peru	F4	82
Ica, dept., Peru	F4	82
Içá (Putumayo), stm., S.A.	I8	84
Içana (Isana), stm., S.A.	G9	84
Icaño, Arg.	E7	80
Icaño, Arg.	E6	80
İçel, Tur.	C3	48
Iceland (Ísland), ctry., Eur.	B4	4
Icém, Braz.	F4	79
Ichaikaronji, India	D3	46
Ichikawa, Japan	L14	36
Ichilo, stm., Bol.	G9	82
Ichinomiya, Japan	L11	36
Ichinoseki, Japan	I16	36
Ich'ŏn, S. Kor.	F15	32
Icó, Braz.	E11	76
Iconha, Braz.	F8	79
Icy Cape, c., Ak., U.S.	A7	109
Ida, co., Ia., U.S.	B2	122
Idabel, Ok., U.S.	D7	143
Ida Grove, Ia., U.S.	B2	122
Idah, Nig.	H13	64
Idaho, co., Id., U.S.	D3	119
Idaho, state, U.S.	E3	119
Idaho City, Id., U.S.	F3	119
Idaho Falls, Id., U.S.	F6	119
Idaho Springs, Co., U.S.	B5	113
Idamay, W.V., U.S.	k10	155
Idanre, Nig.	H12	64
Idar-Oberstein, Ger.	F7	10
Idaville, In., U.S.	C4	121
Ider, Al., U.S.	A4	108
Idfū, Egypt	E7	60
Idi, Indon.	L4	40
Idiofa, Zaire	C3	58
Idlib, Syria	D4	48
Idrica, Russia	E11	22
Idrija, Slvn.	C9	18
Iecava, Latv.	E7	22
Iepê, Braz.	G3	79
Ieper (Ypres), Bel.	G2	12
Ierisós, Grc.	I7	20
Ife, Nig.	H12	64
Ifni, hist. reg., Mor.	F5	62
Ifon-Oshogbo, Nig.	H12	64
Igaporã, Braz.	B7	79
Igarka, Russia	D9	28
Igbasa-Odo, Nig.	H11	64
Iğdır, Tur.	B8	48
Iglesias, Italy	J3	18
Igloolik, N.W. Ter., Can.	C16	96
Ignacio, Co., U.S.	D3	113
Ignacio Zaragoza, Mex.	C6	90
Ignalina, Lith.	F9	22
Iguaçu, stm., S.A.	C12	80
Iguaçu, Cataratas do (Iguassu Falls), wtfl, S.A.	C11	80
Iguaí, Braz.	C8	79
Iguala, Mex.	H10	90
Igualada, Spain	D13	16
Iguape, Braz.	C15	80
Iguassu Falls see Iguaçu, Cataratas do, wtfl, S.A.	C11	80
Iguatemi, Braz.	G1	79
Iguatu, Braz.	E11	76
Ihiala, Nig.	I13	64
Ihosy, Madag.	s22	67b
Ihtiman, Bul.	G7	20
Iida, Japan	L12	36
Iizuka, Japan	N5	36
Ijaji, Eth.	M9	60
Ijebu-Igbo, Nig.	H12	64
IJmuiden, Neth.	D6	12
IJssel, stm., Neth.	C8	12
IJsselmeer (Zuiderzee), Neth.	C7	12
Ijuí, Braz.	E12	80
Ikalamavony, Madag.	r22	67b
Ikirun, Nig.	H12	64
Ikot Ekpene, Nig.	I13	64
Ikša, Russia	E20	22
Īlām, Iran	E9	48
Ilan, Tai.	K10	34
Ilanskij, Russia	F17	26
Ilanz, Switz.	E11	13
Ilaro, Nig.	H11	64
Iława, Pol.	B19	10
Ilderton, Ont., Can.	D3	103
Île-à-la-Crosse, Sask., Can.	m7	105
Île-à-la-Crosse, Lac, l., Sask., Can.	B2	105
Ilebo, Zaire	B4	58
Île-de-France, hist. reg., Fr.	C9	14
Île-Perrot, Que., Can.	q19	104
Ilesha, Nig.	H12	64
Ilford, Man., Can.	A4	100
Ilfracombe, Austl.	D6	70
Ilhabela, Braz.	G6	79
Ilha Grande, Baía da, b., Braz.	G6	79
Ilha Solteira, Reprêsa de, res., Braz.	F3	79
Ilhéus, Braz.	C9	79
Iliamna Lake, l., Ak., U.S.	D8	109
Iliamna Volcano, vol., Ak., U.S.	C9	109
Iligan, Phil.	D7	38
Ilion, N.Y., U.S.	B5	139
Iljinskoje-Chovanskoje, Russia	E22	22
Illampu, Nevado, mtn., Bol.	F7	82
Illapel, Chile	F3	80
Illéla, Niger	D12	64
Iller, stm., Ger.	H10	10
Illimani, Nevado, mtn., Bol.	G8	82
Illinois, state, U.S.	C4	120
Illinois, stm., U.S.	A7	143
Illinois, stm., Il., U.S.	B5	120
Illiopolis, Il., U.S.	D4	120
Illmo, Mo., U.S.	D8	132
Ilo, Peru	G6	82
Ilobasco, El Sal.	D6	92
Iloilo, Phil.	C7	38
Ilora, Nig.	H11	64
Ilorin, Nig.	G12	64
Ilūkste, Lat.	F9	22
Ilwaco, Wa., U.S.	C1	154
Imabari, Japan	M8	36
Imari, Japan	N4	36
Imaruí, Braz.	E14	80
Imatra, Fin.	K21	6
Imbabura, prov., Ec.	G3	84
Imbituba, Braz.	E14	80
Imboden, Ar., U.S.	A4	111
Imeni C'urupy, Russia	F21	22
İmişli, Azer.	B10	48
Imjin-gang, stm., Asia	F14	32
Imlay, Nv., U.S.	C3	135
Imlay City, Mi., U.S.	E7	129
Immokalee, Fl., U.S.	F5	116
Imnaha, stm., Or., U.S.	B10	144
Imola, Italy	E6	18
Imperatriz, Braz.	E9	76
Imperia, Italy	F3	18
Imperial, Sask., Can.	F3	105
Imperial, Peru	E3	82
Imperial, Mo., U.S.	C7	132
Imperial, Ne., U.S.	D4	134
Imperial, Pa., U.S.	k13	145
Imperial, co., Ca., U.S.	F6	112
Imperial Beach, Ca., U.S.	o15	112
Imperial Reservoir, res., U.S.	E1	110
Imperial Valley, val., Ca., U.S.	F6	112
Impfondo, Congo	A3	58
Imphāl, India	H15	44
Imuris, Mex.	B4	90
Iñapari, Peru	D7	82
Inari, Fin.	G20	6
Inarijärvi, l., Fin.	G20	6
Inca, Spain	F14	16
Inch'ŏn, S. Kor.	F14	32
Incline Village, Nv., U.S.	D2	135
Inda Silase, Eth.	J10	60
Indaw, Mya.	C3	40
Independence, Ia., U.S.	B6	122
Independence, Ks., U.S.	E8	123
Independence, Ky., U.S.	B5	124
Independence, La., U.S.	D5	125
Independence, Ms., U.S.	A4	131
Independence, Mo., U.S.	B3	132
Independence, Or., U.S.	C3	144
Independence, Va., U.S.	D1	153
Independence, Wi., U.S.	D2	156
Independence, co., Ar., U.S.	B4	111
Independence National Historical Park, Pa., U.S.	p21	145
Independence Rock, mtn., Wy., U.S.	D5	157
Independencia, Bol.	G8	82
India (Bhārat), ctry., Asia	E10	42
Indiana, Pa., U.S.	E3	145
Indiana, co., Pa., U.S.	E3	145
Indiana, state, U.S.	E5	121
Indiana Dunes National Lakeshore, In., U.S.	A3	121
Indianapolis, In., U.S.	E5	121
Indian Head, Sask., Can.	G4	105
Indian Head, Md., U.S.	C3	127
Indian Mound, Tn., U.S.	A4	149
Indian Neck, Ct., U.S.	D4	114
Indian Ocean	J11	158
Indianola, Ia., U.S.	C4	122
Indianola, Ms., U.S.	B3	131
Indianola, Ne., U.S.	D5	134
Indian River, co., Fl., U.S.	E6	116
Indian River, b., Fl., U.S.	D6	116
Indian River Bay, b., De., U.S.	F5	115
Indian Rocks Beach, Fl., U.S.	p10	116
Indian Springs, Nv., U.S.	G6	135
Indiantown, Fl., U.S.	E6	116
Indian Trail, N.C., U.S.	B2	140
Indiaporã, Braz.	E3	79
Indigirka, stm., Russia	D21	28
Indio, Ca., U.S.	F5	112
Indira Gandhi Canal, India	F5	44
Indochina, reg., Asia	H11	24
Indonesia, ctry., Asia	G7	38
Indore, India	I6	44
Indus, stm., Asia	H2	44
İnegöl, Tur.	I13	20
Infiernillo, Presa del, res., Mex.	H9	90
Ingalls, In., U.S.	E6	121
Ingalls Park, Il., U.S.	B5	120
Ingelheim, Ger.	F8	10
Ingelmunster, Bel.	G3	12
Ingeniero Luiggi, Arg.	H6	80
Ingeniero Luis A. Huergo, Arg.	J5	80
Ingersoll, Ont., Can.	D4	103
Ingham, Austl.	B7	70
Ingham, co., Mi., U.S.	F6	129
Ingleside, Tx., U.S.	F4	150
Inglewood, Ca., U.S.	n12	112
Inglis, Man., Can.	D1	100
Ingolstadt, Ger.	G11	10
Ingonish, N.S., Can.	C9	101
Ingonish Beach, N.S., Can.	C9	101
Ingrāj Bāzār, India	H13	44
Ingram, Pa., U.S.	k13	145
Ingwiller, Fr.	D14	14
Inhambane, Moz.	D12	66
Inhambupe, Braz.	A9	79
Inhapim, Braz.	E7	79
Inharrime, Moz.	E12	66
Inhumas, Braz.	D4	79
Inimutaba, Braz.	E6	79
Inírida, stm., Col.	F8	84
Inisa, Nig.	H12	64
Injune, Austl.	E8	70
Inkom, Id., U.S.	G6	119
Inkster, Mi., U.S.	p15	129
Inland Sea see Seto-naikai, Japan	M7	36
Inle Lake, l., Mya.	D4	40
Inman, Ks., U.S.	D6	123
Inman, S.C., U.S.	A3	147
Inn (En), stm., Eur.	D20	14
Inner Channel, strt., Belize	I15	90
Inner Mongolia see Nei Monggol Zizhiqu, prov., China	C10	30
Innisfail, Austl.	A7	70
Innisfail, Alta., Can.	C4	98
Innisfree, Alta., Can.	C5	98
Innsbruck, Aus.	H11	10
Inola, Ok., U.S.	A6	143
Inongo, Zaire	B3	58
Inowrocław, Pol.	C18	10
In Salah, Alg.	G12	62
Institute, W.V., U.S.	m12	155
Inta, Russia	D10	26
Intendente Alvear, Arg.	H7	80
Interlaken, Switz.	E8	13
International Falls, Mn., U.S.	B5	130
Intervale, N.H., U.S.	B4	136
Inthanon, Doi, mtn., Thai.	E5	40
Intibucá, dept., Hond.	C6	92
Intracoastal Waterway, U.S.	E4	125
Inukjuak, Que., Can.	g11	104
Inuvik, N.W. Ter., Can.	C6	96
Invercargill, N.Z.	G2	72
Inverell, Austl.	G9	70
Invergordon, Scot., U.K.	D9	8
Inver Grove Heights, Mn., U.S.	n12	130
Invermay, Sask., Can.	F4	105
Invermere, B.C., Can.	D9	99
Inverness, Scot., U.K.	D9	8
Inverness, Fl., U.S.	D4	116
Inverness, Ms., U.S.	B3	131
Inverness, Mt., U.S.	B6	133
Investigator Group, is., Austl.	F6	68
Investigator Strait, strt., Austl.	J2	70
Inwood, Man., Can.	D3	100
Inwood, Ia., U.S.	A1	122
Inwood, N.Y., U.S.	k13	139
Inwood, W.V., U.S.	B6	155
Inyangani, mtn., Zimb.	B11	66
Inyo, co., Ca., U.S.	D5	112
Inza, Russia	G7	26
Inžavino, Russia	I25	22
Ioánnina, Grc.	J4	20
Iō-jima (Iwo Jima), i., Japan	F18	158
Iola, Ks., U.S.	E8	123
Iola, Wi., U.S.	D4	156
Iolotan', Turk.	J10	26
Iona, Id., U.S.	F7	119
Ione, Ca., U.S.	C3	112
Ione, Wa., U.S.	A8	154
Ionia, Mi., U.S.	F5	129
Ionia, co., Mi., U.S.	F5	129
Ionian Islands see Iónioi Nísoi, is., Grc.	K4	20
Ionian Sea, Eur.	H11	4
Iónioi Nísoi, is., Grc.	K4	20
Iosco, co., Mi., U.S.	D7	129
Iota, La., U.S.	D3	125
Iowa, La., U.S.	D2	125
Iowa, co., Ia., U.S.	C5	122
Iowa, co., Wi., U.S.	E3	156
Iowa, state, U.S.	C4	122
Iowa, stm., Ia., U.S.	C6	122
Iowa City, Ia., U.S.	C6	122
Iowa Falls, Ia., U.S.	B4	122
Iowa Park, Tx., U.S.	C3	150
Ipameri, Braz.	D4	79
Ipatinga, Braz.	E7	79
Ípeiros, hist. reg., Grc.	J4	20
Ipiales, Col.	G4	84
Ipiaú, Braz.	C9	79
Ipirá, Braz.	B9	79
Ipiranga, Braz.	C13	80
Ipoh, Malay.	L6	40
Iporá, Braz.	D3	79
Iporã, Braz.	G2	79
Ipoti-Ekiti, Nig.	H12	64
Ipswich, Austl.	F10	70
Ipswich, Eng., U.K.	I15	8
Ipswich, Ma., U.S.	A6	128
Ipswich, S.D., U.S.	B6	148
Ipu, Braz.	D10	76
Ipupiara, Braz.	A7	79
Iqaluit, N.W. Ter., Can.	D19	96
Iquique, Chile	G7	74
Iquique, Chile	I6	82
Iquitos, Peru	I6	84
Iraí, Braz.	D12	80
Iráklion, Grc.	N9	20
Iran (Īrān), ctry., Asia	C5	42
Iran, Pegunungan, mts., Asia	E5	38
Īrānshahr, Iran	H16	48
Irapa, Ven.	B11	84
Irapuato, Mex.	G9	90
Iraq (Al-'Irāq), ctry., Asia	C3	42
Irará, Braz.	B9	79
Irasburg, Vt., U.S.	B4	152
Irati, Braz.	C13	80
Irazú, Volcán, vol., C.R.	H11	92
Irbid, Jord.	C5	50
Irbīl, Iraq	C8	48
Irbit, Russia	F10	26
Iredell, co., N.C., U.S.	B2	140
Ireland (Éire), ctry., Eur.	E6	4
Irene, S.D., U.S.	D8	148
Ireng (Maú), stm., S.A.	E13	84
Iri, S. Kor.	H14	32
Iringa, Tan.	C7	58
Irion, co., Tx., U.S.	D2	150
Iriona, Hond.	B9	92
Irish Sea, Eur.	H8	8
Irkutsk, Russia	G12	28
Irma, Alta., Can.	C5	98
Irmo, S.C., U.S.	C5	147
Iron, co., Mi., U.S.	B2	129
Iron, co., Mo., U.S.	D7	132
Iron, co., Ut., U.S.	F2	151
Iron, co., Wi., U.S.	B3	156
Irondale, Al., U.S.	f7	108
Irondequoit, N.Y., U.S.	B3	139
Iron Gate, val., Eur.	E6	20
Iron Gate Reservoir, res., Eur.	E6	20
Iron Knob, Austl.	I2	70
Iron Mountain, Mi., U.S.	C2	129
Iron Mountains, mts., U.S.	D1	153
Iron River, Mi., U.S.	B2	129
Iron River, Wi., U.S.	B2	156
Ironton, Mo., U.S.	D7	132
Ironton, Oh., U.S.	D3	142
Ironwood, Mi., U.S.	n11	129
Iroquois, Ont., Can.	C9	103
Iroquois, S.D., U.S.	C8	148
Iroquois, co., Il., U.S.	C6	120
Iroquois, stm., U.S.	C6	120
Iroquois Falls, Ont., Can.	o19	103
Irrawaddy see Ayeyarwady, stm., Mya.	F3	40
Irricana, Alta., Can.	D4	98
Irrigon, Or., U.S.	B7	144
Irshava, Ukr.	A7	20
Irtyš (Ertix), stm., Asia	E11	26
Irtyšsk, Kaz.	G13	26
Irún, Spain	B10	16
Irvine, Alta., Can.	E5	98
Irvine, Scot., U.K.	F9	8
Irvine, Ca., U.S.	n13	112
Irvine, Ky., U.S.	C6	124
Irving, Tx., U.S.	n10	150
Irvington, Al., U.S.	E1	108
Irvington, Ky., U.S.	C3	124
Irvington, N.J., U.S.	k8	137
Irvington, N.Y., U.S.	g13	139
Irwin, Pa., U.S.	F2	145
Irwin, co., Ga., U.S.	E3	117
Irwinton, Ga., U.S.	D3	117
Isabel, S.D., U.S.	B4	148
Isabelia, Cordillera, mts., Nic.	D9	92
Isabella, co., Mi., U.S.	E6	129
Isaccea, Rom.	D12	20
Ísafjörður, Ice.	A2	6a
Isahaya, Japan	O5	36
Isana (Içana), stm., S.A.	G8	84
Isanti, Mn., U.S.	E5	130
Isanti, co., Mn., U.S.	E5	130
Isar, stm., Eur.	G11	10
Isara, Nig.	H11	64
Ise (Uji-yamada), Japan	M11	36
Iselin, N.J., U.S.	B4	137
Iseo, Lago d', l., Italy	D5	18
Isère, stm., Fr.	G12	14
Iserlohn, Ger.	D7	10
Isernia, Italy	H9	18
Isesaki, Japan	K14	36
Iseyin, Nig.	H11	64
Ishinomaki, Japan	I16	36
Ishpeming, Mi., U.S.	B3	129
Isil'kul', Russia	G12	26
Išim, Russia	F11	26
Išim, stm., Asia	F12	26
Išimbaj, Russia	G9	26
Isiolo, Kenya	A7	58
Isipingo, S. Afr.	G10	66
Isiro, Zaire	H6	56
Isisford, Austl.	E6	70
Iskăr, stm., Bul.	F8	20
İskenderun, Tur.	C4	48
Iskitim, Russia	G8	28
Isla, Mex.	H12	90
Isla Cristina, Spain	H4	16
Islāmābād, Pak.	D5	44
Isla Mujeres, Mex.	G16	90
Island, co., Wa., U.S.	A3	154
Island Beach, N.J., U.S.	D4	137
Island City, Or., U.S.	B8	144
Island Falls, Me., U.S.	B4	126
Island Lake, l., Man., Can.	C4	100
Island Park, R.I., U.S.	E6	146
Island Pond, Vt., U.S.	B5	152
Islands, Bay of, b., Newf., Can.	D2	102
Islas de la Bahía, dept., Hond.	A8	92
Isla Verde, Arg.	G7	80
Isla Vista, Ca., U.S.	E4	112
Islay, Alta., Can.	C5	98
Islay, i., Scot., U.K.	F7	8
Isle-aux-Morts, Newf., Can.	E2	102
Isle of Man, dep., Eur.	E7	4
Isle of Palms, S.C., U.S.	k12	147
Isle of Wight, co., Eng., U.K.	K12	8
Isle of Wight, co., Va., U.S.	D6	153
Isle of Wight Bay, b., Md., U.S.	D7	127
Isle Royale National Park, Mi., U.S.	h9	129
Islesboro Island, i., Me., U.S.	D4	126
Isleta, N.M., U.S.	C3	138
Islington, Ma., U.S.	h11	128
Ismael Cortinas, Ur.	G10	80
Ismailia see Al-Ismā'īlīyah, Egypt	B7	60
Isnā, Egypt	E7	60
Isojoki, Fin.	J17	6
Isola, Ms., U.S.	B3	131
Isparta, Tur.	H14	4
Israel (Yisra'el), ctry., Asia	C2	42
Issaquah, Wa., U.S.	B3	154
Issaquena, co., Ms., U.S.	C2	131
Issoire, Fr.	G10	14
Issoudun, Fr.	F9	14
Is-sur-Tille, Fr.	E12	14
Issyk-Kul', ozero, l., Kyrg.	I13	26
İstanbul, Tur.	H12	20
İstanbul Boğazı (Bosporus), strt., Tur.	H13	20
Isto, Mount, mtn., Ak., U.S.	B11	109
Istokpoga, Lake, l., Fl., U.S.	E5	116
Istra, Russia	F19	22
Itá, Para.	C10	80
Itabaiana, Braz.	F11	76
Itabaiana, Braz.	E11	76
Itabapoana, Braz.	F8	79
Itaberá, Braz.	G4	79
Itaberaba, Braz.	B8	79
Itaberaí, Braz.	D4	79
Itabira, Braz.	E7	79
Itabuna, Braz.	C9	79
Itacoatiara, Braz.	I13	84
Itaeté, Braz.	B8	79
Itagi, Braz.	C8	79
Itaguaçu, Braz.	E8	79
Itaguajé, Braz.	G3	79
Itaguara, Braz.	F6	79
Itaguaru, Braz.	C4	79
Itagüí, Col.	D5	84
Itaí, Braz.	G4	79
Itá-Ibaté, Arg.	D10	80
Itaiópolis, Braz.	D14	80
Itaipu, Reprêsa de, res., S.A.	C11	80
Itaituba, Braz.	D7	76
Itajá, Braz.	E3	79
Itajaí, Braz.	D14	80
Itajubá, Braz.	G6	79
Itajuípe, Braz.	C9	79
Italy (Italia), ctry., Eur.	G10	4
Itamaraju, Braz.	D9	79
Itamarandiba, Braz.	D7	79
Itamari, Braz.	B9	79
Itambacuri, Braz.	E8	79
Itambé, Braz.	C8	79
Itami, Japan	M10	36
Itanhaém, Braz.	H5	79
Itanhém, Braz.	D8	79
Itanhomi, Braz.	E8	79
Itaobim, Braz.	D8	79
Itapaci, Braz.	C4	79
Itapagipe, Braz.	E4	79
Itapé, Braz.	C9	79

Name	Map Ref.	Page
Itapebi, Braz.	C9	79
Itapecerica, Braz.	F6	79
Itapecuru-Mirim, Braz.	D10	76
Itapemirim, Braz.	F8	79
Itaperuna, Braz.	F8	79
Itapetinga, Braz.	C8	79
Itapetininga, Braz.	G4	79
Itapeva, Braz.	G4	79
Itapira, Braz.	G5	79
Itapiranga, Braz.	D12	80
Itapiranga, Braz.	I13	84
Itapirapuã, Braz.	C3	79
Itapitanga, Braz.	C9	79
Itápolis, Braz.	F4	79
Itaporã, Braz.	G1	79
Itaporanga, Braz.	G4	79
Itapúa, dept., Para.	D11	80
Itapuranga, Braz.	C4	79
Itaquara, Braz.	B9	79
Itaquari, Braz.	F8	79
Itaqui, Braz.	E10	80
Itarantim, Braz.	C8	79
Itararé, Braz.	H4	79
Itārsi, India	I7	44
Itasca, Il., U.S.	k8	120
Itasca, co., Mn., U.S.	C5	130
Itasca, Lake, l., Mn., U.S.	C3	130
Itatí, Arg.	D9	80
Itatinga, Braz.	G4	79
Itaúna, Braz.	F6	79
Itawamba, co., Ms., U.S.	A5	131
Itenes (Guaporé), stm., S.A.	E10	82
Ithaca, Mi., U.S.	E6	129
Ithaca, N.Y., U.S.	C4	139
Itinga, Braz.	D8	79
Itirapina, Braz.	G5	79
Itiruçu, Braz.	B8	79
Itō, Japan	M14	36
Itonamas, stm., Bol.	E9	82
Itororó, Braz.	C8	79
Itta Bena, Ms., U.S.	B3	131
Itú, Braz.	G5	79
Ituaçu, Braz.	B8	79
Ituango, Col.	D5	84
Ituberá, Braz.	B9	79
Ituiutaba, Braz.	E4	79
Itumbiara, Braz.	E4	79
Ituna, Sask., Can.	F4	105
Ituporanga, Braz.	D14	80
Iturama, Braz.	E3	79
Iturup, ostrov (Etorofu-tō), i., Russia	c22	36a
Ituverava, Braz.	F5	79
Ituzaingó, Arg.	D10	80
Itzehoe, Ger.	B9	10
Iuka, Ms., U.S.	A5	131
Iúna, Braz.	F8	79
Iva, S.C., U.S.	C2	147
Ivaceviči, Bela.	I8	22
Ivahona, Madag.	s22	67b
Ivaí, stm., Braz.	G2	79
Ivaiporã, Braz.	C13	80
Ivangorod, Russia	B11	22
Ivangrad, Yugo.	G3	20
Ivanhoe, Mn., U.S.	F2	130
Ivano-Frankivs'k, Ukr.	H2	26
Ivanovo, Bela.	I8	22
Ivanovo, Russia	D23	22
Ivato, Madag.	r22	67b
Ivdel', Russia	E10	26
Ivenec, Bela.	H9	22
Ivins, Ut., U.S.	F2	151
Ivje, Bela.	H8	22
Ivory Coast, C. Iv.	I7	64
Ivory Coast see Cote d'Ivoire, ctry., Afr.	G5	54
Ivoryton, Ct., U.S.	D6	114
Ivrea, Italy	D2	18
Iwaki (Taira), Japan	J15	36
Iwakuni, Japan	M7	36
Iwamizawa, Japan	d16	36a
Iwo, Nig.	H12	64
Iwo Jima see Iō-jima, i., Japan	F18	158
Ixiamas, Bol.	E7	82
Ixmiquilpan, Mex.	G10	90
Ixopo, S. Afr.	H10	66
Ixtapa, Mex.	I9	90
Ixtepec, Mex.	I12	90
Ixtlán de Juárez, Mex.	I11	90
Ixtlán del Río, Mex.	G7	90
Izabal, dept., Guat.	B5	92
Izabal, Lago de, l., Guat.	B5	92
Izamal, Mex.	G15	90
Izard, co., Ar., U.S.	A4	111
Izberbaš, Russia	I7	26
Izegem, Bel.	G3	12
Īzeh, Iran	F10	48
Iževsk, Russia	F8	26
Izmail, Ukr.	H3	26
İzmir (Smyrna), Tur.	K11	20
İzmit, Tur.	G13	4
Izoplit, Russia	E19	22
Izozog, Bañados del, sw., Bol.	H10	82
Izra', Syria	C6	50
Iztaccíhuatl, Volcán, vol., Mex.	H10	90
Izúcar de Matamoros, Mex.	H10	90
Izumi, Japan	I15	36
Izumo, Japan	M10	36
Izumo, Japan	L7	36
Izu-shotō, is., Japan	E15	30
Izyum, Ukr.	H5	26

J

Name	Map Ref.	Page
Jabal al-Awliyā', Sud.	J7	60
Jabalpur, India	I8	44
Jabālyah, Gaza	E2	50
Jabiru, Austl.	B6	68
Jablah, Syria	D3	48
Jablonec nad Nisou, Czech Rep.	E15	10
Jablonovyj chrebet, mts., Russia	G14	28
Jaboatão, Braz.	E11	76
Jaborandi, Braz.	F4	79
Jaboticabal, Braz.	F4	79
Jaca, Spain	C11	16
Jacala, Mex.	G10	90
Jacarei, Braz.	G6	79
Jacarezinho, Braz.	G4	79
Jaceel, val., Som.	F11	56
Jachroma, Russia	E20	22
Jaciara, Braz.	C1	79
Jacinto, Braz.	D8	79
Jacinto Aráuz, Arg.	J7	80
Jacinto City, Tx., U.S.	r14	150
Jacinto Machado, Braz.	E14	80
Jack, co., Tx., U.S.	C3	150
Jackman, Me., U.S.	C2	126
Jackman Station, Me., U.S.	C2	126
Jack Mountain, mtn., Mt., U.S.	D4	133
Jack Mountain, mtn., Wa., U.S.	A5	154
Jackpot, Nv., U.S.	B7	135
Jacksboro, Tn., U.S.	C9	149
Jacksboro, Tx., U.S.	C3	150
Jacks Mountain, mtn., Pa., U.S.	E6	145
Jackson, Al., U.S.	D2	108
Jackson, Ga., U.S.	C3	117
Jackson, Ky., U.S.	C6	124
Jackson, La., U.S.	D4	125
Jackson, Mi., U.S.	F6	129
Jackson, Mn., U.S.	G4	130
Jackson, Ms., U.S.	C3	131
Jackson, Mo., U.S.	D8	132
Jackson, N.H., U.S.	B4	136
Jackson, Oh., U.S.	C3	142
Jackson, S.C., U.S.	E4	147
Jackson, Tn., U.S.	B3	149
Jackson, Wi., U.S.	E5	156
Jackson, Wy., U.S.	C2	157
Jackson, co., Al., U.S.	A3	108
Jackson, co., Ar., U.S.	B4	111
Jackson, co., Co., U.S.	A4	113
Jackson, co., Fl., U.S.	B1	116
Jackson, co., Ga., U.S.	B3	117
Jackson, co., Il., U.S.	F4	120
Jackson, co., In., U.S.	G5	121
Jackson, co., Ia., U.S.	B7	122
Jackson, co., Ks., U.S.	C8	123
Jackson, co., Ky., U.S.	C5	124
Jackson, co., La., U.S.	B3	125
Jackson, co., Mi., U.S.	F6	129
Jackson, co., Mn., U.S.	G3	130
Jackson, co., Ms., U.S.	E5	131
Jackson, co., Mo., U.S.	B3	132
Jackson, co., N.C., U.S.	f9	140
Jackson, co., Oh., U.S.	C3	142
Jackson, co., Ok., U.S.	C2	143
Jackson, co., Or., U.S.	E4	144
Jackson, co., S.D., U.S.	D4	148
Jackson, co., Tn., U.S.	C8	149
Jackson, co., Tx., U.S.	E4	150
Jackson, co., W.V., U.S.	C3	155
Jackson, co., Wi., U.S.	D3	156
Jackson, Mount, mtn., Ant.	C12	73
Jackson Lake, res., Wy., U.S.	C2	157
Jackson Mountain, mtn., Me., U.S.	D2	126
Jackson's Arm, Newf., Can.	D3	102
Jacksons Gap, Al., U.S.	C4	108
Jacksonville, Al., U.S.	B4	108
Jacksonville, Ar., U.S.	C3	111
Jacksonville, Fl., U.S.	B5	116
Jacksonville, Il., U.S.	D3	120
Jacksonville, N.C., U.S.	C5	140
Jacksonville, Or., U.S.	E4	144
Jacksonville, Tx., U.S.	D5	150
Jacksonville, Vt., U.S.	F3	152
Jacksonville Beach, Fl., U.S.	B5	116
Jacmel, Haiti	E8	94
Jacobābād, Pak.	F3	44
Jacobina, Braz.	F10	76
Jacques-Cartier, Détroit de, strt., Que., Can.	h8	102
Jacquet River, N.B., Can.	B4	101
Jacupiranga, Braz.	C14	80
Jaén, Peru	A2	82
Jaén, Spain	H8	16
Jaffa, Cape, c., Austl.	K3	70
Jaffa, Tel Aviv- see Tel Aviv-Yafo, Isr.	D3	50
Jaffna, Sri L.	H6	46
Jaffrey, N.H., U.S.	E2	136
Jaffrey Center, N.H., U.S.	E2	136
Jagādhri, India	E7	44
Jagdalpur, India	C7	46
Jagodnoje, Russia	E21	28
Jagtiāl, India	C5	46
Jaguaquara, Braz.	B9	79
Jaguarão, Braz.	G12	80
Jaguarão (Yaguarón), stm., S.A.	G12	80
Jaguari, Braz.	E11	80
Jaguariaíva, Braz.	C14	80
Jaguaruna, Braz.	E14	80
Jagüey Grande, Cuba	C4	94
Jahrom, Iran	G12	48
Jaipur, India	G6	44
Jaja, Russia	F15	26
Jajce, Bos.	E12	18
Jakarta, Indon.	j13	39a
Jakobstad (Pietarsaari), Fin.	E14	6
Jakutija, state, Russia	D18	28
Jakutsk, Russia	E17	28
Jal, N.M., U.S.	E6	138
Jalālābād, Afg.	C4	44
Jalālī, stm., Hond.	C8	92
Jalandhar, India	E6	44
Jalapa, Guat.	C5	92
Jalapa, dept., Guat.	C5	92
Jalapa, Mex.	G8	90
Jalapa, Mex.	G8	90
Jālgaon, India	J6	44
Jālna, India	C3	46
Jalostotitlán, Mex.	G8	90
Jalpa, Mex.	G8	90
Jalpāiguri, India	G13	44
Jalpan, Mex.	G10	90
Jalūlā', Iraq	D8	48
Jalutorovsk, Russia	F11	26
Jamaica, ctry., N.A.	E6	94
Jamaica Bay, b., N.Y., U.S.	k13	139
Jamaica Channel, strt., N.A.	E7	94
Jamāl, poluostrov, pen., Russia	C12	26
Jamalo-Neneckij, state, Russia	D12	26
Jamālpur, Bngl.	H13	44
Jamālpur, India	H12	44
Jambi, Indon.	F3	38
Jambol, Bul.	G10	20
James, stm., U.S.	C7	106
James, stm., Mo., U.S.	E4	132
James, stm., Va., U.S.	C5	153
James, Lake, res., N.C., U.S.	B1	140
James Bay, b., Can.	F16	96
Jamesburg, N.J., U.S.	C4	137
James City, N.C., U.S.	B5	140
James City, co., Va., U.S.	C6	153
James Craik, Arg.	G7	80
James Island, S.C., U.S.	k12	147
Jamesport, Mo., U.S.	B4	132
Jamestown, Austl.	I3	70
Jamestown, Co., U.S.	A5	113
Jamestown, In., U.S.	E4	121
Jamestown, Ky., U.S.	D4	124
Jamestown, N.Y., U.S.	C1	139
Jamestown, N.C., U.S.	B3	140
Jamestown, N.D., U.S.	C7	141
Jamestown, R.I., U.S.	F5	146
Jamestown, Tn., U.S.	C9	149
James Town, Wy., U.S.	E3	157
Jamestown Reservoir, res., N.D., U.S.	C7	141
Jammu, India	D6	44
Jammu and Kashmir, dep., Asia	C10	42
Jamnagar, India	I4	44
Jamshedpur, India	I12	44
Jamuna, stm., Bngl.	H13	44
Janaúba, Braz.	C7	79
Jandaia, Braz.	D3	79
Jandaia do Sul, Braz.	G3	79
Janesville, Ia., U.S.	B5	122
Janesville, Mn., U.S.	F5	130
Janesville, Wi., U.S.	F4	156
Jangijul', Uzb.	I11	26
Janīn, W.B.	D4	50
Jan Kempdorp (Andalusia), S. Afr.	F7	66
Jan Mayen, i., Sval.	A6	52
Janos, Mex.	B5	90
Jánoshalma, Hung.	I19	10
Jansen, Sask., Can.	F3	105
Jansen, Co., U.S.	D6	113
Jantarnyj, Russia	G2	22
Januária, Braz.	C6	79
Japan (Nihon), ctry., Asia	D14	30
Japan, Sea of (Nihon-kai), Asia	K7	36
Japurá (Caquetá), stm., S.A.	H8	84
Jarābulus, Syria	C5	48
Jaraguá, Braz.	C4	79
Jaraguá do Sul, Braz.	D14	80
Jarales, N.M., U.S.	C3	138
Jaramānah, Syria	B6	50
Jaransk, Russia	F7	26
Jarcevo, Russia	F15	22
Jardim, Braz.	I13	82
Jardín América, Arg.	D11	80
Jardines de la Reina, Archipiélago de los, is., Cuba	D5	94
Jardinópolis, Braz.	F5	79
Jarnac, Fr.	G6	14
Jarocin, Pol.	D17	10
Jaroměř, Czech Rep.	E15	10
Jaroslavl', Russia	D22	22
Jarosław, Pol.	E22	10
Jarrettsville, Md., U.S.	A5	127
Jaru, Braz.	D10	82
Järvenpää, Fin.	K19 - 6	
Jarvis Island, i., Oc.	I23	158
Jāsk, Iran	F21	10
Jasmine Estates, Fl., U.S.	D4	116
Jasnogorsk, Russia	G20	22
Jasonville, In., U.S.	F3	121
Jasper, Al., U.S.	B2	108
Jasper, Fl., U.S.	B4	116
Jasper, Ga., U.S.	B2	117
Jasper, In., U.S.	H4	121
Jasper, Mo., U.S.	D3	132
Jasper, Tn., U.S.	D8	149
Jasper, Tx., U.S.	D6	150
Jasper, co., Ga., U.S.	C3	117
Jasper, co., Il., U.S.	D5	120
Jasper, co., In., U.S.	B3	121
Jasper, co., Ia., U.S.	C4	122
Jasper, co., Ms., U.S.	C4	131
Jasper, co., Mo., U.S.	D3	132
Jasper, co., S.C., U.S.	G5	147
Jasper, co., Tx., U.S.	D5	150
Jasper National Park, Alta., Can.	C1	98
Jászberény, Hung.	H19	10
Jataí, Braz.	D3	79
Jaú, Braz.	G4	79
Jauaperi, stm., Braz.	H12	84
Jauja, Peru	D4	82
Jaunjelgava, Lat.	E8	22
Jaunpur, India	H10	44
Javari (Yavari), stm., S.A.	D4	76
Java Sea see Jawa, Laut, Indon.	G5	38
Java Trench	J11	24
Jawa (Java), i., Indon.	j15	39a
Jawa, Laut (Java Sea), Indon.	G5	38
Jawbar, Syria	A6	50
Jawor, Pol.	D16	10
Jaworzno, Pol.	E19	10
Jay, Me., U.S.	D2	126
Jay, Ok., U.S.	A7	143
Jay, co., In., U.S.	D7	121
Jaya, Puncak, mtn., Indon.	F10	38
Jayanca, Peru	B2	82
Jayapura (Sukarnapura), Indon.	F11	38
Jayb, Wādī al- (Ha'Arava), val., Asia	H4	50
Jay Peak, mtn., Vt., U.S.	B3	152
Jaypur, India	C7	46
Jean, Nv., U.S.	H6	135
Jeanerette, La., U.S.	E4	125
Jean Lafitte, La., U.S.	k11	125
Jeannette, Pa., U.S.	F2	145
Jeberos, Peru	A3	82
Jeddore Lake, res., Newf., Can.	D3	102
Jedrzejów, Pol.	E20	10
Jeff, Ky., U.S.	C6	124
Jeff Davis, co., Ga., U.S.	E4	117
Jeff Davis, co., Tx., U.S.	o12	150
Jefferson, Ga., U.S.	B3	117
Jefferson, Ia., U.S.	B3	122
Jefferson, La., U.S.	k11	125
Jefferson, Me., U.S.	D3	126
Jefferson, N.C., U.S.	A1	140
Jefferson, Oh., U.S.	A5	142
Jefferson, Or., U.S.	C3	144
Jefferson, S.D., U.S.	E9	148
Jefferson, Wi., U.S.	E5	156
Jefferson, co., Al., U.S.	B3	108
Jefferson, co., Ar., U.S.	C3	111
Jefferson, co., Co., U.S.	B5	113
Jefferson, co., Fl., U.S.	B3	116
Jefferson, co., Ga., U.S.	C4	117
Jefferson, co., Id., U.S.	F6	119
Jefferson, co., Il., U.S.	E5	120
Jefferson, co., In., U.S.	G6	121
Jefferson, co., Ia., U.S.	C5	122
Jefferson, co., Ks., U.S.	C8	123
Jefferson, co., Ky., U.S.	B4	124
Jefferson, co., La., U.S.	E5	125
Jefferson, co., Ms., U.S.	D2	131
Jefferson, co., Mo., U.S.	C7	132
Jefferson, co., Mt., U.S.	D4	133
Jefferson, co., Ne., U.S.	D8	134
Jefferson, co., N.Y., U.S.	A5	139
Jefferson, co., Oh., U.S.	B5	142
Jefferson, co., Ok., U.S.	C4	143
Jefferson, co., Or., U.S.	C5	144
Jefferson, co., Pa., U.S.	D3	145
Jefferson, co., Tn., U.S.	C10	149
Jefferson, co., Tx., U.S.	E5	150
Jefferson, co., Wa., U.S.	B1	154
Jefferson, co., W.V., U.S.	B7	155
Jefferson, co., Wi., U.S.	E5	156
Jefferson, stm., Mt., U.S.	E5	133
Jefferson, Mount, mtn., Id., U.S.	E7	119
Jefferson, Mount, mtn., Nv., U.S.	E5	135
Jefferson, Mount, mtn., Or., U.S.	C5	144
Jefferson City, Mo., U.S.	C5	132
Jefferson City, Tn., U.S.	C10	149
Jefferson Davis, co., La., U.S.	D3	125
Jefferson Davis, co., Ms., U.S.	D4	131
Jefferson Farms, De., U.S.	i7	115
Jefferson Heights, Md., U.S.	A2	127
Jeffersontown, Ky., U.S.	B4	124
Jeffersonville, Ga., U.S.	D3	117
Jeffersonville, In., U.S.	H6	121
Jeffersonville, Ky., U.S.	C6	124
Jeffersonville, Vt., U.S.	B3	152
Jeffrey, W.V., U.S.	D3	155
Jeffrey City, Wy., U.S.	D5	157
Jefimovskij, Russia	L24	6
Jefremov, Russia	G5	26
Jega, Nig.	E12	64
Jegorjevsk, Russia	F22	22
Jeishou, China	B4	34
Jejsk, Russia	H5	26
Jekaterinburg, Russia	F10	26
Jekyll Island, i., Ga., U.S.	E5	117
Jelabuga, Russia	F8	26
Jelec, Russia	I21	22
Jelenia Góra (Hirschberg), Pol.	E15	10
Jelgava, Lat.	E6	22
Jelizavety, mys., c., Russia	G20	28
Jelizovo, Bela.	H12	22
Jellico, Tn., U.S.	C9	149
Jel'n'a, Russia	G16	22
Jemanželinsk, Russia	G10	26
Jember, Indon.	G5	38
Jemez Pueblo, N.M., U.S.	B3	138
Jemez Springs, N.M., U.S.	B3	138
Jemison, Al., U.S.	C3	108
Jemmal, Tun.	N5	18
Jena, Ger.	E11	10
Jena, La., U.S.	C3	125
Jendouba (Souk el Arba), Tun.	M3	18
Jenisej (Yenisey), stm., Russia	D15	26
Jenisejsk, Russia	F10	28
Jenisejskij zaliv, b., Russia	C8	28
Jenkins, Ky., U.S.	C7	124
Jenkins, co., Ga., U.S.	D5	117
Jenkintown, Pa., U.S.	o21	145
Jenks, Ok., U.S.	A6	143
Jennings, La., U.S.	D3	125
Jennings, Mo., U.S.	f13	132
Jennings, co., In., U.S.	G6	121
Jensen Beach, Fl., U.S.	E6	116
Jeparit, Austl.	K4	70
Jequeri, Braz.	F7	79
Jequié, Braz.	B8	79
Jequitaí, Braz.	D6	79
Jequitinhonha, Braz.	D8	79
Jequitinhonha, stm., Braz.	D9	79
Jerada, Mor.	C9	62
Jerauld, co., S.D., U.S.	C7	148
Jérémie, Haiti	E7	94
Jeremoabo, Braz.	F11	76
Jerevan, Arm.	I6	26
Jerez de García Salinas, Mex.	F8	90
Jerez de la Frontera, Spain	I5	16
Jericho, Vt., U.S.	B3	152
Jericho see Arīhā, W.B.	E4	50
Jerid, Chott, sw., Tun.	D15	62
Jerimoth Hill, hill, R.I., U.S.	C1	146
Jermiš', Russia	G25	22
Jermolajevo, Russia	E19	22
Jermolino, Russia	F19	22
Jermyn, Pa., U.S.	B7	79
Jerofej Pavlovič, Russia	G16	28
Jerome, Az., U.S.	C3	110
Jerome, Id., U.S.	G4	119
Jerome, co., Id., U.S.	G4	119
Jersey, dep., Eur.	F7	4
Jersey City, N.J., U.S.	B4	137
Jersey Shore, Pa., U.S.	D7	145
Jersey Village, Tx., U.S.	r14	150
Jerseyville, Il., U.S.	D3	120
Jerusalem see Yerushalayim, Isr.	E4	50
Jervis, Cape, c., Austl.	J3	70
Jervis Inlet, b., B.C., Can.	D6	99
Jesi, Italy	F8	18
Jesil', Kaz.	G11	26
Jessamine, co., Ky., U.S.	C5	124
Jessentuki, Russia	I6	26
Jessore, Bngl.	I13	44
Jessup, Md., U.S.	B4	127
Jessup, Pa., U.S.	m18	145
Jesup, Ga., U.S.	E5	117
Jesup, Ia., U.S.	B5	122
Jesup, Lake, l., Fl., U.S.	D5	116
Jésus, Île, i., Que., Can.	p19	104
Jesús Carranza, Mex.	I12	90
Jesús María, Arg.	F6	80
Jesús Menéndez, Cuba	D6	94
Jetmore, Ks., U.S.	D4	123
Jetpur, India	J4	44
Jette, Bel.	G5	12
Jeumont, Fr.	B11	14
Jevrej, state, Russia	H18	28
Jewell, Ia., U.S.	B4	122
Jewell, Ks., U.S.	C5	123
Jewell, co., Ks., U.S.	C5	123
Jewett City, Ct., U.S.	C8	114
Jhang Sadar, Pak.	E5	44
Jhānsi, India	H8	44
Jharia, India	I12	44
Jhārsuguda, India	B8	46
Jhelum, Pak.	D5	44
Jhelum, stm., Asia	E5	44
Jhunjhunūn, India	F6	44
Jiading, China	D10	34
Jiamusi, China	B13	30
Ji'an, China	H3	34
Jianchuan, China	A5	40
Jiangduo, China	C9	34
Jiangjin, China	F8	30
Jiangkou, China	G9	30
Jiangmen, China	M2	30
Jiangsu (Kiangsu), prov., China	E10	30
Jiangxi (Kiangsi), prov., China	F10	30
Jiangyin, China	D9	34
Jianli, China	F1	34
Jianning, China	I5	34
Jian'ou, China	H7	34
Jianshui, China	C7	40
Jiaohe, China	C12	30
Jiaoshanhe, China	F1	34
Jiaoxian, China	G7	32
Jiaozuo, China	D9	30
Jiashan, China	C7	34
Jiawang, China	A6	34
Jiaxian, China	B2	34
Jiaxing, China	E9	34
Jiayu, China	F2	34
Jiazi, China	M5	34
Jicatuyo, stm., Hond.	C6	92
Jiddah (Jeddah), Sau. Ar.	D1	47
Jieshou, China	B4	34
Jieyang, China	L5	34
Jieznas, Lith.	G7	22
Jigonazhen, China	A4	34
Jihlava, Czech Rep.	F15	10
Jijel, Alg.	B13	62
Jilib, Som.	A8	58
Jilin, China	C12	30
Jilin (Kirin), prov., China	C12	30
Jill, Kediet ej, mtn., Maur.	I4	62
Jima, Eth.	N9	60
Jimbolia, Rom.	D4	20
Jiménez, Mex.	D7	90
Jim Hogg, co., Tx., U.S.	F3	150
Jimo, China	G8	32
Jim Thorpe, Pa., U.S.	E10	145
Jim Wells, co., Tx., U.S.	F3	150
Jinan (Tsinan), China	G4	32
Jincheng, China	D9	30
Jīnd, India	F7	44
Jindřichův Hradec, Czech Rep.	F15	10
Jingdezhen (Kingtechen), China	F6	34
Jinggang, China	G1	34
Jinggangshan (Ciping), China	I3	34
Jinghai, China	E4	32
Jinghong, China	C6	40
Jingoutun, China	B5	32
Jingxi, China	C9	40
Jingxian, China	F4	32
Jingyu, China	A14	32
Jingzhi, China	G7	32
Jinhua, China	F8	34
Jining, China	C9	30
Jining, China	H4	32
Jinja, Ug.	A6	58
Jinlingzhen, China	B7	40
Jinning, China	B7	40
Jinotega, Nic.	D8	92
Jinotega, dept., Nic.	D9	92
Jinotepe, Nic.	E8	92
Jinping, China	A10	40
Jinsha, stm., China	E10	34
Jinshan, China	F9	30
Jintian, China	H3	34
Jinxi, China	D9	34
Jinxian, China	D9	34
Jinyu, China	F6	30
Jinzhou (Chinchow), China	B9	32
Jipijapa, Ec.	H2	84
Jiquilisco, El Sal.	D6	92
Jiquilisco, Bahía de, b., El Sal.	D6	92
Jirāfī, Wādī al- (Nahal Paran), val.	I3	50
Jirbān, Sud.	L6	60
Jirjā, Egypt	D6	60
Jirkov, Czech Rep.	E13	10
Jiroft, Iran	G14	48
Jisr ash-Shughūr, Syria	D4	48
Jitaúna, Braz.	C9	79
Jiujiang, China	F4	34
Jiuling, China	D6	30
Jiushangshui, China	B3	34
Jiutai, China	C12	30
Jixi, China	B13	30
Jixian, China	H2	32
Jiyang, China	G5	32
Jīzān, Sau. Ar.	F3	47
Joaçaba, Braz.	D13	80
Joaíma, Braz.	D8	79
Joanna, S.C., U.S.	C4	147
João Neiva, Braz.	E8	79
João Pessoa, Braz.	E12	76
João Pinheiro, Braz.	D5	79
Joaquim Távora, Braz.	G4	79
Joaquín V. González, Arg.	C6	80
Job Peak, mtn., Nv., U.S.	D3	135
Jocassee, Lake, res., U.S.	B1	147
Jódar, Spain	H8	16
Jodhpur, India	G5	44
Jodie, W.V., U.S.	m13	155
Joe Batt's Arm [-Barr'd Islands-Shoal Bay], Newf., Can.	D4	102
Joensuu, Fin.	J21	6
Joetsu, Japan	J13	36
Joffre, Mount, mtn., Can.	D3	98
Jõgeva, Est.	C9	22
Jog Falls, wtfl, India	E3	46
Joggins, N.S., Can.	D5	101
Johannesburg, S. Afr.	F9	66
John Day, Or., U.S.	C8	144
John Day, stm., Or., U.S.	B6	144
John F. Kennedy Space Center, sci., Fl., U.S.	D6	116
John H. Kerr Reservoir, res., U.S.	D4	153
John Martin Reservoir, res., Co., U.S.	C7	113
John Redmond Reservoir, res., Ks., U.S.	D8	123
John Sevier, Tn., U.S.	m14	149
Johnson, Ar., U.S.	A1	111
Johnson, Ks., U.S.	E2	123
Johnson, Vt., U.S.	B3	152
Johnson, co., Ar., U.S.	B2	111
Johnson, co., Il., U.S.	F5	120
Johnson, co., In., U.S.	F5	121
Johnson, co., Ia., U.S.	C5	122
Johnson, co., Ks., U.S.	D9	123
Johnson, co., Ky., U.S.	C7	124
Johnson, co., Mo., U.S.	C4	132
Johnson, co., Ne., U.S.	D9	134
Johnson, co., Tn., U.S.	C12	149
Johnson, co., Tx., U.S.	C4	150
Johnson, co., Wy., U.S.	B6	157
Johnsonburg, Pa., U.S.	D4	145
Johnson City, N.Y., U.S.	C5	139
Johnson City, Tn., U.S.	C11	149
Johnson City, Tx., U.S.	D3	150
Johnson Creek, Wi., U.S.	E5	156
Johnsonville, S.C., U.S.	D9	147
Johnston, Ia., U.S.	e8	122
Johnston, R.I., U.S.	C4	146
Johnston, S.C., U.S.	D4	147
Johnston, co., N.C., U.S.	B4	140
Johnston, co., Ok., U.S.	C5	143
Johnston Atoll, atoll, Oc.	G23	158
Johnston City, Il., U.S.	F5	120
Johnstone Strait, strt., B.C., Can.	D4	99
Johnstown, Co., U.S.	A6	113
Johnstown, N.Y., U.S.	B6	139
Johnstown, Oh., U.S.	B3	142
Johnstown, Pa., U.S.	F4	145
John W. Flannagan Reservoir, res., Va., U.S.	e9	153
Johor Baharu, Malay.	N7	40
Joigny, Fr.	E10	14
Joiner, Ar., U.S.	B5	111
Joinvile, Braz.	D14	80
Joinville, Fr.	D12	14
Jokkmokk, Swe.	H16	6
Joliet, Il., U.S.	B5	120
Joliet, Mt., U.S.	E8	133
Joliette, Que., Can.	D4	104
Jolo, Phil.	D7	38
Jonava, Lith.	F7	22
Jones, Ok., U.S.	B4	143
Jones, co., Ga., U.S.	C3	117
Jones, co., Ia., U.S.	B6	122
Jones, co., Ms., U.S.	D4	131
Jones, co., N.C., U.S.	B5	140
Jones, co., S.D., U.S.	D5	148
Jones, co., Tx., U.S.	C3	150
Jonesboro, Ar., U.S.	B5	111
Jonesboro, Ga., U.S.	C2	117
Jonesboro, Il., U.S.	F4	120
Jonesboro, In., U.S.	D6	121
Jonesboro, La., U.S.	B3	125
Jonesborough, Tn., U.S.	C11	149
Jonesburg, Mo., U.S.	C6	132
Jones Mill, Ar., U.S.	C3	111
Jonesport, Me., U.S.	D5	126
Jonestown, Ms., U.S.	A3	131
Jonesville, La., U.S.	C4	125
Jonesville, Mi., U.S.	G6	129
Jonesville, N.C., U.S.	A2	140
Jonesville, S.C., U.S.	B4	147
Jonesville, Vt., U.S.	C3	152
Jonesville, Va., U.S.	f8	153
Jönköping, Swe.	H10	6
Jonquière, Que., Can.	A6	104
Jonuta, Mex.	H13	90
Joplin, Mo., U.S.	D3	132
Joppatowne, Md., U.S.	B5	127
Jordan, Mn., U.S.	F5	130
Jordan, Mt., U.S.	C10	133
Jordan (Al-Urdun), ctry., Asia	C2	42
Jordan (Nahr al-Urdunn) (HaYarden), stm., Asia	E5	50
Jordan, Ut., U.S.	C4	151
Jordânia, Braz.	C8	79
Jornado del Muerto, des., N.M., U.S.	D3	138
Jos, Nig.	G14	64
José Battle y Ordóñez, Ur.	G11	80
José Bonifácio, Braz.	F4	79
José Pedro Varela, Ur.	G11	80
Joseph, Or., U.S.	B9	144
Joseph Bonaparte Gulf, b., Austl.	B5	68
Joseph City, Az., U.S.	C5	110
Josephine, co., Or., U.S.	E3	144
Joshua, Tx., U.S.	n9	150
Joshua Tree National Monument, Ca., U.S.	F6	112
Jöskar-Ola, Russia	F7	26
Joubertina, S. Afr.	I6	66

Name	Map Ref.	Page
Jourdanton, Tx., U.S.	E3	150
Joussard, Alta., Can.	B3	98
Jovellanos, Cuba	C4	94
Joviânia, Braz.	D4	79
J. Percy Priest Lake, res., Tn., U.S.	A5	149
Juab, co., Ut., U.S.	D4	151
Juan Aldama, Mex.	E8	90
Juan Bautista Alberdi, Arg.	D6	80
Juan de Fuca, Strait of, strt., N.A.	A1	154
Juan Fernández, Archipiélago, is., Chile	C1	78
Juan José Castelli, Arg.	C8	80
Juanjuí, Peru	B3	82
Juan L. Lacaze, Ur.	H10	80
Juan N. Fernández, Arg.	J9	80
Juan Viñas, C.R.	H11	92
Juárez see Ciudad Juárez, Mex.	B6	90
Juárez, Sierra de, mts., Mex.	B2	90
Juàzeiro, Braz.	E10	76
Juazeiro do Norte, Braz.	E11	76
Jūbā, Sud.	H7	56
Jūbāl, Maḍīq, strt., Egypt	D7	60
Jubba (Genale), stm., Afr.	H9	56
Juby, Cap, c., Mor.	C4	62
Júcar (Xúquer), stm., Spain	F10	16
Juchipila, Mex.	G8	90
Juchitán de Zaragoza, Mex.	I12	90
Juchnov, Russia	G18	22
Jucuapa, El Sal.	D6	92
Judaea, hist. reg., Asia	E4	50
Judenburg, Aus.	H14	10
Judique, N.S., Can.	D8	101
Judith, Point, c., R.I., U.S.	G4	115
Judith Basin, co., Mt., U.S.	C6	133
Judith Mountains, mts., Mt., U.S.	C7	133
Judsonia, Ar., U.S.	B4	111
Juexi, China	F10	34
Juidongshan, China	L6	34
Juigalpa, Nic.	E9	92
Juiz de Fora, Braz.	F7	79
Jujuy, prov., Arg.	B5	80
Julesburg, Co., U.S.	A8	113
Juliaca, Peru	F6	82
Julia Creek, Austl.	C4	70
Juliaetta, Id., U.S.	C2	119
Julian, W.V., U.S.	C3	155
Julianakanaal, Neth.	F8	12
Julian Alps, mts., Eur.	C8	18
Juliana Top, mtn., Sur.	F14	84
Julianehåb, Grnld.	C15	86
Jülich, Ger.	E6	10
Julimes, Mex.	C7	90
Júlio de Castilhos, Braz.	E12	80
Jumilla, Spain	G10	16
Jūnāgadh, India	J4	44
Junction City, Ar., U.S.	D3	111
Junction City, Ks., U.S.	C7	123
Junction City, Ky., U.S.	C5	124
Junction City, Or., U.S.	C3	144
Jundiaí, Braz.	G5	79
Juneau, Ak., U.S.	D13	109
Juneau, Wi., U.S.	E5	156
Juneau, co., Wi., U.S.	E3	156
Junee, Austl.	J7	70
June in Winter, Lake, l., Fl., U.S.	E5	116
Jungfrau, mtn., Switz.	E8	13
Junggar Pendi, China	B4	30
Juniata, Ne., U.S.	D7	134
Juniata, co., Pa., U.S.	F7	145
Juniata, stm., Pa., U.S.	F7	145
Junín, Arg.	H8	80
Junín, Peru	D3	82
Junín, dept., Peru	D4	82
Junín, Lago de, l., Peru	D3	82
Junior, W.V., U.S.	C5	155
Juniper, N.B., Can.	C2	101
Junqueirópolis, Braz.	F3	79
Junxian, China	E9	30
Juozapinès kalnas, hill, Lith.	G8	22
Jupiter, Fl., U.S.	F6	116
Jupiter Inlet, b., Fl., U.S.	F6	116
Juquiá, Braz.	C15	80
Jur, mtn., Sud.	M5	60
Jura, mts., Eur.	F13	14
Jura, i., Scot., U.K.	F8	8
Jurga, Russia	D26	22
Jurjevec, Russia	E22	22
Jūrmala, Lat.	E6	22
Jurty, Russia	F17	28
Juruá, stm., S.A.	D5	76
Juruena, stm., Braz.	B12	82
Jur'uzan', Russia	G9	26
Justiniano Posse, Arg.	G7	80
Justo Daract, Arg.	G6	80
Jutaí, Braz.	A7	82
Jutiapa, Guat.	C5	92
Jutiapa, dept., Guat.	C5	92
Juticalpa, Hond.	C8	92
Jutiquile, Hond.	C8	92
Jutland see Jylland, pen., Den.	M11	6
Juva, Fin.	K20	6
Juventud, Isla de la (Isla de Pinos), i., Cuba	D3	94
Juža, Russia	E25	22
Južno-Sachalinsk, Russia	H20	28
Južno-Ural'sk, Russia	G10	26
Jwayjá, Leb.	B4	50
Jylland, reg., Den.	M11	6
Jyväskylä, Fin.	J19	6

K

Name	Map Ref.	Page
K2 (Qogir Feng), mtn., Asia	C7	44
Kaaawa, Hi., U.S.	f10	118
Kaachka, Turk.	J9	48
Kaachka, Turk.	C15	48
Kaala, mtn., Hi., U.S.	f9	118
Kaapstad see Cape Town, S. Afr.	I4	66
Kabalega Falls, wtfl, Ug.	H7	56
Kabalo, Zaire	C5	58
Kabardino-Balkarija, state, Russia	I6	26
Kabba, Nig.	H13	64
Kabetogama Lake, l., Mn., U.S.	B5	130
Kabinda, Zaire	C4	58
Kabīr Kūh, mts., Iran	E9	48
Kabkābīyah, Sud.	K3	60
Kābol, Afg.	C3	44
Kabr, Sud.	L4	60
Kābul see Kābol, Afg.	C3	44
Kabwe (Broken Hill), Zam.	D5	58
Kachchh, Gulf of, b., India	I3	44
Kachemak, Ak., U.S.	D9	109
Kachisi, Eth.	M9	60
K'achta, Russia	G13	28
Kačug, Russia	G13	28
Kadaiyanallūr, India	H4	46
Kadiana, Mali	F6	64
Kadina, Austl.	I2	70
Kadirli, Tur.	C4	48
Kadnikov, Russia	B23	22
Kadoka, S.D., U.S.	D4	148
Kadom, Russia	G25	22
Kadoma, Zimb.	B9	66
Kaduj, Russia	B20	22
Kaduna, Nig.	F13	64
Kaduna, stm., Nig.	G12	64
Kāḍuqlī, Sud.	L5	60
Kadyj, Russia	D26	22
Kadžaròn, Russia	E21	28
Kaédi, Maur.	C3	64
Kaena Point, c., Hi., U.S.	B3	118
Kaesòng, N. Kor.	F14	32
Kafan, Arm.	B9	48
Kaffrine, Sen.	D2	64
Kafia Kingi, Sud.	M3	60
Kafin Madaki, Nig.	F14	64
Kafirévs, Ákra, c., Grc.	K8	20
Kafr ad-Dawwār, Egypt	B6	60
Kafr ash-Shaykh, Egypt	B6	60
Kafue, stm., Zam.	E5	58
Kagera, stm., Afr.	B6	58
Kagoshima, Japan	P5	36
Kahaluu, Hi., U.S.	g10	118
Kahaluu, Hi., U.S.	D6	118
Kahemba, Zaire	C3	58
Kahoka, Mo., U.S.	A6	132
Kahoolawe, i., Hi., U.S.	C5	118
Kahramanmaraş, Tur.	C4	48
Kahuku, Hi., U.S.	B4	118
Kahuku Point, c., Hi., U.S.	B4	118
Kahului, Hi., U.S.	C5	118
Kaiapoi, N.Z.	E4	72
Kaibab Plateau, plat., Az., U.S.	A3	110
Kaibito, Az., U.S.	A4	110
Kaifeng, China	I2	32
Kailahun, S.L.	G4	64
Kaili, China	A9	40
Kailu, China	C11	30
Kailua, Hi., U.S.	B4	118
Kailua Kona, Hi., U.S.	D6	118
Kainaliu, Hi., U.S.	D6	118
Kaipara Harbour, b., N.Z.	B5	72
Kaiping, China	G9	30
Kairouan, Tun.	N5	18
Kaiserslautern, Ger.	F7	10
Kaithal, India	F7	44
Kaiwi Channel, strt., Hi., U.S.	B4	118
Kaiyuan, China	A12	32
Kaijaani, Fin.	I20	6
Kajang, Malay.	M6	40
Kaka, Cen. Afr. Rep.	N4	60
Kākā, Sud.	L7	60
Kakamas, S. Afr.	G5	66
Kake, Ak., U.S.	D13	109
Kakegawa, Japan	M13	36
Kakhovs'ke vodoskhovyshche, res., Ukr.	H4	26
Kākināda, India	D6	46
Kakogawa, Japan	M9	36
Kalaa Kebira, Tun.	N5	18
Kalaa Sghira, Tun.	N5	18
Kālābagh, Pak.	D4	44
Kalač, Russia	G6	26
Kalačinsk, Russia	F12	26
Kalač-na-Donu, Russia	H6	26
Kalahari Desert, des., Afr.	E5	66
Kalaheo, Hi., U.S.	B2	118
Kalajoki, Fin.	I18	6
Kalakamate, Bots.	C8	66
Kalama, Wa., U.S.	C3	154
Kálamai, Grc.	L6	20
Kalamazoo, Mi., U.S.	F5	129
Kalamazoo, co., Mi., U.S.	F5	129
Kalamazoo, stm., Mi., U.S.	F5	129
Kalasin, Thai.	F7	40
Kalašnikovo, Russia	D18	22
Kalāt, Pak.	F2	44
Kalaw, Mya.	D4	40
Kalawao, co., Hi., U.S.	B5	118
Kal'azin, Russia	D20	22
Kaleden, B.C., Can.	E8	99
Kalemie (Albertville), Zaire	C5	58
Kalevala, Russia	D4	26
Kalewa, Mya.	C3	40
Kalgan see Zhangjiakou, China	C2	32
Kalgoorlie-Boulder, Austl.	F4	68
Kaliakra, nos, c., Bul.	F12	20
Kalima, Zaire	B5	58
Kálimnos, Grc.	M10	20
Kalinin see Tver', Russia	E18	22
Kaliningrad (Königsberg), Russia	G3	22
Kalinkoviči, Bela.	I12	22
Kalispell, Mt., U.S.	B2	133
Kalisz, Pol.	D18	10
Kalkaska, Mi., U.S.	D5	129
Kalkaska, co., Mi., U.S.	D5	129
Kallaste, Est.	C10	22
Kalmar, Swe.	M15	6
Kalmykija see Kalmykija, state, Russia	H7	26
Kalmykija, state, Russia	H7	26
Kālol, India	I5	44
Kaltag, Ak., U.S.	C8	109
Kaluga, Russia	G19	22
Kalyān, India	C2	46
Kalynivka, Lith.	G6	22
Kama, stm., Russia	F8	26
Kamaishi, Japan	H16	36
Kamakura, Japan	L14	36
Kamanjab, Nmb.	B2	66
Kamas, Ut., U.S.	C4	151
Kamba, Nig.	F11	64
Kambar, Pak.	G3	44
Kambarka, Russia	F8	26
Kambia, S.L.	G3	64
Kamčatka, poluostrov (Kamchatka), pen., Russia	F24	28
Kamchatka see Kamčatka, poluostrov, pen., Russia	F24	28
Kamčija, stm., Bul.	F11	20
Kamenec, Bela.	I6	22
Kamenjak, Rt, c., Cro.	E8	18
Kamen'-na-Obi, Russia	G8	28
Kamennogorsk, Russia	K21	6
Kamensk-Ural'skij, Russia	F10	26
Kameškovo, Russia	E24	22
Kāmet, mtn., Asia	E8	44
Kamiah, Id., U.S.	C2	119
Kamienna Góra, Pol.	E16	10
Kamina, Zaire	C5	58
Kamloops, B.C., Can.	D7	99
Kamo, Arm.	A8	48
Kamooloa, Hi., U.S.	f9	118
Kampala, Ug.	A6	58
Kampar, Malay.	L6	40
Kampen, Neth.	C8	12
Kamphaeng Phet, Thai.	F5	40
Kâmpóng Cham, Camb.	H8	40
Kâmpóng Chhnăng, Camb.	H8	40
Kâmpóng Saôm, Camb.	I7	40
Kâmpóng Thum, Camb.	H8	40
Kâmpôt, Camb.	I8	40
Kamsack, Sask., Can.	F5	105
Kamskoje vodochranilišče, res., Russia	F9	26
Kāmthi, India	B5	46
Kamuela (Waimea), Hi., U.S.	C6	118
Kámuk, Cerro, mtn., C.R.	H11	92
Kam'yanets'-Podil's'kyy, Ukr.	H3	26
Kamyšin, Russia	G7	26
Kamyšlov, Russia	F10	26
Kanab, Ut., U.S.	F3	151
Kanabec, co., Mn., U.S.	E5	130
Kanairiktok, stm., Newf., Can.	g9	102
Kananga (Luluabourg), Zaire	C4	58
Kanaš, Russia	F7	26
Kanata, Ont., Can.	B9	103
Kanawha, Ia., U.S.	B4	122
Kanawha, co., W.V., U.S.	C3	155
Kanawha, stm., W.V., U.S.	C3	155
Kanazawa, Japan	K11	36
Kanchanaburi, Thai.	G5	40
Kānchenjunga, mtn., Asia	G13	44
Kānchipuram, India	F5	46
Kandalakša, Russia	D4	26
Kandangan, Indon.	F6	38
Kandava, Lat.	D5	22
Kandiyohi, co., Mn., U.S.	E3	130
Kandy, Sri L.	I6	46
Kane, co., Il., U.S.	B5	120
Kane, co., Ut., U.S.	F3	151
Kaneohe, Hi., U.S.	B4	118
Kaneohe Bay, b., Hi., U.S.	g10	118
Kang, Bots.	D6	66
Kangaroo Island, i., Austl.	J2	70
Kangāvar, Iran	D9	48
Kangding, China	E7	30
Kanggye, N. Kor.	C14	32
Kangnichumike, China	D9	44
Kangnŭng, S. Kor.	F16	32
Kango, Gabon	A2	58
Kangping, China	A11	32
Kangrinboqê Feng, mtn., China	E9	44
Kangshan, Tai.	M9	34
Kangsŏ, N. Kor.	E13	32
Kani, Mya.	C3	40
Kaniama, Zaire	C4	58
Kanin, poluostrov, pen., Russia	D7	26
Kanin Nos, mys, c., Russia	D6	26
Kaniva, Austl.	K4	70
Kanjiža, Yugo.	C4	20
Kankakee, Il., U.S.	B6	120
Kankakee, co., Il., U.S.	B6	120
Kankakee, stm., Il., U.S.	B5	120
Kankan, Gui.	F5	64
Kankossa, Maur.	D4	64
Kannapolis, N.C., U.S.	B2	140
Kano, Nig.	E14	64
Kanopolis, Ks., U.S.	D5	123
Kanoya, Japan	P5	36
Kānpur, India	G9	44
Kansas, state, U.S.	D5	123
Kansas, co., Ks., U.S.	C7	123
Kansas City, Ks., U.S.	C9	123
Kansas City, Mo., U.S.	B3	132
Kanshan, China	E9	34
Kansk, Russia	F11	28
Kantchè, Niger	E14	64
Kantunilkin, Mex.	G16	90
Kanuma, Japan	K14	36
Kanye, Bots.	E7	66
Kaohsiung, Tai.	M9	34
Kaohsiunghsien, Tai.	M9	34
Kaolack, Sen.	D1	64
Kapaa, Hi., U.S.	A2	118
Kapaau, Hi., U.S.	C6	118
Kapčagaj, Kaz.	I13	26
Kapenberg, Aus.	H15	10
Kapiri Mposhi, Zam.	D5	58
Kapiskasing, Can.	o19	103
Kapoeta, Sud.	H7	56
Kaposvár, Hung.	I17	10
Kapuas, Nmb.	D3	66
Kapuas, stm., Indon.	F4	38
Kapuas Hulu, Pegunungan, mts., Asia	E5	38
Kapuskasing, Can.	o19	103
Kapuvár, Hung.	H17	10
Kara-Balta, Kyrg.	E21	22
Karabanovo, Russia	E21	22
Karabükü, Russia	F10	26
Karabük, Tur.	G14	4
Karacabey, Tur.	I12	20
Karačev, Russia	H18	22
Karāchi, Pak.	H2	44
Karaganda, Kaz.	H12	26
Karaj, Iran	D11	48
Karakol (Prževal'sk), Kyrg.	I13	26
Karakoram Pass, Asia	C7	44
Karakoram Range, mts., Asia	C7	44
Karakumskij kanal, Turk.	C16	48
Karakumy, des., Turk.	J9	26
Karaman, Tur.	C2	48
Karamay, China	B3	30
Karamürsel, Tur.	I13	20
Karapınar, Tur.	C2	48
Karasburg, Nmb.	G4	66
Karasjok, Nor.	G19	6
Karasuk, Russia	G7	28
Karatau, Kaz.	I12	26
Karatsu, Japan	N4	36
Karawang, Indon.	j13	39a
Karażal, Kaz.	H12	26
Karbalā', Iraq	E8	48
Karcag, Hung.	H20	10
Kärdhítsa, Grc.	J5	20
Kärdla, Est.	B5	22
Kardymovo, Russia	G15	22
Kārḍžali, Bul.	H9	20
Karelia see Karelija, state, Russia	E4	26
Karelia, hist. reg., Eur.	J22	6
Karelija, state, Russia	E4	26
Kargopol', Russia	E5	26
Kariba, Zimb.	E5	58
Kariba, Lake, res., Afr.	E5	58
Karibib, Nmb.	C2	66
Karimata, Selat (Karimata Strait), strt., Indon.	F4	38
Karīmnagar, India	C5	46
Karis (Karjaa), Fin.	K18	6
Karisimbi, Volcan, vol., Afr.	B5	58
Kariya, Japan	M11	36
Karkaralinsk, Kaz.	H13	26
Karl-Marx-Stadt see Chemnitz, Ger.	E12	10
Karlovac, Cro.	D10	18
Karlovo, Bul.	G8	20
Karlovy Vary, Czech Rep.	E12	10
Karlskoga, Swe.	L14	6
Karlskrona, Swe.	M14	6
Karlsruhe, Ger.	F8	10
Karlstad, Mn., U.S.	B2	130
Karmah, Sud.	H6	60
Karmel, Har (Mount Carmel), mtn., Isr.	C4	50
Karnak see Al-Karnak, Egypt	E7	60
Karnāl, India	F7	44
Karnātaka, state, India	E3	46
Karnes, co., Tx., U.S.	E4	150
Karnes City, Tx., U.S.	E4	150
Karnobat, Bul.	G10	20
Kärnten, state, Aus.	I13	10
Karonga, Mwi.	C6	58
Karpenísion, Grc.	K5	20
Karpinsk, Russia	F10	26
Karratha, Austl.	D3	68
Kars, Tur.	A7	48
Kārsava, Lat.	E10	22
Karši, Uzb.	J11	26
Karskije Vorota, proliv, strt., Russia	C9	26
Karskoje more (Kara Sea), Russia	C11	26
Kartaly, Russia	G10	26
Karūr, India	G5	46
Karviná, Czech Rep.	F18	10
Karymskoje, Russia	G14	28
Kas, Sud.	K3	60
Kasai (Cassai), stm., Afr.	B3	58
Kasama, Zam.	D6	58
Kasane, Bots.	A7	66
Kasaoka, Japan	M8	36
Kasba-Tadla, Mor.	D7	62
Kasenga, Zaire	D5	58
Kāsganj, India	G8	44
Kashan, Iran	B5	47
Kashgar see Kashi, China	D2	30
Kashi, China	D2	30
Kashihara, Japan	M10	36
Kashima, Japan	F8	24
Kāshīpur, India	F8	44
Kashiwazaki, Japan	J13	36
Kashmar, Iran	D15	48
Kashmir see Jammu and Kashmīr, dep., Asia	C10	42
Kasigluk, Ak., U.S.	C7	109
Kasilof, Ak., U.S.	C9	109
Kasimov, Russia	G24	22
Kašin, Russia	D20	22
Kaskaskia, stm., Il., U.S.	D5	120
Kaskö (Kaskinen), Fin.	J17	6
Kasli, Russia	F10	26
Kaslo, B.C., Can.	E9	99
Kasongo, Zaire	B5	58
Kasongo-Lunda, Zaire	C3	58
Kasota, Mn., U.S.	F5	130
Kaspijsk, Russia	I7	26
Kaspijskij, Russia	H7	26
Kassalā, Sud.	J9	60
Kassel, Ger.	D9	10
Kasserine, Tun.	C15	62
Kasson, Mn., U.S.	F6	130
Kastamonu, Tur.	G14	4
Kastória, Grc.	I5	20
Kasūr, Pak.	E6	44
Katahdin, Mount, mtn., Me., U.S.	C4	126
Katanga, hist. reg., Zaire	D5	58
Katanning, Austl.	F3	68
Katchall, i., India	J2	40
Katerini, Grc.	I6	20
Kates Needle, mtn., Ak., U.S.	m24	109
Katha, Mya.	B4	40
Kathleen, Fl., U.S.	D4	116
Kathmandu see Kāthmāndau, Nepal	G11	44
Katihār, India	H12	44
Katiola, C. Iv.	G7	64
Katmai, Mount, mtn., Ak., U.S.	D9	109
Katmai National Park, Ak., U.S.	D9	109
Kāthmāndau, Nepal	G11	44
Katoomba, Austl.	I9	70
Katoúna, Grc.	K5	20
Katowice, Pol.	E19	10
Kätrīnā, Jabal, mtn., Egypt	C7	60
Katsina, Nig.	E13	64
Katsina Ala, Nig.	H14	64
Katsuta, Japan	K15	36
Kattakurgan, Uzb.	J11	26
Kattegat, strt., Eur.	M12	6
Katwijk aan Zee, Neth.	D5	12
Katy, Tx., U.S.	r14	150
Kauai, co., Hi., U.S.	B1	118
Kauai, i., Hi., U.S.	A2	118
Kauai Channel, strt., Hi., U.S.	B3	118
Kaufbeuren, Ger.	H10	10
Kaufman, Tx., U.S.	C4	150
Kaufman, co., Tx., U.S.	C4	150
Kauiki Head, c., Hi., U.S.	C6	118
Kaukauna, Wi., U.S.	D5	156
Kaukau Veld, plat., Afr.	C5	66
Kaulakahi Channel, strt., Hi., U.S.	A2	118
Kaumakani, Hi., U.S.	B2	118
Kaunakakai, Hi., U.S.	B4	118
Kaunas, Lith.	G6	22
Kaura Namoda, Nig.	E13	64
Kautokeino, Nor.	G18	6
Kavajë, Alb.	H3	20
Kavála, Grc.	I8	20
Kavalerovo, Russia	I19	28
Kāvali, India	E5	46
Kāveri, stm., India	G5	46
Kavieng, Pap. N. Gui.	k17	68a
Kavīr, Dasht-e, des., Iran	D13	48
Kawagoe, Japan	L14	36
Kawaguchi, Japan	L14	36
Kawaikini, mtn., Hi., U.S.	A2	118
Kawailoa Beach, Hi., U.S.	f9	118
Kawasaki, Japan	L14	36
Kaw Lake, res., Ok., U.S.	A5	143
Kawm Umbū, Egypt	E7	60
Kawthaung, Mya.	J5	40
Kay, co., Ok., U.S.	A4	143
Kaya, Burkina	E9	64
Kayan, Mya.	F4	40
Kāyankulam, India	H4	46
Kaycee, Wy., U.S.	C6	157
Kayenta, Az., U.S.	A5	110
Kayes, Mali	D4	64
Kayseri, Tur.	B3	48
Kaysville, Ut., U.S.	B4	151
Kazakhstan, ctry., Asia	H11	26
Kazan', Russia	F7	26
Kazan, stm., N.W. Ter., Can.	D13	96
Kazandžik, Turk.	J9	26
Kazanlâk, Bul.	G9	20
Kāzerūn, Iran	G11	48
Kazincbarcika, Hung.	G20	10
Kazinka, Russia	I22	22
Kazlų Rūda, Lith.	G6	22
Keaau, Hi., U.S.	D6	118
Keahole Point, c., Hi., U.S.	D5	118
Kealakekua, Hi., U.S.	D6	118
Kealia, Hi., U.S.	A2	118
Keams Canyon, Az., U.S.	B5	110
Keansburg, N.J., U.S.	C4	137
Kearney, Ont., Can.	B5	103
Kearney, Mo., U.S.	B3	132
Kearney, Ne., U.S.	D7	134
Kearney, co., Ne., U.S.	D7	134
Kearneysville, W.V., U.S.	B7	155
Kearns, Ut., U.S.	C4	151
Kearny, Az., U.S.	D5	110
Kearny, N.J., U.S.	h8	137
Kearny, co., Ks., U.S.	D2	123
Kearsarge, N.H., U.S.	B4	136
Kébémer, Sen.	D1	64
Kebili, Tun.	D15	62
Kebnekaise, mtn., Swe.	H16	6
Kecel, Hung.	I19	10
Kecskemét, Hung.	I19	10
Kédainiai, Lith.	F7	22
Kedgwick, N.B., Can.	B2	101
Kediri, Indon.	j16	39a
Kédougou, Sen.	F3	64
Kędzierzyn Kozle, Pol.	E18	10
Keego Harbor, Mi., U.S.	o15	129
Keeling Islands see Cocos Islands, dep., Oc.	K10	24
Keene, N.H., U.S.	E2	136
Keene, Tx., U.S.	n9	150
Keenesburg, Co., U.S.	A6	113
Keerbergen, Bel.	F6	12
Keetmanshoop, Nmb.	E4	66
Keewatin, Ont., Can.	E4	100
Keewatin, Mn., U.S.	C5	130
Kefallinía, i., Grc.	K4	20
Kefar Nahum (Capernaum), hist., Isr.	C5	50
Kefar Sava, Isr.	D3	50
Keffi, Nig.	G13	64
Keflavík, Ice.	C2	6a
Kehra, Est.	B8	22
Keila, Est.	B7	22
Keimoes, S. Afr.	G5	66
Keiser, Ar., U.S.	B5	111
Keith, Scot., U.K.	D11	8
Keith, co., Ne., U.S.	C4	134
Keizer, Or., U.S.	B3	144
Kekaha, Hi., U.S.	B2	118
Kékes, mtn., Hung.	H20	10
Kelang, Malay.	M6	40
Kelani, Malay.	M6	40
Kelheim, Ger.	G11	10
Kelibia, Tun.	M5	18
Keller, Tx., U.S.	n9	150
Kelleys Island, i., Oh., U.S.	A3	141
Kellogg, Id., U.S.	B2	119
Kelly, Wy., U.S.	C2	157
Kellyville, N.H., U.S.	D3	136
Kellyville, Ok., U.S.	B5	143
Kelme, Lith.	F5	22
Kelo, Chad	F8	56
Kelowna, B.C., Can.	E8	99
Kelso, Wa., U.S.	C3	154
Keluang, Malay.	M7	40
Kelvington, Sask., Can.	E4	105
Kelwood, Man., Can.	D2	100
Kem', Russia	C4	26
Kemano, B.C., Can.	C4	99
Kemerovo, Russia	F9	28
Kemi, Fin.	I19	6
Kemijärvi, Fin.	H20	6
Kemmerer, Wy., U.S.	E2	157
Kemparana, Mali	E7	64
Kemper, co., Ms., U.S.	C5	131
Kempsey, Austl.	H10	70
Kempten [Allgäu], Ger.	H10	10
Kemptville, Ont., Can.	B9	103
Kenai, Ak., U.S.	C9	109
Kenai Fjords National Park, Ak., U.S.	D10	109
Kenai Mountains, mts., Ak., U.S.	h16	109
Kenai Peninsula, pen., Ak., U.S.	h16	109
Kenaston, Sask., Can.	F2	105
Kenbridge, Va., U.S.	D4	153
Kendall, Fl., U.S.	s13	116
Kendall, co., Il., U.S.	B5	120
Kendall, co., Tx., U.S.	E3	150
Kendall Park, N.J., U.S.	C3	137
Kendallville, In., U.S.	B7	121
Kendari, Indon.	F7	38
Kendrick, Id., U.S.	C2	119
Kenduskeag, Me., U.S.	B4	126
Kenedy, Tx., U.S.	E4	150
Kenedy, co., Tx., U.S.	F4	150
Kenema, S.L.	H4	64
Kenesaw, Ne., U.S.	D7	134
Kenge, Zaire	B3	58
Kēng Tung, Mya.	D5	40
Kenhardt, S. Afr.	G5	66
Kenilworth, Il., U.S.	h9	120
Kenitra, Mor.	C7	62
Kenly, N.C., U.S.	B4	140
Kenmare, N.D., U.S.	A3	141
Kenmore, N.Y., U.S.	C2	139
Kennard, Ne., U.S.	C9	134
Kennebec, co., Me., U.S.	D3	126
Kennebec, stm., Me., U.S.	D3	126
Kennebunk, Me., U.S.	E2	126
Kennebunkport, Me., U.S.	E2	126
Kennedy, Sask., Can.	G4	105
Kennedy, Al., U.S.	B2	108
Kennedy, Mount, mtn., Yukon	D5	96
Kenner, La., U.S.	E5	125
Kennesaw, Ga., U.S.	B2	117
Kennetcook, N.S., Can.	D6	101
Kennett, Mo., U.S.	E7	132
Kennett Square, Pa., U.S.	G10	145
Kennewick, Wa., U.S.	C6	154
Kennydale, Wa., U.S.	e11	154
Keno, Or., U.S.	E5	144
Kénogami, Lac, l., Que., Can.	A6	104
Kenora, Ont., Can.	o16	103
Kenosha, Wi., U.S.	F6	156
Kenosha, co., Wi., U.S.	F5	156
Kenova, W.V., U.S.	C2	155
Kensett, Ar., U.S.	B4	111
Kensington, P.E.I., Can.	C6	101
Kensington, Ct., U.S.	C4	114
Kensington, Ks., U.S.	C5	123
Kensington, Md., U.S.	B3	127
Kent, Al., U.S.	A2	108
Kent, Ct., U.S.	C2	114
Kent, Oh., U.S.	A4	142
Kent, Wa., U.S.	B3	154
Kent, co., Eng., U.K.	J14	8
Kent, co., De., U.S.	D3	115
Kent, co., Md., U.S.	B5	127
Kent, co., Mi., U.S.	E5	129
Kent, co., R.I., U.S.	D3	146
Kent, co., Tx., U.S.	C2	150
Kentau, Kaz.	I11	26
Kent Group, is., Austl.	L7	70
Kent Island, i., Md., U.S.	C5	127
Kentland, In., U.S.	C3	121
Kenton, Man., Can.	E1	100
Kenton, Oh., U.S.	B2	142
Kenton, Tn., U.S.	A2	149
Kenton, co., Ky., U.S.	B5	124
Kent Point, c., Md., U.S.	C5	127
Kentucky, state, U.S.	C4	124
Kentucky, Lake, res., U.S.	D9	106
Kentville, N.S., Can.	D5	101
Kentwood, La., U.S.	D5	125
Kentwood, Mi., U.S.	F5	129
Kenvir, Ky., U.S.	D6	124
Kenya, ctry., Afr.	B7	58
Kenya, Mount see Kirinyaga, mtn., Kenya	B7	58
Kenyon, Mn., U.S.	F6	130
Kenyon, R.I., U.S.	F2	146
Keokea, Hi., U.S.	C5	118
Keokuk, Ia., U.S.	D6	122
Keokuk, co., Ia., U.S.	C5	122
Keo Neua, Col de, Asia	E8	40
Keosauqua, Ia., U.S.	D6	122
Keota, Ia., U.S.	C6	122
Keowee, Lake, res., S.C., U.S.	B2	147
Kerala, state, India	G4	46
Kerang, Austl.	J5	70
Kerch, Ukr.	H5	26
Keremeos, B.C., Can.	E8	99
Keren, Erit.	J10	60
Kerewan, Gam.	E1	64
Kerguélen, Îles, is., F.S.A.T.	M10	158
Kericho, Kenya	B7	58
Kerinci, Gunung, mtn., Indon.	F3	38
Kerkenna, Îles, is., Tun.	C16	62
Kerkhoven, Mn., U.S.	E3	130
Kerki, Turk.	J11	26
Kérkira (Corfu), Grc.	J3	20
Kérkira (Corfu), i., Grc.	J3	20
Kermadec Islands, is., N.Z.	K22	158
Kerman, Iran	J9	48
Kerman, co., Ca., U.S.	D3	112
Kern, co., Ca., U.S.	E4	112
Kern, stm., Ca., U.S.	E4	112
Kernersville, N.C., U.S.	A2	140
Kerr, co., Tx., U.S.	D3	150
Kerrobert, Sask., Can.	F1	105
Kerrville, Tx., U.S.	D3	150
Kerry, co., Ire.	I4	8
Kersey, Co., U.S.	A6	113
Kershaw, S.C., U.S.	B6	147
Kershaw, co., S.C., U.S.	C6	147
Kersley, B.C., Can.	C6	99

Name	Map Ref.	Page

Kerulen (Cherlen) (Herlen), stm., Asia B10 30
Kerzers, Switz. E7 13
Keşan, Tur. I10 20
Kesennuma, Japan I16 36
Keshena, Wi., U.S. D5 156
Keskin, Tur. B2 48
Keski-Suomen lääni, prov., Fin. J19 6
Kesova Gora, Russia D20 22
Keszthely, Hung. I17 10
Keta, Ghana I10 64
Ketchikan, Ak., U.S. D13 109
Ketchum, Id., U.S. F4 119
Kétou, Benin H11 64
Kętrzyn (Rastenburg), Pol. . A21 10
Kettering, Eng., U.K. I13 8
Kettering, Oh., U.S. C1 142
Kettle Falls, Wa., U.S. A7 154
Keuka Lake, l., N.Y., U.S. . . C3 139
Kewanee, Il., U.S. B4 120
Kewanna, In., U.S. B5 121
Kewaskum, Wi., U.S. D5 156
Kewaunee, Wi., U.S. D6 156
Kewaunee, co., Wi., U.S. . D6 156
Keweenaw, co., Mi., U.S. . A2 129
Keweenaw Bay, b., Mi., U.S. B2 129
Keweenaw Peninsula, pen., Mi., U.S. A3 129
Keweenaw Point, c., Mi., U.S. A3 129
Keya Paha, co., Ne., U.S. . B6 134
Keya Paha, stm., U.S. A5 134
Keyhole Reservoir, res., Wy., U.S. B8 157
Key Largo, Fl., U.S. G6 116
Keyport, N.J., U.S. C4 137
Keyser, W.V., U.S. B6 155
Keystone, W.V., U.S. D3 155
Keystone Lake, res., Ok., U.S. A5 143
Keytesville, Mo., U.S. B5 132
Key West, Fl., U.S. H5 116
Kezar Falls, Me., U.S. E2 126
Khadki (Kirkee), India C2 46
Khairpur, Pak. G3 44
Khakassia see Chakassija, state, Russia G15 26
Khakhea, Bots. E6 66
Khalkís, Grc. K7 20
Khambhāt, India I5 44
Khambhāt, Gulf of, b., India J5 44
Khāmgaon, India B4 46
Khamis Mushayt, Sau. Ar. . E3 47
Khammam, India D6 46
Khānābād, Afg. B3 44
Khandwa, India J7 44
Khānewāl, Pak. E4 44
Khaniá, Grc. N8 20
Khānpur, Pak. F4 44
Khān Yūnus, Gaza F2 50
Kharagpur, India I12 44
Kharg Island see Khārk, Jazīreh-ye, i., Iran . . . G11 48
Khargon, India J6 44
Khāriān Cantonment, Pak. . D5 44
Khārk, Jazīreh-ye, i., Iran . G11 48
Kharkiv (Kharkov), Ukr. . . . G5 26
Kharkov see Kharkiv, Ukr. . G5 26
Khartoum see Al-Kharţūm, Sud. J7 60
Khartoum North see Al-Kharţūm Baḥrī, Sud. . . . J7 60
Khartum see Al-Kharţūm, Sud. J7 60
Khashm al-Qirbah, Sud. . . J8 60
Khemis, Alg. B12 62
Khenchla, Alg. C14 62
Khenifra, Mor. D8 62
Kherson, Ukr. H4 26
Khios, Grc. K10 20
Khíos (Chíos), i., Grc. K10 20
Khmel'nyts'kyy, Ukr. H3 26
Kholm, Afg. B2 44
Khomeyn, Iran E11 48
Khomeynīshahr, Iran E11 48
Khon Kaen, Thai. F7 40
Khorramābād, Iran E10 48
Khorramshahr, Iran F10 48
Khotyn, Ukr. A10 20
Khouribga, Mor. D7 62
Khowst, Afg. D3 44
Khuis, Bots. F5 66
Khulna, Bngl. I13 44
Khūnjerāb Pass, Asia B6 44
Khūrīyā Murīyā, Jazā'ir, is., Oman F10 47
Khurja, India F7 44
Khust, Ukr. H2 26
Khuzdār, Pak. G2 44
Khvoy, Iran B8 48
Khwae Noi, stm., Thai. . . . G5 40
Khyber Pass, Asia C4 44
Kiama, Austl. J9 70
Kiamichi, stm., Ok., U.S. . . C6 143
Kiana, Ak., U.S. B7 109
Kibombo, Zaire B5 58
Kibre Mengist, Eth. O10 60
Kigoma, Tan. B5 58
Kihei, Hi., U.S. C5 118
Kikinda, Yugo. D4 20
Kikládhes (Cyclades), is., Grc. L9 20
Kikwit, Zaire C3 58
Kilauea, Hi., U.S. A2 118
Kilauea Crater, crat., Hi., U.S. D6 118

Kilchu, N. Kor. C17 32
Kildare, Ire. H7 8
Kildare, co., Ire. H7 8
Kil'dinstroj, Russia G23 6
Kilgore, Tx., U.S. C5 150
Kilimanjaro, mtn., Tan. . . . B7 58
Kilimavony, Madag. s20 67b
Kilingi-Nõmme, Est. C7 22
Kilis, Tur. C4 48
Kiliya, Ukr. D13 20
Kilkenny, Ire. I6 8
Kilkenny, co., Ire. I6 8
Kilkís, Grc. H6 20
Killala, Alta., Can. C5 98
Killarney, Man., Can. E2 100
Killarney, Ire. I4 8
Killdeer, N.D., U.S. B3 141
Killeen, Tx., U.S. D4 150
Killen, Al., U.S. A2 108
Killington Peak, mtn., Vt., U.S. D3 152
Kilmarnock, Scot., U.K. . . . F9 8
Kilmarnock, Va., U.S. C6 153
Kilmichael, Ms., U.S. B4 131
Kiln, Ms., U.S. E4 131
Kilosa, Tan. C7 58
Kimba, Austl. I2 70
Kimball, Mn., U.S. E4 130
Kimball, Ne., U.S. C2 134
Kimball, S.D., U.S. D7 148
Kimball, W.V., U.S. D3 155
Kimball, co., Ne., U.S. . . . C2 134
Kimberley, B.C., Can. E10 99
Kimberley, S. Afr. G7 66
Kimberley Plateau, plat., Austl. C5 68
Kimberling City, Mo., U.S. . E4 132
Kimberlin Heights, Tn., U.S. n14 149
Kimberly, Al., U.S. B3 108
Kimberly, Id., U.S. G4 119
Kimberly, W.V., U.S. m13 155
Kimberly, Wi., U.S. h9 156
Kimble, co., Tx., U.S. D3 150
Kimch'aek (Sŏngjin), N. Kor. C17 32
Kimch'ŏn, S. Kor. G16 32
Kimje, S. Kor. H14 32
Kimovsk, Russia H21 22
Kimry, Russia E20 22
Kinabalu, Gunong, mtn., Malay. D6 38
Kinbasket Lake, res., B.C., Can. D8 99
Kincaid, Sask., Can. H2 105
Kincaid, Il., U.S. D4 120
Kincaid, W.V., U.S. m13 155
Kincardine, Ont., Can. C3 103
Kinchafoonee Creek, stm., Ga., U.S. E2 117
Kinder, La., U.S. D3 125
Kindersley, Sask., Can. . . . F1 105
Kindia, Gui. F3 64
Kindred, N.D., U.S. C9 141
Kindu, Zaire B5 58
Kinel', Russia G8 26
Kineo, Mount, mtn., Me., U.S. C3 126
Kinešma, Russia D25 22
King, N.C., U.S. A2 140
King, Wi., U.S. D4 156
King, co., Tx., U.S. C2 150
King, co., Wa., U.S. B3 154
King and Queen, co., Va., U.S. C6 153
Kingaroy, Austl. F9 70
King City, Ont., Can. D3 112
King City, Mo., U.S. A3 132
King Cove, Ak., U.S. E7 109
Kingfield, Me., U.S. D2 126
Kingfisher, Ok., U.S. B4 143
Kingfisher, co., Ok., U.S. . . B3 143
King George, co., Va., U.S. . B5 153
King George Island, i., Ant. . B1 73
Kingisepp, Russia B11 22
King Island, i., Austl. L6 70
King Leopold Ranges, mts., Austl. C5 68
Kingman, Az., U.S. B1 110
Kingman, In., U.S. E3 121
Kingman, Ks., U.S. E5 123
Kingman, co., Ks., U.S. . . . E5 123
King of Prussia, Pa., U.S. . . F11 145
Kings, stm., Ca., U.S. D4 112
Kings, co., Ca., U.S. D4 112
Kings, co., N.Y., U.S. E7 139
Kings, stm., Ca., U.S. D4 112
Kings, stm., Nv., U.S. B3 135
King Salmon, Ak., U.S. . . . D8 109
Kingsburg, Ca., U.S. D4 112
Kingsbury, co., S.D., U.S. . C8 148
Kings Canyon National Park, Ca., U.S. D4 112
Kingscote, Austl. J2 70
Kingsey-Falls, Que., Can. . . D5 104
Kingsford, Mi., U.S. C2 129
Kingsland, Ar., U.S. D3 111
Kingsland, Ga., U.S. F5 117
Kingsley, Ia., U.S. B2 122
King's Lynn, Eng., U.K. . . . I14 8
Kings Mountain, N.C., U.S. . B1 140
King Solomon's Mines see Mikhrot Shelomo Hamelekh, hist., Isr. . . I3 50
King Sound, strt., Austl. . . . C4 68
Kings Peak, mtn., Ut., U.S. . C5 151
King's Point, Newf., Can. . . D3 102
Kingsport, Tn., U.S. C11 149
Kingston, Ont., Can. C8 103
Kingston, Jam. E6 94
Kingston, Id., U.S. B2 119
Kingston, Ma., U.S. C6 128
Kingston, N.H., U.S. E4 136
Kingston, N.Y., U.S. D6 139
Kingston, Ok., U.S. D5 143
Kingston, Pa., U.S. D10 145
Kingston, R.I., U.S. F3 146
Kingston, Tn., U.S. D9 149
Kingston Southeast, Austl. . K3 70
Kingston Springs, Tn., U.S. . A4 149
Kingston upon Hull, Eng., U.K. H13 8
Kingstown, St. Vin. H14 94
Kingstree, S.C., U.S. D8 147

Kingsville, Ont., Can. E2 103
Kingsville, Md., U.S. B5 127
Kingsville, Tx., U.S. F4 150
King William, co., Va., U.S. C5 153
King William Island, i., N.W. Ter., Can. C13 96
King William's Town, S. Afr. I8 66
Kingwood, Tx., U.S. q14 150
Kingwood, W.V., U.S. B5 155
Kinistino, Sask., Can. E3 105
Kinkora, P.E.I., Can. C6 101
Kinloch, Mo., U.S. f13 132
Kinnaird Head, c., Scot., U.K. D11 8
Kinnear, Wy., U.S. C4 157
Kinnelon, N.J., U.S. B4 137
Kinneret, Yam (Sea of Galilee), l., Isr. C5 50
Kinney, co., Tx., U.S. E2 150
Kinsey, Al., U.S. D4 108
Kinshasa (Léopoldville), Zaire B3 58
Kinsley, Ks., U.S. E4 123
Kinston, Al., U.S. D3 108
Kinston, N.C., U.S. B5 140
Kintampo, Ghana G9 64
Kintyre, pen., Scot., U.K. . . F8 8
Kintyre, Mull of, c., Scot., U.K. F8 8
Kinuso, Alta., Can. B3 98
Kinyeti, mtn., Sud. H7 56
Kiowa, Co., U.S. B6 113
Kiowa, Ks., U.S. E5 123
Kiowa, Ok., U.S. C6 143
Kiowa, co., Co., U.S. C8 113
Kiowa, co., Ks., U.S. E4 123
Kiowa, co., Ok., U.S. C2 143
Kiowa Creek, stm., Co., U.S. B6 113
Kipling, Sask., Can. G4 105
Kipnuk, Ak., U.S. C7 109
Kipushi, Zaire D5 58
Kirane, Mali D4 64
Kirejevsk, Russia H20 22
Kirensk, Russia F13 28
Kirgizskij chrebet, mts., Asia I12 26
Kiribati, ctry., Oc. F24 2
Kirikhan, Tur. C4 48
Kırıkkale, Tur. B2 48
Kirillov, Russia B21 22
Kirin see Jilin, China C12 30
Kirinyaga, mtn., Kenya B7 58
Kirişi, Russia B15 22
Kırkağaç, Tur. J11 20
Kirkcaldy, Scot., U.K. E10 8
Kirkcudbright, Scot., U.K. . . G9 8
Kirkenes, Nor. G22 6
Kirkland, Il., U.S. A5 120
Kirkland, Wa., U.S. B3 154
Kirkland Lake, Ont., Can. . . o19 103
Kırklareli, Tur. H11 20
Kirklin, In., U.S. D5 121
Kirkpatrick, Mount, mtn., Ant. D8 73
Kirksville, Mo., U.S. A5 132
Kirkūk, Iraq D8 48
Kirkwall, Scot., U.K. C11 8
Kirkwood, S. Afr. I7 66
Kirkwood, De., U.S. B3 115
Kirkwood, Mo., U.S. f13 132
Kirov, Russia G17 22
Kirov, Russia F7 26
Kirovakan, Arm. I6 26
Kirovgrad, Russia F10 26
Kirovohrad, Ukr. H4 26
Kirovsk, Bela. H12 22
Kirovsk, Russia B14 22
Kirovsk, Russia D4 26
Kirovskij, Kaz. I13 26
Kirs, Russia F8 26
Kirsanov, Russia I25 22
Kırşehir, Tur. B3 48
Kirtland, N.M., U.S. A1 138
Kiruna, Swe. H17 6
Kiryū, Japan K14 36
Kiržač, Russia E21 22
Kisangani (Stanleyville), Zaire A5 58
Kisarazu, Japan L14 36
Kisbey, Sask., Can. H4 105
Kisel'ovsk, Russia G9 28
Kishangarh Bās, India G6 44
Kishi, Nig. G11 64
Kishinev see Chişinău, Mol. B12 20
Kishiwada, Japan M10 36
Kisii, Kenya B6 58
Kiska Island, i., Ak., U.S. . . E3 109
Kiskinfélegyháza, Hung. . . I19 10
Kiskunhalas, Hung. I19 10
Kiskunmajsa, Hung. I19 10
Kislovodsk, Russia I6 26
Kismaayo, Som. B8 58
Kismet, Ks., U.S. E3 123
Kissidougou, Gui. G4 64
Kissimmee, Fl., U.S. D5 116
Kissimmee, stm., Fl., U.S. . E5 116
Kissimmee, Lake, l., Fl., U.S. E5 116
Kistler, W.V., U.S. D3 155
Kisújszállás, Hung. H20 10
Kisumu, Kenya B6 58
Kisvárda, Hung. G22 10
Kita, Mali E5 64
Kitaibaraki, Japan K15 36
Kitakyūshū, Japan N5 36
Kitale, Kenya A7 58
Kitami, Japan d18 36a
Kit Carson, Co., U.S. C8 113
Kit Carson, co., Co., U.S. . . B8 113
Kitchener, Ont., Can. D4 103
Kitimat, B.C., Can. B3 99
Kitsap, co., Wa., U.S. B3 154
Kitscoty, Alta., Can. C5 98
Kitsman', Ukr. A9 20
Kittanning, Pa., U.S. E2 145
Kittatinny Mountain, mtn., U.S. B2 137
Kittery, Me., U.S. E2 126
Kittery Point, Me., U.S. . . . E2 126
Kittilä, Fin. H19 6
Kittitas, Wa., U.S. C5 154
Kittitas, co., Wa., U.S. B4 154
Kitts, Ky., U.S. D6 124
Kittson, co., Mn., U.S. B2 130

Kitty Hawk, N.C., U.S. . . . A7 140
Kitty Hawk Bay, b., N.C., U.S. A7 140
Kitui, Kenya B7 58
Kitwe, Zam. D5 58
Kitzbühel, Aus. H12 10
Kiukiang see Jiujiang, China F4 34
Kivalina, Ak., U.S. B7 109
Kiviõli, Est. B9 22
Kivu, Lac, l., Afr. B5 58
Kizel, Russia F9 26
Kızıltepe, Tur. C6 48
Kizl'ar, Russia I7 26
Kizyl-Arvat, Turk. J9 26
Kizyl-Atrek, Turk. J8 26
Kjustendil, Bul. G6 20
Kladno, Czech Rep. E14 10
Klagenfurt, Aus. I14 10
Klaipėda (Memel), Lith. . . . F4 22
Klamath, co., Or., U.S. E5 144
Klamath, stm., U.S. B2 112
Klamath Falls, Or., U.S. . . . E5 144
Klamath Mountains, mts., U.S. E2 144
Klatovy, Czech Rep. F13 10
Klawer, S. Afr. H4 66
Klawock, Ak., U.S. D13 109
Kleberg, co., Tx., U.S. F4 150
Kleck, Bela. H9 22
Klerksdorp, S. Afr. F8 66
Kletn'a, Russia H16 22
Kleve, Ger. D6 10
Kličev, Bela. H12 22
Klickitat, Wa., U.S. D4 154
Klickitat, co., Wa., U.S. . . . D4 154
Klickitat, stm., Wa., U.S. . . C4 154
Klimovič, Bela. H14 22
Klimovo, Russia I15 22
Klimovsk, Russia F20 22
Klin, Russia E19 22
Klincy, Russia I15 22
Kłodzko, Pol. E16 10
Klondike, hist. reg., Yukon, Can. D5 96
Klondike Gold Rush National Historical Park, Ak., U.S. k22 109
Klosterneuburg, Aus. G16 10
Kloster, Switz. E12 13
Kloten, Switz. D10 13
Kluane Lake, l., Yukon, Can. D5 96
Kl'učevskaja Sopka, vulkan, vol., Russia F24 28
Kl'uči, Russia F24 28
Kluczbork, Pol. E18 10
Knee Lake, l., Man., Can. . . B4 100
Kneža, Bul. F8 20
Knightdale, N.C., U.S. B4 140
Knight Inlet, b., B.C., Can. . D5 99
Knightstown, In., U.S. E6 121
Knightsville, In., U.S. E3 121
Knin, Cro. E11 18
Knittelfeld, Aus. H14 10
Knobel, Ar., U.S. A5 111
Knob Noster, Mo., U.S. . . . C4 132
Knokke-Heist, Bel. F3 12
Knollwood, W.V., U.S. m12 155
Knott, co., Ky., U.S. C6 124
Knox, In., U.S. B4 121
Knox, co., Il., U.S. B3 120
Knox, co., In., U.S. G3 121
Knox, co., Ky., U.S. D6 124
Knox, co., Me., U.S. D4 126
Knox, co., Mo., U.S. A5 132
Knox, co., Ne., U.S. B8 134
Knox, co., Oh., U.S. B3 142
Knox, co., Tn., U.S. C10 149
Knox, co., Tx., U.S. C3 150
Knox, Cape, c., B.C., Can. . B1 99
Knoxville, Ia., U.S. C4 122
Knoxville, Il., U.S. B3 120
Knoxville, Tn., U.S. D10 149
Knysna, S. Afr. J6 66
Kobar Sink, depr., Eth. F9 56
Kōbe, Japan M10 36
København (Copenhagen), Den. N13 6
Koblenz, Ger. E7 10
Kobrin, Bela. I7 22
Kobuk Valley National Park, Ak., U.S. B8 109
Kočani, Mac. H6 20
Kočevje, Slvn. D9 18
Kočevje, Slvn. D9 18
Koch Bihār, India G13 44
Kōchi, Japan N8 36
Kochma, Russia E24 22
Koch Peak, mtn., Mt., U.S. . E5 133
Kodiak, Ak., U.S. D9 109
Kodiak Island, i., Ak., U.S. . D9 109
Kodok, Sud. M7 60
Kodyma, Ukr. A13 20
Koekelare, Bel. F2 12
Koes, Nmb. G4 66
Köflach, Aus. H15 10
Koforidua, Ghana H9 64
Kōfu, Japan L13 36
Koga, Japan K14 36
Køge, Den. N13 6
Kogoni, Mali D6 64
Kohāt, Pak. D4 44
Kohila, Est. B7 22
Kohīma, India H16 44
Kohler, Wi., U.S. E6 156
Kohtla-Järve, Est. B10 22
Koidu, S.L. G4 64
Kokand, Uzb. I12 26
Kokčetav, Kaz. G11 26
Koko, Nig. F11 64
Koko Head, c., Hi., U.S. . . . B4 118
Kokomo, In., U.S. C5 121
Kokong, Bots. E6 66
Kokopo, Pap. N. Gui. k17 68a
Koksan, N. Kor. E14 32
Kokstad, S. Afr. H9 66
Kola, Russia G23 6
Kola Peninsula see Kol'skij poluostrov, pen., Russia . D5 26
Kolār, India F5 46
Kolār Gold Fields, India . . . F5 46
Kolchozabad, Taj. B3 44
Kol'čugino, Russia E22 22

Kolda, Sen. E2 64
Kolgujev, ostrov, i., Russia . D7 26
Kolhāpur, India D3 46
Kolin, Czech Rep. E15 10
Kolkasrags, c., Lat. D5 22
Köln (Cologne), Ger. E6 10
Kolo, Niger E11 64
Koło, Pol. C18 10
Koloa, Hi., U.S. B2 118
Kołobrzeg, Pol. A15 10
Kologriv, Russia C27 22
Kolomna, Russia F21 22
Kolomyya, Ukr. H3 26
Kolpaševo, Russia F8 28
Kolpino, Russia B13 22
Kolpny, Russia I20 22
Kol'skij poluostrov (Kola Peninsula), pen., Russia . D5 26
Kolwezi, Zaire D5 58
Kolyma, stm., Russia D22 28
Komadugu Gana, stm., Nig. F9 54
Komadugu Yobe, stm., Afr. . F9 54
Komandorskije ostrova, is., Russia F25 28
Komarichi, Russia I17 22
Komárno, Slvk. H18 10
Komárom, Hung. H18 10
Komatsu, Japan K11 36
Komi, state, Russia E8 26
Komin Yanga, Burkina F10 64
Komló, Hung. I18 10
Kommunizma, pik, mtn., Taj. J12 26
Komodo, Pulau, i., Indon. . . G6 38
Komotiní, Grc. H9 20
Komsomolec, Kaz. G10 26
Komsomolec, ostrov, i., Russia A17 26
Komsomol'sk, Russia D23 22
Komsomol'sk-na-Amure, Russia G19 28
Kondoa, Tan. B7 58
Kondopoga, Russia E4 26
Kondrovo, Russia G18 22
Kondūz, Afg. B3 44
Kongcheng, China D6 34
Kongfang, China H5 34
Kongju, S. Kor. G15 32
Konglong, China F4 34
Kongolo, Zaire C5 58
Kongor, Sud. N6 60
Kongsvinger, Nor. K13 6
Kongur Shan, mtn., China . . D2 30
Königswinter, Ger. E7 10
Konin, Pol. C18 10
Kōniz, Switz. E7 13
Konjic, Bos. F1 20
Konoša, Russia E6 26
Konotop, Ukr. G4 26
Końskie, Pol. D20 10
Konstantinovskij, Russia . . . D22 22
Konstanz, Ger. H9 10
Kontagora, Nig. F12 64
Kontich, Bel. F5 12
Kontiomäki, Fin. I21 6
Kon Tum, Viet. G10 40
Kontum, Plateau du, plat., Viet. H10 40
Konya, Tur. C2 48
Koochiching, co., Mn., U.S. B4 130
Kooskia, Id., U.S. C3 119
Kootenai, co., Id., U.S. B2 119
Kootenay Lake, l., B.C., Can. E9 99
Kopaonik, mtn., Yugo. F4 20
Koper, Slvn. D8 18
Kopetdag, chrebet, mts., Asia C15 48
Kopřivnice, Cro. C11 18
Kopyl', Bela. H10 22
Korab (Maja e Korabit), mtn., Eur. H4 20
Korablino, Russia H23 22
Korba, Tun. M5 18
Korbach, Ger. D8 10
Korçë, Alb. I4 20
Korčula, Otok, i., Cro. G11 18
Korea, North, ctry., Asia . . C12 30
Korea, South, ctry., Asia . . D12 30
Korea Bay, b., Asia E11 32
Korea Strait, strt., Asia I16 32
Korenovsk, Russia H5 26
Korfovskij, Russia H19 28
Korhogo, C. Iv. G7 64
Korinthiakós Kólpos (Gulf of Corinth), b., Grc. . . . K6 20
Kórinthos (Corinth), Grc. . . L6 20
Kōriyama, Japan J15 36
Korkino, Russia G10 26
Korla, China C4 30
Korneuburg, Aus. G16 10
Korogwe, Tan. C7 58
Korosten', Ukr. G3 26
Korovin Volcano, vol., Ak., U.S. E5 109
Korsakov, Russia H20 28
Korsør, Den. N12 6
Kortrijk (Courtrai), Bel. G3 12
Koruçam Burnu, c., N. Cyp. D2 48
Koryukivka, Ukr. G4 26
Kos, Grc. M11 20
Kos, i., Grc. L11 20
Kosa Gora, Russia G20 22
Kościan, Pol. C16 10
Kościerzyna, Pol. B17 10
Kosciusko, Ms., U.S. B4 131
Kosciusko, Mount, mtn., Austl. K8 70
Koshkonong, Lake, l., Wi., U.S. F5 156
Košice, Slvk. G21 10
Kosiv, Ukr. A9 20
Kosovo-Metohija, prov., Yugo. G5 20
Kosovska Mitrovica, Yugo. . G4 20

Kossuth, co., Ia., U.S. . . . A3 122
Koster, S. Afr. E8 66
Kosterevo, Russia F22 22
Kostroma, Russia D23 22
Kost'ukoviči, Bela. H15 22
Kost'ukovka, Bela. I13 22
Kostyantynivka, Ukr. H5 26
Koszalin (Köslin), Pol. A16 10
Kőszeg, Hung. H16 10
Kota, India H6 44
Kota Baharu, Malay. K7 40
Kotabaru, Indon. F6 38
Kotabumi, Indon. F3 38
Kotel'nič, Russia F7 26
Kotel'nikovo, Russia H6 26
Kotel'nyj, ostrov, i., Russia . B19 28
Köthen, Ger. D11 10
Kotka, Fin. K20 6
Kotlas, Russia E7 26
Kotlik, Ak., U.S. C7 109
Koton-Karifi, Nig. G13 64
Kotovsk, Russia I24 22
Kotovs'k, Ukr. H3 26
Kottagūdem, India D6 46
Kotto, stm., Cen. Afr. Rep. . G5 56
Kotzebue, Ak., U.S. B7 109
Kou'an, China C8 34
Kouandé, Benin F10 64
Koudougou, Burkina E8 64
Koulamoutou, Gabon B2 58
Koulikoro, Mali E6 64
Koumra, Chad G4 56
Koundara, Gui. E3 64
Koupéla, Burkina E9 64
Kourousa, Gui. F5 54
Koussané, Mali D4 64
Koussi, Emi, mtn., Chad . . . E4 56
Koutiala, Mali E7 64
Kouts, In., U.S. B3 121
Kovarskas, Lith. F7 22
Kovdor, Russia H22 6
Kovel', Ukr. G2 26
Kovernino, Russia D26 22
Kovilpatti, India H4 46
Kovrov, Russia F6 26
Koyuk, Ak., U.S. C7 109
Koyukuk, stm., Ak., U.S. . . B8 109
Kozan, Tur. C3 48
Kozáni, Grc. I5 20
Kozel'sk, Russia G18 22
Kozlovo, Russia E19 22
Kpandu, Ghana H10 64
Kra, Isthmus of, Asia I5 40
Krâchéh, Camb. H9 40
Kragerø, Nor. L11 6
Kragujevac, Yugo. E4 20
Krakatoa see Rakata, Pulau, i., Indon. j12 39a
Kraków, Pol. E19 10
Kralendijk, Neth. Ant. H10 94
Kraljevo, Yugo. F4 20
Kramators'k, Ukr. H5 26
Kranj, Slvn. C9 18
Kraskino, Russia A18 32
Krāslava, Lat. F10 22
Krasnaja Gorbatka, Russia . F24 22
Kraśnik, Pol. E22 10
Krasnoarmejsk, Russia . . . E21 22
Krasnodar, Russia H5 26
Krasnogorsk, Russia F20 22
Krasnogorsk, Russia H20 28
Krasnoil's'k, Ukr. A9 20
Krasnojarsk, Russia F10 28
Krasnojarskoje vodochranilišče, res., Russia F16 26
Krasnoje-na-Volge, Russia . D24 22
Krasnokamsk, Russia F9 26
Krasnoslobodsk, Russia . . . H6 26
Krasnoturjinsk, Russia F10 26
Krasnoufimsk, Russia D19 4
Krasnoural'sk, Russia F10 26
Krasnovišersk, Russia E8 26
Krasnovodsk, Turk. I8 26
Krasnovodskij poluostrov, pen., Turk. A12 48
Krasnozavodsk, Russia . . . E21 22
Krasnoznamensk, Russia . . G13 22
Krasnyj, Russia C20 22
Krasnyj Cholm, Russia G7 22
Krasnyj Kut, Russia H7 26
Krasnyj Okt'abr', Russia . . . E21 22
Krasnystaw, Pol. E23 10
Krasnyj Luch, Ukr. H5 26
Krebs, Ok., U.S. C6 143
Krefeld, Ger. C12 22
Kremenčuk, Russia D6 10
Kremenchuts'ke vodoskhovyshche, res., Ukr. H4 26
Kremmling, Co., U.S. A4 113
Krems an der Donau, Aus. . G15 10
Krestcy, Russia C15 22
Kretinga, Lith. F4 22
Kribi, Cam. H8 54
Kričev, Bela. H14 22
Kriens, Switz. D9 13
Krishna, stm., India D5 46
Krishnagar, India I13 44
Kristiansand, Nor. L10 6
Kristianstad, Swe. M14 6
Kristiansund, Nor. J10 6
Kríti (Crete), i., Grc. N8 20
Kritikón Pélagos (Sea of Crete), Grc. N8 20
Krk, Otok, i., Cro. D9 18
Kroměříž, Czech Rep. F17 10
Kromy, Russia I18 22
Kronach, Ger. G3 105
Kronštadt, Russia B12 22
Kroonstad, S. Afr. F8 66
Kropotkin, Russia H6 26
Krosno, Pol. D17 10
Krotz Springs, La., U.S. . . . D4 125
Krugersdorp, S. Afr. F8 66
Kruisfontein, S. Afr. J7 66
Krung Thep (Bangkok), Thai. H6 40

Name	Map Ref.	Page
Krupki, Bela.	G12	22
Kruševac, Yugo.	F5	20
Kryms'kyy pivostriv (Crimean Peninsula), pen., Ukr.	H4	26
Kryve Ozero, Ukr.	B14	20
Kryvyy Rih (Krivoy Rog), Ukr.	H4	26
Kryzhopil', Ukr.	A12	20
Ksar Chellala, Alg.	C12	62
Ksar-el-Kebir, Mor.	J6	16
Ksar Hellal, Tun.	N5	18
Ksenjevka, Russia	G15	28
Ksour Essaf, Tun.	N6	18
Kualakapuas, Indon.	F5	38
Kuala Lumpur, Malay.	M6	40
Kualapuu, Hi., U.S.	B4	118
Kuala Terengganu, Malay.	L7	40
Kuantan, Malay.	M7	40
Kubbum, Sud.	L2	60
Kuching, Malay.	N11	40
Kuçovë, Alb.	I3	20
Kudirkos Naumiestis, Lith.	G5	22
Kudus, Indon.	j15	39a
Kudymkar, Russia	F8	26
Kufstein, Aus.	H12	10
Kūhdasht, Iran	E9	48
Kuito, Ang.	D3	58
Kujbyšev see Samara, Russia	G8	26
Kujbyšev, Russia	F13	26
Kujbyševskoje vodochranilišče, res., Russia	G7	26
Kukawa, Nig.	F9	54
Kukuihaele, Hi., U.S.	C6	118
Kula, Hi., U.S.	C5	118
Kula, Yugo.	D3	20
Kul'ab, Taj.	J11	26
Kula Kangri, mtn., Bhu.	F14	44
Kuldīga, Lat.	E4	22
Kule, Bots.	D5	66
Kulebaki, Russia	F25	22
Kulim, Malay.	L6	40
Kulm, N.D., U.S.	C7	141
Kulmbach, Ger.	E11	10
Kuloj, Russia	E6	26
Kulotino, Russia	C16	22
Kulpmont, Pa., U.S.	E9	145
Kul'sary, Kaz.	H8	26
Kulti, India	I12	44
Kumagaya, Japan	K14	36
Kumajri, Arm.	I6	26
Kumamoto, Japan	O5	36
Kumanovo, Mac.	G5	20
Kumasi, Ghana	H9	64
Kumba, Cam.	I14	64
Kumbakonam, India	G5	46
Kümch'ŏn, N. Kor.	E14	32
Kum-Dag, Turk.	J8	26
Kumla, Swe.	L14	6
Kumo, Nig.	F9	54
Kumukahi, Cape, c., Hi., U.S.	D7	118
Kuna, Id., U.S.	F2	119
Kunašir, ostrov (Kunashiri-tō), i., Russia	c21	36a
Kunda, Est.	B9	22
Kunene (Cunene), stm., Afr.	E2	58
Kungsbacka, Swe.	M13	6
Kungur, Russia	F9	26
Kunhegyes, Hung.	H20	10
Kunia, Hi., U.S.	g9	118
Kunja, Russia	E13	22
Kunming, China	B7	40
Kunsan, S. Kor.	H14	32
Kunshan, China	D9	34
Kunszentmárton, Hung.	I20	10
Kuopio, Fin.	J20	6
Kuopion lääni, prov., Fin.	J20	6
Kupang, Indon.	H7	38
Kupino, Russia	G7	28
Kupreanof Island, i., Ak., U.S.	m23	109
Kup'yans'k, Ukr.	H5	26
Kuqa, China	C3	30
Kurashiki, Japan	M8	36
Kuraymah, Sud.	H6	60
Kurayyimah, Jord.	D5	50
Kurdistan, hist. reg., Asia	B4	42
Kure, Japan	M7	36
Kure Island, i., Hi., U.S.	k12	118
Kuressaare, Est.	C5	22
Kurgan, Russia	F11	26
Kurgan-T'ube, Taj.	J11	26
Kuria Muria Islands see Khurīyā Murīyā, is., Oman	F10	47
Kuridala, Austl.	C4	70
Kuril Islands see Kuril'skije ostrova (Kuril Islands), is., Russia	H22	28
Kurkino, Russia	H21	22
Kurlovskij, Russia	F23	22
Kurmuk, Sud.	L8	60
Kurnool, India	E5	46
Kurovskoje, Russia	F21	22
Kursk, Russia	G5	26
Kurtistown, Hi., U.S.	D6	118
Kuruman, S. Afr.	F6	66
Kurume, Japan	N5	36
Kurzeme, hist. reg., Lat.	E5	22
Kusa, Russia	F9	26
Kushiro, Japan	e19	36a
Kuskokwim, stm., Ak., U.S.	C8	109
Kuskokwim Bay, b., Ak., U.S.	D7	109
Kuskokwim Mountains, mts., Ak., U.S.	C8	109
Kušmurun, Kaz.	G10	26
Küsnacht, Switz.	D10	13
Kusŏng, N. Kor.	D13	32
Küssnacht am Rigi, Switz.	D9	13
Kustanaj, Kaz.	G10	26
Küstī, Sud.	K7	60
Kušva, Russia	F9	26
Kuta, Nig.	G13	64
Kütahya, Tur.	H13	4
Kutaisi, Geor.	I6	26
Kutch, Rann of (Rann of Kachchh), reg., Asia	H4	44
Kutina, Cro.	D11	18
Kutná Hora, Czech Rep.	F15	10
Kutno, Pol.	C19	10
Kutu, Zaire	B3	58
Kutum, Sud.	J3	60
Kutztown, Pa., U.S.	E10	145
Kuujjuaq, Que., Can.	g13	104
Kuusamo, Fin.	I21	6
Kuusankoski, Fin.	K20	6
Kuvandyk, Russia	G9	26
Kuvango, Ang.	D3	58
Kuvšinovo, Russia	D17	22
Kuwait see Al-Kuwayt, Kuw.	G9	48
Kuwana, Japan	L11	36
Kuybyshev see Samara, Russia	G8	26
Kuženkino, Russia	D16	22
Kuzneck, Russia	G7	26
Kwai see Khwae Noi, stm., Thai.	G5	40
Kwajok, Sud.	M4	60
Kwando (Cuando), stm., Afr.	E4	58
Kwangchow see Guangzhou, China	L2	34
Kwangju, S. Kor.	H14	32
Kwango (Cuango), stm., Afr.	B3	58
Kwangyang, S. Kor.	I15	32
Kweisui see Hohhot, China	C9	30
Kwekwe, Zimb.	B9	66
Kwethluk, Ak., U.S.	C7	109
Kwidzyn, Pol.	B18	10
Kwigillingok, Ak., U.S.	D7	109
Kwilu (Cuilo), stm., Afr.	B3	58
Kyabram, Austl.	K6	70
Kyaiklat, Mya.	F3	40
Kyaikto, Mya.	F4	40
Kyaukse, Mya.	D4	40
Kyauktaw, Mya.	D2	40
Kyaunggon, Mya.	F3	40
Kyle, Sask., Can.	F12	105
Kymen lääni, prov., Fin.	K20	6
Kyoga, Lake, l., Ug.	A6	58
Kyogle, Austl.	G10	70
Kyŏngju, S. Kor.	H17	32
Kyŏngsan, S. Kor.	H16	32
Kyŏngsŏng, N. Kor.	B17	32
Kyōto, Japan	L10	36
Kyrgyzstan, ctry., Asia	I13	26
Kyštym, Russia	F10	26
Kyūshū, i., Japan	O5	36
Kyyiv (Kiev), Ukr.	G4	26
Kyyivs'ke vodoskhovyshche, res., Ukr.	G4	26
Kyzyl, Russia	G10	28
Kyzylkum, des., Asia	I10	26
Kzyl-Orda, Kaz.	I11	26

L

Name	Map Ref.	Page
Laa an der Thaya, Aus.	G16	10
La Aguja, Cabo de, c., Col.	B5	84
La Algaba, Spain	H5	16
La Araucanía, prov., Chile	J2	80
La Arena, Pan.	J14	92
Laas Caanood, Som.	G10	56
La Asunción, Ven.	B11	84
Labadieville, La., U.S.	E5	125
La Banda, Arg.	D6	80
La Barca, Mex.	G8	90
La Barge, Wy., U.S.	D2	157
La Baule-Escoublac, Fr.	E4	14
Labé, Gui.	F3	64
Labe (Elbe), stm., Eur.	B9	10
La Belle, Fl., U.S.	F5	116
La Belle, Mo., U.S.	A6	132
Labette, co., Ks., U.S.	E8	123
Labin, Cro.	D9	18
Labinsk, Russia	I6	26
Laborde, Arg.	G7	80
Laboulaye, Arg.	H7	80
Labrador, reg., Newf., Can.	g9	102
Labrador City, Newf., Can.	h8	102
Labrador Sea, N.A.	E22	96
Lábrea, Braz.	E6	76
Lábrea, Braz.	B9	82
La Broquerie, Man., Can.	E3	100
Labutta, Mya.	F3	40
Labytnangi, Russia	D11	26
La Calera, Chile	G3	80
La Canada Flintridge, Ca., U.S.	m12	112
Lacantún, stm., Mex.	I14	90
La Carlota, Arg.	G7	80
La Carolina, Spain	G8	16
Lac-Bouchette, Que., Can.	A5	104
Lac-Brome, Que., Can.	D5	104
Laccadive Islands see Lakshadweep, is., India	G2	46
Lac du Bonnet, Man., Can.	D3	100
Lac du Flambeau, Wi., U.S.	B4	156
La Ceiba, Hond.	B8	92
La Ceiba, Ven.	C7	84
La Center, Ky., U.S.	e9	124
Lac-Etchemin, Que., Can.	C7	104
Lacey, Wa., U.S.	B3	154
Laceys Spring, Al., U.S.	A3	108
La Chaux-de-Fonds, Switz.	D6	13
Lachdenpochja, Russia	K22	6
Lachen, Switz.	D10	13
Lachine, Que., Can.	D4	104
Lachlan, stm., Austl.	J6	70
La Chorrera, Col.	H6	84
La Chorrera, Pan.	C3	84
L'achovichi, Bela.	H9	22
Lachute, Que., Can.	D3	104
La Ciotat, Fr.	I12	14
Lackawanna, N.Y., U.S.	C2	139
Lackawanna, co., Pa., U.S.	D10	145
Lac La Biche, Alta., Can.	B5	98
Lac la Hache, B.C., Can.	D7	99
Laclede, Id., U.S.	B5	132
Laclede, co., Mo., U.S.	D5	132
La Clotilde, Arg.	D8	80
Lac-Mégantic, Que., Can.	D7	104
La Cocha, Arg.	D6	80
Lacolle, Que., Can.	D4	104
Lacombe, Alta., Can.	C4	98
Lacombe, La., U.S.	D6	125
Lacon, Il., U.S.	B4	120
La Concepción, Mex.	B7	90
La Concepción, Ven.	B7	84
Laconia, N.H., U.S.	C4	136
La Conner, Wa., U.S.	A3	154
La Consulta, Arg.	G4	80
Lacoochee, Fl., U.S.	D4	116
La Coruña, Spain	B3	16
Lac qui Parle, co., Mn., U.S.	F2	130
La Crescent, Mn., U.S.	G7	130
La Crete, Alta., Can.	f7	98
La Crosse, In., U.S.	B4	121
La Crosse, Ks., U.S.	D4	123
La Crosse, Wi., U.S.	E2	156
La Crosse, co., Wi., U.S.	E2	156
La Cruz, Arg.	E10	80
La Cruz, Col.	G4	84
La Cruz, C.R.	F9	92
La Cruz de Río Grande, Nic.	D10	92
La Cuesta, C.R.	I12	92
La Cumbre, Arg.	F6	80
La Cygne, Ks., U.S.	D9	123
Ladainha, Braz.	D8	79
Ladário, Braz.	H13	82
Ladd, Il., U.S.	B4	120
Laddonia, Mo., U.S.	B6	132
Ladismith, S. Afr.	I5	66
Ladoga, In., U.S.	E4	121
Ladoga, Lake see Ladožskoje ozero, l., Russia	E4	26
La Dorada, Col.	E5	84
La Dormida, Arg.	G5	80
Ladožskoje ozero (Lake Ladoga), l., Russia	E4	26
Ladson, S.C., U.S.	F7	147
Lady Elliot Island, i., Austl.	E10	70
Lady Lake, Fl., U.S.	D5	116
Ladysmith, B.C., Can.	E6	99
Ladysmith, S. Afr.	G6	66
Ladysmith, Wi., U.S.	C2	156
Lae, Pap. N. Gui.	m16	68a
La Esmeralda, Ven.	F10	84
La Esperanza, Hond.	C6	92
La Falda, Arg.	F6	80
Lafayette, Al., U.S.	C4	108
Lafayette, Ca., U.S.	h8	112
Lafayette, Co., U.S.	B5	113
Lafayette, Ga., U.S.	B1	117
Lafayette, In., U.S.	D4	121
Lafayette, La., U.S.	D3	125
Lafayette, N.C., U.S.	B3	144
Lafayette, Or., U.S.	B3	144
Lafayette, R.I., U.S.	E4	146
Lafayette, Tn., U.S.	A5	149
Lafayette, co., Ar., U.S.	D2	111
Lafayette, co., Fl., U.S.	C3	116
Lafayette, co., La., U.S.	D3	125
Lafayette, co., Ms., U.S.	A4	131
Lafayette, co., Mo., U.S.	B4	132
Lafayette, co., Wi., U.S.	F3	156
Lafayette, Mount, mtn., N.H., U.S.	B3	136
Lafe, Ar., U.S.	A5	111
La Feria, Tx., U.S.	F4	150
La Ferté-Bernard, Fr.	D7	14
La Ferté-Gaucher, Fr.	D10	14
La Ferté-Macé, Fr.	D6	14
La Ferté-Saint-Aubin, Fr.	E8	14
Lafia, Nig.	G14	64
Lafitte, La., U.S.	k11	125
Laflèche, Sask., Can.	H2	105
La Flèche, Fr.	E6	14
La Follette, Tn., U.S.	C9	149
La Fontaine, In., U.S.	C6	121
Lafourche, co., La., U.S.	E5	125
Lafourche, Bayou, stm., La., U.S.	E5	125
La Francia, Arg.	F7	80
La Galite, l., Tun.	L3	18
La Gallareta, Arg.	E8	80
Lagangzong, China	F14	44
Lages, Braz.	D13	80
Laghouat, Alg.	D12	62
La Gloria, Col.	C6	84
Lagoa da Prata, Braz.	F6	79
Lagoa Formosa, Braz.	E5	79
Lagoa Santa, Braz.	E7	79
Lagoa Vermelha, Braz.	E13	80
Lagos, Nig.	H11	64
Lagos, Port.	H3	16
Lagos de Moreno, Mex.	G9	90
La Gouèra, W. Sah.	J2	62
La Goulette, Tun.	M5	18
La Grand'Combe, Fr.	H11	14
La Grande, Or., U.S.	B8	144
La Grande, stm., Que., Can.	h11	104
La Grande Deux, Réservoir, res., Que., Can.	h11	104
La Grange, Ga., U.S.	C1	117
La Grange, Il., U.S.	k9	120
La Grange, In., U.S.	A7	121
La Grange, Ky., U.S.	B4	124
La Grange, Mo., U.S.	A6	132
La Grange, N.C., U.S.	B5	140
La Grange, Tx., U.S.	E4	150
Lagrange, Wy., U.S.	E8	157
Lagrange, co., In., U.S.	A7	121
La Grange Park, Il., U.S.	k9	120
La Gran Sabana, pl., Ven.	E12	84
La Guadeloupe (Saint-Evariste), Que., Can.	D7	104
La Guajira, dept., Col.	B6	84
La Guajira, Península de, pen., S.A.	A7	84
La Guerche-de-Bretagne, Fr.	E5	14
Laguna, Braz.	E14	80
Laguna, N.M., U.S.	B2	138
Laguna Beach, Ca., U.S.	F5	112
Laguna Larga, Arg.	F7	80
Laguna Paiva, Arg.	F8	80
Lagunas, Peru	A4	82
Lagunillas, Bol.	H10	82
La Habana (Havana), Cuba	C3	94
La Habra, Ca., U.S.	n13	112
Lahaina, Hi., U.S.	C5	118
La Harpe, Il., U.S.	C2	120
La Harpe, Ks., U.S.	E8	123
Lahat, Indon.	F3	38
Lahij, Yemen	G3	47
Lāhījān, Iran	C11	48
Lahontan Reservoir, res., Nv., U.S.	D2	135
Lahore, Pak.	E6	44
Lahr, Ger.	G7	10
Lahti, Fin.	K19	6
La Huaca, Peru	A1	82
La Huacana, Mex.	H9	90
Laie, Hi., U.S.	B4	118
L'Aigle, Fr.	D7	14
Laingsburg, S. Afr.	I5	66
Laird, Sask., Can.	E2	105
Laishui, China	D3	32
Laiwu, China	G5	32
Laiyang, China	G8	32
Laizhou Wan (Laichow Bay), b., China	F7	32
La Jalca, Peru	B3	82
La Jara, Co., U.S.	D5	113
La Junta, Co., U.S.	D7	113
Lake, co., Ca., U.S.	C2	112
Lake, co., Co., U.S.	B4	113
Lake, co., Fl., U.S.	D5	116
Lake, co., Il., U.S.	A6	120
Lake, co., In., U.S.	B3	121
Lake, co., Mi., U.S.	E5	129
Lake, co., Mn., U.S.	C7	130
Lake, co., Mt., U.S.	C2	133
Lake, co., Oh., U.S.	A4	142
Lake, co., Or., U.S.	E6	144
Lake, co., S.D., U.S.	C8	148
Lake, co., Tn., U.S.	A2	149
Lake Alfred, Fl., U.S.	D5	116
Lake Andes, S.D., U.S.	D7	148
Lake Arrowhead, Ca., U.S.	E5	112
Lake Arthur, La., U.S.	D3	125
Lake Arthur, N.M., U.S.	D5	138
Lake Benton, Mn., U.S.	F2	130
Lake Bluff, Il., U.S.	A6	120
Lake Butler, Fl., U.S.	B4	116
Lake Cargelligo, Austl.	I7	70
Lake Charles, La., U.S.	D2	125
Lake Chelan National Recreation Area, Wa., U.S.	A5	154
Lake City, Ar., U.S.	B5	111
Lake City, Fl., U.S.	B4	116
Lake City, Ia., U.S.	B3	122
Lake City, Mn., U.S.	F6	130
Lake City, Pa., U.S.	B1	145
Lake City, S.C., U.S.	D8	147
Lake City, Tn., U.S.	C9	149
Lake Clark National Park, Ak., U.S.	C9	109
Lake Cowichan, B.C., Can.	g11	99
Lake Crystal, Mn., U.S.	F4	130
Lake Delton, Wi., U.S.	E4	156
Lake Elsinore, Ca., U.S.	F5	112
Lake Erie Beach, N.Y., U.S.	C1	139
Lakefield, Ont., Can.	C6	103
Lakefield, Mn., U.S.	G3	130
Lake Forest, Il., U.S.	A6	120
Lake Geneva, Wi., U.S.	F5	156
Lake George, Co., U.S.	C5	113
Lake Hamilton, Ar., U.S.	g7	111
Lake Harbour, N.W. Ter., Can.	D19	96
Lake Havasu City, Az., U.S.	C1	110
Lake Helen, Fl., U.S.	D5	116
Lake in the Hills, Il., U.S.	h8	120
Lake Jackson, Tx., U.S.	r14	150
Lakeland, Fl., U.S.	D5	116
Lakeland, Ga., U.S.	E3	117
Lakeland, Tn., U.S.	B2	149
Lake Lenore, Sask., Can.	E3	105
Lake Linden, Mi., U.S.	A2	129
Lake Louise, Alta., Can.	D2	98
Lake Magdalene, Fl., U.S.	o11	116
Lake Mary, Fl., U.S.	D5	116
Lake Mead National Recreation Area, U.S.	H7	135
Lake Mills, Ia., U.S.	A4	122
Lake Mills, Wi., U.S.	E5	156
Lakemore, Oh., U.S.	A4	142
Lake Nash, Austl.	C2	70
Lake Nebagamon, Wi., U.S.	B2	156
Lake Norden, S.D., U.S.	C8	148
Lake Odessa, Mi., U.S.	F5	129
Lake of the Woods, co., Mn., U.S.	B4	130
Lake Orion, Mi., U.S.	F7	129
Lake Oswego, Or., U.S.	B4	144
Lake Ozark, Mo., U.S.	C5	132
Lake Park, Fl., U.S.	F6	116
Lake Park, Ia., U.S.	A2	122
Lake Placid, Fl., U.S.	E5	116
Lake Placid, N.Y., U.S.	A7	139
Lake Pontchartrain Causeway, La., U.S.	h11	125
Lake Preston, S.D., U.S.	C8	148
Lake Providence, La., U.S.	B4	125
Lake Shore, Md., U.S.	B5	127
Lakeshore, Ms., U.S.	E4	131
Lakeside, Ca., U.S.	F5	112
Lakeside, Ct., U.S.	C2	136
Lakeside, Mt., U.S.	B2	133
Lakeside, Or., U.S.	D2	144
Lakeside Park, Ky., U.S.	h13	124
Lake Station, In., U.S.	A3	121
Lake Station, In., U.S.	A3	143
Lake Stevens, Wa., U.S.	A3	154
Lake Tansi Village, Tn., U.S.	D8	149
Laketon, In., U.S.	C6	121
Lake View, Ar., U.S.	C5	111
Lake View, Ia., U.S.	B2	122
Lakeview, Or., U.S.	E6	144
Lake Village, Ar., U.S.	D4	111
Lake Village, In., U.S.	B3	121
Lakeville, Ct., U.S.	B2	136
Lakeville, Ma., U.S.	C6	128
Lakeville, Mn., U.S.	F5	130
Lake Wales, Fl., U.S.	E5	116
Lake Worth, Fl., U.S.	F6	116
Lake Zurich, Il., U.S.	h8	120
Lakhīmpur, India	G9	44
Lakin, Ks., U.S.	E2	123
Lakinsk, Russia	E22	22
Lakota, N.D., U.S.	A7	141
Lakshadweep, ter., India	H2	46
Lakshadweep, is., India	G2	46
Lakshadweep Sea, Asia	H3	46
La Leonesa, Arg.	D9	80
Lalibela, Eth.	K10	60
La Libertad, El Sal.	D5	92
La Libertad, Guat.	I14	90
La Libertad, dept., Peru	B2	82
La Ligua, Chile	G3	80
La Lima, Hond.	B7	92
La Línea, Spain	I6	16
Lalitpur, India	H8	44
Lālmanir Hāt, Bngl.	H13	44
La Loche, Sask., Can.	m7	105
La Loupe, Fr.	D8	14
Lalupon, Nig.	H12	64
La Luz, N.M., U.S.	E4	138
La Maddalena, Italy	H4	18
La Malbaie, Que., Can.	B7	104
Lamaline, Newf., Can.	E4	102
La Mancha, reg., Spain	B2	111
Lamar, Ar., U.S.		
Lamar, Co., U.S.	C8	113
Lamar, Mo., U.S.	D3	132
Lamar, S.C., U.S.	C7	147
Lamar, co., Al., U.S.	B1	108
Lamar, co., Ga., U.S.	C2	117
Lamar, co., Ms., U.S.	D4	131
Lamar, co., Tx., U.S.	C5	150
Lamarque, Arg.	J6	80
La Marsa, Tun.	M5	18
Lamas, Peru	B3	82
Lamb, co., Tx., U.S.	B1	150
Lamballe, Fr.	D4	14
Lambaréné, Gabon	B2	58
Lambayeque, Peru	B1	82
Lambayeque, dept., Peru	B1	82
Lambert, Ms., U.S.	A3	131
Lambert Glacier, Ant.	C5	73
Lamberton, Mn., U.S.	F3	130
Lambertville, Mi., U.S.	G7	129
Lambton, Cape, c., N.W. Ter., Can.	B8	96
Lame Deer, Mt., U.S.	E10	133
La Mendieta, Arg.	B5	101
Lamèque, N.B., Can.	B5	101
Lamèque, Île, i., N.B., Can.	B5	101
La Merced, Arg.	E6	80
La Merced, Arg.	C6	80
La Mesa, Arg.	I13	92
La Mesa, Ca., U.S.	F5	112
La Mesa, N.M., U.S.	E3	138
Lamesa, Tx., U.S.	C2	150
La Palma, i., Spain	o23	17b
La Moille, Il., U.S.	B4	120
Lamoille, Nv., U.S.	C6	135
Lamoille, co., Vt., U.S.	B3	152
Lamoille, stm., Vt., U.S.	B3	152
La Moine, stm., Il., U.S.	C3	120
Lamoni, Ia., U.S.	D4	122
Lamont, Alta., Can.	C4	98
Lamont, Ca., U.S.	E4	112
La Monte, Mo., U.S.	C4	132
La Mosquitia, hist. reg., Hond.	B11	92
La Motte, Isle, i., Vt., U.S.	B2	152
Lamotte-Beuvron, Fr.	E9	14
La Moure, N.D., U.S.	C7	141
La Moure, co., N.D., U.S.	C7	141
Lampa, Peru	F6	82
Lampang, Thai.	E5	40
Lampasas, Tx., U.S.	D3	150
Lampasas, co., Tx., U.S.	D3	150
Lampazos de Naranjo, Mex.	D9	90
Lampman, Sask., Can.	H4	105
La Muerte, Cerro, mtn., C.R.	H11	92
Lanai, i., Hi., U.S.	C5	118
Lanai City, Hi., U.S.	C5	118
Lanark, Ont., Can.	B8	103
Lanark, Il., U.S.	A4	120
Lanark, W.V., U.S.	n13	155
Lancashire, co., Eng., U.K.	H11	8
Lancaster, Ont., Can.	B10	103
Lancaster, Eng., U.K.	G11	8
Lancaster, Ca., U.S.	E4	112
Lancaster, Ky., U.S.	C5	124
Lancaster, Mo., U.S.	A5	132
Lancaster, N.H., U.S.	B3	136
Lancaster, N.Y., U.S.	C2	139
Lancaster, Oh., U.S.	C3	142
Lancaster, Pa., U.S.	F9	145
Lancaster, S.C., U.S.	B6	147
Lancaster, Tx., U.S.	n10	150
Lancaster, Wi., U.S.	F3	156
Lancaster, co., Ne., U.S.	D9	134
Lancaster, co., Pa., U.S.	G9	145
Lancaster, co., S.C., U.S.	B6	147
Lancaster, co., Va., U.S.	C6	153
Lancaster Sound, strt., N.W. Ter., Can.	B16	96
Lance Creek, Wy., U.S.	C8	157
Lanciano, Italy	G9	18
Lancun, China	E22	10
Lańcut, Pol.	F5	13
Lancy, Switz.	F8	10
Land Between the Lakes, U.S.	f9	124
Landeck, Aus.	H10	10
Landen, Bel.	G7	12
Lander, Wy., U.S.	D4	157
Lander, co., Nv., U.S.	C4	135
Landerneau, Fr.	D2	14
Landis, Sask., Can.	E1	105
Landis, N.C., U.S.	B2	140
Landisville, Pa., U.S.	F9	145
Landivisiau, Fr.	D2	14
Landrum, S.C., U.S.	A3	147
Land's End, c., Eng., U.K.	K8	8
Landsberg [am Lech], Ger.	G10	10
Landshut, Ger.	G12	10
Landskrona, Swe.	N13	6
Lane, co., Ks., U.S.	D3	123
Lane, co., Or., U.S.	C4	144
Lanesboro, Mn., U.S.	G7	130
Lanesville, In., U.S.	H6	121
Lanett, Al., U.S.	C4	108
Lang, Sask., Can.	H3	105
Langarūd, Iran	C11	48
Lang Bay, B.C., Can.	E5	99
Langdon, Alta., Can.	D4	98
Langdon, N.D., U.S.	A7	141
Langeac, Fr.	G10	14
Langeais, Fr.	E7	14
Langenburg, Sask., Can.	G5	105
Langenhagen, Ger.	C9	10
Langenthal, Switz.	D8	13
Langham, Sask., Can.	E2	105
Langlade, co., Wi., U.S.	C4	156
Langley, B.C., Can.	f13	99
Langley, S.C., U.S.	E4	147
Langley, Wa., U.S.	A3	154
Langley Park, Md., U.S.	f9	127
Langnau, Switz.	E8	13
Langogne, Fr.	H10	14
Langon, Fr.	H6	14
Langøya, i., Nor.	G14	6
Langres, Fr.	E12	14
Langruth, Man., Can.	D2	100
Langsa, Indon.	L4	40
Langston, Ok., U.S.	B4	143
Langxi, China	D8	34
Langzhong, China	E8	30
Lanham, Md., U.S.	C4	127
Lanier, co., Ga., U.S.	E3	117
Lanigan, Sask., Can.	F3	105
Länkäran, Azer.	J7	26
Lannemezan, Fr.	I7	14
Lannion, Fr.	D3	14
Lannon, Wi., U.S.	m11	156
L'Annonciation, Que., Can.	C3	104
Lansdale, Pa., U.S.	F11	145
Lansdowne, Md., U.S.	B4	127
L'Anse, Mi., U.S.	B2	129
L'Anse-au-Loup, Newf., Can.	C3	102
Lansford, N.D., U.S.	A4	141
Lansford, Pa., U.S.	E10	145
Lansing, Il., U.S.	B6	120
Lansing, Ia., U.S.	A6	122
Lansing, Ks., U.S.	C9	123
Lansing, Mi., U.S.	F6	129
Lansing, N.Y., U.S.	C4	139
Lantana, Fl., U.S.	F6	116
Lanxi, China	F8	34
Lanzarote, i., Spain	n27	17b
Lanzhou, China	D7	30
Laoag, Phil.	I19	39b
Laochang, China	B8	40
Laois, co., Ire.	I6	8
Laon, Fr.	C10	14
La Orotava, Spain	o24	17b
La Oroya, Peru	D4	82
Laos (Lao), ctry., Asia	B3	38
Lapa, Braz.	C13	80
Lapalisse, Fr.	F10	14
La Palma, Pan.	C3	84
La Palma, Pan.	D2	84
La Palma, i., Spain	o23	17b
La Paloma, Ur.	H11	80
La Pampa, prov., Arg.	I5	80
La Paragua, Ven.	D11	84
La Pasión, Río de, stm., Guat.	I14	90
La Paz, Arg.	F9	80
La Paz, Arg.	G5	80
La Paz, Bol.	G7	82
La Paz, Col.	B6	84
La Paz, Hond.	C7	92
La Paz, Mex.	E4	90
La Paz, Mex.	F9	90
La Paz, In., U.S.	B5	121
La Paz, dept., Bol.	F7	82
La Paz, dept., Hond.	C7	92
La Paz, co., Az., U.S.	D2	110
La Paz, Bahía, b., Mex.	E4	90
La Pedrera, Col.	H8	84
Lapeer, Mi., U.S.	E7	129
Lapeer, co., Mi., U.S.	E7	129
Lapel, In., U.S.	D6	121
La Perla, Mex.	C7	90
La Perouse Strait (Sōya-kaikyō), strt., Asia	b17	36a
La Piedad de Cabadas, Mex.	G8	90
La Pine, Or., U.S.	D5	144
Lapin lääni, prov., Fin.	H20	6
Lapinlahti, Fin.	J20	6
La Pintada, Pan.	I14	92
La Place, La., U.S.	h11	125
Lapland, hist. reg., Eur.	H18	6
La Plata, Arg.	H10	80
La Plata, Col.	F5	84
La Plata, Md., U.S.	C4	127
La Plata, Mo., U.S.	A5	132
La Plata, co., Co., U.S.	D3	113
La Plata Peak, mtn., Co., U.S.	B4	113
La Pocatière, Que., Can.	B7	104
Laporte, Co., U.S.	A5	113
La Porte, In., U.S.	A4	121
La Porte, Tx., U.S.	r14	150
La Porte, co., In., U.S.	A4	121
La Porte City, Ia., U.S.	B5	122
Lappeenranta, Fin.	K21	6
La Prairie, Que., Can.	D4	104
Laptevych, more (Laptev Sea), Russia	B17	28
La Puebla de Cazalla, Spain	H6	16
La Push, Wa., U.S.	B1	154
La Quiaca, Arg.	B6	80
La Quinta, Ca., U.S.	F5	112
L'Aquila, Italy	G8	18
Lār, Iran	H13	48
Lara, state, Ven.	B8	84
Larache, Mor.	J5	16
Laragne-Montéglin, Fr.	H12	14
Laramie, Wy., U.S.	E7	157
Laramie, co., Wy., U.S.	E8	157
Laramie, stm., U.S.	E7	157
Laramie Mountains, mts., Wy., U.S.	D7	157
Laranjal, Braz.	F7	79
Laranjeiras do Sul, Braz.	C12	80
L'Arbresle, Fr.	G11	14

Name	Map Ref.	Page
Larchmont, N.Y., U.S.	h13	139
Larchwood, Ia., U.S.	A1	122
Laredo, Spain	B8	16
Laredo, Tx., U.S.	F3	150
La Reforma, Mex.	E5	90
Largo, Fl., U.S.	E4	116
Largo, Key, i., Fl., U.S.	G6	116
Largs, Scot., U.K.	F9	8
Larimer, co., Co., U.S.	A5	113
Larimore, N.D., U.S.	B8	141
La Rioja, Arg.	E5	80
La Rioja, prov., Arg.	E5	80
La Rioja, prov., Spain	C9	16
Lárisa, Grc.	J6	20
La Rivière, Man., Can.	E2	100
Lark, Ut., U.S.	C3	151
Lärkäna, Pak.	G3	44
Lark Harbour, Newf., Can.	D2	102
Larkspur, Ca., U.S.	h7	112
Larksville, Pa., U.S.	n17	145
Lárnax (Larnaca), Cyp.	D2	48
Larned, Ks., U.S.	D4	123
La Rochefoucauld, Fr.	G7	14
La Rochelle, Fr.	F5	14
La Roche-sur-Yon, Fr.	F5	14
La Roda, Spain	F9	16
La Romana, Dom. Rep.	E10	94
La Ronge, Sask., Can.	B3	105
Larose, La., U.S.	E5	125
Larroque, Arg.	G9	80
Larsen Ice Shelf, Ant.	B12	73
Larue, co., Ky., U.S.	C4	124
Larvik, Nor.	L12	6
LaSalle, Que., Can.	q19	104
La Salle, Co., U.S.	A6	113
La Salle, Il., U.S.	B4	120
La Salle, co., Il., U.S.	B4	120
La Salle, co., La., U.S.	C3	125
La Salle, co., Tx., U.S.	E3	150
La Sal Mountains, mts., Ut., U.S.	E6	151
Las Animas, Co., U.S.	C7	113
Las Animas, co., Co., U.S.	D6	113
La Sarre, Que., Can.	k11	104
Las Arrias, Arg.	F7	80
Las Ballenas, Canal de, strt., Mex.	C3	90
Las Breñas, Arg.	D8	80
Las Cabezas de San Juan, Spain	I6	16
Las Cabras, Chile	H3	80
Lascano, Ur.	G11	80
Lascar, Volcán, vol., Chile	B5	80
Las Catitas, Arg.	G4	80
Las Cejas, Arg.	D6	80
Las Choapas, Mex.	I12	90
La Scie, Newf., Can.	D4	102
Las Cruces, N.M., U.S.	E3	138
La Selle, Morne, mtn., Haiti	E9	94
La Serena, Chile	E3	80
La Seyne, Fr.	I12	14
Las Flores, Arg.	I9	80
Las Flores, Arg.	F4	80
Las Garcitas, Arg.	D9	80
Lashburn, Sask., Can.	D1	105
Las Heras, Arg.	G4	80
Lashio, Mya.	C4	40
Łask, Pol.	D19	10
L'askel'a, Russia	K22	6
Las Lajas, Arg.	J3	80
Las Lajas, Pan.	C2	84
Las Lajitas, Arg.	C6	80
Las Lomitas, Arg.	C8	80
Las Margaritas, Mex.	I14	90
Las Minas, Cerro, mtn., Hond.	C6	92
La Solana, Spain	G8	16
Las Palmas, Arg.	D9	80
Las Palmas, Pan.	C2	84
Las Palmas, prov., Spain	o26	17b
Las Palmas de Gran Canaria, Spain	o25	17b
La Spezia, Italy	E4	18
Las Piedras, Ur.	H10	80
Las Piedras, Río de, stm., Peru	E7	82
Las Rosas, Arg.	G8	80
Las Rosas, Mex.	I13	90
Lassen, co., Ca., U.S.	B3	112
Lassen Peak, vol., Ca., U.S.	B3	112
Lassen Volcanic National Park, Ca., U.S.	B3	112
L'Assomption, Que., Can.	D4	104
Las Tablas, Pan.	D2	84
Last Mountain Lake, l., Sask., Can.	F3	105
Las Toscas, Arg.	E9	80
Lastoursville, Gabon	B2	58
Las Tunas, Cuba	D6	94
Las Varas, Mex.	C5	90
Las Varas, Mex.	G7	90
Las Varillas, Arg.	F7	80
Las Vegas, Nv., U.S.	G6	135
Las Vegas, N.M., U.S.	B4	138
Latacunga, Ec.	H3	84
Latah, co., Id., U.S.	C2	119
Latakia see Al-Lādhiqīyah, Syria	D3	48
La Teste-de-Buch, Fr.	H5	14
Lathrop, Ca., U.S.	h10	112
Lathrop, Mo., U.S.	B3	132
Lathrop Wells, Nv., U.S.	G5	135
Latimer, co., Ok., U.S.	C6	143
Latina, Italy	H7	18
La Toma, Arg.	G6	80
La Tour-du-Pin, Fr.	G12	14
La Tremblade, Fr.	G5	14
La Trinité, Mart.	G14	94
Latrobe, Pa., U.S.	F3	145
Latta, S.C., U.S.	C9	147
La Tuque, Que., Can.	B5	104
Lätür, India	C4	46
Latvia (Latvija), ctry., Eur.	D8	22
Lauchhammer, Ger.	D13	10
Lauderdale, Ms., U.S.	C5	131
Lauderdale, co., Al., U.S.	A2	108
Lauderdale, co., Ms., U.S.	C5	131
Lauderdale, co., Tn., U.S.	B3	149
Lauderdale Lakes, Fl., U.S.	r13	116
Laufen, Switz.	D8	13
Laughlin, Nv., U.S.	H7	135
Launceston, Austl.	M7	70
La Unión, Chile	E2	78
La Unión, Col.	G4	84
La Unión, El Sal.	D7	92
La Unión, Mex.	I9	90
La Unión, Peru	C3	82
La Unión, Spain	H11	16
Laupahoehoe, Hi., U.S.	D6	118
La Urbana, Ven.	D9	84
Laurel, De., U.S.	F3	115
Laurel, Fl., U.S.	E4	116
Laurel, In., U.S.	F7	121
Laurel, Md., U.S.	B4	127
Laurel, Ms., U.S.	D4	131
Laurel, Mt., U.S.	E8	133
Laurel, Ne., U.S.	B8	134
Laurel, co., Ky., U.S.	C5	124
Laurel Bay, S.C., U.S.	G6	147
Laureldale, Pa., U.S.	F10	145
Laurel Hill, N.C., U.S.	C3	140
Laurel River Lake, res., Ky., U.S.	D5	124
Laurence Harbor, N.J., U.S.	C4	137
Laurens, Ia., U.S.	B3	122
Laurens, S.C., U.S.	C3	147
Laurens, co., Ga., U.S.	D4	117
Laurens, co., S.C., U.S.	C3	147
Laurentides, Que., Can.	D4	104
Laurier, Man., Can.	D2	100
Laurier, Que., Can.	C6	104
Laurinburg, N.C., U.S.	C3	140
Laurium, Mi., U.S.	A2	129
Lausanne, Switz.	E6	13
Lautaro, Chile	J2	80
Lauterbrunnen, Switz.	E8	13
Lavaca, Ar., U.S.	B1	111
Lavaca, co., Tx., U.S.	E4	150
Lava Hot Springs, Id., U.S.	G6	119
Laval, Que., Can.	D4	104
Laval, Fr.	D6	14
La Vale, Md., U.S.	k13	127
La Vall d'Uixo, Spain	F11	16
Lavalle, Arg.	E6	80
Lavalle, Arg.	E9	80
Lavaltrie, Que., Can.	D4	104
Lavapié, Punta, c., Chile	I2	80
Laveen, Az., U.S.	m8	110
La Vega, Dom. Rep.	E9	94
La Vela de Coro, Ven.	B8	84
Lavelanet, Fr.	J8	14
Lavello, Italy	H10	18
La Verde, Arg.	D9	80
La Vergne, Tn., U.S.	A5	149
La Verkin, Ut., U.S.	F2	151
La Verne, Ca., U.S.	m13	112
Laverne, Ok., U.S.	A2	143
Laverton, Austl.	E4	68
La Veta, Co., U.S.	D5	113
La Victoria, Ven.	B9	84
La Vila Joiosa, Spain	G11	16
Lavillette, N.B., Can.	B4	101
La Viña, Arg.	C6	80
La Virginia, Col.	E5	84
La Vista, Ne., U.S.	g12	134
Lavonia, Ga., U.S.	B3	117
La Voulte-sur-Rhône, Fr.	H11	14
Lavras, Braz.	F6	79
Lavras do Sul, Braz.	F12	80
Lavumisa, Swaz.	F10	66
Lawai, Hi., U.S.	B2	118
Lawksawk, Mya.	D4	40
Lawn, Newf., Can.	E4	102
Lawrence, In., U.S.	E5	121
Lawrence, Ks., U.S.	D8	123
Lawrence, Ma., U.S.	A5	128
Lawrence, N.Y., U.S.	k13	139
Lawrence, co., Al., U.S.	A2	108
Lawrence, co., Ar., U.S.	A4	111
Lawrence, co., Il., U.S.	E6	120
Lawrence, co., In., U.S.	G4	121
Lawrence, co., Ky., U.S.	B7	124
Lawrence, co., Ms., U.S.	D3	131
Lawrence, co., Mo., U.S.	D4	132
Lawrence, co., Oh., U.S.	D3	142
Lawrence, co., Pa., U.S.	E1	145
Lawrence, co., S.D., U.S.	C2	148
Lawrence, co., Tn., U.S.	B4	149
Lawrenceburg, In., U.S.	F8	121
Lawrenceburg, Ky., U.S.	B5	124
Lawrenceburg, Tn., U.S.	B4	149
Lawrence Park, Pa., U.S.	B1	145
Lawrencetown, N.S., Can.	E4	101
Lawrenceville, Ga., U.S.	C3	117
Lawrenceville, Il., U.S.	E6	120
Lawrenceville, N.J., U.S.	C3	137
Lawrenceville, Va., U.S.	D5	153
Lawson, Mo., U.S.	B3	132
Lawsonia, Md., U.S.	E6	127
Lawtell, La., U.S.	D3	125
Lawton, Mi., U.S.	F5	129
Lawton, Ok., U.S.	C3	143
Lawz, Jabal al-, mtn., Sau. Ar.	G3	48
Laxå, Swe.	L14	6
Lázaro Cárdenas, Mex.	I8	90
Lázaro Cárdenas, Mex.	B2	90
Lazdijai, Lith.	G6	22
Lazio, prov., Italy	G7	18
Lea, co., N.M., U.S.	D6	138
Leachville, Ar., U.S.	B5	111
Lead, S.D., U.S.	C2	148
Leader, Sask., Can.	G1	105
Leadville, Co., U.S.	B4	113
Leadwood, Mo., U.S.	D7	132
Leaf, stm., Ms., U.S.	D5	131
Leaf Rapids, Man., Can.	A1	100
League City, Tx., U.S.	r14	150
Leake, co., Ms., U.S.	C4	131
Leakesville, Ms., U.S.	D5	131
Lealman, Fl., U.S.	p10	116
Leamington, Ont., Can.	E2	103
Leandro N. Alem, Arg.	D11	80
Leary, Ga., U.S.	E2	117
Leask, Sask., Can.	E2	105
Leatherman Peak, mtn., Id., U.S.	E5	119
Leavenworth, Ks., U.S.	C9	123
Leavenworth, Wa., U.S.	B5	155
Leavenworth, co., Ks., U.S.	C8	123
Leavittsburg, Oh., U.S.	A5	142
Leawood, Ks., U.S.	D9	123
Lebanon, Il., U.S.	E4	120
Lebanon, In., U.S.	D5	121
Lebanon, Ky., U.S.	C4	124
Lebanon, Mo., U.S.	D5	132
Lebanon, N.H., U.S.	C2	136
Lebanon, Oh., U.S.	C1	142
Lebanon, Or., U.S.	C4	144
Lebanon, Pa., U.S.	F9	145
Lebanon, Tn., U.S.	A5	149
Lebanon, Va., U.S.	f9	153
Lebanon, co., Pa., U.S.	F8	145
Lebanon (Lubnān), ctry., Asia	C2	42
Lebanon Junction, Ky., U.S.	C4	124
Lebed'an', Russia	H22	22
Le Blanc, Fr.	F8	14
Lebo, Ks., U.S.	D8	123
Lebombo Mountains, hills, Afr.	E10	66
Łębork, Pol.	A17	10
Lebret, Sask., Can.	G4	105
Lebrija, Spain	I5	16
Lebu, Chile	I2	80
Le Cannet, Fr.	I14	14
Le Cateau, Fr.	B10	14
Lecce, Italy	I13	18
Lecco, Italy	D4	18
Le Center, Mn., U.S.	F5	130
Le Cheylard, Fr.	H11	14
Le Claire, Ia., U.S.	C7	122
Lecompte, La., U.S.	C3	125
Lecompton, Ks., U.S.	C8	123
Leconte, Mount, mtn., Tn., U.S.	D10	149
Le Creusot, Fr.	F11	14
Łęczyca, Pol.	C19	10
Lede, Bel.	G4	12
Ledong, China	E10	40
Leduc, Alta., Can.	C4	98
Lee, Ma., U.S.	B1	128
Lee, co., Al., U.S.	C4	108
Lee, co., Ar., U.S.	C5	111
Lee, co., Fl., U.S.	F5	116
Lee, co., Ga., U.S.	E2	117
Lee, co., Il., U.S.	B4	120
Lee, co., Ia., U.S.	D6	122
Lee, co., Ky., U.S.	C6	124
Lee, co., Ms., U.S.	A5	131
Lee, co., N.C., U.S.	B3	140
Lee, co., S.C., U.S.	C7	147
Lee, co., Tx., U.S.	D4	150
Lee, co., Va., U.S.	f8	153
Leechburg, Pa., U.S.	E2	145
Leech Lake, l., Mn., U.S.	C4	130
Leech Lake Indian Reservation, Mn., U.S.	C4	130
Leeds, Eng., U.K.	H12	8
Leeds, Al., U.S.	B3	108
Leeds, N.D., U.S.	A6	141
Leelanau, co., Mi., U.S.	D5	129
Lee Park, N.J., U.S.	n17	145
Leer, Ger.	B7	10
Leesburg, Fl., U.S.	D5	116
Leesburg, Ga., U.S.	E2	117
Leesburg, Va., U.S.	A5	153
Lees Summit, Mo., U.S.	C3	132
Leesville, La., U.S.	C2	125
Leesville, S.C., U.S.	D4	147
Leeton, Austl.	J7	70
Leeton, Mo., U.S.	C4	132
Leetonia, Oh., U.S.	B5	142
Leeuwarden, Neth.	B8	12
Leeuwin, Cape, c., Austl.	F3	68
Leeward Islands, is., N.A.	F13	94
Leflore, co., Ms., U.S.	B3	131
Le Flore, co., Ok., U.S.	C7	143
Legal, Alta., Can.	C4	98
Legaspi, Phil.	o20	39b
Leghorn see Livorno, Italy	F5	18
Legionowo, Pol.	C20	10
Legnago, Italy	D6	18
Legnano, Italy	D3	18
Legnica (Liegnitz), Pol.	D16	10
Le Grand, Ia., U.S.	B5	122
Le Grau-du-Roi, Fr.	I11	14
Le Havre, Fr.	C7	14
Lehi, Ut., U.S.	C4	151
Lehigh, co., Pa., U.S.	E10	145
Lehigh, stm., Pa., U.S.	E10	145
Lehigh Acres, Fl., U.S.	F5	116
Lehighton, Pa., U.S.	E10	145
Lehrte, Ger.	C9	10
Lehututu, Bots.	D5	66
Leiah, Pak.	E4	44
Leibnitz, Aus.	I15	10
Leicester, Eng., U.K.	I12	8
Leicester, Ma., U.S.	B4	128
Leicestershire, co., Eng., U.K.	I12	8
Leichhardt, stm., Austl.	D7	70
Leiden, Neth.	D6	12
Leigh, Ne., U.S.	C8	134
Leigh Creek, Austl.	H3	70
Leighton, Al., U.S.	A2	108
Leinster, hist. reg., Ire.	H6	8
Leipsic, Oh., U.S.	A2	142
Leipsic, stm., De., U.S.	C3	115
Leipzig, Ger.	D12	10
Leisure City, Fl., U.S.	s13	116
Leitchfield, Ky., U.S.	C3	124
Leitrim, co., Ire.	H5	8
Leiyang, China	I1	34
Leizhou Bandao, pen., China	D11	40
Lek, stm., Neth.	E6	12
Leksand, Swe.	K14	6
Leland, Ms., U.S.	B3	131
Le Locle, Switz.	D6	13
Le Lude, Fr.	E7	14
Le Mans, Fr.	D7	14
Le Mars, Ia., U.S.	B1	122
Lemberg, Sask., Can.	G4	105
Lemdiyya, Alg.	B12	62
Leme, Braz.	G5	79
Lemesós (Limassol), Cyp.	D2	48
Lemgo, Ger.	C8	10
Lemhi, co., Id., U.S.	E4	119
Lemhi, stm., Id., U.S.	E5	119
Lemhi Pass, Id., U.S.	E5	119
Lemhi Range, mts., Id., U.S.	E5	119
Lemitar, N.M., U.S.	C3	138
Lemmon, S.D., U.S.	B3	148
Lemmon, Mount, mtn., Az., U.S.	E5	110
Lemon Valley, Nv., U.S.	D2	135
Lemon Grove, Ca., U.S.	o15	112
Lemont, Il., U.S.	B5	120
Lemont, Pa., U.S.	E6	145
Le Mont-Saint-Michel, Fr.	D5	14
Lemoore, Ca., U.S.	D4	112
Le Moule, Guad.	F14	94
Lempa, stm., N.A.	D6	92
Lempira, dept., Hond.	C6	92
Lemsid, W. Sah.	G4	62
Lena, Il., U.S.	A4	120
Lena, stm., Russia	C17	28
Lenawee, co., Mi., U.S.	G6	129
Lençóis, Braz.	B8	79
Lenexa, Ks., U.S.	D9	123
Lenghu, China	D5	30
Lenina, pik, mtn., Asia	J12	26
Leningrad see Sankt-Peterburg, Russia	B13	22
Leninogorsk, Kaz.	G8	28
Leninogorsk, Russia	G8	26
Leninsk-Kuzneckij, Russia	G9	28
Lennox, S.D., U.S.	D9	148
Lennox, Isla, i., Chile	H3	78
Lennoxville, Que., Can.	D6	104
Lenoir, N.C., U.S.	B1	140
Lenoir, co., N.C., U.S.	B5	140
Lenoir City, Tn., U.S.	D9	149
Lenox, Ga., U.S.	E3	117
Lenox, Ia., U.S.	D3	122
Lenox, Ma., U.S.	B1	128
Lens, Fr.	B9	14
Lensk, Russia	E14	28
Lentini, Italy	L10	18
Lenzburg, Switz.	D9	13
Leo, In., U.S.	B7	121
Leoben, Aus.	H15	10
Léogâne, Haiti	E8	94
Leola, Ar., U.S.	C3	111
Leola, S.D., U.S.	B7	148
Leominster, Ma., U.S.	A4	128
León, Nic.	E8	92
León, Spain	C6	16
León, Ia., U.S.	D4	122
León, dept., Nic.	E8	92
León, Mex.	G9	90
Leon, co., Fl., U.S.	B2	116
Leon, co., Tx., U.S.	D4	150
Leon, stm., Tx., U.S.	D4	150
Leonard, Tx., U.S.	C4	150
Leonardtown, Md., U.S.	D4	127
León [de los Aldamas], Mex.	G9	90
Leones, Arg.	G7	80
Leonforte, Italy	L9	18
Leonia, N.J., U.S.	h9	137
Leonora, Austl.	E4	68
Leopold and Astrid Coast, Ant.	B5	73
Leopoldina, Braz.	F7	79
Leopoldo de Bulhões, Braz.	D4	79
Léopoldville see Kinshasa, Zaire	B3	58
Leoti, Ks., U.S.	D2	123
Leova, Mol.	C12	20
Leoville, Sask., Can.	D2	105
Lepanto, C.R.	H9	92
Lepanto, Ar., U.S.	B5	111
Lepe, Spain	H4	16
Lepel', Bela.	G11	22
Lephepe, Bots.	D7	66
Leping, China	G6	34
L'Épiphanie, Que., Can.	D4	104
Le Port, Reu.	v17	67c
Le Puy, Fr.	G10	14
Lere, Nig.	F14	64
Lerma, stm., Mex.	G9	90
Leroy, Sask., Can.	F3	105
Le Roy, Il., U.S.	C5	120
Le Roy, Ks., U.S.	D8	123
Le Roy, Mn., U.S.	G6	130
Le Roy, N.Y., U.S.	C3	139
Lerwick, Scot., U.K.	A12	8
Léry, Que., Can.	q19	104
Les Andelys, Fr.	C8	14
Lesbos see Lésbos, i., Grc.	J10	20
Les Cayes, Haiti	E8	94
Leshan, China	F7	30
Leskovac, Yugo.	G5	20
Leslie, Ar., U.S.	B3	111
Leslie, Mi., U.S.	F6	129
Leslie, co., Ky., U.S.	C6	124
Lesnoj, Russia	G23	22
Lesogorskij, Russia	K21	6
Lesosibirsk, Russia	F10	28
Lesotho, ctry., Afr.	G5	58
Les Sables-d'Olonne, Fr.	F5	14
Les Saintes, is., Guad.	G14	94
Lesser Antilles, is.	H14	94
Lesser Caucasus, mts., Asia	I6	26
Lesser Slave Lake, l., Alta., Can.	B3	98
Lesser Sunda Islands see Tenggara, Nusa, is., Indon.	G7	38
Lessines (Lessen), Bel.	G4	12
Lester Prairie, Mn., U.S.	F4	130
Lestock, Sask., Can.	F3	105
Le Sueur, Mn., U.S.	F5	130
Le Sueur, co., Mn., U.S.	F5	130
Le Sueur, stm., Mn., U.S.	G5	130
Leszno, Pol.	D16	10
Letcher, co., Ky., U.S.	C7	124
Letellier, Man., Can.	E3	100
Lethbridge, Alta., Can.	E4	98
Lethbridge, Newf., Can.	D5	102
Lethem, Guy.	F13	84
Le Thillot, Fr.	E13	14
Leticia, Col.	J8	84
Letlhakane, Bots.	C7	66
Letlhakeng, Bots.	E7	66
Letpadan, Mya.	F3	40
Le Tréport, Fr.	B8	14
Letterkenny, Ire.	G5	8
Leuk, Switz.	F8	13
Leuven (Louvain), Bel.	G6	12
Levádhia, Grc.	K6	20
Levelland, Tx., U.S.	C1	150
Leveque, Cape, c., Austl.	C4	68
Leverkusen, Ger.	D6	10
Levice, Slvk.	G18	10
Le Vigan, Fr.	I10	14
Levin, N.Z.	D5	72
Lévis [-Lauzon], Que., Can.	C6	104
Levittown, N.Y., U.S.	E7	139
Levittown, Pa., U.S.	F12	145
Levkás, Grc.	K4	20
Lev Tolstoj, Russia	H22	22
Levy, co., Fl., U.S.	C4	116
Lewe, Mya.	E4	40
Lewes, De., U.S.	E5	115
Lewis, Ks., U.S.	E4	123
Lewis, co., Id., U.S.	C2	119
Lewis, co., Ky., U.S.	B6	124
Lewis, co., Mo., U.S.	A6	132
Lewis, co., N.Y., U.S.	B5	139
Lewis, co., Tn., U.S.	B4	149
Lewis, co., Wa., U.S.	C3	154
Lewis, co., W.V., U.S.	C4	155
Lewis, stm., Wa., U.S.	C4	154
Lewis, Butt of, c., Scot., U.K.	C7	8
Lewis, Isle of, i., Scot., U.K.	C7	8
Lewis, Mount, mtn., Nv., U.S.	C5	135
Lewis and Clark, co., Mt., U.S.	C4	133
Lewis and Clark Lake, res., U.S.	E8	148
Lewisburg, Ky., U.S.	D3	124
Lewisburg, Pa., U.S.	E8	145
Lewisburg, Tn., U.S.	B5	149
Lewisburg, W.V., U.S.	D4	155
Lewisport, Ky., U.S.	C3	124
Lewis Smith Lake, res., Al., U.S.	B2	108
Lewiston, Id., U.S.	C1	119
Lewiston, Me., U.S.	D2	126
Lewiston, Mn., U.S.	G7	130
Lewiston, N.Y., U.S.	B1	139
Lewiston, Ut., U.S.	B4	151
Lewistown, Il., U.S.	C3	120
Lewistown, Mt., U.S.	C7	133
Lewistown, Pa., U.S.	E6	145
Lewisville, Ar., U.S.	D2	111
Lewisville, Id., U.S.	F6	119
Lewisville, Tx., U.S.	C4	150
Lewisville Lake, res., Tx., U.S.	C4	150
Lexington, Al., U.S.	A2	108
Lexington, Il., U.S.	C5	120
Lexington, Ky., U.S.	B5	124
Lexington, Ma., U.S.	B5	128
Lexington, Ms., U.S.	B3	131
Lexington, Mo., U.S.	B4	132
Lexington, Ne., U.S.	D6	134
Lexington, N.C., U.S.	B2	140
Lexington, Oh., U.S.	B3	142
Lexington, Ok., U.S.	B4	143
Lexington, S.C., U.S.	D5	147
Lexington, Tn., U.S.	B3	149
Lexington, Va., U.S.	C3	153
Lexington, co., S.C., U.S.	D5	147
Lexington Park, Md., U.S.	D5	127
Leyte, i., Phil.	C7	38
Leyte Gulf, b., Phil.	C8	38
Leżajsk, Pol.	E22	10
Lezha, Alb.	H4	20
Lež'ovo, Russia	E23	22
L'gov, Russia	G5	26
Lhasa, China	F14	44
Lhazê, China	F12	44
Lhokseumawe, Indon.	L4	40
Lhorong, China	E6	30
L'Hospitalet de Llobregat, Spain	D14	16
Lianjiang, China	I8	34
Lianshui, China	B8	34
Lianxian, China	G9	30
Lianyungang, China	I7	32
Lianyungang (Xinpu), China	I7	32
Liao, stm., China	C11	30
Liaocheng, China	G3	32
Liaodong Bandao (Liaotung Peninsula), pen., China	D10	32
Liaodong Wan, b., China	C11	30
Liaoning, prov., China	C11	30
Liaoyang, China	B11	32
Liaoyuan, China	C12	30
Liaozhong, China	B11	32
Liard, stm., Can.	D8	96
Líbano, Col.	E5	84
Libby, Mt., U.S.	B1	133
Libenge, Zaire	H4	56
Liberal, Ks., U.S.	E3	123
Liberal, Mo., U.S.	D3	132
Liberec, Czech Rep.	E15	10
Liberia, C.R.	G9	92
Liberia, ctry., Afr.	G5	54
Libertad, Ven.	C8	84
Libertador General Bernardo O'Higgins, prov., Chile	H3	80
Libertador General San Martín, Arg.	B6	80
Liberty, In., U.S.	E8	121
Liberty, Ky., U.S.	C5	124
Liberty, Mo., U.S.	B3	132
Liberty, N.Y., U.S.	D6	139
Liberty, N.C., U.S.	B3	140
Liberty, S.C., U.S.	B2	147
Liberty, Tx., U.S.	D5	150
Liberty, co., Fl., U.S.	B2	116
Liberty, co., Ga., U.S.	E5	117
Liberty, co., Mt., U.S.	B5	133
Liberty, co., Tx., U.S.	D5	150
Lībīyah, Aş-Şahrā' al- (Libyan Desert), des., Afr.	D6	56
Libourne, Fr.	H6	14
Libramont, Bel.	I7	12
Libres, Mex.	H11	90
Libreville, Gabon	A1	58
Libya (Lībiyā), ctry., Afr.	C4	56
Libyan Desert see Lībiyā, Aş-Şahrā' al-, des., Afr.	D6	56
Licancábur, Volcán, vol., S.A.	J8	82
Licantén, Chile	H2	80
Licata, Italy	L8	18
Lichinga, Moz.	D7	58
Lichoslavl', Russia	D18	22
Lichuan, China	H5	34
Licking, Mo., U.S.	D6	132
Licking, co., Oh., U.S.	B3	142
Licking, stm., Ky., U.S.	B6	124
Lida, Bela.	H8	22
Lidao, China	F10	32
Lidgerwood, N.D., U.S.	C8	141
Lidköping, Swe.	L13	6
Lido, Pan.	C3	84
Liechtenstein, ctry., Eur.	F9	4
Liège (Luik), Bel.	G8	12
Liège, prov., Bel.	G8	12
Liegnitz see Legnica, Pol.	D16	10
Lielvārde, Lat.	E7	22
Lienz, Aus.	I12	10
Liepāja, Lat.	E4	22
Lier (Lierre), Bel.	F6	12
Liestal, Switz.	D8	13
Liévin, Fr.	B9	14
Lièvre, Rivière du, stm., Que., Can.	D2	104
Lighthouse Point, c., Mi., U.S.	C5	129
Lighthouse Reef, rf., Belize	I16	90
Lignite, N.D., U.S.	A3	141
Ligny-en-Barrois, Fr.	D12	14
Ligonier, In., U.S.	B6	121
Ligonier, Pa., U.S.	F3	145
Liguria, prov., Italy	E3	18
Ligurian Sea, Eur.	E4	18
Lihue, Hi., U.S.	B2	118
Lijiang, China	F7	30
Likasi (Jadotville), Zaire	D5	58
Likely, B.C., Can.	C7	99
Likino-Dulevo, Russia	F21	22
Lilbourn, Mo., U.S.	E8	132
Lilburn, Ga., U.S.	h8	117
Liling, China	H2	34
Lille, Fr.	B10	14
Lillebonne, Fr.	C7	14
Lillehammer, Nor.	K12	6
Lillers, Fr.	B9	14
Lillesand, Nor.	L11	6
Lillestrøm, Nor.	L12	6
Lillian, Al., U.S.	E2	108
Lillington, N.C., U.S.	B4	140
Lillinonah, Lake, l., Ct., U.S.	C2	114
Lillooet, B.C., Can.	D7	99
Lillooet, stm., B.C., Can.	D6	99
Lilly Grove, W.V., U.S.	D3	155
Lilongwe, Mwi.	D6	58
Lily, Ky., U.S.	C5	124
Lilydale, Austl.	M7	70
Lima, Para.	B10	79
Lima, Peru	E3	82
Lima, Mt., U.S.	F4	133
Lima, N.Y., U.S.	C3	139
Lima, Oh., U.S.	B1	142
Lima, dept., Peru	D3	82
Limache, Chile	G3	80
Limay, stm., Arg.	J4	80
Limbaži, Lat.	D7	22
Limburg, prov., Bel.	G7	12
Limburg, prov., Neth.	F8	12
Limburg an der Lahn, Ger.	E8	10
Limeira, Braz.	G5	79
Limerick, Ire.	I5	8
Limerick, co., Ire.	I5	8
Limestone, Me., U.S.	B5	126
Limestone, co., Al., U.S.	A2	108
Limestone, co., Tx., U.S.	D4	150
Limoges, Ont., Can.	B9	103
Limoges, Fr.	G8	14
Limón, Hond.	B9	92
Limon, Co., U.S.	B7	113
Limoux, Fr.	I9	14
Limpopo, stm., Afr.	E11	66
Lin'an, China	E8	34
Linares, Chile	H3	80
Linares, Mex.	E10	90
Linares, Spain	G8	16
Lincang, China	C7	40
Linch, Wy., U.S.	C6	157
Lincoln, Eng., U.K.	H13	8
Lincoln, Al., U.S.	B3	108
Lincoln, Ar., U.S.	B1	111
Lincoln, Ca., U.S.	C3	112
Lincoln, De., U.S.	E4	115
Lincoln, Il., U.S.	C4	120
Lincoln, Ks., U.S.	C5	123
Lincoln, Me., U.S.	C4	126
Lincoln, Mo., U.S.	C4	132
Lincoln, Ne., U.S.	D9	134
Lincoln, N.H., U.S.	B3	136
Lincoln, co., Ar., U.S.	D4	111
Lincoln, co., Co., U.S.	C7	113
Lincoln, co., Ga., U.S.	C4	117
Lincoln, co., Id., U.S.	G4	119
Lincoln, co., Ks., U.S.	C5	123
Lincoln, co., Ky., U.S.	C5	124
Lincoln, co., Me., U.S.	D3	126
Lincoln, co., Mn., U.S.	F2	130
Lincoln, co., Mo., U.S.	B7	132
Lincoln, co., Mt., U.S.	B1	133
Lincoln, co., Ne., U.S.	C5	134
Lincoln, co., Nv., U.S.	F6	135
Lincoln, co., N.M., U.S.	D4	138
Lincoln, co., N.C., U.S.	B1	140
Lincoln, co., Ok., U.S.	B5	143
Lincoln, co., Or., U.S.	C3	144
Lincoln, co., S.D., U.S.	D9	148
Lincoln, co., Tn., U.S.	B5	149
Lincoln, co., Wa., U.S.	B7	154
Lincoln, co., W.V., U.S.	C2	155
Lincoln, co., Wi., U.S.	C4	156
Lincoln, co., Wy., U.S.	D2	157
Lincoln Center, Me., U.S.	C3	144
Lincoln Heights, Oh., U.S.	o13	142
Lincoln Park, Co., U.S.	C5	113
Lincoln Park, Ga., U.S.	D2	117
Lincoln Park, Mi., U.S.	p15	129
Lincoln Park, N.J., U.S.	B4	137
Lincoln Sea, N.A.	A14	86
Lincolnshire, Il., U.S.	h9	120
Lincolnshire, co., Eng., U.K.	H13	8
Lincoln Tomb State Memorial, hist., Il., U.S.	D4	120

Name	Map Ref.	Page
Lincolnton, Ga., U.S.	C4	117
Lincolnton, N.C., U.S.	B1	140
Lincolnwood, Il., U.S.	h9	120
Lincroft, N.J., U.S.	C4	137
Lindale, Ga., U.S.	B1	117
Lindau, Ger.	H9	10
Linden, Alta., Can.	D4	98
Linden, Guy.	D13	84
Linden, Al., U.S.	C2	108
Linden, In., U.S.	D4	121
Linden, Mi., U.S.	F7	129
Linden, N.J., U.S.	k8	137
Linden, Tn., U.S.	B4	149
Lindenhurst, Il., U.S.	h8	120
Lindenhurst, N.Y., U.S.	n15	139
Lindenwold, N.J., U.S.	D3	137
Lindi, Tan.	D7	58
Lindon, Ut., U.S.	C4	151
Lindsay, Ont., Can.	C6	103
Lindsay, Ca., U.S.	D4	112
Lindsay, Ok., U.S.	C4	143
Lindsborg, Ks., U.S.	D6	123
Lindstrom, Mn., U.S.	E6	130
Line Islands, is., Oc.	H24	158
Lineville, Al., U.S.	B4	108
Linfen, China	D9	30
Lingao, China	E10	40
Lingayen, Phil.	m19	39b
Lingbi, China	B6	34
Lingen, Ger.	C7	10
Lingga, Kepulauan, is., Indon.	O8	40
Linghu, China	E9	34
Lingle, Wy., U.S.	D8	157
Linglestown, Pa., U.S.	F8	145
Lingling, China	A11	40
Linglongta, China	C7	32
Lingqiu, China	D2	32
Lingshui, China	E11	40
Linguère, Sen.	D2	64
Lingyuan, China	B7	32
Linhai, China	G10	34
Linhares, Braz.	E8	79
Linhe, China	C8	30
Linjiang, China	B14	32
Linköping, Swe.	L14	6
Linkou, China	B13	30
Linkuva, Lith.	E6	22
Linn, Ks., U.S.	C6	123
Linn, Mo., U.S.	C6	132
Linn, co., Ia., U.S.	B6	122
Linn, co., Ks., U.S.	D9	123
Linn, co., Mo., U.S.	B4	132
Linn, co., Or., U.S.	C4	144
Lino Lakes, Mn., U.S.	m12	130
Linqing, China	G3	32
Linqu, China	G6	32
Linquan, China	B4	34
Linru, China	A1	34
Linruzhen, China	A1	34
Lins, Braz.	F4	79
Lintao, China	D7	30
Lintlaw, Sask., Can.	E4	105
Linton, In., U.S.	F3	121
Linton, N.D., U.S.	C5	141
Linwood, Ont., Can.	D4	103
Linwood, Ks., U.S.	m15	123
Linwood, N.J., U.S.	E3	137
Linxia, China	D7	30
Linxiang, China	F2	34
Linyanti, Smb.	B7	66
Linyanti, stm., Afr.	B7	66
Linyi, China	H6	32
Linying, China	B2	34
Linz, Aus.	G14	10
Lion, Golfe du, b., Fr.	F13	22
Liozno, Bela.	F13	22
Lipeck, Russia	I22	22
Lipetsk see Lipeck, Russia	I22	22
Lipki, Russia	H20	22
Lipova, Rom.	C5	20
Lippe, stm., Ger.	D8	10
Lippstadt, Ger.	D8	10
Lipscomb, Al., U.S.	B3	108
Lipscomb, co., Tx., U.S.	A2	150
Lipton, Sask., Can.	G4	105
Liptovský Mikuláš, Slvk.	F19	10
Lircay, Peru	E4	82
Lisala, Zaire	A4	58
Lisboa (Lisbon), Port.	G2	16
Lisbon see Lisboa, Port.	G2	16
Lisbon, Ia., U.S.	C6	122
Lisbon, Me., U.S.	D2	126
Lisbon, Md., U.S.	B3	127
Lisbon, N.H., U.S.	B3	136
Lisbon, N.D., U.S.	C8	141
Lisbon, Oh., U.S.	B5	142
Lisbon Center, Me., U.S.	f7	126
Lisbon Falls, Me., U.S.	E2	126
Lisburn, N. Ire., U.K.	G7	8
Lisburne, Cape, c., Ak., U.S.	B6	109
Lishui, China	G8	34
Lisieux, Fr.	C7	14
Liski (Georgiu-Dež), Russia	G5	26
Lisle, Il., U.S.	k8	120
L'Islet-sur-Mer, Que., Can.	B7	104
Lisman, Al., U.S.	C1	108
Lismore, Austl.	G10	70
Listowel, Ont., Can.	D4	103
Litchfield, Ct., U.S.	C3	114
Litchfield, Il., U.S.	D4	120
Litchfield, Mi., U.S.	F6	129
Litchfield, Mn., U.S.	E4	130
Litchfield, co., Ct., U.S.	B2	114
Litchfield Park, Az., U.S.	m8	110
Lithgow, Austl.	I9	70
Lithia Springs, Ga., U.S.	h7	117
Lithonia, Ga., U.S.	C2	117
Lithuania (Lietuva), ctry., Eur.	F6	22
Lititz, Pa., U.S.	F9	145
Litoměřice, Czech Rep.	E14	10
Litomyšl, Czech Rep.	F16	10
Little, stm., La., U.S.	C3	125
Little, stm., Ok., U.S.	B5	143
Little Acres, Az., U.S.	D5	110
Little America, Wy., U.S.	E3	157
Little Andaman, i., India	I2	40
Little Arkansas, stm., Ks., U.S.	D6	123
Little Belt Mountains, mts., Mt., U.S.	D6	133
Little Bighorn, stm., U.S.	E9	133
Little Blue, stm., U.S.	C6	123
Little Boars Head, N.H., U.S.	E5	136
Little Catalina, Newf., Can.	D5	102
Little Cayman, i., Cay. Is.	E4	94
Little Chute, Wi., U.S.	D5	156
Little Colorado, stm., Az., U.S.	B4	110
Little Compton, R.I., U.S.	E6	146
Little Current, Ont., Can.	B3	103
Little Diomede Island, i., Ak., U.S.	B6	109
Little Eagle, S.D., U.S.	B5	148
Little Egg Harbor, b., N.J., U.S.	D4	137
Little Falls, Mn., U.S.	E4	130
Little Falls, N.J., U.S.	B4	137
Little Falls, N.Y., U.S.	B6	139
Little Ferry, N.J., U.S.	h8	137
Littlefield, Tx., U.S.	C1	150
Littlefork, Mn., U.S.	B5	130
Little Fork, stm., Mn., U.S.	B5	130
Little Gunpowder Falls, stm., Md., U.S.	A4	127
Little Humboldt, stm., Nv., U.S.	C4	135
Little Kanawha, stm., W.V., U.S.	C3	155
Little Lake, l., La., U.S.	E5	125
Little Lynches, stm., S.C., U.S.	C7	147
Little Mecatina, stm., Can.	h9	102
Little Miami, stm., Oh., U.S.	C1	142
Little Missouri, stm., U.S.	B6	106
Little Missouri, stm., Ar., U.S.	D2	111
Little Owyhee, stm., U.S.	B5	135
Little Pee Dee, stm., S.C., U.S.	C9	147
Little Powder, stm., U.S.	F11	133
Little Red, stm., Ar., U.S.	B4	111
Little River, Ks., U.S.	D5	123
Little River, co., Ar., U.S.	D1	111
Little Rock, Ar., U.S.	C3	111
Little Sable Point, c., Mi., U.S.	E4	129
Little Saint Bernard Pass see Petit-Saint-Bernard, Col du, Eur.	G13	14
Little Sandy, stm., Ky., U.S.	B6	124
Little Silver, N.J., U.S.	C4	137
Little Sioux, stm., U.S.	B2	122
Little Smoky, stm., Alta., Can.	B2	98
Littlestown, Pa., U.S.	G7	145
Little Tennessee, stm., U.S.	D9	149
Littleton, Co., U.S.	B6	113
Littleton, Il., U.S.	C3	120
Littleton, Ma., U.S.	B5	126
Littleton, N.H., U.S.	f10	128
Littleton, N.H., U.S.	B3	136
Littleville, Al., U.S.	A2	108
Little Wabash, stm., Il., U.S.	E5	120
Little White, stm., S.D., U.S.	D5	148
Litvínov, Czech Rep.	E13	10
Liuchen, China	C11	40
Liucheng, China	B10	40
Liuhe, China	A13	32
Liuheng, China	C7	34
Liuku, China	B5	40
Liuwangtou, China	I4	32
Liuyang, China	G2	34
Liuzhou, China	B10	40
Līvāni, Lat.	E9	22
Live Oak, Fl., U.S.	B4	116
Live Oak, Ca., U.S.	E3	150
Live Oak, co., Tx., U.S.	E3	150
Livermore, Ca., U.S.	h9	112
Livermore, Ky., U.S.	C2	124
Livermore, Mount, mtn., Tx., U.S.	o12	150
Livermore Falls, Me., U.S.	D2	126
Liverpool, N.S., Can.	E5	101
Liverpool, Eng., U.K.	H11	8
Livingston, Guat.	B6	92
Livingston, Al., U.S.	C1	108
Livingston, Ca., U.S.	D3	112
Livingston, Il., U.S.	E4	120
Livingston, La., U.S.	D5	125
Livingston, Mt., U.S.	E6	133
Livingston, N.J., U.S.	B4	137
Livingston, Tn., U.S.	C8	149
Livingston, Tx., U.S.	D5	150
Livingston, co., Il., U.S.	C5	120
Livingston, co., Ky., U.S.	e9	124
Livingston, co., La., U.S.	D5	125
Livingston, co., Mi., U.S.	F7	129
Livingston, co., Mo., U.S.	B4	132
Livingston, Lake, res., Tx., U.S.	D5	150
Livingstone, Zam.	A7	66
Livingstonia, Zam.	F12	18
Livny, Russia	I20	22
Livonia, La., U.S.	D4	125
Livonia, Mi., U.S.	F7	129
Livorno (Leghorn), Italy	F5	18
Livramento do Brumado, Braz.	B8	79
Lixian, China	E3	32
Liyang, China	D8	34
Lizang, China	J2	34
Lizella, Al., U.S.	D3	117
Lizard Head Pass, Co., U.S.	D3	113
Lizard Head Peak, mtn., Wy., U.S.	D3	157
Lizard Point, c., Eng., U.K.	L8	8
Lizella, Ga., U.S.	D3	117
Ljubljana, Slvn.	C9	18
Ljubuški, Bos.	F11	18
Ljungby, Swe.	M13	6
Ljusdal, Swe.	K15	6
Llancanelo, Laguna, l., Arg.	H4	80
Llandrindod Wells, Wales, U.K.	I10	8
Llanelli, Wales, U.K.	H9	8
Llangollen, Wales, U.K.	I10	8
Llanidloes, Wales, U.K.	I10	8
Llano, co., Tx., U.S.	D3	150
Llano, stm., Tx., U.S.	D3	150
Llanos, pl., S.A.	E7	84
Llata, Peru	C3	82
Lleida, Spain	D12	16
Llico, Chile	H2	80
Lliria, Spain	F11	16
Liorona, Punta, c., C.R.	I11	92
Lloyd, Ky., U.S.	B7	124
Lloydminster, Alta., Can.	C5	98
Lloydminster (Alta. and Sask.), Can.	D1	105
Llucmajor, Spain	F14	16
Llullaillaco, Volcán, vol., S.A.	C4	80
Loa, stm., Chile	I7	82
Loanda, Braz.	G2	79
Lobatse, Bots.	E7	66
Lobelville, Tn., U.S.	B4	149
Lobería, Arg.	J9	80
Lobito, Ang.	D2	58
Lobn'a, Russia	E20	22
Lobos, Arg.	H9	80
Locarno, Switz.	F10	13
Lochearn, Md., U.S.	g10	127
Loches, Fr.	E8	14
Loch Raven Reservoir, res., Md., U.S.	B4	127
Locke Mills, Me., U.S.	D2	126
Lockeport, N.S., Can.	F4	101
Lockerbie, Scot., U.K.	F10	8
Lockesburg, Ar., U.S.	D1	111
Lockhart, Austl.	J7	70
Lockhart, Fl., U.S.	D3	108
Lockhart, Tx., U.S.	E4	150
Lock Haven, Pa., U.S.	D7	145
Lockland, Oh., U.S.	o13	142
Lockport, Man., Can.	D3	100
Lockport, Il., U.S.	B5	120
Lockport, La., U.S.	E5	125
Lockport, N.Y., U.S.	B2	139
Lockwood, Mo., U.S.	D4	132
Lockwood, Mt., U.S.	E8	133
Locumba, Peru	G6	82
Locust, N.C., U.S.	B2	140
Locust Fork, stm., Al., U.S.	B3	108
Locust Grove, Ga., U.S.	C2	117
Locust Grove, Ok., U.S.	A6	143
Lod (Lydda), Isr.	E3	50
Lodejnoje Pole, Russia	A16	22
Lodge Grass, Mt., U.S.	E9	133
Lodgepole, Alta., Can.	C3	98
Lodgepole, Ne., U.S.	C3	134
Lodi, Italy	D4	18
Lodi, Ca., U.S.	C3	112
Lodi, N.J., U.S.	h8	137
Lodi, Oh., U.S.	A3	142
Lodi, Wi., U.S.	E4	156
Lodja, Zaire	B4	58
Łódź, Pol.	D19	10
Loei, Thai.	F6	40
Loeriesfontein, S. Afr.	H4	66
Lofoten, is., Nor.	G13	6
Loga, Niger	E11	64
Logan, Ia., U.S.	C2	122
Logan, Ks., U.S.	C4	123
Logan, N.M., U.S.	B6	138
Logan, Oh., U.S.	C3	142
Logan, Ut., U.S.	B4	151
Logan, W.V., U.S.	D3	155
Logan, co., Ar., U.S.	B2	111
Logan, co., Co., U.S.	A7	113
Logan, co., Il., U.S.	C4	120
Logan, co., Ks., U.S.	D2	123
Logan, co., Ky., U.S.	D3	124
Logan, co., Ne., U.S.	C5	134
Logan, co., N.D., U.S.	C6	141
Logan, co., Oh., U.S.	B2	142
Logan, co., Ok., U.S.	B4	143
Logan, co., W.V., U.S.	D3	155
Logan, Mount, mtn., Yukon, Can.	D4	96
Logan Creek, stm., Ne., U.S.	B9	134
Logandale, Nv., U.S.	G7	135
Logan Lake, B.C., Can.	D7	99
Logan Martin Lake, res., Al., U.S.	B3	108
Logan Pass, Mt., U.S.	B2	133
Logansport, In., U.S.	C5	121
Logansport, La., U.S.	C2	125
Loganville, Ga., U.S.	C3	117
Loggieville, N.B., Can.	B4	101
Log Lane Village, Co., U.S.	A7	113
Logojsk, Bela.	G10	22
Logroño, Spain	C9	16
Loi-kaw, Mya.	E4	40
Loire, stm., Fr.	E5	14
Loja, Ec.	I3	84
Loja, Ec.	J12	86
Loja, Spain	H7	16
Loja, prov., Ec.	J3	84
Lökbatan, Azer.	A10	48
Lokn'a, Russia	E13	22
Lokoja, Nig.	H13	64
Lokot', Russia	I17	22
Lol, Sud.	N5	60
Lola, Gui.	H5	64
Lolo, Mt., U.S.	D2	133
Lolo Pass, U.S.	C4	119
Lom, Bul.	F7	20
Lomas de Zamora, Arg.	H9	80
Lombard, Il., U.S.	k8	120
Lombardia, prov., Italy	D4	18
Lombok, i., Indon.	G6	38
Lomé, Togo	H10	64
Lomira, Wi., U.S.	E5	156
Lommel, Bel.	F7	12
Lomonosov, Russia	B12	22
Łomża, Pol.	k13	127
Lonaconing, Md., U.S.	D2	127
Loncoche, Chile	J3	80
Loncopué, Arg.	J3	80
London, Ont., Can.	E3	103
London, Eng., U.K.	J13	8
London, Ar., U.S.	B2	111
London, Ky., U.S.	C5	124
London, Oh., U.S.	C2	142
Londonderry (Derry), N. Ire., U.K.	F6	8
Londonderry, N.H., U.S.	E4	136
Londonderry, Vt., U.S.	E3	152
Londonderry, Cape, c., Austl.	B5	68
Londontown, Md., U.S.	C4	127
Londres, Arg.	D5	80
Londrina, Braz.	G3	79
Lone Grove, Ok., U.S.	C4	143
Lone Tree, Ia., U.S.	C6	122
Long, co., Ga., U.S.	E5	117
Longa, proliv, strt., Russia	C27	28
Long Beach, Ca., U.S.	F4	112
Long Beach, In., U.S.	A4	121
Long Beach, Ms., U.S.	D5	127
Long Beach, Ms., U.S.	g7	131
Long Beach, N.Y., U.S.	E7	139
Long Beach, Wa., U.S.	C1	154
Longboat Key, Fl., U.S.	q10	116
Long Branch, N.J., U.S.	C5	137
Longbranch, Wa., U.S.	B3	154
Longchuan, China	K4	34
Longdou, China	H6	34
Longford, Austl.	L7	70
Longford, co., Ire.	H6	8
Long Harbour [-Mount Arlington Heights], Newf., Can.	E5	102
Longhua, China	B5	32
Long Island, i., Bah.	C9	94
Long Island, i., N.Y., U.S.	E7	139
Long Island Sound, strt., U.S.	E7	139
Longitudinal, Valle, val., Chile	H3	80
Longjiang, China	B11	30
Long Lake, l., U.S.	h8	120
Long Lake, l., N.D., U.S.	C6	141
Longli, China	F8	30
Longling, China	B5	40
Longmeadow, Ma., U.S.	B2	128
Longmont, Co., U.S.	A5	113
Long Pine, Ne., U.S.	B6	134
Long Point, c., Man., Can.	C2	100
Long Point, c., Newf., Can.	D2	102
Long Point, pen., Ont., Can.	E4	103
Long Prairie, Mn., U.S.	E4	130
Longquan, China	G8	34
Long Range Mountains, mts., Newf., Can.	D3	102
Longreach, Austl.	D6	70
Longsheng, China	B11	40
Longs Peak, mtn., Co., U.S.	A5	113
Longtian, China	J8	34
Longtoupu, China	H2	34
Longueuil, Que., Can.	D4	104
Longuyon, Fr.	C12	14
Longview, Alta., Can.	D3	98
Long View, N.C., U.S.	B1	140
Longview, Tx., U.S.	C5	150
Longview, Wa., U.S.	C3	154
Longwy, Fr.	C12	14
Long Xuyen, Viet.	I8	40
Longyan, China	J6	34
Longzhou, China	C9	40
Lonoke, Ar., U.S.	C4	111
Lonoke, co., Ar., U.S.	C4	111
Lonsdale, Mn., U.S.	F5	130
Lonsdale, R.I., U.S.	B4	146
Lons-le-Saunier, Fr.	F12	14
Loogootee, In., U.S.	G4	121
Lookout, Cape, c., N.C., U.S.	C6	140
Lookout Mountain, Tn., U.S.	h11	149
Lookout Mountain, mtn., U.S.	D8	149
Lookout Pass, U.S.	B3	119
Loomis, Ne., U.S.	D6	134
Loon Lake, Wa., U.S.	A8	154
Loosahatchie, stm., Tn., U.S.	B2	149
Lop, China	B9	44
Lopatka, mys, c., Russia	G23	28
Lop Buri, Thai.	G6	40
López, Mex.	D7	90
López, Cap, c., Gabon	B1	58
Lopez Island, i., Wa., U.S.	A3	154
Lop Nur (Lop Nor), l., China	C5	30
Lora del Río, Spain	H6	16
Lorado, W.V., U.S.	D3	155
Lorain, Oh., U.S.	A3	142
Lorain, co., Oh., U.S.	A3	142
Lorca, Spain	H10	16
Lord Howe Island, i., Austl.	F11	68
Lordsburg, N.M., U.S.	E1	138
Loreauville, La., U.S.	D4	125
Loreburn, Sask., Can.	F2	105
Loreley, Ger.	E7	10
Lorena, Braz.	G6	79
Lorenzo Geyres (Queguay), Ur.	G10	80
Loreto, Arg.	D10	80
Loreto, Braz.	E9	76
Loreto, Mex.	F9	90
Loreto, Mex.	D4	90
Loreto, Para.	B10	80
Loreto, dept., Peru	I5	84
Lorette, Man., Can.	E3	100
Loretteville, Que., Can.	C6	104
Loretto, Ky., U.S.	C4	124
Loretto, Tn., U.S.	B4	149
Lorica, Col.	C5	84
Lorient, Fr.	E3	14
L'Orignal, Ont., Can.	B10	103
Loris, S.C., U.S.	C10	147
Lorman, Ms., U.S.	D2	131
Lorne, N.B., Can.	B3	101
Lörrach, Ger.	H7	10
Lorraine, hist. reg., Fr.	D13	14
Los Alamos, N.M., U.S.	B3	138
Los Alamos, co., N.M., U.S.	B3	138
Los Altos, Ca., U.S.	k8	112
Los Amates, Guat.	B5	92
Los Andes, Chile	G3	80
Los Ángeles, Chile	I2	80
Los Ángeles, Ca., U.S.	E4	112
Los Angeles Aqueduct, Ca., U.S.	E4	112
Los Banos, Ca., U.S.	D3	112
Los Berros, Arg.	F6	80
Los Cerrillos, Arg.	C2	142
Los Chiles, C.R.	F10	92
Los Gatos, Ca., U.S.	D8	80
Los Juries, Arg.	D2	112
Los Lagos, Chile	E7	80
Los Lunas, N.M., U.S.	D7	78
Los Mochis, Mex.	C3	138
Los Ojos, N.M., U.S.	E5	90
Los Palacios, Cuba	A3	138
Los Palacios y Villafranca, Spain	C3	94
	H6	16
Los Quirinchos, Arg.	G8	80
Los Ranchos de Albuquerque, N.M., U.S.	B3	138
Los Ríos, prov., Ec.	H3	84
Los Roques, Islas, is., Ven.	B9	84
Los Santos, prov., Pan.	J14	92
Los Sauces, Chile	I2	80
Lossiemouth, Scot., U.K.	D10	8
Los Taques, Ven.	B7	84
Los Telares, Arg.	E7	80
Los Teques, Ven.	B9	84
Lost River Range, mts., Id., U.S.	E5	119
Lost Trail Pass, U.S.	D5	119
Los Vilos, Chile	F3	80
Lota, Chile	I2	80
Lotung, Tai.	K10	34
Louang Namtha, Laos	D6	40
Louangphrabang, Laos	E7	40
Louchi, Russia	D4	26
Loudéac, Fr.	D4	14
Loudon, Tn., U.S.	D9	149
Loudon, co., Tn., U.S.	D9	149
Loudonville, Oh., U.S.	B3	142
Loudoun, co., Va., U.S.	A5	153
Loudun, Fr.	E7	14
Louga, Sen.	D1	64
Lougheed, Alta., Can.	C5	98
Louhans, Fr.	F12	14
Louisa, Ky., U.S.	B7	124
Louisa, Va., U.S.	B4	153
Louisa, co., Ia., U.S.	C6	122
Louisa, co., Va., U.S.	C5	153
Louisbourg, N.S., Can.	D10	101
Louisburg, N.C., U.S.	A4	140
Louisdale, N.S., Can.	D8	101
Louiseville, Que., Can.	C5	104
Louisiade Archipelago, is., Pap. N. Gui.	B10	68
Louisiana, Mo., U.S.	B6	132
Louisiana, state, U.S.	C3	125
Louisiana Point, c., La., U.S.	E2	125
Louis Trichardt, S. Afr.	D9	66
Louisville, Al., U.S.	D4	108
Louisville, Co., U.S.	B5	113
Louisville, Ga., U.S.	C4	117
Louisville, Il., U.S.	E5	120
Louisville, Ky., U.S.	B4	124
Louisville, Ms., U.S.	B4	131
Louisville, Ne., U.S.	D9	134
Louisville, Oh., U.S.	B4	142
Louis-XIV, Pointe, c., Que., Can.	h11	104
Loup, co., Ne., U.S.	C6	134
Loup, stm., Ne., U.S.	C8	134
Loup City, Ne., U.S.	C7	134
Lourdes, Newf., Can.	D2	102
Lourdes, Fr.	I6	14
Lourenço Marques see Maputo, Moz.	E11	66
Louth, co., Ire.	H7	8
Louviers, Fr.	C8	14
Louviers, Co., U.S.	B6	113
Love, co., Ok., U.S.	D4	143
Loveč, Bul.	F8	20
Loveland, Co., U.S.	A5	113
Loveland, Oh., U.S.	n13	142
Loveland Pass, Co., U.S.	B5	113
Lovell, Wy., U.S.	B4	157
Lovelock, Nv., U.S.	C3	135
Lovely, Ky., U.S.	C7	124
Lovenia, Mount, mtn., Ut., U.S.	C5	151
Love Point, c., Md., U.S.	B5	127
Loves Park, Il., U.S.	A4	120
Lovettsville, Va., U.S.	A5	153
Loving, N.M., U.S.	E5	138
Loving, co., Tx., U.S.	D1	150
Lovington, Il., U.S.	D5	120
Lovington, N.M., U.S.	E6	138
Lovosice, Czech Rep.	E14	10
Lowden, Ia., U.S.	C7	122
Lowe Farm, Man., Can.	E3	100
Lowell, Ar., U.S.	A1	111
Lowell, In., U.S.	B3	121
Lowell, Ma., U.S.	A5	126
Lowell, Mi., U.S.	F5	129
Lowell, N.C., U.S.	B1	140
Lowell, Or., U.S.	D4	144
Lower Arrow Lake, res., B.C., Can.	E8	99
Lower Brule, S.D., U.S.	C6	148
Lower California see Baja California, pen., Mex.	C3	90
Lower Hutt, N.Z.	D5	72
Lower Klamath Lake, l., Ca., U.S.	B3	112
Lower Monumental Lake, res., Wa., U.S.	C7	154
Lower New York Bay, b., N.J., U.S.	k8	137
Lower Paia, Hi., U.S.	C5	118
Lower Red Lake, l., Mn., U.S.	C3	130
Lower Saxony see Niedersachsen, state, Ger.	C8	10
Lower Village, Vt., U.S.	C3	152
Lower West Pubnico, N.S., Can.	F4	101
Lower Woods Harbour, N.S., Can.	F4	101
Lowestoft, Eng., U.K.	I15	8
Łowicz, Pol.	C19	10
Lowndes, co., Al., U.S.	C3	108
Lowndes, co., Ga., U.S.	F3	117
Lowndes, co., Ms., U.S.	B5	131
Lowrah (Pishin Lora), stm., Asia	G18	44
Lowry City, Mo., U.S.	C4	132
Lowville, N.Y., U.S.	B5	139
Loxley, Al., U.S.	E2	108
Loxton, Austl.	J4	70
Loyal, Wi., U.S.	D3	156
Loyall, Ky., U.S.	D6	124
Loznica, Yugo.	E3	20
Lualaba, stm., Zaire	B5	58
Lu'an, China	B5	34
Luan, China, China	C10	30
Luanda, Ang.	C2	58
Luang Prabang Range, mts., Asia	E6	40
Luang Prabang Range, mts., Asia	D5	58
L'uban', Bela.	I10	22
L'uban', Russia	B14	22
Lubango, Ang.	D2	58
Lubbock, Tx., U.S.	C2	150
Lubbock, co., Tx., U.S.	C2	150
Lubec, Me., U.S.	D6	126
Lübeck, Ger.	B10	10
L'ubercy, Russia	F20	22
L'ubim, Russia	C23	22
Lubin, Pol.	D16	10
Lublin, Pol.	D22	10
Lubliniec, Pol.	E18	10
Lubnān, Jabal (Lebanon Mountains), mts., Leb.	A5	50
Lubny, Ukr.	G4	26
Luboń, Pol.	C16	10
Lubudi, Zaire	C5	58
Lubumbashi (Élisabethville), Zaire	D5	58
Lucan, Ont., Can.	D3	103
Lucania, Mount, mtn., Yukon, Can.	D4	96
Lucas, Ks., U.S.	C5	123
Lucas, co., Ia., U.S.	C4	122
Lucas, co., Oh., U.S.	A2	142
Lucas González, Arg.	G9	80
Lucca, Italy	F5	18
Luce, co., Mi., U.S.	B5	129
Lucedale, Ms., U.S.	E5	131
Lucena, Phil.	o19	39b
Lucena, Spain	H7	16
Lučenec, Slvk.	G19	10
Lucera, Italy	H10	18
Lucerne see Luzern, Switz.	D9	13
Luceville, Que., Can.	A9	104
Luchovicy, Russia	G22	22
Luchow see Luzhou, China	F8	30
Luck, Wi., U.S.	C1	156
Luckenwalde, Ger.	C13	10
Lucknow, Ont., Can.	D3	103
Lucknow, India	G9	44
Lucky Lake, Sask., Can.	G2	105
Lucky Peak Lake, res., Id., U.S.	F3	119
Luçon, Fr.	F5	14
Lüda see Dalian, China	E9	32
Lüdenscheid, Ger.	D7	10
Lüderitz, Nmb.	F2	66
Ludhiāna, India	E6	44
Ludington, Mi., U.S.	E4	129
Ludlow, Russia	H17	22
Ludlow, Ky., U.S.	h13	124
Ludlow, Ma., U.S.	B3	128
Ludlow, Vt., U.S.	E3	152
Ludowici, Ga., U.S.	E5	117
Ludvika, Swe.	K14	6
Ludwigsburg, Ger.	G9	10
Ludwigsfelde, Ger.	C13	10
Ludwigshafen, Ger.	F8	10
Ludza, Lat.	E10	22
Luebo, Zaire	C4	58
Luena, Ang.	D3	58
Lufeng, China	M4	34
Lufeng, China	B7	40
Lufkin, Tx., U.S.	D5	150
Luga, Russia	C12	22
Lugano, Switz.	F10	13
Lugano, Lago di, l., Eur.	C4	18
Lugenda, stm., Moz.	D7	58
Lugo, Italy	E6	18
Lugo, Spain	B4	16
Lugoff, S.C., U.S.	C6	147
Lugoj, Rom.	D5	20
Luhans'k, Ukr.	H5	26
Luján, Arg.	G4	80
Luján, Arg.	G6	80
Lukang, Tai.	K9	34
Luke Air Force Base, mil., Az., U.S.	D3	110
Lukolela, Zaire	B3	58
Łuków, Pol.	D22	10
Lula, Ga., U.S.	B3	117
Luleå, Swe.	I18	6
Lüleburgaz, Tur.	H11	20
Lules, Arg.	D6	80
Luliang, China	B7	40
Luling, La., U.S.	k11	125
Luling, Tx., U.S.	E4	150
Lumber, stm., U.S.	C9	147
Lumber City, Ga., U.S.	E4	117
Lumberport, W.V., U.S.	B4	155
Lumberton, Ms., U.S.	D4	131
Lumberton, N.C., U.S.	C3	140
Lumberton, N.M., U.S.	D5	150
Lumbres, Fr.	B9	14
Lumby, B.C., Can.	D8	99
Lumpkin, Ga., U.S.	D2	117
Lumpkin, co., Ga., U.S.	B2	117
Lumsden, Newf., Can.	D5	102
Lumsden, Sask., Can.	G3	105
Luna, N.M., U.S.	D1	138
Luna, co., N.M., U.S.	E2	138
Luna Pier, Mi., U.S.	G7	129
Lund, Swe.	N13	6
Lund, Nv., U.S.	E6	135
Lundale, W.V., U.S.	n12	155
Lundar, Man., Can.	D2	100
Lundazi, Zam.	D6	58
Lundbreck, Alta., Can.	E3	98
Lüneburg, Ger.	B10	10
Lüneburger Heide, reg., Ger.	B10	10
Lunel, Fr.	I11	14
Lünen, Ger.	D7	10
Lunenburg, N.S., Can.	E5	101
Lunenburg, Vt., U.S.	C5	152
Lunenburg, co., Va., U.S.	D4	153
Lunéville, Fr.	D13	14
Lungi, S.L.	G3	64
Luninec, Bela.	I9	22
Lunjiao, China	M2	34
Luohe, China	B3	34
Luoji, China	C6	34
Luoyang, China	E9	30
Lupeni, Rom.	D7	20
Luray, Va., U.S.	B4	153
Lure, Fr.	E13	14
Luribay, Bol.	G8	82
Lúrio, stm., Moz.	D7	58
Lurín, Peru	F3	82
Lusaka, Zam.	D5	58
Lusambo, Zaire	B4	58
Lusby, Md., U.S.	D5	127
Luseland, Sask., Can.	E1	105

Name	Map Ref.	Page
Lushnje, Alb.	I3	20
Lüshun (Port Arthur), China	E9	32
Lüsi, China	C10	34
Lusk, Wy., U.S.	D8	157
Lūt, Dasht-e, des., Iran	E15	48
Lutcher, La., U.S.	D5	125
Luther, Ok., U.S.	B4	143
Luthersville, Ga., U.S.	C2	117
Lutherville-Timonium, Md., U.S.	B4	127
Luton, Eng., U.K.	J13	8
Luts'k, Ukr.	G3	26
Luttrell, Tn., U.S.	C10	149
Lutz, Fl., U.S.	D4	116
Lützow-Holm Bay, b., Ant.	B4	73
Lutzville, S. Afr.	H4	66
Luverne, Al., U.S.	D3	108
Luverne, Mn., U.S.	G2	130
Luxembourg (Luxemburg), Lux.	I9	12
Luxembourg, prov., Bel.	I7	12
Luxembourg, ctry., Eur.	F9	4
Luxemburg, Wi., U.S.	D6	156
Luxeuil-les-Bains, Fr.	E13	14
Luxi (Mangshi), China	B5	40
Lüxia, China	I9	34
Luxomni, Ga., U.S.	h8	117
Luxor see Al-Uqsur, Egypt	E7	60
Luxora, Ar., U.S.	B6	111
Luz, Braz.	E6	79
Luza, Russia	E7	26
Luzern, Switz.	D9	13
Luzerne, Pa., U.S.	n17	145
Luzerne, co., Pa., U.S.	D9	145
Luzhou, China	F8	30
Luziânia, Braz.	D5	79
Luzon, i., Phil.	n19	39b
Luzon Strait, strt., Asia	N9	34
L'viv (L'vov), Ukr.	H2	26
L'vovskij, Russia	F20	22
Lycksele, Swe.	I16	6
Lycoming, co., Pa., U.S.	D7	145
Lydenburg, S. Afr.	E10	66
Lyell, Mount, mtn., Can.	D2	98
Lykens, Pa., U.S.	E8	145
Lyle, Wa., U.S.	D4	154
Lyman, Ne., U.S.	C1	134
Lyman, S.C., U.S.	B3	147
Lyman, Wy., U.S.	E2	157
Lyman, co., S.D., U.S.	D6	148
Lymans'ke, Ukr.	C14	20
Lyme, N.H., U.S.	C2	136
Lynch, Ky., U.S.	D7	124
Lynchburg, Tn., U.S.	B5	149
Lynchburg, Va., U.S.	C3	153
Lynches, stm., S.C., U.S.	D8	147
Lynden, Wa., U.S.	A3	154
Lyndhurst, Austl.	H3	70
Lyndhurst, N.J., U.S.	h8	137
Lyndhurst, Oh., U.S.	g9	142
Lyndon, Ks., U.S.	D8	123
Lyndon, Ky., U.S.	g11	124
Lyndon, Vt., U.S.	B4	152
Lyndon B. Johnson National Historical Site, hist., Tx., U.S.	D3	150
Lyndon B. Johnson Space Center, sci., Tx., U.S.	r14	150
Lyndon Center, Vt., U.S.	B4	152
Lyndonville, Vt., U.S.	B4	152
Lyndora, Pa., U.S.	E2	145
Lynn, Al., U.S.	A2	108
Lynn, In., U.S.	D8	121
Lynn, Ma., U.S.	B6	128
Lynn, co., Tx., U.S.	C2	150
Lynn, Lake, res., W.V., U.S.	B5	155
Lynn Canal, b., Ak., U.S.	k22	109
Lynnfield, Ma., U.S.	f11	128
Lynn Garden, Tn., U.S.	C11	149
Lynn Garden, Tn., U.S.	A9	149
Lynn Haven, Fl., U.S.	u16	116
Lynnville, In., U.S.	H3	121
Lynnwood, Wa., U.S.	B3	154
Lynwood, Ca., U.S.	n12	112
Lyon, Fr.	G11	14
Lyon, co., Ia., U.S.	A1	122
Lyon, co., Ks., U.S.	D7	123
Lyon, co., Ky., U.S.	C1	124
Lyon, co., Mn., U.S.	F3	130
Lyon, co., Nv., U.S.	D2	135
Lyons, Co., U.S.	A5	113
Lyons, Ga., U.S.	D4	117
Lyons, Il., U.S.	k9	120
Lyons, In., U.S.	G3	121
Lyons, Ks., U.S.	D5	123
Lyons, Ne., U.S.	C9	134
Lyons, N.Y., U.S.	B3	139
Lyons, Or., U.S.	C4	144
Lysite, Wy., U.S.	C5	157
Lyster Station, Que., Can.	C6	104
Lys'va, Russia	F9	26
Lysychans'k, Ukr.	H5	26
Lytton, B.C., Can.	D7	99
Lyubashivka, Ukr.	B14	20
Lyubotyn, Ukr.	H5	26

M

Name	Map Ref.	Page
Ma'ān, Jord.	H5	50
Ma'anshan, China	D7	34
Maardu, Est.	B8	22
Ma'arrat an-Nu'mān, Syria	D4	48
Maas (Meuse), stm., Eur.	D5	10
Maaseik, Bel.	F8	12
Maasmechelen, Bel.	G8	12
Maastricht, Neth.	G8	12
Maave, Moz.	C12	66
Maba, China	C7	34
Mababe Depression, depr., Bots.	B7	66
Mabaruma, Guy.	C13	84
Mabel, Mn., U.S.	G7	130
Maben, Ms., U.S.	B4	131
Mabeul, Tun.	M5	18
Mableton, Ga., U.S.	h7	117
Mabou, N.S., Can.	C8	101
Mabrūk, Mali	M5	60
Mabscott, W.V., U.S.	D3	155
Mabton, Wa., U.S.	C5	154
Macachín, Arg.	I7	80
Macaé, Braz.	G8	79
Macajuba, Braz.	B8	79
Macapá, Braz.	C8	76
Macará, Ec.	J3	84
Macarani, Braz.	C8	79
Macas, Ec.	I3	84
Macau, Braz.	E11	76
Macau (Aomen), Macau	M2	34
Macau, dep., Asia	G9	30
Macaúbas, Braz.	B7	79
Maccan, N.S., Can.	D5	101
MacClenny, Fl., U.S.	B4	116
Macclesfield, Eng., U.K.	H11	8
Macdhui, Ben, mtn., Afr.	H8	66
MacDonnell Ranges, mts., Austl.	D6	68
Macduff, Scot., U.K.	D11	8
Macdui, Ben, mtn., Scot., U.K.	D10	8
Macedonia, Oh., U.S.	A4	142
Macedonia, hist. reg., Eur.	H6	20
Macedonia (Makedonija), ctry., Eur.	H5	20
Maceió, Braz.	E11	76
Macenta, Gui.	G5	64
Macerata, Italy	F8	18
MacGregor, Man., Can.	E2	100
Machachi, Ec.	H3	84
Machačkala, Russia	I7	26
Machado, Braz.	F6	79
Machagai, Arg.	D8	80
Machakos, Kenya	B7	58
Machala, Ec.	I3	84
Machaneng, Bots.	D8	66
Machecoul, Fr.	E5	14
Machias, Me., U.S.	D5	126
Machias Bay, b., Me., U.S.	D5	126
Machiasport, Me., U.S.	D5	126
Machilīpatnam (Bandar), India	D6	46
Machiques, Ven.	B6	84
Machupicchu, hist., Peru	E5	82
Maciá, Arg.	G9	80
Mackay, Austl.	C8	70
Mackay, Id., U.S.	F5	119
Mackay, Lake, l., Austl.	D5	68
MacKenzie, B.C., Can.	B6	99
Mackenzie, Guy.	D13	84
Mackenzie, stm., N.W. Ter., Can.	C6	96
Mackenzie Bay, b., Can.	C5	96
Mackenzie Mountains, mts., Can.	D7	96
Mackinac, co., Mi., U.S.	B5	129
Mackinac, Straits of, strt., Mi., U.S.	C6	129
Mackinac Bridge, Mi., U.S.	C6	129
Mackinac Island, i., Mi., U.S.	C6	129
Mackinaw, Il., U.S.	C4	120
Mackinaw City, Mi., U.S.	C6	129
Mackinaw, stm., Il., U.S.	C4	120
Macklin, Sask., Can.	E1	105
Macksville, Austl.	H10	70
Macksville, Ks., U.S.	E5	123
Maclean, Austl.	G10	70
Macomb, Il., U.S.	C3	120
Macomb, co., Mi., U.S.	F8	129
Mâcon, Fr.	F11	14
Macon, Ga., U.S.	C3	111
Macon, Ga., U.S.	D3	117
Macon, Il., U.S.	D5	120
Macon, Ms., U.S.	B5	131
Macon, Mo., U.S.	B5	132
Macon, co., Al., U.S.	C4	108
Macon, co., Ga., U.S.	D2	117
Macon, co., Il., U.S.	D5	120
Macon, co., Mo., U.S.	B5	132
Macon, co., N.C., U.S.	f9	140
Macon, co., Tn., U.S.	A5	149
Macoupin, co., Il., U.S.	D4	120
Macquarie Island, i., Austl.	A8	73
MacTier, Ont., Can.	B5	103
Macuelizo, Hond.	B6	92
Macungie, Pa., U.S.	E10	145
Macuspana, Mex.	I13	90
Macusse, Ang.	A5	66
Macy, Ne., U.S.	B9	134
Ma'dabā, Jord.	E5	50
Madagascar (Madagasikara), ctry., Afr.	E9	58
Madame, Isle i., N.S., Can.	D9	101
Madanapalle, India	F5	46
Madang, Pap. N. Gui.	m16	68a
Madaoua, Niger	F7	64
Madawaska, Me., U.S.	A4	126
Madawaska, stm., Ont., Can.	B7	103
Maddaloni, Italy	H9	18
Maddock, N.D., U.S.	B6	141
Madeira, Oh., U.S.	o13	142
Madeira, stm., S.A.	E6	76
Madeira, Arquipélago da, is., Port.	m21	17a
Madeleine, Îles de la, is., Que., Can.	B8	101
Madelia, Mn., U.S.	F4	130
Madeline Island, i., Wi., U.S.	B3	156
Madera, Mex.	C5	90
Madera, Ca., U.S.	D3	112
Madera, co., Ca., U.S.	D4	112
Madhya Pradesh, state, India	I8	44
Madill, Ok., U.S.	C5	143
Madīnat ash-Sha'b (Al-Ittihad), Yemen	H4	47
Madingou, Congo	B2	58
Madison, Al., U.S.	A3	108
Madison, Ar., U.S.	B5	111
Madison, Ct., U.S.	D5	114
Madison, Fl., U.S.	B3	116
Madison, Ga., U.S.	C3	117
Madison, Il., U.S.	E3	120
Madison, In., U.S.	G7	121
Madison, Ks., U.S.	D7	123
Madison, Me., U.S.	D3	126
Madison, Mn., U.S.	E2	130
Madison, Ms., U.S.	C3	131
Madison, N.J., U.S.	B4	137
Madison, Oh., U.S.	A4	142
Madison, S.D., U.S.	D8	148
Madison, W.V., U.S.	C3	155
Madison, Wi., U.S.	E4	156
Madison, co., Al., U.S.	A3	108
Madison, co., Ar., U.S.	B2	111
Madison, co., Fl., U.S.	B3	116
Madison, co., Ga., U.S.	B3	117
Madison, co., Id., U.S.	F7	119
Madison, co., Il., U.S.	E4	120
Madison, co., In., U.S.	D6	121
Madison, co., Ia., U.S.	C3	122
Madison, co., Ky., U.S.	C5	124
Madison, co., La., U.S.	B4	125
Madison, co., Ms., U.S.	C4	131
Madison, co., Mo., U.S.	D7	132
Madison, co., Mt., U.S.	E5	133
Madison, co., Ne., U.S.	C8	134
Madison, co., N.Y., U.S.	C5	139
Madison, co., N.C., U.S.	f10	140
Madison, co., Oh., U.S.	C2	142
Madison, co., Tn., U.S.	B3	149
Madison, co., Tx., U.S.	D5	150
Madison, co., Va., U.S.	B4	153
Madison, stm., Mt., U.S.	E5	133
Madison Heights, Mi., U.S.	o15	129
Madison Heights, Va., U.S.	C3	153
Madisonville, Ky., U.S.	C2	124
Madisonville, Tn., U.S.	D9	149
Madisonville, Tx., U.S.	D5	150
Madiun, Indon.	j15	39a
Madoc, Ont., Can.	C7	103
Madona, Lat.	E9	22
Madougou, Mali	D8	64
Madras, India	G11	42
Madras, Or., U.S.	C5	144
Madre, Laguna, b., Mex.	E11	90
Madre, Laguna, b., Tx., U.S.	F4	150
Madre, Sierra, mts., Phil.	m20	39b
Madre de Chiapas, Sierra, mts., N.A.		
Madre de Dios, dept., Peru	D6	82
Madre de Dios, stm., S.A.	D8	82
Madre del Sur, Sierra, mts., Mex.	I10	90
Madre Occidental, Sierra, mts., Mex.	E6	90
Madre Oriental, Sierra, mts., Mex.	F9	90
Madrid, Spain	E8	16
Madrid, Ia., U.S.	C4	122
Madrid, prov., Spain	E8	16
Madridejos, Spain	F8	16
Madriz, dept., Nic.	D8	92
Madura, i., Indon.	j16	39a
Madurai, India	H5	46
Maebashi, Japan	K14	36
Maeser, Ut., U.S.	C6	151
Mae Sot, Thai.	F5	40
Maestra, Sierra, mts., Cuba	D6	94
Maevatanana, Madag.	p22	67b
Mafeking, Man., Can.	C1	100
Mafeteng, Leso.	G8	66
Maffra, Austl.	K7	70
Mafia Island, i., Tan.	C7	58
Mafikeng, S. Afr.	G5	58
Mafikeng, S. Afr.	E7	66
Mafra, Braz.	D14	80
Magadan, Russia	F22	28
Magalia, Ca., U.S.	C3	112
Magallanes, Estrecho de (Strait of Magellan), strt., S.A.	G3	78
Magangué, Col.	C5	84
Magazine, Ar., U.S.	B2	111
Magazine Mountain, mtn., Ar., U.S.	B2	111
Magburaka, S.L.	G4	64
Magdagači, Russia	G17	28
Magdalena, Arg.	H10	80
Magdalena, Bol.	E9	82
Magdalena, Mex.	B4	90
Magdalena, N.M., U.S.	C2	138
Magdalena, dept., Col.	B5	84
Magdalena, stm., Col.	C5	84
Magdalena, Bahía, b., Mex.	E3	90
Magdalena, Isla, i., Mex.	E3	90
Magdalena de Kino, Mex.	B4	90
Magdeburg, Ger.	C11	10
Magee, Ms., U.S.	D4	131
Magelang, Indon.	j15	39a
Magellan, Strait of see Magallanes, Estrecho de, strt., S.A.	G3	78
Magenta, Italy	D3	18
Maggiore, Lago, l., Eur.	C3	18
Maghāghah, Egypt	C6	60
Maghama, Maur.	D3	64
Maghnīyya, Alg.	C10	62
Maglaj, Bos.	E2	20
Magna, Ut., U.S.	C3	151
Magnetawan, stm., Ont., Can.	B4	103
Magnet Cove, Ar., U.S.	C3	111
Magnitogorsk, Russia	G9	26
Magnolia, Ar., U.S.	D2	111
Magnolia, Ky., U.S.	C4	124
Magnolia, Ms., U.S.	D3	131
Magnolia Springs, Al., U.S.	E2	108
Magoffin, co., Ky., U.S.	C6	124
Magog, Que., Can.	D5	104
Magrath, Alta., Can.	E4	98
Magway, Mya.	D3	40
Mahābād, Iran	C8	48
Mahabo, Madag.	r21	67b
Mahajanga, Madag.	o22	67b
Mahalatswe, Bots.	D8	66
Mahanoro, Madag.	q23	67b
Mahanoy City, Pa., U.S.	E9	145
Mahārāshtra, state, India	C3	46
Maha Sarakham, Thai.	F7	40
Mahaska, co., Ia., U.S.	C5	122
Mahasolo, Madag.	q22	67b
Mahbūbnagar, India	D5	46
Mahdia, Tun.	N6	18
Mahé, Island, i., Sey.	B11	58
Mahesāna, India	I5	44
Mahnomen, Mn., U.S.	C2	130
Mahnomen, co., Mn., U.S.	C3	130
Mahomet, Il., U.S.	C5	120
Mahone Bay, N.S., Can.	E5	101
Mahopac, N.Y., U.S.	D7	139
Mahoning, co., Oh., U.S.	B5	142
Mahres, Tun.	C16	62
Mahwah, N.J., U.S.	A4	137
Mai Aini, Erit.	J10	60
Maicao, Col.	B6	84
Maîche, Fr.	E13	14
Maiden, N.C., U.S.	B1	140
Maidenhead, Eng., U.K.	J13	8
Maidstone, Sask., Can.	D1	105
Maidstone, Eng., U.K.	J14	8
Maiduguri, Nig.	F9	54
Maili, Hi., U.S.	g9	118
Main, stm., Ger.	F9	10
Main-à-Dieu, N.S., Can.	C10	101
Main Channel, strt., Ont., Can.	B3	103
Mai-Ndombe, Lac, l., Zaire	B3	58
Maine, state, U.S.	C3	126
Maine, Gulf of, b., N.A.	C13	106
Mainpuri, India	G8	44
Maintirano, Madag.	q21	67b
Mainz, Ger.	E8	10
Maipo, Volcán, vol., S.A.	I10	80
Maipú, Arg.	G4	80
Maipú, Chile	G3	80
Maipú, Chile	I10	80
Maiquetía, Ven.	B9	84
Maisonnette, N.B., Can.	B4	101
Maitland, Austl.	I9	70
Maíz, Islas del, is., Nic.	E11	92
Maize, Ks., U.S.	g12	123
Maizuru, Japan	L10	36
Majagual, Col.	C5	84
Majé, Braz.	G7	79
Majkain, Kaz.	G13	26
Majkop, Russia	I6	26
Major, co., Ok., U.S.	A3	143
Majorca see Mallorca, i., Spain	F15	16
Makaha, Hi., U.S.	g9	118
Makakilo City, Hi., U.S.	g9	118
Makalamabedi, Bots.	C6	66
Makallé, Arg.	D9	80
Makālū, mtn., Asia	G12	44
Makanza, Zaire	A3	58
Makapuu Head, c., Hi., U.S.	B4	118
Makarjev, Russia	D26	22
Makarov, Russia	H20	28
Makarska, Cro.	F12	18
Makasar, Selat (Makassar Strait), strt., Indon.	F6	38
Makat, Kaz.	H8	26
Makawao, Hi., U.S.	C5	118
Makaweli, Hi., U.S.	B2	118
Makeni, S.L.	G3	64
Makgadikgadi, pl., Bots.	C7	66
Makinsk, Kaz.	G12	26
Makiyivka, Ukr.	H5	26
Makkah (Mecca), Sau. Ar.	D1	47
Makó, Hung.	I20	10
Makokou, Gabon	A2	58
Makoua, Congo	A3	58
Makran Coast, Asia	I16	48
Maksatiha, Russia	D18	22
Makung (P'enghu), Tai.	L8	34
Makurdi, Nig.	H14	64
Makushin Volcano, vol., Ak., U.S.	E6	109
Mala, Hung.	D3	84
Malabar, Fl., U.S.	D6	116
Malabar Coast, India	G3	46
Malabo, Eq. Gui.	J14	64
Malacacheta, Braz.	D7	79
Malacca, Strait of, strt., Asia	M6	40
Malad City, Id., U.S.	G6	119
Málaga, Col.	D6	84
Málaga, Spain	I7	16
Malaja Kuril'skaja Gr'ada (Habomai-Shotō), is., Russia	d21	36a
Malaja Višera, Russia	C15	22
Malakāl, Sud.	M6	60
Malang, Indon.	j16	39a
Malanje, Ang.	C3	58
Mälaren, l., Swe.	L15	6
Malartic, Que., Can.	k11	104
Malaspina Glacier, Ak., U.S.	D11	109
Malatya, Tur.	B5	48
Malawi, ctry., Afr.	D6	58
Malawi, Lake see Nyasa, Lake, l., Afr.	D6	58
Malāyer, Iran	D10	48
Malay Peninsula, pen., Asia	K6	40
Malaysia, ctry., Asia	E3	38
Malazgirt, Tur.	B7	48
Malbaie, stm., Que., Can.	B7	104
Malbork, Pol.	A19	10
Malbrán, Arg.	E7	80
Maldegem, Bel.	F3	12
Malden, Ma., U.S.	g11	128
Malden, Mo., U.S.	E8	132
Malden, W.V., U.S.	m12	155
Maldives, ctry., Asia	I8	24
Maldonado, Ur.	H12	80
Male', Mald.	I8	24
Maléa, Ákra, c., Grc.	M7	20
Mālegaon, India	B3	46
Māler Kotla, India	E6	44
Malesherbes, Fr.	D9	14
Malha, Sud.	J4	60
Malheur, co., Or., U.S.	D9	144
Malheur, stm., Or., U.S.	D8	144
Malheur Lake, l., Or., U.S.	D7	144
Mali, ctry., Afr.	E6	54
Malik, Wādī al-, val., Sud.	I6	60
Malin, Or., U.S.	E5	144
Malin Head, c., Ire.	F5	8
Malkara, Tur.	I10	20
Mallaig, Scot., U.K.	D7	8
Mallawī, Egypt	C6	60
Mallet, Braz.	C13	80
Malligasta, Arg.	E5	80
Mallorca, i., Spain	F15	16
Mallow, Ire.	I5	8
Malmesbury, S. Afr.	I4	66
Maloarchangel'sk, Russia	I19	22
Malojaroslavec, Russia	F19	22
Malolos, Phil.	n19	39b
Małopolska, reg., Pol.	E21	10
Malpelo, Isla de, i., Col.	C2	76
Malpeque Bay, b., P.E.I., Can.	C6	101
Malta, Il., U.S.	B5	120
Malta, Lat.	E10	22
Malta, Mt., U.S.	B9	133
Malta, ctry., Eur.	H10	4
Maltahöhe, Nmb.	E3	66
Maluku (Moluccas), is., Indon.	F8	38
Maluku, Laut (Molucca Sea), Indon.	F7	38
Malvern, Ar., U.S.	C3	111
Malvern, Ia., U.S.	D2	122
Malvern, Pa., U.S.	o19	145
Malverne, N.Y., U.S.	k13	139
Mamberamo, stm., Indon.	F10	38
Mamers, Fr.	D7	14
Mamfe, Cam.	H13	64
Mamiña, Chile	I7	82
Mammoth, Az., U.S.	E5	110
Mammoth, W.V., U.S.	C3	155
Mammoth Cave National Park, Ky., U.S.	C4	124
Mammoth Lakes, Ca., U.S.	D4	112
Mammoth Spring, Ar., U.S.	A4	111
Mamonovo, Russia	G22	22
Mamou, Gui.	F3	64
Mamou, La., U.S.	D3	125
Mampikony, Madag.	p22	67b
Männedorf, Switz.	D10	13
Mamry, Jezioro, l., Pol.	A21	10
Ma'mūn, Sud.	K2	60
Mamuno, Bots.	D5	66
Man, C. Iv.	H6	64
Man, W.V., U.S.	D3	155
Manabí, prov., Ec.	H2	84
Manacapuru, Braz.	I12	84
Manacor, Spain	F15	16
Manado, Indon.	E7	38
Managua, Nic.	E8	92
Managua, dept., Nic.	E8	92
Managua, Lago de, l., Nic.	E8	92
Manakara, Madag.	s23	67b
Manama see Al-Manāmah, Bahr.	C6	47
Mananara, Madag.	p23	67b
Manangatang, Austl.	J5	70
Mananjary, Madag.	r23	67b
Manantenina, Madag.	t22	67b
Manāslu, mtn., Nepal	F11	44
Manasquan, N.J., U.S.	C4	137
Manassa, Co., U.S.	D5	113
Manassas, Va., U.S.	B5	153
Manassas National Battlefield Park, Va., U.S.	g11	153
Manassas Park, Va., U.S.	B5	153
Manatee, co., Fl., U.S.	E4	116
Manatí, P.R.	E11	94
Manaus, Braz.	I12	84
Manawa, Wi., U.S.	D5	156
Manbij, Syria	C4	48
Mancelona, Mi., U.S.	D5	129
Manchester, Eng., U.K.	H11	8
Manchester, Ct., U.S.	B5	114
Manchester, Ga., U.S.	D2	117
Manchester, Ia., U.S.	B6	122
Manchester, Ky., U.S.	C6	124
Manchester, Me., U.S.	D3	126
Manchester, Md., U.S.	A4	127
Manchester, Mi., U.S.	F6	129
Manchester, Mo., U.S.	f12	132
Manchester, N.H., U.S.	E4	136
Manchester, Oh., U.S.	D2	142
Manchester, Pa., U.S.	F8	145
Manchester, Tn., U.S.	B5	149
Manchester, Vt., U.S.	E2	152
Manchester Center, Vt., U.S.	E2	152
Manchuria, hist. reg., China	B12	30
Mancos, Co., U.S.	D2	113
Mandabe, Madag.	r21	67b
Mandaguari, Braz.	G3	79
Mandal, Nor.	L10	6
Mandalay, Mya.	C4	40
Mandan, N.D., U.S.	C5	141
Mandara Mountains, mts., Afr.	F9	54
Mandaree, N.D., U.S.	B3	141
Mandeb, Bab el, strt.	H3	47
Mandeville, Jam.	E6	94
Mandeville, Ar., U.S.	D2	111
Mandeville, La., U.S.	D5	125
Mandi, India	E7	44
Mandimba, Moz.	D7	58
Mandritsara, Madag.	o23	67b
Mandsaur, India	H6	44
Mandvi, India	I3	44
Mandya, India	F4	46
Manfalūt, Egypt	C6	60
Manfredonia, Italy	H10	18
Manfredonia, Golfo di, b., Italy	H11	18
Manga, Burkina	F9	64
Mangalore, India	F3	46
Manglares, Cabo, c., Col.	G3	84
Mangoche, Mwi.	D7	58
Mangoky, stm., Madag.	r21	67b
Mangueirinha, Braz.	C12	80
Manhattan, Ks., U.S.	C7	123
Manhattan, Mt., U.S.	E5	133
Manhattan Beach, Ca., U.S.	n12	112
Manhattan Island, i., N.Y., U.S.	h13	139
Manhuaçu, Braz.	F7	79
Manhumirim, Braz.	F7	79
Manicoré, Braz.	A11	82
Manicouagan, Réservoir, res., Que., Can.	h13	104
Manigotagan, Man., Can.	D3	100
Manihiki, Phil.	n19	39b
Manila, Ar., U.S.	B5	111
Manila, Phil.	n19	39b
Manila, Austl.	H9	70
Manila, Ut., U.S.	B2	151
Manipur, state, India	H15	44
Manisa, Tur.	K11	20
Manistee, Mi., U.S.	D4	129
Manistee, co., Mi., U.S.	D4	129
Manistee, stm., Mi., U.S.	D5	129
Manistique, Mi., U.S.	B4	129
Manistique, stm., Mi., U.S.	B4	129
Manistique Lake, l., Mi., U.S.	B5	129
Manito, Il., U.S.	C4	120
Manitoba, prov., Can.	C3	100
Manitoba, Lake, l., Man., Can.	D2	100
Manitou, Man., Can.	E2	100
Manitou, Lake, l., Ont., Can.	B3	103
Manitou Island, i., Mi., U.S.	A3	129
Manitoulin Island, i., Ont., Can.	B2	103
Manitou Springs, Co., U.S.	C6	113
Manitowoc, Wi., U.S.	D6	156
Manitowoc, co., Wi., U.S.	D6	156
Maniwaki, Que., Can.	C2	104
Manizales, Col.	E5	84
Manja, Madag.	r21	67b
Manjacaze, Moz.	E11	66
Manjakandriana, Madag.	q22	67b
Manjimup, Austl.	F3	68
Mankato, Ks., U.S.	C5	123
Mankato, Mn., U.S.	F5	130
Mankota, Sask., Can.	H2	105
Manlius, N.Y., U.S.	C5	139
Manlleu, Spain	C14	16
Manly, Ia., U.S.	A4	122
Mannahill, Austl.	I3	70
Mannar, Gulf of, b., Asia	H5	46
Mannford, Ok., U.S.	A5	143
Mannheim, Ger.	F8	10
Manning, Alta., Can.	A2	98
Manning, Ia., U.S.	C2	122
Manning, S.C., U.S.	D7	147
Mannington, W.V., U.S.	B4	155
Mannville, Alta., Can.	C5	98
Manoel Ribas, Braz.	C13	80
Manokotak, Ak., U.S.	D8	109
Manokwari, Indon.	F9	38
Manombo, Madag.	t21	67b
Manono, Zaire	C5	58
Manor, Sask., Can.	H4	105
Manosque, Fr.	I12	14
Manresa, Spain	D13	16
Mansa, Zam.	D5	58
Mansel Island, i., N.W. Ter., Can.	D17	96
Mansfield, Austl.	K7	70
Mansfield, Ar., U.S.	B1	111
Mansfield, Il., U.S.	C5	120
Mansfield, La., U.S.	B2	125
Mansfield, Ma., U.S.	B5	128
Mansfield, Mo., U.S.	D5	132
Mansfield, Oh., U.S.	B3	142
Mansfield, Pa., U.S.	C7	145
Mansfield, Tx., U.S.	n9	150
Mansfield, Mount, mtn., Vt., U.S.	B3	152
Mansfield Center, Ct., U.S.	B7	114
Mansfield Hollow Lake, res., Ct., U.S.	B7	114
Manson, Ia., U.S.	B3	122
Manson, Wa., U.S.	B5	154
Mansura, La., U.S.	C3	125
Mansura see Al-Mansūrah, Egypt	B6	60
Manta, Ec.	H2	84
Mantachie, Ms., U.S.	A5	131
Manteca, Ca., U.S.	D3	112
Mantena, Braz.	B6	120
Mantes-la-Jolie, Fr.	D8	14
Manti, Ut., U.S.	D4	151
Mantiqueira, Serra da, mts., Braz.	G6	79
Manton, Mi., U.S.	D5	129
Mantorville, Mn., U.S.	F6	130
Mantova, Italy	D5	18
Mantua see Mantova, Italy	D5	18
Mantua, Ut., U.S.	B4	151
Manturovo, Russia	C27	22
Mäntyharju, Fin.	K20	6
Manu, Peru	E6	82
Manua Islands, is., Am. Sam.	J23	158
Manus Island, i., Pap. N. Gui.	k16	68a
Manvel, N.D., U.S.	A8	141
Manvel, Tx., U.S.	r14	150
Manville, N.J., U.S.	B3	137
Manville, R.I., U.S.	B3	146
Manville, Wy., U.S.	D8	157
Many, La., U.S.	C2	125
Manyana, Bots.	D5	66
Many Farms, Az., U.S.	A6	110
Manzanares, Spain	F8	16
Manzanillo, Cuba	D6	94
Manzanillo, Mex.	H7	90
Manzanillo, Punta, c., Pan.	H15	92
Manzanillo Bay, b., N.A.	E9	94
Manzanola, Co., U.S.	C7	113
Manzhouli, China	B10	30
Manzini, Swaz.	F10	66
Mao, Chad	F4	56
Maó, Dom. Rep.	E9	94
Maó, Spain	F16	16
Maoke, Pegunungan, mts., Indon.	F10	38
Maoming, China	G9	30
Mapastepec, Mex.	J13	90
Mapimí, Mex.	E8	90
Mapimí, Bolsón de, des., Mex.	D8	90
Maping, China	D2	34
Mapire, Ven.	D10	84
Maple, stm., N.D., U.S.	C8	141
Maple Bluff, Wi., U.S.	E4	156
Maple Creek, Sask., Can.	H1	105
Maple Grove, Mn., U.S.	m12	130
Maple Heights, Oh., U.S.	h9	142
Maple Hill, Ks., U.S.	C7	123
Maple Lake, Mn., U.S.	E5	130
Maple Plain, Mn., U.S.	m11	130
Maple Shade, N.J., U.S.	D2	137
Maplesville, Al., U.S.	C3	108
Mapleton, Ia., U.S.	B2	122
Mapleton, Mn., U.S.	G5	130
Mapleton, N.D., U.S.	C8	141
Mapleton, Or., U.S.	C3	144
Mapleton, Ut., U.S.	C4	151
Maple Valley, Wa., U.S.	f11	154
Mapleville, R.I., U.S.	B2	146
Maplewood, Mn., U.S.	n12	130
Maplewood, Mo., U.S.	f13	132
Maputo, Moz.	E11	66
Maquoketa, Ia., U.S.	B7	122
Maquoketa, stm., Ia., U.S.	B6	122

Name	Map Ref.	Page
Mar, Serra do, clf., Braz.	C14	80
Marabá, Braz.	E9	76
Maracaí, Braz.	G3	79
Maracaibo, Ven.	B7	84
Maracaibo, Lago de, l., Ven.	C7	84
Maracaju, Braz.	F1	79
Maracaju, Serra de, hills, S.A.	F1	79
Maracás, Braz.	B8	79
Maracay, Ven.	B9	84
Maradi, Niger	E13	64
Marāgheh, Iran	C9	48
Maragogipe, Braz.	F11	76
Maragogipe, Braz.	B9	79
Marahuaca, Cerro, mtn., Ven.	F10	84
Marajó, Ilha de, i., Braz.	D9	76
Maralal, Kenya	A7	58
Maralaleng, Bots.	E6	66
Marana, Az., U.S.	E4	110
Marand, Iran	B8	48
Maranguape, Braz.	D11	76
Marañón, stm., Peru	D3	76
Marapanim, Braz.	D9	76
Marathón, Grc.	K7	20
Marathon, Fl., U.S.	H5	116
Marathon, Wi., U.S.	D4	156
Marathon, co., Wi., U.S.	D4	156
Marau, Braz.	E12	80
Maravilha, Braz.	D12	80
Marawī, Sud.	H6	60
Marbella, Spain	I7	16
Marble Bar, Austl.	D3	68
Marble Canyon, val., Az., U.S.	A4	110
Marble Falls, Tx., U.S.	D3	150
Marble Hall, S. Afr.	E9	66
Marblehead, Ma., U.S.	B6	128
Marble Hill, Mo., U.S.	D8	132
Marbleton, Wy., U.S.	D2	157
Marburg, Ger.	E8	10
Marbury, Md., U.S.	C3	127
Marcala, Hond.	C6	92
Marcelin, Sask., Can.	E2	105
Marceline, Mo., U.S.	B5	132
Marcellus, Mi., U.S.	F5	129
March (Morava), stm., Eur.	G16	10
Marchand, Man., Can.	E3	100
Marche, prov., Italy	F8	18
Marche-en-Famenne, Bel.	H7	12
Marchena, Spain	H6	16
Mar Chiquita, Laguna, b., Arg.	I10	80
Marco, Fl., U.S.	G5	116
Marcona, Peru	F4	82
Marcos Juárez, Arg.	G7	80
Marcos Paz, Arg.	H9	80
Marcus, Ia., U.S.	B2	122
Marcus Baker, Mount, mtn., Ak., U.S.	g18	109
Marcus Hook, Pa., U.S.	G11	145
Marcy, Mount, mtn., N.Y., U.S.	A7	139
Mardān, Pak.	C5	44
Mar del Plata, Arg.	J10	80
Mardin, Tur.	C6	48
Marechal Cândido Rondon, Braz.	C11	80
Mareeba, Austl.	A6	70
Marengo, Il., U.S.	A5	120
Marengo, In., U.S.	H5	121
Marengo, Ia., U.S.	C5	122
Marengo, co., Al., U.S.	C2	108
Marfa, Tx., U.S.	o12	150
Margaret, Al., U.S.	B3	108
Margarita, Isla de, i., Ven.	B10	84
Margarita Belén, Arg.	D9	80
Margate, S. Afr.	H10	66
Margate, Eng., U.K.	J15	8
Margate, Fl., U.S.	F6	116
Margate City, N.J., U.S.	E3	137
Margherita Peak, mtn., Afr.	A5	58
Margilan, Uzb.	I12	26
Mārgow, Dasht-e, des., Afg.	F17	48
Marguerite Bay, b., Ant.	B12	73
Marhanets', Ukr.	H4	26
María Ignacia (Vela), Arg.	I9	80
María la Baja, Col.	C5	84
Mariana, Braz.	F7	79
Mariana Islands, is., Oc.	G18	158
Mariana Trench	G18	158
Marianna, Ar., U.S.	C5	111
Marianna, Fl., U.S.	B1	116
Mariano I. Loza, Arg.	E9	80
Mariano Moreno, Arg.	J3	80
Mariánské Lázně, Czech Rep.	F12	10
Mariapolis, Man., Can.	E2	100
Marias, stm., Mt., U.S.	B4	133
Marías, Islas, is., Mex.	G6	90
Marias Pass, Mt., U.S.	B3	133
María Teresa, Arg.	H8	80
Mariato, Punta, c., Pan.	D2	84
Maribor, Slvn.	C10	18
Maricopa, Az., U.S.	E3	110
Maricopa, co., Az., U.S.	D3	110
Maricopa Mountains, mts., Az., U.S.	m7	110
Marie Byrd Land, reg., Ant.	C10	73
Marie-Galante, i., Guad.	G14	94
Mariehamn, Fin.	K16	6
Mari El see Marij El, state, Russia	F7	26
Mariemont, Oh., U.S.	o13	142
Marienbad see Mariánské Lázně, Czech Rep.	F12	10
Mariental, Nmb.	E3	66
Maries, co., Mo., U.S.	C6	132
Mariestad, Swe.	L13	6
Marietta, Ga., U.S.	C2	117
Marietta, Oh., U.S.	C4	142
Marietta, Ok., U.S.	D4	143
Marietta, Wa., U.S.	A3	154
Marieville, Que., Can.	I12	14
Marignane, Fr.	I12	14
Marigot, Dom.	G14	94
Mariinsk, Russia	F9	28
Mariinskij Posad, Russia	F7	26
Marijampole, Lith.	G6	22
Marij El, state, Russia	F7	26
Marília, Braz.	G4	79
Marimba, Ang.	C3	58
Marín, Spain	C3	16
Marin, co., Ca., U.S.	C2	112
Marina, Ca., U.S.	D3	112
Marine, Il., U.S.	E4	120

Name	Map Ref.	Page
Marine City, Mi., U.S.	F8	129
Marinette, Wi., U.S.	C6	156
Marinette, co., Wi., U.S.	C5	156
Maringá, Braz.	G3	79
Maringouin, La., U.S.	D4	125
Marion, Al., U.S.	C2	108
Marion, Ar., U.S.	B5	111
Marion, Ct., U.S.	C4	114
Marion, Il., U.S.	F5	120
Marion, In., U.S.	C6	121
Marion, Ia., U.S.	B6	122
Marion, Ks., U.S.	D6	123
Marion, Ky., U.S.	e9	124
Marion, Ms., U.S.	C5	131
Marion, N.C., U.S.	B1	140
Marion, Oh., U.S.	B2	142
Marion, S.C., U.S.	C9	147
Marion, S.D., U.S.	D8	148
Marion, Va., U.S.	f10	153
Marion, Wi., U.S.	D5	156
Marion, co., Al., U.S.	A2	108
Marion, co., Ar., U.S.	A3	111
Marion, co., Fl., U.S.	C4	116
Marion, co., Ga., U.S.	D2	117
Marion, co., Il., U.S.	E4	120
Marion, co., In., U.S.	E5	121
Marion, co., Ia., U.S.	C4	122
Marion, co., Ks., U.S.	D6	123
Marion, co., Ky., U.S.	C4	124
Marion, co., Ms., U.S.	D4	131
Marion, co., Mo., U.S.	B6	132
Marion, co., Oh., U.S.	B2	142
Marion, co., Or., U.S.	C4	144
Marion, co., S.C., U.S.	C9	147
Marion, co., Tn., U.S.	D8	149
Marion, co., Tx., U.S.	C5	150
Marion, co., W.V., U.S.	B4	155
Marion, Lake, res., S.C., U.S.	E7	147
Marion Station, Md., U.S.	D6	127
Marionville, Mo., U.S.	D4	132
Mariposa, co., Ca., U.S.	D3	112
Marissa, Il., U.S.	E4	120
Mariscal Estigarribia, Para.	B8	80
Maritime Alps, mts., Eur.	H14	14
Mariupol' (Ždanov), Ukr.	H5	26
Marjamaa, Est.	C7	22
Marjina Gorka, Bela.	H11	22
Marka, Som.	H9	56
Markala, Mali	E6	64
Markdale, Ont., Can.	C4	103
Marked Tree, Ar., U.S.	B5	111
Markesan, Wi., U.S.	E5	156
Markham, Ont., Can.	D5	103
Markham, Il., U.S.	k9	120
Markham, Mount, mtn., Ant.	D8	73
Markle, In., U.S.	C7	121
Marks, Russia	G7	26
Marks, Ms., U.S.	A3	131
Marksville, La., U.S.	C3	125
Marktredwitz, Ger.	E12	10
Mark Twain Lake, res., Mo., U.S.	B6	132
Marlboro, Va., U.S.	n17	153
Marlboro, co., S.C., U.S.	B8	147
Marlborough, Austl.	D8	70
Marlborough, Ct., U.S.	C6	114
Marlborough, Ma., U.S.	B4	128
Marlborough, N.H., U.S.	E2	136
Marlette, Mi., U.S.	E7	129
Marley, Md., U.S.	B4	127
Marlin, Tx., U.S.	D4	150
Marlinton, W.V., U.S.	C4	155
Marlow, N.H., U.S.	D2	136
Marlow, Ok., U.S.	C4	143
Marlowe, W.V., U.S.	B7	155
Marlton, N.J., U.S.	D3	137
Marmaduke, Ar., U.S.	A5	111
Marmande, Fr.	H7	14
Marmara Denizi (Sea of Marmara), Tur.	I12	20
Marmet, W.V., U.S.	C3	155
Marmora, Ont., Can.	C7	103
Marne, stm., Fr.	C10	14
Maroa, Il., U.S.	C5	120
Maroa, Ven.	F9	84
Maroantsetra, Madag.	o23	67b
Maromme, Fr.	C8	14
Maromokotro, mtn., Madag.	o23	67b
Marondera, Zimb.	B10	66
Maroni, stm., S.A.	C8	76
Maroseranana, Madag.	q23	67b
Marovoay, Madag.	p22	67b
Marquesas Keys, is., Fl., U.S.	H4	116
Marquette, Ks., U.S.	D6	123
Marquette, Mi., U.S.	B3	129
Marquette, co., Mi., U.S.	B3	129
Marquette, co., Wi., U.S.	E4	156
Marquette Heights, Il., U.S.	B8	14
Marquise, Fr.		
Marquises, Îles (Marquesas Islands), is., Fr. Poly.	I26	158
Marrah, Jabal, mtn., Sud.	K3	60
Marrakech, Mor.	E6	62
Marrero, La., U.S.	E5	125
Marromeu, Moz.	B12	66
Mars, Pa., U.S.	E1	145
Marsá al-Burayqah, Libya	B4	56
Marsabit, Kenya	H8	56
Marsala, Italy	L7	18
Marsá Maţrūḩ, Egypt	B4	60
Marsden, Austl.	I7	70
Marsden, Sask., Can.	E1	105
Marseille, Fr.	I12	14
Marseilles, Il., U.S.	B5	120
Marshall, Lib.	D1	105
Marshall, Lib.	G4	54
Marshall, Ak., U.S.	C7	109
Marshall, Il., U.S.	D6	120
Marshall, In., U.S.	F3	121
Marshall, Mi., U.S.	F6	129
Marshall, Mn., U.S.	F3	130
Marshall, Mo., U.S.	B4	132
Marshall, N.C., U.S.	f10	140
Marshall, Tx., U.S.	C5	150
Marshall, Va., U.S.	B5	153
Marshall, co., Al., U.S.	A3	108
Marshall, co., Il., U.S.	B4	120
Marshall, co., In., U.S.	B5	121
Marshall, co., Ia., U.S.	B4	122
Marshall, co., Ks., U.S.	C7	123
Marshall, co., Ky., U.S.	f9	124
Marshall, co., Mn., U.S.	B2	130

Name	Map Ref.	Page
Marshall, co., Ms., U.S.	A4	131
Marshall, co., Ok., U.S.	C5	143
Marshall, co., S.D., U.S.	B8	148
Marshall, co., Tn., U.S.	B5	149
Marshall, co., W.V., U.S.	B4	155
Marshall Islands, ctry., Oc.	H20	158
Marshallton, De., U.S.	B3	115
Marshalltown, Ia., U.S.	B5	122
Marshallville, Ga., U.S.	D3	117
Marshes Siding, Ky., U.S.	D5	124
Marshfield, Ma., U.S.	B6	128
Marshfield, Mo., U.S.	D5	132
Marshfield, Vt., U.S.	C4	152
Marshfield, Wi., U.S.	D3	156
Marshfield Hills, Ma., U.S.	B6	128
Marsh Harbour, Bah.	A6	94
Mars Hill, Me., U.S.	B5	126
Mars Hill, N.C., U.S.	f10	140
Marsh Island, i., La., U.S.	E4	125
Marsh Peak, mtn., Ut., U.S.	C6	151
Marshville, N.C., U.S.	C2	140
Marsing, Id., U.S.	F2	119
Marston, Mo., U.S.	E8	132
Marstons Mills, Ma., U.S.	C7	128
Martaban, Gulf of, b., Mya.	F4	40
Martapura, Indon.	F5	38
Marthasville, Mo., U.S.	C6	132
Martha's Vineyard, i., Ma., U.S.	D6	128
Martigny, Switz.	F7	13
Martigues, Fr.	I12	14
Martin, Slvk.	F18	10
Martin, Ky., U.S.	C7	124
Martin, S.D., U.S.	D4	148
Martin, Tn., U.S.	A3	149
Martin, co., Fl., U.S.	E6	116
Martin, co., In., U.S.	G4	121
Martin, co., Ky., U.S.	C7	124
Martin, co., Mn., U.S.	G4	130
Martin, co., N.C., U.S.	B5	140
Martin, co., Tx., U.S.	C2	150
Martina Franca, Italy	I12	18
Martin City, Mt., U.S.	B3	133
Martinez, Ca., U.S.	C2	112
Martinez, Ga., U.S.	C4	117
Martínez de la Torre, Mex.	G11	90
Martinho Campos, Braz.	E6	79
Martinique, dep., N.A.	G14	94
Martinique Passage, strt., N.A.	G14	94
Martin Lake, res., Al., U.S.	C4	108
Martinniemi, Fin.	I19	6
Martinsburg, Pa., U.S.	F5	145
Martinsburg, W.V., U.S.	B7	155
Martins Ferry, Oh., U.S.	B5	142
Martinsville, Il., U.S.	D6	120
Martinsville, In., U.S.	F5	121
Martinsville, Va., U.S.	D3	153
Martin Vaz, Ilhas, is., Braz.	G12	74
Martos, Spain	H8	16
Mato Grosso, Braz.	E13	64
Marugame, Japan	M8	36
Marv Dasht, Iran	G12	48
Marvejols, Fr.	H10	14
Marvell, Ar., U.S.	C5	111
Marvine, Mount, mtn., Ut., U.S.	E4	151
Marwayne, Alta., Can.	C5	98
Mary, Turk.	J10	26
Maryborough, Austl.	E10	70
Maryborough, Austl.	K5	70
Marydale, S. Afr.	G6	66
Maryfield, Sask., Can.	H5	105
Mary Kathleen, Austl.	C3	70
Maryland, state, U.S.	B4	127
Maryland City, Md., U.S.	B4	127
Maryland Heights, Mo., U.S.	f13	132
Maryland Point, c., Md., U.S.	D3	127
Marys, stm., Nv., U.S.	B6	135
Marystown, Newf., Can.	E4	102
Marysville, N.B., Can.	C3	112
Marysville, Ks., U.S.	C7	123
Marysville, Mi., U.S.	F8	129
Marysville, Oh., U.S.	B2	142
Marysville, Pa., U.S.	F8	145
Marysville, Wa., U.S.	A3	154
Maryville, Mo., U.S.	A3	132
Maryville, Tn., U.S.	D10	149
Marzūq, Libya	C3	56
Masada see Meẕada, Horvot, hist., Isr.	F4	50
Masaka, Ug.	B6	58
Masan, S. Kor.	H16	32
Masatepe, Nic.	F8	92
Masaya, dept., Nic.	F8	92
Masaya, Nic.	F8	92
Mascara, Alg.	F11	58
Mascarene Islands, is., Afr.	F11	58
Mascoma, stm., N.H., U.S.	C2	136
Mascot, Tn., U.S.	C10	149
Mascota, Mex.	G7	90
Mascouche, Que., Can.	D4	104
Mascoutah, Il., U.S.	E4	120
Maseru, Leso.	G5	66
Mashhad, Iran	C15	48
Mashra'ur-Raqq, Sud.	M5	60
Masi Manimba, Zaire	B3	58
Maṣīrah, Khalīj, b., Oman	E11	47
Masisea, Peru	C4	82
Masjed-e Soleymān, Iran	F10	48
Mask, Lough, l., Ire.	H4	8
Masoala, Presqu'île de, pen., Madag.	o24	67b
Masoarivo, Madag.	q21	67b
Mason, Mi., U.S.	F6	129
Mason, Nv., U.S.	E2	135
Mason, Oh., U.S.	C1	142
Mason, W.V., U.S.	B2	155
Mason, co., Il., U.S.	C4	120
Mason, co., Ky., U.S.	B6	124
Mason, co., Mi., U.S.	D4	129
Mason, co., Tx., U.S.	D3	150
Mason, co., Wa., U.S.	C2	154
Mason, co., W.V., U.S.	C2	155
Mason City, Il., U.S.	C4	120
Mason City, Ia., U.S.	A4	122
Masontown, Pa., U.S.	G2	145
Masontown, W.V., U.S.	B5	155
Masonville, Co., U.S.	A5	113
Masqat (Muscat), Oman	C11	47
Massa, Italy	E5	18
Massac, co., Il., U.S.	f9	124
Massachusetts, state, U.S.	B4	128

Name	Map Ref.	Page
Massachusetts Bay, b., Ma., U.S.	B6	128
Massafra, Italy	I12	18
Massena, N.Y., U.S.	f10	139
Masset, B.C., Can.	C1	99
Massey, Ont., Can.	A2	103
Massillon, Oh., U.S.	B4	142
Massina, reg., Mali	D7	64
Massinga, Moz.	D12	66
Massive, Mount, mtn., Co., U.S.	B4	113
Maṣṭagha, Azer.	I8	26
Masterton, N.Z.	D5	72
Mastic Beach, N.Y., U.S.	n16	139
Mastung, Pak.	F2	44
Masury, Oh., U.S.	A5	142
Masvingo, Zimb.	C10	66
Mata de São João, Braz.	B9	79
Matadi, Zaire	C2	58
Matagalpa, Nic.	E9	92
Matagalpa, dept., Nic.	E9	92
Matagorda, co., Tx., U.S.	E5	150
Matagorda Bay, b., Tx., U.S.	E4	150
Matagorda Island, i., Tx., U.S.	E4	150
Matagorda Peninsula, pen., Tx., U.S.	E5	150
Matale, Sri L.	I6	46
Matam, Sen.	D3	64
Matamoros, Pa., U.S.	D12	145
Matamoros, Mex.	E11	90
Matamoros, Mex.	E8	90
Matane, Que., Can.	k13	104
Matanuska, stm., Ak., U.S.	g18	109
Matanzas, Cuba	C4	94
Matapalo, Cabo, c., C.R.	I11	92
Matara, Sri L.	J6	46
Mataram, Indon.	G6	38
Mataró, Spain	D14	16
Matatiele, S. Afr.	H9	66
Matawan, N.J., U.S.	C4	137
Matehuala, Mex.	F9	90
Matera, Italy	I11	18
Mátészalka, Hung.	H22	10
Mateur, Tun.	L4	18
Matewan, W.V., U.S.	D2	155
Matheson Island, Man., Can.	D3	100
Mathews, co., Va., U.S.	C6	153
Mathews, Va., U.S.	C6	153
Mathis, Tx., U.S.	E4	150
Mathiston, Ms., U.S.	B4	131
Mathura, India	G7	44
Matias Barbosa, Braz.	F7	79
Matías Romero, Mex.	I12	90
Matipó, Braz.	F7	79
Matoaca, Va., U.S.	n18	153
Matočkin Šar, proliv, strt., Russia	C8	26
Mato Grosso, Braz.	D13	82
Mato Grosso, Planalto do, plat., Braz.	G7	76
Mato Grosso do Sul, state, Braz.	G8	76
Matosinhos, Port.	D3	16
Mato Verde, Braz.	C7	79
Matozinhos, Braz.	E6	79
Maṭraḥ, Oman	C11	47
Matru, S.L.	H3	64
Matsqui, B.C., Can.	f13	99
Matsue, Japan	L14	36
Matsue, Japan	L8	36
Matsumoto, Japan	K12	36
Matsu Tao, i., Tai.	I8	34
Matsuyama, Japan	N7	36
Mattancheri, Ma., U.S.	C5	153
Mattaponi, stm., Va., U.S.	C5	153
Mattawa, Ont., Can.	A6	103
Mattawamkeag, Me., U.S.	C4	126
Mattawamkeag, stm., Me., U.S.	C4	126
Matterhorn, mtn., Eur.	G14	14
Matterhorn, mtn., Nv., U.S.	B6	135
Matteson, Il., U.S.	k9	120
Matthews, In., U.S.	D7	121
Matthews, Mo., U.S.	E8	132
Matthews, N.C., U.S.	B2	140
Matthew Town, Bah.	D8	94
Mattituck, N.Y., U.S.	n16	139
Mattoon, Il., U.S.	D5	120
Mattydale, N.Y., U.S.	B4	139
Matucana, Peru	D3	82
Matunuck, R.I., U.S.	G3	146
Maturín, Ven.	C11	84
Matutina, Braz.	E6	79
Maú (Ireng), stm., S.A.	E13	84
Maúa, Moz.	D7	58
Maubeuge, Fr.	B10	14
Maués, Braz.	I14	84
Maugerville, N.B., Can.	D3	101
Maui, co., Hi., U.S.	C5	118
Maui, i., Hi., U.S.	C6	118
Mauldin, S.C., U.S.	B3	147
Maule, prov., Chile	H2	80
Maumee, Oh., U.S.	A2	142
Maumee, stm., U.S.	A2	142
Maumee Bay, b., U.S.	G7	129
Maumelle, Lake, res., Ar., U.S.	C3	111
Maun, Bots.	C6	66
Mauna Kea, vol., Hi., U.S.	D6	118
Maunaloa, Hi., U.S.	B4	118
Mauna Loa, vol., Hi., U.S.	D6	118
Maunawili, Hi., U.S.	g10	118
Maungdaw, Mya.	D2	40
Maurepas, Lake, l., La., U.S.	D5	125
Mauriac, Fr.	G9	14
Maurice, stm., N.J., U.S.	E2	137
Mauritania (Mauritanie), ctry., Afr.	D4	54
Mauritius, ctry., Afr.	F11	58
Maury, co., Tn., U.S.	B4	149
Maury City, Tn., U.S.	B3	149
Mauston, Wi., U.S.	E3	156
Mauterndorf, Aus.	H13	10
Mauthausen, Aus.	G14	10
Maverick, co., Tx., U.S.	E2	150

Name	Map Ref.	Page
Mawlaik, Mya.	C3	40
Mawlamyine (Moulmein), Mya.	F4	40
Max, N.D., U.S.	B4	141
Maxcanú, Mex.	G15	90
Maxton, N.C., U.S.	C3	140
Maxville, Ont., Can.	B10	103
Maxwell, Ca., U.S.	C2	112
Maxwell, Ia., U.S.	C4	122
Maxwell Acres, W.V., U.S.	g8	155
Mayaguana, i., Bah.	C8	94
Mayaguana Passage, strt., Bah.	C8	94
Mayagüez, P.R.	E11	94
Maya Mountains, mts., N.A.	D7	94
Mayarí, Cuba	D9	94
Maybole, Scot., U.K.	F9	8
Mayenne, Fr.	M13	14
Mayer, Az., U.S.	C3	110
Mayerthorpe, Alta., Can.	C3	98
Mayes, co., Ok., U.S.	A6	143
Mayfield, Ky., U.S.	f9	124
Mayfield, Pa., U.S.	C10	145
Mayfield Heights, Oh., U.S.	A4	142
Mayflower, Ar., U.S.	C3	111
Mayhill, N.M., U.S.	E4	138
Mayking, Ky., U.S.	C7	124
Maymont, Sask., Can.	E2	105
Maymyo, Mya.	C4	40
Maynard, Ar., U.S.	A5	111
Maynard, Ma., U.S.	B5	128
Maynardville, Tn., U.S.	C10	149
Mayne, B.C., Can.	g12	99
Mayo, Yukon, Can.	D5	96
Mayo, Md., U.S.	C4	127
Mayo, co., Ire.	H4	8
Mayodan, N.C., U.S.	A3	140
Mayon Volcano, vol., Phil.	o20	39b
Mayotte, dep., Afr.	D9	58
May Park, Or., U.S.	B8	144
May Pen, Jam.	F6	94
Maysville, Ga., U.S.	B3	117
Maysville, Ky., U.S.	B6	124
Maysville, Mo., U.S.	B3	132
Maysville, Ok., U.S.	C4	143
Mayville, N.D., U.S.	B8	141
Mayville, Wi., U.S.	E5	156
Maywood, Il., U.S.	k9	120
Maywood, N.J., U.S.	h8	137
Maza, Arg.	I7	80
Mazabuka, Zam.	E5	58
Mazagan see El-Jadida, Mor.	D6	62
Mazagão, Braz.	D8	76
Mazamet, Fr.	I9	14
Mazara del Vallo, Italy	L7	18
Mazār-e Sharīf, Afg.	B2	44
Mazaruni, stm., Guy.	E13	84
Mazatenango, Guat.	C3	92
Mazatlán, Mex.	F6	90
Mazatzal Mountains, mts., Az., U.S.	C4	110
Mazatzal Peak, mtn., Az., U.S.	C4	110
Mažeikiai, Lith.	E5	22
Mazeppa, Mn., U.S.	F6	130
Mazomanie, Wi., U.S.	E4	156
Mazury, reg., Pol.	B20	10
Mbabane, Swaz.	F10	66
Mbaiki, Cen. Afr. Rep.	H4	56
Mbala, Zam.	C6	58
Mbalmayo, Cam.	H9	54
Mbandaka (Coquilhatville), Zaire	A3	58
Mbanga, Cam.	I14	64
M'banza Congo, Ang.	C2	58
Mbanza-Ngungu, Zaire	C2	58
Mbarara, Ug.	B6	58
Mbeya, Tan.	C6	58
Mbomou (Bomu), stm., Afr.	H5	56
Mbour, Sen.	D1	64
Mbout, Maur.	D2	64
Mbuji-Mayi (Bakwanga), Zaire	C4	58
Mburucuyá, Arg.	E9	80
McAdoo, Pa., U.S.	E9	145
McAfee Peak, mtn., Nv., U.S.	B6	135
McAlester, Ok., U.S.	C6	143
McAllen, Tx., U.S.	F3	150
McAlmont, Ar., U.S.	h10	111
McAlpine, Md., U.S.	B4	127
McAuley, Man., Can.	D1	100
McBride, B.C., Can.	C7	99
McCall, Id., U.S.	E2	119
McCalla, Al., U.S.	g6	108
McCammon, Id., U.S.	G6	119
McCandless, Pa., U.S.	h13	145
McCartys, N.M., U.S.	B2	138
McCaysville, Ga., U.S.	B2	117
McClain, co., Ok., U.S.	C4	143
McCleary, Wa., U.S.	B2	154
McClintock, Mount, mtn., Ant.	D8	73
McClusky, N.D., U.S.	B5	141
McColl, S.C., U.S.	B8	147
McComas, W.V., U.S.	D3	155
McComb, Ms., U.S.	D3	131
McComb, Oh., U.S.	A2	142
McCone, co., Mt., U.S.	C11	133
McCook, Ne., U.S.	D5	134
McCook, co., S.D., U.S.	D8	148
McCook Lake, S.D., U.S.	E9	148
McCool Junction, Ne., U.S.	D8	134
McCool, In., U.S.	B4	121
McCordsville, In., U.S.	E6	121
McCormick, co., S.C., U.S.	D3	147
McCormick, S.C., U.S.	D3	147
McCracken, co., Ky., U.S.	e9	124
McCreary, Man., Can.	D2	100
McCreary, co., Ky., U.S.	D5	124
McCulloch, co., Tx., U.S.	D3	150
McCurtain, co., Ok., U.S.	C7	143
McDonald, co., Mo., U.S.	E3	132
McDonough, Ga., U.S.	C2	117
McDonough, co., Il., U.S.	C3	120
McDowell, co., N.C., U.S.	f10	140
McDowell, co., W.V., U.S.	D3	155
McDowell Peak, mtn., Az., U.S.	k9	110

Name	Map Ref.	Page
McDuffie, co., Ga., U.S.	C4	117
Mcensk, Russia	H19	22
McEwen, Tn., U.S.	A4	149
McFadden, Wy., U.S.	E6	157
McFarland, Ca., U.S.	E4	112
McFarland, Wi., U.S.	E4	156
McGehee, Ar., U.S.	D4	111
McGill, Nv., U.S.	D7	135
McGrath, Ak., U.S.	C8	109
McGregor, Ia., U.S.	A6	122
McGregor, Tx., U.S.	D4	150
McGuire Air Force Base, mil., N.J., U.S.	C3	137
McHenry, Il., U.S.	A5	120
McHenry, co., Il., U.S.	A5	120
McHenry, co., N.D., U.S.	A5	141
McIntosh, Mn., U.S.	C3	130
McIntosh, S.D., U.S.	B4	148
McIntosh, co., Ga., U.S.	E5	117
McIntosh, co., N.D., U.S.	C6	141
McIntosh, co., Ok., U.S.	B6	143
McKean, co., Pa., U.S.	C4	145
McKee, Ky., U.S.	C6	124
McKeesport, Pa., U.S.	F2	145
McKees Rocks, Pa., U.S.	F1	145
McKenzie, Al., U.S.	D3	108
McKenzie, Tn., U.S.	A3	149
McKenzie, co., N.D., U.S.	B2	141
McKenzie, stm., Or., U.S.	C4	144
McKinley, co., N.M., U.S.	B1	138
McKinley, Mount, mtn., Ak., U.S.	C9	109
McKinley Park, Ak., U.S.	C10	109
McKinleyville, Ca., U.S.	B1	112
McKinney, Tx., U.S.	C4	150
McLain, Ms., U.S.	D5	131
McLaughlin, S.D., U.S.	B5	148
McLaurin, Ms., U.S.	D4	131
McLean, Sask., Can.	G3	105
McLean, Va., U.S.	g12	153
McLean, co., Il., U.S.	C4	120
McLean, co., Ky., U.S.	C2	124
McLean, co., N.D., U.S.	B4	141
McLeansboro, Il., U.S.	E5	120
McLennan, Alta., Can.	B2	98
McLennan, co., Tx., U.S.	D4	150
McLeod, co., Mn., U.S.	F4	130
M'Clintock Channel, strt., N.W. Ter., Can.	B12	96
McLoud, Ok., U.S.	B4	143
McLoughlin, Mount, mtn., Or., U.S.	D4	144
McLouth, Ks., U.S.	C8	123
M'Clure Strait, strt., N.W. Ter., Can.	B9	96
McMechen, W.V., U.S.	B4	155
McMillan, Lake, res., N.M., U.S.	E5	138
McMinn, co., Tn., U.S.	D9	149
McMinnville, Or., U.S.	B3	144
McMinnville, Tn., U.S.	D8	149
McMullen, co., Tx., U.S.	E3	150
McMurdo Sound, strt., Ant.	C8	73
McNairy, co., Tn., U.S.	B3	149
McNeill, Ms., U.S.	D4	131
McPherson, Ks., U.S.	D6	123
McPherson, co., Ks., U.S.	D6	123
McPherson, co., Ne., U.S.	C4	134
McPherson, co., S.D., U.S.	B6	148
McRae, Ar., U.S.	B4	111
McRae, Ga., U.S.	D4	117
McRoberts, Ky., U.S.	C7	124
McSherrystown, Pa., U.S.	G7	145
McVille, N.D., U.S.	B7	141
M'Daourouch, Alg.	M2	18
Mead, Co., U.S.	A6	113
Mead, Ne., U.S.	C9	134
Mead, Wa., U.S.	B8	154
Mead, Lake, res., U.S.	A1	110
Meade, Ks., U.S.	E3	123
Meade, co., Ks., U.S.	E3	123
Meade, co., Ky., U.S.	C3	124
Meade, co., S.D., U.S.	C3	148
Meade Peak, mtn., Id., U.S.	G7	119
Meadowbrook, W.V., U.S.	k10	155
Meadow Lake, Sask., Can.	n7	105
Meadowview, Va., U.S.	f10	153
Meadville, Pa., U.S.	C1	145
Meaford, Ont., Can.	C4	103
Meagher, co., Mt., U.S.	D6	133
Meath, co., Ire.	H7	8
Meath, hist. reg., Ire.	H6	8
Meath Park, Sask., Can.	D3	105
Meaux, Fr.	D9	14
Mebane, N.C., U.S.	A3	140
Mecca see Makkah, Sau. Ar.	D1	47
Mechanic Falls, Me., U.S.	D2	126
Mechanicsburg, Pa., U.S.	F7	145
Mechanicsville, Ia., U.S.	C6	122
Mechanicsville, Va., U.S.	C5	153
Mechanicville, N.Y., U.S.	C7	139
Mechelen (Malines), Bel.	F5	12
Mechita, Arg.	H8	80
Mechriyya, Alg.	D10	62
Mecklenburg, co., N.C., U.S.	B2	140
Mecklenburg, co., Va., U.S.	D4	153
Mecklenburger Bucht, b., Ger.	A11	10
Mecklenburg-Vorpommern, state, Ger.	B12	10
Mecosta, co., Mi., U.S.	E5	129
Medan, Indon.	M5	40
Médanos, Arg.	J7	80
Medanosa, Punta, c., Arg.	F3	78
Medaryville, In., U.S.	B4	121
Medeiros Neto, Braz.	D8	79
Medellín, Col.	D5	84
Médenine, Tun.	D16	62
Mederdra, Maur.	h10	128
Medfield, Ma., U.S.	h10	128
Medford, Ma., U.S.	B5	128
Medford, N.J., U.S.	F5	130
Medford, Ok., U.S.	A4	143
Medford, Or., U.S.	E4	144
Medford, Wi., U.S.	C3	156
Medgidia, Rom.	E12	20
Media, Pa., U.S.	G11	145
Mediapolis, Ia., U.S.	C6	122
Medias, Rom.	C8	20
Medical Lake, Wa., U.S.	B8	154
Medicine Bow, Wy., U.S.	E6	157

type

Medi-Miss

Name	Map Ref.	Page

Medicine Bow, stm., Wy., U.S. — E6 157
Medicine Bow Mountains, mts., U.S. — E6 157
Medicine Bow Peak, mtn., Wy., U.S. — E6 157
Medicine Hat, Alta., Can. — D5 98
Medicine Lake, Mt., U.S. — B12 133
Medicine Lodge, Ks., U.S. — E5 123
Medicine Lodge, stm., U.S. — E4 123
Medina, Braz. — D8 79
Medina see Al-Madīnah, Sau. Ar. — B1 47
Medina, N.Y., U.S. — B2 139
Medina, N.D., U.S. — C6 141
Medina, Oh., U.S. — A4 142
Medina, Tn., U.S. — B3 149
Medina, Wa., U.S. — e11 154
Medina, co., Oh., U.S. — A4 142
Medina, co., Tx., U.S. — E3 150
Medina del Campo, Spain — D7 16
Medinīpur, India — I12 44
Mediterranean Sea — E9 52
Medjerda, Monts de la, mts., Afr. — M3 18
Mednogorsk, Russia — G9 26
Medora, In., U.S. — G5 121
Medstead, Sask., Can. — D1 105
Medvežjegorsk, Russia — E4 26
Medway, Me., U.S. — C4 126
Medway, Ma., U.S. — B5 128
Medyn', Russia — G18 22
Meekatharra, Austl. — E3 68
Meeker, Co., U.S. — A3 113
Meeker, Ok., U.S. — B5 143
Meeker, co., Mn., U.S. — E4 130
Meelpaeg Lake, res., Newf., Can. — D3 102
Meerane, Ger. — E12 10
Meerut, India — F7 44
Meeteetse, Wy., U.S. — B4 157
Mega, Eth. — H8 56
Mégantic, Lac, l., Que., Can. — D7 104
Mégara, Grc. — K7 20
Meghālaya, state, India — H14 44
Meghna, stm., Bngl. — H14 44
Mehar, Pak. — G2 44
Mehlville, Mo., U.S. — f13 132
Meigs, Ga., U.S. — E2 117
Meigs, co., Oh., U.S. — C3 142
Meigs, co., Tn., U.S. — D9 149
Meiktila, Mya. — D3 40
Meiningen, Ger. — E10 10
Meiringen, Switz. — E9 13
Meissen, Ger. — D13 10
Meixian, China — K5 34
Meiyino, Sud. — N8 60
Mejerda, Oued (Oued Medjerda), stm., Afr. — M4 18
Mejez el Bab, Tun. — M4 18
Mejicanos, El Sal. — D5 92
Mejillones, Chile — B3 80
Mejillones, Península, pen., Chile — B3 80
Mékambo, Gabon — A2 58
Mekele, Eth. — K10 60
Meknès, Mor. — D8 62
Mekong, stm., Asia — H8 40
Melaka, Malay. — M7 40
Melanesia, is., Oc. — I19 158
Melbourne, Austl. — K6 70
Melbourne, Ar., U.S. — A4 111
Melbourne, Fl., U.S. — D6 116
Melbourne, Ky., U.S. — h14 124
Melbourne Beach, Fl., U.S. — D6 116
Melcher, Ia., U.S. — C4 122
Melchor Múzquiz, Mex. — D9 90
Melechovo, Russia — E24 22
Melenki, Russia — F24 22
Meleuz, Russia — G9 26
Mélèzes, Rivière aux, stm., Que., Can. — g12 104
Melfi, Italy — H10 18
Melfort, Sask., Can. — E3 105
Melghir, Chott, l., Alg. — C14 62
Melilla, Sp. N. Afr. — C9 62
Melincué, Arg. — G8 80
Melipilla, Chile — G3 80
Melita, Man., Can. — E1 100
Melitopol', Ukr. — F15 4
Mellen, Wi., U.S. — B3 156
Mellette, co., S.D., U.S. — D5 148
Mělník, Czech Rep. — E14 10
Melo, Ur. — G11 80
Melocheville Que. Can. — q19 104
Melong, Cam. — I14 64
Melrose, Fl., U.S. — C4 116
Melrose, Ma., U.S. — B5 128
Melrose, Mn., U.S. — E4 130
Melrose, N.M., U.S. — C6 138
Melton Hill Lake, res., Tn., U.S. — D9 149
Melton Mowbray, Eng., U.K. — I13 8
Melun, Fr. — D9 14
Melvern, Ks., U.S. — D8 123
Melville, Sask., Can. — G4 105
Melville, La., U.S. — D4 125
Melville, Lake, l., Newf., Can. — B2 102
Melville Island, i., Austl. — B6 68
Melville Island, i., N.W. Ter., Can. — B8 86
Melville Peninsula, pen., N.W. Ter., Can. — C16 96
Melvin, Ky., U.S. — C7 124
Melvin Village, N.H., U.S. — C4 136
Melyana, Alg. — B12 62
Memel see Nemunas, stm., Eur. — F6 22
Memmingen, Ger. — H10 10
Mempawah, Indon. — N10 40
Memphis, Fl., U.S. — p10 116
Memphis, Mi., U.S. — F8 129
Memphis, Mo., U.S. — A5 132
Memphis, Tn., U.S. — B1 149
Memramcook, N.B., Can. — C5 101
Mena, Ar., U.S. — C1 111
Menagha, Mn., U.S. — D3 130
Ménaka, Mali — D11 64
Menan, Id., U.S. — F7 119
Menands, N.Y., U.S. — C7 139
Menard, co., Il., U.S. — C4 120
Menard, co., Tx., U.S. — D3 150
Menasha, Wi., U.S. — D5 156

Mende, Fr. — H10 14
Mendenhall, Ms., U.S. — D4 131
Méndez, Mex. — E10 90
Mendham, N.J., U.S. — B3 137
Mendi, Eth. — M8 60
Mendi, Pap. N. Gui. — G11 38
Mendocino, co., Ca., U.S. — C2 112
Mendon, Ut., U.S. — B4 151
Mendota, Ca., U.S. — D3 112
Mendota, Il., U.S. — B4 120
Mendota, Lake, l., Wi., U.S. — E4 156
Mendoza, Arg. — G4 80
Mendoza, prov., Arg. — H4 80
Mene de Mauroa, Ven. — B7 84
Mene Grande, Ven. — C7 84
Menemen, Tur. — K11 20
Menen (Menin), Bel. — G3 12
Menfi, Italy — L7 18
Mengcheng, China — E10 30
Menggala, Indon. — F4 38
Menghai, China — C6 40
Mengzi, China — C7 40
Menifee, Ar., U.S. — B3 111
Menifee, co., Ky., U.S. — C6 124
Menindee, Austl. — I5 70
Menlo Park, Ca., U.S. — k8 112
Menno, S.D., U.S. — D8 148
Menominee, Mi., U.S. — C3 129
Menominee, co., Mi., U.S. — C3 129
Menominee, co., Wi., U.S. — C5 156
Menominee, stm., U.S. — C6 156
Menomonee Falls, Wi., U.S. — E5 156
Menomonie, Wi., U.S. — D2 156
Menongue, Ang. — D3 58
Menorca, i., Spain — F16 16
Mentawai, Kepulauan, is., Indon. — F2 38
Mentawai, Selat, strt., Indon. — F3 38
Menton, Fr. — I14 14
Mentone, Al., U.S. — A4 108
Mentone, In., U.S. — B5 121
Mentor, Oh., U.S. — A4 142
Mentor-on-the-Lake, Oh., U.S. — A4 142
Menzel Bourguiba, Tun. — L4 18
Menzel Bou Zelfa, Tun. — M5 18
Menzel Temime, Tun. — M5 18
Menzies, Mount, mtn., Ant. — C5 73
Meoqui, Mex. — C7 90
Meota, Sask., Can. — D1 105
Meppel, Neth. — C9 12
Meppen, Ger. — C7 10
Mequon, Wi., U.S. — E6 156
Mer, Fr. — E8 14
Meramec, stm., Mo., U.S. — C7 132
Merano (Meran), Italy — C6 18
Merasheen Island, i., Newf., Can. — E4 102
Merauke, Indon. — G11 38
Meraux, La., U.S. — k12 125
Merced, Ca., U.S. — D3 112
Merced, co., Ca., U.S. — D3 112
Merced, stm., Ca., U.S. — D3 112
Mercedario, Cerro, mtn., Arg. — F3 80
Mercedes, Arg. — H9 80
Mercedes, Arg. — G6 80
Mercedes, Arg. — E9 80
Mercedes, Tx., U.S. — F4 150
Mercedes, Ur. — G9 80
Mercer, Pa., U.S. — D1 145
Mercer, Wi., U.S. — B3 156
Mercer, co., Il., U.S. — B3 120
Mercer, co., Ky., U.S. — C5 124
Mercer, co., Mo., U.S. — A4 132
Mercer, co., N.J., U.S. — C3 137
Mercer, co., N.D., U.S. — B4 141
Mercer, co., Oh., U.S. — B1 142
Mercer, co., Pa., U.S. — D1 145
Mercer, co., W.V., U.S. — D3 155
Mercer Island, i., Wa., U.S. — B3 154
Mercerville, N.J., U.S. — C3 137
Merchtem, Bel. — G5 12
Mercier, Que., Can. — D3 104
Meredith, N.H., U.S. — C3 136
Meredith, Lake, res., Tx., U.S. — B2 150
Meredosia, Il., U.S. — D3 120
Mergui (Myeik), Mya. — H5 40
Mergui Archipelago, is., Mya. — H5 40
Mérida, Mex. — G15 90
Mérida, Spain — G5 16
Mérida, Ven. — C7 84
Mérida, state, Ven. — C7 84
Mérida, Cordillera de, mts., Ven. — C7 84
Meriden, Ct., U.S. — C4 114
Meriden, Ks., U.S. — C8 123
Meriden, N.H., U.S. — C2 136
Meridian, Id., U.S. — F2 119
Meridian, Ms., U.S. — C5 131
Meridian, Tx., U.S. — D3 150
Meridian Hills, In., U.S. — k10 121
Meridianville, Al., U.S. — A3 108
Mérignac, Fr. — H6 14
Merigold, Ms., U.S. — B3 131
Merimbula, Austl. — K8 70
Merín, Laguna (Lagoa Mirim), b., S.A. — G12 80
Merinos, Ur. — G10 80
Meriwether, co., Ga., U.S. — C2 117
Merlin, Ont., Can. — E2 103
Merlo, Arg. — G6 80
Merna, Ne., U.S. — C6 134
Meron, Hare, mtn., Isr. — C4 50
Merredin, Austl. — F3 68
Merriam, Ks., U.S. — k16 123
Merrick, co., Ne., U.S. — C7 134
Merrickville, Ont., Can. — C9 103
Merrill, Ia., U.S. — B1 122
Merrill, Or., U.S. — E5 144
Merrill, Wi., U.S. — C4 156
Merrillville, In., U.S. — B3 121
Merrimac, Ma., U.S. — A5 128
Merriman, N.H., U.S. — D3 136
Merrimack, co., N.H., U.S. — D3 136
Merrimack, stm., U.S. — A5 128
Merritt, B.C., Can. — D7 99
Merritt Island, Fl., U.S. — D6 116
Merryville, La., U.S. — D2 125
Merseburg, Ger. — D11 10
Merthyr Tydfil, Wales, U.K. — J10 8
Merton, Wi., U.S. — m11 156

Méru, Fr. — C9 14
Meru, Kenya — A7 58
Meru, Mount, mtn., Tan. — B7 58
Merzig, Ger. — F6 10
Mesa, Az., U.S. — D4 110
Mesa, co., Co., U.S. — C2 113
Mesabi Range, hills, Mn., U.S. — C6 130
Mesagne, Italy — I12 18
Mesa Verde National Park, Co., U.S. — D2 113
Mescalero, N.M., U.S. — D4 138
Meschede, Ger. — D8 10
Meščovsk, Russia — G18 22
Meshgīn Shahr, Iran — B9 48
Mesilla, N.M., U.S. — E3 138
Mesita, N.M., U.S. — C2 138
Meskiana, Alg. — C14 62
Mesolóngion, Grc. — K5 20
Mesopotamia, hist. reg., Asia — D8 48
Mesquite, Nv., U.S. — G7 135
Mesquite, N.M., U.S. — E3 138
Mesquite, Tx., U.S. — n10 150
Messina, Italy — K10 18
Messina, S. Afr. — D10 66
Messina, Stretto di, strt., Italy — K10 18
Messini, Grc. — L6 20
Mestghanem, Alg. — C11 62
Mestre, Italy — D7 18
Meta, dept., Col. — F6 84
Meta, stm., S.A. — D9 84
Metairie, La., U.S. — k11 125
Metamora, Il., U.S. — C4 120
Metán, Arg. — C6 80
Metapán, El Sal. — C5 92
Metcalfe, Ont., Can. — B9 103
Metcalfe, Ms., U.S. — B2 131
Metcalfe, co., Ky., U.S. — C4 124
Meteghan, N.S., Can. — E3 101
Meteghan River, N.S., Can. — E3 101
Meteor Crater, crat., Az., U.S. — C4 110
Methow, stm., Wa., U.S. — A5 154
Methuen, Ma., U.S. — A5 128
Metlakatla, Ak., U.S. — D13 109
Metlaoui, Tun. — C15 62
Meto, Bayou, stm., Ar., U.S. — C4 111
Metropolis, Il., U.S. — F5 120
Metter, Ga., U.S. — D4 117
Metu, Eth. — M8 60
Metuchen, N.J., U.S. — B4 137
Metz, Fr. — C13 14
Metzger, Or., U.S. — h12 144
Meulan, Fr. — C8 14
Meurthe, stm., Fr. — D13 14
Meuse (Maas), stm., Eur. — E5 10
Mexia, Tx., U.S. — D4 150
Mexicali, Mex. — A2 90
Mexican Springs, N.M., U.S. — B1 138
Mexico, In., U.S. — C5 121
Mexico, Me., U.S. — D2 126
Mexico, Mo., U.S. — B6 132
México, state, Mex. — H10 90
Mexico (México), ctry., N.A. — F9 90
Mexico, Gulf of, b., N.A. — C6 88
Mexico City see Ciudad de México, Mex. — H10 90
Meximieux, Fr. — G12 14
Meycauayan, Phil. — n19 39b
Meyersdale, Pa., U.S. — G3 145
Meymaneh, Afg. — C1 44
Mezada, Horvot (Masada), hist., Isr. — F4 50
Meždurečensk, Russia — G11 28
Mèze, Fr. — I10 14
Mezen', Russia — D6 26
Mezőberény, Hung. — I21 10
Mezőkövesd, Hung. — H20 10
Mezőtúr, Hung. — H20 10
Mglin, Russia — H15 22
M'goun, Irhil, mtn., Mor. — E7 62
Mhow, India — I6 44
Miahuatlán de Porfirio Díaz, Mex. — I11 90
Miami, Man., Can. — E2 100
Miami, Az., U.S. — D5 110
Miami, Fl., U.S. — G6 116
Miami, Ok., U.S. — A7 143
Miami, co., In., U.S. — C5 121
Miami, co., Ks., U.S. — D9 123
Miami, co., Oh., U.S. — B1 142
Miami Beach, Fl., U.S. — G6 116
Miami Canal, Fl., U.S. — F6 116
Miamisburg, Oh., U.S. — C1 142
Miami Shores, Fl., U.S. — s13 116
Miami Springs, Fl., U.S. — G6 116
Miandoāb, Iran — C9 48
Miandrivazo, Madag. — q21 67b
Mīāneh, Iran — C9 48
Mianhu, China — L5 34
Miānwāli, Pak. — D4 44
Mianyang, China — E7 30
Mianyang, China — E2 34
Miaoli, Tai. — K9 34
Miass, Russia — G10 26
Micco, Fl., U.S. — E6 116
Michajlov, Russia — G22 22
Michajlovka, Russia — G6 26
Michelson, Mount, mtn., Ak., U.S. — B11 109
Michie, Tn., U.S. — B3 149
Michigamme Reservoir, res., Mi., U.S. — B2 129
Michigan, N.D., U.S. — A7 141
Michigan, state, U.S. — E6 129
Michigan, Lake, l., U.S. — C9 106
Michigan Center, Mi., U.S. — F6 129
Michigan City, In., U.S. — A4 121
Michnevo, Russia — F20 22
Michoacán, state, Mex. — H9 90
Mico, stm., Nic. — E10 92
Micronesia, is., Oc. — G19 158
Micronesia, Federated States of, ctry., Oc. — H19 158
Mičurinsk, Russia — I23 22
Midale, Sask., Can. — H4 105
Mid-Atlantic Ridge — F9 160
Middelburg, Neth. — E4 12
Middelburg, S. Afr. — E9 66
Middelburg, S. Afr. — H7 66

Middelfart, Den. — N11 6
Middle America Trench — H10 86
Middle Andaman, i., India — H2 40
Middleboro (Middleborough Center), Ma., U.S. — C6 128
Middlebourne, W.V., U.S. — B4 155
Middleburg, Fl., U.S. — B5 116
Middleburg Heights, Oh., U.S. — h9 142
Middlebury, Ct., U.S. — C3 114
Middlebury, In., U.S. — A6 121
Middlebury, Vt., U.S. — C2 152
Middlefield, Ct., U.S. — C5 114
Middlefield, Oh., U.S. — A4 142
Middle Musquodoboit, N.S., Can. — D6 101
Middleport, Oh., U.S. — C3 142
Middlesboro, Ky., U.S. — D6 124
Middlesbrough, Eng., U.K. — G12 8
Middlesex, Belize — I15 90
Middlesex, N.J., U.S. — B4 137
Middlesex, co., Ct., U.S. — D5 114
Middlesex, co., Ma., U.S. — A5 128
Middlesex, co., N.J., U.S. — C4 137
Middlesex, co., Va., U.S. — C6 153
Middle Stewiacke, N.S., Can. — D6 101
Middleton, N.S., Can. — E4 101
Middleton, Id., U.S. — F2 119
Middleton, Ma., U.S. — A5 128
Middleton, N.H., U.S. — D4 136
Middleton, Wi., U.S. — E4 156
Middletown, Ct., U.S. — C5 114
Middletown, De., U.S. — C3 115
Middletown, In., U.S. — D6 121
Middletown, Ky., U.S. — g11 124
Middletown, Md., U.S. — B2 127
Middletown, N.J., U.S. — C4 137
Middletown, N.Y., U.S. — D6 139
Middletown, Oh., U.S. — C1 142
Middletown, Pa., U.S. — F8 145
Middletown, R.I., U.S. — E5 146
Middletown, Va., U.S. — A4 153
Middletown Springs, Vt., U.S. — E2 152
Middleville, Mi., U.S. — F5 129
Midelt, Mor. — D8 62
Midfield, Al., U.S. — g7 108
Midland, Ont., Can. — C5 103
Midland, Mi., U.S. — E6 129
Midland, Pa., U.S. — E1 145
Midland, co., Mi., U.S. — E6 129
Midland, co., Tx., U.S. — D1 150
Midland City, Al., U.S. — D4 108
Midland Park, Ks., U.S. — g12 123
Midland Park, N.J., U.S. — B4 137
Midland Park, S.C., U.S. — k11 147
Midlothian, Il., U.S. — k9 120
Midlothian, Tx., U.S. — C4 150
Midnapore Sud, Madag. — s22 67b
Midvale, Ut., U.S. — C4 151
Midville, Ga., U.S. — D4 117
Midway, B.C., Can. — E8 99
Midway, Al., U.S. — C4 108
Midway, De., U.S. — F5 115
Midway, Ky., U.S. — B5 124
Midway, Ut., U.S. — C4 151
Midway Islands, dep., Oc. — E1 2
Midwest, Wy., U.S. — C6 157
Midwest City, Ok., U.S. — B4 143
Midyat, Tur. — C6 48
Międzyrzecz, Pol. — C15 10
Mielec, Pol. — E21 10
Mier, Mex. — D10 90
Mieres, Spain — B6 16
Miercurea-Ciuc, Rom. — C9 20
Mieres, Spain — B6 16
Mezen', Russia — I10 14
Mifflin, co., Pa., U.S. — E6 145
Mifflinburg, Pa., U.S. — E7 145
Miguel Alemán, Presa, res., Mex. — H11 90
Miguel Auza, Mex. — E8 90
Miguelópolis, Braz. — F4 79
Miguel Riglos, Arg. — I7 80
Mihara, Japan — M8 36
Mikašević, Bela. — I10 22
Mikhrot Shelomo Hamelekh (Timna') (King Solomon's Mines), hist., Isr. — I3 50
Mikkeli, Fin. — K20 6
Mikkelin lääni, prov., Fin. — J20 6
Mikolów, Pol. — E18 10
Mikonos, Grc. — L9 20
Mikun', Russia — E8 26
Milaca, Mn., U.S. — E5 130
Milagro, Ec. — I3 84
Milam, co., Tx., U.S. — D4 150
Milan see Milano, Italy — D4 18
Milan, Ga., U.S. — D3 117
Milan, Il., U.S. — B3 120
Milan, In., U.S. — F7 121
Milan, Mi., U.S. — F7 129
Milan, Mo., U.S. — A4 132
Milan, N.M., U.S. — B2 138
Milan, Tn., U.S. — B3 149
Milano (Milan), Italy — D4 18
Minas de Corrales, Ur. — F11 80
Minas de Matahambre, Cuba — C3 94
Minas de Oro, Hond. — C7 92
Minas Gerais, state, Braz. — E6 79
Minas Novas, Braz. — D7 79
Minatitlán, Mex. — I12 90
Minbu, Mya. — D3 40
Minco, Ok., U.S. — B4 143
Mindanao, i., Phil. — D8 38
Mindanao, C.V. — k16 64a
Minden, Ont., Can. — C6 103
Minden, Ger. — C8 10
Minden, La., U.S. — B2 125
Minden, Ne., U.S. — D7 134
Minden, Nv., U.S. — E2 135
Minden, W.V., U.S. — n13 155
Mindoro, i., Phil. — C7 38
Mineiros, Braz. — D2 79
Mineola, N.Y., U.S. — E7 139
Mineola, Tx., U.S. — C5 150
Mineral, Wa., U.S. — C3 154
Mineral, co., Co., U.S. — D4 113
Mineral, co., Mt., U.S. — C1 133
Mineral, co., Nv., U.S. — E3 135
Mineral, co., W.V., U.S. — B6 155

Mineral'nyje Vody, Russia — I6 26
Mineral Point, Wi., U.S. — F3 156
Mineral Springs, Ar., U.S. — D2 111
Mineral Wells, Tx., U.S. — C3 150
Minersville, Pa., U.S. — E9 145
Minersville, Ut., U.S. — E3 151
Minerva, Oh., U.S. — B4 142
Minervino Murge, Italy — H11 18
Minfeng, China — D3 30
Mingācevir, Azer. — I7 26
Mingela, Austl. — B7 70
Minggang, China — C3 34
Mingo, co., W.V., U.S. — D2 155
Mingo Junction, Oh., U.S. — B5 142
Minhang, China — D10 34
Minhla, Mya. — F3 40
Minho, hist. reg., Port. — D3 16
Minho, China — I8 30
Miniota, Man., Can. — D1 100
Minidoka, co., Id., U.S. — G5 119
Minier, Il., U.S. — C4 120
Minna, Nig. — G13 64
Minneapolis, Ks., U.S. — C6 123
Minneapolis, Mn., U.S. — F5 130
Minnedosa, Man., Can. — D2 100
Minnehaha, co., S.D., U.S. — D9 148
Minneola, Ks., U.S. — E3 123
Minneota, Mn., U.S. — F3 130
Minnesota, state, U.S. — E4 130
Minnesota, stm., Mn., U.S. — G5 130
Minnesota Lake, Mn., U.S. — G5 130
Minnetonka, Mn., U.S. — n12 130
Minnetonka, Lake, l., Mn., U.S. — n11 130
Minnewaukan, N.D., U.S. — A6 141
Minocqua, Wi., U.S. — C4 156
Minonk, Il., U.S. — C4 120
Minooka, Il., U.S. — B5 120
Minot, N.D., U.S. — A4 141
Minquadale, De., U.S. — i7 115
Minsk, Bela. — H10 22
Mińsk Mazowiecki, Pol. — C21 10
Minster, Oh., U.S. — B1 142
Mintaka Pass, Asia — B6 44
Mint Hill, N.C., U.S. — B2 140
Minto, Man., Can. — E1 100
Minto, N.B., Can. — C3 101
Minto, N.D., U.S. — A8 141
Minturn, Co., U.S. — B4 113
Minturno, Italy — H8 18
Minusinsk, Russia — G10 28
Minute Man National Historical Park, Ma., U.S. — g10 128
Minxian, China — E7 30
Minya see Al-Minyā, Egypt — C6 60
Minya Konka see Gongga Shan, mtn., China — F7 30
Mio, Mi., U.S. — D6 129
Miory, Bela. — F10 22
Mirabel, Que., Can. — D3 104
Miracema do Tocantins, Braz. — E9 76
Mirador, Braz. — E10 76
Miradouro, Braz. — F7 79
Miraflores, Arg. — G6 84
Miraflores, Esclusas de, Pan. — I15 92
Miraj, India — D3 46
Miramar, Arg. — J10 80
Miramar, Fl., U.S. — s13 116
Miramas, Fr. — I12 14
Miramichi Bay, b., N.B., Can. — B5 101
Miranda, Arg. — I13 82
Miranda, Col. — F4 84
Miranda, state, Ven. — B9 84
Miranda de Ebro, Spain — C9 16
Mirande, Fr. — I7 14
Mirandela, Port. — D4 16
Mirante do Paranapanema, Braz. — G3 79
Mirecourt, Fr. — D13 14
Miri, Malay. — E5 38
Miriam, Lagoa, b., S.A. — H9 74
Mirim, Lagoa (Laguna Merín), b., S.A. — G12 80
Mirnyj, Russia — E14 28
Mirpur Khās, Pak. — H3 44
Mirria, Niger — E14 64
Mirror, Alta., Can. — C4 98
Mirror Lake, N.H., U.S. — C4 136
Mirzāpur, India — H10 44
Misanthe, Mex. — H11 90
Miscou Centre, N.B., Can. — B5 101
Miscouche, P.E.I., Can. — C6 101
Miscou Island, i., N.B., Can. — B5 101
Miscou Point, c., N.B., Can. — A5 101
Mishan, China — B13 30
Mishawaka, In., U.S. — A5 121
Mishicot, Wi., U.S. — D6 156
Misiones, prov., Arg. — D11 80
Misiones, dept., Para. — D10 80
Miskī, Sud. — J3 60
Miskolc, Hung. — G20 10
Mislata, Spain — A10 62
Mişlişbon, stm., De., U.S. — E4 115
Misrātah, Libya — B4 56
Missaukee, co., Mi., U.S. — D5 129
Mission, Ks., U.S. — m16 123
Mission, S.D., U.S. — D5 148
Mission, Tx., U.S. — F3 150
Mission Viejo, Ca., U.S. — n13 112
Missisquoi, stm., Vt., U.S. — B3 152
Mississauga, Ont., Can. — D5 103
Mississinewa Lake, res., In., U.S. — C6 121
Mississippi, co., Ar., U.S. — B5 111
Mississippi, co., Mo., U.S. — E8 132
Mississippi, state, U.S. — C4 131
Mississippi, stm., U.S. — E8 106
Mississippi Delta, La., U.S. — E6 125
Mississippi Sound, strt., U.S. — E5 131
Mississippi State, Ms., U.S. — B5 131
Missoula, Mt., U.S. — D2 133
Missoula, co., Mt., U.S. — C2 133
Missouri, state, U.S. — C5 132
Missouri, stm., U.S. — C7 106
Missouri Buttes, mtn., Wy., U.S. — B8 157

192

Name	Map Ref.	Page

Missouri City, Tx., U.S. — r14 150
Missouri Valley, Ia., U.S. — C2 122
Mistassini, Lac, l., Que., Can. — h12 104
Mistelbach, Aus. — G16 10
Misti, Volcán, vol., Peru — G6 82
Mitchell, Austl. — F7 70
Mitchell, Ont., Can. — D3 103
Mitchell, Il., U.S. — E3 120
Mitchell, In., U.S. — G5 121
Mitchell, Ne., U.S. — C2 134
Mitchell, S.D., U.S. — D7 148
Mitchell, co., Ga., U.S. — E2 117
Mitchell, co., Ia., U.S. — A5 122
Mitchell, co., Ks., U.S. — C5 123
Mitchell, co., N.C., U.S. — e10 140
Mitchell, co., Tx., U.S. — C2 150
Mitchell, stm., Austl. — K7 70
Mitchell, Mount, mtn., N.C., U.S. — f10 140
Mitchellville, Ar., U.S. — D4 111
Mitchellville, Ia., U.S. — C4 122
Mitilíni, Grc. — J10 20
Mito, Japan — K15 36
Mitsamiouli, Com. — k15 67a
Mitsinjo, Madag. — p21 67b
Mitsiwa (Massawa), Erit. — J10 60
Mittellandkanal, Ger. — C9 10
Mitú, Col. — G7 84
Mitumba, Monts, mts., Zaire — B5 58
Mitzic, Gabon — A2 58
Miura, Japan — L14 36
Miyako, Japan — H16 36
Miyakonojō, Japan — P6 36
Miyazaki, Japan — P6 36
Miyun, China — C4 32
Mizan Teferi, Eth. — N8 60
Mizdah, Libya — B3 56
Mizen Head, c., Ire. — J4 8
Mizhhir'ya, Ukr. — A7 20
Mizoram, state, India — I15 44
Mizque, Bol. — G9 82
Mjesa, l., Nor. — K12 6
Mladá Boleslav, Czech Rep. — E14 10
Mlanje Peak see Sapitwa, mtn., Mwi. — E7 58
Mława, Pol. — B20 10
Mmabatho, S. Afr. — E7 66
Mmadinare, Bots. — C8 66
Mo, Nor. — H14 6
Moab, Ut., U.S. — E6 151
Moanda, Gabon — B2 58
Moapa, Nv., U.S. — G7 135
Mobara, Japan — L15 36
Mobaye, Cen. Afr. Rep. — H5 56
Moberly, Mo., U.S. — B5 132
Mobile, Al., U.S. — E1 108
Mobile, co., Al., U.S. — E1 108
Mobile, stm., Al., U.S. — E1 108
Mobile Bay, b., Al., U.S. — E1 113
Mobridge, S.D., U.S. — B5 148
Moca, Dom. Rep. — E9 94
Moçambique, Moz. — E8 58
Mocha see Al-Makhā', Yemen — H3 47
Mocha, Isla, i., Chile — J2 80
Mochudi, Bots. — E8 66
Mocksville, N.C., U.S. — B2 140
Moclips, Wa., U.S. — B1 154
Môco, Serra do, mtn., Ang. — D3 58
Mocoa, Col. — G4 84
Mococa, Braz. — F5 79
Mocoduene, Moz. — D12 66
Mocoretá, Arg. — F10 80
Mocorito, Mex. — E6 90
Moctezuma, Mex. — C5 90
Modane, Fr. — G13 14
Modena, Italy — E5 18
Modesto, Ca., U.S. — D3 112
Modica, Italy — M9 18
Mödling, Aus. — G16 10
Modoc, co., Ca., U.S. — B3 112
Moe, Austl. — L7 70
Moema, Braz. — E6 79
Moengo, Sur. — B8 76
Moenkopi, Az., U.S. — A4 110
Moenkopi Plateau, plat., Az., U.S. — B4 110
Moffat, Co., U.S. — A2 113
Moffat Tunnel, Co., U.S. — B5 113
Moga, India — E6 44
Mogadiscio see Muqdisho, Som. — H10 56
Mogadishu see Muqdisho, Som. — H10 56
Mogadore, Oh., U.S. — A4 142
Mogapinyana, Bots. — D8 66
Mogaung, Mya. — B4 40
Mogil'ov, Bela. — H13 22
Mogincual, Moz. — E8 58
Mogoča, Russia — G15 28
Mogogh, Sud. — M6 60
Mogok, Mya. — C4 40
Mogollon Mesa, mtn., Az., U.S. — C5 110
Mogollon Rim, clf, Az., U.S. — C5 110
Mogotón, mtn., N.A. — D8 92
Moguer, Spain — H5 16
Mogzon, Russia — G14 28
Mohács, Hung. — J18 10
Mohall, N.D., U.S. — A4 141
Mohammedia (Fedala), Mor. — D7 62
Mohave, co., Az., U.S. — B1 110
Mohave, Lake, res., U.S. — H7 135
Mohave Valley, Az., U.S. — C1 110
Mohawk, N.Y., U.S. — C5 139
Mohawk, stm., N.Y., U.S. — C5 139
Mohe, China — A11 30
Mohican, stm., Oh., U.S. — B3 142
Mohnton, Pa., U.S. — F10 145
Moho, stm., Belize — A6 92
Mohyliv-Podil's'kyy, Ukr. — H3 26
Moineşti, Rom. — C10 20
Mõisaküla, Est. — C8 22
Moisés Ville, Arg. — F8 80
Moissac, Fr. — H8 14
Mojave, stm., Ca., U.S. — E5 112
Mojave Desert, des., Ca., U.S. — E5 112
Mojimirim, Braz. — G5 79
Mojo, Eth. — M10 60
Mokapu Peninsula, pen., Hi., U.S. — g10 118
Mokelumne, stm., Ca., U.S. — C3 112
Mokena, Il., U.S. — k9 120

Moknine, Tun. — N5 18
Mokp'o, S. Kor. — I14 32
Mol, Bel. — F7 12
Mola di Bari, Italy — H12 18
Molalla, Or., U.S. — B4 144
Moldau see Vltava, stm., Czech Rep. — F14 10
Moldavia, hist. reg., Rom. — B11 20
Moldavia see Moldova, ctry., Eur. — F13 4
Molde, Nor. — J10 6
Moldova, ctry., Eur. — F13 4
Moldoveanu, Vârful, mtn., Rom. — D8 20
Molepolole, Bots. — E7 66
Molėtai, Lith. — F8 22
Molfetta, Italy — H11 18
Molina, Chile — H3 80
Molina de Segura, Spain — G10 16
Moline, Il., U.S. — B3 120
Moline, Ks., U.S. — E7 123
Molins de Rei, Spain — D14 16
Molise, prov., Italy — H9 18
Mollendo, Peru — G5 82
Mölndal, Swe. — M13 6
Moločnoje, Russia — B22 22
Molodečno, Bela. — G9 22
Molokai, i., Hi., U.S. — B5 118
Molopo, stm., Afr. — F5 66
Molotov see Perm', Russia — F9 26
Molsheim, Fr. — D14 14
Molson Lake, l., Man., Can. — B3 100
Moluccas see Maluku, is., Indon. — F8 38
Molucca Sea see Maluku, Laut, Indon. — F7 38
Momanga, Nmb. — B5 66
Mombasa, Kenya — B7 58
Momence, Il., U.S. — B6 120
Mompós, Col. — C5 84
Mona, Ut., U.S. — D4 151
Mona, Canal de la, strt., N.A. — E11 94
Mona, Isla de, i., P.R. — E11 94
Monaca, Pa., U.S. — E1 145
Monaco, ctry., Eur. — G9 4
Monadnock, Mount, mtn., N.H., U.S. — E2 136
Monagas, state, Ven. — C11 84
Monaghan, co., Ire. — G6 8
Monahans, Tx., U.S. — D1 150
Monarch, Alta., Can. — E4 98
Monarch Mills, S.C., U.S. — B4 147
Monarch Pass, Co., U.S. — C4 113
Monashee Mountains, mts., B.C., Can. — D8 99
Monastir see Bitola, Mac. — H5 20
Monastir, Tun. — N5 18
Monastyrščina, Russia — G14 22
Moncalieri, Italy — D2 18
Monção, Braz. — D9 76
Monçegorsk, Russia — D4 26
Mönchengladbach, Ger. — D6 10
Moncks Corner, S.C., U.S. — E7 147
Monclova, Mex. — D9 90
Moncton, N.B., Can. — C5 101
Mondaí, Braz. — D12 80
Mondovi, Wi., U.S. — D2 156
Monee, Il., U.S. — B6 120
Monessen, Pa., U.S. — F2 145
Monett, Mo., U.S. — E4 132
Monette, Ar., U.S. — B5 111
Monfalcone, Italy — D8 18
Monforte de Lemos, Spain — C4 16
Mongaguá, Braz. — H5 79
Mong Cai, Viet. — D9 40
Möng Hsat, Mya. — D5 40
Möng Mit, Mya. — C4 40
Mongo, Chad — F4 56
Mongolia (Mongol Ard Uls), ctry., Asia — B8 30
Mongu, Zam. — E4 58
Möng Yawng, Mya. — D6 40
Monida Pass, U.S. — E6 119
Monino, Russia — F21 22
Moniquirá, Col. — E6 84
Monistrol-sur-Loire, Fr. — G11 14
Moniteau, co., Mo., U.S. — C5 132
Monkey River, Belize — A6 92
Monkton, Ont., Can. — D3 103
Monmouth, Il., U.S. — C3 120
Monmouth, Me., U.S. — D2 126
Monmouth, Or., U.S. — C3 144
Monmouth, co., N.J., U.S. — C4 137
Monmouth Mountain, mtn., B.C., Can. — D6 99
Mono, co., Ca., U.S. — D4 112
Mono, Punta, c., Nic. — F11 92
Monocacy, stm., Md., U.S. — B3 127
Mono Lake, l., Ca., U.S. — D4 112
Monomoy Island, i., Ma., U.S. — C7 128
Monomoy Point, c., Ma., U.S. — C7 128
Monon, In., U.S. — C4 121
Monona, Ia., U.S. — A6 122
Monona, Wi., U.S. — E4 156
Monona, co., Ia., U.S. — B1 122
Monongah, W.V., U.S. — B4 155
Monongahela, Pa., U.S. — F2 145
Monongahela, stm., U.S. — G2 145
Monongalia, co., W.V., U.S. — B4 155
Monopoli, Italy — I12 18
Monòver, Spain — G11 16
Monreale, Italy — K8 18
Monroe, In., U.S. — C8 121
Monroe, Ia., U.S. — C4 122
Monroe, La., U.S. — B3 125
Monroe, Mi., U.S. — G7 129
Monroe, N.C., U.S. — C2 140
Monroe, N.Y., U.S. — D6 139
Monroe, Ut., U.S. — E3 151
Monroe, Wa., U.S. — B4 154
Monroe, Wi., U.S. — F4 156
Monroe, co., Al., U.S. — D2 108
Monroe, co., Ar., U.S. — C4 111
Monroe, co., Fl., U.S. — G5 116
Monroe, co., Ga., U.S. — D3 117
Monroe, co., Il., U.S. — E3 120
Monroe, co., In., U.S. — F4 121
Monroe, co., Ia., U.S. — D5 122
Monroe, co., Ky., U.S. — D4 124

Monroe, co., Mi., U.S. — G7 129
Monroe, co., Ms., U.S. — B5 131
Monroe, co., Mo., U.S. — B5 132
Monroe, co., N.Y., U.S. — B3 139
Monroe, co., Oh., U.S. — C4 142
Monroe, co., Pa., U.S. — D11 145
Monroe, co., Tn., U.S. — D9 149
Monroe, co., W.V., U.S. — D4 155
Monroe, co., Wi., U.S. — E3 156
Monroe Center, Ct., U.S. — D3 114
Monroe City, In., U.S. — G3 121
Monroe City, Mo., U.S. — B6 132
Monroe Lake, res., In., U.S. — F5 121
Monroe Park, De., U.S. — h7 115
Monroeville, Al., U.S. — D2 108
Monroeville, In., U.S. — C8 121
Monroeville, Pa., U.S. — k14 145
Monrovia, Lib. — H4 64
Monrovia, Ca., U.S. — m13 112
Monrovia, In., U.S. — E5 121
Mons (Bergen), Bel. — H4 12
Monsefú, Peru — B2 82
Monson, Me., U.S. — C3 126
Monson, Ma., U.S. — B3 128
Montagu, S. Afr. — I5 66
Montague, P.E.I., Can. — C7 101
Montague, Mi., U.S. — E4 129
Montague, Ca., U.S. — C4 150
Montague Island, i., Ak., U.S. — D10 109
Montaigu, Fr. — F5 14
Montana, Bul. — F7 20
Montana, state, U.S. — D7 133
Montargis, Fr. — D9 14
Montauban, Fr. — H8 14
Montbard, Fr. — E11 14
Montbéliard, Fr. — E13 14
Mont Blanc, Tunnel du, Eur. — G6 13
Montbrison, Fr. — G11 14
Montcalm, co., Mi., U.S. — E5 129
Montceau [-les-Mines], Fr. — F11 14
Montchanin, Fr. — F11 14
Montchanin, De., U.S. — h7 115
Montclair, Ca., U.S. — m13 112
Montclair, N.J., U.S. — B4 137
Mont Clare, Pa., U.S. — o19 145
Mont-de-Marsan, Fr. — I6 14
Montdidier, Fr. — C9 14
Monteagle, Tn., U.S. — D8 149
Monte Alegre, Braz. — D8 76
Monte Alegre de Minas, Braz. — E4 79
Monte Azul, Braz. — C7 79
Monte Azul Paulista, Braz. — F4 79
Monte Bello Islands, is., Austl. — D3 68
Monte Buey, Arg. — G7 80
Montecarlo, Arg. — D11 80
Monte Caseros, Arg. — F10 80
Montecassino, Abbazia di, Italy — H8 18
Montecatini-Terme, Italy — F5 18
Monte Comán, Arg. — H5 80
Montecristi, Ec. — H2 84
Monte Escobedo, Mex. — F8 90
Montego Bay, Jam. — E6 94
Montélimar, Fr. — H11 14
Montelindo, stm., Para. — B9 80
Montello, Nv., U.S. — B7 135
Montello, Wi., U.S. — E4 156
Monte Maíz, Arg. — G7 80
Montemorelos, Mex. — E10 90
Montemor-o-Novo, Port. — G3 16
Montenegro, Braz. — E13 80
Montenegro see Crna Gora, state, Yugo. — G2 20
Monte Patria, Chile — F3 80
Montepuez, Moz. — D7 58
Monte Quemado, Arg. — C7 80
Montereau-Faut-Yonne, Fr. — D9 14
Monterey, Ca., U.S. — D3 112
Monterey, Tn., U.S. — C8 149
Monterey, co., Ca., U.S. — D3 112
Monterey Bay, b., Ca., U.S. — D2 112
Monterey Park, Ca., U.S. — m12 112
Montería, Col. — C5 84
Montero, Bol. — G10 82
Monteros, Arg. — D6 80
Monterotondo, Italy — G7 18
Monterrey, Mex. — E9 90
Monte Sant'Angelo, Italy — H10 18
Montes Claros, Braz. — F10 74
Montes Claros, Braz. — D7 79
Montevallo, Al., U.S. — B3 108
Montevarchi, Italy — F6 18
Montevideo, Mn., U.S. — F3 130
Montevideo, Ur. — H10 80
Monte Vista, Co., U.S. — D4 113
Montezuma, Ga., U.S. — D2 117
Montezuma, In., U.S. — E3 121
Montezuma, Ia., U.S. — C5 122
Montezuma, Ks., U.S. — E3 123
Montezuma, co., Co., U.S. — D2 113
Montfort, Fr. — D5 14
Montgomery, Al., U.S. — C3 108
Montgomery, Il., U.S. — B5 120
Montgomery, Mn., U.S. — F5 130
Montgomery, N.Y., U.S. — D6 139
Montgomery, Pa., U.S. — D8 145
Montgomery, W.V., U.S. — C3 155
Montgomery, co., Al., U.S. — C3 108
Montgomery, co., Ar., U.S. — C2 111
Montgomery, co., Ga., U.S. — D4 117
Montgomery, co., Il., U.S. — D4 120
Montgomery, co., In., U.S. — D4 121
Montgomery, co., Ia., U.S. — C2 122
Montgomery, co., Ks., U.S. — E8 123
Montgomery, co., Ky., U.S. — B6 124
Montgomery, co., Md., U.S. — B3 127
Montgomery, co., Ms., U.S. — B4 131
Montgomery, co., Mo., U.S. — C6 132
Montgomery, co., N.C., U.S. — B3 140
Montgomery, co., Oh., U.S. — C1 142
Montgomery, co., Pa., U.S. — F11 145
Montgomery, co., Tn., U.S. — A4 149
Montgomery, co., Tx., U.S. — D5 150
Montgomery, co., Va., U.S. — C2 153
Montgomery Center, Vt., U.S. — B3 152
Montgomery City, Mo., U.S. — C6 132

Monticello, Ar., U.S. — D4 111
Monticello, Fl., U.S. — B3 116
Monticello, Ga., U.S. — C3 117
Monticello, Il., U.S. — C5 120
Monticello, In., U.S. — C4 121
Monticello, Ia., U.S. — B6 122
Monticello, Ky., U.S. — D5 124
Monticello, Me., U.S. — B5 126
Monticello, Mn., U.S. — E5 130
Monticello, Ms., U.S. — D3 131
Monticello, N.Y., U.S. — D6 139
Monticello, Ut., U.S. — F6 151
Monticello, Wi., U.S. — F4 156
Montijo, Pan. — D2 84
Montijo, Port. — G3 16
Montijo, Spain — G5 16
Montijo, Golfo de, b., Pan. — D2 84
Montilla, Spain — H7 16
Montividiu, Braz. — D3 79
Montivilliers, Fr. — C7 14
Mont-Joli, Que., Can. — A9 104
Mont-Laurier, Que., Can. — C2 104
Montluçon, Fr. — F9 14
Montluel, Fr. — G12 14
Montmagny, Que., Can. — C7 104
Montmartre, Sask., Can. — G4 105
Montmorency, co., Mi., U.S. — C6 129
Montmorillon, Fr. — F7 14
Monto, Austl. — E9 70
Montour, co., Pa., U.S. — D8 145
Montoursville, Pa., U.S. — D8 145
Montpelier, Id., U.S. — G7 119
Montpelier, In., U.S. — C7 121
Montpelier, Oh., U.S. — A1 142
Montpelier, Vt., U.S. — C3 152
Montpellier, Fr. — I10 14
Montpon-Ménesterol, Fr. — G7 14
Montréal, Que., Can. — D4 104
Montréal, Île de, i., Que., Can. — q19 104
Montreal Lake, l., Sask., Can. — C3 105
Montréal-Nord, Que., Can. — p19 104
Montreux, Switz. — F6 13
Mont-Rolland, Que., Can. — D3 104
Montrose, B.C., Can. — E9 99
Montrose, Scot., U.K. — E11 8
Montrose, Al., U.S. — E2 108
Montrose, Ar., U.S. — D4 111
Montrose, Co., U.S. — C3 113
Montrose, Ia., U.S. — D6 122
Montrose, Mi., U.S. — E7 129
Montrose, Pa., U.S. — C10 145
Montrose, S.D., U.S. — D8 148
Montrose, Va., U.S. — m18 153
Montrose, co., Co., U.S. — C2 113
Mont-Royal, Que., Can. — p19 104
Montsaint-Michel see Le Mont-Saint-Michel, Fr. — D5 14
Montserrat, dep., N.A. — F13 94
Montvale, N.J., U.S. — A4 137
Mont Vernon, N.H., U.S. — E3 136
Montville, Ct., U.S. — D7 114
Monument, Co., U.S. — B6 113
Monument Peak, mtn., Id., U.S. — G4 119
Monument Valley, val., Az., U.S. — A5 110
Monywa, Mya. — C3 40
Monza, Italy — D4 18
Monzón, Peru — C3 82
Monzón, Spain — D12 16
Moodus, Ct., U.S. — D6 114
Moody, Me., U.S. — E2 126
Moody, co., S.D., U.S. — C9 148
Mooirivier, S. Afr. — G9 66
Mookane, Bots. — E7 66
Moora, Austl. — F3 68
Moorcroft, Wy., U.S. — B8 157
Moore, Ok., U.S. — B4 143
Moore, co., N.C., U.S. — B3 140
Moore, co., Tn., U.S. — B5 149
Moore, co., Tx., U.S. — B2 150
Moorefield, W.V., U.S. — B6 155
Mooreland, Ok., U.S. — A2 143
Moore Reservoir, res., U.S. — B4 136
Moores Hill, In., U.S. — F7 121
Mooresboro, N.C., U.S. — B1 140
Moorestown, N.J., U.S. — D3 137
Mooresville, In., U.S. — E5 121
Mooresville, N.C., U.S. — B2 140
Moorhead, Mn., U.S. — D2 130
Moorhead, Ms., U.S. — B3 131
Mooringsport, La., U.S. — B2 125
Mooreesburg, S. Afr. — I4 66
Moose, Wy., U.S. — C2 157
Moose Creek, Ont., Can. — B10 103
Moosehead Lake, l., Me., U.S. — C3 126
Moosehorn, Man., Can. — D2 100
Moose Jaw, Sask., Can. — G3 105
Moose Lake, Man., Can. — C1 100
Moose Lake, Mn., U.S. — D6 130
Mooselookmeguntic Lake, l., Me., U.S. — D2 126
Moose Mountain Creek, stm., Sask., Can. — H4 105
Moosic, Pa., U.S. — m18 145
Moosilauke, Mount, mtn., N.H., U.S. — B3 136
Moosomin, Sask., Can. — G5 105
Moosup, Ct., U.S. — C8 114
Mopipi, Bots. — D7 66
Mopti, Mali — D7 64
Moquegua, Peru — G6 82
Moquegua, dept., Peru — G6 82
Mór, Hung. — H18 10
Mora, Spain — F8 16
Mora, Swe. — K14 6
Mora, Mn., U.S. — E5 130
Mora, N.M., U.S. — B4 138
Mora, co., N.M., U.S. — A4 138
Morādābād, India — F8 44
Morada Nova de Minas, Braz. — E6 79
Morafenobe, Madag. — p21 67b
Mor'akovskij Zaton, Russia — F14 26
Moraleda, Canal, strt., Chile — E2 78
Morales, Guat. — B3 92
Moran, Ks., U.S. — E8 123
Moran, Tx., U.S. — C3 150
Morant Bay, Jam. — F9 94
Morant Point, c., Jam. — F9 94
Moratuwa, Sri L. — I5 46
Morava, hist. reg., Czech Rep. — F17 10

Morava (March), stm., Eur. — G16 10
Moravia, C.R. — H11 92
Moravia, Ia., U.S. — D5 122
Mortes, Rio das, stm., Braz. — B3 79
Moravia see Morava, hist. reg., Czech Rep. — F17 10
Moray Firth, est., Scot., U.K. — D10 8
Morbi, India — I4 44
Morcenx, Fr. — H6 14
Morden, Man., Can. — E2 100
Mordovija, state, Russia — G6 26
Mordovo, Russia — I23 22
Mordvinia see Mordovija, state, Russia — G6 26
Moreau, stm., S.D., U.S. — B3 148
Moreauville, La., U.S. — C4 125
Moree, Austl. — G8 70
Morehead, Ky., U.S. — B6 124
Morehead City, N.C., U.S. — C6 140
Morehouse, Mo., U.S. — E8 132
Morehouse, co., La., U.S. — B4 125
Moreland, Id., U.S. — F6 119
Morelia, Mex. — H9 90
Morell, P.E.I., Can. — C7 101
Morelos, state, Mex. — H10 90
Morena, India — G8 44
Morenci, Az., U.S. — D6 110
Morenci, Mi., U.S. — G6 129
Moresby Island, i., B.C., Can. — C2 99
Moreton Island, i., Austl. — F10 70
Moreuil, Fr. — C9 14
Morey Peak, mtn., Nv., U.S. — E5 135
Morez, Fr. — F13 14
Morgan, Mn., U.S. — F4 130
Morgan, Ut., U.S. — B4 151
Morgan, co., Al., U.S. — A3 108
Morgan, co., Co., U.S. — A7 113
Morgan, co., Ga., U.S. — C3 117
Morgan, co., Il., U.S. — D3 120
Morgan, co., In., U.S. — F5 121
Morgan, co., Ky., U.S. — C6 124
Morgan, co., Mo., U.S. — C5 132
Morgan, co., Oh., U.S. — C4 142
Morgan, co., Tn., U.S. — C9 149
Morgan, co., Ut., U.S. — B4 151
Morgan, co., W.V., U.S. — B6 155
Morgan City, La., U.S. — E4 125
Morganfield, Ky., U.S. — C2 124
Morgan Hill, Ca., U.S. — D3 112
Morganton, N.C., U.S. — B1 140
Morgantown, In., U.S. — F5 121
Morgantown, Ky., U.S. — C3 124
Morgantown, Ms., U.S. — D2 131
Morgantown, W.V., U.S. — B5 155
Morghāb (Murgab), stm., Asia — B16 48
Moriah, Mount, mtn., Nv., U.S. — D7 135
Moriah, Mount, mtn., N.H., U.S. — B4 136
Moriarty, N.M., U.S. — C3 138
Moribaya, Gui. — G5 64
Moriki, Nig. — E13 64
Morinville, Alta., Can. — C4 98
Morioka, Japan — H16 36
Morisset, Austl. — I9 70
Morlaix, Fr. — D3 14
Morley, Mo., U.S. — D8 132
Morning Sun, Ia., U.S. — C6 122
Mornington, Austl. — L6 70
Mornington Island, i., Austl. — A3 70
Morocco, In., U.S. — C3 121
Morocco (Al-Magreb), ctry., Afr. — B5 54
Morococha, Peru — D3 82
Morogoro, Tan. — C7 58
Moro Gulf, b., Phil. — D7 38
Moroleón, Mex. — G9 90
Morombe, Madag. — r20 67b
Morón, Arg. — H9 80
Morón, Cuba — C5 94
Mörön, Mong. — B7 30
Morón, Ven. — B8 84
Morona-Santiago, prov., Ec. — I3 84
Morón de la Frontera, Spain — H6 16
Moroni, Com. — k15 67a
Moroni, Ut., U.S. — D4 151
Morozovsk, Russia — H6 26
Morrill, Ne., U.S. — C2 134
Morrill, co., Ne., U.S. — C2 134
Morrilton, Ar., U.S. — B3 111
Morrin, Alta., Can. — D4 98
Morrinhos, Braz. — D4 79
Morrinsville, N.Z. — B5 72
Morris, Man., Can. — E3 100
Morris, Il., U.S. — B5 120
Morris, Mn., U.S. — E3 130
Morris, Ok., U.S. — B6 143
Morris, co., Ks., U.S. — D7 123
Morris, co., N.J., U.S. — B3 137
Morris, co., Tx., U.S. — C5 150
Morrisburg, Ont., Can. — C9 103
Morris Jesup, Kap, c., Grnld. — A16 86
Morrison, Il., U.S. — B4 120
Morrison, co., Mn., U.S. — D4 130
Morrison City, Tn., U.S. — C11 149
Morristown, In., U.S. — E6 121
Morristown, N.J., U.S. — B4 137
Morristown, Tn., U.S. — C10 149
Morrisville, N.Y., U.S. — C5 139
Morrisville, Pa., U.S. — F12 145
Morrisville, Vt., U.S. — B3 152
Morro Bay, Ca., U.S. — E3 112
Morro do Chapéu, Braz. — F10 76
Morrón, Peru — A1 82
Morrosquillo, Golfo de, b., Col. — C5 84
Morrow, Ga., U.S. — C2 117
Morrow, Oh., U.S. — C1 142
Morrow, co., Oh., U.S. — B3 142
Morrow, co., Or., U.S. — B7 144
Moršansk, Russia — H24 22
Morse, Sask., Can. — G2 105
Mortagne, Fr. — D7 14
Mortagne-sur-Sèvre, Fr. — E6 14
Mortara, Italy — D3 18

Morteau, Fr. — E13 14
Morteros, Arg. — F7 80
Mortes, Rio das, stm., Braz. — B3 79
Mortlach, Sask., Can. — G2 105
Morton, Il., U.S. — C4 120
Morton, Ms., U.S. — C4 131
Morton, Wa., U.S. — C3 154
Morton, co., Ks., U.S. — E2 123
Morton, co., N.D., U.S. — C4 141
Morton Grove, Il., U.S. — h9 120
Mortons Gap, Ky., U.S. — C2 124
Morwell, Austl. — L7 70
Mosal'sk, Russia — G17 22
Moscow see Moskva, Russia — F20 22
Moscow, Id., U.S. — C2 119
Moscow, Vt., U.S. — C3 152
Moscow Mills, Mo., U.S. — C7 132
Mosel (Moselle), stm., Eur. — C13 14
Moselle, Ms., U.S. — D4 131
Moselle (Mosel), stm., Eur. — D13 14
Moses Lake, Wa., U.S. — B6 154
Mosetse, Bots. — C8 66
Mosheim, Tn., U.S. — C11 149
Moshi, Tan. — B7 58
Mosinee, Wi., U.S. — D4 156
Mosjøen, Nor. — I13 6
Moskva (Moscow), Russia — F20 22
Mosomane, Bots. — E8 66
Mosonmagyaróvár, Hung. — H17 10
Mosopa, Bots. — E7 66
Mosquera, Col. — F3 84
Mosquito Creek Lake, res., Oh., U.S. — A5 142
Mosquito Lagoon, b., Fl., U.S. — D6 116
Mosquitos, Costa de, hist. reg., Nic. — D11 92
Mosquitos, Golfo de los, b., Pan. — H13 92
Moss, Nor. — L12 6
Mossaka, Congo — B3 58
Mossâmedes, Braz. — D3 79
Mossbank, Sask., Can. — H3 105
Moss Bluff, La., U.S. — D2 125
Mosselbaai, S. Afr. — J6 66
Mossendjo, Congo — B2 58
Mossoró, Braz. — E11 76
Moss Point, Ms., U.S. — E5 131
Moss Vale, Austl. — J9 70
Most, Czech Rep. — E13 10
Mostar, Bos. — F12 18
Mostardas, Braz. — F13 80
Mosty, Bela. — H7 22
Mostys'ka, Ukr. — F23 10
Mosul see Al-Mawsil, Iraq — C7 48
Mota, Eth. — L9 60
Motagua, stm., N.A. — B6 92
Motala, Swe. — L14 6
Motatán, Ven. — C7 84
Motherwell, Scot., U.K. — F9 8
Motihāri, India — G11 44
Motley, co., Tx., U.S. — B2 150
Motloutse, Bots. — C8 66
Motozintla de Mendoza, Mex. — J13 90
Motril, Spain — I8 16
Motru, Rom. — E7 20
Mott, N.D., U.S. — C3 141
Motueka, N.Z. — D4 72
Motul [de Felipe Carrillo Puerto], Mex. — G15 90
Motupe, Peru — B2 82
Mouaskar, Alg. — C11 62
Mouchoir Passage, strt., N.A. — D9 94
Moudjéria, Maur. — C3 64
Moudon, Switz. — E6 13
Mouila, Gabon — B2 58
Moulins, Fr. — F10 14
Moulmein see Mawlamyine, Mya. — F4 40
Moulmeingyun, Mya. — F3 40
Moulouya, Oued, stm., Mor. — C9 62
Moulton, Al., U.S. — A2 108
Moultonboro, N.H., U.S. — C4 136
Moultrie, Ga., U.S. — E3 117
Moultrie, co., Il., U.S. — D5 120
Moultrie, Lake, res., S.C., U.S. — E7 147
Mound, Mn., U.S. — n11 130
Mound Bayou, Ms., U.S. — B3 131
Mound City, Ks., U.S. — D9 123
Mound City, Mo., U.S. — A2 132
Moundou, Chad — G4 56
Moundridge, Ks., U.S. — D6 123
Mounds, Il., U.S. — F4 120
Mounds, Ok., U.S. — B5 143
Mounds View, Mn., U.S. — m12 130
Moundsville, W.V., U.S. — B4 155
Mound Valley, Ks., U.S. — E8 123
Moundville, Al., U.S. — C2 108
Mountainair, N.M., U.S. — C3 138
Mountain Brook, Al., U.S. — g7 108
Mountainburg, Ar., U.S. — B1 111
Mountain City, Ga., U.S. — B3 117
Mountain City, Nv., U.S. — B6 135
Mountain City, Tn., U.S. — C12 149
Mountain Grove, Mo., U.S. — D5 132
Mountain Home, Ar., U.S. — A3 111
Mountain Home, Id., U.S. — F3 119
Mountain Iron, Mn., U.S. — C6 130
Mountain Lake, Mn., U.S. — G4 130
Mountain Lake Park, Md., U.S. — m12 127
Mountain Nile (Bahr al-Jabal), stm., Sud. — M6 60
Mountain Pine, Ar., U.S. — C2 111
Mountainside, N.J., U.S. — B4 137
Mountain View, Ar., U.S. — B3 111
Mountain View, Ca., U.S. — k8 112
Mountain View, Hi., U.S. — D6 118
Mountain View, Mo., U.S. — D6 132
Mountain View, Ok., U.S. — B3 143
Mountain View, Wy., U.S. — E2 157
Mountain Village, Ak., U.S. — C7 109
Mount Airy, Md., U.S. — B3 127
Mount Airy, N.C., U.S. — A2 140
Mount Albert, Ont., Can. — C5 103
Mount Angel, Or., U.S. — B4 144
Mount Ayr, Ia., U.S. — D3 122

Name | Map Ref. | Page

Mount Barker, Austl. J3 70
Mount Carmel, Il., U.S. E6 120
Mount Carmel, Pa., U.S. E9 145
Mount Carmel [-Mitchell's Brook-Saint Catherine's], Newf., Can. E5 102
Mount Carroll, Il., U.S. A4 120
Mount Clare, W.V., U.S. B4 155
Mount Clemens, Mi., U.S. F8 129
Mount Desert Island, i., Me., U.S. D4 126
Mount Dora, Fl., U.S. D5 116
Mount Forest, Ont., Can. D4 103
Mount Gambier, Austl. K4 70
Mount Gay, W.V., U.S. D2 155
Mount Gilead, N.C., U.S. B3 140
Mount Gilead, Oh., U.S. B3 142
Mount Hagen, Pap. N. Gui. G11 38
Mount Healthy, Oh., U.S. o12 142
Mount Holly, Ar., U.S. D3 111
Mount Holly, N.J., U.S. D3 137
Mount Holly, N.C., U.S. B1 140
Mount Holly Springs, Pa., U.S. F7 145
Mount Hope, Ks., U.S. E6 123
Mount Hope, W.V., U.S. D3 155
Mount Horeb, Wi., U.S. E4 156
Mount Ida, Ar., U.S. C2 111
Mount Isa, Austl. C3 70
Mount Jackson, Va., U.S. B4 153
Mount Joy, Pa., U.S. F9 145
Mount Juliet, Tn., U.S. A5 149
Mount Kisco, N.Y., U.S. D7 139
Mount Lebanon, Pa., U.S. F1 145
Mount Magnet, Austl. E3 68
Mount Meigs, Al., U.S. C3 108
Mount Morgan, Austl. D9 70
Mount Morris, Il., U.S. A4 120
Mount Morris, Mi., U.S. E7 129
Mount Morris, N.Y., U.S. C3 139
Mount Olive, Al., U.S. B3 108
Mount Olive, Il., U.S. D4 120
Mount Olive, Ms., U.S. D4 131
Mount Olive, N.C., U.S. B4 140
Mount Olive, Tn., U.S. n14 149
Mount Pearl, Newf., Can. E5 102
Mount Penn, Pa., U.S. F10 145
Mount Perry, Austl. E9 70
Mount Pleasant, Ar., U.S. B4 111
Mount Pleasant, Ia., U.S. D6 122
Mount Pleasant, Mi., U.S. E6 129
Mount Pleasant, Pa., U.S. F2 145
Mount Pleasant, S.C., U.S. F8 147
Mount Pleasant, Tn., U.S. B4 149
Mount Pleasant, Tx., U.S. C5 150
Mount Pleasant, Ut., U.S. D4 151
Mount Pocono, Pa., U.S. D11 145
Mount Prospect, Il., U.S. A6 120
Mount Pulaski, Il., U.S. C4 120
Mountrail, co., N.D., U.S. A3 141
Mount Rainier, Md., U.S. f9 127
Mount Rainier National Park, Wa., U.S. C4 154
Mount Rushmore National Memorial, hist., S.D., U.S. D2 148
Mount Savage, Md., U.S. k13 127
Mount Sterling, Il., U.S. D3 120
Mount Sterling, Ky., U.S. B6 124
Mount Stewart, P.E.I., Can. C7 101
Mount Sunapee, N.H., U.S. D2 136
Mount Uniacke, N.S., Can. E6 101
Mount Union, Pa., U.S. F6 145
Mount Vernon, Al., U.S. D1 108
Mount Vernon, Ga., U.S. D4 117
Mount Vernon, Il., U.S. E5 120
Mount Vernon, In., U.S. I2 121
Mount Vernon, Ia., U.S. C6 122
Mount Vernon, Ky., U.S. C5 124
Mount Vernon, Mo., U.S. D4 132
Mount Vernon, N.Y., U.S. h13 139
Mount Vernon, Oh., U.S. B3 142
Mount Vernon, S.D., U.S. D7 148
Mount Vernon, Wa., U.S. A3 154
Mount View, R.I., U.S. D4 146
Mount Washington, Ky., U.S. B4 124
Mount Zion, Il., U.S. D5 120
Moura, Austl. E8 70
Moura, Port. G4 16
Mourdiah, Mali D6 64
Moussoro, Chad F4 56
Moutier, Switz. D7 13
Moûtiers, Fr. G13 14
Moville, Ia., U.S. B1 122
Moweaqua, Il., U.S. D4 120
Mower, co., Mn., U.S. G6 130
Moxee City, Wa., U.S. C5 154
Moyamba, S.L. G3 64
Moyen Atlas, mts., Mor. D8 62
Moyeuvre-Grande, Fr. C13 14
Moyie Springs, Id., U.S. A2 119
Moyobamba, Peru B3 82
Moyock, N.C., U.S. A6 140
Možajsk, Russia F19 22
Mozambique (Moçambique), ctry., Afr. E7 58
Mozambique Channel, strt., Afr. E8 58
Mozarlândia, Braz. C3 79
Mozdok, Russia I6 26
Možga, Russia F8 26
Mozyr', Bela. G3 26
Mpika, Zam. D6 58
Mrągowo, Pol. B21 10
M'Saken, Tun. N5 18
M'Sila, Alg. C13 62
Mstera, Russia E24 22
Mstislavl', Bela. G14 22
Mtwara, Tan. D8 58
Muanda, Zaire C2 58
Muang Khammouan, Laos F8 40
Muang Không, Laos G8 40
Muang Khôngxédôn, Laos G8 40
Muang Pakxan, Laos E7 40
Muang Sing, Laos D6 40
Muang Xaignabouri, Laos E6 40
Muar (Bandar Maharani), Malay. M7 40
Muchinga Mountains, mts., Zam. D6 58
Muchtolovo, Russia F26 22
Mučkapskij, Russia J25 22
Muconda, Ang. D4 58
Muçum, Braz. E13 80
Mucuri, Braz. E9 79
Mudanjiang, China C12 30
Muddy Boggy Creek, stm., Ok., U.S. C6 143
Mudgee, Austl. I8 70
Mudon, Mya. F4 40
Mudu, China D9 34
Muenster, Sask., Can. E3 105
Mufulira, Zam. D5 58
Mu Gia, Deo, Asia F8 40
Muğla, Tur. L12 20
Muhammad, Ra's, c., Egypt D8 60
Mühlacker, Ger. G8 10
Muhlenberg, co., Ky., U.S. C2 124
Mühlhausen, Ger. D10 10
Muiron Islands, is., Austl. D2 68
Muisne, Ec. G2 84
Mukacheve, Ukr. H2 26
Mukdahan, Thai. F8 40
Mukden see Shenyang, China B11 32
Mukilteo, Wa., U.S. B3 154
Muktsar, India E6 44
Mukwonago, Wi., U.S. F5 156
Mulanje, Mwi. E7 58
Mulberry, Ar., U.S. B1 111
Mulberry, Fl., U.S. E4 116
Mulberry, In., U.S. D4 121
Mulberry, Ks., U.S. E9 123
Mulberry, N.C., U.S. A1 140
Mulberry, stm., Ar., U.S. B1 111
Mulberry Fork, stm., Al., U.S. B3 108
Mulchén, Chile I2 80
Muldraugh, Ky., U.S. C4 124
Muldrow, Ok., U.S. B7 143
Mulegé, Mex. D3 90
Muleshoe, Tx., U.S. B1 150
Mulgrave, N.S., Can. D8 101
Mulhacén, mtn., Spain H8 16
Mulhouse, Fr. E14 14
Mull, Island of, i., Scot., U.K. E7 8
Mullan, Id., U.S. B3 119
Mullen, Ne., U.S. B4 134
Mullens, W.V., U.S. D3 155
Mullett Lake, l., Mi., U.S. C6 129
Mullewa, Austl. E3 68
Mullica, stm., N.J., U.S. D3 137
Mullingar, Ire. H6 8
Mullins, S.C., U.S. C9 147
Multān, Pak. E4 44
Multnomah, co., Or., U.S. B4 144
Mulvane, Ks., U.S. E6 123
Mumu, Sud. K2 60
Mun, stm., Thai. G8 40
Muna, Mex. G15 90
München (Munich), Ger. G11 10
Münchenstein, Switz. C8 13
Munch'ŏn, N. Kor. D15 32
Muncie, In., U.S. D7 121
Muncy, Pa., U.S. D8 145
Mundare, Alta., Can. C4 98
Mundelein, Il., U.S. A5 120
Münden, Ger. D9 10
Mundo Novo, Braz. A8 79
Mundubbera, Austl. E9 70
Munford, Al., U.S. B4 108
Munford, Tn., U.S. B2 149
Munfordville, Ky., U.S. C4 124
Munger, India H12 44
Mungindi, Austl. G8 70
Munhall, Pa., U.S. k14 145
Munich see München, Ger. G11 10
Munich, N.D., U.S. A7 141
Munising, Mi., U.S. B4 129
Muniz Freire, Braz. F8 79
Munsan, S. Kor. F14 32
Münsingen, Switz. E8 13
Munster, Fr. D14 14
Münster, Ger. D7 10
Munster, In., U.S. A2 121
Munster, hist. reg., Ire. I5 8
Muonio, Fin. H18 6
Muqdisho (Mogadishu), Som. H10 56
Muqui, Braz. F8 79
Muraši, Russia F7 26
Murat, stm., Tur. B5 48
Murchison, stm., Austl. E3 68
Murchison, Mount, mtn., N.Z. E3 72
Murchison Falls see Kabalega Falls, wtfl, Ug. H7 56
Murcia, Spain H10 16
Murcia, prov., Spain G10 16
Murderkill, stm., De., U.S. D4 115
Murdo, S.D., U.S. D5 148
Muret, Fr. I8 14
Murfreesboro, Ar., U.S. C2 111
Murfreesboro, N.C., U.S. A5 140
Murfreesboro, Tn., U.S. B5 149
Murgab (Morghāb), stm., Asia B16 48
Murgon, Austl. F9 70
Muri, Switz. E7 13
Muriaé, Braz. F7 79
Murmansk, Russia D4 26
Murmino, Russia G23 22
Murom, Russia F25 22
Muroran, Japan e15 36a
Murphy, Mo., U.S. g13 132
Murphy, N.C., U.S. f8 140
Murphysboro, Il., U.S. F4 120
Murray, Ia., U.S. C4 122
Murray, Ky., U.S. f9 124
Murray, Ne., U.S. D10 134
Murray, Ut., U.S. C4 151
Murray, co., Ga., U.S. B2 117
Murray, co., Mn., U.S. F3 130
Murray, co., Ok., U.S. C4 143
Murray, stm., Austl. J3 70
Murray, Lake, res., Ok., U.S. C4 143
Murray, Lake, res., S.C., U.S. C5 147
Murray Bridge, Austl. J3 70
Murray Harbour, P.E.I., Can. D7 101
Murray Head, c., P.E.I., Can. C7 101
Murray River, P.E.I., Can. C7 101
Murraysburg, S. Afr. H6 66
Murrayville, Ga., U.S. B3 117
Murrells Inlet, S.C., U.S. D9 147
Murrumbidgee, stm., Austl. J6 70
Murrumburrah, Austl. J8 70
Murska Sobota, Slvn. C11 18
Murten, Switz. E7 13
Murwāra, India I9 44
Murwillumbah, Austl. G10 70
Mürzzuschlag, Aus. H15 10
Muş, Tur. B6 48
Mūsā, Jabal (Mount Sinai), mtn., Egypt C7 60
Musala, mtn., Bul. G7 20
Musan, N. Kor. A17 32
Musandam Peninsula, pen., Oman A10 47
Muscat see Masqaṭ, Oman C11 47
Muscatatuck, stm., In., U.S. G5 121
Muscatine, Ia., U.S. C6 122
Muscatine, co., Ia., U.S. C6 122
Muscle Shoals, Al., U.S. A2 108
Muscoda, Wi., U.S. E3 156
Muscogee, co., Ga., U.S. D2 117
Musconetcong, stm., N.J., U.S. B4 137
Musgrave Harbour, Newf., Can. D5 102
Musgravetown, Newf., Can. D5 102
Mushie, Zaire B3 58
Mushin, Nig. H11 64
Muskego, Wi., U.S. F5 156
Muskegon, Mi., U.S. E4 129
Muskegon, co., Mi., U.S. E4 129
Muskegon, stm., Mi., U.S. E4 129
Muskegon Heights, Mi., U.S. E4 129
Muskingum, co., Oh., U.S. B4 142
Muskingum, stm., Oh., U.S. C4 142
Muskogee, Ok., U.S. B6 143
Muskogee, co., Ok., U.S. B6 143
Musoma, Tan. B6 58
Musquodoboit Harbour, N.S., Can. E6 101
Musselshell, co., Mt., U.S. D8 133
Musselshell, stm., Mt., U.S. D9 133
Mustafakemalpaşa, Tur. I12 20
Mustang, Ok., U.S. B4 143
Mustvee, Est. C9 22
Muswellbrook, Austl. I9 70
Mūt, Egypt E5 60
Mut, Tur. C2 48
Mutare, Zimb. B11 66
Mutsamudu, Com. I16 67a
Muttenz, Switz. C8 13
Mutuípe, Braz. B9 79
Mutum, Braz. E8 79
Muzaffarābād, Pak. C5 44
Muzaffarnagar, India F7 44
Muzaffarpur, India G11 44
Muzon, Cape, c., Ak., U.S. n23 109
Muztag, mtn., China B12 44
Muztag, mtn., China B9 44
Mvolo, Sud. N5 60
Mvuma, Zimb. B10 66
Mwali (Mohéli), i., Com. I15 67a
Mwanza, Tan. B6 58
Mweka, Zaire B4 58
Mweru, Lake, l., Afr. C5 58
Myaing, Mya. D3 40
Myanaung, Mya. E3 40
Myanmar (Burma), ctry., Asia A2 38
Myaungmya, Mya. F3 40
Myebon, Mya. D2 40
Myerstown, Pa., U.S. F9 145
Myingyan, Mya. D3 40
Myitkyinā, Mya. B4 40
Myittha, Mya. D4 40
Mykolayiv, Ukr. H4 26
Mymensingh, Bngl. H14 44
Mynämäki, Fin. K18 6
Myrnam, Alta., Can. C5 98
Myrtle Beach, S.C., U.S. D10 147
Myrtle Grove, Fl., U.S. u14 116
Myrtle Point, Or., U.S. D2 144
Myski, Russia G9 28
Myślenice, Pol. F19 10
Mysłowice, Pol. E19 10
Mysore, India F4 46
Mystic, Ct., U.S. D8 114
Myszków, Pol. E19 10
My Tho, Viet. I9 40
Mytišči, Russia F20 22
Mzimba, Mwi. D6 58
Mzuzu, Mwi. D6 58

N

Naalehu, Hi., U.S. D6 118
Naas, Ire. H7 8
Nabā, Jabal an- (Mount Nebo), mtn., Jord. E5 50
Naberežnyje Čelny, Russia F8 26
Nabeul, Tun. M5 18
Nabī Shu'ayb, Jabal an-, mtn., Yemen G3 47
Nabnasset, Ma., U.S. A5 128
Naboomspruit, S. Afr. E9 66
Nābulus, W.B. D4 50
Nacala-Velha, Moz. D8 58
Nacaome, Hond. D7 92
Naches, Wa., U.S. C5 154
Naches, stm., Wa., U.S. C5 154
Náchod, Czech Rep. E16 10
Nachodka, Russia I18 28
Nacimiento, Chile I2 80
Nacmine, Alta., Can. D4 98
Naco, Mex. B5 90
Naco, Az., U.S. F6 110
Nacogdoches, Tx., U.S. D5 150
Nacogdoches, co., Tx., U.S. D5 150
Nacozari de García, Mex. B5 90
Ñacunday, Para. D11 80
Nadiād, India I5 44
Nădlac, Rom. C4 20
Nador, Mor. C9 62
Nadvirna, Ukr. A8 20
Nadvoicy, Russia J24 6
Nadym, Russia D12 26
Näfels, Switz. D11 13
Naga, Phil. o20 39b
Naga Hills, mts., Asia B3 40
Nāgāland, state, India H16 44
Nagano, Japan K13 36
Nagaoka, Japan J13 36
Nagaon, India G15 44
Nāgappattinam, India G5 46
Nagarote, Nic. E8 92
Nagasaki, Japan O4 36
Nāgaur, India G5 44
Nagda, India I6 44
Nāgercoil, India H4 46
Nagold, Ger. G8 10
Nagorno-Karabakh, reg., Azer. A9 48
Nagoya, Japan L11 36
Nāgpur, India J8 44
Nags Head, N.C., U.S. B7 140
Nagua, Dom. Rep. E10 94
Nagyatád, Hung. I17 10
Nagykanizsa, Hung. I17 10
Nagykőrös, Hung. H19 10
Naha, Japan u2 37b
Nahant, Ma., U.S. g12 128
Nahariyya, Isr. B4 50
Nahāvand, Iran D10 48
Nahe, China B11 30
Nahunta, Ga., U.S. E5 117
Naica, Mex. D7 90
Naicam, Sask., Can. E3 105
Nailin, China B7 32
Nain, Newf., Can. g9 102
Nairn, La., U.S. E6 125
Nairobi, Kenya B7 58
Naivasha, Kenya B7 58
Najafābād, Iran E11 48
Naj'Hammādī, Egypt D7 60
Najībābād, India F8 44
Najin, N. Kor. A18 32
Naju, S. Kor. H14 32
Nakape, Sud. O5 60
Nakatsu, Japan N6 36
Nakhon Pathom, Thai. H6 40
Nakhon Phanom, Thai. F8 40
Nakhon Ratchasima, Thai. G7 40
Nakhon Sawan, Thai. G6 40
Nakhon Si Thammarat, Thai. J5 40
Nakina, Ont., Can. o18 103
Nakło nad Notecią, Pol. B17 10
Naknek, Ak., U.S. D8 109
Nakskov, Den. N12 6
Nakuru, Kenya B7 58
Nakusp, B.C., Can. D9 99
Nal'čik, Russia I6 26
Nalgonda, India D5 46
Nālūt, Libya E16 62
Namangan, Uzb. I12 26
Namatanai, Pap. N. Gui. k17 68a
Nambe, N.M., U.S. B4 138
Nambour, Austl. F10 70
Nam Co, l., China E14 44
Nam Dinh, Viet. D9 40
Namekagon, stm., Wi., U.S. B2 156
Namhkam, Mya. C4 40
Namib Desert, des., Nmb. D2 66
Namibe, Ang. E2 58
Namibia, ctry., Afr. F3 58
Namjagbarwa Feng, mtn., China F16 44
Namounou, Burkina F10 64
Nampa, Alta., Can. A2 98
Nampa, Id., U.S. F2 119
Namp'o, N. Kor. E13 32
Nampula, Moz. E7 58
Namsang, Mya. D4 40
Namsos, Nor. I12 6
Namtu, Mya. A2 38
Namur (Namen), Bel. H6 12
Namur, prov., Bel. H6 12
Namwŏn, S. Kor. H15 32
Nan, Thai. E6 40
Nanaimo, B.C., Can. E5 99
Nanakuli, Hi., U.S. B3 118
Nanao, Japan J11 36
Nance, co., Ne., U.S. C7 134
Nanchang, China G4 34
Nancheng, China H5 34
Nanchong, China E8 30
Nancy, Fr. D13 14
Nanda Devi, mtn., India E8 44
Nandaime, Nic. F8 92
Nānded, India C4 46
N'andoma, Russia E6 26
Nandurbār, India J6 44
Nandyāl, India E5 46
Nanga Parbat, mtn., Pak. C6 44
Nang Rong, Thai. G7 40
Nanjing (Nanking), China D7 34
Nankang, China J3 34
Nanking see Nanjing, China C7 34
Nannine, Austl. E3 68
Nanning, China C10 40
Nanpi, China E4 32
Nanping, China I7 34
Nansei-shotō (Ryukyu Islands), is., Japan s4 37b
Nantes, Fr. E5 14
Nanticoke, Ont., Can. E4 103
Nanticoke, Pa., U.S. D10 145
Nanticoke, stm., U.S. D6 127
Nanton, Alta., Can. D4 98
Nantong, China C9 34
Nant'ou, Tai. L9 34
Nantua, Fr. F12 14
Nantucket, Ma., U.S. D7 128
Nantucket, co., Ma., U.S. D7 128
Nantucket Island, i., Ma., U.S. D7 128
Nantucket Sound, strt., Ma., U.S. C7 128
Nanty Glo, Pa., U.S. F4 145
Nanuet, N.Y., U.S. g12 139
Nanuque, Braz. D8 79
Nanwan, China C2 34
Nanxiang, China D10 34
Nanxiong, China J3 34
Nanyang, China B1 34
Nanzhao, China B1 34
Naoma, W.V., U.S. n13 155
Não-me-Toque, Braz. E12 80
Náousa, Grc. I6 20
Napa, Ca., U.S. C2 112
Napa, co., Ca., U.S. C2 112
Napakiak, Ak., U.S. C7 109
Napanee, Ont., Can. C8 103
Napaskiak, Ak., U.S. C7 109
Napatree Point, c., R.I., U.S. G1 146
Napavine, Wa., U.S. C3 154
Napenay, Arg. D8 80
Naperville, Il., U.S. B5 120
Napier, N.Z. C6 72
Napier, S. Afr. J4 66
Napierville, Que., Can. D4 104
Naples see Napoli, Italy I9 18
Naples, Fl., U.S. F5 116
Naples, Me., U.S. E2 126
Naples, Ut., U.S. C6 151
Napo, prov., Ec. H4 84
Napo, stm., S.A. I6 84
Napoleon, N.D., U.S. C6 141
Napoleon, Oh., U.S. A1 142
Napoli (Naples), Italy I9 18
Nappanee, In., U.S. B5 121
Naqadeh, Iran C8 48
Nara, Japan M10 36
Nara, Mali D6 64
Naracoorte, Austl. K4 70
Naramata, B.C., Can. E8 99
Naranja, Fl., U.S. G6 116
Naranjal, Ec. I3 84
Narasaraopet, India D6 46
Narathiwat, Thai. K6 40
Nārāyanganj, Bngl. I14 44
Narberth, Pa., U.S. p20 145
Narbonne, Fr. I10 14
Nardò, Italy I13 18
Nares Strait, strt., N.A. A13 86
Narew, stm., Eur. C21 10
Nariño, dept., Col. G3 84
Narita, Japan L15 36
Nar'jan-Mar, Russia D8 26
Narmada, stm., India J5 44
Narodnaja, gora, mtn., Russia D10 26
Naro-Fominsk, Russia F19 22
Narol, Man., Can. D3 100
Narooma, Austl. K9 70
Narrabri, Austl. H8 70
Narragansett, R.I., U.S. F4 146
Narragansett Bay, b., R.I., U.S. E5 146
Narrandera, Austl. J7 70
Narrogin, Austl. F3 68
Narromine, Austl. I8 70
Narrows, Va., U.S. C2 153
Narva, Est. B11 22
Narvik, Nor. G15 6
Narvskij zaliv (Narva laht), b., Eur. B10 22
Naryškino, Russia I18 22
Naschel, Arg. G6 80
Naselle, Wa., U.S. C2 154
Nash, co., N.C., U.S. A4 140
Nāshik, India C2 46
Nashua, Ia., U.S. B5 122
Nashua, Mt., U.S. B10 133
Nashua, N.H., U.S. E4 136
Nashua, stm., U.S. E3 136
Nashville, Ar., U.S. D2 111
Nashville, Ga., U.S. E3 117
Nashville, Il., U.S. E4 120
Nashville, In., U.S. F5 121
Nashville, Mi., U.S. F5 129
Nashville, N.C., U.S. B5 140
Nashville, Tn., U.S. A5 149
Nashwauk, Mn., U.S. C5 130
Nāṣir, Buḥayrat, res., Afr. D7 56
Naskaupi, stm., Newf., Can. g9 102
Nassau, Bah. B6 94
Nassau, co., Fl., U.S. B5 116
Nassau, co., N.Y., U.S. E7 139
Nasser, Lake see Nāṣir, Buḥayrat, res., Afr. D7 56
Nässjö, Swe. M14 6
Nata, Bots. C8 66
Natá, Pan. C2 84
Natagaima, Col. F5 84
Natal, Braz. E11 76
Natashquan, stm., Can. h9 102
Natchez, Ms., U.S. D2 131
Natchitoches, La., U.S. C2 125
Natchitoches, co., La., U.S. C2 125
Natick, Ma., U.S. B5 128
National City, Ca., U.S. F5 112
Natitingou, Benin F10 64
Natron, Lake, l., Afr. B7 58
Natrona, co., Wy., U.S. D5 157
Natrona Heights, Pa., U.S. E2 145
Natuna Besar, Kepulauan, is., Indon. L10 40
Natural Bridge, Al., U.S. A2 108
Natural Bridge, Va., U.S. C3 153
Natural Bridges National Monument, Ut., U.S. F6 151
Naturaliste, Cape, c., Austl. F3 68
Naturita, Co., U.S. C2 113
Nau, Cap de la, c., Spain G12 16
Nauders, Aus. I10 10
Naugatuck, Ct., U.S. D3 114
Naugatuck, stm., Ct., U.S. D3 114
Naujamiestis, Lith. F7 22
Naujoji Akmenė, Lith. E5 22
Naumburg, Ger. D11 10
Nauru, ctry., Oc. G24 2
Naushon Island, i., Ma., U.S. D6 128
Nauta, Peru J6 84
Nautilus Park, Ct., U.S. D7 114
Nautla, Mex. G11 90
Nauvoo, Il., U.S. C2 120
Nava, Mex. C9 90
Navadwīp, India I13 44
Navajo, N.M., U.S. B1 138
Navajo, co., Az., U.S. B5 110
Navajo Indian Reservation, U.S. A4 110
Navajo Mountain, mtn., Ut., U.S. F5 151
Navajo Reservoir, res., U.S. A2 138
Navalmoral de la Mata, Spain F6 16
Navan, Ont., Can. B9 103
Navarin, mys, c., Russia E27 28
Navarino, Isla, i., Chile H3 78
Navarra, prov., Spain C10 16
Navarro, Arg. H9 80
Navarro, co., Tx., U.S. D4 150
Navašino, Russia F25 22
Navasota, Tx., U.S. D4 150
Navassa Island, i., N.A. E7 94
Navidad, Chile G3 80
Naviraí, Braz. G1 79
Navl'a, Russia I17 22
Năvodari, Rom. E12 20
Navoi, Uzb. I11 26
Navojoa, Mex. D5 90
Navolato, Mex. E6 90
Navoloki, Russia D24 22
Návpaktos, Grc. K5 20
Návplion, Grc. L6 20
Navsāri, India J5 44
Nawābganj, Bngl. H13 44
Nawābshāh, Pak. G3 44
Naxçıvan, Azer. J7 26
Naxçıvan Muxtar Respublikası, state, Azer. B8 48
Náxos, Grc. L9 20
Nayarit, state, Mex. F7 90
Naylor, Mo., U.S. E7 132
Nazaré, Braz. B9 79
Nazaré, Port. F2 16
Nazaré da Mata, Braz. E11 76
Nazareth see Nazerat, Isr. C4 50
Nazareth, Pa., U.S. E11 145
Nazário, Braz. D4 79
Nazarovo, Russia F10 28
Nazas, Mex. E7 90
Nazas, stm., Mex. E7 90
Nazca, Peru F4 82
N'azepetrovsk, Russia F9 26
Nazerat (Nazareth), Isr. C4 50
Nazerat 'Illit, Isr. C4 50
Nazija, Russia B14 22
Nazilli, Tur. L12 20
Nazlini, Az., U.S. B6 110
Nazret, Eth. M10 60
Nazyvajevsk, Russia F12 26
N'dalatando, Ang. C2 58
N'Djamena, Chad F4 56
Ndola, Zam. D5 58
Neagh, Lough, l., N. Ire., U.K. G7 8
Neah Bay, Wa., U.S. A1 154
Near Islands, is., Ak., U.S. E2 109
Nebit-Dag, Turk. J8 26
Neblina, Pico da, mtn., S.A. G9 84
Nebo, Mount, mtn., Ut., U.S. D4 151
Nebraska, state, U.S. C6 134
Nebraska City, Ne., U.S. D10 134
Nechako, stm., B.C., Can. C5 99
Neche, N.D., U.S. A8 141
Nechí, Col. C5 84
Neckar, stm., Ger. F9 10
Neckarsulm, Ger. F9 10
Necochea, Arg. J9 80
Nederland, Co., U.S. B5 113
Nederland, Tx., U.S. E6 150
Neder Rijn, mth., Neth. E8 12
Nédroma, Alg. C10 62
Nedrow, N.Y., U.S. C4 139
Needham, Ma., U.S. g11 128
Needles, Ca., U.S. E6 112
Ñeembucú, dept., Para. D9 80
Neenah, Wi., U.S. D5 156
Neepawa, Man., Can. D2 100
Nefta, Tun. D14 62
Negage, Ang. C3 58
Negaunee, Mi., U.S. B3 129
Negele, Eth. G8 56
Negev Desert see HaNegev, reg., Isr. G3 50
Negombo, Sri L. I5 46
Negotin, Yugo. E6 20
Negritos, Peru J2 84
Negro, stm., Arg. E4 78
Negro, stm., N.A. E7 92
Negro, stm., S.A. G10 80
Negro, stm., S.A. H13 84
Negros, i., Phil. C7 38
Neguac, N.B., Can. B4 101
Nehalem, stm., Or., U.S. A3 144
Neiba, Dom. Rep. E9 94
Neiges, Piton des, mtn., Reu. v17 67c
Neihuang, China H2 32
Neijiang, China F8 30
Neilburg, Sask., Can. E1 105
Neillsville, Wi., U.S. D3 156
Nei Monggol Zizhiqu (Inner Mongolia), prov., China C10 30
Neisse (Nysa Łużycka) (Nisa), stm., Eur. D14 10
Neiva, Col. F5 84
Neja, Russia C26 22
Nejo, Eth. M8 60
Nekemte, Eth. M9 60
Nekoosa, Wi., U.S. D4 156
Nekrasovskoje, Russia D23 22
Nelidovo, Russia E15 22
Neligh, Ne., U.S. B7 134
Nellore, India E5 46
Nelson, B.C., Can. E9 99
Nelson, N.Z. D4 72
Nelson, Ne., U.S. D7 134
Nelson, N.H., U.S. E2 136
Nelson, co., Ky., U.S. C4 124
Nelson, co., N.D., U.S. B7 141
Nelson, co., Va., U.S. C4 153
Nelson, stm., Man., Can. A4 100
Nelson, Cape, c., Austl. L4 70
Nelsonville, Oh., U.S. C3 142
Nelspruit, S. Afr. E10 66
Néma, Maur. C6 64
Nemadji, stm., U.S. B1 156
Nemaha, co., Ks., U.S. C7 123
Nemaha, co., Ne., U.S. D10 134
Neman, Russia F5 22
Nemenčinė, Lith. G8 22
Nemours, Fr. D9 14
Nemunas (Neman), stm., Eur. F6 22
Nemuro, Japan d20 36a
Nemuro Strait, strt., Asia c20 36a
Nenana, Ak., U.S. C10 109
Neneckij, state, Russia D9 26
Nenetsia see Neneckij, state, Russia D9 26
Neodesha, Ks., U.S. E8 123
Neoga, Il., U.S. D5 120
Neola, Ia., U.S. C2 122
Neola, Ut., U.S. C5 151
Neosho, Mo., U.S. E3 132
Neosho, co., Ks., U.S. E8 123
Neosho, stm., Ok., U.S. A6 143
Nepal (Nepāl), ctry., Asia D11 42
Nepālganj, Nepal F9 44
Nepean, Ont., Can. h12 103
Nephi, Ut., U.S. D4 151
Nepisiguit, stm., N.B., Can. B3 101

Name | Map Ref. | Page

Nepisiguit Bay, b., N.B., Can. B4 101
Neponset, stm., Ma., U.S. h11 128
Neptune, N.J., U.S. C4 137
Neptune Beach, Fl., U.S. B5 116
Neptune City, N.J., U.S. C4 137
Nerčinsk, Russia G15 28
Nerechta, Russia D23 22
Nerja, Spain I8 16
Nerópolis, Braz. D4 79
Neshoba, co., Ms., U.S. C4 131
Nesquehoning, Pa., U.S. E10 145
Ness, co., Ks., U.S. D4 123
Ness, Loch, l., Scot., U.K. D9 8
Ness City, Ks., U.S. D4 123
Nesterov, Russia G5 22
Nesviž, Bela. H9 22
Netanya, Isr. D3 50
Netherlands (Nederland), ctry., Eur. E9 4
Netherlands Antilles (Nederlandse Antillen), dep., N.A. H10 94
Nettie, W.V., U.S. C4 155
Nettilling Lake, l., N.W. Ter., Can. C18 96
Nett Lake Indian Reservation, Mn., U.S. B6 130
Nettleton, Ms., U.S. A5 131
Nettuno, Italy H7 18
Neubrandenburg, Ger. B13 10
Neuburg an der Donau, Ger. G11 10
Neuchâtel, Switz. E6 13
Neuchâtel, Lac de, l., Switz. E6 13
Neudorf, Sask., Can. G4 105
Neufchâteau, Bel. I7 12
Neufchâteau, Fr. D12 14
Neufchâtel-en-Bray, Fr. C8 14
Neuhausen, Switz. C10 13
Neu-Isenburg, Ger. E8 10
Neumarkt in der Oberpfalz, Ger. F11 10
Neumünster, Ger. A9 10
Neunkirchen/Saar, Ger. F7 10
Neuquén, Arg. J4 80
Neuquén, prov., Arg. J4 80
Neuquén, stm., Arg. J4 80
Neuruppin, Ger. C12 10
Neuschwanstein, Schloss, Ger. C14 13
Neuse, stm., N.C., U.S. B6 140
Neusiedl am See, Aus. H16 10
Neusiedler See, l., Eur. H16 10
Neustadt, Ont., Can. C4 103
Neustadt an der Weinstrasse, Ger. F8 10
Neustrelitz, Ger. B13 10
Neu-Ulm, Ger. G10 10
Neuville-sur-Saône, Fr. G11 14
Neuwied, Ger. E7 10
Neva, stm., Russia B13 22
Nevada, Ia., U.S. B4 122
Nevada, Mo., U.S. D3 132
Nevada, co., Ar., U.S. D2 111
Nevada, co., Ca., U.S. C3 112
Nevada, state, U.S. D5 135
Nevada, Sierra, mts., Spain H8 16
Nevada, Sierra, mts., Ca., U.S. D4 112
Nevel', Russia E12 22
Nevel'sk, Russia H20 28
Nevers, Fr. E10 14
Nevesinje, Bos. F2 20
Nevinnomyssk, Russia I6 26
Nevis, i., St. K./N. F13 94
Nevis, Ben, mtn., Scot., U.K. E9 8
Nevjansk, Russia F10 26
Nevşehir, Tur. B3 48
New, stm., Belize H15 90
New, stm., Guy. F14 84
New, stm., U.S. C3 155
New, stm., Az., U.S. k8 110
New Albany, In., U.S. H6 121
New Albany, Ms., U.S. A4 131
New Amsterdam, Guy. D14 84
Newark, Ar., U.S. B4 111
Newark, Ca., U.S. h8 112
Newark, De., U.S. B3 115
Newark, N.J., U.S. B4 137
Newark, N.Y., U.S. B3 139
Newark, Oh., U.S. B3 142
New Athens, Il., U.S. E4 120
New Augusta, Ms., U.S. D4 131
Newaygo, Mi., U.S. E5 129
Newaygo, co., Mi., U.S. E5 129
New Baden, Il., U.S. E4 120
New Baltimore, Mi., U.S. F8 129
New Bedford, Ma., U.S. C6 128
Newberg, Or., U.S. B4 144
New Berlin, Wi., U.S. n11 156
New Bern, N.C., U.S. B5 140
Newbern, Tn., U.S. A2 149
Newberry, Fl., U.S. C4 116
Newberry, Mi., U.S. B5 129
Newberry, S.C., U.S. C4 147
Newberry, co., S.C., U.S. C4 147
New Bight, Bah. B7 94
New Boston, Mi., U.S. p15 129
New Boston, N.H., U.S. E3 136
New Boston, Oh., U.S. D3 142
New Boston, Tx., U.S. C5 150
New Braunfels, Tx., U.S. E3 150
New Bremen, Oh., U.S. B1 142
New Brighton, Mn., U.S. m12 130
New Brighton, Pa., U.S. E1 145
New Britain, Ct., U.S. C4 114
New Britain, i., Pap. N. Gui. m17 68a
New Brockton, Al., U.S. D4 108
New Brunswick, N.J., U.S. C4 137
New Brunswick, prov., Can. C3 101
New Buffalo, Mi., U.S. G4 129
Newburg, Mo., U.S. D6 132
Newburgh, Ont., Can. C8 103
Newburgh, In., U.S. I3 121
Newburgh, N.Y., U.S. D6 139
Newburgh Heights, Oh., U.S. h9 142
Newbury, Eng., U.K. J12 8
Newbury, Vt., U.S. C4 152
Newburyport, Ma., U.S. A6 128
New Caledonia, dep., Oc. H24 2
New Canaan, Ct., U.S. E2 114
New Carlisle, In., U.S. A4 121
New Carlisle, Oh., U.S. C1 142
New Carrollton, Md., U.S. C4 127
Newcastle, Austl. I9 70
Newcastle, N.B., Can. C4 101
Newcastle, Ont., Can. D6 103
Newcastle, S. Afr. F9 66
New Castle, Al., U.S. B3 108
New Castle, Co., U.S. B3 113
New Castle, De., U.S. B3 115
New Castle, In., U.S. E7 121
New Castle, Ky., U.S. B4 124
Newcastle, Me., U.S. D3 126
New Castle, N.H., U.S. D5 136
Newcastle, Ok., U.S. B4 143
New Castle, Pa., U.S. D1 145
Newcastle, Wy., U.S. C8 157
New Castle, co., De., U.S. B3 115
Newcastle-under-Lyme, Eng., U.K. H11 8
Newcastle upon Tyne, Eng., U.K. G12 8
New City, N.Y., U.S. D6 139
Newcomerstown, Oh., U.S. B4 142
New Concord, Oh., U.S. C4 142
New Cumberland, Pa., U.S. F8 145
New Cumberland, W.V., U.S. A4 155
Newdale, Man., Can. D1 100
Newdale, Id., U.S. F7 119
Newdegate, Austl. F3 68
New Delhi, India F7 44
New Denver, B.C., Can. D9 99
New Durham, N.H., U.S. D4 136
Newell, Ia., U.S. B2 122
Newell, S.D., U.S. C2 148
Newell, W.V., U.S. A4 155
New Ellenton, S.C., U.S. E4 147
Newellton, La., U.S. B4 125
New England, N.D., U.S. C3 141
New England Range, mts., Austl. H9 70
Newenham, Cape, c., Ak., U.S. D7 109
New Fairfield, Ct., U.S. D2 114
Newfane, N.Y., U.S. B2 139
Newfields, N.H., U.S. D5 136
New Florence, Mo., U.S. C6 132
Newfound Gap, U.S. f9 140
Newfound Lake, l., N.H., U.S. C3 136
Newfoundland, prov., Can. D4 102
New Franklin, Mo., U.S. B5 132
New Freedom, Pa., U.S. G8 145
New Georgia, i., Sol.Is. A11 68
New Germany, N.S., Can. E5 101
New Glarus, Wi., U.S. F4 156
New Glasgow, N.S., Can. D7 101
New Gloucester, Me., U.S. E2 126
New Goshen, In., U.S. E3 121
New Guinea, i. m15 68a
Newhall, Ia., U.S. C6 122
New Hampshire, state, U.S. C3 136
New Hampton, Ia., U.S. A5 122
New Hampton, N.H., U.S. C3 136
New Hanover, co., N.C., U.S. C5 140
New Hanover, i., Pap. N. Gui. k17 68a
New Harbor, Me., U.S. E3 126
New Harbour, Newf., Can. E5 102
New Harmony, In., U.S. H2 121
New Hartford, Ct., U.S. B4 114
New Hartford, Ia., U.S. B5 122
New Haven, Ct., U.S. D4 114
New Haven, In., U.S. B7 121
New Haven, Ky., U.S. C4 124
New Haven, Mi., U.S. F8 129
New Haven, Mo., U.S. C6 132
New Haven, W.V., U.S. C3 155
New Haven, co., Ct., U.S. D4 114
New Hazelton, B.C., Can. B4 99
New Hebrides see Vanuatu, ctry., Oc. H24 2
New Holland, Ga., U.S. B3 117
New Holland, Pa., U.S. F9 145
New Holstein, Wi., U.S. E5 156
New Hope, Al., U.S. A3 108
New Hope, Ky., U.S. C4 124
New Hope, Mn., U.S. m12 130
New Hope, Tn., U.S. D8 149
New Iberia, La., U.S. D4 125
Newington, Ct., U.S. C5 114
New Ipswich, N.H., U.S. E3 136
New Ireland, i., Pap. N. Gui. k17 68a
New Jersey, state, U.S. C4 137
New Johnsonville, Tn., U.S. A4 149
New Kensington, Pa., U.S. E2 145
New Kent, co., Va., U.S. C5 153
Newkirk, Ok., U.S. A4 143
New Kowloon, H.K. M3 34
New Laguna, N.M., U.S. B2 138
New Leipzig, N.D., U.S. C4 141
New Lenox, Il., U.S. B6 120
New Lexington, Oh., U.S. C3 142
New Lisbon, Wi., U.S. E3 156
New Liskeard, Ont., Can. p20 103
Newllano, La., U.S. C2 125
New London, Ct., U.S. D7 114
New London, Ia., U.S. D6 122
New London, Mn., U.S. E4 130
New London, Mo., U.S. B6 132
New London, N.H., U.S. D3 136
New London, Oh., U.S. A3 142
New London, Wi., U.S. D5 156
New London, co., Ct., U.S. C7 114
New Madrid, Mo., U.S. E8 132
New Madrid, co., Mo., U.S. E8 132
Newman, Austl. D3 68
Newman, Il., U.S. D6 120
New Manchester, W.V., U.S. e8 155
Newman Grove, Ne., U.S. C8 134
Newmarket, Ont., Can. C5 103
New Market, Al., U.S. A3 108
New Market, In., U.S. E4 121
Newmarket, N.H., U.S. D5 136
New Market, Tn., U.S. C10 149
New Market, Va., U.S. B4 153
New Martinsville, W.V., U.S. B4 155
New Meadows, Id., U.S. D2 119
New Mexico, state, U.S. C3 138
New Miami, Oh., U.S. C1 142
New Milford, Ct., U.S. C2 114
New Milford, N.J., U.S. h8 137
Newnan, Ga., U.S. C2 117
New Norfolk, Austl. N7 70
New Norway, Alta., Can. C4 98
New Orleans, La., U.S. E5 125
New Palestine, In., U.S. E6 121
New Paltz, N.Y., U.S. D6 139
New Paris, In., U.S. B6 121
New Philadelphia, Oh., U.S. B4 142
New Plymouth, N.Z. C5 72
New Plymouth, Id., U.S. F2 119
New Point Comfort, c., Va., U.S. C6 153
Newport, Wales, U.K. I9 8
Newport, Ar., U.S. B4 111
Newport, De., U.S. B3 115
Newport, In., U.S. E3 121
Newport, Ky., U.S. A5 124
Newport, Me., U.S. D3 126
Newport, Mn., U.S. n13 130
Newport, N.H., U.S. D2 136
Newport, N.C., U.S. C6 140
Newport, Or., U.S. C2 144
Newport, R.I., U.S. F5 146
Newport, Tn., U.S. D10 149
Newport, Vt., U.S. B4 152
Newport, Wa., U.S. A8 154
Newport, co., R.I., U.S. E5 146
Newport Beach, Ca., U.S. n13 112
Newport News, Va., U.S. D6 153
New Port Richey, Fl., U.S. D4 116
Newport Station, N.S., Can. E5 101
New Prague, Mn., U.S. F5 130
New Preston, Ct., U.S. C2 114
New Providence, N.J., U.S. B4 137
New Providence, i., Bah. B6 94
New Richland, Mn., U.S. G5 130
New Richmond, Que., Can. A4 101
New Richmond, Oh., U.S. D1 142
New Richmond, Wi., U.S. C1 156
New Roads, La., U.S. D4 125
New Rochelle, N.Y., U.S. E7 139
New Rockford, N.D., U.S. B6 141
New Ross, N.S., Can. E5 101
New Ross, Ire. I7 8
New Salem, N.D., U.S. C4 141
New Salisbury, In., U.S. H5 121
New Sarepta, Alta., Can. C4 98
New Sarpy, La., U.S. k11 125
New Schwabenland, reg., Ant. C2 73
New Sharon, Ia., U.S. C5 122
New Sharon, Me., U.S. D2 126
New Siberian Islands see Novosibirskije ostrova, is., Russia B20 28
New Site, Al., U.S. B4 108
New Smyrna Beach, Fl., U.S. C6 116
New South Wales, state, Austl. F9 68
New Tazewell, Tn., U.S. C10 149
Newton, Al., U.S. D4 108
Newton, Ga., U.S. E2 117
Newton, Il., U.S. E5 120
Newton, Ia., U.S. C4 122
Newton, Ks., U.S. D6 123
Newton, Ma., U.S. B5 128
Newton, Ms., U.S. C4 131
Newton, N.H., U.S. E4 136
Newton, N.J., U.S. A3 137
Newton, N.C., U.S. B1 140
Newton, Ut., U.S. B4 151
Newton, co., Ar., U.S. B2 111
Newton, co., Ga., U.S. C3 117
Newton, co., In., U.S. B3 121
Newton, co., Ms., U.S. C4 131
Newton, co., Mo., U.S. E3 132
Newton, co., Tx., U.S. D6 150
Newton Abbot, Eng., U.K. K10 8
Newton Falls, Oh., U.S. A5 142
Newton Junction, N.H., U.S. E4 136
Newton Stewart, Scot., U.K. G9 8
Newtown, Newf., Can. D5 102
Newtown, Ct., U.S. D2 114
New Town, N.D., U.S. B3 141
Newtownabbey, N. Ire., U.K. G8 8
Newtown Square, Pa., U.S. p20 145
New Ulm, Mn., U.S. F4 130
New Underwood, S.D., U.S. C3 148
Newville, Al., U.S. D4 108
New Washington, In., U.S. G6 121
New Waterford, N.S., Can. C9 101
New Westminster, B.C., Can. E6 99
New Whiteland, In., U.S. E5 121
New Wilmington, Pa., U.S. D1 145
New Windsor, N.Y., U.S. D6 139
New World Island, i., Newf., Can. D4 102
New York, N.Y., U.S. E7 139
New York, co., N.Y., U.S. k13 139
New York, state, U.S. C6 139
New York Mills, Mn., U.S. D3 130
New Zealand, ctry., Oc. D4 72
Neyrīz, Iran G13 48
Neyshābūr, Iran C15 48
Nezahualcóyotl, Mex. H10 90
Nezahualcóyotl, Presa, res., Mex. I13 90
Nez Perce, co., Id., U.S. C2 119
Ngaoundéré, Cam. G9 54
Nguigmi, Niger F9 54
Nguiroungou, Cen. Afr. Rep. N2 60
Nguru, Nig. F9 54
Nhamundá, Braz. I14 84
Nhandeara, Braz. F3 79
Nha Trang, Viet. H10 40
Nhill, Austl. K4 70
Niafounké, Mali D7 64
Niagara, Wi., U.S. C6 156
Niagara, co., N.Y., U.S. B2 139
Niagara Falls, Ont., Can. D5 103
Niagara Falls, N.Y., U.S. B1 139
Niagara-on-the-Lake, Ont., Can. D5 103
Niamey, Niger E11 64
Niangoloko, Burkina F7 64
Niantic, Ct., U.S. D7 114
Niaro, Sud. L6 60
Nias, Pulau, i., Indon. N4 40
Nibley, Ut., U.S. B4 151
Nicaragua, ctry., N.A. E5 92
Nicaragua, Lago de, l., Nic. F9 92
Nicastro, Italy K11 18
Nice, Fr. I14 14
Niceville, Fl., U.S. u15 116
Nicholas, co., Ky., U.S. B6 124
Nicholas, co., W.V., U.S. C4 155
Nicholas Channel, strt., N.A. C4 94
Nicholasville, Ky., U.S. C5 124
Nicholls, Ga., U.S. E4 117
Nicholl's Town, Bah. B5 94
Nichols Hills, Ok., U.S. B4 143
Nicholson, Ms., U.S. E4 131
Nicholson, stm., Austl. A2 70
Nickajack Lake, res., Tn., U.S. D8 149
Nickel Centre, Ont., Can. p19 103
Nickerie, dept., Sur. E14 84
Nickerson, Ks., U.S. D5 123
Nicobar Islands, is., India J2 40
Nicolet, Que., Can. C5 104
Nicolet, stm., Que., Can. C5 104
Nicollet, Mn., U.S. F4 130
Nicollet, co., Mn., U.S. F4 130
Nicoma Park, Ok., U.S. B4 143
Nicosia, Cyp.-N. Cyp. D2 48
Nicosia, Italy L9 18
Nicoya, C.R. G9 92
Nicoya, Golfo de, b., C.R. H10 92
Nicoya, Península de, pen., C.R. H9 92
Niederbronn-les-Bains, Fr. D14 14
Niederösterreich, state, Aus. G15 10
Niedersachsen, state, Ger. C8 10
Niéna, Mali F6 64
Nienburg, Ger. C9 10
Nieuwegein, Neth. D7 12
Nieuw Nickerie, Sur. E14 84
Nieuwpoort (Nieuport), Bel. F2 12
Nigadoo, N.B., Can. B4 101
Niğde, Tur. C3 48
Niger, ctry., Afr. E8 54
Niger, stm., Afr. G8 54
Nigeria, ctry., Afr. F8 54
Nigrita, Grc. I7 20
Niigata, Japan J14 36
Niihama, Japan N8 36
Niihau, i., Hi., U.S. B1 118
Nijmegen, Neth. E8 12
Nijverdal, Neth. D9 12
Nikel', Russia G22 6
Nikishka, Ak., U.S. g16 109
Nikolajevsk-na-Amure, Russia G20 28
Nikol'sk, Russia F7 26
Nikol'sk, Russia G7 26
Nikopol', Ukr. H4 26
Nikšić, Yugo. G2 20
Nile (Nahr an-Nīl), stm., Afr. C7 56
Niles, Il., U.S. h9 120
Niles, Mi., U.S. G4 129
Niles, Oh., U.S. A5 142
Nīmach, India H6 44
Nimba, Mont, mtn., Afr. G5 54
Nimba Range, mts., Afr. G5 54
Nîmes, Fr. I11 14
Nimrod Lake, res., Ar., U.S. C2 111
Nindigully, Austl. G8 70
Ninette, Man., Can. E2 100
Ninety Mile Beach, Austl. L7 70
Ninety Six, S.C., U.S. C3 147
Ninga, Man., Can. E2 100
Ningari, Mali D8 64
Ningbo, China F10 34
Ningcheng (Tianyi), China B7 32
Ningdu, China I4 34
Ninghai, China F10 34
Ningming, China C9 40
Ningsia see Yinchuan, China D8 30
Ningwu, China D9 30
Ningxiang, China G1 34
Ninilchik, Ak., U.S. C9 109
Ninnescah, stm., Ks., U.S. E6 123
Nioaque, Braz. I14 82
Niobrara, Ne., U.S. B7 134
Niobrara, co., Wy., U.S. C8 157
Niobrara, stm., U.S. B7 134
Nioki, Zaire B3 58
Niono, Mali D6 64
Nioro du Sahel, Mali D5 64
Niort, Fr. F6 14
Niota, Tn., U.S. D9 149
Nipawin, Sask., Can. D4 105
Nipigon, Lake, l., Ont., Can. o17 103
Nipissing, Lake, l., Ont., Can. A5 103
Nipomo, Ca., U.S. E3 112
Niquelândia, Braz. C4 79
Niquero, Cuba D6 94
Niš, Yugo. F5 20
Nisa (Neisse) (Nysa Łużycka), stm., Eur. E15 10
Nishio, Japan M12 36
Niskayuna, N.Y., U.S. C7 139
Nisqually, stm., Wa., U.S. C3 154
Nisswa, Mn., U.S. D4 130
Nistru (Dnister), stm., Eur. H3 26
Niterói, Braz. G7 79
Nitra, Slvk. G18 10
Nitro, W.V., U.S. C3 155
Niubu, China D6 34
Niue, dep., Oc. H1 2
Niuzhuang, China C10 32
Nivelles (Nijvel), Bel. G5 12
Niverville, Man., Can. E3 100
Niwot, Co., U.S. A5 113
Nixa, Mo., U.S. D4 132
Nixon, Nv., U.S. D2 135
Nizāmābād, India C5 46
Nizhyn, Ukr. G4 26
Nizip, Tur. C4 48
Nízke Tatry, mts., Slvk. G19 10
Nižn'aja Pojma, Russia F11 28
Nižn'aja Tura, Russia F9 26
Nižneudinsk, Russia G11 28
Nižnevartovsk, Russia E13 26
Nižnij Novgorod (Gor'kij), Russia E27 22
Nižnij Tagil, Russia F9 26
Nizwá, Oman C10 47
Njazidja (Grande Comore), i., Com. k15 67a
Nkhata Bay, Mwi. D6 58
Nkhotakota, Mwi. D6 58
Nkongsamba, Cam. H8 54
Nkurenkuru, Nmb. A4 66
Noank, Ct., U.S. D8 114
Noatak, Ak., U.S. B7 109
Nobeoka, Japan O6 36
Noble, Ok., U.S. B4 143
Noble, co., In., U.S. B7 121
Noble, co., Oh., U.S. C4 142
Noble, co., Ok., U.S. A4 143
Nobleford, Alta., Can. E4 98
Nobles, co., Mn., U.S. G3 130
Noblesville, In., U.S. D6 121
Noboribetsu, Japan e16 36a
Nobres, Braz. F13 82
Nocera [Inferiore], Italy I9 18
Nockatunga, Austl. F5 70
Nodaway, co., Mo., U.S. A3 132
Nodaway, stm., U.S. A2 132
Noel, Mo., U.S. E3 132
Noelville, Ont., Can. A4 103
Noetinger, Arg. G7 80
Nogales, Mex. B4 90
Nogales, Az., U.S. F5 110
Nōgata, Japan N5 36
Nogent-le-Rotrou, Fr. D7 14
Noginsk, Russia F21 22
Nogoyá, Arg. G9 80
Nokaneng, Bots. B6 66
Nokomis, Sask., Can. F3 105
Nokomis, Fl., U.S. E4 116
Nokomis, Il., U.S. D4 120
Nola, Italy I9 18
Nolan, W.V., U.S. D2 155
Nolan, co., Tx., U.S. C2 150
Nolichucky, stm., Tn., U.S. C10 149
Nolin Lake, res., Ky., U.S. C3 124
Nolinsk, Russia F7 26
Nomans Land, i., Ma., U.S. D6 128
Nombre de Dios, Mex. F7 90
Nome, Ak., U.S. C6 109
Nondweni, S. Afr. G10 66
Nong'an, China C12 30
Nong Khai, Thai. F7 40
Nongoma, S. Afr. F10 66
Nonoai, Braz. D12 80
Nonoava, Mex. D6 90
Nonogasta, Arg. E5 80
Nonsan, S. Kor. G15 32
Nonthaburi, Thai. H6 40
Nontron, Fr. G7 14
Nooksack, Wa., U.S. A3 154
Noonan, N.D., U.S. A2 141
Noord-Brabant, prov., Neth. E6 12
Noord-Holland, prov., Neth. C6 12
Noordoewer, Nmb. G3 66
Noordwijk aan Zee, Neth. D5 12
Noorvik, Ak., U.S. B7 109
No Point, Point, c., Md., U.S. D5 127
Nóqui, Ang. C2 58
Nora Springs, Ia., U.S. A5 122
Norberto de la Riestra, Arg. H9 80
Norborne, Mo., U.S. B4 132
Norco, Ca., U.S. n13 112
Norco, La., U.S. E5 125
Norcross, Ga., U.S. C2 117
Nordaustlandet, i., Sval. B3 24
Norden, Ger. B7 10
Nordenham, Ger. B8 10
Norderstedt, Ger. B10 10
Nordhausen, Ger. D10 10
Nordhorn, Ger. C7 10
Nordkapp, c., Nor. F19 6
Nordland, Wa., U.S. A3 154
Nördlingen, Ger. G10 10
Nord-Ostsee-Kanal, Ger. A9 10
Nordreisa, Nor. G17 6
Nordrhein-Westfalen, state, Ger. D7 10
Norfolk, Ct., U.S. B3 114
Norfolk, Ne., U.S. B8 134
Norfolk, Va., U.S. D6 153
Norfolk, co., Eng., U.K. I15 8
Norfolk, co., Ma., U.S. B5 128
Norfolk Island, dep., Oc. K20 158
Norfork, Ar., U.S. A3 111
Norfork Lake, res., U.S. A3 111
Noril'sk, Russia D9 28
Norland, Fl., U.S. s13 116
Normal, Il., U.S. C5 120
Norman, Ar., U.S. C2 111
Norman, Ok., U.S. B4 143
Norman, co., Mn., U.S. C2 130
Norman, Lake, res., N.C., U.S. B2 140
Normandie, hist. reg., Fr. D6 14
Normandy, Mo., U.S. f13 132
Normandy see Normandie, hist. reg., Fr. D6 14
Norman Park, Ga., U.S. E3 117
Normanton, Austl. A4 70
Norman Wells, N.W. Ter., Can. C7 96
Norphlet, Ar., U.S. D3 111
Norquay, Sask., Can. F4 105
Norridge, Il., U.S. k9 120
Norridgewock, Me., U.S. D3 126
Norris, Tn., U.S. C9 149
Norris Arm, Newf., Can. D4 102
Norris City, Il., U.S. F5 120
Norris Lake, res., Tn., U.S. C10 149
Norris Point, Newf., Can. D3 102
Norristown, Pa., U.S. F11 145
Norrköping, Swe. L15 6
Norrtälje, Swe. L16 6
Norseman, Austl. F4 68
Norte, Canal do, strt., Braz. C8 76
Norte de Santander, state, Col. J8 94
Norte de Santander, dept., Col. C6 84
Nortelândia, Braz. F13 82
North, Cape, c., N.S., Can. B9 101
North Adams, Ma., U.S. A1 128
North Albany, Or., U.S. k11 144
Northam, Austl. F3 68
North America E9 86
North Amherst, Ma., U.S. B2 128
Northampton, Austl. E2 68
Northampton, Eng., U.K. I13 8
Northampton, Ma., U.S. B2 128
Northampton, Pa., U.S. E11 145
Northampton, co., N.C., U.S. A5 140
Northampton, co., Pa., U.S. E11 145
Northampton, co., Va., U.S. C7 153
Northamptonshire, co., Eng., U.K. I13 8
North Andaman, i., India H2 40
North Andover, Ma., U.S. A5 128
North Anson, Me., U.S. D3 126
North Arlington, N.J., U.S. h8 137
North Atlanta, Ga., U.S. h8 117
North Attleboro, Ma., U.S. C5 128
North Augusta, S.C., U.S. D4 147
North Aurora, Il., U.S. k8 120
North Baltimore, Oh., U.S. A2 142
North Battleford, Sask., Can. E1 105
North Bay, Ont., Can. A5 103
North Beach, Md., U.S. C4 127
North Belmont, N.C., U.S. B1 140
North Bend, B.C., Can. E7 99
North Bend, Ne., U.S. C9 134
North Bend, Or., U.S. D2 144
North Bend, Wa., U.S. B4 154
North Bennington, Vt., U.S. F2 152
North Bergen, N.J., U.S. h8 137
North Berwick, Scot., U.K. E11 8
North Berwick, Me., U.S. E2 126
North Billerica, Ma., U.S. A5 128
Northborough, Ma., U.S. B4 128
North Branch, Mn., U.S. E6 130
North Branch, N.H., U.S. D3 136
North Branford, Ct., U.S. D4 114
Northbridge, Ma., U.S. B4 128
North Bridgton, Me., U.S. D2 126
Northbrook, Il., U.S. h9 120
North Brookfield, Ma., U.S. B3 128
North Brother, mtn., Me., U.S. C4 126
North Brunswick, N.J., U.S. C4 137
North Caldwell, N.J., U.S. B4 137
North Canadian, stm., Ok., U.S. A5 143
North Canton, Ga., U.S. B2 117
North Canton, Oh., U.S. B4 142
North Cape, c., P.E.I., Can. B6 101
North Cape, c., N.Z. A4 72
North Cape see Nordkapp, c., Nor. F19 6
North Carolina, state, U.S. B3 140
North Carrollton, Ms., U.S. B4 131
North Cascades National Park, Wa., U.S. A4 154
North Channel, strt., Ont., Can. A2 103
North Channel, strt., U.K. F8 8
North Charleston, S.C., U.S. F8 147
North Chicago, Il., U.S. A6 120
North Clarendon, Vt., U.S. D3 152
North College Hill, Oh., U.S. o12 142
North Conway, N.H., U.S. B4 136
North Corbin, Ky., U.S. D5 124
North Crossett, Ar., U.S. D4 111
North Dakota, state, U.S. B5 141
North Dartmouth, Ma., U.S. C6 128
North Eagle Butte, S.D., U.S. B4 148
North East, Md., U.S. A6 127
North East, Pa., U.S. B2 145
Northeast Cape Fear, stm., N.C., U.S. C5 140
Northeast Harbor, Me., U.S. D4 126
North Easton, Ma., U.S. B5 128
Northeast Providence Channel, strt., Bah. B6 94
Northeim, Ger. D10 10
North English, Ia., U.S. C5 122
North Enid, Ok., U.S. A4 143
Northern Dvina see Severnaja Dvina, stm., Russia E6 26
Northern Ireland, ter., U.K. G7 8
Northern Mariana Islands, dep., Oc. G19 158
Northern Territory, ter., Austl. C6 68
North Falmouth, Ma., U.S. C6 128
Northfield, Mn., U.S. F5 130
Northfield, N.H., U.S. D3 136
Northfield, N.J., U.S. E3 137
Northfield, Oh., U.S. h9 142
Northfield, Vt., U.S. C3 152
Northfield Falls, Vt., U.S. C3 152
North Flinders Range, mts., Austl. H3 70
North Fond du Lac, Wi., U.S. E5 156
Northford, Ct., U.S. D4 114
North Foreland, c., Eng., U.K. J15 8
North Fort Myers, Fl., U.S. F5 116
North Frisian Islands, is., Eur. A8 10
Northglenn, Co., U.S. B6 113
North Grafton, Ma., U.S. B4 128
North Grosvenordale, Ct., U.S. B8 114
North Gulfport, Ms., U.S. E4 131
North Haledon, N.J., U.S. B4 137
North Hampton, N.H., U.S. E5 136
North Hartland, Vt., U.S. D4 152
North Haven, Ct., U.S. D4 114
North Haven, Me., U.S. D4 126
North Haverhill, N.H., U.S. B2 136
North Head, N.B., Can. E3 101
North Hero Island, i., Vt., U.S. B2 152
North Hyde Park, Vt., U.S. B3 152
North Industry, Oh., U.S. B4 142
North Island, i., N.Z. B4 72
North Judson, In., U.S. B4 121
North Kansas City, Mo., U.S. h10 132
North Kingstown, R.I., U.S. E4 146
North Kingsville, Oh., U.S. A5 142
North La Junta, Co., U.S. C7 113
Northlake, Il., U.S. k9 120
North Las Vegas, Nv., U.S. G6 135
North Liberty, In., U.S. A5 121
North Liberty, Ia., U.S. C6 122
North Little Rock, Ar., U.S. C3 111
North Logan, Ut., U.S. B4 151
North Loup, Ne., U.S. C7 134
North Magnetic Pole B9 86
North Manchester, In., U.S. C6 121
North Manitou Island, i., Mi., U.S. C4 129
North Mankato, Mn., U.S. F4 130
North Miami, Fl., U.S. G6 116

Name	Map Ref.	Page

North Miami Beach, Fl., U.S. — s13 116
North Middletown, Ky., U.S. — B5 124
North Monmouth, Me., U.S. — D2 126
North Muskegon, Mi., U.S. — E4 129
North Myrtle Beach, S.C., U.S. — D10 147
North Naples, Fl., U.S. — F5 116
North New Portland, Me., U.S. — D2 126
North New River Canal, Fl., U.S. — F6 116
North Ogden, Ut., U.S. — B4 151
North Olmsted, Oh., U.S. — h9 142
North Ossetia see Severnaja Osetija, state, Russia — I6 26
North Park, Il., U.S. — A4 120
North Pembroke, Ma., U.S. — B6 128
North Plainfield, N.J., U.S. — B5 137
North Plains, Or., U.S. — B4 144
North Platte, Ne., U.S. — C5 134
North Platte, stm., U.S. — C6 106
North Point, c., Mi., U.S. — C7 129
North Pole, Ak., U.S. — C10 109
North Pole — A4 86
Northport, Al., U.S. — B2 108
North Portal, Sask., Can. — H4 105
North Pownal, Vt., U.S. — F2 152
North Prairie, Wi., U.S. — F5 156
North Providence, R.I., U.S. — C4 146
North Raccoon, stm., Ia., U.S. — C3 122
North Reading, Ma., U.S. — f11 128
North Rhine-Westphalia see Nordrhein-Westfalen, state, Ger. — D7 10
North Richland Hills, Tx., U.S. — n9 150
Northridge, Oh., U.S. — C2 142
North Ridgeville, Oh., U.S. — A3 142
North Royalton, Oh., U.S. — h9 142
North Rustico, P.E.I., Can. — C6 101
North Salem, N.H., U.S. — E4 136
North Salt Lake, Ut., U.S. — C4 151
North Sanbornton, N.H., U.S. — C3 136
North Saskatchewan, stm., Can. — F10 96
North Schell Peak, mtn., Nv., U.S. — D7 135
North Scituate, Ma., U.S. — h12 128
North Scituate, R.I., U.S. — C3 146
North Sea, Eur. — D8 4
North Shoshone Peak, mtn., Nv., U.S. — D4 135
North Sioux City, S.D., U.S. — E9 148
North Springfield, Vt., U.S. — E3 152
North Star, De., U.S. — A3 115
North St. Paul, Mn., U.S. — m13 130
North Stradbroke Island, i., Austl. — F10 70
North Stratford, N.H., U.S. — A3 136
North Sudbury, Ma., U.S. — g10 128
North Sutton, N.H., U.S. — D3 136
North Swanzey, N.H., U.S. — E2 136
North Sydney, N.S., Can. — C9 101
North Syracuse, N.Y., U.S. — B4 139
North Tarrytown, N.Y., U.S. — D7 139
North Terre Haute, In., U.S. — E3 121
North Thompson, stm., B.C., Can. — D8 99
North Tonawanda, N.Y., U.S. — B2 139
North Troy, Vt., U.S. — B4 152
North Tunica, Ms., U.S. — A3 131
North Turner Mountain, mtn., Me., U.S. — C4 126
North Uist, i., Scot., U.K. — D6 8
Northumberland, co., Eng., U.K. — F11 8
Northumberland, co., Pa., U.S. — D8 145
Northumberland, co., Va., U.S. — C6 153
Northumberland Isles, is., Austl. — C9 70
Northumberland Strait, strt., Can. — C6 101
Northvale, N.J., U.S. — g9 137
North Vancouver, B.C., Can. — E6 99
North Vassalboro, Me., U.S. — D3 126
North Vernon, In., U.S. — F6 121
Northville, Mi., U.S. — p15 129
North Wales, Pa., U.S. — F11 145
North Walpole, N.H., U.S. — D2 136
North Waterford, Me., U.S. — D2 126
North Webster, In., U.S. — B6 121
North West Cape, c., Austl. — D2 68
North Westminster, Vt., U.S. — E4 152
Northwest Providence Channel, strt., Bah. — A5 94
North West River, Newf., Can. — B1 102
Northwest Territories, prov., Can. — C12 96
North Wildwood, N.J., U.S. — E3 137
North Wilkesboro, N.C., U.S. — A1 140
North Windham, Ct., U.S. — C7 114
North Windham, Me., U.S. — E2 126
Northwood, Ia., U.S. — A4 122
Northwood, N.H., U.S. — D4 136
Northwood, N.D., U.S. — B8 141
Northwood Ridge, N.H., U.S. — D4 136
North Woodstock, N.H., U.S. — B3 136
North York, Ont., Can. — D5 103
North Yorkshire, co., Eng., U.K. — G12 8
Norton, N.B., Can. — D4 101
Norton, Ks., U.S. — C4 123
Norton, Ma., U.S. — C5 128
Norton, Oh., U.S. — A4 142
Norton, Va., U.S. — f9 153
Norton, co., Ks., U.S. — C4 123
Norton Shores, Mi., U.S. — E4 129
Norton Sound, strt., Ak., U.S. — C6 109
Nortonville, Ks., U.S. — C8 123

Nortonville, Ky., U.S. — C2 124
Norvegia, Cape, c., Ant. — C2 73
Norwalk, Ca., U.S. — n12 112
Norwalk, Ct., U.S. — E2 114
Norwalk, Il., U.S. — C4 122
Norwalk, Oh., U.S. — A3 142
Norwalk, stm., Ct., U.S. — E2 114
Norway, Me., U.S. — D2 126
Norway, Mi., U.S. — C3 129
Norway (Norge), ctry., Eur. — C10 4
Norway House, Man., Can. — C3 100
Norwegian Sea, Eur. — C1 24
Norwich, Eng., U.K. — I15 8
Norwich, Ct., U.S. — C7 114
Norwich, Ks., U.S. — E6 123
Norwich, N.Y., U.S. — C5 139
Norwich, Vt., U.S. — D4 152
Norwood, Ont., Can. — C7 103
Norwood, Co., U.S. — C2 113
Norwood, Ma., U.S. — B5 128
Norwood, Mn., U.S. — F5 130
Norwood, N.J., U.S. — h9 137
Norwood, N.C., U.S. — B2 140
Norwood, Oh., U.S. — o13 142
Norwood, Pa., U.S. — p20 145
Norwoodville, Ia., U.S. — e8 122
Nosop (Nossob), stm., Afr. — E5 66
Nossob (Nosop), stm., Afr. — E5 66
Nosy Varika, Madag. — r23 67b
Notasulga, Al., U.S. — C4 108
Noto, Italy — M10 18
Notodden, Nor. — L11 6
Noto-hantō, pen., Japan — J11 36
Notre Dame, Monts, mts., Que., Can. — k13 104
Notre Dame Bay, b., Newf., Can. — D4 102
Notre Dame de Lourdes, Man., Can. — E2 100
Notre-Dame-du-Lac, Que., Can. — B9 104
Nottawasaga Bay, b., Ont., Can. — C5 103
Nottaway, stm., Que., Can. — h11 104
Nottingham, Eng., U.K. — I12 8
Nottinghamshire, co., Eng., U.K. — H12 8
Nottoway, co., Va., U.S. — C4 153
Nottoway, stm., Va., U.S. — D5 153
Notus, Id., U.S. — F2 119
Nouâdhibou, Maur. — J2 62
Nouâdhibou, Râs, c., Afr. — J2 62
Nouakchott, Maur. — B2 64
Nouméa, N. Cal. — H24 2
Nouna, Burkina — E8 64
Noupoort, S. Afr. — H7 66
Nova Andradina, Braz. — G2 79
Nova Caipemba, Ang. — C2 58
Nova Era, Braz. — E7 79
Nova Esperança, Braz. — G2 79
Nova Friburgo, Braz. — G7 79
Nova Gradiška, Cro. — D12 18
Nova Granada, Braz. — F4 79
Nova Iguaçu, Braz. — G7 79
Novaja Ladoga, Russia — A15 22
Novaja Sibir', ostrov, i., Russia — B21 28
Novaja Zeml'a, is., Russia — C9 26
Nova Kachovka, Ukr. — H4 26
Nova Lamego, Gui.-B. — E2 64
Nova Lima, Braz. — E7 79
Nova Olinda do Norte, Braz. — I13 84
Nova Ponte, Braz. — E5 79
Nova Prata, Braz. — E13 80
Novara, Italy — D3 18
Nova Scotia, prov., Can. — D6 101
Nova Sofala, Moz. — C12 66
Novato, Ca., U.S. — C2 112
Nova Venécia, Braz. — E8 79
Nova Zagora, Bul. — G10 20
Novelda, Spain — G11 16
Nové Zámky, Slvk. — H18 10
Novgorod, Russia — C14 22
Novi, Mi., U.S. — p15 129
Novi Bečej, Yugo. — D4 20
Novi Ligure, Italy — E3 18
Novinger, Mo., U.S. — A5 132
Novi Pazar, Bul. — F11 20
Novi Pazar, Yugo. — F4 20
Novi Sad, Yugo. — D3 20
Novoaltajsk, Russia — G8 28
Novoanninskij, Russia — G6 26
Novo Aripuanã, Braz. — J12 84
Novočerkassk, Russia — H6 26
Novo Cruzeiro, Braz. — D8 79
Novodugino, Russia — F17 22
Novodvinsk, Russia — E6 26
Novogrudok, Bela. — H8 22
Novo Hamburgo, Braz. — E13 80
Novo Horizonte, Braz. — F4 79
Novohrad-Volyns'kyy, Ukr. — G3 26
Novojel'n'a, Bela. — H8 22
Novokazalinsk, Kaz. — H10 26
Novokuybyševsk, Russia — G7 26
Novokuzneck, Russia — G9 28
Novo Mesto, Slvn. — D10 18
Novomoskovsk, Russia — G21 22
Novomoskovs'k, Ukr. — H5 26
Novopiscovo, Russia — D24 22
Novopolock, Bela. — F11 22
Novorossijsk, Russia — I5 26
Novoržev, Russia — D12 22
Novošachtinsk, Russia — H5 26
Novoselytsya, Ukr. — A10 20
Novosibirsk, Russia — F8 28
Novosibirskije ostrova, is., Russia — B20 28
Novosibirskoje vodochranilišče, res., Russia — G14 26
Novosil', Russia — I20 22
Novosokol'niki, Russia — E13 22
Novotroick, Russia — G9 26
Novouzensk, Russia — G7 26
Novov'ianskoj, Russia — E25 22
Novovolyns'k, Ukr. — G2 26
Novozavidovskij, Russia — E19 22
Novozybkov, Russia — I14 22
Nový Bohumín, Czech Rep. — F18 10
Nový Jičín, Czech Rep. — F18 10
Novyj Nekouz, Russia — D21 22
Nowa Ruda, Pol. — E16 10
Nowa Sól (Neusalz), Pol. — D15 10
Nowata, Ok., U.S. — A6 143

Nowata, co., Ok., U.S. — A6 143
Nowood, stm., Wy., U.S. — B5 157
Nowra, Austl. — J9 70
Nowshāk, mtn., Asia — B4 44
Nowshera, Pak. — C4 44
Nowy Dwór Mazowiecki, Pol. — C20 10
Nowy Sącz, Pol. — F20 10
Nowy Targ, Pol. — F20 10
Noxon, Mt., U.S. — C1 133
Noxon Reservoir, res., Mt., U.S. — C1 133
Noxubee, co., Ms., U.S. — B5 131
Noxubee, stm., U.S. — B5 131
Noyon, Fr. — C10 14
Nsanje, Mwi. — E7 58
Nsawam, Ghana — I9 64
Nsukka, Nig. — H13 64
Ntakat, Maur. — C4 64
Nubian Desert, des., Sud. — G8 60
Nuckolls, co., Ne., U.S. — D7 134
Nucla, Co., U.S. — C2 113
Nueces, co., Tx., U.S. — F4 150
Nueces, stm., Tx., U.S. — E3 150
Nueltin Lake, l., Can. — D13 96
Nueva, Isla, i., Chile — H3 78
Nueva Asunción, dept., Para. — I11 82
Nueva Ciudad Guerrero, Mex. — D10 90
Nueva Esparta, state, Ven. — B10 84
Nueva Gerona, Cuba — D3 94
Nueva Helvecia, Ur. — H10 80
Nueva Imperial, Chile — J2 80
Nueva Italia de Ruiz, Mex. — H8 90
Nueva Ocotepeque, Hond. — C5 92
Nueva Palmira, Ur. — G9 80
Nueva Rosita, Mex. — D9 90
Nueva San Salvador, El Sal. — D5 92
Nueva Segovia, dept., Nic. — D8 92
Nueve de Julio, Arg. — H8 80
Nuevitas, Cuba — D6 94
Nuevo Berlín, Ur. — G9 80
Nuevo Casas Grandes, Mex. — B6 90
Nuevo Laredo, Mex. — D10 90
Nuevo León, state, Mex. — D9 90
Nuevo Progreso, Mex. — H13 90
Nuits-Saint-Georges, Fr. — E11 14
Nukus, Uzb. — I9 26
Nulato, Ak., U.S. — C8 109
Nullagine, Austl. — D4 68
Nullarbor Plain, pl., Austl. — F5 68
Numazu, Japan — L13 36
Nunivak Island, i., Ak., U.S. — D6 109
Nunjiang, China — B12 30
Nunn, Co., U.S. — A6 113
Nuoro, Italy — I4 18
Nuquí, Col. — E4 84
N'urba, Russia — E15 28
Nürburgring, Ger. — H10 12
Nurek, Taj. — A3 44
Nuremberg see Nürnberg, Ger. — F11 10
Nürnberg (Nuremberg), Ger. — F11 10
Nürtingen, Ger. — G9 10
Nusaybin, Tur. — C6 48
Nushki, Pak. — F2 44
Nutley, N.J., U.S. — B4 137
Nutter Fort, W.V., U.S. — k10 155
Nutting Lake, Ma., U.S. — f10 128
Nxaunxau, Bots. — B5 66
Nyabing, Austl. — F3 68
Nyack, N.Y., U.S. — D7 139
Nyala, Sud. — K3 60
Nyamina, Mali — E6 64
Nyanza, Rw. — B5 58
Nyasa, Lake (Lake Malawi), l., Afr. — D6 58
Nyaunglebin, Mya. — F4 40
Nye, co., Nv., U.S. — E5 135
Nyiel, Sud. — N6 60
Nyírbátor, Hung. — H22 10
Nyíregyháza, Hung. — H21 10
Nykøbing, Den. — N12 6
Nykøbing, Den. — M11 6
Nyköping, Swe. — L15 6
Nylstroom, S. Afr. — E9 66
Nymburk, Czech Rep. — E15 10
Nynäshamn, Swe. — L15 6
Nyngan, Austl. — H7 70
Nyon, Switz. — F5 13
Nysa, Pol. — E17 10
Nyssa, Or., U.S. — D9 144
Nytva, Russia — F9 26
Nzébéla, Gui. — G5 64
Nzérékoré, Gui. — H5 64
N'zeto, Ang. — C2 58
Nzi, stm., C. Iv. — H7 64
Nzwani (Anjouan), i., Com. — I16 67a

O

Oacoma, S.D., U.S. — D6 148
Oahe, Lake, res., U.S. — B6 106
Oahu, i., Hi., U.S. — B4 118
Oak Bay, B.C., Can. — h12 99
Oak Bay, N.B., Can. — D2 101
Oakburn, Man., Can. — D1 100
Oak City, Ut., U.S. — D3 151
Oak Creek, Co., U.S. — A4 113
Oak Creek, Wi., U.S. — n12 156
Oakdale, Ca., U.S. — D3 112
Oakdale, Ct., U.S. — D7 114
Oakdale, Ga., U.S. — h8 117
Oakdale, La., U.S. — D3 125
Oakdale, Ne., U.S. — B8 134
Oakdale, Pa., U.S. — k13 145
Oakes, N.D., U.S. — C7 141
Oakey, Austl. — F9 70
Oakfield, Me., U.S. — B4 126
Oakfield, Wi., U.S. — E5 156
Oak Forest, Il., U.S. — k9 120
Oak Grove, Ky., U.S. — D2 124
Oak Grove, La., U.S. — B4 125
Oak Grove, Or., U.S. — B4 144
Oak Grove Heights, Ar., U.S. — A5 111
Oak Harbor, Oh., U.S. — A2 142
Oak Harbor, Wa., U.S. — A3 154
Oak Hill, Tn., U.S. — A5 149
Oak Hill, W.V., U.S. — D3 155

Oakhurst, Ok., U.S. — A5 143
Oak Lake, Man., Can. — E1 100
Oakland, Ca., U.S. — D2 112
Oakland, Il., U.S. — D5 120
Oakland, Ia., U.S. — C2 122
Oakland, Me., U.S. — D3 126
Oakland, Md., U.S. — m12 127
Oakland, Ms., U.S. — A4 131
Oakland, Ne., U.S. — C9 134
Oakland, N.J., U.S. — A4 137
Oakland, Or., U.S. — D3 144
Oakland, R.I., U.S. — B2 146
Oakland, co., Mi., U.S. — F7 129
Oakland City, In., U.S. — H3 121
Oakland Park, Fl., U.S. — r13 116
Oak Lawn, Il., U.S. — B6 120
Oaklawn, Ks., U.S. — g12 123
Oakley, Id., U.S. — G5 119
Oakley, Ks., U.S. — C3 123
Oakley, Ut., U.S. — C4 151
Oakman, Al., U.S. — B2 108
Oakmont, Pa., U.S. — E2 145
Oak Orchard, De., U.S. — F5 115
Oak Park, Il., U.S. — B6 120
Oak Park, Mi., U.S. — p15 129
Oak Point, Man., Can. — D3 100
Oakridge, Or., U.S. — D4 144
Oak Ridge, Tn., U.S. — C9 149
Oak River, Man., Can. — D1 100
Oakton, Va., U.S. — g12 153
Oaktown, In., U.S. — G3 121
Oak Valley, N.J., U.S. — D2 137
Oakville, Man., Can. — E2 100
Oakville, Ont., Can. — D5 103
Oakville, Ct., U.S. — C3 114
Oakville, Mo., U.S. — g13 132
Oakwood, Ga., U.S. — B3 117
Oakwood, Il., U.S. — C6 120
Oakwood, Oh., U.S. — A1 142
Oamaru, N.Z. — F3 72
Oaxaca, state, Mex. — I11 90
Oaxaca [de Juárez], Mex. — I11 90
Ob', stm., Russia — D11 26
Oban, Austl. — C3 70
Oban, Scot., U.K. — E8 8
Oberá, Arg. — B11 80
Oberhausen, Ger. — D6 10
Oberlin, Ks., U.S. — C3 123
Oberlin, La., U.S. — D3 125
Oberlin, Oh., U.S. — A3 142
Obernai, Fr. — D14 14
Oberösterreich, state, Aus. — G13 10
Oberursel, Ger. — E8 10
Obetz, Oh., U.S. — C3 142
Obi, Nig. — G14 64
Óbidos, Braz. — D7 76
Obihiro, Japan — e18 36a
Obion, Tn., U.S. — A2 149
Obion, co., Tn., U.S. — A2 149
Obion, stm., Tn., U.S. — A2 149
Oblong, Il., U.S. — D6 120
Oblučje, Russia — H18 28
Obninsk, Russia — F19 22
Obol', Bela. — F12 22
Oboz'orskij, Russia — J27 6
O'Brien, co., Ia., U.S. — A2 122
Obskaja guba, b., Russia — D12 26
Obuasi, Ghana — H9 64
Ocala, Fl., U.S. — C4 116
Ocaña, Col. — C6 84
Occidental, Cordillera, mts., Col. — E4 84
Ocean, co., N.J., U.S. — D4 137
Ocean, W.V., U.S. — D3 155
Oceana, co., Mi., U.S. — E4 129
Oceana, W.V., U.S. — D3 155
Ocean Bluff, Ma., U.S. — B6 128
Ocean City, Fl., U.S. — u15 116
Ocean City, Md., U.S. — D7 127
Ocean City, N.J., U.S. — E3 137
Ocean City, Wa., U.S. — B1 154
Ocean Grove, Ma., U.S. — C5 128
Ocean Grove, N.J., U.S. — C4 137
Ocean Park, Wa., U.S. — C1 154
Oceanport, N.J., U.S. — C4 137
Oceanside, Ca., U.S. — F5 112
Ocean Springs, Ms., U.S. — E5 131
Ocean [Township], N.J., U.S. — C4 137
Ocean View, De., U.S. — F5 115
Ocha, Russia — G20 28
Ochiltree, co., Tx., U.S. — A2 150
Ochlockonee, stm., Fl., U.S. — B2 116
Ocho Rios, Jam. — E6 94
Ochre River, Man., Can. — D1 100
Ocilla, Ga., U.S. — E3 117
Ocmulgee, stm., Ga., U.S. — D3 117
Ocnița, Mol. — A11 20
Ocoee, Fl., U.S. — D5 116
Ocoña, Peru — G5 82
Oconee, co., Ga., U.S. — C3 117
Oconee, co., S.C., U.S. — B1 147
Oconee, stm., Ga., U.S. — C3 117
Oconee, Lake, res., Ga., U.S. — C3 117
Oconomowoc, Wi., U.S. — E5 156
Oconto, Wi., U.S. — D6 156
Oconto, co., Wi., U.S. — D5 156
Oconto, stm., Wi., U.S. — D5 156
Oconto Falls, Wi., U.S. — D5 156
Ocós, Guat. — C2 92
Ocosingo, Mex. — I13 90
Ocotal, Nic. — D8 92
Ocotepeque, dept., Hond. — C5 92
Ocotlán, Mex. — G8 90
Ocotlán de Morelos, Mex. — I11 90
Ocozocoautla [de Espinosa], Mex. — I13 90
Ocracoke Island, i., N.C., U.S. — B7 140
Ocros, Peru — D3 82
Ocú, Pan. — J14 92
Ocumare del Tuy, Ven. — B9 84
Oda, Ghana — I9 64
Ōdate, Japan — G15 36
Odawara, Japan — L14 36
Odda, Nor. — K10 6
Odebolt, Ia., U.S. — B2 122
Odell, Il., U.S. — B5 122
Odendaalsrus, S. Afr. — F8 66
Odense, Den. — N12 6
Odenton, Md., U.S. — B4 127
Odenville, Al., U.S. — B3 108
Oder (Odra), stm., Eur. — C14 10

Odesa (Odessa), Ukr. — H4 26
Odessa, Ont., Can. — C8 103
Odessa, Sask., Can. — G4 105
Odessa, Mo., U.S. — C4 132
Odessa, Tx., U.S. — D1 150
Odessa, Wa., U.S. — B7 154
Odienné, C. Iv. — G6 64
Odin, Il., U.S. — E4 120
Odincovo, Russia — F20 22
Odojev, Russia — H19 22
Odon, In., U.S. — G4 121
Odorheiu Secuiesc, Rom. — C9 20
Oeiras, Braz. — E10 76
Oelde, Ger. — D8 10
Oelwein, Ia., U.S. — B6 122
O'Fallon, Il., U.S. — E4 120
O'Fallon, Mo., U.S. — f12 132
Offa, Nig. — G12 64
Offaly, co., Ire. — H6 8
Offenbach, Ger. — E8 10
Offenburg, Ger. — G7 10
Oficina Pedro de Valdivia, Chile — B4 80
Ogaden, reg., Afr. — G9 56
Ōgaki, Japan — L11 36
Ogallala, Ne., U.S. — C4 134
Ogbomosho, Nig. — G12 64
Ogden, Ia., U.S. — B3 122
Ogden, Ks., U.S. — C7 123
Ogden, Ut., U.S. — B4 151
Ogdensburg, N.Y., U.S. — f9 139
Ogeechee, stm., Ga., U.S. — D5 117
Ogema, Sask., Can. — H3 105
Ogemaw, co., Mi., U.S. — D6 129
Ogilvie Mountains, mts., Yukon, Can. — D5 96
Ogle, co., Il., U.S. — A4 120
Oglesby, Il., U.S. — B4 120
Oglethorpe, Ga., U.S. — D2 117
Oglethorpe, co., Ga., U.S. — C3 117
Oglio, stm., Italy — D5 18
Ogmore, Austl. — D8 70
Ognon, stm., Fr. — E12 14
Ogoki, stm., Ont., Can. — o18 103
Ogooué, stm., Afr. — B1 58
Ogre, Lat. — E7 22
Ogulin, Cro. — D10 18
Ogunquit, Me., U.S. — E2 126
Ogwashi-Uku, Nig. — H13 64
Ohatchee, Al., U.S. — B3 108
Ohio, co., In., U.S. — G7 121
Ohio, co., Ky., U.S. — C3 124
Ohio, co., W.V., U.S. — A4 155
Ohio, state, U.S. — B3 142
Ohio, stm., U.S. — D9 106
Ohioville, Pa., U.S. — E1 145
Ohrid, Mac. — H4 20
Ōi, stm., Japan — L11 36
Oil City, La., U.S. — B2 125
Oil City, Pa., U.S. — D2 145
Oil Creek, stm., Pa., U.S. — C2 145
Oil Springs, Ont., Can. — E2 103
Oilton, Ok., U.S. — A5 143
Oil Trough, Ar., U.S. — B4 111
Oise, stm., Eur. — C9 14
Ōita, Japan — N6 36
Ojai, Ca., U.S. — E4 112
Ojinaga, Mex. — C7 90
Ojocaliente, Mex. — F8 90
Ojo Caliente, N.M., U.S. — A4 138
Ojos del Salado, Nevado, mtn., S.A. — D4 80
Oka, stm., Russia — E26 22
Okahandja, Nmb. — C3 66
Okaloosa, co., Fl., U.S. — u15 116
Okanagan Centre, B.C., Can. — D8 99
Okanagan Lake, l., B.C., Can. — D8 99
Okanagan Landing, B.C., Can. — D8 99
Okanogan, Wa., U.S. — A6 154
Okanogan, co., Wa., U.S. — A5 154
Okāra, Pak. — E5 44
Okaukuejo, Nmb. — B2 66
Okavango (Cubango), stm., Afr. — E3 58
Okavango Delta, Bots. — B6 66
Okawville, Il., U.S. — E4 120
Okaya, Japan — K13 36
Okayama, Japan — M8 36
Okazaki, Japan — M12 36
Okeechobee, Fl., U.S. — E6 116
Okeechobee, co., Fl., U.S. — E6 116
Okeechobee, Lake, l., Fl., U.S. — F6 116
Okeene, Ok., U.S. — A3 143
Okefenokee Swamp, sw., U.S. — F4 117
Okemah, Ok., U.S. — B5 143
Okene, Nig. — H13 64
Okfuskee, co., Ok., U.S. — B5 143
Okhotsk, Sea of, Asia — c19 36a
Okhtyrka, Ukr. — G4 26
Okiep, S. Afr. — G3 66
Okinawa, Japan — u2 37b
Okinawa-jima, i., Japan — u2 37b
Oklahoma, state, U.S. — B4 143
Oklahoma City, Ok., U.S. — B4 143
Oklawaha, stm., Fl., U.S. — C5 116
Oklawaha, Lake, res., Fl., U.S. — F6 116
Okmulgee, Ok., U.S. — B6 143
Okmulgee, co., Ok., U.S. — B5 143
Okoboji, Ia., U.S. — A2 122
Okolona, Ms., U.S. — B5 131
Okotoks, Alta., Can. — D4 98
Okrika, Nig. — I13 64
Okt'abr'skij, Bela. — I11 22
Okt'abr'skij, Russia — G21 22
Okt'abr'skij, Russia — G8 26
Okt'abr'skoj Revol'ucii, ostrov, i., Russia — B17 26
Oktibbeha, co., Ms., U.S. — B5 131
Okulovka, Russia — C16 22
Ola, Ar., U.S. — B2 111
Olalla, Wa., U.S. — f10 154
Olanchito, Hond. — B8 92

Olancho, dept., Hond. — C9 92
Öland, i., Swe. — M15 6
Olathe, Co., U.S. — C3 113
Olathe, Ks., U.S. — D9 123
Olavarría, Arg. — I8 80
Oława, Pol. — E17 10
Olbia, Italy — I4 18
Olca, Volcán, vol., S.A. — I7 82
Old Bahama Channel, strt., N.A. — C5 94
Old Bennington, Vt., U.S. — F2 152
Old Bridge, N.J., U.S. — C4 137
Old Crow, Yukon, Can. — C5 96
Old Crow, stm., N.A. — C4 96
Oldenburg, In., U.S. — F7 121
Oldenzaal, Neth. — D10 12
Old Faithful Geyser, Wy., U.S. — B2 157
Old Forge, Pa., U.S. — D10 145
Oldham, co., Ky., U.S. — B4 124
Oldham, co., Tx., U.S. — B1 150
Old Harbor, Ak., U.S. — D9 109
Old Hickory Lake, res., Tn., U.S. — A5 149
Oldman, stm., Alta., Can. — E4 98
Old Man of the Mountain, N.H., U.S. — B3 136
Old Mystic, Ct., U.S. — D8 114
Old Northwood, N.H., U.S. — D4 136
Old Orchard Beach, Me., U.S. — E2 126
Old Perlican, Newf., Can. — D5 102
Old Point Comfort, c., Va., U.S. — h15 153
Olds, Alta., Can. — D3 98
Old Saybrook, Ct., U.S. — D6 114
Oldsmar, Fl., U.S. — o10 116
Old Speck Mountain, mtn., Me., U.S. — D2 126
Old Tampa Bay, b., Fl., U.S. — p10 116
Old Tate, Bots. — C8 66
Old Town, Me., U.S. — D4 126
Old Wives Lake, l., Sask., Can. — G2 105
Olean, N.Y., U.S. — C2 139
O'Leary, P.E.I., Can. — C5 101
Oleksandriya, Ukr. — H4 26
Olen, Bel. — F6 12
Olenegorsk, Russia — D4 26
Olenino, Russia — E16 22
Olentangy, stm., Oh., U.S. — B3 142
Oleśnica, Pol. — D17 10
Ol'ga, Russia — I19 28
Ölgij, Mong. — B4 30
Olhão, Port. — H4 16
Olifants (Rio dos Elefantes), stm., Afr. — E10 66
Ólimbos, mtn., Cyp. — D2 48
Ólimbos, Óros (Mount Olympus), mtn., Grc. — I6 20
Olímpia, Braz. — F4 79
Olin, Ia., U.S. — B6 122
Olinda, Braz. — E12 76
Oliva, Arg. — G7 80
Oliva, Spain — G11 16
Olive Branch, Ms., U.S. — A4 131
Olive Hill, Ky., U.S. — B6 124
Olivehurst, Ca., U.S. — C3 112
Oliveira, Braz. — F6 79
Oliver, B.C., Can. — E8 99
Oliver, co., N.D., U.S. — B4 141
Oliver Springs, Tn., U.S. — C9 149
Olivet, Mi., U.S. — F6 129
Olivia, Mn., U.S. — F4 130
Olla, La., U.S. — C3 125
Ollagüe, Chile — I7 82
Ollagüe, Volcán, vol., S.A. — I7 82
Olmos, Peru — A2 82
Olmsted, co., Mn., U.S. — G6 130
Olmsted Falls, Oh., U.S. — h9 142
Olney, Il., U.S. — E5 120
Olney, Md., U.S. — B3 127
Olney, Tx., U.S. — C3 150
Olney Springs, Co., U.S. — C7 113
Ol'okminsk, Russia — F16 28
Olomouc, Czech Rep. — F17 10
Olonec, Russia — J7 6
Olongapo, Phil. — n19 39b
Oloron-Sainte-Marie, Fr. — I6 14
Olot, Spain — C14 16
Olov'annaja, Russia — G15 28
Olpe, Ger. — D7 10
Olpe, Ks., U.S. — D7 123
Olsztyn (Allenstein), Pol. — B20 10
Olt, stm., Rom. — F8 20
Olta, Arg. — F5 80
Olten, Switz. — E10 13
Oltenița, Rom. — E10 20
Oltu, Tur. — F8 20
Oluan Pi, c., Tai. — N9 34
Olukonda, Nmb. — B3 66
Olustee, Ok., U.S. — C2 143
Ol'utorskij, mys, c., Russia — F26 28
Olympia, Wa., U.S. — B3 154
Olympic Mountains, mts., Wa., U.S. — B2 154
Olympic National Park, Wa., U.S. — B2 154
Olympus, Mount see Ólimbos, Óros, mtn., Grc. — I6 20
Olympus, Mount, mtn., Wa., U.S. — B2 154
Olyphant, Pa., U.S. — D10 145
Omaha, Ne., U.S. — C10 134
Omak, Wa., U.S. — A6 154
Oman ('Umān), ctry., Asia — E6 42
Oman, Gulf of, b., Asia — B10 47
Omaruru, Nmb. — C2 66
Omatako, stm., Nmb. — B5 66
Ombouè, Gabon — B1 58
Omdurman see Umm Durmān, Sud. — J7 60
Omega, Ga., U.S. — E3 117
Omemee, Ont., Can. — C6 103
Omeo, Austl. — K7 70
Omerville, Que., Can. — D5 104
Ometepe, Isla de, i., Nic. — I9 92
Ometepec, Mex. — I10 90
Om Hajer, Erit. — J9 60
Ōmiya, Japan — L14 36

Name — Map Ref. — Page

Omoa, Bahía de, b., N.A. B6 92
Omro, Wi., U.S. D5 156
Omsk, Russia F6 28
Omsukčan, Russia E23 28
Ōmuta, Japan N5 36
Omutninsk, Russia F8 26
Onaga, Ks., U.S. C7 123
Onalaska, Wa., U.S. C3 154
Onalaska, Wi., U.S. E2 156
Onamia, Mn., U.S. D5 130
Onancock, Va., U.S. C7 153
Onanole, Man., Can. D2 100
Onarga, Il., U.S. C6 120
Onawa, Ia., U.S. B1 122
Oncativo, Arg. F7 80
Onda, Spain F11 16
Ondangwa, Nmb. A3 66
Ondo, Nig. H12 64
Öndörchaan, Mong. B9 30
Oneco, Fl., U.S. E4 116
Onega, Russia E5 26
Onega, Lake see Onežskoje ozero, l., Russia E5 26
One Hundred Fifty Mile House, B.C., Can. C7 99
One Hundred Mile House, B.C., Can. D7 99
Oneida, Ky., U.S. C6 124
Oneida, N.Y., U.S. B5 139
Oneida, Tn., U.S. C9 149
Oneida, co., Id., U.S. G6 119
Oneida, co., N.Y., U.S. B5 139
Oneida, co., Wi., U.S. C4 156
Oneida Lake, l., N.Y., U.S. B5 139
O'Neill, Ne., U.S. B7 134
Oneonta, Al., U.S. B3 108
Oneonta, N.Y., U.S. C5 139
Onești, Rom. C10 20
Onežskaja guba, b., Russia I25 6
Onežskoje ozero, l., Russia E5 26
Ongjin, N. Kor. F13 32
Ongole, India E6 46
Onida, S.D., U.S. C5 148
Onitsha, Nig. H13 64
Onomichi, Japan M8 36
Onondaga, co., N.Y., U.S. C4 139
Onoway, Alta., Can. C3 98
Onslow, Austl. D3 68
Onslow, co., N.C., U.S. C5 140
Onslow Bay, b., N.C., U.S. C5 140
Ontario, Ca., U.S. E5 112
Ontario, Oh., U.S. B3 142
Ontario, Or., U.S. C10 144
Ontario, co., N.Y., U.S. C3 139
Ontario, prov., Can. C6 103
Ontario, Lake, l., N.A. C11 106
Ontinyent (Onteniente), Spain G11 16
Ontonagon, Mi., U.S. m12 129
Ontonagon, co., Mi., U.S. m12 129
Ŏnyang, S. Kor. G15 32
Ookala, Hi., U.S. C6 118
Ooldea, Austl. F6 68
Oolitic, In., U.S. G4 121
Oologah, Ok., U.S. A6 143
Oologah Lake, res., Ok., U.S. A6 143
Ooltewah, Tn., U.S. D8 149
Oostburg, Wi., U.S. E6 156
Oostende (Ostende), Bel. F2 12
Oosterhout, Neth. E6 12
Oosterschelde, b., Neth. E4 12
Oost-Vlaanderen, prov., Bel. G4 12
Ootsa Lake, l., B.C., Can. C4 99
Ootsi, Bots. E7 66
Opal, Wy., U.S. E2 157
Opala, Zaire B4 58
Opa-Locka, Fl., U.S. s13 116
Oparino, Russia F7 26
Opava, Czech Rep. F17 10
Opelika, Al., U.S. C4 108
Opelousas, La., U.S. D3 125
Opobo, Nig. I13 64
Opočka, Russia E11 22
Opoczno, Pol. D20 10
Opole (Oppeln), Pol. E17 10
Oporto see Porto, Port. D3 16
Opp, Al., U.S. D3 108
Oppelo, Ar., U.S. B3 111
Opportunity, Wa., U.S. B8 154
Optima Reservoir, res., Ok., U.S. e9 143
Oquawka, Il., U.S. C3 120
Oracle, Az., U.S. E5 110
Oradea, Rom. B5 20
Oradell, N.J., U.S. h8 137
Orai, India H8 44
Oraibi, Az., U.S. B5 110
Oran see Wahran, Alg. A6 54
Oran, Mo., U.S. D8 132
Orange, Austl. I8 70
Orange, Fr. H11 14
Orange, Ca., U.S. n13 112
Orange, Ct., U.S. D3 114
Orange, Ma., U.S. A3 128
Orange, N.J., U.S. B4 137
Orange, Tx., U.S. D6 150
Orange, Va., U.S. B4 153
Orange, co., Ca., U.S. F5 112
Orange, co., Fl., U.S. D5 116
Orange, co., In., U.S. G4 121
Orange, co., N.Y., U.S. D6 139
Orange, co., N.C., U.S. A3 140
Orange, co., Tx., U.S. D6 150
Orange, co., Vt., U.S. D3 152
Orange, co., Va., U.S. B4 153
Orange (Oranje), stm., Afr. G4 66
Orange, Cabo, c., Braz. C8 76
Orange Beach, Al., U.S. E2 108
Orangeburg, S.C., U.S. E6 147
Orangeburg, co., S.C., U.S. E6 147
Orange City, Fl., U.S. D5 116
Orange City, Ia., U.S. B1 122
Orange Grove, Ms., U.S. E5 131
Orange Park, Fl., U.S. B5 116
Orangeville, Ont., Can. D4 103
Orangeville, Ut., U.S. D4 151
Orange Walk, Belize H15 90
Oranienburg, Ger. C13 10
Oranjemund, Nmb. G3 66
Oranjestad, Aruba H9 94
Orăștie, Rom. D7 20
Orbe, Switz. E6 13
Orbost, Austl. K8 70
Orcas Island, i., Wa., U.S. A3 154
Orchard, Ne., U.S. B7 134
Orchard City, Co., U.S. C3 113
Orchard Homes, Mt., U.S. D2 133
Orchard Park, N.Y., U.S. C2 139
Orchards, Wa., U.S. D3 154
Orchard Valley, Wy., U.S. E8 157
Orchies, Fr. B10 14
Orchon, stm., Mong. B7 30
Ord, Ne., U.S. C7 134
Ord, stm., Austl. C5 68
Ord, Mount, mtn., Austl. C5 68
Ordu, Tur. G15 4
Ordway, Co., U.S. C7 113
Oreana, Nv., U.S. C3 135
Örebro, Swe. L14 6
Orechovo-Zujevo, Russia F21 22
Orechovsk, Bela. G13 22
Oregon, Il., U.S. A4 120
Oregon, Mo., U.S. B2 132
Oregon, Oh., U.S. A2 142
Oregon, Wi., U.S. F4 156
Oregon, co., Mo., U.S. E6 132
Oregon, state, U.S. C6 144
Oregon City, Or., U.S. B4 144
Orel, Russia I19 22
Orem, Ut., U.S. C4 151
Orenburg, Russia G9 26
Orense, Arg. J9 80
Orense, Spain C4 16
Orestiás, Grc. H10 20
Orford, N.H., U.S. C2 136
Orfordville, N.H., U.S. C2 136
Orfordville, Wi., U.S. F4 156
Organ, N.M., U.S. E3 138
Orgtrud, Russia E23 22
Orgūn, Afg. D3 44
Orhei, Mol. B12 20
Oriental, Cordillera, mts., Col. E6 84
Oriente, Arg. J8 80
Orillia, Ont., Can. C5 103
Orinoco, stm., S.A. C11 84
Orinoco, Delta del, Ven. C12 84
Oriola (Orihuela), Spain G11 16
Orion, Il., U.S. B3 120
Orissa, state, India B7 46
Oristano, Italy J3 18
Oriximiná, Braz. D7 76
Orizaba, Mex. H11 90
Orizaba, Pico de (Volcán Citlaltépetl), vol., Mex. H11 90
Orizona, Braz. D4 79
Orkney, S. Afr. F8 66
Orkney Islands, is., Scot., U.K. B10 8
Orland, Ca., U.S. C2 112
Orlândia, Braz. F5 79
Orlando, Fl., U.S. D5 116
Orland Park, Il., U.S. k9 120
Orléans, Fr. E8 14
Orleans, In., U.S. G5 121
Orleans, Ne., U.S. D6 134
Orleans, Vt., U.S. B4 152
Orleans, co., La., U.S. E6 125
Orleans, co., N.Y., U.S. B2 139
Orleans, co., Vt., U.S. B4 152
Orléans, Île d', i., Que., Can. C6 104
Orlová, Czech Rep. F18 10
Ormond Beach, Fl., U.S. C5 116
Ormstown, Que., Can. D3 104
Ornans, Fr. E13 14
Orne, stm., Fr. D6 14
Örnsköldsvik, Swe. J16 6
Orocué, Col. E7 84
Orodara, Burkina F7 64
Orofino, Id., U.S. C2 119
Oromocto, N.B., Can. D3 101
Oron, Nig. I14 64
Orono, Me., U.S. D4 126
Oronoco, Mn., U.S. F6 130
Oronogo, Mo., U.S. D3 132
Orosháza, Hung. I20 10
Oroville, Ca., U.S. C3 112
Oroville, Wa., U.S. A6 154
Oroville, Lake, res., Ca., U.S. C3 112
Orrick, Mo., U.S. B3 132
Orrington, Me., U.S. D4 126
Orrs Island, Me., U.S. E3 126
Orrville, Oh., U.S. B4 142
Orša, Bela. G13 22
Orsières, Switz. F7 13
Orsk, Russia G9 26
Orthez, Fr. I6 14
Orthon, stm., Bol. D8 82
Orting, Wa., U.S. B3 154
Ortiz, Mex. C4 90
Ortona, Italy G9 18
Ortonville, Mi., U.S. F7 129
Ortonville, Mn., U.S. E2 130
Orūmīyeh (Reẓā'īyeh), Iran C8 48
Orūmīyeh, Daryācheh-ye (Lake Urmia), l., Iran C8 48
Oruro, Bol. G8 82
Oruro, dept., Bol. H8 82
Orwigsburg, Pa., U.S. E9 145
Oš, Kyrg. I12 26
Osa, Península de, pen., C.R. I11 92
Osage, Ia., U.S. A5 122
Osage, Wy., U.S. C8 157
Osage, co., Ks., U.S. D8 123
Osage, co., Mo., U.S. C6 132
Osage, co., Ok., U.S. A5 143
Osage, stm., Mo., U.S. C3 132
Osage Beach, Mo., U.S. C5 132
Osage City, Ks., U.S. D8 123
Ōsaka, Japan M10 36
Osakis, Mn., U.S. E3 130
Osan, S. Kor. F15 32
Osawatomie, Ks., U.S. D9 123
Osborne, Ks., U.S. C5 123
Osborne, co., Ks., U.S. C5 123
Osburn, Id., U.S. B3 119
Osceola, Ar., U.S. B6 111
Osceola, In., U.S. A5 121
Osceola, Ia., U.S. C4 122
Osceola, Mo., U.S. C4 132
Osceola, Ne., U.S. C8 134
Osceola, Wi., U.S. C1 156
Osceola, co., Fl., U.S. E5 116
Osceola, co., Ia., U.S. A2 122
Osceola, co., Mi., U.S. E5 129
Oschatz, Ger. D13 10
Oscoda, co., Mi., U.S. D6 129
Osgood, In., U.S. F7 121
Oshawa, Ont., Can. D6 103
Oshkosh, Ne., U.S. C3 134
Oshkosh, Wi., U.S. D5 156
Oshogbo, Nig. H12 64
Oshwe, Zaire B3 58
Osijek, Cro. D2 20
Osinniki, Russia G9 28
Osipoviči, Bela. H11 22
Osire, Nmb. C3 66
Oskaloosa, Ia., U.S. C5 122
Oskaloosa, Ks., U.S. C8 123
Oskarshamn, Swe. M15 6
Osler, Sask., Can. E2 105
Oslo, Nor. L12 6
Osmānābād, India C4 46
Osmaniye, Tur. C4 48
Oš'many, Bela. G8 22
Osmond, Ne., U.S. B8 134
Osnabrück, Ger. C8 10
Osorno, Chile E2 78
Osoyoos, B.C., Can. E8 99
Osoyoos Lake, l., Wa., U.S. A6 154
Osprey, Fl., U.S. E4 116
Ossa, Mount, mtn., Austl. M7 70
Ossabaw Island, i., Ga., U.S. E5 117
Osseo, Mn., U.S. m12 130
Osseo, Wi., U.S. D2 156
Ossian, In., U.S. C7 121
Ossian, Ia., U.S. A6 122
Ossining, N.Y., U.S. D7 139
Ossipee, N.H., U.S. C4 136
Ossipee, stm., U.S. C5 136
Ossora, Russia F24 28
Ostaškov, Russia D16 22
Osterode, Ger. D10 10
Östersund, Swe. J14 6
Osterville, Ma., U.S. C7 128
Ostfriesische Inseln, is., Ger. B7 10
Ostrava, Czech Rep. F18 10
Ostróda, Pol. B19 10
Ostrogožsk, Russia G5 26
Ostrołęka, Pol. B21 10
Ostrov, Czech Rep. E12 10
Ostrov, Russia D11 22
Ostrov, i., Slvk. H17 10
Ostrovskoje, Russia D25 22
Ostrowiec Świętokrzyski, Pol. E21 10
Ostrów Mazowiecka, Pol. C21 10
Ostrów Wielkopolski, Pol. D17 10
Ostuni, Italy I12 18
Osuna, Spain H6 16
Osvaldo Cruz, Braz. F3 79
Oswegatchie, stm., N.Y., U.S. f9 139
Oswego, Il., U.S. B5 120
Oswego, Ks., U.S. E8 123
Oswego, N.Y., U.S. B4 139
Oswego, co., N.Y., U.S. B4 139
Oswego, stm., N.Y., U.S. B4 139
Oświęcim, Pol. E19 10
Otaki, N.Z. D5 72
Otaru, Japan d16 36a
Otava, Fin. K20 6
Otavalo, Ec. G3 84
Otavi, Nmb. B3 66
Oteen, N.C., U.S. f10 140
Otepää, Est. C9 22
Otero, co., Co., U.S. D7 113
Otero, co., N.M., U.S. E3 138
Othello, Wa., U.S. C6 154
Otis, Co., U.S. A8 113
Otis Orchards, Wa., U.S. g14 154
Otis Reservoir, res., Ma., U.S. B1 128
Otjiwarongo, Nmb. C3 66
Otočac, Cro. E10 18
Otoe, co., Ne., U.S. D9 134
Otradnyj, Russia G8 26
Otranto, Italy I13 18
Otranto, Strait of, strt., Eur. I2 20
Otsego, Mi., U.S. F5 129
Otsego, co., Mi., U.S. C6 129
Otsego, co., N.Y., U.S. C5 139
Ōtsu, Japan L10 36
Otta, Nor. K11 6
Ottawa, Ont., Can. B9 103
Ottawa, Il., U.S. B5 120
Ottawa, Ks., U.S. D8 123
Ottawa, Oh., U.S. A1 142
Ottawa, co., Ks., U.S. C6 123
Ottawa, co., Mi., U.S. F4 129
Ottawa, co., Oh., U.S. A2 142
Ottawa, co., Ok., U.S. A7 143
Ottawa, stm., Can. G17 96
Ottawa Hills, Oh., U.S. e6 142
Otterbein, In., U.S. D3 121
Otterburne, Man., Can. E3 100
Otter Creek, Me., U.S. D4 126
Otter Creek, stm., Vt., U.S. C2 152
Otter Tail, co., Mn., U.S. D3 130
Otter Tail, stm., Mn., U.S. D2 130
Otter Tail Lake, l., Mn., U.S. D3 130
Otterville, Ont., Can. E4 103
Ottumwa, Ia., U.S. C5 122
Oturkpo, Nig. H14 64
Otway, Cape, c., Austl. L5 70
Otwell, In., U.S. H3 121
Otwock, Pol. C21 10
Ötztaler Alpen, mts., Eur. C5 18
Ou, stm., Laos D7 40
Ouachita, co., Ar., U.S. D3 111
Ouachita, co., La., U.S. B3 125
Ouachita, Lake, res., Ar., U.S. C2 111
Ouachita Mountains, mts., U.S. E8 106
Ouadâne, Maur. J5 62
Ouagadougou, Burkina E9 64
Ouahigouya, Burkina F6 54
Ouahigouya, Burkina E8 64
Oualâta, Maur. C6 64
Ouallam, Niger D11 64
Ouarzazate, Mor. E7 62
Oubangui (Ubangi), stm., Afr. H8 52
Oudenaarde (Audenarde), Bel. G4 12
Oudtshoorn, S. Afr. I6 66
Oued Tlelat, Alg. J11 16
Oued-Zem, Mor. D7 62
Ouémé, stm., Benin H11 64
Ouenza, Alg. N3 18
Ouessant, Île d' (Ushant), i., Fr. D1 14
Ouesso, Congo A3 58
Ouezzane, Mor. C8 62
Ouidah, Benin H11 64
Oujda, Mor. C10 62
Oulainen, Fin. I19 6
Oulu, Fin. I19 6
Oulujärvi, l., Fin. I20 6
Oulun lääni, prov., Fin. I20 6
Oum El Bouagui, Alg. C14 62
Ouray, Co., U.S. C3 113
Ouray, co., Co., U.S. C3 113
Ourinhos, Braz. G4 79
Ouro Fino, Braz. G5 79
Ouro Preto, Braz. F7 79
Ourthe, stm., Bel. H8 12
Ouse, stm., Eng., U.K. H12 8
Outagamie, co., Wi., U.S. D5 156
Outardes Quatre, Réservoir, res., Que., Can. h13 104
Outer Island, i., Wi., U.S. A3 156
Outjo, Nmb. C3 66
Outlook, Sask., Can. F2 105
Outremont, Que., Can. p19 104
Ouyen, Austl. J5 70
Ovalle, Chile F3 80
Overbrook, Ks., U.S. D8 123
Overgaard, Az., U.S. C5 110
Overijssel, prov., Neth. D9 12
Overland, Mo., U.S. f13 132
Overland Park, Ks., U.S. m16 123
Overlea, Md., U.S. B4 127
Overpelt, Bel. F7 12
Overton, Ne., U.S. D6 134
Overton, Nv., U.S. G7 135
Overton, co., Tn., U.S. C8 149
Övertorneå, Swe. H18 6
Ovett, Ms., U.S. D4 131
Ovid, Co., U.S. A8 113
Ovid, Mi., U.S. E6 129
Oviedo, Spain B6 16
Owando, Congo B3 58
Owasco Lake, l., N.Y., U.S. C4 139
Owasso, Ok., U.S. A6 143
Owatonna, Mn., U.S. F5 130
Owbeh, Afg. D17 48
Owego, N.Y., U.S. C4 139
Owen, co., In., U.S. F4 121
Owen, co., Ky., U.S. B5 124
Owens, stm., Ca., U.S. D4 112
Owensboro, Ky., U.S. C2 124
Owens Cross Roads, Al., U.S. A3 108
Owens Lake, l., Ca., U.S. D5 112
Owen Sound, Ont., Can. C4 103
Owen Sound, b., Ont., Can. C4 103
Owen Stanley Range, mts., Pap. N. Gui. m16 68a
Owensville, In., U.S. H2 121
Owensville, Mo., U.S. C6 132
Owenton, Ky., U.S. B5 124
Owerri, Nig. I13 64
Owings Mills, Md., U.S. B4 127
Owingsville, Ky., U.S. B6 124
Owls Head, Me., U.S. D3 126
Owo, Nig. H12 64
Owosso, Mi., U.S. E6 129
Owsley, co., Ky., U.S. C6 124
Owyhee, Nv., U.S. B5 135
Owyhee, co., Id., U.S. G2 119
Owyhee, stm., U.S. E9 144
Owyhee, Lake, res., Or., U.S. D9 144
Owyhee Mountains, mts., U.S. G2 119
Oxbow, Sask., Can. H4 105
Oxford, N.S., Can. D6 101
Oxford, Eng., U.K. J12 8
Oxford, Al., U.S. B4 108
Oxford, Ar., U.S. A4 111
Oxford, Ct., U.S. D3 114
Oxford, Ga., U.S. C3 117
Oxford, In., U.S. C3 121
Oxford, Ia., U.S. C6 122
Oxford, Ks., U.S. E6 123
Oxford, Me., U.S. D2 126
Oxford, Ma., U.S. B4 128
Oxford, Mi., U.S. F7 129
Oxford, Ms., U.S. A4 131
Oxford, Ne., U.S. D6 134
Oxford, N.C., U.S. A4 140
Oxford, Oh., U.S. C1 142
Oxford, Pa., U.S. G10 145
Oxford, co., Me., U.S. D2 126
Oxfordshire, co., Eng., U.K. J12 8
Oxkutzcab, Mex. G15 90
Oxnard, Ca., U.S. E4 112
Oxon Hill, Md., U.S. f9 127
Oyama, B.C., Can. D8 99
Oyama, Japan K14 36
Oyem, Gabon A2 58
Oyen, Alta., Can. D5 98
Oyo, Nig. H11 64
Oyonnax, Fr. F12 14
Oyster Bay, N.Y., U.S. E7 139
Ozamiz, Phil. D7 38
Ozark, Al., U.S. D4 108
Ozark, Ar., U.S. B2 111
Ozark, Mo., U.S. D4 132
Ozark, co., Mo., U.S. E5 132
Ozark Escarpment, clf, U.S. B4 111
Ozark Plateau, plat., U.S. D8 106
Ozark Reservoir, res., Ar., U.S. B1 111
Ozarks, Lake of the, res., Mo., U.S. C5 132
Ozaukee, co., Wi., U.S. E6 156
Ozawkie, Ks., U.S. k15 123
Ózd, Hung. G20 10
Ožerelje, Russia G21 22
Ozery, Russia G21 22
Ozona, Tx., U.S. D2 150
Ozorków, Pol. D19 10
Ozubulu, Nig. I13 64
Ozuluama, Mex. G11 90

P

Paarl, S. Afr. I4 66
Paauhau, Hi., U.S. C6 118
Paauilo, Hi., U.S. C6 118
Pabianice, Pol. D19 10
Pablo, Mt., U.S. C2 133
Pābna, Bngl. H13 44
Pacaembu, Braz. F3 79
Pacaltsdorp, S. Afr. J6 66
Pacasmayo, Peru B2 82
Pace, Fl., U.S. u14 116
Pachuca [de Soto], Mex. G10 90
Pacific, Mo., U.S. C7 132
Pacific, Wa., U.S. f11 154
Pacific, co., Wa., U.S. C2 154
Pacifica, Ca., U.S. h8 112
Pacific Beach, Wa., U.S. B1 154
Pacific City, Or., U.S. B3 144
Pacific Grove, Ca., U.S. D3 112
Pacific Ocean J24 158
Pacific Palisades, Hi., U.S. g10 118
Pacific Ranges, mts., B.C., Can. D4 99
Pacific Rim National Park, B.C., Can. E5 99
Packwood, Wa., U.S. C4 154
Pacolet, S.C., U.S. B4 147
Pacolet, stm., S.C., U.S. A4 147
Pacora, Pan. C3 84
Padang, Indon. O6 40
Padangpanjang, Indon. O6 40
Padangsidempuan, Indon. N5 40
Paddock Lake, Wi., U.S. n11 156
Paddockwood, Sask., Can. D3 105
Paden City, W.V., U.S. B4 155
Paderborn, Ger. D8 10
Padilla, Bol. H9 82
Padova, Italy D6 18
Padre Bernardo, Braz. C4 79
Padre Island, i., Tx., U.S. F4 150
Padre Island National Seashore, Tx., U.S. F4 150
Padre Paraíso, Braz. D8 79
Padua see Padova, Italy D6 18
Paducah, Ky., U.S. e9 124
Paducah, Tx., U.S. B2 150
Paektu-san, mtn., Asia A16 32
Pag, Otok, i., Cro. E10 18
Pagadian, Phil. D7 38
Page, Az., U.S. A4 110
Page, N.D., U.S. B8 141
Page, W.V., U.S. C3 155
Page, co., Ia., U.S. D2 122
Page, co., Va., U.S. B4 153
Pageland, S.C., U.S. B7 147
Pagoda Peak, mtn., Co., U.S. A3 113
Pagoda Point, c., Mya. G3 40
Pagon, Bukit, mtn., Asia E6 38
Pagosa Springs, Co., U.S. D3 113
Paguate, N.M., U.S. B2 138
Pahala, Hi., U.S. D6 118
Pahang, stm., Malay. M7 40
Pahoa, Hi., U.S. D7 118
Pahokee, Fl., U.S. F6 116
Pahrump, Nv., U.S. G6 135
Paia, Hi., U.S. C5 118
Paide, Est. C8 22
Paignton, Eng., U.K. K10 8
Paiján, Peru B2 82
Päijänne, l., Fin. K19 6
Paimpol, Fr. D3 14
Paincourtville, La., U.S. k9 125
Painesville, Oh., U.S. A4 142
Painted Desert, des., Az., U.S. B4 110
Painted Rock Reservoir, res., Az., U.S. D3 110
Paintsville, Ky., U.S. C7 124
Paisley, Ont., Can. C3 103
Paisley, Scot., U.K. F9 8
Paita, Peru A1 82
Paizhou, China E2 34
Pajala, Swe. H18 6
Pajan, Ec. H2 84
Pakaraima Mountains, mts., S.A. E12 84
Pakhoi see Beihai, China G8 30
Pakistan (Pākistān), ctry., Asia C9 42
Pakokku, Mya. D3 40
Pākpattan, Pak. E5 44
Pak Phraek, Thai. J6 40
Pakruojis, Lith. F6 22
Paks, Hung. I18 10
Pakxé, Laos G8 40
Pala, Chad G3 56
Palacios, Tx., U.S. E4 150
Palagruža, Otoci, is., Cro. G11 18
Palana, Russia F23 28
Palanga, Lith. F4 22
Palangkaraya, Indon. F5 38
Palani, India G4 46
Pālanpur, India H5 44
Palapye, Bots. D8 66
Palatine, Il., U.S. A5 120
Palatka, Russia E22 28
Palatka, Fl., U.S. C5 116
Palau, ctry., Oc. H17 158
Palawan, i., Phil. D6 38
Pālayankottai, India H4 46
Paldiski, Est. B7 22
Palech, Russia E24 22
Palembang, Indon. F3 38
Palencia, Spain C7 16
Palenque, Mex. I14 90
Palenque, hist., Mex. I13 90
Palermo, Italy K8 18
Palestina, Braz. F4 79
Palestine, Ar., U.S. C5 111
Palestine, Il., U.S. D6 120
Palestine, Tx., U.S. D5 150
Palestine, hist. reg., Asia D4 50
Palestrina, Italy H7 18
Pālghāt, India G4 46
Pāli, India H5 44
Palisade, Co., U.S. B2 113
Palisade, Ne., U.S. D4 134
Palisades Park, N.J., U.S. h8 137
Palisades Reservoir, res., U.S. F7 119
Paliseul, Bel. I7 12
Palizada, Mex. H13 90
Palk Bay, b., Asia H5 46
Palk Strait, strt., Asia H5 46
Palliser, Cape, c., N.Z. D5 72
Palma, Braz. F7 79
Palma, Moz. D8 58
Palma del Río, Spain H6 16
Palma [de Mallorca], Spain F14 16
Palmar, Lago Artificial del, res., Ur. G10 80
Palmares, Braz. E11 76
Palmares, C.R. G10 92
Palmares do Sul, Braz. F13 80
Palmar Sur, C.R. I11 92
Palmas, Braz. F9 76
Palmas, Braz. D12 80
Palmas Bellas, Pan. C2 84
Palmas de Monte Alto, Braz. C7 79
Palma Soriano, Cuba D6 94
Palm Bay, Fl., U.S. D6 116
Palm Beach, Fl., U.S. F6 116
Palm Beach, co., Fl., U.S. F6 116
Palmdale, Ca., U.S. E4 112
Palm Desert, Ca., U.S. F5 112
Palmeira, Braz. C13 80
Palmeira das Missões, Braz. D12 80
Palmeira d'Oeste, Braz. F3 79
Palmeiras, Braz. B8 79
Palmer, Ak., U.S. C10 109
Palmer, Ma., U.S. B3 128
Palmer, Ms., U.S. D4 131
Palmer, Ne., U.S. C7 134
Palmer, Tn., U.S. D8 149
Palmer Lake, Co., U.S. B6 113
Palmer Land, reg., Ant. C12 73
Palmerston, Ont., Can. D4 103
Palmerston North, N.Z. D5 72
Palmerton, Pa., U.S. E10 145
Palmetto, Fl., U.S. E4 116
Palmetto, Ga., U.S. C2 117
Palm Harbor, Fl., U.S. o10 116
Palmi, Italy K10 18
Palmira, Col. F4 84
Palmira, Cuba C4 94
Palmitas, Ur. G10 80
Palmitos, Braz. D12 80
Palm Springs, Ca., U.S. F5 112
Palm Valley, Fl., U.S. m9 116
Palmyra see Tudmur, Syria D5 48
Palmyra, In., U.S. H5 121
Palmyra, Mo., U.S. B6 132
Palmyra, Ne., U.S. D9 134
Palmyra, N.J., U.S. C2 137
Palmyra, N.Y., U.S. B3 139
Palmyra, Pa., U.S. F8 145
Palmyra, Wi., U.S. F5 156
Palmyra, hist., Syria D5 48
Palmyra Atoll, atoll, Oc. H23 158
Palo Alto, Ca., U.S. D2 112
Palo Alto, co., Ia., U.S. A3 122
Paloich, Sud. L7 60
Palomar Mountain, mtn., Ca., U.S. F5 112
Palo Negro, Ven. B9 84
Palo Pinto, co., Tx., U.S. C3 150
Palopo, Indon. F7 38
Palos see Palos de la Frontera, Spain H5 16
Palos, Cabo de, c., Spain H11 16
Palo Santo, Arg. C9 80
Palos de la Frontera, Spain H5 16
Palos Park, Il., U.S. k9 120
Palos Verdes Estates, Ca., U.S. n12 112
Palouse, Wa., U.S. C8 154
Palouse, stm., Wa., U.S. C7 154
Palpa, Peru F4 82
Palpalá, Arg. C6 80
Palu, Indon. F6 38
Pamekasan, Indon. j16 39a
Pamiers, Fr. I8 14
Pamir, mts., Asia B5 44
Pamlico, co., N.C., U.S. B6 140
Pamlico, stm., N.C., U.S. B6 140
Pamlico Sound, strt., N.C., U.S. B6 140
Pampa, Tx., U.S. B2 150
Pampa, reg., Arg. I6 80
Pampa del Indio, Arg. D9 80
Pampa del Infierno, Arg. D8 80
Pampa de los Guanacos, Arg. D8 80
Pampa Grande, Bol. H9 82
Pampas, Peru E4 82
Pampas, stm., Peru E5 82
Pamplico, S.C., U.S. D8 147
Pamplona, Col. D6 84
Pamplona, Spain C10 16
Pamunkey, stm., Va., U.S. C5 153
Pana, Il., U.S. D4 120
Panabá, Mex. G15 90
Panaca, Nv., U.S. F7 135
Panamá, Pan. C3 84
Panama, Ok., U.S. B7 143
Panamá, prov., Pan. I15 92
Panama (Panamá), ctry., N.A. G8 88
Panamá, Canal de, Pan. H15 92
Panamá, Golfo de, b., Pan. C3 84
Panamá, Istmo de, Pan. C2 84
Panama City, Fl., U.S. u16 116
Panama City Beach, Fl., U.S. u16 116
Panambi, Braz. E12 80
Panao, Peru C3 82
Pančevo, Yugo. E4 20
Pandamatenga, Bots. B7 66
Pan de Azúcar, Ur. H11 80
Pandėlys, Lith. E8 22
Pandharpur, India D3 46
Pando, dept., Bol. D8 82
P'andž (Panj), stm., Asia A4 44
Panevėžys, Lith. F7 22
Panfilov, Kaz. I14 26
Pangalanes, Canal des, Madag. q23 67b
Pangani, Tan. C7 58
Pangburn, Ar., U.S. B4 111
Pangfou see Bengbu, China E10 30
Pangkalpinang, Indon. F4 38
Pangman, Sask., Can. H3 105
Pangnirtung, N.W. Ter., Can. C19 96
Pangong Tso, l., Asia D8 44
Panguitch, Ut., U.S. F3 151
Pānīpat, India F7 44
Panj (P'andž), stm., Asia B4 44
P'anmunjŏm, N. Kor. F14 32
Pannawonica, Austl. D3 68
Panola, co., Ms., U.S. A3 131
Panola, co., Tx., U.S. C5 150

Name	Map Ref.	Page
Panora, Ia., U.S.	C3	122
Panorama, Braz.	F3	79
Pánuco, Mex.	F10	90
Pánuco, stm., Mex.	G10	90
Panxian, China	B8	40
Panyam, Nig.	G14	64
Panyu, China	M2	34
Panzós, Guat.	B5	92
Paola, Italy	J11	18
Paola, Ks., U.S.	D9	123
Paoli, In., U.S.	G5	121
Paoli, Pa., U.S.	o20	145
Paonia, Co., U.S.	C3	113
Paotow see Baotou, China	C8	30
Pápa, Hung.	H17	10
Papaaloa, Hi., U.S.	D6	118
Papagayo, Golfo de, b., C.R.	G9	92
Papaikou, Hi., U.S.	D6	118
Papantla [de Olarte], Mex.	G11	90
Papenburg, Ger.	B7	10
Papillion, Ne., U.S.	C9	134
Papineauville, Que., Can.	D2	104
Paposo, Chile	C3	80
Papua, Gulf of, b., Pap. N. Gui.	m15	68a
Papua New Guinea, ctry., Oc.	m15	68a
Papudo, Chile	G3	80
Papun, Mya.	E4	40
Paquetville, N.B., Can.	B4	101
Pará, state, Braz.	B13	82
Paraburdoo, Austl.	D3	68
Paracatu, Braz.	D5	79
Paracel Islands see Xisha Qundao, is., China	B5	38
Paracho de Verduzco, Mex.	H8	90
Parachute, Co., U.S.	B2	113
Paraćin, Yugo.	F5	20
Paradise, Guy.	D14	84
Paradise, Ca., U.S.	C3	112
Paradise, Mt., U.S.	C2	133
Paradise, Nv., U.S.	G6	135
Paradise, Ut., U.S.	B4	151
Paradise Hill, Sask., Can.	D1	105
Paradise Hills, N.M., U.S.	B3	138
Paradise Valley, Az., U.S.	k9	110
Paradise Valley, Nv., U.S.	B4	135
Paragon, In., U.S.	F4	121
Paragould, Ar., U.S.	A5	111
Paraguá, stm., Bol.	E11	82
Paragua, stm., Ven.	D11	84
Paraguaçu, stm., Braz.	B9	79
Paraguaçu Paulista, Braz.	G3	79
Paraguaná, Península de, pen., Ven.	B8	84
Paraguari, Para.	C10	80
Paraguari, dept., Para.	D10	80
Paraguay, ctry., S.A.	A5	78
Paraguay (Paraguai), stm., S.A.	G9	74
Paraíso, C.R.	H11	92
Paraíso, Mex.	H13	90
Paraíso, Pan.	C3	84
Paraíso do Norte, Braz.	G2	79
Paraisópolis, Braz.	G6	79
Parakou, Benin	G11	64
Paramakkudi, India	H5	46
Paramaribo, Sur.	B7	76
Paramirim, Braz.	B7	79
Paramonga, Peru	D3	82
Paramount, Md., U.S.	A2	127
Paramus, N.J., U.S.	h8	137
Paran, Naḥal (Wādī al-Jirāfī), val.	H3	50
Paraná, Arg.	F8	80
Paraná, state, Braz.	C13	80
Paraná, stm., Braz.	B5	79
Paraná, stm., S.A.	H9	74
Paranaguá, Braz.	C14	80
Paranaíba, Braz.	E3	79
Paranaíba, stm., Braz.	E3	79
Paranapanema, stm., Braz.	G3	79
Paranavaí, Braz.	G2	79
Paranhos, Braz.	G1	79
Paraopeba, Braz.	E6	79
Parapetí, stm., Bol.	H10	82
Paratinga, Braz.	B7	79
Paraúna, Braz.	D3	79
Paray-le-Monial, Fr.	F11	14
Parbhani, India	C4	46
Parchment, Mi., U.S.	F5	129
Pardeeville, Wi., U.S.	E4	156
Pardubice, Czech Rep.	E15	10
Paredón, Mex.	E9	90
Parepare, Indon.	F6	38
Parera, Arg.	H6	80
Parfino, Russia	D14	22
Paria, Gulf of, b.	B11	84
Paria, Península de, pen., Ven.	B11	84
Pariaguán, Ven.	C10	84
Pariaman, Indon.	O6	40
Pariči, Bela.	I12	22
Parima, Sierra, mts., S.A.	F10	84
Pariñas, Punta, c., Peru	J2	84
Parintins, Braz.	I14	84
Pariquera-Açu, Braz.	C15	80
Paris, Ont., Can.	D4	103
Paris, Fr.	D9	14
Paris, Ar., U.S.	B2	111
Paris, Id., U.S.	G7	119
Paris, Il., U.S.	D6	120
Paris, Ky., U.S.	B5	124
Paris, Me., U.S.	D2	126
Paris, Mo., U.S.	B5	132
Paris, Tn., U.S.	A3	149
Paris, Tx., U.S.	C5	150
Parismina, C.R.	G11	92
Parita, Bahía de, b., Pan.	I14	92
Park, co., Co., U.S.	B5	113
Park, co., Mt., U.S.	E6	133
Park, co., Wy., U.S.	B3	157
Parkano, Fin.	J18	6
Park City, Ks., U.S.	E8	123
Park City, Mt., U.S.	E8	133
Park City, Ut., U.S.	C4	151
Parkdale, P.E.I., Can.	C6	101
Parkdale, Ar., U.S.	D4	111
Parke, co., In., U.S.	E3	121
Parker, Az., U.S.	C1	110
Parker, Co., U.S.	B6	113
Parker, Fl., U.S.	u16	116
Parker, S.D., U.S.	D8	148
Parker, co., Tx., U.S.	C4	150
Parker, Cape, c., N.W. Ter., Can.	A17	96
Parker City, In., U.S.	D7	121
Parkersburg, Ia., U.S.	B5	122
Parkersburg, W.V., U.S.	B3	155
Parkers Prairie, Mn., U.S.	D3	130
Parkes, Austl.	I8	70
Parkesburg, Pa., U.S.	G10	145
Park Falls, Wi., U.S.	C3	156
Park Forest, Il., U.S.	B6	120
Parkhill, Ont., Can.	D3	103
Park Hills, Ky., U.S.	h13	124
Parkin, Ar., U.S.	B5	111
Parkland, Wa., U.S.	f11	154
Park Layne, Oh., U.S.	C1	142
Park Range, mts., Co., U.S.	A4	113
Park Rapids, Mn., U.S.	D3	130
Park Ridge, Il., U.S.	B6	120
Park Ridge, N.J., U.S.	g8	137
Park River, N.D., U.S.	A8	141
Parkrose, Or., U.S.	B4	144
Parksley, Va., U.S.	C7	153
Parkston, S.D., U.S.	D8	148
Parksville, B.C., Can.	E5	99
Parkville, Md., U.S.	B4	127
Parkville, Mo., U.S.	B3	132
Parkwater, Wa., U.S.	g14	154
Parkwood, N.C., U.S.	B4	140
Parli, India	C4	46
Parlier, Ca., U.S.	D4	112
Parma, Italy	E5	18
Parma, Id., U.S.	F2	119
Parma, Mo., U.S.	E8	132
Parma, Oh., U.S.	A4	142
Parma Heights, Oh., U.S.	h9	142
Parmelee, S.D., U.S.	D4	148
Parmer, co., Tx., U.S.	B1	150
Parnaíba, Braz.	D10	76
Parnassós, mtn., Grc.	K6	20
Pärnu, Est.	C7	22
Pärnu-Jaagupi, Est.	C7	22
Paro, Bhu.	G13	44
Paroo, stm., Austl.	H5	70
Parowan, Ut., U.S.	F3	151
Parral, Chile	I3	80
Parral see Hidalgo del Parral, Mex.	D7	90
Parramatta, Austl.	I9	70
Parras de la Fuente, Mex.	E8	90
Parrish, Al., U.S.	B2	108
Parrsboro, N.S., Can.	D5	101
Parry Channel, strt., N.W. Ter., Can.	B9	86
Parry Sound, Ont., Can.	B4	103
Parshall, N.D., U.S.	B3	141
Parsons, Ks., U.S.	E8	123
Parsons, Tn., U.S.	B3	149
Parsons, W.V., U.S.	B5	155
Parson's Pond, Newf., Can.	C3	102
Parthenay, Fr.	F6	14
Partinico, Italy	K8	18
Partizansk, Russia	I18	28
Partridge Point, c., Newf., Can.	C3	102
Pasadena, Newf., Can.	D3	102
Pasadena, Ca., U.S.	E4	112
Pasadena, Md., U.S.	B4	127
Pasadena, Tx., U.S.	r14	150
Pasado, Cabo, c., Ec.	H2	84
Pasaje, Ec.	I3	84
Pasaje, stm., Arg.	C6	80
Pascagoula, Ms., U.S.	E5	131
Pascagoula, stm., Ms., U.S.	E5	131
Pașcani, Rom.	B10	20
Pasco, Wa., U.S.	C6	154
Pasco, dept., Peru	D4	82
Pasco, co., Fl., U.S.	D4	116
Pascoag, R.I., U.S.	B2	146
Pascua, Isla de (Easter Island), i., Chile	G4	74
Pasig, Phil.	n19	39b
Pasinler, Tur.	B6	48
Pasni, Pak.	I17	48
Paso de los Libres, Arg.	E10	80
Paso de los Toros, Ur.	G10	80
Paso de Patria, Para.	D9	80
Paso Robles, Ca., U.S.	E3	112
Pasquotank, co., N.C., U.S.	A6	140
Pasrūr, Pak.	D6	44
Passaic, N.J., U.S.	B4	137
Passaic, co., N.J., U.S.	A4	137
Passaic, stm., N.J., U.S.	h8	137
Passamaquoddy Bay, b., Me., U.S.	C6	126
Passau, Ger.	G13	10
Pass Christian, Ms., U.S.	E4	131
Passero, Capo, c., Italy	M10	18
Passo Fundo, Braz.	E12	80
Passos, Braz.	F5	79
Passumpsic, stm., Vt., U.S.	C4	152
Pastaza, prov., Ec.	H4	84
Pastaza, stm., S.A.	J4	84
Pasto, Col.	G4	84
Pasuruan, Indon.	j16	39a
Pasvalys, Lith.	E7	22
Patagonia, Az., U.S.	F5	110
Patagonia, reg., Arg.	F3	78
Pātan, India	I5	44
Patapsco, stm., Md., U.S.	B4	127
Pataskala, Oh., U.S.	C3	142
Pataz, Peru	B3	82
Patchogue, N.Y., U.S.	n15	139
Patea, N.Z.	C5	72
Patensie, S. Afr.	I7	66
Paterna, Spain	F11	16
Paternò, Italy	L9	18
Pateros, Wa., U.S.	A6	154
Paterson, N.J., U.S.	B4	137
Pathānkot, India	D6	44
Pathein (Bassein), Mya.	F3	40
Pathfinder Reservoir, res., Wy., U.S.	D6	157
Pātiāla, India	E7	44
Pativilca, Peru	D3	82
Pātkai Range, mts., Asia	G16	44
Patna, India	H11	44
Pato Branco, Braz.	D12	80
Patoka, In., U.S.	H2	121
Patoka, stm., In., U.S.	H2	121
Patoka Lake, res., In., U.S.	H4	121
Patos, Braz.	E11	76
Patos, Lagoa dos, b., Braz.	F13	80
Patos de Minas, Braz.	E5	79
Patquía, Arg.	F5	80
Pátrai, Grc.	K5	20
Patras see Pátrai, Grc.	K5	20
Patrick, co., Va., U.S.	D2	153
Patrick Air Force Base, mil., Fl., U.S.	D6	116
Patrocínio, Braz.	E5	79
Patrocínio Paulista, Braz.	F5	79
Pattani, Thai.	K6	40
Patten, Me., U.S.	C4	126
Patterson, Ga., U.S.	E4	117
Patterson, La., U.S.	E4	125
Patton, Pa., U.S.	E4	145
Patuca, stm., Hond.	B10	92
Patuxent, stm., Md., U.S.	D4	127
Pátzcuaro, Mex.	H9	90
Patzicía, Guat.	C4	92
Patzún, Guat.	C3	92
Pau, Fr.	I6	14
Pau Brasil, Braz.	C9	79
Paucarbamba, Peru	E4	82
Pauk, Mya.	D3	40
Paul, Id., U.S.	G5	119
Paulaya, stm., Hond.	B9	92
Paulding, Oh., U.S.	A1	142
Paulding, co., Ga., U.S.	C2	117
Paulding, co., Oh., U.S.	A1	142
Paulicéia, Braz.	F3	79
Paulina Peak, mtn., Or., U.S.	E5	144
Paulins Kill, stm., N.J., U.S.	A3	137
Paulista, Braz.	E10	76
Paullina, Ia., U.S.	B2	122
Paulo Afonso, Braz.	E11	76
Paulo de Faria, Braz.	F4	79
Paulsboro, N.J., U.S.	D2	137
Pauls Valley, Ok., U.S.	C4	143
Paungde, Mya.	E3	40
Pauwela, Hi., U.S.	C5	118
Pavelec, Russia	H22	22
Pavia, Italy	D4	18
Pavillion, Wy., U.S.	C4	157
Pavilly, Fr.	C7	14
Pavlodar, Kaz.	G7	28
Pavlof Volcano, vol., Ak., U.S.	D7	109
Pavlovo, Russia	F26	22
Pavlovsk, Russia	B13	22
Pavlovskij Posad, Russia	F21	22
Pavo, Ga., U.S.	F3	117
Pawcatuck, Ct., U.S.	D8	114
Pawcatuck, stm., R.I., U.S.	G1	146
Paw Creek, N.C., U.S.	B2	140
Pawhuska, Ok., U.S.	A5	143
Pawlet, Vt., U.S.	E2	152
Pawnee, Il., U.S.	D4	120
Pawnee, Ok., U.S.	A5	143
Pawnee, co., Ks., U.S.	D4	123
Pawnee, co., Ne., U.S.	D9	134
Pawnee, co., Ok., U.S.	A5	143
Pawnee City, Ne., U.S.	D9	134
Paw Paw, Mi., U.S.	F5	129
Paw Paw, W.V., U.S.	B6	155
Pawtucket, R.I., U.S.	C4	146
Pawtuxet, stm., R.I., U.S.	C4	146
Paxton, Il., U.S.	C5	120
Paxton, Ne., U.S.	C4	134
Payakumbuh, Indon.	O6	40
Payette, Id., U.S.	E2	119
Payette, co., Id., U.S.	E2	119
Payne, co., Ok., U.S.	A4	143
Paynesville, Mn., U.S.	E4	130
Paynton, Sask., Can.	D1	105
Paysandú, Ur.	H9	74
Paysandú, Ur.	G9	80
Payson, Az., U.S.	C4	110
Payson, Il., U.S.	D2	120
Payson, Ut., U.S.	C4	151
Pazardžik, Bul.	G8	20
Pazin, Cro.	D8	18
Pea, stm., U.S.	D3	108
Peabody, Ks., U.S.	D6	123
Peabody, Ma., U.S.	A6	128
Peace, stm., Can.	E10	96
Peace, stm., Fl., U.S.	E5	116
Peace Dale, R.I., U.S.	F3	146
Peace River, Alta., Can.	A2	98
Peach, co., Ga., U.S.	D3	117
Peach Creek, W.V., U.S.	D5	155
Peach Springs, Az., U.S.	B2	110
Peak Hill, Austl.	E3	68
Peale, Mount, mtn., Ut., U.S.	E6	151
Pea Ridge, Ar., U.S.	A1	111
Pearisburg, Va., U.S.	C2	153
Pearl, Ms., U.S.	C3	131
Pearl, stm., U.S.	D3	131
Pearland, Tx., U.S.	r14	150
Pearl City, Hi., U.S.	B4	118
Pearl Harbor, b., Hi., U.S.	B3	118
Pearlington, Ms., U.S.	E4	131
Pearl River, La., U.S.	D6	125
Pearl River, N.Y., U.S.	g12	139
Pearl River, co., Ms., U.S.	E4	131
Pearsall, Tx., U.S.	E3	150
Pearson, Ga., U.S.	E4	117
Pearston, S. Afr.	I7	66
Peary Land, reg., Grnld.	A16	86
Pebas, Peru	I7	84
Pecan Gap, Tx., U.S.	C5	150
Pecatonica, Il., U.S.	A4	120
Pecatonica, stm., U.S.	A4	120
Pechora see Pečora, stm., Russia	D8	26
Pečora, Russia	D9	26
Pečora, stm., Russia	D8	26
Pečory, Russia	D10	22
Pecos, N.M., U.S.	B4	138
Pecos, Tx., U.S.	D1	150
Pecos, co., Tx., U.S.	D1	150
Pecos, stm., U.S.	E6	106
Pécs, Hung.	I18	10
Peculiar, Mo., U.S.	C3	132
Pedasi, Pan.	D2	84
Pedernales, Arg.	H9	80
Pedernales, Ven.	C11	84
Pedra Azul, Braz.	D8	79
Pedra Lume, C.V.	k17	64a
Pedregal, Pan.	C1	84
Pedregal, Ven.	B7	84
Pedregulho, Braz.	F5	79
Pedreiras, Braz.	D10	76
Pedro Afonso, Braz.	E9	76
Pedro Gomes, Braz.	E1	79
Pedro II, Braz.	D10	76
Pedro II, Ilha, i., S.A.	G9	84
Pedro Juan Caballero, Para.	B11	80
Pedro Leopoldo, Braz.	E6	79
Pedro Luro, Arg.	J7	80
Pedro Osório, Braz.	F12	80
Pedro R. Fernández, Arg.	E9	80
Peekskill, N.Y., U.S.	D7	139
Peel, stm., Can.	C5	96
Pe Ell, Wa., U.S.	C2	154
Pegasus Bay, b., N.Z.	E4	72
Pegnitz, stm., Ger.	F11	10
Pego, Spain	G11	16
Pegu see Bago, Mya.	F4	40
Pehuajó, Arg.	H8	80
Peikang, Tai.	L9	34
Peine, Ger.	C10	10
Peiziyan, China	H3	32
Pekalongan, Indon.	j14	39a
Pekanbaru, Indon.	N6	40
Pekin, Il., U.S.	C4	120
Pekin, In., U.S.	G5	121
Peking see Beijing, China	D4	32
Pelagie, Isole, is., Italy	N7	18
Pelahatchie, Ms., U.S.	C4	131
Pelée, Montagne, mtn., Mart.	G14	94
Pelee Island, i., Ont., Can.	F2	103
Pelham, Ont., Can.	D5	103
Pelham, Al., U.S.	B3	108
Pelham, Ga., U.S.	E2	117
Pelham, N.H., U.S.	E4	136
Pelham Manor, N.Y., U.S.	h13	139
Pelhřimov, Czech Rep.	F15	10
Pelican Narrows, Sask., Can.	B4	105
Pelican Rapids, Man., Can.	C1	100
Pelican Rapids, Mn., U.S.	D2	130
Pelileo, Ec.	H3	84
Pella, Ia., U.S.	C5	122
Pell City, Al., U.S.	B3	108
Pell Lake, Wi., U.S.	n11	156
Pellegrini, Arg.	I7	80
Pello, Fin.	H19	6
Pelly, stm., Yukon, Can.	D6	96
Pelly Crossing, Yukon, Can.	D5	96
Pelly Mountains, mts., Yukon, Can.	D6	96
Peloncillo Mountains, mts., U.S.	E1	138
Peloponnesos see Pelopónnisos, pen., Grc.	L6	20
Pelopónnisos (Peloponnesus), pen., Grc.	L6	20
Pelotas, Braz.	F12	80
Pemadumcook Lake, l., Me., U.S.	C3	126
Pemalang, Indon.	j14	39a
Pematangsiantar, Indon.	M5	40
Pemba, Moz.	D8	58
Pemba, i., Tan.	C7	58
Pemberton, Austl.	F3	68
Pemberton, B.C., Can.	D6	99
Pembina, N.D., U.S.	A8	141
Pembina, co., N.D., U.S.	A8	141
Pembina, stm., Alta., Can.	C3	98
Pembroke, Ont., Can.	B7	103
Pembroke, Wales, U.K.	J9	8
Pembroke, Ga., U.S.	D5	117
Pembroke, Ky., U.S.	D2	124
Pembroke, Ma., U.S.	B6	128
Pembroke, N.C., U.S.	C3	140
Pembroke, Va., U.S.	C2	153
Pembroke Pines, Fl., U.S.	r13	116
Pemigewasset, stm., N.H., U.S.	C3	136
Pemiscot, co., Mo., U.S.	E8	132
Pemuco, Chile	I2	80
Peña Barroza, Bol.	J8	82
Peña Blanca, N.M., U.S.	B3	138
Peñafiel, Port.	D3	16
Penápolis, Braz.	F3	79
Pen Argyl, Pa., U.S.	E11	145
Peñarroya-Pueblonuevo, Spain	G6	16
Penas, Golfo de, b., Chile	F2	78
Penasco, N.M., U.S.	A4	138
Peñasco, Rio, stm., N.M., U.S.	E4	138
Penbrook, Pa., U.S.	F8	145
Pendembu, S.L.	G3	64
Pender, Ne., U.S.	B9	134
Pender, co., N.C., U.S.	C4	140
Pendleton, Or., U.S.	B8	144
Pendleton, S.C., U.S.	B2	147
Pendleton, co., Ky., U.S.	B5	124
Pendleton, co., W.V., U.S.	C5	155
Pend Oreille, co., Wa., U.S.	A8	154
Pend Oreille, Lake, l., Id., U.S.	A2	119
Penedo, Braz.	F11	76
Penetanguishene, Ont., Can.	C5	103
Penge, S. Afr.	E10	66
Penglai (Dengzhou), China	F8	32
Pengxian, China	E7	30
Penha, Braz.	D14	80
Penhold, Alta., Can.	C4	98
Peniche, Port.	F2	16
Penjamillo [de Degollado], Mex.	G9	90
Pennant Point, c., N.S., Can.	E6	101
Pennant Station, Sask., Can.	G1	105
Pennell, Mount, mtn., Ut., U.S.	F5	151
Penniac, N.B., Can.	C3	101
Pennington, co., Mn., U.S.	B2	130
Pennington, co., S.D., U.S.	D2	148
Pennington Gap, Va., U.S.	f8	153
Pennsauken, N.J., U.S.	D2	137
Pennsboro, W.V., U.S.	B4	155
Pennsburg, Pa., U.S.	F11	145
Penns Grove, N.J., U.S.	D2	137
Pennsville, N.J., U.S.	D1	137
Pennsylvania, state, U.S.	E7	145
Pennville, In., U.S.	D7	121
Penn Yan, N.Y., U.S.	C3	139
Peno, Russia	E15	22
Penobscot, co., Me., U.S.	C4	126
Penobscot, stm., Me., U.S.	C4	126
Penobscot Bay, b., Me., U.S.	D3	126
Penola, Austl.	K4	70
Penong, Austl.	F6	68
Penonomé, Pan.	C2	84
Penrith, Austl.	I9	70
Pensacola, Fl., U.S.	u14	116
Pensacola Bay, b., Fl., U.S.	u14	116
Pensacola Mountains, mts., Ant.	D1	73
Pense, Sask., Can.	G3	105
Pentagon Mountain, mtn., Mt., U.S.	C3	133
Penticton, B.C., Can.	E8	99
Pentland Firth, strt., Scot., U.K.	C10	8
Penza, Russia	G7	26
Penzance, Eng., U.K.	l13	8
Peoria, Az., U.S.	D3	110
Peoria, Il., U.S.	C4	120
Peoria, co., Il., U.S.	C4	120
Peoria Heights, Il., U.S.	C4	120
Peotone, Il., U.S.	B6	120
Pepeekeo, Hi., U.S.	D6	118
Peper, Sud.	N7	60
Pepin, co., Wi., U.S.	D1	156
Pepin, Lake, l., U.S.	D1	156
Pepperell, Ma., U.S.	A4	128
Pequannock, N.J., U.S.	B4	137
Pequot Lakes, Mn., U.S.	D4	130
Perabumulih, Indon.	F3	38
Percy, Il., U.S.	E4	120
Percy Isles, is., Austl.	C9	70
Perdido, Al., U.S.	D2	108
Perdido, stm., U.S.	E2	108
Perdido, Monte, mtn., Spain	C12	16
Perdido Bay, b., Al., U.S.	E2	108
Perdizes, Braz.	E5	79
Perdue, Sask., Can.	E2	105
Pereira, Col.	F5	84
Pereira Barreto, Braz.	F3	79
Pere Marquette, stm., Mi., U.S.	E4	129
Pereslavl'-Zalesskij, Russia	E21	22
Pérez, Arg.	G8	80
Pergamino, Arg.	G8	80
Perham, Mn., U.S.	D3	130
Perico, Arg.	C6	80
Pericos, Mex.	E6	90
Peridot, Az., U.S.	D5	110
Périgueux, Fr.	G7	14
Perijá, Serranía De, mts., S.A.	B6	84
Perkasie, Pa., U.S.	F11	145
Perkins, Ok., U.S.	B4	143
Perkins, co., Ne., U.S.	D4	134
Perkins, co., S.D., U.S.	B3	148
Perkinston, Ms., U.S.	E4	131
Perlas, Archipiélago de las, is., Pan.	C3	84
Perlas, Laguna de, b., Nic.	E11	92
Perlas, Punta de, c., Nic.	E11	92
Perm', Russia	F9	26
Pernik, Bul.	G7	20
Péronne, Fr.	C9	14
Perote, Mex.	H11	90
Perpignan, Fr.	J9	14
Perquimans, co., N.C., U.S.	A6	140
Perrine, Fl., U.S.	G6	116
Perris, Ca., U.S.	F5	112
Perry, Fl., U.S.	B3	116
Perry, Ga., U.S.	D3	117
Perry, Ia., U.S.	C3	122
Perry, Ks., U.S.	C8	123
Perry, Mi., U.S.	F6	129
Perry, Mo., U.S.	B6	132
Perry, N.Y., U.S.	C2	139
Perry, Ut., U.S.	B3	151
Perry, co., Al., U.S.	C2	108
Perry, co., Ar., U.S.	C3	111
Perry, co., Il., U.S.	E4	120
Perry, co., In., U.S.	H4	121
Perry, co., Ky., U.S.	C6	124
Perry, co., Ms., U.S.	D4	131
Perry, co., Mo., U.S.	D8	132
Perry, co., Oh., U.S.	C3	142
Perry, co., Pa., U.S.	F7	145
Perry, co., Tn., U.S.	B4	149
Perryman, Md., U.S.	B5	127
Perryopolis, Pa., U.S.	F2	145
Perrysburg, Oh., U.S.	A2	142
Perryton, Tx., U.S.	A2	150
Perryville, Ak., U.S.	D8	109
Perryville, Md., U.S.	A5	127
Perryville, Mo., U.S.	D8	132
Pershing, co., Nv., U.S.	C3	135
Persian Gulf (Arabian Gulf), b., Asia	H11	48
Person, co., N.C., U.S.	A3	140
Perth, Austl.	F3	68
Perth, Ont., Can.	C8	103
Perth, Scot., U.K.	E10	8
Perth-Andover, N.B., Can.	D10	101
Peru, Il., U.S.	B4	120
Peru, In., U.S.	C5	121
Peru, Ne., U.S.	D10	134
Peru (Perú), ctry., S.A.	E3	76
Peru-Chile Trench	G7	74
Perugia, Italy	F7	18
Peruíbe, Braz.	C15	80
Pervomajskij, Russia	H23	22
Pervomays'k, Ukr.	H4	26
Pervoural'sk, Russia	F9	26
Pervyj Kuril'skij proliv, strt., Russia	G23	28
Pesaro, Italy	F7	18
Pescadores see P'enghu Ch'üntao, is., Tai.	L8	34
Pescara, Italy	G9	18
Peshastin, Wa., U.S.	B5	154
Pesé, Pan.	D2	84
Peshāwar, Pak.	C4	44
Peshtigo, Wi., U.S.	C6	156
Peshtigo, stm., Wi., U.S.	C5	156
Peski, Russia	F21	22
Pesočnyj, Russia	A13	22
Peso da Régua, Port.	D4	16
Pesqueira, Braz.	E11	76
Pessac, Fr.	H6	14
Pest'aki, Russia	E25	22
Peštera, Bul.	G8	20
Pestovo, Russia	C18	22
Petaḥ Tiqwa, Isr.	D3	50
Petal, Ms., U.S.	D4	131
Petalcingo, Mex.	I13	90
Petaluma, Ca., U.S.	C2	112
Pétange, Lux.	I8	12
Petare, Ven.	B9	84
Petatlán, Mex.	I9	90
Petawawa, Ont., Can.	B7	103
Petén, dept., Guat.	A5	92
Petén Itzá, Lago, l., Guat.	I15	90
Petenwell Lake, res., Wi., U.S.	D4	156
Peterborough, Austl.	I3	70
Peterborough, Ont., Can.	C6	103
Peterborough, Eng., U.K.	I13	8
Peterborough, N.H., U.S.	E3	136
Peterhead, Scot., U.K.	D12	8
Peter I Island, i., Ant.	B11	73
Peterman, Al., U.S.	D2	108
Peter Pond Lake, l., Sask., Can.	m7	105
Petersburg, Ak., U.S.	D13	109
Petersburg, Il., U.S.	C4	120
Petersburg, In., U.S.	H3	121
Petersburg, Mi., U.S.	G7	129
Petersburg, Ne., U.S.	C7	134
Petersburg, Va., U.S.	C5	153
Petersburg, W.V., U.S.	B5	155
Petersfield, Man., Can.	D3	100
Peterson, Al., U.S.	B2	108
Peterstown, W.V., U.S.	D4	155
Petersville, Al., U.S.	A2	108
Pétionville, Haiti	E8	94
Petit Bois Island, i., Ms., U.S.	E5	131
Petitcodiac, N.B., Can.	D4	101
Petit-de-Grat, N.S., Can.	D9	101
Petite Rivière, N.S., Can.	E5	101
Petite Rivière Noire, Piton de la, mtn., Mrts.	v18	67c
Petit-Étang, N.S., Can.	C9	101
Petit-Goâve, Haiti	E8	94
Petit Jean, stm., Ar., U.S.	B2	111
Petitot, stm., Can.	E8	96
Petit-Rocher, N.B., Can.	B4	101
Petit-Saint-Bernard, Col du, Eur.	G13	14
Petitsikapau Lake, l., Newf., Can.	g8	102
Peto, Mex.	G15	90
Petorca, Chile	G3	80
Petoskey, Mi., U.S.	C6	129
Petra see Baṭrā, hist., Jord.	H4	50
Petra Velikogo, zaliv, b., Russia	I18	28
Petrified Forest National Park, Az., U.S.	B6	110
Petrikov, Bela.	I11	22
Petrila, Rom.	D7	20
Petrinja, Cro.	D11	18
Petrodvorec, Russia	B12	22
Petroleum, co., Mt., U.S.	C8	133
Petrolia, Ont., Can.	E2	103
Petrolina, Braz.	E10	76
Petrolina de Goiás, Braz.	D4	79
Petropavlovsk, Kaz.	G11	26
Petropavlovsk-Kamčatskij, Russia	G23	28
Petrópolis, Braz.	G7	79
Petros, Tn., U.S.	C9	149
Petroșani, Rom.	D7	20
Petrovsk, Russia	D22	22
Petrovskoje, Russia	G7	26
Petrovsk-Zabajkal'skij, Russia	G13	28
Petrozavodsk, Russia	E4	26
Petrusville, S. Afr.	H7	66
Pettaquamscutt Lake Shores, R.I., U.S.	F4	146
Pettis, co., Mo., U.S.	C4	132
Petuchovo, Russia	F11	26
Petuški, Russia	F22	22
Pevek, Russia	D26	28
Pevely, Mo., U.S.	g13	132
Pewaukee, Wi., U.S.	E5	156
Pewee Valley, Ky., U.S.	B4	124
Pézenas, Fr.	I10	14
Pfäffikon, Switz.	D10	13
Pforzheim, Ger.	G8	10
Pfungstadt, Ger.	F8	10
Pha-an, Mya.	F4	40
Phagwāra, India	D6	66
Phala, Bots.	D6	66
Phalaborwa, S. Afr.	D10	66
Phalsbourg, Fr.	D14	14
Phanom Dongrak, Thiu Khao, mts., Asia	G7	40
Phan Rang, Viet.	I10	40
Phan Thiet, Viet.	I10	40
Pharr, Tx., U.S.	F3	150
Phatthalung, Thai.	K6	40
Phayao, Thai.	E5	40
Phelps, Ky., U.S.	C7	124
Phelps, Wi., U.S.	C4	156
Phelps, co., Mo., U.S.	D6	132
Phelps, co., Ne., U.S.	D6	134
Phelps Lake, l., N.C., U.S.	B6	140
Phenix City, Al., U.S.	C4	108
Phetchabun, Thai.	F6	40
Phetchaburi, Thai.	H5	40
Phichit, Thai.	F6	40
Philadelphia, Ms., U.S.	C4	131
Philadelphia, Pa., U.S.	G11	145
Philadelphia, co., Pa., U.S.	G12	145
Phil Campbell, Al., U.S.	A2	108
Philip, S.D., U.S.	C4	148
Philippeville, Bel.	H6	12
Philippi, W.V., U.S.	B4	155
Philippines (Pilipinas), ctry., Asia	C7	38
Philippine Sea	G17	158
Philippine Trench	H16	158
Philipsburg, Mt., U.S.	D3	133
Philipsburg, Pa., U.S.	E5	145

Phil-Port

Name	Map Ref.	Page
Phillips, Me., U.S.	D2	126
Phillips, Wi., U.S.	C3	156
Phillips, co., Ar., U.S.	C5	111
Phillips, co., Co., U.S.	A8	113
Phillips, co., Ks., U.S.	C4	123
Phillips, co., Mt., U.S.	B8	133
Phillipsburg, Ks., U.S.	C4	123
Phillipsburg, N.J., U.S.	B2	137
Philo, Il., U.S.	C5	120
Philomath, Or., U.S.	C3	144
Philpott Reservoir, res., Va., U.S.	D2	153
Phitsanulok, Thai.	F6	40
Phnom Penh see Phnum Pénh, Camb.	I8	40
Phnum Pénh, Camb.	I8	40
Phoenix, Az., U.S.	D3	110
Phoenix, Il., U.S.	k9	120
Phoenix, Or., U.S.	E4	144
Phoenix Islands, is., Kir.	I22	158
Phoenixville, Pa., U.S.	F10	145
Phôngsali, Laos	D7	40
Phra Nakhon Si Ayutthaya, Thai.	G6	40
Phuket, Thai.	K5	40
Phu Ly, Viet.	D8	40
Phumĭ Béng, Camb.	H8	40
Phumĭ Chhuk, Camb.	I8	40
Phumĭ Kâmpóng Trâbêk, Camb.	H8	40
Phuoc Binh, Viet.	I9	40
Phu Quoc, Dao, i., Viet.	I8	40
Piacenza, Italy	D4	18
Piaseczno, Pol.	C21	10
Piatra-Neamț, Rom.	C10	20
Piatt, co., Il., U.S.	D5	120
Piave, stm., Italy	D7	18
Piazza Armerina, Italy	L9	18
Picacho, Az., U.S.	E4	110
Picayune, Ms., U.S.	E4	131
Piccadilly, Newf., Can.	D2	102
Pichanal, Arg.	B6	80
Picher, Ok., U.S.	A7	143
Pichilemu, Chile	H2	80
Pichincha, prov., Ec.	H3	84
Pichucalco, Mex.	I13	90
Pickaway, co., Oh., U.S.	C2	142
Pickens, Ms., U.S.	C4	131
Pickens, S.C., U.S.	B2	147
Pickens, co., Al., U.S.	B1	108
Pickens, co., Ga., U.S.	B2	117
Pickens, co., S.C., U.S.	B2	147
Pickering, Ont., Can.	D5	103
Pickerington, Oh., U.S.	C3	142
Pickett, co., Tn., U.S.	C8	149
Pickwick Lake, res., U.S.	A6	131
Pico, i., Port.	k19	62a
Pico Rivera, Ca., U.S.	n12	112
Picos, Braz.	E10	76
Picton, Austl.	J9	70
Picton, Ont., Can.	D7	103
Picton, N.Z.	D5	72
Picton, Isla, i., Chile	H3	78
Pictou, N.S., Can.	D7	101
Pictou Landing, N.S., Can.	D7	101
Picture Butte, Alta., Can.	E4	98
Pictured Rocks National Lakeshore, Mi., U.S.	B4	129
Pidálion, Akrotírion, c., Cyp.	D3	48
Pidurutalagala, mtn., Sri L.	I6	46
Piedecuesta, Col.	D6	84
Piedmont, Al., U.S.	B4	108
Piedmont, Ca., U.S.	h8	112
Piedmont, Mo., U.S.	D7	132
Piedmont, Ok., U.S.	B4	143
Piedmont, S.C., U.S.	B3	147
Piedmont, S.D., U.S.	C2	148
Piedmont, W.V., U.S.	B5	155
Piedmont Lake, res., Oh., U.S.	B4	142
Piedras, Punta, c., Ven.	B12	84
Piedras Blancas, Arg.	F9	80
Piedras Negras, Mex.	C9	90
Pieksämäki, Fin.	J20	6
Piemonte, prov., Italy	E2	18
Piendamó, Col.	F4	84
Pierce, Co., U.S.	A6	113
Pierce, Id., U.S.	C3	119
Pierce, Ne., U.S.	B8	134
Pierce, co., Ga., U.S.	E4	117
Pierce, co., Ne., U.S.	B8	134
Pierce, co., N.D., U.S.	A5	141
Pierce, co., Wa., U.S.	C3	154
Pierce, co., Wi., U.S.	D1	156
Pierce, Lake, l., Fl., U.S.	E5	116
Pierce City, Mo., U.S.	E3	132
Pierceton, In., U.S.	B6	121
Pierre, S.D., U.S.	C5	148
Pierrefonds, Que., Can.	q19	104
Pierre Part, La., U.S.	k9	125
Pierson, Man., Can.	E1	100
Pierson, Fl., U.S.	C5	116
Pierz, Mn., U.S.	E4	130
Piešt'any, Slvk.	G17	10
Pietermaritzburg, S. Afr.	G10	66
Pietersburg, S. Afr.	D9	66
Pietrasanta, Italy	F5	18
Piet Retief, S. Afr.	F10	66
Pigeon, Mi., U.S.	E7	129
Pigeon, stm., U.S.	f9	140
Pigeon Forge, Tn., U.S.	D10	149
Pigeon Point, c., Mn., U.S.	h10	130
Pigg, stm., Va., U.S.	D3	153
Piggott, Ar., U.S.	A5	111
Piggs Peak, Swaz.	E10	66
Pigüé, Arg.	I7	80
Pihtipudas, Fin.	J19	6
Pijijiapan, Mex.	J13	90
Pikal'ovo, Russia	B17	22
Pike, co., Al., U.S.	D4	108
Pike, co., Ar., U.S.	C2	111
Pike, co., Ga., U.S.	C2	117
Pike, co., Il., U.S.	D2	120
Pike, co., In., U.S.	H3	121
Pike, co., Ky., U.S.	C7	124
Pike, co., Ms., U.S.	D3	131
Pike, co., Mo., U.S.	B6	132
Pike, co., Oh., U.S.	C2	142
Pike, co., Pa., U.S.	D11	145
Pike Lake, Mn., U.S.	D6	130
Pikes Peak, mtn., Co., U.S.	C5	113
Pikesville, Md., U.S.	B4	127
Piketberg, S. Afr.	I4	66
Pikeville, Ky., U.S.	C7	124
Pikeville, Tn., U.S.	D8	149
Pikwitonei, Man., Can.	B3	100
Pila, Arg.	I9	80
Piła (Schneidemühl), Pol.	B16	10
Pilar, Arg.	F8	80
Pilar, Arg.	F7	80
Pilar, Para.	D9	80
Pilar do Sul, Braz.	G5	79
Pilaya, stm., Bol.	I9	82
Pilcomayo, stm., S.A.	G8	74
Pilger, Ne., U.S.	B8	134
Pīlībhīt, India	F8	44
Pilica, stm., Pol.	D21	10
Pillaro, Ec.	H3	84
Pilot, mtn., Austl.	K8	70
Pilot Butte, Sask., Can.	G3	105
Pilot Grove, Mo., U.S.	C5	132
Pilot Knob, Mo., U.S.	D7	132
Pilot Mound, Man., Can.	E2	100
Pilot Peak, mtn., Nv., U.S.	B7	135
Pilot Rock, Or., U.S.	B8	144
Pilot Station, Ak., U.S.	C7	109
Pilsen see Plzeň, Czech Rep.	F13	10
Pima, Az., U.S.	E6	110
Pima, co., Az., U.S.	E3	110
Pimmit Hills, Va., U.S.	g12	153
Pinal, co., Az., U.S.	E4	110
Pinalón, Cerro, mtn., Guat.	B5	92
Pinang see George Town, Malay.	L6	40
Pinar del Río, Cuba	C3	94
Pinardville, N.H., U.S.	E3	136
Piñas, Ec.	I3	84
Pincher Creek, Alta., Can.	E4	98
Pinckard, Al., U.S.	D4	108
Pinckney, Mi., U.S.	F7	129
Pinckneyville, Il., U.S.	E4	120
Pinconning, Mi., U.S.	E7	129
Pindamonhangaba, Braz.	G6	79
Píndhos Óros (Pindus Mountains), mts., Grc.	J5	20
Pinduši, Russia	J24	6
Pindus Mountains see Píndhos Óros, mts., Grc.	J5	20
Pine, Az., U.S.	C4	110
Pine, Co., U.S.	B5	113
Pine, co., Mn., U.S.	D6	130
Pine Barrens, reg., N.J., U.S.	D3	137
Pine Bluff, Ar., U.S.	C3	111
Pine Bluffs, Wy., U.S.	E8	157
Pine Bridge, Ct., U.S.	D3	114
Pine Castle, Fl., U.S.	D5	116
Pine City, Mn., U.S.	E6	130
Pine Creek, Austl.	B6	68
Pine Creek, stm., Pa., U.S.	C6	145
Pine Creek Lake, res., Ok., U.S.	C6	143
Pinedale, Wy., U.S.	D3	157
Pine Falls, Man., Can.	D3	100
Pinefield, Md., U.S.	C4	127
Pine Grove, Pa., U.S.	E9	145
Pine Haven, Wy., U.S.	B8	157
Pine Hill, Al., U.S.	D2	108
Pine Hill, N.J., U.S.	D3	137
Pine Hills, Fl., U.S.	D5	116
Pinehouse Lake, Sask., Can.	B2	105
Pinehurst, Ma., U.S.	f11	128
Pinehurst, N.C., U.S.	B3	140
Pine Island, Mn., U.S.	F6	130
Pine Island Bay, b., Ant.	C11	73
Pine Knot, Ky., U.S.	D5	124
Pine Lake, Ga., U.S.	h8	117
Pine Lawn, Mo., U.S.	f13	132
Pine Level, N.C., U.S.	B4	140
Pinellas, co., Fl., U.S.	D4	116
Pinellas Park, Fl., U.S.	E4	116
Pine Mountain, Ga., U.S.	D2	117
Pine Mountain, mtn., U.S.	D6	124
Pine Orchard, Ct., U.S.	D4	114
Pine Point, N.W. Ter., Can.	D10	96
Pine Point, Me., U.S.	E2	126
Pine Ridge, S.D., U.S.	D3	148
Pine River, Man., Can.	D1	100
Pine River, Mn., U.S.	D4	130
Pinerolo, Italy	E2	18
Pines, Lake O' the, res., Tx., U.S.	C5	150
Pinesdale, Mt., U.S.	D2	133
Pinetops, N.C., U.S.	B5	140
Pinetown, S. Afr.	G10	66
Pine Valley, N.H., U.S.	E3	136
Pineville, Ky., U.S.	D6	124
Pineville, La., U.S.	C3	125
Pineville, Mo., U.S.	E3	132
Pineville, N.C., U.S.	B2	140
Pineville, W.V., U.S.	D3	155
Piney, Man., Can.	E4	100
Piney Point, Md., U.S.	D4	127
Piney View, W.V., U.S.	n13	155
Pingdingshan, China	B2	34
Pingdu, China	G7	32
Pinghe, China	K6	34
Pinghu, China	E10	34
Pingjiang, China	G2	34
Pingliang, China	D8	30
Pingquan, China	C6	32
Pingshui, China	F9	34
P'ingtung, Tai.	M9	34
Pingwu, China	E7	30
Pingxiang, China	H2	34
Pingxiang, China	C9	40
Pingyao, China	D9	30
Pingyi, China	H5	32
Pinhal Novo, Port.	G3	16
Pinheiro, Braz.	D9	76
Pinheiro Machado, Braz.	F12	80
Piniós, stm., Grc.	J6	20
Pinjarra, Austl.	F3	68
Pinneberg, Ger.	B9	10
Pinole, Ca., U.S.	h8	112
Pinon, Az., U.S.	A5	110
Pinos, Mex.	F9	90
Pinrang, Indon.	F6	38
Pins, Pointe aux, c., Ont., Can.	E3	103
Pinsk, Bela.	I9	22
Pinson, Al., U.S.	f7	108
Pin'ug, Russia	E7	26
Pioche, Nv., U.S.	F7	135
Piombino, Italy	G5	18
Pionerskij, Russia	G3	22
Pionki, Pol.	D21	10
Piotrków Trybunalski, Pol.	D19	10
Pipestone, Man., Can.	E1	100
Pipestone, Mn., U.S.	G2	130
Pipestone, co., Mn., U.S.	F2	130
Pipestone National Monument, Mn., U.S.	G2	130
Piqua, Oh., U.S.	B1	142
Piracanjuba, Braz.	D4	79
Piracicaba, Braz.	G5	79
Piraçununga, Braz.	F5	79
Piraeus see Piraiévs, Grc.	L7	20
Piraí do Sul, Braz.	C14	80
Piraiévs (Piraeus), Grc.	L7	20
Piraju, Braz.	G4	79
Pirajuí, Braz.	F4	79
Piran, Slvn.	D8	18
Pirané, Arg.	C9	80
Piranga, Braz.	F7	79
Piranhas, Braz.	D3	79
Pirapora, Braz.	D6	79
Piraquara, Braz.	C14	80
Piratini, Braz.	F12	80
Pirenópolis, Braz.	C4	79
Pires do Rio, Braz.	D4	79
Pírgos, Grc.	L5	20
Piriápolis, Ur.	H11	80
Pirmasens, Ger.	F7	10
Pirna, Ger.	E13	10
Pirot, Yugo.	F6	20
Pirovano, Arg.	I8	80
Pīr Panjāl Range, mts., Asia	D6	44
Pirtleville, Az., U.S.	F6	110
Pisa, Italy	F5	18
Pisagua, Chile	H6	82
Piscataquis, co., Me., U.S.	C3	126
Piscataway, N.J., U.S.	B4	137
Pisco, Peru	E3	82
Piscovo, Russia	D23	22
Písek, Czech Rep.	F14	10
Pisgah, Al., U.S.	A4	108
Pisgah, Oh., U.S.	n13	142
Pisgah Forest, N.C., U.S.	f10	140
Pishan, China	B8	44
Pishīn, Pak.	E2	44
Pishīn Lora (Lowrah), stm., Asia	G18	48
Pismo Beach, Ca., U.S.	E3	112
Pisticci, Italy	I11	18
Pistoia, Italy	F5	18
Pistolet Bay, b., Newf., Can.	C4	102
Pisz, Pol.	B21	10
Pit, stm., Ca., U.S.	B3	112
Pitalito, Col.	G4	84
Pitanga, Braz.	C13	80
Pitangueiras, Braz.	F4	79
Pitangui, Braz.	E6	79
Pitcairn, Pa., U.S.	k14	145
Pitcairn, dep., Oc.	K27	158
Piteå, Swe.	I17	6
Pitești, Rom.	E8	20
Pithiviers, Fr.	D9	14
Pitiquito, Mex.	B3	90
Pitk'aranta, Russia	K22	6
Pitkin, co., Co., U.S.	B4	113
Pitman, N.J., U.S.	D2	137
Pitt, co., N.C., U.S.	B5	140
Pitt Island, i., B.C., Can.	C3	99
Pittsboro, In., U.S.	E5	121
Pittsboro, N.C., U.S.	B3	140
Pittsburg, Ca., U.S.	g9	112
Pittsburg, Ks., U.S.	E9	123
Pittsburg, Ky., U.S.	C5	124
Pittsburg, Tx., U.S.	C5	150
Pittsburg, co., Ok., U.S.	C6	143
Pittsburgh, Pa., U.S.	F1	145
Pittsfield, Il., U.S.	D3	120
Pittsfield, Me., U.S.	D3	126
Pittsfield, Ma., U.S.	B1	128
Pittsfield, N.H., U.S.	D4	136
Pittsford, Vt., U.S.	D2	152
Pittston, Pa., U.S.	D10	145
Pittsylvania, co., Va., U.S.	D3	153
Piura, Peru	A1	82
Piura, dept., Peru	A1	82
Piute, co., Ut., U.S.	E3	151
Pivdennyy Buh, stm., Ukr.	H4	26
Placentia, Newf., Can.	E5	102
Placentia Bay, b., Newf., Can.	E4	102
Placer, co., Ca., U.S.	C3	112
Placerville, Ca., U.S.	C3	112
Placetas, Cuba	C5	94
Plácido de Castro, Braz.	D8	82
Plácido Rosas, Ur.	G12	80
Placitas, N.M., U.S.	B3	138
Plain City, Oh., U.S.	B2	142
Plain City, Ut., U.S.	B3	151
Plain Dealing, La., U.S.	B2	125
Plainfield, Ct., U.S.	C8	114
Plainfield, Il., U.S.	B5	120
Plainfield, In., U.S.	E5	121
Plainfield, N.H., U.S.	C2	136
Plainfield, N.J., U.S.	B4	137
Plainfield, Vt., U.S.	C4	152
Plains, Ga., U.S.	D2	117
Plains, Ks., U.S.	E3	123
Plains, Mt., U.S.	C2	133
Plains, Pa., U.S.	n17	145
Plainview, Ar., U.S.	C2	111
Plainview, Mn., U.S.	F6	130
Plainview, Ne., U.S.	B8	134
Plainview, Tx., U.S.	B2	150
Plainville, Ct., U.S.	C4	114
Plainville, Ks., U.S.	C4	123
Plainville, Ma., U.S.	B5	128
Plainwell, Mi., U.S.	F5	129
Plaistow, N.H., U.S.	E4	136
Plamondon, Alta., Can.	B4	98
Planalto, Braz.	C8	79
Planalto, Braz.	D12	80
Planeta Rica, Col.	C5	84
Plankinton, S.D., U.S.	D7	148
Plano, Il., U.S.	B5	120
Plano, Tx., U.S.	C4	150
Plantagenet, Ont., Can.	B9	103
Plantation, Fl., U.S.	r13	116
Plant City, Fl., U.S.	D4	116
Plantersville, Al., U.S.	C3	108
Plantersville, Ms., U.S.	A5	131
Plantsite, Az., U.S.	D6	110
Plantsville, Ct., U.S.	C4	114
Plaquemine, La., U.S.	D4	125
Plaquemines, co., La., U.S.	E6	125
Plasencia, Spain	E5	16
Plast, Russia	G10	26
Plaster Rock, N.B., Can.	C2	101
Plata, Río de la, est., S.A.	H10	80
Plateau, N.S., Can.	C8	101
Plato, Col.	C5	84
Platte, S.D., U.S.	D7	148
Platte, co., Mo., U.S.	B3	132
Platte, co., Ne., U.S.	C8	134
Platte, co., Wy., U.S.	D7	157
Platte, stm., U.S.	B3	132
Platte, stm., Ne., U.S.	D6	134
Platte Center, Ne., U.S.	C8	134
Platte City, Mo., U.S.	B3	132
Platteville, Co., U.S.	A6	113
Platteville, Wi., U.S.	F3	156
Plattsburg, Mo., U.S.	B3	132
Plattsburgh, N.Y., U.S.	f11	139
Plattsmouth, Ne., U.S.	D10	134
Plattsville, Ont., Can.	D4	103
Platveld, Nmb.	B3	66
Plauen, Ger.	E12	10
Pļaviņas, Lat.	E8	22
Plavsk, Russia	H20	22
Playa del Carmen, Mex.	G16	90
Playas, N.M., U.S.	F1	138
Playa Vicente, Mex.	I12	90
Play Cu, Viet.	H10	40
Playgreen Lake, l., Man., Can.	B2	100
Plaza de Caisán, Pan.	I12	92
Plaza Huincul, Arg.	J4	80
Pleasant Bay, N.S., Can.	C9	101
Pleasant Garden, N.C., U.S.	B3	140
Pleasant Grove, Al., U.S.	g7	108
Pleasant Grove, Ut., U.S.	C4	151
Pleasant Hill, Ca., U.S.	h8	112
Pleasant Hill, Il., U.S.	D3	120
Pleasant Hill, Ia., U.S.	e8	122
Pleasant Hill, Mo., U.S.	C3	132
Pleasant Hills, Md., U.S.	A5	127
Pleasant Lake, In., U.S.	A7	121
Pleasanton, Ca., U.S.	h9	112
Pleasanton, Ks., U.S.	D9	123
Pleasanton, Ne., U.S.	D6	134
Pleasanton, Tx., U.S.	E3	150
Pleasant Prairie, Wi., U.S.	n12	156
Pleasants, co., W.V., U.S.	B3	155
Pleasant Valley, Ia., U.S.	g11	122
Pleasant Valley, Mo., U.S.	h11	132
Pleasant View, Ut., U.S.	B3	151
Pleasantville, Ia., U.S.	C4	122
Pleasantville, N.J., U.S.	E3	137
Pleasantville, N.Y., U.S.	D7	139
Pleasure Beach, Ct., U.S.	D7	114
Pleasure Ridge Park, Ky., U.S.	g11	124
Pleasureville, Ky., U.S.	B4	124
Pleiku see Play Cu, Viet.	H10	40
Plenty, Sask., Can.	F1	105
Plenty, Bay of, b., N.Z.	B6	72
Plentywood, Mt., U.S.	B12	133
Pleščenicy, Bela.	G10	22
Pleseck, Russia	E6	26
Plessisville, Que., Can.	C6	104
Pleszew, Pol.	D17	10
Pleven, Bul.	F8	20
Pljevlja, Yugo.	F3	20
Płock, Pol.	C19	10
Ploërmel, Fr.	E4	14
Ploești see Ploiești, Rom.	E10	20
Ploiești, Rom.	E10	20
Plomárion, Grc.	K10	20
Plonge, Lac la, l., Sask., Can.	B2	105
Płońsk, Pol.	C20	10
Pl'os, Russia	D24	22
Plottier, Arg.	J4	80
Plovdiv, Bul.	G8	20
Plover, Wi., U.S.	D4	156
Plum, Pa., U.S.	k14	145
Plumas, Man., Can.	D2	100
Plumas, co., Ca., U.S.	B3	112
Plum Bayou, stm., Ar., U.S.	k10	111
Plum Beach, R.I., U.S.	E4	146
Plum Coulee, Man., Can.	E3	100
Plumerville, Ar., U.S.	B3	111
Plum Island, i., Ma., U.S.	A6	128
Plummer, Id., U.S.	B2	119
Plumtree, Zimb.	C8	66
Plungė, Lith.	F4	22
Pl'ussa, Russia	C12	22
Plymouth, Monts.	F13	94
Plymouth, Eng., U.K.	K9	8
Plymouth, Ct., U.S.	C3	114
Plymouth, Fl., U.S.	D5	116
Plymouth, In., U.S.	B5	121
Plymouth, Ma., U.S.	C6	128
Plymouth, Mi., U.S.	p15	129
Plymouth, Mn., U.S.	m12	130
Plymouth, Ne., U.S.	D9	134
Plymouth, N.H., U.S.	C3	136
Plymouth, N.C., U.S.	B6	140
Plymouth, Oh., U.S.	A3	142
Plymouth, Pa., U.S.	D10	145
Plymouth, Wi., U.S.	E6	156
Plymouth, co., Ia., U.S.	B1	122
Plymouth, co., Ma., U.S.	C6	128
Plymouth Bay, b., Ma., U.S.	C6	128
Plzeň, Czech Rep.	F13	10
Pô, Burkina	F9	64
Po, stm., Italy	E7	18
Pobé, Benin	H11	64
Pobedy, pik, mtn., Asia	I14	26
Pocahontas, Ar., U.S.	A5	111
Pocahontas, Ia., U.S.	B3	122
Pocahontas, co., Ia., U.S.	B3	122
Pocahontas, co., W.V., U.S.	C4	155
Pocasset, Ma., U.S.	C6	128
Pocatalico, W.V., U.S.	C3	155
Pocatello, Id., U.S.	G6	119
Počep, Russia	I16	22
Pochvistnevo, Russia	G8	26
Počinok, Russia	G15	22
Poções, Braz.	C8	79
Pocola, Ok., U.S.	B7	143
Pocomoke, stm., Md., U.S.	D7	127
Pocomoke City, Md., U.S.	D6	127
Pocomoke Sound, strt., Md., U.S.	E6	127
Poconé, Braz.	G13	82
Pocono Mountains, hills, Pa., U.S.	E11	145
Poços de Caldas, Braz.	F5	79
Pocrane, Braz.	E8	79
Pocrí, Pan.	I14	92
Poděbrady, Czech Rep.	E15	10
Podgorica, Yugo.	G3	20
Podol'sk, Russia	F20	22
Podor, Maur.	C2	64
Podporožje, Russia	E4	26
Podsvilje, Bela.	F10	22
Pofadder, S. Afr.	G4	66
Pogar, Russia	I16	22
Poggibonsi, Italy	F6	18
Pograničnyj, Russia	I18	28
P'ohang, S. Kor.	G17	32
Pohénégamook, Que., Can.	B8	104
Pohjois-Karjalan lääni, prov., Fin.	J21	6
Poinsett, co., Ar., U.S.	B5	111
Poinsett, Cape, c., Ant.	B6	73
Point Clear, Al., U.S.	E2	108
Pointe-à-Pitre, Guad.	F14	94
Pointe-Calumet, Que., Can.	p19	104
Pointe-Claire, Que., Can.	D4	104
Pointe Coupee, co., La., U.S.	D4	125
Pointe du Bois, Man., Can.	D4	100
Pointe-du-Chêne, N.B., Can.	C5	101
Point Edward, Ont., Can.	D2	103
Pointe-Noire, Congo	B2	58
Pointe-Verte, N.B., Can.	B4	101
Point Fortin, Trin.	I14	94
Point Hope, Ak., U.S.	B6	109
Point Leamington, Newf., Can.	D4	102
Point of Rocks, Md., U.S.	B2	127
Point of Rocks, Wy., U.S.	E4	157
Point Pleasant, N.J., U.S.	C4	137
Point Pleasant, W.V., U.S.	C2	155
Point Pleasant Beach, N.J., U.S.	C4	137
Point Roberts, Wa., U.S.	A2	154
Poipu, Hi., U.S.	B2	118
Poisson Blanc, Lac du, res., Que., Can.	C2	104
Poissy, Fr.	D9	14
Poitiers, Fr.	F7	14
Pojarkovo, Russia	H17	28
Pojo, Bol.	G9	82
Pojuca, Braz.	B9	79
Pokharā, Nepal	F10	44
Pokrov, Russia	F22	22
Pokrovsk, Russia	E17	28
Pokrovskoje, Russia	I19	22
Polacca, Az., U.S.	B5	110
Poland (Polska), ctry., Eur.	E11	4
Pol'arnyj, Russia	D4	26
Polatlı, Tur.	B2	48
Polcura, Chile	I3	80
Pol-e Khomrī, Afg.	C3	44
Polesje, reg., Eur.	G3	26
Polessk [Labiau], Russia	G4	22
Polevskoj, Russia	F10	26
Pŏlgyo, S. Kor.	I15	32
Police, Pol.	B14	10
Poligny, Fr.	F12	14
Políyiros, Grc.	I7	20
Polk, co., Ar., U.S.	C1	111
Polk, co., Fl., U.S.	E5	116
Polk, co., Ga., U.S.	C1	117
Polk, co., Ia., U.S.	C4	122
Polk, co., Mn., U.S.	C2	130
Polk, co., Mo., U.S.	D4	132
Polk, co., Ne., U.S.	C8	134
Polk, co., N.C., U.S.	f10	140
Polk, co., Or., U.S.	C3	144
Polk, co., Tn., U.S.	D9	149
Polk, co., Tx., U.S.	D5	150
Polk, co., Wi., U.S.	C1	156
Polk City, Ia., U.S.	C4	122
Pollāchi, India	G4	46
Pollards Point, Newf., Can.	D3	102
Pollock, S.D., U.S.	B5	148
Polo, Il., U.S.	B4	120
Polo, Mo., U.S.	B3	132
Polochic, stm., Guat.	B5	92
Polock, Bela.	F11	22
Polson, Mt., U.S.	C2	133
Poltava, Ukr.	H4	26
Põltsamaa, Est.	C8	22
Polunočnoje, Russia	E10	26
Polynesia, is., Oc.	I24	158
Polysajevo, Russia	G15	26
Pomabamba, Peru	C3	82
Pomerania, hist. reg., Pol.	A16	10
Pomeranian Bay, b., Eur.	A14	10
Pomerode, Braz.	D14	80
Pomeroy, Ia., U.S.	B3	122
Pomeroy, Oh., U.S.	C3	142
Pomeroy, Wa., U.S.	C8	154
Pomme de Terre, stm., Mn., U.S.	E3	130
Pomme de Terre Lake, res., Mo., U.S.	D4	132
Pomoho, Hi., U.S.	f9	118
Pomona, Ca., U.S.	E5	112
Pomona, Ks., U.S.	D8	123
Pompano Beach, Fl., U.S.	F6	116
Pompei, hist., Italy	I9	18
Pompéia, Braz.	G3	79
Pompéu, Braz.	E6	79
Pompton Lakes, N.J., U.S.	A4	137
Pomquet, N.S., Can.	D8	101
Ponca, Ne., U.S.	B9	134
Ponca City, Ok., U.S.	A4	143
Ponce, P.R.	E11	94
Ponchatoula, La., U.S.	D5	125
Pond Creek, Ok., U.S.	A3	143
Pondera, co., Mt., U.S.	B4	133
Ponderay, Id., U.S.	A2	119
Pondicherry, India	G5	46
Pondicherry, ter., India	G5	46
Pond Inlet, N.W. Ter., Can.	B17	96
Ponferrada, Spain	C5	16
Ponoka, Alta., Can.	C4	98
Ponorogo, Indon.	j15	39a
Pons, Fr.	G6	14
Ponta Delgada, Port.	m21	62a
Ponta Grossa, Braz.	C13	80
Pontalina, Braz.	D4	79
Ponta Porã, Braz.	G1	79
Pontarlier, Fr.	F13	14
Pont-Audemer, Fr.	C7	14
Pontchartrain, Lake, l., La., U.S.	D5	125
Pontedera, Italy	F5	18
Ponteix, Sask., Can.	H2	105
Ponte Nova, Braz.	F7	79
Ponte Serrada, Braz.	D13	80
Pontevedra, Spain	C3	16
Ponte Vedra Beach, Fl., U.S.	B5	116
Pontiac, Il., U.S.	C5	120
Pontiac, Mi., U.S.	F7	129
Pontianak, Indon.	F4	38
Pontivy, Fr.	D4	14
Pont-l'Abbé, Fr.	E2	14
Pont-l'Évêque, Fr.	C7	14
Pontoise, Fr.	C9	14
Pontorson, Fr.	D5	14
Pontotoc, Ms., U.S.	A4	131
Pontotoc, co., Ms., U.S.	A4	131
Pontotoc, co., Ok., U.S.	C5	143
Pont-Rouge, Que., Can.	C6	104
Pontypridd, Wales, U.K.	J10	8
Ponyri, Russia	I19	22
Poole, Eng., U.K.	K12	8
Pooler, Ga., U.S.	D5	117
Poolesville, Md., U.S.	B3	127
Poona see Pune, India	C2	46
Poopo, Bol.	H8	82
Poopó, Lago, l., Bol.	H8	82
Popayán, Col.	F4	84
Pope, co., Ar., U.S.	B2	111
Pope, co., Il., U.S.	F5	120
Pope, co., Mn., U.S.	E3	130
Poperinge, Bel.	G2	12
Poplar, Mt., U.S.	B11	133
Poplar Bluff, Mo., U.S.	E7	132
Poplar Grove, Ar., U.S.	C5	111
Poplarville, Ms., U.S.	E4	131
Popocatépetl, Volcán, vol., Mex.	H10	90
Popondetta, Pap. N. Gui.	m16	68a
Popovo, Bul.	F10	20
Poppel, Bel.	F7	12
Poprad, Slvk.	F20	10
Poquonock, Ct., U.S.	B5	114
Poquonock Bridge, Ct., U.S.	D7	114
Poquoson, Va., U.S.	C6	153
Porangatu, Braz.	B4	79
Porbandar, India	J3	44
Porcher Island, i., B.C., Can.	C2	99
Porchov, Russia	D12	22
Porciúncula, Braz.	F7	79
Porcupine Mountains, mts., Mi., U.S.	m12	129
Porcupine Plain, Sask., Can.	E4	105
Pordenone, Italy	D7	18
Porecatu, Braz.	G3	79
Pori, Fin.	K17	6
Porlamar, Ven.	B11	84
Poroma, Bol.	H9	82
Poronajsk, Russia	H20	28
Porosozero, Russia	J23	6
Porrentruy, Switz.	D7	13
Portachuelo, Bol.	G10	82
Port Adelaide, Austl.	J3	70
Portadown, N. Ire., U.K.	G7	8
Portage, In., U.S.	A3	121
Portage, Me., U.S.	B4	126
Portage, Mi., U.S.	F5	129
Portage, Pa., U.S.	F4	145
Portage, Wi., U.S.	E4	156
Portage, co., Oh., U.S.	A4	142
Portage, co., Wi., U.S.	D4	156
Portage Lakes, Oh., U.S.	B4	142
Portage la Prairie, Man., Can.	E2	100
Portageville, Mo., U.S.	E8	132
Port Alberni, B.C., Can.	E5	99
Portal del Infierno, wtfl, Hond.	C9	92
Portales, N.M., U.S.	C6	138
Port Alfred (Kowie), S. Afr.	I8	66
Port Alice, B.C., Can.	D4	99
Port Allegany, Pa., U.S.	C5	145
Port Allen, La., U.S.	D4	125
Port Angeles, Wa., U.S.	A2	154
Port Antonio, Jam.	E6	94
Port Aransas, Tx., U.S.	F4	150
Port Arthur see Lüshun, China	E9	32
Port Arthur, Tx., U.S.	E6	150
Port Augusta, Austl.	I2	70
Port au Port Bay, b., Newf., Can.	D2	102
Port au Port [West-Aguathuna-Felix Cove], Newf., Can.	D2	102
Port-au-Prince, Haiti	E8	94
Port-au-Prince, Baie de, b., Haiti	E8	94
Port au Prince Peninsula, pen., Newf., Can.	D2	102
Port Barre, La., U.S.	D4	125
Port-Bergé, Madag.	o22	67b
Port Birmingham, Al., U.S.	B2	108
Port Blair, India	I2	40
Port Blandford, Newf., Can.	D4	102
Port Burwell, Ont., Can.	E4	103
Port Byron, Il., U.S.	B3	120
Port Carbon, Pa., U.S.	E9	145
Port Carling, Ont., Can.	B5	103
Port-Cartier-Ouest, Que., Can.	k13	104
Port Charlotte, Fl., U.S.	F4	116
Port Chester, N.Y., U.S.	E7	139
Port Clements, B.C., Can.	C1	99
Port Clinton, Oh., U.S.	A3	142
Port Clyde, Me., U.S.	E3	126
Port Colborne, Ont., Can.	E5	103
Port Coquitlam, B.C., Can.	E6	99
Port-de-Paix, Haiti	E8	94
Port Deposit, Md., U.S.	A5	127
Port Dickson, Malay.	M6	40
Porte Crayon, Mount, mtn., W.V., U.S.	C5	155
Port Edward, B.C., Can.	B2	99
Port Edward, S. Afr.	H10	66
Port Edwards, Wi., U.S.	D4	156
Portegolpe, C.R.	G9	92
Porteirinha, Braz.	C7	79
Portel, Braz.	D8	76
Port Elgin, N.B., Can.	C5	101
Port Elgin, Ont., Can.	C3	103
Port Elizabeth, S. Afr.	I7	66
Porter, In., U.S.	A3	121
Porter, Tx., U.S.	D5	150
Porter, co., In., U.S.	B3	121
Porterdale, Ga., U.S.	C3	117
Porterville, Ca., U.S.	D4	112

Name	Map Ref.	Page
Port Ewen, N.Y., U.S.	D7	139
Port Fairy, Austl.	L5	70
Port Gentil, Gabon	B1	58
Port Gibson, Ms., U.S.	D3	131
Port Harcourt, Nig.	I13	64
Port Hastings, N.S., Can.	D8	101
Port Hawkesbury, N.S., Can.	D8	101
Port Hedland, Austl.	D3	68
Port Hood, N.S., Can.	C8	101
Port Hope, Ont., Can.	D6	103
Port Hope Simpson, Newf., Can.	B3	102
Port Howe, Bah.	B7	94
Port Hueneme, Ca., U.S.	E4	112
Port Huron, Mi., U.S.	F8	129
Portia, Ar., U.S.	A4	111
Portimão, Port.	H3	16
Port Isabel, Tx., U.S.	F4	150
Port Jefferson, N.Y., U.S.	n15	139
Port Jervis, N.Y., U.S.	D6	139
Port Kembla, Austl.	J9	70
Portland, Austl.	L4	70
Portland, Ar., U.S.	D4	111
Portland, Ct., U.S.	C5	114
Portland, In., U.S.	D8	121
Portland, Me., U.S.	E2	126
Portland, Mi., U.S.	F6	129
Portland, N.D., U.S.	B8	141
Portland, Or., U.S.	B4	144
Portland, Tn., U.S.	A5	149
Portland, Tx., U.S.	E4	150
Portland, Bill of, c., Eng., U.K.	K11	8
Portland Bight, Jam.	F6	94
Portland Inlet, b., B.C., Can.	B2	99
Portland Point, c., Jam.	F6	94
Port Laoise, Ire.	H6	8
Port Lavaca, Tx., U.S.	E4	150
Port Lincoln, Austl.	J1	70
Port Loko, S.L.	G3	64
Port Louis, Mrts.	v18	67c
Port Ludlow, Wa., U.S.	B3	154
Port Macquarie, Austl.	H10	70
Port Maitland, N.S., Can.	F3	101
Port Maria, Jam.	E6	94
Port McNeil, B.C., Can.	D4	99
Port McNicoll, Ont., Can.	C5	103
Port Moresby, Pap. N. Gui.	m16	68a
Port Morien, N.S., Can.	C10	101
Port Neches, Tx., U.S.	E6	150
Portneuf, Que., Can.	C6	104
Port Nolloth, S. Afr.	G3	66
Porto, Port.	D3	16
Porto Alegre, Braz.	F13	80
Porto Amboim, Ang.	D2	58
Porto Belo, Braz.	D14	80
Portobelo, Pan.	C3	84
Porto de Moz, Braz.	D8	76
Porto de Pedras, Braz.	E11	76
Porto Feliz, Braz.	G5	79
Porto Ferreira, Braz.	F5	79
Port of Spain, Trin.	I14	94
Portogruaro, Italy	D7	18
Porto Inglês, C.V.	m17	64a
Porto Murtinho, Braz.	I13	82
Porto Nacional, Braz.	F9	76
Porto-Novo, Benin	H11	64
Port Orange, Fl., U.S.	C6	116
Port Orchard, Wa., U.S.	B3	154
Port Orford, Or., U.S.	E2	144
Porto Seguro, Braz.	D9	79
Porto Torres, Italy	I3	18
Porto União, Braz.	D13	80
Porto-Vecchio, Fr.	m24	15a
Porto Velho, Braz.	C10	82
Portoviejo, Ec.	H2	84
Port Phillip Bay, b., Austl.	L6	70
Port Pirie, Austl.	I3	70
Port Rexton, Newf., Can.	D5	102
Port Richey, Fl., U.S.	D4	116
Port Rowan, Ont., Can.	E4	103
Port Royal, S.C., U.S.	G6	147
Port Royal Island, i., S.C., U.S.	G6	147
Port Royal Sound, strt., S.C., U.S.	G6	147
Port Said see Būr Sa'īd, Egypt	B7	60
Port Saint Joe, Fl., U.S.	C1	116
Port Saint Lucie, Fl., U.S.	E6	116
Port Salerno, Fl., U.S.	E6	116
Port Saunders, Newf., Can.	C3	102
Port Shepstone, S. Afr.	H10	66
Portsmouth, Eng., U.K.	K12	8
Portsmouth, N.H., U.S.	D5	136
Portsmouth, Oh., U.S.	D3	142
Portsmouth, R.I., U.S.	E6	146
Portsmouth, Va., U.S.	D6	153
Port Stanley, Ont., Can.	E3	103
Port Sudan see Būr Sūdān, Sud.	H9	60
Port Sulphur, La., U.S.	E6	125
Port Talbot, Wales, U.K.	J10	8
Port Townsend, Wa., U.S.	A3	154
Portugal, ctry., Eur.	H6	4
Portugalete, Spain	B8	16
Portuguesa, state, Ven.	C8	84
Port Union, Newf., Can.	D5	102
Port-Vendres, Fr.	J10	14
Port Wakefield, Austl.	J3	70
Port Washington, N.Y., U.S.	h13	139
Port Washington, Wi., U.S.	E6	156
Port Wentworth, Ga., U.S.	D5	117
Porum, Ok., U.S.	B6	143
Porvenir, Chile	G2	78
Posadas, Arg.	D11	80
Poschiavo, Switz.	F13	13
Posen see Poznań, Pol.	C16	10
Posen, Il., U.S.	k9	120
Posey, co., In., U.S.	H2	121
Poseyville, In., U.S.	H2	121
Posse, Braz.	C5	79
Post, Tx., U.S.	C2	150
Postavy, Bela.	F9	22
Post Falls, Id., U.S.	B2	119
Post Mills, Vt., U.S.	D4	152
Postojna, Slvn.	D9	18
Postville, Ia., U.S.	A6	122
Pótam, Mex.	D4	90
Potaro-Siparuni, prov., Guy.	E13	84
Poté, Braz.	D8	79
Poteau, Ok., U.S.	B7	143
Poteau, stm., U.S.	B7	143
Poteet, Tx., U.S.	E3	150
Potenza, Italy	I10	18
Potgietersrus, S. Afr.	E9	66
Potholes Reservoir, res., Wa., U.S.	B6	154
Potiraguá, Braz.	C9	79
Potirendaba, Braz.	F4	79
Potiskum, Nig.	F9	54
Potlatch, Id., U.S.	C2	119
Potomac, Md., U.S.	B3	127
Potomac, stm., U.S.	D4	127
Potomac Heights, Md., U.S.	C3	127
Potomac Park, Md., U.S.	k13	127
Potosí, Bol.	F8	74
Potosí, Bol.	H9	82
Potosi, Mo., U.S.	D7	132
Potosí, dept., Bol.	I8	82
Potrerillos, Chile	D4	80
Potrerillos, Hond.	B7	92
Potrerillos Arriba, Pan.	I12	92
Potro, Cerro del, mtn., S.A.	E4	80
Potsdam, Ger.	C13	10
Potsdam, N.Y., U.S.	f10	139
Pottawatomie, co., Ks., U.S.	C7	123
Pottawatomie, co., Ok., U.S.	B4	143
Pottawattamie, co., Ia., U.S.	C2	122
Potter, Ne., U.S.	C9	134
Potter, co., Pa., U.S.	C6	145
Potter, co., S.D., U.S.	B6	148
Potter, co., Tx., U.S.	B2	150
Pottstown, Pa., U.S.	F10	145
Pottsville, Ar., U.S.	B2	111
Pottsville, Pa., U.S.	E9	145
Potwin, Ks., U.S.	E6	123
Pouce Coupe, B.C., Can.	B7	99
Pouch Cove, Newf., Can.	E5	102
Poughkeepsie, N.Y., U.S.	D7	139
Poulan, Ga., U.S.	E3	117
Poulsbo, Wa., U.S.	B3	154
Poultney, Vt., U.S.	D2	152
Pound, Va., U.S.	e9	153
Pound Gap, U.S.	C7	124
Pouso Alegre, Braz.	G6	79
Pouso Redondo, Braz.	D14	80
Pouthisat, Camb.	H7	40
Považská Bystrica, Slvk.	F18	10
Povenec, Russia	J24	6
Póvoa de Varzim, Port.	D3	16
Povorino, Russia	G6	26
Powassan, Ont., Can.	A5	103
Poway, Ca., U.S.	F5	112
Powder, stm., U.S.	B5	106
Powder River, Wy., U.S.	C6	157
Powder River, stm., Or., U.S.	C9	144
Powder Springs, Ga., U.S.	h8	117
Powell, Tn., U.S.	m13	149
Powell, Wy., U.S.	B4	157
Powell, co., Ky., U.S.	C6	124
Powell, co., Mt., U.S.	D4	133
Powell, stm., U.S.	C10	149
Powell, Lake, res., U.S.	F5	151
Powell Mountain, mtn., U.S.	C10	149
Powell River, B.C., Can.	E5	99
Powell's Crossroads, Al., U.S.	A4	108
Powells Crossroads, Tn., U.S.	D8	149
Powellton, W.V., U.S.	C3	155
Power, co., Id., U.S.	G5	119
Powers, Or., U.S.	E2	144
Powers Lake, N.D., U.S.	A3	141
Powerview, Man., Can.	D3	100
Poweshiek, co., Ia., U.S.	C5	122
Powhatan, Va., U.S.	C5	153
Powhatan, co., Va., U.S.	C5	153
Pownal, Vt., U.S.	F2	152
Pownal Center, Vt., U.S.	F2	152
Poxoréo, Braz.	C1	79
Poyang Hu, l., China	F5	34
Poyen, Ar., U.S.	C3	111
Poygan, Lake, l., Wi., U.S.	D5	156
Poynette, Wi., U.S.	E4	156
Požarevac, Yugo.	E5	20
Poza Rica, Mex.	G11	90
Pozoblanco, Spain	G7	16
Pozo Almonte, Chile	I7	82
Pozo del Molle, Arg.	G7	80
Pozo del Tigre, Arg.	C8	80
Pozo Hondo, Arg.	D6	80
Pozuelo de Alarcón, Spain	E8	16
Pozuelos, Ven.	B10	84
Pozzallo, Italy	M9	18
Pozzuoli, Italy	I9	18
Prachin Buri, Thai.	G6	40
Pradera, Col.	F4	84
Prades, Fr.	J9	14
Prado, Braz.	D9	79
Prados, Braz.	F6	79
Prague see Praha, Czech Rep.	E14	10
Prague, Ok., U.S.	B5	143
Praha (Prague), Czech Rep.	E14	10
Praia, C.V.	m17	64a
Praia Grande, Braz.	E14	80
Prairie, co., Ar., U.S.	C4	111
Prairie, co., Mt., U.S.	D11	133
Prairie, stm., Mn., U.S.	C5	130
Prairie City, Ia., U.S.	C4	122
Prairie City, Or., U.S.	C8	144
Prairie du Chien, Wi., U.S.	E2	156
Prairie du Sac, Wi., U.S.	E4	156
Prairie Grove, Ar., U.S.	B1	111
Prairie View, Tx., U.S.	D5	150
Prairie Village, Ks., U.S.	m16	123
Prata, Braz.	E4	79
Pratápolis, Braz.	F5	79
Prato, Italy	F6	18
Pratt, Ks., U.S.	E5	123
Pratt, co., Ks., U.S.	E5	123
Prattville, Al., U.S.	C3	108
Pravdinsk, Russia	G4	22
Pravdinsk, Russia	E26	22
Pravdinskij, Russia	E20	22
Praya, Indon.	G6	38
Pra'ža, Russia	K23	6
Preble, co., Oh., U.S.	C1	142
Prečistoje, Russia	C23	22
Preeceville, Sask., Can.	F4	105
Preili, Lat.	E9	22
Prelate, Sask., Can.	G1	105
Prentiss, Ms., U.S.	D4	131
Prentiss, co., Ms., U.S.	A5	131
Prenzlau, Ger.	B13	10
Preparis North Channel, strt., Mya.	G3	40
Preparis South Channel, strt., Mya.	G3	40
Přerov, Czech Rep.	F17	10
Prescott, Ont., Can.	C9	103
Prescott, Az., U.S.	C3	110
Prescott, Ar., U.S.	D2	111
Prescott, Wi., U.S.	D1	156
Presho, S.D., U.S.	D5	148
Presidencia de la Plaza, Arg.	D9	80
Presidencia Roca, Arg.	D9	80
Presidencia Roque Sáenz Peña, Arg.	D8	80
Presidente Epitácio, Braz.	F2	79
Presidente Getúlio, Braz.	D14	80
Presidente Hayes, dept., Para.	C9	80
Presidente Olegário, Braz.	E5	79
Presidente Prudente, Braz.	G3	79
Presidente Venceslau, Braz.	F3	79
Presidential Range, mts., N.H., U.S.	B4	136
Presidio, Tx., U.S.	p12	150
Presidio, co., Tx., U.S.	o12	150
Prešov, Slvk.	F21	10
Presque Isle, Me., U.S.	B5	126
Presque Isle, co., Mi., U.S.	C6	129
Preston, Eng., U.K.	H11	8
Preston, Id., U.S.	G7	119
Preston, Ia., U.S.	B7	122
Preston, Mn., U.S.	G6	130
Preston, Wa., U.S.	e12	154
Preston, co., W.V., U.S.	B5	155
Preston, co., Ky., U.S.	C7	124
Prestonsburg, Ky., U.S.	C7	124
Prestwick, Scot., U.K.	F8	8
Pretoria, S. Afr.	E9	66
Prettyboy Reservoir, res., Md., U.S.	A4	127
Pretty Prairie, Ks., U.S.	E5	123
Prewitt, N.M., U.S.	B1	138
Prey Vêng, Camb.	I8	40
Pribilof Islands, is., Ak., U.S.	D5	109
Priboj, Yugo.	F3	20
Příbram, Czech Rep.	F14	10
Price, Ut., U.S.	D5	151
Price, co., Wi., U.S.	C3	156
Priceville, Al., U.S.	A3	108
Prichard, Al., U.S.	E1	108
Priego de Córdoba, Spain	H7	16
Priekule, Lat.	E4	22
Priekule, Lith.	F4	22
Prieska, S. Afr.	G6	66
Priest Lake, l., Id., U.S.	A2	119
Priest Rapids Lake, res., Wa., U.S.	C6	154
Priest River, Id., U.S.	A2	119
Prievidza, Slvk.	G18	10
Prijedor, Bos.	E11	18
Prijutovo, Russia	G8	26
Prikaspijskaja nizmennost', pl.	H7	26
Prilep, Mac.	H5	20
Priluki, Ukr.	G4	26
Primeiro de Maio, Braz.	G3	79
Primero, stm., Arg.	F7	80
Primghar, Ia., U.S.	A2	122
Primorsk, Russia	A11	22
Primrose, R.I., U.S.	B3	146
Prince Albert, Sask., Can.	D3	105
Prince Albert, S. Afr.	I6	66
Prince Albert Mountains, mts., Ant.	C8	73
Prince Charles Island, i., N.W. Ter., Can.	C17	96
Prince Edward, co., Va., U.S.	C4	153
Prince Edward Island, prov., Can.	C6	101
Prince Edward Islands, is., S. Afr.	M7	158
Prince Frederick, Md., U.S.	C4	127
Prince George, B.C., Can.	C6	99
Prince Georges, co., Md., U.S.	C4	127
Prince of Wales, Cape, c., Ak., U.S.	B6	109
Prince of Wales Island, i., Austl.	B8	68
Prince of Wales Island, i., N.W. Ter., Can.	B13	96
Prince of Wales Island, i., Ak., U.S.	n23	109
Prince of Wales Strait, strt., N.W. Ter., Can.	B9	96
Prince Olav Coast, Ant.	B4	73
Prince Patrick Island, i., N.W. Ter., Can.	B6	86
Prince Regent Inlet, b., N.W. Ter., Can.	B14	96
Prince Rupert, B.C., Can.	B2	99
Princes Lakes, In., U.S.	F5	121
Princess Anne, Md., U.S.	D6	127
Princess Astrid Coast, Ant.	B2	73
Princess Martha Coast, Ant.	C2	73
Princess Ragnhild Coast, Ant.	C3	73
Princess Royal Channel, strt., B.C., Can.	C3	99
Princess Royal Island, i., B.C., Can.	C3	99
Princes Town, Trin.	I14	94
Princeton, B.C., Can.	E7	99
Princeton, Fl., U.S.	G6	116
Princeton, Il., U.S.	B4	120
Princeton, In., U.S.	H2	121
Princeton, Ia., U.S.	C7	122
Princeton, Ky., U.S.	C2	124
Princeton, Me., U.S.	C5	126
Princeton, Mn., U.S.	E5	130
Princeton, Mo., U.S.	A4	132
Princeton, N.J., U.S.	C3	137
Princeton, W.V., U.S.	D3	155
Princeton, Wi., U.S.	E4	156
Princeton, Mount, mtn., Co., U.S.	C4	113
Princeville, Que., Can.	C6	104
Princeville, Il., U.S.	C4	120
Princeville, N.C., U.S.	B5	140
Prince William, co., Va., U.S.	B5	153
Prince William Sound, strt., Ak., U.S.	g18	109
Príncipe, i., S. Tom./P.	A1	58
Principe Channel, strt., B.C., Can.	C3	99
Prineville, Or., U.S.	C6	144
Prinzapolka, Nic.	D11	92
Prinzapolka, stm., Nic.	D11	92
Prior Lake, Mn., U.S.	F5	130
Priozërsk, Russia	K22	6
Prip'at', stm., Eur.	G3	26
Pripet Marshes see Polesje, reg., Eur.	G3	26
Pristina, Yugo.	G5	20
Privas, Fr.	H11	14
Privolžsk, Russia	D24	22
Privolžskij, Russia	G7	26
Prizren, Yugo.	G4	20
Probolinggo, Indon.	j16	39a
Proctor, Mn., U.S.	D6	130
Proctor, Vt., U.S.	D2	152
Proctorsville, Vt., U.S.	E3	152
Proddatūr, India	E5	46
Progreso, Mex.	G15	90
Progreso, Ur.	H10	80
Prokopjevsk, Russia	G9	28
Prokuplje, Yugo.	F5	20
Proletarij, Russia	C14	22
Proletarskij, Russia	F20	22
Prome (Pyè), Mya.	E3	40
Promissão, Braz.	F4	79
Pronsk, Russia	G22	22
Propriá, Braz.	F11	76
Proserpine, Austl.	C8	70
Prospect, Ct., U.S.	C4	114
Prospect, Ky., U.S.	g11	124
Prospect, Or., U.S.	E4	144
Prospect Harbor, Me., U.S.	D4	126
Prospect Park, N.J., U.S.	B4	137
Prospect Park, Pa., U.S.	p20	145
Prosperity, S.C., U.S.	C4	147
Prosperity, W.V., U.S.	n13	155
Prosser, Wa., U.S.	C6	154
Prostějov, Czech Rep.	F17	10
Protection, Ks., U.S.	E4	123
Provadija, Bul.	F11	20
Provence, hist. reg., Fr.	I13	14
Providence, R.I., U.S.	C4	146
Providence, co., R.I., U.S.	B3	146
Providence, Ut., U.S.	B4	151
Providence, co., R.I., U.S.	C5	146
Providence, Cape, c., N.Z.	F12	72
Providence, Island, i., Sey.	C10	58
Providencia, Isla de, i., Col.	H4	94
Providenija, Russia	E29	28
Provincetown, Ma., U.S.	B7	128
Provins, Fr.	D10	14
Provo, Ut., U.S.	C4	151
Provo, stm., Ut., U.S.	C4	151
Provost, Alta., Can.	C5	98
Prowers, co., Co., U.S.	D8	113
Prudence Island, i., R.I., U.S.	E5	146
Prudentópolis, Braz.	C13	80
Prudhoe Bay, b., Ak., U.S.	A10	109
Prud'homme, Sask., Can.	E3	105
Prudnik, Pol.	E17	10
Pruszków, Pol.	C20	10
Prut, stm., Eur.	D12	20
Pružany, Bela.	I7	22
Pryor, Mt., U.S.	E8	133
Pryor, Ok., U.S.	A6	143
Przemyśl, Pol.	F22	10
Pskov, Russia	D11	22
Pszczyna, Pol.	F18	10
Ptolemaís, Grc.	I5	20
Ptuj, Slvn.	C10	18
Puán, Arg.	I7	80
Pucallpa, Peru	C4	82
Pučež, Russia	E26	22
Pucheng, China	H7	34
Pudož, Russia	E5	26
Pudukkottai, India	G5	46
Puebla [de Zaragoza], Mex.	H10	90
Pueblo, Co., U.S.	C6	113
Pueblo, co., Co., U.S.	C6	113
Pueblo Mountain, mtn., Or., U.S.	E8	144
Pueblo Nuevo, Ven.	B8	84
Pueblo Nuevo Tiquisate, Guat.	C2	92
Pueblo of Acoma, N.M., U.S.	C2	138
Puebloviejo, Ec.	H3	84
Pueblo Yaqui, Mex.	D4	90
Puente Alto, Chile	G3	80
Puente-Genil, Spain	H7	16
Puerco, stm., N.M., U.S.	C6	110
Puerco, Rio, stm., N.M., U.S.	B2	138
Puerto Acosta, Bol.	F7	82
Puerto Aisén, Chile	F2	78
Puerto Armuelles, Pan.	C1	84
Puerto Asís, Col.	G4	84
Puerto Ayacucho, Ven.	E9	84
Puerto Baquerizo Moreno, Ec.	m16	85a
Puerto Barrios, Guat.	B6	92
Puerto Bermejo, Arg.	D9	80
Puerto Bermúdez, Peru	D4	82
Puerto Boyacá, Col.	D5	84
Puerto Busch, Bol.	I13	82
Puerto Cabello, Ven.	B8	84
Puerto Cabezas, Nic.	C11	92
Puerto Carreño, Col.	D9	84
Puerto Chicama, Peru	B2	82
Puerto Colombia, Col.	B5	84
Puerto Cortés, Hond.	B7	92
Puerto Cumarebo, Ven.	B8	84
Puerto de Lomas, Peru	F4	82
Puerto del Rosario, Spain	o27	17b
Puerto Escondido, Mex.	J11	90
Puerto Francisco de Orellana, Ec.	H4	84
Puerto Iguazú, Arg.	C11	80
Puerto Jiménez, C.R.	I11	92
Puerto la Cruz, Ven.	B10	84
Puerto Leguízamo, Col.	H5	84
Puerto Lempira, Hond.	B11	92
Puerto Libertad, Mex.	C3	90
Puerto Limón, C.R.	G11	92
Puertollano, Spain	G7	16
Puerto López, Col.	E6	84
Puerto Madero, Mex.	C2	92
Puerto Maldonado, Peru	E7	82
Puerto Montt, Chile	E2	78
Puerto Morazán, Nic.	E7	92
Puerto Natales, Chile	G2	78
Puerto Padre, Cuba	D6	94
Puerto Páez, Ven.	D9	84
Puerto Peñasco, Mex.	B3	90
Puerto Pilón, Pan.	H15	92
Puerto Piray, Arg.	D11	80
Puerto Plata, Dom. Rep.	E9	94
Puerto Princesa, Phil.	D6	38
Puerto Real, Spain	I5	16
Puerto Rico, Arg.	D11	80
Puerto Rico, dep., N.A.	E11	94
Puerto Rico Trench	G13	86
Puerto Saavedra, Chile	J2	80
Puerto Sandino, Nic.	E8	92
Puerto San José, Guat.	D4	92
Puerto San Julián, Arg.	F3	78
Puerto Santa Cruz, Arg.	G3	78
Puerto Siles, Bol.	E9	82
Puerto Suarez, Bol.	H13	82
Puerto Supe, Peru	D3	82
Puerto Tejada, Col.	F4	84
Puerto Vallarta, Mex.	G7	90
Puerto Varas, Chile	E2	78
Puerto Viejo, C.R.	H12	92
Puerto Viejo, C.R.	G11	92
Puerto Wilches, Col.	D6	84
Pueyrredón, Lago (Lago Cochrane), l., S.A.	F2	78
Pugačov, Russia	G7	26
Puget Sound, strt., Wa., U.S.	B3	154
Puglia, prov., Italy	I11	18
Pugwash, N.S., Can.	D6	101
Puhi, Hi., U.S.	B2	118
Pujiang, China	F8	34
Pujili, Ec.	H3	84
Pukalani, Hi., U.S.	C5	118
Pukch'ŏng, N. Kor.	C16	32
Pukekohe, N.Z.	B5	72
Pukou, China	C7	34
Puksoozero, Russia	J27	6
Pula, Cro.	E8	18
Pulacayo, Bol.	H8	82
Pulaski, N.Y., U.S.	B4	139
Pulaski, Tn., U.S.	B4	149
Pulaski, Va., U.S.	C2	153
Pulaski, Wi., U.S.	D5	156
Pulaski, co., Ar., U.S.	C3	111
Pulaski, co., Ga., U.S.	D3	117
Pulaski, co., Il., U.S.	F4	120
Pulaski, co., In., U.S.	B4	121
Pulaski, co., Ky., U.S.	C5	124
Pulaski, co., Mo., U.S.	D5	132
Pulaski, co., Va., U.S.	C2	153
Puławy, Pol.	D21	10
Pullman, Wa., U.S.	C8	154
Pully, Switz.	E6	13
Pułtusk, Pol.	C21	10
Pumphrey, Md., U.S.	h11	127
Puná, Isla, i., Ec.	I2	84
Punata, Bol.	G5	82
Pune (Poona), India	C2	46
Punia, Zaire	B5	58
Punjab, state, India	E6	44
Punnichy, Sask., Can.	F3	105
Puno, Peru	F5	82
Puno, dept., Peru	F5	82
Punta, Cerro de, mtn., P.R.	E11	94
Punta Alta, Arg.	J7	80
Punta Arenas, Chile	G2	78
Punta Cardón, Ven.	B7	84
Punta del Este, Ur.	H11	80
Punta de Piedras, Ven.	B10	84
Punta Gorda, Belize	I15	90
Punta Gorda, Fl., U.S.	F4	116
Punta Gorda, Nic.	F11	92
Punta Gorda, Bahía de, b., Nic.	F11	92
Puntarenas, C.R.	H10	92
Punto Fijo, Ven.	B7	84
Punxsutawney, Pa., U.S.	E4	145
Puolanka, Fin.	I20	6
Puqi, China	F9	30
Puquio, Peru	E4	82
Purcell, Ok., U.S.	B4	143
Purcellville, Va., U.S.	A5	153
Purdy, Mo., U.S.	E4	132
Purgatoire Peak, mtn., Co., U.S.	D5	113
Puri, India	K11	44
Purmerend, Neth.	C6	12
Pūrnia, India	H12	44
Pursglove, W.V., U.S.	B4	155
Puruliya, India	I12	44
Purus (Purús), stm., S.A.	D6	76
Purvis, Ms., U.S.	D4	131
Purwakarta, Indon.	j13	39a
Purwokerto, Indon.	j14	39a
Pusan, S. Kor.	H17	32
Pushmataha, co., Ok., U.S.	C6	143
Pŭskin, Russia	B13	22
Puškino, Russia	E20	22
Puškinskije Gory, Russia	D11	22
Püspökladány, Hung.	H21	10
Püssi, Est.	B10	22
Pustoška, Russia	E12	22
Putao, Mya.	G17	44
Putian, China	J8	34
Puting, Tanjung, c., Indon.	F5	38
Putnam, Ct., U.S.	B8	114
Putnam, co., Fl., U.S.	C5	116
Putnam, co., Ga., U.S.	C3	117
Putnam, co., Il., U.S.	B4	120
Putnam, co., In., U.S.	E4	121
Putnam, co., Mo., U.S.	A4	132
Putnam, co., N.Y., U.S.	D7	139
Putnam, co., Oh., U.S.	A1	142
Putnam, co., Tn., U.S.	C8	149
Putnam, co., W.V., U.S.	C2	155
Putney, Ga., U.S.	E2	117
Putney, Vt., U.S.	F3	152
Putre, Chile	H7	82
Putumayo, ter., Col.	G4	84
Putumayo (Içá), stm., S.A.	I7	84
Putuo, China	F11	34
Puunene, Hi., U.S.	C5	118
Puxi, China	J8	34
Puxico, Mo., U.S.	E7	132
Puyallup, Wa., U.S.	B3	154
Puyang, China	H2	32
Puyango (Tumbes), stm., S.A.	I3	84
Puyo, Ec.	H4	84
Puyŏ, S. Kor.	G14	32
Pweto, Zaire	C5	58
Pyapon, Mya.	F3	40
Pyinmana, Mya.	E4	40
Pymatuning Reservoir, res., U.S.	C1	145
Pyŏktong, N. Kor.	C13	32
P'yŏngt'aek, S. Kor.	F15	32
P'yŏngyang, N. Kor.	D13	32
Pyramid Lake, l., Nv., U.S.	C2	135
Pyrenees, mts., Eur.	C13	16
Pytalovo, Russia	D10	22
Pyu, Mya.	E4	40

Q

Name	Map Ref.	Page
Qacentina (Constantine), Alg.	B14	62
Qā'emshahr, Iran	C12	48
Qaidam Pendi, China	B16	44
Qalāt, Afg.	D2	44
Qal'at Bīshah, Sau. Ar.	D3	47
Qalqīlya, W.B.	D3	50
Qamar, Ghubbat al-, b., Yemen	F8	47
Qamdo, China	E6	30
Qānā, Leb.	B4	50
Qantur, Sud.	M3	60
Qārūn, Birkat, l., Egypt	C6	60
Qasr el-Boukhari, Alg.	C12	62
Qa'tabah, Yemen	H4	47
Qatanā, Syria	B6	50
Qatar (Qatar), ctry., Asia	D5	42
Qattara Depression see Qattārah, Munkhafad al-, depr., Egypt	B4	60
Qattārah, Munkhafad al- (Qattara Depression), depr., Egypt	B4	60
Qazimämmäd, Azer.	I7	26
Qazvīn, Iran	C11	48
Qeisari, Horbat (Caesarea), hist., Isr.	C3	50
Qeshm, Iran	H14	48
Qeshm, Jazīreh-ye, i., Iran	H13	48
Qezel Owzan, stm., Iran	C10	48
Qianyang, China	F9	30
Qidong, China	D10	34
Qiemo, China	A11	44
Qift (Coptos), Egypt	D7	60
Qijiang, China	F8	30
Qilian Shan, China	D6	30
Qilian Shan, mts., China	D6	30
Qinâ, Egypt	D7	60
Qingchengzi, China	C11	32
Qingdao (Tsingtao), China	G8	32
Qinghai (Tsinghai), prov., China	D6	30
Qinghai Hu, l., China	D7	30
Qingjiang, China	G4	34
Qingjiang, China	B8	34
Qinglian, China	K1	34
Qinglong, China	B8	34
Qingpu, China	D10	34
Qingyang, China	E3	34
Qingyang, China	D8	30
Qingyuan, China	D9	34
Qingyuan, China	G8	30
Qingyuan, China	L2	34
Qinhuangdao (Chinwangtao), China	D7	30
Qin Ling, mts., China	E8	30
Qinzhou, China	D10	40
Qionglai, China	E7	30
Qiongzhong, China	E10	40
Qiqihar (Tsitsihar), China	B11	30
Qiryat Ata, Isr.	C4	50
Qiryat Bialik, Isr.	C4	50
Qiryat Gat, Isr.	D3	50
Qiryat Motzkin, Isr.	C4	50
Qiryat Ono, Isr.	B5	50
Qiryat Shemona, Isr.	B5	50
Qiryat Yam, Isr.	C4	50
Qishuyan, China	D9	34
Qitai, China	A4	30
Qiyang, China	A11	40
Qnadsa, Alg.	E9	62
Qom, Iran	D11	48
Qomsheh, Iran	E11	48
Qondūz, Afg.	J11	26
Qondūz, stm., Afg.	D9	48
Qorveh, Iran	D9	48
Quabbin Reservoir, res., Ma., U.S.	B3	128
Quail Oaks, Va., U.S.	n18	153
Quaker Hill, Ct., U.S.	D7	114
Quakertown, Pa., U.S.	F11	145
Qualicum Beach, B.C., Can.	E5	99
Quanah, Tx., U.S.	B3	150
Quang Ngai, Viet.	G10	40
Quantico, Va., U.S.	B5	153
Quanzhou (Chuanchou), China	K7	34
Quapaw, Ok., U.S.	A7	143
Qu'Appelle, Sask., Can.	G4	105
Qu'Appelle, stm., Can.	G5	105
Quaraí, Braz.	F10	80
Quaraí, stm., Braz.	F10	80
Quartu Sant'Elena, Italy	J4	18
Quartzsite, Az., U.S.	D1	110
Quay, co., N.M., U.S.	C6	138
Quba, Azer.	I7	26
Qūchān, Iran	C15	48
Queanbeyan, Austl.	J8	70
Québec, Que., Can.	C6	104
Quebec, prov., Can.	C5	104
Quebracho, Ur.	F10	80
Quechee, Vt., U.S.	D4	152
Quedlinburg, Ger.	D11	10
Queen Annes, co., Md., U.S.	B5	127
Queen Charlotte, B.C., Can.	C1	99

Name	Map Ref.	Page
Queen Charlotte Islands, is., B.C., Can.	C1	99
Queen Charlotte Strait, strt., B.C., Can.	D4	99
Queen City, Mo., U.S.	A5	132
Queen Creek, Az., U.S.	m9	110
Queen Elizabeth Islands, is., N.W. Ter., Can.	B9	86
Queen Maud Land, reg., Ant.	C3	73
Queen Maud Mountains, mts., Ant.	D9	73
Queens, co., N.Y., U.S.	E7	139
Queensland, state, Austl.	D9	68
Queenstown, Austl.	N6	70
Queenstown, N.Z.	F2	72
Queenstown, S. Afr.	H8	66
Queimadas, Braz.	G7	79
Quelimane, Moz.	A13	66
Quemado, N.M., U.S.	C1	138
Quemado, Punta de, c., Cuba	D7	94
Quemoy see Chinmen Tao, i., Tai.	K7	34
Quemú Quemú, Arg.	I7	80
Quepos, C.R.	H10	92
Quequén, Arg.	J9	80
Querétaro, Mex.	G9	90
Querétaro, state, Mex.	G10	90
Quesada, C.R.	G10	92
Queshan, China	C3	34
Quesnel, B.C., Can.	C6	99
Quesnel, stm., B.C., Can.	C6	99
Quesnel Lake, l., B.C., Can.	C7	99
Questa, N.M., U.S.	A4	138
Quetta, Pak.	E2	44
Quetzaltenango, Guat.	C3	92
Quetzaltenango, dept., Guat.	C3	92
Quevedo, Ec.	H3	84
Quezaltepeque, El Sal.	D5	92
Quezon City, Phil.	n19	39b
Qufu, China	H5	32
Quibdó, Col.	E4	84
Quiberon, Fr.	E3	14
Quíbor, Ven.	C8	84
Quidnessett, R.I., U.S.	E4	146
Quidnick, R.I., U.S.	D3	146
Quiindy, Para.	C10	80
Quila, Mex.	E6	90
Quilcene, Wa., U.S.	B3	154
Quilino, Arg.	F6	80
Quillagua, Chile	I7	82
Quillan, Fr.	J9	14
Quill Lake, Sask., Can.	E3	105
Quillota, Chile	G3	80
Quilon, India	H4	46
Quilpie, Austl.	F6	70
Quilpué, Chile	G3	80
Quimbaya, Col.	E5	84
Quimili, Arg.	D7	80
Quimper, Fr.	D2	14
Quimperlé, Fr.	E3	14
Quinault, stm., Wa., U.S.	B1	154
Quincy, Fl., U.S.	B2	116
Quincy, Il., U.S.	D2	120
Quincy, Ma., U.S.	B5	128
Quincy, Mi., U.S.	G6	129
Quincy, Wa., U.S.	B6	154
Quincy Bay, b., Ma., U.S.	g12	128
Quindío, dept., Col.	E5	84
Quinebaug, Ct., U.S.	A8	114
Quinebaug, stm., Ct., U.S.	C8	114
Quines, Arg.	G6	80
Quinhagak, Ak., U.S.	D7	109
Qui Nhon, Viet.	H10	40
Quinn, stm., Nv., U.S.	B3	135
Quinnipiac, stm., Ct., U.S.	D4	114
Quintana Roo, state, Mex.	H15	90
Quinter, Ks., U.S.	C3	123
Quintero, Chile	G3	80
Quinto de Noviembre, Presa, El Sal.	D6	92
Quinton, Sask., Can.	F3	105
Quinton, Ok., U.S.	B6	143
Quinwood, W.V., U.S.	C4	155
Quirindi, Austl.	H9	70
Quirinópolis, Braz.	E3	79
Quiriquire, Ven.	C11	84
Quiroga, Mex.	H9	90
Quitilipi, Arg.	D8	80
Quitman, Ar., U.S.	B3	111
Quitman, Ga., U.S.	F3	117
Quitman, Ms., U.S.	C5	131
Quitman, co., Ga., U.S.	E1	117
Quitman, co., Ms., U.S.	A3	131
Quito, Ec.	H3	84
Quixadá, Braz.	D11	76
Quijiang, China	K2	34
Quijing, China	B7	40
Quonochontaug, R.I., U.S.	G2	146
Quorn, Austl.	I3	70
Qūs, Egypt	E7	60
Quxi, China	L5	34
Quxian, China	G7	34
Quzhou, China	G2	32

R

Name	Map Ref.	Page
Raahe, Fin.	I19	6
Ra'ananna, Isr.	D3	50
Raba, Indon.	G6	38
Rabat (Victoria), Malta	M9	18
Rabat, Mor.	C7	62
Rabat, P.N. Gui.	k17	68a
Rabbit Lake, Sask., Can.	D2	105
Rābigh, Sau. Ar.	C1	47
Rābigh, Sau. Ar.	J5	48
Râbnița (Rybnica), Mol.	B13	20
Rabun, co., Ga., U.S.	B3	117
Rabyānah, Şaḥrā', des., Libya	D5	56
Raccoon Creek, stm., Oh., U.S.	D3	142
Race, Cape, c., Newf., Can.	E5	102
Raceland, Ky., U.S.	B7	124
Raceland, La., U.S.	E5	125
Race Point, c., Ma., U.S.	B7	128
Rach Gia, Viet.	I8	40
Racibórz (Ratibor), Pol.	E18	10
Racine, W.V., U.S.	C3	155
Racine, Wi., U.S.	F6	156
Racine, co., Wi., U.S.	F5	156
Rădăuți, Rom.	B9	20
Radcliff, Ky., U.S.	C4	124
Radebeul, Ger.	D13	10
Rades, Tun.	B16	62
Radford, Va., U.S.	C2	153
Radisson, Sask., Can.	E2	105
Radium Hot Springs, B.C., Can.	D9	99
Radom, Pol.	D21	10
Radomsko, Pol.	D19	10
Radoškovichi, Bela.	G10	22
Radoviš, Mac.	H6	20
Radviliškis, Lith.	F6	22
Radville, Sask., Can.	H3	105
Rae, N.W. Ter., Can.	D9	96
Rae Bareli, India	G9	44
Raeford, N.C., U.S.	C3	140
Rafaela, Arg.	F8	80
Rafah, Gaza	F2	50
Rafsanjān, Iran	F14	48
Raft, stm., Id., U.S.	G5	119
Raft River Mountains, mts., Ut., U.S.	B2	151
Raga, Sud.	M3	60
Ragged Island Range, is., Bah.	C7	94
Ragland, Al., U.S.	B3	108
Ragusa, Italy	M9	18
Rahīmyār Khān, Pak.	F4	44
Rahway, N.J., U.S.	B4	137
Rahway, stm., N.J., U.S.	k7	137
Rāichūr, India	D4	46
Raigani, India	H13	44
Raigarh, India	J10	44
Rainbow Bridge National Monument, Ut., U.S.	F5	151
Rainelle, W.V., U.S.	D4	155
Rainier, Or., U.S.	A4	144
Rainier, Wa., U.S.	C3	154
Rainier, Mount, mtn., Wa., U.S.	C4	154
Rains, co., Tx., U.S.	C5	150
Rainsville, Al., U.S.	A4	108
Rainy Lake, l., Mn., U.S.	B5	130
Rainy River, Ont., Can.	o16	103
Raipur, India	J9	44
Rājahmundry, India	D6	46
Rajang, stm., Malay.	E5	38
Rājapālaiyam, India	H4	46
Rajasthān, state, India	G5	44
Rajčichinsk, Russia	H17	28
Rājkot, India	I4	44
Rāj Nāndgaon, India	J9	44
Rājshāhi, Bngl.	H13	44
Rakaposhi, mtn., Pak.	B6	44
Rakata, Pulau, i., Indon.	j12	39a
Rakovník, Czech Rep.	E13	10
Rakvere, Est.	B9	22
Raleigh, Ms., U.S.	C4	131
Raleigh, N.C., U.S.	B4	140
Raleigh, W.V., U.S.	n13	155
Raleigh, co., W.V., U.S.	D3	155
Raleigh Bay, b., N.C., U.S.	C6	140
Ralls, co., Mo., U.S.	B6	132
Ralston, Ne., U.S.	g12	134
Ralston, Wy., U.S.	B4	157
Rama, Nic.	E10	92
Ramah, N.M., U.S.	B1	138
Ramallah, W.B.	E4	50
Ramapo, stm., N.J., U.S.	A4	137
Ramat Gan, Isr.	D3	50
Ramat HaSharon, Isr.	D3	50
Ramathlabama, Bots.	E7	66
Rambervillers, Fr.	D13	14
Ramblewood, N.J., U.S.	D3	137
Rambouillet, Fr.	D8	14
Ramea, Newf., Can.	E3	102
Ramenskoje, Russia	F21	22
Ramer, Al., U.S.	C3	108
Rameški, Russia	D19	22
Ramhormoz, Iran	F10	48
Ramiriquí, Col.	E6	84
Ramla, Isr.	E3	50
Ramlu, mtn., Afr.	F9	56
Ramm, Jabal, mtn., Jord.	I4	50
Râmnicu Sărat, Rom.	D11	20
Râmnicu Vâlcea, Rom.	D8	20
Ramona, Ca., U.S.	F5	112
Ramotswa, Bots.	E7	66
Rāmpur, India	F8	44
Ramree Island, i., Mya.	E2	40
Ramsey, I. of Man	G9	8
Ramsey, Il., U.S.	D4	120
Ramsey, Mn., U.S.	*E5	130
Ramsey, N.J., U.S.	A4	137
Ramsey, co., Mn., U.S.	E5	130
Ramsey, co., N.D., U.S.	A7	141
Ramshorn Peak, mtn., Mt., U.S.	E5	133
Ramygala, Lith.	F7	22
Ranburne, Al., U.S.	B4	108
Rancagua, Chile	H3	80
Rancharia, Braz.	G3	79
Ranchester, Wy., U.S.	B5	157
Rānchi, India	I11	44
Ranchillos, Arg.	D6	80
Ranchos de Taos, N.M., U.S.	A4	138
Rancocas Creek, stm., N.J., U.S.	C3	137
Rancul, Arg.	H6	80
Rand, W.V., U.S.	C3	155
Randall, co., Tx., U.S.	B2	150
Randallstown, Md., U.S.	B4	127
Randers, Den.	M12	6
Randle, Wa., U.S.	C4	154
Randleman, N.C., U.S.	B3	140
Randolph, Me., U.S.	D3	126
Randolph, Ma., U.S.	B5	128
Randolph, Ne., U.S.	B8	134
Randolph, Vt., U.S.	D3	152
Randolph, Wi., U.S.	E5	156
Randolph, co., Al., U.S.	B4	108
Randolph, co., Ar., U.S.	A4	111
Randolph, co., Ga., U.S.	E2	117
Randolph, co., Il., U.S.	E4	120
Randolph, co., In., U.S.	D7	121
Randolph, co., Mo., U.S.	B5	132
Randolph, co., N.C., U.S.	B3	140
Randolph, co., W.V., U.S.	C5	155
Randolph Center, Vt., U.S.	D3	152
Randolph Hills, Md., U.S.	B3	127
Random Lake, Wi., U.S.	E6	156
Rāngāmāti, Bngl.	I15	44
Rangeley, Me., U.S.	D2	126
Rangeley Lake, l., Me., U.S.	D2	126
Rangely, Co., U.S.	A2	113
Ranger, Tx., U.S.	C3	150
Rangoon see Yangon, Mya.	B2	38
Rangpur, Bngl.	H13	44
Rānībennur, India	E3	46
Ranken Store, Austl.	B2	70
Rankin,	k14	145
Rankin, co., Ms., U.S.	C4	131
Rankin Inlet, N.W. Ter., Can.	D14	96
Ranomafana, Madag.	t22	67b
Ransom, co., N.D., U.S.	C8	141
Ranson, W.V., U.S.	B7	155
Rantauprapat, Indon.	M5	40
Rantekombola, Bulu, mtn., Indon.	F7	38
Rantoul, Il., U.S.	C5	120
Ranua, Fin.	I20	6
Raoping, China	L6	34
Raoul, Ga., U.S.	B3	117
Rapallo, Italy	E4	18
Rapid, stm., Mn., U.S.	B4	130
Rapid City, Man., Can.	D1	100
Rapid City, S.D., U.S.	C2	148
Rapides, co., La., U.S.	C3	125
Rapids City, Il., U.S.	B3	120
Räpina, Est.	C10	22
Rapla, Est.	B7	22
Rappahannock, co., Va., U.S.	B4	153
Rappahannock, stm., Va., U.S.	B5	153
Rapperswil, Switz.	D10	13
Raquette, stm., N.Y., U.S.	f10	139
Raritan, N.J., U.S.	B3	137
Raritan, stm., N.J., U.S.	C4	137
Raritan Bay, b., N.J., U.S.	C4	137
Rasa, Punta, c., Arg.	I10	80
Ra's al-'Ayn, Syria	C6	48
Ra's al-Khaymah, U.A.E.	B9	47
Ra's an-Naqb, Jord.	H4	50
Râşcani, Mol.	B11	20
Ras Dashen Terara, mtn., Eth.	K10	60
Raseiniai, Lith.	F6	22
Râs el Aïoun, Alg.	N3	18
Ras el Ma, Alg.	C10	62
Rashād, Sud.	L6	60
Rashīd, Egypt	B6	60
Rasht, Iran	C10	48
Rass Jebel, Tun.	L5	18
Rasskazovo, Russia	I24	22
Ra's Tannūrah, Sau. Ar.	H11	48
Rastatt, Ger.	G8	10
Rastede, Ger.	B8	10
Rathbun Lake, res., Ia., U.S.	D5	122
Rathdrum, Id., U.S.	B2	119
Rathenow, Ger.	C12	10
Rathwell, Man., Can.	E2	100
Rat Islands, is., Ak., U.S.	E3	109
Ratlām, India	I6	44
Ratnapura, Sri L.	I6	46
Raton, N.M., U.S.	A5	138
Raton Pass, N.M., U.S.	A5	138
Raub, Malay.	M6	40
Rauch, Arg.	I9	80
Raul Soares, Braz.	F7	79
Rauma, Fin.	K17	6
Raurkela, India	I11	44
Raven, Va., U.S.	e10	153
Ravena, N.Y., U.S.	C7	139
Ravenden, Ar., U.S.	A4	111
Ravenel, S.C., U.S.	k11	147
Ravenna, Italy	E7	18
Ravenna, Ky., U.S.	C6	124
Ravenna, Ne., U.S.	C7	134
Ravenna, Oh., U.S.	A4	142
Ravensburg, Ger.	H9	10
Ravensdale, Wa., U.S.	f12	154
Ravensthorpe, Austl.	F4	68
Ravenswood, W.V., U.S.	C3	155
Rāwalpindi, Pak.	D5	44
Rawdon, Que., Can.	C4	104
Rawicz, Pol.	D16	10
Rawlins, Wy., U.S.	E5	157
Rawlins, co., Ks., U.S.	C2	123
Rawson, Arg.	E3	78
Rawson, Arg.	H8	80
Ray, N.D., U.S.	A2	141
Ray, co., Mo., U.S.	B3	132
Ray, Cape, c., Newf., Can.	E2	102
Raya, Bukit, mtn., Indon.	F5	38
Ray City, Ga., U.S.	E3	117
Raymond, Alta., Can.	E4	98
Raymond, Me., U.S.	E2	126
Raymond, Mn., U.S.	E3	130
Raymond, Ms., U.S.	C3	131
Raymond, N.H., U.S.	D4	136
Raymond, Wa., U.S.	C2	154
Raymond Terrace, Austl.	I9	70
Raymondville, Tx., U.S.	F4	150
Raymore, Sask., Can.	F3	105
Raymore, Mo., U.S.	C3	132
Rayne, La., U.S.	D3	125
Raynham, Ma., U.S.	C5	128
Raynham Center, Ma., U.S.	C5	128
Rayón, Mex.	C4	90
Rayong, Thai.	H6	40
Raytown, Mo., U.S.	h11	132
Rayville, La., U.S.	B4	125
R'azan', Russia	G22	22
Razdan, Arm.	A8	48
Razdil'na, Ukr.	C14	20
Răzeni, Mol.	C12	20
Razgrad, Bul.	F10	20
R'ažsk, Russia	H23	22
Ré, Île de, i., Fr.	F5	14
Reader, W.V., U.S.	B4	155
Readfield, Me., U.S.	D3	126
Reading, Eng., U.K.	J13	8
Reading, Ma., U.S.	A5	128
Reading, Oh., U.S.	C1	142
Reading, Pa., U.S.	F10	145
Readlyn, Ia., U.S.	B5	122
Readsboro, Vt., U.S.	F3	152
Reagan, co., Tx., U.S.	D2	150
Real, co., Tx., U.S.	E3	150
Real, Cordillera, mts., S.A.	H9	82
Real del Padre, Arg.	H5	80
Realicó, Arg.	H6	80
Reamstown, Pa., U.S.	F9	145
Rebouças, Braz.	C13	80
Recanati, Italy	F8	18
Recherche, Archipelago of the, is., Austl.	F4	68
Rečica, Bela.	I13	22
Recife, Braz.	E12	76
Recinto, Chile	I3	80
Recklinghausen, Ger.	D7	10
Reconquista, Arg.	E9	80
Recreio, Braz.	F7	79
Recreo, Arg.	E6	80
Rector, Ar., U.S.	A5	111
Red (Hong) (Yuan), stm., Asia	C8	40
Red, stm., N.A.	B7	106
Red, stm., U.S.	E8	106
Red, stm., Ky., U.S.	C6	124
Red, stm., Tn., U.S.	A4	149
Red Bank, N.J., U.S.	C4	137
Red Bank, S.C., U.S.	D5	147
Red Bank, Tn., U.S.	D8	149
Red Banks, Ms., U.S.	A4	131
Red Bay, Al., U.S.	A1	108
Red Bluff, Ca., U.S.	B2	112
Red Bluff Lake, res., U.S.	o12	150
Red Bluff Reservoir, res., U.S.	B8	90
Red Boiling Springs, Tn., U.S.	C8	149
Red Buttes Village, Wy., U.S.	D6	157
Red Cedar, stm., Wi., U.S.	C2	156
Redcliff, Alta., Can.	D5	98
Redcliff, Co., U.S.	B4	113
Redcliff, Zimb.	B9	66
Redcliffe, Austl.	F10	70
Red Cliffs, Austl.	J5	70
Red Cloud, Ne., U.S.	D7	134
Redcloud Peak, mtn., Co., U.S.	D3	113
Red Deer, Alta., Can.	C4	98
Red Deer, stm., Can.	D4	98
Red Deer, stm., Can.	E4	105
Redding, Ca., U.S.	B2	112
Redding, Ct., U.S.	D2	114
Redfield, Ar., U.S.	C3	111
Redfield, Ia., U.S.	C3	122
Redfield, S.D., U.S.	C7	148
Redford, Mi., U.S.	F7	129
Redgranite, Wi., U.S.	D4	156
Red Jacket, W.V., U.S.	D2	155
Redkey, In., U.S.	D7	121
Redkino, Russia	E19	22
Redlake, Mn., U.S.	C3	130
Red Lake, co., Mn., U.S.	C2	130
Red Lake, l., Az., U.S.	B1	110
Red Lake, l., Mn., U.S.	C2	130
Red Lake Falls, Mn., U.S.	C2	130
Red Lake Indian Reservation, Mn., U.S.	B3	130
Redlands, Ca., U.S.	E5	112
Red Level, Al., U.S.	D3	108
Red Lion, Pa., U.S.	G8	145
Red Lodge, Mt., U.S.	E7	133
Redmond, Or., U.S.	C5	144
Redmond, Ut., U.S.	E4	151
Redmond, Wa., U.S.	e11	154
Red Mountain, mtn., Mt., U.S.	C4	133
Red Oak, Ga., U.S.	h7	117
Red Oak, Ia., U.S.	D2	122
Red Oak, Tx., U.S.	n10	150
Red Oaks, La., U.S.	h9	125
Redon, Fr.	E4	14
Redonda, i., Antig.	F13	94
Redondo, Wa., U.S.	f11	154
Redondo Beach, Ca., U.S.	n12	112
Redoubt Volcano, vol., Ak., U.S.	g15	109
Red River, N.M., U.S.	A4	138
Red River, co., La., U.S.	B2	125
Red River, co., Tx., U.S.	C5	150
Red Rock, Ar., U.S.	F4	133
Red Rock, Lake, res., Ia., U.S.	C4	122
Red Sea	D8	56
Red Springs, N.C., U.S.	C3	140
Redstone, N.H., U.S.	B4	136
Redvers, Sask., Can.	H5	105
Redwater, Alta., Can.	C4	98
Red Willow, co., Ne., U.S.	D5	134
Red Wing, Mn., U.S.	F6	130
Redwood, co., Mn., U.S.	F3	130
Redwood City, Ca., U.S.	D2	112
Redwood Falls, Mn., U.S.	F3	130
Redwood National Park, Ca., U.S.	B2	112
Ree, Lough, l., Ire.	H5	8
Reed, Ky., U.S.	D4	111
Reed City, Mi., U.S.	E5	129
Reeder, N.D., U.S.	C3	141
Reedley, Ca., U.S.	D4	112
Reedsburg, Wi., U.S.	E3	156
Reedsport, Or., U.S.	D2	144
Reedsville, W.V., U.S.	B5	155
Reedsville, Wi., U.S.	D6	156
Reedy, stm., S.C., U.S.	C3	147
Reelfoot Lake, l., Tn., U.S.	A2	149
Reese, Mi., U.S.	E7	129
Reese, stm., Nv., U.S.	C4	135
Reeves, co., Tx., U.S.	o13	150
Reform, Al., U.S.	B1	108
Refugio, Tx., U.S.	E4	150
Refugio, co., Tx., U.S.	E4	150
Regensburg, Ger.	F12	10
Regent, N.D., U.S.	C3	141
Reggio di Calabria, Italy	K10	18
Reggio nell'Emilia, Italy	E5	18
Reghin, Rom.	C8	20
Regina, Fr. Gu.	C8	76
Regina Beach, Sask., Can.	G3	105
Región Metropolitana, prov., Chile	G3	80
Registro, Braz.	C15	80
Rehoboth, Nmb.	D3	66
Rehoboth Bay, b., De., U.S.	F5	115
Rehoboth Beach, De., U.S.	F5	115
Rehovot, Isr.	E3	50
Reichenbach, Ger.	E12	10
Reidland, Ky., U.S.	e9	124
Reidsville, Ga., U.S.	D4	117
Reidsville, N.C., U.S.	A3	140
Reigate, Eng., U.K.	J13	8
Reims, Fr.	C11	14
Reinach, Switz.	C8	13
Reinach, Switz.	D9	13
Reinbeck, Ia., U.S.	B5	122
Reindeer Island, i., Man., Can.	C3	100
Reindeer Lake, l., Can.	m8	105
Reinga, Cape, c., N.Z.	A4	72
Reinosa, Spain	B7	16
Reisterstown, Md., U.S.	B4	127
Reitz, S. Afr.	F9	66
Reliance, Wy., U.S.	E3	157
Remagen, Ger.	E7	10
Remanso, Braz.	E10	76
Rembang, Indon.	j15	39a
Remedios, Pan.	C2	84
Remedios, Punta, c., El Sal.	D5	92
Remington, In., U.S.	C3	121
Remiremont, Fr.	D13	14
Remmel Dam, Ar., U.S.	g8	111
Remscheid, Ger.	D7	10
Remsen, Ia., U.S.	B2	122
Rend Lake, res., Il., U.S.	E5	120
Rendsburg, Ger.	A9	10
Renens, Switz.	E6	13
Renews [-Cappahayden], Newf., Can.	E5	102
Renforth, N.B., Can.	D4	101
Renfrew, Ont., Can.	B8	103
Rengo, Chile	H3	80
Renhua, China	J2	34
Reni, Ukr.	D12	20
Renmark, Austl.	J4	70
Rennes, Fr.	D5	14
Rennie, Man., Can.	E4	100
Reno, Nv., U.S.	D2	135
Reno, co., Ks., U.S.	E5	123
Renous, N.B., Can.	C4	101
Rensselaer, In., U.S.	C3	121
Rensselaer, N.Y., U.S.	C7	139
Rensselaer, co., N.Y., U.S.	C7	139
Rentería, Spain	B10	16
Renton, Wa., U.S.	B3	154
Renville, Mn., U.S.	F3	130
Renville, co., Mn., U.S.	F4	130
Renville, co., N.D., U.S.	A4	141
Repentigny, Que., Can.	D4	104
Repino, Russia	A12	22
Republic, Mo., U.S.	D4	132
Republic, Wa., U.S.	A7	154
Republic, co., Ks., U.S.	C6	123
Republican, stm., U.S.	C6	123
Repulse Bay, N.W. Ter., Can.	C15	96
Requena, Spain	F10	16
Reserva, Braz.	C13	80
Reserve, La., U.S.	h10	125
Reserve, N.M., U.S.	D1	138
Rešetnikovo, Russia	E19	22
Resistencia, Arg.	D9	80
Reşiţa, Rom.	D5	20
Resolute, N.W. Ter., Can.	B14	96
Resplendor, Braz.	E8	79
Restín, Punta, c., Peru	J2	84
Restinga Seca, Braz.	E12	80
Reston, Man., Can.	E1	100
Reston, Va., U.S.	B5	153
Retalhuleu, Guat.	C3	92
Retalhuleu, dept., Guat.	C3	92
Rethel, Fr.	C11	14
Réthimnon, Grc.	N8	20
Reunion (Réunion), dep., Afr.	F11	58
Reus, Spain	D13	16
Reutlingen, Ger.	G9	10
Revda, Russia	F9	26
Revelo, Ky., U.S.	D5	124
Revelstoke, B.C., Can.	D8	99
Revelstoke, Lake, res., B.C., Can.	D8	99
Reventazón, stm., C.R.	G11	92
Revere, Ma., U.S.	g11	128
Revigny-sur-Ornain, Fr.	D11	14
Revillagigedo, Islas, is., Mex.	H4	90
Revillagigedo Island, i., Ak., U.S.	n24	109
Revin, Fr.	C11	14
Revolución Mexicana, Mex.	A1	92
Rewa, India	H9	44
Rewari, India	F7	44
Rex, Ga., U.S.	h8	117
Rexburg, Id., U.S.	F7	119
Rexton, N.B., Can.	C5	101
Rey, Isla del, i., Pan.	C3	84
Reyes, Bol.	F8	82
Reyes, Point, c., Ca., U.S.	C2	112
Reyhanli, Tur.	C4	48
Reykjanes, pen., Ice.	C2	6a
Reykjavík, Ice.	C3	6a
Reyno, Ar., U.S.	A5	111
Reynolds, Ga., U.S.	D2	117
Reynolds, co., Mo., U.S.	D6	132
Reynoldsburg, Oh., U.S.	C3	142
Reynoldsville, Pa., U.S.	D4	145
Reynosa, Mex.	D10	90
Rež, Russia	F10	26
Rezé, Fr.	E5	14
Rēzekne, Lat.	E10	22
Rezina, Mol.	B12	20
Rhaetian Alps, mts., Eur.	F16	14
Rhea, co., Tn., U.S.	D9	149
Rheda-Wiedenbrück, Ger.	D8	10
Rheims see Reims, Fr.	C11	14
Rhein, Sask., Can.	G4	105
Rhein see Rhine, stm., Eur.	D6	10
Rheine, Ger.	C7	10
Rheinland-Pfalz, state, Ger.	E6	10
Rhine (Rhein) (Rhin), stm., Eur.	D6	10
Rhinebeck, N.Y., U.S.	D7	139
Rhinelander, Wi., U.S.	C4	156
Rhir, Cap, c., Mor.	E6	62
Rho, Italy	D4	18
Rhode Island, state, U.S.	D3	146
Rhode Island, i., R.I., U.S.	E5	146
Rhode Island Sound, strt., U.S.	F5	146
Rhodes see Ródhos, i., Grc.	M12	20
Rhodesia see Zimbabwe, ctry., Afr.	E5	58
Rhodope Mountains (Rodopi) (Orosirá Rodhópis), mts., Eur.	H8	20
Rhône, stm., Eur.	H11	14
Riachão, Braz.	E9	76
Riacho de Santana, Braz.	B7	79
Rialma, Braz.	C4	79
Rialto, Ca., U.S.	m14	112
Ribas do Rio Pardo, Braz.	F2	79
Ribeauvillé, Fr.	D14	14
Ribeira Grande, C.V.	k16	64a
Ribeirão do Pinhal, Braz.	G3	79
Ribeirão Preto, Braz.	F5	79
Ribera, Italy	L8	18
Riberalta, Bol.	D8	82
Rib Mountain, mtn., Wi., U.S.	D4	156
Riccione, Italy	F7	18
Rice, co., Ks., U.S.	D5	123
Rice, co., Mn., U.S.	F5	130
Riceboro, Ga., U.S.	E5	117
Rice Lake, Wi., U.S.	C2	156
Rice Lake, l., Ont., Can.	C6	103
Riceville, Ia., U.S.	A5	122
Rich, co., Ut., U.S.	B4	151
Richard's Bay, S. Afr.	G11	66
Richardson, Tx., U.S.	n10	150
Richardson, co., Ne., U.S.	D10	134
Richardson Lakes, l., Me., U.S.	D2	126
Richardson Mountains, mts., Can.	C5	96
Richardton, N.D., U.S.	C3	141
Riche, Pointe, c., Newf., Can.	C3	102
Richer, Man., Can.	E3	100
Richey, Mt., U.S.	C11	133
Richfield, Id., U.S.	F4	119
Richfield, Mn., U.S.	F5	130
Richfield, Ut., U.S.	E3	151
Richford, Vt., U.S.	B3	152
Rich Hill, Mo., U.S.	C3	132
Richibucto, N.B., Can.	C5	101
Richland, Ga., U.S.	D2	117
Richland, Mo., U.S.	D5	132
Richland, Wa., U.S.	C6	154
Richland, co., Il., U.S.	E5	120
Richland, co., La., U.S.	B4	125
Richland, co., Mt., U.S.	C12	133
Richland, co., N.D., U.S.	C8	141
Richland, co., Oh., U.S.	B3	142
Richland, co., S.C., U.S.	D6	147
Richland, co., Wi., U.S.	E3	156
Richland Balsam, mtn., N.C., U.S.	f10	140
Richland Center, Wi., U.S.	E3	156
Richlands, Va., U.S.	e10	153
Richmond, Austl.	C5	70
Richmond, Austl.	I9	70
Richmond, B.C., Can.	E6	99
Richmond, Que., Can.	D5	104
Richmond, N.Z.	D4	72
Richmond, S. Afr.	G10	66
Richmond, S. Afr.	H6	66
Richmond, Ca., U.S.	D2	112
Richmond, Il., U.S.	A5	120
Richmond, In., U.S.	E8	121
Richmond, Ks., U.S.	D8	123
Richmond, Ky., U.S.	C5	124
Richmond, Me., U.S.	D3	126
Richmond, Mi., U.S.	F8	129
Richmond, Mn., U.S.	E4	130
Richmond, Mo., U.S.	B3	132
Richmond, Tx., U.S.	E5	150
Richmond, Ut., U.S.	B4	151
Richmond, Vt., U.S.	C3	152
Richmond, co., Ga., U.S.	C4	117
Richmond, co., N.Y., U.S.	E6	139
Richmond, co., N.C., U.S.	C3	140
Richmond, co., Va., U.S.	C6	153
Richmond Beach, Wa., U.S.	B3	154
Richmond Heights, Fl., U.S.	s13	116
Richmond Heights, Mo., U.S.	f13	132
Richmond Highlands, Wa., U.S.	B3	154
Richmond Hill, Ont., Can.	D5	103
Richmond Hill, Ga., U.S.	E5	117
Richmound, Sask., Can.	G1	105
Richton, Ms., U.S.	D5	131
Richwood, Oh., U.S.	B2	142
Richwood, W.V., U.S.	C4	155
Rickman, Tn., U.S.	C8	149
Riddle, Or., U.S.	E3	144
Rideau, stm., Ont., Can.	B9	103
Ridgecrest, Ca., U.S.	E5	112
Ridge Farm, Il., U.S.	D6	120
Ridgefield, Ct., U.S.	D2	114
Ridgefield, N.J., U.S.	h8	137
Ridgefield, Wa., U.S.	D3	154
Ridgefield Park, N.J., U.S.	h8	137
Ridgeland, Ms., U.S.	C3	131
Ridgeland, S.C., U.S.	G6	147
Ridgely, Md., U.S.	C6	127
Ridgely, Tn., U.S.	A2	149
Ridgetown, Ont., Can.	E3	103
Ridgeville, In., U.S.	D7	121
Ridgeville, S.C., U.S.	E7	147
Ridgeway, Va., U.S.	D3	153
Ridgewood, N.J., U.S.	B4	137
Ridgway, Co., U.S.	C3	113
Ridgway, Il., U.S.	F5	120
Ridgway, Pa., U.S.	D4	145
Riding Mountain, hills, Man., Can.	D1	100
Ridley Park, Pa., U.S.	p20	145
Ried im Innkreis, Aus.	G13	10
Riesa, Ger.	D13	10
Riesco, Isla, i., Chile	G2	78
Rietavas, Lith.	F4	22
Rieti, Italy	G7	18
Rif, mts., Mor.	C8	62
Riffe Lake, res., Wa., U.S.	C3	154
Rifle, Co., U.S.	B3	113
Rift Valley, val., Afr.	I9	52
Riga, Lat.	E7	22
Riga, Gulf of (Rīgas jūras līcis) (Riia laht), b., Eur.	D6	22
Rigaud, Que., Can.	D3	104
Rigby, Id., U.S.	F7	119
Rīgestān, reg., Afg.	E1	44
Riggins, Id., U.S.	D2	119

Name	Map Ref.	Page
Riiser-Larsen Peninsula, pen., Ant.	B4	73
Rijeka, Cro.	D9	18
Rijswijk, Neth.	D5	12
Riley, Ks., U.S.	C7	123
Riley, co., Ks., U.S.	C7	123
Rillito, Az., U.S.	E4	110
Rímac, stm., Peru	D3	82
Rimavská Sobota, Slvk.	G20	10
Rimbey, Alta., Can.	C3	98
Rimi, Nig.	E13	64
Rimini, Italy	E7	18
Rimouski, Que., Can.	A9	104
Rimouski-Est, Que., Can.	A9	104
Rincón, C.R.	I11	92
Rincon, Ga., U.S.	D5	117
Rincon, N.M., U.S.	E2	138
Rincón del Bonete, Lago Artificial de, res., Ur.	G11	80
Rincón de Romos, Mex.	F8	90
Rindge, N.H., U.S.	E2	136
Ringgold, Ga., U.S.	B1	117
Ringgold, La., U.S.	B2	125
Ringgold, co., Ia., U.S.	D3	122
Ringling, Ok., U.S.	C4	143
Ringwood, N.J., U.S.	A4	137
Rinjani, Gunung, mtn., Indon.	G6	38
Rinteln, Ger.	C9	10
Rio Arriba, co., N.M., U.S.	A2	138
Rio Azul, Braz.	C13	80
Riobamba, Ec.	H3	84
Rio Blanco, co., Co., U.S.	B2	113
Rio Branco, Braz.	C8	82
Río Branco, Ur.	G12	80
Rio Brilhante, Braz.	F1	79
Río Caribe, Ven.	B11	84
Rio Casca, Braz.	F7	79
Río Ceballos, Arg.	F6	80
Rio Claro, Braz.	G5	79
Rio Claro, Trin.	I14	94
Río Colorado, Arg.	J6	80
Río Cuarto, Arg.	G6	80
Rio de Janeiro, Braz.	G7	79
Rio de Janeiro, state, Braz.	G7	79
Río de Jesús, Pan.	J13	92
Río de Oro, Col.	C6	84
Rio do Sul, Braz.	D14	80
Río Gallegos, Arg.	G3	78
Rio Grande, Braz.	G12	80
Río Grande, Mex.	F8	90
Rio Grande, Nic.	E8	92
Rio Grande, co., Co., U.S.	D4	113
Rio Grande see Grande, Rio, stm., N.A.	F7	106
Rio Grande City, Tx., U.S.	F3	150
Rio Grande do Sul, state, Braz.	E11	80
Ríohacha, Col.	B6	84
Río Hato, Pan.	C2	84
Rioja, Peru	B3	82
Río Lagartos, Mex.	G15	90
Riolândia, Braz.	E4	79
Rio Largo, Braz.	E11	76
Riom, Fr.	G10	14
Rio Mulatos, Bol.	H8	82
Riondel, B.C., Can.	E9	99
Rio Negro, Braz.	E1	79
Rio Negro, Braz.	D14	80
Ríonegro, Col.	D5	84
Río Negro, prov., Arg.	J6	80
Rionero in Vulture, Italy	I10	18
Rio Novo do Sul, Braz.	F8	79
Rio Pardo, Braz.	E12	80
Rio Pardo de Minas, Braz.	C7	79
Rio Piracicaba, Braz.	E7	79
Rio Pomba, Braz.	F7	79
Rio Preto, Braz.	G7	79
Rio Rancho, N.M., U.S.	B3	138
Río San Juan, dept., Nic.	F10	92
Río Segundo, Col.	F7	80
Ríosucio, Col.	D4	84
Ríosucio, Col.	E5	84
Río Tercero, Arg.	G6	80
Río Tinto, Braz.	E11	76
Rio Verde, Braz.	D3	79
Ríoverde, Mex.	G10	90
Rio Verde de Mato Grosso, Braz.	E1	79
Ripley, Ont., Can.	C3	103
Ripley, Ms., U.S.	A5	131
Ripley, Tn., U.S.	B2	149
Ripley, W.V., U.S.	C3	155
Ripley, co., In., U.S.	F7	121
Ripley, co., Mo., U.S.	E7	132
Ripoll, Spain	C14	16
Ripon, Wi., U.S.	E5	156
Ririe, Id., U.S.	F7	119
Risaralda, dept., Col.	E4	84
Rishon LeZiyyon, Isr.	E3	50
Rising Sun, De., U.S.	D3	115
Rising Sun, In., U.S.	G8	121
Rising Sun, Md., U.S.	A5	127
Rison, Ar., U.S.	D3	111
Risør, Nor.	L11	6
Ritchie, co., W.V., U.S.	B3	155
Ritter, Mount, mtn., Ca., U.S.	D4	112
Rittman, Oh., U.S.	B4	142
Ritzville, Wa., U.S.	B7	154
Riva, Italy	D5	18
Rivadavia, Arg.	G4	80
Rivadavia, Arg.	H7	80
Rivadavia, Arg.	F4	80
Rivadavia, Chile	E3	80
Rivanna, stm., Va., U.S.	C4	153
Rivas, Nic.	F9	92
Rivas, dept., Nic.	F8	92
Rive-de-Gier, Fr.	G11	14
Rivera, Arg.	I7	80
Rivera, Ur.	F11	80
Riverbank, Ca., U.S.	D3	112
River Bourgeois, N.S., Can.	D9	101
River Cess, Lib.	I5	64
Riverdale, Il., U.S.	k9	120
Riverdale, Md., U.S.	C4	127
Riverdale, N.D., U.S.	B4	141
River Edge, N.J., U.S.	h8	137
River Falls, Al., U.S.	D3	108
River Falls, Wi., U.S.	D1	156
River Forest, Il., U.S.	k9	120
River Grove, Il., U.S.	k9	120
Riverhead, N.Y., U.S.	n16	139
River Hebert, N.S., Can.	D5	101
River Heights, Ut., U.S.	B4	151
River Hills, Wi., U.S.	m12	156
Riverhurst, Sask., Can.	G2	105
Riverina, reg., Austl.	J6	70
River John, N.S., Can.	D6	101
River Pines, Ma., U.S.	f10	128
Riverport, N.S., Can.	E5	101
River Ridge, La., U.S.	k11	125
River Road, Or., U.S.	C3	144
River Rouge, Mi., U.S.	p15	129
Rivers, Man., Can.	D1	100
Riversdale, S. Afr.	J5	66
Riverside, Al., U.S.	B3	108
Riverside, Ca., U.S.	F5	112
Riverside, Il., U.S.	k9	120
Riverside, Ia., U.S.	C6	122
Riverside, N.J., U.S.	C3	137
Riverside, Pa., U.S.	E8	145
Riverside, Wy., U.S.	E6	157
Riverside, co., Ca., U.S.	F5	112
Riverside-Albert, N.B., Can.	D5	101
Riverton, Man., Can.	D3	100
Riverton, Il., U.S.	D4	120
Riverton, Ks., U.S.	E9	123
Riverton, Ut., U.S.	C4	151
Riverton, Wy., U.S.	C4	157
Riverton Heights, Wa., U.S.	f11	154
River Vale, N.J., U.S.	h8	137
Riverview, Fl., U.S.	p11	116
Riverview, Mi., U.S.	p15	129
Rivesaltes, Fr.	J9	14
Rivesville, W.V., U.S.	B4	155
Riviera Beach, Fl., U.S.	F6	116
Riviera Beach, Md., U.S.	B4	127
Rivière-du-Loup, Que., Can.	B8	104
Rivière-Verte, N.B., Can.	B1	101
Riviersonderend, S. Afr.	J4	66
Rivne, Ukr.	G3	26
Rivoli, Italy	D2	18
Riyadh see Ar-Riyāḍ, Sau. Ar.	B5	47
Rize, Tur.	G16	4
Rizhao, China	H7	32
Roachdale, In., U.S.	E4	121
Road Town, Br. Vir. Is.	E12	94
Roane, co., Tn., U.S.	D9	149
Roane, co., W.V., U.S.	C3	155
Roan High Knob, mtn., N.C., U.S.	C11	149
Roan Mountain, Tn., U.S.	C11	149
Roanne, Fr.	F11	14
Roanoke, Al., U.S.	B4	108
Roanoke, Il., U.S.	C4	120
Roanoke, In., U.S.	C7	121
Roanoke, Va., U.S.	C3	153
Roanoke, co., Va., U.S.	C2	153
Roanoke, stm., U.S.	A5	140
Roanoke Rapids, N.C., U.S.	A5	140
Roanoke Rapids Lake, res., U.S.	A5	140
Roaring Fork, stm., Co., U.S.	C4	113
Roaring Spring, Pa., U.S.	F5	145
Roatán, Hond.	A8	92
Roatán, Isla de, i., Hond.	A8	92
Robbins, Il., U.S.	k9	120
Robbinsdale, Mn., U.S.	m12	130
Robersonville, N.C., U.S.	B5	140
Roberta, Ga., U.S.	D2	117
Roberts, Id., U.S.	F6	119
Roberts, Mt., U.S.	E7	133
Roberts, Wi., U.S.	C1	156
Roberts, co., S.D., U.S.	B8	148
Roberts, co., Tx., U.S.	B2	150
Robert's Arm, Newf., Can.	D4	102
Robertsdale, Al., U.S.	E2	108
Robert S. Kerr Reservoir, res., Ok., U.S.	B6	143
Roberts Mountain, mtn., Wy., U.S.	D3	157
Robertson, S. Afr.	I4	66
Robertson, co., Ky., U.S.	B5	124
Robertson, co., Tn., U.S.	A5	149
Robertson, co., Tx., U.S.	D4	150
Robertsonville, Que., Can.	C6	104
Robertsport, Lib.	H4	64
Robertville, N.B., Can.	B4	101
Roberval, Que., Can.	A5	104
Robeson, co., N.C., U.S.	C3	140
Robins, Ia., U.S.	B6	122
Robinson, Il., U.S.	D6	120
Róbinson Crusoe, Isla, i., Chile	H7	74
Robinvale, Austl.	J5	70
Roblin, Man., Can.	D1	100
Roboré, Bol.	H12	82
Robson, Mount, mtn., B.C., Can.	C8	99
Robstown, Tx., U.S.	F4	150
Roca, Cabo da, c., Port.	G2	16
Rocafuerte, Ec.	H2	84
Rocanville, Sask., Can.	G5	105
Rocas, Atol das, atoll, Braz.	D12	76
Rocha, Ur.	H9	74
Rocha, Ur.	H11	80
Rochedo, Braz.	E1	79
Rochefort, Bel.	H7	12
Rochefort, Fr.	G6	14
Rochelle, Ga., U.S.	E3	117
Rochelle, Il., U.S.	B4	120
Rochelle Park, N.J., U.S.	h8	137
Rochester, In., U.S.	B5	121
Rochester, Mi., U.S.	F7	129
Rochester, Mn., U.S.	F6	130
Rochester, N.H., U.S.	D5	136
Rochester, N.Y., U.S.	B3	139
Rochester, Pa., U.S.	E1	145
Rochester, Vt., U.S.	D3	152
Rochester, Wa., U.S.	C2	154
Rochester, Wi., U.S.	n11	156
Rock, co., Mn., U.S.	G2	130
Rock, co., Ne., U.S.	B6	134
Rock, co., Wi., U.S.	F4	156
Rock, stm., U.S.	B3	120
Rock, stm., Wi., U.S.	A1	120
Rockall, i., Scot., U.K.	D5	4
Rockaway, N.J., U.S.	B3	137
Rockaway, Or., U.S.	B3	144
Rockbridge, co., Va., U.S.	C3	153
Rockcastle, co., Ky., U.S.	C5	124
Rockcliffe Park, Ont., Can.	h12	103
Rock Creek, U.S.	E6	130
Rock Creek Butte, mtn., Or., U.S.	C8	144
Rockdale, Il., U.S.	B5	120
Rockdale, Md., U.S.	B4	127
Rockdale, Tx., U.S.	D4	150
Rockdale, co., Ga., U.S.	C3	117
Rockfall, Ct., U.S.	C5	114
Rock Falls, Il., U.S.	B4	120
Rockford, Al., U.S.	C3	108
Rockford, Il., U.S.	A4	120
Rockford, Ia., U.S.	A5	122
Rockford, Mi., U.S.	E5	129
Rockford, Mn., U.S.	E5	130
Rockford, Tn., U.S.	D10	149
Rockglen, Sask., Can.	H3	105
Rock Hall, Md., U.S.	B5	127
Rock Hill, S.C., U.S.	B5	147
Rockhampton, Austl.	D9	70
Rockingham, N.C., U.S.	C3	140
Rockingham, co., N.H., U.S.	D5	136
Rockingham, co., N.C., U.S.	A3	140
Rockingham, co., Va., U.S.	B4	153
Rock Island, Il., U.S.	B3	120
Rock Island, Wa., U.S.	B5	154
Rock Island, co., Il., U.S.	B3	120
Rockland, Ont., Can.	B9	103
Rockland, Me., U.S.	D3	126
Rockland, Ma., U.S.	B6	128
Rockland, co., N.Y., U.S.	D6	139
Rockledge, Fl., U.S.	D6	116
Rockledge, Pa., U.S.	o20	145
Rocklin, Ca., U.S.	C3	112
Rockmart, Ga., U.S.	B1	117
Rock Point, Az., U.S.	A6	110
Rockport, Ar., U.S.	g8	111
Rockport, In., U.S.	I3	121
Rockport, Me., U.S.	D3	126
Rockport, Ma., U.S.	A6	128
Rock Port, Mo., U.S.	A2	132
Rockport, Tx., U.S.	F4	150
Rock Rapids, Ia., U.S.	A1	122
Rock River, Wy., U.S.	E7	157
Rock Springs, Wy., U.S.	E3	157
Rockton, Il., U.S.	A4	120
Rockvale, Co., U.S.	C5	113
Rock Valley, Ia., U.S.	A1	122
Rockville, In., U.S.	E3	121
Rockville, Md., U.S.	B3	127
Rockville Centre, N.Y., U.S.	n15	139
Rockwall, Tx., U.S.	C4	150
Rockwall, co., Tx., U.S.	C4	150
Rockwell, Ia., U.S.	B4	122
Rockwell, N.C., U.S.	B2	140
Rockwell City, Ia., U.S.	B3	122
Rockwell Park, N.C., U.S.	B2	140
Rockwood, Mi., U.S.	F7	129
Rockwood, Tn., U.S.	D9	149
Rockyford, Alta., Can.	D4	98
Rocky Ford, Co., U.S.	C7	113
Rocky Hill, Ct., U.S.	C5	114
Rocky Mount, N.C., U.S.	B5	140
Rocky Mount, Va., U.S.	D3	153
Rocky Mountain, mtn., Mt., U.S.	C4	133
Rocky Mountain House, Alta., Can.	C3	98
Rocky Mountain National Park, Co., U.S.	A5	113
Rocky Mountains, mts., N.A.	E8	86
Rocky Ripple, In., U.S.	k10	121
Rocky River, Oh., U.S.	A4	142
Roddickton, Newf., Can.	C3	102
Rodeo, Arg.	F4	80
Rodeo, Mex.	E7	90
Roderfield, W.V., U.S.	D3	155
Rodez, Fr.	H9	14
Ródhos (Rhodes), Grc.	M12	20
Ródhos (Rhodes), i., Grc.	M12	20
Rodney, Ont., Can.	E3	103
Rodney Village, De., U.S.	D3	115
Rodniki, Russia	D24	22
Rodrigues, i., Mrts.	K7	24
Roebourne, Austl.	D3	68
Roebuck, S.C., U.S.	B4	147
Roeland Park, Ks., U.S.	k16	123
Roermond, Neth.	F9	12
Roff, Ok., U.S.	C5	143
Rogačov, Bela.	H13	22
Rogagua, Bos.	F3	20
Roger Mills, co., Ok., U.S.	B2	143
Rogers, Ar., U.S.	A1	111
Rogers, co., Ok., U.S.	A6	143
Rogers, Mount, mtn., Va., U.S.	f10	153
Rogers City, Mi., U.S.	C7	129
Rogersville, N.B., Can.	C4	101
Rogersville, Al., U.S.	A2	108
Rogersville, Mo., U.S.	D4	132
Rogersville, Tn., U.S.	C10	149
Rogue, stm., Or., U.S.	E2	144
Rogue River, Or., U.S.	E3	144
Rohnert Park, Ca., U.S.	C2	112
Rohtak, India	F7	44
Roi Et, Thai.	F7	40
Rojas, Arg.	H8	80
Rojo, Cabo, c., Mex.	G11	90
Rojo, Cabo, c., P.R.	F11	94
Rokiškis, Lith.	F8	22
Rokycany, Czech Rep.	F13	10
Roland, Man., Can.	E3	100
Roland, Ar., U.S.	C3	111
Roland, Ia., U.S.	B4	122
Roland, Ok., U.S.	B7	143
Rolândia, Braz.	G3	79
Roldán, Arg.	G8	80
Rolette, N.D., U.S.	A6	141
Rolette, co., N.D., U.S.	A5	141
Rolfe, Ia., U.S.	B3	122
Rolla, Mo., U.S.	D6	132
Rolla, N.D., U.S.	A6	141
Rolle, Switz.	F5	13
Rollingbay, Wa., U.S.	e10	154
Rolling Fork, Ms., U.S.	C3	131
Rolling Fork, stm., Ky., U.S.	C4	124
Rolling Hills, Wy., U.S.	D7	157
Rolling Meadows, Il., U.S.	h8	120
Rollinsford, N.H., U.S.	D5	136
Roma, Austl.	F8	70
Roma (Rome), Italy	H7	18
Roma, Tx., U.S.	F3	150
Romagna, hist. reg., Italy	H18	14
Romaine, stm., Can.	h9	106
Roman, Rom.	C10	20
Romania (România), ctry., Eur.	F13	4
Roman Nose Mountain, mtn., Md., U.S.	m12	127
Romanshorn, Switz.	C11	13
Romans [-sur-Isère], Fr.	G12	14
Romanzof, Cape, c., Ak., U.S.	C6	109
Rome see Roma, Italy	H7	18
Rome, Ga., U.S.	B1	117
Rome, Il., U.S.	C4	120
Rome, N.Y., U.S.	B5	139
Rome City, In., U.S.	B7	121
Romeo, Co., U.S.	D4	113
Romeo, Mi., U.S.	F7	129
Romeoville, Il., U.S.	k8	120
Romilly-sur-Seine, Fr.	D10	14
Romney, W.V., U.S.	B6	155
Romny, Ukr.	G4	26
Romont, Switz.	E6	13
Romorantin-Lanthenay, Fr.	E8	14
Romulus, Mi., U.S.	p15	129
Ronan, Mt., U.S.	C2	133
Roncador, Serra do, plat., Braz.	F8	76
Ronceverte, W.V., U.S.	D4	155
Ronda, Spain	I6	16
Rondon, Braz.	G2	79
Rondônia, state, Braz.	D10	82
Rondonópolis, Braz.	D1	79
Ronge, Lac la, l., Sask., Can.	B3	105
Rongshui, China	B10	40
Rønne, Den.	N14	6
Ronneby, Swe.	M14	6
Ronne Ice Shelf, Ant.	C12	73
Ronse (Renaix), Bel.	G4	12
Roodhouse, Il., U.S.	D3	120
Rooks, co., Ks., U.S.	C4	123
Roorkee, India	F7	44
Roosendaal, Neth.	E5	12
Roosevelt, Ut., U.S.	C5	151
Roosevelt, co., Mt., U.S.	B11	133
Roosevelt, co., N.M., U.S.	C6	138
Roosevelt Island, i., Ant.	C9	73
Roosevelt Park, Mi., U.S.	E4	129
Root, stm., Mn., U.S.	G7	130
Roper, stm., Austl.	B6	68
Roque Pérez, Arg.	H9	80
Roraima, state, Braz.	G12	84
Roraima, Mount, mtn., S.A.	E12	84
Rorketon, Man., Can.	D2	100
Røros, Nor.	J12	6
Rorschach, Switz.	D12	13
Rosa, Monte, mtn., Eur.	G8	13
Rošal', Russia	F22	22
Rosales, Mex.	C7	90
Rosalia, Wa., U.S.	B8	154
Rosamond, Ca., U.S.	E4	112
Rosamorada, Mex.	F7	90
Rosario, Arg.	G8	80
Rosário, Braz.	D10	76
Rosario, Mex.	F7	90
Rosario, Para.	C10	80
Rosario, Ur.	H10	80
Rosario, Ven.	B6	84
Rosario de la Frontera, Arg.	C6	80
Rosario de Lerma, Arg.	C6	80
Rosario del Tala, Arg.	G9	80
Rosário do Sul, Braz.	F11	80
Rosário Oeste, Braz.	F13	82
Roščino, Russia	A12	22
Roscoe, Il., U.S.	A5	120
Roscoe, S.D., U.S.	B6	148
Roscommon, co., Ire.	H5	8
Roscommon, co., Mi., U.S.	D6	129
Rose, Mount, mtn., Nv., U.S.	D2	135
Roseau, Dom.	G14	94
Roseau, Mn., U.S.	B3	130
Roseau, co., Mn., U.S.	B3	130
Rosebery, Austl.	M6	70
Rose-Blanche [-Harbour le Cou], Newf., Can.	E2	102
Roseboro, N.C., U.S.	C4	140
Rosebud, S.D., U.S.	D5	148
Rosebud, co., Mt., U.S.	D10	133
Roseburg, Or., U.S.	D3	144
Rosedale, Austl.	E3	121
Rosedale, In., U.S.	E3	121
Rosedale, Md., U.S.	g11	127
Rosedale, Ms., U.S.	B2	131
Rose Hill, Ks., U.S.	E6	123
Rose Hill, N.C., U.S.	C4	140
Rose Hill, Va., U.S.	f8	153
Roseland, In., U.S.	A5	121
Roseland, La., U.S.	D5	125
Roseland, Oh., U.S.	B3	142
Roselle, Il., U.S.	k8	120
Roselle, N.J., U.S.	k7	137
Roselle Park, N.J., U.S.	k7	137
Rosemary, Alta., Can.	D4	98
Rosemère, Que., Can.	p19	104
Rosemount, Mn., U.S.	F5	130
Rosenberg, Tx., U.S.	E5	150
Rosenfeld, Man., Can.	E3	100
Rosenheim, Ger.	H12	10
Rosepine, La., U.S.	D2	125
Rose Point, c., B.C., Can.	B2	99
Rosetown, Sask., Can.	F1	105
Rosetta see Rashīd, Egypt	B6	60
Roseville, Ca., U.S.	C3	112
Roseville, Il., U.S.	C3	120
Roseville, Mi., U.S.	o16	129
Roseville, Mn., U.S.	m12	130
Rosewood Heights, Il., U.S.	E3	120
Rosholt, S.D., U.S.	B9	148
Rosiclare, Il., U.S.	F5	120
Roşiori de Vede, Rom.	E9	20
Roslavl', Russia	H15	22
Roslyn, Wa., U.S.	B4	154
Roslyn Heights, N.Y., U.S.	h13	139
Rosporden, Fr.	E3	14
Ross, Austl.	N7	70
Ross, Oh., U.S.	C1	142
Ross, co., Oh., U.S.	C2	142
Rossano, Italy	J11	18
Ross Barnett Reservoir, res., Ms., U.S.	C4	131
Rossburn, Man., Can.	D1	100
Rossford, Oh., U.S.	A2	142
Ross Ice Shelf, Ant.	D9	73
Rossignol, Lake, l., N.S., Can.	E4	101
Rossland, B.C., Can.	E9	99
Rosso, Maur.	C2	64
Rossony, Bela.	F11	22
Rossoš', Russia	G5	26
Ross River, Yukon, Can.	D6	96
Ross Sea, Ant.	C9	73
Rossville, Ga., U.S.	B1	117
Rossville, Il., U.S.	C6	120
Rossville, In., U.S.	D4	121
Rossville, Ks., U.S.	C8	123
Rosthern, Sask., Can.	E2	105
Rostock, Ger.	A12	10
Rostov, Russia	D22	22
Rostov-na-Donu, Russia	H5	26
Roswell, Ga., U.S.	B2	117
Roswell, N.M., U.S.	D5	138
Rota, Spain	I5	16
Rotenburg, Ger.	B9	10
Rothenburg ob der Tauber, Ger.	F10	10
Rothesay, N.B., Can.	D4	101
Rothschild, Wi., U.S.	D4	156
Rothsville, Pa., U.S.	F9	145
Rotorua, N.Z.	C6	72
Rottenburg, Ger.	G8	10
Rottenmann, Aus.	H14	10
Rotterdam, Neth.	E5	12
Rotterdam, N.Y., U.S.	C6	139
Rottweil, Ger.	G8	10
Roubaix, Fr.	B10	14
Roudnice, Czech Rep.	E14	10
Rouen, Fr.	C8	14
Rouge, stm., Que., Can.	D3	104
Rough River Lake, res., Ky., U.S.	C3	124
Rouleau, Sask., Can.	G3	105
Round Lake, Il., U.S.	h8	120
Round Lake Beach, Il., U.S.	h8	120
Round Mountain, Nv., U.S.	E4	135
Round Mountain, mtn., Austl.	H10	70
Round Pond, Me., U.S.	E3	126
Round Rock, Az., U.S.	A6	110
Round Rock, Tx., U.S.	D4	150
Roundup, Mt., U.S.	D8	133
Routt, co., Co., U.S.	A3	113
Rouyn [-Noranda], Que., Can.	k11	104
Rovaniemi, Fin.	H19	6
Rovereto, Italy	D6	18
Rovigo, Italy	D6	18
Rovuma (Ruvuma), stm., Afr.	D7	58
Rowan, co., Ky., U.S.	B6	124
Rowan, co., N.C., U.S.	B2	140
Rowlesburg, W.V., U.S.	B5	155
Roxboro, N.C., U.S.	A4	140
Roxbury, Vt., U.S.	C3	152
Roxie, Ms., U.S.	D2	131
Roxton Falls, Que., Can.	D5	104
Roy, N.M., U.S.	B5	138
Roy, Ut., U.S.	B3	151
Royal Canal, Ire.	H6	8
Royal Center, In., U.S.	C4	121
Royale, Isle, i., Mi., U.S.	h9	129
Royal Gorge, val., Co., U.S.	C5	113
Royal Leamington Spa, Eng., U.K.	I12	8
Royal Oak, Mi., U.S.	F7	129
Royal Pines, N.C., U.S.	f10	140
Royalton, Il., U.S.	F4	120
Royalton, Mn., U.S.	E4	130
Royal Tunbridge Wells, Eng., U.K.	J14	8
Royan, Fr.	G5	14
Roye, Fr.	C9	14
Royersford, Pa., U.S.	F10	145
Royerton, In., U.S.	D7	121
Royston, B.C., Can.	E5	99
Royston, Ga., U.S.	B3	117
Rtiščevo, Russia	G6	26
Ruacana Falls, wtfl, Afr.	A2	66
Ruapehu, mtn., N.Z.	C5	72
Rub' al Khali see Ar-Rub' al-Khālī, des., Asia	D7	47
Rubcovsk, Russia	G8	28
Rubiataba, Braz.	C4	79
Rubidoux, Ca., U.S.	n14	112
Rubim, Braz.	D8	79
Rubino, C. Iv.	H5	64
Rubio, Ven.	D6	84
Rubizhne, Ukr.	H5	26
Ruby Dome, mtn., Nv., U.S.	C6	135
Rudall, Austl.	I2	70
Ruda Śląska, Pol.	E18	10
Rudensk, Bela.	H10	22
Rudnja, Russia	G14	22
Rudnyj, Kaz.	G10	26
Rudolf, Lake (Lake Turkana), l., Afr.	H8	56
Rudolstadt, Ger.	E11	10
Rudong, China	C10	34
Rufā'ah, Sud.	F12	60
Rufino, Arg.	H7	80
Rufisque, Sen.	D1	64
Rufus Woods Lake, res., Wa., U.S.	A6	154
Rugao, China	C9	34
Rugby, Eng., U.K.	I12	8
Rugby, N.D., U.S.	A5	141
Rügen, i., Ger.	A13	10
Rugeley, Eng., U.K.	K12	8
Rui'an, China	H9	34
Ruidoso, N.M., U.S.	D4	138
Ruidoso Downs, N.M., U.S.	D4	138
Ruijin, China	J5	34
Ruiz, Mex.	G7	90
Ruiz, Nevado del, vol., Col.	E5	84
Ruiz de Montoya, Arg.	D11	80
Rūjiena, Lat.	D8	22
Ruleville, Ms., U.S.	B3	131
Ruma, Yugo.	D3	20
Rumbek, Sud.	N5	60
Rumbeke, Bel.	G3	12
Rumford, Me., U.S.	D2	126
Rumia, Pol.	A18	10
Rumney Depot, N.H., U.S.	C3	136
Rumson, N.J., U.S.	C4	137
Runan, China	B3	34
Rundu, Nmb.	A4	66
Runge, co., Tx., U.S.	D3	150
Runnels, co., Tx., U.S.	D3	150
Ruoqiang, China	D4	30
Ruoxi, China	F4	34
Rupert, Id., U.S.	G5	119
Rupert, W.V., U.S.	D4	155
Rupert, Rivière de, stm., Que., Can.	h11	104
Rupununi, stm., Guy.	F13	84
Rural Hall, N.C., U.S.	A2	140
Rural Retreat, Va., U.S.	D1	153
Rurrenabaque, Bol.	F8	82
Rusape, Zimb.	B11	66
Ruse, Bul.	F9	20
Rush, co., In., U.S.	E6	121
Rush, co., Ks., U.S.	D4	123
Rush City, Mn., U.S.	E6	130
Rushford, Mn., U.S.	G7	130
Rushmere, Va., U.S.	h14	153
Rush Springs, Ok., U.S.	C4	143
Rushville, Il., U.S.	C3	120
Rushville, In., U.S.	E7	121
Rushville, Ne., U.S.	B3	134
Rusk, Tx., U.S.	D5	150
Rusk, co., Tx., U.S.	C5	150
Rusk, co., Wi., U.S.	C2	156
Ruskin, Fl., U.S.	E4	116
Russas, Braz.	D11	76
Russell, Man., Can.	D1	100
Russell, Ont., Can.	B9	103
Russell, Ks., U.S.	D5	123
Russell, Ky., U.S.	B7	124
Russell, co., Al., U.S.	C4	108
Russell, co., Ks., U.S.	D5	123
Russell, co., Ky., U.S.	D4	124
Russell, co., Va., U.S.	f9	153
Russell Springs, Ky., U.S.	C4	124
Russellville, Al., U.S.	A2	108
Russellville, Ar., U.S.	B2	111
Russellville, Ky., U.S.	D3	124
Russellville, Mo., U.S.	C5	132
Russellville, Tn., U.S.	C10	149
Rüsselsheim, Ger.	E8	10
Russia, ctry., Eur.	E14	26
Russian, stm., Ca., U.S.	C2	112
Russiaville, In., U.S.	D5	121
Rust, Aus.	H16	10
Rustavi, Geor.	I7	26
Rustburg, Va., U.S.	C3	153
Rustenburg, S. Afr.	E8	66
Ruston, La., U.S.	B3	125
Ruston, Wa., U.S.	B3	154
Ruteng, Indon.	G7	38
Ruth, Nv., U.S.	D6	135
Rutherford, N.J., U.S.	B4	137
Rutherford, Tn., U.S.	A3	149
Rutherford, co., N.C., U.S.	B1	140
Rutherford, co., Tn., U.S.	B5	149
Rutherfordton, N.C., U.S.	B1	140
Ruthven, Ia., U.S.	A3	122
Rüti, Switz.	D10	13
Rutland, Ma., U.S.	B4	128
Rutland, Vt., U.S.	D3	152
Rutland, co., Vt., U.S.	D2	152
Rutledge, Al., U.S.	D3	108
Rutledge, Ga., U.S.	C3	117
Rutledge, Tn., U.S.	C10	149
Rutshuru, Zaire	B5	58
Ruvuma (Ruvuma), stm., Afr.	D7	58
Ruy Barbosa, Braz.	B8	79
Ruza, Russia	F19	22
Ruzajevka, Russia	G6	26
Ružany, Bela.	I7	22
Ružomberok, Slvk.	F19	10
Rwanda, ctry., Afr.	B5	58
Ryan, Ok., U.S.	C4	143
Rybinsk, Russia	C21	22
Rybinskoje vodochranilišče, res., Russia	C21	22
Rybnik, Pol.	E18	10
Rybnoje, Russia	G22	22
Rycroft, Alta., Can.	B1	98
Ryde, Eng., U.K.	K12	8
Rye, N.H., U.S.	D5	136
Rye, N.Y., U.S.	h13	139
Rye Beach, N.H., U.S.	E5	136
Ryegate, Mt., U.S.	D7	133
Rye Patch Reservoir, res., Nv., U.S.	C3	135
Ryley, Alta., Can.	C4	98
Rysy, mtn., Eur.	F20	10
Ryukyu Islands see Nansei-shotō, is., Japan	F12	30
Ržaksa, Russia	I25	22
Rzeszów, Pol.	E22	10
Ržev, Russia	E17	22

S

Name	Map Ref.	Page
Saale, stm., Ger.	D11	10
Saalfeld, Ger.	E11	10
Saar see Saarland, state, Ger.	F6	10
Saarbrücken, Ger.	F6	10
Saaremaa, i., Est.	C5	22
Saarland, state, Ger.	F6	10
Saarlouis, Ger.	F6	10
Saatlı, Azer.	B10	48
Saavedra, Arg.	I7	80
Saba, i., Neth. Ant.	F13	94
Šabac, Yugo.	E3	20
Sabadell, Spain	D14	16
Sabae, Japan	L11	36
Sabana, Archipiélago de, is., Cuba	C4	94
Sabana de La Mar, Dom. Rep.	E10	94
Sabanagrande, Hond.	D7	92
Sabanalarga, Col.	B5	84
Sabancuy, Mex.	H14	90
Sabará, Braz.	E7	79
Sabattus, Me., U.S.	D2	126
Sabetha, Ks., U.S.	C8	123
Sabi (Save), stm., Afr.	C11	66
Sabina, Oh., U.S.	C2	142
Sabinas, Mex.	D9	90
Sabinas, stm., Mex.	D9	90

Name	Map Ref.	Page
Sabinas Hidalgo, Mex. . . .	D9	90
Sabine, co., La., U.S. . . .	C2	125
Sabine, co., Tx., U.S.	D6	150
Sabine, stm., U.S.	D6	150
Sabine Lake, l., U.S.	E2	125
Sabinópolis, Braz.	E7	79
Sabirabad, Azer.	A10	48
Sable, Cape, c., Fl., U.S. .	G5	116
Sable Island, i., N.S., Can.	F10	101
Sablé-sur-Sarthe, Fr.	E6	14
Sabou, Burkina	E8	64
Sabula, Ia., U.S.	B7	122
Sabyā, Sau. Ar.	F3	47
Sabzevār, Iran	C14	48
Sac, co., Ia., U.S.	B2	122
Sacaba, Bol.	G8	82
Sacajawea, Lake, res., Wa., U.S.	C7	154
Sacajawea Peak, mtn., Or., U.S.	B9	144
Sacaton, Az., U.S.	D4	110
Sac City, Ia., U.S.	B2	122
Săcele, Rom.	D9	20
Sachalin, ostrov (Sakhalin), i., Russia	G20	28
Sachayoj, Arg.	D8	80
Šachovskaja, Russia	E18	22
Šachrisabz, Uzb.	J11	26
Sachse, Tx., U.S.	n10	150
Sachsen, state, Ger.	D13	10
Sachsen-Anhalt, state, Ger.	C11	10
Sachs Harbour, N.W. Ter., Can.	B7	96
Šachty, Russia	H6	26
Šachunja, Russia	F7	26
Šack, Russia	G24	22
Sackville, N.B., Can.	D5	101
Saco, Me., U.S.	E2	126
Saco, Mt., U.S.	B9	133
Saco, stm., U.S.	E2	126
Sacramento, Braz.	E5	79
Sacramento, Ca., U.S. . . .	C3	112
Sacramento, Ky., U.S. . . .	C2	124
Sacramento, co., Ca., U.S.	C3	112
Sacramento, stm., Ca., U.S.	C3	112
Sacramento Mountains, mts., N.M., U.S.	E4	138
Sacramento Valley, val., Az., U.S.	B1	110
Sacramento Valley, val., Ca., U.S.	C2	112
Sacré-Coeur-Saguenay, Que., Can.	A8	104
Sa'dah, Yemen	F3	47
Saddle Ball Mountain, mtn., Ma., U.S.	A1	128
Saddle Brook, N.J., U.S. . .	h8	137
Sa Dec, Viet.	I8	40
Sado, i., Japan	I13	36
Šadrinsk, Russia	F10	26
Safety Harbor, Fl., U.S. . .	E4	116
Safford, Az., U.S.	E6	110
Safi, Mor.	D6	62
Safonovo, Russia	F4	26
Saga, Japan	N5	36
Sagadahoc, co., Me., U.S.	E3	126
Sagaing, Mya.	D3	40
Sagamihara, Japan	L14	36
Sagamore, Ma., U.S.	C6	128
Sagamore Hills, Oh., U.S. .	h9	142
Saganaga Lake, l., Mn., U.S.	B7	130
Sāgar, India	I8	44
Saginaw, Al., U.S.	B3	108
Saginaw, Mi., U.S.	E7	129
Saginaw, Tx., U.S.	n9	150
Saginaw, co., Mi., U.S. . .	E6	129
Saginaw Bay, b., Mi., U.S.	E7	129
Sagleipie, Lib.	H5	64
Šagonar, Russia	G16	26
Saguache, Co., U.S.	C4	113
Saguache, co., Co., U.S. .	C4	113
Sagua de Tánamo, Cuba .	D7	94
Sagua la Grande, Cuba . .	C4	94
Saguenay, stm., Que., Can.	A7	104
Sagunt, Spain	F11	16
Sahāb, Jord.	E6	50
Sahagún, Col.	C5	84
Sahara, des., Afr.	F7	52
Sahāranpur, India	F7	44
Sahel see Sudan, reg., Afr.	F11	54
Sāhīwal, Pak.	E5	44
Sahuaripa, Mex.	C5	90
Sahuarita, Az., U.S.	F5	110
Sahuayo de José María Morelos, Mex.	G8	90
Saïda, Alg.	C11	62
Saidpur, Bngl.	H13	44
Saidu, Pak.	C5	44
Saigon see Thanh Pho Ho Chi Minh, Viet.	I9	40
Saijō, Japan	N8	36
Saiki, Japan	O6	36
Saimaa, l., Fin.	K20	6
Saín Alto, Mex.	F8	90
Saint-Affrique, Fr.	I9	14
Saint Agatha, Me., U.S. . .	A4	126
Sainte Agathe, Man., Can.	E3	100
Sainte-Agathe-des-Monts, Que., Can.	C3	104
Saint Alban's, Newf., Can.	E4	102
Saint Albans, Eng., U.K. . .	J13	8
Saint Albans, Vt., U.S. . . .	B2	152
Saint Albans, W.V., U.S. . .	C3	155
Saint Albans Bay, Vt., U.S.	B2	152
Saint Albert, Alta., Can. . .	C4	98
Saint-Alexandre, Que., Can.	D4	104
Saint-Amand-Montrond, Fr.	F9	14
Saint-Ambroise, Que., Can.	A6	104
Saint-Anaclet, Que., Can. .	A9	104
Saint-André, Cap, c., Madag.	p21	67b
Saint-André-Avellin, Que., Can.	D2	104
Saint-André-Est, Que., Can.	D3	104
Saint Andrews, N.B., Can.	D2	101
Saint Andrews, Scot., U.K.	E11	8
Saint Andrews, S.C., U.S. .	C5	147
Saint Andrews, S.C., U.S. .	F7	147
Saint Anne, Il., U.S.	B6	120
Sainte-Anne-de-Beaupré, Que., Can.	B7	104
Sainte-Anne [-de-Bellevue], Que., Can.	q19	104
Sainte Anne-de-Madawaska, N.B., Can. .	B1	101
Sainte Anne-des-Chênes, Man., Can.	E3	100
Saint-Anselme, Que., Can.	C7	104
Saint Ansgar, Ia., U.S. . . .	A5	122
Saint Anthony, Newf., Can.	C4	102
Saint Anthony, Id., U.S. . .	F7	119
Saint Antoine, N.B., Can. .	C5	101
Saint-Antoine [-sur-Richelieu], Que., Can. . .	D4	104
Saint-Apollinaire, Que., Can.	C6	104
Saint Arnaud, Austl.	K5	70
Saint Arthur, N.B., Can. . .	B3	101
Saint Augustin, stm., Can.	C2	102
Saint Augustine, Fl., U.S. .	C5	116
Saint-Avold, Fr.	C13	14
Saint-Barthélemy, i., Guad.	F13	94
Saint Basile, N.B., Can. . .	B1	101
Saint-Basile [-Sud], Que., Can.	C6	104
Saint Bees Head, c., Eng., U.K.	F10	8
Saint-Benoît-Labre, Que., Can.	C7	104
Saint-Bernard, Que., Can.	C6	104
Saint Bernard, Al., U.S. . .	A3	108
Saint Bernard, co., La., U.S.	E6	125
Saint Bernice, In., U.S. . .	E2	121
Saint Bride, Mount, mtn., Alta., Can.	D3	98
Saint Bride's, Newf., Can. .	E4	102
Saint-Brieuc, Fr.	D4	14
Saint Brieux, Sask., Can. .	E3	105
Saint-Bruno, Que., Can. . .	A6	104
Saint-Calais, Fr.	E7	14
Saint-Casimir, Que., Can. .	C5	104
Saint Catharines, Ont., Can.	D5	103
Saint Catherines Island, i., Ga., U.S.	E5	117
Saint-Césaire, Que., Can. .	D4	104
Saint-Chamond, Fr.	G11	14
Saint Charles, Il., U.S. . . .	B5	120
Saint Charles, Md., U.S. . .	C4	127
Saint Charles, Mi., U.S. . .	E6	129
Saint Charles, Mn., U.S. . .	G6	130
Saint Charles, Mo., U.S. . .	C7	132
Saint Charles, co., La., U.S.	E5	125
Saint Charles, co., Mo., U.S.	C7	132
Saint Christopher (Saint Kitts), i., St. K./N. . . .	F13	94
Saint Christopher-Nevis see Saint Kitts and Nevis, ctry., N.A.	F13	94
Saint Clair, Mi., U.S.	F8	129
Saint Clair, Mo., U.S.	C6	132
Saint Clair, Pa., U.S.	E9	145
Saint Clair, co., Al., U.S. . .	B3	108
Saint Clair, co., Il., U.S. . .	E3	120
Saint Clair, co., Mi., U.S. .	F8	129
Saint Clair, co., Mo., U.S. .	C4	132
Saint Clair Shores, Mi., U.S.	p16	129
Saint Clairsville, Oh., U.S. .	B5	142
Saint Claude, Man., Can. .	E2	100
Saint-Claude, Fr.	F12	14
Saint Cloud, Fl., U.S.	D5	116
Saint Cloud, Mn., U.S. . . .	E4	130
Saint-Constant, Que., Can.	q19	104
Sainte-Croix, Que., Can. . .	C6	104
Sainte-Croix, Switz.	E6	13
Saint Croix, co., Wi., U.S. .	C1	156
Saint Croix, i., V.I.U.S. . .	F12	94
Saint Croix, stm., U.S. . . .	C1	156
Saint Croix Falls, Wi., U.S.	C1	156
Saint-Damase, Que., Can.	D4	104
Saint David, Az., U.S. . . .	F5	110
Saint David's Head, c., Wales, U.K.	J8	8
Saint-Denis, Fr.	D9	14
Saint-Denis, Reu.	v17	67c
Saint-Dié, Fr.	D13	14
Saint-Dizier, Fr.	D11	14
Saint-Dominique, Que., Can.	D5	104
Saint Edward, Ne., U.S. . .	C8	134
Saint Eleanor's, P.E.I., Can.	C6	101
Saint Elias, Cape, c., Ak., U.S.	D11	109
Saint Elias, Mount, mtn., N.A.	D4	96
Sainte-Élie, Fr. Gu.	C8	76
Saint Elmo, Al., U.S.	E1	108
Saint Elmo, Il., U.S.	D5	120
Saint-Étienne, Fr.	G11	14
Saint-Eustache, Que., Can.	D4	104
Saint-Félicien, Que., Can. .	A5	104
Saint-Félix-de-Valois, Que., Can.	C4	104
Saint-Ferdinand (Bernierville), Que., Can.	C6	104
Sainte-Ferréol [-les-Neiges], Que., Can.	B7	104
Saint-Flour, Fr.	G10	14
Sainte-Foy, Que., Can. . . .	n17	104
Saint Francis, Ks., U.S. . .	C2	123
Saint Francis, Me., U.S. . .	A4	126
Saint Francis, Mn., U.S. . .	E5	130
Saint Francis, S.D., U.S. . .	D5	148
Saint Francis, Wi., U.S. . .	n12	156
Saint Francis, co., Ar., U.S.	B5	111
Saint Francis, stm., U.S. . .	A5	111
Saint Francis, Cape, c., Newf., Can.	E5	102
Saint Francisville, La., U.S.	D4	125
Saint Francois, co., Mo., U.S.	D7	132
Saint-François, stm., Que., Can.	D5	104
Saint-François, Lac, l., Que., Can.	D6	104
Saint Francois Mountains, hills, Mo., U.S.	D7	132
Saint-Fulgence, Que., Can.	A7	104
Saint-Gabriel, Que., Can. .	C4	104
Saint-Gaudens, Fr.	I7	14
Saint-Gédéon, Que., Can. .	D7	104
Sainte Genevieve, Mo., U.S.	D7	132
Sainte Genevieve, co., Mo., U.S.	D7	132
Saint George, Austl.	G8	70
Saint George, N.B., Can. .	D3	101
Saint George, Ont., Can. .	D4	103
Saint George, Me., U.S. . .	D3	126
Saint George, S.C., U.S. . .	E6	147
Saint George, Ut., U.S. . . .	F2	151
Saint George, Cape, c., Newf., Can.	D2	102
Saint George, Cape, c., Fl., U.S.	C1	116
Saint George Island, i., Ak., U.S.	D6	109
Saint George's, Newf., Can.	D2	102
Saint-Georges, Que., Can.	C5	104
Saint-Georges, Fr. Gu. . . .	C8	76
Saint George's, Gren. . . .	H14	94
Saint George's, De., U.S. .	B3	115
Saint George's Bay, b., Newf., Can.	D2	102
Saint Georges Bay, b., N.S., Can.	D8	101
Saint George's Channel, strt., Eur.	J7	8
Saint-Germain, Fr.	D9	14
Saint-Gilles (Sint-Gillis), Bel.	G5	12
Saint-Gilles, Que., Can. . .	C6	104
Saint-Girons, Fr.	J8	14
Saint Gregory, Mount, mtn., Newf., Can.	D2	102
Saint Helena, i., La., U.S. .	D5	125
Saint Helena, dep., i., Afr. .	J6	52
Saint Helena Island, i., S.C., U.S.	G6	147
Saint Helena Sound, strt., S.C., U.S.	G7	147
Saint Helens, Austl.	M8	70
Saint Helens, Or., U.S. . .	B4	144
Saint Helens, Mount, vol., Wa., U.S.	C3	154
Saint Helier, Jersey	L11	8
Saint-Hilaire-du-Harcouët, Fr.	D5	14
Saint-Hilarion, Que., Can. .	B7	104
Saint-Hubert, Que., Can. .	q20	104
Saint-Hubert-de-Témiscouata, Que., Can.	B8	104
Saint-Hyacinthe, Que., Can.	D5	104
Saint Ignace, N.B., Can. . .	C4	101
Saint Ignace, Mi., U.S. . . .	C6	129
Saint Ignatius, Mt., U.S. . .	C2	133
Saint-Imier, Switz.	D7	13
Saint Isidore de Prescott, Ont., Can.	B10	103
Saint Jacques, N.B., Can. .	B1	101
Saint-Jacques, Que., Can.	D4	104
Saint James, Mn., U.S. . .	G4	130
Saint James, Mo., U.S. . .	D6	132
Saint James, co., La., U.S.	D5	125
Saint James, Cape, c., B.C., Can.	D2	99
Saint-Jean, Lac, l., Que., Can.	A5	104
Saint Jean Baptiste, Man., Can.	E3	100
Saint-Jean-Chrysostome, Que., Can.	o17	104
Saint-Jean-d'Angély, Fr. . .	G6	14
Saint-Jean-de-Luz, Fr. . . .	I5	14
Saint-Jean-sur-Richelieu, Que., Can.	D4	104
Saint-Jérôme, Que., Can. .	D3	104
Saint-Joachim, Que., Can. .	B7	104
Saint Joe, stm., Id., U.S. . .	B3	119
Saint John, N.B., Can. . . .	D3	101
Saint John, In., U.S.	B3	121
Saint John, Ks., U.S.	E5	123
Saint John, i., V.I.U.S. . . .	E12	94
Saint John, Cape, c., Newf., Can.	D4	102
Saint John Bay, b., Newf., Can.	C3	102
Saint John's, Antig.	F14	94
Saint John's, Newf., Can. .	E5	102
Saint Johns, Az., U.S. . . .	C6	110
Saint Johns, Mi., U.S. . . .	F6	129
Saint Johns, co., Fl., U.S. .	C5	116
Saint Johnsbury, Vt., U.S. .	C4	152
Saint Johnsbury Center, Vt., U.S.	C4	152
Saint Jones, stm., De., U.S.	D4	115
Saint Joseph, N.B., Can. . .	D5	101
Saint Joseph, Il., U.S. . . .	C5	120
Saint Joseph, La., U.S. . .	C4	125
Saint Joseph, Mi., U.S. . .	F4	129
Saint Joseph, Mn., U.S. . .	E4	130
Saint Joseph, Mo., U.S. . .	B3	132
Saint Joseph, Tn., U.S. . .	B4	149
Saint Joseph, co., In., U.S.	A5	121
Saint Joseph, co., Mi., U.S.	G5	129
Saint Joseph, Lake, l., Ont., Can.	o17	103
Saint Joseph Bay, b., Fl., U.S.	C1	116
Saint-Joseph-de-Beauce, Que., Can.	C7	104
Saint Joseph Point, c., Fl., U.S.	v16	116
Saint-Jovite, Que., Can. . .	C3	104
Saint-Julien-en-Genevois, Fr.	F13	14
Saint-Junien, Fr.	G7	14
Saint-Just-en-Chaussée, Fr.	C9	14
Saint Kilda, i., Scot., U.K. .	D5	8
Saint Kitts see Saint Christopher, i., St. K./N.	F13	94
Saint Kitts and Nevis, ctry., N.A.	F13	94
Saint-Lambert, Que., Can. .	p19	104
Saint Landry, co., La., U.S.	D3	125
Saint-Laurent, Que., Can. .	p19	104
Saint-Laurent-du-Maroni, Gu.	B8	76
Saint Lawrence, Newf., Can.	E4	102
Saint Lawrence, co., N.Y., U.S.	A5	139
Saint Lawrence, stm., N.A.	G19	96
Saint Lawrence, Cape, c., N.S., Can.	B9	101
Saint Lawrence, Gulf of, b., Can.	G20	96
Saint Lawrence Island, i., Ak., U.S.	C5	109
Saint Lazare, Man., Can. .	D1	100
Saint-Lazare, Que., Can. .	q18	104
Saint Léonard, N.B., Can. .	B2	101
Saint-Lô, Fr.	C5	14
Saint Louis, Sask., Can. . .	E3	105
Saint-Louis, Reu.	v17	67c
Saint-Louis, Sen.	C1	64
Saint Louis, Mi., U.S. . . .	E6	129
Saint Louis, Mo., U.S. . . .	C7	132
Saint Louis, co., Mn., U.S.	C6	130
Saint Louis, co., Mo., U.S.	C7	132
Saint Louis, stm., U.S. . . .	D6	130
Saint Louis Bay, b., Ms., U.S.	f7	131
Saint Louis-de-Kent, N.B., Can.	C5	101
Saint Louis Park, Mn., U.S.	n12	130
Saint-Loup-sur-Semouse, Fr.	E13	14
Saint-Luc, Que., Can. . . .	D4	104
Saint Lucia, ctry., N.A. . .	H14	94
Saint Lucia Channel, strt., N.A.	G14	94
Saint Lucie, co., Fl., U.S. .	E6	116
Saint Lucie Canal, Fl., U.S.	F6	116
Sainte-Madeleine, Que., Can.	D4	104
Saint Malo, Man., Can. . .	E3	100
Saint-Malo, Fr.	D4	14
Saint-Malo, Golfe de, b., Fr.	D4	14
Saint-Marc, Haiti	E8	94
Saint-Marc, Canal de, strt., Haiti	E8	94
Saint-Marc [-des-Carrières], Que., Can.	C5	104
Sainte-Marie, Que., Can. .	C6	104
Sainte-Marie, Cap, c., Madag.	t21	67b
Sainte-Marie-aux-Mines, Fr.	D14	14
Saint Maries, Id., U.S. . . .	B2	119
Sainte Marie-sur-Mer [-Saint Raphaël-sur-Mer], N.B., Can.	B5	101
Saint Martin, co., La., U.S.	D4	125
Saint-Martin (Sint Maarten), i., N.A.	E13	94
Saint Martins, N.B., Can. .	D4	101
Saint Martinville, La., U.S. .	D4	125
Saint Mary, co., La., U.S. .	E4	125
Saint Mary-of-the-Woods, In., U.S.	E3	121
Saint Mary Peak, mtn., Austl.	H3	70
Saint Marys, Austl.	M8	70
Saint Mary's, Newf., Can. .	E5	102
Saint Mary's, Ont., Can. . .	D3	103
Saint Marys, Ak., U.S. . . .	C7	109
Saint Marys, Ga., U.S. . . .	F5	117
Saint Marys, In., U.S. . . .	A5	121
Saint Marys, Ks., U.S. . . .	C7	123
Saint Marys, Oh., U.S. . . .	B1	142
Saint Marys, Pa., U.S. . . .	D4	145
Saint Marys, W.V., U.S. . .	B3	155
Saint Marys, co., Md., U.S.	D4	127
Saint Marys, stm., N.S., Can.	D8	101
Saint Marys, stm., U.S. . .	F5	117
Saint Marys, stm., U.S. . .	C8	121
Saint Mary's Bay, b., Newf., Can.	E5	102
Saint Marys Bay, b., N.S., Can.	E3	101
Saint Marys City, Md., U.S.	D5	127
Saint Matthew Island, i., Ak., U.S.	C5	109
Saint Matthews, Ky., U.S. .	B4	124
Saint Matthews, S.C., U.S.	D6	147
Saint-Maur [-des-Fossés], Fr.	D9	14
Saint-Maurice, Que., Can. .	C5	104
Saint-Maurice, stm., Que., Can.	C5	104
Sainte-Maxime, Fr.	I13	14
Saint-Méen-le-Grand, Fr. .	D4	14
Saint Meinrad, In., U.S. . .	H4	121
Sainte-Menehould, Fr. . . .	C11	14
Saint-Mère-Église, Fr. . . .	C5	14
Saint-Méthode [-de-Frontenac], Que., Can. . .	C6	104
Saint Michael, Ak., U.S. . .	C7	109
Saint Michael, Mn., U.S. . .	E5	130
Saint Michaels, Az., U.S. .	B6	110
Saint Michaels, Md., U.S. .	C5	127
Saint-Michel [-de-Bellechasse], Que., Can.	C7	104
Saint-Mihiel, Fr.	D12	14
Saint-Moritz see Sankt Moritz, Switz.	F16	14
Saint-Nazaire, Fr.	E4	14
Saint-Nicolas, Que., Can. .	o17	104
Saint-Odilon, Que., Can. . .	C7	104
Saint-Omer, Fr.	B9	14
Saint-Pacôme, Que., Can. .	B8	104
Saint-Pamphile, Que., Can.	C8	104
Saint-Pascal, Que., Can. . .	B8	104
Saint Paul, Alta., Can. . . .	B5	98
Saint Paul, In., U.S.	F6	121
Saint Paul, Ks., U.S.	E8	123
Saint Paul, Mn., U.S.	F5	130
Saint Paul, Mo., U.S.	f12	132
Saint Paul, Ne., U.S.	C7	134
Saint Paul, Va., U.S.	f9	153
Saint-Paul, Île, i., F.S.A.T.	L11	158
Saint-Paulin, Que., Can. . .	C4	104
Saint Paul Island, i., Ak., U.S.	D5	109
Saint Paul Park, Mn., U.S.	n12	130
Saint Pauls, N.C., U.S. . . .	C4	140
Sainte-Perpétue-de-L'Islet, Que., Can.	B8	104
Saint Peter, Mn., U.S. . . .	F5	130
Saint Peter Port, Guernsey	C4	14
Saint Peters, N.S., Can. . .	D9	101
Saint Peters, Mo., U.S. . .	q17	132
Saint Petersburg see Sankt-Peterburg, Russia	B13	22
Saint Petersburg, Fl., U.S.	E4	116
Saint Petersburg Beach, Fl., U.S.	p10	116
Saint-Pie, Que., Can. . . .	D5	104
Saint-Pierre, Mart.	G14	94
Saint-Pierre, Reu.	v17	67c
Saint-Pierre, St. P./M. . . .	E3	102
Saint Pierre and Miquelon, dep., N.A.	E3	102
Saint Pierre-Jolys, Man., Can.	E3	100
Saint-Pol-de-Léon, Fr. . . .	D3	14
Saint-Pol-sur-Ternoise, Fr.	B9	14
Saint-Prime, Que., Can. . .	A5	104
Saint Quentin, N.B., Can. .	B2	101
Saint-Quentin, Fr.	C10	14
Saint-Raphaël, Fr.	I13	14
Saint-Raymond, Que., Can.	C6	104
Saint-Rédempteur, Que., Can.	o17	104
Saint Regis, Mt., U.S. . . .	C1	133
Saint-Rémi, Que., Can. . . .	D4	104
Saint-Rémy-de-Provence, Fr.	I11	14
Saint-Romuald, Que., Can.	C6	104
Saint Rose, La., U.S.	k11	125
Saint Rose du Lac, Man., Can.	D2	100
Saint Sauveur, N.B., Can. .	B4	101
Saint-Sauveur-des-Monts, Que., Can.	D3	104
Saint Simons Island, Ga., U.S.	E5	117
Saint Simons Island, i., Ga., U.S.	E5	117
Saint Stephen, N.B., Can. .	D2	101
Saint Stephen, S.C., U.S. .	E8	147
Saint Tammany, co., La., U.S.	D5	125
Sainte-Thècle, Que., Can.	C5	104
Sainte-Thérèse, Que., Can.	D4	104
Saint Thomas, Ont., Can. .	E3	103
Saint Thomas, N.D., U.S. .	A8	141
Saint Thomas, i., V.I.U.S. .	E12	94
Saint Timothée, Que., Can.	q18	104
Saint-Tite, Que., Can. . . .	C5	104
Saint-Tropez, Fr.	I13	14
Saint-Valéry-en-Caux, Fr. .	C7	14
Saint Vincent, Gulf, b., Austl.	J3	70
Saint Vincent and the Grenadines, ctry., N.A. .	H14	94
Saint-Vincent-de-Tyrosse, Fr.	I5	14
Saint Vincent Passage, strt., N.A.	H14	94
Saint Vincent's [-Saint Stephens-Peter's River], Newf., Can.	E5	102
Saint Walburg, Sask., Can.	D1	105
Saint-Zacharie, Que., Can.	C7	104
Sajama, Nevado, mtn., Bol.	H7	82
Sajano-Šušenskoje vodochranilišče, res., Russia	G16	26
Sajat, Turk.	B17	48
Sajnšand, Mong.	C9	30
Sajószentpéter, Hung. . . .	G20	10
Sakai, Japan	M10	36
Sakākah, Sau. Ar.	G6	48
Sakakawea, Lake, res., N.D., U.S.	B3	141
Sakaraha, Madag.	s21	67b
Sakarya, Tur.	G14	4
Sakata, Japan	I14	36
Sakchu, N. Kor.	C13	32
Sakété, Benin	H11	64
Sakhalin see Sachalin, ostrov, i., Russia	G20	28
Sakon Nakhon, Thai.	F8	40
Sakonnet, stm., R.I., U.S. .	E6	146
Sakonnet Point, c., R.I., U.S.	F6	146
Sal, i., C.V.	B7	92
Sala, Swe.	L15	6
Salaberry-de-Valleyfield, Que., Can.	D3	104
Salacgrīva, Lat.	D7	22
Saladas, Arg.	E9	80
Saladillo, Arg.	H9	80
Salado, stm., Arg.	H9	80
Salado, stm., Arg.	F8	80
Salado, stm., Arg.	H5	80
Salado, stm., Mex.	D10	90
Salamá, Guat.	B4	92
Salamá, Hond.	C8	92
Salamanca, Chile	F3	80
Salamanca, Mex.	G9	90
Salamanca, Spain	E6	16
Salamanca, N.Y., U.S. . . .	C2	139
Salamat, Bahr, stm., Chad	F4	56
Salamina, Col.	E5	84
Salamís, Grc.	L7	20
Salamonie, stm., In., U.S. .	C6	121
Salamonie Lake, res., In., U.S.	C6	121
Salatiga, Indon.	j15	39a
Salavat, Russia	G9	26
Salaverry, Peru	C2	82
Sala y Gómez, Isla, i., Chile	K29	158
Salcantay, Nevado, mtn., Peru	E5	82
Saldanha, S. Afr.	I3	66
Saldungaray, Arg.	J8	80
Saldus, Lat.	E5	22
Sale, Austl.	L7	70
Salé, Mor.	C7	62
Salechard, Russia	D5	28
Sale Creek, Tn., U.S.	D8	149
Salem, India	G5	46
Salem, Ar., U.S.	A4	111
Salem, Il., U.S.	E5	120
Salem, In., U.S.	G5	121
Salem, Ky., U.S.	e9	124
Salem, Ma., U.S.	A6	128
Salem, Mo., U.S.	D6	132
Salem, N.H., U.S.	E4	136
Salem, N.J., U.S.	D2	137
Salem, Oh., U.S.	B5	142
Salem, S.D., U.S.	D8	148
Salem, Va., U.S.	C2	153
Salem, W.V., U.S.	B4	155
Salem, Wi., U.S.	n11	156
Salem, co., N.J., U.S. . . .	D2	137
Salemi, Italy	L7	18
Salentina, Penisola, pen., Italy	I13	18
Salerno, Italy	I9	18
Salerno, Golfo di, b., Italy .	I9	18
Salesville, Ar., U.S.	A3	111
Salgótarján, Hung.	G19	10
Salida, Co., U.S.	C5	113
Salies-de-Béarn, Fr.	I5	14
Salihli, Tur.	K12	20
Salima, Mwi.	D6	58
Salina, Ks., U.S.	D6	123
Salina, Ok., U.S.	A6	143
Salina, Ut., U.S.	E4	151
Salina Cruz, Mex.	I12	90
Salinas, Braz.	D7	79
Salinas, Ec.	I2	84
Salinas, Ca., U.S.	D3	112
Salinas de Garci Mendoza, Bol.	H8	82
Salinas de Hidalgo, Mex. .	F9	90
Saline, Mi., U.S.	F7	129
Saline, co., Ar., U.S.	C3	111
Saline, co., Il., U.S.	F5	120
Saline, co., Ks., U.S.	D6	123
Saline, co., Mo., U.S. . . .	B4	132
Saline, co., Ne., U.S.	D8	134
Saline, stm., Ar., U.S. . . .	D4	111
Saline, stm., Ar., U.S. . . .	C1	111
Saline, stm., Ks., U.S. . . .	C3	123
Salingyi, Mya.	D3	40
Salisbury, Austl.	J3	70
Salisbury, N.B., Can.	C4	101
Salisbury, Eng., U.K.	J12	8
Salisbury, Ct., U.S.	B2	114
Salisbury, Md., U.S.	D6	127
Salisbury, Ma., U.S.	A6	128
Salisbury, Mo., U.S.	B5	132
Salisbury, N.H., U.S.	D3	136
Salisbury, N.C., U.S.	B2	140
Salisbury see Harare, Zimb.	A10	66
Salisbury Plain, pl., Eng., U.K.	J12	8
Salkehatchie, stm., S.C., U.S.	E5	147
Salkhad, Syria	D7	50
Sallanches, Fr.	G13	14
Salliqueló, Arg.	I7	80
Sallisaw, Ok., U.S.	B7	143
Sallūm, Khalīj as-, b., Afr. .	B3	60
Salmās, Iran	B8	48
Salmo, B.C., Can.	E9	99
Salmon, Id., U.S.	D5	119
Salmon, stm., Id., U.S. . . .	D3	119
Salmon Creek, Wa., U.S. .	D3	154
Salmon Falls, stm., U.S. . .	D5	136
Salmon Point, c., Ont., Can.	D7	103
Salmon River Mountains, mts., Id., U.S.	E3	119
Salo, Fin.	K18	6
Salon-de-Provence, Fr. . . .	I12	14
Salonika see Thessaloníki, Grc.	I6	20
Salonta, Rom.	C5	20
Saloum, stm., Sen.	D2	64
Sal Rei, C.V.	k17	64a
Salsacate, Arg.	F6	80
Sal'sk, Russia	H6	26
Salsomaggiore Terme, Italy	E4	18
Salt, stm., Az., U.S.	D4	110
Salt, stm., Ky., U.S.	C4	124
Salt, stm., Mo., U.S.	B6	132
Salta, Arg.	C6	80
Salta, prov., Arg.	C5	80
Saltcoats, Sask., Can. . . .	F4	105
Salt Fork Lake, res., Oh., U.S.	B4	142
Saltillo, Mex.	E9	90
Saltillo, Ms., U.S.	A5	131
Salt Lake, co., Ut., U.S. . .	C3	151
Salt Lake, l., Hi., U.S. . . .	g10	118
Salt Lake City, Ut., U.S. . .	C4	151
Salto, Arg.	H8	80
Salto, Ur.	F10	80
Salto da Divisa, Braz. . . .	D9	79
Salto Grande, Braz.	G4	79
Salto Grande, Embalse, res., S.A.	F9	80
Salton Sea, l., Ca., U.S. . .	F5	112
Salt Rock, W.V., U.S. . . .	C2	155
Saltville, Va., U.S.	f10	153
Saluda, S.C., U.S.	C4	147
Saluda, co., S.C., U.S. . . .	C4	147
Saluda, stm., S.C., U.S. . .	C4	147
Saluzzo, Italy	E2	18
Salvador, Braz.	B9	79
Salvador, Lake, l., La., U.S.	E5	125
Salvatierra, Mex.	G9	90
Salween (Nu) (Thanlwin), stm., Asia	D5	40
Salyan, Azer.	A7	48
Salyersville, Ky., U.S. . . .	C6	124
Salzburg, Aus.	H13	10
Salzburg, state, Aus.	H13	10
Salzgitter, Ger.	C10	10
Salzkammergut, reg., Aus.	H13	10
Salzwedel, Ger.	C11	10
Sama [de Langreo], Spain .	B6	16
Samaipata, Bol.	H10	82
Samālūt, Egypt	C6	60
Samaná, Bahía de, b., Dom. Rep.	E10	94
Samaná, Cabo, c., Dom. Rep.	E10	94
Samandağı, Tur.	C3	48
Samaniego, Col.	G4	84
Samara (Kujbyšev), Russia	G8	26
Samarai, Pap. N. Gui. . . .	n17	68a
Samarinda, Indon.	E9	84
Samariapo, Indon.	F6	38
Samarkand, Uzb.	J11	26
Šamaxı, Azer.	A10	48
Sambalpur, India	J10	44
Sambas, Indon.	N10	40
Sambava, Madag.	o24	67b
Sambhal, India	F8	44
Sambir, Ukr.	F23	10
Samborombón, Bahía, b., Arg.	I10	80
Samborondón, Ec.	H3	84
Samch'ŏk, S. Kor.	F17	32
Samch'ŏnp'o, S. Kor. . . .	I16	32
Samedan, Switz.	E12	13
Samoa Islands, is., Oc. . .	J22	158

Name	Map Ref.	Page
Sámos, Grc.	L11	20
Samoset, Fl., U.S.	q10	116
Sampacho, Arg.	G6	80
Sampit, Indon.	F5	38
Sampson, co., N.C., U.S.	B4	140
Sam Rayburn Reservoir, res., Tx., U.S.	D5	150
Samson, Al., U.S.	D3	108
Samsun, Tur.	G15	4
Samtown, La., U.S.	C3	125
Samuels, Id., U.S.	A2	119
Samuhú, Arg.	D8	80
Samui, Ko, i., Thai.	J6	40
Samut Prakan, Thai.	H6	40
Samut Sakhon, Thai.	H6	40
Samut Songkhram, Thai.	H6	40
San, Mali	E7	64
Saña, Peru	B2	82
San'ā', Yemen	G4	47
Sanaga, stm., Cam.	J14	64
San Agustín, Arg.	F6	80
San Agustín, Col.	G4	84
San Agustin, Plains of, pl., N.M., U.S.	C2	138
San Ambrosio, Isla, i., Chile	B1	78
Sanandaj, Iran	D9	48
San Andrés, Col.	H4	94
San Andrés, Pan.	I12	92
San Andrés, Isla de, i., Col.	H4	94
San Andrés de Giles, Arg.	H9	80
San Andrés Tuxtla, Mex.	H12	90
San Andrés y Providencia, ter., Col.	H4	94
Sananduva, Braz.	D13	80
San Angelo, Tx., U.S.	D2	150
San Anselmo, Ca., U.S.	h7	112
San Antonio, Arg.	E6	80
San Antonio, Belize	A5	92
San Antonio, Chile	D3	80
San Antonio, Chile	G3	80
San Antonio, N.M., U.S.	D3	138
San Antonio, Tx., U.S.	E3	150
San Antonio, Cabo, c., Arg.	I10	80
San Antonio, Cabo de, c., Cuba	D2	94
San Antonio Bay, b., Tx., U.S.	E4	150
San Antonio de Areco, Arg.	H9	80
San Antonio de los Baños, Cuba	C3	94
San Antonio de los Cobres, Arg.	C5	80
San Antonio del Táchira, Ven.	D6	84
San Antonio Mountain, mtn., N.M., U.S.	A3	138
Sanatorium, Ms., U.S.	D4	131
San Augustine, co., Tx., U.S.	D5	150
San Benedetto del Tronto, Italy	G8	18
San Benito, Tx., U.S.	F4	150
San Benito, co., Ca., U.S.	D3	112
San Bernardino, Ca., U.S.	E5	112
San Bernardino, co., Ca., U.S.	E5	112
San Bernardo, Arg.	D8	80
San Bernardo, Chile	G3	80
San Blas, Mex.	G7	90
San Blas, Mex.	F5	90
San Blas, Cape, c., Fl., U.S.	v16	116
San Borja, Bol.	F8	82
Sanborn, Ia., U.S.	A2	122
Sanborn, co., S.D., U.S.	D7	148
Sanbornton, N.H., U.S.	D3	136
Sanbornville, N.H., U.S.	C4	136
San Bruno, Ca., U.S.	D2	112
San Buenaventura, Mex.	D9	90
San Carlos, Arg.	C6	80
San Carlos, Arg.	D11	80
San Carlos, Arg.	G4	80
San Carlos, Chile	I3	80
San Carlos, Mex.	C9	90
San Carlos, Nic.	F10	92
San Carlos, Para.	B10	80
San Carlos, Phil.	C7	38
San Carlos, Az., U.S.	D5	110
San Carlos, Ca., U.S.	k8	112
San Carlos, Ur.	H11	80
San Carlos, Ven.	C8	84
San Carlos, stm., C.R.	G10	92
San Carlos Centro, Arg.	F8	80
San Carlos de Bariloche, Arg.	E2	78
San Carlos de Bolívar, Arg.	I8	80
San Carlos del Zulia, Ven.	C7	84
San Carlos de Río Negro, Ven.	G9	84
San Carlos Lake, res., Az., U.S.	D5	110
San Cataldo, Italy	L8	18
San Cayetano, Arg.	J9	80
Sánchez, Dom. Rep.	E10	94
San Ciro de Acosta, Mex.	G10	90
San Clemente, Ca., U.S.	F5	112
San Clemente, Cerro, mtn., Chile	F2	78
San Clemente Island, i., Ca., U.S.	F4	112
San Cosme, Arg.	D9	80
San Cristóbal, Arg.	F8	80
San Cristóbal, Dom. Rep.	E9	94
San Cristóbal, Ven.	D6	84
San Cristóbal, Volcán, vol., Nic.	E7	92
San Cristóbal de la Laguna, Spain	o24	17b
San Cristóbal de las Casas, Mex.	I13	90
Sancti Spíritus, Cuba	D5	94
Sancy, Puy de, mtn., Fr.	G9	14
Sandaré, Mali	D4	64
Sand Coulee, Mt., U.S.	C5	133
Sanders, Az., U.S.	B6	110
Sanders, co., Mt., U.S.	C1	133
Sandersville, Ga., U.S.	D4	117
Sandersville, Ms., U.S.	D4	131
Sandgate, Austl.	F10	70
Sandia, Peru	F7	82
Sandia Mountains, mts., N.M., U.S.	k8	138
Sandia Park, N.M., U.S.	k8	138
San Diego, Ca., U.S.	F5	112
San Diego, Tx., U.S.	F3	150
San Diego, co., Ca., U.S.	F5	112

Name	Map Ref.	Page
San Diego de la Unión, Mex.	G9	90
Sand Island, i., Hi., U.S.	g10	118
Sand Mountain, mtn., U.S.	A3	108
Sandoná, Col.	G4	84
San Donà di Piave, Italy	D7	18
Sandoval, Il., U.S.	E4	120
Sandoval, co., N.M., U.S.	B2	138
Sandovo, Russia	C19	22
Sandoway, Mya.	E3	40
Sandown, N.H., U.S.	E4	136
Sand Point, Ak., U.S.	D7	109
Sandpoint, Id., U.S.	A2	119
Sandspit, B.C., Can.	C2	99
Sand Springs, Ok., U.S.	A5	143
Sandston, Va., U.S.	m18	153
Sandstone, Mn., U.S.	D6	130
Sandusky, Mi., U.S.	E8	129
Sandusky, Oh., U.S.	A3	142
Sandusky, co., Oh., U.S.	A2	142
Sandusky, stm., Oh., U.S.	B2	142
Sandusky Bay, b., Oh., U.S.	A3	142
Sandviken, Swe.	K15	6
Sandwich, Il., U.S.	B5	120
Sandwich, Ma., U.S.	C7	128
Sandwip Island, i., Bngl.	I14	44
Sandy, Or., U.S.	B4	144
Sandy, Ut., U.S.	C4	151
Sandy Cape, c., Austl.	E10	70
Sandy Hook, Ct., U.S.	D2	114
Sandy Hook, spit, N.J., U.S.	C5	137
Sandy Lake, Man., Can.	D1	100
Sandy Springs, Ga., U.S.	h8	117
Sandy Springs, S.C., U.S.	B2	147
San Estanislao, Para.	C10	80
San Esteban, Hond.	B9	92
San Felipe, Chile	G3	80
San Felipe, Mex.	B2	90
San Felipe, Mex.	G9	90
San Felipe, Ven.	B8	84
San Felipe Pueblo, N.M., U.S.	B3	138
San Félix, Isla, i., Chile	K31	158
San Fernando, Chile	H3	80
San Fernando, Mex.	E10	90
San Fernando, Phil.	n19	39b
San Fernando, Phil.	m19	39b
San Fernando, Spain	I5	16
San Fernando, Trin.	I14	94
San Fernando, Ca., U.S.	m12	112
San Fernando, Ven.	D9	84
San Fernando de Atabapo, Ven.	E9	84
San Fernando del Valle de Catamarca, Arg.	E6	80
Sanford, Co., U.S.	D5	113
Sanford, Fl., U.S.	D5	116
Sanford, Me., U.S.	E2	126
Sanford, N.C., U.S.	B3	140
Sanford, Mount, mtn., Ak., U.S.	C11	109
San Francisco, Arg.	F7	80
San Francisco, Col.	G4	84
San Francisco, El Sal.	D6	92
San Francisco, Pan.	I14	92
San Francisco, Ca., U.S.	D2	112
San Francisco, co., Ca., U.S.	D2	112
San Francisco, Paso de, S.A.	D4	80
San Francisco Bay, b., Ca., U.S.	h8	112
San Francisco de Borja, Mex.	D6	90
San Francisco del Chañar, Arg.	E7	80
San Francisco del Monte de Oro, Arg.	G5	80
San Francisco del Oro, Mex.	D7	90
San Francisco del Rincón, Mex.	G9	90
San Francisco de Macoris, Dom. Rep.	E9	94
San Gabriel, Ec.	G4	84
San Gabriel Chilac, Mex.	H11	90
San Gabriel Mountains, mts., Ca., U.S.	m12	112
Sangamon, co., Il., U.S.	D4	120
Sangamon, stm., Il., U.S.	C3	120
Sangay, vol., Ec.	H3	84
Sangchunghsih, Tai.	J10	34
Sanger, Ca., U.S.	D4	112
Sanger, Tx., U.S.	C4	150
Sângera, Mol.	B12	20
Sangerhausen, Ger.	D11	10
San Germán, Cuba	D6	94
San Germán, P.R.	E11	94
Sangerville, Me., U.S.	C3	126
San Gil, Col.	D6	84
San Giovanni in Fiore, Italy	J11	18
Sangju, S. Kor.	G16	32
Sangolquí, Ec.	H3	84
San Gorgonio Mountain, mtn., Ca., U.S.	E5	112
San Gottardo, Passo del, Switz.	E10	13
San Gregorio, Arg.	H7	80
San Gregorio, Ur.	G11	80
Sangre Grande, Trin.	I14	94
Sangudo, Alta., Can.	C3	98
Sanibel, Fl., U.S.	F4	116
Sanibel Island, i., Fl., U.S.	F4	116
San Ignacio, Arg.	D11	80
San Ignacio, C.R.	H10	92
San Ignacio, Para.	D10	80
San Ignacio de Moxo, Bol.	F9	82
San Ignacio de Velasco, Bol.	G11	82
San Ildefonso, Cerro, mtn., Hond.	B6	92
San Isidro, Arg.	H9	80
San Isidro, Arg.	F9	80
San Isidro, C.R.	H11	92
San Jacinto, co., Tx., U.S.	D5	150
San Javier, Arg.	D11	80
San Javier, Arg.	F9	80
San Javier, Arg.	G10	82
San Javier de Loncomilla, Chile	H3	80
San Jerónimo Norte, Arg.	F8	80

Name	Map Ref.	Page
Sanjō, Japan	J13	36
San Joaquín, Para.	C10	80
San Joaquin, co., Ca., U.S.	D3	112
San Joaquin, stm., Ca., U.S.	D3	112
San Joaquin Valley, val., Ca., U.S.	D3	112
San Jon, N.M., U.S.	B6	138
San Jorge, Arg.	F8	80
San Jorge, Golfo, b., Arg.	F3	78
San José, Arg.	D11	80
San José, C.R.	H10	92
San Jose, Ca., U.S.	D3	112
San José, El Sal.	D6	92
San José de Bácum, Mex.	D4	90
San José de Chiquitos, Bol.	G11	82
San José de Feliciano, Arg.	F9	80
San José de Guanipa, Ven.	C10	84
San José de Jáchal, Arg.	F4	80
San José de la Esquina, Arg.	G8	80
San José de las Lajas, Cuba	C3	94
San José del Cabo, Mex.	F5	90
San José del Guaviare, Col.	F6	84
San José de los Molinos, Peru	E4	82
San José de Mayo, Ur.	H10	80
San Jose Island, i., Tx., U.S.	E4	150
San Juan, Arg.	F4	80
San Juan, P.R.	E11	94
San Juan, Tx., U.S.	F3	150
San Juan, prov., Arg.	F4	80
San Juan, co., Co., U.S.	D3	113
San Juan, co., N.M., U.S.	A1	138
San Juan, co., Ut., U.S.	F5	151
San Juan, co., Wa., U.S.	A2	154
San Juan, stm., Arg.	G5	80
San Juan, stm., Mex.	E10	90
San Juan, stm., N.A.	G10	92
San Juan, stm., S.A.	G3	84
San Juan, stm., U.S.	D5	106
San Juan Bautista, Para.	D10	80
San Juan Capistrano, Ca., U.S.	F5	112
San Juan de Abajo, Mex.	G7	90
San Juan de Colón, Ven.	C6	84
San Juan [de la Maguana], Dom. Rep.	E9	94
San Juan del Norte, Nic.	G11	92
San Juan de los Cayos, Ven.	B8	84
San Juan de los Morros, Ven.	C9	84
San Juan del Río, Mex.	G9	90
San Juan del Sur, Nic.	F9	92
San Juan Evangelista, Mex.	I12	90
San Juan Island, i., Wa., U.S.	A2	154
San Juan Mountains, mts., Co., U.S.	D3	113
San Juan Nepomuceno, Col.	C5	84
San Juan Nepomuceno, Para.	D11	80
San Justo, Arg.	F8	80
Sankt Gallen, Switz.	D11	13
Sankt Ingbert, Ger.	F7	10
Sankt Moritz, Switz.	E12	13
Sankt Niklaus, Switz.	F8	13
Sankt-Peterburg (Saint Petersburg), Russia	B13	22
Sankt Pölten, Aus.	G15	10
Sankt Veit an der Glan, Aus.	H9	12
Sankt Vith (Saint-Vith), Bel.	H9	12
Sankt Wendel, Ger.	F7	10
Sanpete, co., Ut., U.S.	D4	151
Sanpoil, stm., Wa., U.S.	A7	154
San Lázaro, Para.	B10	80
San Lázaro, Cabo, c., Mex.	E3	90
San Leandro, Ca., U.S.	h8	112
Şanlıurfa, Tur.	C5	48
San Lorenzo, Arg.	E9	80
San Lorenzo, Arg.	G8	80
San Lorenzo, Ec.	G3	84
San Lorenzo, Hond.	D7	92
San Lorenzo, Bahía de, b., Hond.	D7	92
San Lorenzo, Cabo, c., Mex.	H2	84
San Lorenzo, Isla, i., Peru	E3	82
San Lorenzo de El Escorial, Spain	E7	16
Sanlúcar de Barrameda, Spain	I5	16
San Lucas, Bol.	I9	82
San Lucas, Ec.	I3	84
San Lucas, Mex.	F5	90
San Lucas, Cabo, c., Mex.	F5	90
San Luis, Arg.	G5	80
San Luis, Cuba	D7	94
San Luis, Guat.	A5	92
San Luis, Az., U.S.	E1	110
San Luis, Co., U.S.	D5	113
San Luis, prov., Arg.	H5	80
San Luis de la Paz, Mex.	G9	90
San Luis del Palmar, Arg.	D9	80
San Luis Jilotepeque, Guat.	C5	92
San Luis Obispo, Ca., U.S.	E3	112
San Luis Obispo, co., Ca., U.S.	E3	112
San Luis Potosí, Mex.	F9	90
San Luis Potosí, state, Mex.	F9	90
San Luis Río Colorado, Mex.	A2	90
San Luis Valley, val., Co., U.S.	D4	113
San Manuel, Arg.	I9	80
San Manuel, Az., U.S.	E5	110
San Marcos, Col.	C5	84
San Marcos, C.R.	H10	92
San Marcos, El Sal.	D5	92
San Marcos, Guat.	C3	92
San Marcos, Mex.	I10	90
San Marcos, Tx., U.S.	E4	150
San Marcos, co., dept., Guat.	B3	92
San Marcos de Colón, Hond.	D8	92
San Marino, S. Mar.	F7	18
San Marino, Ca., U.S.	m12	112
San Marino, ctry., Eur.	G10	4
San Martín, Col.	F6	84
San Martín, dept., Peru	B3	82
San Martín, stm., Bol.	E10	82

Name	Map Ref.	Page
San Martín, Lago (Lago O'Higgins), l., S.A.	F2	78
San Martín de los Andes, Arg.	E2	78
San Martín Texmelucan, Mex.	H10	90
San Mateo, Ca., U.S.	D2	112
San Mateo, Ven.	C10	84
San Mateo, co., Ca., U.S.	D2	112
San Matías, Bol.	G12	82
San Matías, Golfo, b., Arg.	E4	78
Sanmenxia, China	E9	30
San Miguel, Arg.	E10	80
San Miguel, El Sal.	D6	92
San Miguel, N.M., U.S.	E3	138
San Miguel, co., Co., U.S.	D2	113
San Miguel, co., N.M., U.S.	B5	138
San Miguel (Cuilco), stm., N.A.	B2	92
San Miguel, Golfo de, b., Pan.	C3	84
San Miguel, Volcán de, vol., El Sal.	D6	92
San Miguel de Allende, Mex.	G9	90
San Miguel del Monte, Arg.	H9	80
San Miguel de Salcedo, Ec.	H3	84
San Miguel de Tucumán, Arg.	D6	80
San Miguel el Alto, Mex.	G8	90
San Nicolás de los Arroyos, Arg.	G8	80
San Nicolás de los Garza, Mex.	E9	90
Sânnicolau Mare, Rom.	C4	20
Sanniquellie, Lib.	H5	64
Sano, Japan	K14	36
Sañogasta, Arg.	E5	80
Sanok, Pol.	F22	10
San Onofre, Col.	C5	84
San Pablo, Col.	G4	84
San Pablo, Phil.	n19	39b
San Pablo, Ca., U.S.	h8	112
San Pablo Bay, b., Ca., U.S.	g8	112
San Patricio, co., Tx., U.S.	E4	150
San Pedro, Arg.	G9	80
San Pedro, Arg.	C6	80
San Pedro, Arg.	D6	80
San Pedro, Para.	C10	80
San Pedro, dept., Para.	C10	80
San Pedro, stm., N.A.	I14	90
San Pedro, Volcán, vol., Chile	A4	80
San Pedro de Atacama, Chile	A4	80
San Pedro de Buena Vista, Bol.	H9	82
San Pedro de las Colonias, Mex.	D8	90
San Pedro de Lloc, Peru	B2	82
San Pedro del Paraná, Para.	D10	80
San Pedro de Macorís, Dom. Rep.	E10	94
San Pedro Peaks, mts., N.M., U.S.	A3	138
San Pedro Pochutla, Mex.	J11	90
San Pedro Sacatepéquez, Guat.	C3	92
San Pedro Sula, Hond.	B6	92
Sanpete, co., Ut., U.S.	D4	151
Sanpoil, stm., Wa., U.S.	A7	154
San Rafael, Arg.	H4	80
San Rafael, Ca., U.S.	D2	112
San Rafael, N.M., U.S.	B2	138
San Rafael, Ven.	B7	84
San Rafael, stm., Ut., U.S.	D5	151
San Rafael del Norte, Nic.	D8	92
San Rafael del Sur, Nic.	F8	92
San Ramón, C.R.	G10	92
San Ramón, Hond.	C10	92
San Ramón, Peru	D4	82
San Ramon, Ca., U.S.	h9	112
San Ramón, Ur.	H11	80
San Ramón de la Nueva Orán, Arg.	B6	80
San Remo, Italy	F2	18
San Román, Cabo, c., Ven.	A7	84
San Roque, Arg.	E9	80
San Roque, Spain	I6	16
San Rosendo, Chile	I2	80
San Saba, co., Tx., U.S.	D3	150
San Salvador, El Sal.	D5	92
San Salvador (Watling Island), i., Bah.	B7	94
San Salvador de Jujuy, Arg.	C6	80
Sansanné-Mango, Togo	F10	64
Sansepolcro, Italy	F7	18
San Severo, Italy	H10	18
Sanshui, China	L1	34
San Simon, Az., U.S.	E6	110
San Simon, stm., Az., U.S.	E6	110
Sanso, Mali	F6	64
Sans-Souci, hist., Haiti	E8	94
Santa, Peru	C2	82
Santa Adélia, Braz.	F4	79
Santa Albertina, Braz.	F3	79
Santa Ana, Bol.	E9	82
Santa Ana, Bol.	H2	84
Santa Ana, El Sal.	D5	92
Santa Ana, Mex.	B4	90
Santa Ana, Ca., U.S.	F5	112
Santa Ana, Volcán de, vol., El Sal.	D5	92
Santa Ana del Alto Beni, Bol.	F8	82
Santa Ana Pueblo, N.M., U.S.	B3	138
Santa Bárbara, Chile	I2	80
Santa Bárbara, Hond.	C6	92
Santa Bárbara, Mex.	D7	90
Santa Barbara, Ca., U.S.	E4	112
Santa Bárbara, dept., Hond.	B6	92
Santa Barbara, co., Ca., U.S.	E3	112
Santa Barbara do Sul, Braz.	E12	80

Name	Map Ref.	Page
Santa Catalina Island, i., Ca., U.S.	F4	112
Santa Catarina, Mex.	E9	90
Santa Catarina, state, Braz.	D13	80
Santa Catarina, Ilha de, i., Braz.	D14	80
Santa Cecília, Braz.	D13	80
Santa Clara, Cuba	C5	94
Santa Clara, Ca., U.S.	D2	112
Santa Clara, Ut., U.S.	F2	151
Santa Clara, co., Ca., U.S.	D3	112
Santa Clara de Olimar, Ur.	G11	80
Santa Claus, In., U.S.	H4	121
Santa Cruz, Braz.	E8	79
Santa Cruz, Chile	H3	80
Santa Cruz, C.R.	G9	92
Santa Cruz, Phil.	n19	39b
Santa Cruz, N.M., U.S.	B3	138
Santa Cruz, dept., Bol.	G11	82
Santa Cruz, co., Az., U.S.	F5	110
Santa Cruz, co., Ca., U.S.	D2	112
Santa Cruz, stm., Arg.	G2	78
Santa Cruz, stm., Az., U.S.	E4	110
Santa Cruz Cabrália, Braz.	D9	79
Santa Cruz de la Palma, Spain	o23	17b
Santa Cruz de la Sierra, Bol.	G10	82
Santa Cruz del Quiché, Guat.	B3	92
Santa Cruz del Sur, Cuba	D5	94
Santa Cruz de Tenerife, Spain	o24	17b
Santa Cruz de Tenerife, prov., Spain	o23	17b
Santa Cruz do Rio Pardo, Braz.	G4	79
Santa Cruz do Sul, Braz.	E12	80
Santa Cruz Island, i., Ca., U.S.	F4	112
Santa Cruz Islands, is., Sol.Is.	J20	158
Santa Elena, Arg.	F9	80
Santa Elena, Ec.	H2	84
Santa Elena, Cabo, c., C.R.	G9	92
Santa Elena, Punta, c., Ec.	I2	84
Santa Elena de Uairén, Ven.	E12	84
Santa Fé, Arg.	F8	80
Santa Fé, Braz.	G3	79
Santa Fe, Spain	H8	16
Santa Fe, N.M., U.S.	B4	138
Santa Fe, Tx., U.S.	r14	150
Santa Fe, prov., Arg.	F8	80
Santa Fe, co., N.M., U.S.	B3	138
Santa Fe Baldy, mtn., N.M., U.S.	A4	138
Santa Fé de Bogotá, Col.	E5	84
Santa Fé do Sul, Braz.	F3	79
Santa Helena de Goiás, Braz.	D3	79
Santai, China	E8	30
Santa Inês, Braz.	B9	79
Santa Inés, Isla, i., Chile	G2	78
Santa Isabel, Arg.	I5	80
Santa Isabel, Arg.	G8	80
Santa Isabel, i., Sol.Is.	I19	158
Santa Isabel de Sihuas, Peru	G5	82
Santa Juliana, Braz.	E5	79
Santa Lucía, Arg.	E9	80
Santa Lucía, Arg.	F4	80
Santa Lucía, Ur.	H10	80
Santa Lucía Cotzumalguapa, Guat.	C3	92
Santa Magdalena, Arg.	H7	80
Santa Margarita, Isla, i., Mex.	E4	90
Santa María, Arg.	D5	80
Santa Maria, Braz.	E12	80
Santa María, C.R.	H11	92
Santa María, Pan.	I14	92
Santa María del Oro, Mex.	E3	112
Santa María del Río, Mex.	G9	90
Santa María, stm., Az., U.S.	C2	110
Santa María, Volcán, vol., Guat.	C3	92
Santa María Asunción Tlaxiaco, Mex.	I11	90
Santa Maria Capua Vetere, Italy	H9	18
Santa Maria da Vitória, Braz.	B6	79
Santa Maria de Itabira, Braz.	E7	79
Santa María do Suaçuí, Braz.	E7	79
Santa Maria Madalena, Braz.	F7	79
Santa Marta, Ciénaga Grande, b., Col.	B5	84
Santa Monica, Ca., U.S.	m12	112
Santana, Braz.	B6	79
Santana, Coxilha de, hills, S.A.	F11	80
Santana do Livramento, Braz.	F11	80
Santander, Spain	B8	16
Santander, dept., Col.	D6	84
Santander Jiménez, Mex.	E10	90
Santanilla, Islas, is., Hond.	F3	94
Santanoni Peak, mtn., N.Y., U.S.	A6	139
Sant Antoni de Portmany, Spain	G13	16
Santaquin, Ut., U.S.	D4	151
Santarém, Braz.	D8	76
Santarém, Port.	F3	16
Santaren Channel, strt., Bah.		
Santa Rita, Ven.	B7	84
Santa Rita de Araguaia, Braz.	D2	79
Santa Rosa, Arg.	B6	78
Santa Rosa, Arg.	D11	80
Santa Rosa, Bol.		
Santa Rosa, Ec.	I3	84

Name	Map Ref.	Page
Santa Rosa, Ca., U.S.	C2	112
Santa Rosa, N.M., U.S.	C5	138
Santa Rosa, dept., Guat.	C4	92
Santa Rosa, co., Fl., U.S.	u14	116
Santa Rosa de Aguán, Hond.	B9	92
Santa Rosa de Cabal, Col.	E5	84
Santa Rosa [de Copán], Hond.	C6	92
Santa Rosa del Conlara, Arg.	G6	80
Santa Rosa de Leales, Arg.	D6	80
Santa Rosa de Osos, Col.	D5	84
Santa Rosa de Río Primero, Arg.	F7	80
Santa Rosa Island, i., Ca., U.S.	F3	112
Santa Rosalía, Mex.	D3	90
Šantarskije ostrova, is., Russia	F19	28
Santa Sylvina, Arg.	D8	80
Santa Teresa, Arg.	E8	79
Santa Teresa, N.M., U.S.	F3	138
Santa Tereza de Goiás, Braz.	B4	79
Santa Vitória, Braz.	E3	79
Santa Vitória do Palmar, Braz.	G12	80
Sant Carles de la Ràpita, Spain	E12	16
Santee, co., S.C., U.S.	o16	112
Santee, Ne., U.S.	B8	134
Santee, stm., S.C., U.S.	E8	147
Sant Feliu de Guíxols, Spain	D15	16
Santiago, Braz.	E11	80
Santiago, Chile	G3	80
Santiago, Pan.	C2	84
Santiago, Para.	D10	80
Santiago, i., C.V.	m17	64a
Santiago, stm., Mex.	E7	90
Santiago, stm., S.A.	I4	84
Santiago Atitlán, Guat.	C3	92
Santiago de Cao, Peru	B2	82
Santiago de Compostela, Spain	C3	16
Santiago de Cuba, Cuba	D7	94
Santiago de Huari, Bol.	H8	82
Santiago del Estero, Arg.	D6	80
Santiago del Estero, prov., Arg.	E7	80
Santiago [de los Caballeros], Dom. Rep.	E9	94
Santiago de Machaca, Bol.	G7	82
Santiago Ixcuintla, Mex.	G7	90
Santiago Jamiltepec, Mex.	I11	90
Santiago Papasquiaro, Mex.	E7	90
Santiaguillo, Laguna, l., Mex.	E7	90
Santiam Pass, Or., U.S.	C4	144
Santo Amaro, Braz.	B9	79
Santo Anastácio, Braz.	F3	79
Santo André, Braz.	G5	79
Santo Ângelo, Braz.	E11	80
Santo Antão, i., C.V.	k16	64a
Santo Antônio da Patrulha, Braz.	E13	80
Santo Antônio de Jesus, Braz.	B9	79
Santo Antônio de Pádua, Braz.	F7	79
Santo Antônio do Amparo, Braz.	F6	79
Santo Antônio do Içá, Braz.	I9	84
Santo Antônio do Leverger, Braz.	F13	82
Santo Antônio do Sudoeste, Braz.	D12	80
Santo Augusto, Braz.	D12	80
Santo Domingo, Dom. Rep.	E10	94
Santo Domingo de los Colorados, Ec.	H3	84
Santo Domingo Pueblo, N.M., U.S.	B3	138
Santo Domingo Tehuantepec, Mex.	I12	90
Santo Domingo Zanatepec, Mex.	I12	90
Santo Estêvão, Braz.	B9	79
Santoña, Spain	B8	16
Santos, Braz.	G5	79
Santos Dumont, Braz.	F7	79
Santo Tomás, Nic.	E9	92
Santo Tomás, Peru	F5	82
Santo Tomé, Braz.	E10	80
San Vicente, El Sal.	D6	92
San Vicente, Volcán de, vol., El Sal.	D6	92
San Vicente de Cañete, Peru	E3	82
San Vicente del Caguán, Col.	F5	84
São Bento do Norte, Braz.	D10	76
São Bento do Sul, Braz.	D14	80
São Borja, Braz.	E10	80
São Caetano do Sul, Braz.	G5	79
São Cristóvão, Braz.	F11	76
São Domingos, Braz.	D12	80
São Felipe, C.V.	m16	64a
São Francisco, Braz.	C6	79
São Francisco, Ilha de, i., Braz.	D14	80
São Francisco de Assis, Braz.	E11	80
São Francisco de Goiás, Braz.	C4	79
São Francisco de Paula, Braz.	E13	80
São Francisco do Sul, Braz.	D14	80
São Gabriel, Braz.	F11	80
São Gabriel da Palha, Braz.	E8	79
São Gonçalo do Abaeté, Braz.	E6	79
São Gonçalo do Sapucaí, Braz.	F6	79
São Gonçalo dos Campos, Braz.	B9	79
São Jerônimo, Braz.	E13	80
São João da Barra, Braz.	F8	79

Name	Map Ref.	Page
São João da Boa Vista, Braz.	F5	79
São João da Madeira, Port.	E3	16
São João da Ponte, Braz.	C6	79
São João del-Rei, Braz.	F6	79
São João do Paraíso, Braz.	C7	79
São João Evangelista, Braz.	E7	79
São Joaquim, Braz.	E14	80
São Joaquim da Barra, Braz.	F5	79
São José, Braz.	D14	80
São José do Cedro, Braz.	D12	80
São José do Rio Preto, Braz.	F4	79
São José dos Campos, Braz.	G6	79
São José dos Pinhais, Braz.	C14	80
São Leopoldo, Braz.	E13	80
São Lourenço, Braz.	G6	79
São Lourenço do Oeste, Braz.	D12	80
São Lourenço do Sul, Braz.	F13	80
São Luís, Braz.	D10	76
São Luís de Montes Belos, Braz.	D3	79
São Luís Gonzaga, Braz.	E11	80
São Manuel, Braz.	G4	79
São Manuel, stm., Braz.	C13	82
São Mateus, Braz.	E9	79
São Mateus do Sul, Braz.	C13	80
São Miguel, i., Port.	m21	62a
São Miguel, stm., Braz.	D8	79
São Miguel do Araguaia, Braz.	B3	79
São Miguel d'Oeste, Braz.	D12	80
Saona, Isla, i., Dom. Rep.	E10	94
São Paulo, Braz.	G5	79
São Paulo, state, Braz.	G4	79
São Paulo de Olivença, Braz.	I8	84
São Pedro do Sul, Braz.	E11	80
São Raimundo Nonato, Braz.	E10	76
São Romão, Braz.	D6	79
São Roque, Braz.	G5	79
São Sebastião, Braz.	G6	79
São Sebastião, Ilha de, i., Braz.	G6	79
São Sebastião, Ponta, c., Moz.	D12	66
São Sebastião do Paraíso, Braz.	F5	79
São Sepé, Braz.	F12	80
São Simão, Braz.	E3	79
São Simão, Braz.	F5	79
São Simão, Représa de, res., Braz.	E3	79
São Tiago, Braz.	F6	79
São Tomé, S. Tom./P.	A1	58
São Tomé, Cabo de, c., Braz.	F8	79
Sao Tome and Principe (São Tomé e Príncipe), ctry., Afr.	A1	58
São Vicente, Braz.	G5	79
São Vicente, i., C.V.	k16	64a
São Vicente, Cabo de (Cape Saint Vincent), c., Port.	H2	16
São Vicente de Minas, Braz.	F6	79
Sapé, Braz.	E11	76
Sapele, Nig.	I12	64
Sapelo Island, i., Ga., U.S.	E5	117
Sapitwa, mtn., Mwi.	E7	58
Sa Pobla, Spain	F15	16
Saposoa, Peru	E2	84
Sapožok, Russia	H23	22
Sapporo, Japan	d16	36a
Sapulpa, Ok., U.S.	B5	143
Saqqez, Iran	C6	48
Saquena, Peru	A5	82
Sarāb, Iran	C9	48
Saraburi, Thai.	G6	40
Saragossa see Zaragoza, Spain	D11	16
Sarai, Russia	H24	22
Sarajevo, Bos.	F2	20
Sarakhs, Iran	C16	48
Saraland, Al., U.S.	E1	108
Saran', Kaz.	H12	26
Saranac, Mi., U.S.	F5	129
Saranac, stm., N.Y., U.S.	F11	139
Saranac Lake, N.Y., U.S.	f10	139
Sarandi, Braz.	D12	80
Sarandí del Yi, Ur.	G11	80
Sarandí Grande, Ur.	G11	80
Saransk, Russia	G7	26
Sarapul, Russia	F8	26
Sara Sara, Nevado, mtn., Peru	F5	82
Sarasota, Fl., U.S.	E4	116
Sarasota, co., Fl., U.S.	E4	116
Sarasota Bay, b., Fl., U.S.	E4	116
Saratoga, Ca., U.S.	k8	112
Saratoga, Wy., U.S.	E6	157
Saratoga, co., N.Y., U.S.	B7	139
Saratoga National Historical Park, N.Y., U.S.	B7	139
Saratoga Springs, N.Y., U.S.	B7	139
Saratov, Russia	G7	26
Saratovskoje vodochranilišče, res., Russia	G7	26
Saravan, Laos	G9	40
Sárbogárd, Hung.	I18	10
Sarcoxie, Mo., U.S.	D3	132
Sardārshahr, India	F6	44
Sardegna, prov., Italy	I4	18
Sardegna (Sardinia), i., Italy	I4	18
Sardinal, C.R.	G9	92
Sardinia see Sardegna, i., Italy	I4	18
Sardis, Ga., U.S.	D5	117
Sardis, Ms., U.S.	A4	131
Sardis Lake, res., Ms., U.S.	A4	131
Sar-e Pol, Afg.	B1	44
Sarepta, La., U.S.	B2	125
Sargans, Switz.	D11	13
Sargasso Sea	F8	160
Sargent, Ga., U.S.	C2	117
Sargent, Ne., U.S.	C6	134
Sargent, co., N.D., U.S.	C8	141
Sargodha, Pak.	D5	44
Sarh, Chad	G4	56
Sārī, Iran	C12	48
Sankamış, Tur.	A7	48
Sarina, Austl.	C8	70
Sariwŏn, N. Kor.	E13	32
Šarja, Russia	F7	26
Šarkovščina, Bela.	F10	22
Sarmiento de Gamboa, Cerro, mtn., Chile	G2	78
Sarnen, Switz.	E9	13
Sarnia, Ont., Can.	E2	103
Sarno, Italy	I9	18
Saron, S. Afr.	I4	66
Saronno, Italy	D4	18
Sárospatak, Hung.	G21	10
Sarpsborg, Nor.	L12	6
Sarpy, co., Ne., U.S.	C9	134
Sarralbe, Fr.	C14	14
Sarrebourg, Fr.	D14	14
Sarreguemines, Fr.	C14	14
Sarro, Mali	E7	64
Sarstoon (Sarstún), stm., N.A.	B5	92
Sarstún (Sarstoon), stm., N.A.	B5	92
Sartell, Mn., U.S.	E4	130
Sárvár, Hung.	H16	10
Saryozek, Kaz.	I13	26
Sarzana, Italy	E4	18
Säsäräm, India	H11	44
Sasebo, Japan	N4	36
Saskatchewan, prov., Can.	E3	105
Saskatchewan, stm., Can.	F12	96
Saskatoon, Sask., Can.	E5	105
Sasolburg, S. Afr.	F8	66
Sasovo, Russia	G24	22
Sassafras Mountain, mtn., U.S.	A2	147
Sassandra, C. Iv.	I6	64
Sassandra, stm., C. Iv.	I6	64
Sassari, Italy	I3	18
S'as stroj, Russia	A15	22
Sassuolo, Italy	E5	18
Sastown, Lib.	I5	64
Sastre, Arg.	F8	80
Sasyk, ozero, l., Ukr.	D13	20
Satanta, Ks., U.S.	E3	123
Sātāra, India	D2	46
Satilla, stm., Ga., U.S.	E5	117
Satipo, Peru	D4	82
Satka, Russia	F9	26
Satna, India	H9	44
Sátoraljaújhely, Hung.	G21	10
Sātpura Range, mts., India	J7	44
Satsuma, Al., U.S.	E1	108
Sattahip, Thai.	H6	40
Satu Mare, Rom.	B6	20
Satun, Thai.	K6	40
Šatura, Russia	F22	22
Saturnino M. Laspiur, Arg.	F7	80
Šaturtorf, Russia	F22	22
Sauce, Arg.	F9	80
Sauce, Ur.	H10	80
Saucillo, Mex.	C7	90
Sauda, Nor.	L10	6
Saudi Arabia (Al-'Arabīyah as-Su'ūdīyah), ctry., Asia	D4	42
Saugerties, N.Y., U.S.	C7	139
Saugus, Ma., U.S.	B5	128
Saujil, Arg.	E5	80
Sauk, co., Wi., U.S.	E4	156
Sauk, stm., Wa., U.S.	A4	154
Sauk Centre, Mn., U.S.	E4	130
Sauk City, Wi., U.S.	E4	156
Sauk Rapids, Mn., U.S.	E4	130
Saukville, Wi., U.S.	E6	156
Saül, Fr. Gu.	C8	76
Saulkrasti, Lat.	D7	22
Saulnierville, N.S., Can.	E3	101
Sault Sainte Marie, Ont., Can.	p18	103
Sault Sainte Marie, Mi., U.S.	B6	129
Saumur, Fr.	E6	14
Saunders, co., Ne., U.S.	C9	134
Saurimo, Ang.	C4	58
Sausalito, Ca., U.S.	D2	112
Savage, Md., U.S.	B4	127
Savage, Mt., U.S.	C12	133
Savaiʻi, i., W. Sam.	k12	127
Savalou, Benin	J22	158
Savanna, Il., U.S.	H10	64
Savanna, Ok., U.S.	A3	120
Savannah, Ga., U.S.	C6	143
Savannah, Mo., U.S.	D5	117
Savannah, Tn., U.S.	B3	132
Savannah, stm., U.S.	B3	149
Savannakhét, Laos	F5	147
Savanna-la-Mar, Jam.	F8	40
Save (Sabi), stm., Afr.	E5	94
Säveh, Iran	C12	66
Saverne, Fr.	D11	48
Savigliano, Italy	D14	14
Savino, Russia	E2	18
Savinskij, Russia	E24	22
Savona, B.C., Can.	J27	6
Savona, Italy	D7	99
Savoonga, Ak., U.S.	E3	18
Savoy, Il., U.S.	C5	109
Savu Sea see Sawu, Laut, Indon.	C5	120
Sawahlunto, Indon.	G7	38
Sawai Mādhopur, India	O6	40
Sawankhalok, Thai.	H7	44
Sawda', Qurnat as-, mtn., Leb.	H9	60
Sawhāj, Sud.	F5	40
Sawhāj, Egypt	D4	48
Sawknah, Libya	J5	60
Sawmill, Az., U.S.	D6	60
Sawtooth Mountains, mts., Id., U.S.	C4	56
Sawu, Laut (Savu Sea), Indon.	B6	110
Sawyer, N.D., U.S.	F4	119
Sawyer, co., Wi., U.S.	G7	38
Saxman, Ak., U.S.	A4	141
Saxon, Switz.	C2	156
Saxony see Sachsen, state, Ger.	n24	109
Saxtons River, Vt., U.S.	F7	13
Say, Niger	C9	10
Sayán, Peru	E3	152
	E11	64
	D3	82
Sayan Mountains (Sajany), mts., Asia	G11	28
Saybrook Manor, Ct., U.S.	D6	114
Saydā (Sidon), Leb.	A4	50
Saydel, Ia., U.S.	e8	122
Sayhūt, Yemen	G7	47
Saylesville, R.I., U.S.	B4	146
Saylorville, Ia., U.S.	e8	122
Saylorville Lake, res., Ia., U.S.	C4	122
Sayre, Al., U.S.	B3	108
Sayre, Ok., U.S.	B2	143
Sayre, Pa., U.S.	C8	145
Sayreville, N.J., U.S.	C4	137
Sayula, Mex.	H8	90
Sayville, N.Y., U.S.	n15	139
Saywūn, Yemen	G6	47
Sazonovo, Russia	B18	22
Sbeïtla, Tun.	N4	18
Scafell Pikes, mtn., Eng., U.K.	G10	8
Scammon, Ks., U.S.	E9	123
Scammon Bay, Ak., U.S.	C6	109
Scandia, Ks., U.S.	C6	123
Scanlon, Mn., U.S.	D6	130
Scapa Flow, b., Scot., U.K.	C10	8
Scapegoat Mountain, mtn., Mt., U.S.	C3	133
Scappoose, Or., U.S.	B4	144
Scarborough, Ont., Can.	m15	103
Scarborough, Trin.	I14	94
Scarborough, Eng., U.K.	G13	8
Scarborough, Me., U.S.	E2	126
Scarbro, W.V., U.S.	n13	155
Scarsdale, N.Y., U.S.	h13	139
Ščelkovo, Russia	F21	22
Sceptre, Sask., Can.	G1	105
Ščerbinka, Russia	F20	22
Schaerbeek (Schaarbeek), Bel.	G5	12
Schaffhausen, Switz.	C10	13
Schaller, Ia., U.S.	h8	120
Schaumburg, Il., U.S.	h8	120
Schefferville, Que., Can.	h13	104
Schelde (Escaut), stm., Eur.	D4	10
Schell Creek Range, mts., Nv., U.S.	D7	135
Schenectady, N.Y., U.S.	C7	139
Schenectady, co., N.Y., U.S.	C6	139
Schererville, In., U.S.	B3	121
Schertz, Tx., U.S.	h7	150
Schiedam, Neth.	E5	12
Schiermonnikoog, i., Neth.	B9	12
Schiller Park, Il., U.S.	k9	120
Schiltigheim, Fr.	D14	14
Schio, Italy	D6	18
Schladming, Aus.	H13	10
Schleicher, co., Tx., U.S.	D2	150
Schleswig, Ger.	A9	10
Schleswig, Ia., U.S.	B2	122
Schleswig-Holstein, state, Ger.	A9	10
Schlieren, Switz.	D9	13
Schodn'a, Russia	F20	22
Schofield, Wi., U.S.	D4	156
Schofield Barracks, mil., Hi., U.S.	g9	118
Schoharie, co., N.Y., U.S.	C6	139
Schoharie Creek, stm., N.Y., U.S.	C6	139
Schönebeck, Ger.	C11	10
Schoolcraft, Mi., U.S.	F5	129
Schoolcraft, co., Mi., U.S.	B4	129
Schorndorf, Ger.	G9	10
Schramberg, Ger.	G8	10
Schulenburg, Tx., U.S.	E4	150
Schüpfheim, Switz.	E9	13
Schurz, Nv., U.S.	E3	135
Schuyler, Ne., U.S.	C8	134
Schuyler, co., Il., U.S.	C3	120
Schuyler, co., Mo., U.S.	A5	132
Schuyler, co., N.Y., U.S.	C4	139
Schuylkill, co., Pa., U.S.	E9	145
Schuylkill, stm., Pa., U.S.	F10	145
Schuylkill Haven, Pa., U.S.	E9	145
Schwabach, Ger.	F11	10
Schwaben, hist. reg., Ger.	G10	10
Schwäbisch Gmünd, Ger.	G9	10
Schwäbisch Hall, Ger.	F9	10
Schwandorf, Ger.	F12	10
Schwarzwald (Black Forest), mts., Ger.	G8	10
Schwaz, Aus.	H11	10
Schwedt, Ger.	B14	10
Schweinfurt, Ger.	E10	10
Schwerin, Ger.	B11	10
Schwyz, Switz.	D10	13
Sciacca, Italy	L8	18
Science Hill, Ky., U.S.	C5	124
Scilly, Isles of, is., Eng., U.K.	L7	8
Scioto, co., Oh., U.S.	D3	142
Scioto, stm., Oh., U.S.	B2	142
Scituate, Ma., U.S.	B6	128
Scituate Reservoir, res., R.I., U.S.	C3	146
Scobey, Mt., U.S.	B11	133
Ščokino, Russia	G20	22
Scone, Austl.	I9	70
Scooba, Ms., U.S.	C5	131
Scotch Plains, N.J., U.S.	B4	137
Scotia, N.Y., U.S.	A1	73
Scotia Sea, S.A.	C7	114
Scotland, Ont., Can.	D7	114
Scotland, Ct., U.S.	D8	148
Scotland, S.D., U.S.	A5	132
Scotland, co., Mo., U.S.	C3	140
Scotland, co., N.C., U.S.	D9	8
Scotland, ter., U.K.	A5	140
Scotland Neck, N.C., U.S.	D7	101
Scotlandville, La., U.S.	D4	125
Scotsburn, N.S., Can.	D3	125
Scott, La., U.S.	C1	111
Scott, co., Ar., U.S.	D3	120
Scott, co., Il., U.S.	G6	121
Scott, co., In., U.S.	C7	122
Scott, co., Ia., U.S.	D3	123
Scott, co., Ks., U.S.	B5	124
Scott, co., Ky., U.S.	F5	130
Scott, co., Mn., U.S.	C4	131
Scott, co., Ms., U.S.	D8	132
Scott, co., Mo., U.S.	C9	149
Scott, co., Tn., U.S.	f9	153
Scott, co., Va., U.S.	D3	99
Scott, Cape, c., B.C., Can.	E4	144
Scott, Mount, mtn., Or., U.S.	C8	73
Scott Base, sci., Ant.	H10	66
Scottburgh, S. Afr.	D3	123
Scott City, Ks., U.S.	D8	132
Scott City, Mo., U.S.	h8	117
Scottdale, Ga., U.S.	F2	145
Scottdale, Pa., U.S.	D3	99
Scott Islands, is., B.C., Can.	C2	134
Scottsbluff, Ne., U.S.	C2	134
Scotts Bluff, co., Ne., U.S.	C2	134
Scotts Bluff National Monument, Ne., U.S.	A3	108
Scottsboro, Al., U.S.	G6	121
Scottsburg, In., U.S.	D4	110
Scottsdale, Az., U.S.	D3	124
Scottsville, Ky., U.S.	E4	129
Scottville, Mi., U.S.	m23	109
Scow Bay, Ak., U.S.	D8	123
Scranton, Ks., U.S.	C2	141
Scranton, Pa., U.S.	D10	145
Screven, Ga., U.S.	E4	117
Screven, co., Ga., U.S.	D5	117
Scribner, Ne., U.S.	C9	134
Ščučin, Bela.	H7	22
Scugog, Lake, l., Ont., Can.	C6	103
Scurry, co., Tx., U.S.	C2	150
Scutari, Lake, l., Eur.	G3	20
Seabreeze, De., U.S.	F5	115
Seabrook, N.H., U.S.	E5	136
Seabrook, Tx., U.S.	r14	150
Seaford, De., U.S.	F3	115
Seaford, Va., U.S.	h15	153
Seaforth, Ont., Can.	D3	103
Seagraves, Tx., U.S.	n10	150
Seahorse Point, c., N.W. Ter., Can.	D16	96
Sea Islands, is., U.S.	E10	106
Sea Lake, Austl.	J5	70
Seal Cove, N.B., Can.	E3	101
Seal Cove, Newf., Can.	D3	102
Seal Harbor, Me., U.S.	D4	126
Seal Rock, Or., U.S.	C2	144
Sealy, Tx., U.S.	E4	150
Seara, Braz.	D12	80
Searchlight, Nv., U.S.	H7	135
Searcy, Ar., U.S.	B4	111
Searcy, co., Ar., U.S.	B3	111
Searsport, Me., U.S.	D4	126
Seaside, Ca., U.S.	D3	112
Seaside, Or., U.S.	B3	144
Seat Pleasant, Md., U.S.	C4	127
Seattle, Wa., U.S.	B3	154
Seaview, Wa., U.S.	C1	154
Sébaco, Nic.	E8	92
Sebago Lake, l., Me., U.S.	E2	126
Sebastian, Fl., U.S.	E6	116
Sebastian, co., Ar., U.S.	B1	111
Sebastián Vizcaíno, Bahía, b., Mex.	C2	90
Sebec Lake, l., Me., U.S.	C3	126
Sebeka, Mn., U.S.	D3	130
Seberi, Braz.	D12	80
Sebeş, Rom.	D7	20
Sebewaing, Mi., U.S.	E7	129
Sebree, Ky., U.S.	C2	124
Sebring, Fl., U.S.	E5	116
Sebring, Oh., U.S.	B4	142
Sebringville, Ont., Can.	D3	103
Secaucus, N.J., U.S.	h8	137
Sechelt, B.C., Can.	E6	99
Sechura, Peru	A1	82
Sechura, Desierto de, des., Peru	A1	82
Second Mesa, Az., U.S.	B5	110
Section, Al., U.S.	A4	108
Sécure, stm., Bol.	F9	82
Security, Co., U.S.	C6	113
Sedalia, Mo., U.S.	C4	132
Sedan, Fr.	C11	14
Sedan, Ks., U.S.	E7	123
Sedgwick, Alta., Can.	C5	98
Sedgwick, Ks., U.S.	E6	123
Sedgwick, co., Co., U.S.	A8	113
Sedgwick, co., Ks., U.S.	E6	123
Sedley, Sask., Can.	G3	105
Sedom (Sodom), hist., Isr.	F4	50
Sedona, Az., U.S.	C4	110
Sedrata, Alg.	M2	18
Sedro Woolley, Wa., U.S.	A3	154
Seduva, Lith.	F6	22
Seeheim, Nmb.	F3	66
Seekonk, Ma., U.S.	C5	128
Seeley Lake, Mt., U.S.	C3	133
Seelyville, In., U.S.	F3	121
Sées, Fr.	D7	14
Seesen, Ger.	D10	10
Sefare, Bots.	D8	66
Sefrou, Mor.	B5	62
Segamat, Malay.	M7	40
Segbana, Benin	F11	64
Segbwema, S.L.	G4	64
Segeža, Russia	E4	26
Ségou, Mali	E6	64
Segovia, Spain	E7	16
Séguéla, C. Iv.	H6	64
Segui, Arg.	F8	80
Seguin, Tx., U.S.	E4	150
Segundo, stm., Arg.	F7	80
Sehithwa, Bots.	C6	66
Seia, Port.	E4	16
Seiling, Ok., U.S.	A3	143
Seinäjoki, Fin.	J18	6
Seine, stm., Fr.	C7	14
Seixal, Port.	G2	16
Sejmčan, Russia	E22	28
Seki, Japan	L11	36
Sekiu, Wa., U.S.	A1	154
Sekoma, Bots.	E6	66
Sekondi-Takoradi, Ghana	I9	64
Sekota, Eth.	K10	60
Šeksna, Russia	B21	22
Selah, Wa., U.S.	C5	154
Selatan, Tanjung, c., Indon.	F5	38
Selawik, Ak., U.S.	B7	109
Selb, Ger.	E12	10
Selbu, Nor.	J12	6
Selby, S.D., U.S.	B5	148
Selbyville, De., U.S.	G5	115
Sel'co, Russia	H17	22
Selebi Phikwe, Bots.	D8	66
Sélestat, Fr.	D14	14
Selfridge, N.D., U.S.	C5	141
Selibaby, Maur.	D3	64
Šelichova, zaliv, b., Russia	F23	28
Seligman, Az., U.S.	B3	110
Seligman, Mo., U.S.	E4	132
Selinsgrove, Pa., U.S.	E8	145
Seližarovo, Russia	E16	22
Selkirk, Man., Can.	D3	100
Selkirk, Scot., U.K.	F11	8
Selkirk Mountains, mts., Can.	D6	96
Sellersburg, In., U.S.	H6	121
Sellersville, Pa., U.S.	F11	145
Sells, Az., U.S.	F4	110
Selm, Ger.	D7	10
Selma, Al., U.S.	C2	108
Selma, Ca., U.S.	D4	112
Selma, In., U.S.	D7	121
Selma, N.C., U.S.	B4	140
Selmer, Tn., U.S.	B3	149
Selva, Arg.	E7	80
Selvas, for., Braz.	E6	76
Selwyn Mountains, mts., Can.	D6	96
Semans, Sask., Can.	F3	105
Semarang, Indon.	j15	39a
Semenivka, Ukr.	I15	22
Semeru, Gunung, mtn., Indon.	k16	39a
Semibratovo, Russia	D22	22
Seminoe Reservoir, res., Wy., U.S.	D6	157
Seminole, Ok., U.S.	B5	143
Seminole, Tx., U.S.	C1	150
Seminole, co., Fl., U.S.	D5	116
Seminole, co., Ga., U.S.	F2	117
Seminole, co., Ok., U.S.	B5	143
Seminole, Lake, res., U.S.	F2	117
Semipalatinsk, Kaz.	G8	28
Semmes, Al., U.S.	E1	108
Semnān, Iran	D12	48
Šemonaicha, Kaz.	G14	26
Sem'onov, Russia	F6	26
Semur-en-Auxois, Fr.	E11	14
Sena, Braz.	D4	79
Senador Canedo, Braz.	D4	79
Senador Firmino, Braz.	F7	79
Senador Pompeu, Braz.	E11	76
Sena Madureira, Braz.	C7	82
Senanga, Zam.	E4	58
Senath, Mo., U.S.	E7	132
Senatobia, Ms., U.S.	A4	131
Sendafa, Eth.	M10	60
Sendai, Japan	I15	36
Sêndo, China	E15	44
Seneca, Il., U.S.	B5	120
Seneca, Ks., U.S.	C7	123
Seneca, Mo., U.S.	E3	132
Seneca, S.C., U.S.	B2	147
Seneca, co., N.Y., U.S.	C4	139
Seneca, co., Oh., U.S.	A2	142
Seneca Falls, N.Y., U.S.	C4	139
Seneca Lake, l., N.Y., U.S.	C4	139
Senecaville Lake, res., Oh., U.S.	C4	142
Senegal (Sénégal), ctry., Afr.	F4	54
Sénégal, stm., Afr.	E4	54
Senekal, S. Afr.	G8	66
Senftenberg, Ger.	D14	10
Sengés, Braz.	F10	76
Senhor do Bonfim, Braz.	G17	10
Senica, Slvk.	F8	10
Senigallia, Italy	E9	18
Senj, Cro.	G15	6
Senja, i., Nor.	E6	26
Senkursk, Russia	C9	14
Senlis, Fr.	H9	40
Senmonorom, Camb.	k11	104
Senneterre, Que., Can.	C2	117
Senoia, Ga., U.S.	D10	14
Sens, Fr.	D4	20
Senta, Yugo.	B2	143
Sentinel, Ok., U.S.	F14	32
Seoul see Sŏul, S. Kor.	k15	68a
Sepik, stm., Pap. N. Gui.	B6	66
Sepopa, Bots.	h13	104
Sept-Îles (Seven Islands), Que., Can.	D8	149
Sequatchie, co., Tn., U.S.	D8	149
Sequatchie, stm., Tn., U.S.	A2	154
Sequim, Wa., U.S.	D4	112
Sequoia National Park, Ca., U.S.	B7	143
Sequoyah, co., Ok., U.S.	C16	48
Serachs, Turk.	H6	26
Serafimovič, Russia	E9	12
Seraing, Bel.	F8	38
Seram (Ceram), i., Indon.	F8	38
Seram, Laut (Ceram Sea), Indon.	j13	39a
Serang, Indon.	F4	20
Serbia see Srbija, state, Yugo.	G6	26
Serdobsk, Russia	G21	22
Sereb'anyje Prudy, Russia	I17	22
Seredina-Buda, Ukr.	M6	40
Seremban, Malay.	B6	58
Serengeti Plain, pl., Tan.	A9	20
Seret (Siret), stm., Eur.	B1	122
Sergeant Bluff, Ia., U.S.	E21	22
Sergijev Posad, Russia	E5	38
Seria, Bru.	F8	80
Serodino, Arg.	F10	26
Serov, Russia	D8	66
Serowe, Bots.	H4	16
Serpa, Port.	E22	28
Serpents Mouth, strt.	I7	26
Serpuchov, Russia	G20	22
Serra do Salitre, Braz.	E5	79
Sêrrai, Grc.	H7	20
Serra Talhada, Braz.	E11	76
Serranópolis, Braz.	F6	80
Serrezuela, Arg.	E7	79
Serrinha, Braz.	E7	79
Serro, Braz.	E11	76
Sertânia, Braz.		
Serule, Bots.	C8	66
Sesfontein, Nmb.	B1	66
Sesheke, Zam.	E4	58
Sesser, Il., U.S.	E4	120
Sestao, Spain	B8	16
Sestri Levante, Italy	E4	18
Sestroreck, Russia	A12	22
Sète, Fr.	I10	14
Sete Barras, Braz.	C15	80
Sete Lagoas, Braz.	E6	79
Seth, W.V., U.S.	C3	155
Seto, Japan	L12	36
Seto-naikai, Japan	M7	36
Settat, Mor.	D7	62
Setúbal, Port.	G3	16
Setúbal, Baía de, b., Port.	G3	16
Seul, Lac, l., Ont., Can.	o16	103
Sevan, Arm.	A8	48
Sevan, ozero, l., Arm.	I7	26
Sévaré, Mali	D7	64
Sevastopol', Ukr.	I4	26
Seven Devils Mountains, mts., Id., U.S.	D2	119
Seven Hills, Oh., U.S.	h9	142
Severance, N.H., U.S.	D4	136
Severn, Md., U.S.	B4	127
Severn, stm., Ont., Can.	n17	103
Severn, stm., U.K.	J11	8
Severnaja Dvina, stm., Russia	E6	26
Severnaja Osetija, state, Russia	I6	26
Severnaja Zeml'a, is., Russia	B17	26
Severna Park, Md., U.S.	B4	127
Severodvinsk, Russia	E5	26
Severomorsk, Russia	D4	26
Severoural'sk, Russia	E9	26
Severo-Zadonsk, Russia	G21	22
Sevier, co., Ar., U.S.	D1	111
Sevier, co., Tn., U.S.	D10	149
Sevier, co., Ut., U.S.	E4	151
Sevier, stm., Ut., U.S.	D3	151
Sevier Bridge Reservoir, res., Ut., U.S.	D4	151
Sevier Lake, l., Ut., U.S.	E2	151
Sevierville, Tn., U.S.	D10	149
Sevilla, Col.	E5	84
Sevilla (Seville), Spain	H6	16
Seville see Sevilla, Spain	H6	16
Sevsk, Russia	I17	22
Sewanee, Tn., U.S.	D8	149
Seward, Ak., U.S.	C10	109
Seward, Ne., U.S.	D8	134
Seward, co., Ks., U.S.	E3	123
Seward, co., Ne., U.S.	D8	134
Seward Peninsula, pen., Ak., U.S.	B7	109
Sewell, Chile	H3	80
Sewickley, Pa., U.S.	E1	145
Sexsmith, Alta., Can.	B1	98
Seybaplaya, Mex.	H14	90
Seychelles, ctry., Afr.	B11	58
Seydisfjörður, Ice.	B6	6a
Seylac, Som.	F9	56
Seymour, Austl.	K6	70
Seymour, Ct., U.S.	D3	114
Seymour, In., U.S.	G6	121
Seymour, Ia., U.S.	D4	122
Seymour, Mo., U.S.	D5	132
Seymour, Tn., U.S.	D10	149
Seymour, Tx., U.S.	C3	150
Seymour, Wi., U.S.	D5	156
Seymourville, La., U.S.	h9	125
Sfântu Gheorghe, Rom.	D9	20
Sfax, Tun.	C16	62
Sfizef, Alg.	C10	62
's-Gravenhage (The Hague), Neth.	D5	12
Shaanxi (Shensi), prov., China	D8	30
Shabeelle (Shebele), stm., Afr.	H9	56
Shache (Yarkand), China	A7	44
Shackelford, co., Tx., U.S.	C3	150
Shādegān, Iran	F10	48
Shady Cove, Or., U.S.	E4	144
Shady Side, Md., U.S.	C4	127
Shadyside, Oh., U.S.	C5	142
Shady Spring, W.V., U.S.	D3	155
Shafter, Ca., U.S.	E4	112
Shagamu, Nig.	H11	64
Shah Alam, Malay.	M6	40
Shahdol, India	J8	44
Shāhjahānpur, India	G8	44
Shahr-e Kord, Iran	E11	48
Shakawee, Bots.	B5	66
Shaker Heights, Oh., U.S.	A4	142
Shaki, Nig.	G11	64
Shakopee, Mn., U.S.	F5	130
Shām, Bādiyat ash- (Syrian Desert), des., Asia	E6	48
Shām, Jabal ash-, mtn., Oman	C10	47
Shambu, Eth.	M9	60
Shāmli, India	F7	44
Shamokin, Pa., U.S.	E8	145
Shamva, Zimb.	E6	58
Shandī, Sud.	I7	60
Shandong (Shantung), prov., China	D10	30
Shandong Bandao (Shantung Peninsula), pen., China	F8	30
Shangcheng, China	D4	34
Shanghai, China	D10	34
Shanghai Shi, China	E11	30
Shanghai (Zhuji), China	A4	34
Shangrao, China	G6	34
Shangxingzhen, China	D8	34
Shanhaiguan, China	C7	32
Shannock, R.I., U.S.	F2	146
Shannon, co., Ms., U.S.	A5	131
Shannon, co., Mo., U.S.	D6	132
Shannon, co., S.D., U.S.	D3	148
Shannon, stm., Ire.	I4	8
Shannon Hills, Ar., U.S.	k10	111
Shannontown, S.C., U.S.	D7	147
Shansi see Shanxi, prov., China	D9	30
Shāntipur, India	I13	44
Shantou (Swatow), China	L5	30

Name	Map Ref.	Page
Shanxi (Shansi), prov., China	D9	30
Shanxian, China	I4	32
Shaoguan, China	K2	34
Shaowu, China	H6	34
Shaoxing, China	E9	34
Shaoyang, China	F9	30
Shaqrā', Sau. Ar.	I8	48
Shaqrā', Yemen	H4	47
Sharkey, co., Ms., U.S.	C3	131
Sharm ash-Shaykh, Egypt	D8	60
Sharon, Ct., U.S.	B2	114
Sharon, Ma., U.S.	B5	128
Sharon, Pa., U.S.	D1	145
Sharon, Tn., U.S.	A3	149
Sharon, Wi., U.S.	F5	156
Sharon Hill, Pa., U.S.	p20	145
Sharon Springs, Ks., U.S.	D2	123
Sharonville, Oh., U.S.	n13	142
Sharp, co., Ar., U.S.	A4	111
Sharpe, Lake, res., S.D., U.S.	C6	148
Sharpes, Fl., U.S.	D6	116
Sharpley, De., U.S.	h7	115
Sharpsburg, N.C., U.S.	B5	140
Sharpsburg, Pa., U.S.	k14	145
Sharpsville, In., U.S.	D5	121
Sharpsville, Pa., U.S.	D1	145
Sharqī, Al-Jabal ash- (Anti-Lebanon), mts., Asia	A6	50
Sharqīyah, As-Ṣaḥrā' ash-(Arabian Desert), des., Egypt	D7	60
Shashemene, Eth.	N10	60
Shashi, China	E9	30
Shasta, co., Ca., U.S.	B3	112
Shasta, Mount, vol., Ca., U.S.	B2	112
Shasta Lake, res., Ca., U.S.	B2	112
Shattuck, Ok., U.S.	A2	143
Shaunavon, Sask., Can.	H1	105
Shaw, Ms., U.S.	B3	131
Shawangunk Mountains, mts., N.Y., U.S.	D6	139
Shawano, Wi., U.S.	D5	156
Shawano, co., Wi., U.S.	D5	156
Shawinigan, Que., Can.	C5	104
Shawinigan Lake, B.C., Can.	g12	99
Shawinigan-Sud, Que., Can.	C5	104
Shawnee, Co., U.S.	B5	113
Shawnee, Ks., U.S.	k16	123
Shawnee, Ok., U.S.	B5	143
Shawnee, co., Ks., U.S.	D8	123
Shawneetown, Il., U.S.	F5	120
Shawo, China	G3	34
Shay Gap, Austl.	D4	68
Shaykh, Jabal ash- (Mount Hermon), mts., Asia	B5	50
Shaykh 'Uthmān, Yemen	H4	47
Shebele (Shabeelle), stm., Afr.	G9	56
Sheberghān, Afg.	B1	44
Sheboygan, Wi., U.S.	E6	156
Sheboygan, co., Wi., U.S.	E6	156
Sheboygan Falls, Wi., U.S.	E6	156
Shechem see Nābulus, W.B.	D4	50
Shediac, N.B., Can.	C5	101
Sheenjek, stm., Ak., U.S.	B11	109
Sheep Peak, mtn., Nv., U.S.	G6	135
Sheet Harbour, N.S., Can.	E7	101
Shefar'am, Isr.	C4	50
Sheffield, Eng., U.K.	H12	8
Sheffield, Al., U.S.	A2	108
Sheffield, Il., U.S.	B4	120
Sheffield, Ia., U.S.	B4	122
Sheffield, Vt., U.S.	B4	152
Sheffield Lake, Oh., U.S.	A3	142
Sheho, Sask., Can.	F4	105
Sheila, N.B., Can.	B5	101
Shekhūpura, Pak.	E5	44
Shelbiana, Ky., U.S.	C7	124
Shelbina, Mo., U.S.	B5	132
Shelburn, In., U.S.	F3	121
Shelburne, N.S., Can.	F4	101
Shelburne, Ont., Can.	C4	103
Shelburne, Vt., U.S.	C2	152
Shelburne Falls, Ma., U.S.	A2	128
Shelby, Al., U.S.	B3	108
Shelby, Ia., U.S.	B3	121
Shelby, In., U.S.	C2	122
Shelby, Mi., U.S.	E4	129
Shelby, Ms., U.S.	B3	131
Shelby, Mt., U.S.	B5	133
Shelby, Ne., U.S.	C8	134
Shelby, N.C., U.S.	B1	140
Shelby, Oh., U.S.	B3	142
Shelby, co., Al., U.S.	B3	108
Shelby, co., Il., U.S.	D5	120
Shelby, co., In., U.S.	E6	121
Shelby, co., Ia., U.S.	C2	122
Shelby, co., Ky., U.S.	B4	124
Shelby, co., Mo., U.S.	B5	132
Shelby, co., Oh., U.S.	B1	142
Shelby, co., Tn., U.S.	B2	149
Shelby, co., Tx., U.S.	D5	150
Shelbyville, Il., U.S.	D5	120
Shelbyville, In., U.S.	F6	121
Shelbyville, Ky., U.S.	B4	124
Shelbyville, Mo., U.S.	B5	132
Shelbyville, Tn., U.S.	B5	149
Shelbyville, Lake, res., Il., U.S.	D5	120
Sheldon, Il., U.S.	C6	120
Sheldon, Ia., U.S.	A2	122
Sheldon, Vt., U.S.	B3	152
Sheldon Springs, Vt., U.S.	B3	152
Shell, Wy., U.S.	B5	157
Shellbrook, Sask., Can.	D2	105
Shelley, Id., U.S.	F6	119
Shell Lake, Sask., Can.	D2	105
Shell Lake, Wi., U.S.	C2	156
Shellman, Ga., U.S.	E2	117
Shell Rock, Ia., U.S.	B5	122
Shellsburg, Ia., U.S.	B6	122
Shelton, Ct., U.S.	D3	114
Shelton, Ne., U.S.	D7	134
Shelton, Wa., U.S.	B2	154
Shemogue, N.B., Can.	C5	101
Shenandoah, Ia., U.S.	D2	122
Shenandoah, Pa., U.S.	E9	145
Shenandoah, Va., U.S.	B4	153
Shenandoah, co., Va., U.S.	B4	153
Shenandoah, stm., U.S.	A5	153
Shenandoah National Park, Va., U.S.	B4	153
Shenandoah Valley, val., U.S.	B4	153
Shendam, Nig.	G14	64
Shengze, China	E9	34
Shenqiu, China	B4	34
Shenyang (Mukden), China	B11	32
Shenzhen, China	M3	34
Shepetivka, Ukr.	G3	26
Shepherd, Mi., U.S.	E6	129
Shepherd, Mt., U.S.	E8	133
Shepherdstown, W.V., U.S.	B7	155
Shepherdsville, Ky., U.S.	C4	124
Shepparton, Austl.	K6	70
Sheqi, China	B1	34
Sherab, Sud.	L3	60
Sherbro Island, i., S.L.	H3	64
Sherbrooke, N.S., Can.	D8	101
Sherbrooke, Que., Can.	D6	104
Sherburn, Mn., U.S.	G4	130
Sherburne, co., Mn., U.S.	E5	130
Sheridan, Ar., U.S.	C3	111
Sheridan, Il., U.S.	B5	120
Sheridan, In., U.S.	D5	121
Sheridan, Mt., U.S.	E4	133
Sheridan, Or., U.S.	B3	144
Sheridan, Wy., U.S.	B6	157
Sheridan, co., Ks., U.S.	C3	123
Sheridan, co., Mt., U.S.	B12	133
Sheridan, co., Ne., U.S.	B3	134
Sheridan, co., N.D., U.S.	B5	141
Sheridan, co., Wy., U.S.	B5	157
Sherman, Ms., U.S.	A5	131
Sherman, Tx., U.S.	C4	150
Sherman, co., Ks., U.S.	C2	123
Sherman, co., Ne., U.S.	C6	134
Sherman, co., Or., U.S.	B6	144
Sherman, co., Tx., U.S.	A2	150
Sherman Mills, Me., U.S.	C4	126
Sherman Reservoir, res., Ne., U.S.	C7	134
Sherman Station, Me., U.S.	C4	126
Sherpur, Bngl.	H14	44
Sherridon, Man., Can.	B1	100
Sherrill, N.Y., U.S.	B5	139
's-Hertogenbosch, Neth.	E7	12
Sherwood, P.E.I., Can.	C6	101
Sherwood, Ar., U.S.	C3	111
Sherwood, N.D., U.S.	A4	141
Sherwood, Or., U.S.	h12	144
Sherwood Manor, Ct., U.S.	A5	114
Sherwood Park, De., U.S.	i7	115
Shetland Islands, is., Scot., U.K.	A12	8
Shetucket, stm., Ct., U.S.	C7	114
Shexian, China	F7	34
Sheyenne, N.D., U.S.	B6	141
Sheyenne, stm., N.D., U.S.	C8	141
Shiawassee, co., Mi., U.S.	F6	129
Shibām, Yemen	G6	47
Shibata, Japan	J14	36
Shibīn al-Kawm, Egypt	B6	60
Shicheng, China	I5	34
Shickley, Ne., U.S.	D8	134
Shigezhuang, China	E4	32
Shijiazhuang, China	E2	32
Shijing, China	K7	34
Shikārpur, Pak.	G3	44
Shikoku, i., Japan	N8	36
Shiliguri, India	G13	44
Shillong, India	H14	44
Shiloh, Oh., U.S.	C1	142
Shiloh National Military Park, Tn., U.S.	B3	149
Shilong, China	L2	34
Shimada, Japan	M13	36
Shimbiris, mtn., Som.	F10	56
Shimizu, Japan	L13	36
Shimoda, Japan	K14	36
Shimoga, India	F3	46
Shimonoseki, Japan	N5	36
Shiner, Tx., U.S.	E4	150
Shinkolobwe, Zaire	D5	58
Shinnston, W.V., U.S.	B4	155
Shinyanga, Tan.	B6	58
Shiocton, Wi., U.S.	D5	156
Shiogama, Japan	I16	36
Shiping, China	C7	40
Shippagan, N.B., Can.	B5	101
Shippensburg, Pa., U.S.	F6	145
Shiprock, N.M., U.S.	A1	138
Ship Rock, mtn., N.M., U.S.	A1	138
Shipshewana, In., U.S.	A6	121
Shipu, China	F10	34
Shīrāz, Iran	G12	48
Shire, stm., Afr.	E6	58
Shirley, Ar., U.S.	B3	111
Shirley, In., U.S.	E6	121
Shirley Basin, Wy., U.S.	D6	157
Shirvān, Iran	C14	48
Shishaldin Volcano, vol., Ak., U.S.	E7	109
Shishmaref, Ak., U.S.	B6	109
Shively, Ky., U.S.	B4	124
Shivpuri, India	H7	44
Shivwits Plateau, plat., Az., U.S.	A2	110
Shizuoka, Japan	M13	36
Shkodër, Alb.	G3	20
Shoal Harbour, Newf., Can.	D4	102
Shoal Lake, Man., Can.	D1	100
Shoals, In., U.S.	G4	121
Shongopovi, Az., U.S.	B5	110
Shoreacres, B.C., Can.	E9	99
Shores Acres, R.I., U.S.	E4	146
Shoreview, Mn., U.S.	m12	130
Shorewood, Il., U.S.	k8	120
Shorewood, Mn., U.S.	n11	130
Shorewood, Wi., U.S.	E6	156
Short Beach, Ct., U.S.	D4	114
Shorter, Al., U.S.	C4	108
Shoshone, Id., U.S.	G4	119
Shoshone, co., Id., U.S.	B2	119
Shoshone, stm., Wy., U.S.	B4	157
Shoshone Falls, wtfl, Id., U.S.	G4	119
Shoshone Mountains, mts., Nv., U.S.	E4	135
Shoshong, Bots.	D8	66
Shoshoni, Wy., U.S.	C4	157
Shostka, Ukr.	G4	26
Shouning, China	H8	34
Shouxian, China	C5	34
Show Low, Az., U.S.	C5	110
Shreveport, La., U.S.	B2	125
Shrewsbury, Eng., U.K.	I11	8
Shrewsbury, Ma., U.S.	B4	128
Shrewsbury, Pa., U.S.	G8	145
Shropshire, hist. reg., Eng., U.K.	I11	8
Shuangcheng, China	B12	30
Shuangliao, China	C11	30
Shuangmiaozi, China	A10	32
Shuangyashan, China	B13	30
Shubenacadie, N.S., Can.	D6	101
Shubrā al-Khaymah, Egypt	B6	60
Shubuta, Ms., U.S.	D5	131
Shuksan, Mount, mtn., Wa., U.S.	A4	154
Shullsburg, Wi., U.S.	F3	156
Shunchang, China	I6	34
Shunde, China	M2	34
Shuqualak, Ms., U.S.	C5	131
Shurugwi, Zimb.	B10	66
Shūsh, Iran	E10	48
Shūshtar, Iran	E10	48
Shuwak, Sud.	J8	60
Shwebo, Mya.	C3	40
Shweli, stm., Asia	E8	30
Si'an, China	E8	34
Si'an see Xi'an, China	E8	30
Šiauliai, Lith.	F6	22
Sibaj, Russia	E19	4
Šibenik, Cro.	F10	18
Siberia see Sibir', reg., Russia	D14	28
Sibi, Pak.	F2	44
Sibir' (Siberia), reg., Russia	D14	28
Sibiti, Congo	B2	58
Sibiu, Rom.	D8	20
Sibley, Ia., U.S.	A2	122
Sibley, La., U.S.	B2	125
Sibley, co., Mn., U.S.	F4	130
Sibolga, Indon.	N5	40
Sibuyan Sea, Phil.	C7	38
Sicamous, B.C., Can.	D8	99
Sichote-Alin', mts., Russia	H19	28
Sichuan (Szechwan), prov., China	E7	30
Sicilia, prov., Italy	L9	18
Sicilia (Sicily), i., Italy	L9	18
Sicily see Sicilia, i., Italy	L9	18
Sicily, Strait of, strt.	L6	18
Sico Tinto, stm., Hond.	B9	92
Sicuani, Peru	F6	82
Sidéropolis, Braz.	E14	80
Sídheros, Ákra, c., Grc.	N10	20
Sidi Aïssa, Alg.	C12	62
Sīdī Barrānī, Egypt	B3	60
Sidi bel Abbès, Alg.	C10	62
Sidi Bennour, Mor.	D6	62
Sidi Bou Zid, Tun.	C15	62
Sidi Ifni, Mor.	F5	62
Sidi Kacem, Mor.	C8	62
Sidikalang, Indon.	M5	40
Sidi Okba, Alg.	C13	62
Sidi Slimane, Mor.	C8	62
Sidley, Mount, mtn., Ant.	C10	73
Sidney, B.C., Can.	E6	99
Sidney, Man., Can.	E2	100
Sidney, Il., U.S.	C5	120
Sidney, Ia., U.S.	D2	122
Sidney, Mt., U.S.	C12	133
Sidney, Ne., U.S.	C3	134
Sidney, N.Y., U.S.	C5	139
Sidney, Oh., U.S.	B1	142
Sidney Lanier, Lake, res., Ga., U.S.	B2	117
Sidon see Saydā, Leb.	A4	50
Sidon, Ms., U.S.	B3	131
Sidra, Gulf of see Surt, Khalīj, b., Libya	B4	56
Sidrolândia, Braz.	F1	79
Siedlce, Pol.	C22	10
Siegburg, Ger.	E7	10
Siegen, Ger.	E8	10
Siemianowice Śląskie, Pol.	E19	10
Siémréab, Camb.	H7	40
Siena, Italy	F6	18
Sieradz, Pol.	D18	10
Sierpc, Pol.	C19	10
Sierra, co., Ca., U.S.	C3	112
Sierra, co., N.M., U.S.	D2	138
Sierra Blanca Peak, mtn., N.M., U.S.	D4	138
Sierra Chica, Arg.	I8	80
Sierra Colorada, Arg.	E3	78
Sierra Gorda, Chile	B4	80
Sierra Leone, ctry., Afr.	G4	54
Sierra Madre, Ca., U.S.	m12	112
Sierra Vista, Az., U.S.	F5	110
Sierre, Switz.	F8	13
Sifton, Man., Can.	D1	100
Sig, Alg.	J11	16
Sighetu Marmației, Rom.	B7	20
Sighișoara, Rom.	C8	20
Sigli, Indon.	L3	40
Siglufjörður, Ice.	A4	6a
Signal Mountain, Tn., U.S.	D8	149
Sigourney, Ia., U.S.	C5	122
Siguatepeque, Hond.	C7	92
Siguiri, Gui.	F5	64
Sigulda, Lat.	D7	22
Sihanoukville see Kâmpóng Saôm, Camb.	I7	40
Sihuas, Peru	C3	82
Siirt, Tur.	C6	48
Sikasso, Mali	F7	64
Sikeston, Mo., U.S.	E8	132
Sikkim, state, India	G13	44
Sīlāle, Lith.	F5	22
Silao, Mex.	G9	90
Silay, Phil.	C7	38
Silchar, India	H15	44
Siler City, N.C., U.S.	B3	140
Silesia, hist. reg., Pol.	D16	10
Siletz, Or., U.S.	C3	144
Siliana, Tun.	M4	18
Silifke, Tur.	C3	48
Siling Co, l., China	E13	44
Silistra, Bul.	E11	20
Silivri, Tur.	H12	20
Šilka, Russia	G15	28
Šilka, stm., Russia	G15	28
Sillamäe, Est.	B10	22
Sillery, Que., Can.	n17	104
Siloam Springs, Ar., U.S.	A1	111
Šilovo, Russia	G23	22
Silsbee, Tx., U.S.	D5	150
Silt, Co., U.S.	B3	113
Šilutė, Lith.	F4	22
Silvan (Miyafarkin), Tur.	B6	48
Silvânia, Braz.	D4	79
Silver Bank Passage, strt., N.A.	D9	94
Silver Bay, Mn., U.S.	C7	130
Silver Bow, co., Mt., U.S.	E4	133
Silver City, Nv., U.S.	D2	135
Silver City, N.M., U.S.	E1	138
Silver Cliff, Co., U.S.	C5	113
Silver Creek, Ne., U.S.	C8	134
Silver Creek, N.Y., U.S.	C1	139
Silver Grove, Ky., U.S.	h14	124
Silver Hill, Md., U.S.	f9	127
Silver Lake, In., U.S.	B6	121
Silver Lake, Ks., U.S.	C8	123
Silver Lake, Ma., U.S.	f11	128
Silver Lake, Mn., U.S.	F4	130
Silver Lake, N.H., U.S.	C4	136
Silver Lake, Wi., U.S.	F5	156
Silverpeak, Nv., U.S.	F4	135
Silver Spring, Md., U.S.	C3	127
Silver Springs, Nv., U.S.	D2	135
Silver Star Mountain, mtn., Wa., U.S.	A5	154
Silvertip Mountain, mtn., Mt., U.S.	C3	133
Silverton, Co., U.S.	D3	113
Silverton, Id., U.S.	B3	119
Silverton, N.J., U.S.	C4	137
Silverton, Oh., U.S.	o13	142
Silverton, Or., U.S.	C4	144
Silvia, Col.	F4	84
Silvies, stm., Or., U.S.	D7	144
Silview, De., U.S.	B3	115
Silvis, Il., U.S.	B3	120
Šimanovsk, Russia	G17	28
Simao, China	G7	30
Simcoe, Ont., Can.	E4	103
Simcoe, Lake, l., Ont., Can.	C5	103
Simeria, Rom.	D7	20
Simferopol', Ukr.	I4	26
Simiri, Niger	D11	64
Simití, Col.	D6	84
Simi Valley, Ca., U.S.	E4	112
Simla, Co., U.S.	B6	113
Simmesport, La., U.S.	D4	125
Simnas, Lith.	G6	22
Simoca, Arg.	D6	80
Simojovel, Mex.	I13	90
Simon's Town, S. Afr.	J4	66
Šimorskoje, Russia	F25	22
Simplon Pass, Switz.	F9	13
Simplon Tunnel, Eur.	F9	13
Simpson, Sask., Can.	F3	105
Simpson, co., Ky., U.S.	D3	124
Simpson, co., Ms., U.S.	D4	131
Simpson Desert, des., Austl.	D7	68
Simpsonville, Ky., U.S.	B4	124
Simpsonville, S.C., U.S.	B3	147
Simsbury, Ct., U.S.	B4	114
Šimsk, Russia	C13	22
Sīnā', Shibh Jazīrat (Sinai Peninsula), pen., Egypt	C7	60
Sinai, Mount see Mūsā, Jabal, mtn., Egypt	C7	60
Sinaia, Rom.	D9	20
Sinai Peninsula see Sīnā', Shibh Jazīrat, pen., Egypt	C7	60
Sinaloa, state, Mex.	F6	90
Sinaloa, stm., Mex.	E5	90
Sinanju, N. Kor.	D13	32
Sincé, Col.	C5	84
Sincelejo, Col.	C5	84
Sinch'ang, N. Kor.	C16	32
Sinch'ŏn, N. Kor.	E13	32
Sinclair, Me., U.S.	A4	126
Sinclair, Wy., U.S.	E5	157
Sinclair, Lake, res., Ga., U.S.	C3	117
Sindelfingen, Ger.	G9	10
Sindi, Est.	C7	22
Sindri, India	I12	44
Sine, val., Sen.	D2	64
Singapore, Sing.	N7	40
Singapore, ctry., Asia	E3	36
Singapore Strait, strt., Asia	N8	40
Singaraja, Indon.	G6	38
Sing Buri, Thai.	G6	40
Singen [Hohentwiel], Ger.	H8	10
Singida, Tan.	B6	58
Singkang, Indon.	F7	38
Singkawang, Indon.	N10	40
Singleton, Austl.	I9	70
Sinhŭng, N. Kor.	C15	32
Sinj, Cro.	F11	18
Sinjah, Sud.	K7	60
Sinkāt, Sud.	H9	60
Sinkiang see Xinjiang Uygur Zizhiqu, prov., China	C3	30
Sinnamary, Fr. Gu.	B8	76
Sinnūris, Egypt	C6	60
Sinop, Tur.	G15	4
Sin'p'o, N. Kor.	C16	32
Sinsheim, Ger.	C15	14
Sintaluta, Sask., Can.	G4	105
Sintang, Indon.	E5	38
Sint Eustatius, i., Neth. Ant.	F13	94
Sint Maarten (Saint-Martin), i., N.A.	E13	94
Sint-Michiels, Bel.	F3	12
Sint-Niklaas (Saint-Nicolas), Bel.	F5	12
Sint-Truiden (Saint-Trond), Bel.	G7	12
Sinŭiju, N. Kor.	C12	32
Siófok, Hung.	I18	10
Sion (Sitten), Switz.	F7	13
Sioux, co., Ia., U.S.	A1	122
Sioux, co., Ne., U.S.	B2	134
Sioux, co., N.D., U.S.	C4	141
Sioux Center, Ia., U.S.	A1	122
Sioux City, Ia., U.S.	B1	122
Sioux Falls, S.D., U.S.	D9	148
Sioux Lookout, Ont., Can.	o17	103
Sioux Rapids, Ia., U.S.	B2	122
Siparia, Trin.	I14	94
Sipiwesk Lake, l., Man., Can.	B3	100
Siple, Mount, mtn., Ant.	C10	73
Sipsey, Al., U.S.	B2	108
Sipsey, stm., Al., U.S.	B2	108
Siquia, stm., Nic.	E10	92
Siqueira Campos, Braz.	G4	79
Siquijor, C.R.	G11	92
Siquirres, C.R.	G11	92
Siquisique, Ven.	B8	84
Siracusa (Syracuse), Italy	L10	18
Sirājganj, Bngl.	H13	44
Sir Douglas, Mount, mtn., Can.	D3	98
Sir Edward Pellew Group, is., Austl.	C7	68
Siret (Sereth), stm., Eur.	D11	20
Sīrjān, Iran	G13	48
Sir James MacBrien, Mount, mtn., N.W. Ter., Can.	D7	96
Sir Joseph Banks Group, is., Austl.	J2	70
Sir Sandford, Mount, mtn., B.C., Can.	D9	99
Sirte, Gulf of see Surt, Khalīj, b., Libya	B4	56
Sirupa, stm., Mex.	C5	90
Širvintos, Lith.	F7	22
Sisak, Cro.	D11	18
Si Sa Ket, Thai.	G8	40
Sishui, China	H5	32
Siskiyou, co., Ca., U.S.	B2	112
Siskiyou Mountains, mts., U.S.	F3	144
Siskiyou Pass, Or., U.S.	E4	144
Sissach, Switz.	D8	13
Sisseton, S.D., U.S.	B8	148
Sisson Branch Reservoir, res., N.B., Can.	B2	101
Sissonville, W.V., U.S.	C3	155
Sīstān, reg., Asia	F17	48
Sisters, Or., U.S.	C5	144
Sistersville, W.V., U.S.	B4	155
Sitāpur, India	G9	44
Sitka, Ak., U.S.	D12	109
Sitka National Historical Park, Ak., U.S.	m22	109
Sitka Sound, strt., Ak., U.S.	m22	109
Sittard, Neth.	F8	12
Sittwe (Akyab), Mya.	D2	40
Siuna, Nic.	D10	92
Sivakāsi, India	H4	46
Sivas, Tur.	B4	48
Sivé, Maur.	D3	64
Siverek, Tur.	C5	48
Siverskij, Russia	B13	22
Siwān, India	G11	44
Sixaola, stm., N.A.	H12	92
Sixitou, China	H8	34
Sjælland, i., Den.	N12	6
Skagen, Den.	M12	6
Skagerrak, strt., Eur.	M11	6
Skagit, co., Wa., U.S.	A4	154
Skagit, stm., Wa., U.S.	A4	154
Skagway, Ak., U.S.	D12	109
Skamania, co., Wa., U.S.	D3	154
Skanderborg, Den.	M11	6
Skaneateles, N.Y., U.S.	C4	139
Skaneateles Lake, l., N.Y., U.S.	C4	139
Skārdu, Pak.	C6	44
Skarzysko-Kamienna, Pol.	D20	10
Skaudvilė, Lith.	F5	22
Skawina, Pol.	F19	10
Skeleton Coast, Nmb.	B1	66
Skeleton Lake, l., Ont., Can.	B5	103
Skellefteå, Swe.	I17	6
Skiatook, Ok., U.S.	A5	143
Skiatook Reservoir, res., Ok., U.S.	A5	143
Skidel', Bela.	H7	22
Skien, Nor.	L11	6
Skierniewice, Pol.	D20	10
Skikda (Philippeville), Alg.	B14	62
Skive, Den.	M11	6
Sklov, Bela.	G13	22
Skokie, Il., U.S.	A6	120
Skopin, Russia	H22	22
Skopje, Mac.	H5	20
Skövde, Swe.	L13	6
Skovorodino, Russia	G16	28
Skowhegan, Me., U.S.	D3	126
Skrīveri, Lat.	E8	22
Skrunda, Lat.	E5	22
Skunk, stm., Ia., U.S.	D6	122
Skuodas, Lith.	E4	22
Skuratovskij, Russia	G20	22
Skye, Island of, i., Scot., U.K.	D7	8
Skykomish, stm., Wa., U.S.	B4	154
Skyland, Nv., U.S.	D2	135
Skyline, Al., U.S.	A3	108
Slamet, Gunung, mtn., Indon.	j14	39a
Slancy, Russia	B11	22
Slaný, Czech Rep.	E14	10
Slater, Ia., U.S.	C4	122
Slater, Mo., U.S.	B4	132
Slater, S.C., U.S.	A3	147
Slatersville, R.I., U.S.	A3	146
Slatina, Rom.	E8	20
Slatington, Pa., U.S.	E10	145
Slaton, Tx., U.S.	C2	150
Slav'ansk-na-Kubani, Russia	H5	26
Slave, stm., Can., U.S.	D10	96
Slave Lake, Alta., Can.	B3	98
Slavgorod, Bela.	H13	22
Slavgorod, Russia	G7	28
Slavonia, hist. reg., Cro.	D12	18
Slavonska Požega, Cro.	D12	18
Slavonski Brod, Cro.	D13	18
Slavsk, Russia	F4	22
Slayton, Mn., U.S.	G3	130
Sledge, Ms., U.S.	A3	131
Sleeping Bear Dunes National Lakeshore, Mi., U.S.	D4	129
Sleepy Eye, Mn., U.S.	F4	130
Slidell, La., U.S.	D6	125
Slide Mountain, mtn., N.Y., U.S.	D6	139
Sliedrecht, Neth.	E6	12
Sligo, Ire.	G5	8
Sligo, co., Ire.	G5	8
Slinger, Wi., U.S.	E5	156
Slippery Rock, Pa., U.S.	D1	145
Sliven, Bul.	G10	20
Sloan, Ia., U.S.	B1	122
Sloan, Nv., U.S.	H6	135
Sloan, N.Y., U.S.	C2	139
Slobodskoj, Russia	F8	26
Slobozia, Mol.	C13	20
Slobozia, Rom.	E11	20
Slobozia, Rom.	F9	20
Slocan, B.C., Can.	E9	99
Slocomb, Al., U.S.	D4	108
Slonim, Bela.	H8	22
Slope, co., N.D., U.S.	C2	141
Slovakia (Slovenská Republika), ctry., Eur.	G20	10
Slovenia (Slovenija), ctry., Eur.	C9	18
Slov'yans'k, Ukr.	H5	26
Sluck, Bela.	H10	22
Slunj, Cro.	D10	18
Słupsk (Stolp), Pol.	A17	10
Smackover, Ar., U.S.	D3	111
Smalininkai, Lith.	F5	22
Smallwood Reservoir, res., Newf., Can.	g8	102
Smara, W. Sah.	G5	62
Smeaton, Sask., Can.	D3	105
Smederevo, Yugo.	E4	20
Smelterville, Id., U.S.	B2	119
Smethport, Pa., U.S.	C5	145
Smidovič, Russia	H18	28
Smila, Ukr.	H4	26
Smiloviči, Bela.	H11	22
Smiltene, Lat.	D8	22
Smith, Alta., Can.	B3	98
Smith, Nv., U.S.	E2	135
Smith, co., Ks., U.S.	C5	123
Smith, co., Ms., U.S.	C4	131
Smith, co., Tn., U.S.	A5	149
Smith, co., Tx., U.S.	C5	150
Smith Center, Ks., U.S.	C5	123
Smithers, B.C., Can.	B4	99
Smithfield, N.C., U.S.	B4	140
Smithfield, Ut., U.S.	B4	151
Smithfield, Va., U.S.	D6	153
Smith Island, i., U.S.	D5	127
Smith Island, i., Va., U.S.	C7	153
Smith Mountain Lake, res., Va., U.S.	C3	153
Smith Point, c., Ma., U.S.	D7	128
Smith Point, c., Va., U.S.	C6	153
Smithsburg, Md., U.S.	A2	127
Smiths Cove, N.S., Can.	E4	101
Smiths Falls, Ont., Can.	C8	103
Smiths Grove, Ky., U.S.	C3	124
Smithton, Austl.	M6	70
Smithton, Il., U.S.	E4	120
Smithton, Mo., U.S.	C5	132
Smithtown, N.Y., U.S.	n15	139
Smithville, Ga., U.S.	E2	117
Smithville, Ms., U.S.	A5	131
Smithville, Mo., U.S.	B3	132
Smithville, Tn., U.S.	D8	149
Smithville, Tx., U.S.	D4	150
Smithville Lake, res., Mo., U.S.	B3	132
Smoky, stm., Alta., Can.	B1	98
Smoky Hill, stm., U.S.	D5	123
Smoky Lake, Alta., Can.	B4	98
Smolensk, Russia	G15	22
Smolevičì, Bela.	G11	22
Smoljan, Bul.	H8	20
Smoot, Wy., U.S.	D2	157
Smooth Rock Falls, Ont., Can.	o19	103
Smoothstone Lake, l., Sask., Can.	C2	105
Smorgon', Bela.	G9	22
Smyrna see İzmir, Tur.	K11	20
Smyrna, De., U.S.	C3	115
Smyrna, Ga., U.S.	C2	117
Smyrna, Tn., U.S.	B5	149
Smyrna Mills, Me., U.S.	B4	126
Smyth, co., Va., U.S.	f10	153
Snake, stm., U.S.	B3	106
Snake, stm., Mn., U.S.	D5	130
Snares Islands, is., N.Z.	M20	158
Snead, Al., U.S.	A3	108
Sneads, Fl., U.S.	B2	116
Sneedville, Tn., U.S.	C10	149
Sneek, Neth.	B8	12
Śniardwy, Jezioro, l., Pol.	B21	10
Snohomish, Wa., U.S.	B3	154
Snohomish, co., Wa., U.S.	A4	154
Snoqualmie, Wa., U.S.	B4	154
Snoqualmie, stm., Wa., U.S.	B4	154
Snoqualmie Pass, Wa., U.S.	B4	154
Snowdon, mtn., Wales, U.K.	H9	8
Snowdrift, N.W. Ter., Can.	D10	96
Snowflake, Az., U.S.	C5	110
Snow Hill, Md., U.S.	D7	127
Snow Hill, N.C., U.S.	B5	140
Snow Lake, Man., Can.	B1	100
Snowmass Mountain, mtn., Co., U.S.	B3	113
Snow Mountain, mtn., Me., U.S.	C2	126
Snowshoe Peak, mtn., Mt., U.S.	B1	133
Snowy, stm., Austl.	K8	70
Snowy Mountain, mtn., N.Y., U.S.	B6	139
Snowy Mountains, mts., Austl.	K8	70
Snyatyn, Ukr.	A9	20
Snyder, Ok., U.S.	C3	143
Snyder, Tx., U.S.	C2	150
Snyder, co., Pa., U.S.	E7	145
Soacha, Col.	E5	84
Soalala, Madag.	p21	67b
Soap Lake, Wa., U.S.	B6	154
Soatá, Col.	D6	84
Soavinandriana, Madag.	q22	67b
Sobat, stm., Sud.	M7	60
Sobinka, Russia	F23	22
Soboko, Cen. Afr. Rep.	N3	60

Name	Map Ref.	Page
Sobradinho, Braz.	E12	80
Sobradinho, Represa de, res., Braz.	E10	76
Sobral, Braz.	D10	76
Socastee, S.C., U.S.	D9	147
Sochaczew, Pol.	C20	10
Sochi see Soči, Russia	G15	4
Soči, Russia	I5	26
Social Circle, Ga., U.S.	C3	117
Société, Archipel de la (Society Islands), is., Fr. Poly.	J24	158
Socoltenango, Mex.	I13	90
Socompa, Paso, S.A.	C4	80
Socorro, Col.	D6	84
Socorro, N.M., U.S.	C3	138
Socorro, Tx., U.S.	o11	150
Socorro, co., N.M., U.S.	D2	138
Socorro, Isla, i., Mex.	H4	90
Socotra see Suquṭrā, i., Yemen	G5	42
Soc Trang, Viet.	J8	40
Socuéllamos, Spain	F9	16
Soda Springs, Id., U.S.	G7	119
Soddy-Daisy, Tn., U.S.	D8	149
Söderhamn, Swe.	K15	6
Södertälje, Swe.	L15	6
Sodo, Eth.	N9	60
Soe, Indon.	G7	38
Soest, Ger.	D8	10
Sofia see Sofija, Bul.	G7	20
Sofia, stm., Madag.	o22	67b
Sofija (Sofia), Bul.	G7	20
Sofrino, Russia	E20	22
Sogamoso, Col.	E6	84
Sognafjorden, Nor.	K9	6
Søgne, Nor.	L10	6
Sointula, B.C., Can.	D4	99
Soissons, Fr.	C10	14
Sokch'o, S. Kor.	E16	32
Söke, Tur.	L11	20
Sokodé, Togo	G10	64
Sokol, Russia	F6	26
Sokółka, Pol.	B23	10
Sokolov, Czech Rep.	E12	10
Sokoto, Nig.	E12	64
Sokyryany, Ukr.	A11	20
Sol, Costa del, Spain	I7	16
Solana Beach, Ca., U.S.	F5	112
Solano, co., Ca., U.S.	C3	112
Solāpur, India	D3	46
Sol'cy, Russia	C13	22
Sol de Julio, Arg.	E7	80
Soldotna, Ak., U.S.	g16	109
Soledad, Col.	B5	84
Soledad, Ca., U.S.	D3	112
Soledad, Ven.	C11	84
Soledade, Braz.	E12	80
Soligalič, Russia	B25	22
Soligorsk, Bela.	I10	22
Solikamsk, Russia	F9	26
Sol'-Ileck, Russia	G8	26
Soliman, Tun.	M5	18
Solingen, Ger.	D7	10
Sollefteå, Swe.	J15	6
Solnečnogorsk, Russia	E19	22
Solok, Indon.	O6	40
Sololá, dept., Guat.	C3	92
Solomon, Az., U.S.	E6	110
Solomon, Ks., U.S.	D6	123
Solomon, stm., Ks., U.S.	C6	123
Solomon Islands, ctry., Oc.	G23	2
Solomons, Md., U.S.	D5	127
Solomon Sea, Oc.	I19	158
Solon, Ia., U.S.	C6	122
Solon, Me., U.S.	D3	126
Solon, Oh., U.S.	A4	142
Solotča, Russia	G22	22
Solothurn, Switz.	D8	13
Solotvyna, Ukr.	B7	20
Solvay, N.Y., U.S.	B4	139
Sol'vyčegodsk, Russia	E7	26
Solway Firth, est., U.K.	G10	8
Solwezi, Zam.	D5	58
Soma, Tur.	J11	20
Somalia (Somaliya), ctry., Afr.	G10	56
Sombor, Yugo.	D3	20
Sombra, Ont., Can.	E2	103
Sombrerete, Mex.	F8	90
Sombrero, i., St. K./N.	E13	94
Sombrio, Braz.	E14	80
Somerdale, N.J., U.S.	D2	137
Somers, Ct., U.S.	B6	114
Somers, Mt., U.S.	B2	133
Somerset, Austl.	M6	70
Somerset, Man., Can.	E2	100
Somerset, Ky., U.S.	C5	124
Somerset, Ma., U.S.	C5	128
Somerset, N.J., U.S.	B3	137
Somerset, Pa., U.S.	F3	145
Somerset, Wi., U.S.	C1	156
Somerset, co., Eng., U.K.	J11	8
Somerset, co., Me., U.S.	C2	126
Somerset, co., Md., U.S.	D6	127
Somerset, co., N.J., U.S.	B3	137
Somerset, co., Pa., U.S.	G3	145
Somerset East, S. Afr.	I7	66
Somerset Island, i., N.W. Ter., Can.	B14	96
Somerset Reservoir, res., Vt., U.S.	E3	152
Somerset West, S. Afr.	J4	66
Somers Point, N.J., U.S.	E3	137
Somersville, Ct., U.S.	B6	114
Somersworth, N.H., U.S.	D5	136
Somerton, Az., U.S.	E1	110
Somervell, co., Tx., U.S.	C4	150
Somerville, Ma., U.S.	B5	128
Somerville, N.J., U.S.	B3	137
Somerville, Tn., U.S.	B2	149
Somme, stm., Fr.	C9	14
Sömmerda, Ger.	D11	10
Somonauk, Il., U.S.	B5	120
Somoto, Nic.	D8	92
Son, stm., India	H10	44
Soná, Pan.	C2	84
Sŏnch'ŏn, N. Kor.	D12	32
Sønderborg, Den.	N11	6
Sondershausen, Ger.	D10	10
Sondrio, Italy	C4	18
Songbu, China	D3	34
Song Cau, Viet.	H10	40
Songea, Tan.	D7	58
Songhua, stm., China	B13	30
Songhua Hu, res., China	C12	30
Songjiang, China	D10	34
Songjiangzhen, China	A14	32
Songjŏng, S. Kor.	H14	32
Songkhla, Thai.	K6	40
Sŏngnam, S. Kor.	F15	32
Songnim, N. Kor.	E13	32
Sonīpat, India	F7	44
Sonkovo, Russia	D20	22
Sonneberg, Ger.	E11	10
Sonoma, Ca., U.S.	C2	112
Sonoma, co., Ca., U.S.	C2	112
Sonoma Peak, mtn., Nv., U.S.	C4	135
Sonora, state, Mex.	C4	90
Sonora, stm., Mex.	C4	90
Sonoran Desert, des., N.A.	F8	86
Sonoyta, Mex.	B3	90
Sonqor, Iran	D9	48
Sonsón, Col.	E5	84
Sonsonate, El Sal.	D5	92
Son Tay, Viet.	D8	40
Soochow see Suzhou, China	D9	34
Soperton, Ga., U.S.	D4	117
Sophia, W.V., U.S.	D3	155
Sopot, Pol.	A18	10
Sopron, Hung.	H16	10
Sora, Italy	H8	18
Sorata, Bol.	F7	82
Sorel, Que., Can.	C4	104
Soria, Spain	D9	16
Soriano, Ur.	G9	80
Soroca, Mol.	A12	20
Sorocaba, Braz.	G5	79
Soročinsk, Russia	G8	26
Sorong, Indon.	F9	38
Soroti, Ug.	H7	56
Sørøya, i., Nor.	F18	6
Sorrento, Italy	I9	18
Sorrento, La., U.S.	D5	125
Sorris Sorris, Nmb.	C2	66
Sorsogon, Phil.	o21	39b
Sortavala, Russia	E4	26
Sŏsan, S. Kor.	G14	32
Sosnogorsk, Russia	E8	26
Sosnovskoje, Russia	F26	22
Sosnovyj Bor, Russia	B12	22
Sosnowiec, Pol.	E19	10
Sos'va, Russia	F10	26
Sotkamo, Fin.	I21	6
Soto la Marina, Mex.	F10	90
Sotteville, Fr.	C8	14
Soucook, stm., N.H., U.S.	D4	136
Soudan, Mn., U.S.	C6	130
Souderton, Pa., U.S.	F11	145
Soufrière, mtn., Guad.	F14	94
Soufrière, mtn., St. Vin.	H14	94
Souguer, Alg.	C11	62
Sŏul (Seoul), S. Kor.	F14	32
Soulougou, Burkina	E10	64
Soúnion, Ákra, c., Grc.	L8	20
Souq Ahras, Alg.	B14	62
Sources, Mont-aux-, mtn., Afr.	G9	66
Sour el Ghozlane, Alg.	B12	62
Souris, Man., Can.	E1	100
Souris, P.E.I., Can.	C7	101
Souris, stm., N.A.	B6	106
Sousa, Braz.	E11	76
Sousse, Tun.	N5	18
South Acton, Ma., U.S.	g10	128
South Africa (Suid-Afrika), ctry., Afr.	H4	58
South Amboy, N.J., U.S.	C4	137
South America	F8	74
South Amherst, Ma., U.S.	B2	128
Southampton, Ont., Can.	C3	103
Southampton, Eng., U.K.	K12	8
Southampton, N.Y., U.S.	n16	139
Southampton, co., Va., U.S.	D5	153
Southampton Island, i., N.W. Ter., Can.	D16	96
South Andaman, i., India	I2	40
South Australia, state, Austl.	F7	68
Southaven, Ms., U.S.	A3	131
South Baldy, mtn., N.M., U.S.	D2	138
South Barnstead, N.H., U.S.	D4	136
South Barre, Vt., U.S.	C3	152
South Bay, Fl., U.S.	F6	116
South Beloit, Il., U.S.	A4	120
South Bend, In., U.S.	A5	121
South Bend, Wa., U.S.	C2	154
South Berwick, Me., U.S.	E2	126
South Boston, Va., U.S.	D4	153
Southbridge, Ma., U.S.	B3	128
South Bristol, Me., U.S.	E3	126
South Britain, Ct., U.S.	D3	114
South Broadway, Wa., U.S.	C5	154
South Bruny Island, i., Austl.	N7	70
South Burlington, Vt., U.S.	C2	152
Southbury, Ct., U.S.	D3	114
South Carolina, state, U.S.	D6	147
South Carthage, Tn., U.S.	C8	149
South Charleston, W.V., U.S.	C3	155
South Chicago Heights, Il., U.S.	m9	120
South China, Me., U.S.	D3	126
South China Sea, Asia	M7	34
South Coffeyville, Ok., U.S.	A6	143
South Congaree, S.C., U.S.	D5	147
South Connellsville, Pa., U.S.	G2	145
South Dakota, state, U.S.	C5	148
South Dartmouth, Ma., U.S.	C6	128
South Daytona, Fl., U.S.	C5	116
South Deerfield, Ma., U.S.	B2	128
South Dennis, Ma., U.S.	C7	128
South Duxbury, Ma., U.S.	B6	128
South East Point, c., Austl.	L7	70
South Elgin, Il., U.S.	B5	120
Southend-on-Sea, Eng., U.K.	J14	8
Southern Alps, mts., N.Z.	E3	72
Southern Cross, Austl.	F3	68
Southern Ghāts, mts., India	H4	46
Southern Indian Lake, l., Man., Can.	f8	100
Southern Pines, N.C., U.S.	B3	140
South Euclid, Oh., U.S.	g9	142
Southey, Sask., Can.	G3	105
Southfield, Mi., U.S.	o15	129
South Foreland, c., Eng., U.K.	J15	8
South Fork, Co., U.S.	D4	113
South Freeport, Me., U.S.	g7	126
South Fulton, Tn., U.S.	A3	149
South Gastonia, N.C., U.S.	B1	140
South Gate, Ca., U.S.	n12	112
Southgate, Ky., U.S.	h14	124
Southgate, Mi., U.S.	p15	129
South Georgia, i., S. Geor.	J11	74
South Georgia and the South Sandwich Islands, dep., S.A.	J11	74
South Glastonbury, Ct., U.S.	C5	114
South Glens Falls, N.Y., U.S.	B7	139
South Grafton, Ma., U.S.	B4	128
South Hadley, Ma., U.S.	B2	128
South Hadley Falls, Ma., U.S.	B2	128
South Hamilton, Ma., U.S.	A6	128
South Hātia Island, i., Bngl.	I14	44
South Haven, In., U.S.	A3	121
South Haven, Ks., U.S.	E6	123
South Haven, Mi., U.S.	F4	129
South Heart, N.D., U.S.	C3	141
South Hero, Vt., U.S.	B2	152
South Hero Island, i., Vt., U.S.	B2	152
South Hill, Va., U.S.	D4	153
South Hingham, Ma., U.S.	h12	128
South Holland, Il., U.S.	k9	120
South Holston Lake, res., U.S.	A9	149
South Hooksett, N.H., U.S.	D4	136
South Hopkinton, R.I., U.S.	F1	146
South Houston, Tx., U.S.	r14	150
South Hutchinson, Ks., U.S.	f11	123
South Indian Lake, Man., Can.	A2	100
Southington, Ct., U.S.	C4	114
South International Falls, Mn., U.S.	B5	130
South Island, i., N.Z.	E2	72
South Jacksonville, Il., U.S.	D3	120
South Jordan, Ut., U.S.	C3	151
South Lake Tahoe, Ca., U.S.	C4	112
South Lebanon, Oh., U.S.	C1	142
South Londonderry, Vt., U.S.	E3	152
South Lyndeborough, N.H., U.S.	E3	136
South Lyon, Mi., U.S.	F7	129
South Magnetic Pole	B7	73
South Manitou Island, i., Mi., U.S.	C4	129
South Marsh Island, i., Md., U.S.	D5	127
South Miami, Fl., U.S.	G6	116
South Miami Heights, Fl., U.S.	s13	116
South Milwaukee, Wi., U.S.	F6	156
South Negril Point, c., Jam.	E5	94
South Ogden, Ut., U.S.	B4	151
Southold, N.Y., U.S.	m16	139
South Orange, N.J., U.S.	B4	137
South Orkney Islands, is., Ant.	B1	73
South Orrington, Me., U.S.	D4	126
South Paris, Me., U.S.	D2	126
South Pass, Wy., U.S.	D4	157
South Pass, strt., La., U.S.	F6	125
South Patrick Shores, Fl., U.S.	D6	116
South Pekin, Il., U.S.	C4	120
South Pittsburg, Tn., U.S.	D8	149
South Plainfield, N.J., U.S.	B4	137
South Platte, stm., U.S.	C6	106
South Pole, Ant.	D4	73
Southport, Austl.	F10	70
Southport, Eng., U.K.	H10	8
Southport, Fl., U.S.	u16	116
Southport, In., U.S.	E5	121
Southport, N.Y., U.S.	C4	139
Southport, N.C., U.S.	D4	140
South Portland, Me., U.S.	E2	126
South Portsmouth, Ky., U.S.	B6	124
South River, Ont., Can.	B5	103
South River, N.J., U.S.	C4	137
South Royalton, Vt., U.S.	D3	152
South Ryegate, Vt., U.S.	C4	152
South Saint Paul, Mn., U.S.	n12	130
South Sandwich Islands, is., S. Geor.	A2	73
South San Francisco, Ca., U.S.	h8	112
South Saskatchewan, stm., Can.	F11	96
South Shetland Islands, is., Ant.	B1	73
Southside, Al., U.S.	B3	108
South Sioux City, Ne., U.S.	B9	134
South Skunk, stm., Ia., U.S.	C4	122
South Slocan, B.C., Can.	E9	99
South Streator, Il., U.S.	B5	120
South Torrington, Wy., U.S.	D8	157
South Tucson, Az., U.S.	E5	110
South Uist, i., Scot., U.K.	D6	8
South Venice, Fl., U.S.	E4	116
South Wellfleet, Ma., U.S.	C8	128
South Wellington, B.C., Can.	f12	99
South West Africa see Namibia, ctry., Afr.	F3	58
South West City, Mo., U.S.	E3	132
Southwest Harbor, Me., U.S.	D4	126
Southwest Pass, strt., La., U.S.	E3	125
Southwest Pass, strt., La., U.S.	F6	125
South Whitley, In., U.S.	B6	121
South Williamson, Ky., U.S.	C7	124
South Williamsport, Pa., U.S.	D7	145
South Windham, Ct., U.S.	C7	114
South Windham, Me., U.S.	E2	126
South Windsor, Ct., U.S.	B5	114
South Wolfeboro, N.H., U.S.	C4	136
Southwood Acres, Ct., U.S.	A5	114
South Woodstock, Ct., U.S.	B8	114
South Yarmouth, Ma., U.S.	C7	128
South Zanesville, Oh., U.S.	C3	142
Sovetsk, Russia	H20	22
Sovetsk, Russia	F7	26
Sovetsk, Russia	F2	26
Sovetskaja Gavan', Russia	H20	28
Sovetskij, Russia	A11	22
Søvik, Nor.	J10	6
Soweto, S. Afr.	F8	66
Soyapango, El Sal.	D5	92
Spa, Bel.	G8	12
Spain (España), ctry., Eur.	G7	4
Spakenburg, Neth.	D7	12
Spalding, Sask., Can.	E3	105
Spalding, Ne., U.S.	C7	134
Spalding, co., Ga., U.S.	C2	117
Spanaway, Wa., U.S.	B3	154
Spangler, Pa., U.S.	E4	145
Spaniard's Bay, Newf., Can.	E5	102
Spanish Fork, Ut., U.S.	C4	151
Spanish Fort, Al., U.S.	E2	108
Spanish Lake, Mo., U.S.	f13	132
Spanish North Africa, dep., Afr.	J6	16
Spanish Sahara see Western Sahara, dep., Afr.	D4	54
Spanish Town, Jam.	F6	94
Sparkman, Ar., U.S.	D3	111
Sparks, Ga., U.S.	E3	117
Sparks, Nv., U.S.	D2	135
Sparta see Spárti, Grc.	L6	20
Sparta, Ga., U.S.	C4	117
Sparta, Il., U.S.	E4	120
Sparta, Mi., U.S.	E5	129
Sparta, Mo., U.S.	D4	132
Sparta (Lake Mohawk), N.J., U.S.	A3	137
Sparta, N.C., U.S.	A1	140
Sparta, Tn., U.S.	D8	149
Sparta, Wi., U.S.	E3	156
Spartanburg, S.C., U.S.	B4	147
Spartanburg, co., S.C., U.S.	B3	147
Spárti (Sparta), Grc.	L6	20
Spartivento, Capo, c., Italy	K3	18
Sparwood, B.C., Can.	E10	99
Spas-Demensk, Russia	G17	22
Spas-Klepiki, Russia	F23	22
Spassk-Dal'nij, Russia	I18	28
Spátha, Ákra, c., Grc.	N7	20
Spear, Cape, c., Newf., Can.	E5	102
Spearfish, S.D., U.S.	C2	148
Spearman, Tx., U.S.	A2	150
Spearville, Ks., U.S.	E4	123
Speed, In., U.S.	H6	121
Speedway, In., U.S.	E5	121
Spence Bay, N.W. Ter., Can.	C14	96
Spencer, In., U.S.	F4	121
Spencer, Ia., U.S.	A2	122
Spencer, Ma., U.S.	B4	128
Spencer, Ne., U.S.	B7	134
Spencer, N.C., U.S.	B2	140
Spencer, S.D., U.S.	D8	148
Spencer, Tn., U.S.	D8	149
Spencer, W.V., U.S.	C3	155
Spencer, Wi., U.S.	D3	156
Spencer, co., In., U.S.	H4	121
Spencer, co., Ky., U.S.	B4	124
Spencer, Cape, c., Austl.	J2	70
Spencer Gulf, b., Austl.	J2	70
Spencerport, N.Y., U.S.	B3	139
Spencerville, Md., U.S.	B4	127
Spencerville, Oh., U.S.	B1	142
Sperry, Ok., U.S.	A6	143
Spesutie Island, i., Md., U.S.	B5	127
Speyer, Ger.	F8	10
Spezia see La Spezia, Italy	E4	18
Spiceland, In., U.S.	E7	121
Spicer, Mn., U.S.	E4	130
Spiez, Switz.	E8	13
Spijkenisse, Neth.	F5	12
Spindale, N.C., U.S.	B1	140
Spink, co., S.D., U.S.	C7	148
Spirit Lake, Id., U.S.	B2	119
Spirit Lake, Ia., U.S.	A2	122
Spirit Lake, l., Wa., U.S.	C3	154
Spirit River, Alta., Can.	B1	98
Spiritwood, Sask., Can.	D2	105
Spiro, Ok., U.S.	B7	143
Spirovo, Russia	D17	22
Spišská Nová Ves, Slvk.	G20	10
Spitsbergen, i., Sval.	B2	24
Spittal an der Drau, Aus.	I13	10
Split, Cro.	F11	18
Split, Cape, c., N.S., Can.	D5	101
Split Lake, l., Man., Can.	A4	100
Spofford, N.H., U.S.	E2	136
Spokane, Wa., U.S.	B8	154
Spokane, co., Wa., U.S.	B8	154
Spokane, stm., U.S.	B8	154
Spoleto, Italy	G7	18
Spoon, stm., Il., U.S.	C3	120
Spooner, Wi., U.S.	C2	156
Spotswood, N.J., U.S.	C4	137
Spotsylvania, Va., U.S.	B5	153
Spotsylvania, co., Va., U.S.	B5	153
Sprague, Man., Can.	E4	100
Sprague, W.V., U.S.	n13	155
Sprague, stm., Or., U.S.	E5	144
Spratly Islands, is., Asia	D5	38
Spremberg, Ger.	D14	10
Spring, Tx., U.S.	q14	150
Spring, stm., Ar., U.S.	A4	111
Spring Arbor, Mi., U.S.	F6	129
Springbok, S. Afr.	G3	66
Springboro, Oh., U.S.	C1	142
Spring City, Pa., U.S.	F10	145
Spring City, Tn., U.S.	D9	149
Spring City, Ut., U.S.	D4	151
Springdale, Newf., Can.	D3	102
Springdale, Ar., U.S.	A1	111
Springdale, Oh., U.S.	n13	142
Springdale, Pa., U.S.	E2	145
Springdale, S.C., U.S.	D5	147
Springe, Ger.	C9	10
Springer, N.M., U.S.	A5	138
Springerville, Az., U.S.	C6	110
Springfield, Ont., Can.	E4	103
Springfield, Co., U.S.	D8	113
Springfield, Fl., U.S.	u16	116
Springfield, Ga., U.S.	D5	117
Springfield, Il., U.S.	D4	120
Springfield, Ky., U.S.	C4	124
Springfield, Ma., U.S.	B2	128
Springfield, Mn., U.S.	F4	130
Springfield, Mo., U.S.	D4	132
Springfield, Ne., U.S.	C9	134
Springfield, N.J., U.S.	B4	137
Springfield, Oh., U.S.	C2	142
Springfield, Or., U.S.	C4	144
Springfield, Pa., U.S.	p20	145
Springfield, S.D., U.S.	E8	148
Springfield, Tn., U.S.	A5	149
Springfield, Vt., U.S.	E4	152
Springfield, Va., U.S.	g12	153
Springfield, Lake, res., Il., U.S.	D4	120
Spring Glen, Ut., U.S.	D5	151
Spring Green, Wi., U.S.	E3	156
Spring Grove, Il., U.S.	h8	120
Spring Grove, Mn., U.S.	G7	130
Spring Grove, Pa., U.S.	G8	145
Springhill, N.S., Can.	D5	101
Spring Hill, Fl., U.S.	D4	116
Spring Hill, Ks., U.S.	D9	123
Springhill, La., U.S.	A2	125
Spring Hill, Tn., U.S.	B5	149
Spring Hope, N.C., U.S.	B4	140
Spring Lake, Mi., U.S.	E4	129
Spring Lake, N.C., U.S.	B4	140
Spring Lake, l., Me., U.S.	C2	126
Spring Lake Heights, N.J., U.S.	C4	137
Spring Mountains, mts., Nv., U.S.	G6	135
Springs, S. Afr.	F9	66
Springside, Sask., Can.	F4	105
Springsure, Austl.	E8	70
Springvale, Me., U.S.	E2	126
Spring Valley, Ca., U.S.	o16	112
Spring Valley, Ca., U.S.	F5	112
Spring Valley, Il., U.S.	B4	120
Spring Valley, Mn., U.S.	G6	130
Spring Valley, N.Y., U.S.	g12	139
Spring Valley, Wi., U.S.	D1	156
Springville, Al., U.S.	B3	108
Springville, Ia., U.S.	B6	122
Springville, N.Y., U.S.	C2	139
Springville, Ut., U.S.	C4	151
Spruce Grove, Alta., Can.	C4	98
Spruce Knob, mtn., W.V., U.S.	C6	155
Spruce Knob-Seneca Rocks National Recreation Area, W.V., U.S.	C5	155
Spruce Mountain, mtn., Nv., U.S.	C7	135
Spruce Pine, Al., U.S.	A2	108
Spruce Pine, N.C., U.S.	f10	140
Spruce Run Reservoir, res., N.J., U.S.	B3	137
Spurr, Mount, mtn., Ak., U.S.	g15	109
Spy Hill, Sask., Can.	G5	105
Squam Lake, l., N.H., U.S.	C4	136
Square Lake, l., Me., U.S.	A4	126
Squatec, Que., Can.	B9	104
Squibnocket Point, c., Ma., U.S.	D6	128
Squire, W.V., U.S.	D3	155
Srbija (Serbia), state, Yugo.	F4	20
Srbobran, Yugo.	D3	20
Sredinnyj chrebet, mts., Russia	F24	28
Srednekolymsk, Russia	D22	28
Śrem, Pol.	C17	10
Sremska Mitrovica, Yugo.	E3	20
Sretensk, Russia	G15	28
Sri Jayawardenepura (Kotte), Sri L.	I5	46
Srīkākulam, India	C7	46
Sri Lanka, ctry., Asia	H11	42
Srīnagar, India	C6	44
Srīrampur, India	C3	46
Srīrangam, India	G5	46
Srīvilliputtūr, India	H4	46
Środa Wielkopolski, Pol.	C17	10
Stade, Ger.	B9	10
Staden, Bel.	G3	12
Stafford, Eng., U.K.	I11	8
Stafford, Ks., U.S.	E5	123
Stafford, Va., U.S.	B5	153
Stafford, co., Ks., U.S.	D5	123
Stafford, co., Va., U.S.	B5	153
Staffordshire, co., Eng., U.K.	I11	8
Stafford Springs, Ct., U.S.	B6	114
Staines, Eng., U.K.	J13	8
Stakhanov, Ukr.	H5	26
Stalingrad see Volgograd, Russia	H6	26
Stalowa Wola, Pol.	E22	10
Stambaugh, Mi., U.S.	B2	129
Stamford, Austl.	C5	70
Stamford, Ct., U.S.	E1	114
Stamford, Tx., U.S.	C3	150
Stamford, Vt., U.S.	F2	152
Stamping Ground, Ky., U.S.	B5	124
Stamps, Ar., U.S.	D2	111
Stanaford, W.V., U.S.	D3	155
Stanberry, Mo., U.S.	A3	132
Standard, Alta., Can.	D4	98
Standerton, S. Afr.	F9	66
Standish, Me., U.S.	E2	126
Standish, Mi., U.S.	E7	129
Stanfield, Az., U.S.	E3	110
Stanfield, Or., U.S.	B7	144
Stanford, Ky., U.S.	C5	124
Stanford, Mt., U.S.	C6	133
Stanislaus, co., Ca., U.S.	D3	112
Stanley, N.B., Can.	C3	101
Stanley, Falk. Is.	G5	78
Stanley, N.C., U.S.	B1	140
Stanley, N.D., U.S.	A3	141
Stanley, Va., U.S.	B4	153
Stanley, Wi., U.S.	D3	156
Stanley, co., S.D., U.S.	C5	148
Stanleytown, Va., U.S.	D3	153
Stanleyville, N.C., U.S.	A2	140
Stanleyville see Kisangani, Zaire	A5	58
Stanly, co., N.C., U.S.	B2	140
Stanovoj chrebet, mts., Russia	F17	28
Stanovoje nagorje (Stanovoy Mountains), mts., Russia	F14	28
Stans, Switz.	E9	13
Stanthorpe, Austl.	G9	70
Stanton, Ia., U.S.	D2	122
Stanton, Ky., U.S.	C6	124
Stanton, Mi., U.S.	E5	129
Stanton, Ne., U.S.	C8	134
Stanton, N.D., U.S.	B4	141
Stanton, co., Ks., U.S.	E2	123
Stanton, co., Ne., U.S.	C8	134
Stanwood, Wa., U.S.	A3	154
Staples, Mn., U.S.	D4	130
Stapleton, Al., U.S.	E2	108
Star, Id., U.S.	F2	119
Star, Ms., U.S.	C3	131
Stará Boleslav, Czech Rep.	E14	10
Starachowice, Pol.	D21	10
Staraja Russa, Russia	C14	22
Staraja Vičuga, Russia	D24	22
Stara Planina (Balkan Mountains), mts., Eur.	G8	20
Stara Zagora, Bul.	G9	20
Starbuck, Man., Can.	E3	100
Starbuck, Mn., U.S.	E3	130
Star City, Sask., Can.	E3	105
Star City, Ar., U.S.	D4	111
Star City, In., U.S.	C4	121
Star City, W.V., U.S.	B5	155
Stargard Szczeciński (Stargard in Pommern), Pol.	B15	10
Stargo, Az., U.S.	D6	110
Starica, Russia	E17	22
Stark, co., Il., U.S.	B4	120
Stark, co., N.D., U.S.	C3	141
Stark, co., Oh., U.S.	B4	142
Starke, Fl., U.S.	C4	116
Starke, co., In., U.S.	B4	121
Starkville, Ms., U.S.	B5	131
Starobin, Bela.	I10	22
Starodub, Russia	I15	22
Starogard Gdański, Pol.	B18	10
Starožilovo, Russia	G22	22
Star Peak, mtn., Nv., U.S.	C3	135
Starr, co., Tx., U.S.	F3	150
Startex, S.C., U.S.	B3	147
Startup, Wa., U.S.	B4	154
Staryje Dorogi, Bela.	H11	22
Staryj Oskol, Russia	G5	26
Stassfurt, Ger.	D11	10
State Center, Ia., U.S.	B4	122
State College, Pa., U.S.	E6	145
Stateline, Nv., U.S.	E2	135
Staten Island, i., N.Y., U.S.	k12	139
Statenville, Ga., U.S.	F4	117
Statesboro, Ga., U.S.	D5	117
Statesville, N.C., U.S.	B2	140
Statham, Ga., U.S.	C3	117
Statue of Liberty National Monument, N.J., U.S.	k8	137
Staunton, Il., U.S.	D4	120
Staunton, In., U.S.	F3	121
Staunton, Va., U.S.	B3	153
Stavanger, Nor.	L9	6
Stavely, Alta., Can.	D4	98
Stavropol', Russia	H6	26
Stawell, Austl.	K5	70
Stayner, Ont., Can.	C4	103
Stayton, Or., U.S.	C4	144
Steamboat, Nv., U.S.	D2	135
Steamboat Canyon, Az., U.S.	B6	110
Steamboat Mountain, mtn., Mt., U.S.	C4	133
Steamboat Springs, Co., U.S.	A4	113
Stearns, Ky., U.S.	D5	124
Stearns, co., Mn., U.S.	E4	130
Stebbins, Ak., U.S.	C7	109
Steele, Al., U.S.	B3	108
Steele, Mo., U.S.	E8	132
Steele, N.D., U.S.	C6	141
Steele, co., Mn., U.S.	F5	130
Steele, co., N.D., U.S.	B8	141
Steeleville, Il., U.S.	E4	120
Steelton, Pa., U.S.	F8	145
Steelville, Mo., U.S.	D6	132
Steens Mountain, mts., Or., U.S.	E8	144
Steep Falls, Me., U.S.	E2	126
Stefansson Island, i., N.W. Ter., Can.	B11	96
Steffisburg, Switz.	E8	13
Steger, Il., U.S.	B6	120
Steiermark, state, Aus.	H15	10
Steilacoom, Wa., U.S.	f10	154
Steinbach, Man., Can.	E3	100
Steinkjer, Nor.	I12	6
Stellarton, N.S., Can.	D7	101
Stellenbosch, S. Afr.	I4	66
Stenay, Fr.	C12	14
Stendal, Ger.	C11	10
Stephen, Mn., U.S.	B2	130
Stephens, Ar., U.S.	D2	111
Stephens, co., Ga., U.S.	B3	117
Stephens, co., Ok., U.S.	C4	143
Stephens, co., Tx., U.S.	C3	150
Stephens City, Va., U.S.	A4	153
Stephens Lake, res., Man., Can.	A4	100
Stephenson, co., Il., U.S.	A4	120
Stephenville, Newf., Can.	D2	102
Stephenville, Tx., U.S.	C3	150
Stephenville Crossing, Newf., Can.	D2	102
Sterling, Ak., U.S.	g16	109
Sterling, Co., U.S.	A7	113
Sterling, Il., U.S.	B4	120
Sterling, Ks., U.S.	D5	123
Sterling, Ne., U.S.	D9	134
Sterling, Va., U.S.	A5	153
Sterling, co., Tx., U.S.	D2	150
Sterling Heights, Mi., U.S.	o15	129
Sterlington, La., U.S.	B3	125
Sterlitamak, Russia	G9	26
Sterrett, Al., U.S.	B3	108
Stettin see Szczecin, Pol.	B14	10
Stettler, Alta., Can.	C4	98
Steuben, co., In., U.S.	A7	121
Steuben, co., N.Y., U.S.	C3	139
Steubenville, Oh., U.S.	B5	142
Stevens, co., Ks., U.S.	E2	123
Stevens, co., Mn., U.S.	E3	130

Name	Map Ref.	Page
Stevens, co., Wa., U.S.	A7	154
Stevenson, Al., U.S.	A4	108
Stevenson, Ct., U.S.	D3	114
Stevenson, Wa., U.S.	D4	154
Stevens Pass, Wa., U.S.	B4	154
Stevens Point, Wi., U.S.	D4	156
Stevensville, Md., U.S.	C5	127
Stevensville, Mi., U.S.	F4	129
Stevensville, Mt., U.S.	D2	133
Stewart, B.C., Can.	B3	99
Stewart, co., Ga., U.S.	D2	117
Stewart, co., Tn., U.S.	A4	149
Stewart, stm., Yukon, Can.	D5	96
Stewart Island, i., N.Z.	G1	72
Stewarton, Scot., U.K.	F9	8
Stewarts Point, Nv., U.S.	G7	135
Stewartsville, B.C., U.S.	B3	132
Stewartville, Mn., U.S.	G6	130
Stewiacke, N.S., Can.	D6	101
Steyr, Aus.	G14	10
Steytlerville, S. Afr.	I7	66
Stickney, S.D., U.S.	D7	148
Stif, Alg.	B13	62
Stigler, Ok., U.S.	B6	143
Stikine, stm., Ak., U.S.	D13	109
Stilbaai, S. Afr.	J5	66
Stilfontein, S. Afr.	F8	66
Stilis, Grc.	K6	20
Stillhouse Hollow Lake, res., Tx., U.S.	D4	150
Stillmore, Ga., U.S.	D4	117
Stillwater, Mn., U.S.	E6	130
Stillwater, Ok., U.S.	A4	143
Stillwater, co., Mt., U.S.	E7	133
Stilwell, Ok., U.S.	B7	143
Stimson, Mount, mtn., Mt., U.S.	B3	133
Štip, Mac.	H6	20
Stirling, Alta., Can.	E4	98
Stirling, Ont., Can.	C7	103
Stirling, Scot., U.K.	E10	8
Stockbridge, Ga., U.S.	C2	117
Stockbridge, Ma., U.S.	B1	128
Stockbridge, Mi., U.S.	F6	129
Stockerau, Aus.	G16	10
Stockholm, Sask., Can.	G4	105
Stockholm, Swe.	L16	6
Stockton, Ca., U.S.	D3	112
Stockton, Il., U.S.	A3	120
Stockton, Ks., U.S.	C4	123
Stockton, Mo., U.S.	D4	132
Stockton Lake, res., Mo., U.S.	D4	132
Stockton [-on-Tees], Eng., U.K.	G12	8
Stockton Springs, Me., U.S.	D4	126
Stockwell, In., U.S.	D4	121
Stoddard, Wi., U.S.	D2	156
Stoddard, co., Mo., U.S.	E8	132
Stœng Trëng, Camb.	H8	40
Stoke-on-Trent, Eng., U.K.	H11	8
Stokes, co., N.C., U.S.	A2	140
Stokesdale, N.C., U.S.	A3	140
Stolac, Bos.	F12	18
Stolboy, Bela.	H9	22
Stolberg, Ger.	E6	10
Stollings, W.V., U.S.	n12	155
Stolp see Słupsk, Pol.	A17	10
Stone, co., Ar., U.S.	B3	111
Stone, co., Ms., U.S.	E4	131
Stone, co., Mo., U.S.	E4	132
Stoneham, Ma., U.S.	g11	128
Stone Mountain, Ga., U.S.	C2	117
Stone Mountains, mts., U.S.	A1	140
Stonewall, Man., Can.	D3	100
Stonewall, La., U.S.	B2	125
Stonewall, Ms., U.S.	C5	131
Stonewall, co., Tx., U.S.	C2	150
Stonewood, W.V., U.S.	k10	155
Stoney Creek, Ont., Can.	D5	103
Stonington, Ct., U.S.	D8	114
Stonington, Il., U.S.	D4	120
Stonington, Me., U.S.	D4	126
Stony Brook, N.Y., U.S.	n15	139
Stony Plain, Alta., Can.	C3	98
Stony Point, N.C., U.S.	B1	140
Stony Rapids, Sask., Can.	m7	105
Storey, co., Nv., U.S.	D2	135
Storm Bay, b., Austl.	N7	70
Storm Lake, Ia., U.S.	B2	122
Stornoway, Scot., U.K.	C7	8
Storozhynets', Ukr.	A9	20
Storrs, Ct., U.S.	B7	114
Storuman, Swe.	I15	6
Story, Wy., U.S.	B6	157
Story, co., Ia., U.S.	B4	122
Story City, Ia., U.S.	B4	122
Stoughton, Sask., Can.	H4	105
Stoughton, Ma., U.S.	B5	128
Stoughton, Wi., U.S.	F4	156
Stover, Mo., U.S.	C5	132
Stow, Oh., U.S.	A4	142
Stowe, Pa., U.S.	F10	145
Stowe, Vt., U.S.	C3	152
Strafford, Mo., U.S.	D4	132
Strafford, N.H., U.S.	D4	136
Strafford, co., N.H., U.S.	D4	136
Straffordville, Ont., Can.	E4	103
Strahan, Austl.	N6	70
Strakonice, Czech Rep.	F13	10
Stralsund, Ger.	A13	10
Strand, S. Afr.	J4	66
Strangford Lough, l., N. Ire., U.K.	G8	8
Stranraer, Scot., U.K.	G8	8
Strasbourg, Sask., Can.	F3	105
Strasbourg, Fr.	D14	14
Strasburg, Co., U.S.	B6	113
Strasburg, N.D., U.S.	C5	141
Strasburg, Pa., U.S.	G9	145
Strasburg, Va., U.S.	B4	153
Stratford, Ont., Can.	D3	103
Stratford, N.Z.	C5	72
Stratford, Ct., U.S.	E3	114
Stratford, Ia., U.S.	B4	122
Stratford, N.J., U.S.	D2	137
Stratford, Ok., U.S.	C5	143
Stratford, Tx., U.S.	D3	156
Stratford Point, c., Ct., U.S.	E3	114
Stratford-upon-Avon, Eng., U.K.	I12	8
Stratham, N.H., U.S.	D5	136
Strathclair, Man., Can.	D1	100
Strathmore, Alta., Can.	D4	98

Strathroy, Ont., Can.	E3	103
Stratton, Co., U.S.	B8	113
Stratton, Me., U.S.	C2	126
Stratton, Ne., U.S.	D4	134
Stratton Mountain, mtn., Vt., U.S.	E3	152
Straubing, Ger.	G12	10
Strausberg, Ger.	C13	10
Strawberry, stm., Ar., U.S.	A4	111
Strawberry, stm., Ut., U.S.	C5	151
Strawberry Mountain, mtn., Or., U.S.	C8	144
Strawberry Point, Ia., U.S.	B6	122
Strawn, Ks., U.S.	D8	123
Streator, Il., U.S.	B5	120
Stroh, In., U.S.	A7	121
Stromboli, Isola, i., Italy	K10	18
Strome, Alta., Can.	C4	98
Stromsburg, Ne., U.S.	C8	134
Strong, Ar., U.S.	D3	111
Strong, Me., U.S.	D2	126
Strong City, Ks., U.S.	D7	123
Strongsville, Oh., U.S.	A4	142
Stroud, Austl.	I9	70
Stroud, Ok., U.S.	B5	143
Stroudsburg, Pa., U.S.	E11	145
Struer, Den.	M11	6
Struga, Mac.	H4	20
Strugi-Krasnyje, Russia	C12	22
Strum, Wi., U.S.	D2	156
Strumica, Mac.	H6	20
Strunino, Russia	E21	22
Struthers, Oh., U.S.	A5	142
Stryy, Ukr.	H2	26
Strzegom, Pol.	E16	10
Strzelce Opolskie, Pol.	E18	10
Strzelecki Desert, des., Austl.	F4	70
Stuart, Fl., U.S.	E6	116
Stuart, Ia., U.S.	C3	122
Stuart, Ne., U.S.	B6	134
Stuart, Va., U.S.	D2	153
Stuart, stm., B.C., Can.	B5	99
Stuart, Mount, mtn., Wa., U.S.	B5	154
Stuart Lake, l., B.C., Can.	B5	99
Stuarts Draft, Va., U.S.	B3	153
Studen Kladenec, Jazovir, res., Bul.	H9	20
Stupino, Russia	G21	22
Sturbridge, Ma., U.S.	B3	128
Sturgeon, Mo., U.S.	B5	132
Sturgeon Bay, Wi., U.S.	D6	156
Sturgeon Falls, Ont., Can.	A5	103
Sturgeon Lake, l., Ont., Can.	C6	103
Sturgis, Sask., Can.	F4	105
Sturgis, Ky., U.S.	e10	124
Sturgis, Mi., U.S.	G5	129
Sturgis, S.D., U.S.	C2	148
Sturtevant, Wi., U.S.	F6	156
Sturt Stony Desert, des., Austl.	G4	70
Stutsman, co., N.D., U.S.	B6	141
Stutterheim, S. Afr.	I8	66
Stuttgart, Ger.	G9	10
Stuttgart, Ar., U.S.	C4	111
Suakin Archipelago, is., Sud.	H10	60
Subiaco, Ar., U.S.	B2	111
Sublette, Ks., U.S.	E3	123
Sublette, co., Wy., U.S.	D2	157
Sublimity, Or., U.S.	C4	144
Subotica, Yugo.	C3	20
Succasunna, N.J., U.S.	B3	137
Suceava, Rom.	B10	20
Süchbaatar, Mong.	A8	30
Suchiniči, Russia	G18	22
Suchitepéquez, dept., Guat.	C3	92
Suchitoto, El Sal.	D5	92
Suchou see Suzhou, China	E11	30
Suchumi, Geor.	I6	26
Sucre, Bol.	H9	82
Sucre, Ec.	H2	84
Sucre, state, Ven.	B11	84
Sucre, dept., Col.	C5	84
Sucúa, Ec.	I3	84
Sucumbíos, prov., Ec.	H4	84
Sud, Canal du, strt., Haiti	E8	94
Suda, Russia	B20	22
Sudan (As-Sūdān), ctry., Afr.	E7	56
Sudan, reg., Afr.	F9	54
Sudbury, Ont., Can.	A4	103
Sudbury, Ma., U.S.	B5	128
Sudbury, stm., Ma., U.S.	B5	128
Sudbury Center, Ma., U.S.	g10	128
Sudogda, Russia	F23	22
Sueca, Spain	F11	16
Suez see As-Suways, Egypt	C7	60
Suez, Gulf of see Suways, Khalīj as-, b., Egypt	C7	60
Suez Canal see Suways, Qanāt as-, Egypt	C7	60
Suffern, N.Y., U.S.	D6	139
Suffield, Ct., U.S.	B5	114
Suffolk, Va., U.S.	D6	153
Suffolk, co., Eng., U.K.	I15	8
Suffolk, co., Ma., U.S.	B5	128
Suffolk, co., N.Y., U.S.	n15	139
Sufu see Kashi, China	D2	30
Sugar, stm., N.H., U.S.	D2	136
Sugar City, Co., U.S.	C7	113
Sugar City, Id., U.S.	F7	119
Sugar Creek, Mo., U.S.	h11	132
Sugarcreek, Pa., U.S.	D2	145
Sugar Grove, Va., U.S.	D1	153
Sugar Hill, Ga., U.S.	B2	117
Sugar Island, i., Mi., U.S.	B6	129
Sugar Land, Tx., U.S.	E5	150
Sugar Loaf, Va., U.S.	C3	153
Sugarloaf Mountain, mtn., Me., U.S.	C2	126
Sugarloaf Mountain, mtn., Mt., U.S.	C4	133
Suḩār, Oman	B10	47
Suhl, Ger.	E10	10
Suhr, Switz.	D9	13
Suiattle, stm., Wa., U.S.	A4	154
Suichuan, China	I3	34
Suifenhe, China	C13	30
Suihua, China	B12	30
Suining, China	E8	30
Suipacha, Arg.	H9	80

Suiping, China	B2	34
Suitland, Md., U.S.	C4	127
Suixian, China	D2	34
Suizhong, China	C8	32
Suizhou, China	E9	30
Šuja, Russia	E24	22
Sujāngarh, India	G6	44
Sujiatun, China	B11	32
Sukabumi, Indon.	j13	39a
Sukhothai, Thai.	F5	40
Sukkur, Pak.	G3	44
Sul, Canal do, strt., Braz.	D9	76
Sulaco, stm., Hond.	B7	92
Sulawesi (Celebes), i., Indon.	F7	38
Sulejówek, Pol.	C21	10
Sullana, Peru	A1	82
Sulligent, Al., U.S.	B1	108
Sullivan, Il., U.S.	D5	120
Sullivan, In., U.S.	F3	121
Sullivan, Mo., U.S.	C6	132
Sullivan, co., In., U.S.	F3	121
Sullivan, co., Mo., U.S.	A4	132
Sullivan, co., N.H., U.S.	D2	136
Sullivan, co., N.Y., U.S.	D6	139
Sullivan, co., Pa., U.S.	D9	145
Sullivan, co., Tn., U.S.	C11	149
Sullivans Island, S.C., U.S.	k12	147
Sully, Fr.	E9	14
Sully, Ia., U.S.	C5	122
Sully, co., S.D., U.S.	C5	148
Sulmona, Italy	G8	18
Sulphur, La., U.S.	D2	125
Sulphur, Ok., U.S.	C5	143
Sulphur Rock, Ar., U.S.	B4	111
Sulphur Springs, Ar., U.S.	A1	111
Sulphur Springs, Tx., U.S.	C5	150
Sulphur Springs Valley, val., Az., U.S.	E6	110
Sultan, Wa., U.S.	B4	154
Sultānpur, India	G10	44
Sulu Archipelago, is., Phil.	D7	38
Sulūq, Libya	B5	56
Sulu Sea, Asia	D6	38
Sulzbach-Rosenberg, Ger.	F11	10
Sumampa, Arg.	E7	80
Sumas, Wa., U.S.	A3	154
Sumatera (Sumatra), i., Indon.	F3	38
Sumatra see Sumatera, i., Indon.	F3	38
Sumayh, Sud.	K6	60
Sumba, i., Indon.	G7	38
Sumbawa, i., Indon.	G6	38
Sumbawa Besar, Indon.	G6	38
Sumbawanga, Tan.	C6	58
Sumbe, Ang.	D2	58
Šumen, Bul.	F10	20
Sumenep, Indon.	j16	39a
Šumicha, Russia	F10	26
Šumperk, Russia	F10	26
Šumiswald, Switz.	D8	13
Sumiton, Al., U.S.	B2	108
Summerdale, Al., U.S.	E2	108
Summerfield, N.C., U.S.	A3	140
Summerford, Newf., Can.	D4	102
Summer Lake, l., Or., U.S.	E6	144
Summerland, B.C., Can.	E8	99
Summers, co., W.V., U.S.	D4	155
Summerside, P.E.I., Can.	C6	101
Summersville, Mo., U.S.	D6	132
Summersville, W.V., U.S.	C4	155
Summersville Lake, res., W.V., U.S.	C4	155
Summerton, S.C., U.S.	D7	147
Summertown, Tn., U.S.	B4	149
Summerville, Ga., U.S.	B1	117
Summerville, S.C., U.S.	E7	147
Summit, Ar., U.S.	A3	111
Summit, Il., U.S.	k9	120
Summit, Ms., U.S.	D3	131
Summit, N.J., U.S.	B4	137
Summit, Tn., U.S.	h11	149
Summit, co., Co., U.S.	B4	113
Summit, co., Oh., U.S.	A4	142
Summit, co., Ut., U.S.	C5	151
Summit Hill, Pa., U.S.	E10	145
Summit Mountain, mtn., Nv., U.S.	D5	135
Summit Point, W.V., U.S.	B7	155
Summitville, In., U.S.	D6	121
Sumner, Il., U.S.	E6	120
Sumner, Ia., U.S.	B5	122
Sumner, Wa., U.S.	B3	154
Sumner, co., Ks., U.S.	E6	123
Sumner, co., Tn., U.S.	A5	149
Šumperk, Czech Rep.	F16	10
Sumqayıt, Azer.	I7	26
Sumrall, Ms., U.S.	D4	131
Sumter, S.C., U.S.	D7	147
Sumter, co., Al., U.S.	C1	108
Sumter, co., Fl., U.S.	D4	116
Sumter, co., Ga., U.S.	D2	117
Sumter, co., S.C., U.S.	D7	147
Sumy, Ukr.	G4	26
Sumzom, China	F17	44
Sunapee, N.H., U.S.	D2	136
Sunapee Lake, l., N.H., U.S.	D2	136
Sunbright, Tn., U.S.	C9	149
Sunburst, Mt., U.S.	B5	133
Sunbury, Austl.	K6	70
Sunbury, Oh., U.S.	B3	142
Sunbury, Pa., U.S.	E8	145
Sunchales, Arg.	F8	80
Suncho Corral, Arg.	D7	80
Sunch'ŏn, N. Kor.	D13	32
Sunch'ŏn, S. Kor.	I15	32
Sun City, Az., U.S.	k8	110
Suncook, N.H., U.S.	D4	136
Sunda, Selat, strt., Indon.	G4	38
Sundance, Wy., U.S.	B8	157
Sundarbans, reg., Asia	J13	44
Sunderland, Ont., Can.	C5	103
Sundre, Alta., Can.	D3	98
Sundridge, Ont., Can.	B5	103
Sundsvall, Swe.	J15	6
Sunflower, Ms., U.S.	B3	131
Sunflower, co., Ms., U.S.	B3	131
Sunflower, Mount, mtn., Ks., U.S.	C2	123
Sungaipenuh, Indon.	F3	38
Sungai Petani, Malay.	L6	40
Sunjiabu, China	E7	34
Sunland Park, N.M., U.S.	F3	138
Sunman, In., U.S.	F7	121

Sunnyside, Newf., Can.	E5	102
Sunnyside, Wa., U.S.	C5	154
Sunnyvale, Ca., U.S.	k8	112
Sun Prairie, Wi., U.S.	E4	156
Sunrise, Wy., U.S.	D8	157
Sunset, La., U.S.	D3	125
Sunset, Ut., U.S.	B4	151
Sunset Beach, Hi., U.S.	f9	118
Sunset Country, reg., Austl.	J4	70
Sunshine, Austl.	K6	70
Sun Valley, Id., U.S.	F4	119
Sun Valley, Nv., U.S.	D2	135
Sunyani, Ghana	H8	64
Suojarvi, Russia	J23	6
Suonenjoki, Fin.	J20	6
Superior, Az., U.S.	D4	110
Superior, Co., U.S.	B5	113
Superior, Mt., U.S.	C2	133
Superior, Ne., U.S.	D7	134
Superior, Wi., U.S.	B1	156
Superior, Wy., U.S.	E4	157
Superior, Lake, l., N.A.	B9	106
Superstition Mountains, mts., Az., U.S.	m10	110
Suphan Buri, Thai.	G6	40
Suponevo, Russia	H17	22
Sūq ash-Shuyūkh, Iraq	F9	48
Suqian, China	B7	34
Suquamish, Wa., U.S.	B3	154
Suqutrā (Socotra), i., Yemen	G5	42
Şūr (Tyre), Leb.	B4	50
Sur, Point, c., Ca., U.S.	D3	112
Surabaya, Indon.	j16	39a
Surakarta, Indon.	j15	39a
Sūrat, India	J5	44
Surat Thani (Ban Don), Thai.	J5	40
Suraž, Russia	H15	22
Surendranagar, India	I4	44
Surfers Paradise, Austl.	G10	70
Surfside, Fl., U.S.	s13	116
Surfside Beach, S.C., U.S.	D10	147
Surgoinsville, Tn., U.S.	C11	149
Surgut, Russia	E6	28
Surigao, Phil.	D8	38
Surin, Thai.	G7	40
Suriname, ctry., S.A.	C7	76
Surprise, Az., U.S.	k8	110
Surrey, N.D., U.S.	A4	141
Surrey, co., Eng., U.K.	J13	8
Surry, co., N.C., U.S.	A2	140
Surry, co., Va., U.S.	C6	153
Sursee, Switz.	D9	13
Surt, Libya	B4	56
Surt, Khalīj, b., Libya	B4	56
Surtsey, í., Ice.	C3	6a
Susanino, Russia	C24	22
Susanville, Ca., U.S.	B3	112
Šušenskoje, Russia	G16	26
Sušice, Czech Rep.	F13	10
Susitna, stm., Ak., U.S.	C10	109
Susquehanna, Pa., U.S.	C10	145
Susquehanna, co., Pa., U.S.	C10	145
Susquehanna, stm., U.S.	A5	127
Sussex, N.B., Can.	D4	101
Sussex, Wi., U.S.	m11	156
Sussex, co., De., U.S.	F4	115
Sussex, co., N.J., U.S.	A3	137
Sussex, co., Va., U.S.	D5	153
Susuman, Russia	E21	28
Susurluk, Tur.	J12	20
Sutcliffe, Nv., U.S.	D2	135
Sutherland, S. Afr.	I5	66
Sutherland, Ia., U.S.	B2	122
Sutherland, Ne., U.S.	C4	134
Sutherlin, Or., U.S.	D3	144
Sutter, co., Ca., U.S.	C3	112
Sutton, Que., Can.	D5	104
Sutton, Ak., U.S.	g17	109
Sutton, Ne., U.S.	D8	134
Sutton, W.V., U.S.	C4	155
Sutton, co., Tx., U.S.	D2	150
Sutton in Ashfield, Eng., U.K.	H12	8
Sutton Lake, res., W.V., U.S.	C4	155
Suurbraak, S. Afr.	J5	66
Suure-Jaani, Est.	C8	22
Suva, Fiji	H24	2
Suvorov, Russia	G19	22
Suwa, Erit.	G2	47
Suwa, Japan	K13	36
Suwałki, Pol.	A22	10
Suwanee, Ga., U.S.	B2	117
Suwannee, co., Fl., U.S.	B3	116
Suwannee, stm., U.S.	C4	116
Suwaylih, Jord.	D5	50
Suways, Khalīj as- (Gulf of Suez), b., Egypt	C7	60
Suways, Qanāt as- (Suez Canal), Egypt	C7	60
Suwŏn, S. Kor.	F15	32
Suyo, Peru	J2	84
Suzdal', Russia	E23	22
Suzhou (Soochow), China	D9	34
Suzuka, Japan	M11	36
Svalbard, dep., Eur.	B2	24
Svalyava, Ukr.	A6	20
Sv'atoj Nos, mys, c., Russia	C20	28
Svay Riĕng, Camb.	I8	40
Svelvik, Nor.	L12	6
Sven', Russia	H17	22
Švenčioneliai, Lith.	F9	22
Sverdlovsk see Jekaterinburg, Russia	F10	26
Sverdlovs'k, Ukr.	H5	26
Svetlogorsk, Bela.	I12	22
Svetlograd, Russia	H6	26
Svetlyj, Russia	I15	22
Svetogorsk, Russia	K21	6
Svilengrad, Bul.	H10	20
Svir', Russia	H10	22
Svisloč, Bela.	H7	22
Svisloč, Bela.	B24	10
Svištov, Bul.	F9	20
Svobodnyj, Russia	G17	28
Svolvær, Nor.	G14	6
Swain, co., N.C., U.S.	f9	140
Swainsboro, Ga., U.S.	D4	117
Swakop, stm., Nmb.	D2	66
Swakopmund, Nmb.	D2	66

Swampscott, Ma., U.S.	B6	128
Swan Hill, Austl.	J5	70
Swan Hills, Alta., Can.	B3	98
Swan Islands see Santanilla, Islas, is., Hond.	F3	94
Swan Lake, Man., Can.	E2	100
Swannanoa, N.C., U.S.	f10	140
Swan Peak, mtn., Mt., U.S.	C3	133
Swan River, Man., Can.	C1	100
Swansea, Wales, U.K.	J10	8
Swansea, Il., U.S.	E4	120
Swans Island, Me., U.S.	D4	126
Swanson Lake, res., Ne., U.S.	D4	134
Swanton, Oh., U.S.	A2	142
Swanton, Vt., U.S.	B2	152
Swanzey Center, N.H., U.S.	E2	136
Swarthmore, Pa., U.S.	p20	145
Swartz Creek, Mi., U.S.	F7	129
Swarzędz, Pol.	C17	10
Swatow see Shantou, China	L5	34
Swayzee, In., U.S.	C6	121
Swaziland, ctry., Afr.	G6	58
Sweden (Sverige), ctry., Eur.	C11	4
Swedesboro, N.J., U.S.	D2	137
Swedru, Ghana	I9	64
Sweeny, Tx., U.S.	r14	150
Sweet Grass, co., Mt., U.S.	E7	133
Sweet Home, Or., U.S.	C4	144
Sweetser, In., U.S.	C6	121
Sweet Springs, Mo., U.S.	C4	132
Sweetwater, Tn., U.S.	D9	149
Sweetwater, Tx., U.S.	C2	150
Sweetwater, co., Wy., U.S.	E3	157
Sweetwater, stm., Wy., U.S.	D4	157
Sweetwater Creek, Fl., U.S.	p10	116
Swellendam, S. Afr.	J5	66
Świdnica (Schweidnitz), Pol.	E16	10
Świdnik, Pol.	D22	10
Świebodzice, Pol.	E16	10
Świebodzin, Pol.	C15	10
Świecie, Pol.	B18	10
Swift, co., Mn., U.S.	E3	130
Swift Creek Reservoir, res., Wa., U.S.	C3	154
Swift Current, Sask., Can.	G2	105
Swifton, Ar., U.S.	B4	111
Swindon, Eng., U.K.	J12	8
Swink, Co., U.S.	C7	113
Świnoujście (Swinemünde), Pol.	B14	10
Swisher, co., Tx., U.S.	B2	150
Swissvale, Pa., U.S.	k14	145
Switzer, W.V., U.S.	D3	155
Switzerland, Fl., U.S.	m8	116
Switzerland, co., In., U.S.	G7	121
Switzerland, ctry., Eur.	F9	4
Swoyerville, Pa., U.S.	D10	145
Sycamore, Al., U.S.	B3	108
Sycamore, Il., U.S.	B5	120
Syčovka, Russia	F17	22
Sydenham, Ont., Can.	C8	103
Sydney, Austl.	I9	70
Sydney, N.S., Can.	C9	101
Sydney Mines, N.S., Can.	C9	101
Sykesville, Md., U.S.	B4	127
Syktyvkar, Russia	E8	26
Sylacauga, Al., U.S.	B3	108
Sylhet, Bngl.	H14	44
Sylt, i., Ger.	A8	10
Sylva, N.C., U.S.	f9	140
Sylvania, Al., U.S.	A4	108
Sylvania, Ga., U.S.	D5	117
Sylvania, Oh., U.S.	A2	142
Sylvan Lake, Alta., Can.	C3	98
Sylvan Lake, Mi., U.S.	o15	129
Sylvester, Ga., U.S.	E3	117
Symsonia, Ky., U.S.	f9	124
Syracuse see Siracusa, Italy	L10	18
Syracuse, In., U.S.	B6	121
Syracuse, Ks., U.S.	E2	123
Syracuse, Ne., U.S.	D9	134
Syracuse, N.Y., U.S.	B4	139
Syracuse, Ut., U.S.	B3	151
Syrdarja (Syr Darya), stm., Asia	H10	26
Syria, ctry., Asia	B2	42
Syriam, Mya.	F4	40
Syrskij, Russia	I22	22
Sysert', Russia	F10	26
Syzran', Russia	G7	26
Szamotuły, Pol.	C16	10
Szarvas, Hung.	I20	10
Szczecin (Stettin), Pol.	B14	10
Szczecinek (Neustettin), Pol.	B16	10
Szczytno, Pol.	B21	10
Szeged, Hung.	I20	10
Székesfehérvár, Hung.	H18	10
Szekszárd, Hung.	I18	10
Szentendre, Hung.	H19	10
Szentes, Hung.	I20	10
Szolnok, Hung.	H20	10
Szombathely, Hung.	H16	10

Táchira, state, Ven.	D6	84
Tachov, Czech Rep.	F12	10
Tacna, Peru	H6	82
Tacna, Az., U.S.	E1	110
Tacna, dept., Peru	G6	82
Tacoma, Wa., U.S.	B3	154
Taconic Range, mts., U.S.	A1	128
Taco Pozo, Arg.	C7	80
Tacuarembó, Ur.	F11	80
Tacuatí, Para.	B10	80
Tacutu (Takutu), stm., S.A.	F12	84
Tâdepallegūdem, India	D6	46
Tadjemout, Alg.	H12	62
Tādpatri, India	E5	46
T'aebaek-sanmaek, mts., Asia	F16	32
Taech'ŏn, S. Kor.	G14	32
Taegu, S. Kor.	H16	32
Taejŏn, S. Kor.	G15	32
Tafalla, Spain	C10	16
Tafí Viejo, Arg.	D6	80
Taft, Ca., U.S.	E4	112
Taft, Tx., U.S.	F4	150
Taganrog, Russia	F15	4
Tagawa, Japan	N5	36
Tagish Lake, l., Can.	E6	96
Taguatinga, Braz.	B5	79
Tagus (Tejo) (Tajo), stm., Eur.	F3	16
Tahat, mtn., Alg.	I13	62
Tahiti, i., Fr. Poly.	J25	158
Tahlequah, Ok., U.S.	B7	143
Tahoe, Lake, l., U.S.	B3	135
Taholah, Wa., U.S.	B1	154
Tahoua, Niger	D12	64
Tahquamenon, stm., Mi., U.S.	B5	129
Tahsis, B.C., Can.	E4	99
Tahtā, Egypt	D6	60
Tai'an, China	G5	32
T'aichung, Tai.	K9	34
Taif see At-Tā'if, Sau. Ar.	D2	47
Taihang Shan, mts., China	D2	32
Taihe, China	B4	34
Tai Hu, l., China	D9	34
Tailai, China	B11	30
Tailem Bend, Austl.	J7	70
T'ainan, Tai.	L9	34
Taínaron, Ákra, c., Grc.	M6	20
Taining, China	I6	34
Taiobeiras, Braz.	C7	79
T'aipei, Tai.	J10	34
T'aipeihsien, Tai.	J10	34
Taiping, China	M2	34
Taiping, Malay.	L6	40
Taishun, China	H8	34
Taitao, Península de, pen., Chile	F1	78
Taitouying, China	C7	32
T'aitung, Tai.	M10	34
Taiwan (T'aiwan), ctry., Asia	G11	30
Taiwan Strait, strt., Asia	K8	34
Taixian, China	C9	34
Taixing, China	C9	34
Taiyiba, Isr.	D4	50
Taiyuan, China	D9	30
Taizhou, China	C8	34
Ta'izz, Yemen	H4	47
Tajerouine, Tun.	N3	18
Tajga, Russia	F9	28
Tajikistan, ctry., Asia	J12	26
Tajimi, Japan	L12	36
Tajšet, Russia	F11	28
Tajumulco, Volcán, vol., Guat.	B3	92
Takāb, Iran	C9	48
Takahe, Mount, mtn., Ant.	C11	73
Takamatsu, Japan	M9	36
Takaoka, Japan	K12	36
Takapuna, N.Z.	B5	72
Takasaki, Japan	K14	36
Takatsuki, Japan	M10	36
Takayama, Japan	K12	36
Takefu, Japan	L11	36
Tākestān, Iran	C10	48
Takêv, Camb.	I8	40
Takhli, Thai.	G6	40
Takla Lake, l., B.C., Can.	B5	99
Taklimakan Shamo, des., China	D3	30
Takoma Park, Md., U.S.	f8	127
Taku Glacier, Ak., U.S.	k22	109
Takutu (Tacutu), stm., S.A.	F13	84
Tala, Ur.	G8	90
Tala, Ur.	H11	80
Talagante, Chile	G3	80
Talamanca, Cordillera de, mts., C.R.	H11	92
Talara, Peru	J2	84
Talata Mafara, Nig.	E13	64
Talavera de la Reina, Spain	F7	16
Talawdī, Sud.	L6	60
Talbot, co., Ga., U.S.	D2	117
Talbot, co., Md., U.S.	C5	127
Talbotton, Ga., U.S.	D2	117
Talca, Chile	H3	80
Talcahuano, Chile	I2	80
Talcott, W.V., U.S.	D4	155
Taldom, Russia	E20	22
Taldy-Kurgan, Kaz.	H13	26
Talca, U.S.	E4	144
Talgar, Kaz.	I13	26
Taliaferro, co., Ga., U.S.	C4	117
Talica, Russia	F10	26
Talihina, Ok., U.S.	C6	143
Talkeetna, Ak., U.S.	C10	109
Talladega, Al., U.S.	B3	108
Talladega, co., Al., U.S.	B3	108
Tall 'Afar, Iraq	C7	48
Talladega, Al., U.S.	B3	108
Tall, Egypt	C6	60
Tallahassee, Fl., U.S.	B2	116
Tallahatchie, co., Ms., U.S.	B3	131
Tallahatchie, stm., Ms., U.S.	B3	131
Tallangatta, Austl.	K7	70
Tallapoosa, Ga., U.S.	C1	117
Tallapoosa, co., Al., U.S.	C4	108
Tallapoosa, stm., Al., U.S.	C3	108
Talleyville, De., U.S.	A3	115
Tallinn, Est.	B7	22
Tall Kalakh, Syria	D4	48

Name	Map Ref.	Page
Tallmadge, Oh., U.S.	A4	142
Tallulah, La., U.S.	B4	125
Tal'menka, Russia	G14	26
Talsi, Lat.	D5	22
Taltal, Chile	C3	80
Tama, Ia., U.S.	C5	122
Tama, co., Ia., U.S.	B5	122
Tamacuarí, Pico, mtn., S.A.	G10	84
Tamalameque, Col.	C6	84
Tamale, Ghana	G9	64
Tamalpais, Mount, mtn., Ca., U.S.	h7	112
Tamano, Japan	M8	36
Tamaqua, Pa., U.S.	E10	145
Tamaulipas, state, Mex.	F10	90
Tamazula de Gordiano, Mex.	H8	90
Tamazulapan del Progreso, Mex.	I11	90
Tamazunchale, Mex.	G10	90
Tambacounda, Sen.	E3	64
Tāmbaram, India	F6	46
Tambo, Austl.	E7	70
Tambo, stm., Peru	D5	82
Tambo Grande, Peru	A1	82
Tambor, C.R.	H9	92
Tambov, Russia	I24	22
Tambura, Sud.	O4	60
Tamchaket, Maur.	C4	64
Tame, Col.	D7	84
Tamenghest, Alg.	I13	62
Tamiahua, Mex.	G11	90
Tamiahua, Laguna de, b., Mex.	G11	90
Tamiami Canal, Fl., U.S.	G6	116
Tamil Nādu, state, India	G5	46
Tam Ky, Viet.	G10	40
Tampa, Fl., U.S.	E4	116
Tampa Bay, b., Fl., U.S.	E4	116
Tampaón, stm., Mex.	G10	90
Tampere, Fin.	K18	6
Tampico, Mex.	F11	90
Tamsalu, Est.	B9	22
Tamworth, Austl.	H9	70
Tamworth, Ont., Can.	C8	103
Tamworth, N.H., U.S.	C4	136
Tana, Lake, l., Eth.	K9	60
Tanabe, Japan	N10	36
Tanabi, Braz.	F4	79
Tanacross, Ak., U.S.	C11	109
Tanami Desert, des., Austl.	C5	68
Tan An, Viet.	I9	40
Tanana, Ak., U.S.	B9	109
Tanana, stm., Ak., U.S.	C10	109
Tananarive see Antananarivo, Madag.	q22	67b
Tancheng, China	I6	32
Tanch'ŏn, N. Kor.	C16	32
Tānda, India	G10	44
Tandaltī, Sud.	K6	60
Tandil, Arg.	I9	80
Taney, co., Mo., U.S.	E4	132
Taneytown, Md., U.S.	A3	127
Tanga, Tan.	C7	58
Tangail, Bngl.	H13	44
Tanganyika, Lake, l., Afr.	C5	58
Tanger (Tangier), Mor.	C8	62
Tanggu, China	B7	34
Tanggu, China	D5	32
Tanggula Shan, mts., China	D13	44
Tangier see Tanger, Mor.	C8	62
Tangier Sound, strt., Md., U.S.	D6	127
Tangipahoa, co., La., U.S.	D5	125
Tangipahoa, stm., La., U.S.	D5	125
Tangjiang, China	E6	34
Tangjin, S. Kor.	G14	32
Tangshan, China	D6	32
Tangxian, China	E2	32
Tanjungbalai, Indon.	M5	40
Tanjungpandan, Indon.	F4	38
Tanjungpinang, Indon.	N8	40
Tānk, Pak.	D4	44
Tanner, Al., U.S.	A3	117
Tannūrah, Ra's, c., Sau. Ar.	H11	48
Tânout, Niger	D14	64
Tanquinho, Braz.	B9	79
Tanshui, Tai.	J10	34
Tantā, Egypt	B6	60
Tantallon, Sask., Can.	G5	105
Tan-Tan, Mor.	F5	62
Tantoyuca, Mex.	G10	90
Tanzania, ctry., Afr.	C6	58
Taolakepa, China	D11	44
Taos, Mo., U.S.	C5	132
Taos, N.M., U.S.	A4	138
Taos, co., N.M., U.S.	A4	138
Taos Pueblo, N.M., U.S.	A4	138
Taoura, Alg.	M3	18
Taourirt, Mor.	C9	62
Tapa, Est.	B8	22
Tapachula, Mex.	J13	90
Tapajós, stm., Braz.	D7	76
Tapalqué, Arg.	I8	80
Tapanahony, stm., Sur.	C7	76
Tapauá, Braz.	A10	82
Tapejara, Braz.	E12	80
Tapera, Braz.	E12	80
Taperoá, Braz.	B9	79
Tapes, Braz.	F13	80
Tapeta, Lib.	H6	64
Taphan Hin, Thai.	F6	40
Tāpi, stm., India	B2	46
Tapolca, Hung.	I17	10
Tappahannock, Va., U.S.	C6	153
Tappan, N.Y., U.S.	g13	139
Tappan Lake, res., Oh., U.S.	B4	142
Tappen, N.D., U.S.	C6	141
Tappi-zaki, c., Japan	F15	36
Taquara, Braz.	E13	80
Taquari, Braz.	E13	80
Taquaritinga, Braz.	F4	79
Tar, stm., N.C., U.S.	B5	140
Tara, Austl.	F9	70
Tara, Ont., Can.	C3	103
Tara, Russia	F6	28
Ṭarābulus (Tripoli), Leb.	D3	48
Ṭarābulus (Tripoli), Libya	B3	56
Ṭarābulus (Tripolitania), hist. reg., Libya	B3	56
Taraclia, Mol.	D12	20
Taranaki, Mount see Egmont, Mount, mtn., N.Z.	C4	72
Tarancón, Spain	E8	16
Taranto, Italy	I12	18
Taranto, Golfo di, b., Italy	I12	18
Tarapacá, Col.	I8	84
Tarapoto, Peru	B3	82
Tarare, Fr.	G11	14
Tarariras, Ur.	H10	80
Tarascon, Fr.	J8	14
Tarascon, Fr.	I11	14
Tarata, Bol.	G8	82
Tarata, Peru	G6	82
Tarauacá, Braz.	C6	82
Tarawa, atoll, Kir.	H21	158
Tarazona, Spain	D10	16
Tarbes, Fr.	I7	14
Tarboro, N.C., U.S.	B5	140
Tarcoola, Austl.	F6	68
Taree, Austl.	H10	70
Tarentum, Pa., U.S.	E2	145
Targhee Pass, U.S.	E7	119
Tărgovište, Bul.	F10	20
Târgoviște, Rom.	E9	20
Târgu Jiu, Rom.	D7	20
Târgu Mureș, Rom.	C8	20
Târgu-Neamț, Rom.	B10	20
Târgu Ocna, Rom.	C10	20
Tarhūnah, Libya	B3	56
Tari, Pap. N. Gui.	G11	38
Tariba, Ven.	D6	84
Tarifa, Punta de, c., Spain	I6	16
Tariffville, Ct., U.S.	B4	114
Tarija, Bol.	I9	82
Tarija, dept., Bol.	I9	82
Tarim, stm., China	C3	30
Tarim Pendi, China	A9	44
Tarkio, Mo., U.S.	A2	132
Tarkwa, Ghana	I9	64
Tarlac, Phil.	n19	39b
Tarma, Peru	D4	82
Târnăveni, Rom.	C8	20
Tarnobrzeg, Pol.	E21	10
Tarnów, Pol.	E21	10
Tarnowskie Góry, Pol.	E18	10
Taroudant, Mor.	E6	62
Tarpon Springs, Fl., U.S.	D4	116
Tarragona, Spain	D13	16
Tarraleah, Austl.	N7	70
Tarrant, Al., U.S.	B3	108
Tarrant, co., Tx., U.S.	C4	150
Tàrrega, Spain	D13	16
Tarrytown, N.Y., U.S.	D7	139
Tarsus, Tur.	C3	48
Tartagal, Arg.	E9	80
Tartagal, Arg.	B7	80
Tartu, Est.	C9	22
Tartūs, Syria	D3	48
Tarumirim, Braz.	E8	79
Tarusa, Russia	G20	22
Tašauz, Turk.	I9	26
Tashkent see Taškent, Uzb.	j14	39a
Tasikmalaya, Indon.	j14	39a
Taškent, Uzb.	I11	26
Tasman Bay, b., N.Z.	D4	72
Tasmania, state, Austl.	H9	68
Tasmania, i., Austl.	N7	70
Tasman Sea, Oc.	L19	158
Tasso, Tn., U.S.	D9	149
Taštagol, Russia	G9	28
Tata, Hung.	H18	10
Tatabánya, Hung.	H18	10
Tataouine, Tun.	D16	62
Tatarbunary, Ukr.	D13	20
Tataria, state, Russia	F8	26
Tatarsk, Russia	F7	28
Tatarskij proliv, strt., Russia	H20	28
Tatarstan see Tatarija, state, Russia	F8	26
Tate, Ga., U.S.	B2	117
Tate, co., Ms., U.S.	A4	131
Tateville, Ky., U.S.	D5	124
Tatnam, Cape, c., Man., Can.	f9	100
Tatta, Pak.	H2	44
Tattnall, co., Ga., U.S.	D4	117
Tatum, N.M., U.S.	D6	138
Tatvan, Tur.	B7	48
Taubaté, Braz.	G6	79
Taumarunui, N.Z.	C5	72
Taum Sauk Mountain, mtn., Mo., U.S.	D6	132
Taungdwingyi, Mya.	D3	40
Taunggyi, Mya.	D4	40
Taungup, Mya.	E3	40
Taunton, Eng., U.K.	J10	8
Taunton, Ma., U.S.	C5	128
Taupo, N.Z.	C6	72
Taupo, Lake, l., N.Z.	C5	72
Tauranga, N.Z.	B6	72
Taurianova, Italy	K11	18
Tauroa Point, c., N.Z.	A4	72
Taurus Mountains see Toros Dağları, mts., Tur.	H14	4
Tavares, Fl., U.S.	D5	116
Tavda, Russia	F11	26
Tavernes de Valldigna, Spain	F11	16
Tavernier, Fl., U.S.	G6	116
Tavira, Port.	H4	16
Tavoy see Dawei, Mya.	G5	40
Tavşanlı, Tur.	J13	20
Tawakoni, Lake, res., Tx., U.S.	C4	150
Tawas City, Mi., U.S.	D7	129
Tawkar, Sud.	H9	60
Taxco de Alarcón, Mex.	H10	90
Tay, Loch, l., Scot., U.K.	E8	8
Tayabamba, Peru	C3	82
Tayabas, Phil.	A7	39
Taylor, B.C., Can.	A7	99
Taylor, Az., U.S.	C5	110
Taylor, Mi., U.S.	p15	129
Taylor, Ne., U.S.	C7	134
Taylor, Pa., U.S.	D10	145
Taylor, Tx., U.S.	D4	150
Taylor, co., Fl., U.S.	B3	116
Taylor, co., Ga., U.S.	D2	117
Taylor, co., Ia., U.S.	D3	122
Taylor, co., Ky., U.S.	C4	124
Taylor, co., Tx., U.S.	C3	150
Taylor, co., W.V., U.S.	B4	155
Taylor, co., Wi., U.S.	C3	156
Taylor, Mount, mtn., N.M., U.S.	B2	138
Taylor Mill, Ky., U.S.	k14	124
Taylor Mountain, mtn., Id., U.S.	E4	119
Taylors, S.C., U.S.	B3	147
Taylors Falls, Mn., U.S.	E6	130
Taylors Island, i., Md., U.S.	D5	127
Taylorsville, In., U.S.	F6	121
Taylorsville, Ky., U.S.	B4	124
Taylorsville, Ms., U.S.	D4	131
Taylorsville, N.C., U.S.	B1	140
Taylorville, Il., U.S.	D4	120
Taymouth, N.B., Can.	C3	101
Tay Ninh, Viet.	I9	40
Tayoltita, Mex.	E7	90
Taza, Mor.	C8	62
Tazewell, Tn., U.S.	C10	149
Tazewell, Va., U.S.	e10	153
Tazewell, co., Il., U.S.	C4	120
Tazewell, co., Va., U.S.	e10	153
Tazin, stm., Can.	D10	96
Tbessa, Alg.	C15	62
Tbilisi, Geor.	I6	26
Tchetti, Benin	H10	64
Tchibanga, Gabon	B2	58
Tchin-Tabáradene, Niger	D12	64
Tchula, Ms., U.S.	B3	131
Tczew, Pol.	A18	10
Tea, S.D., U.S.	D9	148
Teacapan, Mex.	F7	90
Teague, Tx., U.S.	D4	150
Te Anau, Lake, l., N.Z.	F1	72
Teaneck, N.J., U.S.	h8	137
Teapa, Mex.	I13	90
Teaticket, Ma., U.S.	C6	128
Te Awamutu, N.Z.	C5	72
Tebicuary, stm., Para.	D10	84
Tebingtinggi, Indon.	M5	40
Tébourba, Tun.	M4	18
Téboursouk, Tun.	M4	18
Tecalitlán, Mex.	H8	90
Tecate, Mex.	A1	90
Teche, Bayou, stm., La., U.S.	D4	125
Techirghiol, Rom.	E12	20
Tecomán, Mex.	H8	90
Tecpan de Galeana, Mex.	I9	90
Tecuala, Mex.	F7	90
Tecuci, Rom.	D11	20
Tecumseh, Ont., Can.	E2	103
Tecumseh, Ks., U.S.	k14	123
Tecumseh, Mi., U.S.	G7	129
Tecumseh, Ne., U.S.	D9	134
Tecumseh, Ok., U.S.	B5	143
Tedžen, Turk.	J10	26
Teesside see Middlesbrough, Eng., U.K.	G12	8
Teeswater, Ont., Can.	C3	103
Tefé, Braz.	I10	84
Tegal, Indon.	j14	39a
Tegucigalpa, Hond.	C7	92
Tehachapi, Ca., U.S.	E4	112
Tehachapi Mountains, mts., Ca., U.S.	E4	112
Tehama, co., Ca., U.S.	B2	112
Tehrān, Iran	D11	48
Tehuacán, Mex.	H11	90
Tehuantepec, Golfo de, b., Mex.	J12	90
Tehuantepec, Istmo de, Mex.	I12	90
Teide, Pico de, mtn., Spain	o24	17b
Teixeira Pinto, Gui.-B.	E3	64
Teixeira Soares, Braz.	C13	80
Tejkovo, Russia	E23	22
Tejupilco de Hidalgo, Mex.	H9	90
Tekamah, Ne., U.S.	C9	134
Tekax, Mex.	G15	90
Tekeli, Kaz.	I13	26
Tekirdağ, Tur.	I11	20
Tekoa, Wa., U.S.	B8	154
Te Kuiti, N.Z.	C5	72
Tela, Hond.	B7	92
Télagh, Alg.	C10	62
Tel Aviv-Yafo, Isr.	D3	50
Telde, Spain	o25	17b
Telén, Arg.	I6	80
Telescope Peak, mtn., Ca., U.S.	D5	112
Telford, Pa., U.S.	F11	145
Telkwa, B.C., Can.	B4	99
Tell City, In., U.S.	I4	121
Teller, co., Co., U.S.	C5	113
Tellicherry, India	G3	46
Tellico Plains, Tn., U.S.	D9	149
Telluride, Co., U.S.	D3	113
Tel Megiddo (Armageddon), hist., Isr.	C4	50
Telok Anson, Malay.	L6	40
Teloloapan, Mex.	H10	90
Tema, Ghana	I10	64
Temax, Mex.	G15	90
Temecula, Ca., U.S.	F5	112
Temera, Mor.	D7	62
Temirtau, Kaz.	G12	26
Témiscouata, Lac, l., Que., Can.	B9	104
Temora, Austl.	J7	70
Temosachic, Mex.	C6	90
Tempe, Az., U.S.	D4	110
Temperance, Mi., U.S.	G7	129
Tempio Pausania, Italy	I4	18
Tempisque, stm., C.R.	G9	92
Temple, Ga., U.S.	C1	117
Temple, N.H., U.S.	E3	136
Temple, Ok., U.S.	C3	143
Temple, Tx., U.S.	D4	150
Temple Terrace, Fl., U.S.	o11	116
Tempoal de Sánchez, Mex.	G10	90
Temr'uk, Russia	H5	26
Temuco, Chile	J2	80
Tena, Ec.	H4	84
Tenabo, Mex.	G14	90
Tenafly, N.J., U.S.	B5	137
Tenāli, India	D6	46
Tenants Harbor, Me., U.S.	E3	126
Tende, Col de, Eur.	H14	14
Tenente Portela, Braz.	D12	80
Ténéré, des., Niger	E9	54
Tenerife, i., Spain	o24	17b
Ténès, Alg.	B11	62
Teng'aopu, China	B10	32
Tengchong, China	B5	40
Tenggara, Nusa (Lesser Sunda Islands), is., Indon.	G7	38
Tengiz, ozero, l., Kaz.	G11	26
Tengxian, China	H5	32
Tenino, Wa., U.S.	C3	154
Tenkiller Ferry Lake, res., Ok., U.S.	B6	143
Tenkodogo, Burkina	F9	64
Tennant Creek, Austl.	C6	68
Tennessee, state, U.S.	B5	149
Tennessee, stm., U.S.	D9	106
Tennessee Pass, Co., U.S.	B4	113
Tennessee Ridge, Tn., U.S.	A4	149
Tennille, Ga., U.S.	D4	117
Tenosique, Mex.	I14	90
Tensas, co., La., U.S.	B4	125
Tensas, stm., La., U.S.	B4	125
Tensaw, stm., Al., U.S.	E2	108
Ten Sleep, Wy., U.S.	B5	157
Tenterfield, Austl.	G10	70
Ten Thousand Islands, is., Fl., U.S.	G5	116
Teocaltiche, Mex.	G8	90
Teodelina, Arg.	D8	79
Teófilo Otoni, Braz.	D8	79
Teotihuacán, hist., Mex.	H10	90
Tepalcatepec, Mex.	H8	90
Tepeaca, Mex.	H11	90
Tepehuanes, Mex.	E7	90
Tepeji de Ocampo, Mex.	H10	90
Tepelenë, Alb.	I4	20
Tepi, Eth.	N8	60
Teplice, Czech Rep.	E13	10
Téra, Niger	D10	64
Teramo, Italy	G8	18
Terbuny, Russia	I21	22
Terceira, i., Port.	k21	62a
Tercero, stm., Arg.	G7	80
Terek, stm., Russia	I7	26
Terenos, Braz.	F1	79
Teresina, Braz.	E10	76
Teresópolis, Braz.	G7	79
Termas de Río Hondo, Arg.	D6	80
Termez, Uzb.	J11	26
Termini Imerese, Italy	L8	18
Términos, Laguna de, b., Mex.	I14	90
Termoli, Italy	G10	18
Ternate, Indon.	E8	38
Ternej, Russia	H19	28
Terneuzen, Neth.	F4	12
Terni, Italy	G7	18
Ternopil', Ukr.	H3	26
Ternopil, mys, c., Russia	H20	28
Terpenija, zaliv, b., Russia	H20	28
Terra Alta, W.V., U.S.	B5	155
Terrace, B.C., Can.	B3	99
Terracina, Italy	H8	18
Terra Rica, Braz.	G2	79
Terra Santa, Braz.	I14	84
Terrassa, Spain	D14	16
Terrebonne, Que., Can.	D4	104
Terrebonne, Or., U.S.	C5	144
Terrebonne, co., La., U.S.	E5	125
Terrebonne Bay, b., La., U.S.	E5	125
Terre Haute, In., U.S.	F3	121
Terrell, Tx., U.S.	C4	150
Terrell, co., Ga., U.S.	E2	117
Terrell, co., Tx., U.S.	D1	150
Terrell Hills, Tx., U.S.	k7	150
Terrenceville, Newf., Can.	E4	102
Terreton, Id., U.S.	F6	119
Terry, Ms., U.S.	C3	131
Terry, Mt., U.S.	D11	133
Terry, co., Tx., U.S.	C1	150
Terry Peak, mtn., S.D., U.S.	C2	148
Terrytown, Ne., U.S.	C2	134
Terryville, Ct., U.S.	C3	114
Terschelling, i., Neth.	B7	12
Teruel, Col.	F5	84
Teruel, Spain	E10	16
Tešanj, Bos.	E2	20
Teseney, Erit.	J9	60
Teslin, Yukon, Can.	D6	96
Teslin, stm., Can.	D6	96
Teslin Lake, l., Can.	D6	96
Tessalit, Mali	B9	64
Tessaoua, Niger	E13	64
Tessenderlo, Bel.	F7	12
Testour, Tun.	M4	18
Tesuque, N.M., U.S.	B4	138
Tete, Moz.	E6	58
Teton, co., Id., U.S.	F7	119
Teton, co., Mt., U.S.	C4	133
Teton, co., Wy., U.S.	C2	157
Teton Range, mts., Wy., U.S.	C2	157
Teton Village, Wy., U.S.	C2	157
Tétouan, Mor.	C8	62
Tetovo, Mac.	G4	20
Teuco, stm., Arg.	C8	80
Teúl de González Ortega, Mex.	G8	90
Teulon, Man., Can.	D3	100
Teutopolis, Il., U.S.	D5	120
Tevere (Tiber), stm., Italy	G7	18
Teverya (Tiberias), Isr.	C5	50
Tewksbury, Ma., U.S.	A5	128
Texada Island, i., B.C., Can.	E5	99
Texarkana, Ar., U.S.	D1	111
Texarkana, Tx., U.S.	C5	150
Texas, Austl.	G9	70
Texas, co., Mo., U.S.	D5	132
Texas, co., Ok., U.S.	e9	143
Texas, state, U.S.	D5	150
Texas City, Tx., U.S.	E5	150
Texel, i., Neth.	B6	12
Texhoma, Ok., U.S.	e9	143
Texico, N.M., U.S.	C6	138
Texoma, Lake, res., U.S.	D5	143
Teyateyaneng, Leso.	G8	66
Teywarah, Afg.	D1	44
Teziutlán, Mex.	H11	90
Thabana-Ntlenyana, mtn., Leso.	G9	66
Thabazimbi, S. Afr.	E8	66
Thai Binh, Viet.	D9	40
Thailand (Prathet Thai), ctry., Asia	B3	38
Thailand, Gulf of, b., Asia	I6	40
Thai Nguyen, Viet.	D8	40
Thal, Pak.	D4	44
Thala, Tun.	N3	18
Thalwil, Switz.	D10	13
Thames, N.Z.	B5	72
Thames, stm., Ont., Can.	E3	103
Thames, stm., Eng., U.K.	J12	8
Thames, stm., Ct., U.S.	D7	114
Thamesville, Ont., Can.	E3	103
Thāna, India	C2	46
Thanbyuzayat, Mya.	G4	40
Thanh Hoa, Viet.	E8	40
Thanh Pho Ho Chi Minh (Saigon), Viet.	I9	40
Thanjāvūr, India	G5	46
Thann, Fr.	E14	14
Thar Desert (Great Indian Desert), des., Asia	F4	44
Tharrawaddy, Mya.	F3	40
Thatcher, Az., U.S.	E6	110
Thaton, Mya.	F4	40
Thaya (Dyje), stm., Eur.	G15	10
Thayer, Ks., U.S.	E8	123
Thayer, Mo., U.S.	E6	132
Thayer, co., Ne., U.S.	D8	134
Thayetmyo, Mya.	E3	40
Thayne, Wy., U.S.	D1	157
Thazi, Mya.	D4	40
Thealka, Ky., U.S.	C7	124
Thebes see Thívai, Grc.	K7	20
Thebes, Il., U.S.	F4	120
The Dalles, Or., U.S.	B5	144
The Dells, val., Wi., U.S.	E4	156
Thedford, Ont., Can.	D3	103
The English Companys Islands, is., Austl.	B7	68
The Everglades, sw., Fl., U.S.	G6	116
The Fens, reg., Eng., U.K.	I14	8
The Flume, wtfl, N.H., U.S.	B3	136
The Hague see 's-Gravenhage, Neth.	E5	12
The Lynd, Austl.	B6	70
The Narrows, strt., Wa., U.S.	f10	154
The Pas, Man., Can.	B1	100
The Plains, Oh., U.S.	C3	142
The Rand see Witwatersrand, reg., S. Afr.	E8	66
Theniet el Hadd, Alg.	C12	62
Theodore, Austl.	E9	70
Theodore, Sask., Can.	F4	105
Theodore, Al., U.S.	E1	108
Theodore Roosevelt Lake, res., Az., U.S.	D4	110
Theodore Roosevelt National Park (South Unit), N.D., U.S.	C2	141
Theodore Roosevelt National Park (North Unit), N.D., U.S.	B2	141
Thermopílai (Thermopylae), hist., Grc.	K6	20
Thermopolis, Wy., U.S.	C4	157
Thermopylae see Thermopílai, hist., Grc.	K6	20
The Rock, Austl.	J7	70
Thessalon, Ont., Can.	p19	103
Thessaloníki (Salonika), Grc.	I6	20
Thetford Mines, Que., Can.	C6	104
The Valley, Anguilla	E13	94
The Village, Ok., U.S.	B4	143
The Wash, b., Eng., U.K.	I14	8
Thibodaux, La., U.S.	E5	125
Thicket Portage, Man., Can.	B3	100
Thief River Falls, Mn., U.S.	B2	130
Thielsen, Mount, mtn., Or., U.S.	D4	144
Thiensville, Wi., U.S.	E6	156
Thiers, Fr.	G10	14
Thiès, Sen.	D1	64
Thika, Kenya	B7	58
Thimphu, Bhu.	G13	44
Thingvellir, Ice.	C13	6a
Thionville, Fr.	C13	14
Thíra (Santoríni), i., Grc.	M9	20
Thívai (Thebes), Grc.	K7	20
Thohoyandou, S. Afr.	D10	66
Thomas, Ok., U.S.	B3	143
Thomas, W.V., U.S.	B5	155
Thomas, co., Ga., U.S.	F3	117
Thomas, co., Ks., U.S.	C2	123
Thomas, co., Ne., U.S.	C5	134
Thomasboro, Il., U.S.	C5	120
Thomaston, Ct., U.S.	C3	114
Thomaston, Ga., U.S.	D2	117
Thomaston, Me., U.S.	D3	126
Thomasville, Al., U.S.	D2	108
Thomasville, Ga., U.S.	F3	117
Thomasville, N.C., U.S.	B2	140
Thompson, Man., Can.	B3	100
Thompson, N.D., U.S.	B8	141
Thompson, stm., U.S.	A4	132
Thompson Falls, Mt., U.S.	C2	133
Thomson, Ga., U.S.	C4	117
Thongwa, Mya.	F4	40
Thonon-les-Bains, Fr.	F13	14
Thonze, Mya.	F3	40
Thorburn, N.S., Can.	D7	101
Thoreau, N.M., U.S.	B1	138
Thornbury, Ont., Can.	C4	103
Thorne Bay, Ak., U.S.	n23	109
Thornton, Ont., Can.	C5	103
Thornton, Ar., U.S.	D3	111
Thorntown, In., U.S.	D4	121
Thorold, Ont., Can.	D5	103
Thorp, Wi., U.S.	D3	156
Thorsby, Alta., Can.	C3	98
Thorsby, Al., U.S.	C3	108
Thouars, Fr.	F6	14
Thousand Islands, is., N.Y., U.S.	A4	139
Thousand Lake Mountain, mtn., Ut., U.S.	E4	151
Thrace, hist. reg., Eur.	H10	20
Thrakikón Pélagos, Grc.	I8	20
Three Forks, Mt., U.S.	E5	133
Three Hills, Alta., Can.	D4	98
Three Mile Plains, N.S., Can.	E5	101
Three Oaks, Mi., U.S.	G4	129
Three Pagodas Pass, Asia	G5	40
Three Rivers, Ma., U.S.	B3	128
Three Rivers, Mi., U.S.	G5	129
Three Sisters, mtn., Or., U.S.	C5	144
Throckmorton, co., Tx., U.S.	C3	150
Throop, Pa., U.S.	m18	145
Thu Dau Mot, Viet.	I9	40
Thule, Grnld.	B13	86
Thun, Switz.	E8	13
Thunder Bay, Ont., Can.	o17	103
Thunder Bay, b., Mi., U.S.	D7	129
Thunder Bay, stm., Mi., U.S.	D6	129
Thunderbird, Lake, res., Ok., U.S.	B4	143
Thunderbolt, Ga., U.S.	D5	117
Thunersee, l., Switz.	E8	13
Thur, stm., Switz.	C10	13
Thüringen, state, Ger.	D11	10
Thüringer Wald, mts., Ger.	E10	10
Thurmont, Md., U.S.	A3	127
Thursday Island, Austl.	B8	68
Thurso, Que., Can.	D2	104
Thurso, Scot., U.K.	C10	8
Thurston, co., Ne., U.S.	B9	134
Thurston, co., Wa., U.S.	C2	154
Thurston Island, i., Ant.	C11	73
Thusis, Switz.	E11	13
Tianchang, China	C8	34
Tiandong, China	C9	40
Tianjin (Tientsin), China	D5	32
Tianjin Shi, China	D10	30
Tianlin, China	B9	40
Tianmen, China	E2	34
Tianshui, China	E8	30
Tiantai, China	F10	34
Tiantou, China	I4	34
Tibaji, Braz.	C13	80
Tiber see Tevere, stm., Italy	G7	18
Tibesti, mts., Chad	D4	56
Tibet see Xizang Zizhiqu, prov., China	E3	30
Tiburón, Isla, i., Mex.	C3	90
Tice, Fl., U.S.	F5	116
Tichît, Maur.	B5	64
Tichoreck, Russia	H6	26
Tichvin, Russia	B16	22
Ticino, stm., Eur.	D3	18
Tickfaw, stm., La., U.S.	C5	125
Ticonderoga, N.Y., U.S.	B7	139
Ticul, Mex.	G15	90
Tide Head, N.B., Can.	B3	101
Tidjikja, Maur.	B4	64
Tidore, Indon.	E8	38
Tieli, China	B12	30
Tieling, China	A11	32
Tielt, Bel.	F3	12
T'ienchung, Tai.	L9	34
Tien Shan, mts., Asia	C3	30
Tientsin see Tianjin, China	D5	32
Tierra Amarilla, Chile	D3	80
Tierra Amarilla, N.M., U.S.	A3	138
Tierra Blanca, Mex.	H11	90
Tierra del Fuego, Isla Grande de, i., S.A.	G3	78
Tietê, Braz.	G5	79
Tietê, stm., Braz.	F3	79
Tieton, Wa., U.S.	C5	154
Tiffin, Oh., U.S.	A2	142
Tift, co., Ga., U.S.	E3	117
Tifton, Ga., U.S.	E3	117
Tighennif, Alg.	C11	62
Tighina, Mol.	H3	26
Tignall, Ga., U.S.	C4	117
Tignish, P.E.I., Can.	C5	101
Tigre, stm., Peru	J5	84
Tigris (Dicle) (Dijlah), stm., Asia	F9	48
Tihert, Alg.	C11	62
Tihuatlán, Mex.	G11	90
Tijeras, N.M., U.S.	B3	138
Tijuana, Mex.	A1	90
Tijucas, Braz.	D14	80
Tikal, hist., Guat.	I15	90
Tiko, Cam.	I14	64
Tikrīt, Iraq	D7	48
Tilarán, C.R.	G10	92
Tilburg, Neth.	E7	12
Tilbury, Ont., Can.	E2	103
Tilcara, Arg.	B6	80
Tilden, Il., U.S.	E4	120
Tilden, Ne., U.S.	B8	134
Tilden, Tx., U.S.	E3	150
Tilemsi, Vallée du, val., Mali	B10	64
Tilghman, Md., U.S.	C5	127
Tilimsen, Alg.	C10	62
Tilisarao, Arg.	G6	80
Tillabéri, Niger	D10	64
Tillamook, Or., U.S.	B3	144
Tillamook, co., Or., U.S.	B3	144
Tillamook Bay, b., Or., U.S.	B3	144
Tillery, Lake, res., N.C., U.S.	B2	140
Tilley, Alta., Can.	D5	98
Tillman, co., Ok., U.S.	C2	143
Tillmans Corner, Al., U.S.	E1	108
Tillsonburg, Ont., Can.	E4	103
Tilpa, Austl.	H6	70
Tilton, Il., U.S.	C6	120
Tilton, N.H., U.S.	D3	136
Timā, Egypt	D6	60

Name	Map Ref.	Page
Timaná, Col.	G5	84
Timaru, N.Z.	F3	72
Timbalier Island, i., La., U.S.	E5	125
Timbedgha, Maur.	C5	64
Timber Lake, S.D., U.S.	B4	148
Timberlake, Va., U.S.	C3	153
Timberville, Va., U.S.	B4	153
Timbó, Braz.	D14	80
Timbuktu see Tombouctou, Mali	C8	64
Timimoun, Alg.	F11	62
Timir'azevskij, Russia	F14	26
Timirist, Rås, c., Maur.	B1	64
Timişoara, Rom.	D5	20
Timmins, Ont., Can.	o19	103
Timmonsville, S.C., U.S.	C8	147
Timms Hill, hill, Wi., U.S.	C3	156
Timor, i., Indon.	G8	38
Timor Sea	J16	158
Tims Ford Lake, res., Tn., U.S.	B5	149
Tinaca Point, c., Phil.	D8	38
Tinaquillo, Ven.	C8	84
Tindouf, Alg.	G6	62
Tingha, Austl.	G9	70
Tingo María, Peru	C4	82
Tingri, China	F12	44
Tinley Park, Il., U.S.	k9	120
Tinogasta, Arg.	E5	80
Tínos, Grc.	L9	20
Tinquipaya, Bol.	H9	82
Tinsukia, India	G16	44
Tinte, Cerro, mtn., S.A.	J8	82
Tintina, Arg.	D7	80
Tinton Falls, N.J., U.S.	C4	137
Tioga, La., U.S.	C3	125
Tioga, N.D., U.S.	A3	141
Tioga, co., N.Y., U.S.	C4	139
Tioga, co., Pa., U.S.	C7	145
Tioughnioga, stm., N.Y., U.S.	C4	139
Tipitapa, Nic.	E8	92
Tippah, co., Ms., U.S.	A5	131
Tipp City, Oh., U.S.	C1	142
Tippecanoe, co., In., U.S.	D4	121
Tippecanoe, stm., In., U.S.	C4	121
Tipperary, Ire.	I5	8
Tipperary, co., Ire.	I5	8
Tipton, In., U.S.	D5	121
Tipton, Ia., U.S.	C6	122
Tipton, Mo., U.S.	C5	132
Tipton, Ok., U.S.	C2	143
Tipton, co., In., U.S.	D5	121
Tipton, co., Tn., U.S.	B2	149
Tipton, Mount, mtn., Az., U.S.	B1	110
Tiptonville, Tn., U.S.	A2	149
Tip Top Mountain, mtn., Ont., Can.	o18	103
Tiradentes, Braz.	F6	79
Tīrān, Madīq, strt.	D8	60
Tiran, Strait of see Tīrān, Madīq, strt.	D8	60
Tiranë, Alb.	H3	20
Tiraque, Bol.	G9	82
Tiraspol, Mol.	H3	26
Tirat Karmel, Isr.	C3	50
Tírnavos, Grc.	J6	20
Tirol, state, Aus.	H10	10
Tiros, Braz.	E6	79
Tiruchchirāppalli, India	G5	46
Tirunelveli, India	H4	46
Tirupati, India	F5	46
Tiruppur, India	G4	46
Tiruvannāmalai, India	F5	46
Tiruvottiyūr, India	F6	46
Tisa (Tisza) (Tysa), stm., Eur.	C4	20
Tisdale, Sask., Can.	E3	105
Tishomingo, Ok., U.S.	C5	143
Tishomingo, co., Ms., U.S.	A5	131
Tisisat Falls, wtfl, Eth.	L9	60
Tissemsilt, Alg.	C11	62
Tisza (Tisa) (Tysa), stm., Eur.	C4	20
Tiszafüred, Hung.	H20	10
Tiszavasvári, Hung.	H21	10
Titicaca, Lago, l., S.A.	F7	82
Titov Veles, Mac.	H5	20
Titus, co., Tx., U.S.	C5	150
Titusville, Fl., U.S.	D6	116
Titusville, Pa., U.S.	C2	145
Tiverton, Ont., Can.	C3	103
Tiverton, R.I., U.S.	D6	146
Tivoli, Italy	H7	18
Tizimín, Mex.	G15	90
Tizi-Ouzou, Alg.	B13	62
Tiznit, Mor.	F6	62
Tlacotalpan, Mex.	H12	90
Tlacotepec, Mex.	I10	90
Tlahualilo de Zaragoza, Mex.	D8	90
Tlalnepantla, Mex.	H10	90
Tlaltenango de Sánchez Román, Mex.	G8	90
Tlaquepaque, Mex.	G8	90
Tlaxcala [de Xicoténcatl], Mex.	H10	90
Toadlena, N.M., U.S.	A1	138
Toamasina, Madag.	q23	67b
Toano, Va., U.S.	C6	153
Toay, Arg.	I6	80
Toba, Danau, l., Indon.	M5	40
Tobago, i., Trin.	I14	94
Toba Inlet, b., B.C., Can.	D5	99
Tobin, Mount, mtn., Nv., U.S.	C4	135
Tobin Lake, l., Sask., Can.	D4	105
Tobique, stm., N.B., Can.	B2	101
Tobol'sk, Russia	F11	26
Tobruk see Tubruq, Libya	A2	56
Tocantínia, Braz.	E9	76
Tocantinópolis, Braz.	E9	76
Tocantins, stm., Braz.	D9	76
Toccoa, Ga., U.S.	B3	117
Toccoa, stm., Ga., U.S.	B2	117
Toccoa Falls, Ga., U.S.	B3	117
Tochigi, Japan	K14	36
Tocoa, Hond.	B8	92
Tocopilla, Chile	B3	80
Tocumwal, Austl.	J6	70
Todd, co., Ky., U.S.	D2	124
Todd, co., Mn., U.S.	D4	130
Todd, co., S.D., U.S.	D5	148
Todos Santos, Bol.	G9	82
Todos Santos, Mex.	F4	90
Tofield, Alta., Can.	C4	98
Tofino, B.C., Can.	E5	99
Togiak, Ak., U.S.	D7	109
Togo, Sask., Can.	F5	105
Togo, ctry., Afr.	G7	54
Togučin, Russia	F14	26
Togwotee Pass, Wy., U.S.	C2	157
Tohatchi, N.M., U.S.	B1	138
Toinya, Sud.	N5	60
Toiyabe Range, mts., Nv., U.S.	D4	135
Tok, Ak., U.S.	C11	109
Tokar'ovka, Russia	J24	22
Tokat, Tur.	A4	48
Tokelau, dep., Oc.	G1	2
Tokmak, Kyrg.	I13	26
Tokoroa, N.Z.	C5	72
Toksook Bay, Ak., U.S.	C7	109
Toksovo, Russia	A13	22
Tokushima, Japan	M9	36
Tokuyama, Japan	M6	36
Tōkyō, Japan	L14	36
Tokyo Bay see Tōkyō-wan, b., Japan	L14	36
Tōkyō-wan, b., Japan	L14	36
Tolé, Pan.	I13	92
Toledo, Braz.	C12	80
Toledo, Spain	F7	16
Toledo, Il., U.S.	D5	120
Toledo, Ia., U.S.	B5	122
Toledo, Oh., U.S.	A2	142
Toledo, Or., U.S.	C3	144
Toledo, Wa., U.S.	C3	154
Toledo Bend Reservoir, res., U.S.	C2	125
Toler, Ky., U.S.	C7	124
Tolga, Alg.	C13	62
Toliara, Madag.	s20	67b
Tolima, dept., Col.	F5	84
Tolima, Nevado del, mtn., Col.	E5	84
Toljatti, Russia	G7	26
Tolland, Ct., U.S.	B6	114
Tolland, co., Ct., U.S.	B6	114
Tollesboro, Ky., U.S.	B6	124
Tolleson, Az., U.S.	m8	110
Tollette, Ar., U.S.	D2	111
Tolmačovo, Russia	C12	22
Tolmezzo, Italy	C8	18
Tolna, Hung.	I18	10
Tolna, N.D., U.S.	B7	141
Toločin, Bela.	G12	22
Tolono, Il., U.S.	D5	120
Tolosa, Spain	B9	16
Toltén, Chile	D2	78
Tolú, Col.	C5	84
Toluca, Il., U.S.	C4	120
Toluca, Nevado de, vol., Mex.	H10	90
Toluca [de Lerdo], Mex.	H10	90
Tomah, Wi., U.S.	E3	156
Tomahawk, Wi., U.S.	C4	156
Tomakomai, Japan	e16	36a
Tomar, Port.	F3	16
Tomás Gomensoro, Ur.	F10	80
Tomaszów Lubelski, Pol.	E23	10
Tomaszów Mazowiecki, Pol.	D20	10
Tomatlán, Mex.	H7	90
Tomave, Bol.	I8	82
Tomball, Tx., U.S.	D5	150
Tombigbee, stm., U.S.	D1	108
Tombos, Braz.	F7	79
Tombouctou (Timbuktu), Mali	C8	64
Tombstone, Az., U.S.	F5	110
Tombua, Ang.	E2	58
Tomé, Chile	I2	80
Tome, N.M., U.S.	C3	138
Tomelloso, Spain	F8	16
Tom Green, co., Tx., U.S.	D2	150
Tomini, Teluk, b., Indon.	F7	38
Tominian, Mali	E7	64
Tommot, Russia	F17	28
Tom Nevers Head, c., Ma., U.S.	D8	128
Tomo, stm., Col.	E8	84
Tompkins, Sask., Can.	G1	105
Tompkins, co., N.Y., U.S.	C4	139
Tompkinsville, Ky., U.S.	D4	124
Tom Price, Austl.	D3	68
Tomsk, Russia	F8	28
Toms River, N.J., U.S.	C4	137
Tonalá, Mex.	I13	90
Tonasket, Wa., U.S.	A6	154
Tonawanda, N.Y., U.S.	B2	139
Tonbridge, Eng., U.K.	J14	8
Tondano, Indon.	E7	38
Tønder, Den.	N11	6
Tondoro, Nmb.	A4	66
Tonekābon, Iran	C11	48
Tonga, ctry., Oc.	H1	2
Tongaat, S. Afr.	G10	66
Tonganoxie, Ks., U.S.	C8	123
Tongcheng, China	D5	34
Tongchuan, China	D8	30
Tongguan, China	E9	30
Tonghai, China	G1	34
Tonghua, China	B7	40
Tongjosŏn-man, b., N. Kor.	D16	32
Tongliao, China	D9	34
Tongliao, China	C11	30
Tongue, stm., Mt., U.S.	E10	133
Tongxian, China	D4	32
Tongyu, China	C11	30
Tonj, Sud.	N5	60
Tonk, India	G6	44
Tonkin, Gulf of, b., Asia	D10	40
Tonneins, Fr.	H7	14
Tonnerre, Fr.	E10	14
Tonopah, Nv., U.S.	E4	135
Tonosí, Pan.	D2	84
Tonota, Bots.	C8	66
Tønsberg, Nor.	L12	6
Tonumah, Austl.	G8	70
Tooele, Ut., U.S.	C3	151
Tooele, co., Ut., U.S.	C2	151
Toole, co., Mt., U.S.	B5	133
Toombs, co., Ga., U.S.	D4	117
Toomsboro, Ga., U.S.	D3	117
Toowoomba, Austl.	F9	70
Topeka, In., U.S.	A6	121
Topeka, Ks., U.S.	C8	123
Topki, Russia	F9	28
Topock, Az., U.S.	C1	110
Topol'čany, Slvk.	G18	10
Topolobampo, Mex.	E5	90
Toppenish, Wa., U.S.	C5	154
Topsfield, Ma., U.S.	A6	128
Topsham, Me., U.S.	E3	126
Topton, Pa., U.S.	F10	145
Torbat-e Heydarīyeh, Iran	D15	48
Torbat-e Jām, Iran	D16	48
Torbay see Torquay, Eng., U.K.	K10	8
Torbejevo, Russia	G26	22
Torez, Ukr.	H5	26
Torgau, Ger.	D13	10
Torino (Turin), Italy	D2	18
Torit, Sud.	H7	56
Tornio, Fin.	I19	6
Tornquist, Arg.	J7	80
Toro, Spain	D6	16
Törökszentmiklós, Hung.	H20	10
Toroni, Nevado, mtn., S.A.	H7	82
Toronto, Ont., Can.	D5	103
Toronto, Oh., U.S.	B5	142
Toropec, Russia	E14	22
Toros Dağları, mts., Tur.	H14	4
Torquay, Sask., Can.	H4	105
Torquay, Eng., U.K.	K10	8
Torrance, Ca., U.S.	n12	112
Torrance, co., N.M., U.S.	C3	138
Torre del Campo, Spain	H8	16
Torredonjimeno, Spain	H8	16
Torrejón de Ardoz, Spain	E8	16
Torrelavega, Spain	B7	16
Torremaggiore, Italy	H10	18
Torremolinos, Spain	I7	16
Torrens, Lake, l., Austl.	H2	70
Torrent, Spain	F11	16
Torreón, Mex.	E8	90
Torres, Braz.	E14	80
Torres Strait, strt., Oc.	B8	68
Torrevieja, Spain	H11	16
Torrington, Ct., U.S.	B3	114
Torrington, Wy., U.S.	D8	157
Torrinha, Braz.	G4	79
Tórshavn, Faer. Is.	D8	6b
Tórtolas, Cerro de las, mtn., S.A.	E4	80
Tortona, Italy	E3	18
Tortosa, Spain	E12	16
Tortue, Île de la, i., Haiti	D8	94
Toruń, Pol.	B18	10
Torup, Swe.	M13	6
Tõrva, Est.	C8	22
Torzők, Russia	F4	26
Toscana (Tuscany), prov., Italy	F5	18
Tosno, Russia	B13	22
Tostado, Arg.	E8	80
Totana, Spain	H10	16
Toteng, Bots.	C6	66
Tot'ma, Russia	B25	22
Totness, Sur.	E14	84
Totonicapán, Guat.	C3	92
Totonicapán, dept., Guat.	B3	92
Totowa, N.J., U.S.	B4	137
Tototlán, Mex.	G8	90
Tottori, Japan	L9	36
Touba, C. Iv.	G6	64
Toubkal, Jebel, mtn., Mor.	E7	62
Toudaogou, China	A17	32
Tougan, Burkina	E8	64
Touggourt, Alg.	D13	62
Toukoto, Mali	E5	64
Toul, Fr.	D12	14
Touliu, Tai.	L9	34
Toulon, Fr.	I12	14
Toulon, Il., U.S.	B4	120
Toulouse, Fr.	I8	14
Toungoo, Mya.	E4	40
Tourcoing, Fr.	B10	14
Tournai (Doornik), Bel.	G3	12
Tournus, Fr.	F11	14
Tours, Fr.	E7	14
Tousside, Pic, mtn., Chad.	D4	56
Toussvrier, S. Afr.	I5	66
Tovar, Ven.	C7	84
Toverkovskij, Russia	H21	22
Towanda, Ks., U.S.	E7	123
Towanda, Pa., U.S.	C9	145
Towaoc, Co., U.S.	D2	113
Tower City, N.D., U.S.	C8	141
Town Creek, Al., U.S.	A2	108
Towner, N.D., U.S.	A5	141
Towner, co., N.D., U.S.	A6	141
Townley, Al., U.S.	B2	108
Townsend, De., U.S.	C3	115
Townsend, Mt., U.S.	D5	133
Townsend, Mount, mtn., Austl.	K8	70
Townshend Island, i., Austl.	D9	70
Townsville, Austl.	B7	70
Towson, Md., U.S.	B4	155
Toyah, Tx., U.S.	D1	150
Toyama, Japan	K12	36
Toyohashi, Japan	M11	36
Toyokawa, Japan	M12	36
Toyonaka, Japan	M10	36
Toyota, Japan	L11	36
Tozeur, Tun.	D15	62
Trabzon, Tur.	G15	4
Tracadie, N.B., Can.	B5	101
Tracy, N.B., Can.	D3	101
Tracy, Que., Can.	C4	104
Tracy, Mn., U.S.	F3	130
Tracy City, Tn., U.S.	D8	149
Tracyton, Wa., U.S.	e10	154
Tradewater, stm., Ky., U.S.	C2	124
Traer, Ia., U.S.	B5	122
Trafalgar, In., U.S.	F5	121
Trafalgar, Cabo, c., Spain	I5	16
Trafford, Pa., U.S.	k14	145
Traiguén, Chile	J2	80
Trail, B.C., Can.	E9	99
Trail Creek, In., U.S.	A4	121
Traill, co., N.D., U.S.	B8	141
Trakai, Lith.	G7	22
Trakya, hist. reg., Eur.	H13	20
Tralee, Ire.	I6	8
Tramore, Ire.	I6	8
Tranås, Swe.	N12	6
Tranebjerg, Den.	N12	6
Trang, Thai.	K5	40
Trangahy, Madag.	q21	67b
Trani, Italy	H11	18
Tranqueras, Ur.	F11	80
Transantarctic Mountains, mts., Ant.	D9	73
Transkei, hist. reg., S. Afr.	H9	66
Transylvania, co., N.C., U.S.	f10	140
Transylvania, hist. reg., Rom.	C7	20
Transylvanian Alps see Carpaţii Meridionali, mts., Rom.	D8	20
Trapani, Italy	K7	18
Trappe, Md., U.S.	C5	127
Traralgon, Austl.	L7	70
Trasimeno, Lago, l., Italy	F7	18
Traskwood, Ar., U.S.	C3	111
Trás-os-Montes, hist. reg., Port.	D4	16
Traun, Aus.	G14	10
Travelers Rest, S.C., U.S.	B3	147
Traverse, co., Mn., U.S.	E2	130
Traverse, Lake, l., U.S.	B9	148
Traverse City, Mi., U.S.	D5	129
Travis, co., Tx., U.S.	D4	150
Travnik, Bos.	E12	18
Treasure, co., Mt., U.S.	D9	133
Treasure Island Naval Station, mil., Ca., U.S.	h8	112
Třebíč, Czech Rep.	F15	10
Trebinje, Bos.	G2	20
Trebišov, Slvk.	G21	10
Treblinka, Pol.	C22	10
Trego, co., Ks., U.S.	D4	123
Tregosse Islets, is., Austl.	A9	70
Tréguier, Fr.	D3	14
Treherne, Man., Can.	E2	100
Treinta y Tres, Ur.	G11	80
Trélazé, Fr.	E6	14
Trelew, Arg.	E3	78
Trelleborg, Swe.	N13	6
Tremblant, Mont, mtn., Que., Can.	C3	104
Tremont, Il., U.S.	C4	120
Tremont, Pa., U.S.	E9	145
Tremonton, Ut., U.S.	B3	151
Trempealeau, Wi., U.S.	D2	156
Trempealeau, co., Wi., U.S.	D2	156
Trenche, stm., Que., Can.	B5	104
Trenčín, Slvk.	G18	10
Trenel, Arg.	H6	80
Trenque Lauquen, Arg.	H7	80
Trent see Trento, Italy	C6	18
Trente et un Milles, Lac des, l., Que., Can.	C2	104
Trentino-Alto Adige, prov., Italy	C6	18
Trento, Italy	C6	18
Trenton, N.S., Can.	D7	101
Trenton, Ont., Can.	C7	103
Trenton, Ga., U.S.	B1	117
Trenton, Il., U.S.	E4	120
Trenton, Mi., U.S.	F7	129
Trenton, Mo., U.S.	A4	132
Trenton, N.J., U.S.	C3	137
Trenton, N.C., U.S.	C5	142
Trenton, Oh., U.S.	C1	142
Trenton, Tn., U.S.	B3	149
Trenton, Tx., U.S.	C4	150
Trepassey, Newf., Can.	E5	102
Trepassey Bay, b., Newf., Can.	E5	102
Tres Algarrobos, Arg.	H7	80
Tres Arroyos, Arg.	J8	80
Três Corações, Braz.	F6	79
Três Coroas, Braz.	E13	80
Tres de Maio, Braz.	D11	80
Três Fronteiras, Braz.	F3	79
Tres Isletas, Arg.	D8	80
Três Lagoas, Braz.	F3	79
Tres Lomas, Arg.	I7	80
Três Marias, Reprêsa de, res., Braz.	E6	79
Três Passos, Braz.	D12	80
Três Pontas, Braz.	F6	79
Tres Puntas, Cabo, c., Arg.	F3	78
Tres Puntas, Cabo, c., Guat.	B6	92
Três Rios, Braz.	G7	79
Treutlen, co., Ga., U.S.	D4	117
Treviglio, Italy	D4	18
Treviso, Italy	D7	18
Trévoux, Fr.	G11	14
Treynor, Ia., U.S.	C2	122
Trezevant, Tn., U.S.	A3	149
Triabunna, Austl.	N7	70
Triadelphia, W.V., U.S.	A4	155
Triánda, Grc.	M12	20
Triangle, Va., U.S.	B5	153
Tribune, Ks., U.S.	D2	123
Trichardt, S. Afr.	F9	66
Trichūr, India	G4	46
Tri City, Or., U.S.	E3	144
Trier, Ger.	F6	10
Trieste, Italy	D8	18
Trigg, co., Ky., U.S.	D2	124
Triglav, mtn., Slvn.	C8	18
Trigo Mountains, mts., Az., U.S.	D1	110
Trikala, Grc.	J5	20
Trikora, Puncak, mtn., Indon.	F10	38
Trim, Ire.	H6	8
Tri Lakes, In., U.S.	B7	121
Trimble, Tn., U.S.	A2	149
Trimble, co., Ky., U.S.	B4	124
Trimont, Mn., U.S.	G4	130
Trincheras, Mex.	B4	90
Trincomalee, Sri L.	H6	46
Trindade, Braz.	D4	79
Trindade, i., Braz.	G12	74
Třinec, Czech Rep.	F18	10
Tring Jonction, Que., Can.	C6	104
Trinidad, Bol.	F9	82
Trinidad, Col.	E7	84
Trinidad, Cuba	D5	94
Trinidad, Co., U.S.	D6	113
Trinidad, Ur.	G10	80
Trinidad, i., Trin.	I14	94
Trinidad and Tobago, ctry., N.A.	I14	94
Trinity, Newf., Can.	D5	102
Trinity, Al., U.S.	A2	108
Trinity, co., Ca., U.S.	B2	112
Trinity, co., Tx., U.S.	D5	150
Trinity, stm., Ca., U.S.	B2	112
Trinity, stm., Tx., U.S.	D5	150
Trinity Bay, b., Newf., Can.	D5	102
Trion, Ga., U.S.	B1	117
Tripoli see Ṭarābulus, Leb.	D3	48
Tripoli see Ṭarābulus, Libya	B3	56
Tripoli, Ia., U.S.	B5	122
Tripolis, Grc.	L6	20
Tripp, S.D., U.S.	D8	148
Tripp, co., S.D., U.S.	D6	148
Tripura, state, India	I14	44
Tristan da Cunha Group, is., St. Hel.	L5	52
Triumph, La., U.S.	E6	125
Trivandrum, India	H4	46
Trnava, Slvk.	G17	10
Trochu, Alta., Can.	D4	98
Trogir, Cro.	F11	18
Troick, Russia	G10	26
Troicko-Pečorsk, Russia	E9	26
Troisdorf, Ger.	E7	10
Trois-Pistoles, Que., Can.	A8	104
Trois-Rivières, Que., Can.	C5	104
Trois-Rivières-Ouest, Que., Can.	C5	104
Trojan, Bul.	G8	20
Trollhättan, Swe.	L13	6
Trombetas, stm., Braz.	H14	84
Tromsø, Nor.	G16	6
Tronador, Monte, mtn., S.A.	E2	78
Troncoso, Mex.	F8	90
Trondheim, Nor.	J12	6
Troon, Scot., U.K.	F9	8
Trostyanets', Ukr.	A13	20
Trotwood, Oh., U.S.	C1	142
Troup, co., Ga., U.S.	C1	117
Trousdale, co., Tn., U.S.	A5	149
Trout Creek, Ont., Can.	B5	103
Trout Lake, Mi., U.S.	B5	129
Trout Lake, l., Ont., Can.	o16	103
Troutman, N.C., U.S.	B2	140
Trout River, Newf., Can.	D2	102
Trouville [-sur-Mer], Fr.	C7	14
Trowbridge, Eng., U.K.	J11	8
Troy, Al., U.S.	D4	108
Troy, Id., U.S.	C2	119
Troy, Il., U.S.	E4	120
Troy, Ks., U.S.	C8	123
Troy, Mo., U.S.	C7	132
Troy, Mt., U.S.	B1	133
Troy, N.H., U.S.	E2	136
Troy, N.Y., U.S.	C7	139
Troy, N.C., U.S.	B3	140
Troy, Oh., U.S.	B1	142
Troy, Pa., U.S.	C8	145
Troy, Tn., U.S.	A2	149
Troy, Vt., U.S.	B4	152
Troy, hist., Tur.	J10	20
Troy Peak, mtn., Nv., U.S.	E6	135
Trubč'ovsk, Russia	I16	22
Truchas, N.M., U.S.	A4	138
Truchas Peak, mtn., N.M., U.S.	B4	138
Truckee, Ca., U.S.	C3	112
Truckee, stm., U.S.	D2	135
Trujillo, Hond.	B8	92
Trujillo, Peru	B2	82
Trujillo, Spain	F6	16
Trujillo, Ven.	C7	84
Trujillo, state, Ven.	C7	84
Truk Islands, is., Micron.	H19	158
Truman, Mn., U.S.	G4	130
Trumann, Ar., U.S.	B5	111
Trumbull, Ct., U.S.	E3	114
Trumbull, co., Oh., U.S.	A5	142
Trumbull, Mount, mtn., Az., U.S.	A2	110
Truro, N.S., Can.	D6	101
Trussville, Al., U.S.	B3	108
Truth or Consequences (Hot Springs), N.M., U.S.	D2	138
Trutnov, Czech Rep.	E15	10
Tryon, N.C., U.S.	f10	140
Trzebinia, Pol.	E19	10
Tsala Apokka Lake, l., Fl., U.S.	D4	116
Tsaratanana, Madag.	p22	67b
Tsaratanana, Massif du, mts., Madag.	o23	67b
Tsévié, Togo	H10	64
Tshabong, Bots.	F6	66
Tshane, Bots.	E5	66
Tshela, Zaire	C2	58
Tshesebe, Bots.	C8	66
Tshikapa, Zaire	C4	58
Tshwane, S. Afr.	D6	66
Tsiafajavona, mtn., Madag.	q22	67b
Tsiombe, Madag.	t21	67b
Tsiroanomandidy, Madag.	q22	67b
Tsobis, Nmb.	C3	66
Tsu, Japan	M11	36
Tsuchiura, Japan	K15	36
Tsugaru-kaikyō, strt., Japan	f15	36a
Tsumeb, Nmb.	B3	66
Tsumkwe, Nmb.	B5	66
Tsuni see Zunyi, China	F8	30
Tsuruga, Japan	L11	36
Tsuruoka, Japan	I14	36
Tsushima, is., Japan	M4	36
Tsushima-kaikyō (Eastern Channel), strt., Japan	N4	36
Tsuyama, Japan	L9	36
Tual, Indon.	G9	38
Tuamotu, Îles, is., Fr. Poly.	J26	158
Tuanfeng, China	E3	34
Tuanwang, China	G8	32
Tuapse, Russia	I5	26
Tuba City, Az., U.S.	A4	110
Tubarão, Braz.	E14	80
Tübingen, Ger.	G9	10
Tubruq (Tobruk), Libya	A2	60
Tucacas, Ven.	B8	84
Tucacas, Punta, c., Ven.	B8	84
Tucano, Braz.	F11	76
Tuckahoe, N.Y., U.S.	h13	139
Tucker, Ar., U.S.	C4	111
Tucker, Ga., U.S.	h8	117
Tucker, co., W.V., U.S.	B5	155
Tuckerman, Ar., U.S.	B4	111
Tuckerton, N.J., U.S.	D4	137
Tučkovo, Russia	F19	22
Tucson, Az., U.S.	E5	110
Tucumán, prov., Arg.	D6	80
Tucumcari, N.M., U.S.	B6	138
Tucupita, Ven.	C11	84
Tucuruí, Braz.	D9	76
Tudela, Spain	C10	16
Tudmur (Palmyra), Syria	D5	48
Tugaloo Lake, res., U.S.	B1	147
Tug Fork, stm., U.S.	C2	155
Tujmazy, Russia	G8	26
T'ukalinsk, Russia	F12	26
Tuktoyaktuk, N.W. Ter., Can.	C6	96
Tukums, Lat.	D6	22
Tukwila, Wa., U.S.	f11	154
Tula, Mex.	F10	90
Tula, Russia	G20	22
Tulancingo, Mex.	G10	90
Tulare, Ca., U.S.	D4	112
Tulare, co., Ca., U.S.	D4	112
Tularosa, N.M., U.S.	D3	138
Tularosa Valley, val., N.M., U.S.	E3	138
Tulbagh, S. Afr.	I4	66
Tulcán, Ec.	G4	84
Tulcea, Rom.	D12	20
Tulchyn, Ukr.	H3	26
Tülkarm, W.B.	D4	50
Tullahoma, Tn., U.S.	B5	149
Tullamore, Austl.	I7	70
Tullamore, Ire.	H6	8
Tulle, Fr.	G8	14
Tulln, Aus.	G16	10
Tullus, Sud.	L3	60
Tully, Austl.	A6	70
Tulsa, Ok., U.S.	A6	143
Tulsa, co., Ok., U.S.	B6	143
Tuluá, Col.	E4	84
Tulum, Mex.	G16	90
Tulun, Russia	G12	28
Tulungagung, Indon.	k15	39a
Tuma, Russia	F23	22
Tumaco, Col.	G3	84
Tumaco, Rada de, b., Col.	G3	84
Tumbarumba, Austl.	J8	70
Tumbes, Peru	I2	84
Tumbes, dept., Peru	F2	84
Tumbes (Puyango), stm., S.A.	I2	84
Tumble Mountain, mtn., Mt., U.S.	E7	133
Tumbler Ridge, B.C., Can.	B7	99
Tumbotino, Russia	F26	22
Tumen, China	A17	32
Tumeremo, Ven.	D12	84
Tumkūr, India	F4	46
Tumuc-Humac Mountains, mts., S.A.	C7	76
Tumut, Austl.	J8	70
Tumwater, Wa., U.S.	B3	154
Tunapuna, Trin.	I17	94
Tungurahua, prov., Ec.	H3	84
Tunica, Ms., U.S.	A3	131
Tunica, co., Ms., U.S.	A3	131
Tunis, Tun.	M5	18
Tunis, Golfe de, b., Tun.	L5	18
Tunisia (Tunisie), ctry., Afr.	B8	54
Tunja, Col.	E6	84
Tunkás, Mex.	G15	90
Tunkhannock, Pa., U.S.	C10	145
Tunnel Hill, Ga., U.S.	B1	117
Tunnelton, W.V., U.S.	B5	155
Tunuyán, Arg.	G4	80
Tunxi, China	F7	34
Tuolumne, co., Ca., U.S.	D4	112
Tuolumne, stm., Ca., U.S.	D3	112
Tupã, Braz.	F3	79
Tupaciguara, Braz.	E4	79
Tupancireta, Braz.	E12	80
Tupelo, Ms., U.S.	A5	131
Tupi Paulista, Braz.	F3	79
Tupiza, Bol.	I9	82
Tupper Lake, N.Y., U.S.	A6	139
Tupper Lake, l., N.Y., U.S.	A6	139
Tupungato, Arg.	G4	80
Tupungato, Cerro, mtn., S.A.	G4	80
Túquerres, Col.	G3	84
Turabah, Sau. Ar.	E5	48
Turbaco, Col.	B5	84
Turbat, Pak.	I17	48
Turbo, Col.	C4	84
Turda, Rom.	C7	20
Turfan see Turpan, China	C4	30
Turfan Depression see Turpan Pendi, depr., China	C4	30
Turgutlu, Tur.	K11	20
Türi, Est.	C8	22
Turin see Torino, Italy	D2	18
Turinsk, Russia	F10	26
Turka, Ukr.	F23	10

Name — Map Ref. — Page

Turkestan, Kaz. I11 26
Túrkeve, Hung. H20 10
Turkey (Türkiye), ctry., Asia H15 4
Turkey, stm., Ia., U.S. B6 122
Turkey Point, c., Md., U.S. B5 127
Turkmenistan, ctry., Asia I9 26
Turks and Caicos Islands, dep., N.A. D9 94
Turks Islands, is., T./C. Is. D9 94
Turku (Åbo), Fin. K18 6
Turley, Ok., U.S. A6 143
Turlock, Ca., U.S. D3 112
Turmalina, Braz. D7 79
Turnbull, Mount, mtn., Az., U.S. D5 110
Turneffe Islands, is., Belize I16 90
Turner, Me., U.S. D2 126
Turner, Or., U.S. C4 144
Turner, co., Ga., U.S. E3 117
Turner, co., S.D., U.S. D8 148
Turners Falls, Ma., U.S. A2 128
Turner Valley, Alta., Can. D3 98
Turnhout, Bel. F6 12
Turnu Măgurele, Rom. F8 20
Turpan, China C4 30
Turpan Pendi, depr., China C4 30
Turquino, Pico, mtn., Cuba E6 94
Turrell, Ar., U.S. B5 111
Turrialba, C.R. H11 92
Turrialba, Volcán, vol., C.R. G11 92
Turriff, Scot., U.K. D11 8
Turtle Creek, Pa., U.S. k14 145
Turtleford, Sask., Can. D1 105
Turtle Lake, N.D., U.S. B5 141
Turun-Porin lääni, prov., Fin. K18 6
Turvo, Braz. E14 80
Tuscaloosa, Al., U.S. B2 108
Tuscaloosa, co., Al., U.S. B2 108
Tuscany see Toscana, prov., Italy F5 18
Tuscarawas, co., Oh., U.S. B4 142
Tuscarawas, stm., Oh., U.S. B4 142
Tuscarora, Nv., U.S. B5 135
Tuscarora Mountain, mtn., Pa., U.S. F6 145
Tuscola, Il., U.S. D5 120
Tuscola, co., Mi., U.S. E7 129
Tusculum College, Tn., U.S. C11 149
Tuscumbia, Al., U.S. A2 108
Tuskegee, Al., U.S. C4 108
Tusket, N.S., Can. F4 101
Tutajev, Russia D22 22
Tuticorin, India H5 46
Tutóia, Braz. D10 76
Tutrakan, Bul. E10 20
Tuttle, Ok., U.S. B4 143
Tuttle Creek Lake, res., Ks., U.S. C7 123
Tutupaca, Volcán, vol., Peru G6 82
Tutwiler, Ms., U.S. A3 131
Tuva, state, Russia G16 26
Tuvalu, ctry., Oc. G24 2
Tuxedo Park, De., U.S. i7 115
Tuxpan, Mex. G11 90
Tuxpan, Mex. G7 90
Tuxtepec, Mex. H11 90
Tuxtla Gutiérrez, Mex. I13 90
Tuy Hoa, Viet. H10 40
Tuz Gölü, l., Tur. H14 4
Tūz Khurmātū, Iraq D8 48
Tuzla, Bos. E2 20
Tver' (Kalinin), Russia E18 22
Tweed, Ont., Can. C7 103
Tweed, stm., U.K. F11 8
Tweed Heads, Austl. G10 70
Tweedy Mountain, mtn., Mt., U.S. E4 133
Twentynine Palms, Ca., U.S. E5 112
Twiggs, co., Ga., U.S. D3 117
Twillingate, Newf., Can. D4 102
Twin Bridges, Mt., U.S. E4 133
Twin City, Ga., U.S. D4 117
Twin Falls, Id., U.S. G4 119
Twin Falls, co., Id., U.S. G4 119
Twin Knolls, Az., U.S. m9 110
Twin Lakes, Ga., U.S. F3 117
Twin Lakes, In., U.S. B5 121
Twin Lakes, Wi., U.S. F5 156
Twin Mountain, N.H., U.S. B3 136
Twin Rivers, N.J., U.S. C4 137
Twinsburg, Oh., U.S. A4 142
Twin Valley, Mn., U.S. C2 130
Twisp, Wa., U.S. A5 154
Two Harbors, Mn., U.S. C7 130
Two Hills, Alta., Can. C5 98
Two Rivers, Wi., U.S. D6 156
Tyachiv, Ukr. A7 20
Tybee Island, Ga., U.S. D6 117
Tychy, Pol. E18 10
Tygart Lake, res., W.V., U.S. B5 155
Tygart Valley, stm., W.V., U.S. B4 155
Tyger, stm., S.C., U.S. B4 147
Tyler, Mn., U.S. F2 130
Tyler, Tx., U.S. C5 150
Tyler, co., Tx., U.S. D5 150
Tyler, co., W.V., U.S. B4 155
Tyler Heights, W.V., U.S. C3 155
Tylertown, Ms., U.S. D3 131
Tyndall, Man., Can. D3 100
Tyndall, S.D., U.S. E8 148
Tyndinskij, Russia F16 28
Tyne, stm., Eng., U.K. G11 8
Tyre see Ṣūr, Leb. B4 50
Tyrma, Russia G18 28
Tyrone, N.M., U.S. E1 138
Tyrone, Ok., U.S. e9 143
Tyrone, Pa., U.S. E5 145
Tyronza, Ar., U.S. B5 111
Tyrrell, co., N.C., U.S. B6 140
Tyrrhenian Sea (Mare Tirreno), Eur. I7 18
Tysa (Tisa) (Tisza), stm., Eur. A8 20
Tytuvėnai, Lith. F6 22
Tzaneen, S. Afr. D10 66
Tzucacab, Mex. G15 90

U

Uaupés (Vaupés), stm., S.A. G9 84
Ubá, Braz. F7 79
Ubaitaba, Braz. C9 79
Ubangi (Oubangui), stm., Afr. H10 54
Ubatã, Braz. C9 79
Ubatuba, Braz. G6 79
Ube, Japan N6 36
Úbeda, Spain G8 16
Uberaba, Braz. E5 79
Uberaba, Lagoa, l., S.A. G13 82
Uberlândia, Braz. E4 79
Ubon Ratchathani, Thai. G8 40
Ucacha, Arg. G7 80
Ucayali, dept., Peru C4 82
Ucayali, stm., Peru A4 82
Uchiza, Peru C3 82
Uchoa, Braz. F4 79
Ucholovo, Russia H23 22
Uchta, Russia E8 26
Ucluelet, B.C., Can. E5 99
Ucon, Id., U.S. F7 119
Udagamandalam, India G4 46
Udaipur, India H5 44
Udall, Ks., U.S. E6 123
Uddevalla, Swe. L12 6
Udgīr, India C4 46
Udine, Italy C8 18
Udmurtia see Udmurtija, state, Russia F8 26
Udmurtija, state, Russia F8 26
Udoml'a, Russia D18 22
Udon Thani, Thai. F7 40
Ueda, Japan K13 36
Uelzen, Ger. C10 10
Ueno, Japan M11 36
Ufa, Russia G9 26
Ugab, stm., Nmb. C1 66
Uganda, ctry., Afr. A6 58
Ugashik Lakes, l., Ak., U.S. D8 109
Ughaybish, Sud. L6 60
Uglegorsk, Russia H20 28
Uglič, Russia D21 22
Uglovka, Russia C16 22
Ugra, Russia G17 22
Uherské Hradiště, Czech Rep. F17 10
Uherský Brod, Czech Rep. F17 10
Uhrichsville, Oh., U.S. B4 142
Uíge, Ang. C3 58
Uijŏngbu, S. Kor. F15 32
Uiju, N. Kor. C12 32
Uinta, co., Wy., U.S. E2 157
Uintah, co., Ut., U.S. D6 151
Uinta Mountains, mts., Ut., U.S. C5 151
Uitenhage, S. Afr. I7 66
Uithoorn, Neth. D6 12
Ujar, Russia F16 26
Újfehértó, Hung. H21 10
Ujiji, Tan. B5 58
Ujjain, India I6 44
'Ujmān, U.A.E. B9 47
Ujungpandang, Indon. G6 38
Ukiah, Ca., U.S. C2 112
Ukmergė, Lith. F7 22
Ukraine, ctry., Eur. H3 26
Ulaanbaatar, Mong. B8 30
Ulaangom, Mong. B5 30
Ulan Bator see Ulaanbaatar, Mong. B8 30
Ulan-Ude, Russia G13 28
Ulco, S. Afr. G7 66
Ulhāsnagar, India C2 46
Uliastaj, Mong. B6 30
Uljanovka, Russia B13 22
Uljanovsk, Russia G7 26
Ulladulla, Austl. J9 70
Ulm, Ger. G10 10
Ulm, Mt., U.S. C5 133
Ulsan, S. Kor. H17 32
Ulster, co., N.Y., U.S. D6 139
Ulster, hist. reg., Eur. G6 8
Ultraoriental, Cordillera (Serra do Divisor), mts., S.A. C5 82
Ulúa, stm., Hond. B6 92
Ulverstone, Austl. M7 70
Ul'yanovka, Ukr. A14 20
Ulysses, Ks., U.S. E2 123
Umán, Mex. G15 90
Uman', Ukr. H4 26
Umarkot, Pak. H3 44
Umatilla, Fl., U.S. D5 116
Umatilla, Or., U.S. B7 144
Umatilla, co., Or., U.S. B8 144
Umatilla, stm., Or., U.S. B7 144
Umbria, prov., Italy G7 18
Umeå, Swe. J17 6
Umhlanga Rocks, S. Afr. G10 66
Umkomaas, S. Afr. H10 66
Umm Durmān (Omdurman), Sud. J7 60
Umm el Fahm, Isr. C4 50
Umm Kaddādah, Sud. K4 60
Umm Ruwābah, Sud. K6 60
Umnak Island, i., Ak., U.S. E6 109
Um'ot, Russia I25 22
Umpqua, stm., Or., U.S. D3 144
Umtata, S. Afr. H9 66
Umtentweni, S. Afr. H10 66
Umuahia, Nig. I13 64
Umuarama, Braz. G2 79
Una, Braz. C9 79
Unadilla, Ga., U.S. D3 117
Unaí, Braz. D5 79
Unaka Mountains, mts., U.S. C11 149
Unalakleet, Ak., U.S. C7 109
Unalaska, Ak., U.S. E6 109
Unalaska Island, i., Ak., U.S. E6 109
'Unayzah, Sau. Ar. H7 48
Uncasville, Ct., U.S. D7 114
Uncia, Bol. H8 82
Uncompahgre Peak, mtn., Co., U.S. C3 113
Underhill, Vt., U.S. B3 152
Underhill Center, Vt., U.S. B3 152
Underwood, Al., U.S. B3 108
Underwood, N.D., U.S. B4 141
Uneča, Russia I15 22
Ungava, Péninsule d', pen., Que., Can. g12 104
Ungava Bay, b., Can. E19 96
União, Braz. D10 76
União da Vitória, Braz. D13 80
União dos Palmares, Braz. E11 76
Unicoi, Tn., U.S. C11 149
Unicoi, co., Tn., U.S. C11 149
Unicoi Mountains, mts., U.S. D9 149
Unimak Island, i., Ak., U.S. D7 109
Unión, Arg. H6 80
Unión, C.R. I11 92
Unión, Para. C10 80
Union, Ky., U.S. k13 124
Union, Me., U.S. D3 126
Union, Ms., U.S. C4 131
Union, Mo., U.S. C6 132
Union, N.H., U.S. D4 136
Union, Or., U.S. B9 144
Union, S.C., U.S. B4 147
Union, Wa., U.S. B2 154
Union, W.V., U.S. D4 155
Union, co., Ar., U.S. D3 111
Union, co., Fl., U.S. B4 116
Union, co., Ga., U.S. B2 117
Union, co., Il., U.S. F4 120
Union, co., In., U.S. E8 121
Union, co., Ia., U.S. C3 122
Union, co., Ky., U.S. C2 124
Union, co., La., U.S. B3 125
Union, co., Ms., U.S. A4 131
Union, co., N.J., U.S. B4 137
Union, co., N.M., U.S. A6 138
Union, co., N.C., U.S. B2 140
Union, co., Oh., U.S. B2 142
Union, co., Or., U.S. B8 144
Union, co., Pa., U.S. E7 145
Union, co., S.C., U.S. B4 147
Union, co., S.D., U.S. E9 148
Union, co., Tn., U.S. C10 149
Union Bay, B.C., Can. E5 99
Union Beach, N.J., U.S. C4 137
Union Bridge, Md., U.S. A3 127
Union City, Ca., U.S. h8 112
Union City, Ga., U.S. C2 117
Union City, In., U.S. D8 121
Union City, Mi., U.S. F5 129
Union City, N.J., U.S. h8 137
Union City, Oh., U.S. B1 142
Union City, Ok., U.S. B4 143
Union City, Pa., U.S. C2 145
Union City, Tn., U.S. A2 149
Unión de Reyes, Cuba C4 94
Unión de Tula, Mex. H7 90
Union Gap, Wa., U.S. C5 154
Union Grove, Wi., U.S. F5 156
Union Mill, Hi., U.S. C6 118
Union Point, Ga., U.S. C3 117
Union Springs, Al., U.S. C4 108
Uniontown, Al., U.S. C2 108
Uniontown, Ky., U.S. C2 124
Uniontown, Oh., U.S. B4 142
Uniontown, Pa., U.S. G2 145
Union Village, R.I., U.S. B3 146
Unionville, Ct., U.S. B4 114
Unionville, Mo., U.S. A4 132
United Arab Emirates (Al-Imārāt al-'Arabīyah al-Muttaḥidah), ctry., Asia E5 42
United Arab Republic see Egypt, ctry., Afr. C7 56
United Kingdom, ctry., Eur. E7 4
United Nations Headquarters, N.Y., U.S. h12 139
United States, ctry., N.A. D7 106
United States Air Force Academy, mil., Co., U.S. B6 113
United States Military Academy, mil., N.Y., U.S. C6 139
United States Naval Academy, mil., Md., U.S. C4 127
Unity, Sask., Can. E1 105
Unity, Me., U.S. D3 126
University City, Mo., U.S. C7 132
University Heights, Ia., U.S. C6 122
University Heights, Oh., U.S. h9 142
University Park, N.M., U.S. E3 138
University Park, Tx., U.S. n10 150
University Place, Wa., U.S. f10 154
Unquillo, Arg. F6 80
Upata, Ven. C11 84
Upington, S. Afr. G5 66
Upland, Ca., U.S. E5 112
Upland, In., U.S. D7 121
Upolu, i., W. Sam. J22 158
Upolu Point, c., Hi., U.S. C6 118
Upper Arlington, Oh., U.S. B2 142
Upper Arrow Lake, res., B.C., Can. D9 99
Upper Darby, Pa., U.S. G11 145
Upper Demerara-Berbice, prov., Guy. D13 84
Upper Frenchville, Me., U.S. A4 126
Upper Gloucester, Me., U.S. E2 126
Upper Graniteville, Vt., U.S. C4 152
Upper Humber, stm., Newf., Can. D3 102
Upper Iowa, stm., Ia., U.S. A5 122
Upper Island Cove, Newf., Can. E5 102
Upper Klamath Lake, l., Or., U.S. E4 144
Upper Marlboro, Md., U.S. C4 127
Upper Musquodoboit, N.S., Can. D7 101
Upper New York Bay, b., U.S. k8 137
Upper Red Lake, l., Mn., U.S. B4 130
Upper Saddle River, N.J., U.S. A4 137
Upper Sandusky, Oh., U.S. B2 142
Upper Sheila [Haut Sheila], N.B., Can. B5 101
Upper Takutu-Upper Essequibo, prov., Guy. F13 84
Uppsala, Swe. L15 6
Upshur, co., Tx., U.S. C5 150
Upshur, co., W.V., U.S. C4 155
Upson, co., Ga., U.S. D2 117
Upton, Ky., U.S. C4 124
Upton, Wy., U.S. B8 157
Upton, co., Tx., U.S. D2 150
Urabá, Golfo de, b., Col. C4 84
Uracoa, Ven. C11 84
Uraj, Russia E10 26
Ural, stm. H8 26
Uralla, Austl. H9 70
Ural'sk, Kaz. G8 26
Ural'skije gory (Ural Mountains), mts., Russia E9 26
Urandangi, Austl. C3 70
Urandi, Braz. C7 79
Ura-T'ube, Taj. J11 26
Uravan, Co., U.S. C2 113
Urawa, Japan L14 36
Urbana, Il., U.S. C5 120
Urbana, Oh., U.S. B2 142
Urbandale, Ia., U.S. C4 122
Urcos, Peru E6 82
Urdinarrain, Arg. G9 80
Urečje, Bela. I10 22
Ures, Mex. C4 90
Urgenč, Uzb. I10 26
Uriah, Al., U.S. D2 108
Uribia, Col. B6 84
Urique, Mex. D6 90
Urique, stm., Mex. D6 90
Urla, Tur. K10 20
Urmia see Orūmīyeh, Iran C8 48
Urmia, Lake see Orūmīyeh, Daryācheh-ye, l., Iran C8 48
Urrao, Col. D4 84
Uršel'skij, Russia F23 22
Uruaçu, Braz. C4 79
Uruana, Braz. C4 79
Uruapan del Progreso, Mex. H8 90
Urubamba, Peru E5 82
Urubamba, stm., Peru D5 82
Urucará, Braz. I14 84
Uruçuca, Braz. C9 79
Urucurituba, Braz. I14 84
Uruguaiana, Braz. E10 80
Uruguay, ctry., S.A. C5 78
Uruguay (Uruguai), stm., S.A. G9 80
Urumchi see Ürümqi, China C4 30
Ürümqi, China C4 30
Urundel, Arg. B6 80
Urupês, Braz. F4 79
Ur'upinsk, Russia G6 26
Urussanga, Braz. E14 80
Uržum, Russia F8 26
Ušači, Bela. F11 22
Uşak, Tur. K13 20
Usakos, Nmb. D2 66
Usborne, Mount, mtn., Falk. Is. G5 78
Usedom, i., Eur. A14 10
Ushuaia, Arg. G3 78
Usman', Russia I22 22
Usolje-Sibirskoje, Russia G12 28
Uspallata, Arg. G4 80
Ussurijsk, Russia I18 28
Ust'-Barguzin, Russia G13 28
Uster, Switz. D10 13
Ust'-Ilimskoje vodochranilišče, res., Russia F18 26
Ústí nad Labem, Czech Rep. E14 10
Ústí nad Orlicí, Czech Rep. F16 10
Ustka, Pol. A16 10
Ust'-Kamčatsk, Russia F24 28
Ust'-Kamenogorsk, Kaz. H8 28
Ust'-Katav, Russia G9 26
Ust'-Kut, Russia F13 28
Ust'-Nera, Russia E20 28
Uštobe, Kaz. H13 26
Ust'-Omčug, Russia E21 28
Ust'-Ordynskij, Russia G12 28
Ust'urt, plato, plat., Asia I9 26
Ust'užna, Russia C19 22
Usu, China C3 30
Usulután, El Sal. D6 92
Usumacinta, stm., N.A. I14 90
Utah, co., Ut., U.S. C4 151
Utah, state, U.S. D4 151
Utah Lake, l., Ut., U.S. C4 151
Utena, Lith. F8 22
Ute Reservoir, res., N.M., U.S. B6 138
Utica, Mi., U.S. F7 129
Utica, Ms., U.S. C3 131
Utica, Ne., U.S. D8 134
Utica, N.Y., U.S. B5 139
Utica, Oh., U.S. B3 142
Utiel, Spain F10 16
Utikuma Lake, l., Alta., Can. B3 98
Utila, Isla de, i., Hond. A8 92
Utrecht, Neth. D7 12
Utrecht, S. Afr. F10 66
Utrecht, prov., Neth. D7 12
Utrera, Spain H6 16
Utsunomiya, Japan K14 36
Uttaradit, Thai. F6 40
Uttar Pradesh, state, India G9 44
Utuado, P.R. E11 94
Uudenmaan lääni, prov., Fin. K19 6
Uusikaupunki (Nystad), Fin. K17 6
Uvá, stm., Col. F8 84
Uvalde, Tx., U.S. E3 150
Uvalde, co., Tx., U.S. E3 150
Uvarovići, Bela. I13 22
Uvarovka, Russia F18 22
Uvarovo, Russia J25 22
Uvira, Zaire B5 58
Uvs nuur, l., Asia A5 30
Uwajima, Japan N7 36
Uwayl, Sud. M4 60
'Uwaynāt, Jabal al-, mtn., Afr. D5 56
Uxbridge, Ma., U.S. B4 128
Uyuni, Bol. I8 82
Uyuni, Salar de, pl., Bol. I8 82
Uzbekistan, ctry., Asia I10 26
Uzda, Bela. H10 22
Uzhhorod, Ukr. H2 26
Užice, Yugo. F3 20
Uzlovaja, Russia H21 22
Uzunköprü, Tur. H10 20
Užur, Russia F9 28
Užventis, Lith. F5 22

V

Vaanta (Vanda), Fin. K19 6
Vaasa (Vasa), Fin. J17 6
Vaasan lääni, prov., Fin. J18 6
Vabalninkas, Lith. F7 22
Vác, Hung. H19 10
Vača, Russia F25 22
Vacaria, Braz. E13 80
Vacaville, Ca., U.S. C3 112
Vacherie, La., U.S. h10 125
Vachš, stm., Taj. J11 26
Vacoas, Mrts. v18 67c
Vadito, N.M., U.S. A4 138
Vadodara, India I5 44
Vaduz, Liech. E16 14
Vågåmo, Nor. K11 6
Váh, stm., Slvk. G17 10
Vaiden, Ms., U.S. B4 131
Vaihingen, Ger. G8 10
Vail, Co., U.S. B4 113
Vajgač, ostrov, i., Russia C9 26
Valašské Meziříčí, Czech Rep. F17 10
Val-Bélair, Que., Can. n17 104
Valcheta, Arg. E3 78
Valcourt, Que., Can. D5 104
Valdai Hills see Valdajskaja vozvyšennost', hills, Russia D15 22
Valdaj, Russia D16 22
Valdajskaja vozvyšennost', hills, Russia D16 22
Val-David, Que., Can. C3 104
Valdepeñas, Spain G8 16
Valders, Wi., U.S. D6 156
Valdés, Península, pen., Arg. E4 78
Valdese, N.C., U.S. B1 140
Valdéz, Ec. G3 84
Valdez, Ak., U.S. C10 109
Val-d'Isère, Fr. G13 14
Valdivia, Chile D2 78
Valdivia, Col. D5 84
Val-d'Or, Que., Can. k11 104
Valdosta, Ga., U.S. F3 117
Vale, Or., U.S. D9 144
Valemount, B.C., Can. C8 99
Valença, Braz. B9 79
Valença, Braz. G7 79
Valence, Fr. H11 14
València, Spain F11 16
Valencia, Az., U.S. m7 110
Valencia, Ven. B8 84
Valencia, co., N.M., U.S. C3 138
Valencia Heights, S.C., U.S. D6 147
Valenciennes, Fr. B10 14
Valentine, Ne., U.S. B5 134
Valera, Ven. C7 84
Valga, Est. D9 22
Valhalla, N.Y., U.S. D7 139
Valhermoso Springs, Al., U.S. A3 108
Valiente, Península, pen., Pan. C2 84
Valier, Mt., U.S. B4 133
Valjevo, Yugo. E3 20
Valka, Lat. D9 22
Valladolid, Mex. G15 90
Valladolid, Spain D7 16
Valle, dept., Hond. D7 92
Valle d'Aosta, prov., Italy D2 18
Valle de la Pascua, Ven. C9 84
Valle del Cauca, dept., Col. F4 84
Valle de Santiago, Mex. G9 90
Valledupar, Col. B6 84
Vallée-Jonction, Que., Can. C7 104
Vallegrande, Bol. H9 82
Valle Hermoso, Arg. F6 80
Valle Hermoso, Mex. E11 90
Vallejo, Ca., U.S. C2 112
Vallenar, Chile E3 80
Valletta, Malta N9 18
Valley, Ne., U.S. C9 134
Valley, co., Id., U.S. E3 119
Valley, co., Mt., U.S. B10 133
Valley, co., Ne., U.S. C6 134
Valley Center, Ks., U.S. E6 123
Valley City, N.D., U.S. C8 141
Valley Cottage, N.Y., U.S. g13 139
Valley East, Ont., Can. p19 103
Valley Falls, Ks., U.S. C8 123
Valley Falls, R.I., U.S. B4 146
Valley Grove, W.V., U.S. A4 155
Valley Head, Al., U.S. A4 108
Valley Head, W.V., U.S. C4 155
Valley of the Kings, hist., Egypt E7 60
Valley Park, Mo., U.S. f12 132
Valley Springs, S.D., U.S. D9 148
Valley Station, Ky., U.S. g11 124
Valley Stream, N.Y., U.S. n15 139
Valleyview, Alta., Can. B2 98
Valley View, Pa., U.S. E8 145
Valliant, Ok., U.S. D6 143
Vallonia, In., U.S. G5 121
Vallorbe, Switz. E5 13
Valls, Spain D13 16
Vallscreek, W.V., U.S. D3 155
Val Marie, Sask., Can. H2 105
Valmiera, Lat. D8 22
Valmy, Nv., U.S. C4 135
Valognes, Fr. C5 14
Vālpārai, India G4 46
Valparaíso, Braz. F3 79
Valparaíso, Chile G3 80
Valparaiso, Fl., U.S. u15 116
Valparaiso, In., U.S. B3 121
Valparaiso, Ne., U.S. C9 134
Valparaíso, prov., Chile G3 80
Valréas, Fr. H11 14
Vals, Tanjung, c., Indon. G10 38
Valsbaai, b., S. Afr. J4 66
Valujki, Russia G5 26
Val Verda, Ut., U.S. C4 151
Val Verde, co., Tx., U.S. E2 150
Valverde del Camino, Spain H5 16
Van, Tur. B7 48
Van, W.V., U.S. n12 155
Vananda, B.C., Can. E5 99
Van Buren, Ar., U.S. B1 111
Van Buren, In., U.S. C6 121
Van Buren, Me., U.S. A5 126
Van Buren, Mo., U.S. E6 132
Van Buren, co., Ar., U.S. B3 111
Van Buren, co., Ia., U.S. D6 122
Van Buren, co., Mi., U.S. F4 129
Van Buren, co., Tn., U.S. D8 149
Vance, co., N.C., U.S. A4 140
Vanceboro, Me., U.S. C5 126
Vanceburg, Ky., U.S. B6 124
Vancleave, Ms., U.S. E5 131
Vancouver, B.C., Can. E6 99
Vancouver, Wa., U.S. D3 154
Vancouver, Cape, c., Austl. G3 68
Vancouver Island, i., B.C., Can. E4 99
Vandalia, Il., U.S. E4 120
Vandalia, Mo., U.S. B6 132
Vandenberg Air Force Base, mil., Ca., U.S. E3 112
Vanderbijlpark, S. Afr. F8 66
Vanderburgh, co., In., U.S. H2 121
Vandergrift, Pa., U.S. E2 145
Vanderhoof, B.C., Can. C5 99
Vanderwagen, N.M., U.S. B1 138
Van Diemen Gulf, b., Austl. B6 68
Vändra, Est. C8 22
Vanegas, Mex. F9 90
Vänern, l., Swe. L13 6
Vänersborg, Swe. L13 6
Vangaindrano, Madag. s22 67b
Van Gölü, l., Tur. B7 48
Vanguard, Sask., Can. H2 105
Van Horn, Tx., U.S. o12 150
Van Horne, Ia., U.S. B5 122
Vanier, Ont., Can. h12 103
Vanimo, Pap. N. Gui. F11 38
Vanino, Russia H20 28
Vāniyambādi, India F5 46
Vankleek Hill, Ont., Can. B10 103
Van Kull, Kill, stm., N.J., U.S. k8 137
Van Lear, Ky., U.S. C7 124
Van Meter, Ia., U.S. C4 122
Vanndale, Ar., U.S. B5 111
Vannes, Fr. E4 14
Vanrhynsdorp, S. Afr. H4 66
Vansant, Va., U.S. e9 153
Vanscoy, Sask., Can. E2 105
Vanua Levu, i., Fiji J21 158
Vanuatu, ctry., Oc. H24 2
Van Wert, Oh., U.S. B1 142
Van Wert, co., Oh., U.S. B1 142
Van Zandt, co., Tx., U.S. C5 150
Vapnyarka, Ukr. A12 20
Vārānasi (Benares), India H10 44
Varangerfjorden, Nor. G22 6
Varangerhalvøya, pen., Nor. F21 6
Varaždin, Cro. C11 18
Varazze, Italy E3 18
Varberg, Swe. M13 6
Vardaman, Ms., U.S. B4 131
Vardø, Nor. F22 6
Varel, Ger. B8 10
Varėna, Lith. G7 22
Varennes, Que., Can. D4 104
Vareš, Bos. E2 20
Varese, Italy D3 18
Varginha, Braz. F6 79
Varina, Va., U.S. C5 153
Varkaus, Fin. J20 6
Varna, Bul. F11 20
Värnamo, Swe. M14 6
Varnsdorf, Czech Rep. E14 10
Varnville, S.C., U.S. F5 147
Várpalota, Hung. H18 10
Vars, Ont., Can. h13 103
Várzea da Palma, Braz. D6 79
Várzea Grande, Braz. F13 82
Vashkivtsi, Ukr. A11 20
Vashon, Wa., U.S. B3 154
Vashon Island, i., Wa., U.S. f11 154
Vasileviči, Bela. I12 22
Vaslui, Rom. C11 20
Vassar, Man., Can. E4 100
Vassar, Mi., U.S. E7 129
Västerås, Swe. L15 6
Västervik, Swe. M15 6
Vasto, Italy G9 18
Vatican City (Città del Vaticano), ctry., Eur. H7 18
Vatnajökull, Ice. B5 6a
Vatomandry, Madag. q23 67b
Vatra Dornei, Rom. B9 20
V'atskije Pol'any, Russia F8 26
Vättern, l., Swe. L14 6
Vaudreuil, Que., Can. D3 104
Vaughan, Ont., Can. D5 103
Vaughn, Mt., U.S. C5 133
Vaughn, N.M., U.S. C4 138
Vaupés, ter., Col. G7 84
Vaupés (Uaupés), stm., S.A. G7 84
Vauvert, Fr. I11 14
Vauxhall, Alta., Can. D4 98
Vavoua, C. Iv. H6 64
Växjö, Swe. M14 6
Vazante, Braz. E5 79
V'azemskij, Russia H18 28
V'az'ma, Russia F17 22
V'azniki, Russia E25 22
Veazie, Me., U.S. D4 126
Veblen, S.D., U.S. B8 148
Vechta, Ger. C8 10
Vecsés, Hung. H19 10
Vedia, Arg. H8 80
Veedersburg, In., U.S. D3 121
Veendam, Neth. B10 12
Veenendaal, Neth. D8 12
Veghel, Neth. E8 12
Vegreville, Alta., Can. C4 98
Veinticinco de Mayo, Arg. H4 80
Veinticinco de Mayo, Arg. H8 80
Veisiejai, Lith. G6 22

Name	Map Ref.	Page
Vejle, Den.	N11	6
Velarde, N.M., U.S.	A4	138
Velas, Cabo, c., C.R.	G9	92
Velázquez, Ur.	H11	80
Velddrif, S. Afr.	I4	66
Veldhoven, Neth.	F7	12
Vélez, Col.	D6	84
Vélez-Málaga, Spain	I7	16
Velika Morava, stm., Yugo.	E5	20
Velikije Luki, Russia	E13	22
Velikij Ust'ug, Russia	E7	26
Veliko Tărnovo, Bul.	F9	20
Vélingara, Sen.	F4	54
Veliž, Russia	F14	22
Velletri, Italy	H7	18
Vellore, India	F5	46
Velp, Neth.	D8	12
Vel'sk, Russia	E6	26
Velva, N.D., U.S.	A5	141
Venado Tuerto, Arg.	G8	80
Venâncio Aires, Braz.	E12	80
Venango, co., Pa., U.S.	D2	145
Vence, Fr.	I14	14
Venceslau Braz, Braz.	G4	79
Venda, hist. reg., S. Afr.	D10	66
Vendôme, Fr.	E8	14
Veneta, C.R.	G10	92
Veneta, Or., U.S.	C3	144
Veneto, prov., Italy	G18	14
Venev, Russia	G21	22
Venezia (Venice), Italy	D7	18
Venezuela, ctry., S.A.	B5	76
Venezuela, Golfo de, b., S.A.	B7	84
Veniaminof, Mount, mtn., Ak., U.S.	D8	109
Venice see Venezia, Italy	D7	18
Venice, Fl., U.S.	E4	116
Venice, Il., U.S.	E3	120
Venice, Gulf of, b., Eur.	D8	18
Vénissieux, Fr.	G11	14
Venlo, Neth.	F9	12
Ventanas, Ec.	H3	84
Ventersdorp, S. Afr.	F8	66
Venterstad, S. Afr.	H7	66
Ventimiglia, Italy	F2	18
Ventnor City, N.J., U.S.	E4	137
Ventspils, Lat.	D4	22
Ventuari, stm., Ven.	E9	84
Ventura (San Buenaventura), Ca., U.S.	E4	112
Ventura, co., Ca., U.S.	E4	112
Venustiano Carranza, Mex.	H8	90
Venustiano Carranza, Mex.	I13	90
Venustiano Carranza, Presa, res., Mex.	D9	90
Vera, Arg.	E8	80
Veracruz, state, Mex.	H12	90
Veracruz [Llave], Mex.	H11	90
Veraguas, prov., Pan.	I13	92
Veranópolis, Braz.	E13	80
Verāval, India	J4	44
Verbania, Italy	D3	18
Verbena, Al., U.S.	C3	108
Verbilki, Russia	E20	22
Verbovskij, Russia	F25	22
Vercelli, Italy	D3	18
Verchères, Que., Can.	D4	104
Verchn'aja Inta, Russia	D10	26
Verchn'aja Salda, Russia	F10	26
Verchnedneprovskij, Russia	G16	22
Verchnedvinsk, Bela.	F10	22
Verchnij Baskunčak, Russia	H7	26
Verchnij Ufalej, Russia	F10	26
Verchojanskij chrebet, mts., Russia	D17	28
Verchoturje, Russia	F10	26
Verchovje, Russia	I20	22
Verda, Ky., U.S.	D6	124
Verde, stm., Para.	B9	80
Verde, stm., Az., U.S.	C4	110
Verde, Cape, c., Bah.	C7	94
Verden, Ger.	C9	10
Verdi, Nv., U.S.	D2	135
Verdigre, Ne., U.S.	B7	134
Verdigris, Ok., U.S.	A6	143
Verdigris, stm., U.S.	A6	143
Verdi Peak, mtn., Nv., U.S.	C6	135
Verdun, Que., Can.	q19	104
Verdun-sur-Meuse, Fr.	C12	14
Vereeniging, S. Afr.	F8	66
Vereja, Russia	F19	22
Vereščagino, Russia	F8	26
Vergara, Ur.	G12	80
Vergennes, Vt., U.S.	C2	152
Vermilion, Alta., Can.	C5	98
Vermilion, Oh., U.S.	A3	142
Vermilion, co., Il., U.S.	C6	120
Vermilion, co., La., U.S.	E3	125
Vermilion, stm., Alta., Can.	C5	98
Vermilion, stm., Il., U.S.	C5	120
Vermilion, stm., La., U.S.	E3	125
Vermilion Bay, b., La., U.S.	E3	125
Vermilion Lake, l., Mn., U.S.	C6	130
Vermilion Pass, Can.	D2	98
Vermilion Range, hills, Mn., U.S.	C7	130
Vermillion, S.D., U.S.	E9	148
Vermillion, co., In., U.S.	E2	121
Vermont, state, U.S.	D3	152
Vernal, Ut., U.S.	C6	151
Verneuil, Fr.	D7	14
Vernon, B.C., Can.	D8	99
Vernon, Fr.	C8	14
Vernon, Al., U.S.	B1	108
Vernon, Tx., U.S.	B3	150
Vernon, Vt., U.S.	F3	152
Vernon, co., La., U.S.	C2	125
Vernon, co., Mo., U.S.	D3	132
Vernon, co., Wi., U.S.	E3	156
Vernon Hills, Il., U.S.	h9	120
Vernonia, Or., U.S.	B3	144
Vero Beach, Fl., U.S.	E6	116
Véroia, Grc.	I6	20
Verona, Ont., Can.	C8	103
Verona, Italy	D6	18
Verona, Mo., U.S.	A5	131
Verona, Mo., U.S.	E4	132
Verona, N.J., U.S.	B4	137
Verona, Pa., U.S.	k14	145
Verona, Wi., U.S.	E4	156
Verónica, Arg.	H10	80
Verret, N.B., Can.	B1	101
Verret, Lake, l., La., U.S.	E4	125
Versailles, Fr.	D9	14
Versailles, In., U.S.	F7	121
Versailles, Ky., U.S.	B5	124
Versailles, Mo., U.S.	C5	132
Versailles, Oh., U.S.	B1	142
Veršino-Darasunskij, Russia	G15	28
Vert, Cap, c., Sen.	D1	64
Vertientes, Cuba	D5	94
Vertou, Fr.	E5	14
Verviers, Bel.	G8	12
Vesjegonsk, Russia	C20	22
Vesoul, Fr.	E13	14
Vespasiano, Braz.	E7	79
Vestal, N.Y., U.S.	C4	139
Vestavia Hills, Al., U.S.	g7	108
Vesterålen, is., Nor.	G14	6
Vestfjorden, Nor.	H14	6
Vestmannaeyjar, Ice.	C3	6a
Vesuvio, vol., Italy	I9	18
Veszprém, Hung.	H17	10
Vésztő, Hung.	I21	10
Veteran, Alta., Can.	C5	98
Veteran, Wy., U.S.	E8	157
Vetluga, Russia	F7	26
Veurne (Furnes), Bel.	F2	12
Vevay, In., U.S.	G7	121
Vevey, Switz.	F6	13
Viacha, Bol.	G7	82
Viale, Arg.	F8	80
Viamão, Braz.	F13	80
Viamonte, Arg.	G7	80
Vian, Ok., U.S.	B7	143
Viana, Braz.	D9	76
Viana do Alentejo, Port.	G3	16
Viana do Castelo, Port.	D3	16
Viangchan (Vientiane), Laos	F7	40
Viareggio, Italy	F5	18
Vibank, Sask., Can.	G4	105
Viborg, Den.	M11	6
Viborg, S.D., U.S.	D8	148
Vibo Valentia, Italy	K11	18
Viburnum, Mo., U.S.	D6	132
Vic (Vich), Spain	D14	16
Vícam, Mex.	D4	90
Vic-en-Bigorre, Fr.	I7	14
Vicente Guerrero, Mex.	F8	90
Vicente López, Arg.	H9	80
Vicenza, Italy	D6	18
Vichada, dept., Col.	E8	84
Vichada, stm., Col.	E8	84
Vichadero, Ur.	F11	80
Vichuquén, Chile	H2	80
Vichy, Fr.	F10	14
Vici, Ok., U.S.	A2	143
Vicksburg, Mi., U.S.	F5	129
Vicksburg, Ms., U.S.	C3	131
Viçosa, Braz.	F7	79
Victor, Co., U.S.	C5	113
Victor, Ia., U.S.	C5	122
Victor, Mt., U.S.	D2	133
Victor Harbor, Austl.	J3	70
Victoria, Arg.	G8	80
Victoria, Cam.	I14	64
Victoria, B.C., Can.	E6	99
Victoria, Newf., Can.	E5	102
Victoria, Chile	J2	80
Victoria, Gren.	H14	94
Victoria (Xianggang), H.K.	M3	34
Victoria, Sey.	B11	58
Victoria, Ks., U.S.	D4	123
Victoria, Ms., U.S.	A4	131
Victoria, Tx., U.S.	E4	150
Victoria, state, Austl.	G9	68
Victoria, co., Tx., U.S.	E4	150
Victoria, stm., Austl.	C6	68
Victoria, Lake, l., Afr.	B6	58
Victoria, Mount, mtn., Pap. N. Gui.	A9	68
Victoria Beach, Man., Can.	D3	100
Victoria Falls, Zimb.	A7	66
Victoria Falls, wtfl, Afr.	A7	66
Victoria Harbour, Ont., Can.	C5	103
Victoria Island, i., N.W. Ter., Can.	B10	96
Victoria Lake, res., Newf., Can.	D3	102
Victoria Land, reg., Ant.	C8	73
Victoria Nile, stm., Ug.	H7	56
Victoria Peak, mtn., Belize	I15	90
Victoriaville, Que., Can.	C6	104
Victoria West, S. Afr.	H6	66
Victorica, Arg.	I6	80
Victorino, Ven.	F9	84
Victorville, Ca., U.S.	E5	112
Vicuña, Chile	F3	80
Vicuña Mackenna, Arg.	G6	80
Vidalia, Ga., U.S.	D4	117
Vidalia, La., U.S.	C4	125
Videira, Braz.	D13	80
Vidin, Bul.	F6	20
Vidisha, India	I7	44
Vidor, Tx., U.S.	D5	150
Viedma, Arg.	E4	78
Viedma, Lago, l., Arg.	F2	78
Vienna see Wien, Aus.	G16	10
Vienna, Ga., U.S.	D3	117
Vienna, Il., U.S.	F5	120
Vienna, Mo., U.S.	C6	132
Vienna, Va., U.S.	B5	153
Vienna, W.V., U.S.	B3	155
Vienne, Fr.	G11	14
Vienne, stm., Fr.	E7	14
Vientiane see Viangchan, Laos	F7	40
Vieques, P.R.	E12	94
Vieques, Isla de, i., P.R.	E12	94
Vierwaldstättersee, l., Switz.	D9	13
Vierzon, Fr.	E9	14
Viesca, Mex.	E8	90
Vieste, Italy	H11	18
Vietnam, ctry., Asia	B4	38
Viet Tri, Viet.	D8	40
Vieux Fort, St. Luc.	H14	94
Vievis, Lith.	G7	22
Vigan, Phil.	m19	39b
Vigeland, Nor.	L10	6
Vigevano, Italy	D3	18
Vigo, Spain	C3	16
Vigo, co., In., U.S.	F3	121
Vihowa, Pak.	E4	44
Viitasaari, Fin.	J19	6
Vijayawāda, India	D6	46
Vila da Ribeira Brava, C.V.	k16	64a
Vila de Manica, Moz.	B11	66
Vilafranca del Penedès, Spain	D13	16
Vila Gomes da Costa, Moz.	E11	66
Vilanculos, Moz.	D12	66
Vila Nova de Foz Côa, Port.	D4	16
Vila Nova de Gaia, Port.	D3	16
Vilanova i la Geltrú, Spain	D13	16
Vila Real, Port.	D4	16
Vila Real de Santo António, Port.	H4	16
Vilas, co., Wi., U.S.	B4	156
Vila Velha, Braz.	F8	79
Vilejka, Bela.	G9	22
Vilhelmina, Swe.	I15	6
Vilhena, Braz.	E11	82
Viljandi, Est.	C8	22
Viljoenskroon, S. Afr.	F8	66
Vilkaviškis, Lith.	G6	22
Vil'kickogo, proliv, strt., Russia	B18	26
Vilkija, Lith.	F6	22
Villa Abecia, Bol.	I9	82
Villa Aberastain, Arg.	F4	80
Villa Alemana, Chile	G3	80
Villa Ana, Arg.	E9	80
Villa Ángela, Arg.	D8	80
Villa Atamisqui, Arg.	E7	80
Villa Atuel, Arg.	H5	80
Villa Bella, Bol.	D9	82
Villa Berthet, Arg.	D8	80
Villa Bruzual, Ven.	C8	84
Villa Cañás, Arg.	H8	80
Villa Carlos Paz, Arg.	F6	80
Villacarrillo, Spain	G8	16
Villa Castelli, Arg.	E4	80
Villach, Aus.	I13	10
Villacidro, Italy	J3	18
Villa Comaltitlan, Mex.	B2	92
Villa Concepción del Tío, Arg.	F7	80
Villa Constitución, Arg.	G8	80
Villa de Arista, Mex.	F9	90
Villa de Arriaga, Mex.	G9	90
Villa de Cos, Mex.	F8	90
Villa de Cura, Ven.	B9	84
Villa del Rosario, Arg.	F7	80
Villa del Rosario, Arg.	F10	80
Villa del Rosario, Arg.	E7	80
Villa de María, Arg.	E7	80
Villa de Nova Sintra, C.V.	m16	64a
Villa de Soto, Arg.	F6	80
Villa Dolores, Arg.	F6	80
Villa Elisa, Arg.	G9	80
Villa Flores, Mex.	I13	90
Villafranca de los Barros, Spain	G5	16
Villafranca di Verona, Italy	D5	18
Villa Grove, Il., U.S.	D5	120
Villaguay, Arg.	F9	80
Villa Guerrero, Mex.	H10	90
Villa Guillermina, Arg.	E9	80
Villa Hayes, Para.	C10	80
Villahermosa, Mex.	I13	90
Villa Hidalgo, Mex.	G8	90
Villa Huidobro, Arg.	H6	80
Villa Insurgentes, Mex.	E4	90
Villa Iris, Arg.	J7	80
Villa Juárez, Mex.	D5	90
Villa Krause, Arg.	F4	80
Villaldama, Mex.	D9	90
Villalonga, Arg.	D4	78
Villa María, Arg.	G7	80
Villa María Grande, Arg.	F9	80
Villa Mazán, Arg.	E5	80
Villa Media Agua, Arg.	F4	80
Villamontes, Bol.	I10	82
Villa Nueva, Arg.	G4	80
Villa Nueva, Arg.	G7	80
Villanueva, Col.	B6	84
Villanueva, Hond.	C4	92
Villanueva, Mex.	F8	90
Villanueva, N.M., U.S.	B4	138
Villanueva de Córdoba, Spain	G7	16
Villanueva de la Serana, Spain	G6	16
Villa Ocampo, Arg.	E9	80
Villa Ojo de Agua, Arg.	E7	80
Villa Oliva, Para.	D10	80
Villa Oropeza, Bol.	H9	82
Villa Park, Il., U.S.	k8	120
Villa Quinteros, Arg.	D6	80
Villa Regina, Arg.	J5	80
Villa Rica, Ga., U.S.	C2	117
Villarrica, Chile	D2	78
Villarrica, Para.	C10	80
Villarrobledo, Spain	F9	16
Villas, N.J., U.S.	E3	137
Villa San Martín, Arg.	E6	80
Villa Unión, Arg.	E4	80
Villa Unión, Mex.	F6	90
Villa Unión, Mex.	C9	90
Villa Valeria, Arg.	H6	80
Villavicencio, Col.	E6	84
Villa Viscarra, Bol.	G9	82
Villazón, Bol.	J9	82
Villa Zorraquín, Arg.	F9	80
Villedieu, Fr.	D5	14
Villefranche, Fr.	G11	14
Villena, Spain	G11	16
Villeneuve-Saint-Georges, Fr.	D9	14
Villeneuve-sur-Lot, Fr.	H7	14
Ville Platte, La., U.S.	D3	125
Villerupt, Fr.	C12	14
Ville Saint-Georges, Que., Can.	C7	104
Villeurbanne, Fr.	G11	14
Villingen-Schwenningen, Ger.	G8	10
Villisca, Ia., U.S.	D3	122
Vilna, Alta., Can.	B5	98
Vilnius, Lith.	G8	22
Vilonia, Ar., U.S.	B3	111
Vil'uj, stm., Russia	E16	28
Vil'ujsk, Russia	E16	28
Vil'ujskoje vodochranilišče, res., Russia	E20	26
Vimioso, Port.	D7	14
Viña del Mar, Chile	G3	80
Vinalhaven, Me., U.S.	D4	126
Vinalhaven Island, i., Me., U.S.	D4	126
Vincennes, In., U.S.	G2	121
Vincent, Al., U.S.	B3	108
Vinces, Ec.	H3	84
Vinchina, Arg.	E4	80
Vindhya Range, mts., India	I7	44
Vine Grove, Ky., U.S.	C4	124
Vineland, N.J., U.S.	E2	137
Vinemont, Al., U.S.	A3	108
Vineyard Haven, Ma., U.S.	D6	128
Vineyard Sound, strt., Ma., U.S.	D6	128
Vinh, Viet.	E8	40
Vinh Long, Viet.	I8	40
Vinita, Ok., U.S.	A6	143
Vinkovci, Cro.	D2	20
Vinnytsya, Ukr.	H3	26
Vinson Massif, mtn., Ant.	C12	73
Vinton, Ia., U.S.	B5	122
Vinton, La., U.S.	D2	125
Vinton, Va., U.S.	C3	153
Vinton, co., Oh., U.S.	C3	142
Viola, Ar., U.S.	A4	111
Viola, Il., U.S.	B3	120
Violet, La., U.S.	k12	125
Viradouro, Braz.	F4	79
Virangehir, Tur.	C5	48
Virbalis, Lith.	G5	22
Virden, Man., Can.	E1	100
Virden, Il., U.S.	D4	120
Vire, Fr.	D6	14
Virgem da Lapa, Braz.	D7	79
Virgin, stm., U.S.	G8	135
Virgin, stm., U.S.	G8	135
Virginia, S. Afr.	G8	66
Virginia, Al., U.S.	g6	108
Virginia, Il., U.S.	D3	120
Virginia, Mn., U.S.	C6	130
Virginia, state, U.S.	C4	153
Virginia Beach, Va., U.S.	D7	153
Virginia City, Nv., U.S.	D2	135
Virginia Falls, wtfl, N.W. Ter., Can.	D7	96
Virginia Peak, mtn., Nv., U.S.	D2	135
Virgin Islands, dep., N.A.	E12	94
Virgin Mountains, mts., U.S.	A1	110
Virginópolis, Braz.	E7	79
Viroqua, Wi., U.S.	E3	156
Virovitica, Cro.	D12	18
Virrat, Fin.	J18	6
Virú, Peru	C2	82
Virudunagar, India	H4	46
Vis, Cro.	F11	18
Vis, Otok, i., Cro.	F11	18
Visalia, Ca., U.S.	D4	112
Visayan Sea, Phil.	C7	38
Visby, Swe.	M16	6
Viscount, Sask., Can.	F3	105
Viscount Melville Sound, strt., N.W. Ter., Can.	B11	96
Visé (Wezet), Bel.	G8	12
Višegrad, Bos.	F3	20
Viseu, Port.	E4	16
Vishākhapatnam, India	D7	46
Visoko, Bos.	F2	20
Visp, Switz.	F8	13
Vista, Ca., U.S.	F5	112
Vista Flores, Arg.	G3	80
Vistula see Wisła, stm., Pol.	A18	10
Vita, Man., Can.	E3	100
Vitarte, Peru	E3	82
Vitebsk, Bela.	F13	22
Viterbo, Italy	G7	18
Viti Levu, i., Fiji	J21	158
Vitim, stm., Russia	F14	28
Vítor, Peru	G6	82
Vitória, Braz.	F8	79
Vitoria (Gasteiz), Spain	C9	16
Vitória da Conquista, Braz.	C8	79
Vitré, Fr.	D5	14
Vitry-le-François, Fr.	D11	14
Vittel, Fr.	D12	14
Vittoria, Italy	M9	18
Vittorio Veneto, Italy	D7	18
Vivian, La., U.S.	B2	125
Vizcaíno, Desierto de, des., Mex.	D3	90
Vizianagaram, India	C7	46
Vlaardingen, Neth.	E5	12
Vladikavkaz, Russia	I6	26
Vladimir, Russia	E23	22
Vladivostok, Russia	I18	28
Vlasenica, Bos.	E2	20
Vlieland, i., Neth.	B7	12
Vlissingen (Flushing), Neth.	F4	12
Vlonë see Vlorë, Alb.	I3	20
Vlorë, Alb.	I3	20
Vltava, stm., Czech Rep.	F14	10
Vnukovo, Russia	F20	22
Vochtoga, Russia	C24	22
Voghera, Italy	E3	18
Vohibinany, Madag.	q23	67b
Vohimarina, Madag.	n24	67b
Võhma, Est.	C8	22
Voinjama, Lib.	G5	64
Voiron, Fr.	G12	14
Voitsberg, Aus.	H15	10
Volcán, Pan.	B6	80
Volcán, Pan.	C1	84
Volcano, Hi., U.S.	D6	118
Volchov, Russia	B15	22
Volga, Russia	D21	22
Volga, S.D., U.S.	C9	148
Volga, stm., Russia	H7	26
Volgodonsk, Russia	H6	26
Volgograd (Stalingrad), Russia	H6	26
Volgogradskoje vodochranilišče, res., Russia	H7	26
Völklingen, Ger.	F6	10
Volkovysk, Bela.	H7	22
Volksrust, S. Afr.	F9	66
Volodarsk, Russia	E26	22
Vologda, Russia	B22	22
Volokolamsk, Russia	E18	22
Volosovo, Russia	B12	22
Volovo, Russia	H21	22
Vološin, Bela.	G9	22
Vol'sk, Russia	G7	26
Volta, stm., Ghana	H10	64
Volta, Lake, res., Ghana	H9	64
Volta Blanche (White Volta), stm., Afr.	F6	54
Volta Noire (Black Volta), stm., Afr.	F6	54
Volta Redonda, Braz.	G6	79
Volta Rouge, stm., Afr.	F9	64
Volterra, Italy	F5	18
Volusia, co., Fl., U.S.	C5	116
Volžsk, Russia	F7	26
Volžskij, Russia	H6	26
Vondrozo, Madag.	s22	67b
Vonore, Tn., U.S.	D9	149
Vopnafjördur, Ice.	B6	6a
Vorarlberg, state, Aus.	H9	10
Vorder-Grauspitz, mtn., Eur.	D12	13
Vordingborg, Den.	N12	6
Vorkuta, Russia	D10	26
Voronovo, Bela.	G8	22
Voronež, Russia	G5	26
Voropajevo, Bela.	F10	22
Voroshilovsk see Stavropol', Russia	H6	26
Vorsma, Russia	F26	22
Võrtsjärv, l., Est.	C9	22
Võru, Est.	D10	22
Vosges, mts., Fr.	D14	14
Voskresensk, Russia	F21	22
Voss, Nor.	K10	6
Vostočno-Sibirskoje more (East Siberian Sea), Russia	C23	28
Votkinsk, Russia	F8	26
Votuporanga, Braz.	F4	79
Vouziers, Fr.	C11	14
Voyageurs National Park, Mn., U.S.	B5	130
Vožega, Russia	A23	22
Voznesens'k, Ukr.	H4	26
Voznesenskoje, Russia	G25	22
Vraca, Bul.	F7	20
Vrangel'a, ostrov, i., Russia	C28	28
Vranje, Yugo.	G5	20
Vrbas, Yugo.	D3	20
Vrede, S. Afr.	F9	66
Vredenburg, S. Afr.	I3	66
Vredendal, S. Afr.	H4	66
Vreed en Hoop, Guy.	D13	84
Vršac, Yugo.	D5	20
Vryburg, S. Afr.	F7	66
Vryheid, S. Afr.	F10	66
Vsetín, Czech Rep.	F17	10
Vsevidof, Mount, mtn., Ak., U.S.	E6	109
Vukovar, Cro.	D3	20
Vulcan, Alta., Can.	D4	98
Vulcan, Mi., U.S.	C3	129
Vulcănești, Mol.	D12	20
Vung Tau, Viet.	I9	40
Vuoksenniska, Fin.	K21	6
Vyborg, Russia	A11	22
Vyksa, Russia	F25	22
Vylkove, Ukr.	D13	20
Vynohradiv, Ukr.	A7	20
Vypolzovo, Russia	D16	22
Vyrica, Russia	B13	22
Vyškov, Czech Rep.	F17	10
Vyšnij Voloček, Russia	D17	22
Vysoké Tatry, mts., Eur.	F20	10
Vysokogornyj, Russia	G19	28
Vysokoje, Bela.	H5	22
Vysokovsk, Russia	E19	22
Vytegra, Russia	E5	26

W

Name	Map Ref.	Page
Wa, Ghana	F8	64
Waal, stm., Neth.	E7	12
Wabag, Pap. N. Gui.	G11	38
Wabamun, Alta., Can.	C3	98
Wabana (Bell Island), Newf., Can.	E5	102
Wabasca, Alta., Can.	B4	98
Wabasca, stm., Alta., Can.	f1	98
Wabash, In., U.S.	C6	121
Wabash, co., In., U.S.	C6	121
Wabash, co., Il., U.S.	E6	120
Wabash, stm., U.S.	H2	121
Wabasha, Mn., U.S.	F6	130
Wabasha, co., Mn., U.S.	F6	130
Wabasso, Mn., U.S.	F3	130
Wabaunsee, co., Ks., U.S.	D7	123
Wabbaseka, Ar., U.S.	C4	111
Wabeno, Wi., U.S.	C5	156
Wabowden, Man., Can.	B2	100
Wabush, Newf., Can.	h8	102
Waccamaw, Lake, l., N.C., U.S.	C4	140
Wachusett Reservoir, res., Ma., U.S.	B4	128
Waco, Tx., U.S.	D4	150
Waco Lake, res., Tx., U.S.	D4	150
Waconda Lake, res., Ks., U.S.	C5	123
Waconia, Mn., U.S.	F5	130
Waddell, Az., U.S.	k8	110
Waddenzee, Neth.	B7	12
Waddington, Mount, mtn., B.C., Can.	D5	99
Wade, Mount, mtn., Ant.	D9	73
Wadena, Mn., U.S.	D3	130
Wadena, co., Mn., U.S.	D4	130
Wadesboro, N.C., U.S.	C2	140
Wādī as-Sīr, Jord.	E5	50
Wādī Halfā', Sud.	G6	60
Wadley, Al., U.S.	B4	108
Wadley, Ga., U.S.	D4	117
Wad Madanī, Sud.	J7	60
Wadowice, Pol.	F19	10
Wadsworth, Il., U.S.	h9	120
Wadsworth, Nv., U.S.	D2	135
Wadsworth, Oh., U.S.	A4	142
Waegwan, S. Kor.	H16	32
Wageningen, Neth.	E8	12
Wageningen, Sur.	E14	84
Wagga Wagga, Austl.	J7	70
Wagner, S.D., U.S.	D7	148
Wagoner, Ok., U.S.	B6	143
Wagoner, co., Ok., U.S.	B6	143
Wagon Mound, N.M., U.S.	A5	138
Wagrowiec, Pol.	C17	10
Wäh Cantonment, Pak.	D5	44
Wahiawa, Hi., U.S.	B3	118
Wahkiakum, co., Wa., U.S.	C2	154
Wahoo, Ne., U.S.	C9	134
Wahpeton, N.D., U.S.	C9	141
Wahran (Oran), Alg.	C10	62
Waialua, Hi., U.S.	B3	118
Waianae, Hi., U.S.	B3	118
Waiblingen, Ger.	G9	10
Waidhofen an der Thaya, Aus.	G15	10
Waidhofen an der Ybbs, Aus.	H14	10
Waihee, Hi., U.S.	C5	118
Waihi, N.Z.	B5	72
Waikapu, Hi., U.S.	C5	118
Waikato, stm., N.Z.	C5	72
Waikerie, Austl.	J3	70
Waikiki Beach, Hi., U.S.	g10	118
Wailua, Hi., U.S.	A2	118
Wailuku, Hi., U.S.	C5	118
Waimanalo, Hi., U.S.	B4	118
Waimate, N.Z.	F3	72
Waimea, Hi., U.S.	B2	118
Waimea, Hi., U.S.	f9	118
Waingapu, Indon.	G7	38
Wainwright, Alta., Can.	C5	98
Wainwright, Ak., U.S.	A8	109
Waipahu, Hi., U.S.	B3	118
Waipio Acres, Hi., U.S.	g9	118
Waipukurau, N.Z.	C6	72
Wairoa, N.Z.	C6	72
Waitara, N.Z.	C5	72
Waite Park, Mn., U.S.	E4	130
Waitsburg, Wa., U.S.	C7	154
Waitsfield, Vt., U.S.	C3	152
Waiuku, N.Z.	B5	72
Waka, Eth.	N9	60
Wakarusa, In., U.S.	A5	121
Wakaw, Sask., Can.	E3	105
Wakayama, Japan	M10	36
Wake, co., N.C., U.S.	B4	140
WaKeeney, Ks., U.S.	C4	123
Wakefield, Ks., U.S.	C6	123
Wakefield, Ma., U.S.	B5	128
Wakefield, Mi., U.S.	n12	129
Wakefield, Ne., U.S.	B9	134
Wakefield, R.I., U.S.	F3	146
Wakefield, Va., U.S.	D6	153
Wake Forest, N.C., U.S.	B4	140
Wake Island, dep., Oc.	E24	2
Wakema, Mya.	F3	40
Wakonda, S.D., U.S.	D8	148
Waku Kundo, Ang.	D3	58
Wakulla, co., Fl., U.S.	B2	116
Walachia, hist. reg., Rom.	E8	20
Walbridge, Oh., U.S.	e6	142
Wałbrzych (Waldenburg), Pol.	E16	10
Walcott, Ia., U.S.	C7	122
Walcott, Lake, res., Id., U.S.	G5	119
Wałcz, Pol.	B16	10
Wald, Switz.	D10	13
Waldeck, Sask., Can.	G2	105
Walden, Ont., Can.	A3	103
Walden, Co., U.S.	A4	113
Walden, N.Y., U.S.	D6	139
Waldenburg, Ar., U.S.	B5	111
Walden Pond, l., Ma., U.S.	g10	128
Walden Ridge, mtn., Tn., U.S.	D8	149
Waldheim, Sask., Can.	E2	105
Waldo, Ar., U.S.	D2	111
Waldo, co., Me., U.S.	D3	126
Waldoboro, Me., U.S.	D3	126
Waldport, Or., U.S.	C2	144
Waldron, Ar., U.S.	C1	111
Waldron, In., U.S.	F6	121
Waldshut, Ger.	H8	10
Waldwick, N.J., U.S.	A4	137
Walenstadt, Switz.	D11	13
Wales, ter., U.K.	I10	8
Waleska, Ga., U.S.	B2	117
Walgett, Austl.	H8	70
Walhalla, N.D., U.S.	A8	141
Walhalla, S.C., U.S.	B1	147
Walker, Ia., U.S.	B6	122
Walker, La., U.S.	g10	125
Walker, Mi., U.S.	E5	129
Walker, co., Al., U.S.	B2	108
Walker, co., Ga., U.S.	B1	117
Walker, co., Tx., U.S.	D5	150
Walker, stm., Nv., U.S.	D3	135
Walker Lake, l., Nv., U.S.	E3	135
Walkersville, Md., U.S.	B3	127
Walkerton, Ont., Can.	C3	103
Walkerton, In., U.S.	B5	121
Walkertown, N.C., U.S.	A2	140
Walkerville, Mt., U.S.	D3	133
Wall, S.D., U.S.	D3	148
Wallace, Id., U.S.	B3	119
Wallace, N.C., U.S.	C4	140
Wallace, W.V., U.S.	B4	155
Wallace, co., Ks., U.S.	D2	123
Wallaceburg, Ont., Can.	E2	103
Wallaroo, Austl.	I2	70

Name	Map Ref.	Page

Walla Walla, Wa., U.S. C7 154
Walla Walla, co., Wa., U.S. C7 154
Walled Lake, Mi., U.S. . . . o15 129
Wallen, In., U.S. B7 121
Wallenpaupack, Lake, l.,
Pa., U.S. D11 145
Waller, co., Tx., U.S. E4 150
Wallingford, Ct., U.S. D4 114
Wallingford, Vt., U.S. E3 152
Wallington, N.J., U.S. h8 137
Wallis and Futuna, dep.,
Oc. G1 2
Wallisellen, Switz. D10 13
Wall Lake, Ia., U.S. B2 122
Wallowa, Or., U.S. B9 144
Wallowa, co., Or., U.S. . . . B9 144
Wallowa Mountains, mts.,
Or., U.S. B9 144
Wallula, Lake, res., U.S. . . C7 154
Walnut, Il., U.S. B4 120
Walnut, Ia., U.S. C2 122
Walnut, Ms., U.S. A5 131
Walnut, stm., Ks., U.S. . . . E6 123
Walnut Creek, Ca., U.S. . . h8 112
Walnut Grove, Al., U.S. . . . A3 108
Walnut Grove, Mo., U.S. . . D4 132
Walnut Hill, Me., U.S. g7 126
Walnutport, Pa., U.S. E10 145
Walnut Ridge, Ar., U.S. . . . A5 111
Walpole, Ma., U.S. B5 128
Walpole, N.H., U.S. D2 136
Walsenburg, Co., U.S. . . . D6 113
Walsh, Co., U.S. D8 113
Walsh, co., N.D., U.S. A8 141
Walsrode, Ger. C9 10
Walterboro, S.C., U.S. F6 147
Walter F. George Lake,
res., U.S. D4 108
Walters, Ok., U.S. C3 143
Walthall, co., Ms., U.S. . . . D3 131
Waltham, Ma., U.S. B5 128
Walthill, Ne., U.S. B9 134
Walthourville, Ga., U.S. . . . E5 117
Walton, In., U.S. C5 121
Walton, Ky., U.S. B5 124
Walton, N.Y., U.S. C5 139
Walton, Fl., U.S. u15 116
Walton, co., Ga., U.S. C3 117
Walworth, Wi., U.S. F5 156
Walworth, co., S.D., U.S. . . B5 148
Walworth, co., Wi., U.S. . . . F5 156
Wamac, Il., U.S. E4 120
Wamego, Ks., U.S. C7 123
Wamesit, Ma., U.S. A5 128
Wamsutter, Wy., U.S. E5 157
Wanaaring, Austl. G6 70
Wanamingo, Mn., U.S. F6 130
Wan'an, China I3 34
Wanapum Lake, res., Wa.,
U.S. B6 154
Wanaque, N.J., U.S. A4 137
Wanaque Reservoir, res.,
N.J., U.S. A4 137
Wanatah, In., U.S. B4 121
Wanblee, S.D., U.S. D4 148
Wanchese, N.C., U.S. B7 140
Wando Woods, S.C., U.S. . . k11 147
Wanganui, N.Z. C5 72
Wangaratta, Austl. K7 70
Wanghu, China D1 32
Wangjiang, China E5 34
Wanham, Alta., Can. D9 34
Wanli, China F3 68
Wanneroo, Austl. E8 30
Wanxian, China G3 34
Wanzai, China B1 142
Wapakoneta, Oh., U.S. . . . C5 154
Wapato, Wa., U.S. . . . . . .
Wapawekka Lake, l., Sask.,
Can. C3 105
Wapella, Sask., Can. G5 105
Wapello, Ia., U.S. C6 122
Wapello, co., Ia., U.S. C5 122
Wappingers Falls, N.Y.,
U.S. D7 139
Wapsipinicon, stm., Ia., U.S. B6 122
Waqqaş, Jord. C5 50
War, W.V., U.S. D3 155
Warangal, India C5 46
Warbreccan, Austl. E5 70
Warburg, Alta., Can. C3 98
Warburg, Ger. D9 10
Warburton Creek, stm.,
Austl. E7 68
Ward, Ar., U.S. B4 111
Ward, co., N.D., U.S. A4 141
Ward, co., Tx., U.S. D1 150
Warden, Wa., U.S. C6 154
Wardha, India B5 46
Ward Mountain, mtn., Mt.,
U.S. D2 133
Ware, Ma., U.S. B3 128
Ware, co., Ga., U.S. E4 117
Ware, stm., Ma., U.S. B3 128
Waregem, Bel. G3 12
Wareham, Ma., U.S. C6 128
Warehouse Point, Ct., U.S. . B5 114
Waremme (Borgworm), Bel. . G7 12
Waren, Ger. B12 10
Warendorf, Ger. D7 10
Ware Shoals, S.C., U.S. . . . C3 147
Warfield, B.C., U.S. E9 99
Wargla, Alg. E13 62
Warialda, Austl. G9 70
Warin Chamrap, Thai. G8 40
Warkworth, Ont., Can. C7 103
Warman, Sask., Can. G4 66
Warmbad, Nmb. E9 66
Warmbad, S. Afr. E9 66
Warminster, Pa., U.S. F11 145
Warm Springs, Ga., U.S. . . D2 117
Warm Springs Reservoir,
res., Or., U.S. D8 144
Warner, Alta., Can. E4 98
Warner, N.H., U.S. D3 136
Warner, Ok., U.S. B6 143
Warner, S.D., U.S. B7 148
Warner Peak, mtn., Or.,
U.S. E7 144
Warner Robins, Ga., U.S. . . D3 117

Warnes, Bol. G10 82
Warracknabeal, Austl. K5 70
Warr Acres, Ok., U.S. B4 143
Warragul, Austl. L6 70
Warren, Ar., U.S. D3 111
Warren, I., U.S. A4 120
Warren, In., U.S. C7 121
Warren, Me., U.S. D3 126
Warren, Mi., U.S. F7 129
Warren, Mn., U.S. B2 130
Warren, N.H., U.S. C3 136
Warren, Oh., U.S. A5 142
Warren, Or., U.S. B4 144
Warren, Pa., U.S. C3 145
Warren, R.I., U.S. D5 146
Warren, Vt., U.S. C3 152
Warren, co., Ga., U.S. C4 117
Warren, co., Il., U.S. C3 120
Warren, co., In., U.S. D3 121
Warren, co., Ia., U.S. C4 122
Warren, co., Ky., U.S. C3 124
Warren, co., Ms., U.S. C3 131
Warren, co., Mo., U.S. C6 132
Warren, co., N.J., U.S. B3 137
Warren, co., N.Y., U.S. B7 139
Warren, co., N.C., U.S. A4 140
Warren, co., Oh., U.S. C1 142
Warren, co., Pa., U.S. C3 145
Warren, co., Tn., U.S. D8 149
Warren, co., Va., U.S. B4 153
Warren Park, In., U.S. k10 121
Warrensburg, Il., U.S. D4 120
Warrensburg, Mo., U.S. . . . C4 132
Warrensburg, N.Y., U.S. . . . B7 139
Warrensville Heights, Oh.,
U.S. h9 142
Warrenton, S. Afr. G7 66
Warrenton, Ga., U.S. C4 117
Warrenton, Mo., U.S. C6 132
Warrenton, Or., U.S. A3 144
Warrenton, Va., U.S. B5 153
Warrenville, Il., U.S. k8 120
Warrenville, S.C., U.S. D4 147
Warri, Nig. I12 64
Warrick, co., In., U.S. H3 121
Warrington, Fl., U.S. u14 116
Warrior, Al., U.S. B3 108
Warrnambool, Austl. L5 70
Warroad, Mn., U.S. B3 130
Warsaw see Warszawa,
Pol. C21 10
Warsaw, Il., U.S. C2 120
Warsaw, In., U.S. B6 121
Warsaw, Ky., U.S. B5 124
Warsaw, Mo., U.S. C4 132
Warsaw, N.Y., U.S. C2 139
Warsaw, N.C., U.S. B4 140
Warsaw, Va., U.S. C6 153
Warszawa (Warsaw), Pol. . . C21 10
Warta, stm., Pol. C15 10
Wartburg, Tn., U.S. C9 149
Warwick, Austl. G10 70
Warwick, Que., Can. D6 104
Warwick, Eng., U.K. I12 8
Warwick, N.Y., U.S. D6 139
Warwick, R.I., U.S. D4 146
Warwickshire, co., Eng.,
U.K. I12 8
Wasaga Beach, Ont., Can. . . C4 103
Wasatch, co., Ut., U.S. C4 151
Wasco, Ca., U.S. E4 112
Wasco, co., Or., U.S. B5 144
Waseca, Mn., U.S. F5 130
Waseca, co., Mn., U.S. F5 130
Washakie, co., Wy., U.S. . . . C5 157
Washburn, Il., U.S. C4 120
Washburn, Me., U.S. B5 126
Washburn, N.D., U.S. B5 141
Washburn, Wi., U.S. B3 156
Washburn, co., Wi., U.S. . . . C2 156
Washington, D.C., U.S. C3 127
Washington, Ga., U.S. C4 117
Washington, Il., U.S. C4 120
Washington, In., U.S. G3 121
Washington, Ia., U.S. C6 122
Washington, Ks., U.S. C6 123
Washington, Ky., U.S. B6 124
Washington, La., U.S. D3 125
Washington, Mo., U.S. C6 132
Washington, N.J., U.S. B3 137
Washington, N.C., U.S. B5 140
Washington, Pa., U.S. F1 145
Washington, Ut., U.S. F2 151
Washington, Vt., U.S. C4 152
Washington, co., Al., U.S. . . D1 108
Washington, co., Ar., U.S. . . A1 111
Washington, co., Co., U.S. . . B7 113
Washington, co., Fl., U.S. . . u16 116
Washington, co., Ga., U.S. . . C4 117
Washington, co., Id., U.S. . . E2 119
Washington, co., Il., U.S. . . . E4 120
Washington, co., In., U.S. . . G5 121
Washington, co., Ia., U.S. . . C6 122
Washington, co., Ks., U.S. . . C6 123
Washington, co., Ky., U.S. . . C4 124
Washington, co., La., U.S. . . D5 125
Washington, co., Me., U.S. . . D5 126
Washington, co., Md., U.S. . . A2 127
Washington, co., Mn., U.S. . . E6 130
Washington, co., Ms., U.S. . . B3 131
Washington, co., Mo., U.S. . . D7 132
Washington, co., Ne., U.S. . . C9 134
Washington, co., N.Y., U.S. . . B7 139
Washington, co., N.C., U.S. . . B6 140
Washington, co., Oh., U.S. . . C4 142
Washington, co., Ok., U.S. . . A6 143
Washington, co., Or., U.S. . . B3 144
Washington, co., Pa., U.S. . . F1 145
Washington, co., R.I., U.S. . . E2 146
Washington, co., Tn., U.S. . . C11 149
Washington, co., Tx., U.S. . . D4 150
Washington, co., Ut., U.S. . . F2 151
Washington, co., Vt., U.S. . . C3 152
Washington, co., Va., U.S. . . f9 153
Washington, co., Wi., U.S. . . E5 156
Washington, state, U.S. B5 154
Washington, Lake, l., Wa.,
U.S. e11 154

Washington, Mount, mtn.,
N.H., U.S. B4 136
Washington Court House,
Oh., U.S. C2 142
Washington Island, i., Wi.,
U.S. C7 156
Washington Park, Il., U.S. . . E3 120
Washington Terrace, Ut.,
U.S. B4 151
Washita, co., Ok., U.S. B2 143
Washita, stm., Ok., U.S. . . . C4 143
Washoe, co., Nv., U.S. C2 135
Washoe City, Nv., U.S. D2 135
Washougal, Wa., U.S. D3 154
Washtenaw, co., Mi., U.S. . . F7 129
Wasilla, Ak., U.S. C10 109
Waskada, Man., Can. E1 100
Waskatenau, Alta., Can. . . . B4 98
Waspam, Nic. C11 92
Waspuk, stm., Nic. C10 92
Wassenaar, Neth. D5 12
Watampone, Indon. F7 38
Watatic, Mount, mtn., Ma.,
U.S. A4 128
Watauga, co., N.C., U.S. . . . A1 140
Watauga Lake, res., Tn.,
U.S. C12 149
Watch Hill, R.I., U.S. G1 146
Watch Hill Point, c., R.I.,
U.S. G1 146
Watchung, N.J., U.S. B4 137
Waterboro, Me., U.S. E2 126
Waterbury, Ct., U.S. C3 114
Waterbury, Vt., U.S. C3 152
Waterbury Center, Vt., U.S. . C3 152
Wateree, stm., S.C., U.S. . . D6 147
Wateree Lake, res., S.C.,
U.S. C6 147
Waterflow, N.M., U.S. A1 138
Waterford, Ire. I6 8
Waterford, Ct., U.S. D7 114
Waterford, Wi., U.S. F5 156
Waterford, co., Ire. I6 8
Waterloo, Bel. G5 12
Waterloo, Ont., Can. D4 103
Waterloo, Que., Can. D5 104
Waterloo, Il., U.S. E3 120
Waterloo, In., U.S. B7 121
Waterloo, Ia., U.S. B5 122
Waterloo, Ne., U.S. g12 134
Waterloo, N.Y., U.S. C4 139
Waterloo, Wi., U.S. E5 156
Waterman, Il., U.S. B5 120
Waterproof, La., U.S. C4 125
Waterton Lakes National
Park, Alta., Can. E3 98
Watertown, Ct., U.S. C3 114
Watertown, Fl., U.S. B4 116
Watertown, Ma., U.S. g11 128
Watertown, N.Y., U.S. B5 139
Watertown, S.D., U.S. C8 148
Watertown, Tn., U.S. A5 149
Watertown, Wi., U.S. E5 156
Water Valley, Ms., U.S. A4 131
Waterville, Me., U.S. C7 123
Waterville, Me., U.S. D3 126
Waterville, Mn., U.S. F5 130
Waterville, Oh., U.S. A2 142
Waterville, Wa., U.S. B5 154
Watervliet, Mi., U.S. F4 129
Watervliet, N.Y., U.S. C7 139
Watford, Ont., Can. E3 103
Watford City, N.D., U.S. . . . B2 141
Wathena, Ks., U.S. C9 123
Watkins, Mn., U.S. E4 130
Watkins Glen, N.Y., U.S. . . . C4 139
Watkinsville, Ga., U.S. C3 117
Watling Island see San
Salvador, i., Bah. B7 94
Watonga, Ok., U.S. B3 143
Watonwan, co., Mn., U.S. . . F3 130
Watrous, Sask., Can. F3 105
Watseka, Il., U.S. C6 120
Watson, Sask., Can. E3 105
Watson Lake, Yukon, Can. . . D7 96
Watsontown, Pa., U.S. D8 145
Watsonville, Ca., U.S. D3 112
Wattenberg, Co., U.S. A6 113
Watts (part of Los Angeles),
Ca., U.S. n12 112
Watts Bar Lake, res., Tn.,
U.S. D9 149
Wattsville, S.C., U.S. B4 147
Wattwil, Switz. D11 13
Watzmann, mtn., Ger. H12 10
Waubay, S.D., U.S. B8 148
Wauchope, Austl. H10 70
Wauchula, Fl., U.S. E5 116
Wauconda, Il., U.S. h8 120
Waukee, Ia., U.S. C4 122
Waukegan, Il., U.S. A6 120
Waukesha, Wi., U.S. F5 156
Waukesha, co., Wi., U.S. . . . E5 156
Waukomis, Ok., U.S. A4 143
Waukon, Ia., U.S. A6 122
Waunakee, Wi., U.S. E4 156
Wauneta, Ne., U.S. D4 134
Waupaca, Wi., U.S. D5 156
Waupaca, co., Wi., U.S. . . . D5 156
Waupun, Wi., U.S. E5 156
Wauregan, Ct., U.S. C8 114
Waurika, Ok., U.S. C4 143
Wausa, Ne., U.S. B8 134
Wauseon, Oh., U.S. A1 142
Wautoma, Wi., U.S. D4 156
Wauwatosa, Wi., U.S. m12 156
Wave Hill, Austl. C6 68
Waveland, Ms., U.S. E4 131
Waverley, N.S., Can. E6 101
Waverly, Il., U.S. D4 120
Waverly, Ia., U.S. B5 122
Waverly, Ks., U.S. D8 123
Waverly, Mo., U.S. B4 132
Waverly, Ne., U.S. D9 134
Waverly, N.Y., U.S. C4 139
Waverly, Oh., U.S. C3 142
Waverly, Tn., U.S. A4 149
Waverly, Va., U.S. C5 153
Waverly, W.V., U.S. B3 155

Waverly Hall, Ga., U.S. D2 117
Wavre (Waver), Bel. G6 12
Wäw, Sud. N4 60
Wawa, stm., Nic. C11 92
Wawanesa, Man., Can. E2 100
Wawota, Sask., Can. H4 105
Waxahachie, Tx., U.S. C4 150
Waxhaw, N.C., U.S. C2 140
Waycross, Ga., U.S. E4 117
Wayland, Ia., U.S. C6 122
Wayland, Ma., U.S. g10 128
Wayland, Mi., U.S. F5 129
Waylyn, S.C., U.S. k12 147
Wayne, Mi., U.S. p15 129
Wayne, Ne., U.S. B8 134
Wayne, N.J., U.S. B4 137
Wayne, W.V., U.S. C2 155
Wayne, co., Ga., U.S. E5 117
Wayne, co., Il., U.S. E5 120
Wayne, co., In., U.S. E7 121
Wayne, co., Ia., U.S. D4 122
Wayne, co., Ky., U.S. D5 124
Wayne, co., Mi., U.S. F7 129
Wayne, co., Ms., U.S. D5 131
Wayne, co., Mo., U.S. D7 132
Wayne, co., Ne., U.S. B8 134
Wayne, co., N.Y., U.S. B3 139
Wayne, co., N.C., U.S. B4 140
Wayne, co., Oh., U.S. B4 142
Wayne, co., Pa., U.S. C11 145
Wayne, co., Tn., U.S. B4 149
Wayne, co., Ut., U.S. E4 151
Wayne, co., W.V., U.S. C2 155
Wayne City, Il., U.S. E5 120
Waynesboro, Ga., U.S. C4 117
Waynesboro, Ms., U.S. D5 131
Waynesboro, Pa., U.S. G6 145
Waynesboro, Tn., U.S. B4 149
Waynesboro, Va., U.S. B4 153
Waynesburg, Pa., U.S. G1 145
Waynesville, Mo., U.S. D5 132
Waynesville, N.C., U.S. f10 140
Waynesville, Oh., U.S. C1 142
Waynetown, In., U.S. D3 121
Waynewood, Va., U.S. g12 153
Waynoka, Ok., U.S. A3 143
Wayzata, Mn., U.S. n11 130
Wazīrābād, Pak. D6 44
Weakley, co., Tn., U.S. A3 149
Weare, N.H., U.S. D3 136
Weatherford, Ok., U.S. B3 143
Weatherford, Tx., U.S. C4 150
Weatherly, Pa., U.S. E10 145
Weatogue, Ct., U.S. B4 114
Weaver, Al., U.S. B4 108
Weaverville, N.C., U.S. f10 140
Webb, Al., U.S. D4 108
Webb, Ms., U.S. B3 131
Webb, co., Tx., U.S. F3 150
Webb City, Mo., U.S. D3 132
Webberville, Mi., U.S. F6 129
Webberville, Mi., U.S. F6 129
Webbwood, Ont., Can. A3 103
Weber, co., Ut., U.S. B4 151
Weber City, Va., U.S. f9 153
Webster, Ma., U.S. B4 128
Webster, N.Y., U.S. B3 139
Webster, S.D., U.S. B8 148
Webster, co., Ga., U.S. D2 117
Webster, co., Ia., U.S. B3 122
Webster, co., Ky., U.S. C2 124
Webster, co., La., U.S. B2 125
Webster, co., Ms., U.S. B4 131
Webster, co., Mo., U.S. D5 132
Webster, co., Ne., U.S. D7 134
Webster, co., W.V., U.S. . . . C4 155
Webster City, Ia., U.S. B4 122
Webster Groves, Mo., U.S. . f13 132
Webster Springs, W.V.,
U.S. C4 155
Websterville, Vt., U.S. C4 152
Weddell Sea, Ant. B1 73
Wedgeport, N.S., Can. F4 101
Wedgewood, Mo., U.S. f13 132
Wedowee, Al., U.S. B4 108
Wedza, Zimb. B10 66
Weed Heights, Nv., U.S. . . . E2 135
Weedsport, N.Y., U.S. B4 139
Weehawken, N.J., U.S. h8 137
Weeksbury, Ky., U.S. C7 124
Weenen, S. Afr. G10 66
Weeping Water, Ne., U.S. . . D9 134
Weert, Neth. F8 12
Wee Waa, Austl. H8 70
Weiden in der Oberpfalz,
Ger. F12 10
Weifang, China G7 32
Weihai, China F10 32
Weimar, Ger. E11 10
Weinan, China E8 30
Weiner, Ar., U.S. B5 111
Weinfelden, Switz. C11 13
Weinheim, Ger. F8 10
Weipa, Austl. B8 68
Weippe, Id., U.S. C3 119
Weir, Ks., U.S. E9 123
Weir, Ms., U.S. B4 131
Weirton, W.V., U.S. A4 155
Weisbury, Arg. D7 80
Weisburd, Arg. E2 119
Weishan (Xiazhen), China . . I5 32
Weissenfels, Ger. D11 10
Weisshorn, mtn., Switz. F8 13
Weiss Lake, res., U.S. A4 108
Weiz, Aus. H15 10
Wejherowo, Pol. A18 10
Welch, W.V., U.S. D3 155
Welcome, Mn., U.S. G4 130
Welcome, S.C., U.S. B3 147
Weld, co., Co., U.S. A6 113
Weldon, Sask., Can. E3 105
Weldon, N.C., U.S. A5 140
Weldon, stm., U.S. A4 132
Weldon Spring, Mo., U.S. . . f12 132
Weleetka, Ok., U.S. B5 143
Welkite, Eth. M9 60
Welkom, S. Afr. F8 66
Welland, Ont., Can. E5 103
Wellesley, Ont., Can. D4 103
Wellesley Islands, is., Austl. . C7 68
Wellesley Islands, is., Austl. . A3 70
Wellfleet, Ma., U.S. C7 128

Wellford, S.C., U.S. B3 147
Wellington, Austl. I8 70
Wellington, Ont., Can. D7 103
Wellington, N.Z. D5 72
Wellington, S. Afr. I4 66
Wellington, Co., U.S. A5 113
Wellington, Ks., U.S. E6 123
Wellington, Mo., U.S. B4 132
Wellington, Nv., U.S. E2 135
Wellington, Oh., U.S. A3 142
Wellington, Ut., U.S. D5 151
Wellington, Isla, i., Chile . . . F2 78
Wellington Station, P.E.I.,
Can. C5 101
Wellman, Ia., U.S. C6 122
Wells, Me., U.S. E2 126
Wells, Mn., U.S. G5 130
Wells, Nv., U.S. B7 135
Wells, Vt., U.S. E2 152
Wells, co., In., U.S. C7 121
Wells, co., N.D., U.S. B6 141
Wells Beach, Me., U.S. E2 126
Wellsboro, Pa., U.S. C7 145
Wellsburg, Ia., U.S. B5 122
Wellsburg, W.V., U.S. A4 155
Wellston, Oh., U.S. C3 142
Wellston, Ok., U.S. B4 143
Wellsville, Ks., U.S. D8 123
Wellsville, Mo., U.S. B6 132
Wellsville, N.Y., U.S. C3 139
Wellsville, Oh., U.S. B5 142
Wellsville, Ut., U.S. B4 151
Wellton, Az., U.S. E1 110
Wels, Aus. G14 10
Welsh, La., U.S. D3 125
Welwitschia, Nmb. C2 66
Wembley, Alta., Can. B1 98
Wenatchee, Wa., U.S. B5 154
Wenatchee, stm., Wa., U.S. . B5 154
Wenatchee Mountains,
mts., Wa., U.S. B5 154
Wenchow see Wenzhou,
China G9 34
Wendell, Id., U.S. G4 119
Wendell, N.C., U.S. B4 140
Wenden, Az., U.S. D2 110
Wendeng, China F10 32
Wendo, Eth. N10 60
Wendover, Ut., U.S. C1 151
Wengyang, China G9 34
Wengyuan, China K3 34
Wenham, Ma., U.S. A6 128
Wenling, China G10 34
Wenona, Il., U.S. B4 120
Wenshan, China C8 40
Wentworth, Austl. J4 70
Wentworth, N.H., U.S. C3 136
Wentzville, Mo., U.S. C7 132
Wenzhou, China G9 34
Wequetequock, Ct., U.S. . . . C8 114
Werda, Bots. E6 66
Were Ilu, Eth. L10 60
Wernigerode, Ger. D10 10
Werribee, Austl. K6 70
Wesel, Ger. D6 10
Weser, stm., Ger. B8 10
Weslaco, Tx., U.S. F4 150
Wesleyville, Newf., Can. . . . D5 102
Wesleyville, Pa., U.S. B2 145
Wessel, Cape, c., Austl. . . . B7 68
Wessel Islands, is., Austl. . . B7 68
Wessington Springs, S.D.,
U.S. C7 148
Wesson, Ms., U.S. D3 131
West Acton, Ma., U.S. g10 128
West Allis, Wi., U.S. m11 156
West Alton, Mo., U.S. f13 132
West Alton, N.H., U.S. C4 136
West Andover, Ma., U.S. . . . A5 128
West Arichat, N.S., Can. . . . D8 101
West Baden Springs, In.,
U.S. G4 121
West Baton Rouge, co.,
La., U.S. D4 125
West Bend, Ia., U.S. B3 122
West Bend, Wi., U.S. E5 156
West Bengal, state, India . . . I12 44
West Billerica, Ma., U.S. . . . f10 128
West Blocton, Al., U.S. B2 108
West Bountiful, Ut., U.S. . . . C4 151
West Boylston, Ma., U.S. . . . B4 128
West Branch, Ia., U.S. C6 122
West Branch, Mi., U.S. D6 129
West Bridgewater, Ma.,
U.S. B5 128
West Brookfield, Ma., U.S. . . B3 128
West Brooklyn, Me., U.S. . . . E2 126
West Burke, Vt., U.S. B5 152
West Burlington, Ia., U.S. . . . D6 122
West Buxton, Me., U.S. E2 126
Westby, Mt., U.S. B12 133
Westby, Wi., U.S. E3 156
West Caldwell, N.J., U.S. . . . B4 137
West Carroll, co., La., U.S. . . B4 125
West Carrollton, Oh., U.S. . . C1 142
West Charleston, Vt., U.S. . . B4 152
Westchester, Il., U.S. k9 120
Westchester, co., N.Y., U.S. . D7 139
West Chester, Pa., U.S. G10 145
Westchester, co., N.Y., U.S. . D7 139
West Chesterfield, N.H.,
U.S. E1 136
West Chicago, Il., U.S. k8 120
Westcliffe, Co., U.S. D5 113
West College Corner, In.,
U.S. E8 121
West Columbia, S.C., U.S. . . D5 147
West Columbia, Tx., U.S. . . . E5 150
West Concord, Ma., U.S. . . . g10 128
West Concord, Mn., U.S. . . . F6 130
West Cote Blanche Bay, b.,
La., U.S. E4 125
West Covina, Ca., U.S. m13 112
West Crossett, Ar., U.S. D4 111
West Cumberland, Me.,
U.S. E2 126
West Dennis, Ma., U.S. C7 128

West Des Moines, Ia., U.S. . C4 122
West Dover, Vt., U.S. F3 152
West End, Bah. A5 94
West Enfield, Me., U.S. C4 126
West Epping, N.H., U.S. . . . D4 136
Westerlo, Bel. F6 12
Westerly, R.I., U.S. F1 146
Western Australia, state,
Austl. E4 68
Western Channel, strt., Asia . I16 32
Western Desert see
Gharbīyah, Aş-Şahrā' al-,
des., Egypt D4 60
Western Ghāts, mts., India . . D2 46
Western Grove, Ar., U.S. . . . A3 111
Westernport, Md., U.S. m12 127
Western Sahara, dep., Afr. . . D4 54
Western Samoa, ctry., Oc. . . G1 2
Western Springs, Il., U.S. . . . k9 120
Westerschelde, est., Neth. . . F4 12
Westerstede, Ger. B7 10
Westerville, Oh., U.S. B3 142
West Falkland, i., Falk. Is. . . G4 78
West Fargo, N.D., U.S. C9 141
West Farmington, Me., U.S. . D2 126
West Feliciana, co., La.,
U.S. D4 125
Westfield, N.B., Can. D3 101
Westfield, In., U.S. D5 121
Westfield, Ma., U.S. B2 128
Westfield, N.J., U.S. B4 137
Westfield, N.Y., U.S. C1 139
Westfield, Wi., U.S. E4 156
Westfield, stm., Ma., U.S. . . B2 128
West Fork, Ar., U.S. B1 111
West Frankfort, Il., U.S. F5 120
West Freehold, N.J., U.S. . . . C4 137
West Friendship, Md., U.S. . . B4 127
Westgate, Fl., U.S. F6 116
West Glacier, Mt., U.S. B3 133
West Grand Lake, l., Me.,
U.S. C5 126
West Grove, Pa., U.S. G10 145
West Hartford, Ct., U.S. B4 114
West Hartford, Vt., U.S. D4 152
West Haven, Ct., U.S. D4 114
West Hazleton, Pa., U.S. . . . E9 145
West Helena, Ar., U.S. C5 111
West Hill Reservoir, res.,
Ma., U.S. B4 128
Westhope, N.D., U.S. A4 141
West Indies, is. E9 94
West Jefferson, Oh., U.S. . . . C2 142
West Jordan, Ut., U.S. C3 151
West Kennebunk, Me., U.S. . E2 126
West Kingston, R.I., U.S. . . . F3 146
West Lafayette, In., U.S. . . . D4 121
West Lafayette, Oh., U.S. . . . B4 142
Westlake, La., U.S. D2 125
Westlake, Oh., U.S. h9 142
Westland, Mi., U.S. F7 129
West Laramie, Wy., U.S. . . . E7 157
West Lebanon, In., U.S. D3 121
West Liberty, Ia., U.S. C6 122
West Liberty, Ky., U.S. C6 124
West Liberty, W.V., U.S. f8 155
West Linn, Or., U.S. B4 144
Westlock, Alta., Can. B4 98
West Long Branch, N.J.,
U.S. C4 137
West Lorne, Ont., Can. E3 103
West Marion, N.C., U.S. f10 140
Westmeath, co., Ire. H6 8
West Medway, Ma., U.S. . . . B5 128
West Memphis, Ar., U.S. . . . B5 111
West Miami, Fl., U.S. s13 116
West Mifflin, Pa., U.S. F2 145
West Milford, N.J., U.S. A4 137
West Milton, Oh., U.S. C1 142
West Milwaukee, Wi., U.S. . . m12 156
Westminster, Ca., U.S. n12 112
Westminster, Co., U.S. B5 113
Westminster, La., U.S. B4 125
Westminster, Md., U.S. A4 127
Westminster, S.C., U.S. B1 147
Westminster, Vt., U.S. E4 152
West Monroe, La., U.S. B3 125
Westmont, Il., U.S. k9 120
Westmont, N.J., U.S. D2 137
Westmont, Pa., U.S. F4 145
Westmoreland, Ks., U.S. . . . C7 123
Westmoreland, Tn., U.S. . . . A5 149
Westmoreland, co., Pa.,
U.S. F2 145
Westmoreland, co., Va.,
U.S. B6 153
West Mystic, Ct., U.S. D8 114
West Newton, Pa., U.S. F2 145
West New York, N.J., U.S. . . h8 137
West Nicholson, Zimb. C9 66
West Nishnabotna, stm.,
Ia., U.S. C2 122
West Norriton, Pa., U.S. . . . o20 145
Weston, Ct., U.S. E2 114
Weston, Id., U.S. G7 119
Weston, Ma., U.S. g10 128
Weston, Mo., U.S. B3 132
Weston, Vt., U.S. E3 152
Weston, W.V., U.S. B4 155
Weston, co., Wy., U.S. C8 157
Weston-super-Mare, Eng.,
U.K. J11 8
West Orange, N.J., U.S. . . . B4 137
West Ossipee, N.H., U.S. . . . C4 136
Westover, W.V., U.S. B5 155
West Palm Beach, Fl., U.S. . . F6 116
West Paris, Me., U.S. D2 126
West Pawlet, Vt., U.S. E2 152
West Pelzer, S.C., U.S. B3 147
West Pensacola, Fl., U.S. . . . u14 116
West Peoria, Il., U.S. C4 120
West Peru, Me., U.S. D2 126
West Peterborough, N.H.,
U.S. E3 136
West Pittston, Pa., U.S. m17 145
West Plains, Mo., U.S. E6 132
West Point, Ga., U.S. D1 117
West Point, Ia., U.S. D6 122
West Point, Ky., U.S. C4 124
West Point, Ms., U.S. B5 131

West-Word

Name — Map Ref. — Page

West Point, Ne., U.S. C9 134
West Point, N.Y., U.S. D7 139
West Point, Va., U.S. C6 153
West Point, c., Austl. J2 70
West Point Lake, res., U.S. C1 117
Westport, N.S., Can. E3 101
Westport, Ont., Can. C8 103
Westport, N.Z. D3 72
Westport, Ct., U.S. E2 114
Westport, In., U.S. F6 121
Westport, N.H., U.S. E2 136
Westport, Wa., U.S. C1 154
West Portsmouth, Oh., U.S. D2 142
West Quoddy Head, c., Me., U.S. D6 126
West Reading, Pa., U.S. F10 145
West Ridge, Ar., U.S. B5 111
West Rindge, N.H., U.S. E2 136
West Rutland, Vt., U.S. D2 152
West Saint Paul, Mn., U.S. n12 130
West Salem, Il., U.S. E5 120
West Salem, Wi., U.S. E2 156
West Scarborough, Me., U.S. E2 126
West Seneca, N.Y., U.S. C2 139
West Simsbury, Ct., U.S. B4 114
West Slope, Or., U.S. g12 144
West Springfield, Ma., U.S. B2 128
West Springfield, Va., U.S. g12 153
West Sussex, co., Eng., U.K. K13 8
West Swanzey, N.H., U.S. E2 136
West Terre Haute, In., U.S. F3 121
West Union, Ia., U.S. B6 122
West Union, Oh., U.S. D2 142
West Union, W.V., U.S. B4 155
West University Place, Tx., U.S. r14 150
West Valley City, Ut., U.S. C4 151
West Vancouver, B.C., Can. f12 99
West Van Lear, Ky., U.S. C7 124
West View, Pa., U.S. h13 145
Westville, N.S., Can. D7 101
Westville, Il., U.S. C6 120
Westville, In., U.S. A4 121
Westville, N.H., U.S. E4 136
Westville, N.J., U.S. D2 137
Westville, Ok., U.S. A7 143
West Virginia, state, U.S. C4 155
West-Vlaanderen, prov., Bel. F2 12
West Wareham, Ma., U.S. C6 128
West Warwick, R.I., U.S. D3 146
Westwego, La., U.S. k11 125
West Wilton, N.H., U.S. E3 136
Westwold, B.C., Can. D8 99
Westwood, Ks., U.S. k16 123
Westwood, Ky., U.S. B7 124
Westwood, Ma., U.S. B5 128
Westwood, N.J., U.S. B4 137
Westwood Lakes, Fl., U.S. s13 116
West Wyalong, Austl. I7 70
West Wyoming, Pa., U.S. n17 145
West Yarmouth, Ma., U.S. C7 128
West Yellowstone, Mt., U.S. F5 133
West York, Pa., U.S. G8 145
Wetaskiwin, Alta., Can. C4 98
Wete, Tan. C7 58
Wethersfield, Ct., U.S. C5 114
Wet Mountains, mts., Co., U.S. C5 113
Wetteren, Bel. F4 12
Wetumka, Ok., U.S. B5 143
Wetumpka, Al., U.S. C3 108
Wetzel, co., W.V., U.S. B4 155
Wetzikon, Switz. D10 13
Wetzlar, Ger. E8 10
Wewahitchka, Fl., U.S. B1 116
Wewak, Pap. N. Gui. k15 68a
Wewoka, Ok., U.S. B5 143
Wexford, Ire. I7 8
Wexford, co., Ire. I7 8
Wexford, co., Mi., U.S. D5 129
Weyauwega, Wi., U.S. D5 156
Weyburn, Sask., Can. H4 105
Weymouth, N.S., Can. E4 101
Weymouth, Eng., U.K. K11 8
Weymouth, Ma., U.S. B6 128
Whakatane, N.Z. B6 72
Whangarei, N.Z. A5 72
Wharton, N.J., U.S. B3 137
Wharton, Tx., U.S. E4 150
Wharton, co., Tx., U.S. E4 150
What Cheer, Ia., U.S. C5 122
Whatcom, co., Wa., U.S. A4 154
Whatcom, Lake, l., Wa., U.S. A3 154
Whatley, Al., U.S. D2 108
Wheatfield, In., U.S. B3 121
Wheatland, Ia., U.S. C7 122
Wheatland, Wy., U.S. D8 157
Wheatland, co., Mt., U.S. D7 133
Wheatley, Ont., Can. E2 103
Wheatley, Ar., U.S. C4 111
Wheaton, Il., U.S. B5 120
Wheaton, Md., U.S. B3 127
Wheaton, Mn., U.S. E2 130
Wheaton, Mo., U.S. E3 132
Wheat Ridge, Co., U.S. B5 113
Wheeler, In., U.S. B3 121
Wheeler, Ms., U.S. A5 131
Wheeler, co., Ga., U.S. D4 117
Wheeler, co., Ne., U.S. C7 134
Wheeler, co., Or., U.S. C6 144
Wheeler, co., Tx., U.S. B2 150
Wheeler Air Force Base, mil., Hi., U.S. g9 118
Wheeler Lake, res., Al., U.S. A2 108
Wheeler Peak, mtn., Nv., U.S. E7 135
Wheeler Peak, mtn., N.M., U.S. A4 138
Wheelersburg, Oh., U.S. D3 142
Wheeling, Il., U.S. h9 120
Wheeling, W.V., U.S. A4 155
Wheelwright, Arg. G8 80
Wheelwright, Ky., U.S. C7 124
Whidbey Island, i., Wa., U.S. A3 154
Whigham, Ga., U.S. F2 117
Whistler, B.C., Can. D6 99
Whitacres, Ct., U.S. A5 114
Whitbourne, Newf., Can. E5 102
Whitby, Ont., Can. D6 103
Whitchurch-Stouffville, Ont., Can. D5 103
White, S.D., U.S. C9 148
White, co., Ar., U.S. B4 111
White, co., Ga., U.S. B3 117
White, co., Il., U.S. E5 120
White, co., In., U.S. C4 121
White, co., Tn., U.S. D8 149
White, stm., U.S. D8 106
White, stm., U.S. C4 111
White, stm., U.S. D5 148
White, stm., U.S. C7 151
White, stm., Az., U.S. D5 110
White, stm., In., U.S. H2 121
White, stm., Nv., U.S. E6 135
White, stm., Tx., U.S. C2 150
White, stm., Vt., U.S. D4 152
White Bay, b., Newf., Can. D3 102
White Bear Lake, Mn., U.S. E5 130
White Bluff, Tn., U.S. A4 149
White Butte, mtn., N.D., U.S. C2 141
White Cap Mountain, mtn., Me., U.S. C3 126
White Castle, La., U.S. D4 125
White Center, Wa., U.S. e11 154
White City, Ks., U.S. D7 123
White City, Or., U.S. E4 144
White Cliffs, Austl. H5 70
Whitecourt, Alta., Can. B3 98
White Earth Indian Reservation, Mn., U.S. C3 130
Whiteface Mountain, mtn., N.Y., U.S. f11 139
White Face Mountain, mtn., Vt., U.S. B3 152
Whitefield, N.H., U.S. B3 136
Whitefish, Mt., U.S. B2 133
Whitefish Bay, Wi., U.S. m12 156
Whitefish Bay, b., Mi., U.S. B6 129
White Fox, Sask., Can. D3 105
White Hall, Al., U.S. C3 108
White Hall, Ar., U.S. C3 111
White Hall, Il., U.S. D3 120
Whitehall, Mi., U.S. E4 129
Whitehall, Mt., U.S. E4 133
Whitehall, N.Y., U.S. B7 139
Whitehall, Oh., U.S. m11 142
Whitehall, Wi., U.S. D2 156
Whitehorse, Yukon, Can. D5 96
White Horse, N.J., U.S. C3 137
Whitehouse, Oh., U.S. A2 142
White House, Tn., U.S. A5 149
Whitehouse, Tx., U.S. C5 150
White Island Shores, Ma., U.S. C6 128
White Lake, S.D., U.S. D7 148
White Lake, l., La., U.S. E3 125
White Mountain Peak, mtn., Ca., U.S. D4 112
White Mountains, mts., U.S. D4 112
White Mountains, mts., N.H., U.S. B3 136
Whitemouth, Man., Can. E4 100
White Nile (Al-Bahr al-Abyad), stm., Sud. L7 60
White Oak, Oh., U.S. o12 142
White Oak, Tx., U.S. C5 150
White Pigeon, Mi., U.S. G5 129
White Pine, Tn., U.S. C10 149
White Pine, co., Nv., U.S. D6 135
White Plains, Ky., U.S. C2 124
White Plains, Md., U.S. C4 127
White Plains, N.Y., U.S. D7 139
Whiteriver, Az., U.S. D6 110
White River, S.D., U.S. D5 148
White River Junction, Vt., U.S. D4 152
White Rock, B.C., Can. E6 99
White Rock, N.M., U.S. B3 138
White Russia see Belarus, ctry., Eur. H11 26
Whitesail Lake, l., B.C., Can. C4 99
White Salmon, Wa., U.S. D4 154
White Sands Missile Range, mil., N.M., U.S. E3 138
White Sands National Monument, N.M., U.S. E3 138
Whitesboro, N.Y., U.S. B5 139
Whitesboro, Tx., U.S. C4 150
Whitesburg, Ga., U.S. C2 117
Whitesburg, Ky., U.S. C7 124
White Sea see Beloje more, Russia D5 26
Whiteside, co., Il., U.S. B3 120
White Sulphur Springs, Mt., U.S. D6 133
White Sulphur Springs, W.V., U.S. D4 155
Whitesville, Ky., U.S. C3 124
Whitesville, W.V., U.S. D3 155
White Swan, Wa., U.S. C5 154
White Tank Mountains, mts., Az., U.S. k7 110
Whiteville, N.C., U.S. C4 140
Whiteville, Tn., U.S. B2 149
White Volta (Volta Blanche), stm., Afr. F6 54
Whitewater, Co., U.S. C2 113
Whitewater, Ks., U.S. E6 123
Whitewater, Wi., U.S. F5 156
Whitewater, stm., U.S. F7 121
Whitewood, Austl. C5 70
Whitewood, Sask., Can. G4 105
Whitewood, S.D., U.S. C2 148
Whitfield, co., Ga., U.S. B2 117
Whitfield Estates, Fl., U.S. q10 116
Whiting, In., U.S. A3 121
Whiting, Ia., U.S. B1 122
Whiting, Wi., U.S. D4 156
Whitingham, Vt., U.S. F3 152
Whitinsville, Ma., U.S. B4 128
Whitley, co., In., U.S. B6 121
Whitley, co., Ky., U.S. D5 124
Whitley City, Ky., U.S. D5 124
Whitman, Ma., U.S. B6 128
Whitman, W.V., U.S. D2 155
Whitman, co., Wa., U.S. B8 154
Whitmire, S.C., U.S. B4 147
Whitmore Lake, Mi., U.S. p14 129
Whitmore Village, Hi., U.S. f9 118
Whitney, S.C., U.S. B4 147
Whitney, Lake, res., Tx., U.S. D4 150
Whitney, Mount, mtn., Ca., U.S. D4 112
Whitsunday Island, i., Austl. C8 70
Whittier, Ak., U.S. C10 109
Whittier, Ca., U.S. F4 112
Whitwell, Tn., U.S. D8 149
Whyalla, Austl. I2 70
Whycocomagh, N.S., Can. D8 101
Wiarton, Ont., Can. C3 103
Wibaux, Mt., U.S. D12 133
Wibaux, co., Mt., U.S. D12 133
Wichita, Ks., U.S. E6 123
Wichita, co., Ks., U.S. D2 123
Wichita, co., Tx., U.S. B3 150
Wichita Falls, Tx., U.S. C3 150
Wichita Mountains, mts., Ok., U.S. C3 143
Wick, Scot., U.K. C10 8
Wickenburg, Az., U.S. D3 110
Wickes, Ar., U.S. C1 111
Wickiup Reservoir, res., Or., U.S. E5 144
Wickliffe, Ky., U.S. f8 124
Wickliffe, Oh., U.S. A4 142
Wicklow, co., Ire. I7 8
Wicomico, co., Md., U.S. D6 127
Wicomico, stm., Md., U.S. D6 127
Widefield, Co., U.S. C6 113
Widener, Ar., U.S. B5 111
Widerøe, Mount, mtn., Ant. C3 73
Wieliczka, Pol. F20 10
Wielkopolska, reg., Pol. D17 10
Wieluń, Pol. D18 10
Wien (Vienna), Aus. G16 10
Wiener Neustadt, Aus. H16 10
Wienerwald, mts., Aus. G16 10
Wierden, Neth. D10 12
Wiesbaden, Ger. E8 10
Wiesloch, Ger. F8 10
Wigan, Eng., U.K. H11 8
Wiggins, Co., U.S. A6 113
Wiggins, Ms., U.S. E4 131
Wikwemikong, Ont., Can. B3 103
Wil, Switz. D11 13
Wilbarger, co., Tx., U.S. B3 150
Wilber, Ne., U.S. D9 134
Wilberforce, Oh., U.S. C2 142
Wilbraham, Ma., U.S. B3 128
Wilbur, Wa., U.S. B7 154
Wilburton, Ok., U.S. C6 143
Wilcannia, Austl. H5 70
Wilcox, Sask., Can. G3 105
Wilcox, co., Al., U.S. D2 108
Wilcox, co., Ga., U.S. E3 117
Wilder, Id., U.S. F2 119
Wilder, Vt., U.S. D4 152
Wild Rice, stm., Mn., U.S. C2 130
Wild Rice, stm., N.D., U.S. C8 141
Wildwood, Fl., U.S. D4 116
Wildwood, Il., U.S. h9 120
Wiley, Co., U.S. C8 113
Wilhelm, Mount, mtn., Pap. N. Gui. m15 68a
Wilhelmshaven, Ger. B8 10
Wilhoit, Az., U.S. C3 110
Wilkes, co., Ga., U.S. C4 117
Wilkes, co., N.C., U.S. A1 140
Wilkes-Barre, Pa., U.S. D10 145
Wilkesboro, N.C., U.S. A1 140
Wilkes Land, reg., Ant. C7 73
Wilkie, Sask., Can. E1 105
Wilkin, co., Mn., U.S. D2 130
Wilkinsburg, Pa., U.S. F2 145
Wilkinson, W.V., U.S. D3 155
Wilkinson, co., Ga., U.S. D3 117
Wilkinson, co., Ms., U.S. D2 131
Will, co., Il., U.S. B6 120
Willacoochee, Ga., U.S. E3 117
Willacy, co., Tx., U.S. F4 150
Willamette, stm., Or., U.S. C3 144
Willamette Pass, Or., U.S. D4 144
Willamina, Or., U.S. B3 144
Willapa Bay, b., Wa., U.S. C1 154
Willard, Mo., U.S. D4 132
Willard, Oh., U.S. A3 142
Willard, Ut., U.S. B3 151
Willcox, Az., U.S. E6 110
Willcox Playa, l., Az., U.S. E5 110
Willemstad, Neth. Ant. H10 94
William Bill Dannelly Reservoir, res., Al., U.S. C2 108
Williams, Az., U.S. B3 110
Williams, co., N.D., U.S. A2 141
Williams, co., Oh., U.S. A1 142
Williams, stm., W.V., U.S. C4 155
Williams Bay, Wi., U.S. F5 156
Williamsburg, In., U.S. E8 121
Williamsburg, Ia., U.S. C5 122
Williamsburg, Ky., U.S. D5 124
Williamsburg, N.M., U.S. D2 138
Williamsburg, Oh., U.S. C1 142
Williamsburg, Va., U.S. C6 153
Williamsburg, co., S.C., U.S. D8 147
Williams Lake, B.C., Can. C6 99
Williamson, W.V., U.S. D2 155
Williamson, co., Il., U.S. F4 120
Williamson, co., Tn., U.S. B5 149
Williamson, co., Tx., U.S. D4 150
Williamsport, In., U.S. D3 121
Williamsport, Md., U.S. A2 127
Williamsport, Pa., U.S. D7 145
Williamston, Mi., U.S. F6 129
Williamston, N.C., U.S. B5 140
Williamston, S.C., U.S. B3 147
Williamstown, Ky., U.S. B5 124
Williamstown, Ma., U.S. A1 128
Williamstown, N.J., U.S. D3 137
Williamstown, Vt., U.S. C3 152
Williamstown, W.V., U.S. B3 155
Williamsville, Il., U.S. D4 120
Williamsville, N.Y., U.S. C2 139
Willimantic, Ct., U.S. C7 114
Willimantic, stm., Ct., U.S. B6 114
Willingboro, N.J., U.S. C3 137
Willingdon, Alta., Can. C4 98
Willis Group, is., Austl. C10 68
Williston, S. Afr. H5 66
Williston, Fl., U.S. C4 116
Williston, N.D., U.S. A2 141
Williston, S.C., U.S. E5 147
Williston, Vt., U.S. C2 152
Williston Lake, res., B.C., Can. B6 99
Willits, Ca., U.S. C2 112
Willmar, Mn., U.S. E3 130
Willoughby, Oh., U.S. A4 142
Willoughby Hills, Oh., U.S. A4 142
Willow, Ak., U.S. g17 109
Willow Bunch, Sask., Can. H3 105
Willow City, N.D., U.S. A5 141
Willow Grove, Pa., U.S. F11 145
Willowick, Oh., U.S. A4 142
Willow Lake, S.D., U.S. C8 148
Willowmore, S. Afr. I6 66
Willow River, B.C., Can. B6 99
Willow Run, De., U.S. i7 115
Willow Run, Mi., U.S. p14 129
Willows, Ca., U.S. C2 112
Willow Springs, Il., U.S. k9 120
Willow Springs, Mo., U.S. E6 132
Wilmar, Ar., U.S. D4 111
Wilmer, Al., U.S. E1 108
Wilmerding, Pa., U.S. k14 145
Wilmette, Il., U.S. A6 120
Wilmington, Austl. I3 70
Wilmington, De., U.S. B3 115
Wilmington, Il., U.S. B5 120
Wilmington, Ma., U.S. A5 128
Wilmington, N.C., U.S. C5 140
Wilmington, Oh., U.S. C2 142
Wilmington, Vt., U.S. F3 152
Wilmington Manor, De., U.S. i7 115
Wilmore, Ky., U.S. C5 124
Wilmot, N.S., Can. E4 101
Wilmot, Ar., U.S. D4 111
Wilmot, S.D., U.S. B9 148
Wilmot Flat, N.H., U.S. D3 136
Wilson, Ar., U.S. B5 111
Wilson, Ks., U.S. D5 123
Wilson, N.C., U.S. B5 140
Wilson, Ok., U.S. C4 143
Wilson, Pa., U.S. E11 145
Wilson, Wy., U.S. C2 157
Wilson, co., Ks., U.S. E8 123
Wilson, co., N.C., U.S. B5 140
Wilson, co., Tn., U.S. A5 149
Wilson, co., Tx., U.S. E3 150
Wilson, Mount, mtn., Az., U.S. B1 110
Wilson, Mount, mtn., Ca., U.S. m12 112
Wilson Lake, res., Al., U.S. A2 108
Wilsons Beach, N.B., Can. E3 101
Wilsons Promontory, c., Austl. L7 70
Wilsonville, Al., U.S. B3 108
Wilsonville, Or., U.S. h12 144
Wilton, Al., U.S. B3 108
Wilton, Ar., U.S. D1 111
Wilton, Ct., U.S. E2 114
Wilton, Ia., U.S. C6 122
Wilton, Me., U.S. D2 126
Wilton, N.H., U.S. E3 136
Wilton, N.D., U.S. B5 141
Wiltshire, co., Eng., U.K. J12 8
Wiluna, Austl. E4 68
Wimauma, Fl., U.S. E4 116
Wimbledon, N.D., U.S. B7 141
Winamac, In., U.S. B4 121
Winburg, S. Afr. G8 66
Winchendon, Ma., U.S. A3 128
Winchester, Ont., Can. B9 103
Winchester, Eng., U.K. J12 8
Winchester, Il., U.S. D3 120
Winchester, In., U.S. D8 121
Winchester, Ks., U.S. k15 123
Winchester, Ky., U.S. C5 124
Winchester, Ma., U.S. g11 128
Winchester, Nv., U.S. G6 135
Winchester, N.H., U.S. E2 136
Winchester, Tn., U.S. B5 149
Winchester, Va., U.S. A4 153
Winchester Bay, Or., U.S. D2 144
Wind, stm., Wy., U.S. C4 157
Windber, Pa., U.S. F4 145
Winder, Ga., U.S. C3 117
Windermere, B.C., Can. D10 99
Windfall, In., U.S. D6 121
Windgap, Pa., U.S. E11 145
Windham, Ct., U.S. C7 114
Windham, Oh., U.S. A4 142
Windham, co., Ct., U.S. B7 114
Windham, co., Vt., U.S. F3 152
Windhoek, Nmb. D3 66
Wind Lake, Wi., U.S. F5 156
Windmill Point, c., Va., U.S. C6 153
Windom, Mn., U.S. G3 130
Window Rock, Az., U.S. B6 110
Wind Point, Wi., U.S. n12 156
Wind River Peak, mtn., Wy., U.S. D3 157
Wind River Range, mts., Wy., U.S. C3 157
Windsor, Austl. I9 70
Windsor, N.S., Can. E5 101
Windsor, Ont., Can. E1 103
Windsor, Que., Can. D5 104
Windsor, Eng., U.K. J13 8
Windsor, Co., U.S. A6 113
Windsor, Ct., U.S. B5 114
Windsor, Il., U.S. D5 120
Windsor, Mo., U.S. C4 132
Windsor, N.C., U.S. A6 140
Windsor, Vt., U.S. E4 152
Windsor, Va., U.S. D6 153
Windsor, co., Vt., U.S. D3 152
Windsor Heights, Ia., U.S. e8 122
Windsor Locks, Ct., U.S. B5 114
Windthorst, Sask., Can. G4 105
Windward Islands, is., N.A. H14 94
Windward Passage, strt., N.A. E7 94
Windy Hill, S.C., U.S. C8 147
Winfield, Al., U.S. B2 108
Winfield, Ia., U.S. C6 122
Winfield, Ks., U.S. E7 123
Winfield, Mo., U.S. C7 132
Winfield, W.V., U.S. C3 155
Wingate, N.C., U.S. C2 140
Wingene, Bel. F3 12
Wingham, Ont., Can. D3 103
Wingo, Ky., U.S. f9 124
Winifreda, Arg. I6 80
Winifrede, W.V., U.S. m12 155
Winkelman, Az., U.S. E5 110
Winkler, Man., Can. E3 100
Winkler, co., Tx., U.S. D1 150
Winlaw, B.C., Can. E9 99
Winlock, Wa., U.S. C3 154
Winn, co., La., U.S. C3 125
Winneba, Ghana I9 64
Winnebago, Il., U.S. A4 120
Winnebago, Mn., U.S. G4 130
Winnebago, Ne., U.S. B9 134
Winnebago, Wi., U.S. h8 156
Winnebago, co., Il., U.S. A4 120
Winnebago, co., Ia., U.S. A4 122
Winnebago, co., Wi., U.S. D5 156
Winnebago, stm., Ia., U.S. A4 122
Winnebago, Lake, l., Wi., U.S. E5 156
Winneconne, Wi., U.S. D5 156
Winnemucca, Nv., U.S. C4 135
Winnemucca Lake, l., Nv., U.S. C2 135
Winner, S.D., U.S. D6 148
Winneshiek, co., Ia., U.S. A6 122
Winnetka, Il., U.S. A6 120
Winnfield, La., U.S. C3 125
Winnibigoshish, Lake, l., Mn., U.S. C4 130
Winnipeg, Man., Can. E3 100
Winnipeg, stm., Can. D4 100
Winnipeg, Lake, l., Man., Can. C3 100
Winnipeg Beach, Man., Can. D3 100
Winnipegosis, Man., Can. D2 100
Winnipegosis, Lake, l., Man., Can. C2 100
Winnipesaukee, Lake, l., N.H., U.S. C4 136
Winnisquam, N.H., U.S. C3 136
Winnisquam Lake, l., N.H., U.S. C3 136
Winnsboro, La., U.S. B4 125
Winnsboro, S.C., U.S. C5 147
Winnsboro Mills, S.C., U.S. C5 147
Winona, Mn., U.S. F7 130
Winona, Ms., U.S. B4 131
Winona, Mo., U.S. D6 132
Winona, co., Mn., U.S. F7 130
Winona Lake, In., U.S. B6 121
Winooski, Vt., U.S. C2 152
Winooski, stm., Vt., U.S. C3 152
Winschoten, Neth. B11 12
Winside, Ne., U.S. B8 134
Winslow, Az., U.S. C5 110
Winslow, Ar., U.S. B1 111
Winslow, In., U.S. H3 121
Winslow, Me., U.S. D3 126
Winsted, Ct., U.S. B3 114
Winsted, Mn., U.S. F4 130
Winston, Fl., U.S. D4 116
Winston, Or., U.S. D3 144
Winston, co., Al., U.S. A2 108
Winston, co., Ms., U.S. B4 131
Winston-Salem, N.C., U.S. A2 140
Winter Garden, Fl., U.S. D5 116
Winter Harbor, Me., U.S. D4 126
Winter Haven, Fl., U.S. D5 116
Winter Park, Co., U.S. B5 113
Winter Park, Fl., U.S. D5 116
Winter Park, N.C., U.S. C5 140
Winterport, Me., U.S. D4 126
Winterset, Ia., U.S. C4 122
Wintersville, Oh., U.S. B5 142
Winterthur, Switz. C10 13
Winterton, Newf., Can. E5 102
Winterville, Ga., U.S. C3 117
Winterville, N.C., U.S. B5 140
Winthrop, Ia., U.S. B6 122
Winthrop, Me., U.S. D3 126
Winthrop, Ma., U.S. B6 128
Winthrop, Mn., U.S. F4 130
Winthrop Harbor, Il., U.S. A6 120
Winton, Austl. D5 70
Wirātanagar, Nepal G12 44
Wirgañj, Nepal G11 44
Wirral, pen., Eng., U.K. H10 8
Wirt, co., W.V., U.S. B3 155
Wiscasset, Me., U.S. D3 126
Wisconsin, state, U.S. D4 156
Wisconsin, stm., Wi., U.S. E3 156
Wisconsin, Lake, res., Wi., U.S. E4 156
Wisconsin Dells, Wi., U.S. E4 156
Wisconsin Rapids, Wi., U.S. D4 156
Wise, Va., U.S. f9 153
Wise, co., Tx., U.S. C4 150
Wise, co., Va., U.S. e9 153
Wishart, Sask., Can. F3 105
Wishek, N.D., U.S. C6 141
Wishram, Wa., U.S. D4 154
Wisła, stm., Pol. A18 10
Wismar, Ger. B11 10
Wisner, La., U.S. C4 125
Wisner, Ne., U.S. C9 134
Wissembourg, Fr. C14 14
Wister, Ok., U.S. C7 143
Wister Lake, res., Ok., U.S. C7 143
Witbank, S. Afr. E9 66
Withamsville, Oh., U.S. C1 142
Withlacoochee, stm., U.S. B3 116
Withlacoochee, stm., Fl., U.S. C4 116
Witless Bay, Newf., Can. E5 102
Witrivier, S. Afr. E10 66
Wittenberg, Ger. D12 10
Wittenberg, Wi., U.S. D4 156
Wittenberge, Ger. B11 10
Wittmann, Az., U.S. D3 110
Wittmund, Ger. B7 10
Witwatersrant, reg., S. Afr. E8 66
Witzputz, Nmb. F3 66
Wixom, Mi., U.S. o14 129
Wixom Lake, res., Mi., U.S. E6 129
Włocławek, Pol. C19 10
Woburn, Ma., U.S. B5 128
Wodonga, Austl. K7 70
Wohlen, Switz. D9 13
Woking, Eng., U.K. J13 8
Wolcott, Ct., U.S. C4 114
Wolcott, In., U.S. C3 121
Wolcottville, In., U.S. A7 121
Wolf, stm., Wi., U.S. C5 156
Wolf, Volcán, vol., Ec. i13 84a
Wolfe, co., Ky., U.S. C6 124
Wolfeboro, N.H., U.S. C4 136
Wolfeboro Falls, N.H., U.S. C4 136
Wolfen, Ger. D12 10
Wolfenbüttel, Ger. C10 10
Wolf Lake, Mi., U.S. E4 129
Wolf Lake, l., Il., U.S. k9 120
Wolf Point, Mt., U.S. B11 133
Wolfsberg, Aus. I14 10
Wolfsburg, Ger. C10 10
Wolfville, N.S., Can. D5 101
Wolhusen, Switz. D9 13
Wollaston Lake, l., Sask., Can. m8 105
Wollongong, Austl. J9 70
Wolmaransstad, S. Afr. F8 66
Wołomin, Pol. C21 10
Wolseley, Sask., Can. G4 105
Wolseley, S. Afr. I4 66
Wolsey, S.D., U.S. C7 148
Wolvega, Neth. C9 12
Wolverhampton, Eng., U.K. I11 8
Womelsdorf, Pa., U.S. F9 145
Wonder Lake, Il., U.S. A5 120
Wŏnju, S. Kor. F15 32
Wonosobo, Indon. j14 39a
Wŏnsan, N. Kor. D15 32
Wonthaggi, Austl. L6 70
Wood, co., Oh., U.S. A2 142
Wood, co., Tx., U.S. C5 150
Wood, co., W.V., U.S. B3 155
Wood, co., Wi., U.S. D3 156
Wood, stm., Sask., Can. H2 105
Wood, stm., R.I., U.S. F2 146
Wood, Mount, mtn., Mt., U.S. E7 133
Woodall Mountain, mtn., Ms., U.S. A5 131
Woodbine, Ga., U.S. F5 117
Woodbine, Ia., U.S. C2 122
Woodbine, Ky., U.S. D5 124
Woodbridge, Ct., U.S. D3 114
Woodbridge, Va., U.S. B5 153
Woodbridge [Township], N.J., U.S. B4 137
Woodburn, In., U.S. B8 121
Woodburn, Or., U.S. B4 144
Woodbury, Ct., U.S. C3 114
Woodbury, Ga., U.S. D2 117
Woodbury, Mn., U.S. F6 130
Woodbury, N.J., U.S. D2 137
Woodbury, Tn., U.S. B5 149
Woodbury, co., Ia., U.S. B1 122
Woodcliff Lake, N.J., U.S. g8 137
Wood Dale, Il., U.S. k9 120
Woodfield, S.C., U.S. C6 147
Woodford, co., Il., U.S. C4 120
Woodford, co., Ky., U.S. B5 124
Woodlake, Ca., U.S. D4 112
Woodland, Ca., U.S. C3 112
Woodland, Me., U.S. C5 126
Woodland, Wa., U.S. D3 154
Woodland Acres, Co., U.S. D6 113
Woodland Park, Co., U.S. C5 113
Woodlawn, Ky., U.S. e9 124
Woodlawn, Md., U.S. g10 127
Woodlawn, Oh., U.S. n13 142
Woodlawn, Va., U.S. D2 153
Woodmont, Ct., U.S. E4 114
Woodmoor, Md., U.S. B4 127
Woodridge, Man., Can. E3 100
Woodridge, Il., U.S. k8 120
Wood-Ridge, N.J., U.S. h8 137
Wood River, Il., U.S. E3 120
Wood River, Ne., U.S. D7 134
Woodroffe, Mount, mtn., Austl. E6 68
Woodruff, S.C., U.S. B3 147
Woodruff, Wi., U.S. C4 156
Woodruff, co., Ar., U.S. B4 111
Woods, co., Ok., U.S. A3 143
Woods, Lake of the, l., N.A. G14 96
Woods Cross, Ut., U.S. C4 151
Woodsfield, Oh., U.S. C4 142
Woods Hole, Ma., U.S. C6 128
Woodside, Austl. L7 70
Woodson, Ar., U.S. C3 111
Woodson, co., Ks., U.S. E8 123
Woodstock, N.B., Can. C2 101
Woodstock, Ont., Can. D4 103
Woodstock, Ga., U.S. B2 117
Woodstock, Il., U.S. A5 120
Woodstock, Vt., U.S. D3 152
Woodstock, Va., U.S. B4 153
Woodsville, N.H., U.S. B2 136
Woodville, Ont., Can. C5 103
Woodville, Fl., U.S. B2 116
Woodville, Ms., U.S. D2 131
Woodville, Oh., U.S. A2 142
Woodville, Wi., U.S. D1 156
Woodward, Ia., U.S. C4 122
Woodward, Ok., U.S. A2 143
Woodward, co., Ok., U.S. A2 143
Woody Head, c., Austl. G10 70
Woolmarket, Ms., U.S. E5 131
Woolwich, Me., U.S. g8 126
Woomera, Austl. H2 70
Woonsocket, R.I., U.S. A3 146
Woonsocket, S.D., U.S. C7 148
Wooster, Ar., U.S. B3 111
Wooster, Oh., U.S. B4 142
Worb, Switz. E8 13
Worcester, S. Afr. I4 66
Worcester, Eng., U.K. I11 8
Worcester, Ma., U.S. B4 128
Worcester, co., Md., U.S. D7 127
Worcester, co., Ma., U.S. A3 128
Worden, Mt., U.S. E8 133

Name — Map Ref. — Page

Worden Pond, l., R.I., U.S. F3 146
Workington, Eng., U.K. G10 8
Worksop, Eng., U.K. H12 8
Worland, Wy., U.S. B5 157
Wormerveer, Neth. D6 12
Worms, Ger. F8 10
Worth, Il., U.S. k9 120
Worth, co., Ga., U.S. E3 117
Worth, co., Ia., U.S. A4 122
Worth, co., Mo., U.S. A3 132
Worthing, Eng., U.K. K13 8
Worthing, S.D., U.S. D9 148
Worthington, In., U.S. F4 121
Worthington, Ky., U.S. B7 124
Worthington, Mn., U.S. G3 130
Worthington, Oh., U.S. B2 142
Wounded Knee, S.D., U.S. D3 148
Wounta, Laguna de, b., Nic. D11 92
Woy Woy, Austl. I9 70
Wrangell, Ak., U.S. D13 109
Wrangell, Cape, c., Ak., U.S. E2 109
Wrangell, Mount, mtn., Ak., U.S. f19 109
Wrangell Island, i., Ak., U.S. m24 109
Wrangell Mountains, mts., Ak., U.S. C11 109
Wrangell-Saint Elias National Park, Ak., U.S. C11 109
Wrath, Cape, c., Scot., U.K. C8 8
Wray, Co., U.S. A8 113
Wrens, Ga., U.S. C4 117
Wrentham, Ma., U.S. B5 128
Wrexham, Wales, U.K. H10 8
Wright, Wy., U.S. B7 157
Wright, co., Ia., U.S. B4 122
Wright, co., Mn., U.S. E4 130
Wright, co., Mo., U.S. D5 132
Wright, Mount, mtn., Mt., U.S. C4 133
Wright Brothers National Memorial, hist., N.C., U.S. A7 140
Wright City, Mo., U.S. C8 132
Wright City, Ok., U.S. C6 143
Wright-Patterson Air Force Base, mil., Oh., U.S. C1 142
Wrightson, Mount, mtn., Az., U.S. F5 110
Wrightstown, Wi., U.S. D5 156
Wrightsville, Ar., U.S. C3 111
Wrightsville, Ga., U.S. D4 117
Wrightsville, Pa., U.S. F8 145
Wrightsville Beach, N.C., U.S. C5 140
Wrigley, N.W. Ter., Can. D8 96
Wrocław (Breslau), Pol. D17 10
Września, Pol. C17 10
Wuchin see Changzhou, China E10 30
Wuchuan, China D11 40
Wudinna, Austl. I1 70
Wugang, China F9 30
Wuhai, China D8 30
Wuhan, China E3 34
Wuhu, China D7 34
Wuhua, China L4 34
Wuhuanchi, China A9 32
Wuji, China E2 32
Wujiang, China D9 34
Wukari, Nig. H14 64
Wum, Cam. H15 64
Wunstorf, Ger. C9 10
Wuping, China J5 34
Wuppertal, Ger. D7 10
Würzburg, Ger. F9 10
Wurzen, Ger. D12 10
Wushan, China E8 30
Wusheng, China F8 34
Wusong, China D10 34
Wutongqiao, China F7 30
Wuustwezel, Bel. F6 12
Wuwei, China D7 30
Wuwei, China D6 34
Wuxi (Wuhsi), China D9 34
Wuyi Shan, mts., China I5 34
Wuyuan, China C8 30
Wuzhi Shan, mtn., China E10 40
Wuzhong, China D8 30
Wuzhou (Wuchow), China C11 40
Wyandot, co., Oh., U.S. B2 142
Wyandotte, Mi., U.S. F7 129
Wyandotte, co., Ks., U.S. C9 123
Wyanet, Il., U.S. B4 120
Wycheproof, Austl. K5 70
Wye, stm., U.K. J11 8
Wylie, Lake, res., U.S. A5 147
Wymore, Ne., U.S. D9 134
Wyndham, Austl. C5 68
Wyndmere, N.D., U.S. C8 141
Wynndel, B.C., Can. E9 99
Wynne, Ar., U.S. B5 111
Wynnewood, Ok., U.S. C4 143
Wynyard, Austl. M6 70
Wynyard, Sask., Can. F3 105
Wyodak, Wy., U.S. B7 157
Wyoming, Ont., Can. E2 103
Wyoming, De., U.S. D3 115
Wyoming, Il., U.S. B4 120
Wyoming, Mi., U.S. F5 129
Wyoming, Mn., U.S. E6 130
Wyoming, Oh., U.S. o13 142
Wyoming, Pa., U.S. n17 145
Wyoming, R.I., U.S. E2 146
Wyoming, co., N.Y., U.S. C2 139
Wyoming, co., Pa., U.S. D9 145
Wyoming, co., W.V., U.S. D3 155
Wyoming, state, U.S. C5 157
Wyomissing, Pa., U.S. F10 145
Wyszków, Pol. C21 10
Wythe, co., Va., U.S. D1 153
Wytheville, Va., U.S. D1 153

X

Xaclbal, stm., N.A. B3 92
Xaidulla, China D2 30
Xai-Xai, Moz. E11 66
Xalapa, Mex. H11 90
Xam Nua, Laos D8 40
Xankändi (Stepanakert), Azer. J7 26
Xánthi, Grc. H8 20
Xanxerê, Braz. D12 80
Xapuri, Braz. D7 82
Xàtiva (Játiva), Spain G11 16
Xaxim, Braz. D12 80
X-Can, Mex. G16 90
Xenia, Oh., U.S. C2 142
Xhumo, Bots. C7 66
Xi, stm., China G9 30
Xiahe, China D7 30
Xiamen (Amoy), China K7 34
Xi'an (Sian), China E8 30
Xiang, stm., China F9 30
Xiangcheng, China B2 34
Xiangfan, China E9 30
Xiangkhoang, Laos E7 40
Xiangtan, China H1 34
Xianju, China G9 34
Xianxian, China E4 32
Xianyou, China J7 34
Xiaodanyang, China D7 34
Xiaogan, China E2 34
Xiaoji, China C8 34
Xiaolan, China M2 34
Xiaoshan, China E9 34
Xiapu, China I9 34
Xichang, China F7 30
Xicoténcatl, Mex. F10 90
Xielipuke, China E10 44
Xigazê, China F13 44
Xihua, China B3 34
Xin'an, China I5 34
Xingcheng, China C8 32
Xinghua, China C8 34
Xingkai Hu (ozero Chanka), l., Asia B13 30
Xingtai, China F2 32
Xingu, stm., Braz. D8 76
Xinguan, China B7 34
Xingyi, China B8 40
Xinhua, China F9 30
Xinhui, China M2 34
Xining, China D7 30
Xinjiang Uygur Zizhiqu (Sinkiang), prov., China C3 30
Xinle (Dongchangshou), China E2 32
Xinmin, China A10 32
Xinshi, China E9 34
Xinwen (Suncun), China H5 32
Xinxian, China D3 34
Xinxiang, China H1 32
Xinyang, China C3 34
Xinzao, China L2 34
Xinzhangzi, China C5 32
Xiping, China B3 34
Xique-Xique, Braz. F10 76
Xırdalan, Azer. I7 26
Xisha Qundao (Paracel Islands), is., China B5 38
Xiuyan, China C11 32
Xixian, China C4 34
Xizang Zizhiqu (Tibet), prov., China E3 30
Xochistlahuaca, Mex. I10 90
Xuancheng, China E7 34
Xuanhua, China C3 32
Xuchang, China A2 34
Xuji, China D5 34
Xun, stm., China G9 30
Xushui, China D3 32
Xuwen, China D11 40
Xuyong, China F8 30
Xuzhou (Süchow), China A6 34

Y

Yaan, China E7 30
Yablonovy Range see Jablonovyj chrebet, mts., Russia G14 28
Yabluniv, Ukr. A8 20
Yaco (Iaco), stm., S.A. D6 82
Yacolt, Wa., U.S. D3 154
Yacuiba, Bol. J10 82
Yacyretá, Isla, i., Para. D10 80
Yadkin, co., N.C., U.S. A2 140
Yadkin, stm., N.C., U.S. B2 140
Yadkinville, N.C., U.S. A2 140
Yafran, Libya B3 56
Yagoua, Cam. F10 54
Yaguachi Nuevo, Ec. I3 84
Yaguajay, Cuba C5 94
Yaguarón (Jaguarão), stm., S.A. G12 80
Yahualica, Mex. G8 90
Yaizu, Japan M13 36
Yakima, Wa., U.S. C5 154
Yakima, co., Wa., U.S. C4 154
Yakima, stm., Wa., U.S. C6 154
Yako, Burkina E8 64
Yakoma, Zaire H5 56
Yakutat, Ak., U.S. D12 109
Yakutat Bay, b., Ak., U.S. D11 109
Yakutia see Jakutija, state, Russia D18 28
Yakutsk see Jakutsk, Russia E17 28
Yala, Thai. K6 40
Yale, Mi., U.S. E8 129
Yale, Ok., U.S. A5 143
Yale, Mount, mtn., Co., U.S. C5 113
Yalgoo, Austl. E3 68
Yalobusha, co., Ms., U.S. A4 131
Yalova, Tur. I13 20
Yalta, Ukr. I4 26
Yalu (Amnok-kang), stm., Asia C12 32
Yamachiche, Que., Can. C5 104
Yamagata, Japan I15 36
Yamaguchi, Japan M6 36
Yamalia see Jamalo-Neneckij, state, Russia D12 26
Yamba, Austl. G10 70
Yambio, Sud. H6 56
Yamethin, Mya. D4 40
Yamhill, Or., U.S. h11 144
Yamhill, co., Or., U.S. B3 144
Yamoussoukro, C. Iv. H7 64
Yampa, Co., U.S. A4 113
Yampa, stm., Co., U.S. A2 113
Yamparaez, Bol. H9 82
Yampil', Ukr. A12 20
Yamsay Mountain, mtn., Or., U.S. E5 144
Yamuna, stm., India H9 44
Yamzho Yumco, l., China F14 44
Yanahuara, Peru G6 82
Yan'an, China D8 30
Yanaoca, Peru F6 82
Yanbu' al-Bahr, Sau. Ar. I5 48
Yancey, co., N.C., U.S. f10 140
Yanceyville, N.C., U.S. A3 140
Yancheng, China B9 34
Yanco, Austl. J7 70
Yandoon, Mya. F3 40
Yanfolila, Mali F5 64
Yangjiang, China G9 30
Yangkoushi, China G7 34
Yangliuqing, China D5 32
Yangon (Rangoon), Mya. B2 38
Yangquan, China F1 32
Yangsan, S. Kor. H17 32
Yangtze see Chang, stm., China E10 30
Yangzhou, China C8 34
Yanji, China A17 32
Yankdŏk, N. Kor. D14 32
Yankton, S.D., U.S. E8 148
Yankton, co., S.D., U.S. D8 148
Yanqi, China C4 30
Yanqing, China C3 32
Yantabulla, Austl. G6 70
Yantai (Chefoo), China F9 32
Yanzhou, China H4 32
Yao, Japan M10 36
Yaoundé, Cam. H9 54
Yapacaní, Bol. G9 82
Yapeyú, Arg. E10 80
Yaque del Norte, stm., Dom. Rep. E9 94
Yaqui, stm., Mex. C5 90
Yaracuy, state, Ven. B8 84
Yardea, Austl. I1 70
Yardley, Pa., U.S. F12 145
Yardville, N.J., U.S. C3 137
Yaremcha, Ukr. A8 20
Yarí, stm., Col. F6 84
Yarīm, Yemen G4 47
Yaritagua, Ven. B8 84
Yarkand see Shache, China A7 44
Yarkant (Yarkand), stm., China D2 30
Yarker, Ont., Can. C8 103
Yarmouth, N.S., Can. F3 101
Yarmouth, Me., U.S. E2 126
Yarnell, Az., U.S. C3 110
Yarrawonga, Austl. K7 70
Yarumal, Col. D5 84
Yasinya, Ukr. A8 20
Yasothon, Thai. G8 40
Yass, Austl. J8 70
Yates, co., N.Y., U.S. C3 139
Yates Center, Ks., U.S. E8 123
Yatsushiro, Japan O5 36
Yauca, Peru F4 82
Yauco, P.R. E11 94
Yauli, Peru D3 82
Yauri, Peru F6 82
Yautepec, Mex. H10 90
Yauyos, Peru E4 82
Yavapai, co., Az., U.S. C3 110
Yavarí (Javari), stm., S.A. D4 76
Yavaros, Mex. D5 90
Yavatmāl, India B5 46
Yaviza, Pan. C4 84
Yavne, Isr. E3 50
Yaxian, China E10 40
Yayuan, China B14 32
Yazd, Iran F13 48
Yazoo, co., Ms., U.S. C3 131
Yazoo, stm., Ms., U.S. C3 131
Yazoo City, Ms., U.S. C3 131
Ye, Mya. G4 40
Yeadon, Pa., U.S. p21 145
Yecheng, China B7 44
Yecla, Spain G10 16
Yehud, Isr. D3 50
Yei, stm., Sud. N6 60
Yekaterinburg see Jekaterinburg, Russia F10 26
Yelarbon, Austl. G9 70
Yell, co., Ar., U.S. B2 111
Yellow see Huang, stm., China D10 30
Yellow, stm., U.S. u15 116
Yellow, stm., Ga., U.S. h8 117
Yellow, stm., Wi., U.S. C3 156
Yellow, stm., Wi., U.S. D3 156
Yellow Grass, Sask., Can. H3 105
Yellowhead Pass, Can. C1 98
Yellowknife, N.W. Ter., Can. D10 96
Yellow Medicine, co., Mn., U.S. F2 130
Yellow Sea (Huang Hai), Asia B11 34
Yellow Springs, Oh., U.S. C2 142
Yellowstone, co., Mt., U.S. D8 133
Yellowstone, stm., U.S. D10 133
Yellowstone Lake, l., Wy., U.S. B2 157
Yellowstone National Park, Wy., U.S. B2 157
Yellowstone National Park, co., Mt., U.S. E6 133
Yellowstone National Park, U.S. B2 157
Yellville, Ar., U.S. A3 111
Yelm, Wa., U.S. C3 154
Yelwa, Nig. F12 64
Yemen (Al-Yaman), ctry., Asia F3 42
Yenangyaung, Mya. D3 40
Yen Bai, Viet. D8 40
Yenda, Austl. J7 70
Yendi, Ghana G9 64
Yenisey see Jenisej, stm., Russia D15 26
Yeppoon, Austl. D9 70
Yerevan see Jerevan, Arm. I6 26
Yerington, Nv., U.S. E2 135
Yerupaja, Nevado, mtn., Peru D3 82
Yerushalayim (Al-Quds) (Jerusalem), Isr. E4 50
Yesan, S. Kor. G14 32
Ye-u, Mya. C3 40
Yevlax, Azer. I7 26
Yevpatoriya, Ukr. H4 26
Yexian, China B2 34
Yhú, Para. C11 80
Yi, stm., Ur. G10 80
Yi'an, China B12 30
Yiannitsá, Grc. I6 20
Yibin, China F7 30
Yicanghe, China C9 34
Yichang, China E9 30
Yichun, China B12 30
Yichun, China F9 30
Yidu, China G6 32
Yijiangzhen, China E7 34
Yilan, China B12 30
Yiliang, China B7 40
Yinchuan, China D8 30
Yingcheng, China E2 34
Yingde, China K2 34
Yingkou, China C10 32
Yingtan, China G6 34
Yining, China C3 30
Yirga Alem, Eth. N10 60
Yirol, Sud. N6 60
Yishan, China B10 40
Yishui, China H6 32
Yíthion, Grc. M6 20
Yitulihe, China A11 30
Yiwu, China F9 34
Yiyang, China F9 30
Ylivieska, Fin. I19 6
Yoakum, Tx., U.S. E4 150
Yoakum, co., Tx., U.S. C1 150
Yoder, Wy., U.S. E8 157
Yogyakarta, Indon. j15 39a
Yŏju, S. Kor. F15 32
Yokkaichi, Japan M11 36
Yokohama, Japan L14 36
Yokosuka, Japan L14 36
Yolo, co., Ca., U.S. C2 112
Yolyn, W.V., U.S. n12 155
Yonago, Japan L8 36
Yoncalla, Or., U.S. D3 144
Yonezawa, Japan J15 36
Yong'an, China J6 34
Yŏngch'ŏn, S. Kor. H16 32
Yongding, China K5 34
Yŏngdong, S. Kor. G15 32
Yongfeng, China H4 34
Yŏngju, S. Kor. G16 32
Yongkang, China G9 34
Yŏngwŏl, S. Kor. F16 32
Yongxin, China I3 34
Yonkers, N.Y., U.S. E7 139
Yorba Linda, Ca., U.S. n13 112
York, Austl. F3 68
York, Ont., Can. D5 103
York, Eng., U.K. H12 8
York, Al., U.S. C1 108
York, Me., U.S. E2 126
York, Ne., U.S. D8 134
York, Pa., U.S. G8 145
York, S.C., U.S. B5 147
York, co., Me., U.S. E2 126
York, co., Ne., U.S. D8 134
York, co., Pa., U.S. G8 145
York, co., S.C., U.S. A5 147
York, co., Va., U.S. C6 153
York, stm., Va., U.S. C6 153
York, Cape, c., Austl. B8 68
York, Kap, c., Grnld. B13 86
York Beach, Me., U.S. E2 126
Yorke Peninsula, pen., Austl. J2 70
York Harbor, Me., U.S. E2 126
Yorklyn, De., U.S. A3 115
Yorkton, Sask., Can. F4 105
Yorktown, In., U.S. D7 121
Yorktown, Va., U.S. C6 153
Yorktown Manor, R.I., U.S. E4 146
Yorkville, Il., U.S. B5 120
Yorkville, N.Y., U.S. B5 139
Yoro, Hond. B7 92
Yoro, Mali D8 64
Yoro, dept., Hond. B7 92
Yosemite National Park, Ca., U.S. D4 112
Yos Sudarso, Pulau, i., Indon. G10 38
Yŏsu, S. Kor. I15 32
Youbou, B.C., Can. g11 99
Youghiogheny, stm., U.S. F2 145
Youghiogheny River Lake, res., U.S. G3 145
Young, Austl. J8 70
Young, Sask., Can. F3 105
Young, Az., U.S. C5 110
Young, Ur. G10 80
Young, co., Tx., U.S. C3 150
Young Harris, Ga., U.S. B3 117
Younghusband Peninsula, pen., Austl. K3 70
Youngstown, Alta., Can. D5 98
Youngstown, Oh., U.S. A5 142
Youngsville, La., U.S. D3 125
Youngsville, Pa., U.S. C3 145
Youngtown, Az., U.S. k8 110
Youngwood, Pa., U.S. F2 145
Youssoufia, Mor. D6 62
Youxi, China I7 34
Yozgat, Tur. B3 48
Ypacaraí, Para. C10 80
Ypé Jhú, Para. B11 80
Ypres (Ieper), Bel. G2 12
Ypsilanti, Mi., U.S. F7 129
Yreka, Ca., U.S. B2 112
Ystad, Swe. N13 6
Yüanlin, Tai. L9 34
Yuanling, China F9 30
Yuanmou, China B6 40
Yuba, co., Ca., U.S. C3 112
Yuba, stm., Ca., U.S. C3 112
Yuba City, Ca., U.S. C3 112
Yucatán, state, Mex. G15 90
Yucatán, Canal de, strt., N.A. D2 94
Yucatan Peninsula (Península de Yucatán), pen., N.A. H15 90
Yuci, China D9 30
Yuecheng, China C3 34
Yueyang, China F2 34
Yugoslavia (Jugoslavija), ctry., Eur. G11 4
Yukon, Ok., U.S. B4 143
Yukon, W.V., U.S. D3 155
Yukon, prov., Can. D5 96
Yukon, stm., N.A. m19 106a
Yulee, Fl., U.S. B5 116
Yulin, China D8 30
Yulin, China C11 40
Yuma, Az., U.S. E1 110
Yuma, Co., U.S. A8 113
Yuma, co., Az., U.S. E1 110
Yuma, co., Co., U.S. A8 113
Yumbo, Col. F4 84
Yumen, China D6 30
Yuncheng, China D9 30
Yungas, reg., Bol. F8 82
Yungay, Chile I2 80
Yungay, Peru C3 82
Yunhe, China G8 34
Yunnan, prov., China F7 30
Yunxian, China E9 30
Yurimaguas, Peru A3 82
Yuriria, Mex. G9 90
Yuscarán, Hond. D8 92
Yü Shan, mtn., Tai. L9 34
Yushu, China E6 30
Yutan, Ne., U.S. C9 134
Yutian, China B9 44
Yuty, Para. D10 80
Yuxian, China A2 34
Yuyao, China E10 34
Yverdon, Switz. E6 13
Yvetot, Fr. C7 14

Z

Zabajkal'sk, Russia H15 28
Zabīd, Yemen G3 47
Žabinka, Bela. I7 22
Ząbkowice Śląskie, Pol. E16 10
Zābol, Iran F16 48
Zabré, Burkina F9 64
Zabrze (Hindenburg), Pol. E18 10
Zacapa, Guat. C5 92
Zacapa, dept., Guat. B5 92
Zacapu, Mex. H9 90
Zacatecas, Mex. F8 90
Zacatecas, state, Mex. F8 90
Zacatecoluca, El Sal. D6 92
Zacatlán, Mex. H11 90
Zachary, La., U.S. D4 125
Zacoalco de Torres, Mex. G8 90
Zacualtipan, Mex. G10 90
Zadar, Cro. E10 18
Zadonsk, Russia I21 22
Zafer Burnu, c., N. Cyp. D3 48
Zafra, Spain G5 16
Żagań, Pol. D15 10
Žagare, Lith. E6 22
Zaghouan, Tun. M5 18
Zagreb, Cro. D10 18
Zāgros, Kūhhā-ye, mts., Iran E9 48
Zahana, Alg. J11 16
Zāhedān, Iran G16 48
Zahlah, Leb. A5 50
Zaire (Zaïre), ctry., Afr. B4 58
Zaječar, Yugo. F6 20
Zajsan, Kaz. H14 26
Zajsan, ozero, l., Kaz. H14 26
Zakamensk, Russia G12 28
Zākhū, Iraq C7 48
Zákinthos, Grc. L4 20
Zákinthos, i., Grc. L4 20
Zakopane, Pol. F19 10
Zalaegerszeg, Hung. I16 10
Zalanga, Nig. F15 64
Zalău, Rom. B7 20
Zalegošč', Russia I19 22
Zalingei, Sud. K2 60
Zalishchyky, Ukr. A9 20
Zambezi (Zambeze), stm., Afr. E6 58
Zambia, ctry., Afr. D5 58
Zamboanga, Phil. D7 38
Zambrano, Col. C5 84
Zambrów, Pol. B22 10
Zamora, Ec. J3 84
Zamora, Spain D6 16
Zamora-Chinchipe, prov., Ec. J3 84
Zamora de Hidalgo, Mex. H8 90
Zamość, Pol. E23 10
Zandvoort, Circuit Autorace, Neth. D6 12
Zanesville, In., U.S. C7 121
Zanesville, Oh., U.S. C4 142
Zanjān, Iran C10 48
Zanjón, stm., Arg. F4 80
Zanzibar, Tan. C7 58
Zanzibar, i., Tan. C7 58
Zaokskij, Russia G20 22
Zaoxi, China E8 34
Zaozhuang, China I5 32
Zaoz'ornyj, Russia F10 28
Zap, N.D., U.S. B4 141
Zapadnaja Dvina, Russia E15 22
Zapadnaja Dvina (Daugava), stm., Eur. F10 22
Zapala, Arg. J3 80
Zapata, Tx., U.S. F3 150
Zapata, co., Tx., U.S. F3 150
Zapatera, Isla, i., Nic. F9 92
Zapatoca, Col. D6 84
Zapol'arnyj, Russia G22 6
Zapopan, Mex. G8 90
Zaporizhzhya, Ukr. H5 26
Zaprudn'a, Russia E20 22
Zaragoza, Col. D5 84
Zaragoza, Mex. C9 90
Zaragoza, Spain D11 16
Zarajsk, Russia G21 22
Zarand, Iran F14 48
Zarasai, Lith. F9 22
Zárate, Arg. H9 80
Zarautz, Spain B9 16
Zaraza, Ven. C10 84
Zarghūn Shahr, Afg. D3 44
Zaria, Nig. F13 64
Žarkovskij, Russia F15 22
Zarrīn Shahr, Iran E11 48
Zaruma, Ec. I3 84
Zarumilla, Peru I2 84
Żary (Sorau), Pol. D15 10
Zarzal, Col. E4 84
Zarzis, Tun. D16 62
Zāskār Mountains, mts., Asia D7 44
Zaslavl', Bela. G10 22
Zastavna, Ukr. A9 20
Zastron, S. Afr. H8 66
Zavala, co., Tx., U.S. E3 150
Zavitinsk, Russia G17 28
Zavolžje, Russia E26 22
Zavolžsk, Russia D25 22
Zawiercie, Pol. E19 10
Zawiyat Shammās, Egypt B4 60
Zduńska Wola, Pol. D18 10
Zeballos, B.C., Can. D4 99
Zebulon, Ga., U.S. C2 117
Zebulon, N.C., U.S. B4 140
Zeehan, Austl. M6 70
Zeeland, Mi., U.S. F5 129
Zeeland, prov., Neth. F4 12
Zeerust, S. Afr. E8 66
Zege, Eth. L9 60
Zeigler, Il., U.S. F4 120
Zeil, Mount, mtn., Austl. D6 68
Zeist, Neth. D7 12
Zeitz, Ger. D12 10
Zeja, Russia G17 28
Zeja, stm., Russia G17 28
Zejskoje vodochranilišče, res., Russia G17 28
Zelaya, dept., Nic. E10 92
Zele, Bel. F5 12
Zelenoborskij, Russia H23 6
Zelenogorsk, Russia A12 22
Zelenograd, Russia E20 22
Zelenogradsk, Russia G3 22
Železnogorsk, Russia I18 22
Železnogorsk-Ilimskij, Russia F12 28
Zelienople, Pa., U.S. E1 145
Zel'onodol'sk, Russia F7 26
Zel'va, Bela. H7 22
Zelzate, Bel. F4 12
Zemetčino, Russia H25 22
Zémio, Cen. Afr. Rep. G6 56
Zendeh Jān, Afg. D16 48
Zenica, Bos. E1 20
Zenith, Wa., U.S. f11 154
Zenon Park, Sask., Can. D4 105
Zephyr Cove, Nv., U.S. E2 135
Zephyrhills, Fl., U.S. D4 116
Zerbst, Ger. D12 10
Žerdevka, Russia J24 22
Zermatt, Switz. F8 13
Zernograd, Russia H6 26
Zevenaar, Neth. E9 12
Zevenbergen, Neth. E6 12
Zgierz, Pol. D19 10
Zhangjiakou (Kalgan), China C2 32
Zhangmutou, China M3 34
Zhangping, China J6 34
Zhangye, China D7 30
Zhangzhou (Longxi), China K6 34
Zhanjiang, China D11 40
Zhao'an, China L6 34
Zhaoqing, China G9 30
Zhaotong, China F7 30
Zhaoyuan, China F8 32
Zhapu, China E10 34
Zhaxigang, China D8 44
Zhdanov see Mariupol', Ukr. H5 26
Zhejiang (Chekiang), prov., China F11 30
Zhengding, China E2 32
Zhengzhou, China E9 30
Zhenjiang, China C8 34
Zhob, Pak. E3 44
Zhongdian, China F6 30
Zhongmeihe, China D5 34
Zhongshan (Shiqizhen), China M2 34
Zhongxiang, China D1 34
Zhoucun, China G5 32
Zhouning, China H8 34
Zhoushan Qundao, is., China E11 34
Zhovti Vody, Ukr. H4 26
Zhumadian, China C3 34
Zhuoxian, China D3 32
Zhushan, China E9 30
Zhuya, China G6 32
Zhuzhou (Chuchow), China H2 34
Zhytomyr, Ukr. G3 26
Žiar nad Hronom, Slvk. G18 10
Zibo (Zhangdian), China G6 32
Ziebach, co., S.D., U.S. C4 148
Zielona Góra (Grünberg), Pol. D15 10
Ziftā, Egypt B6 60
Žigalovo, Russia G13 28
Zigong, China F7 30
Ziguinchor, Sen. E1 64
Zihuatanejo, Mex. I9 90
Žilina, Slvk. F18 10
Zillah, Libya C4 56
Zillah, Wa., U.S. C5 154
Zilwaukee, Mi., U.S. E7 129
Zima, Russia G12 28
Zimapán, Mex. G10 90
Zimbabwe, ctry., Afr. E5 58
Zimmerman, Mn., U.S. E5 130
Zimnicea, Rom. F9 20
Zinder, Niger E14 64
Zion, Il., U.S. A6 120

Name	Map Ref.	Page
Zion National Park, Ut., U.S.	F3	151
Zionsville, In., U.S.	E5	121
Zipaquirá, Col.	E5	84
Žitkoviči, Bela.	I10	22
Zittau, Ger.	E14	10
Zitundo, Moz.	F11	66
Ziway, Lake, l., Eth.	M10	60
Žizdra, Russia	H17	22
Zizhong, China	F7	30
Zlatoust, Russia	F9	26
Zlín, Czech Rep.	F17	10
Žlobin, Bela.	I13	22
Złotów, Pol.	B17	10
Zlynka, Russia	I14	22
Zmeinogorsk, Russia	G14	26
Zmi'ovka, Russia	I19	22
Znamensk, Russia	G4	22
Znam'yanka, Ukr.	H4	26
Znojmo, Czech Rep.	G16	10
Žodino, Bela.	G11	22
Zofingen, Switz.	D8	13
Zollikofen, Switz.	D7	13
Zollikon, Switz.	D10	13
Zolotkovo, Russia	F24	22
Zolotuchino, Russia	I19	22
Zomba, Mwi.	E7	58
Zonguldak, Tur.	G14	4
Zorgo, Burkina	E9	64
Zorritos, Peru	I2	84
Zouérat, Maur.	I4	62
Zouping, China	G5	32
Zrenjanin, Yugo.	D4	20
Zubcov, Russia	E17	22
Zubova Pol'ana, Russia	G25	22
Zuénoula, C. Iv.	H6	64
Zug, Switz.	D10	13
Zugersee, l., Switz.	D10	13
Zugspitze, mtn., Eur.	H10	10
Zuiderzee see IJsselmeer, Neth.	C7	12
Zuid-Holland, prov., Neth.	D6	12
Zujevka, Russia	F8	26
Žukovka, Russia	H16	22
Žukovskij, Russia	F21	22
Zulia, state, Ven.	B6	84
Zululand, hist. reg., S. Afr.	F10	66
Zumbrota, Mn., U.S.	F6	130
Zuni (Zuni Pueblo), N.M., U.S.	B1	138
Zuni, stm., U.S.	C6	110
Zunyi, China	F8	30
Zuodeng, China	C9	40
Zurich, Ont., Can.	D3	103
Zürich, Switz.	D10	13
Zürichsee, l., Switz.	D10	13
Zuru, Nig.	F12	64
Zutphen, Neth.	D9	12
Zuwārah, Libya	B3	56
Zvenigorod, Russia	F19	22
Zvishavane, Zimb.	C10	66
Zvolen, Slvk.	G19	10
Zvornik, Bos.	E3	20
Zweibrücken, Ger.	F7	10
Zweisimmen, Switz.	E7	13
Zwettl, Aus.	G15	10
Zwickau, Ger.	E12	10
Zwijndrecht, Neth.	E6	12
Zwolle, Neth.	C9	12
Zwolle, La., U.S.	C2	125
Zyr'anovsk, Kaz.	H8	28
Żyrardów, Pol.	C20	10
Żywiec, Pol.	F19	10